¥ ± to And-thuy

B~ orcure 1·8

12 - R.A. coloniz. in some agency | 363. link to earlier coloniz
15 - "mongo". *see also Stark*.
17-18 - nationalist politics of archeology
¥162-3 - yumbo dancing in urban Quito (cf- ritoy men)

280. boats in Ecuador

☆ 326 - extension of verticality.
  Jungle Quichua cattle-
  366 ff pressure from govt RA policy·

404 ff. · irrig. · Jdwz. UCU· 2 parts·

▷ 429· Indian land purchase in Ecuador (>>P, B)
  427. why has. govt. Inds. buy land.
  430· consumption

777. pres. made speech in Q.

Cultural Transformations and
Ethnicity in Modern Ecuador

Cultural Transformations and Ethnicity in Modern Ecuador

Edited by NORMAN E. WHITTEN, JR.

UNIVERSITY OF ILLINOIS PRESS
Urbana Chicago London

Publication of this work was made possible in part by a grant from the National Science Foundation.

Library of Congress Cataloging in Publication Data

Main entry under title:

Cultural transformations and ethnicity in modern
Ecuador.

Includes index.
1. Ecuador—Social conditions. 2. Indians of
South America—Ecuador—Social conditions.
3. Minorities—Ecuador. I. Whitten, Norman E., Jr.,
1937–
HN317.C8   986.6   81-4402
ISBN 0-252-00832-4   AACR2

Contents

Foreword

Ecuador is a privileged country comprised of a unique topographical configuration. In spite of its location right on the equator—from hence its name—its climate varies from the characteristic warmth and high humidity of the lowland tropics to the temperate and dry highlands. The Andean cordillera, which divides the territory into Coast, Sierra, and Oriente, is neither a labyrinth nor a continuous massif, but rather consists of parallel mountainous chains repeatedly united by "knots" into a formation resembling a gigantic staircase. The eastern chain, covered with lush Upper Amazonian vegetation, is a discontinuous cord marked by small mountain systems. The great Andean range articulates a complete ecosystem linked by hydrodynamics and by the mountain spurs, which, like huge buttresses, break into the littoral plain and into Amazonia.

The Coast is drained and watered by large rivers, such as the Santiago, Esmeraldas, Chone, Guayas, and Jubones. The Guayas River Valley, about 40,000 kilometers long, is one of the most fertile agricultural zones in the Americas. Marine currents off the coast—the cold Humboldt Current, originating in the Antarctic, and the warm El Niño Current, with its origin off the Panamanian coast—are determinants of its varied climates and rich sources of fish.

The Sierra, or inter-Andean region, extends from north to south between two great cordilleras, which are characterized by recent volcanic activity in the north, where immense and isolated conical mountains stand like sentries of their valleys. This extraordinary inter-Andean landscape has been called the "Avenue of the Volcanoes," for Cayambe, Antisana, Cotopaxi, Tungurahua, Altar, and Sangay all rise more than 5,000 meters in altitude to the east, and, on the west side of the Avenue, Cotacachi, Pichincha, Atacazo, Corazón, and Illiniza are surpassed by massive Chimborazo, which reaches 6,310 meters above sea level. From the Azuay knot south, the cordillera is of Tertiary formation; the land there is poor, and erosion has produced a mountain profile more like a massif, composed of small valleys and retreats.

The Upper Amazonian Oriente is an extensive rainforest region modified in its most western part by the cordilleras of the Napo-Galeras, Cóndor, and Cutucú. The maximum altitude of 3,900 meters is reached by the Sumaco volcano, which is part of the Napo-Galeras system. One of the most outstanding features of this region is its hydrodynamics, especially its great venous system consisting of innumerable Andean-fed rivers, which, as they unite, form the swelling arteries that increase the flow of water into the Amazon. Their trajectory is predominantly south-southeast, some of their courses covering hundreds of kilometers. Almost half of this vital Ecuadorian territory was cut away by the Protocol of Río de Janeiro in 1942, following a Peruvian military invasion. Before this geopolitical amputation, rivers such as the Napo, Tigre, Pastaza, Morona, and Santiago were completely Ecuadorian.

The Galápagos Islands, an extraordinary reserve of animal and plant life, now consecrated by UNESCO as a "Patrimonio Nacional de Humanidad," are also an important part of Ecuadorian territory.

Ecuador is truly unique. It has served as a marvelous panoramic stage upon which the human drama has been enacted through immemorial epochs. Here snow, jungle, volcanoes, rivers, plains, and beaches formed various interrelated landscapes shared by interacting peoples who modified their environment and administered it appropriately until not so long ago. Then, beginning in the late fifteenth century, a new and overwhelming vital theory with an ancestral (perhaps Mediterranean) world view—one that had been handed down historically from generation to generation—was imposed upon an essentially rustic country.

Anthropological studies in Ecuador are not recent. They began in the nineteenth century, initially with a historical focus. This early anthropology plumbed the sources of knowledge of national ancestry. Later, in the mid-twentieth century, a coherent theory was constructed in which culture-historic epochs and their characteristics were clearly defined. The panorama was broadened to unsuspected limits when considerable antiquity for man and culture in our territory was discovered, and it was learned that the Incaic period, although important in its impact, did not define our pre-Hispanic cultures. It was found that truly Ecuadorian cultures such as Valdivia and Chorrera were precursors to later cultures to the south and north, in their utilization of certain techniques and materials. Such early Ecuadorian cultures also held a particular world view, some of the characteristics of which extended to Mesoamerica and Peru. Anthropological attention in Ecuador has also long been directed to ethnohistory, uncovering important aspects of that initial moment of the syncretic formation of the new indo-Hispanic being.

But it is contemporary Ecuador, the nation in the latter part of the twentieth century, that has been the principal preoccupation of the Instituto Nacional de Antropología e Historia (INAH). We are in the midst of a crisis; its beginning coincides with the incredible process which has, since its beginnings in the 1950s, affected the whole world. The technological revolution in our case has produced a process of "de-mediterraneanization." Its grand agents are modern means of communication, the perfection of aviation, the transistor, television. When we add to this the discovery of oil in our territory and its industrial exploitation in the 1970s, we can affirm that Ecuador has been forcefully infused with an unexpected and dizzying process of change for which it was not prepared. This process altered Ecuadorian life substantially. An essential historic-economic dimension must be added, although its roots are much earlier than the technological revolution of the 1950s that Ecuador faced. This is the dimension of land reform, which became more intense in the 1960s. By the mid-twentieth century, ancestral injustice began to vent itself politically, and the agrarian reform was conceived to resolve both the injustices and the political turmoil. The reform will, in my opinion, bring about the disintegration of productive units, in the long run, and, being poorly conceived, cause the complete abandonment of the land by the *campesinos*.

As soon as the "petroleum era," characterized, among other things, by the construction industry's boom in the principal urban centers of Quito and Guayaquil, reaches its peak, desertion of the countryside could be massive. The city attracts with its incentives, its better means of communication, its better salaries. These will lure the *campesinos*, creating dramatic tensions, underemployment, idleness, and all of the consequences inherent in the process—deculturation, alienation manifest in the loss of identity, the abandonment of such values as speaking the mother tongue—all in order to assimilate into the urban culture, where indigenous peoples are disapproved of. Similarly, an altering of appearance will take place with the amputation of such features as the masculine braid, characteristic of some sierran Quichua ethnic groups, or native dress reflecting the traditional identity of the aboriginal populations. Such physical impoverishment could affect substantially the indigenous world view and social structure.

If this is happening in the inter-Andean region, the situation is no less dramatic in Amazonia. State policy has always called for the need to "colonize" the Oriente of Ecuador; such colonization is considered indispensable for reasons of both national sovereignty and exploitation of vital economic resources. The ancient Catholic missions have contributed since the sixteenth century to the fixing of boundaries of the *audiencia de Quito*'s dominion eastward to the confluence of the Putumayo with the Amazon. Since Ecuadorian independence from Spanish domination, not only the Catholic friars but also the military have been called upon to defend territorial sovereignty and to consolidate the presence of the state in the eastern jungle.

The Ecuadorian Amazon was never a "no-man's land"; it has been inhabited for thousands of years. The first Spaniards who left Quito in search of El Dorado found here a great variety of populations. The missionaries are those who have traditionally been in sustained contact with native Amazonian peoples. Their work has long been important from an evangelical viewpoint and, above all else, to the state, since for a very long time they were the only link between the aboriginal peoples, the nation, and the central government. To be successful, the missionaries had to enter profoundly into indigenous essence, and although from an anthropological perspective their methods may be questionable, the Catholic friars were the only ones whose modus operandi implied a certain mystique, an essential action, and permanent cohabitation.

The state always believed it necessary to colonize the Oriente, which, in turn, has always been thought of as a type of reserve, a panacea to be utilized in solving the republic's problems: shortage of workable lands, crowding in highland cities, lack of refuge from regions devastated by drought or other misfortunes. The state has sought to establish human "colonies" there, without ever considering whether or not this meant the uprooting of the true owners of the land. The problem becomes critical when we consider the scope of this colonization policy, which, among other things, implies the destruction of an ancient ecosystem. This problem was never seriously analyzed, if it was even considered. One consequence of colonization and land grants to large agricultural enterprises was the felling of the pristine forest, which can bring such effects as change in climate, immediate erosion, and soil depletion. Only now do we realize the full implications of former President Galo Plaza's famous phrase, "The Oriente is a myth." Considered from the perspective of an agriculture conceived along western lines, the only one used in Ecuador almost since the beginning of the Spanish colonial period, this proclamation is true. The nation has never undertaken a serious study of endogenous technologies used for thousands of years by indigenous Ecuadorian peoples. For this reason the agricultural systems native to the Amazonian region have been considered absurd. It has never been understood in Quito why Upper Amazonian peoples lacked fixed-field agriculture, why they followed a dispersed settlement pattern, or the reason for horticulture in two or more gardens distant from one another.

But the problem cannot only be confined to the damage perpetrated against nature. Since the discovery of petroleum in the northeast, the Ecuadorian economy has been transformed. This incredible economic injection propels the country toward new and unknown paths with ominous consequences. These consequences are not only political; they also involve the destruction of the moral values which once enlightened the republic. The country was not prepared for that temporary affluence, and instead of "sowing the petroleum" (as it is said), oil revenues were in great part squandered. The petroleum boom served the interests of the few without contributing to the well-being of Ecuadorians in general. Ethnocide began as a consequence of oil exploitation; the state never worried about the results of the utilization of sophisticated machines for oil exploitation in a region that was virtually "virgin" to civilization. A gigantic infrastructure began to spread over a territory which had before remained untouched. Its purpose was to take the offensive directly against men who, by birthright, had lived there for centuries or millennia. Genocide and ethnocide are harsh words, but they must nevertheless be used to define a real situation.

This lengthy preamble seeks to explain the intention of the Instituto Nacional de Antropología e Historia in coordinating research in Ecuador by prominent scientists during this crucial period in the nation's life. It is my duty to point out the high degree of reliability, sensitivity, and professional ethics of the authors of this book, compiled and edited by Norman E. Whitten, Jr., qualities which, collectively—together with the analyses presented by the respective research projects—served as a basis for sponsorship by INAH. Meticulous study and discussion prior to and during the development of the various research projects have been mutually enriching.

Humanistic philosophy allowed us to glimpse the urgent need to save and rescue man's spirit, his world view. Above all else, this philosophy implies a vital theory different from that in which those who claim to belong to western civilization are hopelessly submerged. It is necessary and urgent, if the nation of Ecuador can still rectify its actions, to study profoundly its cultural components and, based on such an autodiagnosis founded in an authentic knowledge of its being, to fulfill its historic destiny.

Hernán Crespo Toral, Executive Director
Instituto Nacional de Antropología e Historia
Quito, August 1980

Acknowledgments

Over the past nineteen years so much goodwill and assistance have been given to me by the peoples of Ecuador that I can but mention a few of the most outstanding: Marcelo F. Naranjo, Hernán Crespo Toral, Olga Fisch, Aurelio Fuentes Contreras, Edelberto Rivera Reascos, Bolívar Arisala, Rudi Masaquiza, Marcelo Santi Simbaña, Faviola Vargas Aranda, Luis Antonio Vargas Canelos, and Joe Brenner. Auspices under which I have worked there, and under which I continue to work, include the Casa de la Cultura Ecuatoriana, the Instituto Nacional de Antropología e Historia, the Museos del Banco Central, and the Oficina de Patrimonio Nacional. I am also grateful to the Pontificia Universidad Católica del Ecuador, Quito, and the Programa de Antropología para el Ecuador for numerous cordial reciprocities and collaborative endeavors, and to the Instituto Otavaleño de Antropología and the Federación Shuar for their verve and goodwill in undertaking the collaborative venture to publish parts of this work in Spanish.

Between early fall, 1977, and mid-fall, 1978, I communicated with more than forty-five possible contributors to this book from ten nations, and I failed to communicate with many others. This number alone perhaps indicates something of the vigor with which Ecuadorianist scholarship is being pursued by anthropologists, among dozens upon dozens of other scholars from many disciplines. The time has definitely passed when one could say that Ecuador represents some sort of terra incognita ethnographically, although it is true that the majority of contributions to such scholarship are often found buried in reports, in doctoral dissertations and master's theses, or in extended typescripts or mimeographed manuscripts in relatively inaccessible locations.

While on the brink of decision-making as to whether or not to undertake this editing task, extended conversations with, or other collegial activity by, a few friends pushed me over the edge into a frame of mind of total commitment, and they must be acknowledged: Sibby Whitten, Marcelo F. Naranjo, Frank Salomon, Ronald Stutzman, Philippe Descola, Anne-Christine Taylor, Hernán Crespo Toral, Elizabeth Dulany, and Richard Wentworth. After the commitment was made, and with a sabbatical semester to be devoted exclusively to editing, writing, and communicating with authors, this task could not have been carried out without the substantial support that was granted to me by a research assistantship allocated by the Research Board of the University of Illinois and, on top of that, by a second grant of funds to allow for final retyping of 40 percent of the final manuscript. When funds ran out or when time pressures accelerated the pace of work, Dorothy Osborne of the Center for Latin American and Caribbean Studies cheerfully typed several hundred pages of manuscript for this book, and we are all indebted to her for pulling us back on schedule on many occasions. Sally McBrearty drew several of the diagrams and figures and Gary Apfelstadt did yeoman service by redrafting and helping editor and authors to conceptualize their territories and concepts, as represented in the final graphics.

I am indebted to each of the contributors to this volume for setting other work aside to give this project top priority in the midst of busy schedules and conflicting commitments, and for being so responsive to my queries and editorial recommendations. I am indeed warmed by the initiative taken on their parts to make this a genuine international endeavor.

Even with the active support of twenty-six different authors communicating effectively with me from six nations, released time, and financial help, I would not have been able to complete this project without the creative and painstaking assistance of Kathleen Fine. Kathy not only provided me with a critical commentary on every author's draft, but also on my own edited version; in a few cases she undertook the editing task herself, contributing creatively and productively to the scholarly venture. She cheerfully retyped many papers, thus sparing expense for both authors and editor. She continued to work with me on this project through the spring of 1980 as we finally delivered what turned out to be about 1,300 pages of revised manuscript to the University of Illinois Press.

Through the years, the "risk assessment" policies of several funding agencies established the various bases leading to this task of compilation and editing. The National Institute of Mental Health took a chance on me as a neophyte graduate student in 1961, thereby facilitating my first exposure to an Andean nation where peoples of Afro-Hispanic culture of a Pacific-coastal province talked of their Amazonian "brothers," and named a new section of their community "Puerto de Manaos." Later, in 1968, NIMH again provided funds through an integrated, interdisciplinary "program" to allow me, together with Sibby Whitten, to explore the possibility of undertaking a study of Amazonian Ecuadorian native peoples undergoing pressures similar to those which *costeños* of the western rainforest were subjected. The National Science Foundation provided the funding for our work in the eastern rainforests of Ecuador between 1970 and 1975, and the John Simon Guggenheim Memorial Foundation, together with the Center for Advanced Study at the University of Illinois, allowed me the necessary flexibility to explore new facets of anthropological thought and action while undertaking both basic and applied research in Ecuador in 1976 and 1977. It was at the end of the Guggenheim year that I formulated the plans and made the decisions leading to this edited work.

Over the past decade funding by the University of Illinois, Urbana, through the Research Board, the Center for International Comparative Studies, the Center for Latin American and Caribbean Studies, and the Office of International Programs and Studies has provided the necessary grants, stipends, and research assistantships for all the bits and pieces of exploratory, interstitial, and "final" projects that facilitated the necessary thirteen separate field trips to Ecuador. Without such support I could not have maintained the continuous set of contacts with Ecuadorian peoples necessary to comfortably undertake this endeavor.

My personal and intellectual debt to Dorothea Scott (Sibby) Whitten cannot be underestimated. We have shared our experiences with Ecuadorian (and other) peoples in diverse settings, and have discussed and analyzed such experiences and the data derived from them, at length. In the actual editing of this work I came to her constantly when I was stuck, and she took time off from her own research project here in Champaign-Urbana to help with one manuscript or another.

In completing this work, and in reflecting on the processes by which it materialized over the past three years, my main regret is that all of the potential contributors could not be represented. Were they to be here, this work could easily run to two or three volumes.

May 1980
Urbana, Illinois

1

Introduction

Norman E. Whitten, Jr.

with the assistance of Kathleen Fine

Ecuador has moved within the past decade from a basically agrarian economy to the status of an "oil rich" industrializing nation. Its territory, which is about the size of Oregon, encompasses contiguous, contrasting ecosystems as varied as any in the world. It is bisected by two cordilleras of the Andes where habitable zones 6,000-12,000 feet high are punctuated by soaring 15,000-20,000-foot volcanic peaks, eight of them perpetually snow-capped. This is the *Sierra*, often called the "highlands," which today has a population of 3,360,000, or 48% of the nation's seven million people. East of the Sierra is the *Oriente*, "Amazonian lowlands," and to its west is the *Litoral* or *Costa*, "Littoral" or "Coast." The Galápagos Islands are 600 miles away in the Pacific, and Ecuador reckons its famous 200-mile fishing territory from these Pacific islands as well as from the mainland. In this book we are concerned only with mainland Ecuador, and so write of but three divisions.

Foreigners and even inexperienced *serranos*, as the people from the Sierra are called, often hold an image of hellish green flatlands stretching throughout the Amazonian east, and of a continuous beach blotched by urban sprawl along the Pacific coast. Actually, much of the topography of the Oriente resembles the Great Smokey Mountains, and the Coast is, in much of its territory, similar in terrain to the Sierra Nevada of California. Where 3,430,000 people, or 49% of Ecuador's population, live west of the Andes, a mere 3% of those enumerated by the national census live in the Oriente.[1]

Ecuador's capital, Quito, situated in a 9,000-foot-high valley between the cordilleras, is a city of about 800,000 people; until recently it could have been described as a charming blend of colonial and modern architecture washed in a perpetual springlike climate of Andean freshness. Today it is in the throes of urban renewal in its colo-

UNITED STATES

MEXICO

CUBA

COLOMBIA

QUITO ⊚

ECUADOR

GUAYAQUIL

TERRITORIAL LOSS

IQUITOS

PERU

CENTRAL AMERICA

VENEZUELA

GUYANA
SURINAM
FRENCH GUIANA

COLOMBIA

ECUADOR

GALAPAGOS ISLANDS

AMAZON

PERU

BRAZIL

PACIFIC OCEAN

BOLIVIA

CHILE

PARAGUAY

ARGENTINA

ATLANTIC OCEAN

URUGUAY

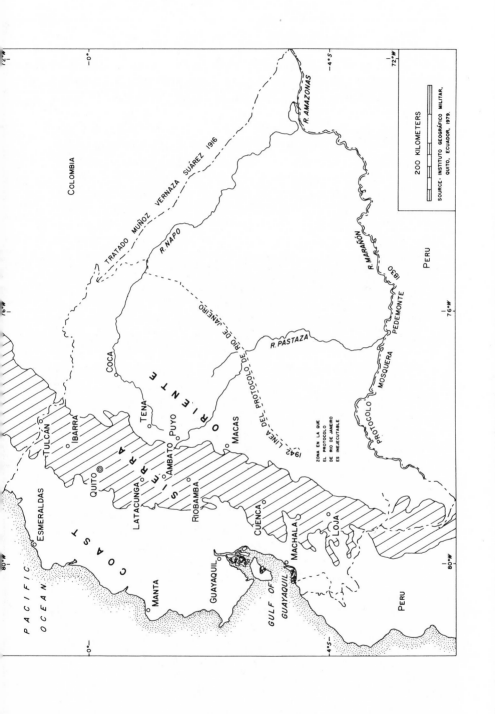

COLOMBIA

TRATADO MUÑOZ VERNAZA SUÁREZ 1916

R. NAPO

R. AMAZONAS

COCA

TENA

R. MARAÑÓN

R. PASTAZA

LÍNEA DEL PROTOCOLO DE RÍO DE JANEIRO 1942

O R I E N T E

AMBATO

PUYO

MACAS

ZONA EN LA QUE
EL PROTOCOLO
DE RÍO DE JANEIRO
ES INEJECUTABLE

S I E R R A

QUITO

LATACUNGA

RIOBAMBA

CUENCA

LOJA

MACHALA

MOSQUERA PEDEMONTE

PROTOCOLO

1830

PERU

C O A S T

TULCÁN

IBARRA

ESMERALDAS

MANTA

GUAYAQUIL

GULF OF GUAYAQUIL

MACHALA

PERU

P A C I F I C
O C E A N

80°W

80°W

76°W

72°W

72°W

0°

0°

4°S

4°S

200 KILOMETERS

SOURCE: INSTITUTO GEOGRÁFICO MILITAR,
QUITO, ECUADOR, 1979.

nial center and in massive construction and territorial expansion on its modern periphery. Some outlying villages consumed by sprawling suburbs are now threatened with demolition to clear space for a new international airport. The present airport is a proposed site for government offices which are being squeezed out of the old downtown area by congestion unrelieved by a lattice of new highways, bypasses, and tunnels. Everywhere cement dust mingles with diesel fumes, and heavy rainfall creates mud slides which block brand new roadways.

The history of Quito is one of transition from a pre-Incaic coordinating hub of trade and agriculture (Salomon 1978), to northern capital of the Inca empire, on through its central *audiencia* position under Spanish colonial rule (Hurtado 1977), to, since 1830, its present seat of national administration.

Throughout its history this urban hierarchy of sacred and social constituents has derived its power from access to Oriente and Littoral resources, as well as from control over rich and varied foodstuffs and other resources from within the Sierra. Today Quito remains a bastion of conservatism and Catholic Christianity.

In sharp contrast to Andean Quito is Guayaquil, the sprawling Pacific port on the turbid Guayas River. As the largest city in Ecuador with a population of over one million, Guayaquil is the locus of commercial, banking, industrial, and agribusiness power. Like Quito, Guayaquil is urbane, but in an open, secular, boisterous, achievement-oriented way. Its pre-Columbian maritime economy was transformed in response to colonial shipping requirements, making its power dependent upon international demand for such raw materials as balsa, kapok, quinine, cotton, and rubber and such food as cacao, coffee, rice, and bananas. Its national strength lies not in preserving Andean hierarchy but in challenging it. Guayaquil, as the metropolitan basis for coastal power, serves not only as ecological-economic counterpoint to Quito but as a challenge to conservatism and Catholicism as well. Guayaquil is liberal, at times revolutionary.

The "tale of two cities"[2] conjoins Pacific Littoral and Andean Sierra in a never-ending series of relationships so that it is nearly impossible to discuss one without the other. The Quito-Guayaquil ecological and economic complementarity and interdependence have generated pervasive sets of mutually reinforcing stereotypes involving coastal and Andean life generally, and it is deceptively easy to draw the conclusion that the Littoral and Sierra are separate worlds, tenuously conjoined but destined to exist forever apart. This is not the case, as we shall see. The articulating relationships between Coast and Sierra are *dialectical*—they are based on a systemization of enduring and emergent regional contrasts which stimulate collective, ideological processes toward nationalist synthesis.[3]

A popular political slogan often emblazoned on official governmental stationery proclaims this synthesis: ¡el *Ecuador ha sido, es y será, país amazónico!* "Ecuador has been, is and will be, an Amazonian country!" This assertion may seem to some a mere ideological masking of harsh geopolitical and economic realities, a stirring nationalist rallying cry for a country caught in an impossible set of contradictory forces between coastal and sierran power bases. Historically, the cry emanates from the loss of Amazonian territory to foreign nations, which has reduced Ecuador by nearly 75% over the past two centuries. Most immediately, it arises from the loss of half its remaining Amazonian territory—the half containing all navigable rivers entering the Amazon River—during Peru's invasion of 1941 and the subsequent tenuous settlement in Río de Janeiro.[4] Although Brazil took the side of Ecuador, Peru prevailed when the United States joined the victor. The Oriente might well be considered an unrealistic, romantic nationalist synthesis to pervasive Andean-coastal sociocultural dialectics. Indeed, one of Ecuador's most famous past presidents, Galo Plaza Lasso, once declared it to be "a myth." But it is mythical only if its population, on the one hand, and its contribution in commercial agricultural produce and raw materials to the gross national product, on the other hand, are considered. Oil was discovered there in the 1930s, and more recent exploration for and exploitation of petroleum in the Oriente have catapulted Ecuador into the world of OPEC nations.[5]

The territory of the Oriente, especially its exploitable subsurface "Texas tea," promises a viable base for an economic resolution of the Sierra-Coast cultural dialectic and political counterpoint. Moreover, the slogan of Amazonian sovereignty ideologically validates the nationalist, developmental, capitalist realpolitik of this Andean nation. Until the undulating 318-mile-long oil pipeline fueled its nation's economy, Quito's administrative power was dependent upon coastal shipping and agribusiness, which, in turn, were partially dependent upon world demand for a few tropical products. Now, Quito's economic power, derived from Amazonian sources, equals or exceeds that of Guayaquil. But this new Quiteño power depends largely on the high energy consumption and industrial demands of the most developed nations.

POLITICAL ECONOMY

The economy of modern Ecuador is aptly summarized in the NACLA Latin America and Empire Report, *Ecuador: Oil up for Grabs* (1975:18):

> . . . industrialization . . . has made great strides over the past five years. But the nature of this process has not signified an improvement in social conditions, and least of all a decline in dependency. The nationalism manifest in the government's policies toward oil, territorial waters and tuna-fishing, has only been extended to industry in the feeblest manner imaginable. . . . The results of industrialization thus far have been the strengthened hegemony of *foreign* capital, increased dependency on *foreign* imports for industry, and the establishment of capital-intensive industries that suit the needs of *foreign* economies.

The basic nationalist strategy to "sow" soaring petroleum revenues in infrastructural development of roads, air transportation, and hydroelectric projects provides precisely what is needed for foreign development of such products as pharmaceuticals, refined petroleum products, and petrochemicals. Although the government took some strong nationalist measures in protecting its oil deposits and territorial waters, it has been more reluctant to extend such controls to industry and agribusiness.

With a growth rate of 3.2 to 3.5%, Ecuador's population may double in less than 22 years, making this one of the world's fastest growing populations. As this expansion of mostly poor people presses extant resources, national dependency on oil revenues will increase greatly. Yet the nation's output is relatively small. According to Sanders (1977:10–11) and various editorials in national newspapers, the country may in fact be forced to meet its burgeoning technological requirements by importing petroleum in the 1980s. Moreover, Ecuador's dependency on industrial demands of other nations is transformed into the politics of the republic through an interlocking oligarchy (Hurtado 1977:175–83). "The dominant economic groups in Ecuador, though not necessarily identified with any particular political parties, are in fact more powerful than any parties" (Sanders 1977:4).

The ideal of the nation, manifest in official statements, in editorials, and as heard everywhere, is to be a democratic, progressive, capitalist country (in Stavenhagen's 1968 terms); but the ideal is seemingly strangled by dependency relations (see, e.g., Galarza 1978; also Cockcroft, Gunder Frank, and Johnson 1972). Overall, Ecuadorian politics oscillates between elections featuring several parties with great internal dissensus, and military takeovers. The time of military rule increased recently to nine years, giving scope to a system of "centralized, technocratic bureaucratic approach to policy making" (Collier 1978).[6] Within this system of oscillating control of the central bureaucracy, presidents tend to be ousted before they complete their elected term. The form of military government, or administration, is likely to undergo further changes—a dictator ousted by a junta, or a junta taken over by a dictator—before free elections are restored. This political periodicity of succession leads most analysts from Blanksten (1951) to Hurtado (1977:143–44) and Sanders (1977) to insist that the republic is among the least stable in Latin America.[7] If, however, one considers the pendulumlike swing from civilian to military, from election to coup, from alliance to realliance, and the continuous re-emergence of familiar personalities, emphases, and complaints, we could consider this to be quite a stable political system. Institutionalized dissensus promotes disequilibrium, which is a central motivating mechanism for stability (see, e.g., Adams 1978).[8]

There are certain contrastive styles to Ecuadorian politics which are worth illustrating, even if they are difficult to "classify" with regard to standard political analysis labels. *Caudillismo* is the ability of a person to draw support from opposing parties and interests in a situation of crisis over particular issues, and to therefore emerge as "leader" of the majority. But the *caudillo* must also contend with the opposition of a majority. For example, the late *caudillo* José María Velasco Ibarra was president of Ecuador five times over a nearly 40-year period, but he only completed one full four-year term of office. During his fifth term he actually staged a military coup to topple his own Velasquista party; this *caudillo*-military alliance was subsequently toppled by another military coup in 1972, placing full control in the hands of the armed forces in the name of the Partido Revolucionario Nacional, Nationalist Revolutionary Party. Later, the military president of this party, General Guillermo Rodríguez Lara, was deposed by a bloodless military countercoup (following a bloody failure the year before), leading NACLA to characterize nationalist political ideology by the slogan "1970s: signal left, turn right." This right-wing counterfaction of the armed forces graciously waited until the end of the president's daughter's wedding, and then allowed him to "escape" to his home in Pujilí prior to making its move (which itself had already been reported earlier that evening on national television).

This is a rather "light" side of political style. On the heavy side lies the specter of naked power wielded from the pinnacle of authority

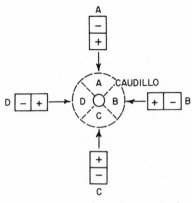

FIGURE 1. *Caudillo* drawing support from factions in four rival parties.

and the locus of bureaucratic control (see, e.g., León Ramírez 1979). For example, on 30 November 1978 the leader of the Frente Radical Alfarista (FRA), the Radical Alfarist Front, was shot in Guayaquil by a man known as "Fat Louie" (*el gordo Lucho*); he died nine days later in a Miami hospital. The trail from Fat Louie to his paymaster allegedly led to the minister of government, General Bolívar Jarrín Cahueñas, a liberal leader within the central, ruling, military junta who had initiated the process of "rational institutionalization" of national political-economic processes some three years earlier. The step-by-step revelations leading to the formal accusation of Jarrín as the person ordering the assassination of a leading spokesman of legitimate, civilian political opposition to the military's own presidential candidate, Sixto Durán Ballén, were published almost daily in the nation's papers and reported continuously, hour by hour, over national radio. In early 1979 the basic issues in Ecuador were whether the military or civilian courts should sit in judgment of Jarrín, and whether his central role within the dictatorship was "active" or "suspended" (see, e.g., *Nueva* 1979). Commenting on the centralized military dictatorship aimed at the immediate use of petroleum revenues to create a "stable" political order, and to return this order to civilian control through "free elections," journalist Jaime Chaves Granja publicly and prominently characterized the political year 1978 as one of "drama, comedy, and farce" (Chaves Granja 1979).

The forces generating order within Ecuadorian politics can be described as a centripetal-centrifugal paradox. The centripetal force centers on a powerful leader (whether individual *caudillo* or corporate military candidate) who arises in a crisis (which he himself may precipitate) to gain a majority of support drawn from opposing forces or

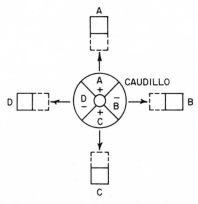

FIGURE 2. *Caudillo* losing support to four rival parties.

factions. This centripetal force is countered by a centrifugal one which develops as the powerful leader consolidates his opponents' alliances. A reduplication or re-creation of factionalism within the *caudillo*'s party occurs, and his opponents' parties are again strengthened. Most Ecuadorian presidents find themselves contending with the continued opposition of all of the sides from which support is initially drawn, as well as with other opposing groups. This phenomenon is illustrated in Figures 1 and 2.

One could dichotomize civilian-political *caudillismo* and military dictatorship as alternative forms of government; the first excessively democratic, promoting anarchy, the second totalitarian. But in Ecuador they tend to complement one another, and even merge from time to time through the centripetal/centrifugal paradox at work in the oscillation born of fundamental institutionalized dissensus producing centralized stability. This portrayal of Ecuadorian political oscillation in no way negates the role of formal political parties, which, just before the elections in April 1979, included various allied or partially allied combinations of conservatives, liberals, independents, and radicals with loose platforms proclaiming the competition of Christian Democracy, Marxist Leninism, Progressive Capitalism, Socialism, and Populism. But this position does stress that the party alliances and oppositions must be seen within the broader framework of *caudillo*-military oscillation, the economic oligarchy, and increasing dependency on industrial nations' demands (Drekonja et al. 1978).

Today the economic transformations brought about by oil exploitation and exportation are producing a tremendous class, status, and lifestyle hiatus between rich and poor (see, e.g., Instituto de Investi-

gaciones Sociales . . . 1977, Moncayo 1977, Stavenhagen 1975). Sanders (1977:3) writes, "The linkages between the economic leaders of
Ecuador have . . . prevented a sharp clash of interests sufficient to
replace more basic cleavages like those between Coast and Sierra or
clerical and anticlerical." The present and potential role of the
"middle class," or "middle sector," remains problematic, just as the
nature of achievement and ascription of roles and statuses within
burgeoning bureaucracies remain unclear (see, e.g., Oszlak 1978).
The gross national product rose nearly 300% in four years (between
1972 and 1976), per capita income little more than doubled during
that period, and current inflation is 15% per year. Imported luxury
and consumer goods have saturated the nation, and subsistence agriculture, for the poor, is as important now as in the recent past. In
spite of being drawn into the vortex of dependency upon cash for
minimal well-being, poor people often have difficulty purchasing the
basic foodstuffs. In turn, the planned, bureaucratic-technocratic efforts of nationalist consolidation are themselves increasingly dependent upon wealthy industrial nations that offer alternative, competing models of political economic control, and impose new ideologies
and constraints. Overall, the political economy which maintained the
oppressively stable multi-ethnic dual society through past centuries
(Hurtado 1977) is extending and re-creating a greater social and economic schism in the revised, modern, dual society under the impress
of development (Galarza 1978).[9]
  Let us now sketch the administrative order through which control
is ideally channeled. The country is divided first into provinces, of
which there are ten in the Sierra, five in the Littoral (one of which,
Los Ríos, is completely inland with no coastline whatsoever), and
four in the Oriente (see map). Each of these has a governor, and each
province is divided into *cantones*, cantons, and subdivided into *parroquias*, parishes. Cantons are headed by a *jefe político*, chief administrative official, and the parish head is called *teniente político*, "political
lieutenant." Fluctuations at national, regional, or local levels tend to
produce changes in personnel in canton and parish structure, and
political parties are involved in such changes even when no election
is held or when the country is under military rule. Although research
is still sorely lacking on this, limited information suggests strongly
that the structure of local and regional political economy is based on
networks of individuals who manipulate economic, social, ethnic,
family, and kinship ties to maintain a strong foothold in groups
which may be in a competitive situation when alteration in the administrative order takes place.

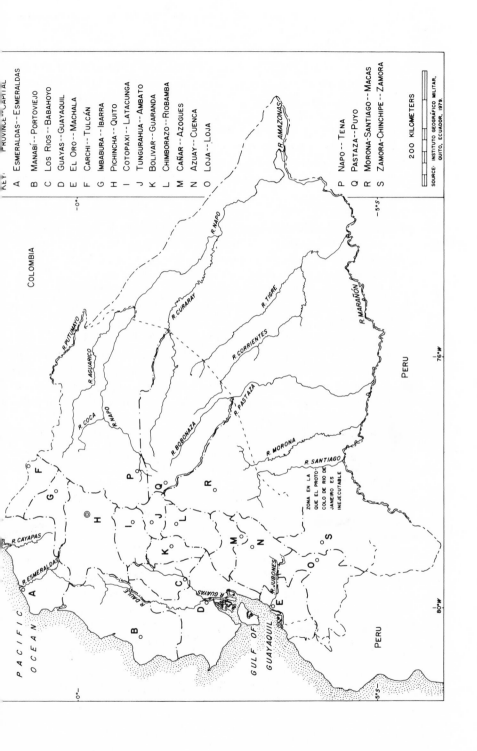

Within the province, canton, and parish subdivisions there are alternative forms of organization, especially cooperatives formed for colonization and the *comunas*, communes, which are putative "self-governing" collective territorial-administrative units under either *de jure* or *de facto* control of a parish or canton. In addition to this administrative set of organization hierarchies, there are the relationships of city-town-*barrio* (neighborhood) divisions, hierarchies of national-regional-local courts, of the national and rural police, of municipal works and public health organizations, and a system of urban and rural markets.

Periodically the military may take over aspects of *de jure* or *de facto* control of any of these administrative systems. In general, the greater the control by the military, the greater the competition between military and police, sometimes resulting in confrontations between police and military personnel.

Finally, there are the great haciendas, landed estates, which have exerted a tremendous political force through all of Ecuador's history. The landholding role and concomitant power of the Catholic church were seriously undermined in the early twentieth century by state expropriation; thereafter church domination was mostly at the parish level. Control over landed forces, private, state, and church, remains in the hands of an oligarchy. Split though the oligarchy may be between agribusiness-oriented kindreds and retrograde prominent gentry (see Hurtado 1977:175–83, Drekonja et al. 1978), its class, ethnic, and family linkages constitute the controlling structure of banking and commerce. This integrated coastal-sierran political-economic structure, in turn, is controlled by a closely knit network of national and international elite (Naranjo 1978).

Both private and state haciendas were confronted by the thrust of modern land redistribution beginning around 1964 with the formation of the Ecuadorian Institute of Agrarian Reform and Colonization (IERAC). In this "revolutionary" reorganization the state mainly changed state haciendas into cooperatives where previously "bound" peasants were allowed to lay claim to unused or underutilized land. On the private haciendas such bound peasants were often given no more than formal title to their traditional meager holdings. Massive colonization into the Oriente and some coastal sectors was encouraged, and a stepped-up promotion of agribusiness and cattle ranching was launched and supported through new systems of bank loans and business incentives. Once again, NACLA is most precise and unequivocal in its portrayal of the revolutionary thrust of agrarian reform against the buttress of oligarchy-controlled land (see also Hurtado 1977, Grayson 1975, Naranjo n.d.):

> The distributive side of agrarian reform in Ecuador has been decidedly abandoned, displaced by a strategy of cooperation between the government and landowners to raise production and revenues. Even the minimal land area that has been distributed since 1973 corresponds in large part to a strategy of colonization. In May, 1975 the President announced that 346,000 hectares had been distributed to 12,500 families. Eighty-six percent of that land, however, represented newly colonized areas brought under cultivation without access to credit or technical assistance. Colonization has, in fact, become the escape valve for the government's promises of land for the peasantry. (NACLA 1975:18)

The *de facto–de jure* relationships between landed forces and the putative counterforces of land reform and colonization also affect the operation of province, canton, and parish.[10]

Velasco Ibarra once said, "Ecuador is a very difficult country to govern." Familiarity with formal administrative units and revolutionary reorganization of land distribution is essential to an understanding of the formal structure of modern Ecuador. Nonetheless, it is impossible to understand much of anything about the nation's transformation without first considering holistically the relationships between ecosystems, modern national infrastructure, and pervasive cultural pluralism.

NATIONALIST DEVELOPMENTALISM AND SURGENT ETHNICITY

Ecuador is a culturally plural country now undergoing centralized, planned integration through uniform nationalist development strategies wherein the discrepancies between rich and poor are heightened by the very programs established to alleviate them (see, e.g., Whitten 1976, Naranjo 1978, Hurtado 1977). The republic's major ethnic groupings, from a nationalist standpoint, include black Ecuadorians (*negro, zambo, moreno*) in lowland and highland settings, Andean Quichua-speaking "Indian" Ecuadorians (*indio, longo, indígena, nativo, Runa*), tropical forest native peoples (*indio, indígena, nativo, ribereños, selváticos, salvajes*) in western and eastern rainforests, and various groupings and categorical sets of putative "mixed racial groups" (*mestizo, cholo, chazo, montuvio, zambo, mulato, claro*). People so tagged, and in some cases so self-identifying, in certain contexts, are especially apparent in their cultural diversity in the regions where resources currently sought after by foreign nations—oil, timber, land for agribusiness—are concentrated. It sometimes seems that there are few "true nationals" in a given Ecuadorian region. To effect a nationalist transformation in the interface between international industrial economic demands and regional and local cultural-ecological, social, and ideological variety, Ecuadorian developers, governed by coherent, doctrinaire political nationalism, attempt to apply strategies of development which are based upon the ideology and designs of North American industrial growth. These designs, their infrastructural basis, and the consequent bureaucratic planning, control, and management are usually quite inadequate in the tropical forest ecosystems, arid coastal-monsoon ecosystems, and Andean ecosystems to which they are applied.

In coastal, sierran, and Amazonian regions people who are ethnically tagged as nonnational (and nonnational*ist*) practice kinds of ecosystem maintenance which are strikingly divergent from techniques recommended by specialists from industrial nations who train Ecuadorian planners. For example, in the rainforest tropical lowlands the complex of polycultural swidden horticulture of starchy crops, extensive use of manioc "beer," hunting strategies permeated with food taboos to regularize a supply of game animals and birds in a dispersed habitat, and concentrated exploitation of insect larvae together with riparian resources such as fish, turtles and their eggs, caimans and their eggs, shrimp, crabs, and other crustaceans, is fundamental to Amazonian ecosystems. This system of "tropical forest cultural ecology" is usually viewed by planners as an undesirable remnant of an archaic past. Ridged field horticulture in sections of the monsoon, semiarid coast, preservation of sections of the mangrove swamp for exploitation of shellfish in the northwest rainforest coast, Andean indigenous forms of irrigation and crop rotation, vertical exploitation of different microecologies (Crespi 1968, Murra 1975, Salomon 1978), and transhumance (Stewart, Belote, and Belote 1976) in the Sierra are all often viewed as archaic systems stemming from the colonial era when ignorance of progressive developmental capitalism led to centuries of stagnation. Blacks, Indians, and all of the stereotypic mixtures of such reputedly inferior groupings are seen as requiring national identity referents and transformation of economy from one harmonious with a given ecosystem to one based on planned, uniform practices producing legally marketable products with specified monetary worth. Modern developmental ideology insists that the worth of a people is bound up in the commercial worth of a region, and the concept of region itself is based on a concentration of marketable products (coffee region, sugar region, banana region). Within a country that contains one of the most complex, diverse sets of contrasting ecosystems in the world, planners adhere to an ideology of development wherein standardization of economic processes has priority over ecosystem parameters.

Ethnically "nonnational" peoples, especially the Afro-Hispanic population of the northwest rainforest-coastal zone of Ecuador-Colombia (Whitten 1965, 1974; Whitten and Friedemann 1974) and the indigenous populations of the Upper Amazon of Ecuador (Harner 1972; Philippe Descola and Anne-Christine Taylor, personal communications; Whitten 1976; Macdonald 1979; Vickers 1976; Robinson 1979) are generally excluded from direct participation in planning changes in their habitat. The nationalization effort of Ecuador, with its Quito-Guayaquil contrapuntal centralization, like that of sister nations struggling in the grip of Euro-American dependency, often proclaims an ideology of ethnic homogenization. The product of homogenization is sometimes called *el hombre ecuatoriano*, but this promise of "inclusion" as "Ecuadorian man" is contradicted by a focus on white supremacy. The practical process of excluding those considered to be nonmixed is carried out by the very persons who espouse an ideology of inclusion based on racial mixture, *mestizaje*, and the resulting contradiction is obvious to ethnically identifiable black *costeño* and black *serrano* Ecuadorians as well as to indigenous Ecuadorian peoples. Additionally, the superficially inclusive claims of *mestizaje* ideology are further undercut by a tacit qualifying clause which ups the price of admission from mere "phenotypical mixture" to cultural *blanqueamiento* ("whitening," in terms of becoming more urban, more Christian, more civilized; less rural, less black, less Indian).[11] This compounds the contradiction by continuously generating internal dissension and dissensus within "mixed categories."

In reaction to nationalist penetration of their ecosystems, denigration of their cosmological principles, and insults to their knowledge, indigenous, "mixed," and Afro-American peoples of contemporary Ecuador may express resistance to ecosystem and social alteration. People may do this directly, through organized or spontaneous protest, or indirectly, through ceremonial enactment and symbolism. In expressive dimensions, allusions to mythical allegories are made so that direct communication can take place within the excluded group while outside "developers" see only puzzlingly nonnational, cultist retentions of supposedly primitive lifeways. The overall effect is that Ecuador seems to be nationalizing and becoming more diverse at the same time. As so-called "primitive" or "tribal" cultures of the Oriente and Coast rapidly disappear, ethnic systems which defy stereotypic pigeonholing emerge. One may see remarkable continuity of form or equally remarkable transformation of form, the apparent paradox being no more than an artifice of conceptual or analytical inadequacy. The more ecosystems, social systems, and public ideological systems are moulded by nationalist developmental strategies, the more intensive and allusive become the countercultural reactions.

Every system in Ecuador is in the throes of cultural transformation; every system seems at some level paradoxical. Here is where the anthropological canons of holism in descriptive ethnography (Adams 1978) and comparative analysis may lead to insight into cultural process and structure. The nation of Ecuador has a relatively small territory (but "normal" by west European standards). Its various convergent and divergent programs for "development" and "progress" are framed by an ideology of planned, centralized, directed change. In this nationalizing context one cannot help but see nationalist ideology within local scenarios, the large scale in the small scale, the macrocosm in the microcosm. Moreover, in the process of cultural transformation within Ecuador there are remarkable continuities. The designation *blanco*, white in terms of national standards, is inextricably linked with high status, wealth, power, national culture, civilization, Christianity, urbanity, and development; its opposites are *indio*, Indian, and *negro*, black. The false resolution of the opposites is found in the doctrine of *mestizaje*, the ideology of racial mixture implying *blanqueamiento*, whitening. *Stereotypically*, the ideology is related to the Sierra-Littoral dialectic, and Oriente ideological resolution, as follows (see, e.g., Estrada Ycaza 1977:31–42).

The Sierra is divided between whites and Indians, the former progressive, the latter backward. Indians are linked as rural bumpkins to the urban centers through the market, and are therefore regarded as the unfortunate result of colonial economic integration. The Coast is already rather well mixed and, except in the northwest, is not culturally plural, but (continuing this *stereotypic* list) the mixture contains sufficient African and Indian blood as to create an unruly, unstable regional character structure. From the *serrano's* standpoint, people there speak "like monkeys" rather than "like Christians," and the urbanity is of the street rather than of "society." In the Oriente, to continue the grossly stereotypic portrayal, tribal Indians have nearly vanished, and the survivors of regrettable ethnocide have "forgotten" their own heritage. Nationally centralized control must, therefore, be exerted over the region if it is not to once again fall beyond the pale of the republic's developmental power. Those who speak for the Oriente are pioneers with their whiteness emerging.

Nationalist synthesis here cannot be held back by Andean pluralism or *costeño* regional character. The continuity of form embedded in these stereotypes emerges strongly: whiteness is superior, the white Sierra is superior, modern Indians are inferior, blacks are essentially nonexistent except in the unruly legacy found in *costeño* blood. These stereotypes permeate the nationalist developmentalism now transforming the republic.

Centralized control of the nation's basic and commercial resources is being facilitated by a rapidly expanding modern infrastructure of roads and air transportation, backed up by regional offices of planned development, including schools, public services, and the like. But this control over resources extends not only to actual observable and material well-being but also to the symbolic life of Ecuador's people. To illustrate, to *work* in a cane field is to be placed in a symbolic environment where upward mobility is nearly impossible, where one is categorically stereotyped as "poor," in need of "development," in need of education, in need of more national governmental support to survive in the modernizing nation. It is to be placed in a symbolic position of personal dependency upon developmental ideology as well as in an economic position of personal dependency upon developmental activity.

Ethnicity and class both interrelate and clash in modern Ecuador, and boundaries between ethnic and class systems sometimes merge, sometimes rigidify, and sometimes dissolve. From the nationalist perspective, poor Indians are poor *because* they are Indians, but wealthier Indians are such in spite of their "race." Poor whites or poor *mestizos*, however, are poor because of the state of the nation, because of its failure to homogenize—the poor non-Indian can blame his poverty on the very fact of continued indigenous existence.

Culture History and Political Episodes

"Indigenous existence" in Ecuador has often been erroneously portrayed as the surviving remnants of ancient marginals who existed in pockets of cultural enclosures on the fringe of the "great areas" of aboriginal development—the high civilizations of Mesoamerica and the Central Andes (see, e.g., Linke 1960:15). Today, thanks to the synthesis which took place during the assemblage of archaeological art treasures from Ecuador, and a debate culminating in fresh field research (e.g., Meggers 1966; Lathrap 1970, 1973; Lathrap, Marcos, and Zeidler 1977; Zevallos et al. 1977), we now know that "intensive farming, permanent villages, and developed ceramics were at least

1,000 years older in Ecuador than in Peru and Mexico . . .[evidence for maize cultivation in the Guayas basin now dates back 5,000 years]. The new information from Ecuador calls for basic revisions of the accepted theories on the origins of New World Civilizations. We see an active trade moving outward from Ecuador between 1800 and 800 B.C., which stimulated the spread of Ecuadorian technology, art motifs, and ideas to Peru and the Pacific coasts of Guatemala and Mexico" (Collier 1975:8). The formative stage of the archaeological record of Ecuador refers to the period during which "a truly effective agricultural system had been achieved, but before fully urban conditions and state-size social units appeared" (Lathrap, Collier, and Chandra 1975:13). This critical period of cultural creativity and technological transformation seems to occur in Ecuador before it makes its appearance elsewhere.

As agricultural efficiency is extended or curtailed by new political controls, the shape of indigenous economies changes until, one after another, new levels of dominance are reached and new relationships forged. To understand this process in ancient Ecuador, two points must be made. The first is that we may think in terms of three major ecological dimensions to culture history of South America—maritime, Andean, and Amazonian. The second point is that in Ecuador these dimensions are forced together by the topography so that innovations in one area may penetrate another rapidly, and so that lattices of communication, trade, and political control can be extended effectively in novel ways as well as by well-known means (see, e.g., Lathrap 1974).

The actual pre-Incaic political episodes are still inchoate (see Jijón y Caamaño 1945 and Meggers 1966 for sequences of culture history). It is certainly clear that Ecuador was blessed by vibrant native cultural systems, some of which undoubtedly sent out stimuli which may have ramified all the way to the Mississippi valley in North America (Lathrap, personal communication).

The Incaic political episode began in the mid-fifteenth century, and by about 1480 Quito was its northern capital (see, e.g., Hemming 1970, Huamán Poma 1978 [ca. 1567], Burgos 1975, Meyers 1976) whence campaigns to subdue other native peoples to the north (near the present border of Colombia) were waged. Fifty years later Francisco Pizarro and 180 Spanish soldiers entered the scene at a time of Incaic civil war when Quiteño Incas, led by Atahualpa, were fighting the Cuzco Incas, ruled by his half-brother Huáscar. With the Spanish crown's rapid decapitation of the Incaic bureaucracy and assumption of imperial control, royal influence from a bureaucratic pinnacle was extended down through chains of relationships in regional and local areas. We know little about these systems except through sparse (but accumulating) archaeological material, fragmentary ethnographic analogies, and reports from the Inca, mixed Spanish-Inca, and especially Spanish chroniclers. The Inca probably introduced the Quechua language, as Quichua, into highland Ecuador, and they certainly promoted its usage as a political lingua franca there. The Spanish introduced Spanish, but Quichua also continued to spread as lingua franca.

As the Spanish took over Quito, began the exploration of the Amazon, and sought to establish a viable Pacific port to link them to the rest of the Spanish empire in the New World and shortly thereafter to Asia, Afro-American peoples began their own conquest of the northern rainforest, in what is now Esmeraldas province. By the mid-sixteenth century self-liberated African slaves and their offspring controlled what was known as the "Zambo Republic." As the "Kingdom of Quito" became a royal *audiencia* of the Spanish crown in 1563, and began to develop bureaucratic controls eastward into Amazonia and westward to the Coast, it was forced to make alliances with the rulers of the Zambo republic, on the latter's terms (see, e.g., Phelan 1967, Whitten 1974). The colonial era lasted for 300 years and bore witness to large-scale depopulation owing to disease, the growth of a caste system, the continued independence of people in most of the tropical lowland areas, and the introduction of new crops and animals (especially sheep) from the Old World. Through it all there were uprisings, revolts, revolutions, movements of self-assertion (Moreno 1976, Albornoz 1976), and, undoubtedly, relationships promoting subsistence, trade, commerce, and cultural coherence below the level of colonial bureaucratic control.

National holidays which proclaim the sequence of events leading to the 150 years of republican history are the 10th of August (1809), "shout for independence," in Quito, and the 24th of May (1822), "Battle of Pichincha," viewed by Quiteños from their houses (after which the *presidencia* of Quito joined the Confederation of Gran Colombia, together with present-day Colombia and Venezuela). In 1830 Ecuador became an independent nation, gained its name, and began a tumultuous history racked with ethnic clashes (see, e.g., Linke 1960:23–26) and dominated by a white minority. A unifying force between about 1860 and 1875 was that of a conservative-Catholic alliance aimed at infrastructural development and consolidation of the *blanco* elite's position, against that of the army, which was rife with blacks and *mestizos*. As conservatism reigned, liberalism grew, the former linked to the Sierra, the latter to the Coast. Twenty years after the assassination of the conservative leader Gabriel García Moreno in Quito, civil war broke out, and, under the leadership of the re-nowned *costeño* liberal Eloy Alfaro, the political pendulum swung left and Alfaro became president of the republic in 1897. During the liberal regime attempts at infrastructural development continued, now with the help of North American, British, and French capital. Alfaro fell to a liberal-conservative coalition during his second term in office, and another civil war erupted. Alfaro and others were arrested and then thrown to a crowd from jail, to be dismembered and burned in Quito on 28 January 1912. Esmeraldas then came back into the national political theater as the former Zambo republic became the bastion of liberalism backed up by military guerrilla resistance.

Decline of dependence on the world market because of World War I, according to Linke (1960:27), calmed the violence and civil disorder and ushered in an era of internal development. But as dependency on world trade reasserted itself, violence again became common until, within the oscillating system of political economic control, "the army, chiefly composed of *serranos* . . . , rebelled like one man and proclaimed the end of the coastal banks' domination and the beginning of a new political era . . ." (Linke 1960:27). Between 1925 and the present, Ecuador's political history is aptly summarized by the system of *caudillo*-military oscillation described above. Its boom-bust economy based on cacao, then bananas, supported a wealthy, learned, internationally oriented elite, but otherwise maintained the people as among the poorest in Latin America, in 1960 (Herring 1961:535–36). Petroleum turned a near bust to boom in the mid-1960s, but the boom itself has peaked. Dependency increases, the oligarchy stays strong, the poor remain without necessary economic wherewithal, but Ecuador's culture history rushes on, awaiting the next political episode.

Language and Culture

Spanish is the national language of Ecuador, but it is spoken very differently depending on region, ethnic group, and socioeconomic class. Quichua, a dialect of Quechua, is also spoken throughout the Sierra, in much of the Oriente, and here and there in the Littoral, but it is not universally understood. Although there are bilingual schools where young children are taught in both Quichua and Spanish, the Ministry of Education does not allow Quichua to be substituted for English, say, as a "second language." Quechua was the lingua franca of the imperial Inca, and it may, or may not, have been spoken in Andean and lowland Ecuador prior to the Incaic conquest. Today its speakers range from Colombia to Argentina and include perhaps eight million people, making it by far the most common indigenous language spoken in the Americas.

Throughout Ecuador there is a creole language, often called *media lengua* in Spanish, *chaupi shimi* in Quichua, or *chaupi lengua* in Chaupilengua (Muysken 1975–76), which is composed of a Spanish vocabulary and Quichua grammatical base. Black *costeños* of Esmeraldas province also speak a somewhat creolized Spanish, sharing this dialect (which has not yet been described by a linguist) and their Afro-Hispanic culture with congeners of the Colombian coast.

In Esmeraldas province and in adjacent areas of Pichincha and Imbabura, there are two groups of people who speak related, mutually intelligible dialects of the Barbacoan division of Chibcha languages which are divided into Cayapa in the north and Tsatchela ("Colorado") in the south. Just north of Cayapa territory live the Coaiquer, who speak a related language which is not understood by the Cayapa and Tsatchela. Moreover, many Cayapa, Tsatchela, and Coaiquer speak Spanish somewhat like black *costeños*, and some also speak other indigenous languages, such as Quichua, Chocó (Colombian Emberá or Noanamá) and perhaps Páez (spoken in southern Colombia).

In the Oriente the spread of Quichua is nearly matched by the Shuar language, to which it is not related. Smaller language groupings include Cofán, Siona-Secoya, Waorani "Auca," and Zaparoan, about which more will be said in Parts I and IV of this work.

One point which must be made as clearly as possible if the bulk of materials presented in this book are to be understood is that indigenous people have no term even remotely resembling "Indian" or *indio* in their native vocabulary. The concept enters their cultural repertoires only as a category imposed by Spanish speakers. Quichua-speaking people consider themselves to be *Runa*, humans; Shuar-speaking people consider themselves to be *Shuar*, humans; Waorani-speaking people consider themselves to be *Waorani*, humans; Cofán-speaking people consider themselves to be *a'i*, humans. Each has its own sets of ethnic terms, which vary considerably according to language spoken, geography, and economic, political, social, cultural, and ethnic relations. These forms do not parallel nationalist categories, although they sometimes reverse or invert them.

Another point which must be understood (using Quichua as exemplar) is that a person, group, or aggregate may speak both Quichua and Spanish without identifying as Runa, without identifying as *indígena*, and without identifying as *blanco* or *mestizo*. Some *cholos* in various parts of Ecuador fit such a situation. Moreover, people such as the Puyo Runa in the Oriente may identify as national, nationa*list*, and Runa all at the same time, intermarry with Shuar people and proclaim themselves utterly distinct from, and alien to, the Shuar world in certain contexts and belonging to the Shuar world in other contexts.

This is not a book about the "white people," "black folk," "Indian and mixed peasants," and "disappearing forest tribes" of Ecuador. The political economy is organized in such a fashion with *mestizaje* as a false synthesis, but the peoples themselves of this small, dynamic nation sort things out in many, many ways. They do so not only within the framework sketched above but also through creative resynthesis of ecology, social structure, and ideology.

CULTURAL TRANSFORMATIONS AND ETHNICITY IN MODERN ECUADOR

This book represents an anthropological exploration of the facets, dimensions, and dynamics of ethnicity, cultural continuity, and cultural change as they converge and diverge within the boundaries of a Third World nation undergoing processes of radical transformation. Most of the papers illustrate what could be called contemporary critical anthropology (e.g., Bonfil Batalla 1970, Bodley 1975, Clastres 1977) in its international dimension. Critical anthropology comments meaningfully on the consequences of nation-state expansion and consolidation for the peoples constituted within its sphere of influence and control. It addresses recognized issues of contemporary relevance for the nation-state or any of its subject peoples. But it also delves into unrecognized or seemingly irrelevant issues to explicate relationships not apparent in the usual process of government planning and development.

Ethnography is fundamental to cultural anthropology. Although sometimes stigmatized as atheoretical in its scope and premises, it is best conceptualized as part and parcel of comparative ethnology which cannot exist in its generalizing dimensions without continuous ethnographic vigor. The ethnographic enterprise itself, of course, is predicated on continuous confrontation of theoretical constructs with fresh data. In turn, ethnographic data "exist" only insofar as methodological sophistication, itself a result of increasing theoretic competence of the investigator, is manifest. Inasmuch as post–World War

II nation-states are cultural systems driven by nationalist forces involving a generative set of ideological premises relating to pervasive incorporation of subject peoples, the ethical purpose implicit in good ethnography (see Goldman 1978) invariably produces explicit data conducive to a critical stance, or perspective, on the expansionist state.

Let us draw this material together in a series of generalizations that should be useful in considering the thrust of most of these papers. Critical anthropology accepts the canons of holistic ethnography and the confrontation of established theories with fresh data in comparative ethnology. Moreover, it seeks to comment upon the *consequences* of political economic control over peoples' lifestyles, lifeways, and life chances. It accepts cultural, ethnic, and individual variation as basic to human nature. But it regards centralized control over either cultural variety or cultural homogenization as an infringement upon human freedom. Critical anthropology accepts, admires, and seeks to illuminate the inner *integrity of a cultural system*—the *structure*—without assuming that it is "functioning on its own," without assuming "retention" from past systems, without assuming "isolation" from larger environing systems, and without assuming "marginality" to a larger system. It accepts *cultural adaptation* without assuming accommodative or assimilationist tendencies, and it accepts *cultural pluralism* without assuming any need for centralized imposition of segmental order (of which racist apartheid of South Africa would be an excellent example). Moreover, it assumes that *cultural transformation*, whether slow or rapid, may take place at any level of any system at any time, and that the need for clarity as to what constitutes change and what constitutes continuity is as problematic today as it has always been. Finally, it assumes that cultural transformation and *social reproduction* (Godelier 1977, Sahlins 1976) must be considered within a unified frame of reference.

The overall organization of the book is wavelike in its presentation. In the first part, *Theoretical and Critical Considerations*, Stutzman, Naranjo, Salomon, and I lead off with four extended essays designed to heighten the reader's sensitivities to issues which are pervasive, though often tacit, in discourse on modern Ecuador. Stutzman begins with major statements on ethnicity in general,[12] based on an extensive review of the literature, and moves on to treat the Ecuadorian nation in terms of its official, mythical charter as manifest in its formal educational system. Although carefully focused on Ibarra, Imbabura, and its sierran hinterland, his essay also contains a holistic, critical perspective on the dynamics of ethnicity and nationalism as contrastive cultural systems: "ethnicity is an idiom of disengagement from the struggle over control of the state apparatus" . . . "ethnicity as a cultural system stands in implicit judgment on the shortcomings of the expansionist state." Naranjo, in the next chapter, continues the theme of seeing the macrocosm of Ecuadorian nationalism within a dynamic microcosm. He focuses directly on dependency theory with special attention to its roots in contemporary Latin American scholarship to provide a general perspective on Ecuadorian modernization and developmentalism through an examination of the port town of Manta, Manabí.

In the fourth chapter N. Whitten turns to the Oriente to describe what he calls an "ethnic interface" in ecological, social, and ideological terms. Here the contemporary native peoples are briefly described, issues regarding their languages and cultures are sketched, and some novel interpretations are offered. He concludes with a discussion of ritual and symbolism inherent in the adaptive dynamics of the Oriente's peoples, asserting that "the knowledge and vision of 10,000 years or more of *cultural* adaptation to the riparian-sylvan, and eventually swidden, habitat is required by those currently contributing to Amazonian 'development,' for so-called progressive development today is destroying nature and culture alike."

With the final chapter in this part we return to the Sierra, to Quito—the pinnacle of official control of the modern republic—to consider Salomon's extensive treatment of a powerful ritual, *yumbada*, which portrays a visit from a group of the Oriente's indigenous people, one of whom is symbolically killed and then restored to life. Enduring ritual expression of massive contradictions is a theme which runs through the ceremonial enactment. On the one hand, the Oriente is "marginal" to everything "national"—it is full of savages smothered by the jungle, in vivid contrast to Quito, which is populated by citizens liberated by urban Christianity. On the other hand, the Oriente represents a potential resolution to nationalist problems, if only its oppositions to nationalist thought can be overcome (the *yumbo* killed) and its potential brought to life (the *yumbo* resurrected). Moreover, those who enact the ritual are *Quito Runa*—they speak Quichua during the extended ritual (though Quito's urbanity, which they symbolize, demands the speaking of Spanish). Salomon turns, as we all eventually must, to culture history with its political overlays to resolve the seeming contradiction. "The little aboriginal communities ringing Quito have for at least five centuries been, in both cultural orientation and economic practices, more thoroughly trans-Andean than any of the imperial civilizations which tried to unify forest and Sierra in a state-centralized scheme of integration. Pantropical cosmopolitans of a multitiered, multi-ethnic landscape, the Quito Runa have been, and still are, the cultural switchboard and economic depot of a transmontane integration unknown to state planners."

Part II, *Infrastructure and Socioeconomic Processes*, is the second wave of the book and is designed to provide more data of a basically materialist nature. Middleton first gives an overall view of the urban anthropology of the nation, drawn from his own field research in Manta, Manabí, and from that of others in sierran, coastal, and Oriente towns and cities. Then Bromley describes the market system of highland Ecuador, Casagrande addresses himself to the critical issues of survival strategies for indigenous *serranos*, and Scrimshaw sketches demographic patterns which relate to in-migration to Guayaquil by highland and coastal groups. After these comparative studies we return to three case studies. In the first, by Brownrigg, we are treated to a view of contemporary migration, ecosystem alteration, and creative adaptation. Brownrigg, like Salomon, turns to culture history to suggest that the hispanicized people from highland Loja migrating to the coastal uplands and lowlands of El Oro may "represent a submerged ethnic group reconstituting an ancient territory." A similar theme is brought forth by Ekstrom's subsequent discussion of the *cholo* population of highland Jima and their "vertical ecological strategies" of adaptation to varied ecosystems from the Andean to the montane jungle abutting Shuara territory in the Oriente. Finally, Macdonald presents the jungle Quijos Quichua adaptive versatility in the total transformation of their ecosystem from one of tropical forest cultural ecology to that of cattlemen. He painstakingly documents the inexorable national pressures on them to effect this transformation, "against their will and better judgment."

In Part III, *Cultural Transformation, Ethnicity, and Adaptation in the Sierra and Littoral*, a series of papers deals directly with varied facets of sierran and coastal ethnicity and racism in contexts of developmental change. Stark's paper focuses on the town of Cotacachi, Imbabura, where land reform is in its infancy and where an unusually high degree of community loyalty is manifest, to make a telling point: *palanca* (access to goods and services, or relative power) correlates remarkably closely with ethnic labeling mechanisms. Ethnicity is further examined by Fock in Juncal, Cañar province, by reference to the dichotomy there between *mestizos* and Runa. Indians are excluded from access to the symbols of national power, which oppresses them, but *mestizos* gain partial access (*palanca*, leverage) through the regional system. His final statement rings a familiar bell for Ecuadorianists who work in both Quichua and Spanish: "political economic imperialism has certainly reached Juncal, but cultural imperialism has as yet been unsuccessful." Salomon, in his article on the famous Otavaleño weavers, demonstrates effectively the creativity that can be unleashed in indigenous communities where nationalist "conquest" is successfully repelled. Far to the south, in Loja, the Belotes continue the theme of ethnic expression, moving us to a context of planned development and the creative response of native Saraguro peoples to ineffectual policies to demonstrate how these indigenous peoples moved into the flow of cultural transformation, essentially on their own terms. Power, self-identity, development, reform, and the expressions of these crucial themes through ritual enactment are the integrated subjects of Crespi's paper, which focuses on a hacienda in Cayambe, Pichincha province, and on the fiesta of St. John the Baptist, which is so strikingly evident in northern Ecuador during the month of June. There St. John's rituals established short-lived and narrowly specialized relationships, which offered whites and Indians mutually acceptable, or tolerable, avenues to their respective objectives within a system of overt racism and castelike stratification. Muratorio then takes us to Colta, Chimborazo, to examine with care the processes of large-scale conversion to fundamentalist, evangelical Protestantism taking place among Indian peasants formerly bound to haciendas. There the native peoples, although oppressed by over 400 years of semiserfdom, "still preserve fundamental aspects of their culture and social organization." Now identifying by their language, Quichua (since Runa there is used pejoratively by *blanco-mestizos* to mean *indio*), these indigenous peoples are caught on the horns of the imposed nationalist stereotypic dilemma where "the ideology of *mestizaje* denies both the existence of social classes and the possibility of incorporation of the Indians with their own identity into the national society." Protestantism, simply, provides an ideology of both class consciousness and ethnic consciousness as part of its political ideology. Indigenous adoption of this political ideology facilitates the cultural transformations taking place "where old modes of production still persist in a complex relationship with capitalism."

With these facets of cultural transformation and ethnicity in the Sierra in mind, we move to the northwest coast, Esmeraldas province, where the republic's majority of black people reside. García-Barrio leads off with an overview of the concepts expressed through Ecuadorian literature of black people, and the qualities of blackness. The prominent themes uncovered include daily life and culture (which are so different from those of both mainstream national Ecuadorian culture found in various classes, and of indigenous cultures of Sierra, Oriente, and Coast), racial mixture and racial identity, conflicts of culture, and commercial exploitation. The latter three of these form what García-Barrio calls "a trilogy of crucial themes." This trilogy is underscored in the next chapter, where Schubert lays bare the cognitive dimensions of surgent racism as expressed through labeling within the changing political economy of San Lorenzo. She concludes that the "gospel of civilization" is being forcefully delivered there: "white is better and black is an offense." As a consequence of the ascendancy of the civilized gospel, "black people's options are now more restricted, and freedom is reduced by powerlessness."

In Part IV we turn to *Cultural Transformation, Ethnicity, and Adaptation in the Oriente*. Salazar first discusses the Shuar Federation, which is today the most powerful native American federation in all of South America, and known throughout the world. Next Descola and Taylor focus directly upon a dynamic, adaptable lowland people, the Achuar, who were virtually unknown to the western (or Andean) world until very recently, to highlight for us processes of change now taking place. James Yost then presents a sober work on one of the world's best-known (stereotypically) and least-known (scientifically or humanistically) lowland indigenous peoples, the Waorani, better known through the Christian world as "Auca," who were made infamous because of the spearing of five North American Protestant evangelists in 1956. The articles by Descola, Taylor, and Yost document significantly the "expansion of scale" (Wilson and Wilson 1945, Barth 1978, Whitten 1980) attendant upon modernization strategies of the Oriente, and the various implications of such expansion on the lifeways of surviving native peoples. They also demonstrate the verve and vigor of indigenous tropical forest cultures in these contexts of radical development-sponsored change. William Vickers then analyzes the material aspects of religious conversion among another of the Oriente's peoples, the Siona-Secoya, and raises the significant question addressed, in one way or another, by all of the above writers on the Oriente: "The government of Ecuador has wisely instituted measures to ensure the survival of the fauna of the Galápagos Islands. Is the survival of unique human cultures of less significance? Native peoples cannot be isolated like museum specimens, but they deserve the legal safeguards afforded to other citizens, including the protection of land rights and the right of cultural self-determination within the social fabric of the nation." The two final chapters in this part try to curb the possible tendency to view the Oriente's native peoples only in terms of their "acculturative" changes by focusing directly on aspects of remarkable continuity of symbolic form within contexts of radical change. Belzner turns to Shuar music and the concept-of-music, and D. Whitten focuses on the ceramic tradition of the Canelos Quichua. These authors deliberately choose settings of extreme pressure to change (Macuma for the Shuara, the Puyo area for the Canelos) and reach similar conclusions, expressed in this summation by D. Whitten: "While Canelos Quichua culture is a repository of ancient symbolism, enacted in ceremonies and portrayed in ceramic design, it is not pristine. Its bearers move between two worlds, maintaining their cultural identity while rationally incorporating some aspects, and rejecting others, of a changing environment and social order."

Most of the articles acknowledge the nationalist and social scientist stereotypes which abound in such situations, but seek to understand the underlying forces which generate them and to avoid using such stereotypes as analytical, tautological conveniences. Some of these papers also express a growing anthropological trend toward paradigms and perspectives (see, e.g., Hsu 1977, Stavenhagen 1968, Nash 1975, Owusu 1978) which eschew the colonial and neocolonial biases embedded in such theoretical views as diffusionism, configurationalism, functionalism, acculturation-assimilationism, or evolutionism. All of them emphatically reassert ethnography as a creative, theory-constructive endeavor. Most of them are holistic (Honigmann 1976, Adams 1978, Sanjek 1978:267) in their handling of data and comparative in their treatment of theoretical relevance. They all deal with the nation both as a cultural system and as a political economy. And, finally, many of them consider "development" to be an ideology as well as a strategy of planned socioeconomic change. The combination of these latter five points relate back to the initial idea, for critical anthropology suggests strongly that governmental ideology, policy, and praxis are powerful, causal factors in the fate of cultures and the state of human conditions.

To understand ethnicity in settings of cultural transformation, concepts of power and ritual are as vital to holism as are concepts of social structure, class, economic hierarchy, and language. Although contributors in this volume follow their own theoretical predilections, some orientation is desirable. Power, according to Dimen-Schein (1977:211), "is encoded in symbols, enacted in relationships, and grounded in things." Power structure, following but paraphrasing Richard N. Adams (1970, 1974, 1975; see also Whitten 1977), is defined as the degree and nature of control, or influence, which one party or actor exerts over the relevant environment of another party or actor, together with the reciprocal recognition of differential control by the respective parties or actors.

Ritual is based on "correspondence structures." According to structuralist Claude Leví-Strauss, and especially as interpreted by James Boon (1972; see also Firth 1973:201), these are replicating sense perceptions from different domains of experience. When people perceive, say, a comparable system of exploitation in their work-a-day lives, within their ceremonial activity, through their system of social protest, and within the structure of family and community, we may speak of a "correspondence structure." Metaphor is the "elementary form" of ritual, for it predicates an identity upon an inchoate subject (see, e.g., Fernandez 1974) and moves people to fill in frames of experience, thereby connecting the unknown future with the mythical, legendary, or remembered past in a "liminal" present (see, e.g., Turner 1974). Ritual launches participants into a domain of creative enactment where they generate their own constraints, where they control the uncontrollable, where they empower their destinies. Performance takes place within an "arena" characterized by oscillation between known social constraints and the boundlessness of being "betwixt and between" positions in a social order. No wonder that Ecuadorian politicians, *caudillos* and military officials alike, often put in an appearance at folk fiestas. They must be perceived as both the guardians of social structure and the embodiment of its dissolution.

In systems of rapid change power structure is revealed as it is transformed, and ritual activity promotes awareness of new levels, new meanings, new syntheses, and new mechanisms of control. Ritual, motivated by metaphoric predication, relates these novelties through correspondence structure to enduring, adaptable systems which are grounded in knowledge transmitted to the present through generations past.

In his exhaustive treatise on power structure Adams (1975, 1978) makes a strong case for higher levels of coordination among disparate groupings emerging at one level, as centralization occurs at another. Fundamental to this process is what he calls "surgent systems"—those which are materially, socially, and mentally in a process of restructuring themselves to cope with an unsatisfactory situation of anticipated dependency. Materials presented in this book suggest that the ritual expressions of various ethnically nonnational people are in the process of resurgence and reorganization. New forms of coordination such as lowland-highland indigenous integration are being expressed through ritual enactment, forms of symbolic expression, and metaphoric predication. Moreover, these forms of coordination are often reworkings of the same ones that existed prior to the colonial, republican, and nationalist centralization which both divided them and, again paradoxically, created the very basis for their resurgence. In Ecuador today we must consider power and ritual as they relate to ethnicity, class, status, and cultural transformation. By so doing transformations back and forth between mundane knowledge and symbolic expression, between day-to-day activity and stylized ritual enactment, between the material and the mental, between the pragmatic and the ideal, are holistically understood. Also, in this way anthropology makes its own contribution to the study of intranational and international cultural dynamics, and perhaps frees itself from perspectives spawned by colonialism and neocolonialism.

NOTES

Acknowledgments: The largely implicit framework for sections of this chapter owes much to the recent theoretical developments of Richard N. Adams. Jane Adams, Edward M. Bruner, Stephen Bunker, Joseph B. Casagrande, Muriel Crespi, Paul Doughty, DeWight Middleton, Marcelo F. Naranjo, Frank Salomon, Grace Schubert, John O. Stewart, Ronald Stutzman, and Dorothea S. Whitten read various drafts of this Introduction and provided very helpful critical commentary. Although the final result is stronger for their efforts, the shape and direction are my responsibility, and I alone must be faulted for errors of interpretation, judgment, presentation, or style. A few pages of this introduction are taken from my article "Ecuador," published in the *Encyclopedia of Developing Nations*, and are published here by permission of McGraw-Hill Book Co.

1. These figures are, at best, inexact and undoubtedly low, in spite of the national census of 1974 and continuing attempts today to come up with reasonable estimates. Because of this, different authors will give different statistics for the same populations, following his or her interpretations of available data. The vast majority of the native peoples of the Oriente, for example, would be the combination of jungle Quichua and Jivaroan groups, and here the combined estimates range from a low of 10,000 or less up to 50,000 or more.

2. I owe this phrase to Hubert Herring (1961:527), who credits it to Arthur Whittaker. Brief historical sketches of Ecuador may be found in Blanksten (1951), Herring (1961), Dozer (1962), and Linke (1960). For more extensive treatments of subjects touched on here, see González Suárez (1969–70), Velasco (1977), Jaramillo Alvarado (1960), Rumazo González (1948–50), and Tobar Donoso (1960).

3. My use of the terms and concepts of "state," "nation," and "nationalism" is more or less standard in political science or political philosophy and in international law. For an adequate discussion see Young (1976:66–97).

Introduction   31

"State" is frequently applied to any form of human government "exhibiting
at least some rudimentary signs of centralization and continuity. . . . The
major universal properties are territoriality and sovereignty" (Young 1976:67).
"Nation" refers to the largest reference group by which collective identity or
loyalty can be engendered. A state may contain more than one nation. "Nationalism" "is an ideological formulation of identity" wherein the state
(nation-state) becomes the locus of loyalty: "Nationalism is a political creed
that underlies the cohesion of modern societies, and legitimizes their claim
to authority. Nationalism centers the supreme loyalty of the overwhelming
majority of the people upon the nation-state, either existing or desired. The
nation-state is regarded not only as the ideal, 'natural,' or 'normal' form of
political organization but also as the indispensable framework for all social,
cultural, and economic activities" (Kohn 1968:63).
     4. For descriptions of the early extent of the "Kingdom of Quito," see Phe-
lan (1967), Velasco (1977), and Salomon (1978). Early disputes with Peru are
discussed in Vacas Galindo (1905) and Tobar Donoso and Luna Tobar (1961).
The Peruvian invasion of 1941, its effects, and its relationship to international
struggles over petroleum control are discussed by Zook (1964), Wood (1966),
Galarza (1972), and Medina Castro (1977). A very succinct review of the history of territory loss is given in El Comercio, 30 Jan. 1979, 1, 12a. Jaime Galarza
(1972:72–99) has written forcefully about the relationship of petroleum companies in the creation of a situation resulting in Peru's 1941 invasion, calling
the political episode of hostility the "petroleum war." For his nationalist
stance Galarza was encarcerated in a military prison for two years (see, e.g.,
Drekonja et al. 1978:378) during the period of the foreign-sponsored and
-dominated petroleum boom.
     5. See, for example, Galarza (1978), Salgado (1978), and other essays in
Drekonja et al. (1978), NACLA (1975), Sanders (1977), Salgado (1979), Ortiz
(1979), and Egüez (1979).
     6. For the most recent synopses on Ecuadorian politics see especially
Chaves Granja (1979) and Villaverde (1979), Hurtado (1977) is required reading for those interested in Ecuadorian power structure and its shifting geo-
economic systems. See also Ortiz Villacís (1977), Muñóz Vicuña (1976), Perez
Concha (1978), and Ayala (1978). Essays on these themes are presented in
Drekonja et al. (1978).
     7. In Ecuador's 149 years as a republic, there have been, officially, 56 dif-
ferent governments and 17 separate constitutions (Villaverde 1979) within a
system which is supposed to enact governmental turnovers by election. According to Sanders, following Hurtado (1977)—who, by the way, is now the
vice-president–elect of the republic, on the Christian Democratic ticket with
Jaime Roldós Aguilera—"Of the 85 governments that held power in the same
period, 21 were dictatorships; 25 were led by people who received the presidential office by constitutional succession or were designated as successors
by the 'notables' of the country; 20 originated from constitutional conven-
tions or congresses dominated by a dictator or caudillo; and only 19 were
elected by popular suffrage" (Sanders 1977:2).
     8. This point of oscillation producing stability has been made repeatedly
by British social anthropologists, notably Fortes (1949), Leach (1954), and
Gluckman (1965), in sharp contrast to perspectives of many political scientists and sociologists. But the British social anthropologists invariably see

"stability" resting on "equilibrium" and the oscillation within "structural time"—the time it takes components in a social system to reorganize back and forth from one form to another (see, e.g., Whitten and Whitten 1972:255–56)—and the political scientists–sociologists see disequilibrium as producing instability. A succinct, penetrating review of contemporary political anthropology is given by Vincent (1978) and should be consulted for further references. Richard N. Adams (1978) firmly views disequilibrium as generating stability and argues his case across the spectrum of levels of sociopolitical complexity to construct a dynamic model of social transformation and change. By so doing he comes in line with other thinkers in contemporary anthropology such as Victor Turner (e.g., 1974), who emerged from the "Manchester School" of social anthropology, led by the late Max Gluckman, to view ritual and power as unified concepts within systems characterized by both change and continuity.

9. Galarza (1978:18) is firm in his rejection of dependency structure and poignant as to his characterization of Ecuador's future if it continues its present course:

"Ecuador will be the Brazil of the Pacific," asserted a minister in his recent trip to West Germany. And he had good reason to say so, since, in 1974, the per capita economic growth of Ecuador surpassed that of Brazil. In the conditions of Ecuador, a country of high strategic value to the United States, small booty but rich and coveted, to be the "Brazil of the Pacific" would mean total dependency, permanent military dictatorship, absence of human rights, and squadrons of death.

10. We should also mention two other major forces in Ecuador, the *sindicatos de choferes* and the students and their movements. The former, composed of all drivers who affiliate with a provincial union with local offices, have the power to bring the nation to a virtual standstill through a general transportation strike. The latter are likely to initiate local and regional *manifestaciones* which heighten and polarize viewpoints and may (or may not) lead to other sorts of political-economic activity.

11. The official position of the new, powerful, military organization, Instituto Nacional de Colonización de la Región Amazónica Ecuatoriana (INCRAE), the National Institute of Colonization of the Amazonion Region of Ecuador, is remarkably similar in its public, published, position to the viewpoint taken here, and therefore strikingly divergent to previous positions taken by IERAC and CREA (see papers in this volume). But, to date, the little I have been able to learn of INCRAE's practices seems to contradict its public ideology and places its modus operandi clearly within the system herein described.

12. Reviews of ethnicity literature, each making its own contribution to clarification and/or obfuscation of the many issues involved, include van den Berghe (1967, 1970), Barth (1969), Schermerhorn (1970), A. Cohen (1974a, 1974b), Bennett (1975), Despres (1975), Glazer and Moynihan (1975), Young (1976), and R. Cohen (1978). Important works on Latin American societies include Wagley (1952), Wagley and Harris (1958), Harris (1964), Mörner (1967, 1970), Aguirre Beltrán (1967), Hoetink (1973), Friede, Friedemann, and Fajardo (1975), Stavenhagen (1975), and van den Berghe and Primov (1977). Monographs which deal directly with ethnicity (including "race relations") in Ecuador are Whitten (1965, 1974, 1976), Burgos (1970), Villavicencio (1973),

Crespi (1968), Stutzman (1974), Naranjo (1978), and Belote (1978). There seem to be a dozen or more studies of ethnicity in preparation, or in a field-work phase, in Ecuador at this time.

Editor's end note. I gained access to the 895-page report on Ecuador compiled by the World Bank and published "for official use only" just as I completed the correction of proofs for this book. Readers of *Cultural Transformations* interested in the blend of ideology, fantasy, and "hard" statistics on "development" are urged to consult this weighty "source." Actual facts and figures on population, migration, urbanization, Gross National Product, and the like vary from those given by authors of articles in *Cultural Transformations*. Most of these variations can be reconciled by judicious and interpretive use of sources cited. But, with regard to many of Ecuador's *peoples*, the World Bank achieves new heights of stereotyping and promulgation of egregious errors. Consider, for example, the following statements about the native peoples of the Oriente: "The 1974 census confirmed that a very sizeable minority (about 40 percent) of the Oriente population are native Amazonian Indians. The main communities are the Shuar in Morona and Zamora provinces (25,000–30,000), and the Yumbo in the Tena-Baeza area of Napo Province (22,000–25,000)" (Document of the World Bank 1979:191). "Reaching beyond their own community, the Shuar Federation is presently working on a Quiche [*sic!*] language radio-school program for the large Yumbo Indian group (22,000) concentrated in the Tena and Baeza area of Napo Province" (Document of the World Bank 1979:194). (Quiché is a Mayan language of Central America unrelated to Quichua, language of the Napo [or Quijos] Quichua of Napo Province, for whom *yumbo* is a pejorative, stereotypic label.) By omitting all Achuar and Canelos Quichua peoples of Pastaza Province and all Napo Quichua peoples living east of Tena, in Napo Province, and by also omitting all Cofán, Siona-Secoya, and Waorani peoples of Napo Province, the World Bank Report cloaks erroneous stereotypes with a tunic of international "scientific reliability." The complete reference to this "source" on Ecuadorian development is: *Development Problems and Prospects of Ecuador: Special Report*. 3 vols. Latin America and the Caribbean Region, Country Programs 1: Report No. 2373-EC. June 18, 1979. No place of publication given.

REFERENCES CITED

Adams, Richard N.
  1970 *Crucifixion by Power*. Austin: University of Texas Press.
  1974 Harnessing Technological Development. In John J. Poggie, Jr., and Robert N. Lynch, eds., *Rethinking Modernization: Anthropological Perspectives*. Westport, Conn.: Greenwood Press, pp. 37–68.
  1975 *Energy and Structure: A Theory of Social Power*. Austin: University of Texas Press.
  1978 Man, Energy, and Anthropology: I Can Feel the Heat, but Where's the Light? *American Anthropologist* 80:297–309.
Aguirre Beltrán, Gonzalo
  1967 *Regiones de Refugio*. Mexico City: Instituto Indigenista Interamericano.

Albornoz P., Oswaldo
  1976? *Las Luchas Indígenas en el Ecuador.* Guayaquil: Editorial Claridad.
Ayala, Enrique
  1978 *Lucha Política y Origen de los Partidos en Ecuador.* Quito: Ediciones de
    la Universidad Católica.
Barth, Fredrik, ed.
  1969 *Ethnic Groups and Boundaries: The Social Organization of Cultural Differ-
    ence.* Boston: Little, Brown.
  1978 *Scale and Social Organization.* New York: Columbia University Press.
Belote, Linda
  1978 Prejudice and Pride: Indian-White Relations in Saraguro, Ecuador.
    Ann Arbor, Mich.: University Microfilms. Ph.D. thesis, University
    of Illinois, Urbana.
Bennett, John W., ed.
  1975 *The New Ethnicity: Perspectives from Ethnology.* 1973 Proceedings of the
    American Ethnological Society. St. Paul, Minn.: West Publishing Co.
Blanksten, George I.
  1951 *Ecuador: Constitutions and Caudillos.* Berkeley: University of Califor-
    nia Press.
Bodley, John H.
  1975 *Victims of Progress.* Menlo Park, Calif.: Cummings Publishing Co.
Bonfil Batalla, G. B.
  1970 Del Indigenismo de la Revolución a la Antropología Crítica. In Bon-
    fil Batalla and Arturo Warman, eds., *De Eso Que Llaman Antropología
    Mexicana.* Mexico City: Editorial Nuestro Tiempo, pp. 39–65.
Boon, James A.
  1972 *From Symbolism to Structuralism: Lévi-Strauss in a Literary Tradition.*
    New York: Harper & Row.
Bromley, Ray
  1977 *Development Planning in Ecuador.* Sussex, Eng.: Latin American Pub-
    lications Fund.
Burgos Guevara, Hugo
  1970 *Relaciones Interétnicas en Riobamba.* Mexico City: Instituto Indigenista
    Interamericano.
  1975 El Guaman, el Puma, y el Amaru: Formación Estructural del Go-
    bierno Indígena en el Ecuador. Ann Arbor, Mich.: University Micro-
    films. Ph.D. thesis, University of Illinois, Urbana.
Chaves Granja, Jaime
  1979 Drama, Comedia y Sainete de la Política en 1978. *El Comercio,* Lunes,
    1 de Enero, Sección D:1, 16.
Clastres, Pierre
  1977 *Society against the State.* New York: Urizen Books. (Trans. Robert
    Hurley from the original French publication of 1974.)
Cockcroft, James D., André Gunder Frank, and Dale L. Johnson, eds.
  1972 *Dependence and Underdevelopment: Latin America's Political Economy.*
    New York: Doubleday.
Cohen, Abner
  1974a Ed. *Urban Ethnicity.* Association of Social Anthropologists, Mono-
    graph 12. London: Tavistock.
  1974b *Two-Dimensional Man.* Berkeley: University of California Press.

Cohen, Ronald
    1978   Ethnicity: Problem and Focus in Anthropology. *Annual Review of An-
            thropology* 7:379–404.
Collier, David
    1978   Industrialization and Authoritarianism in Latin America. *Items, So-
            cial Science Research Council* 31/32 (4/1):5–13.
Collier, Donald
    1975   Ancient Ecuador: Culture, Clay and Creativity, 3000–300 B.C. *Field
            Museum of Natural History Bulletin* 46 (4):7–13.
Crespi, Muriel
    1968   The Patrons and Peons of Pesillo: A Traditional Hacienda System in
            Highland Ecuador. Ann Arbor, Mich.: University Microfilms. Ph.D.
            thesis, University of Illinois, Urbana.
Despres, Leo A., ed.
    1975   *Ethnicity and Resource Competition in Plural Societies*. The Hague:
            Mouton.
Dimen-Schein, Muriel
    1977   *The Anthropological Imagination*. New York: McGraw-Hill.
Dozer, Donald Marquand
    1962   *Latin America: An Interpretive History*. New York: McGraw-Hill.
Drekonja, Gerhard, et al.
    1978   *Ecuador, Hoy*. Bogotá: Siglo Veintiuno Editores.
Egüez T., Marcelo
    1979   Declina Dependencia del Petroleo en la Economia Ecuatoriana: 1978.
            El Comercio, Lunes, 1 de Enero, Sección D:7, 18.
Estrada Ycaza, Julio
    1977   *Regionalismo y Migración*. Guayaquil: Publicaciones del Archivo
            Histórico del Guayas.
Fernandez, James
    1974   The Mission of Metaphor in Expressive Culture. *Current Anthropol-
            ogy* 15 (2):119–45.
Firth, Raymond T.
    1973   *Symbols: Public and Private*. Ithaca, N.Y.: Cornell University Press.
Fortes, Meyer
    1949   Time and Social Structure: An Ashanti Case Study. In Meyer Fortes,
            ed., *Social Structure*. Oxford: Clarendon Press, pp. 54–84.
Friede, Juan, Nina S. de Friedemann, and Dario Fajardo
    1975   *Indigenismo y Aniquilamiento de Indígenas en Colombia*. Bogotá: Uni-
            versidad Nacional de Colombia.
Galarza Zavala, Jaime
    1972   *El Festín del Petróleo*. 2d ed. Quito: "Cicetronic Cía. Ltda." de Pape-
            leriá Moderna.
    1978   Ecuador, el Oro y la Pobreza. In Gerhard Drekonja et al., *Ecuador,
            Hoy*. Bogotá: Siglo Veintiuno Editores, pp. 9–18.
Geertz, Clifford
    1964   Ideology as a Cultural System. In David Apter, ed., *Ideology and Dis-
            content*. New York: Free Press, pp. 47–76.
Glazer, Nathan, and Daniel P. Moynihan, eds.
    1975   *Ethnicity: Theory and Experience*. Cambridge, Mass.: Harvard Univer-
            sity Press.

Gluckman, Max
1965   *Politics, Law, and Ritual in Tribal Society.* Chicago: Aldine.
Godelier, Maurice
1977   *Perspectives in Marxist Anthropology.* New York: Cambridge University Press.
Goldman, Irving
1978   Review of *Sacha Runa: Ethnicity and Adaptation of Ecuadorian Jungle Quichua*, by Norman E. Whitten, Jr. *American Ethnologist* 5 (2):400–403.
González Suárez, Federico
1969–70   *Historia General de la República del Ecuador.* 3 vols. Quito: Casa de la Cultura Ecuatoriana. (Reprint of original 7 vols. published between 1890 and 1903.)
Grayson, George W.
1975   Populism, Petroleum, and Politics in Ecuador. *Current History* 68 (401):15–19, 39–40.
Harner, Michael J.
1972   *The Jívaro: People of the Sacred Waterfalls.* Garden City, N.Y.: Natural History Press.
Harris, Marvin
1964   *Patterns of Race in the Americas.* New York: Walker.
Hemming, John
1970   *The Conquest of the Incas.* New York: Harcourt Brace Jovanovich.
Herring, Hubert
1961   *A History of Latin America.* New York: Alfred A. Knopf.
Hoetink, Harmannus
1973   *Slavery and Race Relations in the Americas.* New York: Harper & Row.
Honigmann, John J.
1976   *The Development of Anthropological Ideas.* Homewood, Ill.: Dorsey Press.
Hsu, Francis L. K.
1977   Role, Affect, and Anthropology. *American Anthropologist* 79:805–8.
Huamán Poma de Ayala, Don Felipe
1978   *Letter to a King.* New York: Dutton. (Translation, rearrangement, and edited version of *Nueva Corónica y Buen Gobierno*, MS ca. 1567–1615, by Christopher Dilke.)
Hurtado, Osvaldo
1977   *El Poder Político en el Ecuador.* Quito: Ediciones de la Universidad Católica.
Instituto de Investigaciones Sociales de la Universidad de Cuenca
1977   Política Económica, Estado y Lucha de Clases en el Ecuador, Período 1972–1975. *Revista Ciencias Sociales (Política Económica y Poder Político en el Ecuador: 1972–1975)* 1 (3–4):13–76. Quito: Universidad Central.
Jaramillo Alvarado, Pio
1960   *Estudios Históricos.* Quito: Casa de la Cultura Ecuatoriana.
Jijón y Caamaño, Jacinto
1945   *Antropología Prehispanica del Ecuador.* Quito: Prensa Católica.
Kohn, Hans
1968   Nationalism. *International Encyclopedia of the Social Sciences* 11:63–70.
Lathrap, Donald W.
1970   *The Upper Amazon.* New York: Praeger.

1973   Summary or Model Building: How Does One Achieve a Meaningful Overview of a Continent's Prehistory? Review of *An Introduction to American Archaeology*, vol. 2, by Gordon R. Willey. *American Anthropologist* 75:1755–67.

1974   The Moist Tropics, the Arid Lands, and the Appearance of Great Art Styles in the New World. In Idris Taylor and M. E. King, eds., *Art and Environment in Native America*. Lubbock: Texas Technological University Museum Special Publication, pp. 115–58.

Lathrap, Donald W., Donald Collier, and Helen Chandra
1975   *Ancient Ecuador: Culture, Clay, and Creativity 3000–300 B.C.* Chicago: Field Museum of Natural History.

Lathrap, Donald W., Jorge G. Marcos, and James Zeidler
1977   Real Alto: An Ancient Ceremonial Center. *Archaeology* 30 (1):3–13.

Leach, Edmund
1954   *Political Systems of Highland Burma.* Boston: Beacon Press.

León Ramírez, Jaime
1979   ¿Intentaron Matar a Roldós?: Piratas y Asesinos en la Costa de Manabí. *Vistazo* :35–38.

Linke, Lilo
1960   *Ecuador: Country of Contrasts.* New York: Oxford University Press.

Macdonald, Theodore, Jr.
1979   Processes of Quijos Quichua Cultural Change. Ann Arbor, Mich.: University Microfilms. Ph.D. thesis, University of Illinois, Urbana.

Medina Castro, Manuel
1977   *La Responsabilidad del Gobierno Norteamericano en el Proceso de la Mutilación Territorial del Ecuador.* Guayaquil: Departamento de Publicaciones de la Universidad de Guayaquil.

Meggers, Betty J.
1966   *Ecuador.* New York: Praeger.

Meyers, Albert
1976   *Die Inka in Ekuador: Untersuchunger Anhand Ihrer Materiellen Hinterlassenschaft.* Bonn: Bonner Amerikanistische Studien 6.

Moncayo, Patricio
1977   Comentario a la Ponencia "Política Económica, Estado y Lucha de Clases en el Ecuador. . . ." *Revista Ciencias Sociales (Política Económica y Poder Político en el Ecuador: 1972–1975)* 1 (3–4):77–92. Quito: Universidad Central.

Moreno Yánez, Segundo
1976   *Sublevaciones Indígenas en la Audiencia de Quito: Desde Comienzos del Siglo XVII Hasta Finales de la Colonia.* Bonn: Bonner Amerikanistische Studien 5.

Mörner, Magnus
1967   *Race Mixture in the History of Latin America.* Boston: Little, Brown.
1970   Ed. *Race and Class in Latin America.* New York: Columbia University Press.

Muñoz Vicuña, Elias
1976   *La Guerra Civil Ecuatoriana de 1895.* Guayaquil: Departamento de Publicaciones de la Universidad de Guayaquil.

Murra, John
1975   *Formaciones Económicas y Políticas del Mundo Andino.* Lima: Instituto de Estudios Peruanos.

Muysken, Pieter C.
   1975–76   La Media Langua: I, II, III. (Three Data Papers.) Salcedo and
   University of Amsterdam: Instituto Inter-Andino de Desarrollo.
NACLA (North American Congress on Latin America)
   1975   *Ecuador: Oil up for Grabs.* Latin America and Empire Report 9 (8),
   November.
Naranjo, Marcelo F.
   In press   Native Peoples and Legal Problems in Eastern Ecuador: Land
   Tenure and Civil Liberties. In Theodore Macdonald, Jr., ed. *Ama-
   zonia: Extinction or Survival?* Madison: University of Wisconsin Press.
   1978   Etnicidad, Estructura Social y Poder en Manta, Occidente Ecuatori-
   ano. Ann Arbor, Mich.: University Microfilms. Ph.D. thesis, Uni-
   versity of Illinois, Urbana.
Naranjo, Marcelo F., José L. Pereira V., and Norman E. Whitten, Jr., eds.
   1977   *Temas sobre la Continuidad y Adaptación Cultural Ecuatoriana.* Quito:
   Prensa de la Pontificia Universidad Católica.
Nash, June
   1975   Nationalism and Fieldwork. *Annual Review of Anthropology* 4:225–45.
Nueva
   1979   Del "Caso Calderón" al "Caso Jarrín"? *Nueva* 55:13–33.
Oberem, Udo
   1976   El Acceso a Recursos Naturales de Diferentes Ecologías de la Sierra
   Ecuatoriana (Siglo XVI). *Actes du XLIIᵉ Congres du Centenaire* 4:51–64.
   Paris.
Ortiz G., Jorge
   1979   Petroleo y Dictaduras Durante la Ultima Etapa Histórica del País. *El
   Comercio*, Lunes, 1 de Enero, Sección D:5, 17.
Ortiz Villacís, Marcelo
   1977   *La Ideología Burguesa en el Ecuador.* Quito: Prensa de la Universidad
   Central.
Oszlak, Oscar
   1978   Notas Críticas para una Teoria de Burocracia Estatal. *Revista Ciencias
   Sociales* 2 (6):57–98. Quito: Universidad Central.
Owusu, Maxwell
   1978   Ethnography of Africa: The Usefulness of the Useless. *American Anthropologist* 80:310–34.
Perez Concha, Jorge
   1978   *Eloy Alfaro: Su Vida y Su Obra.* 2d ed. Guayaquil: Departamento de
   Publicaciones de la Universidad de Guayaquil.
Phelan, John Leddy
   1967   *The Kingdom of Quito in the Seventeenth Century: Bureaucratic Politics in
   the Spanish Empire.* Madison: University of Wisconsin Press.
Redclift, M. R.
   1978   *Agrarian Reform and Peasant Organization on the Ecuadorian Coast.* London: Athlone Press.
Robinson, Scott S.
   1979   Toward an Understanding of Kofán Shamanism. Ann Arbor, Mich.:
   University Microfilms. Ph.D. thesis, Cornell University.
Rumazo González, José
   1948–50   *Documentos para la Historia de la Audiencia de Quito.* 8 vols. Madrid:
   Afrodisio Aguado.

Sahlins, Marshall
1976 *Culture and Practical Reason*. Chicago: University of Chicago Press.
Salgado Peñaherrera, Germánico
1978 Lo Que Fuimos y Lo Que Somos. In Gerhard Drekonja et al., *Ecuador, Hoy*. Bogotá: Siglo Veintiuno Editores, pp. 19–58.
1979 Despúes de la Euforia: Una Economía en Busca de Otros Rumbos. *El Comercio*, Lunes, 1 de Enero, Sección D:3, 18.
Salomon, Frank
1978 Ethnic Lords of Quito in the Age of the Incas: The Political Economy of North-Andean Chiefdoms. Ann Arbor, Mich.: University Microfilms. Ph.D. thesis, Cornell University.
Sanders, Thomas G.
1977 *Ecuador: Politics of Transition*. American Universities Field Staff Reports, West Coast South America Series 24 (1).
Sanjek, Roger
1978 A Network Method and Its Uses in Urban Ethnography. *Human Organization* 37:257–68.
Schermerhorn, Richard A.
1970 *Comparative Ethnic Relations*. Chicago: University of Chicago Press.
Stavenhagen, Rodolfo
1968 Seven Fallacies about Latin America. In James Petras and Maurice Zeitlin, eds., *Latin America: Reform or Revolution?* Greenwich, Conn.: Fawcett Publications, pp. 13–31.
1975 [1969] *Social Classes in Agrarian Societies*. Trans. Judy Adler Hellman. New York: Doubleday.
Stewart, Norman R., Jim Belote, and Linda Belote
1976 Transhumance in the Central Andes. *Annals of the Association of American Geographers* 66 (3):377–97.
Stutzman, Ronald
1974 Black Highlanders: Racism and Ethnic Stratification in the Ecuadorian Sierra. Ann Arbor, Mich.: University Microfilms. Ph.D. thesis, Washington University, St. Louis.
Tobar Donoso, Julio
1960 *Historiadores y Cronistas de las Misiones*. Biblioteca Mínima Ecuatoriana. Puebla, Mexico: Editorial J. M. Cajica, Jr.
Tobar Donoso, Julio, and Alfredo Luna Tobar
1961 *Derecho Territorial Ecuatoriano*. Quito: Editorial La Unión Católica.
Turner, Victor
1974 *Dramas, Fields, and Metaphors: Symbolic Action in Human Society*. Ithaca, N.Y.: Cornell University Press.
Vacas Galindo, Enrique
1905 *Arbitraje de Limites entre el Perú y Ecuador*. Madrid: Imprenta de los Hijos de M. G. Hernández.
van den Berghe, Pierre L.
1967 *Race and Racism: A Comparative Perspective*. New York: Wiley.
1970 *Race and Ethnicity*. New York: Basic Books.
van den Berghe, Pierre L., and George P. Primov (with the assistance of Gladys Becerra Velazque and Narciso Ccahuana Ccohuata)
1977 *Inequality in the Peruvian Andes: Class and Ethnicity in Cuzco*. Columbia: University of Missouri Press.

Vargas, José María
1977   *Historia del Ecuador: Siglo XVI.* Quito: Ediciones de la Universidad Católica.
Velasco, Juan de
1977   *Historia del Reino de Quito en la América Meridional.* Quito: Casa de la Cultura Ecuatoriana. (Reprint of vol. 1 of 3 vols. originally published between 1841 and 1844.)
Vickers, William T.
1976   Cultural Adaptation to Amazonian Habitats: The Siona-Secoya of Eastern Ecuador. Ann Arbor, Mich.: University Microfilms. Ph.D. thesis, University of Florida, Gainesville.
Villavicencio Rivadeneira, Gladys
1973   *Relaciones Interétnicas en Otavalo, Ecuador.* Mexico City: Instituto Indigenista Interamericano.
Vincent, Joan
1978   Political Anthropology: Manipulative Strategies. *Annual Review of Anthropology* 7:175–94.
Wagley, Charles, ed.
1952   *Race and Class in Rural Brazil.* Paris: UNESCO.
Wagley, Charles, and Marvin Harris, eds.
1958   *Minorities in the New World.* New York: Columbia University Press.
Whitten, Norman E., Jr.
1965   *Class, Kinship, and Power in an Ecuadorian Town: The Negroes of San Lorenzo.* Stanford, Calif.: Stanford University Press.
1974   *Black Frontiersmen: A South American Case.* New York: Halsted (Wiley).
1976   (with the assistance of Marcelo F. Naranjo, Marcelo Santi Simbaña, and Dorothea S. Whitten). *Sacha Runa: Ethnicity and Adaptation of Ecuadorian Jungle Quichua.* Urbana: University of Illinois Press.
1977   Structure, Control and the Evolution of Power. Review of *Energy and Structure: A Theory of Social Power*, by Richard N. Adams. *Reviews in Anthropology* 4:567–74.
1980   Scaling Up and Bogging Down. Review of *Scale and Social Organization*, ed. Fredrik Barth. *Reviews in Anthropology* 71:1–19.
Whitten, Norman E., Jr., and Nina S. de Friedemann
1974   La Cultura Negra del Litoral Ecuatoriano y Colombiano: Un Modelo de Adaptación Étnica. *Revista Colombiana de Antropología* (Bogotá) 17:75–115.
Whitten, Norman E., Jr., and Dorothea S. Whitten
1972   Social Strategies and Social Relationships. *Annual Review of Anthropology* 1:247–70.
Wilson, Godfrey, and Monica Wilson
1945   *The Analysis of Social Change.* Cambridge: Cambridge University Press.
Wolf, Teodoro
1892   *Geografía y Geología del Ecuador.* Leipzig: F. A. Brockhaus.
Wood, Bryce
1966   *The United States and Latin American Wars 1932–1942.* New York: Columbia University Press.

Young, Crawford
  1976 *The Politics of Cultural Pluralism.* Madison: University of Wisconsin
      Press.
Zevallos M., Carlos, Waltson C. Galinat, Donald W. Lathrap, Earl R. Leng,
      Jorge G. Marcos, and Kathleen M. Klump
  1977 The San Pablo Corn Kernel and Its Friends. *Science* 196 (4288):385–89.
Zook, David H., Jr.
  1964 *Zarumilla-Marañón: The Ecuador-Peru Dispute.* New York: Bookman.

PART I:
THEORETICAL AND
CRITICAL
CONSIDERATIONS

2

El Mestizaje:
An All-Inclusive Ideology of Exclusion

Ronald Stutzman

A clue to understanding the significance of ethnic identity in the context of national development is found in an incident that occurred on 15 September 1972 in Puyo, a provincial capital located on the western rim of Ecuador's Amazonian interior. General Guillermo Rodríguez Lara, then president of the republic, was in town with his official entourage to discuss with local dignitaries the problems and prospects of regional development. In a lengthy speech the general urged infrastructural transformations of two kinds: (1) construction of roads, schools, and other public facilities and expansion of administrative services in anticipation of population growth and increased commercial activity, and (2) "improved" land utilization, that is, replacing traditional subsistence horticulture with commercial agricultural production for national and export markets. Later the general was asked how indigenous subsistence requirements and indigenous communal rights, already threatened by government-sponsored colonization efforts, could be reconciled with a development policy designed to feed people in the nation's cities, increase export earnings, and relieve population pressure in the Sierra. Instead of responding directly, the general invoked his own legendary ancestry. He emphasized that he had always believed all Ecuadorians to be part indigenous, all sharing something of the blood of the Inca Atahualpa, and that although he did not know how he acquired such blood, he was certain he too was part Indian. "There is no more Indian problem," he insisted; "we all become white when we accept the goals of national culture" (in Whitten 1976b:10–12, 1977:180–82).

While the Rodríguez Lara incident is intimately bound to ecological, demographic, historical, political, economic, and cultural particulars involving human communities on the Amazonian rim, it neatly

frames the more general problem of cultural transformation and social integration that confronts the nation as a whole. Puyo is not the
only town where government officials gather to discuss regional development, nor is it the only setting where ethnicity is lost or denied
when the goals of national culture are accepted. The exchange of ethnicity for nationality, and vice versa, occurs commonly, not only in
Ecuador but in human experience generally. Yet the cultural significance of the trade-off remains poorly understood (see, e.g., Geertz
1973:260–61n, 308–9).

The aim of the present study is to investigate ethnographically the
problem of what it means to exchange ethnic identity for membership in the nation-state, and to inquire into the more general relationship between ethnogenesis (Singer 1962), ethnotransformation
(González 1975), and national integration (Geertz 1963). In analyzing
the place of sierrans of indigenous and African descent in the life of
a *mestizo* Ecuadorian nation, it is assumed that ethnicity and nationality tend to mutual exclusivity and that the cultural aspects of being
ethnic are not simply a function of the national political economy.
These assumptions represent a departure from the more commonly
held views treating ethnicity either as an "adaptive strategy" for gaining a foothold in the control of national affairs (e.g., Cohen 1969) or
as a gloss for material and spiritual poverty of the kind imposed on
subordinate peoples by their oppressors (e.g., Burgos Guevara 1970,
Friedlander 1975).

Here, *ethnicity is construed as an idiom of disengagement from the
struggle over control of the state apparatus* (see, e.g., Aronson 1976, Villavicencio Rivadeneira 1973). Ethnicity is regarded as countercultural, as corresponding to a concept of the nature, meaning, and purpose of human existence at odds with state-sponsored perceptions of
those realities, because we must attend to what General Rodríguez
Lara meant when he said what he said in Puyo. If "all become white
[he meant true Ecuadorians]" who "accept the goals of national culture," then we must ask, What of those who do not accept such
goals? While they are clearly not true Ecuadorians (in the general's
view), their identity and cultural goals remain open to further investigation and evaluation.

The evaluation of the cultural status of nonnational (ethnic) Ecuadorians is divided into three parts. The first is a self-evaluation presented together with a brief ethnographic sketch of the northern
Sierra where persons in five communities were asked to identify
themselves in ethnic/racial terms. Because their responses suggest
that a substantial proportion do not take themselves to be true Ecua-

dorians in General Rodríguez Lara's terms, the second part turns to an evaluation from the national integrationist point of view of the ethnic diversity indicated by our survey. Here the scope of the analysis is broadened to offer an ethnographic account of the major mythic and symbolic components of national culture, gleaned from statements of national leaders, from school-book renderings of national history, and from materials promoting a recent adult literacy campaign. It becomes clear that from the perspective of the nation, contemporary ethnic and cultural diversity is interpreted as a burdensome residue of the republic's colonial past and as an impediment to its future progress.

The third part returns to the contrast between nationalist and ethnic cultural processes, reversing the perspective to permit an evaluation of the nation from the point of view of its ethnic peoples. Arguing that ethnic peoples are such precisely because they persist in their rejection of the legitimacy of the state's claims to sovereignty over their existence, it becomes clear that ethnicity in the context of revolutionary Ecuadorian nationalism entails a reflexive cultural critique: while the proponents of national integration explicitly condemn ethnically distinctive peoples to extinction by naming them in nonviable terms, ethnicity as a cultural system stands in implicit judgment on the shortcomings of the expansionist state.

ETHNIC DIVERSITY IN THE NORTHERN SIERRA

The Ecuadorian Sierra is extraordinarily complex and varied in both its ecological and its human aspects. The northernmost provinces of Carchi and Imbabura are particularly so because of an unusual topography that permits cultivation at temperate elevations between 2,500 and 3,500 meters, and also at subtropical elevations between 1,000 and 2,500 meters along the course of the Chota-Mira River, which divides the two provinces. During the colonial period slave labor was introduced into the arid, subtropical zone along the river to replace an indigenous population decimated, apparently, by tropical diseases (Stutzman 1974:61–74). Because of this circumstance, the northern highlands is one of the few Andean regions that includes a significant black population in addition to persons of European, Amerindian, and mixed descent.[1]

Traditionally, these ethnically diverse peoples have been distributed across the land in a complementary pattern. At lower elevations, where tropical roots, tubers, fruits, and sugar cane are the principal crops, the *campesino*, farm labor, population is predominantly *moreno* or *negro*.[2] At higher elevations, where temperate crops such as potatoes, wheat, barley, maize, beans, and squash are cultivated, the *campesino* population is identified as *mestizo* in Carchi province and as *indígena* and *cholo* in Imbabura province. Those self-identifying as *blancos* or *mestizos* tend to be concentrated in the region's cities and towns, which are located at elevations intermediate between the indigenous communities above and the black communities below.[3]

The major urban center in the northern highlands is San Miguel de Ibarra, founded in 1606 by the Spanish crown as a residence for colonists desiring to live among the indigenous communities of the region. Ibarra today is the capital of Imbabura province and principal market and administrative center between Quito and the Colombian border. In recent years the city's population has swelled from 14,000 in 1950 to 41,000 in 1974 (Terán 1976:242) while at the same time becoming more racially and ethnically diverse. Both demographic changes are attributable to in-migration, most of it from rural communities to the north, and to expansion of the city itself, incorporating within its new limits many formerly rural settlements.

Earlier ethnographic work established that ethnic complementarity, long characteristic of the region as a whole, persists in Ibarra in the form of differential participation in shared institutions.[4] In Ibarra's principal market, for example, product specialization is closely associated with phenotypic characteristics of vendors. *Indígenas* dominate the slaughter of animals and sale of meat. Most of the potatoes, cabbages, carrots, and lettuce are sold by *cholos*. Blacks tend to sell papayas, plantains, and bananas. Outside the market black males dominate occupations such as sugar cane harvesting and cargo handling, while men of indigenous descent predominate in construction trades, garbage collection, and street sweeping. The majority of those who work in the city's shops and offices identify themselves as *blancos* or *mestizos* (Stutzman 1974).

For most countries official statistics are available on the racial or ethnic composition of the population.[5] Not so for Ecuador. It is generally agreed that Ecuador's indigenous population is proportionately one of the largest in the Americas and that Afro-Ecuadorians make up about 15% of the total. But none of Ecuador's three official censuses (1950, 1962, 1974) has attempted to enumerate the population by race or ethnic group. Dr. Gonzalo Rubio Orbe, Ecuadorian scholar and past director of the Instituto Indigenista Interamericano, explains that while criteria for the identification of indigenous groups would not be simple to develop or easy to apply, the reason why no effective criteria exist for Ecuador is that government officials "do not appreciate the importance and significance of enumerating a population culturally different from groups that control and share in the life of the nation . . . " (1974:587).[6] In the absence of official census information a number of students of Ecuadorian society have offered their own estimates, but there is little agreement among them (cf. Hurtado 1969:130, Rubio Orbe 1974:588–89, Terán 1976:18–20).

But the accuracy and uniformity of these estimates matter less than the assumptions that lie behind them. Francisco Terán, for example, has revised his estimate of the country's ethnic composition each of the last three times his widely used *Geografía del Ecuador* has been issued in a new edition. He assumes that the *mestizo* segment of the population is growing most rapidly while the *indígena* and *negro* groups are diminishing in their relative sizes. These shifts are due, he says, to the rapid mixture or hybridization of ethnic types, and to unfavorable socioeconomic and cultural conditions that depress birth rates among Indians and blacks. The *blanco* group is also growing, he believes, because of a limited but significant number of new immigrants, and "because the mixed groups, due to a selective process, are losing their characteristics as such" (Terán 1976:19–20).

Geographer Terán's estimates appear to document a trend assumed to prevail not only in Ecuador but in all multi-ethnic nation-states that boast a single dominant political culture. The assumption is that contemporary cultural and social dynamics are principally a matter of acculturation and assimilation of subordinate peripheral heterogeneity to the dominant homogeneous center. In Ecuador this "selective process" is referred to as *blanqueamiento*—a putative lightening or "whitening" of the population in both the biogenetic and cultural-behavioral senses of the term *blanco*. The cultural goals, the society, and even the physical characteristics of the dominant class are taken by members of that class to be the objective of all cultural, social, and biological movement and change (Grayson 1975, Hurtado 1969:178–80, Whitten 1976a:265–85).

The notion that people are willing and anxious to exchange ethnicity for nationality, to accept the goals of national culture and become *blanco*, has rarely been questioned in Ecuador or the Andes, in the Americas or the world.[7] Review of the literature on acculturation and recruitment of indigenous individuals and groups to the nationalized lower class in Andean countries reveals an equivocal figure called the *cholo* who is believed by social scientists and national elites alike to embody the *blanqueamiento* process (Hurtado 1969:174; Peñaherrera de Costales and Costales Samaniego 1961a, 1961b; Rubio Orbe 1965;

see Bourricaud 1970, 1975, and van den Berghe 1974:16 on a parallel process termed *cholificación* in Peru). The *cholo* is said to have one foot in the indigenous-Quichuan world and the other in the Hispanic-national world because he is in the process of "passing" from one to the other (Crespi 1975, Hickman and Brown 1971, van den Berghe 1968, Whitten 1977). While it is beyond doubt that many persons of indigenous descent find their way out of their natal communities and into the national lower class, the dominant cultural orientation of those labeled *cholos* remained to be investigated. Guided by the hypothesis that *cholo* might designate not a culturally vacuous state of passage from indigenous to national but an alternative way of being in the Ecuadorian world, fieldwork begun in 1977 was designed to make such a determination through a comparative study of *morenos*, *mestizos*, and *cholos* in the northern Sierra.

Ethnic Self-Identification in Five Sierran Communities

Comparative study of *cholo* ethnicity began with sample surveys in two barrios on the outskirts of Ibarra where previous work had indicated that residents self-identify, or are identified by others, in the range of racial/ethnic terms common to the region. The smaller of the two barrios is simply a double file of houses stretching along either side of what once was the main road out of Ibarra to the southwest. A 17% sample of the approximately 168 households in this barrio yielded 25 completed interviews and 3 refusals. The second barrio surveyed had its origin 35 years ago as a similar double file of dwellings along the road out of Ibarra to the northwest. But with the influx of migrants to the city, the barrio expanded so that it now merges with adjacent suburbs that form the city's growing edge. Working out from the core of this barrio as traditionally bounded, a 13% sample of approximately 850 households yielded 103 completed interviews with 7 refusals.

Both barrios are located on, or adjoin, land utilized until recently to produce grain, vegetables, meat, and milk for Ibarra's markets. All of this land was once owned by nationally prominent families and was worked by families of resident laborers who were permitted house sites, garden plots (*huasipungos*), pasture rights, and water rights in return for their labor service on behalf of the owner. In addition to these rights of usufruct that permitted partial self-sufficiency, the *huasipungueros*, peons, were paid a small cash wage for their labor in hacienda fields. The agrarian reform law of 1964 terminated this traditional relationship between hacienda owners and their *huasipungueros* and coincided with the expansion of Ibarra so that most of this land has since been taken out of production. Pastures and cornfields have become housing developments, some planned, some spontaneous. The majority of families now living in these two suburban barrios were once attached as *huasipungueros* to haciendas near Ibarra or elsewhere in northern Imbabura or in Carchi province. Today only 12% of those gainfully employed work in agriculture: 3% farm their own land, usually including the *huasipungo* they received as part of the agrarian reform program, and 9% work as sharecroppers or field hands.

The local construction industry, that builds with mud, cement, adobe, brick, and stone, is the single most important source of employment for those interviewed: 11% work as master masons (independent contractors) and 14% are mason's helpers. Other crafts employ another 25% of those economically active; furniture makers, tailors, seamstresses, shoemakers, and mechanics are most prominent among them. Another 19%, most of them female, maintain stands, shops, and salons selling foodstuffs and beverages on the street, out of the front room of their own homes, or from stalls in the city's central market. The remaining 19% are divided among domestic service workers, taxi and bus drivers or conductors, horsecart operators, policemen, and soldiers. Categorized to reflect relative economic independence-dependence, these same data show 34% of all those economically active to be self-employed; these are mostly artisans and purveyors of foodstuffs and drink. Of those who are employed by others, 80% work under particularistic conditions governed by customary rules and expectations. Only 20% work under the legal protection of collective contracts.

Most of the questions asked of those interviewed dealt with basic demographic and social characteristics such as employment. Since these were generally answered without hesitation when known and remembered, the not uncommon confusion or apparent embarrassment were all the more striking when we came to the question that asked the respondent to identify self and family in terms of racial/ ethnic descent: "¿A cuál de las razas pertenecen Ustedes?" When answered without hesitation the response was usually, "We're *blancos*," "We're *mestizos*," or "We're *morenos*." Otherwise the response was, "What?" "I don't understand," "I really couldn't say."

Interviews were conducted whenever possible with the head of the family or some other adult, and it was usually respondents of the parental or grandparental generation who hesitated most over the question of descent. Generally we pressed for an answer, developing the question, by way of explanation, into a multiple choice. As straightforwardly as possible, we explained that Ecuadorian history teaches that three racial groups—the Spanish, the African, and the indigenous American—each contributed to the formation of the Ecuadorian people, and that it is often possible to say from which of these original groups a particular family or individual is descended. That tack failing, we made the choices more explicit: saying that every day on the streets of Ibarra it is common to hear reference made to persons of many types—*blancos, indígenas, gringos, morenos, cholos, carchenses, místeres, mestizos, negros, otavaleños,* and so on—we asked how they would classify themselves in these terms. On occasion we still got no reply beyond "Don't know/Couldn't say," and the question was dropped. A few times the respondent challenged us to identify him or her, saying, for example, "I am as you see me, *mister.*" Again the matter had to be dropped to avoid being placed in the position of categorizing the respondent ourselves.

But hesitation on the part of the respondent did not usually require elaboration of the question in this way. Bystanders to the interview almost invariably spoke up, when there was a pause, supplying a categorical term that the respondent would accept; or the respondent would ask for advice, as when one perplexed woman ran outside and returned with the word that "¡Es la chola, pues!," "We're *cholos!*" The advice from bystanders, however, was rarely that "We're/You're *cholos.*" The suggestion, rather, was that "We're/You're *mestizos.*" In fact, *mestizo* was the most common response we heard to our questioning. This outcome was unexpected, since we had predicted, on the basis of an earlier survey of blacks (Stutzman 1974:201–7), that *blanco* would be the term most commonly used in reference to self among nonblack respondents. Our assumption that *indígena, cholo,* and *mestizo* would rarely be offered in the interview context was also mistaken (see Table 1).

Each of the communities surveyed exhibits a markedly different pattern of responses, reflecting five distinct ethnic realities. Combined results for the two suburban Ibarra barrios, counting a given household once for each different identity claimed within, show 28% identifying self/family as *mestizo;* 18% self-identified as *blanco;* 15% self-identified as *moreno;* 12% self-identified as *indígena* (even though only one of these families wears what is considered typical indigenous dress); 11% said they didn't know how to characterize their descent line (some subsequently said *mestizo* in response to a suggestion, but only the initial response to our questioning is shown in Table 1); 8% responded with *cholo,* and so on. Statements offered in

TABLE 1. Racial/Ethnic Self-Identification: Sample Populations from Five Mixed Highland Barrios/Communities

Self-Identification by Racial Descent	Suburban Ibarra		Rural Communities		
	South-west Number	North-west Number	Chota Number	Chamanal Number	Río Blanco Number
La raza indígena/india	6	12	0	0	2
La raza chola	3	8	0	1	0
La raza mestiza	9	32	0	0	18
La raza blanca	0	26	0	2	4
La raza mulata/zamba	1	3	3	12	0
La raza morena/negra	1	20	31	4	2
Don't know/Couldn't say	7	9	0	0	11
Place of origin	0	2	0	0	7
Other statements	2	4	0	0	2

place of categorical terms are also given in Table 1, having been tabulated in the most appropriate category.[8]

Tentative results from the suburban barrios led us to backtrack on migration to Ibarra, resulting in similar surveys in three predominantly agricultural communities located along the Chota-Mira River: the community of Chota, 31 interviews, an approximately 20% sample; the community of Chamanal, 16 interviews, a 45% sample; and the Río Blanco area, 33 interviews, a 20% sample. These rural communities, as one might expect, tend to internal homogeneity. The population of Chota, centrally located in the upper Chota-Mira Valley, depended traditionally on nearby haciendas for employment. Today respondents report working in a variety of occupations: 14% farm their own land, 30% work as farm hands, 25% work as employees under collective contract for a sugar mill. The remainder are artisans, operate a small business, or are professional drivers. In this virtually all-black community, few respondents chose to distinguish themselves in terms denoting racial mixture. The community of Chamanal, located farther down the river to the west, was also traditionally associated with the hacienda system. Today three-quarters of those economically active farm land of their own, while most of the remainder are employed as field hands. Though this community is also almost all black, the responses are distinguished by claims to mixed descent.

Río Blanco, located still farther down the river, was a wilderness area until opened, colonized, and brought under cultivation by non-black families who migrated from higher elevations in Carchi province within the last 40 years. Agriculture remains the primary occupation: 49% farm their own land, 19% are employed as field hands, 11% are sharecroppers. The remainder are either artisans or persons who stock small quantities of processed foodstuffs which they sell out of their homes. Thirty-nine percent of the Río Blanco area respondents identified self/family as *mestizo*. Twenty-four percent said they didn't know how to respond to the query on descent. Fifteen percent responded with place designations that reflect the history of the area's colonization.

The significance claimed for our survey results is narrow. Obviously the figures presented in Table 1 do not constitute generalizable statistical documentation of the racial or ethnic makeup of the northern Sierra. Even our limited sampling demonstrates that self-identification varies from one community to the next in ways that do not permit facile generalization. Nor were we striving for an objective assessment of who and what people in these five communities really are. Our purpose, to the contrary, was to obtain—by providing respondents an opportunity to say who and what they take themselves to be—an index of the terms people take to be significant and, by inference from their choice of terms, a rough idea of the degree to which national culture is shared in the communities surveyed. For this reason the documentation presented in Table 1 is the beginning, not the end, of the investigation of ethnicity in the context of Ecuadorian national life. These survey results must now be interpreted first in terms of national culture and then in terms of the ethnic consciousness which they in part signify.

ECUADORIAN NATIONALISM AS A CULTURAL SYSTEM

Throughout most of the nearly 150 years of its history as a republic, those in control of the Ecuadorian state apparatus have been content with the pluralistic heritage of the colonial era. In recent years, however, the national leadership, motivated by the belief that *blanqueamiento* is both necessary and inevitable, has initiated programs designed to reduce the broad cultural, linguistic, and lifestyle differences that still exist. Integrative nationalism of this sort is always "as much cultural, even epistemological, as it [is] political . . . [because national leaders are] attempting to transform the symbolic framework through which people experience social reality, and thus, to the extent that life is what we make of it all, that reality itself" (Geertz 1971:362).

That Geertz's words aptly describe the present Ecuadorian cultural revolution is demonstrated by their echo in a recent statement by General Fernando Dobronsky O., Minister of Education for the Nationalist Revolutionary government in power from 1972 to the present (1979). In a discourse on Ecuadorian political culture the general concluded his remarks by stressing that ". . . the fundamental strategy a policy on national culture must pursue is the raising of consciousness concerning the necessity of such a policy, together with the planning of cultural development, because it is only mental changes [*los cambios mentales*] that will make possible the structural changes our society demands. From this point of view, culture is not simply an end, it is a means, being, without doubt, the beginning of all other human activity" (Dobronsky 1977:145–46).

If revolutionary nationalism entails a fundamental revision of frames of mind—the transformation of people's view of themselves and the definition of the realities they must confront—then any account of ethnic consciousness in the life of the nation must be a cultural account. It begins neither with nationalism nor with ethnicity but with a concept of culture. In that regard I take culture to be neither behavior, nor adaptation, nor cognition, nor the general form of the social order, but a meaningful ordering of persons and things in relation to one another: ". . . culture consists of socially established structures of meaning in terms of which people do . . . things . . . " (Geertz 1973:12).

Viewed as a cultural system, nationalism is a special sort of ideology that attempts to articulate the genius of locally established structures of meaning with symbolic forms selectively drawn from the wider world.[9] Just how the "essentialism" of primordial attachments and sentiments may be combined with what nationalist ideologues take "to be the overall direction and significance of . . . the history of our time" (Geertz 1971:363) is unique to each nation's experience. But in the final analysis nationalistic ideologies serve, as all ideologies do, to provide "maps of problematic social reality and matrices for the creation of collective conscience. . . . Ideologies . . . make empirical claims about the condition and direction of society . . . [naming] the structure of situations in such a way that the attitude toward them is one of commitment. . . . [Ideology] seeks to motivate action" (Geertz 1964:64, 71, 72).

Revolutionary nationalism confronts special problems, however, since it must transform national self-consciousness. Relationships between familiar things, persons, and processes must be redefined and remapped so that people conceive of themselves no longer as an aggregate of disparate groups but, rather, as a single, unified nation with a common past, a common future, and a common sense of how to best achieve the latter given the particular nature of the former. But because ideologies that attempt to produce, or coerce, this kind of social consensus always conglomerate myriad symbols whose power lies precisely in their multivocality, revolutionary nationalism is as likely to inspire opposition and dissensus as create conformity to a common vision. Structures and sentiments, moods and motivations, can indeed be revolutionized. But transformations in national consciousness may well be accompanied by microcosmogony among constituent ethnic groups whose members endeavor to construct or reconstruct their separate realities, "a universe of their own in which to dwell" within the larger sociopolitical order organized by the state (Fernandez 1969:5). It is more accurate, therefore, to conceive of

> . . . the culture of any society at any given moment [as] more like the debris or "fall out" of past ideological systems, than [as] itself a system, a coherent whole. Coherent wholes may exist . . . in individual heads . . . but human social groups tend to find their openness to the future in the variety of their metaphors for what may be the good life and in the contest of their paradigms. If there is order, it is seldom preordained (though transiently bayonets may underpin some political schema); it is achieved—the result of conflicting or concurring wills and intelligences, each relying on some convincing paradigm. (Turner 1974:14)

Marginality: Paradigm for an Expansive Nationalism

In the years since 1972 the claims made by the leaders of Ecuador's Revolutionary Nationalist government concerning the condition and direction of the nation have been clearly and convincingly stated. They have envisioned a movement away from a system of steeply stratified units, defined in racial and ethnic terms and distributed across the land in a complementary, noncompetitive division of labor, and toward a racially and culturally homogeneous, open-class system which will allow for a reshuffling and re-education of the population in such a way as to permit and facilitate national development along the lines of the modern, consumption-oriented world.

The paradigm, or symbolic framework, that names the structure of this situation in a way compelling action has also been clearly and repeatedly outlined by government officials and is widely shared among the national elite including many social scientists.[10] The paradigm hinges on the metaphoric use of margin-center imagery that construes racial and ethnic diversity as standing in relation to the nation as margin or periphery stands with respect to center or core. Thus the correlates of central position—vital activity, growth, and development—become associated by metaphoric correspondence with the nation. Associated with marginality, and corresponding to extant racial and ethnic diversity, are the paired negatives typified by lifelessness, stagnation, and backwardness. The problems of cultural diversity and underdevelopment are paradigmatically resolved, given the realities as posited by the metaphor, by substituting structural conditions of incorporation and integration for margainality, thereby transforming the stagnating margin by bringing it into vital contact with the dynamic center.

A recent analysis by the Ministry of Education applies the marginality paradigm to the problem of illiteracy in the context of national development. "No one can be blamed for being illiterate," the ministry explains in a special supplement to *El Comercio* (10 October 1977). Illiteracy is one of the results of "a long chain of events intimately related to the prejudicial marginalization of the less favored social classes." The range of "geographic, social, economic, political, and administrative factors" are seen by the ministry as being causally implicated in the "long and sorrowful historical process of domination and dependency" that has stripped the marginalized man of his human dignity. But in the last analysis it is "the negligence of the society and the State that have produced this phenomenon [of illiteracy] that so negatively intervenes in the development of peoples." Thus the nonsharing of national culture by the unlettered existing on what are taken to be the margins of national society comes to be interpreted as a major factor contributing to the relative underdevelopment of Ecuador with respect to other nations: *El país no puede levar sus anclas y enrumbarse hacia el progreso porque lo impede un pesado lastre de casi un millón de analfabetos.* "The nation cannot raise anchor and move off toward progress impeded as it is by the ballast of nearly one million illiterates."

The solution, given the paradigm, is obvious. The state, implicated in the creation of the problem out of past negligence, must take responsibility for the integration of marginalized groups and individuals into the active life of the nation. Inasmuch as formal education is the instrumentality by which the backward through resocialization are moved from margin to center, let us examine two aspects of Ecuadorian education—textbook treatment of the nation's history, and adult education and literacy training—that are especially revealing of the linkage perceived between the diffusion of national culture and the economic development of the nation.

Mythic Themes in the Genesis of Ecuadorian Nationality

Since the nation is taken to be sacred by those who believe in it, and since the activities of sacred beings—the Inca and the Christian God and his saints—are essential to the story, it is appropriate to treat Ecuadorian history as myth, a sacred narrative in the classic sense (Thompson 1946:9). Granted, this narrative has been committed to writing and to secular criticism, but careful comparison of successive editions of historical materials used in schools shows that the narrative has been faithfully transmitted to generations of the formally educated since the foundation of Ecuadorian nationhood was laid in the writings of Jesuit Padre Juan de Velasco (first published in Ecuador in 1841–44).[11]

Textbook history of Ecuador also has the same operational value as myth insofar as Lévi-Strauss's commentary on French politicians applies also to proponents of Ecuadorian nationalism: to them national history "is both a sequence [of happenings] belonging to the past . . . and a timeless pattern which can be detected in the contemporary . . . social structure and which provides a clue for its interpretation, a lead from which to infer future developments" (Lévi-Strauss 1963:209). Professor Ligdano Chávez, who in 1943 won a national essay competition on the theme "The Contribution of the Ecuadorian Primary School to the Formation of National Identity," has described the role of the nation's history in parallel terms: "If the past has not bequeathed an Iliad and Odyssey to give us a deep sense of our nationality, then we must review our History and our Geography; there is the greatness of our people, the magnificence of what we were, the hope of what we will be . . . " (Chávez 1952b:54). Unfortunately, from the perspective of those anxious for national development, the marginalized groups have been denied formal schooling, with the result that for them "education has not up to now been able to shape . . . a well-channeled sense, a clear and precise concept, a conscious and self-evident notion of what our nationality is" (Chávez 1952b:52). But for those who have had the opportunity to complete at least the primary grades, textbook accounts of Ecuadorian history communicate a clear concept of the timeless patterns discernible in contemporary life.

El Mestizaje: Condensed Symbol of *Ecuatorianidad*

Those who have received a formal education have a sense of themselves as Ecuadorians which is firmly and frankly rooted in a significant pre-Columbian past. They are not Europeans transplanted to

American soil. The Ecuadorian is a son of Spain *and* of America, "heir of two bloods and two human conditions" (Cevallos García 1974:118). The concept that race mixture has generated a unique mode and manner of being human is nowhere more forthrightly stated than in the opening paragraph of historian Cevallos García's eleventh-grade *Historia del Ecuador*:

> Miscegenation is the point of departure for the history of what we refer to as the Republic of Ecuador. The mixing of human types of diverse origins began thousands of years before the Spaniards landed on American shores, initiating a new genus of miscegenation. The men who arrived in the sixteenth century were *mestizos*; so also were those who had for millennia populated the New World. For this reason the union of these two groups met no resistance; and it is from this fusion that we have acquired the human and the cultural genius, the historic condition, and the physical traits which distinguish us within the universal community of peoples. (Cevallos García 1974:13)

The notion that American history has produced a *mestizo* type—of basically Amerindian descent with European, and perhaps African, admixture—is familiar to most sierrans. That the fusion of which Cevallos García speaks is essentially Amerindian, at least in the Sierra, is based on the supposition that the indigenous component was numerically superior to the Spanish component. That the blend was not and is not uniform is apparent to anyone who compares the physical characteristics of almost any given set of persons presently resident in the region. Often, even within the same family, obvious phenotypic features vary noticeably, suggesting that the ancestral racial stocks are not uniformly represented even within the same family.[12]

If it were simply features of physical appearance that were implicated in *la mezcla de las razas*, any evidence of differential admixture would be of little moment. But as a matter of social fact, the three racial strains—the peninsular *raza blanca*, the Andean *raza india*, the African *raza negra*—customarily distinguished in the northern Sierra are stereotypically associated with certain moral, emotional, motivational, intellectual, and spiritual characteristics believed to have been transmitted more or less intact to present generations despite four centuries of miscegenation (see Faron 1970 on Peruvian folk sociobiology, Pitt-Rivers 1967 and Mörner 1967 on Latin America in general). Miscegenation history, which is the history of the nation, describes the origin of these phenotypic characteristics and accounts for their perceived distribution in the contemporary population as a consequence of that history.

Los Shyris and the Kingdom of Quito

Textbook treatment pushes miscegenation history back into the pre-Columbian epoch. Archaeological remains of regional provenience are interpreted as demonstrating a series of migrations and comminglings of peoples of diverse geographic and cultural origins. The most important development in the history of the nation, according to Padre Velasco, was the conquest of the northern Andes by a powerful and sophisticated people known as the Cara who are said to have arrived on Ecuadorian shores from somewhere over the Pacific about 750 A.D.[13] Having established a city on the coast, an environment they soon found unsatisfactory, they ascended into the highlands where they easily dominated the indigenous agricultural communities. The leaders of the Cara, known as Shyris, or Lords, are said to have organized the tribal units under their domain into a confederation whose capital they located in Quito.

Although the secondary-level texts discuss the legendary Kingdom of Quito at some length, they conclude that Padre Velasco may have exaggerated its significance in the interest of national identity building. One fourth-grade text, however, presenting the Shyris and their kingdom as historic fact, makes them "the foundation of our nationality," because they (1) established the unity and integrity of a political and territorial unit centered on Quito as its capital; (2) established the basic sociopolitical structure of the nation, stratified into social classes led by a *cacique*, chief, or Shyri in the case of the Cara, with classes of warriors, priestly functionaries, the people in general, and the slaves, who were generally prisoners of war, in their respective ranks, below; (3) demonstrated, in their ultimately ill-fated defense of Quiteño territory against the Incaic incursion, an exemplary spirit of liberty and independence (*Colección* L.N.S. 1976:80).

Atahualpa, the Quiteño Inca

Beginning in the 1460s, Incaic domination was gradually extended from south to north as far as Quito as one after another of the Quiteño peoples were subjugated by the armies of Inca Túpac Yupanqui. Conquest of Quiteño territory north of Quito was left to Túpac Yupanqui's son Huayna Cápac in the latter 1490s. It was the peoples of the northern Sierra, above all the Caranquis, who are credited with mounting the final and fiercest phase of Quiteño resistance. These rebellious "friends of liberty" succumbed only after a fearful massacre in which not only the combatants but all males capable of bearing arms, some 30,000 souls, were slain by Huayna Cápac's men in the vicinity of a lake near Ibarra known as Yaguarcocha, the lake of blood.

The penetration of the Kingdom of Quito by the Empire of Cuzco resulted in a further intermingling of indigenous American bloodlines and cultural traditions. Both the soldiers and the *mitimaes* (loyal colonists from Peru and Bolivia settled in Ecuador by the Inca) brought Incaic blood, language, and customs which they apparently shared with the peoples of Quito. Cited in proof of this miscegenation are the cultural, psychological, and emotional similarities said to exist between the present-day *campesino* populations of Ecuador, Peru, and Bolivia (Cevallos García 1974:62–63).

But from the perspective of Ecuadorian nationalism, the most significant development was the subsequent Quiteño "conquest" of the Inca. According to national tradition, Inca Huayna Cápac, who is believed to have been born in Quiteño soil in Cuenca, sought to appease the vanquished Quiteños by establishing his residence in the former Shyri capital and taking Princess Pacha of Caranqui as his wife. The "location of the Emperor's residence in Quito signified the spiritual triumph of Ecuadorian nationality . . . " (Chávez 1952a:49), while the fruit of the union between Inca Huayna Cápac and Princess Pacha became the first Inca of Quiteño parentage as well as the last, owing to the untimely arrival of the Spaniards. The Quiteño Inca Atahualpa thus fills a unique place in national history as the archetype of the indigenous *mestizo* and the root of invidious distinctions between present-day Quiteños and their neighbors to the south. A fourth-grade text characterizes Atahualpa as having been "witty, agile, commanding, and possessed of an excellent memory. His manly character was different from the weakness and submissiveness of his [half-]brother Huáscar [who had a Peruvian mother]" (*Colección* L.N.S. 1976:81).

Spaniards Build Cities; Quiteñas Contribute Their Blood

The Spanish conquest of Quito in the 1530s initiated a new epoch in the formation of the Ecuadorian nation that was to endure for nearly three centuries. Although this new incursion was simply another in the series of imperial penetrations of the northern Andes— first the Cara Kingdom of Quito, then the Inca's *Tahuantinsuyo*, and now the kings and queens of Spain and their *real audiencia de Quito*— the requisites of peninsular civilization differed considerably from those of earlier empires. Chief among the necessities found lacking was the absence of a proper urban ambience. Not that the newly conquered territories were devoid of places where men might dwell, but that the establishment of Spanish cities in the name of God, the crown, and the conquerors themselves represented the institution of an urban, Christian way of life on pagan soil. Thus it was that the

Ecuadorian nation, according to textbook accounts, came to have an urban foundation—the conquistadors turned first, once the Inca lords had been slain, to the laying out of their cities: Quito in 1534, taking over the aboriginal site and name; also in 1534, the city now called Riobamba; Portoviejo in 1535; Guayaquil, on its present site, in 1538, and so on.

While these new cities provided an environment conducive to the lifestyle sought by the conquerors, textbook histories describe these men as wanting for female companionship on account of the scarcity of peninsular women during the early years of the colony. Mixed unions between Spaniard and Quiteña were therefore required if civilized life was to flourish. *La mezcla de las razas* was the natural consequence. Thus, through necessity, urban life and miscegenation became intimately linked as essential to and generative of the life of the nation; "the city was the context within which *el mestizaje* took place, and *el mestizaje* was the social fact that permitted urban life" (Cevallos García 1974:197).

Colonial urban life also required the maintenance of the ancient European and Andean-American tradition of class and ethnic stratification. Conquistadors and others of royal entitlement formed the privileged stratum. A lower stratum, which formed the core of the urban population, was made up of common soldiers of European birth, the *criollos* who were of European descent but born in America, and the *mestizos*. With respect to the social placement of the indigenous Quiteño population, it is necessary to distinguish between two significantly different groups: "those primitives who willfully or through necessity, by force or for lack of caring, came to live within the confines of the Spanish cities, there to be rapidly and definitively absorbed by, or to themselves absorb, their racially opposite counterpart. This group evolved quickly. But those who remained in the countryside . . . stagnated; and it is there, bound to the earth, that they vegetate still" (Cevallos García 1974:118).

Those Quiteños who entered into urban life and the miscegenation that took place there made a lasting contribution to Ecuadorian nationality. As Professor Chávez explains, the Spaniards confronted both cultural and biological challenges in their adaptation to New World conditions. Culturally, their European heritage proved superior to that of the Quiteños. But the aborigines, "in their authentic condition . . . were entities of a perfect race," perfectly adapted, that is to say, to "the forces of the environment . . . in which they lived" (Chávez 1952a:50). They were able to contribute this biological heritage to the new American race, so that in the arteries of every *mestizo*

Ecuadorian there "throbs the genius of the vanquished race . . . "
(Chávez 1952a:50).

The African slave, together with the *mulato* and the *zambo*—product of miscegenation with European and with Quiteño respectively—filled the bottom stratum within colonial society, the status that slaves had traditionally filled in both peninsular and aboriginal Quiteño societies. In all the broad sweep of the historical developments that gave form and content to Ecuadorian nationality, if we follow textbook accounts, the African slave population played the most limited of roles. It is mentioned that *el mestizaje* took on, during certain periods and in certain places, a negroid component. But no positive fruits of this admixture are mentioned. The African contribution seems only to have complicated the amalgam by creating a proliferation of *castas*, terms used to designate the multiplicity of racial crosses that arise when mixed types mate. Beyond that, we learn only that the labor of Africans was utilized in the Sierra where the aborigine could not or was not permitted to work. "These *negros* were not even owners of their own bodies," a seventh-grade textbook recounts; "for them the family did not exist; all were slaves and they were always condemned to the most onerous of labors" (*Colección* L.N.S. ca. 1974:143).

Marginalization and Degeneration of the Indigenous Race

Once the *mestizo* character of the developing nation is firmly established, textbook treatment of the indigenous population changes dramatically. No longer proud, progressive, or heroic figures, the nonurban, unmixed descendants of the Shyris and the Incas are presented as a people whose very soul was crushed by oppressive institutions imposed by greedy colonists to exploit indigenous labor. The result, though lamentable—and, indeed, these were Spanish, not Ecuadorian, institutions—is rationalized as the inevitable consequence of two factors: (1) the nature of the life of the developing nation, given that its developmental course was determined by its nature, and (2) the relative primitiveness of indigenous social and cultural forms.

As an example of the impact of the former, the very exclusion of the nonurban indigenous population from the national mainstream is presented as following logically from the requisites of urban, which is to say national, life:

> Areas of ancient indigenous settlement were taken over for the new urban centers. Land where the aborigine had formerly sown his maize or his

potatoes, his *yuca* or his *camotes*, became the house lots and the agricultural lands of the new citizens. As these areas were always located near a river, with fertile soil and mild climate, the displacement of the aborigine meant an exodus to remote, almost inaccessible fields. One would have to say that with the departure of the *indio* to the rugged slopes or to the desolate *páramo*, America's past departed too, taking refuge in the countryside. (*Colección* L.N.S. ca. 1968:133–34)

The current edition of this text replaces the last sentence with: "There to the countryside he went with his rancor, his sad music, and his Incaic customs . . . " (*Colección* L.N.S. ca. 1974:164).

Although forced to settle on and till the less desirable slopes, the indigenous communities of the Sierra were by no means out of reach of Spanish colonial institutions. These institutions, we are led to believe, drastically and irreversibly altered indigenous life and indigenous character:

> The *indio* was submitted to the most onerous labors, the fruits of which went to the exclusive benefit of the conquerors. From freeman, in control of his destiny, he became a slave; considered as the lowest social class, he had no right to enjoy what was his. *La encomienda* [tribute system], *la mita*, and *los obrajes* [labor service systems] served to make the victors owners of the vanquished. (*Colección* L.N.S. ca. 1968:100)
>
> While preaching the gospel of peace and justice, they took the liberty and the land of the aboriginal American and the new economic institutions caused his ruin. (*Colección* L.N.S. ca. 1974:163)

This reading of the nation's history and this interpretation of the biological, social, and cultural condition of nonnational Ecuadorians clearly lend credence and depth to the center-margin paradigm outlined above. If we take national culture to be a meaningful ordering of persons and things, it can be readily shown that the relation between vital center and vegetating margin serves to neatly classify the highland population by social race; the classification is illustrated in Figure 1, below.

Note also, however, that the isolation of Amerindian- and African-descended peoples is not only geographic—the nation's cities surrounded by the descendants of Atahualpa, nursing their grudges, piping their melancholy tunes, and practicing their ancient customs—but, as is common to the *indigenista*, or Indophile, component of Latin American nationalism in general (see Nash 1975:229–30), indigenous peoples are isolated in both historical and evolutionary time as well. Pre-Columbian peoples are glorified and symbolically appropriated as epitomizing, even as creating, essential features of Ecuadorianness. But, from the perspective of the nation, that which

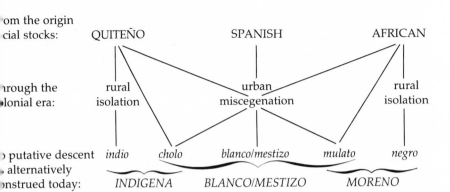

om the origin
cial stocks: QUITEÑO   SPANISH   AFRICAN

rough the   rural   urban   rural
lonial era: isolation   miscegenation   isolation

putative descent   *indio*   *cholo*   *blanco/mestizo*   *mulato*   *negro*
alternatively
nstrued today: *INDIGENA*   *BLANCO/MESTIZO*   *MORENO*

FIGURE 1. Processes of marginalization and miscegenation as presented in
           Ecuadorian national history.

remains of the cultural aspects of the Amerindian heritage can only
be judged as more primitive and, therefore, necessarily inferior to
the culture and the lifestyle of the nation.

One of the more succinctly argued claims that national development must of necessity supersede relatively more primitive indigenous institutions is presented by Ligdano Chávez in his analysis of
the religious aspect of Ecuadorian nationalism:

> In evolutionary terms human religions fall into the following succession of
> types: animism, pantheism, polytheism, and monotheism. It can be
> shown that indigenous religious expression had not reached its full natural
> development before the arrival of the Spaniards. There are manifestations
> of animism, for example, in the practices of the Jívaro tribes of the Oriente.
> Among the pre-Incaic peoples of the highlands one finds pantheistic prac-
> tices: "The Quitus worshiped the Sun; the Puruháes, the high mountains
> . . . ; the Cañaris, snakes, mountains and sacred lakes . . . " [Chávez is
> quoting a litany from Reyes (1934:23) repeated in virtually every Ecuado-
> rian school book]. Incaic civilization, in its turn, had a polytheistic ten-
> dency. But the spontaneous development of American religious forms was
> cut short by the implantation of European monotheism, the product of
> more than twenty centuries of evolution. The indigenous peoples of old
> completely lost their religious reflexes before the Catholic imperative. That
> it was a rude jump for pre-Columbian culture to make was demonstrated
> by the Inca Atahualpa's frank disdain in the presence of Padre Valverde
> [who baptized the Inca before he was slain]. But Catholicism had to im-
> pose itself. As a superior religion and proven as such in the Old World, it
> easily penetrated the Ecuadorian consciousness. Ever since the erection of
> the first church towers in the Colony, it has been common to see the Indian

carrying Saints and *priostazgos* [symbols of festival sponsorship] in the plaza. For the *mestizo* religious adaptation presented no problem; born into Catholicism, he has pursued his development within it. Monotheistic Catholicism corresponds to Ecuadorian nationality; the people, the nation, is very Catholic in its infrastructural essence. (My paraphrase of Chávez 1952a:53–54)

As it was and is with religious belief and expression, so it was and is with other cultural forms. The primitive Quiteño dialects, according to Chávez (1952a:51), blended with the Quichua of the Inca; Quichua, in its turn, collided with the academic language of Castile. With each successive linguistic contribution, the nation is richer in expressive forms, though later forms tend to supersede and replace earlier forms. Today, English, not Quichua, is taught as a second language in Ecuadorian schools. The teaching of English is indicative of a broader Anglo-European invasion of Quiteño territory by what many about-to-be-conquered Ecuadorians take to be more highly evolved cultural forms.

In Step with the Rhythm of Modern Life

It is not possible to know exactly what the native reaction was to the cultural aspects of the Incaic and Spanish invasions. But if valiant defense of Quiteño autonomy indicates resistance to the cultural imperialism that came along with the political subjugation, the current invasion appears to be succeeding without a struggle—at least on the part of those who accept the goals of national culture. This latest chapter in the story of Ecuadorian national development does not yet appear in textbook histories, but its outline can be sketched from journalistic accounts and observations in the northern Sierra.

Willingness to draw on alien cultural forms is, perhaps, common to all nations "in development" that suffer from the double burden of both pride and envy—proud that they are not guilty of the sins of the "over-developed" nations and at the same time envious of the fruits that development brings. In the Ecuadorian case it is a sense of marginality that shapes this ambivalent perspective on the larger world community. The nation's underdeveloped condition is blamed on abuses wrought upon Ecuador by the superpowers, leaving her on the sidelines of major intellectual trends and at the mercy of major economic currents. At the same time, the solution to this marginalization is sought in the form of aid from these same powers—aid in the form of borrowed capital, borrowed technology, borrowed expertise. The assumption operative here is not different from that which informed Professor Chávez's analysis of the evolutionary progression of religious forms: that "developed" economic forms and techniques are generally superior to and must necessarily replace the more "primitive" forms common in "backward," "prejudicially marginalized" regions such as Ecuador. Operating under the assumption that foreign is better, government development planners are and have been attempting to apply strategies and designs borrowed from, and, indeed, not uncommonly imposed by, international corporate concerns, development agencies, and foreign governments. The subject of economic development by infusion is too vast for full treatment here, but a few examples will illustrate how these current trends mesh with the mythic themes in terms of which Ecuadorian nationality is understood.

The first of these major themes, to abstract from our rendering of nationalist history, is that *the nation is a natural political and territorial unit centered in Quito, its capital.* Although the history of border disputes and encroachments is long, and for Ecuador painfully humiliating, current events do not threaten the integrity of the territorial unit so much as the traditional political dominance of Quito and the Sierra with respect to the coastal and interior lowlands. Demographic shifts have given the Coast a slight majority (49%) of the nation's population (INEC 1977:9). The Oriente, while it accounts for only about 3% of the nation's population (INEC 1977:9), includes over half of the national territory.

The relative importance of the lowland regions has also been magnified by recent economic developments. In the Oriente intensive exploitation of Ecuador's oil reserves has been carried out with the collaboration of international concerns. It was a Texaco-Gulf consortium, for example, that laid a 318-mile pipeline from wells in the Amazonian interior, across the Andes, to the Pacific coast port city of Esmeraldas, where a refinery was constructed by a Japanese consortium (NACLA 1975). International financing and investment are involved in timber exploitation on the coast and agribusiness in the Oriente, while Allis-Chalmers of Canada is installing heavy machinery for a cement production facility located near Otavalo for which raw materials will be mined from the rugged interior of the western cordillera.

Nor has the Sierra escaped the impact of internationally assisted development efforts. The Israelis have provided advice on arid-ecology irrigation projects and the formation of agricultural cooperatives which, together with land reform, have aimed at increasing agricultural production in the highlands. That the technologies thus transferred from other ecological and cultural contexts appear ill adapted to Ecuador's delicate arid coastal, tropical forest (both coastal and interior), and microvariable Andean ecosystems seems not to stem the flow of foreign experts. Nor does the existence of cultural systems already well adapted in these ecosystems seem to bear, except negatively as obstacles, on plans to remake Ecuador and Ecuadorians along the lines of the rest of the developed world (on the lowland regions see Whitten 1974b, 1976a, 1978). Economic development efforts have, in fact, reinforced the centralization of labor, investment, and bureaucratic control in Quito and other major urban centers.

Thus the second of the components of Ecuadorian nationality, that *the nation is urban*, has been sustained and strengthened. The business of the nation is conducted in the cities. Nonurban sectors remain the object of the nation's business. The city remains the point where everything converges: "To come here [to Quito] is to arrive. Arrive to become servants of a people who, taking advantage of the advance of modern technology, attempt with all the vigor of their race, to find the path to social well-being for their constituents. . . . Quito is two cities in one: head and mind as the seat of central government, and heart—retaining over the generations her irrevocable vocation as 'Light of America'" (Guillermo Moreno, *El Comercio*, 7 December 1977).

Councilman Moreno's reference to "Light of America" evokes Quito's legendary role as forerunner in the movement for independence from Spanish colonial rule. The light shown on 10 August 1809, when patriots threw local Spanish authorities in jail and proclaimed Quito free. But despite these early declarations of liberty, the third component of Ecuadorian nationality persists: *the nation remains a steeply stratified entity* with a small group of leading families controlling the means by which the remainder of the population is obliged to make its living. The concentration of wealth and power in the hands of an oligarchy (Navarro Jiménez 1976) is generally acknowledged as the factor responsible for 150 years of nonrepresentative, dictatorial governments in Ecuador. The call is for democratic participation in the governance of national affairs. But radical change is unlikely, since modern economic arrangements mesh rather well with Ecuador's five-century tradition of paternalistic rule from distant metropolitan centers through a local privileged elite. What material difference does it made whether the laboring man pays tribute through a local elite to the Inca in Cuzco, the Spanish crown in Seville, Coca-Cola in Atlanta, or Mitsubishi in Tokyo?

The fourth thematic component—that *the nation is mestizo*—is related to the fifth—that *the major initiatives for cultural change have come to the nation from the outside.* The first to come were the Cara from somewhere over the sea, next the Inca from Cuzco, then the Spaniards, and now the world of international development. Textbook history teaches that in each case the conquerors were culturally superior to the native peoples, and that in each case their alien influence was nationalized through miscegenation. One fourth-grade text, for example, describes the impact of the Cara conquest on the native Quiteños in these terms: "It appears certain that the original inhabitants of Quito were weak and little advanced. But men of intelligence and enterprizing race who had settled [on the Coast], ascended [into the Sierra] following the Río Esmeraldas . . . and easily subjugated the Quitus, whose ancient customs they took over, reinvigorating them, but leaving the aboriginal name of this people unchanged" (Arregui de Pazmiño and Carrillo de Landázuri ca. 1975:254).

The ultimate cultural impact of the contemporary invasion is impossible to discern at present, but it is clear that some Ecuadorians are more receptive to outside influences than others. It is these latter, the relatively unmixed *indígena/cholo* and *moreno/mulato* populations, that are seen by the former as the real obstacle to the future well-being of the nation. It is their ways of life and their psychocultural characteristics that are evaluated as less advanced than those that come with technologies imported or imposed from the outside. It is the presence of these nonnationalized groups that is said to give rise to deep internal divisions which must be overcome if the nation is to regain its dignity, find its proper place in the modern world, and win the respect of other nations.

Of the Nation, a School

Under the slogan "Let us make of Ecuador one big school," the military government through the Minister of Education, General Dobronsky O., announced in 1977 a new program of literacy training and adult education designed as a program component of a new law of education and culture. Following a banner page which read, "This is the reality: From a country with deep differences, let us forge a just Ecuador," linkage between education, diffusion of national culture, and socioeconomic development was outlined in an appeal for public commitment to the program (special supplement published with *El Comercio*, 10 October 1977, and attributed to the Ministry of Education). I summarize in paraphrase the rationale offered for popular support as follows:

(1) Development planning must reckon with the capacity of the nation's human capital to assimilate transformations and adapt to the fundamental reforms of economic and social structures currently in progress. In this connection it is well known that those human groups which have existed at the margin of the benefits of the regular educational system create brakes on the development process, since they, just coincidentally, are basically self-sufficient and participate in a limited way in the advance of the nation. (P. 8)

(2) At present, there are over one million persons, at least 28% of the adult population, unlettered, marginalized, and totally incapable of cooperating with the objectives of national development, since illiteracy signifies unemployment, nil or low productivity, conformity, and so on. Most seriously, the illiterate has little motivation for change, has difficulty taking decisive action in the resolution of his own problems, has a limited understanding of cooperative effort and mutual aid, and so cannot contribute effectively to the development of his local community, much less the progress of the nation.

The great mass of illiterates neither produces nor consumes; owing to their lack of knowledge, thousands of *campesinos* do not wear shoes, are unfamiliar with dentifrice, do not use hand soap to wash themselves, and are ignorant of many other of the goods and articles indispensable to life. (P. 7)

(3) From this point of view, adult education takes on economic significance . . . [but] for education to figure as a true factor of change, it must overcome its traditionalist spirit, identify and bind itself to the historic reality of a people in search of new attitudes and postures that facilitate the modification of their structural conditions. (P. 8)

(4) When we extend the right of an education to all, we will find that this million of our marginalized compatriots will not only consume, but also produce, and in this way, by aiding others, we will have helped ourselves. (P. 7)

(5) The Ministry of Education invites all Ecuadorians to take aggressive action toward making of Ecuador one vast school to the end of integrating the illiterate into the life of the country, to recover his dignity . . . and that of the nation.

The development of the nation depends on the culture of its people. (P. 8)

Through text and illustration, this eight-page program announcement clearly spells out the negative characteristics of those who, because of their marginal involvement in national institutions and their failure to share the goals of national culture, have become the ballast which prevents the ship of Ecuadorian development from moving forward. Also clearly spelled out are the characteristics of the "new type of Ecuadorian" who is aware of his civic responsibilities and is

TABLE 2. Psychocultural and Socioeconomic Characteristics Said to Block or
to Facilitate Ecuadorian National Development

The Marginalized Person or Group	The New Type of Ecuadorian
1. He is a *campesino*, rural laborer, including unskilled, unlettered migrants to urban centers.	1. He is a *trabajador*, industrial or technical worker, or anyone who is "working" for national development.
2. He has been deprived of his human dignity.	2. He is confident of his capacities and potentialities.
3. His consciousness is magical in character; he sees his situation in terms of euphemisms and sophistries. He is prejudiced, superstitious, and taboo-ridden.	3. His consciousness is reflective and critical. Everyday realities and problems are seen clearly so they can be dealt with.
4. Waiting for others to do his thinking and acting for him, he has difficulty taking decisive action to resolve his own problems.	4. He thinks as an Ecuadorian, as master of his own destiny, acting with determination to better the environment where he was born and grew up.
5. Forced to sell their labor for pennies, the uneducated see their work as a curse of God.	5. Labor integrated with education becomes a human blessing, liberator from misery, illness, and ignorance.
6. Their illiteracy signifies unemployment, underemployment, backwardness on all levels, conformity, and poverty.	6. The literate individual finds better work opportunities, thus lending his positive support to the development of the country.
7. Long accustomed to the semifeudal hacienda system, the illiterate supplies his own basic needs. He neither produces nor consumes.	7. The new Ecuadorian is integrated into the free world. He exercises his rights and fulfills his obligations. He is disposed to produce and to consume more.

SOURCE: Special supplement announcing "The National Plan for Adult Education and Literacy Training" published with *El Comercio*, Quito, 10 Oct. 1977, and produced, apparently, by the Ecuadorian Ministry of Education, General Fernando Dobronsky Ojeda, Minister of Education. Translation mine.

properly trained and motivated so that he may become positively engaged in national affairs at all levels. Abstracting phraseology used in the announcement, Table 2 contrasts the negative characteristics of the "marginalized person or group" with those of the ideal "new type of Ecuadorian."

It is most significant that in the eight pages of text the announcement makes only one direct racial/ethnic reference—in the context of a discussion citing relatively higher illiteracy rates in rural areas where the "indigenous population" is most numerous. But the several dozen photos and drawings that illustrate the text depict almost exclusively members of the *indígena, cholo, montuvio,* and *moreno* populations. They are shown in both the "marginalized" condition, engaged in "selling their labor for a few pennies," and also in the classroom situation—where their marginalization is to be transformed—as they acquire "the education and the knowledge that will equip them to make a positive contribution to the progress of the nation."

It happens that a substantial portion of the people we interviewed in Ibarra and in the outlying rural communities fit the description of what the Ministry of Education's program announcement depicts in text and illustrations as "marginal." Twenty percent of the adults surveyed were reported to be illiterate; another 23% have received less than four years of formal education. Few of those interviewed would not agree that they are forced to sell their labor for pennies, and if the nation is *mestizo/blanco,* 44% identified themselves in terms that indicate they are nonmembers. Yet if we can catch a glimpse of the nation through the other end of the telescope, interpreting the nation from the point of view of the so-called marginalized groups, what seems to be the center becomes periphery, what seems to be culturelessness becomes ethnicity, and what seems essential to national development becomes a sell-out of *ecuatorianidad.*

ECUADORIAN ETHNICITY AS A CULTURAL SYSTEM

Studies of ethnic minorities in the context of nation-state formation, expansion, and reorganization have been accumulating for over a century, but it has proven difficult for anthropologists and sociologists to discern the cultural significance of being ethnic in the modern world. It has been difficult to reverse the field, to evaluate the encompassing cultural order from the ethnic point of view, because ethnicity has been interpreted either as a vestige of the traditional world on the wane or as a mere sign phenomenon, where ethnic tags, in the manner of bumper stickers, serve to distinguish among social entities that are otherwise culturally homogeneous. When it is believed that a particular minority cultural order is doomed to extinction, it is common to speak of ethnocide (e.g., Bodley 1975, Dostal 1972) or, longer ago, of acculturation (e.g., Broom et al. 1954). When it is found that ethnic diversity persists despite presumed evolutionary trends to higher, more broadly integrative cultural and political systems, it has been common to join the national elites in evaluating cultural pluralism as regressive, or else to treat ethnicity as a vehicle for the achievement of some competitive advantage in the market place or in the political arena.

But in recent years social analysts have begun to notice that in the context of pressures for economic, political, and cultural assimilation, some peoples have been successful in resisting threatened incorporation and cooptation insofar as they have been able to create and maintain separate realities of their own within the larger economic, political, and cultural orders organized and controlled by the nation-state, by state-sponsored international corporations, and by one-world institutions. These instances belie the notion that ethnicity is always epiphenomenal and indicate the need for a theory that will account for the contemporary proliferation of cultural orders. Under the four headings that appear below, elements of such a theory, culled from the literature on ethnogenesis and ethnotransformation in the context of nation-state expansion and integration, are presented parallel to a demonstration of how ethnicity in Ecuador's northern Sierra protests against the larger national situation, not by struggling to take over or overthrow the state apparatus but by refusing to be deceived by the definitions of contemporary realities that the controllers of the state are promoting in the name of national development.

Nation-State Conquest of Tribal and Ethnic Peoples

Nation-state expansion has typically involved the incorporation of formerly autonomous or semiautonomous peoples within a more fully encompassing system of influence and control, often including the internal reordering of such systems to engage more fully peoples who have long lived within the sphere of influence organized by the state but in some different and more limited role (Francis 1948, Fried 1967, Singer 1962, Spicer 1971). In the Ecuadorian case the incorporation of so-called tribal peoples—and peoples on the frontiers of state systems seem always to be perceived as tribal (Fried 1975)—is occurring in the tropical rainforest sectors of the Coast and Oriente as the state attempts to expand its control over these regions and exploit the resources located there for the benefit of national development. In the Sierra national development requires, as the Ministry of Education's literacy program announcement makes clear, a reordering of the engagement of labor. Labor is to be reassigned, through retraining and relocation, away from labor-intensive and cottage industry modes of production, where the laborer or craftsman traditionally had at least partial control over the means, however meager, of production, to more capital-intensive, mechanized means that are wholly owned by parties of another class, place, and disposition. The intent and the effect are to minimize self-sufficiency, archenemy of national development, by eliminating arrangements that allow people to consume primarily what they themselves produce or is produced locally and acquired particularistically, and to maximize consumption of and dependence upon goods that are industrially produced either nationally or abroad.

Class and Ethnicity

In the context of nation-state formation, expansion, or reorganization, competition among subnational allegiances becomes acute, so that individual and collective identity systems take on an increasingly self-conscious and volitional character (Patterson 1975, Valentine 1975). State systems always generate internal differentiation based on differential access to commonly valued resources (Charbonnier 1969, Fried 1967), so that identity—who and what a person or group is—commonly becomes part of a class-based "culture of inequality" (Fallers 1973). But just as commonly ethnicity, as distinct from class and party, becomes or remains an alternative basis of identity claims and commitments (Banton 1974, Bennett 1975:3, Despres 1975, Greeley 1974:290–317, González 1975:120). It is imperative, therefore, that class-based claims and commitments be distinguished from those that are based on ethnicity, since both are commonly present within the encompassing system organized by the state.

The existence of ethnically based conflict over issues of incorporation and assimilation has been documented for the Oriente (Federación de Centros Shuar 1976; Naranjo 1977; Salazar 1977; Whitten 1976b, 1977, 1978). For the Sierra, Frank Salomon has documented the efforts of indigenous Otavaleños to "arrange their relations with the spreading and deepening national institutions in such a way as to protect their own independence and security . . . [by] restricting their dependence to resources over which they have some control," namely, the land (1973:465–66; and see Villavicencio Rivadeneira 1973). This "reconquest of the land," as Salomon has aptly termed it, is also taking place at lower elevations, in the valley of the Río Chota-Mira, where some black former *huasipungueros* have been able to purchase parcels of the hacienda land on which they worked as peons until just a few years ago.

But their numbers are relatively few, and generally in the northern Sierra internal differentiation increasingly is made to turn on class rather than ethnic divisions. As we have seen, national development plans rationalize the reassignment of labor as a necessary step in the integration of the marginalized sierran into the national society and economy. As a class issue this apparent transformation of the status of the sierran workingman is no more than sleight of hand. Members of the so-called marginal populations are well aware that they have for centuries been effectively integrated into the society and the economy of the nation. They have been, quite literally, the backbone, as well as the arms and the legs, of a labor-intensive economy that located its head, heart, and purse strings in Quito and other major urban centers. Under the traditional mode of production labor was permitted sufficient land and other resources so that it could feed and reproduce itself while at the same time rendering up rents and services sufficient to support the dominant classes in the cities. Now that this mixed capitalist-tribute mode of production (I owe this terminology to Wolf 1978) no longer generates the quantity of goods, the kind of consumption, or the amount of return on capital that the national economy is deemed to require, the tribute aspects of the traditional system are being eliminated, labor is being stripped of all direct access to the means of production, and the move is on to transform *indígena, cholo,* and *moreno campesinos* into *mestizo trabajadores*.

One form that resistance to the state's transparent claims has taken is manifest in the proliferation of *campesino* and labor organizations whose varied political colorings are evidenced by international ties ranging all the way from the CIA on the right to the red end of the spectrum on the left (NACLA 1975, Ramirez et al. 1978:45–48). These labor organizations are not, however, ethnic movements, at least not at the level of national and international leadership. They are class-based because they accept the legitimacy of the state's claims to dominance and domain. While they may be at odds with a particular form of government or with the incumbent regime, labor organizations such as these, and class- and party-based groups in general, are competing with the national elites for the goal that both value above all others—control of the state apparatus (Durkheim 1949, Geertz 1963:111, Sahlins 1976:19). A class-based ideology, then, is one that says, in effect, "we [all] agree on the values [goals or valued ends and resources] and we want them (want to keep them, want to share them with you, or want to take them from you)" (Aronson 1976:14–15).

Ethnicity, on the other hand, is an idiom of disengagement from the struggle over control of the encompassing sociopolitical arena organized by the state: "an ethnic ideology says in effect that we do not agree on the ultimate values (or goals or ends) of the system, and we want to be left alone (perhaps with enough resources) to pursue 'our' own ends, whatever you may be doing. Applied to others, it says we will treat you as if you are pursuing different values from those we have" (Aronson 1976:15; cf. Barth 1969:14). Ethnic groups that remain ethnic do not control state systems that include peoples other than themselves (Spicer 1971:797). They stand, rather, as societies against the state (Clastres 1977), rejecting the legitimacy of the state's claims to sovereignty over their existence.

Ethnicity as a Cultural Process

To be ethnic is countercultural because ethnicity entails nonconformity to and dissent from "claims about the condition and direction of society" (Geertz 1964:72) made by those who control it or wish they did. But while ethnicity is self-conscious and chosen, especially in the sense that as a dissident value position it can be abandoned for other alternatives, it is never in its genesis or maintenace a contrived instrumentality. "New ethnic definitions are always grounded in preexisting ethnic realities," making ethnicity both primordial and, because it is an oppositional process, highly changeable (van den Berghe 1976:243; and see Bennett 1975:9).

A primordial attachment is "one that stems from the 'givens'—or, more precisely, as culture is inevitably involved in such matters, the assumed 'givens'—of social existence" (Geertz 1963:109; and see Barth 1969:10, 13). But these givens are not forever fixed, unchanging, and unchangeable. What is given, on the contrary, are beginnings, points of departure, precedents, and anticipations—the elements out of which the future is created (Bennett 1976).

The primordial "given" basic to ethnicity as a self-conscious identity system is "the idea of shared descent, abstracted from the web of kinship" (Keyes 1976:205; and see Francis 1976:6–7). The kinship believed shared among members of an ethnic group is, of course, genealogically untraceable, extending, as it does, far beyond known biological ties. It is, nevertheless, sociologically real (Geertz 1963:112), which is to say that the facts of birth are culturally construed facts. Thus the boundedness of the group within which descent is deemed to be shared is always problematic because "a descent line always breaks up into segments and people identify, in varying circumstances, with units of a different scale" (Banton 1976), and because a given individual can identify as a descendant of as many different genealogical stocks as there are recognized pairs of truncal ancestors when descent reckoning is cognatic (Freeman 1961:204).

The ambiguities inherent in the concept of shared descent are fully illustrated by alternatives available for ethnic identity taking—and denial—in Ecuador's northern Sierra. For those who regard themselves, or are regarded by others, as participating in a relatively unmixed descent line (Figure 1 above is the best representation of this interpretation), identification can be shifted, depending on the circumstances, to units of a different scale. That Quichua-speaking *indígenas*, for example, see their descent line breaking up into segments is clearly indicated by data Weinstock (1970) presents for Otavaleños living in Quito. They differentiate themselves from several other "kinds" of Indians, and they distinguish among themselves on the basis of community of origin. Highland blacks differentiate themselves from other Afro-Americans—accepting the national stereotype that "lighter" is more beautiful. They hold that North American blacks, for example, are "uglier," that is, more negroid, less mixed, than themselves. They distinguish themselves also from coastal Ecuadorian blacks, whose lifestyle black sierrans find baffling. Coastal blacks, for their part, consider highland blacks a distinct race (Whitten, personal communication). Highland blacks further differentiate among themselves depending on the degree of mixture and on the community of origin.

Alternative identifications by social race are also admissible for most persons, given the history of miscegenation posited between the ancestral stocks (compare Figures 1 and 2). *Cholos* may be considered by others and may regard themselves as either *indios* (*indígenas*) or as *mestizos* or *blancos*. *Mulatos* and *zambos* may be classified, alternatively, as either *negros* (*morenos*) or as *mestizos* or *blancos*. If the concept of *el mestizaje* is fully extended (represented by the broken line), as in historian Cevallos García's presentation of both the Indian and

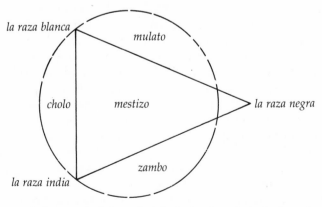

FIGURE 2. Expanded concept of *el mestizaje* includes the relatively "unmixed."

the Spaniard as *mestizos* prior to their contact (1974:13), then every-one who really wants to be a *mestizo* or a *blanco* can be one (recall General Rodríguez Lara's assertion).[14] The *mestizo/blanco* descent cate-gory, representing the nation, can thus be construed as eliminating all other possibilities by encompassing them.

But this extinction of all claims or ascriptions to unmixed descent is only apparent. That the racial descent scheme is equally open to invidiously exclusive distinctions based on the relative absence of mixture is most easily demonstrated by comparing current usage of the terms *mestizo* and *blanco*. Not everyone who self-identifies with the term *mestizo* intends the same meaning. For one of the men who assisted in the surveying of the five highland communities reported above, the term *mestizo* is simply a nonpejorative designation for *cholo*. In a conversational context he customarily used *mestizo* as the term of reference, but, for him, all sierrans, barring black admixture, are really either *cholos* or *indígenas*. Any degree of mixed ancestry is sufficient to distinguish the former from the latter. Proper identifi-cation, and he identifies himself as a *cholo*, depends on a knowledge of a combination of factors including family name, residential history, physical features, and occupation.

For a second assistant, the term *cholo* has no meaning except as an expression of disparagement. Aside from the few unmixed *indígenas* and *negros*, all sierrans are *mestizos*, he believes. That, however, is not to say that they are all the same. The *mestizo* of Carchi province, him-self included, is of Pasto descent and is therefore different from the *mestizo* of Imbabura province, whose aboriginal roots are traceable to the indigenous Caranqui peoples. As the aboriginal Pastos were a more valiant people than their neighbors to the south—the Pastos were never conquered by the Inca in contrast to the Caranquis—so the contemporary *carchense* is commonly reputed to be the most ob-streperous *mestizo* in the country (cf. Peñaherrera de Costales and Costales Samaniego 1961a, 1961b:31–32; Rubio Orbe 1965:131–32). The views of these two assistants represent an extreme range in the usage of the term *mestizo*, from *mestizo* as a polite mask for what is taken to be essential *cholo*ness, to *mestizo* as a name for a complex reality of primordially based phenotypic characteristics differentially distributed in the contemporary population. But, although they label it differently, each of them assigns primary significance to indigenous descent.

Self-identification as *blanco* in the northern Sierra is likewise poly-semic. It can be, first of all, a denial of *negro* admixture in contexts where such might be suspected. It is to say, in effect, "we are not *negros* (and we don't mind letting you know how relieved we are about that)"—relieved, because the character traits stereotypically associated in national culture with *la sangre negra* are almost totally pejorative. Nonblacks say that *los negros* are willing to put forth enough effort only to stay alive; that although they are physically large and strong, they prefer to hurry through their work so as to maximize their relaxation time. It is diversions that *los negros* take seriously, and any real or imagined affronts to their personal dignity. This alleged hot-headedness is said to cause them and everyone else much trouble. In sharp contrast to the character traits of docility and deference attributed in national culture to *los indios*, *los negros* are perceived as hard to get along with when not downright unpleasant and even dangerous (Stutzman (1974).

Second, and similarly, in communities or in situations where indigenous admixture might be suspected, self-identification as *blanco* may be offered as a denial of indigenous descent (David Prucha, personal communication with respect to La Esperanza, Ibarra canton). The logic is the same: social proximity implies genealogical proximity requiring implicit differentiation if not explicit denial.

Third, self-identification as *blanco* represents a claim, in traditional terms, to participation in national culture and society. The key distinction is between those who are deemed to "have" culture and those who do not. To be *inculto*, cultureless, is to be ignorant and uncivilized—the result of having lived on the margins of national life. "Having culture," which is to say, "living the life of a 'proper' human being," is synonymous with being *blanco* because the formally educated elite who have dominated Ecuadorian society for over four centuries have been identified as *blancos*.

Thus, to identify oneself as *blanco* is to say, "I am not a lazy, troublemaking *negro*, nor am I an ignorant, backward *indio*. I am part of what's happening." Ironically, however, to self-identify as *blanco* is to display one's ignorance of what's happening in terms of current nationalist ideology. As we have seen, the textbook ideology of *mestizaje* is based on the premise that, recent immigrants and a few endogamous elite families aside, there are no *blancos* at all among Ecuadorians. Everyone is of mixed descent. Everyone is *mestizo*.

During the survey process we learned just who it is that understands *mestizaje* ideology in terms that deny primordial significance to indigenous descent. In at least one-third of the instances when hesitant respondents agreed to a suggestion that "We're/You're *mestizo*," the suggestion was made by a school-age child or young person. The younger the person, the more obviously anxious he or she was that the question about descent be answered correctly. It soon became apparent that the response "We're *mestizos*" was, in effect, an answer to the question, "What have you learned in school about what it means to be an Ecuadorian?"

Drained of its ethnic content—for no primordially based contrasts exist upon which ethnic claims can be predicated—the textbook ideology of *mestizaje* is made available for predication as "the new type of Ecuadorian" (see, e.g., Forbes 1973:178–205 on Chicano identity). When these young people self-identify as *mestizo* in the textbook sense, they deny the relevance of potential ethnic differentia and affirm their participation in the national mainstream. They divest themselves of any primordial baggage that would prevent them from working in harmony with the goals of national culture. By that token they indeed become *blancos*, as General Rodríguez Lara asserted, or, better, *mestizos*, as suggested here, which in either case indicates that they are ethnically neutral nationals. If the *mestizo* concept can be made to stick as the label for a descent category inclusive of all Ecuadorians, then no distinctions among fellow nationals are relevant except that some of them are contributing to the nation's progress while others are standing in its way. But what, then, becomes of ethnically based claims—claims that dissent from the goals of national culture?

Ecuadorians: Singular or Plural?

If ethnicity in its genesis or transformation is not a *deus ex machina*, neither is nationalism. Nationalistic ideologies do not supersede or replace primordial attachments and sentiments with cultural forms of a more highly evolved order. On the contrary, nation building is an attempt to expand the center by "a progressive extension of the sense of primordial similarity . . . to more broadly defined groups . . . interacting within the framework of the entire national society . . . " (Geertz 1963:153–54; see also Colson 1968). But this effort to expand state influence and control, which in cultural terms involves "a merging of old symbols from diverse cultural patterns into a new and self-conscious ideological framework . . . " (González 1975:120), is as likely to generate differentiation and dissension as it is to produce a shared sense of identity and consensus over the meaning and purpose of collective life (Geertz 1971, Greeley 1974:291–317). Dissensus and disengagement are inevitable because the old symbols upon which nationalism is bound to draw are always multivocal and, when merged into the new ideological framework, many of the voices in which these symbols speak are not included. These alternate voices serve as the cultural raw materials out of which ethnics fashion their metaphors of the good—and separate—life.

The problem of self-identification in racial/ethnic terms is paradigmatic of this tension and trade-off between national culture and *cholo* ethnicity as a cultural system.[15] As a descent claim, *cholo*ness is rooted in a fundamentally indigenous ancestry with some nonindigenous admixture assumed. Note that this is the reverse of General Rodríguez's claim. He insisted he was part Indian, but he did not know how he had acquired such blood. For *cholos*, on the other hand, it is the provenience of the nonindigenous admixture that is uncertain, but surely there. Note also that the general has available several terms to express his sense of shared descent—as *mestizo* or as *blanco*. But there exist no nonpejorative racial/ethnic terms by which a non-Quichua–speaking person of basically indigenous descent may refer to himself or herself. The polite terms, *indígena* and *natural*, are generally used to refer only to Quichua speakers. The terms *indio*, *longo*, and *cholo* are all pejorative and have the same connotations for Spanish speakers as has the term *runa*. In Quichua *runa* is a noun meaning human being, that is, "indigenous person"; in Spanish *runa* is used adjectivally to mean contemptible, worthless, insignificant, ordinary (see, e.g., Tobar Donoso 1961:251). For this reason, as we found when surveying, self-identification in terms of descent categories is done hesitatingly by those whom we may conveniently, but not politely, refer to as *cholos*. In ordinary conversation self-identification in any of these terms is rare.

The preferred form of reference to self, we learned quite inadvertently while surveying, is of an entirely different order. It was not their identification in terms of racial descent nor their sex, age, occupation, or state of material well-being—or poverty—that respondents felt most relevant to the interview situation. It is, rather, their sense of themselves as Catholics. In the midst of explaining the purpose of our visit, one potential respondent told us, for example, that she was Catholic, illiterate, and very busy. Motivated by a similar perception of our respective statuses, another prospective respondent told my companion that she could not talk with me because she feared I would confound her soul. The presumption, of course, is that *gringos* who come knocking are proselytizing for some evangelical faith. It is unwise to agree to study the Bible or the Book of Mormon with *evangelico* missionaries, still another initially hostile and fearful informant subsequently explained, because regrettable incidents have followed in the wake of their visits—someone in the house has fallen sick or died, or the husband has abandoned the family, or the house has been broken into and robbed, and so on (hence the relevance of the above noted denial of literacy and free time). For this reason many with whom we talked were suspicious of our motives and our apparent access to occult powers unavailable to ordinary Catholic Christians.

Cristiano is the preferred form of reference to self. *Cristiano* is the word for human being in the lexicon of *cholo* ethnicity. It designates people as opposed to animals and, by extension, human beings who behave themselves properly rather than as beasts: *¡Qué bestia, no sea mal criado!* Behaving properly includes correct use of the language: *¡Hábleme en cristiano, pues!* "Speak Spanish," that is, "Stop your babbling." *Cristianos* are *gente civilizado*, civilized folk; they observe the holy sacraments. Baptism is the basic rite, the sign that the creature has become human by having entered the moral universe organized by the Creator. Unbaptized children, like the most savage of the pagan Amazonian tribes, are *aucas*, which is to say, amoral beings for whom right and wrong have neither meaning nor consequence. A *cristiano* is a person who believes in God the Father, Christ the Son, the Virgin Mary, and the Saints and who knows that he is dependent upon Their grace and favor for all good things that happen in this life. A proper *cristiano* prefaces all serious claims about future states of affairs with a "God willing." *Si Dios me da vida y salud.* . . . "If God grants life and health, I will. . . ." What happens depends not upon one's own will or upon the will of the national elites, foreign development experts, or international market conditions, but upon the will of God and His Saints.

To identify oneself as *cristiano* thus implies a sense of reality and a theory of behavior determination quite different from the racism implicit in the racial/ethnic terminology of national culture. But it is precisely the view of the world and the particular ethos that the term *cristiano* evokes for *cholos* that the Ministry of Education labels in strongly pejorative terms. Referring back to Table 2, the world view of "marginalized groups" is characterized as being based on a magical consciousness, superstition, and sophistry. Now whether the problem of human social inequality is better solved by making all men *mestizos*, as proponents of national culture would have it, or by making all men equally children of God, the *cristiano*'s solution, is, perhaps, debatable. But from the perspective of *cholo* ethnicity as a cultural system—as a way of construing human experience—to speak of dependence on God's will as magicality, supersitition, and sophistry is blasphemy. So erroneous an attitude toward the way things really are puts the economic planners and proponents of national culture, so far as *cholo* ethnicity is concerned, in the same category with the savage *aucas*, the proselytizers for non-Catholic faiths from Mormons through Baptists to Baha'is, and the irreligious in general, whose access to occult powers is suspect and whose behavior is amoral.

Much that the *cristiano* sees happening around him he interprets as being responsive to powers and forces other than those God would favor: the gradual loss of control over the means of making one's livelihood; the increasing secularization of education and of life in general; increasing scale, bureaucratization, and centralization of social institutions; and the concomitant replacement of personalistic and particularistic relationships by impersonal and rationalistic ones. The ideologues of national culture hold, for their part, that the nation's problem lies precisely in the retrogressive attitude of the marginalized who lack education, are ignorant of modern trends, lack motivation for change, and are totally unprepared for what must inevitably come. From the perspective of the *mestizo* nation, there is something seriously wrong with those who fail to assent to the goals and values of national culture and thus threaten the nationalist future of the republic. If not acting out of utter ignorance or malice, then, the logic of national culture would suggest, they must be sick. We have seen that the racism implicit in the system of descent terminology denies full humanity to those who by choice or necessity are unwilling or unable to exchange their ethnicity for the dominant mode of thought and style of life by naming them in pejorative terms. This racism has also generated scientific interest in finding a cause, in massive genetic damage, that will explain their backwardness (Bonifaz 1976, Varea Terán 1976; see Valentine and Valentine 1975 on scientific justifications of inequality).

But *cholo cristianismo* and *moreno cristianismo*—together with the alternative theories of nature, meaning, and purpose of man's being in the world maintained by other Ecuadorian ethnic groups—are not the retrogressive obstacles to national well-being that the planners of Ecuador's future imagine. Indeed, I submit that the nation will in the long run be fortunate if there remain some who are not ready to exchange their ethnicity for the goals of national culture. In the framing of nationalist ideology there are some obvious niches for ethnics to fill among the gaps left in the definition of who and what constitutes the nation.

If, for example, the nation is indeed urban, and if everyone accepts the goals and values of national culture and goes to join the nation in the cities, what then of the rainforest, *la montaña*, and the countryside in general? Who will till the land to feed an urban nation? The urban bias of Ecuadorian national culture has already had serious material consequences. People in large numbers have moved to the cities. They move for many different reasons, but primarily because of the inability of those in control of the nation to bring themselves to provide the facilities to nonurban areas that the *indígenas, cholos,* and *morenos* living there believe they need. Those who know the land and do not share the nation's pro-urban bias would be happy to stay on as the nation's farmers. But the nation's money is spent on the solution of urban problems, while planners hope that foreign experts and foreign investments will be able to solve the nation's agrarian problems.

If the nation is a stratified system of social relations based on differential privilege and differential access to resources, then accepting the goals and values of national culture means joining the struggle for control of the system or, more realistically, exchanging one sort of privileged class—one set of masters—for another. Many *cholos* are unconvinced that bureaucrats in Quito are going to make better *patrones,* and take better care of the nation's people, than their old *patrones* did under the traditional hacienda system. Then, at least, the master was accessible and could be dealt with on a personal basis, and the peon had some control over the means of producing his own livelihood. I am not saying that this traditional arrangement for the exploitation of *cholo* labor was ideal. But if the choice is between some personal control over one's own well-being and dependency on the nameless new masters who sit behind desks in Quito's, or New York's, or London's glass-fronted offices, the choice is clear. *Cholos* cannot believe that governmental and corporate paternalism is a clear improvement over personalistic paternalism.[16]

Finally, if the nation is *mestizo,* and if everyone accepts the goals and values of national culture and joins the nation in becoming ethnically neutral, then Ecuadorian national history is about to repeat itself. Recall that major cultural advances, according to textbook accounts, have come by invasion from abroad, and that the fusion of elements, as between Spaniard and Quiteña, was facilitated because both parties were *mestizo.* To the degree that *mestizo*ness is culturally inchoate, it is free to be predicated as required by the nation's development needs. It is also open to whatever cultural goods the new conquistadors may import from abroad with their baggage. To the degree that *indígenas, cholos,* and *morenos* of the northern Sierra have not accepted the goals and sensibilities of the *mestizo* nation, they have not opened themselves uncritically to intercourse with the forces of the current invasion. Who but they are in a position to dis-

cern whether the present conquest will not be the disaster for the
Ecuadorian nation that the Spanish conquest was?

NOTES

Acknowledgments: I am grateful to Kathleen Fine, Peter M. Hirsch, Phyllis
Stutzman, Dorothea S. and Norman E. Whitten, Jr., for their critical comments on earlier versions of this paper, and to Patrick M. Browne, Miguel
Angel Minda A., Juan B. Reyes Q., and Juan Tapia B. for their assistance in
the collection of survey data herein cited.

1. The large African-descended population of the Ecuadorian Coast is historically and culturally linked more closely to the black population of Colombia than to the black population of the Ecuadorian Sierra (Pavy 1967; West
1957; Whitten 1965, 1974b; Whitten and Friedemann 1974).

2. Despite the pejorative force of the term, nonblacks customarily refer to
persons of negroid phenotype as *negros*. Blacks self-identify as *morenos*, literally, brown or dark. The usage of *negro* versus *moreno* in the Sierra is thus
parallel to the 1970s usage of "Negro" or "colored" versus "black" in the
United States.

3. Studies of the structure of interethnic relations in the northern Sierra
include the following for *indígena, cholo*, and *mestizo* populations or communities: Beals 1966; Buitrón 1958; Collier and Buitrón 1949; Costales Samaniego
and Theisen 1970; Crespi 1968, 1975; Gillin 1941; Icaza 1934; IEAG 1952; Parsons 1945; Rubio Orbe 1956; Salz 1955; Villavicencio Rivadeneira 1973; Weinstock 1970. Similar studies of black populations or communities include:
Klumpp 1970, Peñaherrera de Costales and Costales Samaniego 1959, Preston 1965, Stutzman 1974.

4. Eighteen months' fieldwork in 1970–72 with sierran *morenos* in Ibarra
was supported by National Institute of Mental Health Fellowship and Research Training Grant no. 49734. Work with *cholos* and *mestizos* in Ibarra and
rural communities of Imbabura and Carchi provinces was begun in June-July
1976 and was supported for two years (1977–79) by National Science Foundation Grant no. 08192. All work in Ecuador has been sponsored by the Instituto Nacional de Antropología e Historia, Quito, Arq. Hernán Crespo
Toral, executive director, and since 1976 has been conducted in affiliation
with the Instituto Otavaleño de Antropología, Plutarco Cisneros A., executive director.

5. It is useful to distinguish between social race (Wagley 1959) and ethnicity, since both are salient to Ecuadorian social organization (Burgos Guevara
1970, Casagrande 1974, Whitten 1974a). In general, following Lyon (1972),
racial group boundaries are maintained by a racist majority group, while ethnic groups maintain their own boundaries vis-à-vis the dominant majority.
In Ecuador's northern Sierra categorical distinctions and structural positions
are maintained by pressures that are both racial and ethnic (Stutzman 1974).

6. This and other translations from Spanish appearing below are my responsibility.

7. Blauner (1972), Clemmer (1972), Isaacs (1975), Nagata (1974), and Valentine (1975) attack the assimilationist bias in the social sciences. Banton

86 *Cultural Transformations and Ethnicity in Modern Ecuador*

(1974:36–40), Bennett (1975), Bohannan (1967), Colombres (1976), González (1975), and Greeley (1974:291–317) discuss the shift to a more dynamic and pluralist view of ethnic and race relations.

8. Statements offered by respondents in place of self-identification in categorical terms were tabulated as follows: *La raza indígena/india*: "children of Atahualpa," "children of *naturales*," "descendants of *los indios*"; *la raza mestiza*: "the American race," "descendants of Atahualpa and of *buenas familias*," "the Ecuadorian race," "nationals," "the new race," "*revueltos*" ("scrambled"), "*trigueños*" (i.e., color of wheat); *la raza blanca*: "descendants of the Spanish," "descendants of *gringos*"; *la raza mulata/zamba*: "*más clara*" ("lighter," i.e., than *morena*); place of origin: "*carchense*" (from Carchi province), "*colombianos*" (from Colombia), "*pastuzos*" (of Carchi province); other statements: "Catholic," "I am as you see me, mister," "*lejos*" ("far out?"), "middle class," "middling," "mountain people," "We're all the same kind of people (in this family)."

9. A symbol is "any object, act, event, quality, or relation which serves as a vehicle for a conception—the conception is the symbol's 'meaning'" (Geertz 1966:5).

10. The "core-periphery" terminology of the "sociology of dependence" school of Latin Americanist analysis (Chilcote and Edelstein 1974; Cockcroft, Gunder Frank, and Johnson 1972; Galtung 1971) is not used, so far as I am aware, in any official government pronouncements or publications. The paradigm and thrust of analysis are, however, similar, and my critique from the perspective of ethnicity as a cultural system applies to both.

11. The first rendering of Ecuadorian "folk history" (Hudson 1966, 1973:133–34) was pieced together from what I heard formally educated informants telling me in 1971 (Stutzman 1974:191–201). The second (Stutzman 1976) supplemented the first with an analysis of seventh-grade (*Colección* L.N.S. ca. 1968) and eleventh-grade (Cevallos García 1974) Ecuadorian history texts. The present rendering is based on a wider consultation of texts, including, in addition to the above: fourth grade: Arregui de Pazmiño and Carrillo de Landázuri (ca. 1975), *Colección* L.N.S. (1976); seventh grade: *Colección* L.N.S. (ca. 1974), García González (ca. 1976), López Monsalve (1976). Curriculum guidelines published by the Ministry of Education, to which all text materials must conform, specify that the formative period of national history be studied in the fourth, seventh, and eleventh grades. For this reason, texts published for these grades cover basically the same ground—origins of man in America, earliest known pre-Incaic inhabitants of what is now Ecuador, Incaic invasion, Spanish invasion, and the colonial period to independence.

12. "Phenotype" is used here to include traits of character and behavior as well as physical appearance. It is "the total of everything that can be observed or inferred about the individual, excepting only his genes" (Dobzhansky 1962:41–42).

13. The López Monsalve (1976) text deviates from the others in his treatment of the Cara. The author relies almost exclusively on archaeological evidence for the pre-Incaic period and rejects P. Velasco's tale as without foundation in either archaeology or documented history (López Monsalve 1976:197–200).

14. *Negros* excepted. By Cevallos García's logic (1974:13, 197) slaves

brought from Africa could also be considered *mestizos*. But neither Cevallos García nor anyone else admits "unmixed" *negros* into the extended *mestizaje*.

15. Although I speak specifically of *cholo* ethnicity, these world-view components are generally applicable to *moreno* ethnicity as well. On the ethos components of highland *moreno* ethnicity, see Stutzman (1974:123–55).

16. On this point *morenos* and *cholos* differ. The former prefer corporate to personalistic paternalism (Stutzman 1974:219).

REFERENCES CITED

Aronson, Dan
    1976 Ethnicity as a Cultural System: An Introductory Essay. In Frances Henry, ed., *Ethnicity in the Americas*. The Hague: Mouton, pp. 9–19.
Arregui de Pazmiño, Fanny, and Rogelia Carrillo de Landázuri
    ca. 1975 *El Libro del Escolar Ecuatoriano: Cuarto Grado*. Quito: Voluntad. (Numerous undated earlier editions.)
Banton, Michael
    1974 1960: A Turning Point in the Study of Race Relations. In Sidney Mintz, ed., *Slavery, Colonialism, and Racism*. New York: Norton, pp. 31–44.
    1976 Choosing Our Relations. Review of *Ethnicity: Theory and Experience*, ed. Nathan Glazer and Daniel P. Moynihan. *Times Literary Supplement*, 6 Feb.
Barth, Fredrik
    1969 Introduction. In Fredrik Barth, ed., *Ethnic Groups and Boundaries: The Social Organization of Cultural Difference*. Boston: Little, Brown, pp. 9–38.
Beals, Ralph
    1966 *Community in Transition: Nayón, Ecuador*. Los Angeles: Latin American Center, UCLA.
Bennett, John W.
    1975 A Guide to the Collection. In John W. Bennett, ed., *The New Ethnicity: Perspectives from Ethnology*. 1973 Proceedings of the American Ethnological Society. St. Paul Minn.: West Publishing Co., pp. 3–10.
    1976 Anticipation, Adaptation, and the Concept of Culture in Anthropology. *Science* 192:847–53.
Blauner, Robert
    1972 *Racial Oppression in America*. New York: Harper & Row.
Bodley, John M.
    1975 *Victims of Progress*. Menlo Park, Calif.: Cummings Publishing Co.
Bohannan, Paul
    1967 Introduction. In Paul Bohannan and Fred Plog, eds., *Beyond the Frontier: Social Process and Cultural Change*. Garden City, N.Y.: Natural History Press, pp. xi–xviii.
Bonifaz, Emilio
    1976 *Los Indígenas de Altura del Ecuador*. 2d ed. Quito: Privately published.
Bourricaud, Francois
    1970 *Power and Society in Contemporary Peru*. New York: Praeger.
    1975 Indian, Mestizo and Cholo as Symbols in the Peruvian System of

Stratification. In Nathan Glazer and Daniel P. Moynihan, eds., *Ethnicity: Theory and Experience*. Cambridge, Mass.: Harvard University Press, pp. 350–87.

Broom, Leonard, et al.
1954   Acculturation: An Exploratory Formulation. *American Anthropologist* 56:973–1000.

Buitrón, Aníbal
1958   Discriminación y Transculturación. *América Indígena* 18:7–15.

Burgos Guevara, Hugo
1970   *Relaciones Interétnicas en Riobamba: Dominio y Dependencia en una Región Indígena Ecuatoriana*. Mexico City: Instituto Indigenista Interamericano.

Casagrande, Joseph B.
1974   Strategies for Survival: The Indians of Highland Ecuador. In Dwight Heath, ed., *Contemporary Cultures and Societies of Latin America: A Reader in the Social Anthropology of Middle and South America*. 2d ed. New York: Random House, pp. 93–107.

Cevallos García, Gabriel
1974   *Historia del Ecuador: Quinto Curso*. 4th ed. Cuenca: Don Bosco.

Charbonnier, G.
1969   *Conversations with Claude Lévi-Strauss*. London: Jonathan Cape.

Chávez, Ligdano
1952a   *Educación y Nacionalidad*. Quito: Casa de la Cultura Ecuatoriana.
1952b   El Contenido de un Nuevo Programa de Historia y Geografía para la Escuela Primaria. *Revista Ecuatoriana de Educación* 22:50–69.

Chilcote, Ronald, and Joel Edelstein
1974   *Latin America: The Struggle with Dependency and Beyond*. New York: Halsted Press.

Clastres, Pierre
1977   *Society against the State*. New York: Urizen Books. (Trans. Robert Hurley from the original French publication of 1974.)

Clemmer, Richard
1972   Truth, Duty, and the Revitalization of Anthropologists: A New Perspective on Cultural Change and Resistance. In Dell Hymes, ed., *Reinventing Anthropology*. New York: Pantheon, pp. 213–47.

Cockcroft, James D., André Gunder Frank, and Dale Johnson, eds.
1972   *Dependence and Underdevelopment: Latin America's Political Economy*. Garden City, N.Y.: Doubleday.

Cohen, Abner
1969   *Custom and Politics in Urban Africa*. Berkeley: University of California Press.

Colección L.N.S.
ca. 1968   *Historia del Ecuador: Primer Curso*. Cuenca: Don Bosco.
ca. 1974   *Ciencias Sociales, Geografía e Historia: Primer Curso*. Cuenca: Don Bosco.
1976   *Enciclopedia Ecuatoriana: Cuarto Grado*. Cuenca: Don Bosco.

Collier, John, Jr., and Aníbal Buitrón
1949   *The Awakening Valley*. Chicago: University of Chicago Press.

Colombres, Adolfo
1976   *La Colonización Cultural de la América Indígena*. Quito: Ediciones del Sol.

Colson, Elizabeth
   1968   Contemporary Tribes and the Development of Nationalism. In June
          Helm, ed., *Essays on the Problem of Tribe*. 1967 Proceedings of the
          American Ethnological Society. Seattle: University of Washington
          Press, pp. 201–6.
Costales Samaniego, Alfredo, and André Theisen
   1970   *Area de Pimampiro*. Oficina de Investigaciones Sociales. Misión An-
          dina del Ecuador.
Crespi, Muriel
   1968   The Patrons and Peons of Pesillo: A Traditional Hacienda System in
          Highland Ecuador. Ann Arbor, Mich.: University Microfilms. Ph.D.
          thesis, University of Illinois, Urbana.
   1975   When *Indios* Become *Cholos*: Some Consequences of the Changing
          Ecuadorian Hacienda. In John W. Bennett, ed., *The New Ethnicity:
          Perspectives from Ethnology*. 1973 Proceedings of the American Eth-
          nological Society. St. Paul, Minn.: West Publishing Co., pp. 148–66.
Despres, Leo A., ed.
   1975   *Ethnicity and Resource Competition in Plural Societies*. The Hague: Mou-
          ton.
Dobronsky O., Fernando
   1977   Política Cultural. *Sarance: Revista del Instituto Otavaleño de Antropo-
          logía* 5:138–47.
Dobzhansky, Theodosius
   1962   *Mankind Evolving: The Evolution of the Human Species*. New Haven,
          Conn.: Yale University Press.
Dostal, W., ed.
   1972   *The Situation of the Indian in South America: Contributions to the Study
          of Inter-Ethnic Conflict in the Non-Andean Regions of South America*. Ge-
          neva: World Council of Churches.
Durkheim, Emile
   1949 [1893]   *The Division of Labor in Society*. Glencoe, Ill.: Free Press.
Fallers, Lloyd
   1973   *Inequality: Social Stratification Reconsidered*. Chicago: University of
          Chicago Press.
Faron, Louis
   1970   Ethnicity and Social Mobility in Chancay Valley, Peru. In Walter
          Goldschmidt and Harry Hoijer, eds., *The Social Anthropology of Latin
          America: Essays in Honor of Ralph Leon Beals*. Los Angeles: Latin
          American Center, UCLA.
Federación de Centros Shuar
   1976   *Solución Original a un Problema Actual*. Quito: Colegio Tecnico, Don
          Bosco.
Fernandez, James
   1969   *Microcosmogony and Modernization in African Religious Movements*.
          Montreal: McGill University Centre of Developing Area Studies, Oc-
          casional Paper 3.
Forbes, Jack
   1973   *Aztecas del Norte: The Chicanos of Aztlán*. Greenwich, Conn.: Fawcett
          Publications.

Francis, E. K.
   1948   Russian Mennonites: From Religious to Ethnic Group. *American Journal of Sociology* 54:101–7.
   1976   *Interethnic Relations: An Essay in Sociological Theory.* New York: Elsevier.
Freeman, J. D.
   1961   On the Concept of the Kindred. *Journal of the Royal Anthropological Institute* 91:192–220.
Fried, Morton
   1967   *The Evolution of Political Society: An Essay in Political Anthropology.* New York: Random House.
   1975   *The Notion of Tribe.* Menlo Park, Calif.: Cummings Publishing Co.
Friedlander, Judith
   1975   *Being Indian in Hueyapan: A Study of Forced Identity in Contemporary Mexico.* New York: St. Martin's.
Galtung, Johan
   1971   A Structural Theory of Imperialism. *Journal of Peace Research* 8:81–117.
García González, Luis
   ca. 1976   *Resumen de Geografía e Historia: Primer Curso.* 4th ed. Quito: Voluntad.
Geertz, Clifford
   1963   The Integrative Revolution: Primordial Sentiments and Civil Politics in the New States. In Clifford Geertz, ed., *Old Societies and New States.* New York: Free Press, pp. 105–57.
   1964   Ideology as a Cultural System. In David Apter, ed., *Ideology and Discontent.* New York: Free Press, pp. 47–76.
   1966   Religion as a Cultural System. In Michael Banton, ed., *Anthropological Approaches ot the Study of Religion.* London: Tavistock, pp. 1–46.
   1971   After the Revolution: The Fate of Nationalism in the New States. In Bernard Barber and Alex Inkeles, eds., *Stability and Social Change.* Boston: Little, Brown, pp. 357–76.
   1973   *The Interpretation of Cultures: Selected Essays.* New York: Basic Books.
Gillin, John
   1941   The Quichua-Speaking Indians of the Province of Imbabura (Ecuador) and Their Anthropometric Relations with the Living Populations of the Andean Area. *Bureau of American Ethnology Bulletin* 128:169–228, Anthropological Papers 16.
González, Nancie
   1975   Patterns of Dominican Ethnicity. In John W. Bennett, ed., *The New Ethnicity: Perspectives from Ethnology.* 1973 Proceedings of the American Ethnological Society. St. Paul, Minn.: West Publishing Co., pp. 110–23.
Grayson, George W.
   1975   Populism, Petroleum, and Politics in Ecuador. *Current History* 68 (401):15ff.
Greeley, Andrew
   1974   *Ethnicity in the United States: A Preliminary Reconnaissance.* New York: John Wiley.
Herskovits, Melville
   1941   *The Myth of the Negro Past.* New York: Harper.

Hickman, John, and Jack Brown
  1971   Adaptation of Aymara and Quechua to the Bicultural Social Context of Bolivian Mines. *Human Organization* 30:359–66.
Hudson, Charles
  1966   Folk History and Ethnohistory. *Ethnohistory* 13:52–70.
  1973   The Historical Approach in Anthropology. In John J. Honigmann, ed., *Handbook of Social and Cultural Anthropology.* Chicago: Rand McNally, pp. 111–41.
Hurtado, Osvaldo
  1969   *Dos Mundos Superpuestos: Ensayo de Diagnóstico de la Realidad Ecuatoriana.* Quito: Offsetec.
Icaza, Jorge
  1934   *Huasipungo.* Quito: Imprenta Nacional.
IEAG (Instituto Ecuatoriano de Antropología y Geografía)
  1952   *La Paz: Un Pueblo Mestizo de la Provincia del Carchi.* Informe 1. Quito.
INEC (Instituto Nacional de Estadística y Censos)
  1977   *División Política Territorial de la Republica del Ecuador.* Quito.
Isaacs, Harold
  1975   Basic Group Identity: The Idols of the Tribe. In Nathan Glazer and Daniel P. Moynihan, eds., *Ethnicity: Theory and Experience.* Cambridge, Mass.: Harvard University Press, pp. 20–52.
Keyes, Charles
  1976   Towards a New Formulation of the Concept of Ethnic Group. *Ethnicity* 3:202–13.
Klumpp, Kathleen
  1970   Black Traders of North Highland Ecuador. In Norman E. Whitten, Jr., and John F. Szwed, eds., *Afro-American Anthropology: Contemporary Perspectives.* New York: Free Press, pp. 245–62.
Lévi-Strauss, Claude
  1963   *Structural Anthropology.* Trans. Claire Jacobsen and Broeke Grundfest Schoepf. London: Penguin.
López Monsalve, Rodrigo
  1976   *Geografía e Historía: Primer Curso.* Cuenca: Offsetcolor.
Lyon, Michael
  1972   Race and Ethnicity in Pluralistic Societies: A Comparison of Minorities in the U.K. and U.S.A. *New Community* (Summer):256–62.
Mörner, Magnus
  1967   *Race Mixture in the History of Latin America.* Boston: Little, Brown.
NACLA (North American Congress on Latin America)
  1975   *Ecuador: Oil up for Grabs.* Latin America and Empire Report 9 (8), November.
Nagata, Judith
  1974   What Is Malay? Situational Selection of Ethnic Identity in a Plural Society. *American Ethnologist* 1:331–50.
Naranjo, Marcelo F.
  1977   Zonas de Refugio y Adaptación Étnica en el Oriente: Siglos XVI-XVII-XVIII. In Marcelo F. Naranjo, José L. Pereira V., and Norman E. Whitten, Jr., eds., *Temas sobre la Continuidad y Adaptación Cultural Ecuatoriana.* Quito: Prensa de la Pontificia Universidad Católica, pp. 105–68.

Nash, June
   1975   Nationalism and Fieldwork. *Annual Review of Anthropology* 4:225–45.
Navarro Jiménez, Guillermo
   1976   *La Concentración de Capitales en el Ecuador.* 2d ed. Quito: Ediciones
          Solitierra.
Parsons, Elsie Clews
   1945   *Peguche, Canton of Otavalo, Province of Imbabura, Ecuador: A Study of
          Andean Indians.* Chicago: University of Chicago Press.
Patterson, Orlando
   1975   Context and Choice in Ethnic Allegiance: A Theoretical Framework
          and Caribbean Case Study. In Nathan Glazer and Daniel P. Moyni-
          han, eds., *Ethnicity: Theory and Experience.* Cambridge, Mass.: Har-
          vard University Press, pp. 305–49.
Pavy, David
   1967   The Provenience of Colombian Negroes. *Journal of Negro History*
          52:35–58.
Peñaherrera de Costales, Piedad, and Alfredo Costales Samaniego
   1959   *Coangue: O Historia Cultural y Social de los Negros del Chota y Salinas.*
          Quito: Instituto Ecuatoriano de Antropología y Geografía, *Llacta* 7.
   1961a *El Chagra: Estudio Socio-Económico del Mestizaje Ecuatoriano.* Quito:
          Instituto Ecuatoriano de Antropología y Geografía, *Llacta* 11.
   1961b *Llacta Runa.* Quito: Instituto Ecuatoriano de Antropología y Geo-
          grafía, *Llacta* 12.
Pitt-Rivers, Julian
   1967   Race, Color, and Class in Central America and the Andes. *Daedalus*
          (Spring). Reprinted in John Hope Franklin, ed., *Color and Race.* Bos-
          ton: Beacon Press, 1968, pp. 264–81.
Preston, David
   1965   Negro, Mestizo, and Indian in an Andean Environment. *Geographi-
          cal Journal* (London) 131:220–34.
Ramirez, Fausto, et al.
   1978   Penetración de la CIA en el Movimiento Indígena. *Nueva* 46:58–65,
          47:43–60.
Reyes, Oscar
   1934   *Breve Historia General del Ecuador.* Vol. 1. Quito: Fray Jodoco Ricke.
          (Available in various later editions.)
Rubio Orbe, Gonzalo
   1956   *Punyaro.* Quito: Casa de la Cultura Ecuatoriana.
   1965   *Aspectos Indígenas.* Quito: Casa de la Cultura Ecuatoriana.
   1974   Ecuador Indígena. *América Indígena* 34:581–603.
Sahlins, Marshall
   1976   *Culture and Practical Reason.* Chicago: University of Chicago Press.
Salazar, Ernesto
   1977   *An Indian Federation in Lowland Ecuador.* Copenhagen: International
          Work Group for Indigenous Affairs, Document 28.
Salomon, Frank
   1973   Weavers of Otavalo. In Danial Gross, ed., *Peoples and Cultures of Na-
          tive South America: An Anthropological Reader.* Garden City, N.Y.:
          Natural History Press, pp. 463–92.

Salz, Beate
1955 *The Human Element in Industrialization: A Hypothetical Case Study of Ecuadorian Indians. American Anthropologist* 57 (3, pt. 2), Memoir 85.
Singer, Lester
1962 Ethnogenesis and Negro-Americans Today. *Social Research* 29:419–32.
Spicer, Edward
1971 Persistent Cultural Systems. *Science* 174:795–800.
Stutzman, Ronald
1974 Black Highlanders: Racism and Ethnic Stratification in the Ecuadorian Sierra. Ann Arbor, Mich.: University Microfilms. Ph.D. thesis, Washington University, St. Louis.
1976 ". . . for without racism physical characteristics are devoid of social significance": An Ecuadorian Case. Paper presented to Central States Anthropological Society, St. Louis.
Terán, Francisco
1976 *Geografía del Ecuador.* 9th ed. Quito: Colón.
Thompson, Stith
1946 *The Folktale.* New York: Dryden.
Tobar Donoso, Julio
1961 *El Lenguaje Rural en la Región Interandina del Ecuador: Lo que Falta y Lo que Sobra.* Quito: La Union Católica.
Turner, Victor
1974 *Dramas, Fields, and Metaphors: Symbolic Action in Human Society.* Ithaca, N.Y.: Cornell University Press.
Valentine, Charles
1975 Voluntary Ethnicity and Social Change: Classism, Racism, Marginality, Mobility, and Revolution with Special Reference to Afro-Americans and Other Third World Peoples. *Journal of Ethnic Studies* 3:1–27.
Valentine, Charles, and Bettylou Valentine
1975 Brain Damage and the Intellectual Defense of Inequality. *Current Anthropology* 16:117–50.
van den Berghe, Pierre L.
1968 Ethnic Membership and Cultural Change in Guatemala. *Social Forces* 44:514–22.
1974 Introduction, and The Use of Ethnic Terms in the Peruvian Social Science Literature. In Pierre L. van den Berghe, ed., *Class and Ethnicity in Peru.* Leiden: Brill, pp. 1–11, 12–22.
1976 Ethnic Pluralism in Industrial Societies: A Special Case? *Ethnicity* 3:242–55.
Varea Terán, José
1976 *El Subdesarrollo Biológico.* Quito: Artes Gráficas.
Velasco, Juan de
1841–44 *Historia del Reino de Quito en la América Meridional.* 3 vols. Quito: Imprenta de Gobierno, por Juan Campuzano. (Various later editions.)
Villavicencio Rivadeneira, Gladys
1973 *Relaciones Interétnicas en Otavalo, Ecuador.* Mexico City: Instituto Indigenista Interamericano.

Wagley, Charles
1959   On the Concept of Social Race in the Americas. *Actas del 33 Congreso Internacional de Americanistas* 1:403–17. San Jose, Costa Rica: Lehmann.
Weinstock, Steven
1970   Ethnic Conceptions and Relations of Otavalo Indian Migrants in Quito, Ecuador. *Anuario Indigenista* 30:157–67.
West, Robert C.
1957   *The Pacific Lowlands of Colombia: A Negroid Area of the American Tropics.* Baton Rouge: Louisiana State University Press.
Whitten, Norman E., Jr.
1965   *Class, Kinship, and Power in an Ecuadorian Town: The Negroes of San Lorenzo.* Stanford, Calif.: Stanford University Press.
1974a The Ecology of Race Relations in Northwest Ecuador. In Dwight Heath, ed., *Contemporary Cultures and Societies of Latin America: A Reader in the Social Anthropology of Middle and South America.* 2d ed. New York: Random House, pp. 327–40.
1974b *Black Frontiersmen: A South American Case.* New York: Halsted (Wiley).
1976a (with the assistance of Marcelo F. Naranjo, Marcelo Santi Simbaña, and Dorothea S. Whitten). *Sacha Runa: Ethnicity and Adaptation of Ecuadorian Jungle Quichua.* Urbana: University of Illinois Press.
1976b *Ecuadorian Ethnocide and Indigenous Ethnogenesis: Amazonian Resurgence amidst Andean Colonialism.* Copenhagen: International Work Group for Indigenous Affairs, Document 23.
1977   Etnocidio Ecuatoriano y Ethnogénesis Indígena: Resurgencia Amazónica ante la Colonización Andina. In Marcelo F. Naranjo, José L. Pereira V., and Norman E. Whitten, Jr., eds., *Temas sobre la Continuidad y Adaptación Cultural Ecuatoriana.* Quito: Prensa de la Pontificia Universidad Católica, pp. 169–213.
1978   *Amazonian Ecuador: An Ethnic Interface in Ecological, Social, and Ideological Perspectives.* Copenhagen: International Work Group for Indigenous Affairs, Document 34.
Whitten, Norman E., Jr., and Nina S. de Friedemann
1974   La Cultura Negra del Litoral Ecuatoriano y Colombiano: Un Modelo de Adaptación Étnica. *Revista Colombiana de Antropología* (Bogotá) 17:75–115.
Wolf, Eric R.
1978   Expanding World, Narrow Vision! Lecture presented at Washington University, St. Louis.

3

Political Dependency, Ethnicity, and Cultural Transformations in Manta

Marcelo F. Naranjo

The industrializing port city of Manta, Manabí, with a population estimated at 60,000 inhabitants, is the focus of this paper. Although based on research carried out during 1976–77, the time depth goes back to the beginning of the 1960s. The study follows the tendency in cultural anthropology to focus on political, economic, and cultural aspects of a particular society, emphasizing such ideas as inequality between, and mutual exploitation of, social groups. Such a political-economic analysis and its ramifications combine with the phenomenon of ethnic segmentation to produce a series of cultural transformations. The perspective on which this paper is based derives from my interest in understanding contemporary cultural transformations in terms of dependency theory.

Three elements—dependency, ethnicity, and cultural transformations—will be treated as the genesis of social phenomena to be discussed below; this treatment will be strictly dynamic. Contemporary cultural anthropology should place greater emphasis on this latter characteristic. Inasmuch as societies have been influenced by the rhythms of modern technology, any static view of internal structure would be empirically false. The political focus of this work is based on dependency theory, which I believe to be of singular value for the study of what is occurring, and has occurred, in Manta. With regard to ethnicity, I would note that Ecuador is a plural society in which diverse groups—whether they are called ethnic groups or social classes—interact and contend for existing subsistence resources. This fact of contention is of primary importance in Manta, where the phenomena of ethnic character (in the sense of group differentiation) and class structure are made more salient and obvious by the relatively reduced geographic habitat of the urban zone.

The cultural transformations herein described are generated by the accelerating processes of urbanization, modernization, and industrialization. I don't wish to claim that had this trilogy of factors not appeared, Manta society would have remained static, without transformations, but rather that these processes precipitated in time and in magnitude the particular series of changes that have occurred. I have arbitrarily isolated these three elements for didactic reasons. In daily life one sees strong connections between the three, each influencing the others, but in the analysis which follows it is appropriate to separate them to examine the major significance and probable projections of each.

POLITICAL FOCUS WITHIN DEPENDENCY THEORY

Before discussing the particular use of dependency theory in the examination of the situation in Manta, it is necessary to establish certain general ideas that will be used throughout this work. These ideas have been used frequently in the literature, often with meanings variable enough to have led to confusion. One of the most basic of these is dependency itself. Castells (1973:82) defines it in this way: ". . . a society is dependent when the articulation of its social structure at the economic, political, and ideological levels expresses asymmetric relationships to another social entity that occupies a position of power in relation to the first."[1] Given this definition, we can begin to examine exactly how two societies enter into contact with each other on asymmetric, or unequal, terms (see, e.g., Dos Santos 1971). The implications of contact based on asymmetric relationship across various domains is important to the society under study; it is equally important to domains external to that society. Relations of asymmetric dependency exist at the international as well as the national levels. Moreover, the notion of dependency alludes directly to the conditions of existence and functioning of economic and political systems, and to the local, regional, national, and international relationships between them (Cardoso and Faletto 1969:24). Other domains of culture must also be examined when discussing dependency between any two social entities. Indeed, one can speak of countries that export cultural elements and countries that import these cultural elements to the detriment of their own cultural values.

Quijano (1973:67) tells us that a dependent culture results from pressure composed of both external and internal mechanisms on the population of a particular society. He concludes by stressing the fact that this is a process of cultural alienation which benefits only the mercantile society (as he calls it) of the international monopolies, and leads inevitably to the perversion of the social conscience. Marcos Kaplan (1973:163–64), in a brilliant analysis of what dependency signifies in the context of cultural colonialism, writes:

> The culture of Euro–North American capitalism proportions to the upper, middle, and lower classes of the large cities, in gradations and with variable shades, the content and focus of their thoughts and actions. They capture and incorporate forms of production and distribution, technology, inventions, images, symbols, patterns of consumption, fashions, customs, ideas, educational methods, values, norms, institutions, and political and social solutions.

These complex processes are occurring in Ecuador. From Quito, the capital, and from Guayaquil, the most populous city—the two immediate receptors of all this accumulation of Euro-American rubbish—this mass of negative elements is re-exported to the smaller cities. In the process of this re-export these elements are further adulterated and made still more grotesque, so that by the time they are received in Manta, they have multiplied and become uglier still. Whether this flow of cultural dependence is imposed subtly or not, the impact is always strongly felt. Contrary to what one would hope, this alienating imposition is generally well received by the majority of the population because they have been convinced that by following the imposed norms, one can *progresar*, progress, and can thereby reduce known ethnic or class differences. I will discuss this aspect of the problem in more detail below.

The reasoning that underlies the idea of cultural dependency can be applied equally well to political and economic domains, the latter being the focal institution in the context of the evolution of the current situation in Manta. These various facets encompassed by the general concept of dependency are what Kaplan (1973:135) denotes by the term "structural dependency." For him, all of these levels and aspects interact, thus influencing, determining, and conditioning global society and the overall process of growth and change.

Parallel to the concept of dependency, and many times as a direct result of it, is the concept of underdevelopment.[2] I will not consider here whether dependency is the result of underdevelopment or vice versa. Such a distinction is of no value to me, since underdevelopment is an empirical fact that must be dealt with in and of itself. Gunder Frank (1970:ix-x), for example, emphasizes the fact that Latin America suffers from a colonial underdevelopment in which its inhabitants are economically, politically, and culturally dependent, not because of Latin American inadequacies but because of metropolitan power. As he says, there exists a true juxtaposition between dependency and underdevelopment because both terms refer to asymmetrical relations and the imposition of a developed society's needs, goals, and institutions onto one that is not developed. Cardoso and Faletto (1969:24–25) take this idea of underdevelopment further when they give as one of its fundamental characteristics "the gradation of differentiation of the productive system without accenting the patterns of control over the decisions of production and consumption, whether internal or external."

Gunder Frank (1970:xii) brings out another element that he feels should be taken into account when dealing with the relations between countries, especially when underdevelopment is a significant factor in this relationship: the historical context of the development of imperialism in the world, which generated dependency in the countries of Latin America. Personally, I don't consider it useful to make the separation between imperialism and dependency because ontologically they would seem to be identical. Imperialist countries of whatever type are the dominant elements in the relation of dependency. It is precisely the character of imperialism that leads to asymmetric relations.

In the Ecuadorian case this is clearly manifest. Ecuador is subjected to relations of dependency on the part of the imperialist countries, especially the United States. Whenever imperialism is canalized, dependency is created, as the case of Ecuador illustrates. Perhaps one could speak of two moments in a single reality in which imperialism would occur first, followed by dependency, but one can never see such a sequence as representing two independent realities. If I differ with Gunder Frank in the importance placed on this separation, I am in complete agreement with him on the importance of understanding Latin American dependency within a world-wide context. Only by looking at the relations of dependency at the local and regional level within the global context can one adequately understand the political, economic, and cultural problems of Latin American societies. Quijano (1973:20) has also found that there exists—although he attempts to correct this—a strong tendency to investigate the phenomenon of dependency as if it occurred in isolated and autonomous societies, despite the fact that the Latin American nations are constitutively and historically dependent on other societies.

The concept of imperialism can be further refined by placing it in the context of center-periphery relations (following the model of Galtung 1971:81, the world consists of central and peripheral nations and each nation at the same time has its center and its periphery). In this way imperialism can be defined as the manner in which the central nation acquires and maintains power over the peripheral nation (Galtung 1971:83), leading inevitably to a harmony of interests between center and center and to a disharmony of interests between centers and peripheries. Ecuador, as a peripheral nation in relation to the center nations of world power, exists in such a relation of dependency. The same division between center and periphery that exists at the international level also exists at the domestic level, that is, between the elite of the dependent country and the economically lower strata.

Authors such as Quijano (1973:23–24) see a transformation taking place from "colonialist dependency" toward "imperialist dependency." The former gave origin to the historical formation of Latin American colonial capitalism; the latter is the actual constitution of dependent national societies within the capitalist industrial system. This entire evolutionary process can be seen in Manta, where a rural domestic economy, the product of colonialist dependency, has been transformed to neocapitalist nascent urban industrialization as a result of imperialist dependency. Economic satellization and underdevelopment are not preliminary stages of capitalism but, rather, the consequences and particular forms of it (Dos Santos 1969:38–61). These forms, in turn, condition the total form and logic of the internal structure of a nation. We return here to the concept of structural dependency that contains various subelements within itself.

Dependency could be "translated" as domination, which, according to Castells (1973:82–83), is of three types arranged along a developmental continuum: "1) colonial domination; 2) colonialist commercial domination; 3) imperialist (industrial and financial) domination." This developmental sequence has occurred in Manta. From colonial domination resulting from contact with Europeans, it has gone on to commercial capitalism fundamentally symbolized by the exportation of cacao and *tagua* (ivory nut), to wind up in a system of imperialism as the result of recent industrialization. These processes are obviously dynamic, since, as Kaplan (1973:134) notes, this development presupposes a permanent interaction between two orders of power. Accepting the existence of imperialism (acceptance of the fact, not of volition) implies actions of intrinsic violence via foreign imposition within a country. Physical force need not occur; only amateur or imperfect imperialists, as Galtung (1971:91) calls them, make use of arms. Professional imperialism is based on structural violence more than on direct physical violence. The line of intrinsic, structural violence has been followed in the imposition of imperialism in Ecuador and, within the nation, in the city of Manta.[3]

Spokesmen for the political-economic-cultural centers of world power are often faced with challenges to, and occasional rejection of, the imposition of imperialist domination. They meet such challenges with the argument that external dependency does not destroy or prevent absolutely the possibility of "development." Kaplan (1973:135) rejects this argument, saying that "it [developmentalism] is a dynamic process towards a type of *dependent capitalism*" (emphasis mine). This line of developmentalist thought, which leads to greater dependency, was followed during the attempted establishment of the Alliance for Progress. The negative experience and ultimate failure of this alliance suggest the invalidity of dependent capitalism as an intermediate phase in a course toward true economic and social independence. Dependent capitalism does not permit, indeed it prevents, the implementation of a force for national development. All of the developmentalist actions undertaken within dependent capitalism are oriented toward the benefit of the dominant countries; the cycle of dependency is thereby reinforced.

This sketch of the concepts of dependency, underdevelopment, imperialism, and domination has been useful in that the recognition of their different foci carries us to a re-evaluation of the general concept of dependency: ". . . as a theoretical instrument to emphasize all of the economic aspects of underdevelopment as the political process of domination of one country over others or of some classes over others, in a context of national dependency" (Cardoso and Faletto 1969: 161–62).

All of the processes analyzed up to this point are now bringing, and will continue to bring, many transformations within the societies in which they occur. But the exact series of changes is carried out by the elite for their own benefit and by means of their own coercive forces within the system that permits them (Bell 1975:162). This is precisely what I observed in Manta, where an elite bearer of power, in all of its manifestations, is imposing the goals and means to obtain them. This is not, however, a movement originated by the national elite in this peripheral country. Rather, the elite of Ecuador (and, within Ecuador, the elite of Manta) act in complete accord with the goals espoused by the elite groups from the dominant, or center, countries. Following Galtung (1971:96), one can say that the peripheral elites are manipulated by the elites from the center countries, since these latter are the ones who impose the directions to follow.

This fact, which appears on the surface to be a contradiction, is not so. The national elites accept this subordination because it implies that, as a class, they can increase their domination at regional and local levels under the protection of the elite of a foreign power. Still further, this manipulation does not greatly affect them, since it does not impede their increasing influence in various sectors, especially that of economic activity at the national level (Quijano 1973:27). One can conclude from this "that the dominant interests within the dependent societies correspond to the total system of dependent relations" (Quijano 1973:22). The important internal role played by the elite of the peripheral countries is important to "external interests" which focus attention increasingly on the sector of production for the internal market, consequently increasing the strength of political alliances with elite groups in urban centers (Cardoso and Faletto 1969:164). By increasing the strength of local elites, usually at the executive level, multinational companies gradually move power and control out of the local economy to loci in the exterior (Kaplan 1973:157).

This phenomenon is best illustrated in Manta by looking at the fishing industry. The three most important companies by economic volume are all foreign-based businesses. All of these companies have acquired the services of certain members of the Manta elite. Two of the companies are subsidiaries of North American companies, Inepaca and Del Monte, and the third, Pesquera Santa Isabel, is a subsidiary of a Spanish company. At the national level the process is the same. Hurtado (1977:175) tells us "that in 1973, of the 1400 companies operating in Ecuador, 60% were controlled by foreign investors." The situation today is essentially the same. The purchase of real estate in dependent countries by foreign companies is one mechanism of penetration and domination that facilitates their establishment. Such administrative techniques facilitate the execution of the policies of the dominant elite (Kaplan 1973:154). These policies, in turn, are carried out by executives and administrators recruited primarily from the largest cities. They serve as nexuses of union between national and international interests. This process can be seen in Manta not only at the executive level but also at the level of the skilled technical worker. Owing to a lack of personnel with the necessary skills to carry out such tasks, such positions are generally filled by persons from outside Manta (Naranjo 1977). Businesses themselves in Manta are "family property," a metaphor used by Furtado (1970:176) to describe most businesses throughout Latin America. In the city of Manta this metaphor is quite accurate, since various industries are identified with different families.

Industrialization is not just an economic process but one of political power, inasmuch as continuation of economic growth is inextricably linked to the central bureaucracy, its policies and activities (Collier

1978:11). Also, in the political sphere, dominant groups seek to reorganize the political regimes to manipulate authoritarian centralization and facilitate the implantation of the capitalist mode of production in the dependent economies so as to consolidate their own domination. Such processes have been analyzed brilliantly by Cardoso and Faletto (1969:153). In Ecuador reorganization of political power is manifest in an ideological movement of the government toward the right, and in the parallel economic emphasis on the idea of national development. I will examine this latter phenomenon below. In this movement toward reorganization the subject of ethnicity grows in importance (Bell 1975:142). We must consider various levels: economic, political, cultural, and social, all of which are strongly interconnected.

I have thus far emphasized dependency at the international level, but the same model of asymmetric dependency relations can be applied to intranational relations. Kaplan (1973:133) thinks there is a tendency to overemphasize the place of external factors and components of dependency in relation to internal ones, and to attribute to the former a total and exclusive function or importance. The elite at the global level do indeed dictate the directions followed by the national elite while disguising the source of their directions, but internal factors must also be analyzed.

According to Quijano (1973:59), the urban system, from the ecological point of view, contains two basic levels: industrial and nonindustrial urbanization in a relation of dependency within the urban economy. What is being expressed by this author could well be complemented by including it within Galtung's (1971) model of the division between the center and the periphery. Such a juxtaposition describes the situation in Manta quite well. There a minority group (or level, in this case) has taken for its own some of the key structural positions within the industrial process, leaving the great majority of people in a dependent relation through lack of opportunity for incorporation. The dichotomy between industrial and nonindustrial urbanization is very apparent in Manta's urban milieu. Van den Berghe and Primov (1977:8) seek to explain phenomena such as this in terms of the existence of one-sided relationships (they try to highlight the asymmetry) between countries. They go on to say that the same model is applicable to relations between different regions of the same country, which yield the same consequences. They conclude that development and underdevelopment are two facets of a single process.

Some cases of internal dependency can be considered as internal colonialism. Van den Berghe and Primov (1977:7) give a list of the conditions that must exist for the concept of internal colonialism to apply. For them, internal colonialism is present when a group is:

> (1) . . . ethnically distinct from the dominant group, (2) spatially segregated in tribal homelands, like Indian reservations, (3) administered through a special governmental machinery like a Bureau of Indian Affairs (United States) or a Ministry or Bantu Administration (South Africa), and (4) subject to a set of laws that give them different status from that of the dominant group members, like a code of Native Law and Custom (South Africa), or a system of communal land tenure.

This list is not exhaustive. There exist other, more subtle and sophisticated forms of creating and maintaining internal dependency or colonialism. In Manta one must take into account the means whereby power is wielded through various political, economic, and social institutions; by whom it is manipulated; how the actual ends are arrived at; and, finally, who gains and who loses in the manipulation of latent and manifest power relations. Domination is always present in Manta and cannot be denied. The systematic and calculated negation of opportunity at all levels by the elite contributes to the creation of a pervasive, dependent dichotomization between the powerful white elite of the industrial sector and the dependent *montuvio* and *cholo* peoples of the nonindustrial sector.

The process of capitalist dependency has been magnified by the nascent industrial stage of developmental economy now occurring in Manta. But the very formation of Latin American societies occurred through the "civilizing" work of the *conquistadores* as they annihilated the pre-Columbian societies, to establish the initial context of colonial dependence (Castells 1973:72). Quijano (1973:23) argues that the emancipation which permitted the emergence of the contemporary nations "did not cancel dependency, but only its modification." Dependency came to be a constituent element in the political-economic-social formation of national Latin American societies (Quijano 1973:21). For Cardoso and Faletto (1969:24), too, dependency began historically with the expansion of the original economies by the colonizers.

HOW DEPENDENCY OPERATES

We turn now to the *modus operandi* of dependency, to the mechanisms that permit the implantation and development of dependent asymmetrical relations. I will also look at the assumed attitudes of persons in those countries that suffer from the imposition of dependency relations.

Furtado (1970:177) says that "national groups align themselves with the foreigners, thus diluting their real autonomy." He means that national groups consciously, from the beginning, know that they are playing a subordinant role within these relations (see also Jaguaribe 1969:188). Quijano (1973:35) stresses this phenomenon by noting that the acceptance of the second (industrial) plane—as he calls it— on the part of the nationals in the process of industrialization is due also to the exigencies of work requiring a high level of technological skill. This is certainly the case in Manta (Naranjo 1978), but it is obviously not the principal ideological reason for the phenomenon.

When a certain degree of industrialization at various levels has been reached, evident restrictions occur in the decision-making process with respect to the national economic system in the context of development (Cardoso and Faletto 1969:149). Consider what happens in the case of the multinational companies discussed above. The danger of economic and political interventionism, though, is not the greatest danger of this process, as Cardoso and Faletto (1969:164) point out: ". . . the formation of an industrial economy on the periphery of the international capitalist system minimizes the effects of typically colonialist exploitation and looks for solidarity not only in the dominant classes, but also in the conjunction of the social groups growing out of modern capitalist production: salaried workers, technologists, businessmen, bureaucrats, etc."

This is the case in Manta, where intelligent maneuvers by businessmen at the executive level create the fiction that *all* of the people who work on tasks of industrialization are active partners, *socios activos*, in it; in reality, only a minority occupies this role and the rest come to be exploited solely so that the minority can become even more powerful. The ideological propaganda of the developmental process constantly stresses joint participation in industrial activities, but this is very far from being true. The fisherman working on a boat of an economically powerful company is far removed from the directors of the company, who are completely unaware of his existence. This same fisherman, though, feels himself to be an active partner in the directors' business, because he *belongs to it*. The mental process operating in this fisherman is dangerous, I think, because it results in a state of acceptance of a dependency relationship that paradoxically removes him more and more as a partner in any action affecting the relationship. The same can be said of a worker in a fish-processing plant, a battery-making plant, or in any factory in Manta; in all cases the process is the same, and the fiction of partnership is created by the same model of developmental change.

Let us now turn to the means by which capitalist dependent industrialization has furthered internal colonialism in the city of Manta.
Dependency here, dichotomized with reference to desired goals, has
created what Quijano (1973:60) calls "a marginalization of growing
sectors of the population."[4] Industrialization has generated a polarization between social groups with reference to economic chances or
opportunities, and a polarization of relative power as a consequence
of economic polarization. The distances between social groups in the
accumulation of wealth and power are becoming greater and greater
as a direct consequence of industrial growth. The generalization
made by Quijano (1973:60) appears to be frighteningly apt: "This dependent industrialization makes it impossible for the following generations, born in the same cities, to incorporate themselves in a stable
and consistent manner into the structure of roles and positions
within the new urban society that emerges with industrialization."
This has happened in Manta, where businesses are all linked to families, but with a further complication. Not only do the people born
there compete for integration into the industrial process, but so do
the large number of people from rural areas who have in-migrated to
Manta in search of work. The poor sector swells, the family businesses endure, and the elite's control grows stronger.

To understand the process of dependency at the internal level, we
must return to the role played by the metropoli at the international
level. Gunder Frank (1970:228), Kaplan (1973:139), and Galtung
(1971:84) agree in assigning to the center metropoli the dual function
of syphoning off capital from the peripheral countries and of using
centralized power to maintain the economic, political, social, and cultural peripherality of these countries. The metropoli perpetuate the
imperialist capitalist system which permits exploitation of the peripheral nations by the center nations. Galtung (1971:84) stresses the fact
that the periphery serves *only* as a means of transmitting valued
goods to the center nations (for detailed studies of the structure of
the international relations between central and peripheral nations,
see Galtung 1971:89 and Cardoso and Faletto 1969:144).

Industrial technology, *per se*, reinforces dependency relations. Continuous incorporation of units of external capital in the form of sophisticated technology is more a necessity of the modern export
economy than of the relatively retarded importing economies. This
technoeconomic asymmetry provides a structure facilitating the economic conditions of increased dependency (Cardoso and Faletto
1969:165). In Manta machinery is imported, technicians to operate it
are usually imported, and all of the spare parts needed for its main-

tenance are imported, thus creating an interminable chain of economic dependency. To return to the famous fishing industry, with the exception of a very few very small ships constructed in small shipyards, all of the rest of the needed fishing equipment is imported from Japan and the United States. At the level of the strictly maritime economy, this results in currency flowing out of the country, contributing to disequilibrium in the balance of payments. The dimension is fundamentally economic, but its repercussions are felt in all aspects of life.

I spoke of the importation of technicians, but at a more basic level one must note the importance of the great lack of local qualified workers. This generates the paradox of Manta having large groups of people who want to work but who lack any knowledge of how to carry out the necessary tasks. Furtado (1970:97) has observed this phenomenon in the majority of Latin American cities and seeks to explain it by noting that the population searching for work has had to move directly from rural agricultural labor requiring little or no sophistication to the completely alien industrial world of urban factories. When they cannot cope with industrial technical demands, people create their own source of entrance to the urban ambience, usually at the lower limits of economic existence (Dwyer 1974:22). One can understand why, in Manta, there are so many roving vendors, shoeshine boys, and small corner stands, *kioskos*, that sell soda pop, ice cream, etc. The only thing that this mass of roving beings can do (according to Castells 1973:75) is to "dissimulate" their condition without any real possibility of obtaining employment, since the available jobs require preparation and training beyond their means.

Just as I have referred to the process of industrialization as structured within the theory of dependency, I also regard contemporary urbanization and urban development as phenomena generated by industrial process. The importance of urbanism is well known; it is superseded only by the problems of nuclear arms and world hunger (Dwyer 1974:9). Because of the saliency of the urban problem, Morse (1971:93) rightly calls for the revision of community studies written in the 1940s and 1950s to include cultural change. This call is quite valid for Manta, since industrialization has clearly generated urbanization and modernization, and a consequent series of changes. Manta was originally just a small community of fishermen (Brooks and Brooks 1965), but its abundance of fish and its deep-water docks attracted capital, which in turn initiated the industrial process resulting in modern urbanization. Here I take issue with Quijano (1973:45), who does not regard urbanization as the result of industrialization.

For Manta, his premise cannot be upheld, as demonstrated by the following fact. In 1976 the tenth anniversary of the founding of the Port Authority of Manta (Autoridad Portuaria 1976) was celebrated. This entity was created at the very beginning of the industrial process, when the docks first began operating commercially. The Port Authority of Manta is also charged with planning and executing all of the infrastructural works for the city. Without the dock yards there would not be a port authority, hence no infrastructural works and no urbanization.

It is important to stress this set of relationships, since in all the other cities of Ecuador the municipal governments are the entities charged with carrying out infrastructural works. The municipal government did exist in Manta in the 1970s, but the increase of infrastructural development dates from ten years before its creation, the date of the establishment of the Port Authority, and the beginning of industrialization. Quijano (1973:43) insists on studying urbanization and industrialization as diverse entities, but to do so in Manta would be to fictitiously and erroneously separate coterminous processes.

To examine the role played by the national government in the face of these problems, it is necessary to go back to the end of the 1960s, a period during which military dictatorships gained power through much of Latin America[5] and consistently promoted accelerated foreign investment. These governments have not followed the traditional form taken by military dictatorships in the past, in which the most important factor was the dictator himself. In these later dictatorships the military institution itself is the locus of power, and the actual persons in leadership positions matter less (see, e.g., Collier 1978:6). In the last four years the Ecuadorian government has passed from the hands of General Rodríguez Lara to a military triumvirate composed of members from the three branches of the armed forces.

The advent of military governments that actively seek foreign investments brings us again to the theme of imperialism, which, according to Galtung (1971:81), segments collectivities within the dependent nation from a harmony of national interest to a disharmony of interests. From this point of view, imperialism is a *species* within the *genus* of domination and power relations (Galtung 1971:81). The transformation of Latin America, according to this analysis, is not a "march towards modernization" (Castells 1973:92) but, rather, the expression of the social contradictions produced by the forms and rhythms of imperialist domination.

With respect to the actions of foreign investors, which the military governments have allowed to impose and increase the strength of domination and imperialism, we can ask (following Castells 1973:99): Do the capitalist businesses, monopolistic or not, national or foreign, ever operate with the goal of meeting the needs of the population? The answer to this question is *no*. All they do is to syphon off resources and take them out of the country, creating the fictions of "progress" and "development." Kaplan (1973:142) stresses the fact that the objective of foreign investments is twofold: (1) satisfaction of the necessities for raw materials, food, minerals, and the like existing in the central, dominant, industrialized countries, and (2) development of the infrastructure and services that increase the realization of the first objective.

This process is observable at the national level and at the regional and local levels focused on the city of Manta. In the national context the type case today is that of oil (in the past it was cacao, later bananas). Foreign investors control all facets of the petroleum industry, proceeding forward toward the satisfaction of foreign needs. The major infrastructural work associated with petroleum is the state refinery. In Manta this process of infrastructural development to meet foreign needs is mirrored in the shipping industry. One marine company, for example, obliged the Port Authority to build a special dock where export goods to foreign markets could flow with greater ease. This infrastructural work fundamentally favors the company.[6] These two examples could easily be multiplied but are sufficient to document Kaplan's (1973:144) thesis.

Propaganda facilitates the advent, reinforcement, and validation of dependency, imperialism, and external and internal colonialism. Such propaganda explicitly expresses an ideology that, in the Ecuadorian case, strongly suggests a true national populist development. The program of industrialization is presented to the nation as a means of providing benefits for all. Ideally, at the governmental level, the ideology of national economic expansion, oriented toward the internal market as a perpetuation of the system of domination, should facilitate the incorporation of the masses into the production and political systems (Cardoso and Faletto 1969:106). In Ecuador developmentalist ideology today saturates communication networks and has the desired result: people generally believe that sooner or later they will actively participate in political-economic power. In reality, economic polarization and all it connotes continue to grow. Collier (1978:7) introduces a new term to describe new Latin American governments: "bureaucratic authoritarianism," which has a technocratic mentality and which uses repression to limit pluralism and at the same time control opposition to the regime. As a counterpoint, he assigns to the general populace an apathetic attitude with respect to the regime.

Obviously, this situation of dependency is far from desirable; it carries with it elements that aggravate extant economic polarization. All attempts by Latin American governments to combat increasing polarization serve only to delay the effects. The problem remains because the causes are not eliminated. This fact has led social scientists interested in Latin America and Third World countries generally to clamor for *structural* change (see Furtado 1970, Gunder Frank 1970, Galtung 1971, Freire 1967, Dos Santos 1971, Cardoso and Faletto 1969), to break out of the constraining model of dependency in which they live daily. The task is not easy since the enemy is powerful, but at least it is known what road should be followed, and some attempts to remedy this problem have been made in various parts of the world. Given the structure of dependency, I consider Bell's (1975:140) opinions about "the movements of romantic liberation and adventure of the countries of the third world" to be malicious and intolerable. If in the fight against oppression, domination, and death he sees these "romantic" characteristics, he must have fallen prey to subconscious intellectual colonialism.

FUNCTION OF ETHNICITY IN THE CONTEXT OF DEPENDENCY

We have seen how dependency has segmented society into various economic strata. As a complement to the economic and social problems thereby generated, it is essential to study the part ethnicity plays within this system of economic strata. Elsewhere (Naranjo 1978) I have shown that Ecuador is a plural society in which one finds clearly differentiated groups which interact economically, politically, and culturally and which recognize among themselves and in others specific identities (which does not necessarily imply acceptance of these identities).

Social ascription of people to plural, differentiated groupings may be called ethnic segmentation or ethnicity. In Manta social cohesion within ethnic groups or categories revolves around *ad hoc* communication (Wallace 1970:111) about ascriptive attributes, which people avoid when it is at all possible to do so. Social pluralism can also be understood in terms of stratified groups or classes. Here I will refer primarily to the structure of groups as a function of ethnicity, but the structure of classes is no less important. Despres (1975:189), following Smith (1969:104), emphasizes that ethnic combinations are strategic in the study of pluralist societies and cultures. Following this criterion, which is certainly applicable to the social structure of Manta, I will refer to pluralism and focus on ethnicity and ethnic segmentation.

The genesis of group formation and its immediate corollary, group integration, stems from the perspective that group integration is preferable to personal interaction. Despres (1975:190–91, citing Barth 1969:15–16), argues that ethnic groups form in such a way that actors use their ethnic identities to categorize others and themselves in order to facilitate intra- and intergroup interaction. In Manta there exist clearly tagged and identifiable ethnic groups: *blancos, montuvios, cholos, negros,* the middle class,[7] *indios,* and *serranos* (Naranjo 1978), members of which may interact among themselves in somewhat identifiable ways. This mosaic of ethnic groups forms an image of pluralism fundamentally grounded in the idea of ascription and autoascription of group membership (Moerman 1965:1218). In the daily life of these ethnic groups autoascription can be observed when individuals refer to their specific ethnic categories as a function of initiating or maintaining patterned group interaction. The reason for this type of behavior is obvious, and must be understood from the perspective of asymmetrical relations that have been created in the entire society. One tagged as *montuvio* (a label denoting class and ethnic inferiority within the context of group relations) will strive to interact with *blancos* as part of a group rather than as an individual. Group identity helps such a person feel less alone and perhaps somewhat more protected. The same can be said with respect to other groups considered inferior within the context of ethnic life in Manta.

The same phenomenon occurs with the ethnic groups—*blancos, clase media*—that occupy superior positions in the social spectrum: they tend to act as a *blanco* ethnic group, or as members of the elite class, never as individuals. They do this not to protect their group structure but, rather, to augment their power and to emphasize their superior political-economic domain. In any case, this acting "as a group" clarifies the concept of pluralism as the hierarchical and vertical segments of Manta's structure emerge constantly in daily interaction.

The practical importance of clarifying the problem of ethnicity lies in the fact that it is intimately tied up with unequal distribution of power and wealth (van den Berghe 1975:71). In the ascription of a particular ethnic group, economic differences are important, and often determinant. In Manta *blancos* constitute the elite group; this group is clearly identified with economic power, leading obviously to the unequal distribution of wealth in relation to the other ethnic groups. In the same way those tagged as *cholos, negros,* or *indios* constitute ethnically segmented groups with strong connotations of economic powerlessness. There are two levels of segmentation here, one of which is the result of the other. At one level is dependency structure, which is the genesis of the problem because it is the element that has polarized the factions into rich and poor, people with power and people without it. At the other level is ethnicity, but it is the result of dependency structure inasmuch as it is the product of polarization. Polarization itself is bound up with unequal distribution of power and wealth (see, e.g., van den Berghe 1975:71).

These levels exist in Manta. The economic situation there generated by dependency has created an asymmetrical set of relationships between the groups within the society. The groups that interact in Manta recognize the magnitude of current economic differentiation and also recognize that the ascription into groups and categories which constitute ethnic group structure follows economic and stereotypic criteria. The case of the *negro* ethnic group clearly exemplifies this. Their low economic situation, a product of dependency organized around a phenotypic trait, has contributed to the formation of a differentiated ethnic group recognized by all as such. *Cholos* and *montuvios* have also been ordered by the same rules of pejorative ascription according to a blend of factors of economic powerlessness and stereotypic labeling.

Van den Berghe and Primov (1977:5) emphasize the idea that ethnic relations and class relations define intergroup relations. In Manta the logic of a dependency-ethnicity dichotomy lets us see how the genesis of ethnicity is the result of a situation originated by dependency. Ethnicity and class relations are interrelated phenomena, but analytically distinct (van den Berghe 1975:73). One cannot juxtapose the two entities; they correspond in some ways but diverge in others. Despres's (1975:195) words illustrate quite well the differentiation that I have tried to make between the two elements: "Ethnic stratifications derive their structural features from categorical status ascriptions. By way of contrast, class stratifications are more evidently based upon status identities which are achieved."

As in Cuzco, Peru (van den Berghe and Primov 1977:4), ethnic groups in Manta are formed by means of ascription; they constitute both distinct and unequal groups. Recognition of ascription and its eventual acceptance imply the noting of differences in the context of social relations. Class, too, based fundamentally on economic power, generates inequality and asymmetry of social relations. Ethnicity and class are both necessary to demarcate inequalities. These two levels of inequality, although representative of different phenomena, are nonetheless manifestations of social inequality within a structure of dependency. Barth (1969:18) emphasizes the fact that marked differences of conduct between groups causes cultural differentiation and its persistence. This is what I observed in group interaction in Manta, where, as a function of cultural differences—which are primarily a product of economic factors—the barriers are maintained and persist in rigid form.[8] In no other way can one understand the profound gap that exists between *blancos* and *montuvios*, or between the elite and the *cholos pescadores*, the *cholo* fishermen, within the economic, political, and social spectrum of Manta.

The element that permits the preservation or breakdown of ethnic barriers does not arise from a uniform model. Thus van den Berghe and Primov (1977) found easy passage from one ethnic group to another in their study of Cuzco. The same authors found that the elite group also accepts new members without major difficulties. This seems to me to be exceptional. The pioneering studies of Mills (1956) in the United States emphasize the closed character of the elite group; this is certainly characteristic of Manta, where the "power elite" is an exclusive, largely endogamous group.

Membership in groups other than the elite is also well delineated in Manta. There is a dual phenomenon with respect to the maintenance of barriers between them. On the one hand, economic, social, and political mobility aspirations to move from one group to another exist; on the other hand, there also exists a tendency to remain in the group to which one belongs and, further still, to reinforce one's ties of affiliation with it. For example, the *cholos pescadores*, who repeatedly emphasize their ethnic identity and say that they do not want to change it, are often in an economic position to change their status if they so chose. This characteristic has been emphasized for other cases by Parsons (1975:57). In the middle class, treated here as though it were an ethnic group, the characteristic sentiment is to avoid downward mobility and promote upward mobility; in reality, most people in that class stay there. This social segment faces great internal conflict, because even to reamin in it requires the exertion of great effort. It is very difficult to rise in status and very easy to fall. This combination of factors creates confusion and great stress in members of this group.

CULTURAL TRANSFORMATIONS IN MANTA

I have alluded repeatedly to the forced implantation of dependency structure and dynamics throughout Ecuador, with its extension to the city of Manta, within the context of internal colonialism, and of the center-periphery global relationships in the context of the periphery countries. I have shown that national governments, instead of fighting dependency, embraced it in the name of "development." I have also noted that when one deals with inequality, ethnic factors play a preponderant part in maintaining and fortifying the *status quo*. In Manta these dynamic processes, with all of their ramifications, have created a series of cultural transformations, to which I now turn.

The process of transformation took place during the 1960s through 1977, the period in which the "industrial revolution" arrived in Manta. Markers of the industrial epoch include construction of the port with deep-water docks, establishment and definitive development of the tuna fleet of Ecuador in the port of Manta, and installation and development of the fishing industry. During this period an extended drought in Manabí province forced rural *campesinos*, tagged *montuvios*, to the city in search of work.

Industrialization has had a disrupting effect. The port and associated industries brought capital but also generated new needs which have not been satisfied. The transition from small town to city life in the process of industrialization has been so abrupt that many inhabitants have not integrated the changes into their daily lives. People there make constant reference to past times in which "life was less complicated and there were not so many problems." The most frequent focus for such statements is the family and the ways by which social relations embedded therein have become diffuse and family ties, in turn, weakened. Although Manta is not overpopulated, as in the case of Chimbote, Peru (Bradfield 1973), change has been so drastic that problems of anonymity have begun to surface, aggravated by the agitation that has taken place in daily life. The frenetic rhythm of life on the docks seems to have become the model on which people pattern all other types of activities. The inhabitants of Manta are not accustomed to this pace of life. A constant complaint is "now there is not time to talk." Not long ago one could pass an entire afternoon in conversation without altering the course of life. But now, if one is employed in an industry, this freedom has been reduced, and tensions are created.

A man who works on a regular daily schedule tries, during the weekend, to compensate for the time he could not pass with his friends during the week. He thereby leaves his home just when other members have the most time to interact with him. This mode of weekend behavior, where male-male friendship interaction supersedes husband-wife and father-children familial interaction, may undermine the harmony of many homes. The fact of receiving a daily wage is also a new dimension in the economic life of the Manta home, especially in its lower economic strata; the earlier model within which households functioned was oriented toward earning enough for the satisfaction of daily necessities. Now daily necessities are more than satisfied at a material level, but family life itself is viewed as problematic in terms of maintenance of satisfying social bonds.

Industrialization of Manta has generated a whole series of new, felt, material needs to satisfy, such as appropriate clothing and better houses. The media continuously impose new needs which collectively act in oppressive form. An example of this is the continuous stress on the consumption of food products such as "American style" bread instead of manioc or plantains. Now popular is the introduction of "lunch" instead of *almuerzo*, composed of "hog dogs" as "in the best places in the United States." Such bread and hot dogs have little to offer in terms of superior nutrition over manioc, plantains, fish, and rice; they represent a new type of desire and the adoption of a new form of life far from that of a coastal Ecuadorian town of the early 1960s.

At another level, the perceived necessity of acquiring certain electrical appliances, such as color television, brings two potential problems. The first is purely economic. Many families cannot buy such appliances because of their high price, and they express frustration because they say they should have them and the media say they should have them. When the economic means are sufficient for the acquisition of these goods, the appliances alter the traditional rhythm of life. It is a constant complaint of husbands and wives that they have little time for conversation because it is all taken up by television.[9]

The attitudes of people between the ages of 25 and 35 are especially interesting, for they live the fiction of being "active partners and participants" in the new industrial process and talk with vigor about the economic benefits that this process brings. But few of these people realize these benefits; the majority suffer most from the consequences of rampant economic inflation. Consciousness of this suffering often transforms one's self-image from "participating partner" to "exploited partner." All of the magic of development disappears, and the frustrations which then surface at the personal level ramify into familial and other social domains.

One of the consequences of the process of domination brought about by dependency is what Quijano (1973:65) calls the "urbanization of culture." Within this expression he includes the process by which expansion and modification of cultural forms (cultural trans-formations) is produced in a society, of alteration of urban-rural cul-tural relations, and of the diffusion of certain cultural elements of urban origin which are carried to a dependent urban culture. This phenomenon can be observed daily in Manta, where cultural norms are being imported directly from the centers of greatest development, Guayaquil and Quito. These norms are integrated into Manta life, usually in a distorted way, but the receptivity of the populace is par-amount. Note that without much difficulty the most developed cen-ters can generate a true acculturative process in a manner much more sophisticated than through the use of force.

Ideology is crucial in the maintenance of cultural dependency, since cities themselves provide a milieu of political economic ambiva-lence (Quijano 1973:68). On the one hand, urban centers serve as mechanisms of penetration and exposition of dependency; on the other, they allow certain groups to concentrate and to become radi-calized by the process, leading to protest and social conflict. In Manta such radical protest and resistance do not exist. The middle class there controls the *sindicatos* and workers' organizations; the actions of constituent groups, as a class, resist drastic changes and aspire to gradual assumption of political-economic rights and privileges con-sonant with the media's propaganda. In the absence of radicalized protest middle-class acquiescence to gradualism actually promotes accelerating change.

I have referred to propaganda as an auspicious element of this ur-banization of culture, but this term must be understood in a wider context, since it is at the level of centralized government that this ideology is generated and spread. Cultural and social standardization of the middle class is a constant theme of official publications and radio broadcasts to which the masses have access. Townspeople who suffer the increasing cost of basic subsistence goods tend to look to the central government as the locus of salvation. Constant repetition of ideological propaganda coming from this locus has the desired ef-fect (from the government's standpoint): people accept the idea that sooner or later economic, political, and social equality will occur, and that all will come to be "happy members of a no less happy middle class."

I place major emphasis on the middle class here because it is in this social segment that one can best observe the dynamics of political economy and society; in a certain sense it is the militant class. The characteristics sketched for this middle class include power of prop-aganda, assumed attitudes, and tendency to uniformity; they also hold true for the subordinate classes of Manta, as they emulate the middle class. Governmental ideology is directed to this middle social segment precisely because of its tendency toward uniformity of culture. This class is also idealized by such propaganda as the goal of maximum aspiration for "inferior" social segments.

CONCLUSIONS

This paper has sought to understand urban dynamics in Manta at three interpenetrating levels. In a global context the world is divided into central and peripheral countries; the central countries have imposed cultural models on the peripheral countries, giving rise to an asymmetrical relationship of dependency of the periphery on the center. Dependency has been imposed by imperialist colonialism, sometimes by means of moral or physical force. Although, at the second level of analysis, one cannot claim that dependency directly causes ethnicity, it does help to perpetuate it, owing especially to the existence—seen in Manta in a clear and pronounced form—of a dependent capitalist colonialism which has structured, ordered, and bounded the ethnic groups. In Manta members of the elite group are descendants of the European conquerors from early colonial times. At the bottom of the class structure are the black, Indian, and especially *montuvio* and *cholo* groups who have always been the subjects of this Euro-white exploiting group. From this point of view, the asymmetric relations defining the parameters of ethnic group daily interaction is a logical extension of the system of dependency.

At the third level of analysis, cultural transformation, dependency processes define the milieu which channels the dynamics of industrialization and modernization. Central countries become rich, leaving the rest for the oligarchies—called the elite group—of the country where the transition to an industrial state occurs. These processes of industrialization and modernization in Manta have created a series of cultural transformations. These have occurred at the personal level (anonymity, the battle for prestige), social level (alteration of the traditional model of the family, new forms of administration of economic resources at the level of hourly wage and salaries), and at the societal level with its overall change in the rhythm and quality of life.

All of these processes at all three levels are dynamic. All are pernicious and concrete: each day the asymmetry of political, economic, and social relations increases, with drastic effects across the entire spectrum of Manta, microcosm of modern Ecuador.

NOTES

Acknowledgments: Funds for the research upon which this article is based were provided by the Research Board of the University of Illinois and by a doctoral dissertation research grant from the National Science Foundation.

1. All translations from the Spanish are my responsibility.

2. By "underdevelopment" I refer to groups which, because they have been subjected to a continuous process of domination, live at a subsistence level without any hope of relieving their situation except by "development."

3. Dominant countries often do not employ brutal physical aggression but instead use a more subtle form of violence. The exportation of Ecuadorian bananas is illustrative. The banana market depended on vicissitudes of demand in the buying country, usually the United States. When the buyer did not want to buy the product, for political reasons, the Ecuadorian economy tottered. This is a type of subtle violence. Today the point of confrontation is petroleum. As a member of OPEC, Ecuador was negatively sanctioned by having certain tariff rights suspended for OPEC's participation in the oil embargo of 1976, even though Ecuador did not participate actively in it. This is another example of the subtle violence to which I have referred.

4. By "marginalization" I mean the process of political economic exclusion from the dominant society of any groups. For a detailed study of marginalization in the context of dependency, see Quijano (1970).

5. It ought to be noted, although already well known, that the installation of military governments is generally decided outside the country of origin; the installation of the military government of Chile is illustrative.

6. The construction of the new dock was the condition demanded by the C.C.T. maritime company in order to continue operating in Manta. This company is the primary beneficiary of this work, not Manta itself, since to accelerate the operations of loading and unloading the rights of port use are reduced in proportion to the invested time. Here one clearly sees that an infrastructural work favors the imposing foreign company more than the national companies.

7. One ought to refer to the middle class in the context of ethnicity, since in Manta the concept of *mestizaje*, which Middleton (1976) uses to delimit this social segment, does not apply. If one speaks of the *mestizo* group, one does so completely subjectively, and this is precisely what I am trying to avoid. [Editor's note: See also note 8. It is precisely because the elite of Manta exclude those not 100% European *blanco* from their sector that Middleton uses the term "mixed" or *mestizo* for their implied ethnic heritage.]

8. The economic element is not the only important factor here. For the case of Manta, one has to take into account the necessity of belonging to a recognized European familial tradition to be a member of the elite. The purely economic factor is not sufficient to characterize this elite group. [Editor's note: This is why Middleton uses the term *mestizo* here.]

9. I refer to the phenomenon of television, *per se*, not to any particular show. If I were to analyze the quality of the shows, this panorama would be made still uglier because of the inherent alienating element of the programs shown, which are mostly dubbed into Spanish from Mexican and U.S. television.

118   *Cultural Transformations and Ethnicity in Modern Ecuador*

REFERENCES CITED

Autoridad Portuaria
   1976   *Puerto de Manta*. Manta, Ecuador.
Barth, Fredrik, ed.
   1969   *Ethnic Groups and Boundaries: The Social Organization of Cultural Differ-ence*. Boston: Little, Brown.
Bell, Daniel
   1975   Ethnicity and Social Change. In Nathan Glazer and Daniel P. Moy-nihan, eds., *Ethnicity: Theory and Experience*. Cambridge, Mass.: Har-vard University Press, pp. 141–74.
Bradfield, Stillman
   1973   Selectivity in Rural-Urban Migrations: The Case of Huaylas, Peru. In Aidan Southall, ed., *Urban Anthropology*. London: Oxford Univer-sity Press, pp. 351–72.
Brooks, Rhoda, and Earle Brooks
   1965   *The Barrios of Manta*. New York: New American Library.
Cardoso, Henrique F., and Enzo Faletto
   1969   *Dependencia y Desarrollo en América Latina*. Mexico City: Siglo Vein-tiuno.
Castells, Manuel
   1973   La Urbanización Dependiente en América Latina. In Martha Schteingart, ed., *Urbanización y Dependencia en América Latina*. Bue-nos Aires: Ediciones S.I.A.P., pp. 70–92.
Collier, David
   1978   Industrialization and Authoritarianism in Latin America. *Items, So-cial Science Research Council* 31/32 (4/1):5–13.
Despres, Leo A.
   1975   Toward a Theory of Ethnic Phenomena. In Leo A. Despres, ed., *Eth-nicity and Resource Competition in Plural Societies*. Chicago: Aldine, pp. 187–207.
Dos Santos, Theotonio
   1969   La Crise de la Théorie du Dévelopement et les Relations de Dépendance en Amérique Latine. *L'Homme et la Societé* 12:43–68.
   1971   The Structure of Dependence. In K. T. Fann and Donald C. Hodges, eds., *Readings in U.S. Imperialism*. Boston: Porter Sargent, pp. 225–36.
Dwyer, D. J.
   1974   Introduction. In D. J. Dwyer, ed., *The City in the Third World*. New York: Harper & Row, pp. 9–25.
Freire, Paulo
   1967   *Pedagogía del Oprimido*. Bogotá: Editorial América Latina.
Furtado, Celso
   1970   *Economic Development of Latin America*. London: Cambridge Univer-sity Press.
Galtung, Johan
   1971   A Structural Theory of Imperialism. *Journal of Peace Research* 8:81–117.
Gunder Frank, André
   1970   *Latin America: Underdevelopment or Revolution*. New York: Monthly Review Press.

Hurtado, Osvaldo
  1977   *El Poder Político en el Ecuador.* Quito: Ediciones de la Universidad
         Católica.
Jaguaribe, Helio
  1969   Causas del Subdesarrollo Latinoamericano. In José Matos Mar, ed.,
         La Crisis del Desarrollismo y la Nueva Dependencia. Buenos Aires:
         Amorrurtu Editores S.C.A., pp. 173–88.
Kaplan, Marcos
  1973   La Ciudad Latinoamericana como Factor de Trasmisión de Poder So-
         cioeconómico y Político hacia el Exterior Durante el Período Con-
         temporáneo. In Martha Schteingart, ed., *Urbanización y Dependencia
         en América Latina.* Buenos Aires: Ediciones S.I.A.P., pp. 132–75.
Middleton, DeWight R.
  1976   The Growth of a City: Urban, Regional, and National Interaction in
         Ecuador. *Urban Anthropology* 5:125–41.
Mills, C. Wright
  1956   *The Power Elite.* Oxford: Oxford University Press.
Moerman, Michael
  1965   Ethnic Identification in a Complex Civilization. Who Are the Lue?
         American Anthropologist 67 (5):1215–30.
Morse, Richard M.
  1971   *La Investigación Urbana Lationamericana: Tendencias y Planteos.* Buenos
         Aires: Ediciones S.I.A.P.
Naranjo, Marcelo F.
  1977   Manta, Ecuador: Structural Dependency and Social Dynamics. Pa-
         per read at the 76th Annual Meeting of the American Anthropo-
         logical Association.
  1978   Etnicidad, Estructura Social y Poder en Manta, Occidente Ecuatori-
         ano. Ann Arbor, Mich.: University Microfilms. Ph.D. thesis, Uni-
         versity of Illinois, Urbana.
Parsons, Talcott
  1975   Some Theoretical Considerations on the Nature and Trends of
         Change of Ethnicity. In Nathan Glazer and Daniel P. Moynihan,
         eds., *Ethnicity: Theory and Experience.* Cambridge, Mass.: Harvard
         University Press, pp. 53–83.
Quijano, Aníbal
  1970   *Redefinición de la Dependencia y Marginalización en América Latina.* San-
         tiago: Publicaciones CESO.
  1973   Dependencia, Cambio Social y Urbanización en América Latina. In
         Martha Schteingart, ed., *Urbanización y Dependencia en América La-
         tina.* Buenos Aires: Ediciones S.I.A.P., pp. 19–69.
Singer, Paul
  1973   Urbanización, Dependencia y Marginalidad en América Latina. In
         Martha Schteingart, ed., *Urbanización y Dependencia en América La-
         tina.* Buenos Aires: Ediciones S.I.A.P., pp. 93–122.
Smith, M. G.
  1969   Pluralism in Precolonial African Societies. In Leo Kuper and M. G.
         Smith, eds., *Pluralism in Africa.* Berkeley: University of California
         Press, pp. 91–151.

van den Berghe, Pierre L.
  1975 Ethnicity and Class in Highland Peru. In Leo A. Despres, ed., *Ethnicity and Resource Competition in Plural Societies*. Chicago: Aldine, pp. 71–85.
van den Berghe, Pierre L., and George P. Primov (with the assistance of Gladys Becerra Velazque and Narciso Ccahuana Ccohuata)
  1977 *Inequality in the Peruvian Andes: Class and Ethnicity in Cuzco*. Columbia: University of Missouri Press.
Wallace, Anthony F. C.
  1970 *Culture and Personality*. New York: Random House.

4

Amazonia Today at the Base of the Andes: An Ethnic Interface in Ecological, Social, and Ideological Perspectives

Norman E. Whitten, Jr.

¡el Ecuador ha sido, es y será, país amazonico! "Ecuador has been, is and will be, an Amazonian country." Thus reads the national rallying cry frequently emblazoned on official stationery within the republic of Ecuador. Ostensibly the motto is a political one which no party would dare to ignore, let alone negate; it protests—and justifiably so—the loss of half of its Amazonian territory to its southern neighbor, Peru, during the early years of World War II. This slogan also validates the nationalist, developmental capitalist realpolitik of an Andean nation—which was, until recently, dependent upon coastal monocultural agribusiness—to incorporate the remaining Upper Amazonian territory within its sphere of burgeoning bureaucratic control with its new economic base of externally sponsored petroleum exploitation.

Incorporation of a territory, even by the gentlest means, is a violent, wrenching episode in national consolidation. This is especially the case when the process follows a century of disruption of the tropical forest peoples and perhaps equal disruption within the Andean-coastal sectors of the country seeking to develop a new Amazonian frontier and to transform that frontier into a tropical image of its changing self. People must be moved into the territory and induced or forced to work in such a manner as to convert energy into modern economic concerns. These concerns—for example, the development of goods which are clearly beneficial to the gross national product, whether or not they feed the new population—generate processes which inevitably involve ecosystem alteration or adjustment, a set of social-jural-political constraints and incentives for resource allocation, and presumably an ideology through which juro-political action is justified, rationalized, and juxtaposed to extant religious thought and evocation.

As I have noted in earlier publications (Whitten 1976a, 1976b, 1977): ". . . the demographic shifts from Andes to lowlands brings the nationalizing population smack into the face of its rainforest inhabitants. This is a profoundly indigenous face, . . . if acknowledged in their richness and adaptable character, the native cultures of the Oriente would contradict the ideology behind the revolutionary force of nationalistic consolidation." In these works I presented an argument that ethnogenesis, or "surgent ethnicity," as I now prefer to call it, was the direct, rational response of the Puyo Runa grouping of Canelos Quichua culture to nationalist-sponsored ethnocidal policies. Here I sketch the indigenous face of the entire Oriente to emphasize the scope of cultural *dynamics*—ecological, economic, social, ideological—as they currently exist in a nationalizing context.

Throughout this work I eschew vacuous gropings to determine "tribal boundaries" and heed the lesson of futility so well documented and argued by Morton Fried (1967, 1975; see also Godelier 1977), for his reasoning is underscored and brought into sharp relief by the ethnic interface of the contemporary Oriente. Among other things, the search for unified "tribes" with their presumptive rigid boundaries and presumed congruence of cultural features and linguistic homogeneity (see, e.g., Harner 1972) strengthens imperialistic imposition of internal colonial "order" (e.g., the "colonial tribe" syndrome described by Helms 1969) and denies panhuman adaptive processes to the rich, changing world of modern Amazonian cultural achievement and potential.

The Introduction to this book, and the papers by Stutzman and Naranjo, establish a set of generalizations about Ecuadorian nationalist development. Among other things, we argue that Ecuadorians everywhere, including the indigenous people of the Oriente—the subjects of our immediate concern—are in the process of surgent reorganization and that this surgency is expressed ecologically, socially, and ideologically. Let us turn now to the reality of contemporary Upper Amazonian peoples caught up in these processes.

INTRODUCTION TO THE ETHNIC INTERFACE OF THE ORIENTE

Because the Oriente lies "east of the Andes," it is common to think of this Ecuadorian rainforest zone in terms of the vastness of Amazonian floodplains and interfluvial territories which rise only hundreds of feet above sea level. In fact, the manifestations of the third Andean cordillera of Ecuador—which rises 3,000–4,000 feet just east of the territory's Andean entrepôts—give us a defining feature of ethnic resurgence of native peoples, in historical and contemporary perspective (as we shall see). The Oriente, as the western fringe of the Upper Amazon, or the southern fringe of the northwest Amazon, or a northern extension of the Peruvian *montaña* (if one wishes to so marginalize it), is most assuredly not one thing—it is not an eastern extension of the Andes in any ecological sense, though it is part of the Andean escarpment in its geological formation.

Much of the Oriente is an interface zone, a domain lying between two forms or structures and forming their common boundary. By placing the Oriente centrally within a common South American Amazonian interface, we strip away the marginal character spuriously attributed to it and draw dynamics of ecological, social, and ideological processes into relief. *Basically, the structures making up the contemporary interface are derived from the contrasts to be drawn between Andean and Amazonian ecologies, stratified bureaucratic and egalitarian social systems, and political nationalist and indigenous ideologies.*

Any traveler beginning a descent of the eastern sierran cordillera, whether via high windswept *páramo* or by deep river cut between majestic Andean slopes, will experience a series of ecosystems which begins with the silent cloud forests featuring the gentle sounds of burbling brooks and the occasional roar of a cataract or small waterfall. A bit farther eastward the burble and occasional torrent crescendo into a more continuous roar of falls and cataracts, accompanied all too often by the crash of landslides. Heavy rainfall brought about as moist Amazonian air currents stroke the cordilleran wall of the towering *montaña* creates a near vertical rainforest in many areas, from which waterfalls gush forth and through which deep riparian ravines are cut.

Farther eastward, but still west of the Oriente's eastern cordillera, in the currently most densely populated areas of the Oriente—Archidona, Tena, Puyo, Macas, Sucúa, Méndez, Gualaquiza—the Andean foothills are encompassed by Upper Amazonian rainforest-montane ecology. Traveling still eastward in one of the most rugged jungles in the world, it is first necessary to wind through a 3,000–4,000-foot-high third cordillera by river pathway, or to ascend and again descend the local manifestation (e.g., Condor, Cutucú, Sigüín, Oglán) of this cordillera before continuing on to lower Amazonia. And as one reaches areas where the rivers become slower, deeper, and more navigable, Ecuador's contemporary border ends in the south and central Oriente, and either Peru, or disputed territory, begins.

Culture history of the Oriente is still inchoate, but we can begin with some general points, moving toward greater specificity with re-

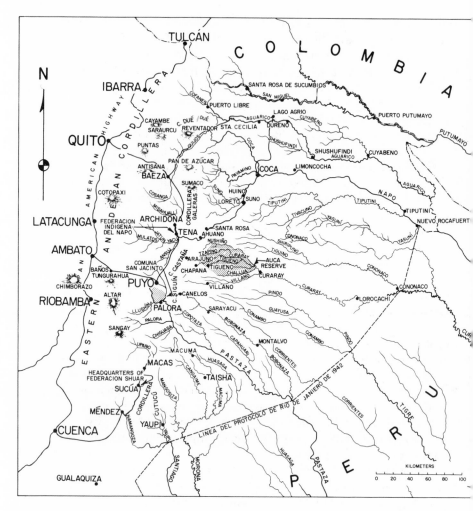

gard to its contemporary inhabitants. Linguistic and archaeological evidence strongly suggests that the first inhabitants were westward-moving tropical forest people who, in the words of Julian Steward (1948:507), "appear to represent a series of migratory waves that had spent their force against the barrier of the Andes, where representatives of many widely distributed linguistic families . . . subsided into comparative isolation. No other area of South America has greater linguistic diversity." Today we must revise this concept of westward colonization out of Amazonia to say that the bearers of native cultures of the Oriente represent successive waves of peoples probably spending their force against the *inhabitants* of the *montaña* (see, e.g.,

Lathrap 1970:176, Porras and Piana 1975:153–60), interdigitating with one another and interacting dynamically to create monolingual and multilingual cultural systems. Some of these systems still exist, but many of them have been obliterated by disease, mission reduction, slave raiding, and the nineteenth-century Amazonian rubber boom, to name only four prominent causes of destruction.

CONTEMPORARY NATIVE LANGUAGES AND CULTURES

The relationship between language and culture is complicated in any region, and this complication presents difficulties when we try to understand the lifeways of a people, their material adaptation to a given habitat and social environment, and their means of communicating. In the Oriente, as in the adjoining northwest Amazon of Colombia, the complexity becomes especially intricate because we find material, social, and ideological commonalities, bonds of kinship and affinity, and political alliances regularly crossing linguistic boundaries. The linguistic boundaries themselves form at the juncture between unrelated native American languages currently existing in the Oriente—Quichua and Jivaroan being the most prominent, with Cofán, Siona, Secoya, Waorani "Auca," and Zaparoan (Záparo-Zapa and Andoa-Shimigae) consisting of small groupings of native speakers. Siona and Secoya are both Tucanoan language dialects associated with the northwest Amazon. None of the other languages are firmly classified in relation to one another, and (with the possible exception of Quichua, which has been postulated to be related to Aymara of highland Bolivia and Peru; see Orr and Longacre 1968) none of these languages are clearly related on linguistic grounds to any other South American language. Furthermore, the stereotype of Quichua as exclusively "of the Andes" and Jivaroan as exclusively "of the jungle" is severely contradicted by data from Ecuador. To understand the contemporary Oriente as an ethnic interface, it is first necessary to consider the various linguistic-cultural groupings.

The Jungle Quichua

Approximately 25,000–35,000 native peoples of the Oriente currently speak Quichua, a dialect of Quechua, which is associated with the Andes and with the Incaic conquest of Ecuador. Because of the "Andean-Incaic" association the majority of Oriente native people have often been thought to represent recent migrations from the Sierra or evidence of "acculturation" of other peoples to Christianity (missionizing friars adopted the language). The director of the National Institute of Anthropology and History of Ecuador, although presumably immersed in data and arguments to the contrary, completely omits these dynamic tropical forest peoples from his view of genuine indigenous (which he calls "polychrome") cultures (Crespo Toral 1978:544). Explanations of the existence of Quichua languages among jungle peoples by slavish adherence to migration and mission reduction assertions are unsatisfactory (Whitten 1976a; Muysken 1974, 1975, 1976). At best, they assume large-scale processes of cultural and linguistic association and transmission for which we have no evidence in the central Oriente; at worst (and, unfortunately, the worst is most often the case, from the academic halls of Quito to the practical decision-making offices of regional towns in the Oriente), they deny the rich, ancient heritage of cultural adaptation to the Oriente's forest and river systems for the majority of her contemporary native people. (An illustrative example of such a denial has recently been given by the North American specialist in tropical forest cultures, Beckerman 1978:18. See also Editor's end note, p. 33.) Let us very briefly review the subject of Quechua, of which Ecuadorian Quichua is a part.

Quechua-Quichua Languages

The Peruvian linguist Alfredo Torero (1965, 1972) and the North American linguist Gary Parker (1963, 1972) both made order of Quechua languages by dividing them into two major groups, which they reconstruct as separating from one another in either coastal or central Peru around 800 A.D. Both Torero and Parker postulate a southward movement of Quechua into the Cuzco area at the time of separation. Seven centuries later Quechua was expanded out of Cuzco by the imperial Inca as a juropolitical lingua franca and spread rapidly, by conquest, southward into Andean Bolivia (where it did not previously exist) and northward into Ecuador (where it may have previously existed; see Guevara 1972, Hartmann n.d.). It continued to spread north without conquest into Colombia and south into Argentina. Today it is the largest native American language in the New World, with more than eight million speakers.

In addition to the Incaic distribution as a lingua franca, and in addition to the Quechuan spread northward and southward beyond Incaic influence, there is evidence that Quechua was spreading in the tropical forests east of the Andes prior to its introduction into the northern highlands by conquest. This expansion, we must stress, was independent of Incaic imperialism (Steward 1948:509; Guevara

1972:17; Orr and Longacre 1968:546; Uriarte 1952:76–77; Muysken 1974, 1975, 1976).

The North American linguist Louisa Stark (1973), probably the best known of Ecuadorianist specialists on Quichua languages, challenges Parker's reconstruction and seeks to move the proto-Quechua time and place to a proto-Quichuan east Ecuadorian hearth at about 600 A.D. She proposes historical explanations regarding Ecuadorian Quichua which are based on her reworking of Parker's proto-Quechua reconstructions, and offers a tentative, but startling, conclusion—that Quichua originally extruded out of the Ecuadorian Oriente and is to be correlated with certain types of ceramics excavated by P. Pedro I. Porras (the Cosanga culture; see Porras 1974, 1975; Porras and Piana 1975). But the Dutch linguist Pieter Muysken (1976), who has studied Ecuadorian Quichua extensively and who has collaborated with Stark on an Ecuadorian dictionary of Quichua dialects (Stark and Muysken 1977), states convincingly, "Stark's reconstruction seems to be an arbitrary way of first recombining and then decomposing terms" (Muysken 1976:26). He firmly and unequivocally rejects her proto-Quechua and proto-Quichua reconstruction on the grounds of both inadequate data base and faulty methodology (see also Hartmann n.d.). This leaves us with the Torero and Parker reconstructions. Again, without in any way detracting from their seminal works, Muysken asserts a caution which is at once serious and humorous: "At this stage of the game the reconstruction of Proto-Quechua is like aiming at the *piñata* (or *olla encantada*) not only blindfolded but also drunk . . . " (Muysken 1976:26).

To gain some reasonable base line for the understanding of jungle Quichua peoples and the relationship of language, society, and culture within their areas, and with regard to their Jivaroan, Waorani "Auca," Zaparoan, Siona-Secoya, and Cofán neighbors, two complementary positions must be considered. First, Incaic Quechua entered or re-entered the Ecuadorian Sierra as a lingua franca. Second, Quichua was probably spreading in the Ecuadorian Oriente prior to the Incaic conquest of the Sierra. Until further *evidence* is brought forth to combine the phenomena of Quichua spread in the Andes and adjacent lowlands, we must keep them analytically separate and seek the relationships between the phenomena without blindly swinging at *ollas encantadas*.

The jungle Quichua are *of* the tropical forest of Ecuador, and no nationalist or academic twisting of facts or creation of fantasies can alter that fact. Quichua *is* their language. Obfuscation of this fundamental point leads to confusion; the projection of this confusion onto the peoples themselves is a common mechanism of cultural denigration in contemporary Ecuador. Because of this I have belabored some obvious points here. Before understanding the possible relationships between language and culture among the contemporary jungle Quichua, let us complete our description of cultural variety and then examine Jivaroan cultures, for the lifeways and histories of Jivaroan and lowland Quichua peoples are intimately interrelated. Within this description I will illustrate the adaptive integration of one grouping of one jungle Quichua culture, once again to strike out against the erroneous and damaging stereotype of nondistinctiveness of the jungle Quichua.

Jungle Quichua Culture

Two jungle Quichua cultures—the Canelos Quichua and the Quijos Quichua—have received considerable attention by scholars from many nations. The former inhabit the area of the Oriente ranging from Puyo over the Sigüín cordillera to the headwaters of the Bobonaza River, and through the area between the Bobonaza and Curaray river areas into Peru. The Canelos Quichua are so named because of the importance of the mission site of Canelos. Like other Quichua speakers, the Canelos Quichua refer to themselves simply as *Runa*, person, indigenous person, and to their language as *runa shimi*, human speech. I (1976a) see the Canelos Quichua as having a basis in a merger of Achuara Jivaroan and Zaparoan peoples, the culture being spread by Quichua speakers:

> Travelers, explorers, and missionaries in this zone seem repeatedly to encounter Canelos Quichua forming out of Zaparoan and Jivaroan intermarriages and alliances, with a mediating Quichua language borne by people in contact with distant sources of valued goods. In the colonial era these goods consisted especially of steel tools. . . . We simply do not know what the bases for the expansion of Canelos Quichua culture within, or prior to, the colonial era were, though re-expansion within the past 100 years can be documented. (Whitten 1976a:8)

The Canelos Quichua seem to be representatives of culture bearers from the east and southeast, probably from the areas drained by the Curaray, Corrientes, Tigre, Pastaza, Marañón, and Huallaga rivers. The contemporary Canelos Quichua represent a rich, dynamic, expanding culture which is today territorially specific, although outwardly ramifying into other culture areas. Many people within the area are bilingual in Achuara Jivaroan, some in Untsuri Shuara Jivaroan and Zaparoan, with a few monolingual Achuara, Untsuri Shuara, and perhaps Zaparoan (Zaparoan-Zapa and/or Andoa-Shimigae) speakers as well.

By apparently sharp contrast with the Canelos Quichua, the Quijos Quichua are seen to have a *montaña* hearth, located somewhere between the contemporary areas of the Quijos valley and Archidona (Oberem 1971, Porras 1974). We have almost no evidence for the original language of the Quijos (Loukotka 1968:249), and the name is not known in indigenous languages today. They have moved eastward at various times as tropical forest Indians were pushed back, enslaved, or obliterated by disease (see, e.g., Oberem 1971). Contemporary native peoples living in and around Tena, and probably those of the Upper Napo feeder rivers such as the Ansuj and Jatun Yacu, represent the contemporary Quijos Quichua, who also refer to themselves as *Runa*. Quijos Quichua culture ranging eastward from Arajuno begins to blend with that of the Canelos Quichua, especially at such sites as Chapana and Villano. A full ethnography of their lifeways is now available (Macdonald 1979).

Many other Quichua speakers live north of the Napo River, from Archidona to the site of Loreto, and extend down the Napo River to Iquitos, Peru. Carolyn Orr and Betsy Wrisley (1965) identify their dialect ("Limoncocha") as separate from that of the Canelos Quichua (the "Bobonaza dialect") and that of the Quijos (the "Tena dialect"), but we do not know what the specific cultural characteristics of these people may be, in relationship to other Oriente native cultures. In the Aguarico basin and in southern Colombia jungle Quichua speakers are called *Ingano*.

All of the jungle Quichua share certain characteristics. They manifest great horticultural sophistication, integrating their knowledge of palm, manioc (cassava, *yuca*), plantain, taro, sweet potato, beans, maize, and peanut cultivation of vegetable carbohydrates and proteins with skillful hunting and fishing techniques for animal protein. *Asua*, a gruel-like drink made from mildly fermented manioc mash, is the mediating force between vegetable carbohydrates and proteins, for the fermentation processes, together with fungi which are sometimes added, provide supplemental protein through bacterial and chemical actions. The jungle Quichua integrate their subsistence base with their social organization and cosmology in rich sets of postulates and propositions which indicate a thorough knowledge of Upper Amazonian ecology and systematics. In addition to this, the Canelos Quichua maintain a tradition of Upper Amazonian ceramics which contain in their multicolor decoration a set of symbols and metaphors expressing pivotal aspects of their enduring structures and adaptive versatility (see D. Whitten, in this volume).

On the whole, the jungle Quichua peoples maintain an adaptive balance between new developments in Andean penetration of the Oriente, and their ecosystem as removed from, although altered by, such developments. To understand jungle Quichua culture and adaptation, one must be familiar with the systematics and dynamics of the ecosystem in a given area, and with the plans, strategies, and activities of Ecuadorian (sierran and coastal) and foreign administrators, businessmen, and colonists in these same areas.

For example, visitors to the Oriente frequently contrast the native people they see in a town such as Puyo or Tena with those they might meet, say, on the Upper Conambo River. In the former setting a man dressed in contemporary western clothes—often new polyester shirt and flared pants, with rubber boots or shoes, accompanied by his wife in a simple dress, with or without shoes—gives an appearance of "near assimilation" to the couple. When one learns that the couple is spending the night in the local church, the notion of a people dependent on Christian missions, and therefore no longer "native," can develop readily. After three days' hard trek to the Upper Conambo, a visitor would encounter a couple in a large oval house with thatched roof and no sides, material paraphernalia including blowguns, baskets, feathered headdresses, multicolor decorated and black pottery ware, and the like, and conclude that here indeed there still exists bona fide indigenous culture. Our traveler might be surprised to learn that he had encountered the *same couple* in the two separate sites.

The striking contrasts between urban and remote jungle life which are characteristic especially of the Puyo Runa grouping of Canelos Quichua culture are manifest through a dichotomy expressed as *alli runa* and *sacha runa*, good (Christian) Indian and jungle (knowledgeable and competent) person. The dichotomy notwithstanding, or perhaps because of its viability, the Canelos Quichua maintain a remarkably integrated system by which they oppose disruptive intrusions and accommodate themselves to their own opposition and resistance.

Modern Organizations

Modern organizations familiar to national officials, and to international agencies, have also sprung from indigenous cultural processes. Just south of Puyo there is a large area (17,000 hectares) organized as the Comuna San Jacinto del Pindo and subdivided into native units called *llacta* which have nuclei in modern hamlets, called *caseríos*. In the Tena-Archidona area there are also *comunas*, but small ones which are nearly coterminous with the *caserío* system. In addition, there is the relatively new Federación Indígena (FOIN), with headquarters in Tena. Cooperatives and *comunas* exist throughout jungle Quichua territory, sometimes with the support of Catholic, Protestant, or secular help, sometimes without such help, sometimes in spite of excessive Catholic and Protestant pressures to develop an utterly undesirable organization, and sometimes in the face of juropolitical maneuvers to destroy them (Whitten 1976a, 1976b, 1977). In all cases for which we have information, particular jungle Quichua organizations are clearly recognizable transformations of indigenous social systems which maintain internal structural integrity while adapting to vicissitudes of an outer world. Cultural adaptation itself, of course, must be understood in terms of real contingencies and constraints on social life and the ecosystem, not in terms of "assimilating" natives yearning after a new social and political order.

Because so much erroneous speculation has characterized nationalist anthropological, governmental, and evangelical pronouncements in recent years, we must again belabor the point here that jungle Quichua lifeways are intricately and intimately bound to subsistence existence within the vast nationally unknown and misunderstood Upper Amazonian–montane rainforest complex, which includes relationships with other indigenous peoples. To understand such a system, we must complete our sketch of linguistic and cultural groupings.

The "Jivaroans"

The 10,000–15,000 Jivaroans currently existing in the Oriente are mostly people self-identifying as *Untsuri Shuara* (or *Shuar*), numerous people, or *Muraiya Shuara* (or *Shuar*), hill people. The term "Jívaro" has no meaning in Shuara language, and it is rejected as a pejorative ethnic designation imposed by nationals and foreigners. The other existing Shuara peoples of the Oriente are the *Achuara Shuara* (or *Achuar*, or *Shuar*), who are often referred to as *Achual* in Peru. The name may be derived from the *achu* ("Buriti" palm, a *Mauritia* species) palm tree with which Achuara associate themselves in certain origin myths. These Ecuadorian Shuara (Untsuri Shuara and Achuara) share their language and cultural characteristics with the contemporary Huambisa Shuara, Aguaruna, Achual, and Maina of Peru, and their culture but perhaps not their language with the Peruvian Candoshi (Shapra and Murato).

Although often thought to be strictly eastern people, living far from contemporary towns in low, swampy jungle areas, the Jivaroan peoples as a whole probably represent interrelated cultures that once extended from the Upper Amazon across the *montaña*, through the Andes, and perhaps to the Gulf of Guayaquil (Karsten 1935, Jijón y Caamaño 1951). In the southern Ecuadorian Andes the Palta and Malacata may have spoken Jivaroan (Steward 1948:617–18). Farther north, the Cañari may have spoken a related language. Between the Sierra and the Oriente the Bracamoro and the Huamboyamay have provided the Jivaroan language bridge cementing the region of trade and war from Andes to Upper Amazonia prior to the Incaic invasion. With the Incaic conquest (and the Spanish conquest hard on its heels) in the Sierra, Jivaroan and other languages were replaced by Quichua (Murra 1946:808–12); as I have argued elsewhere (Whitten 1976a), this lingua franca of the Andes stimulated the spread of Quichua in the Oriente. By spread I do not mean replacement in the Oriente, merely that peoples formerly using Jivaroan or other languages as a lingua franca with highland traders were forced either to use Quichua, or to have more intensive relationships with people who were spreading Quichua, or both.

Contemporary Ecuadorian Shuara peoples have been described by the anthropologist Michael J. Harner (1972) as consisting of the Macabeos, frontier Jívaro, interior Jívaro, and the Achuara. The Macabeos are people long inhabiting the town and immediate environs of Macas who know the Jivaroan language but have evolved their own set of beliefs about "wild Jívaros" of the interior which they often repeat to "explorers," travelers, writers, and anthropologists. The frontier Jívaro are true bearers of Untsuri Shuara culture who live between the eastern slopes of the Cordillera de Cutucú and the western rim of the Upano valley. They have been in long, sustained contact with nonnative settlers and the Macabeos. The interior Jívaro are the Untsuri Shuara of the east side of the Cordillera de Cutucú, who, until recent times, were isolated from direct contact with any cultures other than their eastern native neighbors (Achuara, Huambisa, Candoshi; see, e.g., Varese 1972), with whom they traded for goods which they then exchanged with the frontier Jívaro.

The Achuara are seen as a separate "tribe" by Harner—a people with clearcut language and cultural differences—with whom the Untsuri Shuara waged war and from whom they took heads to make the famous *tsantsa*, shrunken heads. The contemporary Achuara range widely in the Oriente, in some areas intermarrying with the Canelos Quichua, in some areas with Untsuri Shuara, and in some with the Peruvian Maina and Huambisa. Many of them are bilingual in Quichua, and some in Candoshi. In addition to this, some Candoshi use Achuara as a trade language when dealing with the Achuara and perhaps with the Untsuri Shuara.

When immediate ecological factors of a given habitat are taken into consideration, we can say that the various Shuara peoples have the same subsistence base as that of the jungle Quichua. Their ceramic tradition, especially that of the Untsuri Shuara, is distinct, and Untsuri Shuara resemblances to Canelos Quichua multicolor decorated ceramics occur only as a result of intermarriage of a Shuara man and Canelos Quichua woman. Almost all decorated ware sold today in the Sierra as "Jívaro pottery" comes from the Canelos Quichua. The Achuara specialize in the manufacture of blowguns and curare dart poison, and trade these goods with the Untsuri Shuara, the Canelos Quichua, and some of the Quijos Quichua as well. The relationship between the spirit worlds of the Jivaroan peoples and the jungle Quichua peoples is complex and varies from area to area. At a general level, however, we can say that there is great similarity in elements but that the specifics of beliefs and practices configurate differently (see Harner 1972, Whitten 1976a, Macdonald 1979).

Jivaroans far from towns, missions, or trade sites recently lived in dispersed "neighborhoods" with each large oval house representing a microcosm of social life; today most Shuara and Achuara settlements have adopted *caserío* existence (see Descola and Taylor, in this volume). Summing up the changes in Untsuri Shuara culture as he observed them between 1957 and 1969, Harner (1972:211) wrote:

> While the traditional culture and society of the Jívaro are on the wane, their existence as a population certainly is not. Modern medical treatment and drugs provided primarily by missionaries have significantly contributed to a decline in mortality rates, especially among infants, and the estimated 7,830 untsuri suará [Untsuri Shuara] of 1956–57 have now grown to a population for which estimates in 1969 ranged in the neighborhood of 15,000 persons. It is clear that the Jívaro have "turned the corner" demographically, and . . . the prognosis would seem to be for a sustained growth.

The Untsuri Shuara are also making their dynamic presence felt in the rural Upano valley frontier zone, where they have turned heavily to cattle ranching, and in urbanizing Sucúa, which has become the site of the Federación Provincial de Centros Shuaros de Morona-Santiago. This federation has recently received world-wide recognition in the form of publicity through articles and a film, *The Sound of Rushing Water*, for it is the largest, most effectively organized indigenous association in South America. Later in this volume Salazar and Descola focus on the federation, and Belzner and Taylor describe its Protestant analog, AIPSE, with its Macuma locus, so I will not elaborate here.

Other Indigenous Language and Culture Groupings with Small Populations

The combination of Jivaroan and jungle Quichua peoples of the Oriente gives us the vast majority—between 35,000 and 45,000 people—of native culture bearers existing in the mid-1970s. Unlike these two expanding populations, the rest of the Oriente's native peoples are at best holding a steady population and in some cases may be declining. Our discussion will be relatively brief in regard to each of the following peoples, ranging more or less from north to south: Cofán, Siona, Secoya, Waorani "Auca," and Zaparoan; we will also mention other groups which may or may not have contemporary representatives in the Oriente.

The Cofán

The Cofán number but 200–250 individuals in the Oriente, with perhaps 250–300 more in Colombia (Fugler and Swanson 1971, citing SIL linguist Borman; Robinson 1971). Their recent homeland was centered on the Upper Aguarico River, where they lived in small villages and from which sites they ranged widely, including hunting trips westward into the Andes. Their language is currently regarded as unrelated to any other native American language, on linguistic grounds. Culturally, however, they share many characteristics with Siona and Secoya, discussed below, and intermarry with these people as well.

In 1970 Cofán territory was treated to cataclysmic change when the Texaco-Gulf consortium established its base camp at Santa Cecilia. Planes and helicopters bearing foreign and national explorers with their tents, guns, dynamite, motors, canned food, and the like descended. Within months oil bases with new airstrips, more planes and helicopters, and then oil drilling equipment followed, after which came rigs and then a road and a 315-mile pipeline cutting the Cofán territory into ribbons of nationalized infrastructure. Ecuador capitalized on the external exploitation of petroleum to send waves of colonists and businessmen into the territory. While Quito planners and developers and SIL linguists talked of protecting the Cofán and of creating a park for them so that they could be exploited more effectively for tourism, the colonists were flown into their territory and proceeded to take over the native gardens. Given the devastation of Cofán culture and territory (see, e.g., the film *Sky Chief*), it is nothing short of remarkable that anything exists today of the Cofán. But apparently they are still coping with the disaster and eking out an existence which now involves new strategies and alliances, none of which have been described, as far as I am aware (see Robinson 1971 for more information).

The Siona and Secoya

These peoples number about 300 in Ecuador; they are often lumped together with the Cofán as *cushmas* because of their common tunics. They share the Aguarico valley with the native Cofán and today with jungle Quichua colonists, non-Indian colonists, businessmen, and oil crews. Their language is of the western Tucanoan family, once referred to as *Encabellado* or *Piojé*. Also within this language are the Tetete, an isolated group who seem to have separated from the Secoya earlier in the century (Vickers 1972:2, Robinson 1971).

The Siona were settled in their area of the Aguarico prior to the recent immigration of Secoya from the Santa María and Angusilla rivers of Peru, and their population still outnumbers that of the Secoya (Vickers, personal communication). Like the Cofán, the Siona and the Secoya balance subsistence life between relatively settled swidden horticulture fairly near their nucleated riverine villages and seminomadic hunting, fishing, and turtle egg–gathering quests. Against a peaceful, careful, productive exploitation of their natural habitat, with coordinate social system and cosmological structure (Vickers 1972, 1975a, 1975b), is pitted the new force of national conquest of the ecosphere featuring from 10,000 to 15,000 colonists, on the one hand, and the petroleum industry with its new towns and modern camps, on the other. Although not as cataclysmic in immediate effect, perhaps, as the Cofán case, the entire Aguarico area of these few native people must be seen as a new system of poorly planned destruction, with no one taking responsibility for the fate of the indigenous peoples. Vickers gives us an account of religious change later in this volume.

The Waorani "Auca"

Unfortunately, it is impossible to consider these native peoples without reference to North American evangelical drama. On 3 January 1956 five North American evangelical missionaries piloted by Nate Saint flew into "Auca" (the word is a somewhat pejorative multivocalic Quichua term meaning non-Quichua–speaking, jungle-oriented, native people) territory, where they were speared to death on 8 January. Thus began a saga of Christian dialogue with the evangelists on the side of the Lord, and the Auca representing His antithesis, the Devil. This dialogue developed into a well-publicized, highly financed campaign to convert the devil of Ecuador's forests, and, inter alia, to make the evangelical missionaries self- and government-appointed guardians of the Waorani people.

The so-called "Auca" call their language *waodãdi apãedekã*, people's speech (Peeke 1973:3); their self-identifying "people" term is usually written *Huarani* in Ecuador. They are also known as *Aushiri* from the Quichua *Ahuashiri; Awishiri* or *Tahuashiri*, ridge people; and as *Sabela* or *Ssabela*, an extinct South American language known by 30 words (Tessman 1930, Peeke 1973:3). Other names for these people (and, perhaps, for others) include place names designating various rivers in the territory between the Curaray and Napo rivers which was protected by Waorani spears from the time of the Amazonian rubber boom to the coming of the evangelists. Peeke (1973:4) is careful to note:

> Confusion of Auca with Awishiri possibly stems from the local use of both terms to refer to any hostile group. A short Awishiri (Auschiri, Auishiris, Abijiras, Avigiras, Auxiras, Ahuishiri, Ahuisiri, Avixiras) word list provided by Tessman (1930:486) shows clear Záparo affiliation, which the Ssabela word list does not. Thus, while some later compilers (cf. Steward and Métraux 1948:629) have correctly included Awishiri as Zaparoan, there is no basis for the assumption that Ssabela, too, is Zaparoan. . . .

This point is given an ethnohistoric underscoring by Marcelo F. Naranjo's (1974, 1976) exhaustive ethnohistorical search for ethnic correspondences. Naranjo also makes a case for certain "Encabellados"—Siona and Secoya, as noted above—to have been lumped together by evangelizing Catholic friars with Zaparoans under certain circumstances, again cautioning us about equating ethnic labels and language groupings. We return to this point below when discussing the Zaparoans.

To even approach the literature of peoples between the Curaray and Napo rivers, two gross generalizations must be firmly understood. The first of these is that Zaparoan-speaking peoples once in-habited the territory (probably with other peoples, speaking other languages, such as Tupian [see, e.g., Oberem 1967–68]), but they were decimated by a combination of slavery, mission reduction, and especially disease. The second is that the Waorani, also ravaged by the Amazonian rubber boom (Bravo 1920:124) began to expand out of the Upper Tiputini River area around 1920–30, moving into the Za-paroan-inhabited sites and enforcing rights of usufruct at certain ter-ritorial boundary markers at or near the current sites of Misahuallí, Ahuano, Coca, Tiputini, Cononaco, Shiripuno, Curaray, Villano, and Chapana. First, and continuing, mission evangelical efforts were made by the Josephine order at Curaray, but the Waorani-evangelical world dialogue began during the 1950s when numerous Protestant missions attempted to establish stable contact with the Waorani. From the end of World War II to the present, most of the reports on these people come from mission writers (e.g., Elliot 1957, 1961; Wallis 1960, 1973; Spiller 1974, 1:262). The first permanent Protestant mis-sion was established when Brethren Missionaries (MAF) and SIL es-tablished a base at Tigüeno following the drama of the spearing epi-sode and the equally dramatic return of the wife of one missionary, and sister of another, to sustain the evangelical movement.

The contemporary Waorani number about 500 people and we can consider them in terms of three crude divisions: those living with, or within the clear sphere of influence of, evangelical missionaries at Tigüeno; those farther east who maintain a hostile relationship with this group; and those who have left the missionary control zone to establish contact on their own terms with native and nonnative people. Those farthest from the mission sphere are characterized (to western eyes) by their nearly complete lack of clothing; major adorn-ment of these people seems to rest with their large ear plugs and small feathered headpieces. Their black pottery tradition is similar to that of the Quijos Quichua living in the vicinity of Archidona. It con-trasts in form, design, and texture with Canelos Quichua–Jivaroan black ware. Their material culture and ecological adaptation are oth-erwise similar to those of the jungle Quichua and Jivaroan peoples.

The Waorani are the only jungle peoples of Ecuador to exist on a reserve, the boundaries of which were established in 1968 by agree-ment between North American evangelists and the Ecuadorian gov-ernment, and violated apparently without evangelical protest by the oil exploration companies beginning in 1970. Today Waorani contact with indigenous and nonindigenous outsiders is fairly frequent and varied in some areas; in other areas it is still nonexistent, for there are still groups who protect rights of usufruct to their jungle-riverine domain. Recent rumors of armed clashes between the Ecuadorian military and the Waorani in the Cononaco area stress killings on both sides. The nature of "incorporation" of the Waorani into the nation is not at all clear, and perhaps the concept of unit ("tribal") incorporation of the Waorani is wholly fallacious.

Some individual Waorani have been flown to the United States to testify in Madison Square Garden at Billy Graham fund-raising campaigns and other "block busting" fund-raising campaigns throughout the United States (apparently billed as "Rachel Saint and her Auca murderers"; see Bledsoe 1972:127). A dozen or so Waorani today are crippled by poliomyelitis, allegedly because they were protected from vaccine which would have been made available to them had access not been blocked by evangelical judgment (Bledsoe 1972:151). Multilingualism of some (more often women than men) in diverse languages (including Quichua, Zaparoan, Spanish, and English) currently exists, and the greater number of women able to negotiate with "outsiders" gives the false impression of a "matriarchical" society divided into female-led tribes.

More than any other native people of the Oriente, the contemporary Waorani exist not only as a people facing new cataclysmic change in their territory but also as a people known primarily by false and distorted myths which present their culture through the eyes of those seeking to convert and subvert it.

The Zaparoans

The number of people speaking a Zaparoan language in the contemporary Oriente is difficult to state. Known speakers are said to number as few as seven (Stark 1976:1), although I am certain that the actual number of speakers, most if not all of whom are bilingual in jungle Quichua, Waorani, and perhaps Jivaroan, is larger. (Descola and Taylor, personal communication, emphatically confirm my certainty.) Within contemporary Ecuador Záparo and Andoa (also known as Shimigae, from the Quichua "*Gae*" or "*Gayes* speech") constitute the two principal, known dialects of what was once a very large language family extending from the Río Marañón to the Napo (Steward and Métraux 1948, Loukotka 1968, Sweet 1969, Naranjo 1974, Costales 1975, Stark 1976). Other contemporary dialects in Peru are Iquitos and Arabela, the latter of whom may travel into eastern Ecuador, at times. The Zaparoan language, like Cofán, Waorani, and Jivaroan, is not known to be related to any other native American language family, on linguistic grounds. Zaparoan speakers apparently suffered massive annihilation (60–100%, depending on the particular group and location) owing to disease, missionary reduction, and enslavement during the sixteenth through eighteenth centuries (Sweet 1969, Naranjo 1974), and survivors began to live in settlements on affluents of the major rivers, sharing, or competing for, their hunting, fishing, and swidden horticulture territory with Achuara and perhaps Waorani. More decimation through disease occurred around 1930 (Macdonald, personal communication). This decimation, probably accelerated by a Dominican effort to congregate them at Chapana, facilitated Waorani expansion into their area (Macdonald, personal communication). Today culture bearers of former Zaparoans are manifest in Canelos Quichua (especially Andoa-Shimigae), Quijos Quichua (especially Záparo), and perhaps in Waorani lifeways. There are no known "Zaparoan settlements" in Ecuador, but there are peoples within clan segments of contemporary Canelos Quichua who impart knowledge of Zaparoan language to their offspring. Because of their desire to keep the sites of such transmission from the outside world, however, it seems appropriate to respect their wishes.

The decline of perhaps 100,000 or more Zaparoan language-culture bearers to a piddling number in the Oriente, and that part of the Oriente that is now in Peru, bears awful testimony to the results of western contact, and cautions us about being too optimistic about contemporary cultures facing similar pressures.

Summary

The Oriente is characterized by the current existence of two very large, distinct, language families: jungle Quichua and Jivaroan. The former are separated into Canelos Quichua culture and Quijos Quichua culture, the latter into Shuara and Achuara. The Canelos Quichua intermarry with Jivaroans, and all jungle Quichua and Jivaroans share many aspects of their respective lifeways; their languages, however, are not related. In addition to these peoples, Cofán, Siona-Secoya, Waorani "Auca," and Zaparoan constitute separate language families, three of which are not known to be related to each other or to any other existing language, on linguistic grounds. Culturally, however, Cofán and Siona-Secoya are very similar, and the peoples intermarry. Waorani "Auca" life and exposure to national and international dynamics range from complete isolation for some to total influence of the evangelical mission for others. Zaparoan speakers are rare and in some cases "hidden" within Canelos Quichua clans with bilingual representatives.

Obviously, if Ecuador "has been, is and will be an Amazonian country," its Oriente's people cannot be ignored. The clash of cultures, as I argue elsewhere, "exists at all levels of ecology, society, and ideology, and establishes its own system of articulation to national cultures, one juxtaposed upon that created by continuous [in the case of which I was writing, Canelos Quichua] adjustment to the outer world" (Whitten 1976a:28). I also wrote, and continue to assert after eight additional field trips to the Oriente between 1973 and 1979, "In cases such as that presented by the rapid expansion of the Puyo Runa, where cultural integrity and social integration are maintained by people in the process of rapid change and population expansion, the validity of policies which assert a unified 'national culture' for all peoples within consolidated [nation-]state boundaries is doubly challenged" (Whitten 1976a:27).

Let us continue to explore the ramifications of the ethnic interface of the Oriente, using the concepts of power and ethnicity, before returning to symbolism, ritual, and knowledge in our concluding section. It is critical to understand the *recent* history of the Oriente if we are to understand the adaptive viability and versatility of ancient custom within a context of real, cataclysmic, change.

HISTORIC DIMENSIONS OF THE ETHNIC INTERFACE

Technological invention sometimes spawns terrible social malignancies of political-economic growth which spread through an ecosystem in such a way as to permanently alter, cripple, and kill it. European mercantilism with its gold extraction based on refined shipping and communication was one such system: perhaps 90–96% of the native American population was destroyed by its impact in the sixteenth century (see, e.g., Dobyns 1966; Sweet 1969, 1975; Crosby 1972; Wilbert 1972; Denevan 1976). The African slave trade feeding insatiable demands for new cash crops was another such malignancy, the effects of which need not be elaborated here. Lesser known, but equally savage in its effects on Amazonia, was the Amazonian rubber boom.

When Goodyear invented vulcanization in 1839, world demand for rubber soared. Amazonia was at that time the center of wild rubber, and those who sought to control the outflow of latex had but to control the territories and harness labor to tap the wild trees. Native peoples and *mestizo* colonists were cajoled, tricked, and eventually enslaved into service. By the late 1800s the boom was at its peak. Although rubber seeds had been exported from Brazil and were growing in greenhouses in England to be transplanted far from their disease vectors on plantations in Asia and Africa (Collier 1968), the elaborate system of collection, centralization, and shipment of the latex outward from inner Amazonia to the United States and Europe was expanding exponentially.

The *caucheros* (from the extinct east Ecuadorian Omagua term *cahuchu*; see Collier 1968:42), as the rubber searchers were called, developed a system of reciprocal raiding and terrorism as they attempted to control a jungle zone and maintain a captive labor force to exploit wild latex. "Constant thefts of Indians by one 'cauchero' from another led to reprisals more bloody and murderous than anything the Indian had ever wrought upon his fellow Indian. The primary aim of rubber-getting, which could only be obtained from the labor of the Indian, was often lost sight of in these desperate conflicts" (Casement 1912:10). Rubber was the product to be sold on the world markets. But on the tributaries of the Upper Amazon the native peoples were the immediate prize and the target of the rubber-boom social malignancy. "The object of the 'civilized' intruders, in the first instance, was not to annihilate the Indians, but to 'conquistar,' i.e., to subjugate them, and put them to what was termed civilized, or at any rate profitable, occupation to their subduers" (Casement 1912:10).

International activity within the borders of a sovereign state inevitably sets up national processes of consolidation of international boundaries. The expansion of the rubber boom not only wreaked havoc upon native peoples of Upper Amazonia but also stimulated the Andean-coastal based governments of Ecuador and Peru to renew waning interest in their tropical lowlands. The Oriente is so placed as to require enormous energy to extract and transport products to sources of demand. Goods must either flow upward over *montaña* and Sierra (and downward again to the coast), or eastward over waterfalls, rapids, and cataracts to the navigable rivers of the Amazon basin. The rubber boom consolidated the network of river transportation, and a little later the Panama Canal provided the necessary connecting link for Andean countries through their western Pacific ports.

Ecuador's national strategy of infrastructural territorial and resource consolidation during the late nineteenth and early twentieth centuries was to create linkages to both eastern and western waterways, and to provide access from coastal and Oriente to sierran cities and towns (Linke 1960:112–17, Hegen 1966:60–62, Garces 1942, Whitten 1965:29). With stepped-up national, secular interest in the

Oriente, various Catholic missions also re-established sporadic contact with native peoples in many areas (see, e.g., Whitten 1976a for a
discussion of the impact on Canelos Quichua culture). From the late
1800s through the 1920s native peoples of the Upper Amazon experienced war and atrocity; they were pitted against one another and
removed from their territories. Many fled to the few refuge zones
beyond the control of the rubber barons and their guerrilla inslave-
ment squads. *From such refuge zones (Cutucú sierra for the Untsuri
Shuara, the Upper Conambo-Corrientes-Bobonaza-Pindo-Copotaza river system and territory for the Canelos Quichua and Achuara, the Nushiño-Tza-
pino-Tigüeno-Curaray-Challua and Tiputini-Tivacuno drainages for the
western Waorani, the Cononaco river area for eastern Waorani, the Upper
Aguarico for Cofán and Siona-Secoya) the contemporary native cultural-lin-
guistic systems of the Oriente appear to radiate.*

But the refuge zones, too, were soon penetrated, this time by petroleum exploration of the late 1920s. Royal Dutch Shell Oil corporation began exploration around 1920 and in 1928 began the construction of the Baños-Puyo road (see, e.g., Galarza 1972). By the late
1930s the Oriente was characterized by wide-flung oil exploration
and, in some areas, a large intrusion of well-to-do non-Ecuadorians
and a flood of poor nationals. As oil exploration, the establishment of
plantations (many based on foreign capital), and mission activity expanded, World War II erupted, and in July 1941 Peru invaded Ecuador. Following the routes of the *caucheros*, the Peruvian army thrust
up the various Oriente rivers. The result of the invasion was the loss
of half of the Oriente to Peru, that critical half including all of the
easily navigable areas of the major rivers.

This sketch of a few historical episodes over a mere half-century is
given to caution severely the reader who may think that native
peoples of the Oriente are just now encountering "civilization." Quite
the contrary is the case. Native peoples of the moist tropics of east
lowland Ecuador have witnessed repeatedly and convincingly the
destructive might of western civilization on the frontier territories.
Through knowledge, creativity, and perseverance some have survived, while witnessing the disappearance of other native cultures.
All credit for such survival belongs to the native peoples.

CONTEMPORARY DIMENSIONS OF THE ETHNIC INTERFACE

It should be quite clear that culture and language of native Oriente
peoples cannot be discussed without reference to cataclysmic forces
of an outer world. The examples of the Cofán, Siona-Secoya, Waorani

"Auca," and Zaparoans are particularly if dramatically revealing in that regard. We turn now to the ethnic interface itself, the total frontier ecosystem embracing its native peoples and national colonists with a set of paradoxes brought about by a new political economy within which lie the swelling misunderstandings of a new social malignancy. This interface exists at three analytically distinct, though obviously interpenetrating and mutually reinforcing, levels: ecology, social organization, and ideology.

Ecology

Native cultures of the Oriente are characterized by what ecologist David Harris (1971, 1972:249) calls "permanent settlement swidden cultivation." This form of swidden cultivation utilizes the Oriente's lush natural vegetation to release the nitrogen, phosphoric acid, and potash through decay of leaves, stems, vines, and wood, to planted crops, while allowing other forest areas to restore themselves in a cyclical fallow. Differentiation between soil and growth made by western agronomists familiar with temperate zones or arid regions resolves in indigenous swiddens of the moist tropics as the growing matter itself is utilized to provide the soil nutrients. All indigenous peoples of the Oriente manage a complex ecosystem which might be seen to descend from the nitrogen fixation by lightning in the canopy through the nitrogen-capturing epiphytes and other jungle plants through steady release into the mulch-soil of the newly "cleared" *chagra*. The mature *chagra* contains three vertical layers of polycultural crops, replicating in microcosm the forest ecosystem with continuous canopy above to break and diffuse rainfall, filter sunlight, and provide an undersoil root lattice to retard leaching of vital nutrients. Eventually the forest is allowed to return as fallow.

Writing about such swidden systems, Harris (1972:247) states unequivocally:

> . . . contrary to the common assumption that swidden is an inefficient method of cultivation, it can be shown that such systems are often highly productive. Western observers of contemporary swidden cultivators in the tropics have tended to judge the system from the standpoint of their own European tradition of fixed- and clean-field farming and to condemn it as unproductive and wasteful of forest resources. It is an unproductive system per unit area of land cultivated, but in terms of yields per unit of labour expended its productivity can equal or even exceed that of some types of permanent, fixed-field agriculture. *Provided that no land shortage threatens the maintenance of an optimum cycle of cultivation and fallowing, swid-*

den plots can yield as much or more than comparable fields under continuous cultivation. (Emphasis added)

Storage of principal foods—especially manioc—consists of either leaving the root crops in the ground until they are needed, or making a fermented gruel, which is stored in large pottery jars within which the protein and vitamin content is enhanced through bacterial and fungal action. Hunting for game and fishing provide animal protein, supplemented by turtle and turtle egg–gathering, the raising of native ducks, and now chickens. A multitude of fruits, nuts, roots, insects, insect larvae, crustaceans, and snails provides a broad dietary spectrum for indigenous cultures with the requisite repertoire of knowledge of forest and riverine resources.

To understand the growing and spreading social malignancy of the contemporary ethnic interface, it is essential to grasp the fundamental point that all the native peoples of the Oriente—jungle Quichua, Jivaroan, Cofán, Siona, Secoya, Waorani "Auca," Zaparoan—know and practice with technological expertise the swidden horticulture essential to human and vegetative life in their moist tropical zone. The common, general stereotype that some Oriente natives "know nothing" of agriculture is categorically false, and it is equally false that their agricultural knowledge is recently acquired, crude, and primitive. This ancient, productive system (see especially Lathrap 1970), which scientists are beginning to realize needs to be studied in its own terms to understand its contribution to botanical science and resource management (e.g., Conklin 1957; Harris 1972; Berlin 1973, 1976), is viewed as something to be destroyed by contemporary "developers" of the Oriente. Destruction stems from the planning ideology consisting of two points of political-economic propaganda: (1) there is *no shortage of land for colonization* of the Oriente, and (2) the land of the Oriente must be brought under technological "control" by enforcement of a system of *continuous cultivation* of cash crops. Strategic application of this propaganda generates critical conflicts within the ethnic interface.

The easiest way to understand these conflicts is to contrast the successful strategies of continuous cultivation of cash crops (especially sugar and tea) with the swidden system of production of basic food crops (especially palm, manioc, plantain, taro, yam, sweet potato, peanuts, maize). The former is dependent on large-scale capitalization and intensive, cheap, continuous labor, the latter on no capitalization and intensive, sporadic labor. The strategy favored by national development schemes in the Oriente is clearly favoring those large-scale (sometimes absentee) farmers of sugar and tea, many of whom are backed by foreign capital and all of whom rely on cheap labor. Most nonnative colonists are caught between a system of debt peonage to plantations, on the one hand, and the need to learn swidden techniques (from native people) to grow food crops while confined to nonswidden, fixed-plot governmental grants, on the other hand.

Another conflict is generated because *land shortage is severe* near the loci of national infrastructure—the major towns from which radiate roads and smaller towns serving plantations—just beyond which cluster the colonist settlements. Since colonists depend on infrastructural support, they are forced into a system of land shortage; without large capital backing they must work as *peones* for plantations or sell their land to larger-scale, more highly capitalized, interests. Their own opportunities as colonists, then, in areas where they are dependent upon infrastructural support, hinge on the strategy of land and labor acquisition of plantation interests. In the absence of infrastructural support they must learn and apply swidden techniques to raise necessary foodstuffs. These techniques derive from the knowledge and experience of native peoples. More often than not, colonists are forced into a system of land shortage, made dependent upon plantation strategies, and taught the myth that there is abundant land if the indigenous swidden system can be brought under nationalist control.

A mechanism of such control is currently seen in the explosive expansion of cattle ranching (see Brownrigg, Ekstrom, Descola, Taylor, Salazar, and Macdonald, in this volume). The most common technique is to use indigenous labor to completely destroy the forest; thereafter Cuban grass is planted. This high grass is about 90% water and therefore must be consumed in enormous amounts by the cattle to gain their basic nutrition. The devastation of the forest in the cattle-raising areas (which extend straight across the zone east of the Andean mountains and west of the Oriente's cordillera) is depressing in its heat, smell of urine and manure, and ubiquitous botflies which lay their eggs and grow their larvae in human as well as cattle hosts. Where once the night sounds were dominated by tropical whippoorwill cries, hoots of owls, the peeping and croaks of frogs and toads, and where sharp ears could pick up the sounds of nocturnal animal activity, raucous bull bellows and cow responses jab the air. Where once gentle flute music combined with predawn small bird life, the same bellowing greets the day.

Control of the relevant environment of indigenous (and nonindigenous) peoples through cattle raising has banking as its major mechanism. Loans are made to people, and land is the most common collateral. Dependence upon loans, and upon the mechanisms of the enforcement of regular payment, strengthens asymmetric social ties to mission bases and development agencies.

Social Organization

The social organization of indigenous peoples of the Oriente manages a system of resource allocation bound up with social categories of descent and affinity and a division of labor by sex. Fundamental to all social systems which have been described are basic concepts of symmetrical, delayed reciprocity both within ethnic boundaries (e.g., those boundaries established by various combinations of language, custom, marriage, territoriality, trade, and political alliances) and across such boundaries (e.g., dyadic relationships between individuals which cut across recognized divisions and do not bind others of their respective language, custom, marriage, territorial, trade, or political alliance). Such symmetrical reciprocity includes exchange of goods for goods, help received for help given, refuge for refuge, and information for information, and underscores various sorts of marriage systems. It also includes a system of exchange of retort for tort, including, at times, revenge sought through collective or individual juropolitical action both within and beyond other extant boundaries (see Harner 1972, Whitten 1976a, and Macdonald 1979 for illustrative material).

Currently juxtaposed to this system, depressing it but not replacing it, is an elaborate set of social relationships which are based on a system of differential power and wealth extant at national, provincial, and local levels. These power relationships stem from bureaucratic position and from personal wealth and social standing. The society of nonnative peoples is intricately tied to concepts of asymmetrical reciprocity, patronage, and the promise of socioeconomic and ethnic mobility (see, e.g., Casagrande 1974; Whitten 1965, 1976a, 1976b; Naranjo 1978). Embracing these contrastive systems, depressing the former (native) and accelerating the positions of inequality of the latter (national), is a turn toward national internal colonialism (van den Berghe 1967; Robinson 1972; Whitten 1975, 1976b; van den Berghe and Primov 1977) where a sharp distinction is made between those classed as "Indian" and those classed (at least potentially) as "non-Indian" (*blanco, cholo, mestizo*). For the former, governmental strategies stress vague concepts of "civilization" and the end to "margination"; for the latter, a major national concern is given to a productive economic future, albeit one of poverty and often of malnutrition, to "produce" a higher regional and gross national product.

Ideology

Native cultures of the Oriente are rich and varied in their respective world views and cosmologies. Whether or not overt signs of stereotypic "indigenousness" (face and body painting, use of feather headdresses, use of ear, nasal, or lip inserted decoration) are present, all of the cultures discussed seem to share concepts of ionosphere, biosphere, and lithosphere dynamics through celestial, rainforest, riverine, earth, and underearth metaphors of sentience. (Compare, for example, cosmology as set forth by Harner 1972, Whitten 1976a, 1978, Macdonald 1979, and Vickers 1975b, 1976, with works in this volume.) All of these cultures combine vision and knowledge to live in a compatible relationship with their known and unknown habitat, and seek to transcend their immediate work-a-day environment through experiences which integrate dreams, hallucinogenic vision, and trance. Mythology, design, ritual performance, and shamanism configurate in various ways within and between the native cultures, and each configuration has much which is unique, and perhaps is at the same time part of a larger transcultural, metalinguistic, and meta-cosmological transformation system which is as yet not understood. In all ways, though, the native peoples of the Oriente manifest a cultural adaptation to the rainforest and to the hydrospheric system of natural power which controls it. They continuously create a symbolic template and transformational structure of humanity (see, e.g., Reichel-Dolmatoff 1971, 1976; Vickers 1976; Whitten 1978) which is strikingly antithetical, in its richness and in its adaptive capacity, to temperate zone and Andean-based concepts of the moist tropics.

In stark contrast to the indigenous ideologies of the Oriente lies the contemporary working philosophy of nationalist reclamation of "land"—seen within Ecuador as an unexploited natural resource, encompassed by unwanted forest. Political nationalism in Ecuador is back up by nationalist politics under the aegis of military rule (though this is now presumably changing) and supported by the capital of foreign oil, tea, and timber exploitation.

Central to such public ideology is a double image—or dual sets of contradictory imagery. On the one hand, there is the public imagery of bureaucratized efficiency in administration reflecting the ideal of a *mestizo* society with emerging open class system. This ideal is contradicted, on the other hand, by the equally apparent and equally public (if not propagandized) imagery of personalized transaction within bureaucracies. Personalized transactions are facilitated by a web of sinecures where favoritism and clientage are direct reflections of continued class closure and an ideology of white supremacy (see Whitten 1976a, 1976b; Whitten and Friedemann 1976; Naranjo 1978; and Stutzman, Naranjo, and Salomon, in this volume). There are tendencies toward openness in the class-ethnic hierarchy *and* contrary tendencies toward a stratified, paternalist, ethnic-class system. In the latter whites are on top and Indians and blacks are on the bottom, with those classed as mixed moving upward through "whitening" processes of presumptive genetic and cultural "progress" (see, e.g., Stutzman 1974 and in this volume) within a dual economy where the upper limits of the lower sector is the best that can be hoped for. The contradiction is partially buffered in contemporary Upper Amazonian Ecuador by blaming the native peoples for their own reputed plight, and holding up the opposite of their lifeways as a goal for all nonindigenous peoples. But attainment of the goal of being nonindigenous places one right in the contradiction. The ideology is at best transparent, and this very transparency may contribute to the materialist, exploitative ethos by which in-migrating colonists justify the denigration of native cultures and peoples.

The contrast, within national bureaucracies affecting the Oriente, between the public image formally projected (open society with efficient bureaucracy reflecting achievement-based class divisions) and the public image maintained through actual transactions (a web of sinecures with radiating favoritism and clientage) combines with pernicious, pervasive ethnic pluralism based on concepts and applications of wealth, power, family background, regional background, and phenotype. The contrast generates an irreconcilable set of internal contradictions through which the ecological and social organizational interface must often be expressed. The resolution of contradictions through Ecuadorian society are currently being worked out within the realpolitik of that nation; to speculate on the direction of resolution or further conflict is beyond the scope of this chapter. But, today, regardless of formal public image or the inadvertently projected image of internal dynamics, all national agencies and organizations direct their attention toward maintenance of a basic antithesis between themselves, as "developed," "progressive," "civilized," or "white," and peoples who are of the rainforest-riparian-swidden zone, viewed as "undeveloped," "backward," "uncivilized," or "Indian."

The indigenous cultural adaptations to biosphere and hydrosphere

dynamics are all in a deep sense antithetical to the nationally espoused ideology of "development" and the emergence of national
"cultural politics (policy)" (see, e.g., Whitten 1976a, Cisneros 1977,
Stutzman in this volume) with its locus in processes of urbanization
and urbanism (see, e.g., Whitten 1975, 1976a). Yet they are as inescapably part of the contemporary Oriente as their very nationalist
denial, or nationalist assertion, that they (native cultures) are disappearing. The reality of jungle Quichua and Jivaroan cultural surgency
and population expansion in the face of planned and unplanned ethnocide, for example, and their adaptability in seeking new forms of
exploitation of an altered biosphere while at the same time preserving pivotal aspects of their habitat and environment, bear continuing
testimony to the contribution which they may make to nationalization of their respective territories, on their own terms. Herein lies the
base of the paradox of the Oriente as an ethnic interface: nationalization itself, in many areas, is intimately related to the competence
of native peoples to devise new success strategies which link the inescapable parameters of rainforest existence with the threatening
presence of national infrastructure. But the continuing, dogmatic, nationalist *denial* of ultimate cognitive dependence on certain indigenous concepts and sets of knowledge creates the pinnacle of contradiction within the current interface. Although the contradiction is
recognized by international scholarship (see, e.g., articles in Wagley
1974), there is no evidence whatsoever of such awareness diffusing
into the Oriente.

As the United States imports more and more Polynesian poi to be
used for baby food and experiments with manioc to feed part of its
population, Ecuadorian nationalists deplore the drinking of manioc
chicha (which is essentially like poi) and even talk of destroying all
chicha storage containers to stamp out the life-sustaining stored gruel.
As failure after failure of introduced cultivars is noted, nationalists
nonetheless forge on with their deprecation of manioc, plantain, and
palm cultivation, even as poor and well-to-do colonists call for more
and more of these essential foodstuffs. As native peoples demonstrate their superior nutritional base, propaganda mounts that they
suffer brain damage through inadequate nutrition; as their horticultural system is written about and discussed in the world's centers of
tropical ecology, nationalist planners envision its ultimate destruction.

The pinnacle contradiction is swelling in contemporary eastern
Ecuador, and analysis and comprehension of its basic paradox are
not a mere intellectual exercise. Ecological, social, and ideological

ramifications of the contradiction based on the paradox, which permeate all levels and facets of the interface of ethnic relationships, are
already triggering ecosystem destruction, human degradation, and
ethnic, cultural, and biological annihilation.

RITUAL, SYMBOLISM, AND COSMOLOGY

We have explored dimensions of power and ethnicity with their
ecological, social, and ideological ramifications in contemporary
Amazonian Ecuador, focusing on the adaptive versatility of her native peoples and their plight in the face of severe disruption. To complete the sketch of Amazonian Ecuador's indigenous face, we must
move from ideology to the more allusive, symbolic dimensions of
human culture. According to the anthropologist Clifford Geertz
(1973:216–17) in one of his many pioneering studies:

> . . . cognitive and . . . expressive symbols or symbol-systems have . . . at
> least one thing in common: *they are extrinsic sources of information in terms of
> which human life can be patterned*—extrapersonal mechanisms for the percep-
> tion, understanding, judgment, and manipulation of the world, *culture pat-*
> *terns*—religious, philosophical, aesthetic, scientific, ideological—are "pro-
> grams"; they provide a template or blueprint for the organization of social
> and psychological processes. . . .
> The reason such symbolic templates are necessary is that . . . human
> behavior is inherently extremely plastic. Not strictly but only very broadly
> controlled by genetic programs or models—intrinsic sources of informa-
> tion—such behavior must, if it is to have any effective form at all, be con-
> trolled to a significant extent by extrinsic ones. (Emphasis added)

Control over the relevant environment, remember, is the way to
power in the terminology which we have been using. The extrinsic
symbolic template to which Geertz alludes must have referential
bases. The nationalist bureaucratic system cannot provide a symbolic
template for adaptation to the tropical forest ecosystem, for it is internally contradictory, excludes indigenous participation, and denies
indigenous adaptability.

Christian evangelism is also a highly improbable symbolic template
by which to give extrinsic significance to indigenous thought and lifeways in modern Ecuador. The religion is presented by so many contradictory, combative, and incompatible perspectives—Salesian, Dominican, Josephine Catholic, evangelical Protestant, Episcopalian,
with Italian, French, German, Spanish, U.S., Canadian, Ecuadorian,
and Colombian variants—as to inspire indigenous skepticism about
a coherent set of evocative postulates by which knowledge and vi-

sionary experience can be organized. Moreover, and more to the point, Christianity relies on sets of premises alien to indigenous thought and divorced from the force of ecological animism which permeates it.

It is in the sphere of ecological animism, or spiritism, that we uncover the anchoring, referential basis for Geertz's extrinsic symbolic template in the contemporary ethnic interface of Amazonian Ecuador. Simply put, as the Colombian anthropologist Gerardo Reichel-Dolmatoff (1971, 1976) has been insisting for over a decade, and which analysts of the great art styles of the New World continuously uncover (Lathrap 1970, Cordy-Collins and Sten 1977, Linares 1977), *the ecological system of Amazonia itself provides a generative system for metaphoric predication or symbolic expression.* This does not mean, in any sense, that native Americans of the moist tropics—Amazonia in this case—are to be viewed as adaptive biota stagnating in lush forests. Quite the contrary is implied, and we must make this as explicit as possible to a western readership. Christianity has exerted a powerful force upon the western world, and it is still less than 2,000 years old. Among other things, bloody crusades, atrocities against "heathens," the African slave trade, and the "spirit" of western capitalism have in one manner or another garnered strength from its teachings of peace among "men" and "conversion" to its doctrines of those who think differently.

Native peoples of the New World developed their own cosmological premises for perhaps 30,000 years prior to exposure to doctrines of western salvation; for perhaps 10,000 years or more native American cosmological systems were worked through by indigenous philosophers, shamans, and questing individuals within the rainforest setting, which provides the densest set of intricate observable ecological dynamics in the entire world. And for perhaps 4,000 or more years (Lathrap 1970) these symbolic templates have developed in fine detail to the tropical forest cultural ecology of strategic use of riparian-swidden-selvan resources. Gerardo Reichel-Dolmatoff (1976) argues that Amazonian cultures present us with abstract philosophies and ecological theory. I certainly agree with this perspective, as do others. But evidence from the contemporary Oriente suggests that "equilibrium" of native cultures, implying stagnation in the ethnic interface (though Reichel never intended the concept of equilibrium to be so used), is an inappropriate concept. Dynamic, creative, innovative preservation of an ecosystem as it is increasingly threatened by national bureaucratic, international resource-extractive, and Christian evangelical maneuvers toward control of land and people, is certainly a thrust of indigenous cosmology. Its very saturation with animated concepts stressing the dynamics of inner essences and their intricate relationships subsumed by master images of spirit power (see Whitten 1978) allows individuals and groups to communicate effectively within their known biosphere and to cope with contradictions in the ethnic interface. It also allows individuals and groups to reflect deeply on their common beliefs and knowledge, and thereby to transcend the boundaries of their biosphere and their interface situation when the need arises.

Herein, then, we find the extrinsic source of information about which Geertz writes. The cosmological systems of Amazonian peoples must be understood by reference to the intricate, complex web of natural *and cultural* relationships—the ecology—which provides such a vivid referential basis for human thought, reflection, and religious experience, even within the ethnic interface. We find no masking superstructure here, perhaps to the dismay of more doctrinaire Marxists. Rather, we find a revealing cosmological logic providing the impetus for control of power itself, and by which social protest may be ordered and enacted. This does not mean that native peoples so spiritually motivated by ecological imagery and cognitively guided by ecological knowledge are incapable of working within the confines of modern bureaucracies (whether of the rational, efficiency model or that of the web of sinecures). Quite the opposite, once again, is implied. This does not mean, to continue our negative list, that native peoples so motivated and guided cannot fulfill evangelical roles as carriers of new religious messages, for they most certainly can and do so act upon occasion. By now the message must be clear: to understand more about Amazonian systems—ecological, social, ideological—*we must listen to the native peoples of Amazonia.* Their voices must not continue to go unheeded, disregarded, rejected, and ridiculed as has usually been the case except through the technical writing of a few anthropologists. To heed these voices implies a deep philosophical, epistemological, and scientific concern with, and commitment to, another cosmology. Just as Buddhist and Hindu religions have made a great impact upon some of the world's foremost thinkers, philosophers, scholars, scientists, and statesmen, themselves alien to South or Southeast Asian lifeways, so too could Amazonian religions, and their native American spokesmen there and in other regions, make inroads on the social malignancy currently devouring the core of the world's great ecosystems. Malignancy can overwhelm the healthiest of biological systems, and a social malignancy may be seen as having the same proclivity. The "remedy," to carry through the metaphor, cannot be found without continuing attention to the actual system in which it exists. That system, we have argued above, is not only one of the natural order but a profoundly human one generating a deep cultural order predicated on control of observed and postulated dynamics.

Terrible problems confront national colonists and indigenous cultures alike in the contemporary Ecuadorian Oriente owing to the infrastructure of dependency underlying (and perhaps undercutting?) modern Ecuador. *These dependency processes generate degredation of the Upper Amazonian biosphere and exacerbate the asymmetric power system and ethnic prejudices and misunderstandings of national exploitation.* The problem is embedded in the western system of resource exploitation (see, e.g., Commoner 1976), and it is entirely possible that the solution is also so embedded that it will be consumed by western expansion before it is revealed to its "consumers."

The knowledge and vision of 10,000 years or more of *cultural* adaptation to the riparian-selvan, and eventually swidden, habitat are required by those currently contributing to Amazonian "development," for so-called "progressive development" today is destroying nature and culture alike. Again, we return to the theme of listening to the native people. This is more difficult than it seems, because it means attention to their symbols and their referents as set out in their languages, enacted in their ritual, and given form through their lifeways.

There is but one way to "decode" and "reveal" ecological principles embedded in native cosmology (for we must come back to these principles if the biosphere of Amazonia is not to be obliterated) and to apply them to contemporary life. Native peoples of Amazonia must be brought into the process of planning, on their own terms, and with total respect for their underlying premises (see Corry 1978 for a similar argument). This means that planners must go to them, in many cases, and invest the time necessary to learn systemically what the cosmos of Amazonia in its ideological, social, and ecological dimensions really "means." There are some glimmers that this may be happening today in parts of the Ecuadorian Oriente, particularly with a few developers and missionaries face to face with jungle Quichua and Jivaroan peoples over extended periods of time. But the contemporary ethnic interface is also generating stand-offs and contradictions in myriad ways. This paper is designed to heighten the awareness of analytical possibilities within an ethnic interface situation, and to point to the indigenous power source of biosphere knowledge as a logical alternative to developmentalism leading to destruction, degradation, and annihilation.

NOTES

Acknowledgments: Although I am critical of aspects of developmental ideology, strategy, and practice in a country which is not my own, I wish to record here that I do so in great respect for its people, indigenous and non-indigenous, and register my commentary with some force because of United States's history of exploitative destruction of its native peoples. The Andean countries of South America, and their current deep involvement with their Amazonian territories in situations where petroleum exploitation is dominated by foreign capitalist concerns, offer the world the possibility for a new solution to problems of human misery and misunderstanding. By documenting the current viability of native American peoples within a modern republic, as these peoples may contribute positively, productively, and creatively to the solution of the social injustices currently bound to development, I offer my Ecuadorian hosts and sponsors, and those to whom they are responsible, the critical judgment of serious research, not a carping criticism.

This paper is a condensed and slightly modified version of my International Work Group for Indigenous Affairs Document 34. The first draft was written under the auspices of a John Simon Guggenheim Memorial Fellowship during and following research supported by that fellowship. Funds supporting the initial research were provided by National Science Foundation Grant no. GS-2999; more recently, a Wenner-Gren Foundation for Anthropological Research Grant facilitated the study of symbolism. Supplemental funds to these grants have been made available between 1970 and 1978 by the University of Illinois, Urbana, through the Research Board, Center for International Comparative Studies, and Center for Latin American and Caribbean Studies. Research itself was sponsored by the joint auspices of the Ecuadorian Instituto Nacional de Antropología e Historia, Museo del Banco Central, and the Casa de la Cultura Ecuatoriana. I am particularly indebted to Hernán Crespo Toral, Dorothea S. Whitten, Marcelo F. Naranjo, Theodore Macdonald, Joe Brenner, Marcelo Santi Simbaña, Faviola Vargas Aranda, Luis Vargas Canelos, Julian Santi Vargas, Rubén Santi, Alberto Chango, Teresa Santi, Camilo Santi Simbaña, Soledad Vargas, and the late Virgilio Santi for their contributions to this research, and for the various sorts of assistance which they have given to preparation of this paper. Kathleen Fine, Marshall Durbin, Theodore Macdonald, Marcelo F. Naranjo, Ronald Stutzman, William T. Vickers, and Dorothea S. Whitten read earlier drafts and contributed suggestions for revision. Conversations with, and encouragement by, Helge Kleivan led to the preparation of the penultimate manuscript for publication by IWGIA. All errors of omission or commission in interpretation, presentation, and generalization are attributable only to me, most certainly not to those who have generously assisted my intellectual endeavor. Opinions and expressions of values are also attributable only to me.

REFERENCES CITED

Adams, Richard N.
  1975 *Energy and Structure: A Theory of Social Power*. Austin: University of Texas Press.
Beckerman, Stephen
  1978 Comment on: Food Taboos, Diet, and Hunting Strategy, by Eric Ross. *Current Anthropology* 19:17–19.
Berlin, Brent
  1973 Implications of Aguaruna Jívaro Phytosystematics for General Principles of Folk Biological Classification. Paper presented at the 75th Annual Meeting of the American Anthropological Association.
  1976 The Concept of Rank in Ethnobiological Classification: Some Evidence from Aguaruna Folk Botany. *American Ethnologist* 3 (3):381–99.
Bledsoe, Jerry
  1972 Saint. *Esquire: The Magazine for Men*. 78 (1, whole no. 464):127–54.
Boon, James A.
  1972 *From Symbolism to Structuralism: Lévi-Strauss in a Literary Tradition*. New York: Harper & Row.
Bravo, Vicente M.
  1920 *Viaje al Oriente, Segunda Parte: En la Region del Curaray, 1906*. Quito.
Casagrande, Joseph B.
  1974 Strategies for Survival: The Indians of Highland Ecuador. In Dwight Heath, ed., *Contemporary Cultures and Societies of Latin America: A Reader in the Social Anthropology of Middle and South America*. 2d ed. New York: Random House, pp. 93–107.
Casement, Roger
  1912 *Correspondence Reflecting the Treatment of the British Colonial Subjects and Native Indians Employed in the Collection of Rubber in the Putumayo District*. Miscellaneous Publication 8, published by His Majesty's Stationery House. London: Harrison and Sons.
Cisneros A., Plutarco, ed.
  1977 *Política Cultural. SARANCE: Revista del Instituto Otavaleño de Antropología* 5.
Collier, Richard
  1968 *The River That God Forgot: The Story of the Amazon Rubber Boom*. New York: Dutton.
Commoner, Barry
  1976 *The Poverty of Power: Energy and the Economic Crisis*. New York: Bantam Books.
Conklin, Harold C.
  1957 The Relation of Hanunóo Culture to the Plant World. Ann Arbor, Mich.: University Microfilms. Ph.D. thesis, Yale University.
Cordy-Collins, Alana, and Jean Sten, eds.
  1977 *Pre-Columbian Art History: Selected Readings*. Palo Alto, Calif.: Peek Publications.
Corry, Stephen
  1978 *Self-Determination: Rhetoric or Reality?* London: Survival International Document.
Costales, Piedad y Alfredo
  1975 La Familia Etno-Lingüística Zápara. *Ethos* 1:3–30.

Crespi, Muriel
  1968 The Patrons and Peons of Pesillo: A Traditional Hacienda System in Highland Ecuador. Ann Arbor, Mich.: University Microfilms. Ph.D. thesis, University of Illinois, Urbana.
Crespo Toral, Hernán
  1978 El Hombre y su Ambiente. In Hector Merino Valencia, coordinator, *Ecuador: La Naturaleza y el Hombre* 2:539–50. Quito: Ediciones Paralelo Cero.
Crosby, Alfred W., Jr.
  1972 *The Columbian Exchange: Biological and Cultural Consequences of 1492.* Contributions in American Studies 2. Westport, Conn.: Greenwood Press.
Denevan, William N., ed.
  1976 *The Native Population of the Americas in 1492.* Madison: University of Wisconsin Press.
Dimen-Schein, Muriel
  1977 *The Anthropological Imagination.* New York: McGraw-Hill.
Dobyns, Henry F.
  1966 Estimating Aboriginal American Population: An Appraisal of Techniques with a New Hemispheric Estimate. *Current Anthropology* 7 (4):395–449.
Dostal, W., ed.
  1972 *The Situation of the Indian in South America.* Geneva: World Council of Churches.
Elliot, Elisabeth
  1957 *Through Gates of Splendor.* New York: Harper.
  1961 *The Savage My Kinsman.* New York: Harper.
Federación de Centros Shuar
  1976 *Solucíon Original a un Problema Actual.* Sucúa, Ecuador.
Fried, Morton
  1967 *The Evolution of Political Society: An Essay in Political Anthropology.* New York: Random House.
  1975 *The Notion of Tribe.* Menlo Park, Calif.: Cummings Publishing Co.
Fugler, Charles M., and Wallace L. Swanson
  1971 Biological and Ethnological Observations on the Cofán, Secoya, and Awishiri Indians of Eastern Tropical Ecuador. *Proceedings of the Oklahoma Academy of Science* 51:106–19.
Galarza Zavala, Jaime
  1972 *El Festín del Petróleo.* 2d ed. Quito: "Cicetronic Cía., Ltda." de Papelería Moderna.
Garces G., Jorge A.
  1942 *Plan del Camino de Quito al Río Esmeraldas.* Quito: Publicaciones del Archivo Municipal 19.
Gartelmann, Karl Dieter
  1977 *El Mundo Perdido de los Aucas.* Quito: Imprenta Mariscal.
Geertz, Clifford
  1973 [1964] Ideology as a Cultural System. In Clifford Geertz, *The Interpretation of Cultures.* New York: Basic Books, pp. 193–229.
Godelier, Maurice
  1977 *Perspectives in Marxist Anthropology.* New York: Cambridge University Press.

Guevara, Dario
   1972   *El Castellano y el Quichua en el Ecuador.* Quito: Casa de la Cultura
          Ecuatoriana.
Harner, Michael J.
   1972   *The Jívaro: People of the Sacred Waterfalls.* Garden City, N.Y.: Natural
          History Press.
Harris, David P.
   1971   The Ecology of Swidden Cultivation in the Upper Orinoco Rain-
          forest, Venezuela. *Geographical Review* 61 (4):475–95.
   1972   Swidden Systems and Settlement. In Peter J. Ecko, Ruth Tringham,
          and C. W. Dimbleby, eds., *Man, Settlement and Urbanism.* Cam-
          bridge, Mass.: Schenkman, pp. 245–62.
Harris, Marvin
   1974   *Cows, Pigs, Wars and Witches.* New York: Random House.
   1975   *Culture, People, Nature.* New York: Crowell.
Hartmann, Roswith
   n.d.   La Problemática de los Estudios Históricos del Quichua—El caso del
          Ecuador; Las Fuentes a Disposición. Paper delivered at the 1978 Lin-
          guistic Institute Workshop on Andean Linguistics, Urbana, Ill., July
          1978.
Hegen, Edmund Eduard
   1966   *Highways into the Upper Amazon Basin: Pioneer Lands in Southern Co-
          lombia, Ecuador, and Northern Peru.* Gainesville: Center for Latin
          American Studies, University of Florida.
Helms, Mary J.
   1969   The Cultural Ecology of a Colonial Tribe. *Ethnology* 8:76–84.
Hurtado, Osvaldo
   1973   *Dos Mundos Superpuestos: Ensayo de Diagnóstico de la Realidad Ecuato-
          riana.* Quito: Instituto Ecuatoriano de Planificación para el Desa-
          rrollo Social (INEDES).
   1977   *El Poder Político en el Ecuador.* Quito: Ediciones de la Universidad
          Católica.
Jijón y Caamaño, Jacinto
   1951 [1945]   *Antropología Prehispanica del Ecuador.* Quito: Prensa Católica.
Karsten, Rafael
   1935   *The Head-Hunters of Western Amazonas: The Life and Culture of the Jíbaro
          Indians of Eastern Ecuador and Peru.* Helsinki: Societas Scientiarum
          Fennica, Commentationes Humanarum Litterarum 2 (1).
Lathrap, Donald W.
   1970   *The Upper Amazon.* New York: Praeger.
Linares, Olga
   1977   *Ecology and the Arts in Ancient Panama.* Washington, D.C.: Dumbar-
          ton Oaks Studies in Pre-Columbian Art and Archaeology 17.
Linke, Lilo
   1960   *Ecuador: Country of Contrasts.* New York: Oxford University Press.
Loukotka, Čestmír
   1968   *Classification of South American Indian Languages.* Los Angeles: Latin
          American Center, UCLA.
Macdonald, Theodore, Jr.
   1979   Processes of Quijos Quichua Cultural Change. Ann Arbor, Mich.:
          University Microfilms. Ph.D. thesis, University of Illinois, Urbana.

Murra, John
  1946 The Historic Tribes of Ecuador. In Julian H. Steward, ed., *Handbook of South American Indians*, vol. 2.: *The Andean Civilizations*. Bureau of American Ethnology Bulletin 143:705–822.
  1975 *Formaciones Económicas y Políticas del Mundo Andino*. Lima: Instituto de Estudios Peruanos.
Muysken, Pieter C.
  1974 Creolized Features of the Quechua of the Lowlands of Eastern Ecuador. Paper presented at the International Conference on Pidgins and Creoles, University of Hawaii, Jan. 1975.
  1975 The Comparative Construction in Ecuadorian Quichua. Mimeo. Salcedo, Ecuador: Instituto Inter-Andino de Desarrollo.
  1976 One Case in Ecuadorian Quechua. Mimeo. Salcedo, Ecuador: Instituto Inter-Andino de Desarrollo.
NACLA (North American Congress on Latin America)
  1975 *Ecuador: Oil up for Grabs*. Latin America and Empire Report 9 (8), November.
Naranjo, Marcelo F.
  1974 Ethnohistoria de la Zona Central del Alto Amazonas: Siglos 16–17–18. Papel Número 1 del Proyecto de Quichuas Selváticos. Urbana: Department of Anthropology, University of Illinois.
  1977 Zonas de Refugio y Adaptación Étnica en el Oriente. In Marcelo F. Naranjo, José L. Pereira V., and Norman E. Whitten, Jr., eds., *Temas sobre la Continuidad y Adaptación Cultural Ecuatoriana*. Quito: Prensa de la Pontificia Universidad Católica, pp. 105–68.
  In press Native Peoples and Legal Problems in Eastern Ecuador: Land Tenure and Civil Liberties. In Theodore Macdonald, Jr., ed., *Amazonia: Extinction or Survival?* Madison: University of Wisconsin Press.
  1978 Etnicidad, Estructura Social y Poder en Manta, Occidente Ecuatoriano. Ann Arbor, Mich.: University Microfilms. Ph.D. thesis, University of Illinois, Urbana.
Oberem, Udo
  1967–68 Un Grupo Indígena Desaparecido del Oriente Ecuatoriano. *Revista de Antropología* (São Paulo) 15–16:149–70.
  1971 *Los Quijos: Historia de la Transculturación de un Grupo Indígena en el Oriente Ecuatoriano (1538–1956)*. 2 vols. Madrid: Facultad de Filosofía y Letras de la Universidad de Madrid, Memórias del Departamento de Antropología y Etnología de América.
Orr, Carolyn, and Robert E. Longacre
  1968 Proto-Quechumaran. *Language: Journal of the Linguistic Society of America* 44 (3):528–55.
Orr, Carolyn, and Betsy Wrisley
  1965 *Vocabulario Quichua del Oriente del Ecuador*. Quito: Instituto Lingüístico de Verano, Serie de Vocabularios Indígenas 11.
Parker, Gary J.
  1963 Clasificación Genética de los Dialectos Quechuas. *Revista del Museo Nacional* (Lima) 32:241–52.
  1972 Falacias y Verdades Acerca del Quechua. In Alberto Escobar, ed., *El Reto del Multilingüísmo en el Peru* 9:111–21. Lima: Instituto de Estudios Peruanos.

Patzelt, Erwin
    1973 *Hijos de la Selva Ecuatoriana.* Guayaquil: Colegio Alemán Humbolt.
    1976 *Libre como el Jaguar: Los Aucas y su Enigmático Mundo.* Quito: Imprenta
          Europa.
Peeke, Catherine M.
    1973 *Preliminary Grammar of Auca.* Norman, Okla.: Summer Institute of
          Linguistics, Publications in Linguistics and Related Fields 39.
Porras Garces, P. Pedro I.
    1974 *Historia y Arqueología de Ciudad España Baeza de los Quijos, Siglo XVI:
          Estudios Científicos sobre el Oriente Ecuatoriano.* Vol. 1. Quito: Centro
          de Publicaciones de la Pontificia Universidad Católica del Ecuador.
    1975 *Fase Cosanga: Estudios Científicos sobre el Oriente Ecuatoriano. Vol. 2.
          Quito: Centro de Publicaciones de la Pontificia Universidad Católica del
          Ecuador.*
Porras Garces, P. Pedro I., and Luis Piana Bruno
    1975 *Ecuador Prehistórico.* Quito: Imprenta y Ediciones Lexigrama.
Reichel-Dolmatoff, Gerardo
    1971 *Amazonian Cosmos.* Chicago: University of Chicago Press.
    1976 Cosmology as Ecological Analysis: The View from the Rainforest.
          Man: Journal of the Royal Anthropological Institute 11:307–18.
Robinson, Scott S.
    1971 *El Etnocidio Ecuatoriano.* Mexico City: Universidad Iberoamericana.
    1972 Some Aspects of the Spontaneous Colonization of the Selva Com-
          munities of Ecuador. In W. Dostal, ed., *The Situation of the Indian in
          South America.* Geneva: World Council of Churches, pp. 108–13.
Salazar, Ernesto
    1977 *An Indian Federation in Lowland Ecuador.* Copenhagen: International
          Work Group for Indigenous Affairs, Document 28.
Salomon, Frank
    1978 Ethnic Lords of Quito in the Age of the Incas: The Political Economy
          of North-Andean Chiefdoms. Ann Arbor, Mich.: University Micro-
          films. Ph.D. thesis, Cornell University.
Sanders, Thomas G.
    1977 *Ecuador: Politics of Transition.* American Universities Field Staff Re-
          ports, West Coast South America Series 24 (1).
Spiller, Mons. Maxmiliano
    1974 *Historia de la Misión Josefina del Napo.* 2 vols. Quito: Equinoccio.
Stark, Louisa R.
    1973 Historia y Distribución de los Dialectos Quichua en la Sierra Ecuato-
          riana. Paper presented at the Primer Seminario de la Educación Bi-
          lingüe, Quito.
    1976 La Lengua Zapara del Ecuador. Madison, Wis.: Instituto Inter-
          Andino de Desarrollo (Ambato, Tungurahua).
Stark, Louisa R., and Pieter C. Muysken
    1977 *Diccionario Español-Quichua, Quichua-Español.* Quito and Guayaquil:
          Publicaciones de los Museos del Banco Central del Ecuador 1.
Steward, Julian H.
    1948 Tribes of the Montaña and Bolivian East Andes. In Julian H. Stew-
          ard, ed., *Handbook of South American Indians,* vol. 3: *The Tropical Forest
          Tribes. Bureau of American Ethnology Bulletin* 143:507–34.

Steward, Julian H., and Alfred Métraux
  1948 Tribes of the Ecuadorian and Peruvian Montana. In Julian H. Steward, ed., *Handbook of South American Indians*, vol. 3: *The Tropical Forest Tribes. Bureau of American Ethnology Bulletin* 143:535–656.
Stutzman, Ronald
  1974 Black Highlanders: Racism and Ethnic Stratification in the Ecuadorian Sierra. Ann Arbor, Mich.: University Microfilms. Ph.D. thesis, Washington University, St. Louis.
Sweet, David G.
  1969 The Population of the Upper Amazon Valley, 17th and 18th Centuries. M.A. thesis, University of Wisconsin, Madison.
  1975 A Rich Realm of Nature Destroyed: The Middle Amazon Valley, 1640–1750. Ann Arbor, Mich.: University Microfilms. Ph.D. thesis, University of Wisconsin, Madison.
Tessman, Günter
  1930 *Die Indianer Nordost-Perus.* Hamburg: Cram, de Gruyter and Co.
Torero, Alfredo
  1965 Los Dialectos Quechuas. *Anales Científicos de la Universidad Agraria* (Lima) 2:446–78.
  1972 Lingüística e Historia de la Sociedad Andina. In Alberto Escobar, ed., *El Reto del Multilingüismo en el Peru* 9:51–106. Lima: Instituto de Estudios Peruanos.
Uriarte, P. Manuel J., S.J.
  1952 *Diario de un Misionero de Mainas: Transcripción, Introducción y Notas del P. Constantino Bayle, S.J.* Madrid: Consejo Superior de Investigaciones Científicas, Instituto Santo Toribio de Mongrovejo.
van den Berghe, Pierre L.
  1967 *Race and Racism: A Comparative Perspective.* New York: Wiley.
van den Berghe, Pierre L., and George P. Primov (with the assistance of Gladys Becerra Valazque and Narciso Ccahuana Ccohuata)
  1977 *Inequality in the Peruvian Andes: Class and Ethnicity in Cuzco.* Columbia: University of Missouri Press.
Varese, Stéfano
  1972 *The Forest Indians in the Present Political Situation of Peru.* Copenhagen: International Work Group for Indigenous Affairs, Document 8.
Vickers, William T.
  1972 Indians, Oil, and Colonists: Contrasting Systems of Man-Land Relations in the Aguarico River Valley of Eastern Ecuador. *Latinamericanist* 8 (2). Gainesville: Center for Latin American Studies, University of Florida.
  1975a Meat Is Meat: The Siona-Secoya and the Hunting Prowess–Sexual Reward Hypothesis. *Latinamericanist* 11 (1). Gainesville: Center for Latin American Studies, University of Florida.
  1975b El Mundo Espiritual de los Sionas. *Periplo: Revista del Instituto de la Caza Fotografica y Ciencias de la Naturalez* (Madrid) 4:13–23.
  1976 Cultural Adaptation to Amazonian Habitats: The Siona-Secoya of Eastern Ecuador. Ann Arbor, Mich.: University Microfilms. Ph.D. thesis, University of Florida, Gainesville.
Wagley, Charles, ed.
  1974 *Man in the Amazon.* Gainesville: Center for Latin American Studies and the University Presses of Florida.

Wallis, Ethel E.
1960   *The Dayuma Story.* New York: Harper & Row.
1973   *Aucas Downriver.* New York: Harper & Row.
Whitten, Dorothea S., and Norman E. Whitten, Jr.
1978   Ceramics of the Canelos Quichua. *Natural History Magazine* 87 (8):90–99, 152.
Whitten, Norman E., Jr.
1965   *Class, Kinship, and Power in an Ecuadorian Town: The Negroes of San Lorenzo.* Stanford, Calif.: Stanford University Press.
1974   *Black Frontiersmen: A South American Case.* New York: Halsted (Wiley).
1975   Jungle Quechua Ethnicity: An Ecuadorian Case Study. In Leo A. Despres, ed., *Ethnicity and Resource Competition in Plural Societies.* The Hague: Mouton, pp. 41–69.
1976a (with the assistance of Marcelo F. Naranjo, Marcelo Santi Simbaña, and Dorothea S. Whitten). *Sacha Runa: Ethnicity and Adaptation of Ecuadorian Jungle Quichua.* Urbana: University of Illinois Press.
1976b *Ecuadorian Ethnocide and Indigenous Ethnogenesis: Amazonian Resurgence amidst Andean Colonialism.* Copenhagen: International Work Group for Indigenous Affairs, Document 23.
1977   Structure, Control and the Evolution of Power. Review of *Energy and Structure: A Theory of Social Power,* by Richard N. Adams. *Reviews in Anthropology* 4:567–74.
1978   Ecological Imagery and Cultural Adaptability: The Canelos Quichua of Eastern Ecuador. *American Anthropologist* 80 (4):836–59.
Whitten, Norman E., Jr., and Nina S. de Friedemann
1974   La Cultura Negra del Litoral Ecuatoriano y Colombiano: Un Modelo de Adaptación Etnica. *Revista Colombiana de Antropología* 17 (2):75–115.
Wilbert, Johannes
1972   *Survivors of El Dorado.* Englewood Cliffs, N.J.: Prentice-Hall.

5

Killing the Yumbo: A Ritual Drama of Northern Quito

Frank Salomon

From his post as caretaker of the radio masts that guide air traffic in and out of Quito, Segundo Salazar Inapanta looks both outward, toward the luminous snowcaps fencing the Andean *altiplano* off from the Amazonian and Pacific rainforests, and downward, toward the white skyline of the highland metropolis. The land he stands on is his own home, one of the Quichua-speaking settlements which form an aboriginal fringe around the capital and which are now absorbing its expansion. Urban Quito has captured a great part of his imagination; to him, it is the master metaphor for a human being, with the airport as a head from which a "breath of people" moves in and out, the cathedral as heart, the central market as stomach, roads as blood vessels, and power lines as nerves. In the eyes of this Andean Quiteño, who speaks Quichua but who expresses through his gray suit, glasses, and mustache a strong conscious liking for all that is urban and urbane, it is the glory of a human being to constitute "a walking city."

One might guess, then, that the Amazonian artifacts decorating the walls of his house—black chonta palm lances, a feather crown— are simply exotica. It is common for Quiteños who themselves repudiate any non-Hispanic identity to fortify their sense of connection with a largely non-Hispanic country by collecting mementos of what they see as Quito's polar opposite: the jungle. But this is very far from being the destiny of Segundo's crown and lance. They are not impotent mementos; on the contrary, they are the means by which a foreign reality, the world of the native *montaña* dweller, called *yumbo*, and more specifically of the forest shaman, periodically invades his own mind and body. To him, the great lance Reina Infinita Chihuanta, his companion in each summer's yumbo dances, is a living being in her own right, charged with the still greater power of an *urcu mama*, a mountain mother, who grants or withholds the shaman-istic gift. "The mountain accompanies the lance, and the lance accom-panies me; the lance and I are one single being when we are danc-ing."

Dancing in lowland costume is an almost pan-Andean tradition, from the Cuzco region (Roel Pineda 1950, Vásquez 1950–51, Gow 1974, Sallnow 1974, Gow and Condori 1976:93–94) through Imbabura province in northern Ecuador (Moreno 1972:209–15; Buitrón 1949:62–66; Costales 1968, 2:168; Santiana 1948–49:238–74). Its asso-ciations, seasons, and ceremonial functions vary widely.[1] In the Quito region yumbo dancing is associated primarily with Corpus Christi and secondarily with various other dry-season festivities.[2] Perhaps the most distinctive trait of the yumbo complex in the Quito area is the development of an elaborate symbolic antiphony between the play of the "savage" yumbos, which culminates in the ritual combat, slaughter, and resurrection called *yumbo huañuchiy* or *matanza*, and the performance of folk-Catholic rites on the themes of religiously sanctioned hierarchy and community, which culminate in the display of the Host, token of Christian resurrection. Within this overall scheme there are two major variants, one performed in parishes of the Valle de los Chillos, southeast of Quito, and another in the par-ishes bordering the north and northeast of the city.[3] It is the latter which is described here.

Costume dancing has been stereotyped as an essentially rural phe-nomenon, which supposedly withers at the first intrusion of urban culture and economy. Yumbo dancing totally belies this idea. It flour-ishes most where the headlong expansion of oil-rich Quito has brought a sudden and dramatic invasion of formerly rural commu-nities.

As of 1975–78 the hotbed of north Quito yumbo ceremonial was a strip along both sides of the Pan-American Highway from the city airport to the rim of the Guayllabamba canyon. Indeed, the highway, prime artery of Quito's industrial zone, is also a prime theater for yumbo dancing; dancers in full plumage delight in obstructing its traffic with mock ambushes and monkey antics. Some of the chief yumbo-dancing locales are urban-route bus stops, in neighborhoods already completely overrun by and integrated into the industrial belt. Most yumbo dancers in daily life are thoroughly urban people, work-ers in surrounding factories, construction hands, or service person-nel in business and military institutions. Newly paved and equipped with sewers, their streets are turning into valuable residential real estate for the housing of factory workers' families. Multistory buildings are no longer rare. Some households, already active both as proletarians and as market gardeners, also develop an investment in rentable property. By contrast, in communities farther from the highway, yumbo dancing appears to be in sharp decline.

The continued vitality of yumbo dancing is thus the exception to a general rule. In industrial Quito fiesta-*cargo* systems have been drastically simplified and many eliminated. A generation ago the only advancement available to a Quito Quichua speaker was the intracommunal prestige and high credit standing which could be won by sponsoring fiestas. Today such gains must be weighed against the more tangible and reliable rewards of educating one's children or investing in capital goods. These pressures have not, however, eroded all ceremonials at an even pace. In effect, communities have been selecting the ceremonials most significant to them, building these up, and discarding the rest. The dazzling vitality of yumbo play in zones already engulfed by a population which actively scorns everything "Indian" strongly suggests that in some way the yumbo complex makes specific sense to people whose biographies have brought peasant-indigenous (Runa) and urban-Hispanic experiences into the sharpest possible juxtaposition.

Yumbo dancing might be considered as an exploration, in the compact synoptic vehicle of a ritual drama, of its practitioners' peculiar position as an unnamed, unrecognized, but nonetheless distinctive group, poised in the space between two cultures which have long been spotlighted by folk consciousness as the polar extreme of primally "savage" and primally "civilized" identity: the jungle "tribes," on the one hand, and the highland's sacred and secular power center, on the other. This location has been of fateful importance for suburban Quiteños over a very long time. Even under Incaic rule circumQuito aborigines were at the same time builders of "another Cuzco", in the highlands, heavily acculturated toward Inca norms and close partners of the western and Amazonian lowland tribes not only through barter systems but also through politically sanctioned intermarriage and, probably, through shared religious concerns (Burgos Guevara 1975, Salomon 1978:202–66). Yet in this period they retained their distinctive language and polity, borrowed from neither side. Under the Spanish colony indigenous Quito became lodged chiefly in nonnucleated neighborhoods around artificially created nuclear parishes. With the consequent loss of political self-definition, ceremonial life and kindred became paramount in marking off the "authentic" inhabitants from *mestizo* and native intruders. Day labor in Quito evolved from Incaic corvée through Spanish *mita* toward the proletarian forms of today. Simultaneously, contacts with the two lowland zones became increasingly monetarized, where both material and magical transactions were concerned, and emptied of overtly political content. By the nineteenth century aboriginal Quito had found new uses for its situation in the field of tension and mutual dependency between city and forest, without ceasing to be, if clothing and livelihood are any index, an instantly recognizable third presence (Castro y Velásquez 1976).

Segundo Salazar's own life reflects on a private scale this historic bipolarity. As a young soldier in the Oriente he was fascinated by shamanistic lore and tried to learn it. In later life he became no less attached to the technocratic milieu of aviation. His oscillation between a Quiteño persona, based on a sincere adherence to urban, Catholic, and nationalist values, and a yumbo alter ego, whose symbols are those of a shamanism beyond the reach of state or church, thus manifests on a personal level the experience of his people. But the twentieth century has brought drastic changes in the terms on which this bipolar orientation can be lived out: the two outer poles have, so to speak, moved closer, invading the home community and circumscribing ever further the ground on which a distinctive Quito Runa identity can be expressed.

On the one hand, urban Quito has become expansive and aggressive. It no longer readily tolerates the presence of aboriginal enclaves on its margins. Not only has industry physically invaded their space, but schools and church institutions under Hispanic domination have invaded their cultural life so intimately as to force Quichua language and Runa dress out of public life. The native Quiteño who works in the city pays an unacceptable penalty for any visible Indianness. To the degree that he retains any attachment to the Quito Runa identity as something apart from all other possible selves, a native Quiteño is under pressure to live in disguise. Meanwhile the crowding in of newcomers is an irritant factor, posing the problem of how the "authentic" kindreds can enforce their claim to local eminence. Circumstances invite the Quito Runa identity to disappear. At fiestas it reasserts itself by segregating itself in ceremonial functions to which only the local families contribute. Newcomers are admitted as spectators, whose very noncomprehension heightens the esoteric value of the proceedings and labels them as marginal figures.

But if the urban pole has come closer to the Quito Runa homeland, so has the jungle, and the highland-forest confrontation matters much more. Until recently forest peoples were, to urbanites, queer, distant figures on a green horizon. But with the boom in Amazonian oil, the promotion of lowland cattle industry, and the well-publicized struggle over the terms on which lowland peoples are to be "integrated" into the nation-state, they have come continuously into the public eye: themes of shattering emotional import (ethnocide, the national wealth, antiforeign feelings) come to mind at the sight of a feathered headdress. Meanwhile, Quito area natives, who have long been in personal contact with lowlanders, find it increasingly easy to remain so as highways and airplanes put the yumbos' real-life counterparts within weekend travel reach.

It is not only a hypothetical confrontation of lowlander with urbanite which forms the background of the dance, but also a practical and tangible one, whose results, everyone agrees, are of the utmost importance for Ecuador's future. This historical turn gives the yumbo dance, for all its *opera buffa* surface texture, a resonance that is not altogether comic.

YUMBOS AND THEIR SPONSORS

Although yumbo dancing is associated with Corpus Christi, *priostes* or sponsors of any major dry-season fiesta may recruit a yumbo corps as one of the various performing troupes that make up their entourage. *Priostes*, male and female, are named by the parish priest a year in advance. Coercive nominations are now unknown. In neighborhoods close to the Pan-American Highway volunteers are rarely lacking, and it is not unusual for some neighborhoods to have two or more complete *yumbadas* in one year.

Priostes themselves play a central but restrained role during the ceremonies. Although in reality they feel emotional and intellectual stress, it would be bad form for them to appear busy or worried. The ceremony should seem to run by itself. Dressed in plain garments, similar to street clothes save for newness and superior quality, they sit in focal positions from which they act as figures of perfect piety, modesty, and generosity.

Yumbos are the most spectacular of the *priostes'* performing retinue, but there are other troupes as well. The *bracerantes*, senior men who have already carried the greatest *cargos*, endorse the newly won prestige of the sponsors with their presence. As they accompany the sponsors, they toss flower petals in the path and perfume the air with incense. They wear somber business suits and sashes with the national colors. The *loa*, a child dressed in white satin, rides a white-caparisoned horse and declaims a poem of praise appropriate to the Catholic theme of the day at the main processional stations. Four *negros de Esmeraldas,* or *molecañas,* men disguised as blacks of the north coast, guard the *loa.* Their inky masks glitter with golden eyebrows and scarlet lips. Their clothing is that of the backwoods rough rider; their motif is the violence and raunchy humor attributed to coastal blacks. Against their blasphemy and roughhousing the *alumbrantas,* women bearing giant white candles for the church, radiate a feeling of cleanliness, quiet, and modesty. Minor comic dancers—the fire-horned "crazy cow" and his burlesque bullfighters, the broom dancers, capering like deranged street sweepers, and the clowns—provide entertainment between major ceremonial acts.

Priostes may themselves organize the yumbo troupe or may recruit a "deputy" to do so. The "deputy" may, in turn, assume the performing leadership of the troupe as *cabecilla,* "headman," or choose another to lead it. Finally, the performing leader may either be a yumbo first among equals or a distinct costumed character called *rucu,* old man. The formal title of the performing director is *gobernador* (this term is applied also at times to *priostes*). He generally names one of the yumbos as *trasgobernador,* understudy, to take over should he become too drunk to dance. These, however, are backstage terms. As they live out their roles, yumbos always employ kin terms: all the yumbos are "brothers and sisters" to each other and use the four Quichua terms of sibling address. Similarly they address *rucu* as *taita,* father, and he them as *huahuaguna,* children.

The *rucu* of the easterly communities wears a snow-white papier-mâché mask with red-daubed cheeks, brows, and nose, a fedora, a patchwork-quilt poncho, a scarf or flowing bandanna, dark pants, and white fiber sandals. Around his neck, over the poncho, hangs a small round-bottomed bag containing toasted stone-ground barley and a wooden spoon. This represents the highway viands which he provides for his yumbo "children." Under his poncho he carries a rosary of seed beads or snail shells, ending in a pectoral cross, which serves him as a mnemonic *quipu* for taking yumbo attendance. From his wrist dangles a whip with a deer's-foot handle (or formerly one made from a bull's penis) for disciplining his "children."

Whether *rucu* or lead yumbo, the leader must keep the yumbos on their feet in motion all the time—superhuman stamina is a yumbo trademark—and must call the steps with cries such as *pecho pecho!,* which tells the two lines to advance "chest to chest," or *tupanajushun!,* "let's meet!," which signals them to advance, clash lances, and change sides. Periodically, with the cry *sona mano huahuaguna!* he evokes the sound-signature of the *yumbada,* a hooting, sinking whistle made by blowing into the cupped hand. They sound it whenever something agreeable happens, such as a tobacco or liquor gift from a spectator.

Because yumbos never rest while in public view, they must dance to whatever music is being played at the moment. But their favorite music is that of their own *mamaco* or *mama*, "mother," a man who plays both the reed flute, *pingullu*, and a bass drum. His several tunes and their respective rhythms correspond to different phases of the drama (Jiménez de la Espada 1881). Transitions are signaled by sharp taps on the rim of the drum. Yumbos often compare the drumbeat to the distant thunder of the mountains, which in turn is felt to be the voice of the "mountain mothers." At the sound of the drum a yumbo may remark, *Ñuca mama cayan*, "my mother calls."

Perhaps the most demanding roles are those of the two *monos*, monkeys. The monkey is a cavorting buffoon, a thieving trickster and troublemaker, but at the same time a figure of authority. Speaking always in falsetto, he chastises onlookers who crowd the dancers, not only verbally with lewd and insulting wisecracks but by lashing them with his long ropelike tail. Into the huge cloth belly of his par-ticolored woollen coveralls, decorated in symmetrical motley or in plain fur brown with a protruding red tongue, he stuffs the audi-ence's gifts and whatever he can swipe from vendors' kiosks. Then he shares the loot out to his yumbos with a great show of greed and excitement. He humiliates guests who fail to contribute by pretend-ing to urinate on them or by attacking them with a simian coital spasm. He protects generous guests and makes sure they get a good view. Gifts to the dancers must pass through his hands. *Mono* usually carries a woollen doll exactly in his own image, which he calls his baby, and with whom he plays adoringly in the dirt.

The yumbos themselves are ideally 12 or 24 in number, though in practice any even number from 8 up will do. Two yumbo costumes are in common use,[4] and most *yumbadas* contain some of each.

The *mate yumbo*, always male, wears a mask of metal wire mesh with "white" coloration and facial hair (this may be related to local legends about "white" natives of Amazonia). The head is covered with a wig of dark brown, disheveled hair over the shoulders, tied in place with a bright kerchief. The feather crown or *incha*, a genuine import from Amazonia, aflame with the luminous blues, yellows, and greens of macaw and parrot feathers, is sometimes decorated around the headband with alternating strips of yellow and scarlet feather fluff. The *mate yumbo* wears tight, light-colored pants to calf length; traditionally barefoot or shod in fiber sandals, he is today more likely to wear basketball sneakers. Like all yumbos, he carries a black lance at least two meters long, of chonta palm wood or painted to look like it, decorated with ruffs of multicolored cellophane and sometimes painted silver at the point. The garment which gives the *mate yumbo* his name is a cape completely covered with sewn-on halves of dried gourds, *mates*. It gives a bizarre appearance of hulking girth and makes a loud clashing noise with every step, rendered onomatopoetically as *chal-chal, chal-chal*. The half-gourd dish for eating peach palm mush is part of the lowlander's travel kit.

Lluchu (naked) yumbos are, on the contrary, male or female. (All yumbo dancers are men, but many cross-dress for the dance.) The male *lluchu* wears the same headgear as the *mate* and carries the same lance, but no cape. Instead, over a pullover or sweater he drapes many strands of forest-collected seed beads, both gray "San Pedros" and red-and-black "corales," diagonally from shoulder to waist and around the waist. These are often decorated with pieces of feather. His pants are of shiny satin, pink, mauve, or blue, festooned with sequins, calf-length, contrasting in color with his long socks and sneakers. Hung diagonally on his side or back he displays an open-work basket called *ashanga*. Onto this basket not only tropical beads and feathers but stuffed forest animals are sewn: monkeys, parrots, or stump-tailed weasels.

The female *lluchu yumba* wears, instead of pullover and pants, the richly embroidered blouse of north sierran women, white calf-length cotton slips, and, over them, brightly colored satin wraparounds tied in place with one or more embroidered belts. In addition to diagonal bead strands, yumbas may wear the golden necklaces formerly popular among Canelos and Sarayacu women and currently among those of the northern Sierra. In the course of a full *yumbada* each dancer uses two complete costumes, a new one to glorify the climactic day and a used one for the remaining days, so it is unusual to own sufficient clothing in one's own right. But those most experienced and enthusiastic about yumbo dancing do, like Segundo Salazar, make a point of collecting genuine Oriente artifacts which add to the power, panache, and subjective reality of their performances.

How deeply the self-transformation from urbanite to yumbo is felt varies sharply from dancer to dancer. At one extreme the *yumbada* includes novices, prepubescent boys who dance at their parents' urging, often without enough knowledge of Quichua to appreciate the dramatic content of the cycle. For them, what is "real" about yumbo dancing is its comic and dionysian dimension: the excitement of the spotlight, the mad sacrileges of monkeys and drunks, the license to brag and fight, the sumptuous excess of feast and spectacle. For young men in their teens or twenties, the *yumbada* is a chance to act out a heroic self, partly in burlesque and partly in earnest. Proving his fortitude in the teeth of an alcoholic onslaught and exhausting physical demands, the young yumbo warrior tries to excel in the combination of fierceness, humor, and athletic virtuosity which make a fine ritual combat. Younger yumbos tend to heighten comic and athletic play at the expense of dramatic and verbal clarity, distancing themselves from the esoteric content of the dance, as though to set it firmly between quotation marks. They like to excel as performers, to do something glamorous and amusing that no one but a north Quito native can do. But they also feel some anxiety lest their factory mates and *mestizo* neighbors, who are likely to be in the audience, see them as believing too much in something "primitive." Such dancers reach a compromise by making the dance a lighthearted *genre* performance, validating their local authenticity without proclaiming it an impenetrably separate human category.

Dancers from their thirties upward, however, sometimes criticize this attitude. Such veterans say it leads to hammy improvisations that violate the discipline of ritual combat. Worse, it misses the point altogether. A *yumbada* in their eyes is no more defined by its spectacular aspect than a lecture is defined by the gestures of the speaker. Although they would never put it so, they seem to feel that the dancer, rather than using his performance to dramatize himself, should use it to demonstrate something beyond and outside himself: the *yumbada* is a formal art, with a content of its own to which individuals should submit themselves. What is expressed in this way cannot be expressed in any other way, and it cannot be expressed at all if the ritual language gets muddied. In practice, such feelings lead to a primary concern with tight, clear ensemble performance rather than with spontaneity. It is the presence of fiesta veterans well into middle age, unafraid to teach and rebuke, that maintains technical standards.

Some young dancers thus rest content with making the *yumbada* a celebration of local idiosyncrasy and personal valor. Some older ones, with the same unconscious constancy of purpose, use the dance to work out formally the ideal content of shamanistic combat. Both of these latent purposes could be served by purely feigned performances; they demand no self-transformation. But a yumbo troupe gets its vitality, in the last resort, from a few members who, like Segundo Salazar, are in neither way inwardly detached from the dance.

Highland society has long recognized that there are among its members people whose talents lean more toward one cultural pole or the other: virtuosi of Catholicism, who are capable of playing *prioste* or prayer leader or beadle roles to perfection, and virtuosi of Catholicism's unnameable but self-evidently real opposite, who, though not so gifted as the great *yachaj* or *samiyuj* (shamans)[5] of the lowlands, are able to become wizards. Such persons always play the corresponding festal roles with special conviction and energy. To overreach one's daily self in either direction transforms the ritual-as-diagram into something far greater, an ordered confrontation of genuine outer forces which radiate compellingly from the performers. If they do not become so wholly absorbed in their special bent as to secede from the fiesta complex altogether (serious shamans may object to fictive treatment of the theme, and serious Catholics may take church roles so demanding as to impede performance), such persons give their communities' fiestas a momentum stronger than mere showmanship.

Segundo Salazar Inapanta is a member of the latter minority. He experiences the conflict of surrounding spheres not just as an outside, cognitive, structural, or scientific problem but as an inner clash, a volcanic conflict of two worlds that both exist within him, exerting contrary demands with urgency and irresistible fascination. Always prone to insomnia, restless wandering, and half-manic talking jags full of strangely brilliant metaphorical thinking, eaten up with greed for the knowledge that is power (everything from gossip to revelation), he finds in himself no quiet island halfway between the forest and the city. The power and polish, the stateliness and sanctity of Quito are not just outer facts but a force that wells up within him. So too is the sense of a wild green universe, a shamanistic world, in which "all lives, all dances, and all is loud" (Rothenberg 1968:38). For him, the representational aspect of yumbo dancing, the posing of a formal opposition between savage forest people as polar archetype of "Indian" America and its primordial powers, and town or urban-centered Christianity with its heightening of powers that are "white," is no more than stage-setting. It is the precondition to a necessary cataclysm. Fifty-one weeks a year he wears the clothes of people who, to his parents, were foreign, and inwardly is in a continuous process of absorbing foreign lore. On Corpus the compass of existence (a metaphor of which he is fond) turns 180°, and the effort of becoming is turned in an opposite direction, returning not to the ancestral world—it is lost beyond recall—but toward that contrary *alter*, the jungle into which the powers of persecuted America have withdrawn. In him a sense of ethnic distinctiveness deprived of its original ground survives as an electric tension between two equally unrealizable potential selves.

Segundo cannot understand why some people dance yumbo list-
lessly, without conviction. On fire with drunken excitement, he
drives his fellow yumbos to the limit of their endurance, drinking
more, stomping harder, insisting that every verse of the yumbos'
song be sung loudly and with feeling, bitterly resenting any defect in
the ritual and transforming his resentment into the inspired ferocity
of the killer shaman.

A *yumbada* is therefore an assembly of performers who differ not
only in the real-life uses they have made of the city-jungle bipolar
environment but in their attitudes on how one should explore it symbolically. Consequently, there is normally a visible amount of friction
among them. A historic change, the invasion of the Quito Runa communities by the city, impinges on the fiesta tradition in the form of a
generational conflict. Not all the anger which yumbos unleash on
each other during the climactic fight, therefore, is feigned. Within the
restricted confines of the yumbo troupe, resentments are generated
and fought out as they cannot otherwise be. These resentments arise
within ritual context but faithfully reflect and are fueled by larger
conflicts rooted in different attitudes about the problem of ethnicity.
The process might be compared to the way in which a psychoanalytic
relationship produces miniature formal replicas of the major conflicts
in a person's life, so that a small fictive struggle can break the dead-
lock in a larger, realer one.

While the yumbos work out the problem of intracommunal stress
in terms of intimacy and anger (fratricide), the *priostes* and their entourage seek to set the diverse and disagreeing members of the community in order in a different fashion, not by conflict and catharsis
but by decree and consensus. The many conflicts within the collectivity, which cannot be solved on cultural "home ground" because that
ground itself is precisely what is in question, are projected outward
in two opposed directions, onto the two screens of extreme Christianity and extreme paganism. Conflict is dislocated into ceremonial
spheres where, for the duration, tokens replace real stakes. In each
sphere the problem is tried out under a different set of assumptions.
This venture affords an opportunity to explore, in a setting of heightened and yet disguised consciousness, the question of how people in
a state of potential discord can live together.

A YUMBO CEREMONIAL CYCLE

Two nights before Corpus the *cabecilla* assembles the yumbos in the
dead of night to shed their secular selves and become *auca*: unbap-

tised, unsocialized, akin to animals and the spirits of mountains and springs.[6] Making the rounds of yumbo houses, he picks up *mamaco* first and then, as the booming voice of mountain mother calls her "children" to wake up and dress, he gathers the *yumbada* one by one. The growing band hurries from house to house in darkness at a brisk jog, pounding lances and whistling. When the headman has gathered the whole troupe, he brings them to his house for a predawn breakfast. Then he sets them to dancing, helping them enter into the spirit of their roles. In the words of a dance veteran:

> . . . as they do this (begin to dance), they smoke tobacco together while (each) says, "Brother, smoke. Brother, smoke up." . . . And that father of theirs says, "Children, children, let's dance. Move it, move it, child," and as he speaks he holds the whip like so underneath (his poncho). With it he lashes them, saying, "Move it, child, move it! Work, child!" and "Whistle in your hands, children!" and "You, ill-bred brat, your dancing is disgraceful!" Saying "(Dance) lively! Show some enthusiasm!," the one called the father dances along whipping them, whom he addresses with "Ay, my children! Ay, my sons!" . . . And a woman (i.e. man in yumba costume) comes forward in her slip and overskirt . . . and says, "I know (lowland magic), I am a yumba, I am this woman yumba, what I have already worked you will not be able to do"; making jokes like this, they talk to each other. So after that, saying, "Whistle in your hands, children, whistle in your hands," they blow into their hands together over and over again.

Under the dramatic premise that they are shamans from the eastern and the Pacific rainforests who have come to Quito to sell animals and practice medicine, they talk about their journeys and the hazards of the *montaña* trails:

> "Brother, what time did you arrive?" "I'm just arriving right now; the rain caught me three or four *tambos* back, so I've come like this, drying off from it. I'm just bringing this *guacamayo* (tropical bird), and I'm bringing the parrots that I bought, loaded in this carrying cloth, dead; this lot died already, on the road. So that's why I've only just arrived, praise to Santo Domingo (de los Colorados)."

This speech rationalizes the fact that the bird sewn on this dancer's basket is stuffed, not alive, and suggests that he wishes to dance the role of a Tsátchela shaman from Santo Domingo.

Still before dawn, the yumbos undergo a ceremony which establishes their rank and position in the performing array and which bestows the dance names that manifest their spirit affiliations.[7] While the yumbos form a single file facing their chief's house, the *cabecilla*, *mamaco*, and *monos* go into a huddle and emerge with a plan for or-

dering the yumbos; one by one they move each to his place in performing array, wordlessly. They then return to the head of the line
and ask each yumbo what spirit name he wishes to assume:

"What is your name?"
"Isabel Tunguragua."
"Next?"
"Saraurco."

There is variation in the category of spirit names taken. In some
places names of mountain spirits, *urcuguna*, predominate, and this is
the commonest practice by far. In others names of forest animals are
common: *Oso* (bear), *León* (puma), *Guayas Tigre* (coastal jaguar), *Chu-
curi* (stump-tailed weasel).

More experienced dancers will usually have one or two stable spirit
affiliations, whose symbols are named lances, and will choose the
same names every year. For others, name-taking may be capricious.
In general, dancers take names of mountains whose mythological
gender corresponds to that of the costume they are wearing. Names
of the mightiest mountains are reserved for accomplished dancers,
and if a beginner claims a name too grand for him, it may not be
ratified.

From this point on the yumbos will speak of themselves as children
of the mountains in whose names they dance: "I am a son of Iliniza,
I have come from Iliniza to visit the *apu* ("lord," i.e. *prioste*), to cure.
I give good luck." All their powers, of athletic stamina, fighting cour-
age, curing, and the ability to give luck, are favors of the mountains
who protect and discipline their sons and daughters. In extrafiesta
contexts it is felt that the mountains love lowlanders; for example,
when thunder is heard at sundown from Mount Guamaní, it is said
that Guamaní is weeping because his Quijos shamans are passing
him by, going away on the road to Quito.

At or shortly before dawn of the first festal day, the yumbos set out
at a brisk skipping pace, jingling, stomping, and whistling in their
hands to the *priostes'* house. While rockets signaling their arrival are
fired (every change of scene is punctuated with fireworks, partly in
order to help groups preparing at other houses adjust their timing),
they dance circles in the road with a leaping gait, expressing elation
at the end of their journey. Coming to rest in double dancing file in
the *priostes'* patio, they receive rum, *chicha*, and their hosts' greetings.
Breakfast and the dancing that follows are occasions for further thematic conversation, conducted as much as possible in an imitation of
jungle Quichua:

Then, when the people called prioste and priosta say, "May God repay you, God of heavens," and while the band plays, they rise up and dance; they don't say "long live the prioste!" nor "long live the priosta!" or anything like that. They say, "Move it for Mountain Mother, put (the flute) to your mouth, play!" It's as Mountain Mother that I play (drum and flute); as Mountain Mother, saying "tun-tún, tun-tún." That's why I don't drink very much, drinking at a measured pace so as not to get drunk. Doing these things, they go to the prioste's house and the priosta's house, saying, "Ah brother, mother, how is your life?," and to all their relatives, "Are you doing well? Are you doing well? By what miracle (have we come together)? I've come, I've arrived with my Mountain Mother. What is it that you desire? Do you want a cure, or do you want to kill?" . . . Thus they feel for the pulse in their hands: "You are a sick man. Do you want a cure? I will cure you at night. I am the one who knows how." And next a yumba says, "I too know. What I have worked, he won't be able to do. My brother can't do it."

At the church a short service of songs and preaching has been scheduled. While waiting for the sacristan the yumbos dance figures and skirmishes before the portal. Entering the church, the celebrants hear a modern-style informal service in which the poncho-clad priest uses a didactic question-and-answer format. Songs of mixed theological and Catholic-reformist political import are sung: "A people which walks through the world crying, "Come, Lord" / A people which seeks in this life the great liberation." The dawn service ends with more dancing by the yumbos while the *priostes* serve *mestizo* townsmen the customary breakfast of hot spiced rum and bread. *Mono,* reading the morning paper upside down in falsetto, gives the townspeople an insane account of the news.

The yumbos must return to the *priostes'* house to dance in double-line formation until midday, when the hosts feed everyone again. By this time overfed, tipsy, and tired, some yumbos may sneak away for a nap. This is winked at provided their wives or a monkey dancer gets them on their feet by 2:30 P.M., when the entire party must mobilize to fetch the *loa-molecaña* component. At the house of the *loa* the four *molecañas* have prepared the child *loa* in snowy finery and a fresh permanent, and guard her as she waits astride a horse. The *priostes,* with attendants, musicians, yumbos, and guests, present the *loa* sponsor with a substantial gift of liquor, fine breads, pastries, and fruit, which is reciprocated with a full service of food and drinks. The *loa* declaims, the black dancers dance and joke, and blessings are given. Then the reinvigorated fiesta returns to the *priostes'* house for further *loa*-centered ceremonies.

Toward sundown the entire party sets out once again to the parish center, this time accompanied by trucks carrying a mountain of brushwood for the vespers bonfire. Coinciding as it does with the evening rush hour, this procession provides a splendid opportunity to stop traffic for monkey raids and show off to amused, angry, or nonplussed drivers. The *priostes* and their guests hear a "Santo Rosario" similar to the morning service in the church. Costume dancers entertain the town public until it is dark enough to set off fireworks and to launch paper hot-air balloons that float through the night like small painted moons or come to grief among telephone wires. The fireworks attract an enormous audience of townspeople, as do the titanic bonfire that follows, the broom dancers and clowns, and the games of "crazy cow" bullfighting and greased-pole-shinnying.

About 11:00 P.M. the fiesta returns to the *priostes'* house. The yumbos bid barewell to the *priostes*, saying, "May God repay you. Now we have drunk, now we have eaten, and now we go to our mountain. To our mountain *tambo*, to sleep in our *tambo*." Having escorted the *bracerantes* to their headman's house, they return to that of the yumbo headman. From here they have the option of going home to their individual houses. But if the yumbo spirit is running high, they will want to spend the night together:

> He (headman) serves *trago* there, and as he serves *chicha* we (*mamaco* and yumbos) drink. And drinking now, already getting half drunk, he speaks, saying, "Whistle in your hands, children." So then they dance beautifully, and as they're dancing there together, he says, "Let's not break up yet. Let's not break up yet, so we'll be together tomorrow. That's what I say, children. Let's spend the whole night with me, from five to five. Like this, not getting too drunk, let's not get drunk, let's not get mad at each other. Let's stay till five in the morning, and when it dawns at five, if God chooses to wake us we wake (even if we're) drunk."

The second festal day, ideally Corpus proper, is the climax of the cycle from a Catholic point of view and also the part most open to public view. At dawn the yumbos and the band go out to greet the *alumbrantas* at their sponsor's house. After a short yumbo dance in the patio the *alumbrantas*, in single file and conversing softly among themselves, lead the yumbos and the band along the brightening lanes back to the *priostes'* house, where child waiters welcome them with hot spiced rum and bread and where the large floral standards for the procession, religious emblems rendered in blossoms tied to a wire frame, are on display. The yumbos may then absent themselves to dance at the houses of deputies (e.g., of fireworks) who require

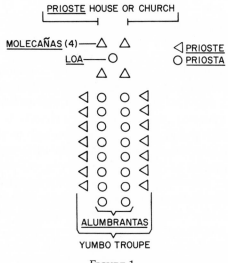

FIGURE 1

special recognition. By about 8:30 A.M. the yumbos have returned, and all costume groups are on hand to receive breakfast. There follows a maximal rendering of the *loa*'s ceremony: the *alumbrantas* form a double file face to face which makes a corridor to the door, and dance a soft two-step in place, just enough to wobble their candles a little, while the yumbos form more vigorously dancing lines behind them. From the street the mounted *loa*, escorted by her guardians the black rough riders, slowly advances down the quadruple aisle to the doorway, where she delivers her poem and flings white paper streamers over the house. In the aisle the *priostes* then dance in couples with her sponsors (see Figure 1).

About an hour before the scheduled mass[8] the entire fiesta, at its apogee of glory—rested, sober, in brand-new costumes—sets out for the parish center. The yumbos lead the parade, running rings or tracing advance-retreat patterns on their path and continually sounding their hands, so active that *mamaco* is hard put to keep up. Silent, queenly *loa* rides among her ebullient *molecañas*; then the *priostes*, with or without *bracerantes*, bearing the floral standards, lead a decorous single file of *alumbrantas* with their candles. Behind these come the *priostes'* duet and the band oompah-ing from a truck, with guests and spectators tagging behind and alongside.

As the fiesta party enters the church—which is festooned with swags and bosses of colored paper, and newly enriched with some major gift from the *priostes*—the floral standards are set by the altar and the massed candles lit. The *priostes* advance to the altar rail to take communion.

The yumbos, on the other hand, are *auca* and must flee the church. They go to a sheltered place such as a tavern courtyard, where they are out of public view. While the *priostes* take wine and wafer, the yumbos eat their viands in a fashion which is formally similar to the *santa mesa*, consecrated meal, but which parodies its substance. In place of the wooden frame used in a *mesa*,[9] the yumbos lay down their lances on the ground, in parallel, so as to form two long rails. Over them they place, instead of the white *mandilis* strip proper to a *mesa*, carrying cloths which the *mono* has borrowed from yumbos' wives. At the head the *monos* pile, not the fresh bread used in a *mesa*, but scraps begged or stolen from the vendors: a picked-clean pig skull, a bag of potato chips, a raw cabbage, a bottle of liquor. While *mamaco* plays and the yumbos dance alongside, *monos* gather the prepared food contributed by the yumbos' wives and spill it out along the cloth strip. If vendors contribute additional food, it is spread evenly. At the head of the table *mamaco* and a senior man knowledgeable in Catholicism, the *rezachidor*, are seated. The *rezachidor* delivers a normal *mesa* blessing, asking three times the benediction of the Trinity. But the yumbos do not eat; instead *mono* leaps up behind the *rezachidor*'s shoulders and burlesques him in falsetto, shrieking, "This man doesn't know how to talk! Blessed God is up there in the heavens and we're down here, so just sit right down! (You'll have to pay, though!)" The reference to paying concerns the next phase, the yumbos' money gifts to *mamaco*, which takes place after the yumbos have eaten a little and left the rest with their wives. Before leaving their places, they must pass bills up the line to *mamaco*, who classifies them by denomination, tucks them under the leather thong of his drum, counts them, and, when satisfied, resumes playing. Money is not mentioned or touched in a true *mesa*.

By this time the yumbos will have heard the rockets which signal the approaching end of the mass, and hurry back to take their place in the procession of the Host. The processional order is the same as that of the parade into town, save that the priest, under a white canopy held by four bearers, walks behind the *priostes* holding the monstrance. The procession halts at the portal to hear the *loa* pronounce her speech, then re-enters and is discharged by the priest.

As the crowd leaves the church, one feels a transition from solemnity to euphoria. *Charoles*,[10] the following act, are the dancers' offerings to their *priostes*, each offering consisting of two parts. The male

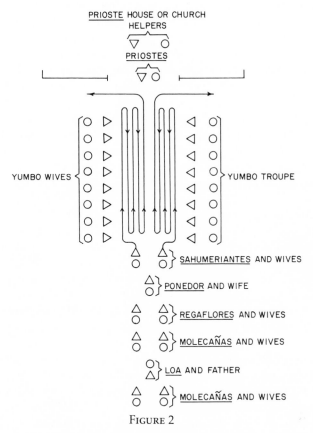

FIGURE 2

part comprises a large bowl full to overflowing with luxury delicacies including, at a minimum, two bottles of fine liquor, bread (which may be fantastically ornate in shape and can even have a written legend stating the names of the *priostes* and the dates of their *cargo*), tropical fruits, sugar wafers, and the candy called *colación*. The female part consists of pots, dishes, or other durables for preparing food, wrapped up in colored cellophane. The delivery of *charoles* is exceedingly formal. The donors advance and retreat in couples, dancing, three times before their gifts are accepted and the blessing given (see Figure 2).

Entradas, the next act, paraphrases the procession of the Host but is altogether secular and euphoric. In it the costume dancers sling over their shoulders large cloths full of lowland delicacies: oranges, small bananas, chunks of sugar cane, and candy called *mishqui muyu*, "sweet seeds." The dancers hurl sweets into the air, causing everyone to scramble and dive for them so that the square becomes a boiling sea of frantic children and dogs.

The remainder of Corpus day varies by locale. A *matanza* (as described below) is often performed for the town public. The return to the house of the *priostes* and the farewell to the leaders of costume groups are essentially the same as on the first day, and, as on the first night, the yumbos have the option of spending the night in company and in character. But by this time they may be too drunk and exhausted to do so.

MATANZA: KILLING THE YUMBO

The third festal day, in all variants, marks a retreat from the public eye and the parish center to the home neighborhood and the social circle defined by celebrants' personal networks. Depending in part on neighborhood tradition and in part on the amount of free time available, it may be a leisurely day in which the *priostes* assemble, slowly and with expansive courtesy, a grand *mesa* of their kin and supporters; or it may be a day of frantic and varied activity in which all the ceremonies that fill two days of a slow-paced cycle are telescoped into one.

In the "slow" variant the morning fiesta divides into three parts, two mobile and one stationary. The stationary part is a quiet and relaxed assembly of the *priostes'* kin and supporters, together with the *bracerantes*, a band—usually a neighborhood amateur band—and the *molecañas*, who entertain with a particularly unbuttoned display of roughhousing. After breakfast people dance in couples and discuss the previous day's doings. Meanwhile, the *priostes'* duo and the yumbos are roaming the neighborhood roads and footpaths. The duo act as a traveling embassy of the *priostes*, walking from house to house, visiting one by one the families that make up the *priostes'* kindred, inviting each to the afternoon *santa mesa*. Meanwhile, as the yumbos roam, every household of *prioste* kin and supporters asks them to grace the house with a short performance and receive hospitality. To have yumbos in the house is a special treat, especially for children, and an honor. If one thinks of the locales of the fiesta dancing as forming a hierarchy of places sanctified, with the church at the apex followed in order by the *prioste* house and the various headmen's houses, then this series of visits has the effect of spreading the fiesta and its feeling downward until it touches almost all the houses of the neighborhood, fixing it in collective memory.

In a fast or compact rendering there is time only to send delegations to the most important households, all performers having to unite at the *prioste*'s house in time for an early-afternoon *matanza*.

From a yumbo point of view *matanza*—also known as *yumbo huañuchiy*, yumbo killing, or *sacha cuchi huañuchiy*, peccary killing—is the climax of the whole cycle. Over the preceding days the *yumbada* has developed a genuine *esprit de corps*; the *rucu* has addressed them tenderly ("My children, you have loved me well"), and the "brothers and sisters," buffered from the rest of the world by the *monos*, have enjoyed commensality always and only with each other. But, as shamans, they also brag and threaten each other incessantly, and friction builds up, exacerbated by fatigue and hangover. In double-file dancing they clash lances more and even jab each other provocatively. In conversation they champion their own homes—Santo Domingo de los Colorados, Archidona, Macas, Arajuno—and boast of their ability to control weather or to kill. They begin to demand favors of each other in a challenging way.

At the moment when *mamaco* taps his drum and breaks into the melancholy, insistent tune of the *matanza*, a tense expectant mood spreads from the yumbos into the crowd. While *monos* clear a field for the dance, the yumbos align themselves in a line along their *cancha*, a strip whose "head" is toward the door of the *priostes'* house (or the church). Two yumbos plant their lance points in the dirt and charge forward, plowing parallel lines. At this moment a sacred but undifferentiated space, likened to the rainforest, is created. Next it is divided among the yumbos, who use their lances to cut transverse lines of division. Then each box is given a center, called a *tambo*, way station, by the intersection of diagonals from two corners (see Figure 3). Although this is the commonest *cancha*, it is not the only kind, and *cancha* design is often an occasion for the kind of genuine disputes that at once endanger and energize the coming climax. The yumbos then take their *tambos* by planting lances, points up, at the X's, all facing the head of the strip, while *rucu*, to the side and near the center of the strip, continues to exhort the yumbos to dance nicely and not get enraged. From the sidelines, too, *mamaco* pounds out a beat to which the yumbos begin to swing their lances in 45° arcs in front of their bodies with a point at belt level as fulcrum. The monkeys, capering in and out of the line, help the *priostes'* people hand out rum and *chicha*, mooch favors from the pressing crowd, and bother the musicians. Two yumbos, partly stripped of their costume for the sake of agility, are chosen for the fateful roles of killer (*huañuchij, huañuchingaj yumbo, cazador, verdugo*) and victim (*huañuj,*

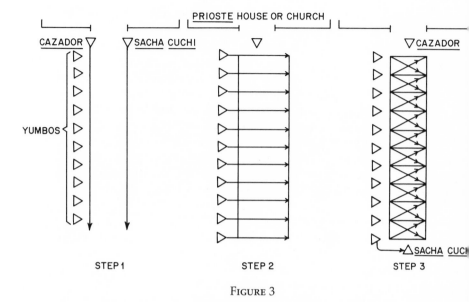

FIGURE 3

huañungaj, sacha cuchi). Killer takes his stance at the head of the line, behind the first *tambo*, and his unarmed victim the opposite post (see Figure 4).

The premise is that the killer, for reasons that are not salient or even explicit (though accusations may be improvised), feels rage against his sibling. Since both are shamans, the battle takes the form of a magic flight and magic pursuit: the victim has taken on the shape of a male *sacha cuchi* (*puerco saíno*, or white-lipped peccary) or, in other performances, a bear, and the killer must catch this animal-person by divination as he chases it through the forest *tambos*. The brother and sister yumbos are compared to the trees of the jungle, rooted to their place but able to fight by swinging their lance-branches, and determined to stop their sibling from being killed. The *cazador* begins his pursuit by asking each in turn whether the hated animal-person has passed by:

> "Hail, Santo Domingo de los Colorados, I am coming!"
> "Hail, brother! Come here, brother."
> "And what news have you, brother? Haven't you seen somebody come by here with his feet and toes twisted backward, with his whole ass and his balls all full of fleas, with maybe a short rope tied around his neck? Didn't you see somebody like that passing by?"
> "Huuu! That one has already gone by here. It was back yesterday that he passed, yesterday around this time he passed by. By now, who knows

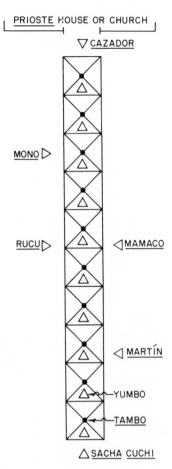

FIGURE 4

where he's going? Huuu! Right now he must have passed ahead three or four *tambos* at least!"

"Right, brother. Thanks. Well, then, at which *tambo* shall I catch him?"

"Brother, I don't know; if you walk fast, brother, you might just catch him."

"Thanks," he says. Leaping, leaping, leaping, going on to another *tambo*, he says, "Hail, brother!"

"Come here, brother."

"Brother, what news have you? Brother, here I come. Haven't you seen somebody with a long nose, somebody with his balls and his ass all full of nits, somebody with all his fangs twisted upward and downward like so maybe, like so, hasn't he passed by here?"

"Yes, brother, he already passed by here, huu, you won't catch him, no."

"Won't I catch him?"

"Well, you might catch him, you might just. Right now he must be advancing two *tambos* ahead already. He's gone by."

"Thanks, brother."

"Right, brother."

Leaping, leaping, leaping, arriving a little farther on at still another (*tambo*), he says: "Hail Santo Domingo, here I come. Haven't you seen a piglike person, chomping potato skins, with potato skins stuffed in his mouth, passing by here? Somebody with a washboard-ribbed belly, it might be?"

"He already passed by here already, huu, just now, just now, but you're getting close now. He'll be passing ahead just one *tambo*."

At this point, just as the hunter approaches the center of the *cancha*, his victim is approaching from the opposite end, crouching behind his brothers and moving up in short dashes. Sensing *sacha cuchi*'s nearness, the hunter takes liquor into his mouth to conduct a divination; he spits the liquor—which is called *ayahuasca*, soul vine, or *jayac huasca*, bitter vine, or *yana yacu*, black water (all terms refer to shamanistic use of *Banisteriopsis*)—over his lance in order to tell from the way the wind carries it which way his enemy has gone. Like a Jívaro shaman, it is said, the killer can tell from wind, from smells, from the motion of branches, and from the buzzing of insects where to hunt in the imaginary forest:

> "Those who are standing there, it's as if they were trees, or underbrush, something to hide in; and it's exactly as if (the killer) had climbed a tree or stood behind an enormous trunk. . . . So (the killer) is walking, and searching, and the wild peccary is right around there tangling in the vegetation. It's just the same as if they were in a rainforest."

At this tense moment in mid-chase, the *sacha cuchi* suddenly lunges into view, and the killer attacks. But *sacha cuchi* is too quick. He spits a mouthful of chewed maize into his persecutor's face, blinding him, and dashes off to a safe *tambo* to the cheers and laughter of the crowd. The killer doggedly continues his hunt down the line: arriving at another *tambo*, in just the same fashion, he says, "Hail, brother!"

"Come here, brother!"

"Brother, haven't you seen a hairy person, nappy-haired, all kinked upward like so, with a squashed snouty nose like so, didn't he go by here? It could be there's a bit of rope tied around his neck?"

"Yes, brother, that one has already gone by here. He must be passing the *tambo* just about now."

As he asks each yumbo in turn, down to the end of the line, he continues to get different answers, and phrases his question in different ways, sometimes hinting that his prey is really a human being: "Someone with the heels of his feet all split, somebody with pants from his knees upward, with his pants all pissed, with his pants all dripping wet. He went by like that, and now he must be arriving at a *tambo*." But by the time the killer reaches the foot of the line, *sacha cuchi* has escaped to the head.

At this moment the chase breaks into headlong combat. No longer moving step by step, both hunter and prey race in and out among the heavy swinging lances of the brothers, always dodging and zig-zagging. The brothers let *sacha cuchi* pass freely but try to block the killer's way by swinging lances across his path, so that at every step the killer must battle his way through with energetic quarter-stave fighting, often spraying liquor into the brothers' eyes so as to blind them, dealing tremendous blows lance on lance, and shouting threats of murder and cannibalism: "I need to eat that person, to murder and eat him is my desire!" Meanwhile the two monkeys have taken sides, one seeking to trip up the killer with his long tail or tackle him, shrieking and chattering, while his counterpart does the same to *sacha cuchi* and the defenders. Infuriating to the dancers but delightful to the spectators, the *monos* are continually sent crashing to the dust, kicked and stabbed, only to rise and interfere again. The chase rages up and down the entire course three or four times, and the maddened killer has narrowly missed murdering his enemy more than once by the time he finally catches up with him. He lunges at *sacha cuchi* with his lance, deals him a deadly stab, and sprints away from the *cancha* with his lance held aloft. The victim crumples face down, dead, and *rucu* breaks into a wail of lament.

Instantly the crowd surges in on the fallen yumbo. One monkey slashes at onlookers' legs with his tail to keep them from crushing the corpse. The other shrouds it with a woollen blanket, under which he hides a corncob; when the blanket is tightened over the cob with a string, it gives the appearance of a swelling. Since the dead *sacha cuchi* lies face down, he thus comes to look like the peccary, which, in the eyes of Acosta or his informants (1954[1590]:133), "is remarkable in having its navel on its spine." According to the same source this animal contains in its spinal navel an essence of corruption: "They are very good eating; but one must first remove that round object which they have in their spinal navel, because otherwise they rot within one day." Correspondingly the modern yumbo dancer feels that his death—which he experiences as a suffocation and faint-ing, caused by being wrapped in hot wool while utterly exhausted,

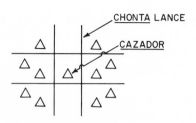

FIGURE 5

drunk, and dizzy—is reversible provided the cure begins before corruption from the cob-navel rots his flesh. If for any reason the sibling yumbos fail to untie it within a quarter-hour or less, *sacha cuchi* will die for real. The sibling yumbos must therefore catch the killer and begin the cure right away. There is an air of terrible urgency. To drag out the remainder of the ceremoney unnecessarily is a transgression that provokes lasting rancor. Segundo Salazar as *sacha cuchi* once suffered such neglect and remains bitter about it years afterward.

While *rucu* stands over his dead child sobbing to the tune of a *mamaco* lament, the triumphant killer has raced beyond view and hidden himself, usually in a neighborhood barroom. His brothers dash off in pursuit and soon catch up with him. He does not resist violently, but denies guilt or blames the victim, and haughtily tries to bribe his brothers with a gift of rum. But they tie his hands behind his back and lock him into a cordon of lances held around his body from four sides (see Figure 5). Taking him captive, they shout *yana yacu!* As he is led back a prisoner, the killer continues to drink and call out to his spirit patron, and even tries to escape. The yumbos demand restitution: " 'You killed my brother. Why did you kill him?'; saying this they lead him back. As they lead him back, they say, 'You are bound to cure my brother, you are the one who will cure my brother'; the woman yumba says, 'It is you who will cure my brother; because you killed him you must bring him back to life.' " Ever hopeful, the yumbo's father has prepared a bowl of fine food, saying, "If he returns to life, he may eat it."

The killer agrees to resuscitate the dead yumbo and is brought the items needed for the cure: liquor, cigarettes, and large branches of leaves, usually *huanduj* (*Datura*, also called *floripondio* or *pelorifondo*) or eucalyptus, standing for *tsini*, nettle. Brought to the corpse, and still held between lances, he prods the corpse and picks loose the string of the spinal navel. Then he begins to clean the cadaver by brushing and whipping it with branches, blowing smoke over it or sucking supernatural dirt and intrusions from the skin. But this helps not at all, because his spirit is clearly not in it. He demands payment from his brothers, and they negotiate a price in cash. Leaves or slips of paper representing the fee change hands, and the killer is now ready to cure in earnest: "Now I will bring him back to life. It's true that I killed him but now I myself will make him live again." Released from his bondage, he holds his lance above the centerline of the dead body and blows liquor over it, then gently tosses the lance from the head end down to the feet so that it skids to a halt in the dust; next he does the same from the other sides. He then directs all the brothers to slip their lances gently underneath the body, from side to side, forming a pallet of lances and therefore a support of mountain forces, on which to heave the dead man upright. As they do this, the shroud falls, his eyes open, and he returns to life. In another version all the brothers give the body a shake, and with a sound like "aaaauuuuussssshhhhh" the breath of life comes back into him.

Now killer and victim must be reconciled and made to drink recip-rocally. As they do, the brothers ask about the journey from the realm of the dead: "Brother, where have you come from?" "What did you see?" "What have you brought?" To these questions the returned yumbo must answer in a soft voice, too soft for the public to hear, "Brothers, I walked over the entire world; I saw all the animals and I saw all my brothers, and now I have brought back the sweet seeds. I went to another world and I brought back what was there: oranges, *colación*, and every fruit." With this the yumbos whistle into their hands and bring *yumbo huañuchiy* to a close.

The epilogue to *yumbo huañuchiy* is a series of minor game-dances. Yumbos may also improvise other pastimes, such as making a rustic barbecue of sheep tripe and calling it monkey meat,[11] a forest deli-cacy.

Following the *matanza* the yumbos conduct a series of rituals which emphasize peacefulness, benign feeling, and integration into the circle of the *priostes'* guests. In each of these the space which was once the *cancha* of combat is transformed into an arena of "civilized" conduct. Two of these, *charoles* and *entradas*, are substantially repeats of earlier acts. The third, *despedida*, "farewell," follows a choreo-graphic routine like that of *charoles*, but in the "farewell" it is a song that is offered by the yumbos, who are beginning to think of their return to the forest. In front of the *priostes'* doorway seats a design is scratched on the ground (see Figure 6). Each pair (or trio, if a yumbo song-leader is chosen to help each pair remember the words) must plant the points of its lances successively at the top, middle, and bottom nodes of the sketch as they sing:

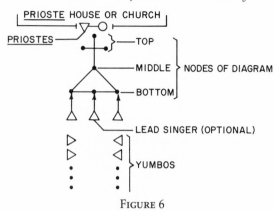

FIGURE 6

Dioselopay Gobernador (2)	May God repay you, *Gobernador*
Tanto tanto agradecini (2)	I thank you so much, so much
Chay tucuyda agradecini (2)	I thank you for all that (you've done)
Huatan huatan urmamunchi (2)	From year to year we drop by
Veranero pishcushina (2)	Like the bird *veranero.*
Ajay ya ves, ojoy ya ves	Ah, now you see, oh, now you see
Huañuy ya ves, causay ya ves	Death now you see, life now you see
Ay no, sí! Eso, sí!	Ay no, yes! That's so, yes!

There are, in theory, 24 stanzas.[12] Because it is a farewell, this is felt to be a melancholy song. The *priostes* are expected to—and in fact are inclined to—weep during its performance.

Late in the day the *priostes* clear the space in front of their house. The former *cancha de matanza* now becomes the *santa mesa*, "sacred table" (see Figure 7). While some variants demand *mesas* in other phases, the *mesa* of the third day is the indispensable and definitive one. From the *priostes'* point of view it is the summit of their hospitality and the global declaration of their rank-structuring of the current fiesta, the moment at which their and the other guests' newly changed places in the communal fiesta hierarchy are consolidated. For the yumbos it is the point when they finally step outside their role and enter into the compact of peace which brings the *priostazgo* to a morally satisfying close.

Preparations for the *santa mesa* include the cooking of immense stores of food and *chicha* and the purchase of fine liquor, sometimes over a hundred bottles. A table is set at the head position. From it,

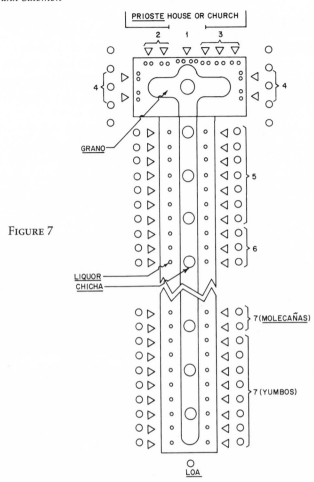

PRIOSTE HOUSE OR CHURCH

GRANO

LIQUOR
CHICHA

7 (MOLECAÑAS)

7 (YUMBOS)

LOA

FIGURE 7

down the *cancha*, extend long, low trestles made of withes tied together on a frame. Logs serve as benches. Sponsors themselves only
watch from the sidelines. Through the intervening authority of a respected elder, each guest is ushered to a seat appropriate to his rank.
Seat-ranking is a diplomatic task requiring a delicate sense of equity.
High seats are highly valued; if a man named to one sometimes plays
coy about taking it, this is only to draw attention to the honor done
him.

During the seating ceremonies the yumbos dance alongside as an
honor guard. At the head table the supreme place goes to the elder
who serves as *rezachidor* (see no. 1 in Figure 7). He is flanked by the
bracerantes (2, 3), in those communities which provide them, and by
the headmen of troupes (4). Those who have provided important

loans, or endorsed the fiesta with the prestige of their own past fiestas, are seated in the upper part of the stem table (5). Men invited for other reasons follow (6), and then the dancers (7). In every case the wife sits a short distance behind her husband, usually on the ground.

All *mesas* segregate food into three categories: the *buda*, food served and eaten on the spot; the *grano*, a sacred food eaten in token amounts; and the *mediano*, food offered exclusively for future consumption away from the *priostes'* house. The *rezachidor* opens the *mesa* with a short speech evoking the Catholic theme of the fiesta, usually the Host as the body of Jesus, and a Hail Mary followed by an Our Father and a blessing of the Trinity. He opens the first bottle of *mesa* liquor, drinks a shot, and sends it down the line with the helpers. Simultaneously the first of many pails of *chicha* is brought from the *priostes'* kitchen and served in rank order. Guests receive *buda*, the more secular part of the feast, in clay bowls. Protein delicacies in *buda* are rank-rationed. While the guests eat *buda* and the soup that goes with it, relatives of the *priostes* are free to do homage by serving liquor to everyone. Normally this results in an onslaught of compulsory drinking such that the rest of the *mesa* becomes a race between solemnity and oblivion.

Meanwhile the helpers bring cooked *grano*, usually hominy of unshelled maize, in great steaming basket-loads which are carefully spilled out over the white cloth center strip. At intervals down the table large clay tureens of *chicha* are placed, and all along the edges gift bottles of brilliant-colored liqueurs form a jewel-like border. The remaining spaces are filled with stacks of sugar-breads and fruit. The prayer leader once again stands, recites a blessing over the grain, asks the seated people to join in a few prayers, and begins the sharing out of the consecrated food. This interval is distinctly solemn. One should not act visibly drunk, crack jokes, or leave the table until it is over. The diners eat only a token handful of *grano*. The prayer leader, and then other men further down, share out nearly all of it in double handfuls to wives, who advance one by one to receive it in carrying cloths. Later their families will eat it at home.

Medianos, dispensed toward the end, are the *priostes'* food gifts to their main collaborators. Consisting of a large enamel basin full of rich food—a whole cooked chicken, a roasted guinea pig, a dozen boiled eggs, fine bread—they are accompanied by at least a jug of *chicha* and a bottle of liquor. They must not be eaten or even tasted until the following day, when, out of the presence of the *priostes*, they will serve as a commemoration of festal generosity. The *mesa* closes with a final performance by a drowsy, out-of-costume *loa*. Dancing in couples to modern *cumbia* and *salsa* played on electric instruments may continue far into the night, but the fiesta now begins, very gradually, to disperse.

The yumbos, however, must last until the very end. Only when the band is ready to pack up and the dancers are few may they make their farewells to the *prioste*:

> "Now we (must) go to our *tambo*, to our home. Now our mountain is calling to us, now our mountain is playing. When our mountain plays, we go away, our mountain does not let us stay. And so each of us has to go to his country, each of us to his hill. Now to our *tambo*—now because of the mountain we must go to our place, toward our *tambo*, we have to work."

The "playing" of the mountains is the flickering of lightning on the far side of the mountains, visible from Quito as a pale glow backlighting the cordilleras' black profiles.

In fact, the end of the *mesa* is not the end of the fiesta cycle, only of that part in which the *priostes* are paramount. In the succeeding days all the major ceremonies are to be repeated at the house of the yumbos' headman, who recapitulates the fiesta on a reduced scale. The yumbo context is dissolved only when they bid each other goodbye:

> "Farewell, farewell, my mountain doesn't let me stay. We're going away to our *tambos* to live. Mountain Mother, play for us, play it sadly. Now we are separating from our brothers; we are leaving our brothers. Farewell, farewell."

"I SAW ALL MY BROTHERS"

Belote and Belote point out that since the suppression of the last vestiges of Indian political authority, "the fiesta *cargo* system is the *only* important institution existing today which serves to integrate the indigenous social structure . . . and to differentiate it from non-indigenous systems" (Belote and Belote 1977:49; my translation, emphasis added). If the *yumbada* has flourished where other ceremonies languish, one may guess that it makes some particularly convincing statement about that structure—that it makes people want to renew a commitment which, in many ways, it would be opportune to repudiate.

We may wring a preliminary clue about this statement from an examination of what is peculiar to this "indigenous social structure." In the first place, it is exceedingly poor in the sort of overt boundary markers which are usually thought to give social structure an ethnic coloration. While there are outward insignia of the Quito Runa identity, these have become intolerably expensive in terms of opportunity cost and are disappearing or being replaced by in-group signals. Nor is this reluctance about giving outsiders handles for ethnic typing entirely new. As far back as the verbal record reaches, there has been no tag-term for Quito natives comparable to *Cañari, Puruhá, Pasto,* or other historic "tribal" terms. (*Panzaleo* is factitious.) So effective has the protective coloration of native Quiteños been that, while there is a literature which speaks of their greater or lesser "assimilation," attempts to define what they assimilate *from* have been half-hearted (Costales 1960, Beals 1966). Yet this camouflaged, almost crypto-Andean population does exist in many places as a social-structural fact in its own right — an assembly of "authentic," or local-rooted, kindreds — and as such has interests to assert vis-à-vis other sectors as well as internal issues to settle. The development of festal play on the theme of ethnicity, to an extreme rare even in Ecuador, today may serve this group as a means of dealing with such issues without endangering the useful property of nonexplicitness.

Second, although the statement made by a ritual is not a statement of fact, a ritual is built of images that derive from experience. On the way to a deeper purpose the *yumbada* offers some reminders about the empirical world in which Quito Runa social structure has adapted itself. Specifically, it expresses a simple historical truth which is not noted in textbooks, and which has powerfully shaped Ecuadorian prehistory and history. The little aboriginal communities ringing Quito have for at least five centuries been, in both cultural orientation and economic practice, more thoroughly trans-Andean than any of the imperial civilizations which tried to unify forest and Sierra in a state-centralized scheme of integration. Pantropical cosmopolitans of a multitiered, multi-ethnic landscape, the Quito Runa have been, and still are, the cultural switchboard and economic depot of a transmontane integration unknown to state planners.

From Experience to Image

Perhaps since the sierran formative era, and certainly since Incaic times, the circum-Quito communities have maintained close and at times conflicting ties with Quito and with the forested lowlands of both Amazonia and the Pacific littoral. Under Tawantinsuyu, the main axis of exchange was that leading through the western *bocas de montaña,* "mouths of the jungle," into what is now called the Noroccidente de Pichincha but was formerly known as the Yumbo country

(Porras 1974:165–76, Cabello 1945 [1579?]:56–66). In the west-slope rainforest a system of barter supplied highlanders with such tropical staples as cotton, capsicum, and salt and, in all likelihood, the general concept of "yumbo" as a lowlander who deals with highlanders. The Yumbos proper, though overtaken by Spanish colonialism only late and incompletely, nonetheless were devastated by its effects and appear to have neared extinction by the 1620s. Although aboriginal Quiteños had long maintained contact with the Amazonian east via the Papallacta-Quijos route (Oberem 1971, 1:175), the decline of the western, or true, Yumbos seems to have led to an intensification of trade with nearer Amazonia and to the generalization of the term *yumbo* to include all lowlanders. As late as the 1740s Spaniards still applied the word *yumbo* to west-slope peoples (Magnin 1940:153–54), and among Quichua speakers, who by the eighteenth century had converted the former barter alliances into stable commercial routes, it has survived until today as a generic term for forest natives both east and west. Many men alive today, including some yumbo dancers, traveled into the Quijos, Canelos, Shuar, and Colorado countries along the colonial routes with mule-loads of textile, food, and manufactured merchandise, and have detailed first-hand knowledge of lowland peoples. It is possible to trace most traits of yumbo dancers' costume and speech to perceived characteristics of the people such travelers observed. While the *lluchu* and *mate* yumbos are in themselves fanciful, they are as "ideal types" the precipitate of centuries of empirical experience. Interest in the *montaña* continues at high levels today, and many people own or hope to own forest land.

Historic involvement with *montaña* peoples, however, goes far beyond economic interdependency. Sixteenth-century evidence not only proves intermarriage between Quito area aborigines and Yumbos proper but strongly suggests some degree of lowland ideological sway over highlanders. The stateless peoples of Amazonia regularly provided leadership for revolts against the Spanish state. The shaman-led rebellion of the Pendes (1579; AGI/S Quito 8:f.lr) was expected to have severe repercussions even in the areas of maximum Inca and Spanish penetration. The great lowland shamans were and are figures of awe to Quito area highlanders. Families that appear thoroughly hispanicized have sent members into the forest zone to contract shamanic services. Nor is it unusual for a young man of Hispanic outward appearance to spend his weekend and his spare cash on shamanic instruction in Amazonia. Another "modernizing" factor which has augmented the salience of shamanism to highlanders is military conscription. Men who learned literacy or technical skills in army training may well also have learned a modicum of shamanistic lore while stationed on the Amazon tributaries.

Conversely, visits by forest shamans to highlanders, such as form the plot of the *yumbada*, correspond to an emotionally charged reality. Many circum-Quito highlanders remember having been cured of childhood illnesses by visiting lowlanders. They also recall awaiting their arrival with gifts or, in the hope of winning their magical favor, helping to get them out of jail when persecuted by government officials.

The tendency to think of Amazonia as remote, inhospitable, and culturally impoverished, far from being an ingrained trait of highland aboriginal civilization, is almost exclusively characteristic of Inca and European groups which have tried, and failed, to impose a state-centered and highland-centered governance upon it (Francisco 1971). The character of lowland nature and lowland peoples, in the eyes of highlanders who have never tried or wanted to dominate the lowlands politically but who, rather, have cultivated "vertical" relationships of economic interdependency and spiritual clientship, differs radically from both the "green hell" and "green paradise" stereotypes.

Alongside these lowland ties the Runa have also maintained a long and intimate association with the Catholicism of Quito. Colonial records show the circum-Quito peoples to have been the builders and devotees of the great cult centers. Nonetheless, their Catholicism is misunderstood. Most writers tend to take Quichua speakers' participation in Catholic ritual either as a demonstration of a religious consciousness essentially identical to that of urban Catholics or else as a mere veneer which coercion has imposed over a non-Christian world view. Priests who serve Quichua parishes know that the first view is unrealistic, and their parishioners would consider the second (if any fieldworker were candid enough to acknowledge it) profoundly insulting. One way to envision the peculiar character of Andean Catholicism might be to highlight the fact that in terms of historical experience Christianity, no less than jungle shamanism, is the religious aspect of a foreign society with which one's own stands in a relation of intimate interdependency. One may say of Christian (or Inca) conquerers and Quito dwellers, as of shamans, that the earthly powers they command and the transcendent powers they worship constitute parts of the ground of Runas' existence. Their effects are everywhere palpable, their reality undeniable. Andeans need neither pretend nor refuse to believe in Christian deities. They are self-evident realities.

The task is rather to locate them within a more inclusive map of the sacred universe.

In such an overall view one might think of the sacred as a concentric space. Its center is Quito, which is the focus of hierarchical, legal earthly power and of the Church, which offers shelter, warmth, and illumination but also confinement and submission. Quito is the home of great saints and the scene of Christianity's mightiest rituals. Runa people, inhabiting the space all around it, partake of Quito's sacredness, are beholden and devoted to it. But in the other direction, looking outward from the ring of Runa parishes around Quito (or any other highland city), there extends a vast space rising out and up to the crags of the Mountain Mothers and beyond, into the forest. Christian holiness is centripetal toward Quito, but another kind of holiness is centrifugal, radiating outward in the immense periphery beyond state and church.

Time and again foreign peoples, conquering and sanctifying Quito with their own powers, exert force outward. This force subjugates the aborigines of the surrounding highlands and in turn expels the aboriginal powers still farther outward, over the brim of the cordilleras, into the refuge of the outer forests. Thus the forest becomes— is forever becoming — the refuge of the ancient, the aboriginal, the autocthonous. It is a reservoir for the kind of knowledge which the powers of the center wish only to expel and replace. To live between the outer forest and the central city, therefore, is a location in time as well as in space. All Quito Runa people are professed and wholly sincere Christians. But they know, in a way too self-evident to require discussion, that, unlike "white" people, they have come from a prior state into Christianity rather than simply having been there from the beginning. Moreover, this prior state still exists beyond and behind Christianity. It makes a claim that cannot be forgotten. One is always primordially indebted to it; unlike the Hispanic Christian for whom paganism is an empty illusion, the yumbo dancer thinks, or feels somewhere beneath his thoughts, that beyond Christianity there is a more general sacred sphere within which Christianity exists. The Church and its city may be a center and a light, but around them stretches a huge holy space, to the Mountain Mothers and beyond, in which it is a Runa's calling to travel.

From Image to Ceremony

This sketch of the shape of Quito Runa experience suggests the range of connotations loaded onto the two polar images of the

fiesta—the center-rooted, Christian, civilized *priostes*, and the periph-
ery-rooted, *auca*, pagan, savage yumbos—but it does not clarify how
or why these personages perform as they do. In historical terms it is
likely that the two contrapuntally opposed ceremonial complexes derive from heterogeneous, largely extraneous sources, and that the
feat of *bricolage* by which they are brought into orderly relation with
each other is the ceremonial counterpart to the historical achievement
of an ethnicity defined not only by internal idiosyncrasy but by its
orderly and vital relations with other cultures.

The yumbo performance manifests a twining together of the Inca-
endorsed, but probably pre-Incaic, fiesta of *Itu*, with the widespread
Andean myth of a spirit flight entailing human-nonhuman interro-
gation. Of the latter myth the *locus classicus* is the second chapter of
the Huarochirí manuscript (Ávila 1966:22–29). Polo de Ondegardo
tells us (1916:25–26) that *Itu*, like the *yumbada*, was a moveable feast
rather than a calendrically fixed one, and Cobo gives details which
leave little room for doubt that its celebrants wore yumbo costumes:

> Itu . . . they did only at irregular intervals, according to the necessity of
> the moment, and so it was not allowed to all to perform it in a single
> standard manner. In the city of Cuzco it was celebrated in the following
> way. . . . After the sacrifice those who were to celebrate it dressed in the
> garments and ornaments consecrated to the solemn act, namely, red *cumbi*
> tunics with long fringes of the same color; onto these they tied some long
> coarse braids which hung to their feet; on their heads large feather dia-
> dems, well-worked, of many colors, and some strings of shell beads
> around the neck; in their hands they carried a small pouch which they
> called *sondorpauca*, and some a dried green bird with its plumage, and a
> small white drum, very well-made. (1956, 2:220–21; translation supplied)

The myth of a magical flight and pursuit in which the pursuer asks
animals where his prey has gone occurs all over the Andes and may
well be pre-Incaic. Some *yumbadas* gave each yumbo an animal identity. An outstanding recent exploration of the theme by Ortiz Rescaniere (1973:35–39) interprets it as showing how the victims' departure from this life makes it possible for earth to provide the means for
human subsistence, a reading compatible with the revived yumbo's
gift of "sweet seeds," that is, tropical produce, to his brothers and to
the audience.

The Catholic portion of the ritual, the *priostes'* role as such, is probably also a historical composite. It juxtaposes aboriginal and Hispanic
practices whose common denominator is an emphasis on the act of
demonstrating centric hierarchy and civic peace. The recurring *santa*

mesa module (which occurs at other seasons but reaches a lavish extreme at Corpus) probably derives from a form of commensality aboriginal to Quito (Atienza 1931:41–42).

Its merger with Corpus was apparently made possible not only by calendric coincidence but by certain surface likenesses. This probably began early in the colonial era. In 1584 Pedro Venegas de Cañaveral (AGI/S Quito 8:f.3v) and in 1590 Martín de Murúa (1946:349) complained that Corpus had been heavily infiltrated by Andean religion. This is not surprising, since Corpus as practiced by Old World Spaniards was already lavish in the use of exotic costume, drama, and stylized combat. Corpus sword dancing, one of the variants of which, from Segovia, has survived into modern times, strikingly resembles yumbo dancing:

> Sword dancers click castanets as they weave their intricate steps in front of the image of the Virgin. The eight youths who dance are dressed in white skirts trimmed in red worn over white shirts, pants, stockings, and sneakers. Plumed mitres cover their heads and colored ribbons and handkerchiefs fly from their shoulders and sleeves. . . . Sword dancers also appear to have been common in southern Spain; a Sevilla decree in 1532 prohibited *cofradía* and guild sword dancers from preceding the custodia. (Foster 1960:196)

By exploiting superficial relationships among available ingredients, it has been possible to combine elements from European Corpus, Andean *Itu*, and lowland traditions of spiritual combat, reorder them, and produce a pair of counterbalanced ceremonial themes—*priostazgo* and *yumbada*—which are uniquely adequate to the celebrants' situation. The superficial likenesses between Corpus and native American ceremonies have provided a shield for the preservation of an Andean tradition in a strikingly conservative form. We know from old pictures that for at least 125 years the *lluchu yumbo* costume has changed hardly at all (Castro y Velásquez 1976; Anonymous 1853). But these coincidences in and of themselves would not have interested anyone if they had not been intrinsically provocative opportunities for re-exploring the nature of Quito Runa existence.

From Ceremony to Reunion

The point, however, is not merely that an array of images from historically complex experience is assembled into a pair of counterbalanced ceremonies, nor how this is done, but to what effect? Is the mere piquancy of the contrast reason enough for the immense effort? Or is there an inner relationship between the two themes such that they comment on each other and illuminate the space between them, that is, the space in which Quito Runa live?

Since Quito Runa culture partakes of both aboriginal and Hispanic norms, most families and neighborhoods feel torn between conflicting desires. The matched ceremonies tease apart aspirations that in daily life are intertwined, projecting them outward onto the twin screens of the middle of the world and the edge of the world. At this remove one can work out experimentally the properties of the primordially "Indian" powers hypostatized as *auca*ness (shamanism, the warrior ethic, intimacy with an untamed nature) and of total *civilización* (Catholicism, submission to laws of state and church, dominion over a tamed nature).

"Civilized" people live together in hierarchical, pacific order by virtue of submission to central authority, secular and ecclesiastical. The state and the church bind people to each other in a condition of civility, but they do so by enclosing humanity upon itself and banishing all else to the foreign realms of subhuman nature and superhuman divinity. One may dominate the former, one must submit to the latter, but one can be intimate with neither. In order that human affairs may be protected by superhumans and dominate subhumans, humanity renounces any social or kinship bond with earth, animals, plants, or spirits. Each person is kin (real, metaphorical, or potential) with every other *cristiano* (a word commonly used to mean "human being"), and this bond ideally allows people to be, literally, civilized, that is, "citizens" or "cities." The social sphere is that of the human only, but potentially panhuman.

The *auca*, by radical contrast, inhabits a social sphere that repudiates all hierarchy, peace, and authority. The *yumbada* is a fragment of a kindred radiating out from the union of *rucu* and *mamaco*, man and mountain, which ultimately includes not only people but all animals, plants, and earth itself. The yumbo can persuade all of nature, borrow any of its forces and features in reciprocity. Within the vast forest kindred all transformations are possible. But if there is no special barrier between human and nonhuman, neither is there any special bond between human and human. By the very fact that the social sphere includes the nonhuman, it becomes inhuman. Full of valor and holiness, this world is also full of fear and sudden danger; all beings live in the tenderest intimacy and the most merciless enmity at the same time. The shaman in ecstasy can see the *auca* world whole, radiant and terrible. In this world no civility is possible. It may be that shamans understand each other as perfectly as human minds can, yet they must live far apart in the forests, for no being's action, whether friendly or hostile, is limited by anything other than the forces of the other beings around it. The civilized person's safety is in concentration, but the *auca*'s is in dispersion.

The two concepts of the human condition are not, however, lacking in common ground. All humans, whether *auca* or *civilizado*, need other humans in order to exist (for reproductive and productive reasons), yet all humans are also in a position to further their own existence at the expense of others; therefore the problem of mutual dependency–mutual transgression is universal. It takes on different forms under the two premises but may be explored by parallel means. For the *auca*, it is not the means to live in spite of murder that is problematic, because all transformations are possible, even from death to life. The problem for *aucas* is that of the means to life in this world: given dispersion and constant war, how can there be a society and an economy here and now? For civilized people, on the other hand, the problem of transgression has opposite results: given civil, nature-dominating conditions, murder will not by itself destroy economy or society. The city can mend the rents in its fabric. But what of the loss of life itself, irretrievable and terrible for purely human society in a way that it cannot be for the shaman?

Within this general antithesis the contrast between the Passion and the yumbo murder is a specific case, a test case. Each concerns a band of sworn companions, pilgrims in search of what is needed to complete life. For the yumbos this means earning the means to earthly life, while for the Apostles it means winning salvation beyond this life. Both pilgrimages are disrupted by a fratricidal crime, born of greed and the decision by one to live against, rather than in, the group. In both the symbol for food appears to represent the means of life: for the yumbos, life here and now; for the Christians, life beyond death. The common denominator is evident: transgression and murder against a magical person, followed by his return to life and a promise of reconciliation whose token is a treasured food. (So much is present at the margin of dancers' consciousness, and if provoked by people who dislike the *yumbada*, they will defend it with such exegesis.) The community, constituted as an audience, lives during the fiesta in the space between two formally parallel treatments of a single theme:

Passion of Jesus	*Yumbo Huañuchiy*
1. A superhuman father and an earthly mother	1. A superhuman mother and an earthly father
2. have a son, outwardly human but latently superhuman,	2. have a son, outwardly human but latently subhuman,
3. who is superior to twelve companions recruited outside his kindred.	3. who is one of twelve equal companions within his kindred.
4. They travel to a city ruled by unbelievers, who are hostile,	4. They travel to a city ruled by Christians, who are friendly,
5. entering its holiest place, and	5. shunning its holiest place, and
6. rebuking the rulers of the place.	6. saluting the rulers of the place.
7. Because of the enmity of outsiders	7. Because of internal discord
8. the son is secretly betrayed.	8. the son is openly attacked.
9. He voluntarily offers his flesh as magical food.	9. The enemy threatens to devour his flesh as magical food.
10. His companions consider him superhuman	10. His companions consider him subhuman
11. but fail to defend him	11. but defend him
12. as he is led submissively	12. as he flees defiantly
13. to a cold-blooded execution, and dies.	13. from an impassioned murderer, and dies.
14. The betrayer, renouncing the profit of his crime,	14. The killer, demanding the profit of his crime,
15. accepts his own just death;	15. undoes his victim's unjust death;
16. the revenant brings the means to eternal life in another world.	16. the revenant brings the means to mortal life in this world.

Jesus promises to his people, whose heirs are the "civilized," food from this life (wafer and wine) which is the means to live in the other; *sacha cuchi* brings from the other life food (*mishqui muyu*) which is the means to life in this one. It is easy now to see why the double festal play, which centers entirely on murder, is nonetheless joyful in feeling. Insofar as it is possible to inhabit both worlds, the problem of transgression is soluble in ways that are not only complementary (as the material economic contributions of the worlds are complementary) but formally congruent. They may be superimposed upon each other, and one may behold both at once without confusion. A radical opposition, fearlessly confronted, ends in a reunion.

From Reunion to Action

But onlookers, like Jesus or the *sacha cuchi*, leave this life only to return to it. They act out the double festal play at projected, hypothetical extremes of ecology and philosophy precisely because in local terms no resolution was evident. The sense of being situated between sacred center and sacred wilderness has been vindicated, without this in itself clarifying directly the matter of how one is to behave in such a situation. In what way does the venture return to earth with a new impulse for forward motion? In what way does it propel the collectivity into the future?

One might look for two kinds of answers, depending on how one conceives of the nature of ritual itself. One alternative is to consider ritual as time set apart from history, to see it as the prolonged instant in which the bare elements of existence, beyond and behind the flux of events, become visible. In this static sense, *sub specie aeternitatis*, the Corpus cycle elucidates two opposed ideas about how society can exist on and beyond the earth. In the "civilized," Christian, centripetal version, all depends, first, on the voluntary act of forgiveness by Jesus and, second, on all peoples' sincerely submitting to the authority which bases itself on the legacy. To live as "civilized" people therefore demands an act of faith not only in one's God but in one's neighbor, and an act of submission not only to the spirit but to the literal fact of the law. In the *auca* version of the human condition, on the other hand, resuscitation takes place not through a voluntary, but through a purchased, act of forgiveness. Since the premises of *auca* existence exclude both submission to law (the *rucu's* wishes are wholly contravened) and renunciation of victory (the shaman is a spirit warrior), the "thirty pieces of silver" which are the vehicle of damnation in Christian thought are the vehicle of salvation in *auca* thought. The autonomy of each shaman is restored; he can go back to his *tambo* with ego intact. The wages of what in the Christian world would be sin are profit to the killer and life to his fellows. The continuance of life under this law demands not only dispersion (the opposite of urbanity), but an everlasting balance of rivalries without central control (the opposite of the state) and strictly symmetrical reciprocity, for good or evil, in both spirit and material transactions (the opposite of Christian charity).

In this static, instantaneous vision, one sees that while the two ideas may be formally congruent, their practical implications are incompatible. It is this incompatibility between two equally real sides of human existence which one experiences in daily life, in the secular round within and without one's own community, as practical evils. The enmities of shamans are innocent, for they live in a world where murder can be a part of a valid order. But what is one to say of *auca*-like transgressions among urban neighbors, or abuse of power by the elite of palaces and cathedrals? Conversely, what does one say when, in an egalitarian context, one's own personal power and autonomy are violated by outsiders who pull rank? The incompatible practical implications of the two visions are irreducible. On earth no final resolution is possible, and to be a Runa means occupying a field of tension. The profit of exploring a double *auca*-Christian vision lies in understanding the dilemma, not in removing it.

Within a purely Christian world view "savage" behavior is simply evil, something to be repressed and forgotten. The *auca* play, however, brings into the sphere of the meaningful exactly what Christianity expels from it; in the interstices of an imperfect civilization, another world reasserts itself. Out of place and incomplete, intruding itself through human error, it is evil. Outside Corpus season, nobody likes to be called a yumbo. Yet insofar as one understands yumboness, what is outside the law, what urbanites see as atavistic and savage, is not outside meaning, or worthless, or even in any final sense wrong. The world of the yumbo dancer does not contain a borderline dividing the known, the good, and the meaningful from outer darkness. In principle, for all that it is a tense and divided world, it is one doubly illuminated.

But another view is possible. Ceremonies do not stand entirely outside history; every performance is an event in the history of the ceremony, an idiosyncratic, never-to-be-repeated moment. If on one hand the *yumbada* and the *priostazgo* contrast atemporal aspects of the Runa situation, on the other hand the working out of each as an arrangement of persons in a particular, temporary rank order has particular, temporary emotional and social results. The way any two yumbos fraternize and fight with each other expresses under the aegis of *auca* ethics relations and conflicts rooted in secular experience, and will have repercussions when they return to the secular. Segundo Salazar, for example, explains his problems with a number of his neighbors by recalling what happened between them in past *yum-*

badas, not by rehearsing the morally pointless secular wrangles that accompanied them. Conversely, the way, *par excellence*, to articulate the Christian and civic aspect of a person's life is to talk about his deeds as *prioste*, the *mesas* he arranged, and the merit of his vows, even though it may be that his secular doings were of more "practical" import. What happens on the projection screens of the *auca*-sacred and the Christian-sacred is not secular history, but it is really historical: it compresses the effects of past events and proposes in supercharged miniature the course of future ones. It is the final grand *mesa*, where the last and most synoptic treatment of the theme Christian/*auca*/sacred food occurs, that one also sees the *priostes'* summation of neighborhood social structure and the state of relationships which will be the raw material of the "authentic" kindreds' historical action in the coming year.

Yumbo dancing, in short, probably serves its practitioners on several planes. Psychologically, it may help one to recognize and come to terms with anger and aggression in an ambience that allows it few secular outlets. Religiously, it generates a bipolar vision which infuses sacred meaning into precisely those parts of existence which Christianity tends to expel from the sphere of the meaningful. Cognitively, it clarifies the complex situation of a community with no openly recognized ethnic standing and many inter-ethnic dependencies. Socially, it concentrates and reinforces the indigenous core of neighborhoods awash in outside population movements. Philosophically, if one may use the word of a process that involves almost no cogitation, it raises and solves theoretically the question of how a person lives both in and against society. It probably has some effect toward consolidating and energizing local solidarity in the face of pressing civic needs.

That all these functions cluster around the image of an intranational cultural minority points up a difference between folk and nationalist tendencies in the defining of a total or national society. Nationalists hope for the subordination of regional and ethnic differences to a more global identity, which they posit at an almost purely theoretical level of generality. Starting from an inventory of what they take to be the nation's needs and potentials, their definition of a common cultural ground proceeds deductively downward toward the endorsement of a *mestizaje* whose only perceptible characteristic is the absence of all subnational identity. By contrast, the folk definition of a person of truly national consciousness, a person aware of all relevant environments, is one who has a rich empirical knowledge of differences and relationships among subnational groups—one who, in short, has seen all his brothers. Such a person is in a position to build up the sense of a whole by working inductively upward from the experience of diversity. The concept of trans-Andean unity existed in local myth and ritual long before it became an administrative project in the minds of state builders or an intellectual one for anthropologists.

NOTES

Acknowledgments: Among the informants whose kind help made this study possible were Manuel Antonio Quilachamín, Segundo Salazar Inapanta, Ignacio Lincango, Manuel Guañuna, Manuel Gualoto, Angel Gualoto, and José Ignacio Cóndor. To these and to many other dancers, cordial thanks are due. It was Kathleen Klumpp who originally called my attention to the *yumbada*. I am also indebted to the Instituto Nacional de Antropología e Historia in Quito, and to the Center for Latin American and Caribbean Studies as well as the Scholars' Travel Fund at the University of Illinois, which supported the research.

1. While the specific *yumbada* culminating in *yumbo huañuchiy* seems to be peculiar to the Quito area, the term *yumbo* is applied to a large number of costumed dance figures whose identification with the selva is more or less explicit. Moreno (1949:134–44) describes an Imbabura version from Cotacachi danced in September, characterized by white dress and elaborate dance figures. Santiana (1948–49:238–74) mentions a yumbo dance in honor of San Luís, observed in Mojanda, whose costumes share with Pichincha yumbos' the pale mask, short pants, and feather crown (see also Buitrón 1949). Costales (1968, 1:186, 196–97, 419–20; 2:168, 172, 175, 185–90, 489–92; 1960:350) summarizes yumbo dances in Cumbas, Pomasqui, Quizapincha, and Tizaleo. Coba Robalino (1929:171, translation supplied) witnessed yumbo dances in Píllaro characterized by "masquerades of people disguised as members of other tribes, as animals, and as birds. Nor were sham battles lacking . . . on the eight days of Corpus, in the streets and plazas of San Miguelito." Both Costales and Coba believe yumbo dancing to represent a folk memory of the same prehistoric invasion of the Sierra by *montaña* peoples emerging from Amazonia through the Pastaza gorge, which González Suárez and later archaeologists have posited on the evidence of material remains. The nineteenth-century observer Pedro Fermín Cevallos (1889:132) seems to have seen yumbo dancers somewhere near Quito, as did Osculati (1959[1850]:309, translation supplied), who says they were "daubed with many colors and adorned with guacamayo plumes, with little seashells, seeds, and other beads, imitating the yumbo savages." The *sacha runa* and *yumbito* ensemble seen by Osculati is still in use in Otón in connection with the Vírgen del Carmen.

2. Characteristically, but not invariably, the patron saints of neighborhood chapels.

3. The parishes where personal observations were conducted include San

Isidro de el Inca, with its *anejos* (nonnucleated Quichua-speaking neighborhoods) of Amagasí and La Victoria (the latter now partly swallowed by the
urban development Ciudadela Kennedy); the *anejo* Carretas of Rumiñahui
parish and nearby *anejo* La Ponciana; *anejo* San Luís of Calderón (Quichua:
Karapungu) parish; and *anejo* Santo Domingo, also of Calderón. Informants
supplied information on performances in places where the *yumbada* is now
rare or defunct, notably Zámbiza, Cotocollao, and Pomasqui, and on certain
zones which I did not visit during Corpus season, including Lloa, Nono, and
Pifo.

4. Both are markedly different from the yumbo costume used in the Valle
de los Chillos variant, which is predominantly white and uses a blond wig.

5. *Yachij* or *yachaj*, literally "one who knows," is a common term meaning
a person who cures disease through use of spirit powers. *Samiyuj*, literally
"possessor of *sami*," means one who is superior to ordinary people by virtue
of exhibiting spirit-bestowed strength and wisdom. The concrete sense of
sami is air or breath. But: "The word *sami* . . . in its verbal form (*saminchay*)
primarily means to bestow a favor which at the same time gives happiness
and does one honor. Lira specifies: 'giving of favors and help by God', possibly from a colonial Quechua adapted to the translation of Christian
thought. This same sense is attested in Paucartambo, in the traditions which
we compiled, within a context that defines it. *Sami* is an attribute of the elite;
or rather, it is that which makes the elite a dominant group and explains its
wisdom and power. . . . It is experience that allows one to detect whether
someone has *sami* or not. . . . The legitimacy of power derives from *sami* as
a gift of God and proof of a privileged relation between God and the Chief.
And if God gives *sami*, he can also take it away" (Delrán 1974:23, translation
supplied). *Sami* continues to exist when it is not invested in a human being,
as the virtue of a plant which absorbs the power of a departed *samiyuj*.

6. In yumbo dancers' descriptions of their experience, personal or vicari-
ous, of lowland shamanistic training, the trainee must bathe repeatedly in a
spring, *pugyu*. Springs are themselves inhabited by female spirits, and in the
water of the spring the bather will find a material gift—"something thrilling,
a beautiful stone, a stone axe, bone, a bottle, a stone with a face"—from the
mountain spirit which favors him.

7. Highly developed in the communities west of the Pan-American Highway, less so or absent in the parishes northeast of Quito.

8. In some performances the *albazo* takes place on the second festal day
before the mass.

9. In communities east of the Pan-American Highway most *mesas* are
served on the ground except for a small table at the head end. In westerly
communities the entire *mesa* is laid out on a line of low trestles.

10. *Charoles* vary considerably by neighborhood. In eastern communities
and in Carretas they are highly developed and performed both in public and
at the *priostes'* houses; in Calderón they are apt to be less lavish and less
public. In Zámbiza they are a "modular" ceremony practiced at most fiestas.

11. Thereby neatly inverting a Canelos Quichua festal game, eating monkey meat and calling it mutton, the archetypal meat of sierran cuisine (Norman E. Whitten, Jr., personal communication).

12. Costales (1968, 2:175) gives additional stanzas of the Pomasqui yumbo
song, some of which are also heard in Calderón area performances.

206 *Cultural Transformations and Ethnicity in Modern Ecuador*

REFERENCES CITED

Acosta, José de
1954[1590] *Historia Natural y Moral de las Indias.* Biblioteca de Autores Españoles 73. Madrid: Ediciones Atlas.
AGI/S (Archivo General de Indias, Sevilla) Quito 8
1580 Carta remitida por la Audiencia de Quito a Su Majestad, tocante a recientes rebeliones en el Oriente, firmada por Francisco de Hinojosa y Francisco de Auncibay. Unpublished.
1584 Carta dirigida a Su Majestad por la Audiencia de Quito, en la cual se presentan recomendaciones para legislación protectora de naturales, firmada por Pedro Venegas de Cañaveral. Unpublished.
Anonymous
1853 Viaje por el Ecuador, por el Napo y el Río de las Esmeraldas. *El Correo de Ultramar, Parte Literaria e Ilustrada* (Paris) 12 (35):556.
Atienza, Lope de
1931[1575?] *Compendio Historial del Estado de los Indios del Perú.* Quito: Editorial Salesiana.
Ávila, Francisco de, comp.
1966[1598?] *Dioses y Hombres de Huarochirí.* Trans. José Maria Arguedas. Lima: Museo Nacional de Historia e Instituto de Estudios Peruanos.
Beals, Ralph
1966 *Community in Transition: Nayón, Ecuador.* Los Angeles: Latin American Center, UCLA.
Belote, Jim, and Linda Belote
1977 El Sistema de Cargos de Fiestas en Saraguro. Trans. V. Sotomayor de Bahnak. In Marcelo F. Naranjo, José L. Pereira V., and Norman E. Whitten, Jr., eds., *Temas sobre la Continuidad y Adaptación Cultural Ecuatoriana.* Quito: Centro de Publicaciones, Pontificia Universidad Católica del Ecuador, pp. 47–73.
Buitrón, Aníbal
1949 Fiestas Indígenas en Otavalo: San Luís. *Boletín de Informaciones Científicas Nacionales* (Quito) 20–21:62–66.
Burgos Guevara, Hugo
1975 El Guaman, el Puma y el Amaru: Formación Estructural del Gobierno Indígena en el Ecuador. Ann Arbor, Mich.: University Microfilms. Ph.D. thesis, University of Illinois, Urbana.
Cabello de Balboa, Miguel
1945[1579?] *Verdadera Descripción y Relación Larga de la Provincia y Tierra de las Esmeraldas, Contenida desde el Cabo Comunmente Llamado Pasao hasta la Bahía de la Buenaventura, que es en la Costa del Mar del Sur, del Reino del Peru. . . .* In Jacinto Jijón y Caamaño, ed., *Obras de Miguel Cabello de Balboa,* vol. 1. Quito: Editorial Ecuatoriana.
1950[1586] *Miscelánea Antártica.* Lima: Facultad de Letras, Universidad Nacional Mayor de San Marcos.
Carvalho-Neto, Paulo de
1964 *Diccionario del Folklore Ecuatoriano.* Quito: Casa de la Cultura Ecuatoriana.
Castro y Velásquez, Juan R.
1976 La Colección Castro: Evaluación Histórico-Etnológico de una Serie

de Pinturas Costumbristas Ecuatorianas del Siglo XIX. M.A. thesis, Seminar for Ethnology, University of Bonn.

Cevallos, Pedro Fermín
1889 *Resumen de la Historia del Ecuador desde su Origen hasta 1845*. Vol. 6. Guayaquil.

Coba Robalino, José Maria
1929 *Monografía General del Cantón Píllaro*. Quito: Tipografía Prensa Católica.

Cobo, Bernabé
1956[1653] *Historia del Nuevo Mundo*. Vol. 2. Biblioteca de Autores Españoles 92. Madrid: Ediciones Atlas.

Costales Samaniego, Alfredo
1960 *Karapungo*. Mexico City: Instituto Panamericano de Geografía e Historia, Publicación 242.
1968 *El Quishihuar, o el Arbol de Diós*. 2 vols. Quito: Instituto Ecuatoriano de Antropología y Geografía, *Llacta* 23–24.

Delrán C., Guido Gerardo
1974 El Sentido de la Historia, Según Tradiciones Campesinas de Paucartambo. *Allpanchis Phuturinqa* (Cuzco) 6:13–28.

Foster, George M.
1960 *Culture and Conquest, America's Spanish Heritage*. Viking Fund Publications in Anthropology 27. Chicago: Quadrangle.

Francisco, Alicia E. de
1971 Factores Culturales en la Historia de las Relaciones entre Sierra y Oriente del Ecuador. *Cuadernos de Historia y Arqueología* (Guayaquil) 21 (38):202–28.

Gow, David D.
1974 Taytacha Ooyllur Rit'i. *Allpanchis Phuturinqa* (Cuzco) 7:49–100.

Gow, Rosalind, and Bernabé Condori
1976 *Kay Pacha*. Cuzco: Centro de Estudios Rurales Andinos "Bartolomé de las Casas."

Jiménez de la Espada, Marcos
1881 Yaravíes Quiteños. *Actas del Cuarto Congreso Internacional de Americanistas* 2:162, i–lxxxxiii. Madrid.

Magnin, Juan
1940[1750] *Breve Descripción de la Provincia de Quito en la America Meridional. Revista de Indias* I. Madrid.

Moreno, Segundo Luís
1949 *Música y Danzas Autóctonas del Ecuador*. Quito: Editorial Fray Jodoco Ricke.
1972 *La Música en el Ecuador*. Vol. 1: *Prehistoria*. Quito: Casa de la Cultura Ecuatoriana.

Murúa, Martín de
1946[1590] *Historia del Origen y Genealogía Real de los Incas*. Madrid.

Oberem, Udo
1971 *Los Quijos: Historia de la Transculturación de un Grupo Indígena en el Oriente Ecuatoriano (1538–1956)*. 2 vols. Madrid: Facultad de Filosofía y Letras, Universidad de Madrid, Departamento de Antropología y Etnología de America, Memorias 1.

Ortiz Rescaniere, Alejandro
1973　*De Adaneva a Inkarrí, una Visión Indígena del Perú.* Lima: Ediciones Retablo de Papel.
Osculati, Gaetano
1959[1850]　(Excerpts from) *Esplorazione delle Regioni Equatoriali lungo il Napo ed il Fiume delle Amazzoni.* In Humberto Toscano, ed., *El Ecuador Visto por los Extranjeros. Viajeros de los Siglos XVIII y XIX.* Puebla, Mexico: Editorial J. M. Cajica.
Polo de Ondegardo, Juan
1916[1559]　*Los Errores y Supersticiones de los Indios, Sacadas del Tratado y Averiguación que Hizo el Licenciado Polo.* Ed. Horacio H. Urteaga. Colección de libros y documentos referentes a la historia del Perú, vol. 3: *Informaciones acerca de la Religión y Gobierno de los Incas por el Licenciado Polo de Ondegardo.* Lima: Imprenta Sanmartí.
Porras, Pedro
1974　*Historia y Arqueología de la Ciudad Española Baeza de los Quijos.* Estudios Científicos sobre el Oriente Ecuatoriano 1. Quito: Centro de Publicaciones, Pontificia Universidad Católica del Ecuador.
Roel Pineda, Josafat
1950　La Danza de los "C'uncos" [sic] de Paucartambo. *Tradición* (Cuzco) 1 (1):59–70.
Rothenberg, Jerome
1968　*Technicians of the Sacred.* Garden City, N.Y.: Doubleday.
Sallnow, Michael J.
1974　La Peregrinación Andina. *Allpanchis Phuturinqa* (Cuzco) 7:101–42.
Salomon, Frank
1978　Ethnic Lords of Quito in the Age of the Incas: The Political Economy of North-Andean Chiefdoms. Ann Arbor, Mich.: University Microfilms. Ph.D. thesis, Cornell University.
Santiana, Antonio
1948–49　Los Indios Mojanda, Etnografía y Folklore. *Revista Filosofía y Letras* (Quito) 4–5:238–74.
Vásquez, Emilio
1950–51　Los Ch'unchos. *Revista del Museo Nacional* (Lima) 19–20:283–98.

PART II:
INFRASTRUCTURE AND
SOCIOECONOMIC PROCESSES

6

Ecuadorian Transformations: An Urban View

DeWight R. Middleton

Ecuador, a country of the Third World, appears today to be a rapidly developing nation. Oil is flowing from her Amazonian provinces, her tuna fleet is growing, modern machinery of various kinds is being imported as never before, and the construction industry is thriving. Like many other developing countries, however, these appearances can be deceiving, for beneath this apparent growth lurks the real world of finite resources, political intrigue, unbalanced regional development, and marked ethnic and class divisions.

The striking socioeconomic forces now transforming Ecuadorian culture and society in particular regions and at various levels must ultimately be understood in the context of national economic development and the national system of urban centers. Urban centers are often crucibles of rapid change, or "theatres of modernization" (Morse 1974:485), because they are centers of innovation, influence, and power, and because the problems of change are focused in dramatic ways. Urban centers are growth poles of development and relay points for the transmission of national culture throughout the urban system and into the hinterlands. This urban view of Ecuadorian national development is not intended to relegate to the hinterlands the character of a passive, inert domain, because such a view is neither conceptually warranted nor empirically accurate. Indeed, neither social scientists nor the people they study can avoid the imposing work-a-day reality of the rural-urban dynamic, perhaps most visible in the magnitude of cityward migration throughout much of Ecuador. Moreover, an urban view of Ecuadorian change does not necessarily restrict discussion to the few large cities of the nation but, rather, includes potentially any population concentration that radiates political, economic, and cultural influence into its surrounding region. Puyo, for example, has only recently attained a population of 10,000, but in the sparsely populated jungles of the Oriente it is a growth pole and the principal purveyor of national culture. On a national level, however, Puyo has none of the influence wielded by the coastal port city of Guayaquil or the highland capital of Quito.

In developing an urban view of Ecuadorian development, this analysis will proceed in the following stages. First, an abstract model of the basic features of an urban system will be presented. Second, this abstract model will provide an analytical guide for explicating the details of the urban system in Ecuador. Third, the role of the urban system in Ecuadorian development will be examined with respect to theories of dependency and development.

THE URBAN SYSTEM

Before constructing a detailed model of the urban system in Ecuador, it would be useful to look at some of the key elements of urban systems in more abstract terms (Friedmann 1971:170–71). First, an urban system links together settlements of various size and importance and degree of independence, which are not uniformly distributed over the landscape (nor are they randomly distributed because of historical and ecological variables). Second, some of these localities may be sources of development, while others simply relay or respond to the impulses for development which emanate from elsewhere. Thus Puyo largely responds to impulses generated in Quito. Third, each region contains a core from which vectors of power and influence pulsate outward to the periphery. Although dependent on Quito, Puyo is the core of its region and wields power and influence. Fourth, internal migration is one form of communication between the nodes of the system, and is a primary mechanism by which manpower can be mobilized for development (Hoselitz 1969:233). Finally, an urban system is linked by networks of communication and transportation.

Delineating a system of urban centers and its role in national development offers several advantages over the more common restricted view that focuses on a primate city or a pair of dominant cities. The more restricted view, however, does reflect a degree of reality and is worth exploring for a moment in anticipation of later arguments.

Many underdeveloped nations of the world emerged from their colonial dependence with a single, dominant metropolis—a primate city—that functions as the center of national economic, political, and cultural influence. Such an urban center is generally also the political capital of the country. In advanced countries Paris is an example of a primate city. In Latin America Buenos Aires, Lima, Montevideo, and Santiago are primate cities as well as political capitals. Quito and Guayaquil, and Río de Janeiro and São Paulo, are examples of twin primate cities, and Guayaquil and both Brazilian cities are examples of cities that are larger than the capitals of Quito and Brazilia. Primacy is a characteristic of underdeveloped countries, usually with a colonial past, that are small in size, dependent on agriculture and exports, have a low per capita income, and feature a rapid rate of growth. Once a city has established sufficient dominance, it draws unto itself even more influence, thus hindering the development of cities in other regions of the country (see Jefferson 1939). The primate city acts as a magnet with an unusually large field of force that captures increasing increments of industry, services, capital, and people; the center continues to grow at the expense of the periphery. If the highly publicized urban problems of squatter settlements, housing shortages, crime, and poverty are combined with primacy, then it is easy to explain why the great cities of Latin America have received the greater share of interest among urban scholars. Conceding that there has been sufficient and compelling reason to lavish scholarly attention on cities of the first rank, however, is not to endorse this approach as the only, or the most desirable, course of action. Such a conceptualization is far too limited to produce full understanding of the complex dynamics of national development in the context of underdevelopment, as the case of Ecuador will demonstrate.

THE URBAN SYSTEM OF ECUADOR

The urban system of Ecuador today has roots firmly imbedded in the colonial past. The location of urban centers and the direction of lines of communication and transportation give stark testimony to the consuming interests of Spain: the extraction of raw materials and the establishment of administrative control through various urban centers. Colonial urban centers were often highly dependent on regional mineral and agricultural resources, and went into decline as productivity dropped. Because urban centers were located and connected in a manner calculated to remove efficiently the various resources of the hinterlands to the major ports of the coast and thence to Europe, the urban systems of Latin America, including Ecuador, were outward-looking.

Guayaquil was founded in 1537 to serve as an outlet for Quito and the mining centers of the southern highlands of Ecuador. The extensive network of major rivers and estuaries merging to form the

Guayas River provided an easy and inexpensive avenue of travel inland until reaching the treacherous foothills of the Andes, where mule tracks became the only means of transportation. For more than two centuries Guayaquil was dominated by Lima, the principal political center of the vice-royalty of Peru, and its satellite port, Callao. Yet the citizens struggled tenaciously to develop their fledgling port and to expand the city's influence. Guayaquil's shipyards became famous throughout the Americas, and the port engaged in illicit as well as legal trade with Panama, Mexico, and other Latin American colonies. By the eighteenth century the city reached a population of 8,000 (Hamerly 1970:12). In the nineteenth century the city's growth was stimulated particularly by increasing production in cacao planted along the rivers of the Guayas basin. Early varieties of cacao thrived on river banks, and thus cultivation assumed a linear configuration, and the presence of the river for transportation made capital investments low and planting financially attractive (Weinman 1970:56). Settlement patterns naturally followed the riparian pattern, although owners of upriver estates usually maintained permanent residence in Guayaquil. Cacao production reached its peak from 1890 to 1925—Ecuador was the world's leading exporter of cacao—but the boom busted in the 1920s, precipitating the migration of workers to Guayaquil (Moore 1978:184).

Although other small ports such as Manta, Bahía de Caráquez, and Esmeraldas existed to the north of Guayaquil, none approached Guayaquil's importance. One reason for their relative unimportance was that their hinterlands did not support sustained commercial or agricultural development. Bahía was the site of experiments in the production of cacao, but they were largely unsuccessful. Much of the province of Manabí, located on Ecuador's arid central coast, was devoid of large agricultural interests. These ports were also more susceptible to pirate attacks than was Guayaquil, which lay about 55 kilometers up the Guayas River.

As Guayaquil continued to develop and cacao production accelerated, the city, and the Guayas basin generally, began to attract substantial numbers of migrants from the highlands and from other parts of the coast. As a result of her economic prosperity, Guayaquil surpassed Quito in population in the late 1800s (Estrada 1977:x, Moore 1978:183), and the Coast doubled its share of the total population from 7% in 1765 to 14% by 1825 (Hamerly 1970:71).

In contrast to Guayaquil, the highland capital of Quito was an administrative outpost of the Inca. And where the Spanish colonial empire was outward-looking, the Inca state was internally inspired and its hegemony extended throughout the highlands. Although it is possible that the Inca conducted trade with the Coast, it is not at all clear whether there was any formal political relationship between the Inca and coastal peoples (Murra 1963:804). The hinterlands of Quito were not rich in agricultural resources, and the importance of Quito was largely political and administrative. Moreover, in the eighteenth and nineteenth centuries the highlands became economically stagnant, experienced declining agricultural productivity, and suffered numerous and damaging earthquakes (Hamerly 1970:68–71). In addition, mines throughout the highlands began to peter out. As the highlands declined, productivity of the Coast in cacao and sugar, and later in bananas, became the dominant economic force in the republic.

The urban pattern which emerged under colonial rule was consolidated during the republican period and exhibited the following characteristics: two dominant cities, one administrative in function and the other commercial; poorly developed interregional ties of commerce and transportation; early establishment of major migration routes from the highlands and other parts of the coast to Guayaquil; and the early commitment of the Coast to monoculture for export. With these basic features in mind, it is now convenient to examine the elements of the contemporary urban system.

Ecuador is a nation of some seven million (Wilkie 1976:15) inhabitants, with an annual average growth rate now calculated at 3.5%, placing it in the sixth rank among all nations in this respect in spite of the fact that it ranks 69th in total population (Wilkie 1976:29). The regional imbalances in Ecuador's development are also reflected in the distribution of the population. The coastal province of Guayas contains 23% (1,512,832) of the total population, while the highland province of Pichincha, where Quito is located, has 15% (981,053), closely followed by Manabí on the central coast at 12% (808,615) (Wilkie 1976:29). In these three provinces live one-half of the total population of Ecuador. None of the other 17 provinces exceeds 6%, and those of the Oriente fall below 1% each. The emerging urban character of this underdeveloped country is seen in the fact that the percentage of the urban population rose from almost 26% in 1960 to 30% in 1970 (Wilkie 1976:30).

Guayaquil has grown from a population of nearly 90,000 in 1864 to 860,000 in the early 1970s, almost 14% of the national population. Quito has grown from about 95,000 in 1864 to 564,000, or almost 9% of the national figure. The third largest city is the highland center of Cuenca at 104,667, followed by another highland center, Ambato, at

77,052 (Moore 1978:182). The coastal cities of Machala (68,379), Manta (63,514), and Portoviejo (59,404) are of intermediate size, with the highland centers of Riobamba (58,029) and Loja (47,268) falling at the lower end of the category (Moore 1978:182).

The rate of growth of each of these centers is for the most part high. Between 1950 and 1974 the population of Guayaquil trebled (Moore 1978). While calculations of growth rate can vary several percentage points, Guayaquil's rate is put generally at 6% or better for the period 1950–62 (Moore 1978:186, Hurtado 1969:23, Estrada 1977:217); it appears to have fallen off a percentage point or two in recent years (Moore 1978:186, Estrada 1977:217). Other coastal cities have experienced growth rates of similar magnitude, exceeding all highland cities except Quito and Ambato (the latter is an important link to the developing Amazonian provinces). Much of the growth of these coastal centers was stimulated by the extension of banana production to the north and south of the Guayas basin. North of Guayaquil, for example, Quevedo's growth rate between 1950 and 1962 was nearly 14% and the port city of Esmeraldas about 8%, and to the south Machala had a rate of growth of 12% (Hurtado 1969:23). The Manabí capital of Portoviejo demonstrated a growth of nearly 6% during the intercensal period and the booming Manabí port of Manta nearly 5%, but Manta has since overtaken Portoviejo in total population.

The urban system of Ecuador manifests regionalism on two levels. On the first level regionalism is expressed in terms of different core urban centers and their peripheral regions reinforced by marked geographical variations; on the second level these regions are collected together in the dominating regionalism of the highland/coastal distinction, with Quito and Guayaquil at the centers. Because of Quito's desire for a northern port to lessen its dependence on Guayaquil, even this national expression of regionalism is overlain by a northern/southern political split (Whitten 1965), suggesting that a third level of regionalism is well within the bounds of accurate conceptualization. These multiple layers of Ecuadorian regionalism have real and dramatic impact on national politics and development, a point that will be explored further in the next section.

Highland urban centers are distributed north to south in a series of intermontane basins formed by the two cordilleras of the Andes, and are linked to each other by air routes and by the Pan-American Highway. The core urban centers of these basins constitute administrative and major retail distribution centers, fed by secondary Indian markets controlled by *mestizos* (Burgos 1970, Bromley 1973). A hierarchy of regional markets is one of the most effective organizers of people and landscape, and often is an indicator of the actual source of political power and economic control in the region (Johnson 1970:3). Burgos (1970) substantiates this view in his study of Riobamba and its region. He is able to delineate the articulation of rural Indians with urban *mestizos* through the mechanism of the regional market system. Burgos argues that rather than being isolated in peripheral communities, rural Indians are actually an integral part of the national political and economic system; since this system is one of internal colonialism, however, their participation is decidedly unequal.

In his study of ethnic identity and stratification in the northern highlands, Stutzman (1974) notes the steady movement of Indians and blacks from the haciendas of the region to the barrios of the city of Ibarra (see Bromley 1974 for historical perspective on migration in the central highlands). Cityward migration is caused by the attraction of higher wages combined with negative rural factors such as surplus agricultural labor and a restrictive land tenure system. Although wages are higher in the city, this fact is offset by inflation and by the loss of subsistence farming as a basis of survival—something to which migrants were entitled on the hacienda. Hoe labor, cane cutting, cargo handling, and construction labor are the main sources of income for lower-class blacks. Only 5% of the blacks qualify objectively for middle-class status. The white urban elite dominates the region as they have since the colonial period.

On the coast six urban centers are particularly important as dynamic centers of growth: Guayaquil, Manta, Esmeraldas, Santo Domingo, Quevedo, and Machala. Little ethnographic information is available for the latter two. The dominance of Guayaquil is a function of its terminal position in a "dendritic system" (Johnson 1970:87–89). That is, all transportation routes, and consequently the flow of natural resources, are directed to the port. Dendritic systems are usually the legacy of colonial exploitation, where a "vertical" market operates to supply the colonial power with raw materials, with the consequence of retarding the development of "horizontal" (internal) markets based on regional interdependency.[1] Guayaquil's explosive growth during the cacao-exporting era was renewed with the production of bananas, which reached a total of 63% of total exports by 1959 (Watkins 1967:2). In the mid-1960s the banana boom collapsed and migration to Guayaquil increased further, as it had in the aftermath of the cacao bust, because workers had few alternatives in the rural areas. Although Guayaquil has developed a substantial industrial sector compared to the remainder of the country, it is not sufficient to meet the demand of migrants from producing areas who leave with each plunge in the level of production. As a consequence of this set of factors, peripheral settlements have since 1950 grown at double the rate of the city, and now constitute over 50% of the city population (Moore 1978:186), overwhelming labor demand and housing supply (Moore 1978:187).

The port city of Manta is one of the most dynamic urban centers in Ecuador (Middleton 1974, 1976, 1977; Naranjo 1978). Home of the Ecuadorian tuna fishing fleet, and a primary outlet for agro-industrial enterprises of the central interior coast, Manta is an industrial city that has experienced a decade of boom in construction and economic development. The proportion of the urban population devoted to traditional fishing, once the bulk of the citizenry, has dwindled sharply as fishermen increasingly seek work on the industrial tuna boats or take other wage labor. Most of the remaining traditional canoes are now equipped with motors, and the fishermen are deep in debt. The growth of Manta has attracted migrants from Manabí and other parts of the coast, and a few, especially technical experts, from the highlands. Some squatter settlements have appeared lately. The relationship of Manta to nearby Portoviejo replicates on small scale the relationship that attains between Quito and Guayaquil. Portoviejo is the provincial administrative center, while Manta is the booming commercial and port city. Indeed, a lively animosity pervades their relationship: Mantenses feel that they generate capital while bureaucrats in Portoviejo seek ways to appropriate it. Exactly what problems this rivalry has presented regional development is uncertain, but in one case it delayed the construction of an all-weather road from Portoviejo to Manta for several years.

The major urban center of the northwest coast is Esmeraldas. No ethnographic data are available on this area except from Whitten's (1974) general work on the region. In spite of the increasing urbanization of Esmeraldas, Whitten (1974:93) observed the "ruralization" of the black barrios—a persistence of rural settlement life in music and ritual. This persistence of rural life in the urban context is encouraged by the exclusion of blacks from full participation in the national and urban culture because of their ethnic identity. Whitten further describes the liveliness of boom towns which flash briefly in the resource frontiers of the rainforest but are quickly extinguished for lack of a constant supply of economic fuel and become decaying bust towns. Social mobility in the city of Esmeraldas and in towns like its satellite, San Lorenzo, depends on personal networks of kin and friend spatially well spread throughout the periphery and frontier regions. Maintaining these networks demands incessant river travel among the city, towns, and hamlets of the heavily forested and swampy area of the northwest coast region. In his earlier work on San Lorenzo, Whitten (1965) writes of the structural and cultural ramifications of the arrival of white and *mestizo* highlanders in the essentially black town, resulting in the reorganization of ethnic diversity into a replication of highland, that is to say national, patterns of stratification. Such reorganization included the idea of the exclusion of blacks from access to power and capital, as well as from the opportunity to live in some parts of town (see Schubert, in this volume).

Santo Domingo de los Colorados, located in the foothills of the Andes where the rainfall is heavy and the rivers are rapid and boiling, was until the mid-twentieth century linked to Quito only by foot trail and mule track. By the 1950s a dirt road had been carved out of the treacherous flanks of the western cordillera, and the trickle of migrants from the highlands and the Coast turned into a flood. A new, all-weather road was finished in 1962, and the frontier town of 3,000–5,000 (Casagrande, Thompson, and Young 1964:307) is today an urban center exceeding 40,000. Banana production in the Santo Domingo region was increased first for internal markets, particularly Quito, and then for export through the port of Esmeraldas. Migration to the area has been encouraged by national agricultural development programs with varying success.

Another frontier town being transformed into a node of the national urban system is Puyo, in the Oriente. Whitten (1976) has provided an account of development and population movement in this area. From Baños to Puyo, and thence throughout the Oriente, highlanders and rich foreigners came during the 1930s to exploit the jungle. In the era following World War II the town of Puyo was the "locus for most brokerage functions between eastern jungles and expanding nationalistic controls" (Whitten 1976:235). With the discovery of oil and government sponsorship of planned colonization, Puyo, a town of about 4,000 in 1962, attained a population of 10,000 by 1972. The competition of the national bureaucracy and expanding foreign interests in plantations and oil exploration seriously threatens the Indian population. Almost all Indians, in fact, have been forced out of Puyo back to their hamlets where they creatively seek to maintain their identity and to ensure cultural survival while selectively interacting with bearers of urban and national culture (see D. Whitten, in this volume).

The major patterns of internal migration were established during the colonial period in the movement from the highlands to the Coast, coastal migrations to Guayaquil, and highland migrations to Quito. Coastward migration from the highlands has been ample but not always permanent. A pattern of circular migration to the Coast and back to the highland point of origin traditionally was channeled through the *enganchador* (Lang 1968), a system of labor recruitment for coastal haciendas in which foremen from the haciendas recruited workers from the same communities each year. Migrants then, as now, complained about the humid lowland climate, the threats to health, and the different customs, not to mention the animosity they were shown by *costeños.* Yet they still came because the opportunity to acquire cash was better than in the highlands. This remains the case today.

It is estimated that between 1950 and 1962 30% of the population migrated internally (Estrada 1977:262). During this period Quito received 95,000 migrants and Guayaquil 145,000. Quito received 20% of her migrants from the Coast in this period, and Guayaquil received 36% from the highlands. In 1975 (Estrada 1977:265) 23% of Guayaquil's population originated on the Coast, particularly from the adjacent provinces of Manabí and Los Rios, and over 9% from the highlands; only 4% of the total population of Quito came from the Coast, and 36% from the highlands.

A second pattern is the movement of rural individuals to the immediate regional urban center. Stutzman (1974) documents this pattern for Ibarra, Whitten (1965, 1974) for the northwest coast centers of San Lorenzo and Esmeraldas, and Middleton (1974) and Naranjo (1978) for Manta. An undetermined number of these intraregional migrants come not from rural hamlets and their own garden plots but directly from smaller towns and villages.

A third pattern of migration is associated with development of frontier areas such as Santo Domingo and Puyo. The pioneer settlement program for the Santo Domingo area was begun in 1957 by the Instituto Nacional de Colonización (INC) as a joint American-Ecuadorian plan to colonize the area, but was generally a failure (Hurtado 1969:67, Eisenlohr 1969). Encouraged by the Ecuadorian government, spontaneous settlement began in 1963 and has been more successful. In addition to the influx of workers and independent colonists, the Oriente has been developed by the Instituto Ecuatoriano de Reforma Agraria y Colonización (IERAC), and in the early 1970s some 10,000 settlers, mostly from the drought-stricken southern province of Loja, poured into the Aguarico area north of Puyo (Crist and Nissly 1973:82). The motivations for migrating are not difficult to ascertain, nor are they unusual. They generally are combinations of lack of land, low agricultural productivity, and better opportunities in the city with respect to work, education, and health. Burgos (1970:88–89) reports that the principal direction of out-migration in Riobamba is to the Coast. Lacking land, migrants seek to earn cash on the Coast in order to return to their highland community, to purchase land, and to participate more effectively in the community fiestas. Scrimshaw (1974:41) reports that migrants enter Guayaquil at a young age (between 15 and 25) to look for work which they usually find through a network of friends (see also Scrimshaw, in this volume).

In the past decade the amount and quality of social science information on Ecuador have vastly improved. This brief survey of the basic features of the urban system, however, reveals some important gaps. One would like to know more, for example, about such urban centers as Machala, Quevedo, and Cuenca. Nevertheless, enough has been done to see not only the growth of particular cities and regions but also how they are linked together in a national system. The growth of intermediate cities such as Manta and Esmeraldas unfortunately seems to be due to a combination of limited opportunity in the city and stagnation in other towns and rural areas. The magnitude of these problems is better visualized in a discussion of planning and development.

CITIES, DEVELOPMENT, AND DEPENDENCY

Many planners have stressed the need to strengthen regional development as a means of equalizing spatial and economic opportunities to offset cityward migration. Their agreement applies particularly to Ecuadorian cities where lack of industry is related to inadequate employment opportunities. As Bromley (1977:30) notes, urbanization in Ecuador is due partly to the undeveloped agriculture sector, particularly the end of the banana boom, and partly to the failure of real agrarian reform in providing land in the eastern and coastal lowlands. The classic western model of urbanization, of course, would require increasing productivity in the rural sector through the use of machines and fertilizers, and outward migration to the industrializing city. But development is never uniformly distributed even in advanced nations. The American South is only now experiencing the growth of industry, cities, and crime, while areas of the Northeast are declining in these aspects. Development plans often call for the encouragement of a thriving urban center in each region from which technology and material rewards will diffuse to lower-rank cities, towns, and peripheral areas. Regional planning calls for the location of industries, where they might not otherwise want to locate, through the inducement of tax breaks or other considerations to compensate for their distance from large cities and major routes of transportation.

Many of the development plans of the Third World have been designed with the intention of removing "obstacles" to change, but on closer examination most of these obstacles appear to represent merely departures from the western European and American models of urbanization and industrialization. Indeed, some development experts believe that many of these obstacles were either nonexistent, neutral, or actually positive for change (Hirschman 1972).

Development plans abound throughout Latin America but often seem ineffective in performance. The reasons for their failure are many and complex (see Hardoy 1975, Browning and Portes 1976, Cornelius and Kemper 1978, Friedmann 1966, Gakenheimer and Miller 1971, Herrick 1965), as will be seen in the case of Ecuador, but many of these reasons have been collected as interlinked phenomena under the rubric of dependency theory. There are several varieties of dependency theory (see Chilcote 1978, Smith 1978, and Walton 1975), including internal colonialism. Gunder Frank (1969) formulated one of the earliest and most influential statements on dependency, and Stavenhagen (1969) contributed the notion of internal colonialism. Generally dependency theorists argue, and few critics quarrel with the fact, that since the colonial period the countries of Latin America have been dependent on the capitalistic world, continuing to supply it with the natural resources to feed their insatiable industries. Elite Latin Americans benefited from this dependent relationship and found it to their advantage to continue the relationship after separation, failing thus to capitalize local industry, to promote interregional linkages, and to develop an adequate national infrastructure. The countries of Latin America lie on the periphery of the capitalistic world and are unequally integrated into it.

This model of center and periphery is replicated internally in a given country where cities are centers, or cores, and the hinterlands the periphery. The view of the role of the city in this formulation is quite different from that advocated by development planners. Instead of being the generator of development, the city becomes the machinery of underdevelopment. Cities are the centers not of technological diffusion but of power and influence that leave their peripheral regions decapitalized, thus forcing peasants into the city in search of low-paying jobs. Moreover, because national capitalists are not really nationalistic, they make economic decisions based on non-local interests. Thus Gunder Frank (1969:69) argues that the very nature of capitalistic economic development contains within it the seeds of underdevelopment. Underdevelopment will not disappear in the face of planning because it is a function of international capitalism.

A number of criticisms and modifications of dependency theory have appeared recently (Chilcote 1978, Gonzalez 1974, Ray 1973, Smith 1978, Walton 1975), but regardless of one's theoretical predilection, it is clear to many that dependency theorists have exposed some blind spots in the philosophical and theoretical underpinnings of development planning, and have cast a cold, analytical eye on the harsh disparity between rhetoric and achievement. Unfortunately, dependency theorists assiduously adhere to a rhetoric of their own which sometimes obfuscates issues. In any event, the case of Ecuador reveals the substance of many of their concerns.

Marked regional disparities and deep social divisions are two of the profound problems with which plans of development must cope in Ecuador. The highland-coastal regionalism is a very real one as reflected in differences in population, productivity, investments, and industrial establishments. By 1972 the Coast contained 54.3% of the population (Bromley 1977:27, 29) and produced over half of the food consumed by Eduadorians. The provincial distribution of investments also clearly indicates regional imbalance, as does the establishment of industry primarily in Pichincha, Guayas, and Manabí (Bromley 1977:34, Hurtado 1969:93). The regional attitudes and animosities mentioned previously also hinder development (Bromley 1977:28)— the northern highlands are a particularly relevant case of this (Bromley 1977:99)—and persist in spite of improved travel and telecommunications which have reduced physical isolation. Generally, investments and industrialization have been allowed to follow the wishes of the private sector rather than those of planners, and government investments have largely followed the same laissez-faire policy (Bromley 1977:9, Moore 1978:194).

Ecuadorian social stratification is characterized by severe economic and status distinctions complicated further by ethnic and racial discrimination. It features a small, poorly organized elite, a small and amorphous middle class, and a huge lower class. Bromley (1977:40) cites evidence by Torres Caicedo (1960:28) that gives the following class distribution: upper class 1.2%, middle class 20.7%, and lower class 78.1%. Since rural and urban dimensions of class structure are important, Hurtado (1969:176) puts the *urban* upper class at 1%, the urban middle class at 13%, and the urban lower class at 36%. Perhaps

75% of the urban population, however, might be better characterized as subproletariat because of the prevalence of unemployment and underemployment (Bromley 1977:42). The middle class has little identity because it emulates the upper class, which in turn emulates foreign values and interests. These class divisions are exacerbated by hostility toward blacks and Indians and their exclusion from full participation in development. These processes of discrimination are amply documented throughout this volume.

Bromley (1977:v) notes in his cogent analysis of Ecuadorian development plans that development and planning are disjointed but that dependency is a common element of both. Dependency is seen not only in the nature of development and planning but also in the values and interests of the elite. Hence development in Ecuador is really a case of changing dependency relationships (Bromley 1977:iii). Planning in Ecuador began in the 1940s, and since then five major plans have been promulgated, in 1958, 1961, 1963, 1969, and 1972. Under the best of circumstances, Ecuador would be a difficult country to develop because of interregional rivalry, wide social and ethnic divisions, and economic instability. But long-term planning has been encouraged by such nonlocal organizations as the United Nations Economic Commission for Latin America, the World Bank, the Organization of American States, and the Alliance for Progress (1961–66). Generally, these plans have been ineffective.

Several general problems plague Ecuadorian development schemes. Initially, they were concerned with import substitution, but this action has not proved to be effective for the general good of Ecuador (Bromley 1977:15). Indeed, during the first four years of the 1963 plan the import restrictions were guided more by the foreign exchange balance, owing to the decline of banana production, than by the success of the plan (Moore 1978:193). A second problem is the overemphasis on technical details and diagnostic statements and insufficient attention to social and political realities (Bromley 1977:68, Moore 1978:193). A third general problem is the lack of coordination among different levels of government or, worse, between planning agencies and those responsible for implementation (Bromley 1977:68, Moore 1978:193–95). Development planning demands a high degree of economic expertise, bureaucratic coordination, and political support that most Third World countries find difficult to achieve (Cornelius 1975:21), and this is certainly true of Ecuador. It should be noted, however, that the planners in various countries of Latin America are technically quite competent with regard to western techniques; many trained in the United States (Bottomley 1972). Unfortunately, technical perfection is little guarantee of success. One of the more difficult problems in planning, for example, is controlling the private economy sector where the decision processes normally lie outside the domain of government. Finally, these plans show no real commitment to change or allowance for popular participation in the planning process, either at the national or the urban level (Bromley 1977:70, Moore 1978:197). The rhetoric and accompanying lack of achievement suggest that these plans often have more political than economic significance. Shifting development from the center to the periphery simply has lacked commitment and coordinated effort, to the continuing benefit of the center (Bromley 1977:33).

The failure of development plans in Ecuador is partly due to the "metropolitan attitudes and technocratic approach of the planners" (Bromley 1977:72). An analysis of the details of some of the plans reveals one reason why they fail. The execution of the plan is left largely to the private sector, which controls the technical skill to develop local programs by which the national scheme is implemented. The plan of 1963, for example, called for "development poles" but did not specify which urban centers would be involved (Moore 1978:174). As a result, the initiative for local planning and coordination was left to cantonal councils. The rhetoric of the plan was industrial decentralization, but the only centers with the technical and administrative ability to devise such a plan were Guayaquil and Quito. As Moore (1978:195) notes, those "high need, low technical and resource zones cannot compete with the existing development poles." A specific example of this reinforcement of present strengths is seen in the Banco Ecuatoriano de Vivienda (BEV) housing program in cities initiated in 1962. By 1974 Guayaquil and Quito accounted for 88% of all BEV housing (Moore 1978:195).

Metropolitan planning, where it has existed at all, has been plagued with some of the same problems as general planning. Typically, urban plans have been "reactive" rather than innovative (Moore 1978:198). Plans for urban development in Guayaquil have been technically sophisticated but politically and socially naive—although this condition certainly is not unique to Ecuador or to Latin America. Such plans concentrate on the physical problems of the city such as unsightly housing, transportation, and services, and ignore the reasons for their existence in the first place; they assume that the city is a self-contained unit. Attempts to remedy problems of the inner city ghetto, *turgurio*, and peripheral invasion settlements, *suburbios*, have not only been inadequate to deal with the specific problems but also have not been linked with regional development and to the growth of intermediate cities, and thus ignore the opportunity to alleviate some of the external sources of Guayaquil's growth.

The expansion of the tertiary service sector throughout the urban system unfortunately reflects not an increase in per capita income or a new affluence but the lack of sufficient industrialization to provide adequate jobs. The jobs of the poor lie in the domain of underemployment and include shoe shining, domestic service, porterage, and petty commercial activity. A steady supply of migrants contributes to a cheap labor supply, and native Guayaquileños complain about the willingness of highland peasants to work for lower wages (Estrada 1977:11).

The military, like civil servants and politicians, has been generally developmentalist in its approach to coping with Ecuador's many problems. The military junta of 1963–66 and the recent military regime of Rodríguez Lara have been heavily involved in planning. Bromley (1977:61) notes that "the armed forces have been granted substantial areas of land for urban housing schemes, rural colonization projects, and whole neighborhoods are now inhabited by serving and retired military personnel." A program commenced in 1972 by the military (the Integrated Plan of National Transformation and Development 1973–77) included the allotment of 563 million sucres for public housing in Guayaquil, but most of it went, in fact, for middle-class housing, with little finally finding its way to lower-class neighborhoods (Moore 1978:195). In addition, rural land invasions of Guayaquil have not been tolerated by the military. Other efforts by the armed forces include physical improvements of the *suburbios*, provision of "grocery stores on wheels," and sponsorship of weekend markets—all accompanied by signs exclaiming that the armed forces are working for the Ecuadorian people. In 1975 the government began the Plan Integrado para la Rehabilitación de Areas Marginales (PREDAM), which is ambitious and does include social and economic projects to accompany physical rehabilitation. This plan, as others, is imposed from above without popular participation.

DEVELOPMENT AND LEGITIMACY

The development process is never just an economic endeavor, but is always a complex interplay of economic, social, political, and spatial factors. For it to be implemented effectively, the cooperation and support of various parts of the private and public sectors must be secured. This support is seldom an integral part of planned development, but politicians seek it instinctively with varying degrees of success. Boulding (1972:24) defines legitimacy as covering diverse social phenomena but ". . . centering around the concept of acceptance of an institution or an organization as right, proper, justified and acceptable." From an economic perspective, legitimacy may be considered a resource—if legitimacy building is successful, groups will make sacrifices as they are called for by authorities, and the expenditure of other resources is thus not required. Building legitimacy is essentially a process of manipulating values and incentives. National elite groups seek to transform rural traditional values and symbols, often considered obstacles to change, into modern ones more useful to the aims of national development. Legitimacy is an important ingredient in nation building and in rallying support to get jobs done in the public sector, but obviously it can also be used as an end in itself, without necessarily bringing general good to those called upon to sacrifice. Although Ecuadorian development plans have been overwhelmingly technical and economic until recently, Bromley's point above with respect to the largely political significance of economic development cannot be ignored.

The national rhetoric surrounding the "tuna war" and the enforcement of the Ecuadorian 200-mile territorial limit is an example of legitimacy building to the degree that it enhanced the national pride and soothed internal conflicts.[2] Another example of the process is the motto referring to Ecuador as an Amazonian country, which reasserts Ecuador's claim on Amazonian territory (including disputed land with Peru) and reinforces programs of colonization, settlement, infrastructural development, oil exploration, and agricultural development. The military government recently created the "Ecuadorian worker" in an effort to deny the existence of ethnicity as a primary factor in social and class distinctions, in sharp contrast to harsh reality (Casagrande 1974; Naranjo 1978; Stutzman 1974; Whitten 1976:265–69, 1978). It is particularly clear in this case that those in the least favorable position are being asked to sacrifice the most. Those who strive to improve their position may be blocked on the "illegitimate" grounds of ethnicity or class, but will still be required to sacrifice as an "Ecuadorian worker" by working harder for less for the sake of development.

The efficacy of legitimacy building in Ecuador may be questioned because of the disorganized elite, because of constantly shifting political allegiances, and because of the proliferation and capricious use of national constitutions as sources of legitimacy (Bromley 1977:40). The strong regional flavor of politics enters on almost every major issue, and interferes with building national consensus. Entrenched class and ethnic divisions continue unameliorated. Metropolitan planning shows no improvement over national planning because the two are inextricably linked in fact. The problems of underdevelopment are neither urban nor rural; they are national. They are, however, often more sharply focused in the city and they are usually more visible there. The urban centers of Quito and Guayaquil, Manta and Ibarra, San Lorenzo and Puyo, radiate change and development, and yet they are national pressure points, microcosms of the national condition. In this sense, then, cities are truly "theatres of modernization," the stage upon which the drama of change is unfolding.

NOTES

Acknowledgments: I would like to thank Kathleen Fine, Dorothea S. Whitten, and Norman Whitten for their perceptive comments and helpful suggestions on an earlier draft of this paper. I alone am responsible, of course, for whatever deficiencies remain. My own work in Manta on various occasions has been greatly facilitated by the kind and effective assistance of Arquitecto Hernán Crespo Toral and the Instituto Nacional de Antropología e Historia in Quito, and by Viliulfo Cedeño Sanchez in Manta. The 1968 visit was made possible by the Latin American Studies Committee, Washington University, St. Louis. The 1970–71 visit was supported by PHS Fellowship MH40146-01A 1S1 from the National Institute of Mental Health, and the 1973 visit was supported by a State University of New York research fellowship.

1. The concept of dendritic system attempts to explain how and why wholesale marketing and export trade follow different channels from those of retail market distributions, the latter of which conform to central-place theory. G. W. Skinner has observed that dendritic-primate configurations are commonly found in riverine or bounded locations where peripheral development would be retarded or constricted (Smith 1976:34–36). Johnson (1970:82–93) developed the concept, but whether it does, in the final analysis, apply to Guayaquil remains to be shown. As long as major sociological investigations of marketing in Ecuador are restricted to the highlands, we are not likely to reach a very clear understanding of the coastal system.

2. Since Ecuador participates with Chile and Peru in defending an expanded territorial limit, these nations probably could be said to engage in legitimacy building to a degree.

REFERENCES CITED

Bottomley, Anthony
  1972 Planning in an Underutilization Economy: The Case of Ecuador. In Norman T. Uphoff and Warren F. Ilchman, eds., *The Political Economy of Development*. Berkeley: University of California Press, pp. 213–19.

Boulding, Kenneth E.
   1972 The Legitimacy of Economics. In Norman T. Uphoff and Warren F.
         Ilchman, eds., *The Political Economy of Development*. Berkeley: Uni-
         versity of California Press, pp. 24–30.
Bromley, Ray
   1973 Inter-regional Marketing Chains in Ecuador. In R. P. Momsen, Jr.,
         ed., *Geographical Analysis for Development in Latin America and the
         Caribbean*. Chapel Hill, N.C.: CLAG Publications, pp. 115–17.
   1977 *Development Planning in Ecuador*. Sussex, Eng.: Latin American Pub-
         lications Fund.
Bromley, Rosemary D. F.
   1974 Urban-Rural Interrelationships in Colonial Hispanic America: A
         Case Study of Three Andean Towns. *Swansea Geographer* 12:15–22.
Browning, H. L., and A. Portes, eds.
   1976 *Current Perspectives in Latin American Urban Research*. Austin: Institute
         of Latin American Studies and University of Texas Press.
Burgos Guevara, Hugo
   1970 *Relaciones Interétnicas en Riobamba: Dominio y Dependencia en una Re-
         gión Indígena Ecuatoriana*. Mexico City: Instituto Indigenista Inter-
         americano.
Casagrande, Joseph B.
   1974 Strategies for Survival: The Indians of Highland Ecuador. In Dwight
         Heath, ed., *Contemporary Cultures and Societies of Latin America*. 2d
         ed. New York: Random House, pp. 93–107.
Casagrande, Joseph B., Stephen I. Thompson, and Philip D. Young
   1964 Colonization as a Research Frontier: The Ecuadorian Case. In Robert
         A. Manners, ed., *Process and Pattern in Culture: Essays in Honor of
         Julian H. Steward*. Chicago: Aldine, pp. 281–325.
Chilcote, Ronald
   1978 A Question of Dependency. *Latin American Research Review* 13:55–68.
Cornelius, Wayne A.
   1975 Introduction. In Wayne A. Cornelius and Felicity M. Trueblood,
         eds., *Urbanization and Inequality: The Political Economy of Urban and
         Rural Development in Latin America*. Beverly Hills, Calif.: Sage, pp.
         9–25.
Cornelius, Wayne A., and Robert V. Kemper, eds.
   1978 *Metropolitan Latin America: The Challenge and the Response*. Beverly
         Hills, Calif.: Sage.
Crist, Raymond E., and Charles M. Nissly
   1973 *East from the Andes: Pioneer Settlements in the South American Heart-
         land*. Gainesville: University of Florida Press.
Eisenlohr, Edda
   1969 *Agrarreform in Ecuador in Entwicklunas-Politischen Kraftspiel*. Dort-
         mund, West Germany: COSAL.
Estrada Ycaza, Julio
   1977 *Regionalismo y Migración*. Guayaquil: Publicaciones del Archivo
         Histórico del Guayas.
Friedmann, John
   1966 *Regional Dvelopment Policy: A Case Study of Venezuela*. Cambridge:
         MIT Press.

1971   The Role of Cities in National Development. In Ralph A. Gakenhei-
        mer and John Miller, eds., *Latin American Urban Policies and the Social
        Sciences*. Beverly Hills, Calif.: Sage, pp. 167–88.
Gakenheimer, Ralph A., and John Miller, eds.
1971   *Latin American Urban Policies and the Social Sciences*. Beverly Hills,
        Calif.: Sage.
Gonzalez, G.
1974   A Critique of the Internal Colony Model. *Latin American Perspectives*
        1:154–61.
Gunder Frank, André
1969   *Capitalism and Underdevelopment in Latin America: Historical Studies of
        Chile and Brazil*. New York: Monthly Review Press.
Hamerly, Michael T.
1970   A Social and Economic History of the City and District of Guayaquil
        during the Late Colonial and Independence Periods. Ann Arbor,
        Mich.: University Microfilms. Ph.D. thesis, University of Florida.
Hardoy, Jorge, ed.
1975   *Urbanization in Latin America: Approaches and Issues*. Garden City,
        N.Y.: Doubleday.
Herrick, Bruce H.
1965   *Urban Migration and Economic Development in Chile*. Cambridge: MIT
        Press.
Hirschman, Albert O.
1972   Obstacles to Development: A Classification and a Quasi-Vanishing
        Act. In Norman T. Uphoff and Warren F. Ilchman, eds., *The Political
        Economy of Development*. Berkeley: University of California Press, pp.
        55–62.
Hoselitz, Bert F.
1969   The Role of Cities in the Economic Growth of Underdeveloped
        Countries. In Gerald Breese, ed., *The City in Newly Developing Coun-
        tries: Readings on Urbanism and Urbanization*. Englewood Cliffs, N.J.:
        Prentice-Hall, pp. 232–45.
Hurtado, Osvaldo
1969   *Dos Mundos Superpuestos: Ensayo de Diagnóstico de la Realidad Ecuato-
        riana*. Quito: Instituto Ecuatoriano de Planificación para el Desa-
        rrollo Social (INEDES).
Jefferson, Mark
1939   The Law of the Primate Cities. *Geographical Review* 29:226–32.
Johnson, E. A. J.
1970   *The Organization of Space in Developing Countries*. Cambridge, Mass.:
        Harvard University Press.
Lang, Norris
1969   Plutocrats, Managers and Workers: An Analysis of the Social Struc-
        ture of a Coastal Ecuadorian Plantation. Ann Arbor, Mich.: Univer-
        sity Microfilms. Ph.D. thesis, University of Illinois, Urbana.
Middleton, DeWight R.
1974   Neighborhood and City in Coastal Ecuador. *Urban Anthropology*
        3:184–99.
1976   The Growth of a City: Urban, Regional, and National Interaction in
        Ecuador. *Urban Anthropology* 5:125–41.

1977   Changing Economics in an Ecuadorian Maritime Community. In M. Estellie Smith, ed., *Those Who Live from the Sea: A Study in Maritime Anthropology.* Monograph of the American Ethnological Society. New York: West Publishing Co., pp. 114–24.

Moore, Richard J.
1978   Urban Problems and Policy Responses for Metropolitan Guayaquil. In Wayne A. Cornelius and Robert V. Kemper, eds., *Metropolitan Latin America: The Challenge and the Response.* Beverly Hills, Calif.: Sage, pp. 181–203.

Morse, Richard M.
1974   The Claims of Tradition in Urban Latin America. In Dwight Heath, ed., *Contemporary Cultures and Societies of Latin America.* 2d ed. New York: Random House, pp. 480–94.

Murra, John
1948   The Historic Tribes of Ecuador. In Julian H. Steward, ed., *Handbook of South American Indians,* vol. 2: *The Andean Civilizations. Bureau of American Ethnology Bulletin* 143:705–822.

Naranjo, Marcelo F.
1978   Etnicidad, Estructura Social y Poder en Manta, Occidente Ecuatoriano. Ann Arbor, Mich.: University Microfilms. Ph.D. thesis, University of Illinois, Urbana.

Ray, David
1973   The Dependency Model of Latin American Underdevelopment: Three Basic Fallacies. *Journal of Interamerican Studies and World Affairs* 15:4–20.

Scrimshaw, Susan M.
1974   Culture, Environment and Family Size: A Study of Urban In-migrants in Guayaquil, Ecuador. Ann Arbor, Mich.: University Microfilms. Ph.D. thesis, Columbia University.

Smith, Carol A.
1976   *Regional Analysis.* Vol. 1. New York: Academic Press.
1978   Beyond Dependency Theory: National and Regional Patterns of Underdevelopment in Guatemala. *American Ethnologist* 5:574–616.

Stavenhagen, Rodolfo
1975[1969]   *Social Classes in Agrarian Society.* Garden City, N.Y.: Doubleday.

Stutzman, Ronald
1974   Black Highlanders: Racism and Ethnic Stratification in the Ecuadorian Sierra. Ann Arbor, Mich.: University Microfilms. Ph.D. thesis, Washington University, St. Louis.

Walton, John
1975   Internal Colonialism: Problems of Definition and Measurement. In Wayne A. Cornelius and Felicity M. Trueblood, eds., *Urbanization and Inequality: The Political Economy of Urban and Rural Development in Latin America.* Beverly Hills, Calif.: Sage, pp. 29–50.

Watkins, R.
1967   *Expanding Ecuador's Exports.* New York: Praeger.

Weinman, Lois
1970   Ecuador and Cacao: Domestic Response to the Boom-Collapse Mono Export Cycle. Ann Arbor, Mich.: University Microfilms. Ph.D. thesis, UCLA.

Whitten, Norman E., Jr.
  1965   *Class, Kinship, and Power in an Ecuadorian Town: The Negroes of San Lorenzo*. Stanford, Calif.: Stanford University Press.
  1974   *Black Frontiersmen: A South American Case*. New York: Halsted (Wiley).
  1976   (with the assistance of Marcelo F. Naranjo, Marcelo Santi Simbaña, and Dorothea S. Whitten). *Sacha Runa: Ethnicity and Adaptation of Ecuadorian Jungle Quichua*. Urbana: University of Illinois Press.
  1978   *Amazonian Ecuador: An Ethnic Interface in Ecological, Social, and Ideological Perspectives*. Copenhagen: International Work Group for Indigenous Affairs, Document 34.
Wilkie, James W.
  1976   *Statistical Abstract of Latin America*. Vol. 17. Los Angeles: Latin American Center, UCLA.

7

Market Center and Market Place in Highland Ecuador: A Study of Organization, Regulation, and Ethnic Discrimination

Ray Bromley

The aim of this essay is to describe the various forms of organization and regulation found in highland Ecuadorian markets, and the roles played by local officials and entrepreneurial traders in initiating and controlling market activity. It is based upon my 18 months of field research in highland Ecuador in 1970–72; all data are described in the present tense. A market place is any location on public land where ten or more traders[1] gather together one or more times each week for commercial purposes; "market" refers to each regular gathering of traders and consumers. All markets in highland Ecuador are held in nucleated settlements, and each settlement with one or more market places is described as a "market center." The study of organization and regulation within individual market centers and market places was conducted within the framework of a much broader study of periodic and daily markets[2] in highland Ecuador (Bromley 1975a), and included the identification of all the market centers in the highlands, an assessment of their levels of activity and periodicity (Bromley 1975b, 1976), and studies of their origins and historical development (Bromley 1978a, 1978b; Bromley and Bromley 1975). "Highland Ecuador" is defined as the area of Ecuador above an altitude of 1,500 meters which forms a continuous mountain belt averaging 120 kilometers in width and which stretches about 620 kilometers from the Colombian to the Peruvian frontiers.

There are 164 market centers (1971 data) in highland Ecuador, markets being held in all settlements with populations of over 2,200 and in many smaller settlements. All markets are held in nucleated settlements, the great majority of which have at least 600 inhabitants. There are, however, a few cases of markets being held in very small settlements, the smallest of all being Salarón in Chimborazo province, a nucleated settlement with only 13 houses and about 65 inhabitants. The markets themselves range from relatively insignificant weekly gatherings of 10–20 traders and a few local consumers in many small villages and hamlets, to massive gatherings involving from hundreds to thousands of traders and many thousands of consumers. The two largest market centers in the highlands—"size" being measured in terms of volume of market activity—are Quito and Ambato. Quito has primarily daily markets, with substantial periodic fluctuations, averaging about 4,800 traders per day. Ambato has only small daily markets but is famous for its Monday periodic market, which attracts about 50,000 people from outside the city specifically for the market and which has about 6,500 traders (Bromley 1975a:262).

In general, there is a fairly strong correlation between the population of the market centers and their total amounts of market activity each week, and between these two variables and the administrative status of the market centers (Bromley 1975a:153–73). Of the 164 market centers, one, Quito, is the national capital as well as the capital of Pichincha province. Nine others are provincial capitals as well as capitals of their own cantons. Thirty-six others are cantonal capitals, and 107 others are rural parish capitals. Finally, 11 market centers have the lowest possible administrative status, that of *anejo*, rural neighborhood, a subdivision of a rural parish.[3] All of the provincial and cantonal capitals in highland Ecuador have markets, but only just under a third of the parish capitals (107 out of 329) and only a minute proportion of the thousands of *anejos* have them.

The principal administrative bodies dealing with market organization are the municipalities, *municipios*, which are the main governmental authorities for all cantonal capitals. Each municipality has a municipal council, presided over by a mayor, *alcalde*, in the towns which are provincial capitals and by a president in the settlements which are merely cantonal capitals. The municipalities have authority throughout their cantons, though they tend to focus most of their attention upon the cantonal capital. Both the rural parish councils and the communal councils of the *anejos* tend to be very weak and have few powers or resources. At a nationally higher level than the municipalities are the provincial councils, which are based in the provincial capitals. They play an important role in constructing and maintaining intercantonal and local roads but have little to do with markets.

Separate from and parallel to this hierarchy of provincial, municipal, and parish councils is an administrative hierarchy headed by the governor of the province, who is appointed by the national government and is concerned primarily with the maintenance of law and order. The governor is represented in each canton, including the canton of the provincial capital, by a *jefe político*, political chief, and in every rural parish by a *teniente político*, political lieutenant. The dual civil hierarchies are paralleled by the ecclesiastical hierarchy of the Catholic church, with provinces generally being equivalent to dioceses and with most of the rural parishes also being ecclesiastical parishes.

MARKET ADMINISTRATION

In the provincial and cantonal capitals of highland Ecuador, most forms of market-place commercial activity are to some extent controlled, regulated, and taxed by the municipal authorities. Most of the market regulations are derived from colonial (see, e.g., Borah 1951:24–31, Levillier 1929, and Moore 1954:168–78) and nineteenth-century models, prohibiting and imposing penalties for such offenses as using inaccurate weights and measures, giving short weight or short measure, selling impure or rotten foodstuffs, forming oligopolies, selling in forbidden areas, obstructing public rights-of-way, failing to pay market taxes, and trading without the necessary licenses and permits. Many of the more recent market regulations are derived from twentieth-century public health legislation designed to control epidemic diseases and to ensure the sale of hygienic foodstuffs. The main responsibility for the administration of the markets lies with the municipal police, who work under the orders of the municipal commissary, one of the principal employees of the municipal council. The municipal police act as caretakers and officials in the market places, although they are almost untrained, in many cases barely literate, and poorly paid. Wages as low as 400–600 sucres per month are not unusual in many municipalities, and it is not surprising that a substantial number of municipal policemen supplement their incomes by accepting bribes and keeping fines for themselves. Indeed, many municipal councils tacitly accept this as the norm, using it as a justification for not paying the municipal police more. Small cantonal capitals with relatively little market activity, such as Tabacundo, Pichincha, usually only have one or two municipal policemen. Larger cantonal capitals with important markets, such as Pelileo, Tungurahua, have three to eight municipal policemen, and each of the largest provincial capitals has several dozen. In some municipalities officials from the municipal or provincial departments of hygiene and public health also inspect the markets and enforce regulations. Particularly in the provincial capitals the national police force, which is considerably better paid and trained than any municipal police force, also intervenes in market administration. The national police are usually especially concerned to keep traders and stalls away from the main traffic routes, and to prevent theft and violence in the markets, or at least to apprehend offenders. Both municipal and national police have the right to fine or arrest traders and to confiscate trading licenses; offending traders may receive short sentences of imprisonment.

In market administration and taxation in the more important market centers, a major distinction is usually made between the daily market traders who trade in the same place on most days of the week, *puestos fijos*, and the periodic market traders who only trade in any particular place on one, two, or three days of the week, *feriantes*. This distinction is linked to the normal division of the week's market activity into periodic market days, *días feriados*, and ordinary days, *días normales*. The municipal officials usually maintain a close control over market activity on the ordinary days when relatively little trading takes place, but have great difficulty in achieving a similar degree of control on the periodic market days when there is usually a much greater amount of trading activity. Thus virtually all daily traders who work on both ordinary and periodic market days are licensed, inspected, and taxed. By contrast, many periodic traders escape such controls through their skill in avoiding the officials or, in the case of petty traders, because of the small scale of their operations, which are not considered worthy of official attention.

Daily traders are usually expected to pay a monthly rent ranging from 20 to 200 sucres, depending on the size and position of their stalls and the type of merchandise handled. Most of the larger-scale periodic traders are expected to pay a tax of between 0.20 and 5.00 sucres for every day that they spend trading in any market, and in some provincial and cantonal centers daily taxes as high as 10–20 sucres may be charged to a few traders. Market taxes are also charged on every head of livestock sold in most of the livestock markets in provincial and cantonal capitals, and on the weighing of goods on the public scale, *romana*, which is set up in many market places. The use of the *romana* by traders and purchasers varies considerably from one market center to another. In some cases public weighing on the *romana* is compulsory for every *quintal*, 46-kilogram, unit sold in the main wholesaling market places. In other cases the use of the *romana* is completely voluntary, or no public *romana* is provided. The tax on weighing at the *romana* usually varies from 0.20 to 1.00 sucre for each *quintal* weighed. Apart from the tax on the *romana*, market taxes are basically a rent for the use of public land and buildings and a contribution toward the cost of administering and cleaning the markets and constructing any public works in the market place.

Municipal revenues from market taxation vary considerably from market center to market center. In some of the smaller cantonal capitals with particularly large markets, such as Saquisilí, Cotopaxi, market taxation makes up over half the total revenue of the municipal council. In these cases the markets usually produce a substantial profit for the municipal councils, and the surplus of income over expenditure is used to finance other activities such as street paving and road construction. In most provincial and cantonal capitals, however, the markets are considerably smaller in relation to the size of the settlement, and market revenues make up a correspondingly smaller proportion of total municipal income. In most municipalities the main form of taxation is the rating of urban and rural properties, *avalúos y catastros*. In many cases some or all of the market taxes are collected indirectly by a system known as *remate*. The right to collect market taxes is auctioned publicly, and the highest bidder, the *rematista*, is given the right to collect the taxes, usually for a year. The *rematista* must pay the municipal council in advance the sum that he has bid for the right to collect taxes, and can then keep any profit that he makes from collecting the taxes. Most *rematistas* employ assistants to help with tax collection or they form tax-collecting partnerships. A *rematista* may take a loss, but market tax collection is more often a lucrative occupation for some of the *blanco* population in the market center.

In theory, direct tax collection by municipal employees allows the municipal council to absorb the profits which are usually made by the *rematistas*. In practice, however, municipal councils find it difficult to control the inefficiency or corruption of their own tax-collecting officials, and revenues from direct market taxation may prove lower than from the indirect system of *remate*. In many cases *rematistas* abuse their powers by charging illegally high taxes, by bullying traders, or by discriminating against Indian (and occasionally black) traders. Because taxes on *feriantes* are usually flexible according to the scale of operations of the trader, there is ample scope for abuses in the determination of what tax to charge.

Market tax revenues are poor data sources for comparing the importance of different market centers, or for comparing the amounts of market activity in the same market center at different points in time. The charges made, the system of charging, and the efficiency

of tax collection all vary considerably from municipality to municipality and from time to time. Furthermore, municipal accounts are
relatively difficult to obtain in most municipalities, and they are often
presented in such a way that the different types of taxes, or the taxes
on market-place and nonmarket-place commerce, cannot be separated from one another.

In the provincial and cantonal capitals trading licenses are normally compulsory for all, or most, daily traders and for a proportion
of the periodic traders. These licenses are usually given on an annual
basis, and cost between 5 and 50 sucres. They normally restrict traders to a particular type or range of merchandise (e.g., fruit and vegetables) and to a particular market place or street within the market
center. Food sellers are often also expected to have a health permit
from the municipal or provincial department of hygiene and public
health, and the possession of such a permit is frequently a condition
for obtaining a trading license from the municipal commissary's office. Health permits usually cost between 5 and 20 sucres and last a
year. They are given to traders who show a clean bill of health after
a medical examination, which may include blood test (mainly for ve-
nereal diseases), chest X-ray, and vaccination against smallpox and
tuberculosis. To obtain a health permit and a trading license, traders
must be prepared to fill out various forms, to make the necessary
payments, and to wait for several days, weeks, or even months before the required documents are issued. In some cases traders may
pay for professional assistance from unqualified lawyers, called *tin-
toreros*. More frequently, networks of friendship and kinship are exploited to gain a sympathetic and rapid hearing, and occasionally
bribes may be used to speed the process.

Market organization is generally much less comprehensive in parish capitals and *anejos* than in cantonal and provincial centers. Administrative responsibilities for parish and *anejo* markets are not
clearly defined by law, and in practice the majority of these markets,
and particularly the small ones, go untaxed and almost unregulated.
In the case of large parish markets, such as the one in La Toma, Loja
province, and large *anejo* markets, such as those in Zumbahua, Cotopaxi, and Salarón, however, the volume of commercial activity offers a substantial potential tax revenue, and taxes are collected by
cantonal, parish, or communal councils. Thus, in Salarón, for example, market taxes are collected by *rematistas* from the cantonal capital of Cajabamba who pay an annual rent to the municipality of Cajabamba, Colta canton. The *rematistas* ride from Cajabamba to Salarón

every Friday to collect taxes in the weekly market. In Zumbahua in 1970 the communal council, *cabildo*, began to charge market taxes, but within a few months a market day riot ensued and the taxes were abandoned.

MUNICIPAL MARKET BUILDINGS

Since 1920, and particularly since 1950, a considerable number of market buildings have been constructed in highland Ecuador. These buildings vary from small structures accommodating 5-20 stalls to large one- or two-story buildings accommodating several hundred stalls. They are generally constructed with municipal funds, and the cost of a single market building can range from under 60,000 to several million sucres. Because of their high cost, they tend to have high stall rents, and traders often have to be compelled by municipal regulations to take up the space provided inside the buildings. Those municipal councils which have invested heavily in market buildings often find that their total receipts from market taxes are considerably smaller than their expenditures on the construction and maintenance of market buildings, the cleaning of market places and buildings, and the wages of market officials. Market buildings are not constructed for profit. Statements on the motivations for their construction stress a concern for public health and hygiene through sale of clean food and a desire to enhance civic dignity through public works. The sale of certain critical foodstuffs such as meat, flour, and cooked dishes is often prohibited or controlled outside the market buildings to force their retailers to occupy stalls inside.

Although enclosed market buildings give greater security for merchandise and more protection from the elements than open-air stalls in the market place, they are not always popular with traders. High rents and the compulsion to pay monthly rather than daily rates tend to discourage part-time and small-scale traders from using the market buildings. Sellers of durable goods often prefer an open-air location where they are clearly visible from a distance to an enclosed location where many consumers may not even notice their presence. Municipal market buildings are mainly used for the sale of meat, flour, cooked foodstuffs, fruit, and vegetables; in most cases they are principally used by full-time daily traders rather than part-time periodic traders. No medium- or large-size market center in highland Ecuador has sufficient space in its market building or buildings to accommodate more than half the total trading activity in its produce markets,[4] and most market centers could not even accommodate a tenth of their market activity in market buildings.

There are 57 official market buildings in use in highland Ecuador, and at least another ten in construction. Apart from Quito, which has 17 municipal market buildings, no other market center has more than three. All provincial capitals, slightly under half the cantonal capitals, and only six parish capitals have one or more market buildings (all 1971 data). The principal factors behind this situation are the cost of constructing official market buildings, which can usually only be borne by provincial or cantonal capitals, and the tendency of market buildings to be oriented toward a regular, daily trade rather than weekly or twice-weekly periodic marketing. Thus market buildings are concentrated in the larger market centers with a substantial urban population and a strong local administration. The few market buildings which have been constructed in parish capitals are generally small and financed by the cantonal authorities rather than the parish authorities. Most of the few market buildings in parish capitals have been constructed in Quito canton, where municipal finances and hygienic standards are particularly high.

In most of the larger market centers of highland Ecuador, and in a few of the smaller ones, a limited number of traders have been allowed to erect and retain semipermanent stalls on public land. These stalls are usually wooden huts with corrugated iron roofs, a lockable door, and a lockable lift-up or flap-down window. Normally described as *kioscos*, kiosks, they are most frequently used for the daily sale of groceries or light refreshments. In a few cases, the most important and famous one being the Ipiales market near the National Palace in downtown Quito, a considerable number of kiosks have been erected in close proximity; together they have the capacity of a substantial municipal market building. Kiosks are usually liable to a monthly or annual tax for the occupation of public land. Because of this tax, and the considerable personal investment required for their construction and maintenance, they are only viable when there is a fairly dependable daily demand. They tend to be found in the larger urban centers and, in particular, close to transport terminals and wayside stopping points along transport routes. Kiosks are only important in a few small market centers which rely heavily on passing road traffic. Examples are the clusters of kiosks at Empalme Aloag at the junction of the Pan-American Highway South and the Santo Domingo road, which link central and southern Ecuador to Quito, and at Guayllabamba on the Pan-American Highway North between Quito and Ibarra.

PROCESSES OF MARKET FOUNDATION

Over the last 30 years the foundation of new markets by formal, organized means and by spontaneous activity has been important in parish capitals and in a few strategically located *anejos*. Markets founded by formal meetings involving municipal and parish officials, local clergy, and prominent citizens are usually administered and taxed by local authorities from inception. Markets founded spontaneously (e.g., when a strategically placed roadside site is utilized by peddlers and merchants on a systematic, predictable basis), however, may continue for several years before succumbing to market administration or taxation.

A central location is necessary, but not sufficient, to lead to the development of a thriving market. Equally necessary are adequate transport facilities or an inducement sufficient to attract transporters. The location must be, or appear to be, convenient and profitable to outside traders, and it is clearly advantageous for a potential market location to have authorities who favor, and are prepared to support actively, the development of a market. The perception of commercial advantages and opportunities by the local population or by outside entrepreneurs may be more important than any real advantage in terms of location or number of inhabitants. Vigorous local efforts to found a market may fail, of course, if the market's location is poor and the population to be served is relatively low. Failure is particularly likely if the support of local and outside traders and transporters is not forthcoming. At least 30 parish capitals presently without markets have witnessed unsuccessful attempts to found them in this century.

An important factor in understanding the pattern of market founding and the growth and decline of market centers in highland Ecuador is the rivalry of neighboring settlements. This ranges from national and regional rivalries, for example between Guayaquil and Quito or between Cuenca and Loja, to local rivalries between neighboring towns, villages, and hamlets. The commercial competition and rivalry between neighboring market centers may be paralleled by sociopolitical animosity. Three twentieth-century cases will serve to illustrate the effects of such rivalries on market activity: Quero, made a cantonal capital in 1972, and Cevallos, a parish capital four kilometers away, in Tungurahua province; Cajabamba, a cantonal capital, and Majipamba, an *anejo* 4.5 kilometers to the south, in Chimborazo province; and Julio Andrade and Guaca, two parish capitals three kilometers apart in Carchi province. In each of these cases animosity has been encouraged by the close proximity of the two settlements and by the economic advantages which the population of a market center gains from having a strong market.

Quero and Cevallos

Quero's Sunday market is one of the older markets in Tungurahua province and was well established as a major commercial focus in the southern part of the province by 1900. While Quero was a parish capital and a moderately important village in the colonial period and the nineteenth century, Cevallos was not made a parish until the last decade of the nineteenth century. In 1908, however, Cevallos received a considerable stimulus to its growth through the completion of the Guayaquil-Quito railway, which passed through Cevallos but not through Quero. After the completion of its station in the 1910s Cevallos increased in commercial importance, and a market foundation was organized by the parish authorities before 1920. Thursday was chosen as market day because it was temporally well separated from Quero's Sunday periodic market and from Ambato's Monday periodic market. Even with this temporal separation of Quero's and Cevallos's markets, however, the spatial proximity of the two market centers inevitably led to some rivalry. After Cevallos's market was founded, most people living closer to Cevallos than to Quero reduced the frequency of their visits to Quero or stopped buying and selling in Quero altogether. Quero now has substantial produce and livestock markets, while Cevallos has a moderate produce market and no livestock market. The competition between the two centers has been somewhat reduced by a high degree of functional specialization in wholesale trading. While Quero has a large livestock market and is a major wholesaling center for grain, Cevallos concentrates on the wholesaling of potatoes, onions, and apples. This situation seems to have developed in an unplanned fashion through the preferences of individual wholesale traders dealing in different products.

Cajabamba and Majipamba

Cajabamba has had a Sunday periodic market since the early or middle colonial period.[5] The most important zone supplying products and customers to its market is the Colta Lake area to the south. The lakeshore is very densely populated (see A.I.C.R.D.P. 1965) and includes several important *anejos*. In 1968 Majipamba, an *anejo* on the western side of the lake by the main Pan-American Highway, established a Sunday market. This market was founded through the initiative of Protestant Indians and missionaries in the *anejo*, and it was designed to coincide with religious services at the Majipamba mission, probably in the hope that it would increase the material welfare of the local inhabitants and the number of converts to the Protestant faith. The cantonal authorities in Cajabamba acted swiftly to close the Majipamba market by presenting a legal case to the provincial authorities claiming that the market was illegal, and refusing to give permission for its continuation. Majipamba's market never grew to be more than a very small gathering of produce traders, and it died out within two months.

Guaca and Julio Andrade

Guaca and Julio Andrade are two roughly equal-sized villages, each with populations of about 1,000. Guaca established Sunday produce and livestock markets in the late 1930s or early 1940s, and Julio Andrade followed suit in the early 1950s. It appears that Julio Andrade's authorities chose Sunday as their market day precisely because it would clash with Guaca's market and hence might capture commercial activity from Guaca. From its inception Julio Andrade's Sunday market was a success. Little by little it attracted produce and livestock buyers and sellers who had previously traded in Guaca, so that Guaca's market went into rapid decline. The parish authorities in Guaca made various protests to the cantonal and provincial authorities in Tulcán, attempting unsuccessfully to get Julio Andrade's market closed and, later, to get its day changed to Thursday. Several times the authorities in Guaca arranged roadblocks between the two villages to try to prevent the people of Guaca and other areas to the south of Julio Andrade from attending its market. A number of violent clashes ensued, and police and troops were called to the two villages on several occasions. Guaca's authorities successfully petitioned for the construction of a market building in the village, but even this failed to arrest the decline of its market. In the late 1960s Guaca's animal market finally faded out of existence, and by 1971 its produce market was less than one-eighth the size of Julio Andrade's.

The rise of Julio Andrade and the decline of Guaca as market centers are related to two major factors: the attitudes of the respective authorities, and the relative locations of the two villages. It appears that Julio Andrade's authorities adopted a more liberal attitude in market administration than those of Guaca, and that they devoted a considerable amount of effort and enthusiasm to founding and encouraging the market in its earliest years. Julio Andrade proved more conveniently located than Guaca for the legal and illegal cattle traders bringing in livestock from Colombia.

These case studies of market foundations and of rivalries between market centers illustrate the importance of social, political, and historical factors in determining the scale and spatiotemporal distribution of market-place trade. The rivalries between neighboring settlements may lead to conflictive or integrative choices of market day[6] and to complementary or competitive functional specializations. Local authorities and local or outside entrepreneurs may exploit or neglect locational advantages related to population distribution or accessibility. The energy of these authorities and entrepreneurs, combined with the wisdom of their choices of market days, specializations, and regulations, plays a major role in the success or failure of individual market centers.

THE SPATIAL ORGANIZATION OF THE MARKET PLACE

In all the market centers of highland Ecuador there is a moderate degree of spatial differentiation between different types of trading activity and between traders dealing in different types of merchandise. Collecting wholesalers, distributing wholesalers, and retailers tend to trade in separate parts of the market place or in different market places, and traders dealing in any particular type of merchandise tend to agglomerate. These features of highland Ecuadorian market places are well illustrated in Figure 1, a sketch map of the only market place in the village of Ilumán, Imbabura, drawn in January 1971 while the weekly periodic market was near its peak of activity. This map of Ilumán's market place can be compared with Hartmann's (1968:113) description of the market in September 1965, when the spatial arrangement of sellers was broadly similar to that found in 1971. Both Hartmann's description and my Figure 1 show the considerable degree of agglomeration of traders selling the same types of merchandise and the clear arrangement of traders in rows. Most of the traders in Ilumán's market are female, Indian, small-scale retailers without proper stalls, who sit on the ground and display their merchandise on the ground in front of themselves.

In many market centers spatial differentiation by type of trader and merchandise is encouraged or enforced by the market authorities. Differentiation is convenient for market administration and cleaning and gives the market place an orderly appearance. Market administrators usually argue that spatial differentiation aids the customer to

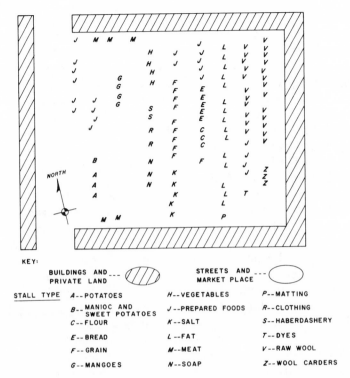

KEY:

BUILDINGS AND ___   STREETS AND ___
PRIVATE LAND   MARKET PLACE

STALL TYPE			
A--POTATOES	H--VEGETABLES	P--MATTING
B--MANIOC AND SWEET POTATOES	J--PREPARED FOODS	R--CLOTHING
C--FLOUR	K--SALT	S--HABERDASHERY
E--BREAD	L--FAT	T--DYES
F--GRAIN	M--MEAT	V--RAW WOOL
G--MANGOES	N--SOAP	Z--WOOL CARDERS

FIGURE 1. Ilumán's market place at 8:30 A.M., Sunday, 10 January 1971.

find what he or she wants quickly and to compare prices efficiently. However, spatial differentiation sometimes encourages the formation of oligopsonies and oligopolies by groups of neighboring traders who cooperate to arrange prices to their own advantage. An illustrative case occurs between August and December in Zumbahua's main Saturday periodic market among the wholesale barley buyers. Each Saturday between 5 and 20 wholesalers travel to Zumbahua to buy barley. They arrange themselves in a line to facilitate communication, and they generally cooperate with one another to ensure that the buying price is held to a low level. These strategies are facilitated by the remoteness of Zumbahua, the relatively small number of large-scale buyers, and the very large numbers of exploitable small-scale Indian producers in the area surrounding the market center.

In some markets, then, spatial order of the market place can be attributed to the work of market officials who try to persuade or coerce traders to arrange their stalls and merchandise in neat rows and to group themselves according to the types of goods handled.

Even in "uncontrolled" parish and *anejo* markets, however, traders arrange themselves in rows and with some degree of spatial differentiation. This enables customers to circulate freely while traders can compare prices and watch the activities of their competitors. Often people of a given community specialize in producing and/or marketing a particular type of merchandise; such traders from the same place share the same background and may also be friends, relatives, or *compadres*. Even in the large urban markets family specializations play an important role. Of the 62 registered meat sellers (61 of them women) in the La Merced (Mariano Borja) market building in Riobamba, there are five Quisaguiña sisters, five Ramos sisters, four Tubón sisters, and three members each of the Ríos, López, Vega, and Chafla families.[7] The market place is a lively center for gossip, and traders sit together for purely social reasons. Agglomeration is particularly pronounced among members of ethnically recognizable and stigmatized indigenous and black low-status groups who are often excluded from free and open social interaction with *blancos*.

There is a countertendency to aggregation by product, as some traders strive to differentiate themselves from the mass of traders dealing in the same goods. Thus retailing forestallers usually try to locate themselves on the main routes of access to the market place to persuade customers that they can save time and effort, and get a bargain, by buying before they even reach the market. Early in the day collecting forestallers try to buy products from the farmers traveling into market from rural areas, and later in the day they take the products to the market place or to wholesale warehouses, reselling the goods at a profit.

FUNCTIONAL DIFFERENTIATION BETWEEN MARKET PLACES

Market activity is often sufficiently extensive to be divided between two or more market places. Quito has 25, Riobamba has 13, Cuenca has 11, and Saquisilí has seven. The number of market places in a market center, however, is not a good measure of market activity, since market places vary markedly in size and in crowdedness. In almost all market centers with more than one market place, there is some degree of functional differentiation between the various market places. Livestock is usually sold apart from other merchandise, sometimes divided between two or more market places, separating pigs, sheep, and goats (*ganado menor*), from cattle, horses, mules, and donkeys (*ganado mayor*). Some market places may be given over to particular products or types of products, such as the Plaza General

Dávalos in Riobamba, which specializes in artisan raw materials and products made of *cabuya*, agave fiber, and *totora*, dried reeds, and the Plaza El Centenario in Otavalo, which specializes in textiles. Even in specialist market places, however, a few food sellers offer refreshments, and there may be a few sellers of such commonplace goods as fruit, vegetables, potatoes, and grain. In the larger market centers, such as Quito, Ambato, and Ibarra, each market place serves a particular barrio with lower-order goods, and many of them also serve the whole urban area for a particular range of specialist higher-order goods. In Quito different market places often have different periodic market days, but this phenomenon is not found to any great extent elsewhere. In Ambato, for example, all of the 18 market places are in use on Monday (the main periodic market day), eight of the market places are in use on Wednesday and Friday (the two secondary periodic market days), and six of the market places are in limited use on the other days of the week when there is a much reduced level of market activity.

The spatial distribution of the different market places in the larger market centers is well illustrated by the examples of Ambato, second only to Quito among the market centers in the highlands (Figure 2); Azogues, in Cañar province, a major regional/local center with nine market places (Figure 3); and Penipe, in Chimborazo, a moderately important local center with two market places (Figure 4). In these three market centers, as in the overwhelming majority of the market centers of highland Ecuador, produce market activity is concentrated toward the center of the settlement, reflecting the importance of accessibility to the local population and agglomeration with other commercial establishments.

The central areas of Ecuadorian settlements usually have higher residential densities and much greater amounts of tertiary economic activity than the peripheral areas. Thus the central market places are usually surrounded by, or in close proximity to, the main shops and warehouses as well as the main public offices and churches. In the larger market centers with various market places, traders generally prefer to operate in the more central market places where commercial activity is greatest. Attempts by local authorities to move markets toward the urban periphery usually encounter resistance from traders and customers, and such moves may be followed by marked drops in market tax revenues. In spite of such resistance, however, the citizens of peripheral barrios in the larger towns and cities often petition the municipal authorities to establish market places in their neighborhoods. A thriving neighborhood market increases the turn-

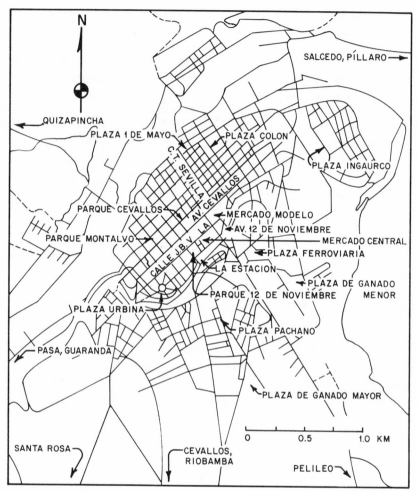

FIGURE 2. The distribution of market places in Ambato, 1971.

over of local shopkeepers, provides commercial income opportunities for local residents, and reduces the distance that local consumers
have to travel to obtain goods and services.

In Ambato, Azogues, and Penipe, as in most livestock market centers, livestock trading takes place in a market place on or close to the
periphery of the settlement. Such a location is preferred by the local
authorities because it reduces the dangers caused by livestock to public health and safety. In many market centers livestock owners are
prohibited from driving or leading their animals through the central
streets to avoid impeding the flow of pedestrians and vehicles, and

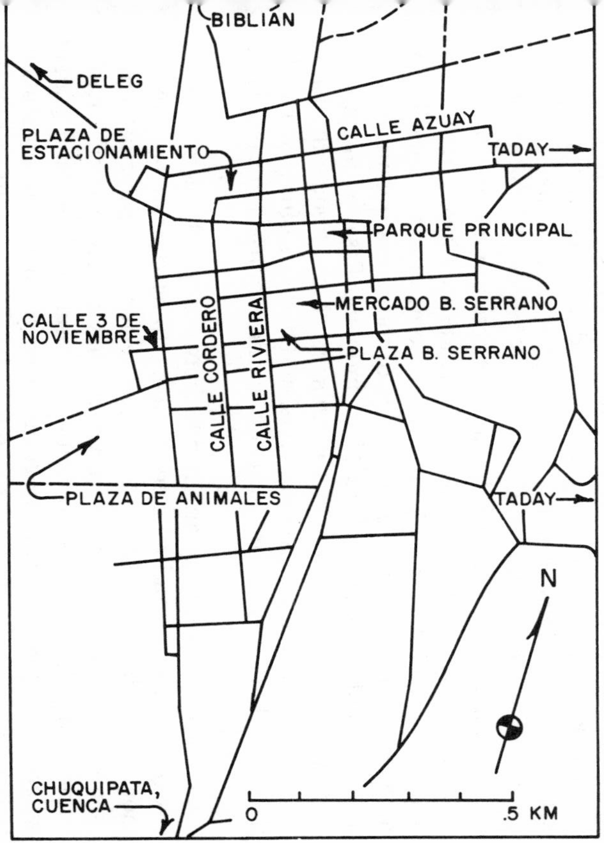

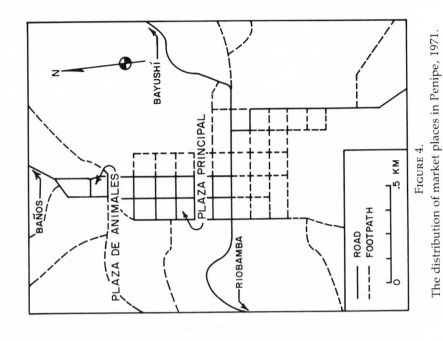

FIGURE 4.

The distribution of market places in Penipe, 1971.

FIGURE 3.

The distribution of market places in Azogues, 1971.

to prevent animal droppings from fouling the streets and contaminating food and water supplies.

COMMERCIAL ACTIVITY IN THE MARKET PLACE

The great majority of retail transactions are cash sales. Transactions are usually preceded by some argument over prices. Prices are rarely fixed or marked in writing, and sellers may vary their prices according to the appearance, knowledge, and bargaining skill of the buyer and according to the time of day, the condition of the merchandise, and whether or not they expect to be able to sell on succeeding days. Regular customers make their purchases with less time lost in bargaining than outsiders, and sellers may extend credit or give special favors to buyers who are, or may well become, regulars. Buyers who are not regular customers of a particular seller often bargain with two or more sellers to test prices. Weights and measures used in retail trade include metric units such as the kilogram and the meter, traditional colonial Hispanic units such as the *vara* and the *fanega*, imperial units such as the pound and the gallon, and locally accepted approximate measures such as the bunch and the mule-load. The situation is further complicated by the widespread custom of *yapa*, a bonus quantity given on top of the amount originally offered. Bargaining may occur in two stages, first over the price and then over the amount.

Barter transactions are rare in the larger market centers and in the areas without substantial indigenous populations. Barter mainly occurs in transactions between Indians, or between Indians and *mestizos*, when only small amounts of merchandise are involved. The best markets in which to observe barter are some of the smaller village markets in the more indigenous areas of the central highlands such as Cusubamba in Cotopaxi, San Fernando and Pasa in Tungurahua, and Columbe and Punín in Chimborazo. Most frequently, barter trading occurs in local food products, and barley is often used as the basic standard of value or "currency" in these transactions (see Hartmann 1971).

Credit transactions occur mainly between wholesalers and between wholesalers and retailers. In these transactions large sums of money may be involved, and informal or formal contractual agreements are made to cover risks. Credit may be given even for relatively minor transactions involving wholesalers. Street and market sellers of oranges and tangerines are often given a hundred fruits to sell by a wholesaler on the condition that they return to pay for the fruits when they are sold. Only if the retailers return and pay for the first hundred can they be given a second hundred. A rolling credit is maintained until the retailer eventually defaults. Credit transactions are facilitated by the existence of complex social networks of friendship, kinship, and *compadrazgo* linking the longer established market traders.

Market-place transactions often include elements of discrimination against ethnically identified and tagged social categories, especially against rural Indians and rural blacks. Most traders are urban *blancos*, whites, and favors are extended by these traders to nonblack and non-Indian urban dwellers and to others classed as *blanco*. In giving *yapa* or in allowing credit, traders favor those they know and trust, and who are nonblack and non-Indian, by giving more generous terms and often by asking lower prices. Rural visitors to the market centers often find that they have to pay a little more, or to receive a little less, than the urban dwellers. Rural traders have particular difficulty in obtaining credit from urban wholesalers, and rural producers and intermediaries have problems in coping with urban regulations on trading licenses, health permits, and commercial practices. The social organization and the administrative organization of the markets combine to discriminate against the poorest, least educated, most rural, and ethnically Indian and black traders and customers. Because of the complexity of municipal licensing policies and the social cohesion of the urban market traders, the more socially and economically disadvantaged traders are usually forced to work periodically, to maintain only small-scale operations, and to trade in types of goods where licenses, permits, and large amounts of credit are not so often required.

The problems encountered by rural Indians in the market place are well illustrated by the following translation of an extract from an interview with an Indian peasant leader in Chimborazo province, recorded by Hammock and Ashe (1970:28–29):

> There are also problems in marketing. We sell some products in our own communities to people who come from the towns to the community and buy from us there. Some of us sell in the village, or in the town of Riobamba.
>
> In the market, the wholesale buyers say: "How much is this?," and we tell them the price without any attempt to deceive or be difficult [*no sea animal o en grano*]. But they insult us: "*Indio*, why are you so like an animal; how can you ask so much for this?," talking very aggressively. Another buyer comes, and he says the same, so that, in the end, the *campesino* has to sell at the price that they offer. Sometimes, they call the police and make us sell by force. They lie and say: "This *indio* offered to sell at this price, but

now that I give him the money, he won't sell." As the policeman is a relative or friend of the buyer, he forces us to sell. If we don't want to sell, he
threatens to send us to jail unless we sell for the price offered. I had a
chance to see this when one Saturday a woman from the community went
to sell a sheep, and I was also there selling a pig, and we were side by
side. Then a buyer came and asked me how much my pig was, and I told
him the price. Then he said to me: "You're just like the *indios*; if only you
were rational [like a *blanco*]." And I replied, "I'm sorry I'm not *blanco*, I am
indio," and he didn't say anything in reply, but just went over to the
woman and said: "How much is this sheep?" She said so much, and he
swore at her, grabbed the sheep, thrust much less than she had asked into
her hand, and walked away. . . . The *campesino* does not protest because
the *campesinos* are dominated by the *blancos*. . . . They have the right to say
that we are *indios*, and because we are *indios*, we are worth less than the
gente del pueblo ["white" townsfolk].

Such cases of blatant discrimination against Indians in Ecuadorian
market places are also described by Fox (1960:2–4), Dubly (1973),
Burgos (1970:262–76), and Villavicencio (1973:115), and similar discrimination against highland blacks is described by Klumpp
(1970:256–57). In general, the *blanco* adopts a paternalistic form of
address to Indians, blacks, and other poor countryfolk, addressing
them as *tu* or *vos* but expecting them to reply with the more respectful
usted. It is mutually accepted that the "white" may insult or even
strike an Indian, but never vice versa. Municipal authorities may
even formally accept the unequal treatment of Indians in the market
place, as in the example of the separate measures used for selling
cloth to "whites" and to Indians in Riobamba: the Indians received
several centimeters less cloth in each yard, *vara*, than the "whites,"
for the same price (Burgos 1970:227).

In most market places, apart from the livestock plazas, over three-
quarters of traders and of customers are women. Women play a
dominant role in the retailing of fresh foodstuffs, where they usually
make up 85 to 95% of the traders (Bromley 1975a:208–10). Some of
these traders have one to three assistants or partners, but the majority work alone. On average, men have slightly larger-scale operations than women. In most market centers men dominate the three
most lucrative fields of operation in the markets: wholesale trading,
the retailing of the more expensive factory-made durable goods, and
livestock trading. A few types of goods and services are handled almost exclusively by one sex, and there is often an element of prejudice against, or ridicule for, members of the opposite sex entering
these trades. For example, men and boys dominate ice cream retail-

ing, shoe shining, and cattle trading, while women are almost the exclusive purveyors of soups and hot meals.[8]

Market-place trade takes place mainly in the daylight hours of the morning with the peak period of activity occurring between 8:00 A.M. and noon. In a few large market centers trading begins well before dawn. In Ambato the wholesaling of potatoes, onions, garlic, fruit, and vegetables runs continuously from Sunday evening to Monday morning, and the wholesaling and retailing of textiles in the Plaza El Centenario of Otavalo starts at about 4:00 A.M. every Saturday. Generally, the larger the market the earlier it begins and the later it finishes. Some trading activity continues in large markets until the evening, while many small village markets are over by 1:00 or 2:00 P.M.

THE RELATIONSHIP BETWEEN THE AMOUNT OF MARKET ACTIVITY AND THE RANGE OF GOODS

Several thousand different products are sold in highland Ecuadorian markets. Two-thirds of the turnover in produce markets is in perishable goods, almost all of them foodstuffs. The remaining third is in durable goods and services, especially clothing, footwear, and textiles. The percentage of perishable goods is highest in the smallest market centers, where it usually exceeds 80%. For medium to large market centers, however, perishable goods account on average for 67% of turnover. Durable goods and services are proportionately almost twice as important in medium to large centers as in small centers. This is because they are higher-order and less frequently consumed goods than perishable foodstuffs.

There are more significant variations between different market centers when we consider merchandise by actual product. The largest centers have a high proportion of fruit, vegetables, meat, fish, eggs, milk, cheese, small animals, and industrially produced consumer durable goods available in their markets. This reflects the concentration of upper- and middle-class consumers in the larger towns and cities, particularly in Quito, Ambato, and Cuenca, the three largest produce market centers. These consumers present a concentrated demand for protein-rich foodstuffs and industrial products, and a correspondingly low proportionate demand for starchy foods and artisan products. Each market center has some concentration in particular categories of merchandise reflecting the presence or absence of local production and commercial specializations.

Artisan products and raw materials, composed mainly of *cabuya*, *totora*, wood, and leather, are most important in the indigenous areas of the central highlands, where traditional rural handicrafts are highly developed. Most of the markets in these areas have relatively low percentages of traders in textiles, clothing, and footwear because a substantial proportion of clothing is woven in the home and because many people go barefoot or wear sandals. By contrast, the predominantly "white" areas of the highlands such as Carchi and Loja have high proportions of textiles, clothing, and footwear in their markets. Percentages of textiles, clothing, and footwear are particularly high in Carchi because of the importance of the contraband trade of Colombian manufactured goods into the province.

Because of the low attraction of the smaller village markets, and because of the high urban population in the largest market centers, most produce markets in the smallest and largest centers cater mainly to the populations of the market centers themselves. By contrast, most markets in medium-size centers cater mainly to the population of the surrounding rural areas and only secondarily to the populations of the market centers. The goods bought and sold by rural dwellers figure most prominently in the trading of medium-size centers and least prominently in the trading of the smallest and largest centers. Medium-size market centers have relatively low levels of trading in fruit and vegetables because most rural dwellers consume only small quantities or rely mainly on their own subsistence production of these goods. Rural dwellers both buy and sell large amounts of grains, root crops, fuel and fodder, artisan products, and raw materials, and they are major buyers of preserves, flour, bread, sugar, salt, and fats, commodities which they usually do not produce themselves. As one would expect, large-scale traders are mainly concentrated in the larger market centers and in the sale of industrially produced durable goods.

THE LIVESTOCK MARKETS

Livestock markets deal mainly in cattle, pigs, and sheep and occasionally also in horses, mules, donkeys, llamas, and goats. Cattle make up about 80% of the total value of all livestock transacted in highland Ecuadorian markets (Bromley 1975a:337), though in the central highlands there are small livestock markets which deal mainly or entirely in pigs and sheep. Livestock markets are always periodic rather than daily. They are usually held in separate market places away from most produce trading, and they are less closely related to the population size and economic structure of the market centers than the produce markets. The animals involved may be sold several times on the same day, or in some cases they may remain unsold. None of the livestock market places in highland Ecuador have stalls, and most of the animals are either tethered to stakes or controlled by a rope held in their owner's hand.

Seventy-two of the 164 market centers in highland Ecuador have one or more livestock markets each week. Livestock trading is particularly important relative to produce trading in some of the market centers closest to the cattle-producing zones in southern Colombia, and in some centers in the southern highlands which deal in cattle from the Oriente provinces of Morona-Santiago and Zamora-Chinchipe, and are involved in the movements of cattle to Guayaquil and to Peru. The flows of cattle from north to south, and from the highlands to Guayaquil, are major elements influencing levels of activity. Variations in the extent of governmental control of livestock movements, both within Ecuador and on the Colombian and Peruvian frontiers, lead to large fluctuations in the levels of activity of those livestock markets which are most involved in this long-distance cattle trade, for example Tulcán, Julio Andrade, and San Gabriel in Carchi province and Loja, Las Juntas, and Solamar in Loja province. Outside the areas most affected by the long-distance cattle trade, livestock trading is important in most of the largest produce market centers, with the notable exception of Quito, and in some of the less densely populated areas with substantial amounts of livestock production, such as the central and southern parts of Chimborazo province and the northern part of Cañar province.

Livestock markets are mainly patronized by small- to medium-scale livestock producers and by their intermediaries. Livestock market trading, then, is notable in areas with large numbers of small-scale livestock producers. Important livestock-producing areas where almost all livestock are produced on large estates generally have no livestock markets. This phenomenon is particularly notable in the Cayambe area of Pichincha province. Although the area around Cayambe is famous for its dairy haciendas, there is no livestock market in the town. Pedigreed cattle, sheep, and pigs are often kept on haciendas but are rarely found on small farms in highland Ecuador. Because the livestock markets are mainly used by small-scale livestock producers, the animals on display are usually low-quality crossbred stock. Small-scale livestock producers usually retain female stock for breeding and sell male stock before or after fattening. Since castration is not normally practiced, a high proportion of all the livestock on display, particularly of cattle, is male.

CONCLUDING COMMENTS

Market-place trade plays an important role in the economic, social, and spatial organization of human activity in highland Ecuador. The region is one of great physical, cultural, and socioeconomic diversity, with marked variations in population density, settlement patterns, and productive activities. These variations are reflected in differences in the location, size, periodicity, and characteristics of market-place trade.

Since the early colonial period, and probably since precolonial times (Hartmann 1968, Bromley 1978b), market activity has been closely supervised and regulated by local authorities. Highland Ecuadorian market places are not "perfect markets," where prices are determined by the unimpeded interplay of the forces of supply and demand. Under certain conditions (Bromley 1974) groups of wholesalers, or occasionally of large-scale producers, may play a part in controlling prices through their hold on supply, bulking, and distribution. The entry of new traders into the market is partially controlled by official licensing policies and, to a lesser extent, by social organizations among traders which, in a few cases, may bar outsiders from participation. Retailers may adopt discriminatory strategies in pricing goods sold to people ethnically tagged *indio* or *negro*, and short-lived monopolies and monopsonies may develop in particular market places for the sale of particular products. Occasionally, local and national authorities may intervene in trading activities to attempt to limit price rises or to prevent long-distance or international commodity flows. While profit is undoubtedly the main motivation inducing most market-place traders to trade, other forms of economic and noneconomic rationality may also play an important role. Working in the market place facilitates social interaction, gives the trader a certain security and status in society, and allows a convenient mixture of part-time work in the market with other occupations.

Highland Ecuadorian markets are complex institutions showing a wide range of different forms of organization. Purely economic models are inadequate for their interpretation, and only a combination of economic, sociocultural, and politico-administrative perspectives, both on contemporary situations and on their historical development, can yield a comprehensive understanding.

NOTES

Acknowledgments: Thanks are due to all those in Ecuador, too numerous to mention individually, who collaborated with this investigation. Without their help it would have been impossible to complete the research. Full acknowledgments are given in Bromley (1975a:iii–v).

1. "Traders" are people who buy and/or sell goods or services in the market place for business purposes or who display merchandise in the hope of making a sale. By contrast, "consumers" are people who buy goods or services for consumption or use rather than for resale.

2. Daily markets take place every day of the week. Periodic markets occur regularly on one to four fixed days each week.

3. Since 1971 several market centers have been upgraded in administrative status, so that the numbers at each status level are no longer valid, even when there has been no change in the number of market centers.

4. The term "produce" is used to indicate all goods and services sold in markets apart from livestock.

5. Until 1797 what is now Cajabamba was part of the town of Riobamba. In that year a major earthquake caused a landslide which destroyed much of the town and led to the shifting of Riobamba to its present site.

6. By adopting an integrative approach, the organizers of a market choose a day on which none of the neighboring market centers holds a market. By adopting a conflictive approach, they deliberately choose the same market day as that of one or more of the neighboring market centers (Symanski and Bromley 1974:386).

7. Data were obtained in 1971 from the Dirección Municipal de Higiene. Even when legally married, most of the market women continue to register in their maiden names.

8. Boys under ten years of age often work as shoe shiners and petty food retailers. In general, children are not prevented from working in the market place, providing they do not trade inside official market buildings or deal in types of merchandise where health permits and trading licenses are required.

REFERENCES CITED

A.I.C.R.D.P. (Andean Indian Community Research and Development Project)
    1965   *Indians in Misery: A Preliminary Report on the Colta Lake Zone, Chimborazo, Ecuador.* Ithaca, N.Y.: Department of Anthropology, Cornell University.
Borah, Woodrow
    1951   *New Spain's Century of Depression.* Ibero-Americana 35. Berkeley: University of California Press.
Bromley, Ray
    1974   Interregional Marketing and Alternative Reform Strategies in Ecuador. *European Journal of Marketing* 8 (3):245–64.
    1975a Periodic and Daily Markets in Highland Ecuador. Ph.D. thesis, Cambridge University. University Microfilms Order No. 76–21,058.

1975b   *Guia a los Mercados y a las Ferias Semanales de la Sierra Ecuatoriana.* Quito: Junta Nacional de Planificación y Coordinación Económica.
1976   Contemporary Market Periodicity in Highland Ecuador. In Carol A. Smith, ed., *Regional Analysis*, vol. 1: *Economic Systems*. New York: Academic Press, pp. 91–122.
1978a   Traditional and Modern Change in the Growth of Systems of Market Centres in Highland Ecuador. In Robert H. T. Smith, ed., *Market-Place Trade: Periodic Markets, Hawkers, and Traders in Africa, Asia, and Latin America.* Vancouver: Centre for Transportation Studies, University of British Columbia, pp. 31–47.
1978b   Precolonial Trade and the Transition to a Colonial Market System in the Audiencia of Quito. *Nova Americana* 1:269–83.

Bromley, Rosemary D. F., and Ray Bromley
1975   The Debate on Sunday Markets in Nineteenth Century Ecuador. *Journal of Latin American Studies* 7 (1):85–108. (Republished in 1976 in Spanish in *Revista del Archivo Histórico del Guayas* 5 (9):7–32.)

Burgos Guevara, Hugo
1970   *Relaciones Interétnicas en Riobamba.* Mexico City: Instituto Indigenista Interamericano.

Dubly, Alain
1973   Exposición para la Humanización de las Plazas Comerciales de Riobamba. *América Indígena* 33:405–30.

Fox, Richard
1960   The Markets of Riobamba. Mimeo. New York: Department of Anthropology, Columbia University.

Hammock, John C., and Jeffrey A. Ashe, eds.
1970   *Hablan Líderes Campesinos del Ecuador.* Quito: Talleres "Gráficas Morillo."

Hartmann, Roswith
1968   Märkte im alten Peru. Bonn: Inaugural Dissertation zur Erlangung der Doktorwürde der Philosophischen Fakultät der Rheinischen Friedrich-Wilhelms-Universität.
1971   Algunas Observaciones Respecto al Trueque y Otras Prácticas en las Ferias de la Sierra Ecuatoriana. *Archiv für Volkerkunde* 25:43–55.

Klumpp, Kathleen
1970   Black Traders of North Highland Ecuador. In Norman E. Whitten, Jr., and John F. Szwed, eds., *Afro-American Anthropology: Contemporary Perspectives.* New York: Free Press, pp. 245–62.

Levillier, Roberto, ed.
1929   *Ordenanzas de Don Francisco de Toledo, Virrey del Perú, 1569–1581.* Madrid.

Marshall, Gloria A.
1970   In a World of Women: Fieldwork in a Yoruba Community. In Peggy Golde, ed., *Women in the Field: Anthropological Experiences.* Chicago: Aldine, pp. 165–91.

Mintz, Sidney W.
1971   Men, Women, and Trade. *Comparative Studies in Society and History* 13:247–69.

Moore, John Preston
1954   *The Cabildo in Peru under the Hapsburgs.* Durham, N.C.: Duke University Press.

Symanski, Richard, and Ray Bromley
  1974 Market Development and the Ecological Complex. *Professional Geographer* 26 (4):382–88.
Tax, Sol
  1953 *Penny Capitalism: A Guatemalan Indian Economy.* Washington, D.C.: Smithsonian Institution, Institute of Social Anthropology, Publication 16.
Villavicencio Rivadeneira, Gladys
  1973 *Relaciones Interétnicas en Otavalo, Ecuador.* Mexico City: Instituto Indigenista Interamericano.

8

Strategies for Survival: The Indians of Highland Ecuador

Joseph B. Casagrande

THE POSITION OF THE SIERRA INDIAN

Like several of its neighbors, Ecuador is characterized by a sharply stratified, dual society in which there is a castelike division between Indians and non-Indians. Estimates of the Indian population of the Sierra vary greatly depending upon the criteria of Indianness employed,[1] but a figure of one million would probably not be far off the mark. By Ecuadorian standards some Indians are well off. Nevertheless, the overwhelming majority of the indigenous population bears the classic stigmata that mark them among the disinherited peoples of the world: poverty, illiteracy, high infant mortality and low life expectancy, a variety of deficiency diseases, low participation in local and national institutions, and limited opportunities for social mobility. Many *mestizos* are no better off—the case is comparable to that of rural blacks and whites in the southern United States. However, the Indians' situation is aggravated by their relegation to the lowest stratum of Ecuadorian society.

In the universal dialectic of racism Indians are endowed with the very traits disesteemed by whites. Even the kindliest among the whites tend to look upon Indians as children perpetually held at a developmental stage lower than that of full adult human beings, or they regard them simply as brutes little better than any other animal capable of carrying a heavy load. Perhaps most insidious of all is the attitude of benevolent condescension that characterizes the *patrón* of classic mold and many would-be benefactors. The fact that some Indian groups in Ecuador are singled out for special comment or praise—the Otavaleños, for example, are said to be proud, clean, industrious, intelligent, and so on—is in effect to commend them for having qualities that one is surprised to find among Indians and at the same time to damn other Indian groups with the implication that these are precisely the qualities *they* don't have. Thus most Indians are generally regarded by whites as being lazy, drunken, dirty, stupid, dishonest, or having other flaws of character. And so is fed the stereotype of the Indians that both keeps them at a distance and gives warrant to the ill treatment accorded them.

If in the earlier colonial period there were recognized *caciques* and noble Indian families (some even granted coats of arms by the king), these status differences have been leveled off with the passage of time. It is noteworthy, too, that little public honor is paid the symbols of Indian ethnicity. The ingredients are at hand, but neither the Indians nor the nation has constructed a believable history or heritage in which both can take pride and with which the Indians can identify.[2]

Racism in Ecuador is institutionalized to a degree that would shock many oppressed peoples elsewhere. Today Indians may not be flogged, jailed for debts, or impressed into menial service. Nevertheless, they are still often the victims of the more insidious if impersonal structural violence done them by a dominant white society whose fundaments were established during the colonial period. In interactions with non-Indians those classed as *indios* (Indians) are constantly and inescapably forced to face the fact of their ethnic stigma and adapt to the profaneness of their own persons (Goffman 1963). That there have been few racial confrontations in highland Ecuador in recent years eloquently bespeaks the fact that Sierra Indians and non-Indians have learned their respective roles of submission and dominance extremely well and almost unthinkingly put them into practice. Others, including the writer Jorge Icaza[3] and the painters Oswaldo Guayasamin and Eduardo Kingman, have voiced outrage against the oppression of the Indians, but as yet no indigenous spokesman has emerged to fan the fires of their own inarticulate, smoldering indignation.

THE RESEARCH APPROACH

Despite the Indians' general low estate, there are marked differences in the adaptive strategies various groups have evolved to defend themselves against the pressures of the dominant society. In our research we have undertaken (1) to describe these differences in full ethnographic detail, (2) to explain the observed differences, and (3) to trace their consequences with regard to self-image, styles of self-presentation, social mobility, acceptance of innovations, and the like.

At the most fundamental level these adaptive responses are expressed in the particular social, economic, and political institutions devised to cope with the dominant sector. They are also expressed in the basic stances groups take vis-à-vis the larger society and in the behavioral strategies employed in interpersonal relationships with members of the dominant sector. These strategies may range from withdrawal or a posture of defensive hostility, through servile deference or feigned ignorance of expected or prescribed behavior, to "realistic" accommodation to the dominant society and manipulation of its representatives. At the cognitive or conceptual level these differences are expressed in varying notions of one's self and others, of the social structure in which one is enmeshed, of one's life chances, man's fate, and the like. Foster's (1965) "image of limited good" is one of the possibilities at this conceptual level.

While there are individual differences, these adaptive strategies are widely shared by members of particular groups. Moreover, individual responses are "summed" as group responses on those occasions when actions or decisions are taken on behalf of a community by a representative group such as the *cabildo*, village council. These strategies differ, sometimes quite dramatically, from one group to another. Indeed, some behaviors are discontinuously distributed among the six communities that figure in our study. For example, such ritualized deference behaviors as kneeling before and kissing the hand of a secular authority, which one may observe in some groups (Atahualpa or San Francisco), are virtually unthinkable in others (Salasaca or Peguche).

It is hypothesized that differences in the adaptive responses observable among various groups, whether at the institutional, behavioral, or cognitive level, are largely determined by, or at least consistent with, differences in the "structures of dominance" that impinge upon them. By "structures of dominance" I mean the ways in which power[4] emanating from the dominant *mestizo*-white sector is brought to bear on an Indian community in various domains—economic, political, social, and religious. For many Indians today, as in the past, this domination is mediated by and symbolized in the persons of the parish priest, the *hacendado*, and the *teniente político* and by other *mestizos* such as the *chicheros* and *tinterillos* who live in the towns. In their respective spheres priest, *hacendado*, and *teniente político* (or their alter egos) still wield great power over the lives of the Indians and the fate that befalls them.[5]

In the economic realm major dimensions of a group's plight are (1) the extent to which it is involved with and dependent on the larger society, (2) the nature of the goods and services exchanged with the outside society, and (3) the degree to which a group has control over the basic resources (land, water, pasture, fuel) necessary to maintain its social and economic integrity at even the minimum level that has for centuries been deemed adequate for Ecuador's impoverished people. With regard to control over basic resources, a major contrast is between those who have long been referred to in Ecuador as *indios proprios*, owned Indians, and *indios libres*, free Indians. Free Indians own their own land, as contrasted with *huasipungueros*, who have rights of usufruct to small plots, *huasipungos*, on the large traditional haciendas together with certain perquisites such as access to pasture and firewood, in exchange for their labor on the estate and a small cash wage.

THE SIX COMMUNITIES[6]

Peguche

Peguche is one of the most prosperous of several communities in the canton of Otavalo, Imbabura province, devoted to weaving.[7] There is evidence that the Indians of Otavalo specialized in weaving even before the conquest (Salomon 1973); until they were outlawed, the textile *obrajes* (workshops in which forced labor was done) were famous just as the products of the present weaving industry are to-day. It is just and not a little ironic that present-day Otavaleños have been able to turn to their own advantage the skills learned by their forebears in the hard schools of the *obrajes*; the communities in which the *obrajes* flourished are precisely those that are best known today for their textiles.

Negociantes, traders, from Otavalo venture as far afield as Venezuela, Puerto Rico, and even the United States to sell their textiles, and they are a familiar sight in the larger cities and weekly markets throughout Ecuador, particularly where tourists are to be found. They do a lively business selling ponchos, scarves, shawls, and the like to passengers and crew members of ships calling at Guayaquil, Ecuador's largest city and principal port. There is a sizable colony of Otaveleños resident in Bogotá, where they weave and sell their wares. Most younger men and a good many of the older ones have lived outside Peguche for periods ranging up to ten years or so. All are bilingual in Spanish and Quichua.

Virtually all adult men and most boys 14 and older, as well as many girls and women, are engaged in a cottage weaving industry that has expanded rapidly in the last few decades. The majority are independent weavers, but a significant number are employed as wage workers by Indian entrepreneurs who operate small-scale factories. One man runs a factory in which 60 workers are employed in two around-the-clock shifts. Most of the goods he produces are exported to the United States and sold in large stores such as Macy's in New York City. The more enterprising are quick to accept innovations. Orlon has all but displaced wool, and the traditional hand looms are giving way to power-operated ones. Bright colors and new styles mark the goods now being produced for the growing export market and the tourist trade.

Within the limits of his identity as an Indian, the Otavaleño's relationship to those non-Indians with whom he deals is impersonal. He sells the products of his own acknowledged skills, not raw labor. It is the impersonal force of the market that comes to bear upon him, not the personal force of the *hacendado* or *patrón*. The greater freedom and invulnerability of the Otavaleño are readily apparent in his demeanor. His way of presenting himself stands in sharp contrast to the subservience of the hacienda-dominated *huasipunguero*. In the presence of authority the peon stands at a distance, knees bent, hunched over the hat clutched to his breast. The man from Peguche stands proudly erect. Where the peon strings together self-deprecating diminutives and utters them in a voice tuned to supplication, the Otavaleño is forthright and direct. Where the peon may not even be conscious that he is unkempt and dirty, the Otavaleño is impeccably groomed.

Although deeply engaged in the larger society and attuned to many of its values, the Otavaleño nevertheless stands apart and aloof from it; he is in it but not really of it. He tends not to intermarry, and he takes a certain pride in his Indian identity and dress, signaled in part by the braid he wears. Indeed, his Indianness has a commercial value; he uses it as a hallmark of the goods he would sell.

From a secure and expanding economic base, the Otavaleño has evolved what might be described as a strategy of selective engagement. The more affluent have adopted many of the amenities of middle-class Ecuadorian life while still preserving traditional culture forms, for example, the pattern of Indian sociability and participation in fiestas. He must be polite, but he need not be servile, nor is servility expected of him. As an Indian his social mobility is restricted, and there are many doors he cannot enter without mutual discomfiture. He most certainly is not immune to the subtle poisons of prejudice, let alone its grosser manifestations. I was present in a restaurant in

Otavalo when a man from Peguche's leading family, Otavalo's wealthiest textile entrepreneur and a complete gentleman, was forced to suffer the loud-mouthed insults of an insignificant town *mestizo*. Even for a person of his stature, the possibility of such treatment exists. Nevertheless, the Otavaleño does have a large measure of respect if not general acceptance.

Atahualpa

Founded by the Order of La Merced in the sixteenth century, Atahualpa is a traditional hacienda located in Cayambe canton, Pichincha province. A combined residential community and commercial enterprise producing barley, wheat, and potatoes for the domestic market, Atahualpa has a population of about 1,500. Of its largely Indian population 1,237 persons live on 135 separate *huasipungos* averaging 3.7 hectares in size. Another 200 are either squatters along the sides of the roads and ravines or resident sharecroppers whose presence on the estate has long been tolerated. The white administrative, technical, and service personnel all live in the central hacienda compound. One-third of the Indians on the *huasipungo* are *apegados* (relatives "attached" to the *huasipunguero*) who live in 105 separate households on the plots.

Following the expropriation of church lands in the early 1900s, Atahualpa was controlled by a government agency, the Asistencia Social, and leased to a succession of individual and institutional patrons, including one of Ecuador's leading breweries. In 1964, in the wake of the agrarian reform law promulgated by the military junta then in power, the *huasipungo* system was abolished and the Indians received title to their small holdings. The hacienda has since been transformed into two cooperatives, one managed by former *huasipungueros* and the other by white ex-employees.

Until very recently, however, in a pattern widely prevalent on other large estates, Atahualpa's Indians were bound to the hacienda in a tightly ordered and relatively self-contained social system presided over by the patron or his surrogate. It was a system sharply divided between those who commanded and those who obeyed. Orders and work assignments flowed down to the workers from the administrator through the *mayordomo* and a number of Indian *mayorales*, overseers.

In encounters between a peon and the patron or other authority figure one could often see acted out a grotesque charade of ceremonial deference as stylized as any ritual behavior ethologists delight in describing. It is a shattering experience to have a man fall on his knees before you, grasp you with a gnarled old root of a hand, and say, with tears streaming down his cheeks, "We who wear the red poncho are nothing. We are animals, brutes who know only how to work. We have nothing. We are poor, poor and ignorant. Look at me!"

Not all Atahualpans are scarred by servitude, however. There are a few exceptional men, including an acknowledged Communist who has visited Cuba and has been in and out of jail in Ecuador. Several of these men have assumed positions of power in the new cooperative. Now they are the *macho* patrons, and they play the part.

However, the simple peon is not defenseless. He has entered into an intricate system of reciprocal relationships for the exchange of various goods and services with kinsmen, *compadres*, and townspeople from Olmedo, the neighboring parish center or *cabecera*. He forms ties of *compadrazgo* with people from the town, and in return for their services as *tinterillos*, intercessors with authorities, and the like, or in exchange for credit extended to him, the peon grazes his *compadres'* animals with his own on hacienda pastures. He also forms sharecropping partnerships with *mestizos* from the town in a system called *chaquihuasca*. The *mestizos* provide seed and gifts of clothing, *aguardiente*, food, and a small amount of money, and the Indians contribute the land and labor. Both share equally in the harvest. Beyond this, the peon connives with white hacienda employees to illicitly exploit the estate's resources to their common gain.

As long as he fulfills his obligations at some minimal acceptable level, the *huasipunguero* has a certain basic security. His situation and his defenses are not unlike those of the army private. His response to orders may be sullen and grudging; he may feign ignorance of expectations or orders; he may loaf on the job and in other ways test the limits of the system; but he will usually be careful to stay within its limits. Despite his low estate, the *huasipunguero* is well aware that there are others who are landless and worse off than he is. And always lurking in the background is the threat of the brute force that the Indian can apply. Since the hacienda depends so heavily on the Indians' labor, it is vulnerable to work stoppages, particularly at crucial periods during the harvest. The organization for concerted political action is foreshadowed by the hierarchical structure of the hacienda; there are visible targets for the application of force, and there are common grievances to impel revolt. It is not surprising, then, that there has been a history of strikes, work stoppages, and violence—to the point of killing several patrons—on the haciendas of Cayambe.

Salasaca

The Salasaca[8] contrast dramatically with the peons of Atahualpa. About 4,000 of them live in a widely dispersed community of essentially independent subsistence farmers situated about 14 kilometers southeast of the city of Ambato in Tungurahua province. Although removed from immediate contact with large haciendas (there is one small estate bordering Salasaca that employs about 20 Indians), the Salasaca are almost completely surrounded by small-scale *mestizo* farmers. Despite their proximity to these *mestizos*, contacts between the two groups are shallow and occur primarily in the economic sphere. Occasionally they drink together at a local *chichería*, *cantina*, or fiesta, but the rule of social distance between the two groups still obtains. Intermarriage is rare.

The Salasaca have for centuries fended off encroachment by non-Indians. They claim that they are *mitimaes* brought to Ecuador from Bolivia by the Inca conquerors, a belief shared by non-Indians as well. Whether true or not, the story serves to justify the reputation of the Salasaca as a different and distinctive people. Their basic stance against outsiders is aggressively defensive. Strangers who venture off the few main paths and roads open to them are likely to be challenged by an abrupt ¿*A donde va?*, "Where are you going?," and menaced by snarling dogs. Little deference, whether signaled by posture, gesture, or form of address, is shown to whites. The Salasaca's reputation as being *muy bravo*, very fierce, is perpetuated by both themselves and others through a number of oft-told tales of violence. One of these involves the killing of a census taker, another the burning of the Catholic mission, yet another a pitched battle with *mestizos* over rights to scarce water. Each of these incidents is symbolic in its own way of resistance to various kinds of outside threats. However, Salasaca bravado is perhaps most aptly symbolized by their bulls. These animals, too, are widely known to be *muy bravo*, and they are eagerly sought for *juegos de toros*, bull baiting, at local fiestas and even in coastal towns.

The Salasaca pride themselves on not accepting menial jobs as *cargadores*, carriers, or domestic servants, and they are scornful of other Indians who do. In recent years a number of younger men have joined the seasonal exodus of highland Indians to the Coast to work on the large plantations there. However, they can work on the Coast as comparatively anonymous individuals (they shed their distinctive black ponchos and heavy, broad-brimmed felt hats) and earn what they regard as a decent wage for honorable labor.

Even more significant has been the introduction of commercial weaving. In 1957, with the help of several agencies including the former Point IV Program, three men were taught to weave small tapestries embellished with colorful traditional designs. The original three took on others as apprentices, and today 200-300 Salasaca, mostly young men and boys in their teens, are engaged in weaving and selling tapestries, largely to tourists and for a small export market. In the manner of the Otavaleños, a few of the more enterprising have established small shops in which they employ several weavers who work at piece rates. They have, in fact, albeit in a less sophisticated way, developed many of the same strategies in interethnic relations evident among the Otavalo weavers. In large degree, weaving has displaced the former making of cordage from *cabuya* fiber as a source of cash income, especially for the younger men.

Except for the introduction of commercial weaving, the only agency to gain a solid foothold in Salasaca is the Catholic church; a Protestant mission has been present for some years but has gained only a handful of converts. The mission and school that were founded by the Madres Lauritas from Colombia in 1943 have had their own vicissitudes. The Misión Andina, an Ecuadorian community development agency, has made several overtures but has been consistently rebuffed. A succession of Peace Corps volunteers has worked in Salasaca. They have had only very modest successes, primarily among the weavers. A weavers' cooperative shakily established by one volunteer some years ago foundered and subsequently failed to be resurrected again a few years later. Today there are many changes as Salasaca moves increasingly into the larger society, but the basic attitude is, "Leave us in peace." They have learned how to defend themselves effectively, and even today the majority follow an essentially traditional style of life.

San Francisco

San Francisco is a nucleated agricultural village of some 540 persons situated on the western rim of the valley of Riobamba in Chimborazo province.[9] All families own some land, but few have enough to subsist on. What land is available is of poor quality, and much of it is badly eroded. Rainfall is often inadequate, and there is not sufficient water to irrigate regularly. Hail is a constant threat to cereal crops, and a blight called *lancha* is another scourge. Equal inheritance among all heirs has led to great fragmentation of land—some families have as many as 25 or 30 minuscule plots. Such fragmentation does, however, permit the spreading of risks where farming is precarious at best.

Given these uncertainties and the scarcity of land, San Francis-queños are forced to go out of the community to survive. Except for small amounts of produce such as alfalfa, barley, peas, and pyre-thrum, a few scrawny sheep, and small baskets woven by the women, they have nothing to offer but their labor in a society where labor is abundant and cheap. Thus about 30 families have a contrac-tual arrangement to provide labor once a week as *ayudas*, helpers, on lands owned by a hacienda in a neighboring valley. In exchange, they are granted access to hacienda pastures for their small flocks of sheep, a ration of potatoes at harvest time, and the like. A number of men are employed as day laborers for periods of several weeks or more on two large estates owned by a wealthy *hacendado* from Am-bato. One of these is a sugar cane plantation on the Coast, the other a highland hacienda. The village itself is a sort of collective client for this particular patron.

Others have established individual patron-client relationships with employers in the larger cities. One man who is especially adroit at managing such relationships has patrons in Riobamba, Ambato, and Quito and has used his influence to find jobs for others from San Francisco, including a number of girls employed as domestics. Many have established similar patron-client relationships with *mestizo* farm-ers from the nearby town of San Juan. Several have solidified ties with patrons by entering into sharecropping arrangements with them. The Indian supplies the land and labor, the patron *partidario* the seed. Both share equally in the harvest—a bad bargain for the Indian, but a good stratagem to secure an ally. San Francisqueños are frequently forced to mortgage their land at extortionate rates, with half the crop demanded as interest in addition to repayment of the principal.

The patron-client relationship, highly asymmetrical and with strong overtones of dependency, is the prototype for all relationships with authority figures who are potential benefactors, including an-thropologists and community development agents. The basic strategy in such a relationship is for the Indian to present himself as a poor, humble, willing, deserving person. Embedded in the relationship, and within the limits of what the patron will tolerate, the Indian em-ploys what might be called a strategy of counterexploitation. In rela-tionships with Ecuadorian patrons the lines are quite clearly drawn, but this is not the case with visiting gringo anthropologists. My role among the people of San Francisco was not sharply defined, nor at the outset did I seek to clarify it or to set limits. I was as a consequence fair game for a variety of exploitative maneuvers, including requests for food, loans, transportation, jobs, and services as intermediary in securing jobs or favors elsewhere. Begging (not the rule in Peguche, Salasaca, or Saraguro) was an especially troublesome problem until I established that I wanted to decide for myself when largess was to be distributed. Perhaps the most poignant example of such behavior was a solemn and tearful leave-taking with a key informant. I count him a true friend, but on parting, and without anticipating any gift I might make him, he asked for my flashlight and a substantial advance against wages for work in a future summer.

The need to establish patron-client relationships can be a source of great competition and envy. I was "captured" early in the game by one man who at first, unbeknownst to me, controlled access to me by his fellow villagers. Jealousy of his relationship with me led to exaggerated stories of the money he got from me, to deep resentment, and to a fight in which he was badly beaten and almost had a thumb bitten off. In San Francisco envy is a gnawing, ever-present emotion, and "the image of limited good" is a harsh reality.

Guabug

Guabug,[10] which lies only a few kilometers to the west across an intervening hill, is like San Francisco in many respects. Yet it has many advantages, and circumstances have conspired to make it a village chosen for progress. Rainfall is more abundant and predictable. The soil is richer and well suited to raising onions, which have become an important cash crop. There have been more and better opportunities for outside employment. A number of men, for example, are employed in a nearby limestone quarry and cement factory established in 1954. There are, moreover, a number of neighboring haciendas which, again in exchange for labor, provide access to their resources and a small cash wage. Although often flagrantly exploitative, such ties are better than none at all, and they are much more regularized than is the case for San Franciso. A number of people have left Guabug, some for well-paying jobs such as school teacher, agronomist, and shopkeeper.

The basic strategies employed in Guabug, both economic and interpersonal, are much like those in San Franciso. The same patterns of deference are shown to authority figures, and the same sorts of alliances are sought with persons outside the community. San Francisco is, however, much more conservative in its general outlook. The fiesta system that still flourishes in San Francisco[11] has disappeared from Guabug, and many men in the latter community have given up Indian dress for western-style clothes while still proclaiming their Indian identity. At the field seminar to be described below, for example, the two from Guabug came nattily dressed in tweed jackets and regular trousers while the two from San Francisco wore ponchos and the traditional small round felt hat. In short, Guabug is much further along the path to cultural mestization and integration into the national culture than is San Francisco.

Saraguro

Like the Otavaleños in the north, the Saraguro are a large group of more than 10,000 who live in a number of communities in Ecuador's southernmost province, Loja. Both the landscape and the people of Saraguro have a different aspect. There are no snowy peaks. Instead there are rolling wooded hills, many of them cleared for fields and pasture, and intensively cultivated valleys devoted largely to corn farming. Unlike the central and northern highlands, there are no large haciendas. *Mestizo* farms in the area are on the same scale as those owned by the Indians. In fact, the average Indian farmer is at least as well off as his white counterpart. Nor is there the same pressure on the land. The best valley land is expensive, as expensive as corn land in central Illinois, but communal, "free" land is available in the hills for the clearing.

Most important is the fact that the Saraguro have colonized the Oriente. Since the turn of the century Saraguro in increasing numbers have settled in the Yacuambi River valley, expropriating the native Shuar. Here they have cleared extensive tracts for pasture and a few other crops such as manioc, sugar cane, and bananas and have recently become engaged in cattle raising (see Stewart, Belote, and Belote 1976). Many Saraguro are thus transmigrant, even transhumant, maintaining land and homes in both the Oriente and the Sierra. To be sure, these circumstances are exceptional in Ecuador, but the concept of "limited good" would have as little meaning for the Saraguro as it would have had for Andrew Carnegie.

Given the absence of systematic exploitation, the greater abundance of land, and greater economic parity in Saraguro, Indian-white relationships are more egalitarian there than they are in most parts of the Sierra (Belote 1978). In some communities Indians and whites live side by side at the same level, and cordial relations are maintained between them. There are, in fact, some curious reversals. Poor whites are often employed by Indians as laborers, and there is an institutionalized pattern of whites begging from Indians. Indians can and do "become" whites (*laichu*, as they are known in Saraguro), simply by changing their costume and, for the men, by cutting their hair. They can change their identity and, unlike most of Ecuador, still openly and unashamedly retain ties with their own Indian families. It is not unusual for one or more children in a family to become *laichu* while their siblings remain Indian, and many genealogies reveal marriages between Indians and *laichu*. Unlike the disavowal of one's racial origins involved in "passing," Saraguro can publicly change their identity and do so without recrimination. The advantage for those who change their identity is that they are able thereby to enlarge their circle of social relations and enter more readily into the world of the whites.

Good farmers, the Saraguro have been quick to accept technological innovations—seed, fertilizer, implements—whatever their source. Their approach to agents of change is pragmatic: "What have you to offer that I can use?" As incipient capitalists and entrepreneurs, they are highly individualistic and little concerned with community development programs unless they have a personal stake in them. In Erasmus's (1961) terms, conspicuous ownership takes precedence over conspicuous giving (or, one might add, over conspicuous involvement), and invidious comparison and emulation are important motivating factors. Like the weavers of Peguche, the Saraguro are an open and proud people who confront their white and *mestizo* compatriots without humility or fear.

THE GUASLÁN SEMINAR

In the summer of 1968 my students and I brought together two men from each of the six communities for an experimental field seminar held at the Misión Andina's training center, Guaslán, near Riobamba. Our purpose was to collect additional data, but especially to test some of our hypotheses and interpretations about the differences among the several groups.

For two weeks we lived closely together. We ate together, drank together, socialized and worked together, so that we came to know each other very well. Each morning and afternoon we held formal meetings lasting three hours. We began by asking each pair of men to describe in detail the style of life in their own community—how they earned their living, the political organization, the fiestas celebrated, relations with neighboring villages and towns, and so on. All paid close attention to the presentations and asked a great many questions. We also asked each pair to discuss a series of special topics, such as the nature of interethnic relationships, the terms used to distinguish various social and racial categories, the recent presidential elections, religious beliefs and practices, what they felt were the principal problems in their respective communities, and what the government might do to solve them.

They were also asked to present small sociodramas in which one man took the role of a priest, *hacendado*, *teniente político*, or the like and the other that of a simple Indian. The selection of the roles they would play was left largely to the Indians themselves. For example, the two men from Saraguro presented a long and very interesting and entertaining sketch between a Saraguro colonist and a Shuar; the two from Salasaca acted out an encounter between a *chichero* and an Indian requesting a loan. In similar fashion we also asked them to give a demonstration of the styles of greeting, in both gestures and words, used in their communities between persons of different social levels.

In many less formal occasions, such as in the dining room or at our small fiestas in the evenings, there were many opportunities to observe differences in behavior among the six groups. For example, the men from Atahualpa, San Francisco, and Guabug showed much more deference to us and to the director of the Guaslán center than those from Peguche, Salasaca, and Saraguro. The two from San Francisco were shocked when the Salasaca greeted the students by their first names only instead of using a more formal title. When there was hard work to be done such as unloading a truck or killing and dressing a pig for our farewell party, it was those from Guabug, San Francisco, and Atahualpa who volunteered while the others stood idly by as observers. Many similar examples could be cited, but, in short, we were able to observe daily in their ordinary behavior many of the differences among the groups that we had hypothesized.

The Indians themselves were sensitive to many of the same differences. On the last day of the seminar we held private interviews with each of the 12 men. Each man was asked to characterize the men from each of the other communities and to compare them with the others. We asked them to tell us which group was most like or most different from themselves, which was the most Indian, the least Indian, the richest, the most "civilized," and so on. In response to such questions, a perceptive and highly intelligent man from Peguche made the following observations:

Question: Which group would you say is most similar to you?

Answer: The group most similar to us are the Saraguros, because they don't have to beg from anyone or ask favors, not from the priest, the *teniente político*, or the *apu*.[12] They know how to speak directly with anyone, while the others ask someone to speak to the priest or the *teniente político* for them. The Saraguros aren't afraid. After the Saraguros perhaps the Salasaca are most like us. Those from Guabug and San Francisco are the same and have the same ideas. The Salasaca weren't bothered with *apus*, and they don't beg from the whites.

Question: Are there differences among those from Atahualpa, Guabug, and San Francisco?

Answer: Yes, there are a few differences. Those from Atahualpa work on a hacienda. Those from Guabug and San Francisco work on haciendas without any real benefits, for no more than a few pieces of straw. They get little from their land. Those from Chimborazo have to beg more than the Salasacas; they are used to begging from the *hacendados*, or rather from the white people.

Question: Why do you think they have had to beg more than the Saraguros and you?

Answer: We have always spoken Spanish and can go directly to the priest and the *teniente político* for what we want. And we haven't been afraid like the others.

Question: Why have they been afraid?

Answer: Perhaps because they don't know how to speak, or because they have always been timid, and because they live under the domination of the hacienda. But we are independent and don't have to look to the haciendas because we have our own industries. The Saraguros also have their own work of cattle raising and their own industry. They have a lot of cattle and land in the Oriente and they don't have to beg from anyone.

The words of this man eloquently express the essential nature of the differences among the six communities with which we have been concerned. And his insight into the causes of these differences is the best confirmation I can offer of the validity of our own "scientific" explanation of them.

NOTES

Acknowledgments: This paper is printed here by kind permission of Random House, in essentially the same form in which it was originally published (Casagrande 1974). A preliminary version was presented at the XXXIX International Congress of Americanists in Lima, Peru, Aug. 1970.

The research has been supported by grants from the National Science Foundation (GS–1224 and GS–3049), the National Institute of Mental Health, and the Center for International Comparative Studies of the University of

Illinois, Urbana. I wish also to acknowledge the contributions of my associates in this research and give them my grateful thanks: Linda and James Belote (Saraguro), Muriel Crespi (Atahualpa), Kathleen Klumpp (Peguche), and Arthur R. Piper (Guabug). Mrs. Crespi's doctoral dissertation (1968) provides a full account of the hacienda.

1. The basic question "Who is an Indian?" is very difficult to answer. The answers vary depending on whether one uses as criteria self-identification, categorization of a person as Indian by others both Indian and non-Indian, or some combination of "objective" measures such as knowledge of Quichua, clothing, type of dwelling, or natal community. Physical appearance is not unimportant in Ecuador; many Indians themselves value a light complexion. However, skin color and other physical traits are not the all-but-indelible markers of race they are for blacks in the United States. There are many *mestizos*, and *blancos*, so acknowledged by themselves and others, who are darker in complexion than many Indians. Race in Ecuador is, then, primarily a social and cultural and not a physical category.

For the Indian, clothing (hat, poncho, trousers, skirt, footwear or the lack of it) and hair style (whether braids of the Otavaleño and Saraguro men or the long-cut hair of the Salasaca) are the public symbols of Indian identity. As elsewhere in the world, costume is used in manifold ways to express one's self-identity, both consciously and unconsciously. One notes a sharp contrast between Indians from Otavalo, Saraguro, and Salasaca on the one hand and Atahualpa, Guabug, or San Francisco on the other. When asked to pose for a photograph, the former will typically *put on* his best Indian clothes while the latter will divest himself of Indian dress and put on western-style clothes if he has them. In Ecuador one can then, knowing passable Spanish, shed these public symbols of Indianness and slip with little notice into the rural or urban proletariat. Thousands do.

2. On several occasions I took Indians on a tour of the magnificent archaeological collections in the Museum of the Central Bank of Ecuador. My Indian friends evinced only mild interest and saw no connection between themselves and these relics of the past.

3. See especially Icaza's novel *Huasipungo*.

4. I use the terms "power" and "domain" in the sense employed by Richard N. Adams (1970).

5. *Hacendado* means owner of a large estate or hacienda; *teniente político*, a political deputy, the appointed parish civil officer; *chichero*, a man who sells *chicha*, a mildly intoxicating beverage made from fermented corn and brown sugar; *tinterillo*, a kind of legal clerk or scribe who draws up documents, writes letters, and the like.

6. The six communities here described represent a considerable range of variation in the degree to which they control essential economic resources, the nature of those resources, and the extent of their involvement in the larger society. Nevertheless, we cannot assume that they cover the full spectrum of adaptive strategies resorted to by the Indians of highland Ecuador. There are other groups—herders who live in the high *páramo* (bleak, barren plateau) and isolated agriculturalists—who presumably have evolved other strategies for survival in their particular, perhaps even harsher, circumstances.

7. There are upward of 40,000 Indians living in scores of separate communities in the Otavalo area. While there are many similarities, one may observe among them many of the same differences we have noted for Ecuador as a whole. Thus some groups are primarily agriculturalists; others are full-time artisans making such products as rush mats, pottery, and bricks; and some are tied to haciendas. Otavalo is the best-described area in highland Ecuador (e.g., Parsons 1945, Collier and Buitrón 1949, Rubio Orbe 1956, Salomon 1973, Villavicencio 1973, Casagrande 1977).

8. The Salasaca are described by Costales and Costales (1959).

9. Burgos Guevara (1970) provides a good account of interethnic relations in the Riobamba area.

10. For a more complete account of Guabug and the parish to which it pertains, see Casagrande and Piper (1969).

11. Casagrande (1978) discusses the subsequent demise of the fiesta system in San Franciso, partly as a consequence of the conversion of a major portion of the population to evangelical Protestantism.

12. *Apu*: a lay religious leader and hereditary intermediary for the Indian in his dealings with the priest and *teniente político*.

REFERENCES CITED

Adams, Richard N.
    1970   *Crucifixion by Power*. Austin: University of Texas Press.
Bateson, Gregory
    1958   *Naven*. 2d ed. Stanford, Calif.: Stanford University Press.
Belote, Linda
    1978   Prejudice and Pride: Indian-White Relations in Saraguro, Ecuador.
            Ann Arbor, Mich.: University Microfilms. Ph.D. thesis, University
            of Illinois, Urbana.
Burgos Guevara, Hugo
    1970   *Relaciones Interétnicas en Riobamba*. Mexico City: Instituto Indigenista
            Interamericano.
Casagrande, Joseph B.
    1974   Strategies for Survival: The Indians of Highland Ecuador. In Dwight
            Heath, ed., *Contemporary Cultures and Societies of Latin America*. 2d
            ed. New York: Random House, pp. 93–107.
    1977   Looms of Otavalo. *Natural History* 86 (8):48–59.
    1978   Religious Conversion and Social Change in an Indian Community
            of Highland Ecuador. In Roswith Hartmann and Udo Oberem, eds.,
            Amerikanistische Studien: Festschrift für Hermann Trimborn, vol. 1. St.
            Augustin: Haus Völker und Kulturen, Anthropos Institut.
Casagrande, Joseph B., and Arthur R. Piper
    1969   La Transformación Estructural de una Parroquia Rural en las Tierras
            Altas del Ecuador. *América Indígena* 29:1039–64.
Collier, John, Jr., and Aníbal Buitrón
    1949   *The Awakening Valley*. Chicago: University of Chicago Press.
Costales, Piedad P. de, and Alfredo Costales Samaniego
    1959   *Los Salasacas*. Quito: Instituto Ecuatoriano de Antropología.

Crespi, Muriel
   1969   The Patrons and Peons of Pesillo: A Traditional Hacienda System in Highland Ecuador. Ann Arbor, Mich.: University Microfilms. Ph.D. thesis, University of Illinois, Urbana.
Erasmus, Charles J.
   1961   *Man Takes Control: Cultural Development and American Aid.* Minneapolis: University of Minnesota Press.
Foster, George M.
   1965   Peasant Society and the Image of Limited Good. *American Anthropologist* 67:293–315.
Goffman, Erving
   1963   *Stigma: Notes on the Management of Spoiled Identity.* Englewood Cliffs, N.J.: Prentice-Hall.
Klumpp, Kathleen
   1974   El Retorno del Inga: Una Expresión Ecuatoriana de la Ideología Mesiánica Andina. *Cuadernos de Historia y Arquelogía* (Guayaquil) 41:99–136.
Ossio A., Juan M.
   1973   *Ideología Mesiánica del Mundo Andina.* Lima: Ignacio Prado Pastor.
Parsons, Elsie Clews
   1945   *Peguche: A Study of Andean Indians.* Chicago: University of Chicago Press.
Rubio Orbe, Gonzalo
   1956   *Punyaro.* Quito: Casa de la Cultura Ecuatoriana.
Salomon, Frank
   1973   Weavers of Otavalo. In Daniel Gross, ed., *Peoples and Cultures of Native South America.* Garden City, N.Y.: Natural History Press, pp. 463–92.
Stewart, Norman R., Jim Belote, and Linda Belote
   1976   Transhumance in the Central Andes. *Annals of the Association of American Geographers* 66 (3):377–97.
Turner, Victor
   1969   *The Ritual Process: Structure and Anti-Structure.* Chicago: Aldine.
Villavicencio Rivadeneira, Gladys
   1973   *Relaciones Interétnicas en Otavalo, Ecuador.* Mexico City: Instituto Indigenista Interamericano.

9

Adaptation and Family Size from Rural Ecuador to Guayaquil

Susan C. M. Scrimshaw

Ethnicity, in Ecuador as everywhere else, carries a corresponding set of beliefs and behaviors that comprises the adaptation of a particular culture group to its environment. Culture has been described as humanity's most powerful adaptation, and culture change has been analyzed as an evolutionary process (Alland 1973:274, Cohen 1968), yet demographic analyses of fertility change and migration tend to ignore social or cultural factors which may affect the processes they study (Nag 1968:7, Polgar 1972:209). Fertility and family size lend themselves to the holistic approach of anthropology particularly well because they are the result of a combination of cultural and biological factors. As Wagley, Polgar, and others have demonstrated, every culture has an implicit or explicit "population policy," a set of practices which affects fertility and family size, with the result that completed family size is not random or merely the result of biological factors (Wagley 1951, Polgar 1972:210). As Alland states, " . . . in any adaptive system, cultural and biological factors can each modify behavior and each other, and these modifications can then affect the state of the system or act to transform it into another system" (1973:274).

Data collected in Guayaquil, and in two rural Ecuadorian communities in 1971, appear to indicate that ethnicity is an important factor in the adaptation of urban in-migrants from rural Ecuador to Guayaquil. Migrants from the rural Ecuadorian Coast and Sierra tend to come from very different environments and ethnic groups. Using changes in fertility behavior as an index, this paper examines factors related to adaptation in the rural environment, the characteristics of migrants in comparison to those who stay behind, and behaviors in the city as they affect adaptation to the urban environment.

The rate and amount of rural-to-urban migration in Latin America have increased rapidly in the past 30 years (Balán 1969:3; Davis and

Casis 1946:196, 199–201; Cardona and Simmons 1975). Ecuador's two primate cities, Quito and Guayaquil, have both been subjected to heavy urban in-migration, estimated to be at least 4% and 5% respectively in the decade from 1965 to 1975 (Merlo et al. 1975; Junta de Planificación, personal communication). In 1970, approximately 35% of Ecuador's 6.5 million people lived in urban centers of 10,000 or more (Macintosh 1972:1, 4). The largest city, Guayaquil, had a population of approximately one million people when the research reported here was undertaken.

Major factors contributing to urban in-migration in Latin America include the rapid population increase as death rates have dropped and birth rates have remained high (Schulz 1970:1). This led to a lack of land and work for the excess population, an increased awareness of urban areas and the many perceived benefits there (Hawley 1969:12, Schulz 1970:7), and a search for upward socioeconomic mobility and education, particularly for the children (Matos Mar 1961:182, Mangin 1959:23, Lewis 1960:972).

The explosive growth in the rate of rural-urban migration in Latin America in the years since World War II has stimulated questions about the effects of urbanization on the fertility behavior of migrants (Kiser 1971:381, Stycos 1963:266). While the validity of the widely accepted belief that rural fertility generally is higher than urban fertility has been questioned (Robinson 1963:292), many researchers present strong cases for the existence of such a differential under most conditions (Carleton 1965:20, Davis and Casis 1946:199, United Nations 1961:91, Micklin 1969:461, Weller and Macisco 1970:3, Pool 1969:1, Mertens and Miro 1969:7).

Given a rural-urban fertility differential, do rural immigrants to cities reproduce at higher "rural" rates, or do they adopt some or all of the urban attitudes and behavior which are related to the relatively lower urban fertility patterns? If the exposure to the urbanization process does affect the fertility of urban in-migrants, how soon after immigration is fertility behavior modified? In the past observers felt that lower fertility as a result of acculturation to the urban milieu occurs after about two generations (Hawley 1969:25, Goldberg 1959:214).

In a 1970 article Weller and Macisco suggest that selective migration may provide an explanation for the relatively low fertility of urban in-migrants in some countries. "Perhaps migration itself is selective of low fertility." Similarly, Goldstein writes, ". . . urban places either attract those with much lower fertility levels, or migrants fairly rapidly assimilate the general patterns of fertility behavior in the place of destination" (1971:35). Both patterns described by Goldstein appear in Ecuador, and depend heavily on the place of origin and thus on the ethnic identity or ethnic classification of the migrant and the migrant's sexual partner, and on their interaction with the urban environment.

METHODOLOGY

The data discussed here were collected in 1971 during six months of enthnographic fieldwork in the squatter settlements, *suburbios*, of Guayaquil, followed by a survey of 2,294 households in the squatter settlements and in the central city slums, *tugurios*. The survey sample was drawn by Professor Albino Bocaz of CELADE with the assistance of Ernesto Pinto Rojas, using the 1962 census distribution as a base. The sample was drawn with probability proportionate to the size of the population in each area, based on estimates made by projecting growth since the 1962 census. Individuals refused interviews for anyone in their household in only 1.65% of the cases.

In each household all women between the ages of 15 and 45 and all men currently in a sexual union with women in that age range were interviewed on such subjects as housing; job histories; economic factors; union and fertility histories; knowledge, attitudes, and practice of contraception; and migration (if migrants). The 2,294 households yielded usable interviews with 2,936 women and 1,119 of their male partners. One hundred households in each of two rural villages also were interviewed. One village was in the sierran province of Tungurahua, the other in the coastal province of Guayas. These two provinces had contributed proportionately more migrants from their region to the sample studied during the urban ethnographic phase of fieldwork.

GEOGRAPHIC AND CULTURAL DIVERSITY

The Introduction to this volume provides a detailed description of Ecuador's geographic and cultural variations. The following few paragraphs highlight factors which are particularly important to the discussion in this paper.

The Sierra

For the purposes of the arguments presented here, it is important to note that the Sierra Indians represent a variety of linguistic and cultural groups which share the common experience of four centuries of subjugation by the Spaniards and their descendants and a resultant low socioeconomic status in many cases.

When some of the few available descriptions of Sierra Indian communities are examined, it is apparent that many such communities have the characteristics common to "closed corporate" peasant communities as described by Wolf (1957). These include a relatively small, stable population, subsistence agriculture with little dependence on cash income, village endogamy, and a resistance to outsiders and outside influences (Casagrande 1972:1–2, Erickson 1966:75–84). According to Casagrande, the population stability is due to relatively late marriage, a high rate of infant and child mortality, a "very low" rate of in-migration, and possibly to induced abortion (1972:3). My own data based on conversations with Indian migrants to Guayaquil and with Indians in the Sierra village studied agree with this.

Because land is limited in these communities and inheritance is shared equally by siblings, it appears that a large family is not adaptive in cultural or environmental terms. In fact, Casagrande (1972:3) says that families are "small," attributing this to high infant death rates, low life expectancy (and therefore shorter reproductive periods), and induced abortion. In addition to similar circumstances in the Sierra village studied (although there were no admitted induced abortions), there was possible evidence of female infanticide. The sex ratios for first pregnancies were significantly disproportionate (43 males to 20 females). The probability of this occurring naturally is less than .01, since normal ratios at birth are about 51 males to 49 females. The ratios in second pregnancies (26 males to 23 females) and subsequent ones were not unusual. It is quite likely that women were often "collapsing" their first and second pregnancies and that the child born first in these cases was usually a girl.

Table 1 shows mean pregnancies and living children by age for women in the Sierra village. Both are relatively low for women at all age groups. The jump in nearly two children for women aged 40–45 over women aged 30–35 is surprising, but this may be simply an artifact owing to the relatively small sample size.

One of the few other studies in the Sierra where some demographic data were collected was done by Peggy Barlett in 1970. In the village where she worked (near Otavalo) the average number of living children for women of all ages was only 2.45 (out of a sample of 158). The average number of live births was 3.67. She also reports a mean age at marriage of 18.4 for women (personal communication 1974). Her findings are consistent with Casagrande's and with my own.

Such a clustering of behavior traits resulting in a relatively small

TABLE 1. Mean Number of Pregnancies and Living Children by Age for Urban Migra and Nonmigrant Women and Women in Two Rural Villages.

	Mean Pregnancies				Mean Living Children			
Age	Coastal Village	Sierra Village	Mi-grant	Urban Non-migrant	Coastal Village	Sierra Village	Mi-grant	Urban Non-migran
Lowest – 19	2.4	1.0	0.5	0.4	2.3	1.0	0.5	0.3
20 – 24	3.7	1.9	1.9	1.7	3.0	1.8	1.6	1.4
25 – 29	6.0	2.6	3.6	3.7	5.1	2.4	2.8	2.9
30 – 34	5.8	4.1	4.6	5.2	4.4	3.4	3.7	3.9
35 – 39	8.1	4.0	6.6	6.5	6.5	3.6	4.9	4.8
40 – 45	6.8	6.2	7.1	6.9	6.0	5.3	5.4	5.1
Total	4.4	3.4	4.2	3.4	3.2	3.0	3.6	2.6
N	80	69	711	2,170	80	69	711	2,170

family size under limited environmental conditions (in this case a scarcity of land and other resources) has been explained as adaptive behavior by Alland (1973:301). Many of the Indian communities of highland Ecuador appear to have values and behavioral systems which lead to relatively small completed families. While such values are often implicit rather than explicit, there was a mean desired family size of three among the Indians in the Sierra village. This is two children less than the mean number of living children (5.3) for 14 women who have probably completed their families (women aged 40–45).

There are other types of communities in highland Ecuador. Besides the Indian villages, there are villages containing *mestizos* and Indians in an uneasy coexistence, and larger towns and cities dominated by *mestizos* and *blanco* upper-class Ecuadorians. While information is scarce, birth and death rates in rural areas and in towns appear to be nearly as high among *mestizos* as among Indians. The larger urban areas in the Sierra may differ from the towns and rural villages in this respect, but migrants who say they are from cities are often originally from rural areas and have spent some months or years in a city before migrating on to Guayaquil.

The Coast

Rural coastal communities are either peasant villages or plantation villages, considerably more open to outside influences than in the

Sierra. This is partly because rural coastal peoples have largely lost their Indian identity. Only a few tribal Indian groups remain, and there are virtually no modern Indians (as described in Wagley and Harris 1968:83). Most *costeños* are subsistence farmers, fishermen, wage-labor plantation workers, or a combination of these.

While living conditions in the Coast are characterized by poverty as in the Sierra, the environment is less forbidding and subsistence somewhat easier. A major difference between the two areas appears to be the greater integration into the national life on the part of the coastal dweller. The "open" peasant subculture and the greater ease of transportation over a longer period of time appear to be partly responsible for this. While travel in the rugged Sierra has always been a major undertaking, the coastal "roads" were rivers, estuaries, and the sea itself. The result is that rural coastal life is not as dependent on the physical and cultural environment as in the Sierra. Wage labor is a possibility if there is not enough land or if the crops fail, and leaving the village is not so difficult.

Under such conditions, the theoretical position that fertility and family size are based on adaptations to the physical and cultural environment would predict that a relatively small family size would not be as important on the Coast. The limitations imposed by limited land in the Sierra are overcome by a greater dependence on cash wages from the big plantations (banana, cacao, etc.) and the greater openness and mobility of the culture. While there is little information (ethnographic *or* demographic) available on rural coastal areas, the data from the coastal village studied show women having approximately two (living) children more than their sierran counterparts. There is not the evidence for infanticide in the coastal village that there is in the Sierra village, although two coastal women (out of 78) reported having had induced abortions.

The numbers of pregnancies and living children by age for women in the coastal village studied are also shown in Table 1. These figures are consistently higher than those for the Sierra village, but the degree of difference lessens in the 40–45 age group, when the mean number of pregnancies drops to 6.8 and the mean number of living children drops to 6.0. It is possible that the memory of older women may be at fault, or perhaps the small sample size is again a problem. My impressions of the rural coastal areas, based on migrants' accounts and a brief stay in one village, is that family size is simply not as important as in the Sierra.

Some additional data for Coast and Sierra are presented by Heer (1964), who shows that the child-woman ratio (ratio of children under 5 to women 15 to 45 years old) differs between Coast and Sierra (his data are actually for linguistic groups). The ratio is higher for coastal provinces. For example, in Guayas, location of the coastal village studied (and Guayaquil), the ratio is 699; in Tungurahua, province of the Sierra village studied, it is 622 (Heer 1964:83).

The research described here did not extend to a study of a rural village in Esmeraldas, where another ethnic group described by Whitten (1974) as Afro-Hispanic predominates. While it has not been possible to obtain precise demographic data for this group, Whitten's descriptions of family life and the value of children would indicate a high-fertility, large-family population, similar to the rest of the Coast, although slightly different values may be operating such as the strength of the mother-child relationship (Whitten 1974:150–53). Because of the similarities in terms of fertility and family size, the migrants from Esmeraldas are considered along with other coastal migrants when fertility patterns are examined.

TABLE 2. Male and Female Migrants to Guayaquil by Province of Origin.

		Male		Female		Total	
	Province	Number	%	Number	%	Number	%
Coast	Cañar	11	2.9	13	1.5	24	1.9
	El Oro	20	5.3	34	4.0	54	4.4
	Esmeraldas	19	4.9	44	5.2	63	5.1
	Guayas	104	27.3	238	28.0	·342	27.8
	Los Ríos	27	7.1	110	12.9	137	11.1
	Manabí	58	15.2	181	21.3	239	19.4
	Subtotal	239	62.7	620	72.9	859	69.7
Sierra	Azuay	25	6.6	61	7.2	86	6.9
	Bolivar	6	1.6	12	1.4	18	1.5
	Carchi	2	0.5	4	0.5	6	0.5
	Cotopaxi	9	2.4	10	1.2	19	1.5
	Chimborazo	27	7.1	51	6.0	78	6.3
	Imbabura	2	0.5	4	0.5	6	0.5
	Loja	15	3.9	23	2.7	38	3.1
	Pichincha	29	7.6	21	2.5	50	4.1
	Tungurahua	19	4.9	34	4.0	53	4.3
	Subtotal	134	35.1	220	26.0	354	28.7
Oriente	Santiago Zamora	8	2.1	10	1.2	18	1.5
	Total	381	99.9	850	100.1	1,231	99.9

MIGRATION AND MIGRANTS

The proportion of long-term urban dwellers (born in Guayaquil or migrated before age 15) to migrants was approximately three to one. Twenty-four percent of the 2,936 women and 25% of the 1,119 men had migrated to Guayaquil at age 15 or older. Despite the fact that (as of 1962) slightly more than half of Ecuador's population live in the Sierra (Erickson et al. 1966:60), 69% of the 1,231 migrants surveyed came from the Coast. Table 2 shows the proportions of men and women from each province. Guayas and Manabí on the Coast and Azuay and Chimborazo in the Sierra contribute the most migrants from their respective regions. This larger proportion of migrants from the Coast can be attributed in part to the proximity of coastal areas to Guayaquil, but other factors may also be involved.

In a paper on migration in Chile, Arthur Conning discusses what he calls "community orientation" in relation to migration. He demonstrates that communities with a greater degree of differentiation (integration into national life) are more likely to contribute migrants to urban areas (Conning 1971:297, 311). Conning's descriptions of communities with greater and lesser differentiation correspond to descriptions of open peasant and closed corporate communities.

In his article on closed corporate peasant communities in Central America and Java, Wolf says that such communities will tend to push off surplus population (1957:12). However, as discussed earlier, population increase owing to births is lower in Sierra villages than in coastal villages. While land is "an absolutely limited good" in many Sierra villages (Casagrande 1972:2), population is relatively stable. Language and cultural differences (from the rest of the country), relative lack of population pressure, and distrust of people beyond the village probably all combine to discourage migration to the Coast.

Table 2 also shows that proportionately more female migrants come from the Coast than from the Sierra. These differences in place of origin for male and female migrants may be due in part to differential roles between men and women. Sierra women are more restricted in their freedom of movement than coastal women and are probably less likely to migrate alone. Women who do migrate alone from both areas are more likely to be from cities where they have learned to be more independent. This is reflected in the fact that proportionately more women than men come from cities over 10,000. As can be seen in Table 3, 28% of the men from all regions and 41% of the women from all regions come from large cities.

More than three-quarters of both men and women migrated between the ages of 15 and 25. In fact, nearly half of both sierran and

TABLE 3. Size of Place of Birth for Migrants.

	Men						Women						Row Total	
	Sierra		Coast		Oriente		Sierra		Coast		Oriente			
	N	%	N	%	N	%	N	%	N	%	N	%	N	%
Cities over 10,000	77	20	70	18	–	–	115	14	230	27	–	–	492	40
Towns under 10,000	26	7	49	13	7	2	39	5	136	16	8	1	265	22
Rural	47	12	104	27	–	–	66	8	254	30	–	–	471	38
Column Totals	150	39	223	59	7	2	220	26	620	73	8	1	1,231	100
Total	Men — 381 — 100%						Women — 850 — 100%							

coastal women arrived in Guayaquil between the ages of 15 and 19. Most men (65%) are single when they migrate, as are nearly half the women (48%). About a third of the women (36%) bring children with them, but most of those who do bring only one or two. Occasionally, children are left behind with relatives.

Nearly three-fourths of the men made the decision to migrate themselves, while only a little over one-third of the women did. In fact, 42% of the women migrated with their partners. Others migrated with other relatives or friends. The dependence of Ecuadorian women on their husbands and other relatives is illustrated by the fact that women migrated with relatives or friends significantly more than men did (p < .01).

The migrants studied were motivated primarily by what are called "pull" factors: the perceived opportunities in the city for jobs, education, and "a better life." Significantly more men are motivated by jobs and the opportunity to advance, while women seek education and a better life (p < .01). Beyond these obvious reasons emerging from the survey data, the migrants I knew, especially the men, had a deep concern with making a better life for their children. Because schools in the rural areas may not even go through the primary grades, migrating to the city has definite advantages. Women who migrated alone often were motivated by boredom and restriction on their activities in the villages, and the complementary attractions of independence and excitement in the city. Both men and women expected better health care in the cities.

Migration in Latin America sometimes involves several steps, where migrants move first to a town or small nearby city before moving to a major city (Macisco n.d.:3). In the current study 46% of the men and 32% of the women who came to Guayaquil had lived in a town or city other than their birthplace before migrating. Thus less than half of all migrants had participated in step migration. This does not necessarily mean that most migrants came straight from their birthplace to reside in Guayaquil, with no previous experience beyond their home town. More than half of the men and women (69% and 56% respectively) had visited Guayaquil before migrating there. This finding bears out an impression gained during the intensive study that a great deal of visiting goes on between relatives in the city and the country.

These relatives also provided vital help for migrants during the adaptation process. Three-fourths (76%) of the men and two-thirds (66%) of the women knew someone in Guayaquil before migrating, and over half stayed with friends or relatives after arrival. This type of help appears to have produced a different migration pattern for some migrants to Guayaquil. In the classic pattern migrants usually move first to the central city slums and only later to the squatter settlements, where they can build a home and hope to eventually own the land (Mangin 1967:68). While more than half of the migrants now living in the *suburbios* originally came by way of the *tugurios*, staying there from a few days to over eight years, as many as a third migrated directly to the *suburbios* and their adaptation was facilitated by friends and relatives there to welcome them.

Despite this, Guayaquil does not, in general, exhibit the pattern described by Doughty (1970) for Lima, Peru, where people from the same area may cluster together or form clubs. The Guayaquil squatter settlement is extended a few lots at a time rather than through mass invasions as in Lima, thus preventing the formation of large clusters of people from the same region. An exception to this is an area of the squatter settlement called La Marimba, where most of the inhabitants are black Esmeraldeños.

While there are few economic differences between migrants and nonmigrants, the 200 rural dwellers studied were not as well off. The people in the coastal village appeared to be better off economically than the people in the sierran village, but both villages ranked below all the urban sample areas in terms of the variables used to estimate economic status. Nor did the migrants feel they had all come from the top economic strata in their villages or towns. A third felt they had been better off than their neighbors, 24% felt they had been "worse off," and the remainder felt their situation had been about average.

Migrants appear to be positively selected in terms of education. While the rural school system is reportedly far less complete and extensive than the urban (Erickson 1966:157), there is no statistically significant difference between the years of schooling for migrant and nonmigrant males (p > .05).

The data on education from the two rural villages support the idea that migrants, especially male migrants, as a group are more highly educated than the rural residents left behind. In both rural villages 9% of the adults had received no formal schooling as compared with 5% of long-term urban dwellers and 7% of urban in-migrants. Ninety-seven percent of the Sierra village residents and 98% of the coastal village residents had stopped their education after six grades or less, as compared with 67% of long-term urban dwellers and 91% of urban in-migrants.

There is a significant difference in reported educational levels for migrant and nonmigrant females (p < .01). This is not surprising in view of the relatively greater differences between male and female roles in the urban areas. The differences in educational levels of migrant males and females are statistically significant (p < .02), but the same is true for urban men and women (p < .05). This means that women in both the rural and urban settings have different (usually lower) educational levels than men, but that urban women have received significantly more education than migrant women, while men in both groups are roughly on a par. While over three-quarters of migrant women from all regions had completed three grades or less of schooling, slightly higher proportions of Sierra women (21% as opposed to 14%) had completed fifth and sixth grades as compared to coastal women.

There were no statistically significant differences between migrant men and urban nonmigrant men for the variables probably related to aspiration such as desire for change in their own lives and hopes for children.

ADAPTATION TO GUAYAQUIL

Life in the City

Emile Durkheim describes the city as containing the greatest division of labor in society. Theoretically, specialization can go on ceaselessly, but where crowding occurs, there is fierce competition for occupational niches (Durkheim 1933:266–67). For the in-migrant this

TABLE 4. Monthly Family Income by Sample Area.

Sucres	Urban Total		Ethnographic Study Area		Coastal Village		Sierra Village	
	N	%	N	%	N	%	N	%
Below 1,000	851	38	19	41	66	69	47	66
1,000–1,999	685	31	12	26	18	19	19	27
2,000–2,999	336	15	7	15	4	4	3	4
3,000–3,999	160	7	2	4	2	2	1	1
4,000–4,999	92	4	2	4	3	3	1	1
5,000–9,999	100	4	4	9	2	2	0	0
10,000+	12	1	0	0	0	0	0	0
Total	2,236	100	46	100	95	99	71	99

p < .01.

competitive arena—where work can be the means to upward mobility, but more often simply permits survival—is the new environment which replaces the scarce land or serfdom in the Sierra or the wage labor on someone else's land on the Coast. For many migrants the adaptation to this new environment was greatly facilitated by friends and relatives already in the city. For example, 64% of the 381 male migrants said they got their first jobs in the city through friends and relatives.

In Guayaquil jobs are often essential for sheer survival as well as a means to upward mobility. The families I lived among in the *suburbio* said they were spending around 90% of their income on food (figure obtained by subtracting from reported daily income reported amount spent daily on food). Although there was probably underreporting of income, the existence of many of these families was based on a daily struggle for enough money to eat, and the scarcity of jobs was a constant topic of conversation. This scarcity was reflected more in underemployment than in unemployment. Of the 1,103 men (both migrants and long-term urban dwellers) who were employed, 14% of these did not work a full eight-hour day, 7.8% did not work a full five-day week, and 9.6% worked ten months or less a year.

Table 4 describes the monthly family income for Guayaquil and the two rural villages studied. Thirty-eight percent of the urban families made less than 1,000 sucres a month as compared with over two-thirds of the sample in the two rural villages. Few people anywhere made over 2,000 sucres in one month. To put this in perspective, 1,000 sucres a month is about 33 sucres a day for a family. The mean amount reportedly spent on food was 40 sucres daily. Clearly the families in the lower-income brackets are living at a very marginal level.

Migrants, however, were doing about as well as their urban-reared neighbors. Male migrants and long-term urban dwellers were similar in many characteristics related to economic status. There was no statistically significant difference between the types of jobs held by the two groups, or for most of the variables used in constructing a socioeconomic scale. The three exceptions were related to housing. Significantly more migrants than nonmigrants had poorer housing (usually bamboo), slightly more living space, and no electricity ($p < .05$, $p < .01$, $p < .05$). Also, fewer migrants had television sets than did nonmigrants.

The likely explanation for these differences is that significantly more migrants live in the recently settled areas of the *suburbios* ($p < .05$), where most of the houses are still bamboo and electricity has not yet reached all homes. However, there is more space per family because the squatters have established as much space as possible for themselves. Thus the recently built house of cheap materials (which later will be replaced by a better one) is correlated with more living space. The difference in television set ownership could be due to the scarcity of electricity rather than to economic factors, as migrants and nonmigrants do not differ significantly in their overall economic situation. The newly settled *suburbio* areas may lack some amenities, but they usually represent a step up for those who move there because they have a chance to claim a piece of the swamp and build their own homes.

Men's aspirations are related to reality in this difficult economic situation. They generally felt that there was relatively little they could do to greatly improve their own standard of living, but that their children had a chance for a better future. Most felt this could be accomplished by giving their children as good an education as possible. Hard work on their part and the part of their children was also stressed.

Coastal residents of *suburbios* differentiated *costeños* and *serranos* with regard to "hard work" and upward mobility. *Serranos* were seen as clever, hard-working, and successful but also as cold, hostile, and "uppity." I, too, found them withdrawn, slow to trust strangers, quiet, and very earnest. Assimilation seemed more difficult for people of Sierra origin. One *serrano* man said: "All is strange here, we know nothing. When I was sick, we didn't know where to find a doctor. . . .In the Sierra there is more honesty, the people are better. Here it is not the same."

It took me several months to really get to know that family, to be trusted by them to some extent. None of my other neighbors knew them at all. It had only taken weeks at most to get to know coastal informants, even the difficult ones. Sometimes I would learn of a Sierra neighbor through gossip. "The widower across the way brought a new wife from the Sierra, but no one ever sees her. They say she is pretty and his children call her 'mother' already." This woman turned out to be so withdrawn that I was able to begin to make friends with her only at her husband's insistence (he had been in the city many years by then). Months later we could converse comfortably and she would even wave me in for a chat as I walked by. She still didn't know anyone else on the street.

In general, migrants from the Sierra had many more adjustments to make than those from the Coast. The coastal migrant must cope with the complexity of the city, the competition for work, housing, and a "better life," but many aspects of life in Guayaquil are comfortingly the same or similar to the village situation, such as climate, foods, dwellings, language, and dress.

The staple in Guayaquil and on the rest of the Coast is rice, instead of maize as in the Sierra. The cool, bright days and chilly nights of the Sierra are a contrast with the hot muggy weather on the Coast. The coastal dwellers build their houses of bamboo and place them on stilts, while Sierra dwellings are of earth and stone and hug the hillsides. Guayaquil, and the rest of the Coast, are Spanish-speaking. Not only are Indian tongues rarely heard (and then from *serranos*), but even the Spanish is different. The sibilants of the Sierra accent are laughed at on the Coast; even some of the vocabulary is different. The unspoken rules of human interaction are different.

Many have appeared to "solve" the problem in a familiar way. They remain somewhat isolated, although this is not a firm policy and marriages with coastal dwellers occur without apparent obstacles. *Serranos* are also mistrusted partly because of their success. They are identified as the entrepreneurs, the shopkeepers, the landlords, the merchants (nearly all on a very small scale). They are classified by their neighbors as the "small businessmen" of the area.

There are implications for values related to fertility and family size in these different patterns of adaptation. The coastal people, with their higher fertility and larger family sizes, are encountering a relatively familiar environment. Consequently, we might expect little or very slow changes in their behavior. However, they are migrants. Most of them are positively selected. They have already taken one step to improve their lot, and are likely to take others.

As previously demonstrated, the Sierra people have values and practices which lead to relatively small completed family size. They arrive in a more alien environment, where some of the reasons for maintaining a small family size, such as limited land, no longer exist. However, in the city new pressures come into play, such as limited income and the cost of children's education. In addition to new pressures, there are new means available to curtail fertility.

Sierra and coastal migrants share aspirations for their own and their children's future. Both groups have shown enterprise and determination by migrating and establishing a foothold in the city. However, as discussed earlier in this paper, it is my impression that people of Sierra origin have been more successful in becoming upwardly mobile. The continuation of relatively smaller families among people of Sierra origin and the change to smaller families among people of coastal origin would not be surprising, given these factors.

Fertility and Family Size

Types of sexual unions in Ecuador fall primarily into two categories: those formalized by both church and state (formal marriages) and *compromisos*, sexual unions recognized by family and neighbors in which a man is expected to take responsibility for his partner and their children. In a *compromiso*, as in a formal marriage, the family unit is known by a composite name composed of the last names of both partners. Partners in a *compromiso* do not always live together. If the man already has another union, he will divide his time (not always equally) between the two households. Where he can, he will set up each woman in a separate household. If that is impossible (usually for financial reasons) there are nearly always relatives for one of the women to live with. The patterns of union formation and dissolution and their relationships to fertility in this population have been discussed elsewhere (Chen, Wishik, and Scrimshaw 1974; Scrimshaw 1978a, 1978b).

Women begin to enter sexual unions as early as ages 12 and 13. Nonmigrant women are significantly younger when they first enter a union than are migrant women (p <. 01). The mean age at first union is 18.4 for nonmigrants and 19.6 for migrants. For the two rural villages, the mean ages at first alliance are 17.7 in the coastal village and 19.10 in the Sierra village (in all situations the age at first union ranges from 12 to 25). Since around half of the migrant women were single at migration, the process of migrating probably delayed their first union.

In order to look at fertility patterns within unions despite the fact that unions may be interrupted, a measure was developed called "years in alliance." Years in alliance is defined as "the number of years . . . engaged in any alliance . . . alliance span minus the total time periods spent in no alliance at all" (Chen, Wishik, and Scrimshaw 1974:12).

Years in alliance differs for migrants and nonmigrants in Guayaquil. The mean for migrants is 11.31 years in alliance, and for nonmigrants the mean is 10.08 years. Since migrants begin their unions later, it is not surprising to find that they are older and thus have spent more time in alliance. The mean age for migrant women is 31.6, while the mean for nonmigrant women is 27.3. The difference is statistically significant (p < .01) when a chi-square test is performed (Scrimshaw 1973:138, 144). When the current ages of migrant women from Sierra and Coast are compared and a chi-square test is performed, there are no statistically significant differences (p < .05).

Another "involuntary" factor possibly affecting fertility is whether an alliance is with someone of the same background or not, as people may have different behavior patterns. The survey data show that out of 1,131 couples interviewed, 26% (300) were migrants married to long-term urban dwellers and 12% (140) were migrants married to other migrants. Nearly all of the latter were both from the same region. In fact, three-fourths of such couples were married before they migrated. Thus most migrants who marry after migration marry someone from a different background (usually urban).

In order to explore this further, the men and women interviewed were matched with their respective spouses and four types of couples were designated: migrant men married to migrant women, migrant men married to nonmigrant women, nonmigrant men married to migrant women, and nonmigrant men married to nonmigrant women. After establishing that there were no significant differences in the number of pregnancies and living children among families in the various sample areas ($p < .05$), multiple stepwise regression[1] was performed using the combined data from all sample areas for the four types of couples. The number of pregnancies and the number of living children in the *current* union were considered the dependent variables (each in a separate run). The independent variables included the four marriage types already described; the duration of the current union; economic status; aspirations; education; and knowledge, attitudes, and use of contraception. Except for a very slight negative correlation between economic status and the dependent variables (.037), none of the variables affected pregnancies or living children except the duration of the current union. This varied among the four marriage types (see Table 5). Migrants married to migrants had current unions about two years longer than the other three marriage types, which resembled each other very closely. They also had about one more child than the other three groups.

Analyses of covariance were performed to see if the differences in the number of pregnancies were significant when controlling for the duration of the current union. In one case the dependent variable was the number of pregnancies; in the second run it was the number of living children. The covariates were duration of current union. As Table 5 shows, controlling for the duration of union eliminates any significant difference in the number of pregnancies among the four groups. The same held true when number of living children was considered.

Migrants "married" to migrants have been in their unions longer because three-fourths of them started their unions before migration.

TABLE 5. Adjusted Means and Standard Errors for Analysis of Covariance
Using Pregnancies in Current Union as the Dependent Variable.

Treatment Group[1]	Mean Duration of Union	Treatment Mean[2]	Adjusted Mean	SE Adjusted
1	11.96	5.2086	4.5540	0.1899
2	9.92	4.1094	4.1279	0.1970
3	9.59	4.0814	4.2087	0.1700
4	9.69	4.0766	4.1730	0.0848

[1] 1 = Migrants "married" to migrants.
2 = Migrant men "married" to nonmigrant women.
3 = Nonmigrant men "married" to migrant women.
4 = Nonmigrants "married" to nonmigrants.
[2] Mean number of pregnancies.

As has been discussed, migration delayed the age of first union for those who migrated single. What is so surprising is that even those migrants who married while in their villages show no significant differences ($p < .05$) in fertility from the other three groups, including long-term urban dwellers, when the differences in length of union are adjusted for. That is very fast adaptation indeed, particularly because the data from the rural villages show a mean family size of several children more than the urban family-size mean.

The women whose partners were also interviewed are only a portion of the sample, since men were harder to locate for interviews and not all women were currently in union. To look at the larger sample, it is necessary to turn again to Table 1. From those data it would appear at first that migrants have higher fertility than nonmigrants. While the mean pregnancies and living children for both groups as a whole differ by about one child (3.4 pregnancies and 2.6 living children for nonmigrants as opposed to 4.2 pregnancies and 3.6 living children for migrants), when the means are compared age group by age group the differences are slight.

While the fertility of all migrant women studied is looked at by region of origin, there is no statistically significant difference, although the fertility of the coastal women would appear slightly higher (chi-square $p < .05$). Thus, whatever the differences in place of origin, in the city both groups resemble urban women in terms of fertility behavior.

The similarity between the two groups is surprising because of the different values and behavior in the rural Sierra and Coast, but also because the family size ideals for the two groups in the survey sample are significantly different (the chi-square shows p < .05). While nearly half of each group (46% from the Coast and 45% from the Sierra) would like two children, more of the remaining coastal women would like four children and more of the remaining Sierra women would like three children (the difference is about 6% in both cases). A few women in both groups would like more than four children or fewer than two.

Both migrants and nonmigrants showed awareness of "modern" contraceptive methods. While there was no statistically significant difference between the knowledge of migrants and nonmigrants (p < .05), the people in the two rural villages have less knowledge about family planning methods. In fact, most (over 90%) rural people refused to answer questions about contraception because "they are too embarrassing—I don't know about any of those things." This was particularly true of the Sierra village. Apparently, migrants' knowledge of contraception, no different from that of urban nonmigrants at time of interview, is mainly acquired after they arrive in Guayaquil.

In order to see if migrants from the two areas have different levels of knowledge of contraception, we can look at and compare the survey data on knowledge for women from the two regions. Significantly more of the coastal women knew about several methods: the IUD, foam tablets, the douche, rhythm, and injections (p < .05, .01, .05, .01 respectively, when the chi-square test is applied). Coastal women also mentioned more additional methods (those not probed for—mostly "folk" methods). Of these other methods, coastal women mentioned aspirin in the vagina and *tallo*, a root used to produce abortions, more often. Sierra women mentioned eating lemons and male sterilization more often. Coastal women have more knowledge of some contraceptive methods than Sierra women.

How often is this knowledge applied? About 22% of all women (and 27% of migrant women) are currently using one form or another of contraception. Forty-four percent of the women are even users of one or more methods (13.5% have only used one method, 31% have used more than one). While not all the methods used are the most effective, nearly half the women have actually tried to prevent pregnancy (Scrimshaw 1973:169–75).

When sierran and coastal migrant women are compared for past or current use of each method (using the chi-square technique), there are no significant differences (p < .05 in all instances). This suggests that while coastal women have relatively more knowledge of contraception, both groups make equal use of the various methods. In the two rural villages virtually no methods of contraception were used, with the occasional exception of rhythm or withdrawal. So the roughly one-fourth (27%) of all migrant women who are currently actively trying to control their fertility have adopted this behavior in Guayaquil.

One final difference between sierran and coastal migrant women which may have a slight effect on fertility is that women of sierran origin believe in breast-feeding their babies longer than do coastal migrants or long-term urban dwellers. This difference is statistically significant when a chi-square test is performed (p < .01).

RAPID ADAPTATION OR PREADAPTATION?

This paper has discussed cultural and environmental factors in the Sierra which interact to provide good "reasons" for a relatively small family size (approximately three living children being desirable) and has shown that completed family size in the few villages where some data are available is relatively small, with a mean of five children. Coastal residents, by contrast, experience cultural and environmental factors which place fewer restrictions on family size; this is reflected both in my data from the coastal village and in Heer's child-woman ratios from the 1950 Ecuadorian census data (1964:83). Some additional insight on these coastal and sierran family size differentials may be obtained by looking at migration to Quito.

The Ecuadorian Center for Demographic Analysis (CAD) produced a monograph on migration to Quito based on the 1950 census data. While this analysis is only roughly comparable to the information discussed here, there are some interesting comparisons to be made between the two cities. In 1950 migrants to Quito, like Guayaquil 20 years later, were young adults, single, and comparatively well educated. Their educational levels were higher than rural and about on a par with urban dwellers of the same socioeconomic status. Their reasons for migrating were the same as for migrants to Guayaquil: to find work and obtain an education for their children. Unlike Guayaquil, 80% of the migrants to Quito were from the Sierra. This may have helped contribute to the fact that they appeared to adapt rapidly (Centro de Análises Demográfico 1975:15–18, 20–23).

More recent data on Quito indicate a continued high rate of in-migration. Preliminary findings show that while sierran rural family-size levels are similar to coastal urban levels, or even lower for younger women, sierran urban levels (Quito) are lower than rural levels (Billsburro 1978, personal communication). Thus urban-rural fertility differentials *do* appear to exist in Ecuador, if region is held constant. For *serranos*, family size need not change when they migrate to Guayaquil, but it does appear to change when they migrate to Quito.

Coming to the city with varied backgrounds, some migrants appear to change rapidly. They are helped in their rapid assimilation by friends and relatives, and by the often permanent nature of migration. The city becomes home and they wish to blend with its people. So rapid is this assimilation that married migrants do not differ significantly from nonmigrants in most respects, including fertility and family size. The very fact of migration involuntarily affects fertility for single migrants, though, for they take time to find a partner in the city, thus delaying the onset of childbearing.

In summary, Sierra migrants have values related to relatively small family size, but must acquire new reasons for maintaining those values and new means for doing so when they migrate to Guayaquil. Coastal migrants to Guayaquil do not value small families, but they are preadapted to the coastal city in many other ways which facilitate the rapid change in family size values.

Sierra migrants come from a situation where scarce land and tight-knit villages make small families important, and go to a situation where the capital needed to improve their own and their children's lives can accomplish more if it provides for fewer people. In Guayaquil their family size is slightly reduced. The coastal migrants also aspire to a better situation, and reduce their family size considerably to accomplish it. Of course, both groups are highly selected and motivated, so such behavior is not surprising. The adaptiveness of these values in the urban environment is clear. Smaller families *do* stand a better chance of realizing their goals of socioeconomic mobility. Money can be used for more than just subsistence, and people are quick to realize this. Unlike the two-generation estimates by Hawley and Goldberg, migrants from the Sierra and the Coast change within a few years of arrival.

"Rural" and "urban" are general terms, too general when the importance of cultural factors is considered. In this case people from highland Ecuador come to Guayaquil with values, practices, and expectations leading to a smaller family, but with language and cultural barriers that make adaptation to the city more difficult. Coastal groups have practices and values leading to larger families, but have the off-setting advantage of linguistic and cultural familiarity with the coastal city. Preadaptation based on cultural familiarity, the positive self-selectivity of migrants, the migration process itself, and the continued high aspirations of migrants for the next generation combine to produce rapid adaptation and assimilation in Guayaquil, and probably in Quito as well.

It is, of course, difficult to predict the eventual success of migrants in attaining the upward mobility they desire. They do not differ economically from their nonmigrant urban neighbors who are at or near the bottom of the class structure, but the migrants have moved up on the socioeconomic scale simply by coming to the city. The characteristics which have aided them in migration and adaptation thus far are likely to help them compete successfully in the urban environment.

NOTES

Acknowledgments: This paper is based on a study supported by USAID (contract number 0113–26332–00, AID'csd-2479 task order number 3B) and by the Ford Foundation. The original research and data analysis were carried out while I was a research associate with the Center for Population and Family Health, Columbia University School of Public Health.

The original invitation to work in Ecuador was extended by Dr. Francisco Parra Gil, the Ecuadorian Minister of Health at the time, and by Dr. Pablo Marangoni of the University of Guayaquil and head of the Asociacion Pro-Bienestar de la Familia Ecuatoriana (APROFE). I deeply appreciate both their invitation to carry out this study and their support throughout its duration. Dr. Felipe Aroca, then director of Health Services for the Ministry of Health, also greatly facilitated the fieldwork, as did many others.

1. All multivariate analyses were run by using the computer programs available in the Statistical Package for the Social Sciences (SPSS) and by the Biomedical Division of the University of California, Los Angeles (BMD).

REFERENCES CITED

Alland, Alexander
  1973   *Evolution and Human Behavior: An Introduction to Darwinian Anthropology*. 2d ed. New York: Doubleday.
Balán, Jorge
  1969   Migrant-Native Socioeconomic Differences in Latin American Cities: A Structural Analysis. *Latin American Research Review* 4:3–29.
Cardona, Ramiro, and Alan Simmons
  1975   Toward a Model of Migration in Latin America. In B. du Toit and H. Safa, eds., *Migration and Urbanization*. The Hague: Mouton, pp. 19–48.
Carleton, R. O.
  1965   Fertility Trends and Differentials in Latin America. *Milbank Memorial Fund Quarterly* 43 (4):15–35.

Casagrande, Joseph B.
1972   Closing Vicious Circles: An Ecological Model for Understanding Population Biology in Indian Communities of Highland Ecuador. Paper presented at the 71st Annual Meeting of the American Anthropological Association.

Chen, Kwan Hwa, Samuel Wishik, and Susan C. M. Scrimshaw
1974   The Effects of Unstable Sexual Unions on Fertility in Guayaquil, Ecuador. *Human Biology* 21 (Winter):353–59.

Cohen, Yehudi, ed.
1968   *Man in Adaptation: The Biosocial Background*. Chicago: Aldine.

Conning, Arthur M.
1971   Rural Community Differentiation and the Rate of Rural-Urban Migration in Chile. *Rural Sociology* 36 (3):296–314.

Davis, Kingsley, and Ana Casis
1946   Urbanization in Latin America. *Milbank Memorial Fund Quarterly* 24 (3):186–207.

Doughty, Paul L.
1970   Behind the Back of the City: "Provincial" Life in Lima, Peru. In William Mangin, ed., *Peasants in Cities: Readings in the Anthropology of Urbanization*. Boston: Houghton Mifflin, pp. 30–46.

Durkheim, Emile
1933   *The Division of Labor in Society*. New York: Free Press.

Erickson, Edwin E.
1966   *Area Handbook for Ecuador*. Washington, D.C.: U.S. Superintendent of Documents.

Goldberg, David
1959   The Fertility of Two-Generation Urbanites. *Population Studies* 12 (3):214–22.

Goldstein, Sidney
1971   *Interrelations between Migration and Fertility in Population Redistribution in Thailand*. Bangkok, Thailand: Institute of Population Studies, Chulalongkorn University, Research Report 5.

Hawley, Amos H.
1969   Population Growth and Urbanization in Developing Countries. Unpublished paper prepared for National Academy of Science, Woods Hole Conference, 27 July–8 Aug.

Heer, David M.
1964   Fertility Differences between Indian and Spanish-Speaking Parts of Andean Countries. *Population Studies* 18 (1):71–84.

Kiser, C. V.
1971   Unresolved Issues in Research on Fertility in Latin America. *Milbank Memorial Fund Quarterly* 49 (3, pt. 1):379–88.

Lewis, Oscar
1960   The Culture of Poverty in Mexico City. *Economic Weekly of Bombay*: 965–72.

Macintosh, Duncan
1972   The Politics of Primacy—Political Factors in the Development of Ecuador's Largest City, Guayaquil. M.A. thesis, Columbia University.

Macisco, John J., Jr.
   n.d.   Some Thoughts on an Analytical Framework for Rural to Urban Mi-
          gration. Unpublished paper prepared for CELADE, Santiago, Chile.
Macisco, John J., Jr., Robert H. Weller, and Leon F. Bouvier
   1969   Some General Considerations of Migrations, Urbanization, and Fer-
          tility in Latin America. In The Family in Transition: A Round Table
          Conference Sponsored by the John E. Fogarty International Center
          for Advanced Study in the Health Sciences, National Institutes of
          Health, 3–6 Nov., Bethesda, Md. *Fogarty International Center Proceed-
          ings* 3:285–97.
Mangin, William
   1959   The Role of Regional Association in the Adaptation of Rural Mi-
          grants to Cities in Peru. *Sociologies* 9:23–26.
   1967   Latin American Squatter Settlements: A Problem and a Solution.
          Latin American Research Review 2 (3):65–98.
Matos Mar, José
   1961   Migration and Urbanization. In Philip Hauser, ed., *Urbanization in
          Latin America*. New York: International Documents Service, pp.
          170–80.
Merlo, Pedro, et al.
   1975   *Migraciones hacia Quito y Proyecciones de la Población*. Quito: Junta Na-
          cional de Planificación y Coordinación.
Mertens, Walter, and Carmen Miro
   1969   Influences Affecting Fertility in Urban and Rural Latin America. *Mil-
          bank Memorial Fund Quarterly* 46 (3):89–120.
Micklin, Michael
   1969   Urban Life and Differential Fertility: Specification of an Aspect of
          the Theory of the Demographic Transition. *Sociological Quarterly* 10
          (4):480–500.
Nag, Moni
   1968   *Factors Affecting Human Fertility in Non-Industrial Societies: A Cross-
          Cultural Study*. New Haven, Conn.: Yale University Publications in
          Anthropology 66.
Polgar, Steven
   1972   Population History and Population Policies from an Anthropological
          Perspective. *Current Anthropology* 13 (2):203–11.
Pool, D. I.
   1969   The Rural-Urban Fertility Differential in Ghana. *Proceedings*, 16th
          General Conference, International Union for the Scientific Study of
          Population, London.
Population Reference Bureau
   1973   *World Population Data Sheet*. Washington, D.C.
Robinson, W. C.
   1963   Urbanization and Fertility: The Non-Western Experience. *Milbank
          Memorial Fund Quarterly* 41 (3):291–308.
Schultz, T. Paul
   1970   *Rural-Urban Migration in Colombia*. Santa Monica, Calif.: Rand Corp.
Scrimshaw, Susan C. M.
   1965   Analysis of Infant Feeding Practices in Sorata, Bolivia. Mimeo. New
          York: Research Institute for the Study of Man.

1973 Migration, Urban Living and the Family: A Study among Residents in the Suburbios and Tugurios of Guayaquil, Ecuador. Mimeo. New York: International Institute for the Study of Human Reproduction, Columbia University.

1978a Family Formation and First Birth in Ecuador. In W. B. Miller and L. F. Newman, eds., *The First Child and Family Formation*. Chapel Hill: Carolina Population Center, University of North Carolina, pp. 108–27.

1978b Stages in Women's Lives and Reproductive Decision-Making in Latin America. *Medical Anthropology* 2 (3):41–58.

Stycos, J. M.
1963 Culture and Differential Fertility of Peru. *Population Studies* 16 (3):257–70.

United Nations Bureau of Social Affairs
1961 Demographic Aspects of Urbanization in Latin America. In Philip Hauser, ed., *Urbanization in Latin America*. New York: International Documents Service, pp. 91–115.

Wagley, Charles
1951 Cultural Influences on Population: A Comparison of Two Tupi Tribes. Reprinted in Andrew P. Vayda, ed., *Environment and Cultural Behavior*. New York: Natural History Press, 1969, pp. 268–79.

Wagley, Charles, and Marvin Harris
1955 A Typology of Latin American Subcultures. *American Anthropologist* 57 (3):428–51.

Weller, Robert H., and John J. Macisco, Jr.
1970 *Migration, Aspirations for Social Mobility, and Fertility in Developing Countries: Suggestions for Further Research*. Providence, R.I.: Population Research and Training Center, Department of Sociology, Brown University.

Whitten, Norman E., Jr.
1974 *Black Frontiersmen: A South American Case*. New York: Halsted (Wiley).

Wolf, Eric R.
1957 Closed Corporate Peasant Communities in Mesoamerica and Central Java. *Southwestern Journal of Anthropology* 13 (1):1–12.

Zarate, Alvan O.
1967 Community of Origin, Migration and Completed Marital Fertility in Metropolitan Monterrey. Paper presented at the Annual Meeting of the Population Association of America, April, Cincinnati, Ohio.

10

Economic and Ecological Strategies of Lojano Migrants to El Oro

Leslie A. Brownrigg

The spontaneous pioneer colonization of the forested foothills of the western slope of the Andes in Arenillas and Piñas cantons of El Oro province by migrants from the southern Andean province of Loja has dramatically changed land use in this frontier area. The Lojano migrants are settling a sparsely populated region between the two long-inhabited areas of El Oro: the commercial agricultural coastal plain with its urban centers of Pasaje, Machala, Santa Rosa, and Arenillas; and the upland interior mining/coffee/cattle-ranching region with its urban centers of Zaruma, Portovelo, and Piñas. This spontaneous settler colonization of the El Oro foothills is itself part of a much larger pattern of Lojano out-migration to all parts of Ecuador.

The population and economy of the coastal province of El Oro, the migration target discussed in this paper, have been growing rapidly in the past decade and a half. Loja, the origin area discussed here, has contributed over twice as many migrants as Azuay, ten times as many as Pichincha, and fifty times as many as Cañar—the three Ecuadorian provinces which follow Loja's lead as the birthplace of new El Oro residents (INEC 1976:12 [El Oro] Cuadro 4). The purpose of this paper is to demonstrate the ways by which Lojano colonization has changed land use in the Andean-Pacific slope and to note the integration and interdependence of ecological, demographic, economic, and social factors necessary to understand a common process of spontaneous pioneer colonization in contemporary Ecuador. I sketch push-pull factors, set forth a replicating sequence of ecological economic exploitation, suggest the colonization strategies revolving around each phase of the sequence, and conclude by noting that contemporary spontaneous pioneer colonization in the Loja–El Oro system is remarkably compatible with the ancient cultural-ecological

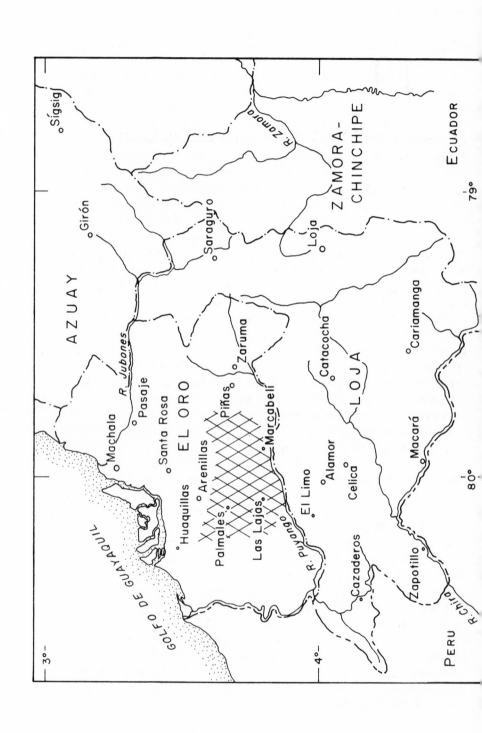

indigenous strategy known as "verticality" (see, e.g., Murra 1972; Brownrigg 1973:106ff., 1975:128ff.; Orlove 1977).

Lojano migration to the upland interior centers of El Oro is a centuries-old process. The mines at Zaruma and at Portovelo functioned as early centers of acculturation to Hispanic lifeways. The *repartimiento* of Capitán Mercadillo, who founded the Spanish gold mining at Zaruma, drew labor from Loja (Wolf 1892:600). The upland El Oro centers of Portovelo and Piñas include Loja areas of Alamor and Catacocha in their urban hinterlands, providing commercial, educational, and professional services to Lojano residents. Villages of the region are socially, spatially, and architecturally organized in manners more similar to Loja communities than to those of the El Oro coastal plain. Lojano migration to the El Oro uplands, though interprovincial, is clearly intraregional. The Pindo and Puyango rivers which form the provincial boundary between Loja and El Oro do not demark social barriers. Members of the same communities may have land in both provinces.

The third Ecuadorian census (INEC 1976), taken in 1974, recorded the presence of 26,585 Loja-born residents living in El Oro (see Table 1). Although these census data do not tell us where in El Oro the Lojanos migrated, it does show that while the population of the upland interior parishes has been relatively stable, the population of the foothills, lower-altitude basins, and coastal plain regions has more than doubled between censuses, and that Lojano migration to El Oro is a steady and continuing process. Of the total number of Loja-born residents enumerated by the census in El Oro, 57.1% were residing in rural areas there, meaning outside provincial, cantonal, or parish capitals. Of these rural Lojano residents in El Oro, 30.4% came from rural areas of Loja, as indicated in Table 2. The intra-urban (26.3%)

TABLE 1. Lojano Migration to El Oro (1974).

Year of Arrival	Total	
1974–73	2,923	
1973–72	1,723	
1972–71	1,850	
1971–70	2,040	
1969–65	6,742	{ Rural origin: 2,977 Urban origin: 3,765
1964–62	3,597	
Before 1961	5,674	
No information	333	

Source: INEC 1976: V (El Oro):14.

TABLE 2. Lojano Migrants to El Oro by "Urban" and Rural Residential Characteristics (1974).

	Urban in El Oro		Rural in El Oro	
Total	11,398	(42.9%)	15,187	(57.1%)
Formerly urban residents	6,981	(26.3%)	7,104	(26.7%)
Formerly rural residents	4,417	(16.6%)	8,083	(30.4%)

Source: INEC 1976: XII (El Oro).

and rural-to-urban (16.6%) migration figures paint an inaccurate and misleading picture (cf. Quijano 1977:71–83). The so-called "urban" capitals of parishes in the El Oro upland regions, where Lojanos prefer to locate, are actually nucleated settlements often forming villages of less than 2,000 inhabitants, with services limited to a primary school, a chapel, and a few stores.[1] In sum, Lojano migration to El Oro is mainly intraregional, rural to rural.

Lojano migration has changed the character of El Oro secondary coastal centers. Of the urban population of Arenillas (5,551 in 1974), 47% were from Loja, Azuay, or other places in Ecuador and 27% were their El Oro–born children (Jaramillo J. and Castro 1975:180). Periurban barrios such as El Cisne–Macará and Pueblo Neuvo–Las Mercedes, founded and settled mainly by Lojanos squatting on municipal land, have added sprawl to Arenillas's town plan. In the growing commercial border town of Huaquillas, 77% of the heads of family are migrants from Loja or Azuay (Jaramillo J. and Castro 1975:245). One of Huaquillas's five formal barrios is named La Lojana.

Lojano settlers have had an important demographic and social-economic impact on older freehold villages and hacienda communities in the El Oro coastal rural areas. Seventy percent of the population of rural Chacras parish are migrants. In one decade Lojano "invasion" has doubled the population of Palmales's parish center, which is located in a coastal basin. Lojanos' residential constructions in San Antonio–El Bunque have revitalized the villages.

The Lojano colonies on the El Oro coast are closely related to spontaneous colonization and land development in the El Oro foothills. The coastal colonies serve both as staging points for inland settlement and as residential bases for settler-colonists in their short-term, seasonal labor migrations to points of coastal employment. The settlers of the remote nucleated spontaneous colonists' villages and outlying dispersed homesteads in the foothills are contributing members to a broad network of self-identifying Lojanos. Their colonization areas are geographically intermediate between the essentially closed microsocieties of referrent natal parishes in Loja and the open coastal community. Community and mutuality are created by a recognition of shared experiences to Lojano out-migration, as well as by formal ties of kinship, *compadrazgo*, and neighborhood bonds formed in the communities or origin.

PUSH AND PULL FACTORS IN LOJANO MIGRATION

Natural Disasters

A popular Ecuadorian explanation of Lojano out-migration focuses on a single "push" factor: the drought of 1968. The *sequía* was a severe incident of a well-known climatic fluctuation which occurs in approximately seven-year cycles (Murphy 1926; Rudolf 1953:565; Sarma 1974:94, 97). During 1968–70 rain, which usually falls inland in the highland southerly mountains of Loja, was displaced westward, causing unusual flooding and pluvial interruptions of harvest and planting cycles in areas of the Guayas and El Oro lowlands and in southern Azuay province.

In Loja dessication after two rainless years was most severe in areas which had a history of deforestation or overgrazing on high-altitude *páramo* pastures. In the drought-affected areas at least two annual harvest cycles failed. Permanent cultivations such as coffee were destroyed. Herds of cattle starved on withered pastures, and hoof and mouth disease spread rapidly where cattle were concentrated in surviving pasture areas. Subsistence agriculturalists, whether freehold peasants or hacienda tenants, also starved. Even in the major centers of population few emergency food rations were distributed in those years of *la quinta Velasquista*.

Lojanos, particularly male heads of families, migrated throughout Ecuador during this period. Some sought wage work in the cities or coastal plantations; others sought a piece of land to cultivate outside the stricken area. Two nearby regions which attracted settler-style migration were the colonization areas of Santiago Morona[2] (Galarza Zavala 1976:25ff.) and the wet and dry tropical forests in the foothills of El Oro.

In certain localities earthquakes are another category of natural disaster which added impetus for migration. The major seismotic events are recorded in Table 3. El Limo, in western Loja, experienced an earthquake in 1970 after 20 rainless months during 1967–68. All of its predominantly adobe and hardwood timber houses and civic build-

TABLE 3. Earthquakes in Loja (1962–72).

Date	Approximate Location	Richter	Depth in kilometers
28 July 1962	Between Catacocha and Alamor 04.?? S	?	70–200
6 Nov. 1962	West of Alamor 04. S		70–200
10 May 1967	Northeast of Alamor	4.1	0–70
25 Apr. 1970	Near Puyango River, 03.904 S 080.070 W	4.7	70–200
21 Dec. 1970	Near Alamor, 03.916 S 080.740 W	4.7	200 and below
27 Jan. 1971	Northeast of Alamor, between 080 and 079 W 04. and 03. S	5.2	70–200

Source: Earthquake Data File Summary, National Geophysical and Solar Terrestrial Data Center (25 Apr. 1977 printout); Mapa Sismológico Preliminar,
CIPT componente peruana.

ings fell or were severely damaged, few of the outlying homesteads
on ridges remained standing, and three persons died. Cariamanga,
on the other side of the province, had the same experience and five
persons died there in a 1970 earthquake. Two persons died in the
December 1970 earthquake in Alamor, and as Table 3 shows, the area
between the Puyango River, Alamor, and Catacocha experienced a
number of earthquakes, both before and just after the drought.

But natural catastrophes such as drought and earthquake are not
themselves "explanations" for Lojano out-migration. We turn now to
socioeconomic factors influencing the process of out-migration and
pioneer settlement.

Socioeconomic Factors

Much of the land base of southwestern Loja was owned in large
private estates. These units included timberlands and higher-altitude
pastures. Such estates were worked under lease arrangements by *ar-
rendatarios* or by service tenants, *arrimados*. *Arrimados* effectively received only usufructory use of land in return for their labor, their
fictive wages going as payments on long-standing debts owed to
landowners and merchants.

Changes since 1964 in the legal structure of land tenancy encouraged the migration of Lojanos to El Oro. Decreto Supremo No. 2172,
the Law of Vacant Lands and Colonization, declared certain classes

of land as vacant, *baldío*, or abandoned, *revertido*. Tracts so classified were detached legally from the title of estates and, together with former state lands, *tierras del estado*, were formally opened for colonization. The Law of Agrarian Reform and Colonization (1964 and subsequent amendments) specified the initial grant of only a provisional title to claims in colonization areas. A claim on a specific plot, popularly called a *posición* and formally termed a *lote* or *prédio*, could be registered and surveyed, but the grant of a title, *adjudicación*, was subject to the claimant's development of 50% of the *posición* within five years and a variety of other conditions.

Provisional titles to subsistence cultivation plots and pasture areas were also made available to long-term service tenants on estates. Provisional titles to these expropriated properties, also called *posiciónes*, were empirically and legally subject to more stringent conditions: personal use of 100% of the *posición*, residence on the plot, compliance with a payment schedule, and fulfillment of other conditions of the provisional title over a five-year period. On paper, land was opened to colonization within Loja. However, the political economic constraints of Loja provided more incentives to out-migration than to actual land redistribution within the province. The traditional landlords, addressed locally by the honorific term *Don*, manipulated broad networks of interpersonal dependents: clients for patronage. The owners of estates in Loja universally contest the provision for the nationalization of vacant and abandoned tracts. Local landlords have registered counterclaims in the courts to dispute the classification as unused of land to which they once held title. The *dons* continue to assert *de facto* rights over lands severed from their estates. In some cases a *don's de facto* rights and unresolved legal counterclaims are enforced by the local political authorities. More generally, Lojanos have been socialized to respect the ownership ideology and land use traditions among co-members of their microregional society. Potential local colonists or their immediate relatives may be dependent on a *don* for credit, for employment, or as the sole source of merchandise. These dependencies would be compromised by asserting colonization claims on land formerly owned *de jure* by the local patron.

Colonization opportunities on unworked or state lands in El Oro lay outside the *de facto* control of the *dons* of Loja parishes. These lands were therefore more attractive to Lojanos. El Oro landlords also registered counterclaims for the foothill "reserves" of coastal plantations. Indeed, part of the area open to colonization in El Oro is in tenure disputes with claims predating the Peruvian invasion of 1941. But for the Lojanos the conflict of land rights was with "outsiders" in

El Oro. No relatives in natal villages could be compromised by the continuing struggle. Local respect for known persons' resources implied no constraints on the exploitation of "outsiders'" land, even when the Lojanos were themselves in the land of the outsiders.

Land tenure restraints were not as severe in the southern and western areas of Loja (Cazaderos, Zapotillo, Sabanilla, Macará, Alamor, Celica, and Catacocha), where the majority of migrants to El Oro originated, as they were in the northeastern pre-reform areas of Loja, Calvas, Paltas, or Chuquiribamba cantons (Galarza Zavala 1976:88–203). The majority of the residents of the southern and western cantons had access to freehold cultivation plots and to communal pasture. Several western parishes were organized with communal plots and pasture available for rent by residents. Landlords in the postreform period increasingly made land available for sale, lease, or rent to avoid higher labor costs. It is important to understand that *approximately 90% of the Lojano migrants to El Oro were freeholders in Loja.* Contrary to expectation, it is not by any means an out-migration of the landless making up the dominant stream of El Oro colonists. Moreover, the landless poor who were service tenants in Loja are concentrated in the sector of salaried workers in El Oro cattle-ranching operations, not in the stream of spontaneous settlements.

In the Loja area affected by drought and earthquake, natural disasters neutralized the advantages of the more equitable traditional land tenure and the opportunities to obtain *posiciónes* for service tenants under agrarian reform. Land could not be improved in quality. The effects of the drought could not be reversed. Crops will simply not grow on baked earth, and grasses do not grow on parched pasture lands. Freehold ownership or provisional title to such land is a vacuous social construct if the land can produce nothing. Freeholders and ex-tenants who also lost a home in earthquakes saw little reason to rebuild there and greater reason to migrate away. By abandoning residence, ex-tenants on provisional titles jeopardized their opportunity to receive permanent titles, but the freeholders' titles remained secure if they migrated. By moving to newly created colonization areas away from their natal settlement, Lojano migrants expanded into new territory and preserved their home socioeconomic structure. Lojano freeholders in particular were able to conjoin Lojano natal adaptive strategies with migratory strategies, creating a system of interprovincial exploitation across ecosystems, as they literally weathered out the natural rejuvenation of the land of Loja.

Ecologically, the scarcity of tropical hardwoods in southern and western Loja contributed another economic push for migration. Though remaining hardwoods are actively gleaned for parquet (wood-tile) factories and lumber operations, the valuable tropical hardwoods are at the brink of extinction in Loja. Near villages settled 50 or more years ago in the southwestern area of the province, the tropical hardwoods suitable for house construction in the Loja folk architectural styles are unavailable. Postearthquake reconstruction was possible in some villages only with the provision of relief funds for cast concrete beams to replace traditional hardwoods in frame and lintel elements.

Opportunities for wage labor in the southern and western parishes of Loja, where the majority of the El Oro migrants originate, are few and highly seasonal. Both wages and day-labor positions peak in August when demand for coffee pickers is high among growers. The remaining estates are organized on the basis of a fixed permanent resident labor force. The peasant agricultural and small-scale commercial sectors are premised upon the work force of immediate and unpaid family members. There are few government salaried posts. There is no major industry. The active program of road building initiated in 1976 now offers employment to a limited number of skilled and unskilled laborers.

The depressed economy of upland Loja contrasts sharply with the boom economy of the El Oro coast, where a variety of rural and urban, skilled and unskilled, seasonal and permanent, wage and salaried opportunities exist.

A problem faced by cash crop farmers in southwestern Loja is the underdevelopment of the transportation infrastructure. The broken topography, *accidentado*, is traversed only by narrow dirt roads which are so poor that it may take a vehicle two hours to move 15 to 20 kilometers. The truckers and middle merchants who respond to the challenges of the area cut into farmers' profits. The underdeveloped infrastructure creates an overhead cost which eliminates many possible areal products from competition in the national market. Perishables such as oranges or bananas can be shipped by truck to the city of Loja from lowland Guayas or El Oro as fast or faster, and cheaper, than from such Loja province parishes as Manga Urcu or El Limo. Other Lojano centers, such as Progreso and Cazaderos, are not even connected to the rudimentary road system. For this reason remote villages specialize in wood products and dried produce such as coffee, maize, and *sarandaja*, the white seed of a leguminous bush.

Social conditions in Loja serve as additional push factors. *Pueblo chico, infierno grande,* "small town, big hell," is a folk saying which summarizes an aspect of village microsociety. Social control and socioeconomic rankings are strictly enforced in the small polities. Enforcement is informal—the Hispanic ritual deference patterns—and also formally applied by each parish's *teniente político,* who is here judge, jury, and sheriff in one. The *teniente's* authority is backed up by the rural police. Because the area is near a national border, there are more police and military personnel per capita than is usual in peasant, rural areas elsewhere in Ecuador. Jails are kept occupied. One act of village justice which I observed during my survey was the sentencing of a 17-year-old youth to ten lashes and a week in jail for having been boisterously intoxicated the night before. In the face of the strictures of the strong social control in each population center, the siren songs of the coastal radio stations, Ondas del Pacífico or Radio Mambo, communicate the location of a more relaxed sociocultural system.

Opportunities for secondary education provide another pull factor for migration. In Loja secondary schools are generally limited to canton capitals, and only the wealthier or better connected can afford to support the pension arrangements of high-school-age children in Celica, Loja, or further afield. In El Oro, by contrast, high schools are more conveniently located on bus routes which allow many rural residents to send their children to central high schools while living at home.

The opportunity to marry is limited in the remote villages by the density of close kinship relationships, by social ranking which separates suitable age mates of the opposite sex into prohibited categories, and by the strong preference for neolocal, independent household formation upon marriage, which is difficult to achieve under extant economic conditions of Loja. Sexual mores are highly traditional; premarital sexual relations are ideally prohibited to both sexes. Institutionalized prostitution near the army posts and the behavior of soldiers serve as negative out-group models against which Lojanos define their own morality. Marriage occurs at age 20 or older for women and around 25 for men. Marital unions are strong, more commonly broken by the death of a spouse than by desertion.

The loyalty of Lojano marriage partners to each other and to their joint labor participation in creating and maintaining self-sufficiency proves highly adaptive in the pioneering socioeconomic situations of spontaneous colonization. Most Lojano migrants to the spontaneous colonization areas in El Oro settle in nuclear family groups as couples with minor children. Among the Lojano settler-colonists in El Oro, few marriage partners were from the same natal parishes. Commonly the spouses were from different areas of Loja or one spouse was from the El Oro uplands. Minor children with the couple had been born at places different from either parent's natal parish, tracing steps in the period of wage migration before colonization settling. Dependent elderly are rarely attached to settler households, though a nondependent extra male (brother or brother-in-law) is fairly common in the initial stages. Collaterally extended households (e.g., two nuclear families linked by a sibling bond) also occur, and common resource exploitation by a male work group linked by sibling bond, affinal bond, or neighborhood bond is the social unit for land development (see the Appendix, p. 323).

ECOLOGICAL STRATEGIES IN MIGRATION

Lojanos settling the tropical very dry, premontane humid, and subtropical humid forests of El Oro originate disproportionately from parishes which contain similar ecological zones in Loja: the protected subtropical valleys such as those near Cazaderos, Zapotillo, Sabanilla, Pindal, El Limo, Macará, Cariamanga, Quilanga, Marcadillo, Alamor, and Catacocha parishes. Successful stabilization through steady maintenance of cultivation plots and pastures in the subtropical premontane requires greater labor input than in clearing new land. Overambitious timber cutting resulted in deforestation in Loja prior to the devastating drought, and demonstrably tipped the ecological balance during the 1968–70 pluvial fluctuation (cf. Sarma 1979). Unless deforested zones are extensively developed with terraces and irrigation systems, a high ratio of forested areas must be maintained. Given the social, economic, and natural constraints of Loja, development of similar ecological zones in El Oro is clearly more labor-efficient and more suitable to the small, entrepreneurial work groups and households of Lojano social organization. I turn now to a brief general sketch of the developmental sequence of ecological strategies in Lojano migration to El Oro.

Land Development and Land Use in the Pioneer Area

In the El Oro foothills a 20- to 30-year cyclical system of land utilization has developed. This cycle is not completed on every plot, but understanding it is essential to provide a background to Lojano migrants' ecological and economic strategies.

Clearing

The forest growing on the chosen site for planting is cleared by male work groups of three or more individuals. These work groups select locations in legally vacant land, giving special consideration to the commercial potential of the trees in an area. The work group first cuts tall "pilot" trees with broad root systems spaced at about one per one-half hectare. The dispersed distribution of the more valuable trees[3] determines the subsequent scattered distribution of plots.

Trees of commercial value are sold by the foot as logs, *rolos*, to industrial lumber mills and wood-tile factories or are cut into planks or lintel timbers either in place or at a nearby roadside location with two-man cross-cut hand saws. Branches are cut, sold for firewood or as wall construction material, or burned for charcoal. Charcoal is also sold in sacks and is the major source of domestic fuel in this corner of petroleum-rich Ecuador, as in many other areas of the country. If the plot is to be further developed, underbrush and smaller trees are cleared by slash and burn swidden techniques. The process of clearing may last a year, as medium-sized trees may be scored at the time pilot trees are cut. Scored trees then die in about six months, providing dry firewood.

Clearings next to developed areas often preclude economic exploitation of wood resources. A kapok tree (*Ceiba pentandra*), which has no commercial value, may occupy the pilot tree niche, but it must be cut and burned to extend the area of clean pasture or cultivation.

Swidden—Subsistence Orientation

For a year after clearing and up to a maximum of three years thereafter, agricultural plots can produce short-cycle, *ciclo corto* or *ciclo de temporado*, subsistence crops. The number of seasons varies according to soil type, surrounding natural vegetation, and crop characteristics. Maize and manioc are the staples of the short cycle. Legumes such as peanuts and *sarandaja*[4] (*Phaseolus alvus*?) extend the number of years a field may be used. *Sarandaja* is especially adapted to drier microclimates.

This phase of land use applies a variation of the type of agriculture known as swidden, shifting, or slash and burn (Pelzer 1945:17). Shifting cultivation is regarded as responding to tropical soil depletion or its reduced fertility after natural growth is cleared (Nye and Greenland 1960; Meggers 1957, 1971:20–22). The precise variables in the ecology of swidden have been debated in the technical literature (cf. Carneiro 1960, 1961; Dumond 1961). The hypothesis advanced by

Conklin (1957) and Morley (1974) that less time is required to clear new garden plots than to weed cultivated plots after a few years because of weed invasion, especially by herbaceous plants, is especially relevant in the El Oro foothills, where takeover by grasses is one desired result of clearing.

Cultivation of Fruits and Seeds—Cash Crop Orientation

Some cleared slope plots are suitable for the cultivation of pineapples or for multicrop combinations involving bananas, plantains, coffee, and/or cacao. Pineapples may be planted for only a few years in sequence and *Musae* may fail before mature fruits are produced. Coffee, particularly above 400 meters, and cacao are more successful if shade trees, called *madres*, can be established.

Plantings may fail in this phase of land use for a variety of reasons. Pineapples, plantains, and bananas are typically planted in rows of vertical furrows, thus exposing the soil to erosion. The cultigens selected do not have the root systems of the natural vegetation. As the root systems of the cleared forest rot, the soil is no longer held in place. A great number of the trees and bushes associated in the natural vegetation of the foothills are Leguminosae (Macey 1976:49). The natural vegetation pattern mixes a great number of species with differing requirements and contributions to soil nutrients (cf. Meggers 1971:16–18 for the similar eastern slope zones). The limited inventory of El Oro crops does not so enrich the soil. Simple contour planting and terracing, which could mitigate erosion, are not practiced. The life of this phase is extended by conservation of surrounding or crest top vegetation. Generally this phase of land use is abandoned when productivity of cash crops falls below economically viable thresholds. The few years of both subsistence swidden cultivation and commercial cultivation of fruits and seed crops are simply inserted between the two economically more important phases of land use: timber exploitation and cattle ranching.

Pasture

The main use of land developed in this pioneer zone is pasture. Labor resources permitting, pastures are systematically maintained and renewed by annual reclearing and burning of any regenerated underbrush and by deliberate reseeding of pastures. The most desired type of grass is *pasto chileño* (*Panicum maximum*), which thrives only in the more humid premontane microzones. Fields which are kept "clean" may be described as "*pasto chileño*" when in fact their vegetation is made up of *grama*, *yaragua*, or *kikuyo*, which are grasses more common in the low montane, humid premontane, and higher montane.

Regrowth

In some areas near older settlements pastures have not been maintained. The basic cycle begins anew as pastures are taken over first by second-growth *wilco* and *chamana* and then by trees. This phase can be observed in the lower-altitude foothills where vegetation at climax should be of the dry tropical savannah or dry tropical forest premontane type. Many of these old pasture areas are in Santa Rosa canton and were originally owned by extensive haciendas; marginal maintenance and sporadic use incurred national expropriation as abandoned *tierras baldías*.

The sequence of land use phases—clearing to swidden to fruit and seed cultivation to pasture to regrowth and back to clearing—has been carried through the full cycle in specific areas of the El Oro foothills in Las Lajas, Palmales, and Arenillas parishes. At present, communities of spontaneous colonists and isolated households are attempting to bring a defined land base through the cycle. The Lojano migrant settlements on the Quebrada Palo de Oro south of the Palmales basin have plots in each of the first four phases: clearing, swidden, fruit and seed cultivation, and pasture. Members of these communities are simultaneously pursuing the economic strategies relevant to each phase. The village of Puyango in Las Lajas represents the residue population in one area where productive pastures failed to develop on a deforested mountainside, and the land is now entering the phase of regrowth.

This potentially replicating forest-agricultural-grazing-forest cycle represents a potential in interaction with specific cultural ecological and economic strategies. The cycle may be "short-circuited" because subsets of land users, committed to more specialized economic strategies, are involved. Foremost in the specialized economic strategies of land use are timber exploitation and cattle ranching.

ECONOMIC STRATEGIES

Timber Exploitation

A mobile community of groups of predominantly Lojano lumberjacks operates in the El Oro foothills. The economic livelihood of these groups is based on the sale of wood and wood by-products.

They are most attracted to areas of climax vegetation where stands of the more valuable tropical hardwoods are preserved. Lumberjacks build temporary houses as a residential base to exploit a new area. These houses are typically constructed of *tabique*, planks, or of split bamboo if *caña guadua* is available in the area. Swidden short-cycle subsistence cultivation, hunting, fishing, and occasional day labor are complementary secondary strategies. Income either from the sale of vaguely defined rights of usufruct to cleared plots and house sites or from the rental of pastures on plots they originally cleared may also enter the total economic strategy.

Part of this community is permanently established in Marcabelí and in Arenillas. The lumberjack community overlaps with those of spontaneous colonists who are committed to permanent settlement and land development in a restricted geographical area. These colonists include among their initial economic strategies the exploitation of wood resources in the areas they are settling. Both communities share the same skills, compete for markets, and depend on cash income from timber exploitation. The two communities can be distinguished by their settlement patterns and mobility.

Besides the free-lance primary resource extraction strategy producing woodsmen of both types (mobile lumberjacks and permanent settlers), commercial logging and timber operations are located in the El Oro foothills. These operations own relocatable milling and wood-tile manufacturing equipment. Their operators buy logs piecemeal (by the *rolo*) from free-lance lumberjacks and mount their own lumbering activities with salaried workers, power saws, and tractors. The mill and logging equipment which located in Palmales in 1977 was previously operated in Loja from as early as 1955.

Commercial lumber mills have no economic interest in further developing the land they incidentally clear. Settler-colonists, by contrast, are primarily interested in the development of cleared land into stable cultivation zones. The lumberjack community has various interests in the cleared land and in forest land.

The lumberjacks prefer to engage in supplementary swidden subsistence cultivation activities along with primary timber-cutting activities. A small group will abandon a temporary house as soon as their lumbering activities expand beyond a radius of comfortable walking distance from this base. If a potential colonist-settler farming family so requests, these lumberjacks may sell house and cleared land on the spot. Larger lumberjack work groups may work their cleared plots through a phase of pineapple cash crop cultivation. Eventual development of cleared plots into pasture rental units is the most labor-efficient means of further capitalizing upon their initial and continuing activities of timber exploitation.

Especially around Marcabelí, in the middle Arenillas River basin and in less isolated level basins, demand for pasture is growing steadily. Lumberjacks may be hired to clear land for pasture use, but, more important, they plan a pivotal role in ranching; they are the pioneer pasture land developers and eventual owners of rentable pastures.

Cattle Ranching

The system of cattle ranching which has developed in the foothills of El Oro represents an innovation. It is an ecological adaptation and an entrepreneurial development within the system of economic constraints and incentives of southern Ecuador.

The traditional cattle-ranching operations on the El Oro coast are land-extensive and labor-intensive. Grazing in xerophobic or dry tropical savannah vegetation pastures owned by the ranch is combined with supplemental use of local feedlots. Private haciendas employ migrants to work as guards, *cuidadores*, or cowhands, *vaqueros*. Such employment may be offered on a permanent salaried basis or for temporary manual labor. In the latter, *peones* work as day laborers to maintain pastures or prepare feedlot forage.

In the Sierra of Loja traditional cattle ranches are land-extensive, labor-unintensive, and inefficient. Thousands of hectares were once locked in large estates where cattle were grazed on low bushes and on the straw grasses of the *páramo* (*paja de páramo*: *Neurolepsis tesselata*, *Neurolepsis sp.*, *Calamangrostis macrophyllum*, and *Carex bomplandii*).

The emerging system of cattle ranching in the foothills and previously undeveloped uplands of El Oro can be termed "rotation grazing in developed pastures" (Brownrigg 1977a). The personnel of the system are usually Lojanos, though Zaruma- and Arenillas-born individuals are also involved.

The system is characterized by a division of the capital investment, risks, labor costs, and profits between cattle herd owners and pasture owners. Cattle herd owners generally possess a small base pasture of about one and one-half hectares per head; they must rent additional pasture from pasture owners at 80 sucres/head/month/hectare (1977 price). They also assume the labor costs of about 1,200 sucres to move grazing herds of about 30 head from one rented pasture to another, and they assume the cost of herd development. Cattle owners have developed a new breed by crossing the basic *criollo* stock of Loja with Brahmans. Brahman stock is adapted to tropical conditions and is now common on the El Oro coast. Each successive generation is bred with Brahman bulls.

The pasture owners assume the labor value or costs of the original development of pastures, the labor costs of annual burnings and re-seedings, estimated at 1,250 sucres/hectare/year (1977 data), and rental transaction costs as credit to cattle herd owners. The system provides two separate, interdependent ladders of capital accumulation: in cattle or in land. Elsewhere in Ecuador, and absolutely in Loja, cattle ranchers control both stock and land. The El Oro system of rotation grazing, also practiced in adjacent Alamor, creates two paths of upward economic mobility and jobs for migrants. With regard to the migrants themselves, the critical economic underpinning of this entire system of cattle ranching is *the availability of Lojano migrants as a cheap labor force* for the work of clearing pasture and herding cattle. These Lojano migrants, by and large, are of the 10% of landless poor, discussed on pp. 309–10 above, who were without freeholdings in their natal parishes.

Significantly, some of the larger cattle herds in Ecuador are being developed in this area. According to the 1968 agricultural census, "233,000 farmers raised some cattle, including dairy, but only 7,500 had more than 50 head and only 165 were ranchers owning more than 500 a piece. Over 188,000 farmers ran less than 10 head of cattle" (Weil et al. 1973:277). While no herd in the system of rotation grazing surveyed in El Oro approached 500, a number of herds in the 150–300-head range were discovered (Santa Rosa IERAC field survey records).

Peasant Agriculture

A minority of the Lojanos in El Oro are involved in, or caught up in, the timber exploitation or cattle-ranching economic strategies. The goal of the majority is to reproduce the small-scale mixed farming freehold pattern of their homeland. Lojano migrants established near La Victoria (Las Lajas) and Marcabelí and in scattered areas such as the Tahüín basin have achieved that goal. Many more Lojanos remain primarily dependent upon wages from agricultural work, live in urban areas, and are only beginning to stake claims to *posiciónes*.

The villages of the Quebradas Chiroquite, Palo de Oro, and El Guineo are representative of Lojano migrants' initiative. The villages of Unión Lojano, Manabí del Oro, La Florida, and El Guineo, each established about a decade ago, were built to last. Houses and communally built civic buildings (school, chapel) were built of locally fired bricks and tiles and the strongest of the hardwoods, *guayacán*. The settlers are adult couples and their young children. Permanent cultivation areas have been established on the natural terraces of the streams. Dessert bananas called *guineo*, cooking plantains called *plátanos*, citrus and other fruit trees, and sugar cane are grown. Maize, manioc, beans, but little *sarandaja*—here known by the variant common name *grandaja*—and few fresh vegetables such as tomatoes and squash are cultivated on upland swidden and better-established plots. Pastures for goats, a few cows, and, inappropriately, sheep have been cleared and are fenced with elaborate *circos* of split logs. Fishing in the streams and hunting for birds and mammals contribute more animal protein to the local settler's diet than domesticated animals. Wild mammals hunted include the *quatusa*, an agouti (*Dasyprocta agouti?*); the *quanta* (elsewhere in Ecuador the common name for the spotted cavy but here tentatively identified as the molluskeating, web-footed giant rodent *Hydrochoerus hidrochoaerus*, called *ronsoco* in the Peruvian Amazon basin); two types of peccaries (*P. tajucu* and *Dicotykes* sp.), deer (*Cervos* sp.); the *cabeza de mate*, a weasel (*Eira barbara*); and a fox (*Canis azarae*). Despite the amount of time devoted to subsistence agriculture, herding, fishing, and hunting by the settlers, about half of the average settler household budget is spent purchasing additional food.

Households' cash income derives largely from the sale of wood and day-labor wages from work on farms in the foothills and haciendas on the El Oro coast. Attempts have been made to establish cash crops, especially coffee. Several households from these villages, along with other Lojano settlers in El Oro, travel back to Loja to harvest coffee on their freeholds there, leaving some relative in the El Oro homestead. Others travel back more frequently to plant, tend, and harvest maize and *sarandaja* in January, March, and August.

The communities have experienced major setbacks ranging from endemic illness caused by intestinal parasites, epidemics such as measles which caused the death of 17 children of the 80 families in Manabí del Oro in 1973, hoof and mouth disease among domestic animals in 1976, and natural disasters such as the flooding of the town center of El Guineo in 1974.

Despite communal features of their village social organization, raising buildings for common purposes and raising community funds with fairs, *kermess*, the settlers resent and resist the requirement that they organize formally in cooperatives to secure clear title, *adjudicación*, to the *posiciones*. Insecurity of land tenure and social, rather than clearly legal, usufructory rights are also general, continuing, problems. Lojanos who colonized early have received individual land titles. This local precedent and the background cultural pattern of freehold status suggest that other forms of group organization, such as the *comuna*—a combination of privately owned tracts of differing size and communal land resource areas—may be more appropriate than the formal cooperative in current government favor.

Other Strategies

The three broad economic strategies sketched above have established pioneering land use patterns on thousands of hectares in the foothills of El Oro. While the application of these strategies in this locale has not been exclusively carried out by Lojano migrants, they have taken the lead. Lojano migrants to El Oro have, of course, also entered other sectors of the El Oro economy. The role of migrants as permanent and seasonal agricultural workers on larger units has been noted in passing. Additional Lojano migrant roles will now be sketched.

Lojano migrants carry artisanal skills in brick and tile making, bread baking, carpentry, and wood fabrication. Individual Lojanos have developed these skills into specialized primary occupations or businesses in El Oro where such artisanship was not well represented in the resident population.

Small-scale entrepreneurs among the Lojano migrants have established *tiendas de primera necesidad*, which are shops for a clientele of fellow migrants and neighbors in each barrio or rural hamlet where Lojanos are concentrated. In general, the commercial sector in El Oro is dominated by native-born residents and merchant migrants from Azuay or Pichincha. These groups have greater capital resources than the collectively and individually marginal Lojanos.

The majority of the Lojano migrants over 15 years of age have completed three or more years of education. The education of both young men and young women is a valued goal among the migrant Lojano families. The emergence of professionally trained Lojanos has already begun among those who migrated as young children to El Oro by the mid-1960s. This investment in the education of youth realizes Lojano aspirations for upward mobility.

CONCLUDING COMMENTS

The dynamism of the settler-colonists and land use pioneers represents an important human resource for El Oro. The present economic and ecological strategies are appropriate to the stage of initial, short-run land development and the pioneering, capital-poor, labor-intensive, small work groups. The long-run land development process in the El Oro foothills, however, depends on the degree of ecological degradation and transformation caused by deforestation and the expansion of cattle raising. If the cylical pattern of land utilization from forest clearing through reforestation is maintained, then ecosystem homeostasis is anticipated. Failure, however, to complete the ecological-economic cycle could replicate the disastrous effects of Loja overexploitation which led, in part, to the colonization of El Oro.

Strategies sketched above falsely presume the limitlessness of finite resources, notably the virgin forest and wild tropical tree species. Forestry research has begun in El Oro, but the experimental cultivation of the commercially important wild tropical trees native to the zone requires a special program. Enforced preservation of forests along upland ridges and on important watersheds along with well-planned reforestation campaigns must also become a government policy initiative. Such steps would extend through time the economic value of the forests and secure other forms of land use.

Stabilization of agricultural land use in the foothills in pastures and mixed-grove tree crops has the greatest short-term potential. In the long term, perhaps a half-century away, massive terracing together with the construction of sophisticated irrigation systems could achieve maximal agricultural land use.

While the Lojano migration to El Oro depends on many features of the modern economy—wage labor opportunities, motor vehicles, the national market structure—it can also be suggested that the migration is asserting anew an ancient territory of a pre-Columbian ethnic group. Aspects of Cieza de Leon's description of the immediate post-colonial territory of the Paltas (LVI, LVIII) describe them as occupying the Tumbes River headwaters (i.e., the Pindo and Puyango), an area south of Zaruma (cf. Segarra Iñiguez 1976), a town named Piedras (Piedras, Arenillas?), and the mountain between the Puyango and Catamayo drainages (southwestern Loja).

Though hispanicized in most aspects of their culture by the end of the seventeenth century, the Lojanos migrating into El Oro may represent a submerged ethnic group reconstituting an ancient territory. The thrust of the migration, while primarily aimed at ecological zones

familiar to the specific settlers, is also adding new zones for manipulation in a vertical ecology strategy (see, e.g., Murra 1972, Orlove
1977) and connecting Lojanos to the nexus of national modern Ecuadorian markets, communications, and civil life.

APPENDIX. Age Structure of Lojano Migrants in El Oro (1974).

Age:	0–4	5–9	10–14	15–19	20–24	
Total	610	2,054	3,120*N.B.	3,765*N.B.	3,555*	
Urban	313	1,008	1,606	2,003	1,963	Generation
Rural	297	1,046	1,514	1,762	1,592	of children

Age:	25–29	30–34	35–39	40–49	50–59	
Total	2,751	2,291	1,999	3,059*N.B.	1,739	Generation
Urban	1,493	1,233	1,087	1,631	929	of heads of
Rural	1,258	1,058	912	1,428	810	household/par- ents

Age:	60–69	70+	
Total	1,003	639	Generation
Urban	490	329	of dependent
Rural	513	310	elderly/grandpar- ents

SOURCE: INEC 1976: IV (Loja).

NOTES

Acknowledgments: This paper is based on research, including fieldwork, in El
Oro and Loja, which I conducted as the consulting anthropologist of the Consorcio Internacional Puyango-Tumbes, under a contract from Harza Engi-
neering Company (Chicago), a member firm of the consortium. Access to
other studies of the CIPT, to the IERAC records at Santa Rosa, and to the
PREDESUR-Machala library provided important information. I am especially
grateful to those co-workers whose insights, information, and supportive attitudes enhanced the anthropological research process in the Ecuadorian
area: Dr. Hector Ayón, geologist; Dr. Peter Ames, terrestrial ecologist; Jerry
Knapp, economist and project manager; Dr. Angel Jijón, sociologist; Dr.
James Thrall, aquatic biologist; Dow Nichols, planning engineer; Dr. Sviato-
slav Krochin, civil engineer and Ecuadorian project director; and Dr. Marcel
Bitouin, civil engineer and Harza branch manager.

1. Examples include La Avanzada, population 1,280; San Antonio, population 490; La Victoria (Las Lajas), population 566 (INEC 1976:XII (El Oro):569).

2. Lojanos in the Oriente have come into conflict with the native inhabitants such as the Jívaro-Shuara of Morona-Santiago and Zamora-Chinchipe. For analogous examples of such conflict see Salazar (in this volume) and Whitten (1976).

3. The common names and tentative species identifications of the valuable trees of the dry or wet tropical forests of El Oro are as follows (*guayacán*, a hardwood, is most avidly sought; balsa, known by the common name *huampo*, is now rare): "Guayacan" (*Guaiacum lignum*); "Laurel" (*Cordia allidora*); "Palo Santo" or "Balsamo" (*Bursera graveolens* or a *Guaiacum* sp.?); "Palo de vaca" (*Alseis egeersili*); "Amarillo" (*Berberis latifolia* or *lutea*); "Barbasco" (*Cassia* of various species); "Fernandez Sanches" or "Fernan Sanchez" (*Triplalaris guayaquilensis*); "Ebano" (*Diospyros* sp.?, *Zizphus thysiflora* or *piurensis*); "Charan" (*Caesalpinia corymbosa*); "Palo de diente" (*Guaiacum* sp.?); "Hilaco" or "Laco" (?); "Huampo" (*Uchroma lagopus*).

4. *Sarandaja* could not be positively identified by CIPT agronomists except as a legume. *Sarandaja* may be a lupine; another lupine, *chochos*, has been identified in Ecuador. My colleague, the Peruvian anthropologist Javier Pulgar Vidal, suggests that *sarandaja* may be a variety of *Phaseolus alvus*, the tentative species identification he ascribes to similar plants which bear red or brown seeds, called *santo somo* in Colocas, *pushko* in Huancayo, and *vocán*, *lanteja*, or *pucatoro* elsewhere in Peru. The seed of *sarandaja*, *sanardaja*, or *grandaja* is white; its bush is a tall, free-standing annual which is monocropped in Loja. In El Oro no extensive plots of *sarandaja* were observed; rather, it alternated with manioc in plots of maize or was grown close to house sites. Pulgar Vidal reports that *Phaseolus alvus* has a higher vegetable protein content than lentils. In this area of Loja the crop is definitely a staple, like maize, for the Quechua. Its distribution extends into Huancabamba in the Peruvian highlands due south of Loja. Its distribution may define a distinct ecological adaptation, which is consistent with the thesis that the Lojanos represent a submerged ethnicity dating to pre-Columbian times.

REFERENCES CITED

Brownrigg, Leslie A.
1973   Ethnology South America: Highlands. *Handbook of Latin American Studies* 35:104–26.
1975   Ethnology South America: Highlands. *Handbook of Latin American Studies* 37:126–50.
1977a   Anthropological Aspects of the Puyango-Tumbes Project Benefit (Irrigation and Flood Control) Zone, Impact Zone and Sub-region in Peru and Ecuador. I: Settlement Pattern, II: Cultural Ecology. Machala-Tumbes-Chicago: Consorcio Internacional Puyango-Tumbes.
1977b   Socio-Economic Comparison of Proposed Reservoir Sites. Report to the Comision Mixta. Machala-Tumbes-Chicago: Consorcio Internacional Puyango-Tumbes.

Carneiro, Robert L.
1960 Slash and Burn Agriculture: A Closer Look at Its Implications for Settlement Patterns. In Anthony F. C. Wallace, ed., *Men and Cultures*. Philadelphia: University of Pennsylvania Press, pp. 229–34.
1961 Slash and Burn Cultivation among the Kuikuru and Its Implications for Cultural Development in the Amazon Basin. In Johannes Wilbert, ed., *The Evolution of Horticultural Systems in Native South America; Causes and Consequences: A Symposium. Antropológica*, supplement 2. Caracas: Sociedad de Ciencias Naturales La Salle, pp. 47–65.

Cieza de Leon, Pedro
1962 [1553] *La Crónica del Perú*. Tercera Edición. Madrid: Espasa-Calpa, S.A., Colección Austral.

Conklin, H. C.
1957 *Hanunóo Agriculture*. Rome: FAO, Forestry Paper 12.

Dumond, Donald E.
1961 Swidden Agriculture and the Rise of Maya Civilization. *Southwestern Journal of Anthropology* 17 (4):301–16.

Galarza Zavala, Jaime
1976 *Los Campesinos de Loja y Zamora*. Quito: Ediciones Solitierra.

IERAC (Instituto Ecuatoriano de Reforma Agraria y Colonización)
1964 Ley de Reforma Agraria y Colonización; Ley de Tierras Baldías y Colonización. Quito.

INEC (Instituto Nacional de Estadística y Censos)
1976 *III Censo de la Población (1974)—Resultados Definitivos—El Oro*. Vol. 12. Quito.

Jaramillo J., Alfredo, and Alfredo Castro A.
1975 *Informe de la Investigación Socio-económica Prioritaria en las Provincias de Loja y El Oro*. Quito: PREDESUR, Publicación 45.

Macey, Ann
1976 *Mapa Ecológico y Uso Potencial de la Cuenca Piloto (Pindo-Calvas, Prov. Loja)*. Quito: PREDESUR, Publicación 47.

Meggers, Betty J.
1957 Environment and Culture in the Amazon Basin: An Appraisal of the Theory of Environmental Determinism. In *Studies in Human Ecology*. Social Science Monograph 3. Washington, D.C.: Pan American Union, pp. 71–113.
1971 *Amazonia: Man and Culture in a Counterfeit Paradise*. Chicago and New York: Aldine/Atherton.

Morley, Sylvanus G.
1974 *The Ancient Maya*. Stanford, Calif.: Stanford University Press.

Murphy, Robert Cushman
1926 Oceanic and Climatic Phenomena along the West Coast of South America during 1925. *Geographical Review* 16:26–45.

Murra, John
1972 El "Control Vertical" de un Máximo de Pisos Ecológicos en la Economía de las Sociedades Andinas. In John Murra, ed., *Visita de la Provincia de León de Huánuco en 1562*, vol. 2. Huánuco, Peru: Facultad de Letras y Ciencias, Universidad Nacional Hermilio Valdizán, pp. 429–76.

Nye, P. H., and D. J. Greenland
   1960   *The Soil under Shifting Cultivation.* Harpenden: Commonwealth Bureau of Soils, Technical Communications 51.
Orlove, Benjamin S.
   1977   Integration through Production: The Use of Zonation in Espinar. *American Ethnologist* 4 (1):84–101.
Pelzer, K. J.
   1945   *Pioneer Settlement in the Asiatic Tropics.* American Geographical Society Special Publication 29. New York: Institute of Pacific Relations.
Quijano, Aníbal
   1977   *Dependencia, Urbanización y Cambio Social en Latinoamérica.* Lima: Mosca Azul Editores.
Rudolf, William
   1953   Weather Cycles from South America's West Coast. *Geographical Review* 43 (4):565–66.
Sarma, Akkaraju
   1974   Holocene Paleoecology of South Coastal Ecuador. *Proceedings of the American Philosophical Society* 118 (1):93–134.
   1979   Recent Environmental Changes and Archeological Implications in South West Coastal South America. Paper presented at the 43rd International Congress of Americanists, Vancouver, Canada.
Segarra Iñiguez, Guillermo
   1976   *Probanza de don Joan Bistancela, Cacique de Toctesi . . . (1594).* Cuaderno Guapnondelig 1. Quito: Comintur.
Weil, A., et al.
   1973   *Area Handbook for Ecuador.* Foreign Area Studies Division, Special Operations Research Office of the American University. Washington, D.C.: Government Printing Office.
Whitten, Norman E., Jr. (with the assistance of Marcelo F. Naranjo, Marcelo Santi Simbaña, and Dorothea S. Whitten)
   1976   *Sacha Runa: Ethnicity and Adaptation of Ecuadorian Jungle Quichua.* Urbana: University of Illinois Press.
Wolf, I.
   1892   *Geografía y Geología del Ecuador.* Leipaig.

11

Colonist Strategies of Verticality in an Eastern Valley

J. Peter Ekstrom

Colonists from the Sierra village of Jima are exploiting multiple ecological zones in the adjacent Cuyes valley on the eastern slopes of the Andes. Out-migrants from Jima have established three satellite communities, San Miguel, Amazonas, and Nueva Tarqui, within the several zones of the valley. In the process of colonizing the Cuyes valley and exploiting its multiple habitats, the colonists have developed a series of interrelated strategies to utilize the vertical pattern of contiguous ecological zones. This exploitation includes zones not only within the Cuyes valley itself but also in the Jima valley. The area of origin of the colonists and the colonization areas comprise one vertical system of continuously connected ecological zones. The environmental parameters of the several zones act as a physical grid, shaping and controlling the adaptive strategies utilized by the colonists.

The exploitation of multiple ecological zones is a recurrent theme in Andean adaptation. The ethnohistorical implications of this theme led Murra (1972) to develop a socioeconomic model of "verticality" that has been the foundation for most studies involving zonation in the Andes (Brush 1973, 1977; Ekstrom 1975; Flores 1975; Fonseca 1972; Mitchell 1973, 1976; Orlove 1977; Rhoades and Thompson 1975; Webster 1973). Murra's (1972) ethnohistoric data support the main thrust of his argument that there is a native Andean complex of adaptation to the vertical nature of Andean habitats which places a premium on control by a single village or ethnic group of the productive capacity of as many different ecological zones as possible. Murra (1972:430) states that these zones form "vertical archipelagoes" containing a string of distinct productive islands separated some distance from one another by nonproductive wasteland.

Brush (1973:165–76, 1977:10–16), expanding on Murra's model of verticality, has broadened the concept of vertical archipelagoes. He recognizes three patterns of Andean zonation, called compressed, archipelago, and extended. The compressed type is characterized by a very steep environmental gradient, a continuous blending of one zone into another, and relatively short distances involved in travel from the controlling village to the most distant zones. There is no need for long-term migrations or complex exchange networks to exploit all the zones. The archipelago type corresponds to Murra's (1972) conception, emphasizing noncontinuous zones separated by wastelands and the establishment of "satellite" communities of colonists or elaborate exchange networks with other groups in the various zones to exploit and control all production. The extended type's diagnostic features include a rather gradual environmental gradient, continuous zones located in relatively large valleys, population spread evenly throughout the zones, and the existence of elaborate exchange networks and market systems needed to efficiently exploit all the zones.

Orlove's (1977) analysis of zonation in the southern Peruvian community of Espinar stresses the importance of an integrated production system involving two ecological zones. His emphasis differs from other studies of zonation and verticality in that production, not distribution, is paramount in the integration of different zones. Espinar also differs from Murra's model in that the " . . . aim [of given communities] is to control lands in two zones rather than in a 'maximum' number of zones . . ." (Orlove 1977:89).

Rhoades and Thompson recognize two major adaptive strategies common to mountainous regions throughout the world. In their view a generalized strategy " . . . involves a single population which, through agro-pastoral transhumance, directly exploits a series of microniches or ecozones at several altitudinal levels. . . ." In a second specialized strategy " . . . a population locks into a single zone and specializes in the agricultural or pastoral activities suitable to that altitude, developing elaborate trade relations with populations in other zones which are also involved in specialized production" (1975:547). Rhoades and Thompson (1975:547) also point out that studies in the Andes, as compared to other mountainous regions, have emphasized the specialized adaptive strategy to the virtual exclusion of the general; that is, Andean studies have focused on Murra's (1972) verticality model stressing elaborate trade networks and systems of reciprocity. Studies such as those by Webster (1973) on pastoralism in the southern Peruvian Andes, Brush (1973, 1977), and Orlove (1977) seem to be redressing this imbalance of emphasis.

In this study of the Jima-Cuyes valleys I will follow an expanded view of Murra's model, taking into account Brush's more detailed differentiation of patterns of zonation, Orlove's emphasis on the integrative function of production, and Rhoades and Thompson's concern with two major strategy types of "mountain procurement systems." In so doing I will endeavor to identify, interpret, and explain the complex of strategies adapted to the vertical arrangement of ecological zones of the Jima-Cuyes valleys. The focus of the study will be on the colonists who reside in the satellite communities in the Cuyes valley. Thus it will be pertinent not only to the study of verticality in mountainous regions but also to the study of colonization as " . . . a process whereby one type of organism establishes itself in a new ecological niche" (Casagrande, Thompson, and Young 1964:283).

PHYSICAL ENVIRONMENT

The description of the physical environment (Figure 1) will focus on the Oriente region in which the Cuyes valley is located and will dwell only briefly on the physical parameters of the Jima valley.

The village of Jima is located in a small inter-Andean valley at the headwaters of the Río Pamar. The elevation at the town center is 2,850 meters. Elevations to the east and west reach 3,600 meters in the *páramos* (cold, humid, grassy areas above 3,000 meters). Jima is about 300 meters higher than Cuenca, 40 kilometers to the north, the nearest city with climatic statistics. Cuenca has an annual average temperature of 13.9°C and receives 862.1 millimeters of rainfall (Ferdon 1950:73). Jima temperatures are probably colder, and it receives more rain owing to its location near the eastern Andean crest. There is a cold dry period from May through August and a peak in rainfall from February through April. Two ecological zones comprise the Jima valley: the inter-Andean and the *páramo*. To the east of the *páramo* the zones of the Oriente begin.

The Oriente represents a varied and complex tropical environment. Climate, forest cover, soil, topography, and geology vary considerably with altitude and geographic position. The axis of greatest variation extends from west to east; at the western extreme are the high, cool,. and damp cloud forests and to the east are the tall gallery forests of the relatively flat Amazonian plain. Variation from north to south, although not as drastic, is significant, especially near the base of the Andes. In the north the Andean wall sharply abuts the Amazonian plain with only a minor development of foothills. In the south, however, the remnants of a third Andean range (cordilleras of Cutucú and Condor), which reach nearly 3,000 meters, result in a far

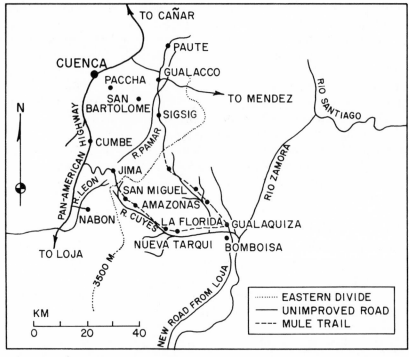

FIGURE 1

more rugged topography and a correspondingly altered climatic regime.

Relatively few published studies exist on the physical geography of the Oriente or, for that matter, the whole Upper Amazon basin. Hegen (1966:18–19) proposes a three-fold division or zonation of the Upper Amazon basin based primarily on altitude and forest cover. This division is very general, with much variation existing within the different zones. The *ceja* zone is a cloud forest occurring at elevations between 4,000 and 2,500 meters. The climate is very damp and the topography is rugged with narrow valleys and steep river profiles. The *montaña* zone of elevations between 2,500 and 1,000 meters is also a humid zone of continuous forest characterized by warmer temperatures and less undergrowth than the *ceja*. The third major zone is the *hylea*, which occurs in the Amazon basin proper below elevations of 1,000 meters. Hegen (1966:19) divides the *hylea* into two subzones: the *eté*, or land above the active floodplains of the rivers, and the *várzea*, the land within the active floodplains which is characterized by periodically renewed alluvium. The contact between the three major zones is gradational; their correspondence to altitude is only approximate and depends on local conditions.

A more detailed subdivision into natural regions has been attempted by Tosi (1960:196) for eastern Peru, who delimits "natural life zones" based on the Holdridge system of ecological analysis. These life zones represent natural plant associations and are determined primarily by physiographic conditions such as climate, topography, and altitude (Tosi and Voertman 1964:191–93).

Unfortunately, there are no detailed life zone studies of Ecuador similar to Tosi's work in Peru. A beginning in this direction has been made by Acosta-Solis (1965), who divided Ecuador into 15 "geobotanical" formations and 18 "ecovegetive" plant formations. Four of the plant formations are located in the Oriente.

Grubb et al. (1963:596) and Grubb and Whitmore (1966:303) divide the Oriente into zones of forest formation types, following closely the forest formation types suggested by Richards (1952) for tropical mountain areas. These formation types are lowland, lower montane, and upper montane rainforest. These three forest formation types generally parallel altitudinally the *hylea*, *montaña*, and *ceja* ecological zones of Hegen (1966). Throughout this study I will utilize the terminology used by Hegen for natural ecological zones in the Oriente unless stated otherwise. To analyze the adaptive strategies, it is first necessary to understand the basic physical parameters of the tropical environment within the various zones of the Oriente (see Figure 2).

Ceja

Traversing west to east, the first ecological zone encountered beyond the Andean crest is the *ceja*. The vegetative cover is a very dense cloud forest, a tangled mass of plants and trees. This zone is characterized by the epiphytes, especially bromeliads, ferns, mosses, and bamboolike cane, *carrizo*. Compared to lower zones, trees are small-leaved, nonbuttressed, ranging in height from 5 to 18 meters, and are arranged in one stratum (Grubb et al. 1963:596). In the lower altitudes of the *ceja* zone, and especially in the southern Oriente, there are many species of the Rubiaceae family, particularly *Cinchona* sp., which has been exploited for the extraction of quinine (Acosta-Solis 1965:135–63), which comes from its bark.

The mountainous topography of the *ceja* is characterized by steep, narrow, V-shaped valleys cut by very swift mountain streams. The steep slopes aid in keeping the soils well drained and supplying vast amounts of run-off to the streams. Much of the *ceja* in Ecuador is

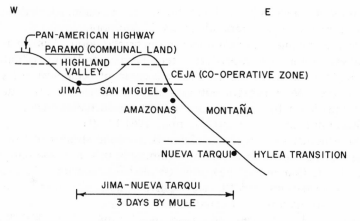

FIGURE 2. Jima-Cuyes zonation.

underlain by a variety of metamorphic rock; there are also small areas underlain by volcanics. Little is known of the soils of this zone, but they are generally thought to be very acidic, of low fertility, and of moderate depth (Hegen 1966:90).

One of the most important parameters of climate in the *ceja* is the pervasiveness of cloud cover and low-lying fog. Grubb and Whitmore (1966:322) believe the degree of low-lying cloud cover is the most important factor in differentiating forest formation types in the Oriente. They contend (1966:326) that the fog and cloud cover alter the aerial environment and thus the forest vegetation by changing the light, temperature, and water regimes to a significant degree.

There are no accurate figures for annual rainfall within the *ceja* zone in Ecuador. For Peru, Tosi (1960:148) estimates that rainfall varies between 1,000 and 2,000 millimeters. Because of the reduced influence of rain shadow effects for much of the Ecuadorian *ceja*, the 2,000-millimeter annual rainfall is probably the closer estimate. Although the temperatures are relatively cooler compared to the zones at lower altitudes, no temperature data are available for the *ceja*.

Montaña

It is in the *montaña* zone that much of the colonization in the Cuyes valley has taken place. Forests in this zone have large trees up to heights of 27 meters; some have small buttresses. The upper part of the *montaña* as it grades into the *ceja* is a vegetative jumble. The upper *montaña* contains an abundance of species of the Rubiaceae family

(Acosta-Solis 1966:407, 437). Throughout the zone epiphytes are abundant. In lower altitudes, especially as it grades into the *hylea*, palms become more abundant (Acosta-Solis 1966:408). The *montaña* is a rugged zone topographically; steep slopes and narrow valleys dominate. Landslide scars are common on many of the steep slopes. Water seems to be everywhere, collecting in mountain streams and plunging down the narrow east-west–oriented valleys toward the Amazonian plain.

The types of soils in the *montaña* are partially determined by the underlying geology. Those soils derived from volcanics are generally more fertile than those derived from the metamorphic rocks. Soils derived from similar rock types change gradually with altitude, showing the increasing effects of the processes of laterization. At higher altitudes humidity and lower temperatures inhibit those same processes. One of the most striking features of *montaña* climate is the very high annual rainfall, especially at the lower elevations on the eastern slopes. Cloud cover and fog are common throughout the year in the *montaña*, much more prevalent than in the *hylea* but not as common as in the *ceja*. Average annual temperatures vary with local topography and, more important, altitude.

Hylea

The *hylea* comprises by far the largest ecological zone in the Oriente. The part of the *hylea* relevant to this study is that which grades into the *montaña* zone at the base of the Andes. Moving farther to the east from this gradational zone certain ecological parameters gradually change.

Topographically, the Andean foothills, with their fast-moving mountain streams, quickly give way to a seemingly monotonous plain characterized by low relief and a heavily dissected hydrographic regime. Eastward the forests become less dense, but the trees are more heavily buttressed and taller; their tops form a continuous canopy which limits the light reaching the forest floor and inhibits the density of the undergrowth. Pure stands of a single species are rare and the number of different forest species great. Soils here are also varied; the greatest variation exists between the fertile recent alluvial soils of the *várzea* subzone and the predominantly lateritic soils of the *eté*. Rainfall decreases eastward as average annual temperatures increase; low clouds and fog are rare compared to the other two zones.

SETTING

The rural parish of Jima has a total population of around 6,000 people, but the actual town center contains approximately 40 households. It is situated in a small valley with an average elevation of 3,000 meters, 40 kilometers southeast of Cuenca. The people consider themselves to be *cholos*, non-Indian peasants. Other ethnic differentiations are made; Jimeños who live in the town center, especially on the plaza, are sometimes referred to by other Jimeños as *blancos*— urban oriented, Spanish speaking, non-Indian. When referring to some rural neighborhoods of Jima, other Jimeños consider them as basically composed of *runas*, Indians. When identifying themselves in relation to outsiders, however, the designation *cholo* is used to refer to all Jimeños. Even internally the separate categories of *cholo*, *blanco*, and *runa* are rarely used. If asked to place themselves in a social category, the word *cholo* is the one that is inevitably employed.

The people work their own agricultural land, as there are only two small haciendas in the Jima valley which are primarily agricultural. The main crops raised are corn, wheat, and broad beans. Cattle, sheep, pigs, chickens, and guinea pigs comprise the livestock inventory. The area is known regionally for its production of milk and cheese. Jima is considered a rather prosperous community for its size in the Andean region south of Cuenca.

As the main focus of this paper is on the Río Cuyes colonization area, only a brief description of the Jima valley has been given. A more detailed description of the colonization area in the Cuyes valley follows.

The ecological zones within the Cuyes valley include the *páramo*, *ceja*, *montaña*, and the beginning of the *hylea*. The zones grade into one another, and there are no sharp boundaries except at the interface of the *páramo* and *ceja*. The zones exploited most by the colonists are the *montaña* and upper *hylea*. San Miguel is located in the lower *ceja* and the upper forests of the *montaña*. Amazonas is entirely within the *montaña* zone. Nueva Tarqui is within the transition zone between *montaña* and *hylea*. The various resources utilized from the several zones will be discussed in relation to the various adaptive strategies.

San Miguel

The journey from Jima to San Miguel in the Cuyes valley is a full day's walk in good weather. It takes about four hours to reach the Andean crest of Moriré, a distance of only about 16 kilometers but an altitude change of almost 1,000 meters. The first hour is spent following the village trails between fields of corn and pasture land, but as altitude is gained one travels only in the windy *páramo*, occasionally passing children guarding herds of sheep and goats grazing on the coarse *ichu* grasses. All the *páramo* areas in Jima are considered community land and may not be appropriated by anyone permanently. Wild animals, principally deer, infrequently puma, and mountain woolly tapir, inhabit the bleak landscape. When the summit of Moriré is reached, and if the day is exceptionally clear, a vast panorama can be seen. To the northeast the smoking and snowcapped crown of the volcano Sangay is clearly visible. To the west the jagged peaks of the *páramo* of Soldados rim the edge of the Cuenca basin. To the east is the most spectacular view: almost the entire Cuyes valley can be seen, the light green patches of the colonists' fields contrasting with the dark green of the tropical forests, and the blue-green heights of the Cordillera del Condor on the far side of the Río Zamora stand out; beyond the cordillera is Peru. For the next seven hours one descends precipitously on a rough mule trail into the Cuyes valley. An indication of the difficulty of the trail is revealed by some of the place names: *infiernillos*, "little hell," *Moriré*, "Will I die?," and *suspiros*, "gasps."

Immediately beyond the crest of Moriré lie the cloud forests of the *ceja*. The low forest is a jumble of moss-covered branches and a multitude of parasitic and epiphytic plants. Because of the steep slopes and the tangled growth, walking in the cloud forest is similar to climbing in the branches of a huge moss-covered tree.

For the first four hours or so of travel in the *ceja* one encounters no signs of colonist habitation. Often, however, colonists and *contrabandistas*, moonshiners, with mules laden with rubber bags filled with *trago*, crude rum, are passed on the trail. The colonists may be herding several head of cattle to be sold in the mountains, or they may be returning to their Jima homes after spending several months tending their Oriente properties, in which case they may have several mules packed with their personal effects or boxes of cheese.

As one continues to descend into the valley, the vegetation of the cloud forest gives way to larger trees and the first colonist pastures appear; in three hours more one arrives at San Miguel. The town center is very small, comprised of only about a dozen buildings surrounding an unfinished plaza perched on the steep northern slope about 170 meters above the Río Cuyes. The population of the entire parish is approximately 350. Among the buildings in San Miguel are a large chapel and a community building used as a combination schoolhouse and *teniente político*'s office. A makeshift store sells rice, raw sugar, salt, noodles, candles, hard candies, and at times soft drinks and beer. All of these goods are brought in by mule from Jima.

A telephone line connects San Miguel back to Jima and also to Amazonas farther down the valley. One of the practical uses of the telephone is as an early warning system to alert the communities to the government liquor tax guards coming over the mountains for a raid.

Amazonas

The trail from San Miguel to Amazonas winds down the valley through cleared pasture lands, corn fields, and forested ravines. It is about a two-and-a-half hour walk.

The town center of Amazonas is located on a steeper slope than San Miguel and is composed of two parts, one 30 meters lower than the other. The altitude is approximately 2,000 meters, about 570 meters lower than San Miguel. Amazonas parish is extensive in area and spans a large change in altitude, from 2,000 to 1,200 meters. It is a seven-hour walk down the valley from one end of the *parroquia* to the other, although the land distance is only about 20 kilometers. Dramatic changes in ecology occur in this interval as the entire *montaña* zone is traversed.

The population of Amazonas is approximately 400, and the town center is similar to that of San Miguel. About half of the dozen buildings are constructed of wood planking, including the rather large chapel and two-story schoolhouse. Most of the town's buildings are located in the upper sector, only the school and three houses in the lower sector. The trail from San Miguel forks outside of town and passes through both sectors. As in San Miguel, the town appears deserted unless church or school is in session. A small store features a similar but better stocked inventory than the one in San Miguel. The *teniente*'s office is a two-story wood structure housing the office, telephone, and small jail (principally used for drunks). Another public building in the upper sector houses a meeting room for the town council and serves as a storeroom for the town's tools (shovels, picks, wheelbarrows, etc.) and for government food storage (CARE food).

A half-hour farther down the trail from Amazonas town center and 200 meters lower in elevation is a settled area called Ganazhuma, located on a small floodplain on the opposite bank of the Río Cuyes. This area is beginning to rival the official town center as the true center of parish interaction. There are only five buildings in Ganazhuma, but more families live within walking distance of Gana-zhuma than the town center. The change in altitude between the town center and Ganazhuma is reflected in the warmer temperature, the greater productivity and shorter growing time of such cash crops as sugar cane, bananas, and citrus fruits, and the increase of such tropical pests as rats, other large rodents (agouti, paca), and snakes.

The eastern, and lowest, extent of Amazonas is an area called Cue-vas de Belén. The "caves" are actually a narrowing of the Cuyes val-ley owing to its passage through a narrow zone of igneous rock. After the Río Cuyes passes through this zone, the valley widens and only foothills of the Andean cordillera remain. The "caves" act as a door opening into the Oriente proper. Vegetation becomes more typical of the canopy forests of the *hylea*. As the Cuyes passes through the caves, it makes a sharp bend to the northeast. On the far side of the river most of the land is inhabited by native Shuar (Jivaroans) who live on land controlled by the Salesian mission of Bomboisa. Colonist lands are scattered all along the main trail and in the major tributary valleys of the Cuyes. However, from about an hour above the Cuevas de Belén to the sharp northeast turn in the Río Cuyes the area is uninhabited, probably because of its steep slopes and isolation.

Nueva Tarqui

Beyond the Cuevas de Belén is the *parroquia* of Nueva Tarqui, which extends along the left bank of the Cuyes to its confluence with the Río Negro, a mere three-hour walk from Gualaquiza. At this con-fluence the Cuyes changes its name to the Río Bomboisa. The major part of Nueva Tarqui lies between 1,200 and 800 meters in elevation. Most of the 350 inhabitants have settled in the fertile, but narrow, floodplain of the Cuyes. Nueva Tarqui has grown rapidly; a third of its population has immigrated in the last seven years. Just below the Cuevas de Belén is the first settlement area, called La Florida. Seven years ago La Florida consisted of one house; today there are ten houses and a school. There are large fields of sugar cane and grass-lands for cattle. Gardens of mixed sweet manioc, taro, and plantains are numerous. Cattle are raised for beef, only secondarily for milk and cheese production, in marked contrast to Amazonas and San Miguel. There are many colonist farms along the three-hour trail be-tween La Florida and the town center of Nueva Tarqui. The topogra-phy is hilly but not mountainous.

Composed overwhelmingly of colonists from Jima, the town lies on an old floodplain of the Cuyes; the eastern Andean cordillera is at its back. It is built around a large central plaza 100 meters square. Seven years ago only four houses flanked the plaza, but today there are 20. The impetus for this increase in population is undoubtedly the new road which connects the Sierra, by way of Loja, with Guala-quiza. The climate here is much warmer than, but not nearly as wet as, in Amazonas and San Miguel.

ETHNOHISTORY

Some archaeological evidence exists to indicate a pre-Spanish utilization of the entire Cuyes valley by Andean peoples, possibly for the extraction of placer gold (Ekstrom 1975:30–32). Ruins of fortifications are present on prominent hills at various points throughout the length of the Cuyes valley. Furthermore, the sites appear to be fortified from attack down valley. Their strategic location, with clear views from one lookout to another, and their similar construction argue for an integrated defense by one group of people in the valley. In addition to the fortifications, there is some archaeological evidence of exploitation of ancient river gravels for gold in the hills behind Nueva Tarqui. A Sierra origin of these people is suggested by the down-valley orientation of the defenses, the possible interest in gold mining, and a similarity in pottery sherds between those found in the Cuyes valley and those from the Jima valley.

Fray Domingo do los Angeles (1965:270–71) relates that in 1582 some 90 Indians from Cuyes were brought to the Sierra near Jima to be included with tribute-paying Indians from the nearby village of San Bartolomé. There is no way of knowing if the Cuyes people mentioned by Domingo de los Angeles are related to the people whose archaeological remains have been referred to. Domingo's reference does indicate, however, the probable utilization and settlement of the Cuyes valley by Sierra peoples in the early part of the sixteenth century.

The exploitation of placer gold also brought the Spanish to the Cuyes valley in the last part of the sixteenth century. The Spaniards mined the gold until they were driven out of the Oriente by Jivaroan uprisings of 1599 (see, e.g., Harner 1972:18–25). There is a rich folk history in Jima and Cuyes describing the flight of the Spaniards out of the Cuyes valley to their eventual settlement in the Jima valley (Ekstrom 1975:32–33). Specific reference is made to an oil painting of the "Virgin del Rosario" which the Spaniards carried as they fled the Cuyes valley. While they were camping just over the *páramo* in the

Jima valley, the painting supposedly was found turned upside down, as if the Virgin were standing on her head. This inversion was taken as a sign to stop running and settle in the Jima area. The painting is now in the Jima church and is venerated annually in October during the fiesta of Santo Rosario by the residents of both Jima and the satellite towns in the Cuyes valley.

From the beginning of the seventeenth century, when the Spaniards fled the Oriente and established Jima, to the last part of the nineteenth century, there is no account of Jimeños occupying any part of the Cuyes valley. It is not known who occupied the valley during this long period, although native Jivaroans probably used the area for hunting. In the oral history of Jima the earliest date of colonist travel to the Cuyes valley is sometime in the 1880s, when two Jimeños successfully settled and farmed in the area near San Miguel. This part of the Cuyes valley was then used only occasionally by native Jivaroans to hunt howler monkeys. The two Jimeños produced a variety of foods, particularly chili peppers and squash, often of large size. Others attempted to follow their example of settling in the Oriente but most failed to cope with the hardships encountered, and a folklore based on fear of the Oriente gradually developed.

Not until the mid-1930s, when news of successful mining of placer gold deposits in the streams draining the eastern Andean slopes reached southern Ecuador, was this fear overcome. Something of a gold rush ensued, and large numbers of people from Jima and neighboring towns converged on the Cuyes valley. They came not to settle but to exploit the gold. Simply washing the sands along the Río Cuyes could produce three or four grams of gold per day, and digging three to four meters down into the loose gravels produced larger quantities. Most miners planted only enough crops for their own subsistence; a few even resorted to robbing the fields of the few colonists who already lived in the area.

Most miners left when the accessible gold gravels sharply diminished or were exhausted, but a number of people from Jima remained and became colonists in the Cuyes valley. At the end of the 1930s they were joined by many other families from Jima as a combination of inflation and a severe drought accompanied by killing frosts made life in the Sierra particularly difficult.

A few years later a new influx into the Cuyes valley occurred as a by-product of World War II. The great need for quinine to treat malaria in the Pacific theater stimulated commercial *Cinchona* bark collecting in the Oriente, especially in southern Ecuador. Although there may have been over 400 quinine bark pickers at the height of the search, very few stayed to colonize the *ceja, montaña,* and *hylea* forests.

The commercial productivity in gold and quinine reacquainted Jima area people with the Cuyes valley and its potential for settled pioneer colonization. Much of the fear of the Oriente dissolved as large numbers of highland people spent at least a transient period there, and colonization of the Cuyes valley became a viable option for many Jimeños experiencing socioeconomic difficulties in the Sierra. The bottom fell out of the quinine market after World War II, and a gradual increase in colonization aimed at settled life in the Cuyes valley ensued. From a population of a little over 700 for the entire valley in the early 1950s (Vega Toral 1958:74), the population increased to approximately 1,100 ten years ago (my estimate) and remains the same today, demonstrating a balance between in- and out-migrations.

EXPLOITATION OF MULTIPLE ZONES

The Jima-Cuyes pattern of zonation is most like Brush's (1973, 1977) compressed type but also includes features of a "vertical archipelago." The environmental gradient is steep, and contiguous, contrasting, zones grade into one another. Although exploitation of *Cinchona* took place there for a brief period, the upper part of the *ceja* is at present nonproductive.

In spite of the distance, the three-day walk from the Sierra valley of Jima to the base of the Cuyes valley at Nueva Tarqui falls within the criteria set out by Brush (1973, 1977) for his compressed type. The distances and the requirements of labor are such that major migrations from zone to zone are necessary and, more important, require the establishment of "satellite" communities of colonists (San Miguel, Amazonas, and Nueva Tarqui). In these features Jima-Cuyes more closely resembles the archipelago type. Nonsubsistence production from the zones is predominantly oriented toward local markets in Jima and regional markets in Cuenca. Exchange networks between the various zones have developed but are mainly concerned with the mobilization of labor. The Jima-Cuyes area also corresponds to the main features of Murra's (1972) model where control of multiple production zones by one group combines with an attempt to exploit as many zones as possible. This latter combination of characteristic features of verticality overlies the pattern of zonation described above. The overwhelming majority of those exploiting the various ecological zones are Jimeños who, even though they are pioneer, settled colonists residing most of the time in the Cuyes valley, orient themselves toward Jima, their town of origin. There is a concerted effort to exploit as many zones as possible, limited only by the labor resources of each individual colonist family.

Adaptive consequences of multiple zone exploitation include the flexibility inherent in the ability to market a large variety of products, the possibility of dividing economic risks between several zones, and the ability to use the resources of one zone to better exploit another zone or zones. Fundamentally, in the Cuyes valley the importance of the various zones lies in the production of nonsubsistence commercially valuable resources for local and regional markets in the Sierra where gold and quinine were the products stimulating short-term migration into the area. The present commercial resources are dairy cattle, beef cattle, sugar cane for *trago* and unrefined sugar cakes (*panela, raspadura*), and *naranjilla* (*Solanum quitoense*).

Each of these resources is concentrated in one or more of the three colonization zones: dairy cattle in San Miguel and Amazonas, beef cattle predominantly in Nueva Tarqui but to a lesser degree in Amazonas, sugar cane in Nueva Tarqui, *naranjilla* in Nueva Tarqui, placer gold in San Miguel and Amazonas, and quinine in San Miguel. In addition to the resources and products of the Cuyes valley zones, the colonists also have access to the resources of the highland valley of Jima, with its dairy cattle, sheep, pigs, corn, wheat, and potatoes as major nonsubsistence, marketable products. By exploiting the resources of more than one ecological zone, colonists produce a greater variety of marketable goods than is possible in one zone. Moreover, exploitation of multiple ecological zones increases greatly the productive *potential* of a settler, family, or group, since failure in one zone can be offset by success in another. Besides producing a large variety of goods and spreading the risks of frontier agriculture, multiple zone exploitation is conducive to intensified, concentrated exploitation of a single zone. By growing sugar cane in Nueva Tarqui and producing *trago*, a multizone colonist can use the return on his *trago* sale in Jima to buy dairy cattle there and pasture them on his land in Amazonas. Similar types of feedback effects are activated by money earned from selling *naranjillas*, cheese, or gold. The important fact is that, when controlled by a single unit of vertical exploitation, production in one zone has a clear effect on production in the other zones a colonist may be exploiting. Finally, it is essential to point out that almost all colonists who exploit more than one lowland zone retain some property in highland Jima, retaining access to the resources of a traditional Sierra subsistence and sociocultural base and to nearby Sierra markets.

STRATEGIES OF PRODUCTION

One of the key strategies involved in the productive system of the Cuyes valley is that of concentrating convertible resources into transportable products of low bulk and high value. The resources used in this production, in order of their contribution to the total economy, are sugar cane, dairy cows, and *naranjilla*. This adaptive strategy has been created to deal with the isolation of the frontier environment and its lack of connecting infrastructure with population centers in the highlands and other developed areas of Ecuador. Only low bulk–high value resources can be transported out of the frontier zone and into the national economy. Similar methods have been employed in Peru in the production and distribution of coca (Hanna 1974:291–92).

The product best representing this strategy is raw, unaged, distilled cane rum, called *trago*. Because of the relatively large profits involved and the relatively small amount of time needed to realize a profit, dealing in one of the phases of the process of production and distribution of *trago* is one of the most successful capital acquisition activities. After several years in the *trago* trade, especially in its transport to the Sierra, an individual can make enough money to buy and raise cattle, the ultimate economic goal of most colonists.

A complex economic network has been established which encompasses growing the sugar cane, reducing it to a liquid ready for fermentation, distilling the fermented liquid, transporting the distillate to the highlands, and finally distributing the *trago* to the consumer. It is rare for any one colonist to be involved in the entire process. Before distribution four to 20 individuals, or more, may be involved; the most important variable is the amount of *trago* involved, since this may vary from approximately 200 liters (one mule-load) to 6,000 liters.

To illustrate the networks and processes instrumental in the production and distribution of *trago*, assume that a relatively new colonist in the La Florida area wants eventually to own a herd of cattle. He has only a few hectares of land cleared on which he has, in addition to his subsistence crops, a crop of mature sugar cane. The colonist has access to a still (a crude affair made from a 55-gallon oil drum) owned by his cousin in Amazonas. He makes a deal with his cousin to bring the still to La Florida and to split the profits from the *trago* they distill. To augment the sugar cane from his own field, the colonist buys cane from a neighbor's field and publicizes his plans to begin distillation shortly.

By the time the process starts, another colonist in the La Florida area has contracted to sell his cane to the two cousins. While the still is being assembled, the cane is pressed in a mill and the liquid is placed in a large wooden box to ferment. Fermentation takes three days to a week; *guarapo*, fermented juice, is then put in the still, and the distillation process turns out high-proof (80–90% alcohol) *trago* at the rate of about three liters per hour. A typical distillation run to produce 1,000 liters of *trago* lasts for three and one-half weeks. After distillation the *trago* is poured into *perras*, 100-liter rubber-coated bags, which are transported to the Sierra either by *contrabandistas*, rum runners, or by the distillers themselves. The *contrabandistas* can double their investment by selling to distributors in Jima. The distributor then cuts the *trago* by as much as one-third to one-half. The *trago* is usually diluted by simply adding water, but some unscrupulous distributors add ammonia or even urine.

The network does not necessarily end once the *trago* arrives in Jima. The *contrabandistas* may try for a better return on their labor by transporting the *trago* to other nearby towns or even to the city of Cuenca. The risks in further transport, however, increase dramatically as larger centers of population are approached. If the *contrabandistas* decide to take the ultimate risk and sell the *trago* in Cuenca, they must arrange with one of the Jima bus owners to hide the bags of *trago* under the floorboards of the bus. The bus owner will then be paid a share of the profits after successful delivery of the *trago*.

The potentially great returns from *trago* production and distribution are matched by considerable risk; *trago* traffic is as illegal in Ecuador as moonshining is in the United States. Raids by government liquor tax agents during the production of *trago* within the Cuyes valley are very infrequent, but they have taken place. The remoteness of the distillation sites and the lack of roads discourage them. The greatest risks are taken by the *contrabandistas* as they guide their mule-loads of *trago* through the mountain passes. Liquor agents frequently hide near the head of the Cuyes valley as it begins to narrow. A confrontation with the *guardas*, liquor agents, can be a serious affair, ranging from a simple "pay-off" to a gun battle. Being caught by *guardas* who refuse to accept a cash settlement can result in confiscation of the *contrabandistas*' cargo animals, appropriation of the *trago* by the *guardas*, a stiff fine for each liter of *trago*, and a possible jail sentence; the result is often economic ruin.

The economic network involved in the various aspects of the *trago* trade is reinforced by a social network of dyadic relationships between the various participants in the trade. The ramifying economic networks of the *trago* trade, in turn, reinforce a strategy of socioeconomic incorporation of the Jima-Cuyes valleys to be discussed later. The ramifying dyadic relationships between individual sugar cane producers and distillers, distillers and *contrabandistas*, and *contrabandistas* and distributors form a lattice of economic and social linkages connecting the people of the Jima and Cuyes valleys into a single economic, political, and social unit. Each member of the network is dependent on the others for the ultimate success of the whole system of *trago* trade. Collaboration of those not directly involved in the *trago* trade is also needed to protect those involved from interference by the government *guardas*. The whole pattern of involvement and collaboration is, then, an important factor in solidifying the two valleys.

Dairy cattle are a resource used to produce cheese, another transportable product of low bulk and high value. Cheese is an especially suitable product for the colonists as it is produced in quantity in the Jima valley, and the knowledge of its production was part of the cultural baggage brought into the Cuyes valley from the Sierra.

The networks involved in cheese production and distribution are much less extensive and complex than those of the *trago* trade. Transportation of the cheese from Cuyes up to Jima is by mule or horse accompanied by the producer or one of the members of his nuclear family. The frequency of trips varies with the number of producing cows that a colonist possesses. In Jima cheese is sold either directly to other individuals or to one of the small stores in the town center; it may be transported by bus to Cuenca where it will sell for a higher price.

In that the husbanding of dairy cattle is one of the most important economic activities of the colonists in the upper zones of the Cuyes valley, as it is in Jima, the number of head of cattle a colonist has is a sure gauge of his relative economic position in the colonization area. Dairy cattle herds vary in size between two and 30 head. Most herds are under a dozen head. A cow produces one to three gallons of milk daily. Bulls are used as studs and sold for meat only under unusual circumstances. However, they are often driven up over the mountains into the Jima valley to serve as draft animals on property owned by the colonists. In the Cuyes area they are not used to plow the fields owing to the steepness of the valley sides and the small size of the subsistence plots, which are more easily tilled by hand plows.

Although most of the interest in raising dairy cattle is in the San Miguel and Amazonas areas, there are some colonists in Nueva Tarqui who are building up small dairy herds in addition to their beef cattle. Until recently the several-day trip to Jima was too long and arduous for profitable cheese transportation to the Sierra. Cheese production became profitable when the road from Loja to Gualaquiza was completed. With the road, cheese could be transported to Gualaquiza within a day and either sold there or shipped by bus to towns along the new road or eventually to Loja province. For the first time an Oriente market was opened to the sierran colonists to the area. Most Nueva Tarqui colonists do not transport their cheese to Gualaquiza themselves but sell it to middlemen, *negociantes*, who transport it there and on up the Loja road.

A third utilization of the strategy of concentrating convertible resources into transportable products of low bulk and high value is of *naranjilla* production. This is confined to the Nueva Tarqui area, even though the fruit is more productive in Amazonas. Transportation difficulties are too great to make *naranjilla* production economically important in the upper Cuyes valley. The proximity of the Loja-Gualaquiza road to Nueva Tarqui, however, does allow for relatively easy transport of the fruit to the Sierra. The new road has a two-fold impact on Nueva Tarqui *naranjilla* production. Besides making transportation of *naranjilla* to the Sierra a realistic possibility, the road has also made it more dangerous to produce *trago* in the Nueva Tarqui area because of its improved accessibility to authorities from the outside. As a result, the *trago* trade has fallen off rather sharply in the last several years and the production of *naranjillas* has increased proportionately.

The colonists in the area say that even though the profits are not as great as in dealing in *trago*, the risks are much less. *Naranjilla* production also serves an economic need very similar to that of *trago* production, the accumulation of relatively large amounts of capital quickly in order to start or increase one's cattle herd. *Naranjillas* are one of the first crops planted on newly cleared land. *Naranjillas* require maximum soil fertility and minimum pest or blight exposure, and give the colonist a relatively quick return on his labor. Such a return facilitates cattle purchase and exploitation of a new production dimension.

Beef cattle production for markets in the Sierra is the fourth major economic strategy emphasized by the Cuyes colonists. Raising beef cattle is a predominant economic goal of most Cuyes colonists, particularly those in the La Florida–Nueva Tarqui area. Many of the other adaptive strategies utilized by the colonists are directed toward the development of large herds of beef cattle. There are combination dairy and beef cattle herds in the San Miguel–Amazonas areas of up to 60–70 head, but in the Nueva Tarqui zone there are a few herds up to 150 head, though most herds there range from ten to 30 head.

In the Nueva Tarqui area cleared land destined for eventual use as pasture is quite often planted first in *naranjillas*. After several harvests of the *naranjilla* crop the land is then planted in pasture grass by broadcasting the seed. The preferred pasture grass is *gramalote* (*Panicum maximum*), although *elefante* (*Pennisetum purpureum*) is grown in the wetter, semiswampy areas. If care is taken in grazing the cattle, *gramalote* rarely needs replanting. Colonists say that in the Gualaquiza area there are productive pastures of *gramalote* that are still being used after 35 years.

Grazing is very carefully controlled. Most colonists agreed that only two to three head of cattle could be productively grazed per hectare of pasture. The cattle are staked out on a 20-foot tether and moved to a new grazing zone twice a day. As the colonist moves the cattle to new pasture, he uses his machete to clean the area just grazed of weeds and unwanted jungle growth. By this continuous process of moving cattle and cleaning recently grazed pasture, the *gramalote* grows strong and healthy in a relatively short time. The tethering prevents the destructive trampling of pasture land by herds of cattle roaming at will. It also concentrates the cattle manure, which enriches the soil and helps the grass to recover quickly from the grazing. The technique of grazing cattle by tethering is part of the cultural heritage brought down by the colonists from the Sierra. Cattle, sheep, goats, and even pigs are tethered in the same way on pasture land in Jima. There are indications that the continual cleaning of pasture to retard the growth of natural vegetation may deprive the cattle of needed nourishment not supplied by the *gramalote*, which is 90% water (Whitten, personal communication). This problem is less severe for those colonists who can periodically move their cattle to land in the higher zones where different pasture grasses are used.

The role of the *trago* trade and the cultivation of *naranjillas* have been mentioned as a means of raising needed capital to acquire a herd of cattle. Another means intimately involved with the strategy of cattle production is the system of *medias*, a system that also facilitates the exploitation of more than one zone. A colonist who has cattle in more than one zone can enter into a *medias* agreement with another colonist to care for his cattle in another zone. The colonist caring for the cattle is entitled to half of all calves born in the herd. This arrangement works to the benefit of both parties; the owner of the cattle can raise his animals on property in more than one zone, and the colonist who takes care of his cattle can increase or start his own herd. In a frontier zone such as the Cuyes valley there are large amounts of land that can be cleared, put into pasture, and occupied, but very few means to acquire cash to buy cattle. The *medias* system allows the poorer colonists to gradually build a herd of cattle without the need to raise the necessary cash. Margolis (1973:990) emphasizes the adaptive value of this type of system in frontier environments when specifically referring to a similar arrangement in northern Brazil called *sorte*.

Marketing of cattle is handled either directly by driving cattle up the Cuyes valley to Jima and then trucking them to the Cumbe market (about 25 kilometers from Jima), or by selling to a *negociante* who will eventually transport them to the Sierra markets. To drive cattle from Nueva Tarqui up to Jima takes from six to eight days under good conditions. The cattle lose so much weight during the journey that most cattle from the Nueva Tarqui region are now driven to Gualaquiza and then trucked to the Sierra. The need to get cattle rapidly and easily up to the Sierra from anywhere in the Cuyes valley has been a basic reason Jimeños and colonists continue to agitate for a road linking Jima with all parts of the Cuyes valley.

SOCIOCULTURAL STRATEGIES

Some of the most crucial adaptive strategies in the Cuyes valley are those involved in providing the labor necessary to exploit more than one zone. A single nuclear family is the basic unit of social organization and source of labor in the colonization zones. This does not mean, however, that members of a nuclear family reside together at all times, or even most of the time. With the high value placed on exploiting more than one ecological zone, it is necessary to utilize the manpower of the nuclear family in a most flexible manner. Thus at any one time the nuclear family may be split up between two or even three locations. The mother and small children may be residing in Jima, the father in Amazonas, and an older son taking care of cattle on a newly cleared and remote *entable*, pasture land.

What constitutes a household at any one time or location is extremely variable, depending on the time of year, the type of work needed in a particular location, the health and size of the family, the need to move products to market, and the meeting of political or social obligations. Unless the family is very large and has many unmarried, adult male members, the type of mobility and flexibility needed to exploit multiple zones places a great deal of stress on the nuclear family. In most cases the labor needs are greater than the resources of the family, and help must be recruited by utilizing affinal ties, *compadrazgo* ties, *medias* agreements, and reciprocal or festive work groups, *mingas*.

The following example illustrates the problems of labor recruitment and their solution by a colonist with a small nuclear family. Genaro L.'s first trip into the Cuyes valley was as a *contrabandista* in 1957. After this initiation he decided to buy land in the Amazonas area. He settled on a small tract near his present property in Trincheros. After a few years he sold this property and acquired 100 hectares of land on the upper slopes of Trincheros. Genaro also owns a small piece of land near the town center of Amazonas. As he cleared his land, he planted it in sugar cane, then distilled *trago* from the cane, carried it up the mountains to Jima, and sold it for a good profit. In this way he has been able to acquire a herd of nearly 60 head of cattle (mixed dairy and beef). Owing to the risks of the *trago* trade, he has no more plans to raise sugar cane and devotes all his efforts to raising cattle. Genaro's nuclear family consists of himself, his wife, and two small children. A significant fact is that Genaro's wife is the daughter of Don Rodríquez, a wealthy and long-established colonist. Genaro bought some of his land in Trincheros from Don Rodríquez. During a land dispute with the school teacher (a Cuencano) in Amazonas over part of this property in Trincheros, Genaro was supported by Don Rodríquez and his large family, who between them owned most of the land in Trincheros. Genaro was also for many years *teniente* in Amazonas, again with the support of Don Rodríquez. Thus, in spite of a small nuclear family, Genaro could capitalize both politically and economically by allying himself with a powerful Jima-Cuyes family through the dyadic social bond of a single affinal tie.

In addition to his Amazonas land, Genaro owns farm land in Jima and a small store in the town center. His wife and children remain most of the year in Jima taking care of the store. Genaro also spends four or five months of the year in Jima taking care of his land, bringing cattle to market, and in the past selling and distributing *trago*. His family is too small to take care of his land and cattle in Amazonas when he is in the Sierra. In response to this need, he has become a *compadre* to one of his poorer neighbors at Trincheros and has entered into a *medias* agreement with him. The terms of the agreement are that Luis, his *compadre*, will take care of his cattle and generally man- · age Genaro's property while he is in Jima in return for half of all newborn calves. In addition to this lateral relationship with Luis,

Genaro has hired Luis's son as peon on a five-year contract, paying him 500 sucres per year. Besides these more formal agreements Genaro can often count on Don Rodríquez's sons for help when short-term labor is needed or when political support is necessary. With the limited labor force of his nuclear family, Genaro cannot exploit as many ecological zones or as many hectares as Don Rodríquez, who has a large nuclear family and exploits three zones, but by manipulating his affinal relationships and utilizing ramifying dyadic ties, reinforced by ties of co-parenthood, which form networks centering on himself, he has exploited two zones and has become established as one of the more successful colonists in the Cuyes valley.

This example also illustrates the common practice of sons and daughters of colonists who intermarry, the use of co-parenthood relationships to reinforce lateral exchange networks, and the constant need of nuclear families to shuttle their members between zones. Most of the lateral ramifying networks based on symmetrical, dyadic, exchange relationships involving kinship, marriage, and co-parenthood are built upon previous network ties developed in the Sierra and are used and extended to more efficiently and effectively exploit the several zones of the Cuyes valley.

Different forms of cooperative labor, all subsumed under the general term *minga*, are part of the cultural baggage of every colonist from Jima. *Mingas* can be used for an individual colonist's needs, for community projects, or even for tasks involving the entire Jima-Cuyes valley system. In frontier areas such as the Cuyes valley, where labor is chronically in short supply, the extension of cooperative labor strategies used in the Sierra, such as the *minga*, have very positive adaptive value. Not only are community and individual work needs met, but a feeling of community solidarity and cooperation is emphasized for a dispersed colonist population in an isolated geographic setting.

When an individual colonist has a task which requires more labor than he or his family can provide, he will often organize a *minga* to accomplish it. Depending on the size of the task and the amount of labor needed, the *minga* will be of either the festive or the exchange form (Erasmus 1965:174). In the Cuyes valley the exchange form is the more common. According to Erasmus (1965:175), exchange labor requires a high degree of obligation to reciprocate labor and food or drink, while in festive labor the more elaborate feasting and drinking rules out the obligation to reciprocate in kind. Exchange labor *mingas* are used for such tasks as clearing land and agricultural work; here one to six workers are needed. The workers are usually related by kinship or *compadrazgo* ties, thereby reinforcing the obligation to re-ciprocate in kind by the host.

The *minga* system also is used to meet community-wide labor needs. Various tools for use on civil projects are stored in the *teniente's* office. Work projects may include construction and repair of public buildings, trail and bridge repair, or work on the town plaza. The size of the *mingas* varies according to the demand of the project.

The most impressive *minga* is the annual intercommunity festive work party to maintain the trail from Jima to Nueva Tarqui. The *minga* attracts 50–400 people every year. A site along the trail in particular need of repair is chosen. Repairs include widening and straighten-ing, cleaning up debris and vegetation, and repairing bridges. Often the work site is at an isolated spot, and the *mingueros* have to be prepared to spend a night or two sleeping in the open. Each satellite town, plus Jima, sends workers to the chosen site equipped with the needed tools. The *teniente político* from each town is responsible for organizing the work groups to be sent. He appoints a *vocal*, represen-tative, for each section of the community who is responsible for stimulating enthusiasm for the *minga* and encouraging volunteers. In addition to sending *minga* workers, the towns also supply food and drink for the workers. No formal sanctions are taken against those who refuse to cooperate, but there is very strong community pres-sure to support the *minga* in some way. There is also an annual inter-community *minga* to undertake a major task, during which time vast amounts of *trago* are drunk, the ubiquitous status of highland Jimeño is stressed, and the contiguity of sierran Jima and Oriente Cuyes val-leys as a unified sociopolitical unit is reaffirmed.

A final strategy employed by the colonists in their exploitation of the Cuyes valley is that of incorporation. This involves the preserva-tion of the area as a homogeneous extension of the Jima valley where as much land as possible can be controlled by Jimeños who, thereby, consciously prohibit "outsiders," including nearby Jivaroans, from establishing themselves within the Cuyes colonization zone. In so doing, mechanisms of integration have been developed among the various colonization zones within the Cuyes valley and the commu-nity of origin. Associated with this need for integration is a corre-sponding need to develop ways to defend the integrity of the valley from outsiders. Although there is no direct community control over land, very strong pressure is exerted by the colonists to limit land transactions with outsiders. The Cuyes valley, with only a few excep-tions, has maintained itself as a homogeneous sierran Jima popula-tion residing in the eastern tropical lowlands.

Constant social, political, and economic interaction between the colonists and Jima is reinforced by their relationship to outsiders, whom they perceive as threats to their valley. As an example, the people of the Jima-Cuyes valleys have distrusted and have had negative relations with the people of Sig Sig. The distrust originates in the Sierra where the *parroquia* of Jima is under the administrative jurisdiction of the cantonal capital of Sig Sig. Jima has always felt that Sig Sig has been unresponsive to its administrative needs, and has attempted to develop ways to deal directly with higher levels of articulation (Adams 1970:53–54) to minimize its administrative subordination. An intense rivalry has developed between the people of the two communities with regard to colonization of the Oriente. Colonists from Sig Sig have settled in the Río Negro valley, adjacent on the north to the Río Cuyes valley; more important, they make up the majority of the population of Gualaquiza. An administrative and political situation parallel to that between Jima and Sig Sig exists between the Cuyes *parroquias* and their cantonal capital of Gualaquiza. A further intensification of the rivalry involves competition between Sig Sig and Jima along with their colonization satellites for political and economic support in each of their quests for a road to connect Gualaquiza to Cuenca. The competition involves a need for strategic access to power brokers (Adams 1975:50–52) and, ultimately, access to higher levels of articulation and the resources they control.

This outside threat perceived by the Jima colonists has helped to reinforce their conception of themselves as a unified, *cholo*, sierran, ethnically homogeneous megacommunity bounded by potentially hostile lowland and highland, Indian, *cholo*, and white neighbors. It has also intensified the need for unified action by the colonists of the Cuyes valley through Jima, instead of Gualaquiza, to satisfy their political and administrative needs. To the east, across the Río Cuyes from Nueva Tarqui, are the Shuar (Jívaro proper; see Harner 1972). Although the Cuyes towns of San Miguel, Amazonas, and Nueva Tarqui are independent *parroquias* in an adjacent province, actual political power is closely tied with Jima, three days' trek to the Sierra.

Colonists holding political office or having strong political influence are members of the same families who have similar political power in Jima. In some cases the same person holds the same political office in Cuyes as he previously held in Jima. The ability of politically prominent Jima families to continue to exert their influence in the Oriente is reinforced by the demographic patterns in the Cuyes valley. These patterns not only tend to perpetuate political and social patterns of the Jima valley but also facilitate the integration of the

Jima and Cuyes valleys. Some of the same family, kinship, and *compadrazgo* relationships utilized in the Sierra can be used by extension in the colonization zone. These ties, of course, aid in communication with Jima and, by extension, to higher levels of articulation in the Sierra. Because of this relationship to the Río Cuyes area, Jima has taken on the role of administrative and political broker (Wolf 1956) between the colonization area and regional, national, and international bureaucracies. It also serves economically as an entrepôt (Casagrande, Thompson, and Young 1964:312) linking the colonization zone with the metropolitan area of Cuenca.

Jima's role of broker and entrepôt is further strengthened by the politico-religious festival of the Virgen del Rosario, held annually in October. The local folk history recounts a common origin for Spanish occupation of the Cuyes valley and the founding of Jima, tying both areas together with the account of the miracle associated with the painting of the Virgin del Rosario. Colonists owning property in Jima spend the end of August and September planting their crops in the Sierra and stay through the October fiesta. Scores of other Cuyes colonists make the annual trip to Jima for this fiesta. The fiesta is a time for visiting with family and friends in Jima and renewing political and social ties in the Sierra, but, most important, it is an event, socially, politically, and religiously sanctioned, stressing the common heritage and ethnic *cholo* homogeneity of the Jima and Cuyes valleys.

CONCLUSION

Out-migrants from Jima are successfully exploiting multiple ecological zones in the Cuyes valley. They have developed a series of adaptive strategies to cope with this type of exploitation in the setting of a tropical frontier environment. The adaptations include an interrelated productive system for the different zones, a series of social and economic arrangements designed to meet the labor requirements of multiple zone exploitation, as well as methods for dealing with the problem of preserving the Cuyes valley as a homogeneous extension of the Jima valley. It has been argued that the situation in the Jima-Cuyes area has many features in common with an expanded version of Murra's model of "verticality," and that colonization within the Cuyes valley cannot be fully understood without an understanding of the vertical ecological zonation of the valley.

NOTES

Acknowledgments: The fieldwork upon which this paper is based was carried out from September to December 1972, and was supported by a National Science Foundation doctoral dissertation research grant and a University of Illinois research assistantship under the directorship of Norman E. Whitten, Jr. In Ecuador, the fieldwork was carried out under the auspices of the Instituto Nacional de Anthropología e Historia, whose director, Hernán Crespo Toral, provided support and timely help. I owe a profound debt of gratitude to Norman E. Whitten, Jr., for his expert guidance and continued support.

REFERENCES CITED

Acosta-Solis, Misael
  1965 *Los Recursos Naturales del Ecuador y su Conservación*. Pt. 1. Mexico City: Instituto Panamericano de Georgrafía e Historia.
  1966 *Los Recursos Naturales del Ecuador y Su Conservación*. Pt. 2. Mexico City: Instituto Panamericano de Geografía e Historia.
Adams, Richard N.
  1970 *Crucifixion by Power: Essays on Guatamalan National Social Structure, 1944–1966*. Austin: University of Texas Press.
  1975 *Energy and Structure: A Theory of Social Power*. Austin: University of Texas Press.
Bromley, Ray
  n.d. Agricultural Colonization in the Upper Amazon Basin: The Impact of Oil Discoveries. Unpublished manuscript.
Brush, Stephen B.
  1973 Subsistence Strategies and Vertical Ecology in an Andean Community: Uchucmarca, Peru. Ph.D. thesis, University of Wisconsin, Madison.
  1977 *Mountain Field and Family: The Economy and Human Ecology of an Andean Valley*. Philadelphia: University of Pennsylvania Press.
Casagrande, Joseph B., Stephen I. Thompson, and Philip D. Young
  1964 Colonization as a Research Frontier: The Ecuadorian Case. In Robert A. Manners, ed., *Process and Pattern in Culture: Essays in Honor of Julian H. Steward*. Chicago: Aldine, pp. 281–325.
Ekstrom, J. Peter
  1975 Responding to a New Ecology: Adaptations of Colonists in Eastern Ecuador. *Papers in Anthropology* 16 (1):25–38.
Erasmus, Charles J.
  1965 The Occurrence and Disappearance of Reciprocal Farm Labor in Latin America. In Dwight Heath and Richard N. Adams, eds., *Contemporary Cultures and Societies of Latin America: A Reader in the Social Anthropology of Middle and South America and the Caribbean*. New York: Random House, pp. 173–99.
Ferdon, Edwin N.
  1950 *Studies in Ecuadorian Geography*. Santa Fe: School of American Research and Museum of New Mexico, Monographs of the School of American Research 15.

Flores, Jorge A.
1975 Sociedad y Cultura en la Puna Alta de los Andes. *América Indígena* 35 (2):297–319.

Fonseca, Cesar
1972 La Economía Vertical y la Economía de Mercado en las Comunidades Compesinas del Perú. In John Murra, ed., *Visita de la Provincia de León de Huánuco en 1562*, vol. 2. Huánuco, Peru: Facultad de Letras y Ciencias, Universidad Nacional Hermilio Valdizán, pp. 315–38.

Grubb, P. J., et al.
1963 A Comparison of Montane and Lowland Rain Forest in Ecuador. I. The Forest Structure, Physiognomy, and Floristics. *Journal of Ecology* 51 (3):567–601.

Grubb, P. J., and T. C. Whitmore
1966 A Comparison of Montane and Lowland Rain Forest in Ecuador. II. The Climate and Its Effects on the Distribution and Physiognomy of the Forests. *Journal of Ecology* 54 (2):303–33.

Hanna, Joel M.
1974 Coca Leaf Use in Southern Peru: Some Biosocial Aspects. *American Anthropologist* 76 (2):281–96.

Harner, Michael J.
1972 *The Jívaro: People of the Sacred Waterfalls*. Garden City, N.Y.: Natural History Press.

Hegen, Edmund Eduard
1966 *Highways into the Upper Amazon Basin: Pioneer Lands in Southern Colombia, Ecuador, and Northern Peru*. Gainesville: Center for Latin American Studies, University of Florida.

Los Angeles, Fray Domingo de
1965 [1582] San Francisco de Pacha y San Bartolomé de Arocxapa. In Marcos-Jiménez de la Espada, ed., *Relaciones Geográficas de Indias*, vol. 2. Biblioteca de Autores Españoles 184, Madrid: Ediciones Atlas, pp. 270–71.

Margolis, Maxine
1973 Reivew of *The Forgotten Frontier: Ranchers of Northern Brazil*, by Peter Rivière. *American Anthropologist* 75 (4):990–91.

Mitchell, William
1973 A Preliminary Report on Irrigation and Community in the Central Peruvian Highlands. Paper presented at the 72nd Annual Meeting of the American Anthropological Association, New Orleans.
1976 Irrigation and Community in the Central Peruvian Highlands. *American Anthropologist* 78 (1):25–44.

Murra, John
1972 El "Control Vertical" de un Máximo de Pisos Ecológicos en la Economía de las Sociedades Andinas. In John Murra, ed., *Visita de la Provincia de León de Huánuco en 1562*, vol. 2. Huánuco, Peru: Facultad de Letras y Ciencias, Universidad Nacional Hermilio Valdizán, pp. 429–76.

Orlove, Benjamin S.
1977 Integration through Production: The Use of Zonation in Espinar. *American Ethnologist* 4 (1):84–101.

Rhoades, Robert E., and Stephen I. Thompson
  1975 Adaptive Strategies in Alpine Environments: Beyond Ecological Particularism. *American Ethnologist* 2 (3):535–51.
Richards, P. W.
  1952 *The Tropical Rain Forest*. New York: Cambridge University Press.
Tosi, Joseph
  1960 *Zonas de Vida Natural en el Perú*. Lima: Instituto Inter-Americano de Ciencias Agrícolas de la OEA: Zona Andina, Boletín Technico 5.
Tosi, Joseph, and R. F. Voertman
  1964 Some Environmental Factors in the Economic Development of the Tropics. *Economic Geography* 40:189–205.
Vega Toral, Tomas
  1958 *Algunas Consideraciones sobre Nuestra Oriente Amazonica y Monographia del Canton Gualaquiza*. Cuenca.
Webster, Steven
  1973 Native Pastoralism in the South Andes. *Ethnology* 12 (2):115–33.
Wolf, Eric R.
  1956 Aspects of Group Relations in a Complex Society: Mexico. *American Anthropologist* 58 (6):1065–78.

12

Indigenous Response to an Expanding Frontier: Jungle Quichua Economic Conversion to Cattle Ranching

Theodore Macdonald, Jr.

Between 1972 and 1974 the landscape changed in Pasu Urcu, a small tropical forest settlement in Amazonian Ecuador. Quijos Quichua Indians cleared large tracts of forest from individually owned lots which they had acquired almost ten years earlier. Then the Runa, as the Quijos Quichua call themselves, planted tough grass known as *gramalote*. When the grass established itself, the Runa herded cattle onto the new pastures. Abruptly, an indigenous social formation of mixed economies was transformed from one dominated (in terms of allocation of time and resources) by subsistence swidden horticulture, hunting, and fishing to one dominated by a market-oriented mode of production. Subsistence horticulturalists became cattlemen.

The Runa, however, did not eagerly embrace their fate. They loathed the size, smell, and appearance of cattle. And they resented the new work schedule which robbed them of time previously allocated to hunting and fishing. They turned to animal husbandry because Ecuadorian national economic and political policies forced them to do so. Cattle raising was a strategy for survival, not an experiment in economic entrepreneurship. At the time, similar patterns of economic and ecological change were underway in other areas of eastern Ecuador, as in Amazonia in general (Davis 1977, Denevan 1973, Fosberg 1973, Goodland and Irwin 1975, Parsons 1975, Salazar 1977, Whitten 1976). Since then the process has rapidly expanded. Numerous scientists, including several of those cited above, argue that the conversion of tropical forest to pasture land is ecologically dangerous, perhaps disastrous. As such, the Runa's acceptance of cattle seems to run against the acknowledged indigenous wisdom with regard to man's place in the complex forest ecosystem. However, by considering the local events in Pasu Urcu and the national trends in Ecuador, I will demonstrate why the Runa, against their will and better judgment, became cattlemen. I will then briefly describe how such actions immediately affected traditional economic activities and social life.

THEORETICAL CONSIDERATIONS

This paper is largely descriptive. Nevertheless, four interrelated theoretical considerations shape the organization and interpretation of data. They are: (1) the concept of mixed economies, (2) the idea that rapid social and economic changes occur when a new mode of production rises to dominate a mixed economy, (3) the observation that agricultural intensification requires increased man-hours of labor, and (4) the belief that social and economic changes become institutionalized when new allocations of time and resources are established.

(1) Societies are frequently characterized as economically uniform systems—hunting and gathering, subsistence horticulture, feudal, industrial, or any one of a number of additional labels. But many societies deny singular classification. Godelier (1977:18) writes, "It is often the case that certain societies are organized on the basis of several modes of production all interconnected in a specific way and dominated by one." Pasu Urcu has had a mixed economic base since at least the turn of the century. I am concerned here with how, during the 1970s, one mode of production became dominant.

(2) Social change is not necessarily a slow cumulative development. Radical restructuring can occur quickly. O'Laughlin (1975:350) writes that, for Marxists, "the basic movement of human history is the dialectical development of the forces and relations of production. Marx did not see this movement as an even, progressive, and harmonious development of the division of labor, but as an uneven, periodized, qualitative change, marked by revolutionary transitions from one epoch of production to another." I will indicate how, in Pasu Urcu, the sudden rise of a new mode of production—market-oriented cattle raising—produced radical economic and social change.

(3) When swidden horticulture dominated economics in Pasu Urcu, garden plots were abandoned whenever the Runa thought that it would be less work to clear a new plot than to weed and maintain an old garden (Carneiro 1961). This usually happened after one or two croppings. By contrast, I will show that tropical forest cattle raising requires multicropping of the same plot. Boserup (1965:43) writes

that "when a piece of land is cropped more frequently—under prein-dustrial techniques—it will usually be necessary to devote more ag-ricultural labor to each crop hectare than before." This paper will con-sider the causes and implications of such labor intensification in Pasu Urcu.

(4) Barth (1967:662) writes: "If we look at social behavior as an al-location of time and resources, we can depict the pattern whereby people allocate their time and resources. . . . New allocations are ob-servable as concrete events that may have systematic effects and thus generate important changes." He later adds that "if you have a sys-tem of allocations going—as you always must when you speak of change—it will be the rate and kind of pay-offs of alternative alloca-tions within that system that determine whether they are adopted, that is, institutionalized" (Barth 1967:668). Cattle raising, as a means for assuring land tenure, produced the "pay-offs" which led to the institutionalized reallocation of time and resources in Pasu Urcu.

THE SETTING: PASU URCU BEFORE CATTLE

Until the late 1960s most of the Pasu Urcu Runa clustered in mul-tifamily dwellings along a half-mile section of the Arajuno River's west bank. They practiced swidden horticulture on an area of recent alluvium, known as the *isla*, which was adjacent to their settlement. Pasu Urcu was their *quiquin llacta*, true settlement, but each Runa family also maintained one or more additional household and garden sites—known as *purina llacta*, travel settlements, on either the Oglán or Nushiño rivers—which were located farther into the eastern inte-rior forest. Here relatively low population density permitted more productive hunting and fishing. The forest surrounding each *llacta*, delimited and protected by local spirit beings, was said to be the ex-clusive property of the *llacta* residents. By periodically shifting resi-dence from one *llacta* to another—hunting, fishing, and gardening on a small scale at each site—the Runa maintained a balanced and de-pendable food supply.

Residence privileges, access to fish and game, and rights of usu-fruct for horticulture within each *llacta* were restricted to members of a residence-based stem kindred known as a *muntun*. Each *muntun* had a powerful shaman, *shinzhi yachaj*, as its reference point. The focal shaman was understood to maintain strong and intense rela-tions with local spirit beings, masters of fish and game, whose do-main was coterminous with the *muntun's* claimed territory. As such, the focal shaman had privileged access to fish and game which he shared with the *muntun* members. The spirit beings also, upon the shaman's request, protected and avenged *muntun* members when illness or other misfortune occurred among them. In return for supernatural protection, cures, and access to fish and game provided through the shaman, the other *muntun* members were expected to support and protect him. They accompanied the shaman during his hallucinogenic voyages, acting as his symbolic "soldiers" in inter-*muntun* disputes. Such support, expressed metaphorically in symbolic journeys, extended to everyday life when members of the *muntun* accompanied the shaman whenever he was threatened with hostile attack. All members of the *muntun* accepted these obligations to the resident shaman as acts of reciprocity to an authority figure, not as demonstrations of obedience to a power figure (Fried 1967). As the focus for concepts of territoriality, social relations, and world view, the shaman-centered *muntun* was the principal organizing unit in Pasu Urcu, as it was throughout much of the upper Napo River.

Just as the Runa's residence schedule was flexible and varied, so was their daily work schedule. They planted and maintained three to five swidden plots each year. Clearing, planting, weeding, and harvesting demanded regular allocations of time and energy. Nevertheless the Runa always found time for hunting and fishing, the other elements in their subsistence mode of production. Most men hunted and fished near the settlement four or five times each week. At least twice a year the entire *muntun* left the settlement and traveled to isolated interior regions where they hunted and fished for several weeks.

Even on days when they were not hunting or fishing, the Runa's work on the gardens ended at about mid-day. After that people returned home, prepared a meal, and performed household chores. They also used the afternoon to visit with other members of the *muntun*—borrowing things, exchanging gossip, and reaffirming friendships. These visits also provided opportunities to recruit assistance or labor service. Such groups, or "action sets" (Gulliver 1971:18–19), were activated by individuals who used the entire *muntun* as their field. Households were so close and visits so frequent that, during an afternoon, an individual could easily find enough people to form a work party. Patterns of reciprocity were such that anyone asked to provide labor service usually agreed. The focal shaman activated action sets of ceremonial supporters in much the same way. Consequently a strong sense of *muntun* unity often prevailed.

The Runa were also part of the larger Ecuadorian society. Since the sixteenth century they had been in fairly close contact with Spanish-

American Ecuadorians (Oberem 1971). But at about the turn of the present century, economic ties with the national society increased. *Blanco* patrons became the sole suppliers of essential goods such as cloth, machetes, shotguns, and ammunition which they exchanged for gold, rubber, food, or labor. Although truly exploitative debt peonage evolved, the labor demands incurred by the patrons did not force the Runa to subordinate their subsistence mode of production to the demands of the market-oriented mode of production. Neither the nature of patron-organized labor nor the time allocated to perform it demanded a drastic reallocation of time and energy. A mixed economy developed in which gold panning, rubber gathering, and short-term labor were accommodated into the dominant subsistence mode of production. But by the mid-1970s the Runa's pattern of social, economic, and territorial life had been radically altered. Steps leading to this rapid change began in early 1960.

THE 1960s—COLONISTS

Early in 1960 two *blancos* left the town of Shell and rode a bus north for 30 kilometers. From there they walked into the forest and tried to locate Pasu Urcu. Unsuccessful, they wandered for three days before they finally found their way back to Shell. On their second attempt several weeks later, they finally arrived in Pasu Urcu, explored the settlement for three days, and then returned to Shell. Their unspectacular arrival in Pasu Urcu marked the onset of a new era for the Runa. The two *blancos* were the vanguard for 30 families who were preparing to colonize the middle Arajuno River.

The colonists' organizer, who had worked near Pasu Urcu in the late 1940s while Shell Oil Company explored for petroleum in the area, promised abundant fertile land and also spoke of a road which would soon cut through the forest to end Pasu Urcu's isolation. Within a year the entire group, buoyed by hope and sponsored by the National Institute of Colonization, had made several trips to Pasu Urcu and had established subsistence gardens. At this time the Runa, despite the fact that most of them had originally lived near the city of Tena, where they had witnessed a progressive dislocation of Indians, saw the colonists not as threats but rather as welcomed deterrents to hostile Waorani "Auca" attack. But shortly afterward, when the colonists, organized under the name Colonia Arajuno, asked government topographers to measure and assign individual lots for each colonist family, the Runa realized that Pasu Urcu had become part of the same expanding alien frontier which had forced other Runa out of the frontier town of Tena. The Runa also knew that they could not keep relocating indefinitely. Most of the land west, north, and south of Pasu Urcu was occupied, and the Waorani threatened all settlements east of the Arajuno River. So several Runa asked the local Protestant and Catholic missionaries to help the Indians acquire legal title to their land. At that time both sects were openly competing for converts and violently denouncing each other. Consequently both Protestant and Catholic missionaries, hoping to gain spiritual dominance in Pasu Urcu, agreed to support the Runa. Each missionary suggested that the Runa request communal (global) titles for a series of contiguous lots which, the missionaries hoped, would function as church-affiliated cooperatives. The Runa, however, had witnessed several unsuccessful cooperatives near Tena and rejected the missionaries' suggestion. They insisted on individual lots.[1] When the topographers arrived, they measured most of the land near Pasu Urcu and assigned 50-hectare lots to most heads of household.

Measuring and dividing land in Pasu Urcu was easy; obtaining legal title was another matter. For both the Runa and the colonists, the 1960s were years of frustrated attempts to gain legal possession of land. During this time several survey teams visited Pasu Urcu; colonists, missionaries, and Runa made numerous trips to Quito to inquire about the progress of the titles; and several Runa even wrote a letter of complaint to the Ecuadorian president. Finally, in the late 1960s, legal titles arrived and formally divided more than 3,000 hectares on either side of the middle Arajuno River.

However, several years of frustrated efforts had disillusioned many of the original colonists and those from four other groups who entered Pasu Urcu during that decade. In addition, the colonists also realized that the anticipated road, which had stimulated each of the five groups of colonists, was not about to materialize. Consequently, of the 55–60 colonist families who entered Pasu Urcu between 1960 and the early 1970s, only eight families were there in 1975. Nevertheless, the colonists provoked the transformation of more then 3,000 hectares of communal land into privately owned lots. As a result, tropical forest Indians, aroused by colonization and the prospect of dispossession, suddenly and unexpectedly became landowners.

While most of their land was being parceled into individual lots, the Runa asked that one section remain communal. This was the area of recent alluvium known as the *isla*, where, from the first Runa settlement near Pasu Urcu, principal subsistence plots had been planted. Throughout the 1960s most of the Runa maintained their principal gardens on the *isla*. They utilized their large, privately owned lots only as locations for secondary gardens, not as sites for intensive exploitation. Therefore, although the system of *land tenure* changed radically, the traditional patterns of *land use* continued. Indigenous economic practices and preferences, however, do not entirely explain the persistence of swidden horticulture on small plots of communal land amidst large tracts of privately owned land. National economic trends and political policies of the 1960s also influenced this situation.

THE 1960s—PASU URCU AND NATIONAL POLICIES

Colonization in Pasu Urcu resulted from Ecuadorian agrarian reform programs initiated in the 1950s. The persistence of indigenous land use patterns reflected, in part, the priorities of those programs as they developed through the 1960s.

Agrarian reform was conceived as a solution to glaring land tenure problems in the Ecuadorian coastal and highland regions. Since the colonial period a small, landed elite controlled most of the valuable arable land; the highland hacienda was seen as the archetypal symbol of inequitable land distribution.[2] Numerous outcries and clamors for reform occurred prior to 1950 (Peñaherrera and Costales 1971:57–82). But movement toward active agrarian reform followed the publication (1956) of the first national agricultural census (1954), which revealed one of the most imbalanced distributions of land in Latin America. In Ecuador 1% of the total agricultural landholdings contained 56% of the cultivated land, while 73.1% of the remaining farms shared only 7.2% of the cultivated land (Ecuador 1964:6). To achieve a more democratic balance, two alternatives existed: (1) divest the large landowner of his property and distribute it among the landless or relatively landless, or (2) encourage the landless to colonize unclaimed and unutilized land. It was far easier to encourage colonization than it was to institute coercive divestiture, so in 1957, as a concession to agrarian reform interests, the Instituto Nacional de Colonización was formed within the Ministerio de Agricultura. The institute was established to develop and support communities organized as agricultural cooperatives. But with the exception of one heavily supported pilot program in Santo Domingo de los Colorados, most colonists did not receive sufficient financial aid or technical support to develop successful cooperatives. Left on their own, settlements such as the Colonia Arajuno were cooperatives in name only.

Internal organization and cooperation hardly existed. During the late 1950s and early 1960s such groups organized on their own initiative, limped along for several years, and eventually died unnoticed. Most members affiliated themselves in cooperatives only to acquire land (Hurtado and Herudek 1974:23). Successive governments up to 1964 did little to organize, implement, or support active colonization programs.

The Cuban revolution, which quickly eliminated large privately owned landholdings, stimulated a concern for more active agrarian reform (Feder 1971:18). Representatives at the 1961 Organization of American States conference at Punta del Este, still startled by the Cuban revolution, produced the Alliance for Progress. Stimulated by the United States' promises of financial and technical aid for development, the alliance encouraged more equitable and efficient utilization of arable lands. Consequently, legislation aimed at altering patterns of land tenure was promulgated throughout Latin America. In 1964 the Ecuadorian military government wrote and passed the Law of Agrarian Reform and Colonization (*Ley de Reforma Agraria y Colonización* 1964). The Ecuadorian Institute of Agrarian Reform and Colonization (IERAC), which superseded the previous Instituto de Colonización, was established to carry out the program.

The introduction to the agrarian reform laws states that Ecuador cannot "progress" without changes in the anachronistic system of land tenure. To change the system, the laws detailed an ambitious two-part plan which would redistribute land more equitably and promote increased production of basic foods for domestic consumption (Ecuador 1964:6). As a complement to the agrarian reform laws, colonization was mentioned. In areas where the landless could not be accommodated onto redistributed land, these people would be encouraged to settle on *tierras baldías*, uncultivated and unused lands. So the 1936 *Ley de Tierras Baldiás y Colonización* was appended to the laws.

Priorities and Problems of Agrarian Reform in the 1960s

While the 1964 laws recognized that existing large landholdings were both socially unjust and economically underproductive, agrarian reform action in the 1960s stressed redistribution rather than production. But large landowners' violent opposition to reform produced obstructive activity and prolonged litigation; redistribution of highland haciendas was a difficult and slow process (NACLA 1975:13).

Consequently colonization, conceived initially as a minor complement to larger agrarian reform activities, became the most active program of land distribution. Seventy-five percent of the land assigned by IERAC from 1964 to 1973 went to colonists; by 1970, 11,808 colonist families had titles to 415,802 hectares (Martz 1972:173). In Pasu Urcu the change in local land tenure patterns illustrates the Runa's incorporation into the dominant land reform program of the 1960s.

But after the land was divided and titled, neither the Ecuadorian government nor any other extralocal organization required, or even encouraged, intensive production. The same was true for landholdings throughout Ecuador. Feder (1971:202) writes:

> Ecuador's decree of 1964 provided first for expropriation of land unused for three consecutive years, *then that of inadequately used land.* However, even these areas can be taken out of the land reform program if the owners present "investment plans," presumably for the improvement of the estates. But there is no provision which determines what is to occur if these plans are not carried out and the decree contains no deadlines with respect to the intensity of land use under the investment plans.

Nor did large landholders voluntarily increase production. They argued that since their land was in precarious tenure, they would not invest money or labor to improve land or increase production. NACLA (1975:15) wrote that "the surplus generated by large agricultural holdings in the highlands was not reinvested to raise productivity but was filtered into urban land speculation, construction and luxurious consumption" (see also Banco Nacional de Fomento et al. 1974:5).

Colonization, the most active agrarian reform program of the decade, allowed large portions of Runa territory to be treated as *tierras baldías* and therefore opened to colonization. This land was then divided and apportioned, giving the appearance of an equitable balance between arable land and landowners. However, what appeared to be democratization was actually the creation of an "escape valve" which relieved some of the pressures created by demands for redistribution of highland haciendas. Meanwhile IERAC made few, if any, demands on the new Runa landowners. Nor was there any incentive to utilize the newly acquired land. Rich and easily cultivated *isla* land provided adequate space for subsistence plots. Even if one of the Runa wanted to increase production by expanding cultivation onto assigned lots, small-farmer credit was unavailable at the time.[3] In the absence of either local or supralocal demands or incentives, most of the Pasu Urcu Runa's private land remained as tropical forest.

THE 1970s—CATTLE, PETROLEUM, AND THE AGRARIAN
REFORM LAWS OF 1974

From 1973 to 1974 land use patterns in Pasu Urcu changed radically. All landowners cleared extensive portions of their holdings and planted pasture. Then each of them purchased cattle, over one hundred head in total, and gradually herded them over a long, narrow trail to Pasu Urcu. Since then pastures have been expanded and cattle have multiplied.[4] By 1975 all private land in the main settlement was pasture, except for approximately ten hectares which was reserved for subsistence swidden plots within each assigned lot. Most Runa had also begun to secure titles for lots on their more distant hunting and fishing territories. Several men had already cleared part of this land for pasture.

Catholic missionaries, fundamentalist Protestant missionaries, and colonists all claimed to have inspired and influenced the Runa's shift to market-oriented economic activities. For a few of the Runa this was true; missionaries and colonists not only encouraged cattle raising but even provided the capital which allowed five or six Runa to start their herds.[5] However, such limited aid and encouragement does not explain (1) the Runa's *complete* shift to cattle raising, (2) the *suddenness* with which cattle tending was adopted, or (3) how *all* of the Runa obtained the capital necessary for such activities.

The shift to cattle, as with the acquisition of individual lots, was another response to current national policies and programs. The two most important influences were: (1) a new set of agrarian reform laws promulgated in 1973, and (2) a government-sponsored program which provided abundant and accessible credit. Both the laws and credit were heavily influenced by large-scale oil exploitation which began in June 1972. Early in that month crude oil began to be pumped from rich oil fields near Lago Agrio in the northern Oriente to the coastal port of Esmeraldas. Within a year Ecuador became the continent's second largest producer of petroleum and quickly accumulated extensive capital reserves. Meanwhile, Ecuadorians were importing most of their basic foodstuffs.

Less than a year after oil began to flow out of the tropical forest, a recently installed military government drew up and promulgated a new set of agrarian reform laws (Ecuador 1974). New agrarian reform legislation was essential. By the late 1960s not only were large landowners unwilling to improve their land or their technology to increase production, but they were actually producing less food for domestic consumption than they did during the pre-agrarian reform period. Between 1965 and 1973 real per capita agricultural output *declined* by 14% (Zuvekas 1976:3). "In 1967, basic imports of wheat, barley, rice, corn and sugar amounted to 370 million sucres [$15 million]. By 1972 they reached 700 million [$28 million]" (Banco Nacional de Fomento et al. 1974:10). Between 1970 and 1973 the cost of agricultural imports rose from $1.9 to $3 million. IERAC was either unable or, most would agree, unwilling to force the large landowners to increase production. Thus, as oil profits raised salaries for the urban middle and upper classes, skyrocketing inflation and scarce food supplies plagued the unhappy urban and rural poor.

Consequently, the 1973 agrarian reform laws were designed to increase national food production, and they did not emphasize expropriation or redistribution of land. While the introduction to the 1964 *Ley de Reforma Agraria y Colonización* contained 22 pages of general statements proclaiming the need for democratic land distribution, the 1973 *Ley de Reforma Agraria* was prefaced with a concise two-paragraph introduction stating the need to utilize land efficiently (Ecuador 1974:5).

The military government also decided that increased agricultural production throughout the country required substantial investments to improve arable land and standardize production through modern technology, neither of which would occur while a landowner's tenure was precarious. To encourage investment by large landowners, the government modified the laws concerning expropriation. Whereas both the 1964 and 1973 laws permitted expropriation of lands which were "inefficiently exploited," only the 1964 legislation limited the size of individual landholdings. Under the new laws population pressure and monopolization of land through family ties were the only causes, other than underproduction, for expropriation (Ecuador 1974:19–20). In general, landowners were told that the only way to lose land was to let it lie idle.

The Pasu Urcu Runa quickly learned of the priorities established by the 1973 *Ley de Reforma Agraria*. IERAC officials, aware that lots were still forested in Pasu Urcu, told the Runa that their land was liable for expropriation if they failed to cultivate or otherwise improve one-half of their holdings within five years.[6] At the time the *isla* could no longer support the growing population and the Runa had already begun to garden on their assigned lots. But subsistence swidden horticulture would never require one-half of a 50-hectare family plot; ten hectares were sufficient. The Runa had to improve at least 25 hectares in order to guarantee their tenure.

Several alternatives were available. The Runa could have begun intensive cash cropping of traditional food sources such as manioc, maize, beans, or peanuts. Lemon and orange orchards were another possibility, as was *naranjilla* fruit, a common cash crop in other parts of the Oriente (Casagrande, Thompson, and Young 1964:291; Whitten 1976:240). Other small farmers in the Oriente had successfully planted tea which they sold to either of two large tea plantations in the area.

But in Pasu Urcu marketing such goods was difficult. Travel to the nearest road, the Puyo-Napo road, required an arduous eight-to-ten-hour walk. The return on most cash crops does not warrant such a journey. In 1974–75 high-value commodities such as beans or peanuts sold for 600–700 sucres ($24–28) per hundred pounds. Maize was worth only 120–200 sucres per hundred pounds. During a short period in 1974 cacao beans were sold for 1,000-2,000 sucres per hundred pounds. At that time several Runa carried 50-pound sacks of cacao over the trail and sold them in Tena. With this single exception, commodities were never transported over the trail to a market.

All transport of commodities was done by small aircraft, which, for large-scale commodity marketing, was unsatisfactory. Freight charges were expensive (1975 rates were .60 sucre per pound), flights were irregular, and pilots always gave preference to passengers rather than freight. Finally, there were no shipping and receiving services available at either end. Each consignee had to meet the plane in Pasu Urcu, load his cargo, and make arrangements for someone to receive the cargo in Shell. Under such conditions large-scale marketing of agricultural commodities was uneconomical, time-consuming, and logistically uncertain and complicated.

Cattle, by contrast, could be sold to traveling buyers who periodically walked over the trail to Pasu Urcu, purchased several head of cattle, and then walked the animals back to the Puyo-Napo road where they were trucked to the provincial capital. In addition, IERAC officials recommended that the Runa convert their land into pasture. Cattle raising, however, required a large initial capital outlay. Prior to the 1970s the Runa could never have acquired such funds, but in the early 1970s they suddenly gained access to new economic means.

Petroleum: Wages and Agricultural Credit

From the late 1960s to 1973 almost every Pasu Urcu male over 18 years worked for oil companies throughout the Oriente. Long-term workers sometimes accumulated considerable savings. However, of the total adult male work force (approximately 40–50), only five or six purchased cattle with their earnings and none of these purchased all of the animals they owned by 1974. Most of the Runa spent their wages on "luxury" goods such as watches, radios, and bell-bottom pants. Wages, therefore, did not cause the sudden and complete conversion to cattle raising. Again, government policies and programs precipitated the major changes.

In 1973 the Ecuadorian government developed a five-year "Integral Plan for Transformation and Development" (*Plan Integral para Transformación y Desarrollo*) which stressed agricultural production and modernization, particularly for small farmers. To stimulate development, private banks (notoriously hesitant to extend credit to small agriculturalists) were required to assign 20–25% of their commercial credit to the agricultural sector (Banco Nacional de Fomento et al. 1974:23). From 1972 to mid-1974 private banks processed $21.1 million of credit for agriculture. Numerous other organizations also increased their loans for agriculture.

The most influential institution of this period was the Banco Nacional de Fomento, a public development bank which had always been the principal, but nontheless limited, source of agricultural credit. In March 1974 the bank instituted a new program to aid small farmers. Credit of up to 100% of the proposed investment (i.e., the borrower did not have to put up any of the initial capital) and with a low interest rate of 9% (institutional credit frequently runs to 15% or more in Ecuador) was made available to all adult property owners. In the same year the Ecuadorian Central Bank, using rapidly accumulating oil profits, tripled the capital reserves of the Banco de Fomento (from 1 to 3,000 million sucres) (Banco Nacional de Fomento et al. 1974:29). The following year both the volume of credit and the number of loans were the largest in the bank's ten-year history.

Of these loans, 73% went to agriculture. Total agricultural credit *doubled* from 1972 to 1973, and by September 1974 it appeared that they would more than double in that year. Credit assigned to pastures and cattle rose 48% in 1973 (from 278.4 million to 412.0 million sucres). Of the total, 78% constituted small loans of less than 50,000 sucres and an additional 12.9% were between 50,000 and 100,000 sucres. Thus over 90% of the Banco Nacional de Fomento's vastly expanded loans went to small farmers.

In Pasu Urcu the Banco Nacional de Fomento extended loans to anyone who could put up his land title as collateral. Following the recommendations of IERAC, the bank earmarked all of its loans for cattle raising and established relatively liberal repayment policies to encourage loans.[7] Such policies permitted the Runa to establish pastures and purchase breeding cattle, even though profits from these investments could not be expected for several years. Cattle, therefore, were the easiest commodity to acquire, establish, and market. By 1974 the Runa of Pasu Urcu, being landowners, were *required* to intensively exploit their recently acquired landholdings, were told to raise cattle, and were provided with the economic means to do so. Almost immediately new economic patterns developed and social relations were adapted to the new mode of production.

THE RUNA AS INCIPIENT CATTLEMEN

As the Pasu Urcu Runa began to purchase cattle, they studied the behavior of those who already understood animal husbandry—the colonists, the missionaries, and the three or four Runa who already owned cattle. The Runa quickly learned how to prepare and plant pasture grass, keep pasture relatively free of weeds, control the cattle, and cure the animals' minor wounds and illnesses. But when they put their education into practice, they immediately realized that cattle raising was a major chore. Their entire schedule of economic activities had to be adjusted to the newly introduced mode of production.

To feed the cattle, they had to prepare and maintain pastures. Since no natural forage existed in the tropical forest, pastures, like gardens, had to be carved out of the forest and created on cleared land. First they cleared the forest and transplanted small bunches of grass from other pastures. After the grass was established, cattle were allowed to consume the limited pasture and the animals were then transferred to another plot. The Runa, with their machetes, then thoroughly cleaned the used pasture, removing all of the weeds and mowing all of the trampled or partially consumed grass. They said that if they failed to clean the pasture, weeds and thorns quickly invaded to compete with the grass. Even when a pasture was fully established after several such cleanings, the strenuous and time-consuming weeding, which was usually the cause for abandoning a swidden plot, was not avoided. Weeds and thorns were always waiting to move onto cleared land. So pasture maintenance became a form of multicropping (Boserup 1965:16). As a result, cattle raising immediately pushed the Runa's economic system into a more intensive stage of agricultural evolution.

After pastures were established, each cattle owner had to consider feeding and controlling his animals. Three methods were commonly utilized: free roaming, tethering, and fencing. Free-roaming animals were simply set loose in unfenced areas. While this was obviously the most economical control technique, in terms of both time and money, cattle often wandered into neighboring pastures or gardens. For the cattle owner this often produced serious disputes and de- mands for remuneration. So cattle grazed uncontrolled only on a few isolated pastures. Tethered animals were easier to control, but since they had to be moved two or three times each day, their care was more time-consuming. Even though adolescent children often moved the animals, the adult owners usually checked their tethered cattle at least once each day. This was essential because the Runa quickly learned that restrained animals could, and often did, stumble into streams and gullies where they became entangled in their tether and, if unattended, injured themselves or died. Fencing, either split palm rail or barbed wire, prevented cattle from wandering into adjacent lots. Fences also eliminated the need for potentially dangerous and time-consuming tethering. However, when cattle roamed about in fenced pastures, they trampled the tall grass and destroyed part of their own food supply, a problem which did not occur with tethering. Thus productivity per hectare decreased as one shifted cattle from tethers to fenced pasture.[8] The Runa were keenly aware of this and they frequently commented on the rapid depletion of fenced pas- tures. Most Runa therefore combined tethering, which demanded frequent attention, with fencing, which, although an inefficient use of grass, gave them more free time.

Cattle and Subsistence: Aspects of a Mixed Economy

Careful consideration of the time and energy dedicated to cattle was essential because cattle raising did not eliminate the man-hours required for subsistence horticulture. In Pasu Urcu cattle were not sources of subsistence; they were commodities raised for sale in the market. As of 1975, cattle sales never provided cash for basic subsis- tence. Nor were cattle ever slaughtered to provide meat for local con- sumption. Horticulture, hunting, and fishing continued to provide subsistence. As mentioned earlier, the Runa had managed a dual economy before; under the patrons they managed market-oriented labor without disrupting their dominant subsistence mode of produc- tion. Gathering rubber and panning for gold were part-time activi- ties.

Maintaining five to 15 head of cattle (the range for most Runa in Pasu Urcu as of 1975) under the conditions described above was also a part-time job. Most families did not work in their pastures all day every week. Cattle raising, however, did require labor at least three or four times each week, often more frequently. As such, animal husbandry did not exclude subsistence horticulture but, when combined with horticulture, it noticeably increased the number of man-hours of labor in the average workday. Boserup (1965), while noting that increased man-hours always accompanied agricultural intensification, also recognized that farmers do not accept an increased work load if more leisurely alternatives are available. Agricultural intensification, she writes, is a response, often a coerced response, to the demands of new social or demographic situations. In Pasu Urcu the politics of agrarian reform indirectly required an increased frequency of cropping and a rise in man-hours of labor.

Cattle, Hunting, and Fishing

Cattle also occasioned qualitative changes in the Runa's economic life. Whereas combining the labor demands of cattle raising with those of subsistence horticulture was largely a matter of organizing a daily schedule, hunting and fishing were more difficult to accommodate into a relatively sedentary existence. Spontaneous or planned hunting trips near the main settlement were either (1) short early-morning or late-afternoon hunts close to home, or (2) day-long trips into the forest. Short trips were convenient only for those living on the periphery of the settlement or in some other location which permitted quick access to the forest. Others had to travel 45 minutes to an hour through pastures before reaching the forest. From there they had to walk even farther if they hoped to see game. The additional time converted a short trip into a longer one, so the use of time had to be carefully considered.

The frequency of day-long hunting trips was inversely related to the size of one's cattle herd. Men said that in previous times they had undertaken such hunts three or four times each week. In 1974–75 the average cattle owner, caring for five to 15 head, rarely hunted more than once a week. Moreover, they went hunting only when there was strong evidence that large game was in the vicinity. During the 18 months that I lived in Pasu Urcu, large game appeared in the immediate vicinity no more than six times. While such infrequent occurrence allowed men to fit hunting into their work schedule, hunting near Pasu Urcu was not a major activity.

Hunting and fishing trips which ranged far from the *quiquin llacta* required more complex scheduling. Previously, seasonality determined the scheduling. During February and September, which are usually the driest months of the year, the largest gardens were usually cleared and planted; for the next two or three months they did not require any maintenance. At the same time, the water level of the rivers begins to drop, exposing large sandy beaches and leaving the water relatively clear and slow-moving. The exposed river banks become nesting areas for river turtles who deposited 15–25 eggs each into the sand. These oily eggs are one of the most prized foods of the Quijos Quichua, as they are throughout Amazonia. The eggs alone motivated long trips to scour the beaches. At the same time the low water level in the rivers forced fish to congregate in small, clear pools. Fishing, done either by dynamiting the clear pools or by poisoning shallow stretches of slow-moving water, became relatively easy and quite productive. Thus twice each year there were periods during which horticulture tasks were minimal and natural foods were abundant.

Previously, large groups from Pasu Urcu—men, women, children, and elders—would slowly travel down the Curaray River for several weeks while they hunted, fished, and gathered turtle eggs. Non-cattle-owning Runa in other settlements still take such trips. But for those of Pasu Urcu these large and extended movements of people have ended. Only once during 1974–75 did a group take advantage of the biannual turtle nesting; four men went to the Curaray while their wives and children remained home to tend their cattle. For most of the Runa of Pasu Urcu, the regular care of cattle institutionalized a maintenance schedule which prohibited family units from leaving their animals for more than a few days. Flannery (1968:82) writes that ". . . in regions of year-round agriculture, certain seasonal activities are curtailed or even abandoned and emphasis is placed on those year-round resources that do not conflict with farming schedules." In Pasu Urcu small-scale cattle ranching demanded limited but nonetheless year-round care. The lack of mobility virtually eliminated turtle egg–hunting and decreased the opportunities to accumulate large amounts of smoked fish.

Cattle therefore provoked a radical reconsideration of priorities in Runa economic life. If we consider only horticulture and cattle raising, we see that the latter caused an increase in daily man-hours of labor. However, since the labor requirements of one activity were accommodated into the labor schedule of the other, neither activity clearly revealed itself as dominant. But when horticulture is combined with fishing and hunting, and considered as a single, integrated mode of production—which it is throughout most of indigenous Amazonia—priorities are clearly visible. By eliminating much hunting and fishing, a market-oriented activity emerged as the dominant mode of production. Subsistence economic activities either had to be accommodated to the demands of cattle raising or else eliminated. As of 1975, the Runa's individually maintained subsistence security was not threatened, but they had clearly become more closely integrated into Ecuadorian political and economic life than they ever had before.

SOCIAL ADJUSTMENTS TO CATTLE RAISING

Barth (1967:663) writes that when people allocate most of their labor to their own fields, reciprocal labor services decrease and, in general, neighborliness and community life fade away. In Pasu Urcu, where cattle raising forced the Runa to allocate more time and labor to individually owned land, neighborliness and reciprocal labor services did not disappear. However, new household spacing and labor scheduling quickly altered the patterns of labor recruitment mentioned earlier. In general, an individual's active "personal set" (Whitten and Wolfe 1973:724) became smaller and simpler. This affected both the cohesiveness of the *muntun* and the authority of the *muntun*'s focal shaman.

The Muntun and Reciprocal Labor

In 1975 most cattle-owning Runa returned from their fields and pastures between four and six o'clock in the afternoon. With only an hour or so before darkness set in, individuals were forced to limit the range of their afternoon visits. They only dropped in on their closest neighbors. Consequently, action sets were usually mustered from within this limited, residentially defined field. Spontaneously activated reciprocal labor parties were usually groups of close neighbors, not individuals drawn from the *muntun* as a whole, such as had occurred when visiting patterns were more extensive and complex.

Spontaneous action sets were not the only groups affected. Even if a work party or other communal activity were scheduled in advance, conceivably permitting the recruitment of a wider range of *muntun* members as they mingled around the settlement each Sunday, individuals rarely attempted to recruit those from outside their close neighborhood set. Previously, patterns of reciprocity kept individuals flowing in and out of numerous action sets, and since each individual participated in many others' sets, he in turn assumed that his own recruiting efforts would be similarly successful. But by 1975 most

Runa realized that their labor services were no longer part of the *muntun*-wide field. A recruiter was therefore hesitant to ask someone to participate in his set when he, the recruiter, might never have the chance to reciprocate. Consequently individuals tended to recruit only those with whom they most frequently cooperated; dyadic reciprocity became the norm. Action sets became fixed groups, reactivated rather than activated anew. They were permanent work groups rather than *ad hoc* action sets. As a result, interaction among *muntun* members as a whole was more restricted.

A family's decreased dependence on the *muntun* was even more noticeable in the secondary settlements, *purina llacta*, such as those on the Nushiño where numerous individuals from outside the original *muntun* had settled. By 1975 the Nushiño population had become so heterogeneous with regard to kinship ties that co-residence eventually became the principal focus of group identification. Autonomous behavior on the Nushiño appeared, not only in the activation of communal labor groups but in the formation of ritual groups and in patterns of interaction in general. This was particularly noticeable for those *muntun* members who were beginning to establish more permanent residence along the Nushiño River. Since they spent little time in the *quiquin llacta*, they depended less and less on those individuals who continued to maintain their principal residence in Pasu Urcu. Consequently, the Nushiño settlement shifted from a residence-based kin group (*muntun*) to an amorphous nascent group, or quasi-group, in which co-residence, more than any other factor, linked the members.[9]

Fragmentation or Fission?

The fragmentation of the Pasu Urcu *muntun*, particularly among those living in the Nushiño area, implies that the non-kin residence-based groups which formed the field for ritual and reciprocal labor sets were not incipient *muntuns*. It assumes that the apparent fragmentation was not fission, a process which has been recorded with considerable consistency in Amazonia (Goldman 1963, Chagnon 1977, Maybury-Lewis 1967, Whitten 1976, Descola in this volume). Fission, however, is not a simple splitting but, rather, a process characterized by continuity and replication of form. If these incipient groups were to become structurally equivalent to the parent *muntun*, a shaman-centered residence-based kin group should have emerged.

Theoretically, at least, the absence of kin ties need not have impeded the development of a *muntun*. I have detailed elsewhere how Quijos Quichua manipulated kin terms and permitted non-kin to incorporate themselves into the kindreds which the Runa call *muntuns* (Macdonald 1979). But, as of 1975, there was no indication that non-kin were attempting to establish kin status by manipulating kinship terminology; only given names were utilized within the incipient groups. More important, the defining feature of any *muntun*, incipient or otherwise, was its focal shaman. None of the incipient groups centered around a shaman. Whenever an individual needed a shaman, he invariably returned to his original *muntun*.

Pasu Urcu's Focal Shaman in 1975

By late 1975 the Pasu Urcu focal shaman's behavior and the *muntun's* reaction to that behavior also indicated a weakening of traditional *muntun* unity. Although the shaman still served as the principal ritual curer, and did so quite frequently, the "role set" (Merton 1968) of most Quijos Quichua shamans included many more roles than that of curer. The role set was so large that the resulting status was usually a combination of knowledge, authority, and respect which tied the shaman to other members of the *muntun* through a network of reciprocal supernatural and social ties mentioned earlier. By 1975 this supernatural and social reciprocity was weakened.

As occurred with cooperative labor service recruitment, when a person arrived at a shaman's house to request his services, the others present in the house were asked to accompany the shaman. But by 1975 the focal shaman, as he attempted to activate such ritual action sets, encountered problems identical to those which other Runa experienced when recruiting labor service. The new spatial and labor conditions produced a smaller and more consistent group of supporters; only those who lived close to the shaman accompanied him regularly.

Support of the shaman and recognition of his authority were also acknowledged through communal care of a plaza–soccer field. This site was the recognized center of the shaman's spirit shield, *lurira*, which circumscribed the fertile garden sites of the *isla* and previously had included the houses of most Pasu Urcu Runa. At least twice each year the shaman organized work parties to clear the growth away from the plaza and paths which led up to it. The members of the *muntun*, by providing their labor, acknowledged and confirmed the shaman's authority.

But by 1975 demographic, economic, and land tenure changes had altered the *muntun's* attitude toward maintaining the plaza. Their dispersal onto individual lots left few permanent residents within the shaman's *lurira*. Nonetheless, the *isla* was still a highly regarded site for gardens. Until the mid-1970s most members of the *muntun* maintained at least one of their gardens on the *isla* and continued to provide labor to maintain the plaza. But as gardens and pastures were established on individual lots, the horticulture primacy of the *isla* diminished, and so did the Runa's sense of obligation to maintain the plaza. So they occasionally failed to provide their labor.

The shaman reacted to such negligence by violently berating those who failed to appear. The Runa, in turn, had a very low tolerance for such abuse; to speak harshly was a violent, critical, and socially unacceptable act, totally inappropriate for an authority figure. When all members of the *muntun* were in daily face-to-face interaction, apologies or equivalent symbolic acts quickly and easily settled minor disputes before they led to irresolvable conflict. But as increased distance and extended work schedules diminished daily social interaction, the aggressive behavior of the shaman became more difficult to resolve. Thus the offended Runa began to avoid additional conflicts by distancing themselves from the shaman. Among other things, they would not attend his work parties. As this schizmogenesis-like (Bateson 1958) process continued, some Runa began to abandon their regrowth plots on the *isla*. In doing so, they severed a visible tie with the rest of the *muntun* members.

The shaman's subsequent behavior worsened this situation. He began to usurp the *isla* land. Until this time the relatively fertile *isla* was used solely for individual garden plots. As the last remaining sector of communal land in Pasu Urcu, the *isla* continued to reflect the previous tenure system, one which permitted only temporary rights of usufruct. But as people failed to exercise their rights of usufruct, the focal shaman converted several upriver fallow plots into permanent pasture for his cattle. Meanwhile, he and those members of the *muntun* who still continued to garden on the *isla* rotated their gardens on another section of recent alluvium downstream from his pastures. By 1975, even on the downstream plots the shaman and his sons, without consulting with any of those who claimed rights of usufruct on the *isla*, began to plant large gardens on sites which were the acknowledged fallow plots of others. Those Runa who still claimed rights of usufruct and actually utilized the relatively fertile *isla* land interpreted this behavior as outright encroachment.

Simmering tensions rose to a boil in late 1975 when members of IERAC were surveying in Pasu Urcu. During this time one of the Runa who was particularly angered by the shaman's actions attempted to utilize the topographer's externally derived authority to resolve the situation which had developed on the *isla*. The Runa suggested to the topographer that the *isla* be divided in half—one section would be given, as titled land, to the shaman and his immediate family, while the other section would remain as communal land. Although such a division would have given the shaman a much larger and more secure portion of the *isla* than he was utilizing at the time, he reacted violently when he heard of the plan and he moved quickly to convince IERAC that such a division was unacceptable. The shaman insisted that the entire *isla* was communal land; rather than divide it, members of the *muntun* should be made to realize their obligation to maintain it. Thus, while he gradually appropriated more and more land for his own use, he argued that the *isla* should still reflect the organization of a *muntun* within which he was the internal authority figure.

It was ironical, yet fully comprehensible, that a man who daily seesawed between subsistence horticulture and production for a market, private and communal land, the *muntun* and the national state, should rage at anyone's actions which whittled away at the symbols of his previous authority and status while he acted in a manner which encouraged such behavior. Perhaps more noticeably than other members of the *muntun* (but certainly not unlike them), the shaman was caught between contradictory desires to maintain a previous role set and the system of social organization and prestige which supported it and at the same time attempting to maximize his position within the new socioeconomic order. By late 1975 many people in Pasu Urcu were angered by the shaman's behavior. It was not surprising that individual families began to experiment with alternative forms of social organization.

BEYOND 1975

By 1975, even though the Pasu Urcu Runa had already adapted their subsistence needs to the demands of a dominant mode of production and were experimenting with forms of social organization which were compatible with the new economic system, it was still too early to predict the future of the shaman-centered *muntun* or to conceive of patterns of social organization which might replace it. One could only identify the economic and political forces which produced a need for new patterns. Ecological conditions, changing national politics and economics, and the Runa themselves will determine the activities which eventually generate new social forms.

Whatever happens, some unique form of Runa society will probably persist. The Quijos Quichua, like many other indigenous groups
living along the eastern flank of the Andes, are an expanding population. The 1974 Ecuadorian national census, when compared to the
previous census, recorded a substantial population increase in Napo
province.[10] Also, in 1973, a group of Quijos Quichua from Tena established the Federation of Indigenous Organizations of the Napo, Federación de Organizaciones Indígenas del Napo, usually called
FOIN, through which they eventually hope to federate local Quijos
Quichua communities throughout the upper Napo, encourage a frequently submerged sense of ethnic pride, and establish agricultural
production and marketing cooperatives (Instituto Ecuatoriano de
Formación Social 1973). Equally important, as I have detailed elsewhere (Macdonald 1979), the Runa order experience, create moods,
and motivate actions by means of a unique logico-symbolic system
which persisted in Pasu Urcu despite radical social and economic
change (see also Descola, Taylor, N. Whitten, D. Whitten, in this volume). This world view need never disappear, for it is a completely
adequate cognitive scheme which will permit the Runa to comprehend and cope with any future change. The children of Pasu Urcu
can still grow up as Runa.

Adaptation to change is one thing; long-term survival is another.
When the Runa were forced to accept cattle raising, they were simultaneously forced to alter the tropical forest landscape in an ecologically absurd manner. Many writers claim that large-scale cattle ranching will rapidly destroy the Amazonian ecosystem (Denevan 1973,
Fosberg 1973, Goodland and Irwin 1975, Parsons 1975). Moreover,
they stress that on-going change is not simply replacing one workable land use system with another equally viable system. Fosberg
(1973:348) clearly expresses the opinion of many ecologists, botanists,
and geographers: "It is doubtful if anywhere in the humid tropics
[cattle] grazing on a large scale could have evolved as an indigenous
cultural pattern, as traits which seriously degrade the habitat are
non-adaptive and would be selected against." If the current emphasis
on cattle raising persists, it could result in a vast savannah landscape
which will never support the people and domesticated animals currently flooding into Amazonia. Other scientists are more optimistic
(Bishop and Blakeslee 1975:14–15). Sánchez (1976) argues that, contrary to popular belief, there is relatively little difference between the
soils of temperate zones and certain areas of Amazonia. He therefore
suggests that intensive land use with high-yield crops is both possible and, given the current population problems, advisable in Ama-

zonia. To test such ideas, long-term controlled experiments are underway in many areas.

But while the debates and experiments continue, the Runa of Pasu Urcu, like most other cattlemen in Amazonia (Davis 1977), continue to clear forest, plant pasture, and tend cattle in a manner which most people agree is ecologically disastrous. Indians have been forced to adopt alien land use systems which may soon produce an unproductive, perhaps unlivable, ecosystem. The Runa know that extensive pasture land (not small plots which can easily be refertilized with animal excrement) will deteriorate quickly. By 1975 they had already noticed that grass planted three or four years earlier was becoming thin and patchy. But they were powerless to avoid the situation.

Compared to the ominous future which looms over Amazonia, the Pasu Urcu Runa's successful adaptation to change could seem futile and insignificant. But this is not true. Their rapid adjustment illustrates how enormously creative, intelligent, aware, and resourceful they are. Their biggest problem is that they are unheard. If they could be included in the policy decisions concerning the fate of Amazonia, they could contribute a wealth of knowledge based on centuries of accumulated experience. If they are excluded, Ecuador's hope for improved agricultural self-sufficiency, which, ironically, was the idea that triggered change in Pasu Urcu, may disappear along with the forest.

NOTES

Acknowledgments: Initial field research for this paper began during June-Aug. 1972 and was supported by a grant from the Center for International Comparative Studies at the University of Illinois, Urbana. Subsequent research in Ecuador, from May 1974 to Dec. 1975, was supported by a doctoral dissertation fellowship from the Social Science Research Council, Foreign Area Fellowship Program.

1. At the time there was no effort to obtain, nor as far as I could determine to consider, communal titles for large tracts of land which could be adjusted to cope with local demographic change. Directly south of Pasu Urcu such communal landholdings exist for the Shuar centers (Salazar 1977, Harner 1972) and for the Puyo Runa *comuna* of San Jacinto, near Puyo (Whitten 1976:240–48).

2. The "classic" highland haciendas were usually seen as self-sufficient but underproductive estates which did little more than provide their owners with a comfortable and genteel existence. Mörner (1973), by contrast, demonstrates that the origin, development, and function of haciendas were more complex and varied than earlier writers assumed. For the purposes of this

paper, however, the stereotype is more important, for it was the image which stimulated the architects of agrarian reform.

3. From 1965 to 1973 private banks in Ecuador extended only 9% of their credit to the agricultural sector. Of this credit, 94.5% was in the form of short-term loans (less than one year) which served mainly to cover the planting and harvesting expenses of large landowners (Banco Nacional de Fomento et al. 1974:22). Likewise, during the 1960s the public Banco Nacional de Fomento extended very little credit to small farmers.

4. In 1974 the second national agriculture and animal husbandry census (Segundo Censo Agropecuario, 1974) reported 629 head of cattle pasturing on 4,847 hectares of cleared land in Pasu Urcu (Ecuador—Instituto Nacional de Estadística y Censos n.d.:47).

5. Two men started their herds with wages earned through missionaries. Three or four others were share-herders with either missionaries or colonists. When share-herding, the missionaries or colonists provided the initial breeding or fattening stock and the Runa provided pasture and labor. Profits, in the form of either calves or cash, were shared equally.

6. The 1973 agrarian reform law (Ecuador 1974) states otherwise. Underproductive lands were understood to be those which did not "tener al 1° de enero de 1976 explotación económica eficiente de acuerdo con las condiciones geográficas, ecologicas, y de infraestructura de zona—no menos del 80% de la superficie agropecuaria aprovechable del predio" (Ecuador 1974:18). The actual amount of usable land within a landholding was determined by local conditions and terrain. For most of Pasu Urcu, 50% of the landholding had to be worked within five years. If the landowner wanted a second lot, the Runa were told that 75% of the first lot had to be under cultivation.

7. On loans extended to purchase cattle for fattening, the borrower paid only the annual interest (8% per annum) for the first two years. In the third year, when the animal was expected to be ready for sale, the owner began paying off the capital; two years were allowed to pay off the capital. Loans secured to purchase breeding stock were extended over a much longer time. For the first seven years borrowers paid only the interest, and they had an additional two years to pay off the capital.

8. To illustrate, one Runa family had a total of 15 hectares of pasture land. Ten of these were surrounded by barbed wire and subdivided into two and one-half hectare sections. The family could pasture their ten head of cattle in each fenced section for three weeks to a month; the entire fenced area could support the herd for no more than four months. The family's remaining five hectares were unfenced and cattle were pastured there on tethers. The unfenced area could support the cattle for up to six months. In brief, the unfenced area, half the size of the fenced area, supported the herd for twice as long as the fenced area.

9. Brief preliminary investigation in 1975 indicated that settlement and interaction patterns such as those on the Nushiño were developed in other areas of eastern Ecuador, particularly in the Lago Agrio–Santa Cecilia region of the Upper Aguarico River, where Quijos Quichua from the Tena-Archidona area had begun to colonize.

10. At the time of the 1962 census the population of Napo province was 24,253 and that of Pastaza province was 13,693 (Ecuador—Junta Nacional de Planificación y Coordinación Económica, División de Estadística y Censos,

n.d.: Segundo Censo). By the time of the 1974 census the population of Napo province had risen to 59,751 and that of Pastaza province to 23,058 (Ecuador—Junta Nacional de Planificación, Oficina de los Censos Nacionales, n.d.: Tercer Censo).

Most of the Quijos Quichua live within the province of Napo. Pasu Urcu, however, is located just across the southern border of that province, on the northern edge of Pastaza province.

The 1974 census, unlike that of 1962, did not attempt to differentiate ethnic and racial groups within the population. However, even a superficial glance at the ethnic composition of the upper Napo area reveals that colonists alone have not caused the population to double. The Runa are still the majority and they are a rapidly increasing population.

REFERENCES CITED

Banco Nacional de Fomento, Ministerio de Agricultura y Ganadería, Banco del Ecuador, and Junta Nacional de Planificación y Coordinación Económica
  1974   *El Crédito Agrícola en el Ecuador.* Quito.
Barth, Fredrik
  1967   On the Study of Social Change. *American Anthropologist* 69 (6):661–69.
Bateson, Gregory
  1958   *Naven.* 2d ed. Stanford, Calif.: Stanford University Press.
Bishop, John P., and Joe Blakeslee
  1975   *Development of a Sustained-Yield Tropical Agroecosystem: Integration of Crop, Livestock, and Forest Production System in a "Mixed" Small Farm Production System in the Upper Amazon Basin.* Quito: Summer Institute of Linguistics.
Boserup, Esther
  1965   *The Conditions of Agricultural Growth.* Chicago: Aldine.
Carneiro, Robert L.
  1961   Slash-and-Burn Cultivation among the Kuikurù and Its Implications for Cultural Development in the Amazon Basin. In J. Wilbert, ed., *The Evolution of Horticultural Systems in Native South America, Causes and Consequences: A Symposium. Antropólgica* Supplement Publication 2, pp. 47–67.
Casagrande, Joseph B., Stephen I. Thompson, and Philip D. Young
  1964   Colonization as a Research Frontier: The Ecuadorian Case. In Robert A. Manners, ed., *Process and Pattern in Culture: Essays in Honor of Julian H. Steward.* Chicago: Aldine, pp. 281–325.
Chagnon, Napoleon A.
  1977   *Yanomamö: The Fierce People.* New York: Holt, Rinehart and Winston.
Davis, Shelton H.
  1977   *Victims of the Miracle: Development and the Indians of Brazil.* New York: Cambridge University Press.
Denevan, William M.
  1973   Development and the Imminent Demise of the Amazon Rainforest. *Professional Geographer* 25:130–35.

Ecuador
  1964   *Decreto Supremo N° 1480: Ley de Reforma Agraria y Colonización.* Quito: Talleres Graficos "Minerva."
Ecuador—Ministerio de Agricultura y Ganadería
  1974   *Reforma Agraria: Ley y Reglamento.* Quito: Cencotap.
Ecuador—Instituto National de Estadística y Censos
  n.d.   Segundo Censo Agropecuario, 1974. Resultados Provisionales, Resumen Nacional. 2d ed. Quito.
Ecuador—Junta Nacional de Planificación y Coordinación Económica, División de Estadística y Censos
  n.d.   Segundo Censo de Población y Primer Censo de Vivienda, 1962. Vol. 1. Quito.
Ecuador—Junta Nacional de Planificación, Oficina de los Censos Nacionales
  n.d.   Tercer Censo de Población; Segundo de Vivienda: Resultados Provisionales. Quito.
Ecuador—Secretaría General de Planeación Económica
  n.d.   El Crédito Agropecuaria en el Periodo 1964–1967. Documento 08–03–24–X–68.
Feder, Ernest
  1971   *The Rape of the Peasantry.* Garden City, N.Y.: Doubleday.
Flannery, Kent V.
  1968   Archeological Systems Theory and Early Mesoamerica. In Betty J. Meggers, ed., *Anthropological Archeology in the Americas.* Washington, D.C.: Anthropological Society of Washington, pp. 67–87.
Fosberg, F. R.
  1973   Temperate Zone Influence on Tropical Forest Land Use: A Plea for Sanity. In Betty J. Meggers, Edward S. Ayensu, and Donald W. Duckworth, eds., *Tropical Forest Ecosystems in Africa and South America: A Comparative Review.* Washington, D.C.: Smithsonian Institution, pp. 345–50.
Fried, Morton
  1967   *The Evolution of Political Society: An Essay in Political Anthropology.* New York: Random House.
Godelier, Maurice
  1977   *Perspectives in Marxist Anthropology.* New York: Cambridge University Press.
Goldman, Irving
  1963   *The Cubeo: Indians of the Northwest Amazon.* Urbana: University of Illinois Press.
Goodland, R. J. A., and H. S. Irwin
  1975   *Amazon Jungle: Green Hell to Red Desert.* Amsterdam: Elsevier.
Gulliver, P. H.
  1971   *Neighbors and Networks: The Idiom of Kinship in Social Action among the Ndendeuli of Tanzania.* Berkeley: University of California Press.
Harner, Michael J.
  1972   *The Jívaro: People of the Sacred Waterfalls.* Garden City, N.Y.: Natural History Press.
Hurtado, Osvaldo, and Joachim Herudek
  1974   *La Organización Popular en el Ecuador.* Quito: Editorial "Fray Jodoco Ricke."

Instituto Ecuatoriano de Formación Social
1973 *Curso para Promotores Campesinos de la Provincia del Napo, 17–20 de Noviembre 1973*. Ecuador.

Macdonald, Theodore, Jr.
1979 Processes of Change in Amazonian Ecuador: Quijos Quichua Indians Become Cattlemen. Ann Arbor, Mich.: University Microfilms. Ph.D. thesis, University of Illinois, Urbana.

Martz, John D.
1972 *Ecuador: Conflicting Political Culture and the Quest for Progress*. Boston: Allyn and Bacon.

Maybury-Lewis, David
1967 *Akwẽ-Shavante Society*. London: Oxford University Press.

Merton, Robert King
1968 *Social Theory and Social Structure*. New York: Free Press.

Mörner, Magnus
1973 The Spanish American Hacienda: A Survey of Recent Research and Debate. *Hispanic American Historical Review* 53 (2):183–216.

NACLA (North American Congress on Latin America)
1975 *Ecuador: Oil up for Grabs*. Latin America and Empire Report 9 (8), November.

Oberem, Udo
1971 *Los Quijos: Historia de la Transculturación de un Grupo Indígena en el Oriente Ecuatoriano (1538–1956)*. 2 vols. Madrid: Facultad de Filosofía y Letras, Universidad de Madrid.

O'Laughlin, Bridget
1975 Marxist Approaches in Anthropology. *Annual Review of Anthropology* 4:341–70.

Parsons, James J.
1975 The Changing Nature of the New World Tropical Forests since European Colonization. *Papers and Proceedings of the Conference*, Ecological Guidelines for Development in the American Humid Tropics, Caracas, Venezuela, 20–22 Feb. 1974.

Peñaherrera de Costales, Piedad, and Alfredo Costales Samaniego
1971 *Historia Social del Ecuador*, vol. 4: *Reforma Agraria*. Quito: Casa de la Cultura Ecuatoriana.

Salazar, Ernesto
1977 *An Indian Federation in Lowland Ecuador*. Copenhagen: International Work Group for Indigenous Affairs, Document 28.

Sánchez, Pedro
1976 *Properties and Management of Soils in the Tropics*. New York: Wiley.

Whitten, Norman E., Jr. (with the assistance of Marcelo F. Naranjo, Marcelo Santi Simbaña, and Dorothea S. Whitten)
1976 *Sacha Runa: Ethnicity and Adaptation of Ecuadorian Jungle Quichua*. Urbana: University of Illinois Press.

Whitten, Norman E., Jr., and Alvin W. Wolfe
1973 Network Analysis. In John J. Honigmann, ed., *Handbook of Social and Cultural Anthropology*. Chicago: Rand McNally, pp. 717–46.

Zuvekas, Clarence, Jr.
1976 Agrarian Reform in Ecuador's Guayas River Basin. *Land Economics* 52 (3):314–29.

PART III:
CULTURAL TRANSFORMATION,
ETHNICITY, AND ADAPTATION IN
THE SIERRA AND LITTORAL

13

Folk Models of Stratification and Ethnicity in the Highlands of Northern Ecuador

Louisa R. Stark

Studies of Andean social stratification and ethnicity have documented the fact that identification and labeling of individuals and groups in ethnic or "racial" categories often depend upon the identity of the speaker using the label. Labeling is at least partially correlated with the position occupied by the speaker within the social hierarchy of a particular geographical area (van den Berghe 1974:21). This paper focuses on the classificatory system[1] used by residents of a circumscribed geographical and political area, the Sector of Cotacachi[2] in the province of Imbabura, to establish sets of ethnic contrasts consonant with relative power within the social structure.

SETTING

The Sector of Cotacachi is located in the west-central part of the province of Imbabura, in the northern highlands of Ecuador. The area covers 72 square kilometers. The eastern part of the sector is located at an altitude of approximately 2,500 meters. Moving northwest, the terrain spreads upward along the slopes of Mount Cotacachi, which rises to 4,937 meters at its highest elevation (Sampedro V. 1975–76:35). Located in the eastern part of the sector is the administrative center of the area, the town of Cotacachi, with a population of 4,788. The rest of the sector has a population of 5,035 (Oficina de Censos Nacionales 1975).

The town of Cotacachi is connected to the Pan-American Highway by five kilometers of two-lane paved road. By means of the Pan-American Highway Cotacacheños have easy access to Ibarra, 20 kilometers to the north, and to Quito, 80 kilometers to the south. There is constant contact between the town and the political centers of the province and nation through frequent bus service, taxis, and the increasing number of private vehicles owned by its residents.

Besides good public transportation systems, Cotacachi has electricity and potable water. It also boasts two large churches, a kindergarten, five primary schools (three public, two parochial), one high school, a town hall, police station, and jail, and a large new stadium; the town is currently in the process of constructing its own hospital.

Economically, Cotacachi is unlike many other Andean towns of the same size in that it does not have a well-developed weekly market. In fact, fresh produce coming from the small farms in the rural areas around the town is sold on Saturdays in the Otavalo market, eight kilometers to the southeast. Agricultural products which are not sold in Otavalo may be brought to a small market held in Cotacachi on Sundays. But it is agreed that such produce generally consists of leftovers, so that enterprising Cotacacheños usually go to the Saturday market in Otavalo for their purchases.

The lack of an important market in Cotacachi is related to the fact that the town does not have the shops and institutions that usually provide goods and services for those rural inhabitants who come to a market town to sell their produce and to purchase those products that they cannot manufacture themselves. Cotacachi has traditionally not supplied these goods and services because the majority of the inhabitants who would normally be involved in this sector of the economy have been engaged in other occupations. Among these is the production of leather goods, which are sold in Quito and Guayaquil and exported to foreign countries. There are also several small factories engaged in the forging of articles made of bronze and brass.

The town is also known for the high level of education of its inhabitants, as well as for their professional involvement in the educational system on local, provincial, and national levels. In fact, there is a disproportionately large number of townspeople who have received high school and university training in Quito. Moreover, they generally return to Cotacachi to live and teach on a local level, or they commute to Ibarra or Quito to participate in the nation's educational system on provincial and national levels. The town also has a reputation for having many residents who are talented musically; it has an excellent high school which specializes in teaching music.

Generally among the residents of Cotacachi there is an *esprit de corps* and loyalty to the town not encountered in other communities of the same size in highland Ecuador. It has been observed in other small towns that the youth want to out-migrate as soon as they possibly can (Basile 1974:103). The opposite seems to occur in Cotacachi, where there is the saying that "Cotacacheños always return here to live," no matter how much time they have spent away from the community.

On the periphery of the town there are several barrios where houses are smaller than those in the center of the urban area, and which have small plots of land adjacent to them. The inhabitants of these barrios cultivate corn, beans, and other vegetables in their fields, while at the same time they own small stores and bars, or participate in such occupations as tailoring, stone masonry, carpentry, and shoemaking. A bit farther outside the town one finds individuals cultivating slightly larger fields on a full-time basis and selling their surplus produce in the market in Otavalo. The inhabitants of both the barrios and the rural areas abutting the town generally speak Spanish and are at least functionally literate.

Finally, as one moves away from the town and passes into the more rural areas at higher elevations, one comes across small *comunas* (communities) ranging from 200 to 1,200 individuals. These are formed of clusters of houses, with a small plot of land near each dwelling used for the cultivation of corn, squash, beans, and other vegetables. Generally each family unit also possesses fields at a somewhat higher altitude above the community for the cultivation of root crops such as potatoes, ocas and mellocas, and barley. Each community has communal lands situated at even higher altitudes for the pasturing of animals and the gathering of firewood. Inhabitants of these communities usually speak only Quichua and, for the most part, are illiterate. They tend to be involved in a subsistence economy, consuming what they produce and making their own homespun clothing. When they need cash for a fiesta, they work on neighboring haciendas. The latter stretch up the slopes of the mountains and produce sugar cane at lower elevations and barley at higher altitudes. These products are generally sold directly to the distilleries and breweries of Quito and Guayaquil.

Haciendas in the Sector of Cotacachi have not yet been greatly affected by the country's land reform policies. Their owners tend to delegate the administration of the haciendas to professional managers, coming up from Quito to visit their properties over weekends and vacations.

THE FOLK TAXONOMY OF SOCIAL STRATIFICATION

In the analysis of any folk classification system the anthropologist must first look for the terms which are significant to the native culture bearers with whom he or she is working. This can be done simply by listening to informal conversations between individuals to pick up what terms seem to be used frequently in certain sociocultural contexts. In Cotacachi one term emerged frequently in discussions of the relationship of people to one another: *palanca* (lit. lever, handle), which can be translated figuratively as *access to goods and services*, or *relative power*. Adams (1967), in discussing class sectors in Latin America, talks of a lower, or work-wealth–based, sector which is internally stratified in terms of what can be bought. He contrasts it to an upper, or power-based, sector which is internally stratified in terms of differing access to specific prestige symbols. Both sectors articulate through wealth, which serves as a prestige symbol in the upper sector and as the principal means of mobility in the lower sector (Adams 1967:48). In the Sector of Cotacachi perceptions of social stratification seemed to be related almost totally to power-prestige, *palanca*; work-wealth, as a folk conceptual basis for social stratification, was rarely ever mentioned in either directed or undirected conversations.

Specified Palanca

Palanca may be referred to in specific terms, or it may be normative. On a specific level the word *palanca* was almost always modified with the prepositions *con*, with, and *para*, for, in order to. In contrast, when the word was used without these prepositions, we may assume that the speaker was referring to *palanca* in its normative form.

Specified *palanca* appears to be of two kinds, institutional and personal. An example of institutional *palanca* is that of the school teacher who had *palanca with* the director of education *in order to* have a new school built in the community in which she taught. It would be assumed that because of her position as a teacher she would have the institutional relationship with the director of education that would enable her to have the school built. This latter assumption would coincide with the normative degree of *palanca* which is generally ascribed to all teachers.

The other kind of specified *palanca* is personal. An example would be the rural agriculturalist who, through *compadrazgo*, had personal *palanca with* the director of public works in the province *in order to* get access to a bulldozer to grade the road into his community. His access to the bulldozer was exceptional, since it was assumed normatively that rural agriculturalists did not have the *palanca* to do such things.

There is much in the conceptualization of specified *palanca* which is analogous to, and at times overlaps with, a patron-client system. Where the two coincide most is in their function in the distribution of the society's goods and services. As Wolf (1966:17) has pointed out, patronage systems evolve in societies in which most goods and services are centralized, with their distribution to outlying areas both limited and irregular. To gain access to goods and services, one must have special connections with those who dispense them. When such connections are institutionalized, such as between a teacher and a director of education, the *palanca* which the teacher would have with the director in order to build a new school is considered part of a normal, professional relationship. On the other hand, when a person has a personal relationship of *palanca* with another individual which is not considered normative, the relationship would be described as one of patron to client. Such would be the case of the rural agriculturalist who would not normally have *palanca* with the director of public works but who, because of a personal relationship of *compadrazgo* is able to secure the loan of a bulldozer for his community.

Normative *palanca* is related to actions in the public domain, and as such is strongly associated with relationships based on occupation. However, as we have seen, such relationships may be modified through the personal actions of an individual. But it is normative conceptions of *palanca* which serve as a basis for the perceptions of social stratification in the Sector of Cotacachi.

Normative Palanca

When general, open-ended questions were directed to informants about *palanca*, it soon became apparent that all inhabitants of the Sector of Cotacachi could be defined in some manner in terms of *palanca*. They were generally categorized as possessing: a great deal of *palanca* (high access to goods and services); a good deal of *palanca* (middling access to goods and services); a little *palanca* (low access to goods and services); no *palanca* (no access to goods and services). These degrees of *palanca* were interpreted as the distinctive features that differentiated people from one another within the social hierarchy. As such, they were used as implicit markers, rather than explicit labels, of social categories.

To find out how people from the sector fit into the social hierarchy as defined by *palanca*, a group of 40 randomly selected persons from a variety of occupations and areas of the sector was asked in their first language, Spanish or Quichua, how they would define each individual as to degree of *palanca* possessed by that person. Another 42 informants, again randomly selected from a variety of occupations and areas of the sector, were asked the following open-ended series of questions in Spanish or in Quichua:

(1) Who would you say has a great deal of *palanca* here in the Sector of Cotacachi?
(2) Who would you say has a good deal of *palanca* here in the Sector of Cotacachi?
(3) Who would you say has a little *palanca* here in the Sector of Cotacachi?
(4) Who would you say has no *palanca* here in the Sector of Cotacachi?

Even though the two sets of questions associated with status reputation (Warner 1949:37) were asked differently, and to different informants, there was almost complete agreement in the placing of individuals in the same categories. When the question "Who would you say has a great deal of *palanca* here in the Sector of Cotacachi?" was asked, one of the first people mentioned was Don Luis, the mayor of the town of Cotacachi. And when other informants were asked to rank Don Luis as to degree of *palanca*, he inevitably was described as possessing a great deal of it. The two sets of questions, then, although asked differently, elicited the same information in their responses.

To determine how people ranked degree of possession of *palanca*, informants were asked the following questions:

(1) Who has more prestige, a person with a great deal of *palanca*, or one with a good deal of *palanca*?
(2) Who has more prestige, a person with a good deal of *palanca*, or one with a little *palanca*?
(3) Who has more prestige, a person with a little *palanca*, or one with no *palanca*?

In this way it was possible to place the varying degrees of *palanca* in a hierarchy, going from high prestige correlated with possession of a great deal of *palanca* to no prestige correlated with lack of *palanca*.

Social Stratification in the Sector of Cotacachi

Homogeneity of responses characterized our results whether the respondent was a resident of the most rural part of the sector living on a subsistence basis or was the supervisor of education for that part of the province. There was rarely any disagreement at all between informants as to the degree of *palanca* associated with an individual in the area or in the ranking of the various levels of *palanca*. This seems to indicate that there was enough communication between individuals living in the different parts of the sector that they could reach consensus as to the relationship between *palanca* and social status. It also seems to indicate that people stayed long enough in one stratum of the society that there was no confusion as to which category they belonged.

We turn now to the residents of the sector to see how they were classified. Those holding a high degree of *palanca* made up a small group consisting of the mayor of the town, the *jefe político*, the priest, and the local hacienda owners. Those who did not have as much *palanca*, yet still possessed a good deal of it, consisted of the local doctors, the sector's police, the professional agronomists managing some of the haciendas in the sector, the secretary to the *jefe político*, members of the town council, owners of stores including those producing and selling leather and brass goods, and carpenters and tailors living in the center of the town. Those with less *palanca* consisted of the sacristan of the church, owners of shops and bars in the barrios, tailors and carpenters established in the barrios, stonemasons, employees of the leather-making establishments and foundries, local livestock dealers, tractor drivers on the haciendas, and those small agriculturalists who had enough capital from surplus crops to be able to participate to a limited extent in a cash economy. Finally, those described as being generally without *palanca* were the largest group, consisting of agriculturalists living in the more isolated rural areas who were involved in a substantially subsistence-based economy.[3]

These groupings, as defined by *palanca*, form a pyramid with a small apex (those with a great deal of *palanca*) and a large base (those without *palanca*), as indicated in Figure 1. There is also an implicit urban-rural continuum here. Those at the apex of the pyramid are associated with the urban area of Cotacachi, as are those in the band just below them. Those in the next section generally lived in the barrios surrounding the town (including the livestock dealers and the tractor drivers, who worked in the countryside but lived in the barrios) or in the rural areas abutting the town. The group at the bottom of the pyramid was to be found in the most isolated rural areas of the sector. This urban-rural continuum in social ranking has been described in Peru by van den Berghe (1975:73). In Cotacachi those at the apex of the triangle had a great deal of *palanca* because they participated most in the national political, economic, and cultural life. As we go further down the pyramid we find that people participated less and less in the national life of the country, until we reach the lowest group, which is composed of those people who were most marginal to the national picture and lacked any *palanca*.

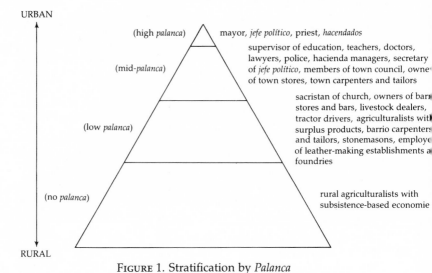

FIGURE 1. Stratification by *Palanca*

THE FOLK TAXONOMY OF ETHNICITY AND ITS RELATIONSHIP TO SOCIAL CATEGORIES

In the Sector of Cotacachi there is a variety of referential terms for individuals and groups, such as *runa, longo, natural, indígena, chulu, cholo, mishu, mestizo, blanco,* and *amu.*[4] The same person might be called *runa, longo, natural,* or *indígena,* the term differing according to the identity of the speaker. For example, a person who lived in a *comuna* in an isolated area might call himself *runa* but might be called *longo* by the tractor driver of the neighboring hacienda, *natural* by the manager of the hacienda, and *indígena* by the owner of the hacienda. The tractor driver himself would self-identify as *blanco* but be called *chulu* by an agricultural worker from the *comuna* and *cholo* by the manager and owner of the hacienda. The manager of the hacienda, too, would self-identify as *blanco* but would be called *mishu* by the worker from the *comuna, blanco* by the tractor driver, and *mestizo* by the owner of the hacienda. Finally, the owner of the hacienda would call himself *blanco,* as would the tractor driver and the manager of the hacienda, but the member of the *comuna* would call him *amu.* See Figure 2. The use of ethnic terms in this area is clearly contingent on the identities of the speaker as well as the person labeled.

In deciding to investigate further the terms used for referring to individual members of the community, it was necessary to return to the informants who had been questioned in the analysis of social

	Referent			
	Member of *Comuna*	Tractor Driver	Manager of Hacienda	Owner of Hacienda
Speaker Member of *comuna*	*runa*	*chulu*	*mishu*	*amu*
Tractor driver	*longo*	*blanco*	*blanco*	*blanco*
Manager of hacienda	*natural*	*cholo*	*blanco*	*blanco*
Owner of hacienda	*indígena*	*cholo*	*mestizo*	*blanco*

FIGURE 2. Referential terms.

stratification. They were asked how they would label, ethnically, the same individuals they had classified in terms of *palanca*. These labels, when used by those at the top and at the bottom of the social hierarchy, correlated almost perfectly with the social groupings based on the criteria of *palanca*, as indicated in Figure 3. However, agreement between ethnic labels and social groups was more disparate when the informant was a member of one of the middle levels, as indicated in Figure 4.

One who was identified as a *cholo* by a person at the apex of the social pyramid identified himself, and all those in the social hierarchy above him, as *blanco*; one who was identified as *mestizo* by a person at the apex of the social pyramid self-identified as *blanco* and labeled those in the social group above him by the same term. In both cases such individuals, when referring to themselves, were using the term that was the self-referent of those at the apex of the social structure and in so doing were collapsing their own ethnic category with those associated with the social strata above them. See Figure 4.

To better understand the criteria employed to make up the various ethnic labels, half of the informants were asked the following question: "How do you recognize a ———?" The other half was asked more specifically: "How do you know that ——— is a ———?" Almost all of the informants based their criteria for ethnic labeling on the following features: language (whether the person spoke Quichua or Spanish), dress (whether the person wore clothing made of homespun or of factory-produced cloth), and whether the person

FIGURE 3. Correlation between ethnic labels and social stratification.		
ETHNIC LABELS*		SOCIAL CLASSIFICATION

FIGURE 3. Correlation between ethnic labels and social stratification.

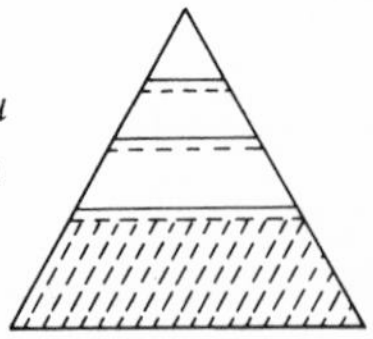

ETHNIC LABELS* — SOCIAL CLASSIFICATION

amu / mishu / chulu / runa — blanco / mestizo / cholo / indígena — high *palanca* / mid-*palanca* / low *palanca* / no *palanca*

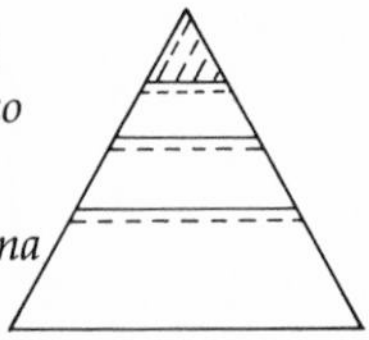

*Self-referent of speaker is underlined. Solid line indicates ethnic identification; broken line indicates class affiliation.

FIGURE 4. Correlation between ethnic labels and social stratification.

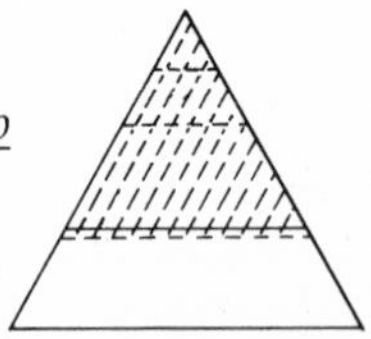

ETHNIC LABELS* — SOCIAL CLASSIFICATION

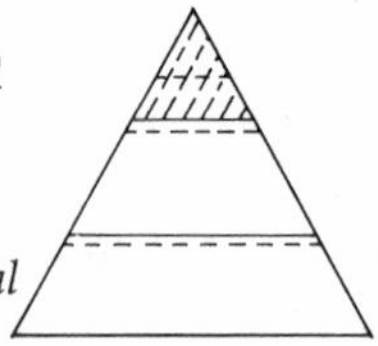

blanco / longo — blanco / cholo / natural — high *palanca* / mid-*palanca* / low *palanca* / no *palanca*

*Self-referent of speaker is underlined. Solid line indicates ethnic identification; broken line indicates class affiliation.

was *bien educado* or not. By *bien educado*, well educated, is meant not degree of formal education but degree of genteel behavior, based on personal qualities of generosity and courtesy, fashionable clothing and housing, refined manners, nondialectal speech, and access to national public and social life; this last factor overlaps with possession of *palanca*.

If an informant was a member of the highest or lowest category of the social hierarchy, he or she identified an individual as a *runa/indígena* if that person spoke Quichua, wore homespun clothing, but wasn't *bien educado*; a *chulu/cholo* was a person who spoke Quichua, wore clothing made of commercially produced cloth, but wasn't *bien educado*; a *mishu/mestizo* spoke Spanish only, wore clothing made of commercially produced cloth, yet wasn't *bien educado*; and an *amu/blanco* spoke Spanish only, wore clothing made of factory-produced cloth, and was *bien educado*.[5] See Figure 5.

FIGURE 5. Distinctive features—*runa/blanco* speaker.

	Speaks Quichua	Wears Homespun Clothing	*Bien Educado*
Speaker: *runa/blanco*			
runa/indígena	+	+	−
chulu/cholo	+	−	−
mishu/mestizo	−	−	−
amu/blanco	−	−	+

FIGURE 6. Distinctive features—*chulu/cholo* speaker.

	Speaks Quinchua	Wears Homespun Clothing	*Bien Educado*
Speaker: *chulu/cholo*			
*longo (runa/indígena)**	+	+	−
blanco (chulu/cholo)	−	−	+
blanco (mishu/mestizo)	−	−	+
blanco (amu/blanco)	−	−	+

FIGURE 7. Distinctive features—*mishu/mestizo* speaker.

	Speaks Quichua	Wears Homespun Clothing	*Bien Educado*
Speaker: *mishu/mestizo*			
*natural (runa/indígena)**	+	+	−
cholo (chulu/cholo)	+	−	−
blanco (mishu/mestizo)	−	−	+
blanco (amu/blanco)	−	−	+

*Labels within parentheses refer to those used by the lowest and highest groups in the social hierarchy.

Both the middle groups in the social hierarchy used the same criteria for defining the various ethnic groups, yet in a somewhat different way. For example, a *chulu/cholo* removed the boundaries used to separate him from the ethnic groups above him in the definitions made by those of the highest and lowest social categories. This was done by denying that he spoke Quichua and asserting that he was *bien educado*. See Figure 6. For example, a tractor driver asserted: "We *blancos* aren't like the *longos*. We don't speak their language, we speak Spanish. But besides that, they're not *bien educado*. They're not even rational." The person in question, although denying that he spoke Quichua to the anthropologist and to the school teacher accompanying her, was overheard speaking the language with the laborers with whom he was working. The same occurred with a barrio store owner who, after waiting on a customer and conversing with him in Quichua, denied that she spoke the language and asserted: "Only the *longos* speak Quichua. We *blancos* speak only Spanish." Later she added: "The *longos* simply aren't rational people. They're not cultured. They're different from us *blancos*. They're not *bien educado*." In their definitions of the putative ethnic group occupying the social strata below them, as contrasted to their own self-definition, both the tractor driver and the store keeper identified themselves as *blancos*, asserting that they spoke only Spanish and were *bien educado*, qualities of the self-identifying *blancos* above them.

Where the *chulu/cholo* identified himself ethnically as a *blanco* by asserting that he did not speak Quichua and was *bien educado*, the *mishu/mestizo* identified himself with those at the apex of the social hierarchy by asserting that he was *bien educado* and by labeling himself *blanco*. See Figure 7. The wife of a policeman asserted: "We *blancos* aren't like the *cholos* who live in the outlying neighborhoods. We're *bien educados*. For them, their life is there in their neighborhood. They're content to work during the week in order to get drunk over the weekends." While the woman was speaking, her husband was drinking heavily with his friends, engaging in the same behavior that she had criticized in speaking of the *cholos*. By denying a behavior which might link her with a category she considered to lack prestige, she negated any possible identification with them. At the same time she asserted that she was *bien educada*, and a *blanca*, and in so doing identified herself with members of a more prestigious group, those at the apex of the social hierarchy.

In studies of social stratification it has often been noted that there is a tendency to minimize distinctions between groups immediately above one's own and to maximize differences below (Davis, Gardner, and Gardner 1941:71–73). In Cotacachi members of the middle groups did not discriminate ethnically between themselves and those above them but did rigidly maintain boundaries between themselves and those below them. Those at the apex of the social hierarchy were content to be where they were. They were the most powerful members of the social structure, and generally the most wealthy. There was no reason for them to move into another social or ethnic category. This is evident in the exceptional endogamy in their marriage patterns. At the other extreme, those who formed the base of the social hierarchy also had no wish to move into another ethnic category. They had an extremely strong ethnic identity which they were intent upon maintaining. In addition, they were actively discouraged either from marrying outside the group or otherwise from leaving it. Those in the middle were anxious to move upward into the ethnic categories above them. They actively solicited marriage partners for their children from the more prestigious groups above them while discouraging the selection of mates from those below them, or, in the case of the *chulu/cholos*, often from among their own group. This drive for upward mobility was most overtly indicated by their refusal to use the ethnic labels used by the other groups to differentially tag them. The wish by the middle groups to separate themselves from those below was manifest through maintenance of ethnic labels that distinguished those less prestigious individuals from themselves. Barth (1969:15) observed that:

> The identification of another person as a fellow member of an ethnic group implies a sharing of criteria for evaluation and judgment. It thus entails the assumption that the two are fundamentally "playing the same game," and this means that there is between them a potential for diversification and expansion of the relationship to cover eventually all different sectors and domains of activity. On the other hand, a dichotomization of others as strangers, as members of another ethnic group implies a recognition of limitations of shared understandings, differences in criteria for judgment of value and performance, and a restriction of interaction to sectors of assumed common understanding and mutual interest.

In the case of the middle sectors of the social hierarchy of Cotacachi, this dichotomization was accomplished by manipulating the distinctive features that made up ethnic categories so as to separate themselves from members of less respected social and ethnic groups while identifying with the more prestigious sectors of the society.

To conclude, we find in the Sector of Cotacachi that: (1) social classification and stratification were based primarily on *palanca*, leverage or access to goods and services, or potential power; (2) ethnic and social categories were most closely correlated with one another by members at the uppermost and lowermost strata of the social hierarchy, and at least closely correlated by members of the middle; and (3) when individuals wish to move upward socially, they use the same ethnic labels to refer to themselves as they do to refer to those *above* them, while at the same time maintaining different labels for those *below* them. In short, a person's position within the social structure affects his interpretation of other domains, in particular that of ethnic identity.

NOTES

Acknowledgments: This article is based on data gathered between 1972 and 1977. During this period I was affiliated with the Programa de Educación Bilingüe in Cotacachi, under the auspices of the Ministerio de Educación Pública and the Instituto Inter-Andino de Desarrollo. I wish to thank the people of Cotacachi who served as my informants, as well as Joseph B. Casagrande, Donald W. Wilworth, Laura Goldman, Pam Hunte, Judith T. Irvine, Theodore Macdonald, Jr., Grace Schubert, Arnold Strickon, and Norman E. Whitten, Jr., for their helpful comments on earlier drafts of this paper. However, full responsibility for the views and interpretations presented here is my own.

1. Studies of folk classification have emphasized botanical, zoological, numerical, color, ethnomedical, and kinship taxonomies (Conklin 1972); there has been a general lack of ethnoscientific studies dealing with the domains of social stratification and ethnic identification. The few exceptions include Moerman (1965), Sanjek (1977), Silverman (1966), and Strickon (1967).

2. "Sector of Cotacachi" refers to the geographical area which is denoted as "la Jurisdicción de Cotacachi" in the national census of Ecuador of 1974 (Oficina de Censos Nacionales 1975).

3. There are gradations within each of these categories. In the cagegory defined by mid-*palanca*, the local supervisor of education would have more *palanca* than one of the sector's school teachers and thus more prestige. Discussion of gradations within the larger units of social stratification lies outside the scope of this paper.

4. These terms were used nonpejoratively to label other individuals as well as for self-identification. There is also a full range of words, which at times overlap with some of those mentioned above, which may be used in a derogatory manner to denote an individual's ethnic, or presumed ethnic, background.

5. Those labeled *runa/indígena* occupy the most rural areas of the sector; those labeled *chulu/cholo* occupy the rural areas and barrios at the edge of the town of Cotacachi; those labeled *mishu/mestizo* live in the town, as do those labeled *amu/blanco*, who might also reside in Quito. Thus any change in social or ethnic category must in all probability entail a move away from one's place of origin toward a more urban locale.

REFERENCES CITED

Adams, Richard N.
   1967   *The Second Sowing: Power and Secondary Development in Latin America.*
          Chicago: Chandler.

Barth, Fredrik, ed.
  1969 *Ethnic Groups and Boundaries: The Social Organization of Cultural Differ-*
        ence. Boston: Little, Brown.
Basile, David G.
  1974 *Tillers of the Andes: Farmers and Farming in the Quito Basin.* Chapel
        Hill: University of North Carolina Studies in Geography 8.
Casagrande, Joseph B.
  1974 Strategies for Survival: The Indians of Highland Ecuador. In Dwight
        Heath, ed., *Contemporary Cultures and Societies of Latin America.* 2d
        ed. New York: Random House, pp. 93–107.
Conklin, Harold C.
  1972 *Folk Classification: A Topically Arranged Bibliography of Contemporary*
        and Background References through 1971. New Haven, Conn.: Depart-
        ment of Anthropology, Yale University.
Davis, Allison, Burleigh B. Gardner, and Mary A. Gardner
  1941 *Deep South: A Social-Anthropological Study of Caste and Class.* Chicago:
        University of Chicago Press.
Moerman, Michael
  1965 Ethnic Identification in a Complex Civilization. Who Are the Lue?
        American Anthropologist 67 (5):1215–30.
Oficina de Censos Nacionales
  1975 *Compendio de Información Socio-Económica de las Provincias del Ecuador,*
        vol. 2: *Imbabura.* Quito.
Sampedro V., Francisco
  1975–76 *Atlas Geográfico del Ecuador.* Quito.
Sanjek, Roger
  1977 Cognitive Maps of the Ethnic Domain in Urban Ghana: Reflections
        on Variability and Change. *American Ethnologist* 4 (4):603–22.
Silverman, Sydel F.
  1966 An Ethnographic Approach to Social Stratification in a Central Ital-
        ian Community. *American Anthropologist* 68 (4): 899–921.
Strickon, Arnold
  1967 Folk Models of Stratification, Political Ideology, and Socio-Cultural
        Systems. *Sociological Review Monographs* 11:93–117.
van den Berghe, Pierre L.
  1974 The Use of Ethnic Terms in the Peruvian Social Science Literature.
        In Pierre L. van den Berghe, ed., *Class and Ethnicity in Peru.* Leiden:
        Brill, pp. 12–22.
  1975 Ethnicity and Class in Highland Peru. In Leo A. Despres, ed., *Eth-*
        nicity and Resource Competition in Plural Societies. The Hague: Mouton,
        pp. 71–86.
Warner, W. Lloyd
  1949 *Social Class in America: A Manual of Procedure for the Measurement of*
        Social Status. Chicago: Science Research Associates.
Wolf, Eric R.
  1966 Kinship, Friendship, and Patron-Client Relations in Complex Socie-
        ties. In Michael Banton, ed., *The Social Anthropology of Complex Socie-*
        ties. London: Tavistock, pp. 1–22.

14

Ethnicity and Alternative Identification: An Example from Cañar

Niels Fock

The theme of the eighth Nordic conference of anthropologists covered a wide field, ranging from cultural imperialism to cultural identity, from the mechanism of mass culture to the identity of individuals. I will try to bring these divergent themes together by choosing a central starting point, the ethnic group. There is reason to suppose that the ethnic group is the natural object of study for the anthropologist, and that it should be on this basis that cultural imperialism and other influences should be evaluated.

The question which Salvador Palomino Flores and I addressed in a previous article (Fock and Palomino 1973) was the following: how is it possible for quite a large number of Latin America communities, ranging from Mexico to Bolivia, to preserve and continue their Indian tradition—to survive as an ethnic group—in spite of an immensely powerful Spanish influence of national and imperialistic character? We found the answer in what we characterized as the Indians' seeming acceptance of the institutions introduced by the Spanish, such as Catholicism with the *compadrazgo* system, the *cargo*-fiesta system, the *vara*-authority system, and the patron-client and market system. As to the whole area it appeared characteristic to us that the indigenous local communities had adopted the enforced system far more willingly and wholeheartedly than could be expected. It was remarkable, too, that the evident exploitation which was exercised from ecclesiastical quarters at the same time gave occasion to an Indian transformation into a rich ritual life, which was capable of maintaining the most dominant Indian symbols.

If we take the view that culture is to be understood as a system of communication, which both verbally and nonverbally articulates the value norms of the ethnic group in varying situations, then we can say that, analytically, the enforced Spanish institutions can be seen as possessing partly a plane of expression and partly a plane of content. The Indians adopted the plane of expression of the systems but redefined the content in accordance with traditional ideas. It would probably have meant physical extinction for the Indians had they not formally accepted the systems (e.g., Catholicism); had they adopted both the content and the expressive forms, it would have meant cultural destruction. The cultural defense has thus been based structurally on a strategy which can be described as superficial, or shallow, acceptance.

The enforced institutions act as broker institutions between the local level and the national level. A cognitive transformation takes place within the institution itself depending on whether it is viewed from the national level or from within the ethnic group (see, e.g., Osborne 1968). Ann Osborne's (1968) work on *compadrazgo* relations obtaining among the Coaiquer of southern Colombia provides an illustrative model. The *mestizos*, representing the national level, view *compadre* relations as a sort of patronage, a hierarchical taxonomic system of quantitative nature. The Indians, by contrast, view the very same *compadre* relation within the framework of a mechanical kinship model determined by two variables, as a paradigmatic system in which the categories are qualitatively different.

These two conceptually different models explain in a satisfying manner the *compadre* relations as a set of relations which, for the Indians, are necessary but burdensome but which, for the *mestizos*, are means to a greater or lesser economic exploitation.

With this example in mind, the classification of the categories became essential to an understanding of the mutual relations between the ethnic groups. We found that the same distinction between one-dimensional taxonomic and two-dimensional paradigmatic classification was essential for the analysis of the political problems in the Andes today.

Concerning the folk categories, the model used "from within" was different from the model in use "from without." From without, viewed from the national level, the Andes population was conceived of as divided in classes, the number of which depended on one's own place in the hierarchy. On the whole, these classes are constituted by the *blancos*, the *mestizos*, the *cholos*, and the *Indians*. The *mestizos* and the *cholos* are looked upon as mixtures only quantitatively different, fitting into a scale model of vertical stratification that expresses a continuous decline with regard to western influence (see Figure 1). Looked upon from within, from the Indian group, the picture is quite different; the hierarchical one-dimensionality has been replaced by a

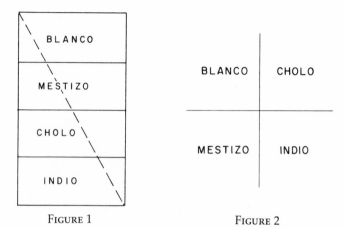

FIGURE 1   FIGURE 2

two-dimensional system, which means, fundamentally, that the folk categories are essentially different.

Palomino and I did not fully perceive the distinctive traits of this paradigm, but I now realize that they are based on a principle of descent and a principle of locality respectively. The horizontal line of Figure 2 expresses the difference between the lower local and the upper nonlocal or national categories; the vertical line divides between Indian descent (to the right) and non-Indian, or postulated white, descent (to the left).

The fact that the *mestizos* and the Indians, both parts meeting at the local level, have different models as a basis for their strategies has far-reaching consequences. In general, it can be said that the *mestizos*, according to the one-dimensional class model, tend to define disagreements as conflicts of interests about land or political power. The Indians, on the other hand, perceiving themselves as an ethnic group, articulate discrepancies chiefly as unbridgeable conflicts of values concerning cultural norms, symbols, and ideology.

GEOGRAPHY, TOPOGRAPHY, AND SOCIAL STRUCTURE

From September 1973 to August 1974 I carried out fieldwork among the Cañar Indians of Ecuador to try to verify these points. I took up residence in an indigenous community, Juncal, situated in the northern part of the Cañar basin. The community is the smallest of all basins in Ecuador. It is also situated highest up in the mountains, at an altitude of 3,000 meters above sea level. The total population amounts to 70,000, about half of which are Indians and the

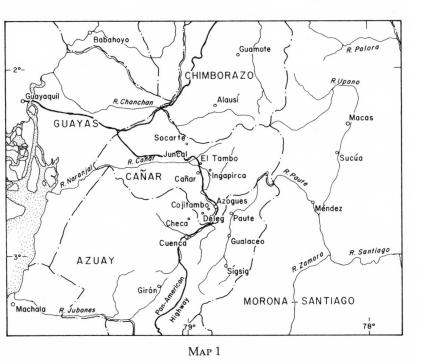

MAP 1

other half *mestizos*. There are very few whites living on the estates or in the town, and *cholos*, deculturated Indians, are likewise found only as dispersed individuals (see Map 1).

The two groups in question are therefore the Indians and the *mestizos*; in some of the hundred or so local communities they are evenly distributed, while in others there are very few of one category. Comuna de Juncal, which constitutes one-third of the entire Juncal parish, is inhabited by some 800 Indians and about 50 *mestizos*. Comuna de Juncal is bounded to the west and east by the neighboring communities of Charcay and San Antonio respectively; to the north lies the *páramo* (4,000 meters above sea level), and to the south the Culebrillas River bounds the entire parish at an altitude of 2,400 meters (see Map 2).

I will now trace some of the more important consequences of the territorial and spatial divisions of Juncal, and illustrate how its basically dualistic character derives from the irrigation system with its principle of diversion and bifurcation. The question of water means one or two yields per year, and thereby is—in a densely populated area with about 200 persons per square kilometer—a question of life

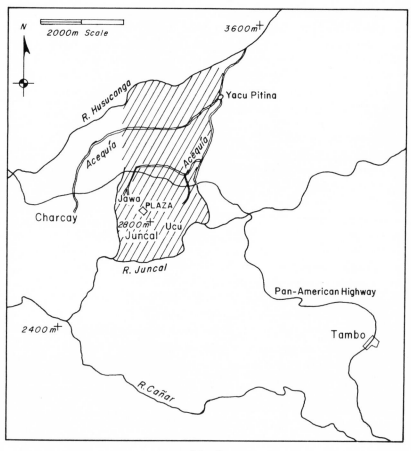

MAP 2

or death. The allocation of water is not, however, centrally regulated or controlled, because the society does not possess the authority necessary for the handling of such conflicts as would arise. It is noticeable, however, that the *mestizos* tend to occupy leading positions; at the annual rinsing of the canals, for instance, they act as overseers—naturally, they think, because of their "greater intelligence." It also appears that the Indians accept this state of affairs because it solves for them a segmentary dilemma. This is due to the fact that Comuna de Juncal on the one side is divided in two localized groupings, *jawa*, upper, above, superior, and *ucu*, lower, below, inferior. But on the other side Comuna de Juncal stands in an analogous opposition to the neighboring community of Charcay.

The irrigation water is diverted from the Río Huallcanga, which in the *páramo* flows to the north of Juncal about 700 meters higher than Río Culebrillas. Where the canal hits the northeastern corner of Comuna de Juncal, it bifurcates at Yacu Pitina; the right branch is led farther on to Charcay, and the left branch falls steeply into the inhabited areas of Comuna de Juncal. This branch bifurcates again into an upper branch, which leads on westward, and a lower one which falls toward the south.

We now see that the area which is watered by the upper and right branch is *jawa* territory and that which is watered by the lower and left branch is *ucu* territory. Thus we may conclude that it is the partition of the water that gives rise to the sociopolitical segmentation and the existing oppositions.

An irrigation system in a politically weakly organized society will always create problems of mutual suspicion regarding both the consumption of water and the fulfillment of obligations of maintenance of the canals. However, *jawa* and *ucu* hold the part of the canal up to Yacu Pitina in common, and they therefore have to act in solidarity vis-à-vis Charcay. Furthermore, once a year the people of Charcay and Comuna de Juncal meet at Yacu Pitina in order to cooperate in the rinsing of the main canal up to Río Huallcanga. It can be argued that these specific local circumstances and the general properties of an irrigation system combine to produce the ambivalent attitudes that govern the relations between the segments of Charcay and Comuna de Juncal and the subsegments of *jawa* and *ucu*.

The inhabitants of *ucu* territory, who live in the southeast part of the area, entertain a deep-rooted suspicion of the people of *jawa* territory; they say that the Juncalese of *jawa* consider themselves superior to the people of *ucu*, that they are probably richer and have more land. The situation, however, is one of mutual suspicion, and one result is that people are very reluctant to visit each other's part of the *comuna* when there is a feast going on, as the consumption of alcohol often leads to fighting. Now, taken as a whole, *jawa* territory does not lie at a higher altitude than *ucu* territory and we are thus presented with a purely social convention expressed in a spatial idiom.

A similar asymmetrical structure is repeated in the relation between two of the three divisions of the parish of Juncal: Charcay and Comuna Juncal. Charcay is regarded as superior to Comuna Juncal but, topographically, they are at the same level. Charcay, however, is characterized as *blanco* (white, i.e., with many *mestizos*), even though the majority of its population is Indian, related to the Indians of Comuna Juncal. The third division of the parish, San Antonio, is completely dominated by white haciendas and in comparison, therefore, Charcay appears relatively non*blanco*. The label *blanco* here expresses the general acceptance of social superiority.

It is now possible to elucidate further the structure of the territory of Comuna Juncal. Besides the two primary categories *jawa* and *ucu*, there are two others, one which is both *jawa* and *ucu* and one which is neither *jawa* nor *ucu*. The *jawa* and *ucu* category comprises primarily the area from Yacu Pitina down to the bifurcation of the canals; a secondary *jawa* and *ucu* area is also established around the drainage of the two main branches of the canal from the plaza down toward Ramran-Huaycu, which is the most important—though by far not the only—drainage which runs to Río Culebrillas and farther to Río Cañar.

Northeast of the plaza there is a ridge, Warawin, that cannot be irrigated and therefore only yields once a year. This ridge belongs to the neither-*jawa*-nor-*ucu* category and two characteristic functions seem to be associated with it. First, it is the place of the cemetery, in the present Catholic era as well as (as far as I can tell) in prehistoric Cañar times. Second, it is the place where the ritual sling-fights were fought; the place name of the cemetery is Waracana (*waraca* means sling).

In Juncal we can then clearly draw a line from northeast to southwest over Yacu Pitina, Warawin, the plaza, and Ramran-Huaycu, a line that divides *jawa* territory from *ucu* territory. The territory along the line itself is a sort of no-man's-land, or no-man's-water-land, and the *mestizos* of the colonial period seem to have taken advantage of this fact. The traditional and the most frequently used entry into the Juncal area is a path that runs exactly from San Antonio over Warawin, and so it is no accident that the plaza is situated on this line in both the *jawa* and *ucu* territory. A former plaza was situated on the same line, only a little farther to the southwest. The *mestizos*, then, have squeezed in between the two territories and thus have been able to exploit the situation of latent conflict between *jawa* and *ucu*.

ETHNICITY AND COGNITIVE ORDERING

The Indians and the *mestizos* have essentially different conceptions of their territorial (spatial) placing which is of fundamental importance for the two groups. The *mestizos* see themselves as part of a wider network of communication manifested by the Pan-American Highway, to which they are linked by a new side road from the locality of Empalme (which means precisely "connection").

They therefore feel marginally situated, but they seek comfort from the fact that the Runas are still more peripheral in relation to the metropolis. The Runas, on the other hand, regard themselves as living in the center; they live in a social community and so constitute a self-sufficient "group-structure," while the *mestizos* are clearly a rather unimportant link in an impersonal "series-structure" (to adopt Sartre's usage of these terms). A *mestizo* who told the story of his life stressed that he had well-off relatives in Cuenca (the largest city in southern Ecuador) but that he himself had come off rather badly because his father had married here in Cañar. One perceives hierarchical and historical undertones which are very far from the ecological foundation of the Runas.

As a consequence of these two very different cosmologies, the relationship between *mestizos* and Runas is loaded with misunderstandings. The strategic position of the *mestizos* on the plaza appears to function as a double-edged sword. Even though it was possible for them to penetrate the area along the invisible line dividing *jawa* and *ucu* territory, it has, on the other hand, been impossible for them to establish the plaza as a parochical center. The Runas from *jawa* and *ucu* territories meet in church for the mass but they drift away again to their respective domains, and they never willingly cross the plaza on their way somewhere else. This is, of course, also due to the fact that the *mestizos* are generally hated because they act as overlords in exercising their various administrative offices, but it is just as much rooted in the traditional observation of a borderline which is itself avoided. *Mestizos* by their localization belong to both *jawa* and *ucu* territories and thereby constitute a superior category. As a result, *mestizos* may be employed as mediators in order to terminate the conflicts between people of *jawa* territory and *ucu* territory because they are regarded as principally disinterested. At times it can be rather grotesque to witness Runas involved in disputes over inheritance call in a *mestizo* to guarantee a correct procedure in the winding up and dividing of the estate. The *mestizos* demand both money and gifts to carry out this task, and one's first thought is that the *mestizos* are exploiting the Runas. From one point of view this is so, but the Runas have asked the *mestizo* to act because the likelihood of reaching an agreement without the help of a mediator is minimal owing to the strong and permanent suspicion between *jawa* and *ucu* territories. It may as well be said, then, that the Runas use the *mestizo* as a pawn in their own private game, in which he does not otherwise participate and which he does not understand.

We have to bear in mind here that, on the national level, it is cus-

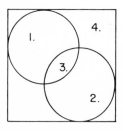

FIGURE 3

tomary to classify *mestizos* and Runas together as the rural proletariat, *campesinos*. The *mestizos* employ a two-class classification, *blancos* and *indios*. They classify themselves as *blancos* and, relating to a center-periphery model, they see it as their right to politically dominate and economically exploit the more "peripheral" Runas. The *mestizos* thus employ a hierarchical and quantitative model which allows them to profit by the inequality which is present in the relationship between themselves and the Runas (see Fock and Palomino 1973). As might be expected, this is not the way the Runas see the situation. The Juncalese Runas' view of their situation may be fairly precisely illustrated by a Venn diagram (Figure 3). The Runas are either 1 or 2, either *jawa* or *ucu*, while the *mestizos* are marginal, category 3. What happens, then, is that the Runas regard the *mestizos* as belonging to a totally different category. Their mutual relation is one of difference rather than of inequality, and the Runas do not, therefore, see themselves as involved in any competition with the *mestizos*. For them the relation is either one of symbiosis or of complete segregation. The position of the *mestizos* on the plaza is an exact expression of these two kinds of relations. Either the Runas avoid them or they use them in the positions which are inaccessible to themselves as a result of their dualistic structure.

Referring to a previous paper (Fock and Palomino 1973), I shall generalize the situation illustrated by the above Venn diagram. What emerges is a paradigm, the four categories of which are characterized as follows: 1 and 2 are either-or, 3 is both-and, and 4 is neither-nor. This paradigm provides an unequivocal description of the ethnic groups in Cañar, and it holds for the entire Andes region. As will be remembered, the relation between Charcay and Juncal is similar to that which obtains between *jawa* and *ucu*, but the people of Charcay were classed as *blancos* by the Juncalese.

Blancos in the narrow sense of the term are called *ame*, referring predominantly to the white *hacendados*. The *mestizos* are called *chazo*. The concept of *cholo* exists here under the name of *ruto*, a category

AMO	RUTO
1.	4.
CHAZO	RUNA
3.	2.

FIGURE 4

the members of which are racially Indian but who have departed from the Indian way of life; the *rutos* are attempting to carve a niche for themselves in an external, national context. We find, then, that *ruto* corresponds closely to the category of our Venn diagram. *Rutos* are neither *jawa* nor *ucu* because they do not make common cause with the local population (they are employed mostly outside Juncal), and in the larger perspective they are neither *amo* nor Runa (see Figure 4).

NATIONALITY AND ETHNICITY

I shall now move from Latin America to find a reasonable and useful general definition of ethnic group and ethnicity. Obviously such a definition must include imperialism and the global system. If one takes a look at the natural positions into which a human being is born, it must be a question of a hierarchy from humanity over nationality and ethnicity to personality. Humanity and personality close the system, and I shall deal here with nationality and ethnicity.

Ethnicity is understood here as the cultural articulation of the ethnic group; since the ethnic group today is looked upon unambiguously as a subsystem within a larger system, for instance the national system, it is the power relations between the dominated subsystem and the dominating national system which determine the way of articulation of the ethnic group.

Abner Cohen (1974) stresses the point that ethnic groups as subsystems within a nation are created by increased interaction between the groups, and not by isolation. The ethnicity expressed by the group is to be understood as a cultural consciousness vis-à-vis the dominating culture. Consequently, he considers ethnicity as a political phenomenon and the symbolic stress on tradition and continuity as an articulation of a specific political affiliation.

Cohen also emphasizes the fact that ethnic groups are weak and informal in their organizations. Precisely because of their informal character, they must make use of a highly developed symbol system to solve the organizational problems of the group. One only has to think of the symbolic mobilization taking place, for instance, in revivalistic religious movements (which are called prepolitical) to see how they serve political aims.

The fact that many peasant groups have endogamous inclinations, thereby tending toward bilateral descent systems of the network type, encourages such mobilization in the absence of a firm organizing device. The kinship relations are often extended by way of ritual kinship such as *compadrazgo* and through elaborated friendship relations, which support group solidarity on an informal basis. It is Cohen's opinion that ethnic groups can change their character to merely regional groups, provided that their organizational forms become externally formalized.

If we look at the Cañar area, with its *mestizos* and Indians, it is clear that the Indians must be characterized as an ethnic group and the *mestizos* as a regional group. The *mestizos* subscribe to the value norms of the Ecuadorian middle class and consequently express themselves in an symbol system essentially different from that used by the Indians. But contrary to Cohen, I do not think that these two symbol systems articulate themselves with reference to the same political power. The two groups have far from the same political goals, and so it is of vital importance to analyze the kind of political power relations that each of the two groups expresses.

If we make use of Cohen's two dimensions, the political and the symbolic, it is possible to view the situation of the *mestizos* as being one in which a merging takes place and thereby to consider them as one-dimensional. As they pre-embedded in a class system, they are also included in the upper level of the hierarchy (the elite of the nation), the objectives of which have validity also for the *mestizos* on the local level. The attitude of the *mestizos* to cultural imperialism is that they cannot get enough of it! They want the priest and the school teacher to take up residence in the community, and they throw themselves open to the greater society in relation to which they feel marginal.

In the economic and the political fields the situation is such that, though poor and weak, the *mestizos* are far better off than the Indians, because they are themselves in charge of regional-level nationalist exploitation through which they exercise authority at the local level. *Mestizos* can evade the burdens of the tithe duty and avoid unfavorable terms of trade or adverse legal proceedings. The reason why they feel impoverished and powerless is not to be found in the system itself but only in the national fact that they are far from its power center.

If the regional *mestizos* are to be conceived as one-dimensional, then two-dimensionality is precisely characteristic of the Indians. Although this refers to the two systems, the political and the symbolic, my conclusion will be different from that of Cohen. The structural trait which I find primarily characteristic of ethnic groups is their potential for alternative identification and classification. What I mean is simply that—speaking of the Cañar Indians—the group has two different possibilities for placing itself within humanity. First, Indians can consider themselves as a rural population in a region within the Ecuadorian nation. Second, they can identify with all neighboring Indian groups, on through the adjacent Quechua-speaking peoples in Peru, and farther on to the whole indigenous Andes population. The two corresponding designations are *campesino* and Runa respectively.

In the case of the group of Cañar Indians which I studied, there is no doubt about their identity: they identify as Runas. But they do so only through their symbol system, for they are unambigously subject to the Ecuadorian power structure, regardless of their own wishes. The variable for defining ethnic groups is thus the symbol system. The national symbolic identification is a latent possibility for Ecuadorian Indians, and for most groups it reveals itself through the process of national integration or incorporation wherein the groups lose one indigenous dimension and are incorporated in the one-dimensional national class system. What takes place in "cholification" as a first step toward "mestization" is that the *cholo* first turns his back on his traditional indigenous symbol system, goes through a phase of dislocalization, and emerges a "regional" *mestizo*.

The alternative symbolic identification seems to be a general principle for ethnic groups. For example, Greenlanders can choose a Danish identity within humanity. Alternatively, they can choose a general identity which is based on Eskimo culture and, together with the Canadian Eskimos and the Canadian Indians, express a pan-indigenous, nonnational identification. The same holds true for the Lapps. At the national level, Denmark herself shows the same features of ethnicity when our self-identification in ideological matters is an obstacle to political solidarity with the European Economic Community and instead goes round by Scandinavia. In this example nationality is a special case of ethnicity.

CULTURE AND ETHNICITY

It should be clear by now that I consider ethnicity a quantitative conception, where the intensity and conformity of the symbolic system have to be seen in its relation to the political system. But whereas the national political system is clearly and unequivocally expressed, the symbolic system is complex and unwieldy. We must, therefore, try to uncover its significance.

In general, ethnic groups are defined as cultural groups, and Isajiw (1974) compared 27 different definitions of synthetic character to find an acceptable determination. The attributes most frequently used, and those given the greatest importance, are common descent, common culture, common religion, common race, and common language. There are qualitative differences among these attributes, especially in that the ethnic group is one of the identities into which one is born. I therefore insist, as does Keyes (1976), on the significant attribute that supports and symbolizes the *principle of descent*. The important thing is not the biological or genealogical fact of descent but *cultural consciousness* of this idea.

The structuring principle for an ethnic group is a cultural counterpart to the concept of species. One is born into it, it shows tendencies to endogamy, and ethnic groups are, in principle, distinct and equal. The boundary between ethnic groups lies in the areas where the mutual differences within the group are suppressed at the expense of stressing the differences between the groups.

Two basic elements for ethnic groups as analogous to species are the body and the name. Body refers to the physical characteristics which are culturally accentuated and which need not have to do with biological race. We find this, of course, in such designations as *blanco* (the whites) and partly in *mestizos* (the mixed), but the culturally shaped distinctions such as long hair braided in pigtails which characterizes the Runa in Cañar are more important. What separates the Indians from each other in local communities is, next to hair style, elements of costume which symbolically articulate physical differences. A subtle semiological code acts as a substitute for a genetic one. *Mestizos*, who are simply badly dressed in an anonymous western style, in a similar manner articulate their position in a class society.

The name is also an essential identity marker for the ethnic group; in the case of the Cañari the word *runa* means man, besides being the designation for a person and for the ethnic group. The set of personal names used by a group also reflects its position, but in this matter the Cañar Indians show a sort of negative confirmation. Through the political system the use of a Christian first name has imposed on them names which are culturally alien. Consequently, the Cañar people hardly ever use their first names as prescribed; they partly quichuacize them (Geronomo = Gerucho, Andrea = Andica, Gregorio = Rigucho), they frequently exchange name identities, and some simply forget the Catholic name received at baptism.

The *mestizos* of Juncal generally know the names of the Indians, but they seldom use them. In addressing the Indians they often use words like *hijito*, little son, and it is characteristic to refer metaphorically to an ethnic group as children. I believe that this usage, which also clearly expresses a paternalistic attitude, refers to a classificatory dilemma as well. The potential and efficiency of a child are less than that of an adult, but at the same time the child is different by virtue of its irrational behavior.

I now return to the starting point of this part of the discussion to uncover the signification of the symbol system. I have tried to show that the variety of cultural attributes characteristic of an ethnic group refers to the idea of common descent. The two-dimensionality of the ethnic group is therefore expressed as an intersection of the political power relations and the symbolic descent relations. The political system expands regionally from the side of the nation and the global system, while descent can trace its course around the nation, the state, and a certain culture area up to humanity. The two dimensions thus express chiefly spatial and temporal perspectives respectively.

ETHNICITY AND CULTURAL IMPERIALISM

I shall now try to generalize the paradigm, which I earlier worked out by means of theoretical considerations on the concept of "ethnic group." Most important for me has been the objectification of the paradigm which has taken place. In the course of the analysis the emphasis has shifted from a model of an unconscious structure among Indians of the Andes to a logical necessity as a consequence of the possibility for alternative identification and two-dimensionality. We can immediately replace Runa with ethnic group, *blanco* with nationally dominant group, and *mestizo* with regional group; for lack of a more precise term, we can for the time being designate *cholo* as marginal group (see Figure 2). The whole set can be said to represent modern Ecuador, and we will see that the left and the right columns of Figure 5 respectively represent descent systems for those who maintain white ancestry and those who are of Indian ancestry.

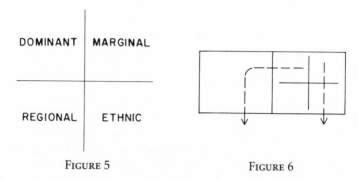

FIGURE 5   FIGURE 6

Facing the dominant white conquest culture, it appears natural that the Indians through their symbol system express identity by means of their alternative identification. The one-dimensionality of the *mestizos* is due to the fact that power and descent coincide, while the two-dimensionality among the Indians can be illustrated as a two-way communication, or combination, in space and time (see Figure 6).

There are, therefore, two possible causes for the decline of ethnicity; the negative one is that, as Indian, one denies the Indian heritage (as in cases from the Andes and the Incas), thereby placing oneself marginally as *cholo*. The positive cause rests in the desire to affirm one's regional affiliation, which could take place in a solidarization with the *mestizos* as, for instance, in a class struggle. In the Cañar area there are at present no definite signs of either of these two possibilities for declining ethnicity; a prerequisite for that would be a quite new and hitherto unknown Indian polity.

I am of the opinion, however, that declining ethnicity must be equivalent to what has been called cultural imperialism. This concept seems to lack a precise definition because, among other things, its composition of words implies a clear contradiction: the analytical incompatibility of conflicts of interests and conflicts of values. The only way to use the concept of cultural imperialism is as a measure for the cultural influences to which an ethnic group is subject from the dominant national elite culture by virtue of the prevailing power system. As previously mentioned, I do not regard the *mestizos*, as a regional group, to be exposed to cultural imperialism. They are certainly subordinate within a political system which originates in the white elite, but their descent ideology, which is within the power structure, legitimizes the cultural influences from above.

It is quite another matter with the Runa ethnic state in Juncal. The national power structure affects them through *mestizos* and results in a series of organized institutions. These institutions automatically bring cultural goods that influence their symbolic system, which had its roots outside the nation. One example is the evangelical medical mission, which is legalized nationally for political reasons but which functions in two ways beyond its medical charter. On the one side, it undermines the Indians' own disease theory according to which cold and hot must be kept in balance, an important part of their total world view. On the other side, it supplies the Indians with the notion of a merciful God and an incomprehensible theory of science.

Cultural imperialism has had surprisingly little effect in the local community in Juncal which I studied. It is clear, of course, that Christianity and the Catholic church organization have influenced the Juncal people strongly, but the influence is not so much through Christian ideology as by the church's organizational expressions. But even where the Christian ideas have advanced, they seem mostly to be formal framework categories, inside which the indigenous world of ideas still prospers. One could say, paradoxically, that cultural imperialism has indeed had effect, but that it has not had any cultural imperialistic influence on the ethnic group.

Consequently, I find ethnicity a more useful concept than cultural imperialism. Today the Cañar Indians have neither a Spanish Catholicism nor an indigenous religion, but quite a third construction, built on available elements of ideology and organization. Taken in relation to the political situation of the group, this construction plays its part in ethnic consciousness and expression.

Other important parts of Runa ethnicity are the judicial system, based on certain essential ideological premises, and the educational system with its glorification of national history, national language, and the western view of knowledge. But just as in the case of the church, these institutions have had little influence in Juncal, where the Indians in general have turned their backs on them in conscious disrespect for law and literacy. This Runa ethnic group shows strong immunity from cultural imperialism. Its natural ethnicity is intact in spite of the political subjection.

The notion of descent, by which the Cañar Indians remain an ethnic group in Ecuador, refers to the Incas as the legitimate ancestors. This is in a way strange, since the Incas brought the Cañar Indians into subjection only 60 years before the Spanish conquest. Cultural imperialism seems exactly to have been the business of the Incas, and they were much more effective than the Spanish and national Ecuadorians. There is no doubt that the Cañar people, in contrast to many other conquered people, maintained their identity as an ethnic group under Inca rule. Those so identifying as Cañaris, non-Inca, were the ones to make alliances with the Spanish conquerers. What has happened from the time of the conquest up to now is that the Cañar Indians have come to identify with their pre-Hispanic, Incaic oppressors, and not with their Spanish or modern oppressors. I am not able to account in a more detailed way for the manner in which this ethnicity process took place, but in an article about the history and historical view of the Cañaris, Eva Krener and I (1978) have tried to describe the course of events.

First of all there was the name itself, Inca, which was extended to cover all the subjects of the Inca state, so that the Cañar Indians, too, were Incas. But they lost that identity in the course of the Spanish conquest; then all Incas became Runas, or decentralized Andes Indians at the local community level. The Incas evidently made strong efforts to create a common identity between the center of the empire and the recently oppressed tribes at its peripheries. The Incas built a sun temple in the Cañar area and they used, symbolically, some stones from the capitol of Cuzco to indicate the identity between Cuzco and the Cañar locality, *Inca-pirca*, which literally means "Inca-stone."

These two examples must suffice here to demonstrate a very interesting difference between Spanish and Inca cultural imperialism. The Spanish imperialism was characterized by an extension of secular power to more and more peripheral areas, while Inca imperialism attempted to replicate its sacred power to create a qualitatively identical system and abolish peripheries. This Incaic strategy, taken together with the fact that after the Spanish conquest the Incas no longer were regarded as the master people, probably made the Cañaris come in time to identify wholeheartedly with the hereditary enemy.

There still exists in Cañar territory a living faith in a close spiritual connection with the Incas, partly found in the notion about Inca Rey, or Ante Cristo. According to this notion the Inca ruler, and possibly several persons with him, literally went underground and, among other things, took with them all the gold. This myth acts as a latent revivalistic hope that now and then flares up in the Andes. At the present, however, it has no political relevance for the Cañaris. More important today is that Inca is identified with the gold that is found in the earth, which, for the Cañar indigenous people, is a symbol of luck and prosperity. Gold, which is always regarded as Inca gold, is virtually a dominating symbol in Juncal, and it articulates in a very precise manner the notion of the Juncalese about an origin from Inca, which is an extranational identification.

I shall end by pointing out that for the Cañaris in Juncal the gold cannot be converted, for, in their view, conversion inevitably causes bad luck. In total opposition to the Runa idea of nonconvertibility of gold is its concept and valuation among the *mestizos*, and within national Ecuadorian society, where gold is the dominant expression of money, the basic medium of exchange. This contrast illustrates better than anything else that political economic imperialism has certainly reached Juncal, but that cultural imperialism has as yet been unsuccessful.

NOTES

Acknowledgments: This paper is an edited version of an article published in the *Transactions of the Finnish Anthropological Society* 2 (1977), reprinted by kind permission of author and publisher.

REFERENCES CITED

Cohen, Abner
    1974   *Two-Dimensional Man: An Essay on the Anthropology of Power and Symbolism in Complex Society.* Berkeley: University of California Press.
Fock, Niels
    in press   Ecology and Mind in an Andean Irrigation Culture. *Yearbook of Symbolic Anthropology*, vol. 2. London: C. Hurst and Co.
Fock, Niels, and Eva Krener
    1978   Los Cañaris del Ecuador y Sus Conceptos Etnohistóricos sobre los Incas. In Roswith Hartmann and Udo Oberem, eds., *Amerikanistische Studien: Festschrift für Hermann Trimborn*, vol. 1. St. Augustin: Haus Völker und Kulturen, Anthropos-Institut, pp. 170–81.
Fock, Niels, and Salvador Palomino Fiores
    1973   Cultural Defense in the Indoamerican Area. In *The Rural Society of Latinamerica Today*. Scandinavian Studies in Latin America 2. Stockholm, pp. 13–25.
Isaacs, Harold
    1974   Basic Group Identity: The Idols of the Tribe. *Ethnicity* 1:15–41.
Isajiw, Wsevolod W.
    1974   Definitions of Ethnicity. *Ethnicity* 1:111–24.
Keyes, Charles
    1976   Towards a New Formulation of the Concept of Ethnic Group. *Ethnicity* 3:202–13.
Osborne, Ann
    1968   Compadrazgo and Patronage: A Colombian Case. *Man, Journal of the Royal Anthropological Institute* 3 (4):593–608.

15

Weavers of Otavalo

Frank Salomon

"I never saw a race of finer looking people than an assembly of Ota-valeños on a Sunday," wrote an English visitor to the Ecuador of a century and a half ago (Stevenson 1825:vii, 347), and many other travelers in the Ecuadorian highlands, from Cieza de León in conquest times up to the anthropologists of our own, have likewise admired Otavalo canton as the home of a people whose prosperity and ethnic pride stand out handsomely amid the Andean spectacle of misery. Today textile merchants from Otavalo, neartly dressed in white pants and shirts under gray or blue ponchos, wearing broad-brimmed hats over long braids, travel as far as Argentina, Colombia, Panama, and even Miami in the conduct of a weaving economy which has distinguished Otavalo as far back as documentation reaches. Yet Otavalo canton, a spacious, fertile valley about thirty-five miles north of the capital city of Quito, looks like anything but a modern manufacturing center; its textile economy remains firmly embedded in an indigenous ("Indian" by the local criteria, Quichua speech and dress) peasant culture which cottage industry has strengthened rather than supplanted.

This symbiosis of a manufacturing economy tied into national and even international market structures with a localistic agricultural system and a community structure that resists out-marriage, permanent out-migration, and the erosion of native norms, is not entirely unique. Several other peoples of the Ecuadorian Sierra have invented functionally parallel adaptations to repeated conquest (Salz 1955:128, Casagrande 1969:6–7) and, like the Otavalans, have intermittently resisted Hispanic domination with violence (Moreno Yánez 1976: 162–221). But this best-studied and best-developed example of a smallholding-cum-cottage industry adaptation offers a particularly impressive instance of the occasional ability of small-scale social and economic formations to survive, and even take advantage of, a ponderous succession of superimposed large-scale systems of domination.

So Otavalo is of double interest to the people of the world's richest nation. First, it serves as a counterexample to the popular stereotype of Indian societies as hermetically sealed, static, and historically doomed, a stereotype which the anthropologists' traditional preference for remote and unacculturated societies did little to erase. Otavalans, like the vast majority of both South and North American Indians, belie this notion. They are not a tribe but a regionally distinct ethnic group with a four-century history of intimate culture contact; to study them is to see that, increasingly, indigenist studies must belong to the social anthropology of complex societies. Second, Otavalo contradicts the steamroller image of modernization, the assumption that traditional societies are critically vulnerable to the slightest touch of outside influence and wholly passive under its impact, devoid of policy for coping with it beyond a futile initial resistance. The view of modern forms of social organizations as a dynamic force acting on the inert mass of older societies, however benevolently voiced, is a reflection of imperialist ideologies of "progress." A postimperialist social science must embody the view from the village as well as that from the metropolis; it must recognize the possibility that what looks like irrationality or conservatism from the master's point of view may be, from the victim's, an activist response to the social problem posed by conquest. Otavalo demonstrates particularly clearly the dynamism of some outwardly traditional societies.

My study of the Otavalan adaptation began with an attempt to gather from ethnographic sources more than what my short visits could teach me about the textile industry in its present form, and the resulting synchronic view forms the first part of this article. But in following up the origins of market weaving, it became clear that the Otavalan market of today is a successor to a long history of local textile economies. The region's cottage industry has been drafted into the service of each of the imperial and national systems that have in turn subjugated native Ecuador. Yet in certain ways Otavalo's productivity, at the same time as it has beckoned exploiters, has enabled it to endure oppression and contempt more successfully than most Indian cultures. This history is the subject of the rest of this paper; the emphasis of the historical presentation is upon pointing out events which have contributed uniquely to Otavalo's integral survival and on suggesting the conditions of its relative good fortune in recent times.

THE VILLAGE IN THE NATION

Aníbal Buitrón (1945), Gonzalo Rubio Orbe (1956), Elsie Clews Parsons (1945), and the collaborators of the Instituto Ecuatoriano de Antropología y Geografía (1953) have supplied a quartet of Otavalan village enthnographies; the first two are native sons of the area, and, by their sensitivity to the differences among the canton's villages, *parcialidades*, not only afford representative or typical community portraits but also explain the directions and range of variation among communities. Joseph Casagrande and his associates have, since 1966, been furthering the comparative study of highland Ecuadorian villages. From these and many specialized sources there emerges a composite picture of the canton as a many-sided reality (e.g. Villavicencio 1973). Depending on what interests us, we can see it as a vast multitude of tiny family subsistence units, each striving for autonomy, or as a constellation of village communities, each an endogamous band of families, or as a single centralized market system in which all the villages act as specialists in a regional economy, or as a regional unit, political or economic, integrated into overarching national and international institutions. To accommodate all these realities, I have pictured it as a nest of systems within systems, a set of concentric productive and political units with the nuclear family at the center.

It is a commonplace of political science that the building of national political and economic institutions demands the integration of old, local systems into bigger, newer ones, even at the price of violent and politically explosive breakup and reconstitution. If we look at the process from the point of view of the traditional peasant, however, and not from that of the state-building elite, the problem appears quite different: how can local collectivities—the family, the village—arrange their relations with the spreading and deepening national institutions in such a way as to protect their own independence and security? What appears to urbanites as traditionalism, stubborness, or irrational identification with the land is simply the peasants' way of doing exactly what the nation builders are also trying to do, namely, restrict their dependence to resources over which they have some influence. This is the question to which the Otavalan farming-manufacturing complex is an answer. In the terms of the nest analogy, how is the tiny central unit to relate to the changing demands of the larger systems around it?

The Farming-Weaving Household

Otavalo canton comprises a high, well-watered valley, walled by extinct volcanoes and freshened by deep, cold lakes. A railroad and a highway connect the city of Otavalo, administrative seat of the region, with Quito to the south and Colombia to the north. Most of the city's 8,600-odd people are white (*blanco*, more a cultural than a racial designation) or *mestizo*. The remaining 37,000 Otavaleños form an overwhelmingly agricultural and Indian population dwelling on family farms in rural *parcialidades* (Cooper 1965:15).

The farming-weaving household, at the center of the nest of structures, is the smallest and the most enduring of Indian socioeconomic institutions. Dependent on the plot for most of their food except spices, meats, cheese, and a few vegetables, they devote tireless labor to its intensive cultivation. The commitment to land is fundamental; other involvements in larger systems "succeed" only insofar as they enhance and protect the family holding. Husband and wife unite their lands to form a productive unit, but each wills his or her portion separately to his or her chosen heirs. Land is alienable property in a sense similar to the white understanding of property, but its emotional and prestige value is so great that families almost never sell out. Children live with parents until they inherit land or marry an inheritor. Those who lack land or cannot farm attach themselves to landed households in a variety of adoption relationships appropriate to paupers, orphans, infirm people, or the very old (Rubio Orbe 1956:372–76, Parsons 1945:33–38).

The farming household, which we have been considering as the smallest unit of the subsistence economy, is also the unit of textile production; weaving takes place almost exclusively within the walls of the home. In weaving, unlike farming, technology is varied and as modern as circumstances allow. For traditional-style woolens weavers use a belt loom of pre-Hispanic design, but families which weave for the market as well as for village consumption also own wooden frame looms, and most augment the portable spindle with Spanish-style spinning wheels. Major textile entrepreneurs own power looms. Families divide the labor roughly by sex and age (for instance, spinning on the wheel is a masculine job, while spindles are women's tools), but each individual can do several tasks. The day's work consists of many short shifts at various textile and agricultural jobs: "for them, rest consists of exchanging one task for another" (Buitrón 1947:52). (A fine photographic record of weaving technique appears in a children's book by Bernard Wolf, *The Little Weaver of Agato.*) Some families especially active in the textile trade hire help, usually landless neighbors, to do piecework, and a few maintain workshops in town near the market, but the true textile factories (Otavalo has had three in recent times) are always *blanco*-owned. Indian factory hands also own or rent family plots; there is as yet no Otavalan textile proletariat.

Technical arrangements and the division of labor within the family do not vary much from place to place within the region, but the prosperity of families and the degree of their involvement in textile trade do vary a great deal, not only between *parcialidades* but even within them. In some places the typical home is a spacious building with a tile roof and broad fields, while in others the landscape of thatched huts and exhausted plots hardly differs from the scenes of misery characteristic of debt peon settlements. The overall differences between Otavalo and poorer regions, as well as the differences in wealth between and within its settlements, all arise from Otavalo's complex land tenure situation.

The parts of the valley vary sharply in the extent and quality of farmlands. Valley-floor land is the most fertile, producing squash, vegetables, corn, and beans; higher slopes yield wheat and barley, while the cold, foggy grasslands over 11,000 feet are good only for quinoa, tiny potatoes, and pasture. Nowhere is land abundant enough for weavers to grow their own wool; it is brought mostly from regions father south (Parsons 1945:16–26, Collier and Buitrón 1949:33). Position in the valley powerfully affects the fortunes of a family or village, specifically, the degree to which it can enter into the cottage manufacturing economy. Farmers whose holdings extend up the poorer slopes must sow and harvest different fields at different times. Extra work then consumes time potentially useful for weaving, and poverty precludes saving money for investment in crafts supplies (Buitrón 1947:45–67). Buitrón holds this to be the chief determinant of the growth of cottage industry. Within the single parish of Ilumán, the weaving industry sorts itself out into weaving households dwelling on the lower richer fields and families upon the higher slopes who spin thread to sell to weavers (IEAG 1953:163).

Although the area overall can be considered a zone of smallholding peasantry, land is far from uniformly distributed, and the quantity as well as the quality of land a family owns affects its place in the textile economy. Not all Otavalan farmers own the land they cultivate, and although nearly all those who do own land fall into the *minifundio* bracket—holdings too small to yield a complete livelihood for a family—there is plenty of variation within that bracket. For instance, Gonzalo Rubio Orbe (1956) found that in Punyaro, a *parcialidad* where land is scarce, "the distribution of lands is irregular: while there are families having two, two and a half, or three *cuadras* [that is, 1.4 to 2.1 hectares], many have a quarter, or less than a quarter, of a *solar* [that is, under .04 of an acre]." There were 23 landless families (in Punyaro), 16 of them homeless and dwelling two or three families to a roof (Rubio Orbe 1956:31, 108n). Seventy-six percent of Punyaro families had less than half a *cuadra*, that is, under .36 hectare (Rubio Orbe 1956:108).

Those who own only *microparcelas* too tiny to live off make do with a variety of other tenures. Some rent extra plots; a more common arrangement is *partido*, sharecropping for an absentee owner. "Collective or communal property is completely unknown in regard to land," Rubio Orbe reports, because, given the custom that only landholders or renters are marriageable, "there is not enough land to provide any. Punyareños consider some brushland in the ravines communal, so as to avail themselves of the firewood. But it's not unusual for a neighbor to declare himself the owner" (1956:31). Pasture land must be sought afar, usually at a price.

In Otavalo as elsewhere minifundism goes hand in hand with latifundism. Yet Otavalo's latifundia appear scarce and precarious when compared to those farther south in the Andes. Several big farms employing landless Indians do own tracts of the valley's finest land; in Punyaro when Rubio Orbe studied it, for instance, absentees owned (but did not cultivate) fields so rich and convenient to the city of Otavalo that Punyareños had no hope of buying them (Rubio Orbe 1956:110–11). And in the 1940s even Peguche, among the most prosperous *parcialidades*, had a few families that farmed only *huasipungos*, small plots of hacienda property allotted in payment for heavy hacienda labor obligations (Parsons 1945:8). In spite of these facts, however, big valley farms stand out by their growing weakness more than their power. Buitrón (n.d.:36) sums up this situation, so contrary to Ecuadorian and foreign stereotypes of highland agriculture: "A good part of the most fertile and best situated lands still belong to the haciendas. But little by little the Indians are buying them up, first the high grasslands, later the hillsides around the valley, and finally the valleys themselves, in short, the whole hacienda . . . abandoned and uncultivated for a long time, [hacienda lands] have been plowed and sown at once on passing into Indian hands." In another study (Buitrón and Buitrón 1945:196) the same observer illustrates the momentum of advancing minifundism:

The Indians of Pucará (another *parcialidad*), with a white man from Otavalo as an intermediary and backer, tried to buy the hacienda of Santa Rosa. They had already offered the hacienda owners 130,000 sucres, a pretty high price in the opinion of everyone. While the sale was being negotiated, to the intermediary's great surprise, about a hundred Indians came to his house to see him one afternoon. They had come from the *parcialidad* of Cumbas, near the hacienda in question, to tell him that they did not want Indians from other places in their territory, much less whites. Each of the hundred had contributed 2,000 sucres and they had already bought the hacienda for 200,00 sucres.

In Punyaro, on the other hand, local bidders lost out to people from the textile-wealthy *parcialidades* of Peguche and Ilumán in nearly all of the 700 transactions that dismantled a neighboring hacienda; this suggests, as we will see later, that the wealth generated by weaving produces social stratification among localities. Otavalo has moved so far in the direction of minifundism that, in 1946, only 31% of residents surveyed did any work on land other than their own, while, for the highlands as a whole, about one-third of the population worked *exclusively* on land owned by others; many more worked both their own and rented fields (Salz 1955:32, 36). But the reasons for the breakup of haciendas, a tendency of which Otavalo is only the most conspicuous example, are not well understood. Beate Salz (1955:41) offers three explanations. First, haciendas are in general low-profit businesses because of high irrigation and other service costs, hazardous production, and scarce labor (crafts, urban labor, and seasonal work in the lowlands all compete for the land-hungry worker's time). Second, the farm products market is unstable (less stable, for instance, than income from city rental properties). For instance, in 1942 the coincidence of new price controls on meat with rising corn prices gave incentive for a shift in land use from pasture to crops, but since an independent farmer can hardly be persuaded to turn peon, hacienda owners failed to raise from the countryside labor forces adequate to the greater need for field hands. Third, cultural change has demoted the hacienda owner; today, "everyone wants to have a Chevrolet and live in Quito." The knowledge that Indians will pay high prices for land encourages landowners to follow this impulse. It might be added as a fourth reason that Ecuadorian legislation now mandates the government to redistribute underused lands, a law which, even when not immediately applied, acts as an incentive for absentees to sell while the selling is good.

The flow of land from latifundists to Indians has taken place through money transactions, typically with *blanco* intermediaries such as lawyers, banks, or government agencies. Thus land hunger, an expression of desires for local autonomy, has paradoxically brought Otavaleños into closer contact with the large-scale institutions of the nation-state. It has put them in need of large amounts of cash and given a seeming incentive to mestization or abandonment of the community. It has erased all possibility of a retreatist or enclave adaptation. Yet, unlike similar encounters in other places, it has not weakened the land-based household by draining its manpower or vitiating the commitment to Indian-ness; and this rare outcome, as we will see later, arises from the historical opportunity to turn a craft tradition of long standing to a new end, the piecemeal reconquest of the land.

The Parcialidad

Although it approaches economic independence, the farming household has economic as well as purely social ties to the *parcialidad* (village, a local usage) of which it forms a part. At harvests and house raisings it depends on cooperative work parties. Reciprocal arrangements also take care of many smaller tasks. The *parcialidad* is an inward-looking system. Buitrón and Buitrón (1945:205) found that, of civilly registered marriages (which include virtually all marriages), 93% of those contracted between two Indians united a man and a woman of the same parish, while the comparable figure for *blancos* was 45% and for *mestizos* 25%. The parish, *parroquia*, encloses several *parcialidades*, but most marriages occur within one village or between contiguous ones. By contrast, relations between nonneighboring *parcialidades* are remote; the weekly market in Otavalo city affords an exchange of greetings and specialty products, but villages have ideological traditions of localism, and the entire history of the region is full of intervillage conflicts, some legalistic, some violent. Ritualized fighting between villages is a feature of the largest annual festival (Hartmann 1972).

The *parcialidad* as such is not an administrative unit but an unofficial subdivision of the *parroquia*; the parochial towns in Otavalo canton form subsidiary centers of non-Indian population and minor governmental and commercial centers. The bulk of Indians live in *parcialidades* of 80 to several thousand people, each consisting of a tract of land with houses scattered among the fields rather than forming a nucleated village. Footpaths, ravines, or rows of *cabuya* plants demarcate *parcialidad* and property boundaries. Buitrón and Buitrón (1945:192) takes a rigidly indigenist approach in defining the *parciali-*

dad as "a portion of territory perfectly delimited, whose inhabitants form perfectly homogeneous groups, not only in regard to material culture, but also in social and economic organization." In fact, however, many *parcialidades* also house a culturally distinct *mestizo* minority which rarely joins Indian families in marriage or cooperative labor. In many places the *mestizos* are poorer than Indians and looked down on with the same contempt that Indians endure in most of Educador.

The *parcialidad* is held together largely by kinship and cooperation; its authority structures are few and not mandated to exercise control outside their narrow specialties. In no single individual are power and authority decisively combined. Even the landlord, if the area is one where much land is rented, exercises dominion only in specifically economic dealings, a sharp contrast to the status of the *hacendado*, "landlord," as ultimate secular authority observed in other parts of Ecuador (Casagrande 1969:5). The power of the *jambidur*, "healer," commands respect in personal matters, but he is no politician. Insofar as the *parcialidad* has any general authority roles, they are representative of more encompassing social structures, the state and the church. Traditionally, each village had at least two *alcaldes*, "mayors," *de doctrina* or religious, and *de justicia* or political. These unpaid part-time officials, appointed by the priest of the parish and the *teniente político* respectively, were to extract labor for various imposed duties such as maintaining churches and roads, and intervene as justices of the peace in minor disputes, tasks which earn more opprobrium than authority. The village *cabildo* or council of aldermen, which the *alcaldes* were supposed to organize, rarely functioned well and in some places became a dead letter (Rubio Orbe 1956:337, 341).

Regional and National Integration

Looking at the social location of the Otavalan as a spot in the center of several nested systems of trust, power, and authority, there appears a discontinuity between arrangements at the village and at the regional and national level. Even when deeply enmeshed in extralocal markets, the locality functions not as a political subsystem of the bigger system but, as much as possible, in isolation from it. This preference finds face-to-face expression in the social distance norms Indians uphold (and which white Ecuadorians are in no hurry to ease) in dealing with white officials and buyers at market: stiff, taciturn courtesy and a complete absence of spontaneity or joking prevail.

The relation of local community to the state remains passive and peripheral.

So long as land supplies could meet the demand posed by natural increase, this preference for enclave living was nonproblematic. However, land hunger profoundly endangers autonomy, and the *minifundio* complex here, as in many parts of Latin America, seems to generate irreversible social change. New plots can be obtained in only a few ways: increasing sharecropping and peonage; land invasions and political revolution, as occurred in Cochabamba, Bolivia; or purchase of lands on the open market. The first implies loss of autonomy; the second a gamble on the chances of violence or politics and, in the event of victory, a commitment to national political institutions; the third a commitment to whatever will give the community a reliable source of cash. The first of these alternatives has been the commonest all over the Andes, while the second stands out much less in Ecuadorian history than in that of Boliva or Peru. But Indians in several parts of the highlands besides Otavalo have moved in the third direction. Ralph Beals (1966:78) describes a village near Quito which adapted to a land squeeze early in the twentieth century by turning to the growing of fruit and vegetables for the city market, so as to expand enough to remain self-sufficient. In Cañar and Azuay provinces during the 1950s Indians developed the manufacture of what the world knows as Panama hats in order to escape from desperate landless poverty (Salz 1955:104n). Throughout the Ecuadorian Sierra, Indians have entered onto the stage of national history almost exclusively in economic roles.

In contrast to its weakness as a political center, the city of Otavalo, and especially its market place, has long acted as an economic nexus unifying the whole canton. Before dawn every Saturday families from every *parcialidad* hike into town with their week's production of textiles, basketry, pots, and produce to do a few intense hours of business and then enjoy an afternoon of drinking, dancing, watching medicine shows, socializing, and eating meats or other delicacies at the stalls in the plaza. Insofar as this exhaustingly lively gathering exchanges mostly local specialty products, it functions as what Eric Wolf calls a sectional market (Wolf 1966:40), a central point among interdependent but autonomous villages "scattered around it in a radial fashion, like the planets of the solar system around the sun." Like planets with satellites of their own, the parochial towns conduct smaller markets, partly remnant sales, the day after the Otavalo city market (IEAG 1953:65). But the weekly market also works as a link integrating the villages into the larger economic system from which they are politically and socially separated by a racial animosity even more intense than that familiar to North Americans, as well as by class and language barriers and the Indians' own disinclination to take part. Buyers of Otavalan craft products include Ecuadorian *mestizos*, both as consumers and as middlemen, some *blancos*, and an ever-increasing number of foreign, chiefly North American, tourists. In turn, manufactured goods from other countries and other parts of Ecuador—pots and pans, glazed stoneware, dyes, sewing machines—find Indian buyers, although the average rural family buys only one of each major item per generation (Rubio Orbe 1956:49–58). Most prominent among extralocal goods are the raw materials of weaving, tools, and trimmings.

At the market the display of village-made products far exceeds that of manufactured goods. Indians have not followed the *mestizos* in becoming indiscriminant consumers of *blanco*-style goods. Money made at market tends to be saved for land buying. Otavalans deal regularly with *mestizos* and *blancos* of all classes. They travel all over Ecuador and into neighboring countries, even overseas, as traders and lately as textile experts; in 1950 a delegation from Peguche visited UN headquarters in New York to speak for and about Ecuador (Rubio Orbe 1957:331). Hardly any indigenous people has had more opportunity to become acculturated, at least in terms of consumption patterns; yet the one point on which all accounts of the region agree is that Otavaleños have adopted a limited body of *blanco* material culture and, aside from religion, little of the nonmaterial. Often traits actively promoted by whites are taken in only reluctantly and slowly. Indeed, those writers who, like Rubio Orbe, believe that a quicker pace of acculturation would be to the Indians' advantage find this reluctance problematic and explainable only in terms of a generalized traditionalism. Yet how can one attribute generally conservative attitudes to a social system which has innovated so aggressively in its external relations?

In "Tappers and Trappers" Robert Murphy and Julian Steward (1956:353) have posited what they consider to be a universal rule: "When goods manufactured by industrialized nations with modern techniques become available through trade to the aboriginal populations, the native people increasingly give up their home crafts in order to devote their efforts to producing specialized cash crops or other trade items in order to obtain more of the industrially made articles. The consequences of this simple though world-wide factor are enormous, even though they vary in local manifestation. The

phenomenon is of such a high order of regularity that special explanations must be sought for the few departures from it." Apparently
Otavalo is such an exception. Buitrón (1962:315) remarks on the Otavalans' "great attachment to their traditional garments. . . . The
young Indians who have been drafted and who for a year have worn
military uniforms, on returning home abandon all these new garments . . . to return to their pants and shirts of white cotton and their
ponchos." But is the explanation needed special, or can we take the
Otavalan experience to mean that Murphy and Steward's generalization is true only given conditions which need to be specified?

Manufactured goods as such possess no special virtue. Sol Tax,
working from Guatemalan highland evidence, holds that even when
Indians accept many non-indigenous practices,

> they have nevertheless maintained a total pattern that is dinstinctively
> their own. The evidence appears to be that the major changes occurred in
> the first generation after the sixteenth-century conquest, and that the new
> pattern crystallized early and has maintained itself since with relatively
> minor changes. It seems easiest to explain this history on the hypotheses
> that alternatives were presented in large numbers when the Spanish first
> came, that the Indians adopted many, and that in the ensuing hundreds
> of years few new alternatives appeared. Colonial Guatemala settled down
> to a fairly stable set of Indian cultures coexisting with an equally stable
> Ladino culture. (1957:105).

We cannot account for acculturation by reading into Indian behavior
pro or con value judgments about white practices as things in themselves; rather, we have to interpret selection and rejection of practices
as expressing estimates of their usefulness in living out already held
values. If a change seems useful, Tax observes, it will take hold
quickly, not slowly.

Otavalans too show a "total pattern that is distinctively their own."
The most conspicuous institutional "acculturations" have in fact a
history of coercion. Among these one might mention the legal authority of native *alcaldes* and *cabildos*, civil registry of births, marriages, and deaths, settlement of land claims in courts, channeling of
ceremonial life through the parish church, and the use of Spanish—
but even coerced innovations tend to be remodeled and reinterpreted
as they become woven into local norms. Many borrowings in areas of
expressive culture and play, for example in sports, children's games,
and stories or myths, even when easily recognizable by outsiders,
are not felt from within as steps away from indigenous indentity. In
any given community the boundary between acceptable behavior

and ethnically over-foreign behavior is sharply drawn, but a good many European-derived traits fall on the acceptable side. Much the same is true in the area of consumption: metal cooking equipment, glazed ceramics, radios, bicycles, and, of late, cars are considered desirable even within an ethos of cultural conservatism. But the indigenous management of the acculturation problem is most interesting and original in the area of production, where borrowings are welcome insofar as they provide means to strengthen one's household's position vis-à-vis the outside world without becoming estranged from neighbors. Use of European-designed looms and knitting machines, German and Japanese dyes, sewing machines, and synthetic fibers enhances productivity immediately, and the sending of children to school, even at the risk of exposure to cultural hostility, is acceptable for the sake of enhancing it in the long run (Rubio Orbe 1956:389–91, 1957:318–34; Buitrón 1962:314–20; IEAG 1953:143; Parsons 1945:181, 190). The drawing of decisions about acceptable versus deviant acculturation, a continuous historical process on the local scale, takes place largely on the plane of conscious discussion.

If one accepts Murphy and Steward's generalization, it becomes hard to see how the lines between acceptable and deviant acculturation are drawn, or why different populations in similar situations of culture contact draw them differently. In Nayón, a formerly Quichua-speaking community near Quito, land-poor Indians turned to truck farming, trading, and outside wage labor in the early twentieth century, and since then have acculturated so rapidly that Ralph Beals (1966:73) sees them as virtually bypassing the *mestizo* stage altogether. Men of Nayón wear suits and short hair, while in Otavalo, which has been in at least as favorable a position to buy into *blanco* culture, Indians draw the line at the use of factory-made ponchos of characteristically Indian design. Apparently the desirability of white-style goods cannot be considered self-evident, even when, as in Ecuador, fidelity to indigenous culture invites oppression.

The most parsimonious explanation of the Otavalans' choices among available innovations (excluding those which have a history of compulsion), as well as of the persistence of villages as enclaves in the political and social nation in spite of their economic involvements, is that economic security and autonomy in the form of land ownership is paramount over the enjoyment of consumer goods. Historically, the reason is not hard to see; the loss of land to *blancos* has almost always left Indians dependent and defenseless. Given this criterion of usefulness, Tax's theory yields cogent explanation of the choices. In an example from Rubio Orbe (1956:216), a young man

who could have supported his future wife well in the city was refused until he agreed to go back to farming. Innovations which further the quest for land are welcome, on the other hand; Buitrón
(1956:228–93) reports that when a North American textile expert introduced a simple device for making wide cloths more easily, it was
not Indian conservatism that prevented wide distribution of the invention—the device was eagerly received—but the noncooperation
of Ecuadorian and foreign officials.

The harnessing of cottage industry to the national market for the
purpose of buying land is the current solution to problems of long
standing, the problems of achieving independence in the face of subjugation. Twentieth-century circumstances, as we will see later, have
made the craft-marketing adaptation outstandingly successful in recent times, but even in the region's worst periods of oppression its
ancient pre-eminence in textile making has paradoxically acted as a
buffer against total cultural demise at the same time that it has invited
exploitation. The historical record, incomplete as it is, allows us to
glimpse several successive relationships between Otavalo and its
conquerors.

WEAVING IN OTAVALAN HISTORY

Archaeological evidence shows that Otavalo between A.D. 500 and
1500 was the home of a people dwelling in small city-states, socially
stratified to about the same extent and in the same manner as the
Chibchans to the north (Murra 1946:792): "The chief and his retain-
ers, priests, and various craftsmen probably lived in a town supported by the produce of farmers scattered over the surrounding
countryside. The latter came to town to exchange goods at the market, to participate in festivals, and to offer prayers and sacrifices at
the temple" (Meggers 1966:159). This population, known as the Cara
or Caranqui tribe or nation, was linguistically similar to the Cayapa-
Colorado Indians to its west; both peoples' tongues are of the
Barbácoa Chibchan group, related to Colombian, not Peruvian,
speech (Loukotka 1968:250).

Incaic and Spanish superimpositions have made it hard to reconstruct Cara sociopolitical arrangements. The only history of Cara territory written before the extinction of the Cara language in the eighteenth century, that of the Jesuit Juan de Velasco, sets forth a picture
so rich in extravagant but undocumented detail that its portrait of the
Cara as empire-building centralizers must be discounted as mostly
regional chauvinism (Szászdi 1964).

One of the few aspects of Cara civilization of which we can be fairly sure, however, is its craft life. "The textile culture of the Otavaleños goes back to the earliest history of the Andean Indians. Before the conquest, before the coming of the Incas, the Otavalo . . . were weaving blankets and cloaks from cotton they obtained in trade with the people of the Amazon jungle" (Collier and Buitrón 1949:163). John Murra writes (1946:794) that "trade relations were maintained with the peoples of the eastern lowlands, who brought achiote (a red coloring powder), parrots, monkeys and even children to exchange for blankets, salt, and dogs. Cotton was also imported from the east." As early as 1552, royal officials commented that the Otavalans "have all the business, or the better part of it, in all of Quito and its environs" (AGI/S Cámara 922 pieza 3ª:f. 165v). The *corregidor* Sancho de Paz Ponce de León, whose 1573 report to the crown is the best early Otavalan document, says that Indians of the area carried on trade with "pagan Indians from lands which have not yet been conquered." Traders enjoyed special prestige, according to Ponce de León: "In the old days, the people of each town or village in this entire *corregimiento* (of Otavalo) had their *cacique* who governed them as a tyrant, because he was the most able and valient. They had him for a master, and obeyed and respected him and paid tribute; and the Indians owned no more than what the *cacique* might let them have, so that he was the master of all the Indians possessed as well as of their wives and children. They served him as if they were his slaves, *except the merchant Indians, who did not serve their chief like the others, but only paid a tribute of gold, blankets, and red or white bone beads*" (Ponce de León 1897:111; italics added).

No single pre-Incaic political unit ever dominated the area north of Quito; even after the Incaic conquest, wars between localities persisted (Cieza de León 1959:22). Nonetheless this region resisted the Peruvians' offensive more tenaciously than any other except Araucanian Chile. Inca invasion of the area began about 1450, but when Huayna Capac's troops finally subjugated it, 45 years had elapsed and Columbus had already set foot on Hispaniola. As a result, the Inca period in Otavalo lasted only some 40 years, and although the Inca empire concentrated much manpower and administrative attention on integrating this rich area—a more fertile and inviting zone than Cuzco, the seat of the empire—its impact proved, in some respects, shallow.

Among towns in the Cara region, only Sarance—the modern city of Otavalo—and Caranqui became Inca administrative centers. Accounts of the building of a formidable temple and a northward extension of the imperial road through Sarance (which must have meant mobilizing large numbers of locals in labor brigades), the removal of local nobles to Cuzco to be trained in Quechua language and imperial ideology, and the reshuffling of land tenures in order to impose the famous tripartite management basic to the integrated Andean economy all suggest that conquest must have completely rebuilt Cara society. But some indicators point in the opposite direction. The large-scale killing of captives suggests an uncertain hold on the political structure, as do the introduction of *mitimaes*, transplanted labor forces, from long-subdued Bolivia and the erection of a fortress in Sarance "to deal with revolts in time of war and peace" (Cieza de León 1959:21). Quechua language did not fully replace Cara for another 200 years, and the ideology and mythology expressed in it never replaced local lore generally (Buitrón and Buitrón 1966:55–79). It is true that the region paid tribute heavily and regularly, and that the upper levels of Cara stratification merged with the middle levels of the Inca hierarchy. Yet "the Inca conquest had not caused major changes in the autochthonous nuclei of population . . . [or] destroyed the social and economic organization of the conquered peoples" (Vargas 1957:71). Apparently, as one descends from wider levels of coordination to local structures, Inca control becomes weaker, so that while Sarance became an Incaic outpost, villages bought relative autonomy by rendering tributes. The introduction of wool-bearing camellids by the Incas must have greatly enhanced Otavalo's productivity in this period (Buitrón 1956:287) and its value as a revenue source. There is a parallel to the modern system in this acquiescence to the material demands of large-scale structures as a proxy for social involvement in them. The price of the accommodation in both cases is the yielding up of whatever is produced beyond subsistence, whether to a market as today or to a fully managed economy as under the Incas. Otavalo has worked hard to remain on the periphery of the political world.

The demands of the next wave of invaders, the Spanish, were far harsher. Aside from the most obvious causes of misery, disease, and brutality, the Spanish conquest created a situation which, even with the best intentions, had to hurt. A fast-growing Spanish immigrant population, largely urban, had to be fed by a labor force which at the same time was being drained by disease and the head-long expansion of mining enterprises. Moreover, the system contained the seeds of its own deterioration in that it drained off in the form of goods and metal exports to Spain much of the value created by Indian labor. The exploitation of the natives did not even succeed in capitalizing the colonial economy with money or social-overhead goods; instead it created a society addicted to the buying of European products. As a result, the answer to every economic problem was to squeeze still greater production from Indian labor. Otavalo fared better in this bind than many other places, but colonial times brought terrible suffering to the region (Reyes 1938:345–57), first through the exploitation of its labor and later through the piecemeal theft of its lands.

Sebastián de Benalcázar and his followers, who conquered modern Ecuador in 1534 in the wake of Pizarro's assault on the war-torn Inca empire, were disappointed in their hopes of finding another gold-rich Peru. Throughout colonial history Ecuador remained politically an appendage to the vice-royalties, first of Peru and after 1720 of New Granada (modern Colombia). This reflected its economic status as supplier of goods to other parts of the empire. Nonetheless the institutions of conquest, and many of their results, resembled those in more politically potent colonies. The evolution of land tenures from usufruct grants to latifundia, and of Indian labor obligations from *encomienda* to *mita* to debt peonage, parallels Peruvian developments.

The newly founded *cabildo*, city council, of Quito granted three forms of agricultural land tenures, limited, from 1535 onward, to fairly small holdings: *solares*, gardens in or near the city; *estancias* for the encouragement of ranching (which proved so successful that seventeenth-century Quito was famous for cheap livestock); and *tierras para sembradura*, land for crops. Not landholding proper, however, but rather the exploitation of a nonterritorial grant, the *encomienda*, yielded up early colonial fortunes. The *encomienda*, consisting of the assignment to a Spanish *encomendero* of a varying number of Indians to be protected and catechized, and, in return for these services, to pay him tribute in goods or labor, specifically required that the *encomendero* should not live on the lands of his *encomendados*. But many managed to acquire land grants neighboring their *encomendado* villages and to extort excessive labor from them under the name of tribute. Otavalo fell into the hands of a violent and adventurous conquistador, Rodrigo de Salazar, in one of the earliest and largest *encomiendas*, and the surrounding areas were divided into a series of much smaller ones. Because the terms of *encomienda* granted the privilege for only two generations, these first grants reverted to the crown relatively early (Salazar's in 1581). The crown chose to set aside this community, so rich in skilled labor, as a crown tributary area. That Otavalan Indians became workers for the Spanish state instead of being reassigned in new *encomiendas* is one reason for their relative good fortune in this era (Reyes 1938:315–22, Vargas 1957: 160–62).

Since the Otavalo area is poor in minerals and under pre-automotive conditions not advantageously placed for truck farming, *encomenderos* and officials extracted private wealth and crown revenue from the area chiefly by putting the yoke of forced labor on the indigenous textile culture. The highly successful introduction of sheep to the Andes and the expansion of cotton growing and other fiber culture in the lowlands supplied Otavalo with the raw materials for making a very large part of the colonial world's supply of textiles, from rope and sackcloth to fine handkerchiefs, but, above all, of ordinary shirt cloth, woolen blankets, and ponchos. Tribute laws of 1612 required every man of 18 through 50 years to render two white cotton cloaks to the crown as well as money and livestock payments (Municipalidad de Otavalo 1909:35–36). Textiles from the Ecuadorian highlands clothed the mine labor forces of Peru and Colombia and paid for the wine and imported goods that Quiteño Spaniards enjoyed. Indeed, the cloth trade, as John Phelan explains in his admirable history *The Kingdom of Quito in the Seventeenth Century* (1967:66–85), became the backbone of Ecuador's colonial economy and made it "the sweatshop of South America."

The Spanish achieved the expansion of weaving from a local craft to an export industry not chiefly through technological reorganization (although the use of the Spanish frame loom did take root quickly throughout the Andes) but through the concentration and merciless overworking of Indians in primitive factories, or *obrajes*, where amid filth, darkness, and hunger, overseers forced them to work hours far beyond what royal legislation theoretically permitted. *Obrajes* ranged downward in size and quality from those operated as crown enterprises (later leased to contractors); to vice-royally licensed private shops, some of which were assigned quotas of forced *mita* labor while others hired weavers; to unlicensed shops run by *encomenderos*, city entrepreneurs, powerful Indians, and, not uncommonly, religious orders. A few *obrajes* belonged to corporate Indian communities which used them to pay their tributes. The most concentrated area of *obraje* production was not Otavalo but Riobamba, a region south of Quito where sheep raising flourished. After the *encomienda* including Otavalo reverted to the crown in 1581, the large *obraje* in Otavalo city was reorganized as a crown enterprise and under corrupt management declined; when a change of royal policy in 1620 put it on the market as a leased concession, it quickly appreciated and by 1623 had become the most valuable in Ecuador (Phelen 1967:69–74; Vargas 1957:235, 303). Also in 1620, another crown *obraje* was opened at Peguche.

The continuing struggle which crown officials waged to put limits to the abuse and wastage of life that colonists were always ready to visit on the king's Indian subjects was resisted tirelessly by colonists who saw no other way to wring a decent living from Ecudador's soil. Amid this conflict, conditions in the *obrajes* proved a perennial bone of contention. From the earliest times of the Ecuadorian *audiencia* (the ruling body immediately subject to the viceroy of Peru), royal correspondence deals with the issues of nonpayment of weavers, overwork, child labor, the question of whether *obrajes* should serve as debtor's prisons, usurpation of Indian lands by *obraje* owners, and myriad forms of cruelty, starvation, and neglect (Landázuri Soto 1959:28, 31, 32, 75–76, 82). Otavalo, by virtue of its status as a crown holding, repeatedly had the good luck to become a test case in *obraje* reform, the decision to lease it in 1620 being one such experiment.

The Otavalo reforms of 1620, planned by the dynamic president of the *audiencia*, Dr. Antonio de Morga, constituted one of the earliest and wisest plans for Indian reconstruction. Its terms included the restoration of all lands whether stolen or bought, provision of a plot and a house for every Indian, exemption from the forced labor of the *mita*, segregation of non-Indians and traders in the town of Ibarra, and a number of measures to ensure administrative honesty and efficiency (Phelan 1967:76). But subsequent presidents could not make them stick, and abuses recurred; a 1648 royal order refers to Otavalo Indians fleeing to the mountains for fear of debtor's prison or because their lands had been stolen (Vargas 1957:95). By 1680 mounting protest prodded King Charles II to a draconian reform which would have decimated textile production by destroying all unlicensed shops. President Munive of the Quito *audiencia* convinced the crown that this reform could only wreck the economy (Phelan 1967:78–79), but in doing so he admitted that the crown tributary areas once again needed protection if they were to prosper:

> [Weavers at Otavalo] live in and are accustomed to the city of Otavalo with their homes and their families there, going to work without any coercion or violence, which condition does not prevail at the *obraje* of Peguche because of the inconvenient distance of 6 to 9 miles from the villages where they live to the workshops, where they enter at four in the morning and leave at six in the evening, resulting in the harm and nuisance of having to walk 18 miles every day to and from work, without a chance to rest . . . they despair . . . three of them threw themselves under a bridge and were pulled out dead, and so I propose to Your Majesty that the only remedy is to demolish this *obraje*. . . . (Landázuri Soto 1959:144–45)

The crown *obraje* at Peguche employed 200 workers; that at Otavalo, 498. The abuses which these workers suffered were far less horrible than those inflicted on inmates of some private shops (Landázuri Soto 1959:171–72).

By this period the crown, through cumulative partial measures, had radically weakened the *encomienda*. However, measures such as the (rarely enforced) ban on tributes payable only in labor and the non-redistribution of *encomiendas* had not brought labor conditions up to the standards of Spanish law, and during the period 1690–1720 the already much-vitiated remaining *encomiendas* were reclaimed for the crown and the institution liquidated (Vargas 1957:163–65). Instead of relieving the Indians of their exploiters, however, the abolition of crown usufruct gave Spaniards and *criollos* an aditional incentive to invest the profits from *obrajes* in land purchases or to indulge in seizures of land which *corregidores* (officials charged with the protection of Indians) could be persuaded to tolerate. It is in the middle and later colony—not the conquest—that we find the seeds of latifundism. Otavalo had and still has some sizable latifundia, but these did not, as happened farther south in the Andes, convert whole villages into captive colonies of landless debt peons; rather, they have bordered on freehold *parcialidades*, so that *huasipungeros* of the big farm nonetheless remained socially attached to independently landed neighbors. Possibly because Otavalo's relatively gentle climate allows farming high up on the mountain sides, and consequently permits victims of land-grabbing to resettle, latifundia of the Otavalo region have had to rely more on hired labor done part time by *minifundistas* and less on fixed colonies of indebted Indians than those elsewhere.

The decline of the *encomienda* also heightened the demand for *mita* labor. The *mita*, an Incaic institution of which nothing Incaic but the name remained by 1700, had become a functional equivalent for slavery. Every village had to supply a quota of workers conscripted for a fixed period (six months was the legal limit) who were marched off to mines or *obrajes*, usually far from their homes, and exploited mercilessly. According to Jorge Juan and Antonio de Ulloa (1918: 288–316), visitors to Ecuador in 1736, few survived the hunger, brutality, and exposure to cold inflicted on *mitayos*. Although a minor debt or offense might incur conscription, it amounted to a sentence of death. "Often on the roads one meets Indians with their braids tied to the tail of a horse, on which a mounted mesitzo leads them to the *obrajes*; and this perhaps for the slight offense of having fled . . . for fear of the cruelties (their masters) inflict on them" (Juan and

Ulloa 1918:311). *Mita* gangs had long been assigned to some licensed *obrajes*, but after 1700 the abolition of the *encomienda* obligation created pressure on the authorities to grant many more operators conscript labor, pressure which they could hardly resist without endangering Quito's place in intercolonial trade.

Even while *obraje* production and the *mita* drained their work force, however, eighteenth-century Otavalans were able to do independent business, and it is in another report of Juan and Ulloa (1806:301–2) that we hear of Otavalans as adapting to domination and the theft of their resources by becoming suppliers to a supralocal open market: " . . . a multitude of Indians residing in its villages . . . seem to have an innate inclination to weaving; for besides the stuffs made at the common manufactories (i.e. *obrajes*), such Indians as are not Mitayos, or who are independent, make, on their own account, a variety of goods, as cottons, carpets, pavillons for beds, quilts in damask work, wholly of cotton, either white, blue, or variegated with different colours; but all in great repute, both in the province of Quito and other parts, where they are sold to great advantage."

During the century following Juan and Ulloa's visit latifundism sank deep roots in the highlands. The traveler William Bennett Stevenson (1825:348) tells of haciendas with 400 or 500 Indians attached either to their fields or *obrajes*, and reports that near Otavalo the Count of Casa Xijón had "brought several mechanics and artisans from Europe for the purpose of establishing a manufactory of fine cloths, woolens, and cottons; also for printing calicoes, and other goods," but the *real audiencia* forbade his plan and forced him to send the mechanics home.

The Creole elites of the Otavalo area sided for the most part with the forces of independence in the war against Napoleonic Spain, and "from its famous workshops came the cloaks that warmed the army in its campaigns" (Jaramillo 1953:4, 22). From them also came the porters of the independence armies' cargos, abducted from their villages in what is still remembered as the *cogida de gente*—the seizure of people—(Rubio Orbe 1956:29) which caused a mass flight to the mountains.

Newly independent and until 1830 a part of the federation of Gran Colombia, Ecuador suddenly became an open market for imports from England, and the resulting flood of cheap factory-made cloth dealt a blow to the *obraje* industry from which, Phelan says (1967:68), it never recovered. Nonetheless several nineteenth-century land magnates tried to revive local weaving in competition with English industry by combining technical modernization with the cheap labor which debt peons provided. Among these was the grandson of the Count of Casa Xijón, Don José Manuel Jijón y Carrión, whose prosperous Peguche hacienda the U.S. diplomat Friedrich Hassaurek visited in 1863. Here hacienda peasants made ponchos and shawls for Indians as well as material for European vests and pants on modern looms, all for shipment to Colombia or the Pacific coast (Vargas 1957:122, Hassaurek 1967:151). Two other latifundia, the Quinta Otavalo and the Quinta de San Pedro, were equipped with European machines, for weaving and for thread making respectively. An earthquake in 1864 destroyed much of this machinery (Municipalidad de Otavalo 1909:294). An unmodernized *parcialidad*, Cotacachi, was doing well with coarse ponchos and silks (products without industrial competition) for sale in other parts of Gran Colombia, while nearby a landowner had imported an industrial cotton mill from New Jersey but went bankrupt on the venture (Hassaurek 1967:175–77). Thus in the later nineteenth century Indian weavers working outside hacienda workshops could profit by the making of clothes for other Indians, but the technologically fortified vestiges of the *obraje* system still dominated whatever share of the city clothing market had not fallen to the English.

The farming-weaving complex in its modern form did not arise until the early twentieth century, when villagers found that the duplication of machine-made luxury textiles on primitive equipment enabled them to undersell the quality import trade even though they could not compete in the making of cheap stuffs. Once introduced, this business became the mainstay of cottage industry. The weaving boom of this period reflected the mounting urgency of land problems and signals the beginning of the land-hunger dynamic described above.

For Otavaleños to own land has double importance: first, it is the only reliable and autonomous way of earning a living; and second, it is a *sine qua non* of full participation in Indian society, since the alternatives are to abandon the community, become a permanent debtor, or live as a dependent of another household. In order to provide every family with a plot, parents will their land partibly, that is, divide it among all the children. We do not know when this practice began, though Murra (1946:794) thinks the system "was greatly influenced by post conquest ideas." But we do know how it worked in the time of the childhood of Elsie Parsons's informant Rosita Lema, when quarter shares of already tiny plots might be all a person inherited. And we know from her testimony how partible inheritance, after centuries of slow population increase, produced a land crisis:

Formerly, my mother tells as her parents tell her, there were not as many families as today, and only two or three little straw houses. The families cultivated land according to their capacity, the rest was common land, untilled, unenclosed, an enormous plain. As the families increased it was customary to upturn land as a kind of deed, always with witnesses or the *curaca* (village headman) to direct it. This made a man owner and lord of this land where he built a house and lived independently of his parents. In the course of time, ambitious for land, families spread over the whole plain, becoming landowners, *and there was no longer common land to turn up.*" (Parsons 1945:186; italics added)

This must have occurred in the middle or late nineteenth century. From the time when lands gave out, the ability to save cash and buy land became the prerequisite for survival as a free peasant: "Then those who had too much land or for other reasons would sell land, a cuadra for five pesos, ten pesos, twenty pesos according to the situation or fertility. Today (1945), if the lot is located on the main street and the soil is fertile, it costs 1,500 sucres; a lot less fertile and far from the main street will cost as little as 400 sucres" (Parsons 1945:186). By 1909 the trend toward land buying by Indians had gone far enough to alarm the anonymous author of Otavalo's municipal history, who saw things from the latifundists' point of view:

By forming societies they have bought *fundos* of the value of twenty-three thousand sucres, of twenty thousand, et cetera . . . Day by day, the Indian is taking over the lands of the Canton, albeit by fair purchase; having taken possession of them on a larger scale, by cultivating them with care he will achieve a well-being that will make him scorn the laborer's wage. Then who will till [the latifundists'] fields? . . . Even now . . . the Indians do not volunteer for government works; it is necessary to round them up with the *alcaldes* or the police, or take their belongings hostage [*quitarles prendas*, an abuse practiced by townsmen], or threaten to throw them in jail, in order to force them to work. (Municipalidad de Otavalo 1909:254–57)

Into this environment of land hunger and rising prices, local *blancos* in 1917 introduced the germ of the modern textile trade. A lady of the hacienda of Cusín, bordering on Peguche, gave her Quiteño son-in-law, F. A. Uribe, a beautifully woven poncho as a wedding gift. Impressed with its quality, rivaling that of costly imported clothes. Uribe sought out its maker, a Peguche native named José Cajas, and offered him the use of a Spanish loom to try his skill at making fine fabric after Scottish patterns. Cajas found that he could profitably undersell imports with his imitation tweeds (*casimires*), and soon had a business in Quito. His descendants are still among the leading weavers of the area (Parsons 1945:25–26).

Thus Otavalo smallholders found a major entrée into the money economy at the precise time when it served to defend, not supplant, the bases of the local economy (IEAG 1953:98). In subsequent decades the *casimir* trade spread to many other villages, although by no means all (in reading Collier and Buitrón's 1949 optimistic account of the weaving renaissance, one must bear in mind that the weaving boom left some *parcialidades* still land-poor and overworked). Since World War II the growth of Ecuadorian textile factories has greatly weakened Otavalo's position in the market for suit fabrics, but the burgeoning of the tourist market in autochthonous and not so autochthonous designs has offset this damage considerably.

Both the Ecuadorian indigenist movement and U.S. foreign aid agencies have sought to encourage cottage industry in capturing foreign money, the former through the programs of the Instituto Ecuatoriano de Antropología y Geografía, which have encouraged the weaving of authentic rather than imitative designs for the market (Salinas 1954:315–26), and the latter through the *Centro Textil* in Otavalo city, which Ecuadorians have consistently criticized as poorly integrated with village life and in fact of use only to *mestizos*. (Rubio Orbe 1957:335–60 offers a detailed critique.) Other recent innovations in textile economy center on marketing; Otavaleños own several shops in downtown Quito while others crisscross the country as traveling merchants.

Because of this interest in modernizing business technique, the children of weaving families attend public schools (though the great majority of families still value home training). Travel needs have involved some villagers in local transportation businesses; others have learned skilled and semiskilled agricultural jobs, or become mechanics in textile factories; and the first generation of Indian nurses, teachers, and lawyers is starting to emerge from universities (Cooper 1965:45–56, Buitrón 1962, Casagrande 1966:9). Most of these changes, large or small, can be understood in the light of Sol Tax's observation that "traditional" populations will innovate readily, provided that innovation promises to be useful within the context of already accepted norms.

But can Otavalo continue to turn large-scale societal conditions to its own local advantage without suffering unintended consequences that will gradually take the pace and direction of change out of the reach of its own mechanisms of social policy? Points of stress are already visible. It may be true that the organization of production in household units sets limits on the scale and complexity of production (Nash 1966:71), but nothing has prevented some families from developing as adjuncts to the household workshops approaching a factory form of organization (Casagrande 1969:4). As a result the textile industry has probably increased rather than moderated the inequality of landholdings and standards of living. It is true that the employment of land-poor villagers by other Indians as spinners, weavers, or farm helpers may share out some of the wealth, but the ascendancy of a few entrepreneurially active families in business is conspicuous. If most textile wealth continues to go into the buying up of lands, partible inheritance and the deprecation of greed central to Otavalan ethics may not prevail against the dynamics of private ownership, and the Indian communities will have agrarian problems of their own. Second, although Otavalans have usually relied on judicial rather than political resolution of power and property struggles, both the increased integration and visibility of the community and the trend in law toward the inclusion of Indians in the effective electorate will bring the area more, though not necessarily more beneficial, government attention. Can the combination of market integration with sociopolitical isolation endure this?

It is by no means a foregone conclusion that any such change would do the *parcialidades* harm, or at any rate harm enough to outbalance the enriching benefits that ideally follow from the modernization of production and the penetration of the nation-state into previously isolated localities. But the human costs of these changes weigh heavy on every people that has undergone them. Early industrial society everywhere seems to be inseparably connected with traumatic reorganizations, brutal demands on workers, and wholesale loss of much of what people live for. Humanly satisfying and varied labor, the solidarity and continuity of small communities, and the preservation of a rationality beyond that of maximizing production at the expense of everything else are the first casualties of every industrial revolution. While the "Awakening Valley" looks poor in the eyes of visitors from the United States, it is a fortunate place not only compared to almost every other Andean region but also compared to areas in the throes of early industrialization. The pride of manner and handsome appearance of its men and women testify to a relation to the modern world that deserves more recognition. It is a great feat to industrialize rapidly; it is also a great feat not to.

Both sides of this paradox find expression in North American youth politics, a politics growing in response to the apparent exhaustion in our country of the very same notion of development that the U.S. government promotes in places like Ecuador. The Marxist left, proclaiming itself an ally of the Third World, advocates the redistribution of industrial wealth and the seizure of control over its machinery and resource bases by neocolonized peoples within and without the U.S.A.; the central aim is to counteract the growth of inequality between rich and proletarized countries and make of the industrial revolution a worldwide egalitarian revolution. But, uneasily in step with the Third World movement, cultural revolutionaries follow a post- or even anti-industrial vision. Seeing industrial society as a Frankenstein monster capable only of following an inflexible track to complete wastage of man and earth, they concentrate on ways of liberating people from the life of economic rationality itself by inventing social forms which can break production into decentralized operations, automate and cleanse industry, and make room for those who want to subsist outside the orbit of modernity altogether. Their mutual lack of confidence reflects a real dilemma; given industry as we know it, how are we to put machines at our service without becoming servants of machines?

Equations of the North American new left with Latin American revolutionary nationalism, and of neotribal communes with indigenous peoples, are obviously specious. Yet the comparison is of some interest. Ecuador is still far from facing any postindustrial problems, but already the question arises of how Ecuador's Indians—nearly half the nation—can be enlisted in the struggle to raise national productivity (under any political regime) without making the supposed beneficiaries mere tools of the effort. Beate Salz (1955:215–19) has answered by proposing, as an alternative to a smallhold agrarian reform which would still further restrict productivity to household subsistence, the implanting of "interstitial industry"—small industrial enterprises which would fit into the "interstices" of rural economy by employing the land-poor while giving them plots as a job benefit. This plan seeks to avoid abruptly destroying rooted social units and agrarian bases, the guaranteed availability of which would form an incentive for workers to stay "until they have sloughed off a traditional predilection for cultivation of land." Thus from a modernist point of view the idea is to uproot tradition in a humane way.

But the Otavaleños have, in effect, carried out Salz's plan of their own accord, for the reverse purpose; they have used an "interstitial" industry, weaving, as a way of preserving their rooted way of life. It may come to pass that the dynamics of their industrialism will eventually weaken land-based organization, as Salz foresees. But this would not signify the loss of local society, for the change could be achieved at least in part on the actors' own terms. The significant point is that Otavalans have found an alternative to exploitation and cultural extinction on the one hand and dire poverty on the other, by creating a nationally integrated small industry distinct from the *Gesellschaft* model. From this both the Marxist and the culture-radical may have something to learn.

In the development-versus-stagnation stereotype, too much is taken for granted. Otavalo, with a minimum of technological aid and little outside sympathy, has succeeded in creating a flexible technology tailored to the changing needs of small groups. Once technologists produce a range of tools suited to small projects, and revolutionaries make their use a high priority, places less historically fortunate may have similar opportunities, as may communal alternatives in rich nations. A broader conception of industry will afford broader alternatives of engagement and autonomy. In both the most advanced and the newest industrial economies, smallness of scale, far from signifying obsolescence, has rationality of its own. In the economies of rich nations communal forms have begun to find a niche by providing labor-intensive products (crafts) and, increasingly, services (such as experimental and special education) to the larger whole on a basis of partial autonomy; the technical and economic possibilities of these forms are just now coming into view. For revolutionists and technicians, it will be a time to cease thinking of how to manage other peoples' livelihoods, and to begin thinking how livelihood can become less a matter of management and more a fruit of local creativity.

NOTES

Acknowledgments: The present essay is a slightly revised version of the text originally published in Daniel Gross, ed., *Peoples and Cultures of Native South America* (Garden City, N.Y.: Natural History Press, 1973), included here by permission of editor and publisher. Based on data of the 1960s, it has been updated only by mention of a few recent publications. No attempt has been made to provide a report on current (1979) Otavalan society.

REFERENCES CITED

AGI/S (Archivo General de Indias, Sevilla)
    1548–83   Cámara 922A. Doña Leonor de Balenzuela muger del capitan Rodrigo de Salazar con el fiscal y la comunidad de los indios del repartimiento de Otavalo. Unpublished.
Beals, Ralph
    1966   *Community in Transition: Nayón, Ecuador.* Los Angeles: Latin American Center, UCLA.

Buitrón, Aníbal
1947 Situación Económica y Social del Indio Otavaleño. *América Indígena* 7:45–67.
1956 La Tecnificación de la Industria Textil Manual de los Indios del Ecuador. In Eusebio Dávalos Hurtado and Ignacio Bernal, eds., *Estudios Antropológicos en Homenaje al Dr. Manuel Gamio*. Mexico City: Universidad Nacional Autónoma de México, Dirección General de Publicaciones, pp. 287–95.
1962 Panorama de la Aculturación en Otavalo, Ecuador. *América Indígena* 22:313–22.
n.d. *Taita Imbabura, Vida Indígena en los Andes*. Quito: Misión Andina.
Buitrón, Aníbal, and Barbara Salisbury Buitrón
1945 Indios, Blancos, y Mestizos en Otavalo, Ecuador. *Acta Americana* 3:190–216.
1966 Leyendas y Supersticiones Indígenas de Otavalo. *América Indígena* 26:53–79.
Casagrande, Joseph B.
1966 Proposal for Research on Intergroup Relations in Ecuador. Unpublished manuscript.
1969 The Implications of Community Differences for Development Programs: An Ecuadorian Example. Paper presented at the Society for Applied Anthropology Meetings, Mexico City, 9–16 Apr.
Cieza de León, Pedro
1959 *The Incas of Pedro de Cieza de León*. Trans. Harriet de Onis, ed. Victor Wolfgang von Hagen. Norman: University of Oklahoma Press.
Collier, John, Jr., and Aníbal Buitrón
1949 *The Awakening Valley*. Chicago: University of Chicago Press.
Cooper, Jed Arthur
1965 *The School in Otavalo Indian Society*. Tucson: Panguitch Publications.
Hartmann, Roswith
1972 Otros Datos sobre las Llamadas "Batallas Rituales." *Actas del XXXIX Congreso Internacional de Americanistas* 6:127–35. Lima.
Hassaurek, Friedrich
1967 *Four Years among the Ecuadoreans*. Ed. C. Harvey Gardner. Carbondale: Southern Illinois University Press.
Instituto Ecuatoriano de Antropología y Geografía (IEAG)
1953 *Ilumán, una Comunidad Indígena Aculturada*. Quito: Instituto Nacional de Previsión, Serie Informes 3.
Jaramillo, Victor Alejandro
1953 *Participación de Otavalo en la Guerra de Independencia*. Otavalo: Editorial Cultura.
Juan, Jorge, and Antonio de Ulloa
1806 *A Voyage to South America: Describing at Large the Spanish Cities, Towns, Provinces, etc. on That Extensive Continent*. Vol. 1. London.
1826 *Noticias Secretas de América*. London.
1918 *Noticias Secretas de America (Siglo XVIII)*. Vol. 1. Madrid: Editorial America, Serie "Biblioteca Ayacucho."
Landázuri Soto, Alberto
1959 *El Régimen Indígena Laboral en la Real Audiencia de Quito*. Madrid: Imprenta de Aldecoa.

Loukotka, Čestmír
1968   *Classification of South American Indian Languages.* Los Angeles: Latin American Center, UCLA.
Meggers, Betty J.
1966   *Ecuador.* New York: Praeger.
Moreno Yánez, Segundo
1976   *Sublevaciones Indígenas en la Audiencia de Quito.* Bonn: Bonner Amerikanistische Studien 5.
Municipalidad de Otavalo
1909   *Monografía del Cantón de Otavalo, Edición Costeada por la Municipalidad.* Quito: Tipografía Salesiana.
Murphy, Robert, and Julian H. Steward
1956   Tappers and Trappers: Parallel Processes in Acculturation. *Economic Development and Culture Change* 4:335–55. (Bobbs-Merrill Reprint #A-167.)
Murra, John
1946   The Historic Tribes of Ecuador. In Julian H. Steward, ed., *Handbook of South American Indians,* vol. 2: *The Andean Civilizations.* Washington, D.C.: Smithsonian Institution, pp. 785–821.
Nash, Manning
1966   *Primitive and Peasant Economic Systems.* San Francisco: Chandler Publishing Co.
Parsons, Elsie Clews
1945   *Peguche, Canton of Otavalo, Province of Imbabura, Ecuador: A Study of Andean Indians.* Chicago: University of Chicago Press.
Phelan, John Leddy
1967   *The Kingdom of Quito in the Seventeenth Century: Bureaucratic Politics in the Spanish Empire.* Madison: University of Wisconsin Press.
Ponce de León, Sancho de Paz
1897   Relación y Descripción de los Pueblos del Partido de Otavalo . . . 1582. In *Relaciones Geográficas de Indias* 3:105–20. Madrid: Ministerio de Fomento.
Reyes, Oscar Efren
1938   *Breve Historia General del Ecuador.* Vol. 1. Quito: Imprenta de la Universidad Central.
1826   *Noticias Secretas de América.* London
Rubio Orbe, Gonzalo
1956   *Punyaro, Estudio de Antropología Social y Cultural de Una Comunidad Indígena y Mestiza.* Quito: Casa de la Cultura Ecuatoriana.
1957   *Promociones Indígenas en América.* Quito: Casa de la Cultura Ecuatoriana.
Salinas, Raúl
1954   Manual Arts in Ecuador. *América Indígena* 14:315–26.
Salz, Beate
1955   *The Human Element in Industrialization: A Hypothetical Case Study of Ecuadorian Indians.* Washington, D.C.: American Anthropological Association, Memoir 85.
Stevenson, William Bennett
1825   *A Historical and Descriptive Narrative of Twenty Years' Residence in South America.* Vol. 2. London: Hurst, Robinson, and Co.

Szászdi, Adam
  1964 The Historiography of the Republic of Ecuador. *Hispanic American Historical Review* 44:503–50.
Tax, Sol
  1957 Changing Consumption in Indian Guatemala. *Economic Development and Culture Change* 5:147–58.
Vargas, José María
  1957 *La Economía Política del Ecuador durante la Colonia.* Quito: Editorial Universitaria.
Villavicencio Rivadeneira, Gladys
  1973 *Relaciones Interétnicas en Otavalo, Ecuador.* Mexico City: Instituto Indigenista Interamericano.
Wolf, Bernard
  1969 *The Little Weaver of Agato.* New York: Cowles Book Co.
Wolf, Eric R.
  1966 *Peasants.* Englewood Cliffs, N.J.: Prentice-Hall.

16

Development in Spite of Itself: The Saraguro Case

Linda Smith Belote and Jim Belote

Between the late 1950s and the early 1970s the Indians of Saraguro experienced many changes. Their expressed self-image became much more positive and they became more assertive in claiming their rights as individuals and as members of a distinct ethnic community.[1] For the first time in recent years nonfamily-based special- and general-interest groups were formed, some of which became involved in local and national politics and other activities in an attempt by Saraguros to gain more control over their own destinies. Adult literacy became much more widespread and a greater number of young people began to attend school through higher grade levels. A few went on to seek university education. The Saraguros gained not only more access to better medical care but a more active awareness of health-related issues.

We will examine the roles that various outside agencies and individuals played during these two decades in stimulating, facilitating, or actually bringing about these and other developments. The agencies to be examined include the Roman Catholic church, an evangelical Protestant mission, and the Andean Mission, Misión Andina, a governmental community development organization. The external agencies and individuals concerned did not necessarily operate in an efficient, productive, and consistent manner with the Saraguros. Our observations of their day-to-day operations, especially those of the Andean Mission, often revealed a discouraging picture of recurrent impatience, frustration, exploitation for personal gain, lack of understanding, little willingness to let the Saraguros have much voice in the changes being attempted, strong desires to take credit where none was due, discontinuity of programs, inadequate support from national headquarters, and application of programs inappropriate to Saraguro. Furthermore, there was a good deal of competition and conflict, especially, but not only, between and among Catholic and Protestant groups. Many of the stated objectives of these various agencies were not fulfilled, and the positive developments set forth above were not necessarily those desired or sought by the agencies. These developments were, nevertheless, influenced or stimulated by the outside agencies, in spite of the many problems in their methods of operation, as we shall show in this paper.

Saraguro is a town of roughly 1,600 inhabitants (1970) located at 2,550 meters' elevation in the province of Loja, Ecuador. The inhabitants of the town, known as "Saragurenses," are non-Indians, locally called *blancos*, whites. These townspeople earn their living primarily from crafts, services, shops, and government employment; owing to a paucity of economic opportunity and lack of a land base, they are not, on the average, as economically secure as the rural inhabitants of the surrounding region.

In the countryside within the greater boundaries of the *parroquia* of Saraguro live about 3,000 *indígenas*, Indians. These represent approximately one-third of the members of the indigenous population of the northern sector of Loja province, who are known as the Saraguros. This study is concerned only with the residents of Saraguro parish. Saraguros wear distinctive clothing and hair styles as ethnic markers which set them off not only from non-Indians but from other Ecuadorian lowland and highland indigenous peoples. A third group of people—non-Indian farmers, called locally *blancos del campo*, rural whites, or more vulgarly *chazos*—also lives in Saraguro parish. While important for an analysis of ethnic relations in Saraguro—their ethnic identity is white but their economic lifestyle is essentially that of the Indians—they are beyond the scope of this paper (see Belote 1978, Schmitz 1977, Masson 1977). All residents of the Saraguro region classify themselves as either *indígenas* or *blancos*. No "intermediate" groups such as *mestizos* or *cholos* are recognized locally.

By Ecuadorian standards the *indígenas* of Saraguro parish are reasonably well off. Most nuclear families own more than 15 hectares of agricultural land in scattered plots. On this land they raise subsistence crops and cattle for cash. Many are engaged in colonization of the Oriente, for the purposes of cattle raising (see Stewart, Belote, and Belote 1976).

CATHOLIC AND PROTESTANT ACTIVITY IN SARAGURO

The Roman Catholic church is beyond question the agency with the greatest influence in Saraguro Indian life. The clergy of the period when this study began inherited a congregation with a long history[2] of devout Catholicism expressed primarily in strict adherence to fast day observation, extensive (and expensive) feast and saints' days celebrations (see Belote and Belote 1977b), absolute conviction of the sanctity of and necessity for religious sacraments, attendance at weekly mass, and payment of *primicias*, first fruits, and *diezmos*, tithes.[3] They also freely contributed time, food, and labor to the clergy as well as a substantial amount of money.

The Church's stated objective was to provide spiritual leadership and religious education to the people. Town whites, particularly young and middle-aged males, while nominally Catholic, tended to view the principal religious figure, the *cura*, parish priest, with cynicism and some hostility and often expressed the view that the main objective of the *cura* was to enrich himself. Similarly, *blancos* often ridiculed the religiosity of the Saraguros and the degree to which they were subject to the influence of the Church.

At the time of this study there were three Catholic units operating in Saraguro: the parish priest; a convent of Marianita nuns, *madres*, whose primary responsibility was a girls' elementary school; and a Franciscan mission, headed by a *padre*, monk, which was originally established in the 1930s as a highland support base for missionary operations in the Oriente but which in the late 1960s assumed the direction of an Indian elementary school as its principal interest.

The Marianitas serve under the direction of the *cura*, and both he and they are subject to the authority of the bishop of Loja. The Franciscans, on the other hand, are under the jurisdiction of a bishop, *monseñor*, of their order, with headquarters in the Oriente town of Zamora. The relationships between the Franciscans and the other representatives of the Church in Saraguro at the time under study ranged from cooperation to conflict at different times and over various issues, owing both to the policies and directives of their respective superiors and to the personal characteristics of the individuals concerned. All three Catholic representatives, however, fostered the spiritual leadership image and encouraged the dutiful obedience which so typified the Saraguros.

It can easily be said that with all its power and influence in the area, the Church had done little in return for the Saraguros' devotion other than provide services of a religious nature.

In the late 1950s an evangelical Protestant mission, the Interamerican Mission, established a medical clinic in Saraguro. This group included a doctor and nurses among its personnel, and the clinic soon gained a good reputation throughout southern Ecuador. The missionaries, who came from North America and Europe, had a two-fold objective: to bring to the people their understanding of Christianity (to provide spiritual leadership) and to provide good, inexpensive health service in the area.

This new agency from the outside was perceived as a serious threat by the Catholic clergy in Saraguro, particularly by the *cura*, who feared erosion of his flock and hence diminution of his power. His response was primarily one of preaching strong sermons condemning the Protestant missionaries and exhorting the congregation to refrain from all contact with them. In some of his more extreme diatribes from the pulpit he proclaimed that anyone whose life was extended by the foreign missionary, or who was injected with the missionary's medicine, was tainted with Protestantism and would thus automatically and eternally be condemned to hell. "Better die now and let your children die now with immediate access to Heaven than live a few years longer only to burn forever," was one of his proclamations. In one local Church publication Protestantism and Communism were identified with each other and the work of the Devil (*El Campanario* 1962).

The antagonism of the Catholic clergy toward the Protestants seemed to have little influence on many town *blancos*, who freely associated with the missionaries and sought their medical help. Few of these *blancos*, however, attended Protestant religious services, and fewer still converted. Saraguros, on the other hand, either reflected the ecclesiastical antagonism or were afraid to indicate any other attitude for fear of rebuke by the clergy or hostility from neighbors. Many would not seek medical attention under any circumstances; others would do so only late at night when, they hoped, no one would learn of it and report it to the *cura*. However, the quality of the medical attention given and the manner in which it was provided (for example, all persons were treated in a friendly manner and in order of arrival, regardless of ethnic group membership or socioeconomic status) began to result in a gradual increase in Indian patronage of the clinic.

This slowly growing acceptance of the presence of the Protestant medical services on the part of the Saraguros, in spite of the *cura*'s warnings to the contrary, apparently led him to take more drastic action in the early 1960s. First, rumors and indications were spread that the *cura* would leave the area and remain absent until the missionaries were "removed." Without the *cura* there would be no provision of essential services such as the performance of baptisms and extreme unction for the local inhabitants. Then he did leave town.

Some ardently devout townspeople together with some respected Indian leaders immediately traveled throughout the countryside to spread the word of the *cura*'s departure. Early the next morning several hundred machete- and stone-wielding Saraguros assembled in town to attack the Protestant mission. Intervention by some town whites and the arrival of army troops from Loja later in the day kept the incident from resulting in bloodshed or other serious consequences. Within the year this *cura* was reassigned to another area.

With the arrival of another *cura* the strategy of the Church in Saraguro began to change. The new *cura* first tried to have the mission removed from town by having parishioners sign a petition stating that the missionaries were disturbing the peace. This petition was hand-carried to Quito by a delegation of both Indians and whites, headed by the *cura*. The petition was presented to an official of the ruling *junta militar*, who scanned the document, gave the delegation a stern lecture on religious freedom in Ecuador, and dismissed them.

Recognizing that the Protestant mission could not be driven out of Saraguro, this *cura* and those who followed began to implement a competitive strategy of far greater consequence to the Saraguros. Attempts to expand the nature of the relationships between the Church and the Indians were begun by various means. The Catholic church could not compete successfully with the Protestants in terms of medical care, but it did compete in other ways.

The *cura* claimed indigenous heritage himself (albeit from Inca nobility)[4] in an attempt to identify with his flock. While his predecessors had offered local whites personal attention and recognition, he was the first to address his Indian parishioners by name. He proclaimed the brotherhood of man, regardless of "racial" or ethnic affiliation. And he instituted in Saraguro a branch of the Legion de María organization which attracted several hundred Indian and *blanco* members. The legion served to reinforce and increase the understanding of the Catholic faith of its members by holding adult religious education classes in the Marianitas' convent on Sundays and in the rural communities throughout the week. It also showed that Indian and *blanco* Catholics could interact with each other on a more equal basis than had been the case in the past. The legion also sponsored nonreligious social events such as the annual election of a *reina indígena*, Indian queen, integrated variety shows, and banquets in which Saraguros and *blancos* ate together and were served together by members of both groups. All efforts of the legion in these social, integrated events were consciously designed to promote the imagery of "white cultural standards" as the "proper" forms of entertainment. White standards were the national standards; to be of the Ecuadorian nation was to be white. The legion was unsuccessful in its *blanqueamiento*, whitening, and nationalizing effort; its activities were well attended, but they only expanded the *indígenas'* social activities rather than supplanting the traditional ones.

In addition, in the late 1960s the *cura* participated in another area of the Indians' life when he became involved in the first attempt by Saraguros to hold local political office. Saraguros had first voted in large numbers in the election of 1956. At that time several townspeople campaigned extensively among the Indians to get them to show up at the polls and vote for Camilo Ponce, the conservative, Church-backed candidate for president of Ecuador. Their campaign included teaching many of the Saraguros to sign their names so they could vote. Although there was strong opposition to their efforts by many town whites, most of whom favored Huerta, hundreds of Indians did vote for Ponce. When Ponce won, he gave great credit to the voting contribution of the Saraguros and invited a delegation of young Indians to visit him at his hacienda north of Quito as a means of showing his gratitude. From this time forward Saraguros continued to participate in elections. However, their participation consisted in little more than voting a straight conservative or Poncista ticket, frequently expressing that this was the dictum of the Catholic church and to do otherwise would be a sin.

The *cura's* involvement in political affairs came through affiliation with a Saraguro Indian man who had been absent from the area for several years. His return in 1968 sparked diverse rumors but no general knowledge about where he had been or what he had been doing. This young man was very outspoken about the injustices suffered by the Saraguros and their need to seek greater control over their own destinies, particularly through political activities. He and the *cura* and a group of young Saraguros began to cooperate in attempts to involve the Indians in political action.

In this year Ponce himself was again a presidential candidate. He came to Saraguro on a campaign trip where he received a warm public welcome. The young Saraguro activist made an eloquent speech in which he presented Indian grievances and problems to Ponce. Ponce, in his response, alienated some of the Indians in the audience by stating that their problems were not Indian problems but those of *campesinos*[5] in general, showing a lack of sensitivity to Indian issues and to local language usage (*campesino* is used for *blanco* farmers only). Shortly thereafter an activist native Saraguro group entered a slate of candidates for municipal council seats, aligned with the party of Ponce's opponent, Dr. José María Velasco Ibarra. This was done out of disenchantment with Ponce and because the incumbent council members, all town whites, were already registered for Ponce's party ticket.

With the strong support of the priest, and the large number of Saraguro voters in the area, the Indian candidates felt confident of victory. However, Velasco was regarded with suspicion by many conservative Catholics, and word was spread among the Indians that the Loja Catholic hierarchy was insistent that good Catholics could vote only for Ponce. The Saraguro vote was split, resulting in defeat for the indigenous slate. While the loss was demoralizing for the candidates, an education regarding the political process was acquired and native Saraguro consciousness was raised to new levels. The town *blancos*, meanwhile, were shaken by their own narrow victory and offered one permanent Indian seat on the council if the Saraguros would agree not to seek more. The Saraguros refused the offer, leaving open the option that they might sometime again try to take control.

Another area of the *cura*'s involvement in Indian "development" was education. The *cura* alone was not responsible for all the advances made in Indian education. The Andean Mission's rural school construction program, rural teachers, understanding parents, and far-sighted children all played a part. The priest, however, in his strong encouragement of education in general, and personal sponsorship of partial scholarships for six young Indian women to pursue secondary education at a convent school in Quito, played an important role in expanding the Saraguros' view of career opportunities other than farming.[6]

Roughly 60% of the Saraguros are fluently bilingual (Spanish and Quichua), over 30% are monolingual Spanish speakers, and the remainder—mainly women and children in the communities most distant from town—are fluent in Quichua only. A significant impetus for Spanish language acquisition came with the arrival of the Pan-American Highway in the 1940s, as the Saraguros increased their engagement in a cash and market economy and their contact with outsiders. Land transactions, cattle sales, the borrowing of money, etc., all required negotiations in Spanish and written contracts and other documents, and the Saraguros realized the value of learning Spanish and of learning to read and do arithmetic as important strategies for economic survival and advancement. Basic schooling was thus viewed positively in Saraguro. In fact, a number of adults had become functionally literate without formal education by studying with their school-age children at home. However, formal education was not seen as an end value in itself, nor was it a symbol of great social prestige within the native Saraguro cultural context. Furthermore, school was not viewed as the place to receive agricultural training, physical education, or lessons on morality, hygiene, or history. When these topics were studied, parents often complained that their children were wasting valuable time—time that should have been used to learn to read, write, and do math, or time they could have been using to help their parents in the fields or around the house. Most Saraguro parents believed three years' education was sufficient for their children to acquire the skills necessary for the career of farmer/ cattle raiser. In fact, most parents did need their children's help with the crops and with the cattle, and it did, indeed, work a hardship on the families who chose to let their children study for more than the customarily accepted time. The *cura*'s influence and advice to parents of children desiring higher education played a key role in their acceptance of their children's absence.

THE ANDEAN MISSION AND COMMUNITY DEVELOPMENT

The *cura* did not become actively involved in projects which could be termed community development or economic development. Several development agencies have practiced their skills in Saraguro over the years for varying lengths of time: 4-F (4-H), agricultural extension, Hiefer project, and the Andean Mission. During the time of this study the Andean Mission was present in Saraguro, and the major portion of the discussion thus relates to this organization.

Analyses of community development projects, successes and failures, are numerous, and there still remains, as Lance and McKenna (1975) attest, "an apparent lack of theoretical foundation for the introduction of changes in the non-Western world." Erasmus (1968), after careful analysis of community development literature, came to the conclusion that "natural" (i.e., without the intervention of outsiders) community development is the only type of successful community development. Casagrande (1974a) pointed out the necessity for community development personnel to be attuned to the total ecology of the community which is the object of change. The history of community development bears strong witness that this has seldom been done anywhere. It certainly has not in Saraguro. We turn now to an analysis of development carried out in Saraguro by the Andean Mission.

Founded and supported originally by agencies of the United Nations, the Andean Mission had as its objectives the development and integration into national life of the mainly indigenous populations of rural areas of the Andean nations (International Labor Organization 1961:16-22). In the 1960s the Andean Mission became an agency of the Ecuadorian government within the Ministerio de Previsión Social, with the United Nations retaining an advisory capacity.[7]

The Andean Mission's approach was to send a team consisting of a zone coordinator, a social worker, an agronomist, and a community development specialist to various communities for several hours a week per community. Occasionally a medical doctor and nurse would be added to the group. The goals of the local team were goals pursued equally throughout Ecuador by all Andean Mission teams and were established by personnel in Quito, not by people in the field. These goals included, to follow Lance and McKenna's (1975) classification system, mechanical (i.e. material) innovations, agricultural innovations, labor cooperation, community organization, and to a minor extent therapeutic innovations. A goal not mentioned by Lance and McKenna but pursued by the Andean Mission was nonagricultural job skill training. We will examine some of these in more depth, in an attempt to clarify the "successes" and "failures" of the Andean Mission approach.

A latrine construction project promoted by the Andean Mission in the mid-1960s is one of many examples belonging to the material innovation category. The field team employees constructed several units in various communities, at the schools and at the homes of willing collaborators, hoping the example would spur emulation. It did not. The Saraguros did have an evaluation of the latrines: they were a waste of time and materials, the privacy heralded by the mission was regarded as unnecessary, and they were smelly, dirty, and attracted flies. Within three years after construction only those standing beside schools were in use and intact. All the others had fallen into disuse; their doors, which had been provided by the Andean Mission, had all been removed and installed in homes.

Sanitation emphasis by the Andean Mission personnel resulted in negative health benefits in some cases. For example, the latrines at one school were moved to a new location directly over a small stream when they became full, so that the latrines would not have to be moved again. The stream served as the principal source of water for many of the community residents. When we questioned the Andean Mission zone coordinator about the advisability of adding such pollutants to drinking water, he acknowledged it was unhealthy but indicated that the Andean Mission had abandoned the latrine promotion; it was now involved in other projects and sanitation was no longer its concern.

In contrast, a household furniture promotion was well received. The Andean Mission hired a carpenter to construct furniture—rustic benches and tables—for Indian homes. The Saraguros were only obliged to supply the wood, which they willingly did. Previously they had to pay local carpenters for the construction. This project terminated, though, when a new zone coordinator arrived and said he was appalled that the Indians were being taught to expect "handouts" from the Andean Mission.

Elevated cooking fire platforms and homemade grass-stuffed mattresses were two other innovations which were tried by some Saraguros, after a demonstration by mission employees, and then rejected. The stove platforms were disliked by the women who tried them because their feet got cold, and they preferred to cook sitting on the floor; the mattresses were found to be lumpy and less comfortable than the mats already in use. In addition, they took much longer to dry out from infants' nighttime wetting and they harbored many more insects than did the mats.

The introduction of sewing machines met with moderate success. Treadle machines were placed in a private home in each of several communities. The home owner was to make the machine available and provide instruction to all the women of her community. The Andean Mission social worker also provided sewing lessons to girls' clubs which met in the communities on a weekly basis. The machines were seldom used by members of the community other than the home owner, however, owing to the Saraguros' mutual respect for individuality. No one wanted to ask the machines' keepers to use that which appeared to be their personal property. Interestingly, men were never provided a format in which they could learn machine sewing, even though it is the men of Saraguro who do all of the sewing of their traditional clothing items—skirts, ponchos, short pants, and *cushmas*, men's tunics. The women who did learn machine sewing did not assume the sewing of these items; rather, they confected apparel which had been purchased previously from local white seamstresses, i.e. women's blouses, children's shirts, and a decorative border on *pulleras*, underskirts. In time a number of women did buy sewing machines for their own use so that they would not have to rely on local town seamstresses.

Although the Andean Mission focused considerable attention on agricultural development, efforts in this area did not result in significant change. This was due primarily to a lack of understanding of the

Saraguros' agricultural system and economy. A pre–Andean Mission experiment exemplifies many projects that the Andean Mission attempted, and it helped set the stage for the Saraguros' pragmatic and somewhat cynical assessment of similar projects initiated by the Andean Mission.

All Saraguro households raise guinea pigs and sheep for subsistence purposes. Guinea pigs are eaten, while the main value of the sheep is in the wool from which most family clothing is made. Wool is rarely bought or sold, as each family maintains about the right number of sheep for its own needs. Saraguro sheep are quite scrawny and have rather thin coats of long, relatively straight-fibered wool. Before the women spin the wool, it is washed and preshrunk, giving it the right amount of curl for Saraguro spinning techniques. Also, many Saraguro sheep are "black" (dark brown), requiring less of the black or indigo dyes which the Saraguros use for much of their clothing. Into this context an agency brought fat, white, thick-coated, expensive Merino sheep, in the hopes of improving local breeding stock and thus wool production. For people to whom wool was an important source of cash this project might have worked. It did not in the Saraguro case. When processed by Saraguro methods, Merino wool curled up much too tightly to be spun. Alternative processing methods which could compensate for this problem were not introduced. Thus what might have been a beneficial market-oriented introduction elsewhere was a failure in terms of the local subsistence orientation. The Merino sheep were soon sold to the local butcher or slaughtered for household consumption.

The Andean Mission's introduction of rabbits in an area where nearly all families, Indian and non-Indian, raise guinea pigs for household consumption, with little involvement of expense or effort, was as inappropriate an innovation as that of the Merino sheep. Not only were rabbits more expensive and time-consuming to raise, but there was no significant internal or external market for them.

One livestock improvement project did meet with initial enthusiastic response. The Andean Mission offered to obtain a fine bull for a reasonable price to breed with local stock. Cattle are the Saraguros' prime cash economy interest, and they immediately saw the merits of the mission's offer. The Saraguros already practiced controlled selective breeding of cattle, reserving their finest bulls (but not cows) for breeding purposes. Persons without fine bulls obtained services of such bulls from persons who owned them, paying an agreed-upon fee at the live birth of a calf. The mission insisted, however, that the bull would be provided only if a cooperative could be organized to collectively purchase and manage it. Saraguros rejected this form of cooperative ownership. Several Saraguros offered to buy and manage the bull themselves, providing access to reproductive services to others according to the established practice. This counteroffer was rejected by the mission; field and office workers branded the Saraguros *egoistas*, and asserted that Saraguros were unable to "cooperate" in any developmental venture. This judgment was erroneous, as we will demonstrate below.

There have been some mixed successes with new crops, though not necessarily in the intended ways. As with sheep and guinea pigs, agriculture is almost entirely subsistence-oriented among the Saraguros. The development agencies, by contrast, were primarily interested in cash crop production, though they did not ignore subsistence factors. They have had very little success in encouraging production of such cash crops as corn and potatoes.

Saraguros are not interested in selling their basic, subsistence crops, and are quite explicit about this. Their crops are seen as an essential component of the subsistence system, and only with radical change in land and time allocation could their crops become commercially significant. The basic staple, corn, is eaten daily, primarily in the form of *mote*, hominy. Corn stores almost indefinitely, and every household strives to produce at least enough to carry it through the year. Families with a two-year supply are regarded as fortunate. Demands on the subsistence crop beyond household maintenance include contributions to charity, the Church, and the fiesta system.

The Saraguros did accept a number of recommended agricultural innovations. Many of them quite readily established vegetable gardens and purchased pesticides and fertilizers where they perceived the value of these items in making their subsistence base more secure and dependable, where little or no perceptible risk or change of the subsistence system was involved.[8] However, more radical introductions such as hybrid corn did not achieve long-term acceptance. These involve an annual purchase of seeds, differences in fertilizer, and more intensive care requirements. In other words, the more radical innovations would have been a risk to Saraguro "security maximization" (cf. Johnson 1971, Scott 1976, Wharton 1971).

Marketing of livestock—pigs, chickens, and especially cattle—and their produce is an area in which the Saraguros participate significantly in the national economy. The arrival of the highway in the 1940s, the establishment of a Sunday market including a *plaza de ganados*, cattle market, in Saraguro shortly after the road came in, and participation of cattle dealers from other parts of Ecuador in the Saraguro market have been the major non-Indian contributions to the local development of cattle as a business enterprise. Other than the offer of a stud bull, development agencies have never become involved in the area of the Saraguros' lives which is directly involved with national economy. The Indians themselves have on occasion sought (but rarely found) veterinary skills and advice on cattle management. Rather than support development in this sphere of Saraguro interest and competence, the development agencies have often railed *against* the "excessive" attention and time devoted to cattle care by the Saraguros. Development agency personnel lamented the disruption of children's education and the lack of participation in agency-sponsored community work projects caused by the exigencies of cattle management in pastures located in the Oriente or other areas at considerable distances from the community of residence.

Labor cooperation and community organization are interrelated areas in which the Andean Mission exerted major emphasis in Saraguro. At the time of the initiation of their work the indigenous communities had only a loose organization beyond the family unit. Each community was served by traditional leaders, generally three per community, called *mayorales*. Always older males, these were officially appointed by the parish *teniente político*, a local *blanco*, for a lifetime position. The *teniente*, however, took no role in the selection of *mayorales*; he merely recorded the name given him by the other *mayorales* of the community.

The *mayorales* of any one community were all of equal rank and generally functioned independently of each other. Each commanded the respect, if not the loyalty, of only a segment of his community. This was not necessarily a localized area, and was very undefined. The *mayoral* had no enforcement powers, and he regarded his role as advisory; he was dependent on his personal influence for the fulfillment of his duties. His specific responsibility was for trail and bridge maintenance. His badge of office was a *quipa*, bullhorn, blown to summon people to come and work on these projects. However, his influence on many matters within the community could be quite strong. He was often consulted on a variety of matters, and the prestige of a *mayoral* was high. As each Saraguro built his own network of relationships with both whites and other Indians, the *mayoral*'s role as a mediator with the outside was minimal. Both the *cura* and the Franciscan *padre* used the *mayorales* to call people for volunteer work at their churches, but people felt they had a right to refuse, and *mayorales* defended this right.

The Andean Mission, in its initial entry into the area, began by enlisting the cooperation of the *mayorales*. In the main this was given with little hesitation. Early projects of the Andean Mission were rather well received. One involved trail improvement so that Andean Mission vehicles had easy entry into the communities, and the other was a school construction project. In both of these the Andean Mission sought and received widespread community labor cooperation. The trail *mingas*, cooperative labor, that were summoned were, of course, within the traditional jurisdiction of the *mayorales*. The Andean Mission added another incentive which the people enjoyed— all workers were "paid" for their efforts with a variety of CARE and Alliance for Progress foodstuffs.

While school construction was not a traditional area of responsibility for the *mayorales*, in the main the people did understand the benefit of this type of structure, as their children were being educated in vacant windowless Indian homes. Here, too, cooperative labor for building construction was customary for the Saraguros, who at that time spent much of the month of August building new homes for neighbors and kin by the *minga* system (see Belote and Belote 1977a). The Andean Mission provided the materials, as any indigenous home builder would, and also provided meals on labor-intensive days, again just as an Indian home builder would.

Through the 1960s support for the Andean Mission began to dwindle on the part of some of the *mayorales* and the community members. The Andean Mission had tried to get the *mayorales* to blow their *quipas* to call people to meetings and to *mingas* for digging wells, building latrines, and making irrigation canals, areas outside the *mayorales'* traditional ken. For some who complied, it weakened the influence that they once had held. Some *mayorales* declared themselves "enemies" of the Andean Mission. Many community members began to ignore the *quipa*, even for trail *mingas*, which were, in their minds, being called much too often. Maintaining a road for vehicular use, it had become clear, was not the same as keeping trails open for human and animal circulation. The Andean Mission employees argued that only with a road could their visits to the communities continue, and it would facilitate the trucking out of crops as well. Neither of these arguments impressed the Saraguros.

The Andean Mission meanwhile began to seek other ways to control the community members and, in keeping with the policy of integration into national society, urged the formation of legally organized *comunas* with annually elected officials forming a *cabildo*, community council, as specified in the *Ley de las Comunas* of the Ministerio de Previsión Social of the national government. Several communities did form such *cabildos*, though enthusiasm for them was quite low and elections often had to be held several times until sufficient voter turnout was achieved. In most communities the *cabildo* concept was not well understood, and most often it was the *mayorales* who continuously won election to the *cabildo* presidency. The Andean Mission, however, repeatedly emphasized that the *mayorales* were inadequate, and that each community should write its own constitution that empowered the president with the legal right to fine community members for lack of attendance at meetings and for failure to participate in community work projects. The Saraguros consistently resisted this measure, holding strong to their concept of an individual's freedom of choice regarding participation or nonparticipation in Andean Mission–sponsored projects.

The lack of Saraguro enthusiasm for the establishment of strong community organization under the aegis of the Andean Mission was also due to a long history of burdensome administrative interference in Saraguro affairs by outsiders. For example, prior to the building of the Pan-American Highway there had been an Indian administration system which was responsible for the maintenance of a *tambo*, way station, for travelers, mainly soldiers. Memories of this system are still fresh in the minds of older people who remember being coerced into giving food and fresh mounts to those traveling through. This system was abandoned when the highway allowed travelers to reach their destination without an overnight stop in Saraguro.[9] At the time of the *tambos* the *mayorales* had been under the jurisdiction of the *teniente político*, who, through the *mayorales*, periodically summoned community members to work in town in jobs such as street sweeping. President Velasco Ibarra halted this practice in the 1940s on a trip made to Saraguro, insisting that Indians be paid for such work. This was done until the early 1960s, when the practice was totally discontinued.

In the late 1950s, riding on the euphoria of the first Ponce election, the Saraguros of one community allowed the *teniente*, a Poncista activist, to organize a savings and loan cooperative in their community. By all accounts initial enthusiasm was great, as Saraguros then had little access to banks and felt they were at the mercy of town whites, who lent them money at interest rates between 3 and 10% per month. A large number of community members made initial deposits ranging from two to several hundred sucres. The money was deposited in a Loja bank, and signatures of both the *teniente* and a respected *mayoral* were required to make withdrawals. In all, a sum of around

100,000 sucres was collected. Before the first loan was made, however, the *teniente* left the area. When inquiries were made about withdrawals from the new account, the Saraguros learned that the entire
sum had already been withdrawn. The cooperative savings and loan
was then defunct.[10]

The Andean Mission's insistence on controlling community affairs
in such ways as establishing community work goals and *cabildo* meeting calendars and agendas appeared to the Saraguros as having the
potential to engender similar situations. The field team demanded
full compliance and cooperation on all projects, however ill conceived or unsuited. This the Saraguros would not grant.

Some Saraguros thought that their lack of unity and organization
was disadvantageous in some respects. For example, the communities had no means of protecting their members from abuses suffered
at the hands of local officials, and from thieves (mainly town whites)
who roamed the Indian communities. The Saraguros frequently commented on their inability to prevent such abuses, and found themselves wanting in comparison with some of the more unified white
campesino communities of the region. The Andean Mission did not
effectively respond to the expressions of need for help with this type
of problem. By the late 1960s the Saraguros began to take political
action to protect their own interests.

The meeting format, so strongly utilized by the Andean Mission,
was an innovation which the Saraguros came to appreciate. Community meetings were always called by the Andean Mission to coincide with their visits to a given community. Eventually members of
one community decided that meetings directed by the Andean Mission were unsatisfactory vehicles for solving their problems, since a
forum was not provided for their suggestions. They began to hold
their own "secret" (i.e., the Andean Mission was not informed) meetings to discuss community problems, safe from the interference and
direction of outsiders.

At one secret *cabildo* meeting the use of some community-owned
land in a forested mountain area nearby was discussed. It was decided to clear a certain amount of land and rent it out as pasture to
members of a rural *blanco* community located in an adjoining *parroquia*. In this way their community would gain funds which could be
used in any way the people decided. A large, well-attended *minga*
was arranged to get the work done. Interestingly, when they learned
about it, the *cura*, the Franciscan *padre*, and members of the Andean
Mission team all showed up at the *minga*, and all offered suggestions
as to what should be done and how it should be done. In addition,

they all attempted to take some of the credit for what was being accomplished.

The Andean Mission could have legitimately regarded the "secret" meetings as a successful achievement: members of the community recognizing a problem and meeting to solve it; but instead resentment grew because of the Indians' attempt to bypass mission authority and direction. In another "secret" meeting the members of the same community addressed a problem which various agencies—the Andean Mission, Peace Corps volunteers, and the Protestant missionary doctor—had been telling the people about for some years: the need for potable water for improved health. Fifty families of the community decided that piped potable water distributed throughout the area was a worthwhile and achievable goal, for they were aware that the Andean Mission had a supply of tubing on hand for such projects. A legal document was drawn up in which each family pledged manual labor and a contribution of 100 sucres. The document, specifying their need for the tubing and technical advice on installation, was presented to the Andean Mission zone coordinator. He turned them down completely. He later told us that "those people" had failed to cooperate with his projects in the past and that therefore he was not going to cooperate with them in the future. This refusal was tied to a general "get tough" policy implemented by the Andean Mission. All Food for Peace distributions for work groups and women's clubs were halted. It was said this was to undo the "spoiling" that the free handouts had caused, and to make the Indians realize the value of cooperative labor per se. Left in a warehouse for many months to be consumed by vermin, the remaining foodstuffs were eventually trucked out of the area. Personal pique therefore got in the way of what could have been another legitimate success for the Andean Mission.

Personal pique, on the part of both Indians and Andean Mission personnel, characterized other relations between the two groups. This sometimes centered around who was to be credited for originating and implementing such aspects of development as "home improvement" or new agricultural techniques. One of the clearest examples of this problem occurred in home improvement activities.

Painting house walls, installing windows, and laying wood floors were all projects encouraged and partially financed by the Andean Mission. Many Indians, however, made these home improvements entirely on their own initiative. They were quite emphatic in denying that the Andean Mission had anything to do with their projects and expressed irritation to us when they heard Andean Mission personnel point out their homes to visiting dignitaries as examples of their success. Some of them were opposed to all Andean Mission intervention in the area, and it appeared to us that they engaged in innovative activities in order to spite the mission—to show that it was not needed in the area because the Saraguros could develop on their own. The Andean Mission failed to appreciate the role of this group of "spiteful" innovators in promoting and implementing many of the mission's goals. And these Saraguros were unwilling to recognize the role of the Andean Mission in at least providing an initial stimulus to various changes.

While some Saraguros were openly opposed to the mission, the majority were either uninvolved with it or supported its presence in the area as a source of benefits if it could be carefully manipulated. The activities of the latter group are exemplified by the following incident.

In 1970 difficulties between the Andean Mission and the Saraguros led the local field team to a decision to move their center of operations to the city of Loja, 60 kilometers to the south. Some Indians opposed this move. They felt the mission should be available to provide them with help, on their own terms. In a showdown the mission team loaded their vehicles and left town under the cover of darkness. Informed Saraguros set up a roadblock just south of town, intercepted the vehicles, lifted them off the ground, and turned them around. The Andean Mission remained in Saraguro until 1973, when it ceased operations in Ecuador.

Although integration was listed as one of the Andean Mission's two prime objectives, it can be seen that it worked primarily against this objective. By refusing to work with livestock management and marketing, it made no contribution to indigenous incorporation into the national economy and, albeit somewhat unintentionally, worked on strengthening subsistence. The work that was accomplished in education (namely school construction) can be called "successful" integrative work, for larger numbers of children and adults are literate in the Spanish language than ever before. However, this facility has been employed by the Saraguros to better manipulate local and national representatives of the dominant national society and to strengthen indigenous identity rather than encourage assimilation.

The training of Saraguros at centers located in central Ecuador was also considered by the Andean Mission as integrative. Young women received training as auxiliary nurses, the men in weaving on upright looms, carpentry, and metalwork. Of these job training endeavors, the weaving and the nursing programs were somewhat successful, as those trained pursued their new careers as sources of supplemental income in their home area. Carpentry and metalworking were not utilized. A workshop was built by the Andean Mission for practice of these trades but was never equipped with any tools. Those who had acquired the skills used them in their own households, but they did not market them or train others.

Ultimately, the goal of "integration" is ethnocide/assimilation (see Whitten 1976:265–85). Within the area of Saraguro parish are a number of transculturated persons who were once Indians and are now *blancos*.[11] These people are obviously integrated into Ecuadorian national society, and while they may represent an end goal of the Andean Mission, they find themselves beyond the sphere of its assistance. On a number of occasions transculturated persons living in town were refused aid from the Andean Mission on the basis that its aid was intended for rural people only.

THE RISE OF A "FOLKLORE" TROUPE IN SARAGURO

The creation of a successful folklore troupe in Saraguro must now be discussed, for it encapsulates some of the changes that occurred during the period under discussion. The troupe was begun as a collaboration between the *cura* and the activist young man mentioned above; together they believed that the way to achieve solutions to the problems of the native Saraguros was to reach young people. Attempts to bring them together through volleyball games met with limited response, but a musical group was more positively viewed, and the group soon consisted of about 20 young members from several different communities, directed by a town white musician. They began as a church choir but soon expanded their repertoire to include performance of traditional Christmas and wedding dances, oratory, and poetry recitation. They were then ready for a larger audience and took their show to the provincial capital of Loja. Favorable response led them to undertake a tour of the country—performing whenever and wherever audiences would pay to hear them. They returned a poorer but more worldly group. Meanwhile, conflict developed between the white musician and the *cura*, and the Franciscan *padre* stepped in to sponsor the group, retaining the musician. Eventually, however, the conflict developed into a split, with one group affiliated with the *cura* and the other with the *padre*.

The Andean Mission, which had in no way participated in the groups, requested that the *cura* send his group to Quito to represent Saraguro and the Andean Mission at the festivals for the national celebration of the anniversary of the founding of the capital. In Quito the Andean Mission heralded the group as its own creation and took them around from barrio to barrio and park to park like zoo animals on display, with little concern for their personal needs. Nevertheless, while in Quito the Saraguros were featured in a front-page photo in the city's major newspaper and, at their own initiative, gained two television spots. While visiting a private white girls' school, the Saraguros were very well received, especially their young male master of ceremonies, who was mobbed by girls seeking his autograph. He wrote in English, "I love you," for most of them. Some members of the troupe also gained an audience with President Velasco Ibarra, and later, during the gala parade, the entire folklore troupe was called over to the president's viewing stand where it was promised financial aid.

In early performances the troupe sought to maintain as much "authenticity" as possible, for the members felt it important to be genuine representatives of the *indígenas* of Saraguro. This was not always easy, as the long and repetitious nature of many Saraguro traditional performances diminished audience appeal. But the folklore troupes of Saraguro have a greater significance than entertainment and the maintenance of tradition. In the first place, participation provided young Saraguros the opportunity to see and experience much more of the outside world.[12] Second, in many of their performances they took the opportunity to inform the outside world about Saraguro from an *indígena* point of view. This they did with eloquence, discussing the social injustice and exploitation suffered by the Saraguros.[13] Finally, they became the nucleus of activism in the Saraguro area and the first indigenous, nonfamily, noncommunity-based formal organization in recent times.

SUMMARY AND CONCLUSION

The changes which occurred among the Saraguros between the late 1950s and the early 1970s can be attributed not to any single factor, agency, or individual but, rather, to a complex interplay of outside influences and Saraguro responses. We offer, in conclusion, a brief summary of the major themes involved in this interplay.

Individualism and egalitarianism. The lack of strong pre-existing forms of nonfamily-based unity, combined with stress on egalitarianism and self-sufficiency, can be viewed as a serious weakness in Saraguro social organization (and is so viewed by many Saraguros). However, under certain circumstances individualism and egalitari-

anism, which promote a lack of unity, contributed to the overall independence of the Saraguros from efficient outside manipulation in
that no powerful indigenous leaders or groups were available to outsiders to be coopted, threatened, bought off, or otherwise induced to
effect the broadly applied changes desired by the outsiders.

Competition. Paralleling Saraguro individualism and egalitarianism
was competition between outside agencies and individuals attempting to direct change in Saraguro life. This competition provided the
Saraguros with a wider range of options and opportunities from
which to select and, in some cases, encouraged outsiders to deal with
Saraguros in a more egalitarian manner.

Manipulation. While Saraguros did not particularly agree with all
the development and change efforts directed to them by the outside,
they did see that outside agencies and individuals could be a resource
for beneficial activities the Saraguros desired. They learned how to
manipulate the change agents to get what they wanted without
either giving up too much or losing the "resource" altogether (cf.
Castile 1976).

Success of failure. The virtual absence of unified, consistent, and
successful implementation of the goals of outside agencies and individuals had the positive effect of preventing the Saraguros from
being seduced into surrendering greater control over their destinies
to these outsiders. They did not become seriously dependent on outside resources but, rather, managed to achieve something close to
what Erasmus called "natural development" (1968:69–70).

Ethnicity and attention. Ethnic pride has been a difficult thing for
most indigenous groups to maintain in highland Ecuador (see Casagrande 1974a, 1974b). However, in recent years Saraguros became
the focus of increasing attention by outsiders such as development
agencies, religious groups, Peace Corps volunteers, anthropologists,
geographers, politicians, tourists, and others. A major reason for this
focus has been the clearcut and unique ethnic identity of the Saraguros. This identity elicited responses ranging from attempts to
eliminate it (see the assimilation/ethnocide strategies discussed by
Whitten 1976:277–81) to attempts to promote it. One twist in these
efforts involved attempts to have the Saraguros assimilate to the national society in every way except for the "show" portion of their
lives (see Friedlander 1975:128–64). Saraguros have become aware
that they receive as much attention as they do (and its occasional
benefits such as financial and technical aid, scholarships, medical
care, etc.) *because* they are ethnically distinct. Thus, whatever inten-

tions lie behind it, attention from the outside has served to reinforce the boundaries promoting Saraguro ethnicity within a context of change. Furthermore, attention in and of itself can be considered a source of change analogous to the so-called "Hawthorne effect" (Roethlisberger and Dickson 1939), in which the subjects of observation or experimentation alter their behavior in response to being observed and not just to the manipulation of variables in their environment.[14]

Expanding perspectives. Activities of change agents, attention by other outsiders, increasing literacy, increasing travel, and the universal spread of the transistor radio among Saraguros in the 1960s have all served to expand Saraguro awareness of the outside world—of national life in general and their place in it, of the struggles of other peoples, of the dangers and opportunities available in the outside world. These expanding perspectives have helped the Saraguros to devise their own strategies of survival and to maintain and promote positive ethnic identity in the broader national context.

Expanding nonlocal contacts. One of the most significant correlates of expanding perspectives is the increasing extent to which Saraguros are able to bypass local, non-Indian sources of authority. In all domains (religious, social, economic, political, educational) the Saraguros began to deal with higher levels of regional and national authority which could either circumvent local non-Indian authority or provide benefits that local authorities could or would not (cf. the corresponding change of focus in institutional relationships in Yungay, Peru, following the earthquakes and avalanches of 1970, Oliver-Smith 1977:11). While some of the response undoubtedly was due to "tokenism," this does not negate all its beneficial consequences.

Economic resources. The underlying theme in the examination of the Saraguro situation is the relative strength of the Saraguro subsistence and market economies. A strong subsistence economy has permitted the Saraguros to avoid involvement with the outside where it did not suit their purposes, while their cash economy has provided the resources to permit self-controlled engagement where that was so desired. In short, the Saraguro economy provided a context in which the Saraguros could maintain a significant degree of control over the course of change in their lives.

It should be apparent from our discussion that the outside agencies and individuals working in Saraguro have served only to facilitate change and development in Saraguro—sometimes because of their anti-Saraguro strategies, sometimes in spite of their mistakes. The native Saraguros themselves have exerted, in their own way, the most important influence on development in their area. But Saraguros, like all peoples in Ecuador, exist in a changing national context. While some of the portents are positive, only the future can determine the extent to which Saraguros can maintain a satisfactory degree of control over their own destinies.

NOTES

Acknowledgments: This is a revised form of a paper presented at the 1977 American Anthropological Association Meetings in the symposium "Local-Level Responses to National Policies and Regional Development in Ecuador: Insights to the Workings of Complex Systems." We were Peace Corps volunteers affiliated with the Andean Mission in Saraguro from 1962 to 1964. Formal research for this study was done in various periods between 1968 and 1972. The cooperation and assistance provided by Arq. Hernán Crespo Toral of INAH made this research possible. Support from the University of Illinois (Department of Anthropology), the Midwest Universities Consortium for International Activities, Inc. (Internship E–1–144), and the National Institute of Mental Health (Fellowship 1 FOI MH 48824–01s1) is also gratefully acknowledged.

1. Erasmus (1968) described this change as a movement from the *encojido* syndrome to the *entron* syndrome, based on terminology used in Sonora, Mexico. In Saraguro the terms used are *timido*, timid, and *sin miedo*, unafraid, but the analogy is apt.

2. By 1582 a member of the regular clergy was resident in the area (Jiménez de la Espada 1965:195). The most complete published history of the Catholic church in Saraguro is found in the *Monografia de la Diocesis de Loja* (Anonymous 1966:251–69).

3. While the Indians dutifully paid the *primicias* and *diezmos*, the local *cura* and the Loja-based bishop did not collect them. Rather, they sold their rights to the highest bidders (always town whites) for collection and profiteering. In the 1940s the collection of *primicias* and *diezmos* was officially declared illegal. However, by the early 1970s only the local priest (but not the bishop) had actually terminated the practice.

4. Claiming descent from indigenous nobility is not unusual among Ecuadorian elites (cf. Whitten 1976:268).

5. *Campesino* is generally translated as "peasant." As such it entails all of the difficulty that the English term does (cf. Foster 1967, Erasmus 1970:317). The attempts to gloss over ethnic distinctions and give preference to occupational titles (such as *campesino*) are not limited to Ponce in Ecuador. Government officials in Peru (see van den Berghe 1975:75) and Bolivia (see Erasmus 1968:72) have utilized a similar approach in modern times.

6. There were two previous times in Saraguro history when a few Indians were sent off by the clergy to become educated. The first was during the presidency of García Moreno (1869–75) and the second was in the 1940s.

Older informants remember the return of one man from the latter group quite well, for they say he was an excellent teacher. No one followed in his footsteps, however, in part owing to lack of interest, in part because the clergy itself changed personnel. This possibility seems highly unlikely today, as the Indian youth themselves are beginning to seek the opportunity. The priest who followed the initiator of the current secondary education thrust was as enthusiastic as his predecessor about the program. In addition to the six young women studying outside, four young men also did so, at about the same time, on their own initiative. All spoke at the time of study of returning to Saraguro as Indians to serve their people, and some have since done so.

7. See Linke and Albornoz (1961) and Misión Andina (1963) for discussion of Andean Mission programs in Ecuador. Célleri (1966:269–73) provides a short discussion of the Andean Mission in Saraguro up to 1965. The Andean Mission ceased to exist in 1973. Its work of community development has been continued by the Ecuadorian Ministerio de Agricultura.

8. Gore (1971) administered lengthy questionnaires to 51 respondents in Saraguro as part of his attempt to elucidate factors relevant to agricultural modernization. While he found, for example, that about half of those interviewed used commercial fertilizers, his research in the area was of little use to us because he did not distinguish between Indian and non-Indian respondents, nor between those who produce crops primarily for subsistence and those town whites who reside in Saraguro but own large commercial wheat holdings in areas outside the Saraguro parish.

9. The system had also mediated between Indians and outsiders, both local and nonlocal. Its demise meant that Saraguro relations with outsiders became more individualized—each individual or family had to pursue its own interests without the aid of Indian officials acting as "cultural brokers" (cf. Silverman 1967, Wolf 1956, and Casagrande and Piper 1969).

10. A branch of the Banco Nacional de Fomento was inaugurated in Saraguro in the summer of 1978 (Joseph B. Casagrande, personal communication).

11. They are identified by themselves and others, Indian and *blanco*, as *blancos*. During the course of our experience in Saraguro we were able to learn the identities of 79 transculturated persons. Of these, 63 had changed from Indian to white; nine had gone from white to Indian; and five, born as Indians, had spent from two to 14 years living as whites and had then returned to their natal identity. The remaining two should be considered fully bicultural. Both were Indians while living in Saraguro, but they continuously crossed the ethnic boundary for periods of time each year when they went outside the area to work. For further details see Belote 1978.

12. Since Quito, folklore performances have taken Saraguros to other parts of Ecuador and to Colombia and Peru.

13. According to Walter Schmitz (1978, personal communication), in 1974 there were "three troupes and none of them had in its repertoire a single traditional dance or piece of music from the Saraguro region." He also stated, "To me these troupes are examples of the whites' manipulative strategies wherein Indians play the part of an exotic attraction which shall help the whites to earn their money."

14. For a recent re-evaluation of the Hawthorne effect, see Franke and Kaul (1978).

REFERENCES CITED

Anonymous
1966 Síntesis Histórica de Saraguro. In José María Vargas et al., eds., *Monografía de la Diocesis de Loja*. Quito: Editorial Santo Domingo, pp. 251–69.

Belote, Jim
n.d. Corn, Cattle and Colonization. Ph.D. thesis in preparation, University of Illinois, Urbana.

Belote, Jim, and Linda Smith Belote
1977a The Limitation of Obligation in Saraguro Kinship. In Ralph Bolton and Enrique Mayer, eds., *Andean Kinship and Marriage*. Washington, D.C.: American Anthropological Association, Special Publication 7, pp. 106–16.
1977b El Sistema de Cargos de Fiesta en Saraguro. In Marcelo F. Naranjo, José L. Pereira V., and Norman E. Whitten, Jr., eds., *Temas sobre la Continuidad y Adaptación Cultural Ecuatoriana*. Quito: Centro de Publicaciones, Pontificia Universidad Católica del Ecuador, pp. 47–73.

Belote, Linda Smith
1978 Prejudice and Pride: Indian-White Relations in Saraguro, Ecuador. Ann Arbor, Mich.: University Microfilms. Ph.D. thesis, University of Illinois, Urbana.

El Campanario
1963 Nos. 1–6. Vicaria Foranea de Saraguro.

Casagrande, Joseph B.
1969 The Implications of Community Differences for Development Programs: An Ecuadorian Example. Paper presented at the Society for Applied Anthropology Meetings, Mexico City.
1974a To Be or Not to Be an Indian—in Ecuador. Paper presented at the XLI International Congress of Americanists, Mexico City.
1974b Strategies for Survival: The Indians of Highland Ecuador. In Dwight Heath, ed., *Contemporary Cultures and Societies of Latin America*. 2d ed. New York: Random House, pp. 93–107.

Casagrande, Joseph B., and Arthur R. Piper
1969 La Transformación Estructural de una Parroquia Rural en las Tierras Altas del Ecuador. *América Indígena* 29:1039–64.

Castile, George P.
1976 Mau Mau in the Mechanism: The Adaptations of Urban Hunters and Gatherers. *Human Organization* 35:394–97.

Célleri, José R.
1966 Misión Andina en el Ecuador: Su Existencia en la Zona de Loja—Saraguro. In José María Vargas et al., eds., *Monografía de la Diocesis de Loja*. Quito: Editorial Santo Domingo, pp. 269–73.

Erasmus, Charles J.
1968 Community Development and the Encogido Syndrome. *Human Organization* 27:65–74.
1970 Comments [Comments on Huizer]. *Human Organization* 29:314–20.

Foster, George M.
1967 What Is a Peasant? In Jack Potter, May Diaz, and George M. Foster, eds., *Peasant Society*. Boston: Little, Brown, pp. 2–14.

Franke, Richard Herbert, and James D. Kaul
   1978   The Hawthorne Experiments: First Statistical Interpretation. *American Sociological Review* 43:623–43.
Friedlander, Judith
   1975   *Being Indian in Hueyapan: A Study of Forced Identity in Contemporary Mexico.* New York: St. Martin's.
Gore, Peter H.
   1971   The Highland Campesino, Backward Peasant or Reluctant Pawn: A Study of the Social and Economic Factors Affecting Small Farmer Modernization in Four Highland Ecuadorian Communities. Ann Arbor, Mich.: University Microfilms. Ph.D. thesis, Cornell University.
International Labor Organization
   1961   *El Programa Andina.* Geneva.
Jiménez de la Espada, Marcos
   1965   *Relaciones Geográficas de Indias.* Vol. 2. Madrid: Biblioteca de Autores Españolas.
Johnson, Allen W.
   1971   Security and Risk Taking among Poor Peasants: A Brazilian Case. In George Dalton, ed., *Studies in Economic Anthropology.* Washington, D.C.: American Anthropological Association, pp. 122–50.
Lance, Larry M., and Edward E. McKenna
   1975   Analysis of Cases Pertaining to the Impact of Western Technology on the Non-Western World. *Human Organization* 3:87–94.
Linke, Lilo, and Miguel Albornoz
   1961   *La Misión Andina del Ecuador.* Quito: El Comercio.
Masson, Peter
   1977   "Cholo" y "China": Contenidos Situacionales, de dos Terminos Interétnicos en Saraguro (Ecuador). *Journal de la Société des Américanistes* 64:107–14.
Misión Andina
   1963   Informe de Actividades: Trimestre Octobre-Diecembre. Quito: Ministerio de Previsión Social.
Oliver-Smith, Anthony
   1977   Disaster Rehabilitation and Social Change in Yungay, Peru. *Human Organization* 36:5–13
Roethlisberger, F. J., and William Dickson
   1939   *Management and the Worker.* Cambridge, Mass.: Harvard University Press.
Schmitz, H. Walter
   1977   Interethnic Relations in Saraguro (Ecuador) from the Point of View of an Anthropology of Communication. *Sociologus* 27 (1):64–84.
Scott, James C.
   1976   *The Moral Economy of the Peasant: Rebellion and Subsistence in Southeast Asia.* New Haven, Conn.: Yale University Press.
Silverman, Sydel F.
   1967   The Community-Nation Mediator in Traditional Central Italy. In Jack Potter, May Diaz, and George M. Foster, eds., *Peasant Society.* Boston: Little, Brown, pp. 279–95.
Stewart, Norman R., Jim Belote, and Linda Smith Belote
   1976   Transhumance in the Central Andes. *Annals of the Association of American Geographers* 66 (3):377–97.

van den Berghe, Pierre L.
  1975   Ethnicity and Class in Highland Peru. In Leo A. Despres, ed., *Ethnicity and Resource Competition in Plural Societies*. The Hague: Mouton, pp. 71–86.
Wharton, Clifton R., Jr.
  1971   Risk, Uncertainty and the Subsistence Farmer: Technological Innovation and Resistance to Change in the Context of Survival. In George Dalton, ed., *Studies in Economic Anthropology*. Washington, D.C.: American Anthropological Association, pp. 151–78.
Whitten, Norman E., Jr. (with the assistance of Marcelo F. Naranjo, Marcelo Santi Simbaña, and Dorothea S. Whitten)
  1976   *Sacha Runa: Ethnicity and Adaptation of Ecuadorian Jungle Quichua*. Urbana: University of Illinois Press.
Wolf, Eric R.
  1956   Aspects of Group Relations in a Complex Society: Mexico. *American Anthropologist* 58 (6):1065–78.

17

St. John the Baptist: The Ritual Looking Glass of Hacienda Indian Ethnic and Power Relations

Muriel Crespi

This chapter draws attention to some neglected interrelationships among ethnicity, saint's day rituals, and the changing political environments of hacienda Indians in northern Ecuador. I shall consider the changing managerial policies at Atahualpa hacienda before and since the 1964 agrarian reforms, and the impact of such policies on Indian laborers and their relationships with white landholders, especially as they are reflected in the Fiesta de San Juan, annual ceremonial enactments to honor St. John the Baptist.

Although Europeans had imposed Catholic celebrations on Indian peasants, and evidence suggests that even contemporary fiestas express the Indians' "political vassalage" (Harris 1964:29), new political contexts may induce change in communal rituals (Friedrich 1966). The power dimension of Indian fiestas, however, is virtually unexplored. With few exceptions (e.g. Smith 1977, Warren 1978, Salomon in this volume) research has veered toward the economic and social correlates of fiestas within ethnically homogeneous communities (e.g. Wolf 1955, Cancian 1965, Reina 1966). In this paper I focus specifically on a stratified hacienda community and the asymmetry of power relations embedded in rituals that engage Indians and powerful non-Indians.

Indian behavior is viewed here as purposive; in some ceremonial contexts it is directed toward establishing vertical relationships with whites which offer both partners maximum advantages with minimum risks. Festivities may also dramatize the changing relationships between Indians and white powerholders through liminal rituals that invert the usual interaction rules (Turner 1974, Babcock 1978). Some Indian communities in Peru and elsewhere in Latin America symbolically express their perception of political subordination to the Spanish *conquistadores* through the ritual "Dance of the Conquest" (Wachtel 1971:65–98). At Atahualpa the theme of subordination is expressed in more local terms. Indians mimic their personal history of servitude to successive Church and state patrons who held prebendal domain over the hacienda land and people. When the 1964 agrarian reforms at state haciendas such as Atahualpa transformed these manorial enterprises into landholding cooperatives, Indians gained more than land. They also gained power through responsibility for determining policy (see, e.g., Swartz 1968). I argue that this new political configuration is triggering change in Indian ethnic identification and in the rituals that customarily mediated and symbolized asymmetrical ethnic relationships between Indians (*indígenas*) and whites (*blancos*).[1]

I begin this account by briefly describing the setting of the hacienda I call Atahualpa. Next I discuss managerial policies from the turn of the present century until 1979, and then consider ethnic interrelations and the fiesta of St. John.

SETTING

Atahualpa lies in a northern *parroquia* of Cayambe canton, Pichincha province, where elevations range from around 2,800 to well above 3,450 meters. The parish is comprised of six communities which have 5,240 inhabitants according to the 1974 census. Approximately 35% live at Atahualpa. Like Atahualpa, five of the six communities are former state haciendas that were reorganized after 1964 into free agricultural settlements comprised of private and cooperative landholdings. The sixth is the town—the local service and administrative *pueblo*—where occupational specialists including artisans and merchants live. In addition to their commercial activities, townspeople also cultivate small plots using seasonal laborers recruited from surrounding communities.

Residents at the former haciendas devote their private hillside holdings, whose size rarely exceeds four hectares, to the barley, wheat, and potatoes that customarily dominate crop inventories at these elevations. The same crops prevail on the several thousand hectares of cooperatively held valley lands, which also support dairy cattle. Natural *páramo* grasslands above 3,450 meters are left to the residents' individually owned sheep. Yields both from cooperative and private holdings serve multiple ends. Although cooperative produce moves primarily toward the highland market, the cooperatives' members commonly borrow from it to meet food and seed shortages. Smallholder production furnishes family staples, and may meet exchange ends as well by flowing between parish communities, sometimes to communities in different parishes, and sometimes to regional markets.

Complementary ecologies, economies, and survival strategies knit the town and the agricultural communities together into a parish-level system. Goods, services, credit, and cash flow from the town shopkeepers and artisans toward the new-style communities in exchange for agricultural products, labor, and indirect access to natural resources. For example, to accumulate animal stock with minimal risk or cash outlay, the cultivators would shepherd town sheep on *páramo* grasslands in return for newborn lambs. In the absence of stabilizing kinship ties between townspeople and cultivators, fictive kinship generates the constraints and social bonds that regularize these otherwise precarious transactions.

Until the turn of the present century the parish represented a single vast estate, *latifundio*, known entirely as Atahualpa. It was linked to political and economic nerve centers in Quito via the articulating roles played by priest-managers of the Mercedarian order, one of the major landholding monastic orders within the Catholic church.

MANAGERIAL PHASES

The Church: Tradition Initiated, 1560–1904

A small crown land grant to the Mercedarians in 1560 initiated the Church occupancy of the Atahualpa region (Monroy 1938:220). Property gifts and the Mercedarians' judicious land purchases during the subsequent century increased the inauspicious ranch to more than 20,000 hectares (Monroy 1932, 1933, 1938), an estate equal in size to the present-day parish. In the pattern characteristic of Andean *latifundios*, expansion ran both a horizontal and a vertical course to bring the ecologically varied resources of valleys, hillsides, and *páramo* under the Mercedarians' control.

Typical of traditional management practices, the relatively unproductive resources that were incorporated during the expansionist phase became a medium of exchange in acquiring agricultural laborers, *huasipungueros* (see, e.g., Wolf and Mintz 1957, Miller 1967). Landless Indian men who became *huasipungueros* received usufructory rights to house-and-garden sites called *huasipungos*, *páramo* grazing areas, and other perquisites in return for their own and their families' labor throughout the week. This asymmetrical exchange of estate resources for indigenous labor gave management a cheap resident labor force which was subject to ramifying forms of coercion.

The pinnacle command center for Atahualpa was the Mercedarians' monastery in Quito, home of upper-echelon members of the ecclesiastical hierarchy. Preoccupied with the order's urban interests, however, the ranking policy makers delegated rural management largely to *de facto* patrons or priest-managers living at the hacienda. These priest-managers controlled the hacienda from a small monastery and ceremonial-administrative center at Atahualpa proper, the oldest section of the estate. Following guidelines set in Quito, they determined working conditions, the distribution of subsistence plots to Indians, and the punitive sanctions for breaking hacienda rules. But, except for ceremonial events and adjudicative functions, they remained aloof from the hacienda community, eschewing *compadrazgo* or other social ties with Indians and leaving sustained interaction with laborers to employees at a lower, secular level in the chain of command.

The priest-managers depended on white skilled employees including *mayordomos*, foremen, to relay instructions downward and report effects upward. But *mayordomos* were no mere messengers. Initiation of the upward flow of information, together with the license to physically punish recalcitrant workers, gave *mayordomos* considerable power. The *compadrazgo* relationships that asymmetrically bound employees and Indians presumably constrained the *mayordomos* from arbitrary sanctions and disclosures of Indian misconduct. But when informed priests ordered them to do so, employees are known to have burned Indian huts and household goods, incarcerated Indians in Atahualpa's jail, and inflicted more serious damage.

In addition to cultivating hacienda fields, Indian families invested their labor in *huasipungo* cultivation to maintain themselves and numerous outsiders. Poor landless whites[2] living at Atahualpa proper (*Registro Civil* 1912) at the turn of the century bartered specialized goods and *chicha* for Indian produce or, using Indian labor, sharecropped the *huasipungos*. More demanding claims on the *huasipungo* yields came from the bishopric, represented in the Cayambe canton seat, which levied obligatory crop taxes, *primicias*, each year. When demands outweighed the harvests, Indians borrowed food and seed crops from the management, charging them against future labor, produce, or cash incomes. Although providing relief in crisis situations, this credit system inevitably drew Indians into insurmountable debt—and debt peonage—to the estate.

Indians had no effective legitimate means of contributing to hacienda policy or redressing grievances. Not even the Indian "mayor," *alcalde*, performed a spokesman's role. Instead, appointed by the priests to conduct obligatory Catholic ceremonies, the *alcalde* extended the priests' politico-religious authority into the interstices of Indian community organization. Although Indian labor might have constituted a power base in an era of labor shortage, even work slow-downs brought retaliation ranging from physical abuse to property losses.[3] Opportunities to leave were blocked by the practice of debt inheritance, which transmitted parental debts to new generations, and by debtor's prisons, which confined laborers who attempted to leave before canceling their debts (Hassaurek 1868:301–3).

The State: Tradition Modified, 1904–64

This theocratic regime was abruptly ended early in this century by the wave of government expropriations that brought Mercedarian and other monastic estates throughout Ecuador under national control.[4] Atahualpa was brought into the nation's geoadministrative network when the area was designated a parish. Secular peace-keeping officers were introduced to the parish center, provisionally located at Atahualpa proper until 1931. In that year the site for a territorially independent town or parish center was cut from Atahualpa proper, and most poor whites moved to town as landed founders (*Registro Oficial* 1931). The state also subdivided the *latifundio* into five separate haciendas, the largest of which remained known as Atahualpa. Some Indian families shifted their residence from Atahualpa proper to the newly established units, and their obligations from the Atahualpa managers to the patrons at each unit.

The national government created the managerial bureaucracy known as the Asistencia Social, social welfare agency, to administer its newly acquired holdings. Despite disruptions in the customary chain of command caused by expulsion of the religious authorities and introduction of secular ones, the state agency maintained intact the asymmetric land-labor exchange and usual hierarchical relationships. Absentee management also continued, but with the agency's control more attenuated by the practice of leasing Atahualpa and its laborers to private or corporate concerns. Leases customarily ran eight years. A major exception was the 24-year lease to a family that nearly converted the hacienda into a personal fiefdom. Lessees themselves were absentee patrons who went to the countryside for fiestas and other special events but otherwise left management to their rural *de facto* patrons.

Two different configurations are discernible in management's production strategies during the approximately 60 years of control by the welfare agency. In the first, which overlaps with the extended period of family management, the exclusive commitment to preindustrial agriculture continued. Working conditions showed little improvement despite some reduction of the former constraints. Cash wages were introduced, but their benefits were eroded by the rising inflation that plagued the country (Linke 1960:27). *Primicia* crop taxes became voluntary, but the Cayambe church collected them until 1964, although in continually declining amounts. Liberalizing legislation abolished debtor's prisons and by the 1930s recognized labor's right to strike. Nevertheless, the *de facto* patrons not only evicted widows from their husbands' *huasipungos* and subdivided already established *huasipungos* to accommodate new workers but also had labor activists beaten and evicted from the hacienda community. Eviction or threat of eviction at a time of increasing competition for external employment severely hindered labor's efforts to formally affect hacienda decision-making but did not prevent the formation of a union, *sindicato*.

The second configuration, in which managerial strategies clearly broke with certain established patterns, was ushered in by a corporation, the final lessee, in the early 1950s. Reflecting the trend that would emerge in this decade among Sierra *hacendados* (see, e.g., Barsky 1978), the corporation was bent on maximum commercial exploitation of Atahualpa. During its tenure the corporation put an unprecedented amount of land into production and introduced mechanized farming, new and improved seed, and new and improved breeds of sheep and cattle. Consistent with its rising commercialism, management reduced the perquisites ordinarily associated with the traditional labor arrangements. It severely curtailed cash advances, eliminated advances of food and seed crops, and gradually halted the creation of new labor contracts. Except for the son who inherited his father's status and obligations, young men were being denied *huasipungo* positions and subsistence plots. This relatively surplus population of landless *apegados* (fig. "stuck on") turned toward *huasipunguero* kin for access to their subsistence sites. At about the same time *huasipungueros* became more dependent on employee and town *compadres* for seed, cash loans, and other assistance in return for asymmetric sharecropping partnerships. The union was too weak to change hacienda hiring practices; still, it had nudged hacienda policies toward alignment with the four-day work week, paid vacations, women's wages, and other conditions mandated by the labor code (Crespi 1976).

The Agrarian Reform Institute: Tradition Disrupted, 1964–Present

In 1964 the long-pending Law of Agrarian Reform and Colonization brought to an end the traditional hacienda system. Explicitly
aimed at stimulating national economic development through agrarian
change, this law mandated ceilings on the size of landholdings, expropriation and redistribution of unutilized and underutilized land,
and the abolition of *huasipungo* arrangements (see, e.g., Blankstein
and Zuvekas 1973). The law differentially affected private and state
owners. It merely required the former to grant *huasipungueros* the
ownership of their subsistence plots, thereby rupturing the traditional land-labor exchange, and to reimburse all subsequent free laborers with cash wages. But the state was fully expected to surrender
its *hacendado* role. The law provided for the transfer of state-owned
haciendas from the social welfare agency to the newly created reform
institute, IERAC. An elaborate development plan implemented under IERAC's auspices would transform Atahualpa and other state haciendas into free communities based on private and cooperative tenure (*Registro Oficial* 1964).

Atahualpa *huasipungueros* received legal titles to their subsistence
plots within a year of the law's establishment and with little ceremony became independent landholders. Landless Indian *apegados*,
white *mayordomos* and other former employees of the welfare agency,
a few white former sharecroppers of the agency, and townspeople all
received small plots in subsequent years. Except for the latter, most
smallholdings were distributed without charge. The remaining fields
and pastures became the resource base for two organizationally separate cooperatives, the largest with an all-Indian membership and the
other ethnically mixed and composed of Indians, white former employees, and sharecroppers. Each cooperative carried a low-interest,
long-term mortgage on its land.

During the tumultuous postreform years a coterie of white econo-
mists and other IERAC specialists remained at Atahualpa to expedite
land redistribution and launch the cooperative enterprises. They cajoled men into membership, appointed managers to the cooperatives, and, in tandem with the managers, directed the enterprises
until 1972. Since then, no ranking IERAC agents have lived permanently at Atahualpa and no cooperative member has continually monopolized the same managerial post. Nor has the Cayambe church
collected *primicias*.

Managerial policy for Atahualpa is no longer centralized or made
for the community as a whole. By 1979 IERAC's role had been re-

duced to providing assistance with major fiscal and land-related legal issues. In the evolving new hierarchy a locally elected board of directors controls the most influential positions. Annually, each cooperative usually elects six literate young men to fill managerial and other posts on the boards and share in making the decisions traditionally controlled by the patron and, briefly, by IERAC. They appoint skilled personnel, design production strategies, determine punitive measures for breaches of cooperative rules, and make decisions about extending credit and loans to members. Managers, and all members, earn a share of the cooperatives' incomes, paid in cash and in kind, commensurate with their positions and the number of days worked. Although all members vote on major issues, the managers help fashion the issues and determine the outcomes.

Land redistribution left the new managers without coercive bases for exacting membership-wide compliance with cooperative policies. However small the plots that former *huasipungueros* and others now control, they afford unprecedented protection from threatened or actual eviction. Persuasion, and the lure of continuing easy access to credit, loans, and other services offered by the cooperatives, must suffice to elicit a member's minimal conformance with management's expectations.

Cash loans, agricultural credit, and services which cooperatives provide make sharecropping arrangements with town whites unnecessary for many members. Some members earn sufficiently greater cash incomes to permit increased market-place purchases and reduced dependence on town shopkeepers for credit lines.[5] New forms of interdependence are emerging between Atahualpa and the town, but with cooperative members in considerably stronger bargaining positions. But Atahualpa residents who are unaffiliated with a cooperative confront serious new problems.

Many residents had initially refused to join the cooperatives; others cannot join now because membership rolls are being closed, and in any case the present cost of joining is beyond most people's means. Consequently, membership in the community and in the cooperative is not overlapping. In 1979 the community included: (1) smallholders consisting of former *huasipungueros*, *apegados*, employees, and sharecroppers; (2) smallholders with the same mixed origins who simultaneously belong to a cooperative; and (3) landless young adults representing the current wave of surplus *apegados* who migrate seasonally or permanently to find wage work.

ETHNIC RELATIONS SHORTLY BEFORE AND AFTER REFORMS

As parish residents perceive their social universe, Indians, non-Indian *cholos*, and whites represent increasingly important people.[6] Stereotypically regarded as powerful natural managers, and "civilized" in the sense of educated, sophisticated, and mannerly, persons defined as white (*blancos, señores*) command privilege and respect denied to all others. Indians (called *naturales, indígenas, runa*, or the pejorative *indio*) are conventionally viewed, and view themselves, as uncivilized, poor, and characterized by exotic customs including the Quichua language and localized clothing styles. *Cholos* (*mestizo* is infrequently used), from their own and others' standpoints, are literate, occupationally skilled, monolingual Spanish speaking, and more rustic than exotic. Residents tend to use skin color to substantiate the ethnic identifications they first make on the basis of occupation, dress, and other behavioral features.

These labeled categories have long coincided with differences in locality and control over productive resources in the form of land and social and occupational skills. Thus townspeople and skilled hacienda employees regarded themselves and were regarded by Indians as white, but the large class of cultivators living at haciendas was concomitant with *naturales*. *Cholos* were also associated with haciendas, not with the town.

The ethnic labels that residents chose for themselves and that others chose for them tended to coincide, but only in the aggregate. When ethnic labels were applied in relation to the users' definitions of their own ranks, reciprocal labeling could not be taken for granted. Hacienda managers, for instance, regarded only themselves as "legitimate" or blood-line whites, born of two white parents; they regarded townspeople as nonlegitimate whites whose status derived from adopting white culture. At worst, hacienda elites offended townspeople by calling them *cholos*, a term clearly implying Indian ancestry. Like the whites, *cholos* may or may not be legitimate. The children of Indian-white matings called themselves *cholos legítimos* and would be so recognized by others if white paternity (blood) were acknowledged. Agriculturalists who abandoned Indian dress and other behaviors also called themselves *cholos*, but other parish residents still called them Indians. Only in situations which Mitchell (1966) calls categorical, when strangers in ephemeral encounters use visual cues to identify one another, were others likely to regard self-defined *cholos* as non-Indians (Crespi 1975).

The rules that regulated interethnic encounters stressed asymmetry and distance, modified by *compadrazgo* relationships, ceremonial events, and the sex and relative age of the participants. Indians invariably used titular addresses and formal Spanish pronouns to whites who, in turn, usually ignored titles and regularly selected informal pronouns. If they were *compadres*, both used fictive kinship terms while maintaining pronoun asymmetry. Whites might address elderly Indians with the honorifics *taita* (Quichua, father and respected male elder) or *mama* (Quichua, mother and respected female elder). More often, if whites used kinship language to Indians, they selected *hijo*, child, in situations requiring persuasiveness. Indians themselves might call patrons *taitico*, *papacito*, or even *mamacita* when, after days of festive drinking, they pleaded for the patrons' blessings, reminding them that as "guardians" of hacienda land they represented the land and "the Indians' parents and source of sustenance."

No intermarriage of Indians and whites occurred under traditional hacienda conditions. This effectively limited the number of offspring who would be categorized as *cholos legítimos* and stand to inherit the assets that the white parent controlled. Although white men were free to initiate illicit sexual relations with indigenous women, the offspring of these unions were assigned to their mother's ethnic category. Such undisclosed white paternity, and endogamy, had successfully perpetuated the social boundaries and distance between ethnic strata. Social distance had its physical counterpart in the segregated settlement pattern which found whites pre-empting the valleys while relegating Indians to the hillsides. Whites also claimed valued areas in public or private buildings and conveyances. For example, on the one hand, whites took front seats in local buses and churches but pushed Indians to the rear. White living space usually was so sacrosanct that, except to perform chores, Indians were excluded from the patrons' quarters and even the homes of town *compadres*. On the other hand, ceremonial events such as Indian baptisms, which generated vertical *compadrazgo* ties with whites, drew townspeople and hacienda employees to Indian huts. There, as honored guests, whites were seated and fed separately.

The endogamy, ascription, and rigid etiquette that generally describe interethnic relations in Latin America have prompted analogies to the Hindu caste and European estate systems (Colby and van den Berghe 1969, Salz 1955). Data from Atahualpa suggest that a more basic analogy to these traditional stratification systems rested with the practice of merging ethnic labels with occupational roles.

Within the hacienda context, the white label was concomitant with the powerful and influential roles of patron or employee, and Indian with powerless laborer. Inevitably, as Gould (1971) noted for stratification systems in agrarian states, occupational roles became synonymous with the role occupants. Thus, in inheriting their parents' ethnic labels, Atahualpa children also inherited, and were socialized to, their parents' occupational roles and the character stereotypes they generated. "Indian" came to signal one who had a menial occupation and was an inferior person. Given the large number of compliant manual laborers required by preindustrial farming and the comparatively limited demand for specialists, birth ascription had offered a device for ensuring automatic succession into the lowest occupational stratum while simultaneously regulating competition for prestigious specialized positions.

Ascribed roles at Atahualpa tended to be enduring, but local conceptions of ethnicity granted the mutability of birth roles and movement across ethnic boundaries. Indians who exchanged their occupation, garb, and other cultural markers for white attributes were called *choliados*, and according to local ideology were engaged in the process of "becoming white." In practice, however, only some white attributes such as dress were ever readily accessible. The critical feature in ethnic transformation was an influential specialized occupation. This, until recently, was denied to most Indians at Atahualpa.

Indians could mitigate the effects of subordination by adopting public strategies that non-Indians favored. The "good Indian" role, which entailed being soft-spoken, jocular, and reasonable, was one successful technique for "impression management," in Goffman's (1959:229) terms. Approving attention was guaranteed by wearing *típica*, Indian dress. Ponchos and white trousers for men and richly embroidered blouses, long pleated dark wool skirts, and mounds of gold-colored glass beads for women identified parish Indians. Indians who won approval might maneuver themselves into favored positions that advanced their private goals. Approval brought *compadrazgo* ties with employees and townspeople. Hacienda managers, though rejecting *compadrazgo* with Indians, might have supported a contender for a vacant *huasipungo* or found employment for an *apegado*.

Organizational changes since 1964 have been eroding the appropriateness of the "good Indian" strategy, not because the labeled hierarchy has changed so that being Indian is more prestigious, but because circumstances no longer compel it. Men who acquire specialized positions in the cooperatives enjoy positions that are roughly equivalent to, or more influential than, those formerly monopolized by the hacienda's white employees. In 1979 men's clothing choices were communicating unmistakable messages about these new local opportunities. Displaying what Terence Turner (1969) might call new social skins, men wear dungarees, tailored trousers, or even suits for special occasions and, except for the coldest days, sweaters and jackets rather than ponchos. But for the differences in the quality of clothing, young Atahualpa men are nearly indistinguishable from townsmen. Correspondingly, more men call themselves *cholos* and more are addressed as *señor* by people who are still called *naturales*. Women have not been offered dramatically new occupational choices, and tend to maintain their distinctive clothing style although modifying it according to changing local fashion.

Townspeople are grudingly modifying their relationships with, and perceptions of, the people they customarily called *naturales*. Marriage and consensual unions involving white women and Atahualpa men, though infrequent, offer telling evidence of change. Despite continuing antagonism to these alliances, townspeople comment that the men have sound economic prospects and are in any case more *cholo* than Indian, that is, becoming more like "us."

Being Indian traditionally meant celebrating the fiesta of San Juan, St. John the Baptist, beginning on the eve of 24 June and continuing until Cayambe canton celebrates St. Peter the following week. Atahualpa recognized other saint's days, including that of Our Lady of Mercy, patron saint for the Mercedarian order and historically the parish's highest ranked saint. But no saint has been celebrated, or is celebrated, as popularly or uniquely as St. John. Festivities for other saints bring *priostes*, sponsors, together on the community's behalf. Some of them are volunteers, but most are selected by each year's outgoing *priostes*. They pay for the mass and for a band or other embellishments if finances permit. For St. John, there are as many *priostes* as there are extended patrilocal families who perform the *rama* ceremony (described below) to honor this "Indian Saint."[7]

THE FIESTA OF ST. JOHN

Under Church Management

Management and labor were unequal partners in co-sponsoring the annual festivities.[8] The priest-managers discharged their responsibilities by distributing a meal, *comida*, and sweet unfermented maize *chicha*, and holding mass for laborers who also brought their household images of St. John. But the most onerous ritual and material burdens fell to laborers, who culminated two sets of cyclical household activities: *huasipungo* cultivation leading to summer harvests and compulsory *primicia* payments, and family feasting and preparations leading to ceremonies which included the obligatory *rama* and *loa* offerings.[9]

The plaza facing the Atahualpa monastery became a ritual arena for the occasion. Although Indians drank and feasted in ethnically exclusive groups at the hillside huts, most festive highlights occurred at the plaza either in view of, or with the cooperation of, whites. At dawn on 24 June the *Día Grande*, teams of masked and costumed families from throughout the hacienda, began assembling just outside the plaza. Flanked by men bearing lances, women led elaborately decorated horses carrying the *rama* and the prepubescent boy, called *innocente*, who would recite the *loa*. Each family team, directed by a *prioste*, made its separate entrance, *entrada*, to the plaza in a quasi-military procession. They must "win the plaza," *ganar la plaza*, by pushing aside previous entrants, to clear and hold a center-stage position before the assembled priests. Pressures from newly arriving teams often escalated the mock battles into bloody confrontations between and among the sexes, and especially between families from different sections of the extensive landholding.

Family teams—now unmasked—climaxed these preliminaries with their solemn presentation of the *loa*, praise, and *rama de gallos*. The youthful orator approached the priests to recite the lengthy *loa* prose recounting St. John's miraculous origins, his capacity to forgive sinners, and his divine intervention to ease misfortunes.[10] Finally tossing a beribboned dove that "carries the peoples' message of faith" to the priests, the boy signaled the presentation of the *rama*. Shouting the givers' name, the team paraded its *rama* before the spectators. The *rama* refers to the two poles, each of which carried six live roosters, *gallos*. After receiving everyone's offerings, the priests awarded outstanding performers with food and cloth.

Masked dancing, the *baile disfrasado*, gained momentum at the plaza as family teams completed their presentations. Gradually, not only the plaza but the nearby *chicherías* of white *compadres* became scenes of frenetic dancing, drinking, and mocking games by Indians who demanded *primicias* from kin, *compadres*, and friends paid in the form of fermented *chicha*. Employees and other whites wearing borrowed or rented Indian costumes joined Indians at the plaza or celebrated in their own segregated groups.

Later that same week the families visited the priests again, both to terminate the *rama* ceremony of the past year and to initiate the ritual for the coming year. Termination required the priests, as *rama* recipients, to feast the Indian families. Each *prioste* received food and *chicha* which he redistributed to his entourage. Initiation required the priests to give each family the obligatory starter rooster, *obligación*, for the following year's offering.

The *prioste* or *capitán de gallos* who received the rooster in his family's name assumed responsibility for organizing the coming year's presentation. He initiated a series of interhousehold exchanges after the summer festivities by inviting kin to a ceremonial meal. That first meal included chickens bred from the "marriage" of the priest's rooster and the *prioste's* hen. Accepting the meal had obligated each guest to contribute roosters, drink, and other items required for feasting at the *prioste's* home before the following year's presentation and for the *rama* itself. *Priostes* ensured abundant household feasts by borrowing sheep from the hacienda flock, charging the costs against future household stock or labor.

Under State Management

Following the geoadministrative changes of the early 1900s, celebrants began gravitating to the *chicherías* in the new town, and families living at the separated haciendas began focusing ritual attention on their own managers. Families at Atahualpa still offered *ramas* and *loas* to the managers and paid harvest taxes, although the *rama*, like the *primicia*, had become voluntary.

The corporate lessees put an end to the *rama* and *loa* ceremonies. Support was withdrawn when the manager rejected his traditional roles as initiator and recipient of the offerings. He found the ritual drinking and personal attention demanded by hundreds of dancers who kissed his hand and sought his blessings both offensive and physically intolerable. In addition, the costs of tending hundreds of roosters, to be later redistributed among friends, employees, and new *priostes*, and of selling fine sheep to *priostes* below market price, became untenable. Equally costly were the labor losses this week meant for management whose grain fields were ready for harvest.

Eliminating the *rama* did not curtail the week-long celebrations. But the severing of the personal ceremonial exchange with the patron generated considerable resentment. The introduction of a dance band, the foods distributed to all families, and the fermented *chicha* given to all comers at the plaza did little to assuage the laborers' anger. They viewed the patron's rejection of the *rama* as symbolizing his rejection of them and disregard for their welfare as Christians. They argued that the exchange as well as the dancing and drinking in St. John's name assured all participants of salvation. "San Juan forgives Indian and white sinners alike . . . his roosters' wings put out the fires of hell." As one *loa* says, "His dove carries the message of love and faith." The patron's acceptance of the offering was the vital link in transmitting that message. Indians claimed that if the patron ignored the dangers of hell for himself, that was unfortunate and his problem. What was unconscionable was that, by rejecting the *rama*, he had endangered the Indians' salvation.

The widespread distress provoked by suspension of the ceremony apparently reflected more than concern for the afterlife. The asymmetrical exchange also brought the patron's "affection and understanding" and had been the only channel, ceremonial or otherwise, to do so. With this avenue blocked, Indians turned to their town *compadres* for partners to the exchange, shifting the *rama* offering from a single dominant recipient to several influential town families.

The masked and costumed dancing continued despite these changes. "Celebrating San Juan" had meant, by all local standards, that Indians assumed certain disguises along with the behavioral characteristics that the disguises required. In effect, festive attire facilitated the transformation into, or possession by, new social identities. On one hand, no legitimate festive role was conceivable for Indians in ordinary dress. On the other, no explicit ethnic ideology compelled whites to conform to a dress code for this "Indian fiesta." Indians welcomed whites in festive costume, but could not demand it. Whether or not whites masqueraded as San Juan characters, however, their behavior was often extraordinary and antithetical to customary norms. In these respects, white ceremonial behavior was consistent with the symbolism of liminal rituals.

When I first observed the ritual events in 1964, on the eve of agrarian reforms, the masked teams largely consisted of male and female kin and *novios*, sweethearts. Males and females occasionally danced in segregated teams. Team members selected their ceremonial identities from among the following, primarily male, roles: devil, *diablo-uma* (devil-head); clown, *payaso*; old man, *viejo*; male transvestite, *hombre vestido de mujer*; male guitarists and flutists, *aruchicos*; women, *chinas*, sometimes called flowers, *sisas*; and male or female caretakers, *huasicamas*.

The participants' faces and voices remained unrecognizable for as long as revelers were sober enough to control their disguises. Kerchiefs covered womens' faces, and cloth hoods with facial features stitched on both sides concealed the devils' heads. Most men wore wire masks painted with facial features of whites including blue eyes and blonde hair and mustaches, but some clowns chose papier-mâché masks portraying animals and national or international celebrities.[11] Devils had vowed to be silent or suffer the misfortunes caused by their accompanying devil spirit, but other dancers chattered in falsettos, often in stylized, distorted Quichua phrases (see also Salomon, in this volume).

Aruchicos were the teams' principal noisemakers. They wore 12 brass bells which were tied to leather thongs and suspended from a belt around their waists. The bells resonated against a leather apron as the men danced and jogged; ordinary walking was considered unacceptable. The most colorful males too, *aruchicos* covered their hats, worn back to front, with a profusion of mirrors and multicolored ribbons that rivaled the roosters' plumage. Devils, clowns, and old men were the most physically aggressive characters. Devils and old men brandished whips while clowns wielded *chorizos*, old socks stuffed hard with rags, to strike their "enemies," people who were really their friends.

Rather than portray comic or menacing characters, women were expected to be pretty, to look, as the Quichua term *sisa* implies, like "flowers." Granted sexual license during this fiesta, unmarried women in their newest and most attractive clothing could freely entice new lovers and potential future mates; married women used discretion. Caretakers were more responsible for protecting dancers that fell drunk by the wayside than for chaperoning young women.

Plaza activities were exuberant in 1964. Singing to the accompaniment of guitars and flutes, masked teams were streaming down the hillsides to the plaza by dawn. By mid-afternoon more than 700 masked dancers had flooded the plaza. Employees were busy serving *chicha* by the gourdful to dancers, who were exchanging drinks with employees and everyone else from their own bottles of *trago*. As the day progressed, brief skirmishes broke out between and among the sexes, demands for *primicias* became more aggressive, and even payments became aggressive as bottles of *trago* were shoved to the mouths of sometimes reluctant recipients.

Whites from town, the Cayambe canton seat, and elsewhere, along with visiting Indians, watched the tumultuous activities from the sidelines. White vendors sold foods and *trago*, desperately trying to observe the goings-on while protecting their wares from dancers who gleefully stole and fled, shouting *"policía, policía,* catch me if you can." Alternating between being the amused or exasperated targets of Indian pranks and powerful religious intermediaries, locally important whites murmured *Dios le bendigo* as they made the sign of the cross over Indians who sought their blessings. Toward late afternoon the spectators, joined by whites in Indian costume, pushed their way into the plaza.

Movement into the crowded plaza signaled white intentions to take counterpart roles in the ribald and jesting play. Whites laughingly sidestepped the light blows delivered by Indian whips and *chorizos*. They traded verbal insults with Indians who audaciously addressed them by first names and used personal pronouns while taunting them with obscenities. White women tossed aside the improprieties of bold indigenous men who playfully lifted their skirts, pinched their buttocks, and, speaking partly in Quichua, invited them to make love. Yielding to Indians who loudly proclaimed their rights over the plaza, whites met the demands for *primicias* with drink, coins, and cigarettes.

The same mocking aggression drove the patron's Indian servants into the hacienda house and other dancers into the homes of white *compadres*. The scenes were similar whether played at the patron's home, homes of employees and townspeople, or even Indian huts. Their coming announced by bells and songs, masked teams danced into white homes toward the kitchens. At each stop in their rounds they called in distorted Quichua for the *primicia* that was due this day. Hosts retorted by ordering the teams to "work," that is, "dance," before being paid. Refusing, the dancers threatened to burn the house, beat the occupants, and send sickness to the occupants, their animals, and their crops unless payment was immediate. Clowns terrified small children with kidnapping threats while *aruchicos* danced around, their bells flying out to nudge the hosts. Satisfied hosts began distributing bowls of *chicha* and sometimes rich soups as well, taken from the stores prepared for Indians who would come in the solemn *rama* procession.

After the Agrarian Reforms

The all-Indian cooperative has assumed responsibility for what had previously been management's economic contributions to the festivities. After several years of paying for the band and for food and drink from cooperative funds, the managers sought external sources of funding. Adopting a pattern common to many towns, the managers began to solicit prizes and funds from relatively prosperous outsiders to defray the usual costs. The patrons of the fiesta were invited to observe the events from the hacienda house, largely converted to offices, and join the managers for a ceremonial meal in the house. New forms of entertainment were introduced by the IERAC co-managers who organized competitive and spectator events such as popular bullfights on the *Día Grande*, and contests to select Indian beauty queens, to catch greased pigs, and to climb greased poles.

In 1979 the number of appropriately dressed men at the plaza has dwindled to between 100 and 125. Most arrive late, stopping first to watch or participate in the bullfights that run concurrently with the plaza dancing. The number of non-Indian observers is correspondingly increased by Atahualpa men who have discarded their masks and festive identities. They take their place with white visitors. Women, left with relatively few partners, may remain with men on the sidelines, assemble more all-women teams, or join the growing number of women in male-female teams. The composition of dance teams reflects another new principle of recruitment: proximity. Neolocal residence patterns generated by the distribution of land to *apegados* are bringing distantly related families together and leading to the incorporation of neighbors into the remaining teams.

The number of white partners is also declining. Siphoned off by parades, dances, bullfights, and other attractions that the town itself has begun to sponsor, fewer whites play the customary festive roles at Atahualpa, or even in town. The dwindling number of Indian teams who still make house-to-house calls for the *primicias* find that town *compadres* more often lock their homes while they leave to enjoy one of the town's events. Although the kitchen in the hacienda house at Atahualpa is nearly bare, a cook, hired to prepare the managers' ceremonial meal, scrapes what she can for the dancers from limited stores.

A resurgence of tradition seemed to be in the offing when the *rama* ceremony reappeared in the active ritual repertoire at Atahualpa. The ceremony was reintroduced in 1968 when the *rama* went to the Indian and IERAC co-managers. They continued to receive the offering until 1972. The new managers voted into office in 1973 and 1974 received the *rama* too, but by mutual agreement none were given since 1974 nor planned for 1980. Nor have townspeople received the *ramas* for a number of years.[12]

Former *priostes* and recipients of their goods and favors in the cooperative and in town comment that present costs of the ritual have made the price of giving and receiving unreasonable. Considerations of costs aside, people add, "Anyway, the cooperative management changes so often, why should we bother with the work and expense of the *rama*? Besides, now that we are members of the cooperative, we are all like patrons, so what's the point?" Townspeople typically comment, "We have to serve food and drink to everyone that comes with the *rama*, which may be 25 or more people. Then what do we get besides 12 skinny, sick, roosters. It just isn't worth it anymore."

No one suggests that salvation is easier to achieve than it used to be, or that it has ceased to be worthwhile. Atahualpa residents still regard themselves as Catholics and take their miniature saints to mass on St. John's day, and continue to celebrate other saints. They are even increasing the number of festivities by reviving the celebrations to a saint that had been dormant for several years and adding a saint that, previously, had been celebrated only by townspeople.

DISCUSSION

Regardless of their other effects, St. John festivities remain local expressions of Catholicism. A panoramic view of the events indicates the dramatization of religious themes. One finds hints of the scenario revealed in the *loa* origin myth about St. John, of the 12 Disciples in the dancers' 12 bells and the 12 *rama* roosters, of the Eucharist in numerous forms of food giving, and of the holy dove that appeared when Christ baptized John, in the *loa* dove. Participants in the ritual offerings thus simulate the baptismal process that strips away polluting spiritual and material properties. Cleansed of sin, Indians as well as whites are transformed and elevated from heathens into true Christians who share a fleeting condition of *communitas* (Turner 1974:53) as spiritual equals in the Kingdom of God.

The festivities also offer an expressive medium for worldly inequities. These are symbolically affirmed and renewed each year through alternating duplication and inversion of the traditional hierarchy. Indian subordination is expressed ritually as a dependence on whites to act as their brokers, or priests, in transmitting absolution from St. John. The apical position in the ordered universe is, however, St. John's, whose divine grace abrogates the negative consequences of being Indian or being the Indians' oppressors. While these sacred powers operate, they override the constraints imposed by ordinary, mundane interaction rules. During the resulting liminal interim (Turner 1974:13) Indians may reverently approach the powerholders or become powerholders themselves by inverting with impunity the very hierarchy they solemnly celebrate. Whether Indian and white celebrants agree to symbolically invert the hierarchy or leave it "upright," their behavior reflects present and past relationships of dom-

TABLE 1. Summarized Aspects of Management, Ethnicity, and St. John Festivities.

Aspects	TURN OF THE CENTURY	Traditional Church	1904 EXPROPRIATION	Modified Family Corporate	1964 AGRARIAN REFORMS	Free Mixed Tenure
Managerial Policies						
Huasipungo arrangements						... .
Exclusively labor-intensive				------------	--	-- -- -----------
Unskilled laborers in demand				------------	--	-- -- -----------
Severe repression of laborers				------------	--	.. ..
Cash and seed advances				------------	--	
Land redistribution		....	:	....	:	
Indian Strategies						
Compadres with whites, not patrons						-----------
"Good Indian" public stance						-----------
Dependence on town		....		------------		-----------
Unionization		....		------------ ------------	--	....
Ethnic-Occupational Hierarchy						
Ideology of indigenous inferiority						
Ideology of ethnic mobility						
Pyramidal centralized power						-- ....
Whites in apical position						-- ....
Primarily ascribed statuses						-- ....

Table 1. (Cont'd)

Aspects	TURN OF THE CENTURY	Traditional Church	1904 EXPROPRIATION	Modified Family Corporate	1964 AGRARIAN REFORMS	Free Mixed Tenure
St. John Festivities						
Co-sponsored by management						
Masked status reversals						----------
Obligatory *primicia* and *rama*				....		.. ..
Voluntary *primicia*		....				....
Voluntary *rama* to patrons		....		————		
Voluntary *rama* to town whites		....		————		....
Nontraditional organization, events		....	....	....		.. ————
Town sponsorship of festivities		....	....	....		.. ————

………absent   ---------- weak   _____present

inance and, some evidence suggests (e.g. Rubio Orbe 1956), continuities with pre-Hispanic ritual enactments.

The pyramidal hierarchy with sharply contrastive strata that had fostered these rituals no longer exists (see Table 1). As Atahualpa residents began to approximate in dress, occupation, and ethnic orientation the non-Indians they had previously mocked or to whom they offered ritual homage, discordance between the new situation and the traditional rituals of hierarchy maintenance or reversal inevitably increased.

The *rama* ceremony also afforded Indians and whites a basis for temporary but annually renewable relationships that promised material advantages to both classes of participants. It is noteworthy that Indians unmasked during this ritual. By surrendering the anonymity characterizing participation in other rituals, they personally and individually called the patron's attention to themselves. Families could distinguish themselves even when the *rama* was obligatory by excelling in the competitive presentations to the priests. Conceivably, the sympathetic recognition that successful competitors won was converted into personal credit which weighed in the Indians' favor when patrons judged critical issues. The ceremonial exchange also ensured assistance from townspeople once the corporate management curtailed the perquisites it had customarily distributed to laborers. The instrumental value of the ritual was further indicated both by presentations to cooperative and IERAC co-managers who held office for several consecutive years and by its subsequent lapse when the offices were rotated. The *rama* to townspeople showed the same demise once cash and credit became available to members of the cooperative.

These congruences suggest that Indian decisions to give the *rama* were influenced by the estimated duration of the recipients' influence or power. *Priostes* requested starter roosters with the expectation that recipients would be in office when delivery was made. They also expected recipients to hold the same or better office long enough to extend favors. The longer the recipients held important offices, the greater were the possible pay-offs for *priostes*. In view of the cooperative's changing managers and their relatively reduced power once land was redistributed, few compelling reasons motivated givers to continue the ceremony, especially when the value of cash investments was rising. Inflation has seriously increased the cost of living over the past decade. It has also driven incomes up, but not by the same margin. It is reasonable to infer, then, that local comments regarding the presently prohibitive costs of the *rama* leave unspoken the notion that costs are too high in relation to the meagerness of presently available returns.

The *rama* also offered management a channel through which easy access to a cheap maleable labor force could be maintained with minimal conflict. *Ramas* were anticipatory offerings from *priostes* who hoped to turn future managerial decisions their way, an outcome that was uncertain until favors were received. Meanwhile, it behooved *priostes* to publicly support the powerholders, to trade loyalty for possible favor. Presumably, managers who encouraged more laborers to bring *ramas* could presumably control more laborers without consistently resorting to overt coercion which might ultimately prove to be counterproductive. Management's investments in entertainment thus brought returns in the form of pliant workers. When the corporate lessees mechanized agricultural production and the number of unskilled laborers exceeded needs, the ritual as both symbol and facilitator of white control became irrelevant to hacienda objectives.

Harris (1964:29–33) suggests that *priostes* who must borrow goods and cash from *hacendados* to meet their festive obligations to the community become snared into the *hacendados'* debt and eventually into the haciendas' permanent work force. In the present case management assumed some festive expenses. Nevertheless, Indian families were lured into debt for the *rama* ceremony during the Church occupancy and early state management. Aside from economic traps, however, St. John's ceremonies offered whites a covert strategy for exercising social control by enticing Indians into a "waiting game" that promised valuable and otherwise unobtainable rewards to the best public performers.

CONCLUSION

Diachronic data show that St. John's fiesta had articulated with the hierarchical organization of the traditional hacienda system in several respects. To the observer, it symbolically revealed the course of hacienda Indian subordination, and through role exchanges between Indians and whites it mirrored for Indian participants the power they never had, and for whites the inequities they regularly perpetrated. The process undoubtedly afforded Indians the recreational and psychological release that tempered "the castigations of a harsh and cruel world" (Holmberg 1965:3). But such respites from routine events were brief, and the status transformations they entailed were illusory. The ritual process had a continuous affect nevertheless, for it fostered the social context of patronage relationships with whites. Considering the absence of formal personalized ties between elite and subordinate members of traditional hacienda society, coupled with their mutual need to guarantee the delivery of elusive goods and services, the ceremonially endorsed forms of patronage created in St. John's name granted Indians and whites access to otherwise unavailable resources in one another's personal environment (see, e.g., Adams 1975). In addition, in view of the many dependent Indians and the limited number of powerholders, the *rama* ceremony also offered a channel for regularizing the distribution of white patronage among competing Indian claimants while sanctifying white control over them. Thus the language, ideology, and rituals of Catholicism offer pertinent resources to persons placed high and low in traditional society. St. John's rituals established short-lived and narrowly specialized relationships which offered whites and Indians mutually acceptable, or tolerable, avenues to their respective objectives within a system of overt racism and castelike stratification.

For decades, and presumably since the sixteenth century, the festivities have responded to changes in the constraints that formed the matrix of asymmetrical interdependence between Indians and whites. The introduction of capital-intensive strategies of production that reduced management's need for unskilled labor had been reflected in the patron's own withdrawal from the ceremonial exchanges. The centuries-old bases for dependence were favorably reduced for Indians only when the agrarian reforms destroyed the state's land monopoly, truncated the pyramidal hierarchy, and redistributed land and influence. Aspects of indigenous ethnicity that were dynamically linked to the traditional system yielded to the exigencies of the new political economy.

Today, rather than express sharply inequitable Indian-white relationships and stereotypic hacienda Indian features, the festivities increasingly offer a secularized spectator event that shares several features with non-Indian celebrations. The fiesta, in its reflective dimensions, still reiterates political and ethnic relationships between townspeople and cultivators, but these are in many respects more equitable and at the same time more competitive. While the newly emerging system is unable to accommodate indigenous practices as these were defined within the traditional context, newly conceived expressions of indigenous ethnicity, dependency relationships, and economic, social, and political inequities cannot be discounted in the future.

NOTES

Acknowledgments: Data for this paper were collected during several field seasons between 1964 and 1979. I appreciate the research funds provided at different times by the National Institute of Mental Health, City University of New York, Fulbright Commission, and the Foundation for Inter-Andean Development. Joseph B. Casagrande's project on comparative ethnic relations, funded by the National Science Foundation, supported my work in 1968, for which I am grateful. The Ecuadorian Instituto Nacional de Antropología e Historia has been consistently helpful. I am indebted to Barbara W. Lex, Stephen I. Thompson, Norman E. Whitten, Jr., and Kathleen Fine for their constructive criticisms of an earlier draft of this paper.

1. Peruvian and Bolivian data suggest that when estate Indians sponsor fiestas, they may establish ties with estate and town whites (Carter 1964:42, Doughty 1971:99, Miller 1967:166), and Burgos Guevara (1970:193) mentions that Chimborazo Indians in Ecuador ritually offer foodstuffs to *hacendados*. The field returns do not, however, reveal any clear pattern regarding the responses of ritual to changes in hacienda organization, but note that Peruvian and Bolivian hacienda fiestas continue sometimes with greater and

sometimes with lesser intensity following change (Carter 1964, Doughty 1971, Erasmus 1967, Simmons 1974).

2. I use ethnic terms for Indians and non-Indians in their most common local sense. The people called whites here are identified as white by themselves and by Indians, although hacienda elites and residents of the Cayambe canton seat would call them *cholos*, a term similar in meaning to *mestizo*.

3. I do not wish to suggest that Atahualpa or other Indians have passively or universally accepted their working conditions. Overt protests were not unknown, but they were rare. In the eighteenth century, for example, Indians at haciendas in Cayambe canton and at haciendas and textile mills, *obrajes*, in adjacent cantons of Imbabura province violently rebelled against patrons. Atahualpa Indians participated in these uprisings, although not to any known degree (Moreno Yánez 1976). Contemporary data indicate that covert efforts to circumvent hacienda rules are daily occurrences. Moreover, at any one time while the public behavior of most Indians falls within the range tolerable to management, the behavior of some Indians does not. People involved in union activities clearly did not conform to management's expectations.

4. Government records indicate that expropriation occurred in 1904, but the archivist at La Merced Monastery claims that it occurred in 1906. The law, *Ley de Beneficencia*, that empowered the state to expropriate monastic holdings was not promulgated until 1908.

5. Atahualpa residents joined the cooperatives with different personal material and social resources at their disposal. Initial variations in subsistence plots, leadership abilities, degree of literacy, and familiarity with non-Indian institutions, although not always marked, affected a member's ability to maximize access to the cooperatives' benefits. Some members are still as poor as *huasipungueros* were, while others, especially former managers, are obviously more successful.

6. For regional variations in interethnic relations, and ethnic roles and categories, see Casagrande (1974) and Whitten (1976), as well as other essays in this volume.

7. St. John's widespread popularity in Cayambe and at haciendas and free communities in adjoining Imbabura province, but reduced significance elsewhere, suggests a "St. John culture area" at the Cayambe-Imbabura interface. Rituals and costumes vary within the area, however, especially between haciendas and free communities. Indians employed at private haciendas in Ibarra canton, Imbabura, continue to offer *ramas* to the patrons, while Indians in free landholding communities of the same canton give *ramas* to the canton priest. For descriptions of St. John in the free communities of Otavalo canton, Imbabura, see Buitrón (n.d.), Parsons (1945), Salz (1955), Rubio Orbe (1956), and Villavicencio (1973).

8. Management and the hacienda's white residents co-sponsored the celebrations for Our Lady of Mercy. The whites were exclusively responsible for other saint's day festivities. Following their move to the new town, whites continued to celebrate some saints and divided the responsibility for others among residents at the five haciendas.

9. Investigators have suggested that St. John festivities also coincide with Inti Raymi, the Incaic celebration of the harvest or summer solstice (e.g., Parsons 1945, Rubio Orbe 1956, Villavicencio 1973). Other syncretisms mark

the fiesta, but a discussion of them is beyond the scope of this paper. [Editor's note: I tentatively offer the opinion that St. John the Baptist, and the fiesta offered in his name, assume paramount importance in this setting, and other analogous ones, because the concept of baptism itself stresses a process of status transformation from savage (sinner) to civilized (absolved Christian). Immersed Indians should (but don't) emerge *blanco* as they accept the One True Faith (Catholic Christianity). Hence the fiesta of St. John symbolizes both transformation and continuity.]

10. Several slightly different versions of the *loa* have been used in the Atahualpa area during the past 25 years, if not longer. The same set is shared by residents at neighboring haciendas in Ibarra canton, Imbabura. Each *loa* draws partly on information and sentiments expressed in the gospels according to St. Mark and St. Luke, and in biblical stories about the New Testament. Despite differing amounts of details, the *loas* all note the birth of St. John to the long-barren Elizabeth and the mute Zacharias, and the saint's divine powers to baptize and liberate people from misfortune. Close associations are drawn between the saint and the roosters and dove, and between the saint and other elements of the festivities, the drinking, dancing, and so on. Some orations refer to the fateful dinner when King Herod agreed to behead the saint. Each *loa* praises the particular hacienda, its patron, and the saint.

11. Indians purchase their wire and papier-mâché masks from non-Indians in the Cayambe market. The wire masks have shown little stylistic variation from one year to another, but papier-mâché masks which portray figures of national and international importance change each year in response to current events. In 1977, for example, masks of President Jimmy Carter graced the faces of numerous clowns. The Indian buyers, however, usually select from the range of available masks without knowing their political significance.

12. *Ramas* are given occasionally within the community to Indian *compadres* of relatively high standing, and the white owners of *chicherías* in some Cayambe towns may request *ramas* from Indians in the Atahualpa parish.

REFERENCES CITED

Adams, Richard N.
    1975   *Energy and Structure: A Theory of Social Power*. Austin: University of Texas Press.
Babcock, Barbara B.
    1978   Introduction. In Barbara A. Babcock, ed., *The Reversible World: Symbolic Inversion in Art and Society*. Ithaca, N.Y.: Cornell University Press.
Barsky, Osvaldo
    1978   Iniciativa Terrateniente en la Reestructuracion de las Relaciones Sociales en la Sierra Ecuatoriana: 1959–1964. *Transformaciones Agrarias en el Altiplano Andino* 2:74–126.
Blankstein, Charles S., and Clarence Zuvekas, Jr.
    1973   Agrarian Reforms in Ecuador: An Evaluation of Past Efforts and the Development of a New Approach. *Economic Development and Cultural Change* 22:73–94.

Buitrón, Aníbal
n.d.   *Taita Imbabura, Vida Indígena en los Andes.* Quito: Misión Andina.
Burgos Guevara, Hugo
1970   *Relaciones Interétnicas en Riobamba.* Mexico City: Instituto Indigenista Interamericano.
Cancian, Frank
1965   *Economics and Prestige in a Maya Community.* Stanford, Calif.: Stanford University Press.
Carter, William E.
1964   *Aymara Communities and the Bolivian Agrarian Reform.* Gainesville: University of Florida Press, Monograph 24.
Casagrande, Joseph B.
1974   Strategies for Survival: The Indians of Highland Ecuador. In Dwight Heath, ed., *Contemporary Cultures and Societies of Latin America.* 2d ed. New York: Random House, pp. 93–107.
Colby, Benjamin N., and Pierre L. van den Berghe
1969   *Ixil Country: A Plural Society in Highland Guatemala.* Berkeley: University of California Press.
Crespi, Muriel
1975   When *Indios* Become *Cholos*: Some Consequences of the Changing Ecuadorian Hacienda. In John W. Bennett, ed., *The New Ethnicity: Perspectives from Ethnology.* 1973 Proceedings of the American Ethnological Society. St. Paul, Minn.: West Publishing Co., pp. 148–65.
1976   Mujeres Campesinas como Líderes Sindicales. *Estudios Andinos* 5:151–71.
Doughty, Paul L.
1971   Human Relations: Affection, Rectitude, and Respect. In Henry F. Dobyns, Paul L. Doughty, and Harold D. Lasswell, eds., *Peasants, Power, and Applied Social Change: Vicos as a Model.* Beverly Hills, Calif.: Sage, pp. 88–113.
Ecuador—Oficina de los Censos Nacionales
1974   *III Censo de Población.* Junta Nacional de Planificación, Republica del Ecuador.
Erasmus, Charles J.
1967   Upper Limits of Peasantry and Agrarian Reform: Bolivia, Venezuela and Mexico Compared. *Ethnology* 6:349–80.
Friedrich, Paul
1966   Revolutionary Politics and Communal Ritual. In Marc J. Swartz, Victor Turner, and Arthur Tuden, eds., *Political Anthropology.* Chicago: Aldine, pp. 191–220.
Goffman, Erving
1959   *The Presentation of Self in Everyday Life.* New York: Doubleday.
Gould, Harold
1971   *Caste and Class: A Comparative View.* Reading, Mass.: Addison-Wesley, Modular Publication 11.
Harris, Marvin
1964   *Patterns of Race in the Americas.* New York: Walker.
Hassaurek, Friedrich
1868   *Four Years among the Spanish-Americans.* New York: Hurd and Houghton.

Holmberg, Allan R.
    1965 The Changing Values and Institutions of Vicos in the Context of National Development. *American Behavioral Scientist* 8:3–8.
Linke, Lilo
    1960 *Ecuador: Country of Contrast*. London: Oxford University Press.
Miller, Solomon
    1967 Hacienda to Plantation in Northern Peru. In Julian H. Steward, ed., *Contemporary Change in Traditional Societies*, vol. 3. Urbana: University of Illinois Press, pp. 135–225.
Mitchell, Clyde J.
    1966 Theoretical Orientations in African Urban Studies. In Michael Banton, ed., *The Social Anthropology of Complex Societies*. London: Tavistock, pp. 37–68.
Monroy, Joel L.
    1932 *El Convento de la Merced de Quito (de 1616–1700)*. Quito: Editorial Labor.
    1933 *La Santisma Virgen de la Merced de Quito y Su Santuario*. Quito: Editorial Labor.
    1938 *El Convento de la Merced de Quito de 1534–1617*. Quito: Editorial Labor.
Moreno Yánez, Segundo
    1976 *Sublevaciones Indígenas en la Audiencia de Quito: Desde Comienzos del Siglo XVIII hasta Finales de la Colonia*. Bonn: Bonner Amerikanistische Studien 5.
Parsons, Elsie Clews
    1945 *Peguche: A Study of Andean Indians*. Chicago: University of Chicago Press.
Registro Civil
    1912 Olmedo.
Registro Oficial
    1931 No. 603. Quito.
    1964 No. 297. *Ley de Reforma Agraria y Colonización. Decreto Supremo 1480*. Quito.
Reina, Ruben
    1966 *Law of the Saints: A Pokomam Pueblo and Its Community Culture*. Indianapolis: Bobbs-Merrill.
Rubio Orbe, Gonzalo
    1956 *Punyaro*. Quito: Casa de la Cultura Ecuatoriana.
Salz, Beate
    1955 *The Human Element in Industrialization: A Hypothetical Case Study of Ecuadorian Indians*. Washington, D.C.: American Anthropological Association, Memoir 85.
Simmons, Roger A.
    1974 *Palca and Pucara: A Study of the Effects of Revolution on Two Bolivian Haciendas*. Berkeley: University of California Press.
Smith, Waldemar R.
    1977 *The Fiesta System and Economic Change*. New York: Columbia University Press.
Swartz, Marc J., ed.
    1968 *Local-Level Politics: Social and Cultural Perspectives*. Chicago: Aldine.

Turner, Terence S.
  1969   Tchikrin: A Central Brazilian Tribe and Its Symbolic Language of
         Bodily Adornment. *Natural History* 8:50–70.
Turner, Victor
  1974   *Dramas, Fields, and Metaphors: Symbolic Action in Human Society.* Ith-
         aca, N.Y.: Cornell University Press.
Villavicencio Rivadeneira, Gladys
  1973   *Relaciones Interétnicas en Otavalo, Ecuador.* Mexico City: Instituto In-
         digenista Interamericano.
Wachtel, Nathan
  1971   *La Vision des Vaincus: Les Indiens du Pérou devant la Conquête Espagnole
         1530–1570.* Paris: Gaillimard.
Warren, Kay B.
  1978   *The Symbolism of Subordination: Ethnic Identity in a Guatemalan Town.*
         Austin: University of Texas Press.
Whitten, Norman E., Jr. (with the assistance of Marcelo F. Naranjo, Marcelo
         Santi Simbaña, and Dorothea S. Whitten)
  1976   *Sacha Runa: Ethnicity and Adaptation of Ecuadorian Jungle Quichua.* Ur-
         bana: University of Illinois Press.
Wolf, Eric R.
  1955   Types of Latin American Peasantry: A Preliminary Discussion.
         American Anthropologist 57:452–71.
Wolf, Eric R., and Sidney W. Mintz
  1957   Haciendas and Plantations in Middle America and the Antilles. *So-
         cial and Economic Studies* 6:380–412.

18

Protestantism, Ethnicity, and Class in Chimborazo

Blanca Muratorio

Although discussion of the folk Catholicism of Andean Indian peasants has a long tradition in the anthropological literature, only a few social scientists[1] have dealt with the problem of Protestantism in South America. Their studies have focused either on large urban centers in Brazil, Chile (Willems 1967, Lalive D'Espinay 1969), and Colombia (Flora 1976) or on relatively small Indian populations in the Brazilian tropical forest (Ribeiro 1973) and the Argentine Chaco (Miller 1971, 1974, 1975).

This paper examines the emergence and development of evangelical Protestantism among a group of Indian peasants in the Ecuadorian highlands. These Indian peasants still preserve fundamental aspects of their culture and social organization, although they have been for more than 400 years an integral part of a class society as semiserfs and now as freeholders. Consequently, I will discuss the effects of the adoption of Protestantism on both ethnic and class consciousness. Furthermore, since the previous religious ideology of Catholicism professed by the peasants was closely tied to the hacienda system of domination, it is necessary to analyze how the breakdown of that system made possible the penetration of Protestantism, which now operates in the context of changing social and economic conditions in the highlands.

The transformation of the traditional hacienda system of the Ecuadorian highlands gathered momentum after the first and rather lukewarm agrarian reform law of 1964 and the abolition of *precarismos*[2] in 1970, and after the new agrarian reform law, passed in 1973, eliminated rent in labor and gave the peasants legal ownership of their plots. Concurrently, the decade of the 1960s witnessed an important ideological change in the position of the Catholic church vis-à-vis social and economic issues. These developments played a significant

role in undermining the hegemony of the landowning class traditionally legitimized by the Catholic church, and they must be taken into
account in order to understand how a new religious ideology "interacts" with the new relations of production. In order to clarify this last
statement, I will say that I do not assume that ideologies occupy a
secondary role in social life or that they may be explained by reducing
them to a passive reflection of economic or other aspects of society.
The ideological sphere has a certain degree of autonomy and articulates in complex ways with the productive activities in a concrete
social formation (see Williams 1977:55–71, 75–82). This paper is an
attempt to understand some of those complexities.

The peasant population to be discussed is primarily that living in a
region known as Colta, which comprises several Indian peasant communities located around or near the Colta Lake in the province of
Chimborazo. Riobamba, the capital of the province and an important
market town, is located about 22 kilometers from Colta.[3]

Because this area, and particularly the community of Majipamba,
where I was stationed, is the major center for the diffusion of Protestantism in the highlands, other peasants frequently visit the area,
and references will be made to them in the course of the argument.
All Protestant peasants discussed are known as *evangélicos* or "Quichuas" and have been converted by the Gospel Missionary Union,
which includes missionaries from a variety of Protestant denomina-
tions.

CATHOLIC IDEOLOGY AND HACIENDA: THEIR
TRANSFORMATIONS

In the hacienda system the landowning class had the actual monopoly of the land and granted the peasants usufruct of small plots
known as *huasipungos*. Consequently, as direct producers the peasants had effective possession of the means of production necessary
to meet their subsistence needs and thus reproduce themselves as a
labor force. Under these conditions the extraction of surplus by the
landowning class was possible only through forms of extra-economic
coercion over the direct producers (Marx 1962:771, Guerrero 1975:28–35
et passim). This surplus appropriation was accomplished effectively
first because the landowning class had political control of the state.
Its members occupied the highest political offices in the country and
could call the police and the army to impose order in the hacienda
whenever there was peasant unrest. Morever, appropriation was ac-

complished effectively because the existing social relations of production were legitimized by the ideological apparatus of the Catholic church.

Until the first decades of this century the Church was one of the largest landowners and shared with the rest of the dominant class the control of the state. Priests could hold political offices as legislators and state councillors. Even more important, the Church had a dominant ideological role in the state, recognized in the Constitution of 1830, which accepted Roman Catholicism as the official religion of the state, excluding all others (Hurtado 1977:66–67). In addition to its specific religious functions, the Church had control over all levels of the educational system and the exclusive right to register births, marriages, and deaths. Catholic ideology regarded the hierarchical order of the universe as ordained by God; poverty existed in the world as a blessing to be accepted with resignation, thereby transforming the existing class structure of the hacienda into a "sacred" order. Furthermore, the belief in the racial inferiority of the Indians—taken for granted in colonial times and still prevalent in the nineteenth century—contributed to the disguising of class relationships, legitimizing the social order of the hacienda as "natural." The link between these two components of the ideology was recognized as part of the legal order. The Constitution of 1830 put the Indians under the control of the Church, ordering that parish priests be nominated "tutors and natural fathers of the innocent, servile and miserable indigenous race" (Hurtado 1977:69). Ethnicity, defined in these terms, was appropriated by the dominant ideological apparatus to set the conditions under which the Indians were incorporated and reproduced as a labor force within the existing class structure.

Furthermore, the state used this same ideological justification—the definition of the Indian population as a special race—to impose on the peasants the payment of the tribute, abolished only in 1857 (Jácome and Llumiquinga 1977:115). On the same grounds the Church could expropriate part of the Indians' surplus primarily through the tithe and *primicias*—a form of rent in kind. The local priest could also extract rent in labor through the *minga*—a form of collective work—and in cash or kind in payment for the religious services of baptisms, marriages, and funerals. One of the main methods of the local priests for extracting surplus from the Indians was the fiesta complex, in which the *priostes*, sponsors, had to pay for all the necessary religious services. The fiesta complex of Andean Indian communities has been extensively discussed in the anthropological literature. The only aspect I would like to examine here is the way in which the fiesta actually helped, directly and indirectly, to increase the different forms of surplus extracted from the peasants by the Church and the landowners.

In order to pay for the religious services of the fiesta, the peasants asked the landowners for advances in money, *suplidos*, and in kind, *socorros*. These advances were difficult to repay and frequently resulted in a form of labor contract that tied the peasant permanently to the hacienda (*concertaje*; see Peñaherrera and Costales 1964, Moreno Yánez 1977:313–16), unless he accepted imprisonment for debt. The following statement about *concertaje* by a member of the landowning class, quoted by Hurtado, is revealing: "What would be the fate of the agricultural class if suddenly the bases of *concertaje* are destroyed? The most horrible misery, a proletariat worse than the one produced in Europe by large industry" (1977:65). *Concertaje* was abolished only in 1918, but debt peonage continued to be enforced. Furthermore, the fiesta guaranteed the landowners that part of the surplus produced by the peasants in their *huasipungos* would be consumed rather than marketed. Then the peasant family would have only the necessary means for its own reproduction, and some of its members would be forced to sell their labor power for wages to the haciendas.[4]

Casagrande and Piper's study (1969) conducted in Chimborazo province provides an interesting example of the collaboration between Church and *hacendados* in using the fiesta complex to tie the Indian peasants to the hacienda. In 1908 the bishop of Riobamba intervened to grant the ecclesiastical status of "parish" to a *población*, hamlet, next to a large hacienda. Having the status of a parish, the *población* could be the center for the yearly cycle of fiestas. Thus the peasantry did not have to leave the area for days, and even weeks, to attend the celebrations somewhere else. The *hacendado* could then have more effective control of *his* Indians and their labor, and the new parish could benefit through the above-mentioned forms of extracting surplus from the peasantry.

Finally, the fiesta complex also contributed indirectly to the extraction of surplus from the peasantry for the benefit of the dominant class. The *alcalde*, an important authority in the peasant communities, was generally selected with the approval of the priest. One of his functions was to nominate the *priostes* and to organize the fiestas. But he also used his prestige and power to recruit Indian labor for the *mingas* called by priests, landowners, or state officials. An informant in Colta remembers how the police chief from Cajabamba helped the *alcalde* by jailing those who refused to be *priostes*, this in exchange for the *alcalde*'s influence in recruiting people from Colta to work in *min-gas* for him and his relatives.

At the beginning of this century the reforms of the liberal govern-ment of Eloy Alfaro started with a direct attack on the economic power of the Church in the highlands. In 1908 the liberals passed the mortmain law, expropriating some of the largest landholdings of the Church and the religious orders. Since these properties reverted to the state and were rented to powerful landowners from the region, this policy did not particularly affect the power of the landowning class.

Most of the legislation passed by the liberals, such as public edu-cation, civil marriage and divorce, and the formal separation of church and state, can be regarded as attempts to destroy the ideo-logical domination of the Church over the state apparatus and to cre-ate the juridical conditions of a secular bourgeois state. None of these policies directly affected the highland Indians, nor did they weaken the ideological control of the Church over them. As I will show later, at the beginning of this century the Church had the power to prevent the introduction of Protestantism among highland Indians despite the freedom of worship supposedly established in the liberals' 1906 Constitution (Hurtado 1977:120).

The possibilities of proletarization for the highland peasantry started with the abolition of *concertaje* in 1918. In the 1950s, under the presidency of Galo Plaza Lasso, the introduction of capitalist agricul-ture on the Coast and the improvement of the country road network created conditions for a large migration of manpower. Some highland landowners were then forced to pay regular wages to their peons and to rationalize the use of the labor force by introducing various tech-nical changes. Nevertheless, the great majority of the landowners continued to extract surplus from the peasants by the traditional means already described. Only the agrarian reforms of the 1960s and 1970s created structural conditions for the disappearance of forced labor.

In the decade of the 1960s the encyclicals of popes John XXIII and Paul VI inspired significant changes in the social and political ide-ology of the Latin American Catholic church. The new orientation called for the liberation of the poor from social injustices and for an active role of the Church in helping them to change the structure of exploitation. In 1963 the Ecuadorian Church demanded agrarian re-form and soon after started to implement it in its remaining highland properties. In Chimborazo, Leonidas Proaño, bishop of Riobamba, initiated a series of social action programs directly concerned with improving the material and social conditions of the peasantry (see Proaño 1974).

Although in 1977 there were still many "traditional" parish priests left in the province, the new social and political action of the Church finally broke its holy alliance with the landowning class. At present, some of the worst indictments against the new Catholic clergy come from the remaining landowners, who see the action of the Church as "class treason." Having lost their main source of ideological legitimation, only their remaining influence on the state apparatus allows the landowners to block the action of those peasant groups who try to have their rights recognized through the implementation of the agrarian reform law.[5]

The liberalization of Catholicism was decisive in opening up the area for the Protestant churches. Systematic action against Protestantism by the Catholic church no longer exists. Nevertheless, there are still conflicts between Catholic and Protestant peasants, sometimes involving violence. Religious factionalism brings about ideological antagonism *within* the Indian peasantry, weakening class unity and hindering the development of ethnic and class ideologies which might challenge the existing political and ideological relations of domination.

Changes in the Social Relations of Production

In Chimborazo the hacienda system has been succeeded not by full-fledged agrarian capitalism but by an economy increasingly dominated by small peasant freeholders, *minifundios*. Still, sharecropping, traditional and modernized haciendas, and communally owned land coexist with peasant freeholders in complex interrelationships. The data I will discuss here refer specifically to the Colta area. What is happening there is similar to developments in many other areas, however, as I found in discussing aspects of the agrarian reform law with peasants from other parts of Chimborazo and in following several land disputes in the Institute of Agrarian Reform and Colonization (IERAC) offices in Riobamba.

The fact that peasant *minifundios* are further subdivided by inheritance results in a constant demand for more land to meet subsistence needs, bringing about an increase in land prices. As a consequence, the number of sharecropping arrangements has increased, primarily between peasants who bought or were granted land after the agrarian reform and those who do not own enough land to produce for subsistence. Besides, many peasants still maintain old sharecropping arrangements with landlords from Cajabamba, Sicalpa, and Riobamba. Under the new agrarian reform law arrangements with these landlords are illegal. In order to legalize this situation with IERAC and the Ministry of Labor, peasants are spending huge sums of money on lawyers, and many are ridden with debts (Muratorio 1976).

The Colta peasants have always preferred the common Andean pattern of having several small plots of land located in different ecological microzones in order to minimize risks and diversify production. However, given the increasingly smaller size of the plots and land erosion in the Colta area, some peasants are now producing in as many as six or seven scattered tiny plots which do not add up to an acreage large enough either to engage the labor power of the whole family or to produce its total subsistence requirements. Young and adult male members of these families are then forced to seek employment outside the area. Some become itinerant merchants; others work as *cargadores*, carriers, or as unskilled construction workers in the urban areas; still others work as wage laborers in the sugar mills of San Carlos and Milagro or on the coastal plantations, thus becoming incorporated in marginal occupations or into the dominant capitalist mode of production as cheap seasonal labor, because part of their own reproduction still takes place in their family plots.

The seasonal migration of part of the labor force leaves agricultural production mostly in the hands of women and older members of the family. This creates a demand for additional labor, generally performed for wages, by those landless people who did not migrate. The fact that these peons are landless puts them outside the forms of reciprocal labor exchange that are still quite prevalent in the area and highly valued by the peasants. However, because most peasants are short of cash, the peons' wages are, to a large extent, paid in kind.

On the one hand, by consolidating the *minifundios* the new agrarian legislation favors inequalities, competition, and individualism. On the other, in order to subsist, the peasants resort to reciprocity in goods and labor as the prevalent form of mutual help in the relations of production. As I will show later, they have even adapted the new religious ideology to the old ceremonial practices which strengthened reciprocity.

Most communities in the area have some acres of land in the *páramo* for pasturing sheep and cattle. When animals have to be left to pasture for longer than a day, peasants in Colta enter into reciprocity arrangements with other peasants living in higher-altitude communities where pasture is better and more abundant.

The development of a capitalist market is increasingly creating new needs for manufactured goods. Synthetic textiles are displacing many of the traditional peasant crafts such as *bayeta*, handwoven woolen cloth, and woolen ponchos. Peasants of the Colta area are still able to sell *esteras*, mats, woven with the *totora* reeds which grow in the lake. To a large extent the transportation and marketing of agricultural produce are controlled by *mestizos* in the Riobamba market (see Burgos Guevara 1977). Peasants try to avoid dependence on the *mestizo* market by diversifying production in their own plots rather than specializing in cash crops. They increase the output for market purchases mostly by intensifying family labor. Part of the output of barley, potatoes, and *quinoa*, for instance, is sold in the market but not in large quantities. The reproduction of the peasants' means of production and the maintenance of their plots do not depend primarily on the market.

As far as the peasant freeholders are concerned, the national agrarian policies of prices, credits, and technical aid favor the accumulation of capital not in their hands but rather in the hands of the largest agricultural capitalists (Báez 1976:260, Hurtado 1977:244). The highland peasants are not turning into effective small capitalist farmers but instead are increasing the size of the proletariat and subproletariat in the cities. The recent policy of emphasizing colonization in the Amazon region at the cost of undermining agrarian reform and the role of IERAC in the highlands (see LAER, 28 Apr. 1978, 6 (16):125, and 10 Nov. 1978, 6 (44):347) is not likely to help change that situation.

HISTORY OF PROTESTANTISM IN THE COLTA AREA

When the first members of the American Bible Society arrived in Ecuador in 1838, they were banished for circulating the Scriptures. It is reported that, rejecting a cargo of Bibles, a customs officer declared: "Protestant Bibles shall not enter into Ecuador so long as Chimborazo stands" (Nickel 1965:12). Well, Mount Chimborazo still stands, and right in the highland province with the highest rate of growth of Protestant converts (Reed 1975:5). It is in front of Colta Lake in Chimborazo where the Gospel Missionary Union (GMU) has its main headquarters for the highland provinces.

The GMU opened its first missionary station in Caliata, south of Riobamba, in 1902. Two American missionary women were chosen to work among the Quichuas because it was thought that it would be easier for women to gain the confidence of the Indians. They encountered strong resistance from the local priests, who even organized processions sprinkling holy water along the roads to scare away the missionaries' "evil spirits" (Nickel 1965:25–27). The Protestant pioneers in the Colta area were the Seventh-Day Adventists (SDA). A married couple arrived there from the United States in 1921, rented a peasant hut, and started their missionary work preaching, treating the sick, and opening a school. None of these strategies proved to be very successful. The Indians viewed the missionaries' modern medicine as a form of miracle healing from the "white witchdoctors," *viracocha yachaj*, and prayed in front of their Ford T-model car, debating among themselves if the devil or an angel was responsible for making it run. Besides, the priest had threatened with excommunication anyone who dared ask for a ride (Westphal 1962:35–43). Catholic opposition to the missionaries' work was consistent and effective. They were accused, among other things, of being "heretics" and "white devils" and of "causing local droughts." After five years in Colta they were able to baptize only two men. One of them, presently living in Colta, still remembers those days: "I went to the missionaries' school only during rainy days when I was not working with my father. I felt proud because Indians did not go to school then. But everybody went to (Catholic) church on Sundays, and I was praying on Saturdays. I felt very lonely."

The SDA abandoned their work among the Quichuas and sold their Colta station to the Christian and Missionary Alliance in 1933. Because of lack of personnel, this mission had to sell to the GMU in 1953 (Nickel 1965:77). The Canadian missionary couple who started the GMU mission 25 years ago is still in charge. Since, like many other peasants, the Indians of the highlands distrust outsiders, this stability of the core personnel has been a great asset in the success of the mission in Colta and in other areas. Its missionary work was also greatly facilitated by the medical mobile teams who visited different communities ministering to the sick. In 1958 the mission opened a hospital where, for the first time, Indians could receive medical attention from physicians fluent in Quichua. The importance of this step cannot be overemphasized. In 1976, when I accompanied many Quichuas to the local state hospital in Cajabamba, I witnessed their fear and apprehension because no member of the staff spoke Quichua. The American physician of the mission hospital and some of the Quichua assistants he trained preached the Gospel to the Quichua patients.

In 1961 the mission started the operation of the radio station HCUE-5 in Colta, now called *La Voz de la Laguna de Colta*, "The Voice of Colta Lake," broadcasting in Quichua. Pretuned receivers were sold to the Indians for a nominal price. Some of the older people in Colta still remember the feeling of awe when they listened to the radio for the first time, and in their own language. No wonder Nickel reports one Indian as saying: "I want to belong to Jesus Christ as that box says" (Nickel 1965:100).

Another strategy used by the GMU to reach the Indians was education. In 1956 the missionaries started basic literacy night classes for women. In 1957 they opened a boarding school where regular classes were taught in Spanish by an Ecuadorian teacher and Bible classes were taught in Quichua by the foreign missionaries (Nickel 1965:107). Many of the children became converted and taught their parents the new religion. The indigenous churches, which may be considered one of the most important strategies for the diffusion of Protestantism in the area, were started by the GMU in 1961. Missionary work by native preachers using a 1954 Quichua translation of the New Testament helped considerably to attract Quichua peasants to the new faith, but resistance from the Catholics was still strong. By 1966 there were only 330 baptized members of the GMU church in all of Chimborazo, 480 in 1967 (Klassen 1974:105), and 8,054 by 1977 (H. Klassen, personal communication). Converts have increased at the rate of nearly 33% per year for the last ten years. The present (1977) figure of 8,054 baptized members would mean an evangelical community of around 24,000 members, if we accept the GMU calculation of at least two believers for every baptized member, or 16% of the Quichua population of the province as estimated by GMU.[6]

I have mentioned the implementation of the agrarian reform and the ideological changes in the Catholic church in accounting for the growth of Protestantism beginning in the late 1960s. Its further growth in the 1970s may be explained, in part, by the fact that a new translation of the New Testament into the Quichua dialect of Chimborazo was published in 1973. As reported by one of the missionaries, the reaction of the Quichuas was: "This is our language, God is speaking to us. God actually loves the Indian as well as the Spanish" (quoted in Klassen 1974:72).

In a society like Ecuador, where the mass media are directed exclusively at a white or *mestizo* audience, a Quichua radio station becomes a very powerful form of ideological penetration among the Indian population. *La Voz de la Laguna de Colta* broadcasts for eight hours a day, five days a week. Every peasant family in the area, Protestant or Catholic, listens to it. Only two and a half hours of the programs are in Spanish, consisting of musical, educational, and evangelical programs. Except when it plays Ecuadorian music, attention decreases, especially among women, when the radio turns to Spanish. Through the transmission in Quichua, everybody is kept informed of local, national, and international news. A good deal of time is used to broadcast readings and explanations of the New Testament performed by groups coming from the different native churches in the province. All the programs, however, are preceded by everybody's favorite show—known locally as *saludos*, greetings—in which every member of the group participating in the program greets every member of his or her extended kinship network by name and kin term wherever they may be. Given the amount of internal and external migration, this program certainly helps to keep the kinship network alive and serves as a bond among small and isolated communities. Quichua songs, hymns, and singing lessons constitute the second most popular program. The majority of these songs have been written by Quichuas from the Colta area using native tunes. "Witness bands," usually composed of young people, use music and dramatization to spread the Gospel. The popularity of the new music has attracted many converts and has begun what the Quichuas define as "a revival of our own music." The periodic Bible conferences, which assemble hundreds of Quichuas from Chimborazo and other provinces, are another important source of new converts and help cement bonds among the congregation of believers. I will have more to say about those conferences later.

Two institutions—the Leadership Training Institute and the Association of Evangelical Indians of Chimborazo (AIECH)—are crucial to an understanding of the more formal organization of the GMU church in the area. Training of lay leaders is done at the institute five or six times a year. One week at a time, designated leaders from each of the Quichua churches attend classes that deal primarily with the interpretation of the Bible and with local church administration. The classes are taught by the missionaries and by some of the older Quichua pastors. The emphasis is on training lay people who can "witness" in their own communities and through the radio. The foreign missionaries see their role now as that of advisors or consultants. The hospital has been replaced by a mobile clinic and the elementary school has been turned over to the state authorities.

The native churches, once organized, join the AIECH, which is the most important political organization in terms of the relationship of the evangelical peasants with state authorities and other national institutions. The AIECH was constituted in 1967, so that the church could legally demand or purchase land for the church building and for the Colta Protestant cemetery. It was instrumental in defending the religious rights of the *evangélicos* when they were harassed and persecuted in the 1960s. By 1977 there were 137 churches in AIECH and three other similar associations in the provinces of Bolívar, Cotopaxi, and Pastaza. The goal seems to be to constitute a national association of evangelical peasants (president of AIECH, personal communication).

Finally, the GMU church is extending its scope in order to reach those highland Quichuas who migrate to the cities. It now has two organized churches in Quito and Guayaquil. These churches serve as meeting places and as centers of information for new and old migrants. In fact, the network of GMU *evangélicos* reaches the eastern jungle of Ecuador and even Colombia, mostly through the Quichua commercial peddlers, who travel continuously, spreading the Gospel, and who become the trusted carriers of money, letters, and greetings for other highland Quichuas who are already living there permanently.

PROTESTANTISM AND ETHNIC IDENTITY

Although the majority of the Protestant Quichuas in Chimborazo belong to the GMU church, there are other Protestant churches active in the province.[7] It is beyond my competence and the scope of this paper to discuss the theological complexities which distinguish the GMU from the other versions of Protestantism. I will therefore limit my comments to the aspects of the GMU version of Protestantism which seem to play a significant role in the on-going process of social, economic, and political transformation in Chimborazo and, in particular, to the ways in which elements of this religious ideology articulate with the dynamics of ethnic and class ideologies among the Indian peasantry.

Even to a lay observer, there are some characteristic beliefs and religious practices introduced by Protestantism that distinguish it from the version of folk Catholicism professed by the Quichuas before conversion. Those beliefs and practices center around the doctrine of "religious individualism," which Lukes defines as "the view that the individual believer does not need intermediaries, that he has the primary responsibility for his own spiritual destiny, that he has the right and the duty to come to his own relationship with God in his own way and by his own effort" (1973:94). Other important articles of faith are: salvation and justification only by God's bestowal of faith in Christ, as opposed to salvation by works and observances; the Bible as the sole reliable authority for the knowledge of God; the universal priesthood of all believers, as well as the idea of the individual's intrinsic worth and dignity under the will of God; and the belief that the secular government is ordained by God (see Dickens 1966, Chadwick 1964). The ethical principles involved derive from the Calvinist tradition, or what is commonly known as the "Protestant ethic." The moral precepts strongly emphasize discipline and abstention from alcohol, tobacco, premarital and extramarital sex, and from all "excesses" believed to be sinful. Finally, the Quichua Protestants have enthusiastically adopted the congregational hymn, that "greatest liturgical innovation of the reformation" (Chadwick 1964:439).

In addition to presenting itself as a way of knowing and explaining reality, religion implies a series of social practices as ways of acquiring power to influence postulated supernatural forces with the purpose of transforming the world (Godelier 1977:179). When they were Catholics, the Quichuas used the cult of the saints and the different folk versions of the Virgin as the main social practice by which they attempted to reach those extrahuman powers which they perceived as dominating them. Prayers, ritual drinking, and dancing with lavish costumes were practices performed to exert pressure on God's intermediaries.[8] The fiesta was a community affair, staged mostly with the purpose of obtaining benefits for the entire group, such as good harvests, rains, and protection for domestic animals.

In contrast, Protestantism emphasizes an individualized religious experience. The Quichuas have been taught about the "inadequacy" and "powerlessness" of the old intermediaries. The saints are now nervously laughed at and regarded as "mere wooden idols" or "senseless painted dolls." The Virgin Mary is acknowledged as the mother of Christ but has lost her powers as an intermediary. The individual is alone with his God. In order to acquire influence with the supernatural, the believer has to become worthy of God's mercy by inflicting on himself or herself a series of taboos and prohibitions to transform his or her body into a "clean temple" where God can dwell. Consequently, the emphasis is put on external cleanliness and on internal purity by avoiding drinking and by observing sexual taboos. These practices transform the Quichuas' "presentation of the self" (Goffman 1959). Changes are particularly evident among young Protestant women; unlike other women in the area, they do not cover their faces with the *baita*, woolen shawl, and are more willing to initiate face-to-face interaction with whites and *mestizos* and to speak and sing in public places.

Giving public "testimony," a ritual in which the new believer recounts his previous life as a sinner, is a regular feature of *conferencias*, meetings, and other *cultos*, religious services. It serves as an example to other participants. The community becomes a witness of these "testimonies," but as a group it cannot influence the supernatural powers—only the individual can.

Unlike the members of some revivalist sects, such as Pentecostalists, these Quichua Protestants are looking not for an instant or even future ecstasy but rather for present tranquility, a type of conformity arrived at by avoiding excesses and searching for a new self-identity. There is a small group of Quichua Pentecostalists in Colta. The *evangélicos* criticize them because "they act crazy, very much like ourselves when we were Catholics. They shout, clap, bang their heads against the wall, drink, and have more than one woman."[9]

Talking about their religious conversion, informants consistently identified their previous everyday life experiences as "animal behavior," with such expressions as "we were like dogs," "like brutes," "like beasts." Self-control and freedom from behavior which is now regarded as "degrading" are the bases for their newly acquired self-respect and dignity. As one informant expressed it: "If I don't behave like an animal I can love and respect myself and, therefore, reject those who despise me and call me Indian."

This new self-image is also a rejection of the previous exploitative relations in which the Indians were literally treated as "beasts of burden" and "less than human." These are not only images of the past; Protestant peasants—like other Indians in the area—are still subjected to discrimination and abuses by *mestizos* and whites. But the *evangélicos* are searching for a new identity to liberate them from a condition of humiliation. As Ribeiro says of Protestantism among the Xóbleng, "Conversion is a moving attempt to achieve ethnic transformation . . . a new consciousness as civilized Indians" (1973:302–3). But unlike the Xóbleng, the Quichuas are not trying to become non-Indians, i.e. *mestizos*. They are caught in a series of conflicts in which their religious experience and their relationship with the GMU move them both toward assimilation and toward efforts to define an ethnic consciousness in the context of a class society. What they wish is both to be and be seen as *gente*, human beings, and to be and be seen as Quichuas. They do not seek a *mestizo* identity as such—indeed, *mestizos* are despised by most Indians—yet the patterns of behavior inspired by Protestantism, the very basis of their self-perception as *gente* and of their new Quichua identity, may lead them toward assimilation. The situation is thus ambiguous.

The majority of Protestant Indians identify themselves as "Quichuas" rather than as *runas*, which means "men" in Quichua but is still used in a deprecatory sense by whites and *mestizos* to refer to all Indians and by some Indians to refer to themselves (see Burgos Guevara 1970:61). If the Indians of Chimborazo were originally Puruhá (Murra 1946:796–98), that is no longer a reality for them. First the Inca conquest and later the Spanish have contributed to the obliteration of an original ethnic identity, such as that which may still be claimed by members of tropical forest cultures of the Ecuadorian Oriente (e.g. Canelos Quichua, Shuara) and even by other highland Indian groups (e.g. Salasaca, Otavaleños, or Saraguros). More than any other, the Indians of Chimborazo were transformed into "generic Indians" (see Ribeiro 1973:16). Speaking the Quichua language, which clearly distinguishes them from *mestizos* and whites, has become the central means for enacting their ethnic identity. Furthermore, the Quichuas have several pejorative terms to refer to whites and *mestizos*, such as *tzala* and *'toto*. The connotation of both terms is that whites and *mestizos* are "rude" and "vulgar" because, lacking competence in Quichua, they cannot convey the subtleties of respect, humor, and feeling that this language allows.

Protestantism has been of fundamental importance in reviving the Quichuas' interest in their language, and they talk about it with a renewed sense of pride. The revalorization of Quichua is also perceived by them as a form of strengthening their identity vis-à-vis the dominant elements of the national society as a whole, to whom the speaking of Quichua as the first language is a *de facto* sign of social and intellectual inferiority.

Although instruction in public schools is conducted exclusively in Spanish, the evangelical Quichuas are showing increasing interest in sending their children to school. Formal schooling is becoming a new symbol of prestige among Protestant leaders and young people. Adult men and women are making an enormous effort to teach themselves to read, and all listen to the basic education programs broadcast in Quichua through the local station. The major goal is to be able to read the Bible instead of merely learning passages by heart as they usually do now. When traveling, men and women carry their Bibles carefully protected in plastic bags. They do not use their Bibles as a fetish, as Miller (1974:396) reports the Pentecostalist Tobas of Argentina used to do, but they see the Bible as containing "the Word" and as a "model for their new lives." As Reyburn has pointed out for the Protestant Tobas in Argentina (quoted in Miller 1971:156), it is also easier for the Quichuas to accept the impersonal authority of the Bible than that of another human being—such as a white Catholic priest—who might be perceived as coercing them. But, in addition, owning a Bible has specific social meaning for the Quichuas because it shows to the outside world that they now know how to read, and it gives them a special sense of dignity in front of all those who once had a monopoly of information, education, and religious interpretation. Through the reading of the Bible, the representation of biblical dramas, and the viewing of religious films, the Quichuas are beginning to understand other cultures and to see themselves incorporated into a common humanity of equals.

Burridge (1973:14) has pointed out the importance of the Bible as a means of breaking down cultural boundaries, thus bringing a variety of European communities into a common humanity. In one of the many *cultos* I observed, the pastor read parts of Paul's Epistle to the Romans on the equality of divine punishment and interpreted it to the audience by saying: "Whites, Quichuas, Mestizos, Blacks, and Gringos will be judged equally before God's law." Although it contrasts with the previous ethnic ideology as manipulated by the Catholic church, this interpretation of the Bible stresses only equality before God. Like many other religious ideologies, this version of Protestantism neutralizes actual antagonisms, postponing their resolution to an afterlife.

As Cardoso de Oliveira (1976:24) points out, in class societies ideologies of ethnicity develop out of relations of domination and subordination. The ethnic ideologies reflect this opposition and are manipulated differently by the various groups in conflict. As I have tried to show in the first part of this paper, in the traditional hacienda system ethnicity was a crucial element of the hegemonic ideology for the reproduction of the relations of production based on serf labor. However, especially during the eighteenth and nineteenth centuries, ethnicity was also used by the peasantry as the rallying ideological principle in the organization of Indian rebellions. The ideology of those rebellions took different forms—reformist, millenarian, nativistic—but, insofar as the rebellions always made explicit the antagonism between Indians and whites, they expressed the reaction of the Indian peasantry against the existing relations of domination. In the context of those rebellions the ideology of ethnicity became a subversive element and was perceived as such by the dominant class, who used brute military force in punishing the Indian leaders and the ideological support of the Church in bringing the Indian masses back into submission (see Moreno Yánez 1977:353–79).

The crisis of both the hacienda system and the dominant ideology opened up the possibilities for the different social sectors in conflict to elaborate and re-elaborate their ideologies. Some sectors among the Indian peasantry have adopted a political ideology of opposition to the present bourgeois system of domination. For other Indian peasants, Protestantism has become an alternative ideology. The state has opted for an ideology of *mestizaje*, which legitimizes the present social relations of domination. It is only with Protestant peasants and the state that I am concerned here.

Presently in Ecuador, as in other Latin American countries, the state defines all members of the national society as *mestizos*, assuming that everyone has some Indian ancestry. If all are *mestizos*, by implication they can be equals in a homogeneous national society. The ideology of *mestizaje* denies both the existence of social classes and the possibility of incorporating the Indians with their own identity into the national society.[10] Thus, by adopting this ideology, the state attempts to neutralize other ideological forms through which the peasantry may express its opposition to the existing relations of domination.

Earlier I discussed how among the Protestant peasants a new presentation of self, pride in their own language, a sense of belonging to a common humanity, and a desire for education became part of a new ethnic identity as a direct result of their conversion to Protestantism. The particular ways in which this identity is going to be manipulated or enacted will depend on the concrete situations of interethnic contact which develop out of the changing relations of production. Indian peasants, Indian proletarians, and Indian petty merchants, although all of them Protestants, may act out their ethnic identity very differently vis-à-vis non-Indians. Because the conversion of the peasants to Protestantism is still quite recent, and because the socioeconomic conditions in the rural highlands are changing from the increasing penetration of capitalism, I have indicated that the relationship between Protestantism and ethnicity is somehow ambiguous. Many of the "traits" and social practices which the Quichuas now value may actually lead them toward assimilation, that is, to the acceptance of a new identity that is not defined by them but is the whites' or *mestizos'* image of what "civilized Indians" should be.

However, among Protestant peasants religious ideology is not only a source of identity but also the main structuring principle of their familial, economic, and political practices. This ideological role of Protestantism in the reorganization of important aspects of the peasants' lives, and the complex relations between Protestantism and ethnic and class consciousness, are discussed in the final sections of this paper.

Protestantism, Family, and Kinship: Relations among Equals

Although Protestantism stresses conversion as an individual religious experience, Colta is a peasant society where the social pressures that have always regulated peasants' lives, such as kinship, friendship, and community obligations, are still binding.

Recruitment of new converts takes place predominantly along kinship lines. Usually whole families become converted as a group, and then their extended kin are convinced to join. Several of the life histories of converts reveal the sense of relief they felt when they became converted because it meant re-establishing family and kinship ties with other members who were already believers. As Protestantism grows, fewer families want to be on their own.

Protestantism has had a strong influence on the Quichua family, mainly because it has reduced the level of mutual violence among its members. Both men and women informants reported how they used to beat each other when they were drunk. More peaceful family relationships have led to more egalitarian participation in domestic chores and in agricultural labor. It is now often possible to find husbands teaching their wives reading and some rudiments of arithmetic. Women informants pointed out that such knowledge gives them more independence when going alone to the market and more self-confidence when confronting *mestizo* merchants.

Commensality has always been an important factor in cementing family and kinship ties among the Quichuas. Most evangelical families insisted in pointing out to me that their meals are now more peaceful and enjoyable. The evening meal, when the whole family eats together, is always preceded by common prayers and singing. The Protestant Quichuas feel that this ritual helps to create an atmosphere of gentleness more conducive to family understanding.

What the Quichuas call the "family service," *culto familiar*, is the ritual that best expresses, in a new symbolic form, this renewed solidarity among family, extended kin, and neighbors. These *cultos* take place generally once a week and consist of singing, praying, and studying the Bible together. They are initiated by one family, which invites close neighbors and kin. The house is specially cleaned for the occasion. Food is offered after the service. The *culto* is led by the household head, but he conducts it as a dialogue so that everybody can participate. The *culto familiar* and commensality help reinforce important ties with those who are in the network of reciprocal labor exchange. Besides, this *culto* transforms the peasants' hut into a sacred place, in contrast with the hierarchy of space created by Catholicism, in which the church was the only place of worship and the sacred was controlled by the priest. Now the peasants feel in full control of the sacred within their own homes. This "democratizing" effect of Protestantism over the religious experience is, of course, not peculiar to the highlands. It has been pointed out repeatedly by students of the European Reformation (see George and George 1968:158).

I have already said that for the Colta peasants reciprocity is still an important pattern in the relations of production. When the peasants were Catholic, they used relationships of *compadrazgo* as a way of extending their reciprocity network. Within the Catholic ideological system these relationships of *compadrazgo* were ritually made sacred, and therefore strengthened, mainly through the sacraments of baptism and marriage. Protestantism has eliminated the godparents for baptism, and usually the parents of the groom are selected as godparents for marriage. Need for labor beyond that of the family still exists, however, and Protestant peasants now use the relationship of "brother in the faith," *hermanos,* to engage others in the same social and economic relationships previously assumed by *compadres.* *Hermanos* are now preferred in sharecropping arrangements. They are also asked for help when building a house and in harvesting, threshing, and other agricultural tasks. *Hermanos* are sought after in areas near the *páramo* to take care of pasturing sheep and cattle. In exchange, those *hermanos* are housed and fed when they come down to Colta. *Hermanos* are also asked for money loans and to act as witnesses in lawsuits. The reasons formerly given by the Quichuas for these preferences are the same as those given for selecting *compadres* in traditional reciprocal arrangements: "they can be trusted," "they act like real brothers," and "they are willing to share." In addition, some of the "Protestant virtues" are now added to the explanation: "they are more honest," "they work harder," and "they don't drink and are more reliable."

Protestantism has also enlarged the reciprocity network of the Quichua migrants in the big cities and wherever their jobs may take them. They can obtain room and board cheaper—sometimes for free—if they lodge with *hermanos.* If need be, merchandise can also be left with them because "they can be trusted." Even those migrants who work as wage earners in the coastal plantations or in sugar mills have established a system of "substitutes" between *hermanos* by which they will replace one another in the job while one of them returns to the countryside to take care of his plot. Thus, in a labor market where supply exceeds demand, the relationship of *hermano* has been transformed into a form of job security. It is then possible to say that in several ways the Quichuas are enacting the ideological relationship of "brother in Christ" as a social relationship of production. As fiestas and other rituals were used before to strengthen kin and fictive kin relationships, the *culto familiar*, conferences, and other forms of Protestant rituals are used now to confirm and sanctify the "new sibling" relationship.

Protestantism and Class Relationships

In the preceding section I discussed how the Quichuas have adapted aspects of Protestantism to maintain those relationships among equals which are meaningful within their culture. My data do not suggest that Protestantism is directly related to an internal differentiation of the peasant class in the region or that Weber's famous thesis on the relationship between Protestantism and the spirit of capitalism (1958) is relevant in understanding the effects of Protestantism among highland peasants in Ecuador.

The majority of evangelical peasants do not have a standard of living drastically higher than non-Protestant peasants. The virtues emphasized by the Protestant ethic, such as "industriousness," "thrift," and "dedication to work," are not new to peasants who have always lived close to subsistence level. Generally, in order to increase his output, the peasant has no alternatives other than intensifying his labor by prolonging the working day, or what Chayanov (1966) calls the "self-exploitation" of labor power within the peasant economy. Furthermore, Protestant peasants do not save but, if possible, try to spend whatever cash they may have on education, modern medicine, zinc roofs for their houses, radios, and bicycles. What Protestantism has done is to remove the social pressures for ceremonial consumption. As Wolf (1966:14–15) argues, when the peasants can escape those demands, they may reduce ceremonial consumption as one of the possible strategies to achieve economic betterment for their families. The peasants changed their consumption patterns from what the new religious ideology defines as "pagan," "extravagant," and "wasteful" to what the same ideology regards as "responsible" and "proper" consumption. These patterns of consumption may put Protestant peasants somewhat ahead of non-Protestant peasants in terms of their participation in the capitalist market for commodities. Differential consumption patterns, however, do not constitute a basis for class relations.

As I have shown already, in this area of Chimborazo there are structural limitations—lack of land, high land prices, scattered small plots, debts—that prevent the emergence of a class of small capitalist farmers, Protestant or other, who might start exploiting the labor power of poorer peasants. However, regarding the participation of Protestant peasants in the wage-labor market, my data show that landowners in the area are beginning to appreciate the value of a "puritanical" labor force. It seems that Protestants acquire everywhere (Willems 1967:177) a reputation for being "dependable," "honest," and "sober," but, most important, they are also well known for not joining unions or other "troublesome" groups. Commenting on the fact that *evangélicos* comprise 90% of his labor force, the owner of one of the largest traditional haciendas still in operation in Chimborazo had this to say: "At first I was extremely upset about all my peons becoming Protestants and blamed the priest for not doing his job properly, but now I have come to realize that the Protestant Indians are more rational, more reliable than those in the hacienda X—for instance—who are organized, mutinous, and rebellious, that is, nonrational."

Furthermore, if the situation that Willems (1967:177) describes for the Protestant urban migrants in Brazil and Chile is repeated in Ecuador, the "Protestant virtues" of the peasant migrants could be used by urban capitalists to keep a more "docile," "quiet," and "efficient" labor force.

Ethnic Consciousness and Class Consciousness

In most instances analyzed so far—individual, family, and kinship and relations among equals—the Protestant peasants have adapted the new religious ideology to social practices which revive and reinforce their cultural and social identity as Quichuas. In order to understand other aspects of Quichua ethnicity in relation to class consciousness, I will turn now to the analysis of two ritual occasions where evangelical peasants are mobilized to act as a group. When examined together, these rituals manifest the ambiguities which permeate the process of incorporation of the Quichuas—as an *etnia* and as a class—into the modern bourgeois state. Here the Quichuas are caught, along with other Andean and Amazonian native peoples, in the predicament of asserting their ethnic identity while confronting the ethnocidal policies of the dominant elements of the national society. It is an intricate and difficult dilemma where, as Whitten has argued, "the complementarity of ethnocide and ethnogenesis exists in the most tenuous balance" (1976:285).

First, I want to examine the religious event known to the *evangélicos* as *conferencia*, a ritual occasion which assembles for a period of three days large numbers of Quichuas (200 to 3,000) from a multitude of peasant communities often from different provinces. They gather to pray, sing, listen to the message of the Gospel, and engage in enjoyable socializing and sports.

Because the Protestant leadership recognizes the competitive attraction which traditional fiestas may still have for recent converts, the largest conferences are scheduled to coincide with Catholic festivals such as Corpus Christi, Christmas, and Holy Week. The peasants themselves perceive the conferences as substitutes for the fiestas, without the hangovers or the large expenses. The improvement of the means of transportation in the region and the popularity of the Protestant radio have made these events possible.

Any community can hold a conference, thus becoming the "sacred" place of congregation for all the others. Conferences take place outdoors in a large tent provided by the missionaries. The community responsible for calling the conference is in charge of preparing the food for all the participants, although a minimal amount of around $1.20 is paid by each person for the right to eat three meals a day and to sleep in the tent for the duration of the conference.

An experience of the sacred is expected to occur, and usually several people "receive the Lord" during the course of the three days. However, there are no sacred influential intermediaries to make it happen. The emphasis is on the inner transformation of the individual. Religious testimonials from old converts are heard in order to give confidence and encourage the newcomers. The new believers are assured that there is a "normative communitas" (Turner 1974:169) of the faithful to support them.

Through a complex system of formal ranked offices of ritual sponsorship, the traditional fiesta was an enactment of the social, political, and economic hierarchy that controlled the affairs of each peasant community. Ceremonial redistribution became the source of authority and power for those who could pay the expenses involved. In contrast, the conference creates that "ritual of inclusiveness" which Turner describes as part of religious pilgrimages, where "the other" becomes the generic human "brother" and "specific siblingship is extended to all who share a system of beliefs" (1974:186). However, if in the more abstract ideological sense the "brotherhood of all mankind" is emphasized, the conferences are kept within the ethnic boundaries (Barth 1969:15–16) of the Quichua population. All aspects of the event, including praying, singing, preaching, and instruction, are conducted in Quichua. *Mestizo* merchants are conspicuously absent. For at least three days, during the conference, Quichua peasants remove themselves from those everyday social interactions where they are continuously being reminded of their "inferiority" as Indians by *mestizo* and white merchants, landowners, bus drivers, and local bureaucrats. In that sense conferences also create a kind of "ethnic communitas" by which a considerable number of peasants can experience a feeling of brotherhood and sisterhood as Quichuas and actually reinforce ties of kinship and friendship.

One could argue that, by generating this kind of solidarity, the conferences could be instrumental in overcoming the fragmentation and isolation of the peasantry which many scholars regard as one of the main sources of the "low classness" (Shanin 1971:253) of the peasantry as a class and, consequently, as an important obstacle for its political action (Marx 1963, Wolf 1969, Hobsbawm 1973). Nevertheless, the conference only *removes* the peasants from social situations where they are exploited as peasants and as Indians, and by clouding class solidarity into a religious experience, it conceals the oppressive nature of the larger system of social relations. In this sense we can say that the function of the ideology is resolving the contradictions by excluding them (Poulantzas 1975:208).

As Turner points out for religious sects and schismatic movements, in general, "when they attract great numbers and persist for many years, they often find it necessary to compromise with structure once again, both in their relations with the wider society and in their own internal concerns, both liturgical and organizational" (1974:267).

In order to understand how the Protestant Quichuas "compromise with structure," we have to analyze another ritual performance, where as a formal organization the *evangélicos* confront the rest of the national society. This is the yearly meeting organized by the Association of Evangelical Indians of Chimborazo mainly to maintain their relations with local and national authorities. Evangelical peasants of the GMU from all parts of Ecuador congregate in Colta for a one-day event which is very similar in structure to the celebration of national civic fiestas, with music followed by speeches, parades, and a large display of banners. Usually children sing the Ecuadorian national anthem in Quichua. They present the authorities with "typical" gifts—

shigras, ponchos, sombreros—and offer them "typical" Quichua food. In the parade "typical" Quichua music is played, and participants wear their best "typical" dress. In this event ethnic consciousness is transformed into expressive folkloric consciousness. This form of ethnic consciousness does not conflict with the state ideology of assimilation, because ethnicity becomes just another commodity to be sold to tourists and provides the Indians with an alienated identity.[11] In a similar way the state has appropriated the Otavaleño Indians' ability for handicrafts and personal characteristics of "cleanliness" and "industriousness," transforming them into the trademarks of Ecuador's tourist industry, which is, of course, not controlled by Otavaleños.

In the speeches addressed to the authorities during this celebration, the leaders present the demands of the Protestant peasants as a group. They ask for better roads, better schools, for drinking water supplies and sewage systems for rural communities, for modern medical care to do away with the Indian witchdoctors—who are satirized in sketches—and for better treatment of the Quichuas by the bureaucratic structure. None of these petitions implies an actual confrontation with the "modernizing" goals of the bourgeois state. On the contrary, those demands assure the representatives of the state that the Protestant Quichuas as a group want to become "acculturated" by working within the existing political institutions. No references are made to land claims and working conditions, which are the main problems peasants as a class are facing. This celebration can be seen as a stage where the Protestant Quichuas express their identity as "good citizens" demonstrating their adherence to the dominant national ideology.

I discussed earlier how, in a semifeudal class structure, the Catholic church legitimized an ideological definition of ethnicity that kept the Indians as servile labor. The version of Protestant political ideology manifested in the meeting described above legitimizes that aspect of the bourgeois political ideology in which the state appears as representing the general interests of equal and free citizens, concealing their distribution in the class structure (see Marx 1975:211–41).

However, not all Protestant peasants accept unconditionally that version of Protestant political ideology. Many Quichua informants with whom I discussed these problems described how, as members of the peasant class and as Indians, they enter into daily confrontations with a society that exploits them. The ambiguity between a Protestant political ideology of acceptance of the status quo and the perception by many Quichuas of their class position is already causing tension and actual conflicts within the Protestant peasant community. These conflicts take place mainly between Protestant leaders of peasant *comunas* (legal organization of peasant communities) and those of the indigenous churches. The former see the need to fight for land rights and against all forms of exploitation of the Quichuas as a peasant class; they give priority to the needs of the peasants over religious diversions, and they see their role as one of service to the peasant class fighting for its rights. The latter define most conflicts as "moral individual issues" so that they can be controlled within the church. When asked how they solve possible confrontations with the authorities, their answer is invariably an abbreviated version of Paul's Epistle to the Romans (chap. 13:1–2): "The authorities have been established by God and should be respected."

The ideological arguments intrinsic to the conflict between these two types of leaders reflect the ambiguities that I have tried to examine in this paper, ambiguities which involve the different levels of articulation of religious, ethnic, and class ideologies in a social formation where old modes of production still persist in complex relationships with capitalism.

NOTES

Acknowledgments: I would like to thank David Aberle, Kathleen Gough, Martin Silverman, and Ricardo Muratorio for helpful comments on and criticisms of a previous version of this paper.

The research on which this essay is based was conducted in Chimborazo between 1975 and 1977 for a period of 12 months. It was supported by two Canada Council grants (S75–0111 and S76–1199). I want to acknowledge my continuing debt to the faculty of the Department of Anthropology of the Pontificia Universidad Católica in Ecuador for their sympathy and support. Three students of that department, Fernando García, Ana María Granja, and Noris de Maldonado, worked as my research assistants in collecting the general ethnographic information. I am grateful for the interest and respect the GMU missionaries showed for my work. They openly provided me with helpful information and friendly assistance. I am also grateful to the leaders of the Association of Evangelical Indians of Chimborazo, with whom I signed a contract of mutual collaboration that allowed me to work in the area. Many Quichuas helped my research along, but I owe a special debt to two Colta families who prefer to remain anonymous. Their wonderful generosity, patience, and sense of humor were my best reward in the field. The interpretations, conclusions, and possible factual errors in this paper are, of course, my exclusive responsibility.

1. There is, however, a substantial amount of literature on Protestantism in Latin America written by Protestant missionaries and Catholic priests. For

the purpose of this paper I only used some of the sources that deal specifically with Ecuador, and they are quoted in the text.

2. In the Ecuadorian highlands *precarismos* refer to those forms of land tenure by which the agricultural workers hold land in usufruct, paying for its use in labor, services, or produce, e.g., *huasipungo* (see Hurtado 1973:31–33).

3. In 1966 a team from the Department of Anthropology of Cornell University did fieldwork in the Colta area in collaboration with the Ecuadorian Institute of Agrarian Reform and Colonization. Their ethnographic work makes for interesting comparison because it deals with this area when a majority of the peasants were still Catholics, and just before the agrarian reform was actually implemented (see Maynard 1966 and Cornell University 1965).

4. For a good discussion of the use of wage labor in the highland haciendas, see Guerrero (1975).

5. In 1976–77 there were at least seven different agencies—from Catholic action groups to unions and associations connected with political parties—trying to mobilize the peasants of Chimborazo. Their efforts resulted in several political meetings of peasant unions and associations in Riobamba, in peasants' land claims, and in land invasions mostly to demand access to pasture land. The landowners retaliated by constituting the "Committee for the Defense of the Land." The peasants accused the local state authorities for allegedly backing the landowners by jailing peasant leaders and closing radio programs broadcast by peasant unions (see *El Comercio*, 30 Jan. 1976).

6. To the best of my knowledge, the GMU missionaries in the area are extremely careful in collecting statistics and cautious in their assessment of the growth of the church. Totally accurate statistics, however, are difficult to obtain because it is almost impossible for the missionaries to have full control over the number of conversions and baptisms performed by the relatively autonomous indigenous churches. The 1974 national census gives the total rural population of Chimborazo as 226,145. It is impossible to deduce from this figure how many are Quichua speakers, but a figure of 150,000, as estimated by the GMU, seems reasonable.

7. To the best of my knowledge, there were at least ten other Protestant missions working in Chimborazo at the time I did my fieldwork. It is difficult to have an accurate and up-to-date estimate of their success in converting the Quichuas, relative to that of the GMU, because the number of converts is changing so fast. All my data suggest that the GMU was better organized and much more visible to the peasants in the area.

8. The two major traditional fiestas in the Colta area were in honor of St. Michael and of the Virgin of Balvanera. The Catholic peasants from Colta do not hold these fiestas anymore because—as they explain—now that many of their relatives are *evangélicos*, they do not find the same incentives and support. It must be added that some of the "new priests" working in the area discourage peasants from holding traditional fiestas because of the costs involved.

9. This type of behavior during *cultos* is common among the members of Pentecostalist sects. Nevertheless, the particular description quoted here portrays the *evangélicos'* own perception of the behavior of Pentecostalists in the Colta area. I do not have independent evidence on their drinking behavior or their marital and extramarital practices.

10. For a detailed discussion of the ideology of *mestizaje* and its implications for the tropical forest Indians of Ecuador, see Whitten (1976:265–85).

11. Cardoso de Oliveira (1976:46–49) refers to "alienating ethnic ideologies" and to "alienated identities" in discussing the Tükúna of the Solimoēs River, who identify themselves as *caboclos*, an ethnic category which presents them as "demoralized" and "lazy" Indians completely tied to the labor relations imposed by the whites. A *caboclo* is thus a Tükúna who sees himself only as the whites see him.

REFERENCES CITED

Báez, René
  1976 Hacia un Subdesarrollo "Moderno." In I. Mejía et al., *Ecuador: Pasado y Presente*. Quito: Universidad Central, pp. 249–71.
Barth, Fredrik, ed.
  1969 *Ethnic Groups and Boundaries: The Social Organization of Cultural Difference*. Boston: Little, Brown.
Burgos Guevara, Hugo
  1977 *Relaciones Interétnicas en Riobamba*. 2d ed. Mexico: Instituto Indigenista Interamericano.
Burridge, Kenelm
  1973 *Encountering Aborigines. A Case Study: Anthropology and the Australian Aboriginal*. New York: Pergamon Press.
Cardoso de Oliveira, Roberto
  1976 *Identidade, Etnia e Estrutura Social*. São Paulo: Livraria Pioneira Editora.
Casagrande, Joseph B.
  1974 Strategies for Survival: The Indians of Highland Ecuador. In Dwight Heath, ed., *Contemporary Cultures and Societies of Latin America*. 2d ed. New York: Random House, pp. 93–107.
Casagrande, Joseph B., and Arthur R. Piper
  1969 La Transformación Estructural de una Parroquia Rural en las Tierras Altas del Ecuador. *América Indígena* 29:1039–64.
Chadwick, Owen
  1964 *The Reformation*. Baltimore: Penguin Books.
Chayanov, A. V.
  1966 *The Theory of Peasant Economy*. Homewood, Ill.: Richard D. Irwin.
Cornell University, Department of Anthropology
  1965 *Indians in Misery*. A report prepared for and in collaboration with the Ecuadorian Institute of Agrarian Reform and Colonization. Quito.
Dickens, A. G.
  1966 *Reformation and Society in Sixteenth Century Europe*. London: Thames and Hudson.
Flora, Cornelia Butler
  1976 *Pentecostalism in Colombia: Baptism by Fire and Spirit*. Cranbury, N.J.: Associated University Presses.
George, Charles, and Katherine George
  1968 Protestantism and Capitalism in Pre-Revolutionary England. In

S. N. Eisenstadt, ed., *The Protestant Ethic and Modernization*. New York: Basic Books, pp. 155–76.

Godelier, Maurice
1977   *Perspectives in Marxist Anthropology*. New York: Cambridge University Press.

Goffman, Erving
1959   *The Presentation of Self in Everyday Life*. New York: Doubleday.

Guerrero, Andrés
1975   *La Hacienda Precapitalista y la Clase Terrateniente en America Latina y su Inserción en el Modo de Producción Capitalista: El Caso Ecuatoriano*. Quito: Universidad Central.

Hobsbawm, E. J.
1973   Peasants and Politics. *Journal of Peasant Studies* 1 (1):3–22.

Hurtado, Osvaldo
1973   *Dos Mundos Superpuestos: Ensayo de Diagnóstico de la Realidad Ecuatoriana*. Quito: Instituto Ecuatoriano para el Desarrollo Social (INEDES).
1977   *El Poder Político en el Ecuador*. Quito: Centro de Publicaciones, Pontificia Universidad Católica del Ecuador.

Jácome, Nicanor, and Inés Llumiquinga
1977   Ecuador: The Indigenous Tribute System as a Mechanism of Exploitation during the Colonial Period and the First Years of Independence. In Elias Sevilla-Casas, ed., *Western Expansion and Indigenous Peoples: The Heritage of Las Casas*. The Hague: Mouton, pp. 87–119.

Klassen, Jacob Peter
1974   Fire on the Páramo. M.A. thesis, Faculty of the School of World Mission and Institute of Church Growth, Fuller Theological Seminary.

Lalive D'Espinay, Christian
1969   *Haven of the Masses: A Study of the Pentecostalist Movement in Chile*. London: Lutterworth Press.

Lukes, Steven
1973   *Individualism*. Oxford: Basil Blackwell.

Marx, Karl
1962   *Capital*. Vol. 3. Moscow: Foreign Languages Publishing House.
1963   *The Eighteenth Brumaire of Louis Bonaparte*. New York: International Publishers.
1975   On the Jewish Question. In Karl Marx, *Early Writings*. Baltimore: Penguin Books, pp. 211–41.

Maynard, Eileen, ed.
1966   *The Indians of Colta: Essays on the Colta Lake Zone, Chimborazo (Ecuador)*. Ithaca, N.Y.: Department of Anthropology, Cornell University.

Miller, Elmer S.
1971   The Argentine Toba Evangelical Religious Service. *Ethnology* 10 (2):149–59.
1974   The Christian Missionary, Agent of Secularization. In Patricia J. Lyon, ed., *Native South Americans: Ethnology of the Least Known Continent*. Boston: Little, Brown, pp. 391–97.
1975   Shamans, Power Symbols, and Change in Argentine Toba Culture. *American Ethnologist* 2 (3):477–96.

Moreno Yánez, Segundo
   1977   *Sublevaciones Indígenas en la Audiencia de Quito.* Quito: Centro de Pub-
          licaciones, Pontificia Universidad Católica del Ecuador.
Muratorio, Blanca
   1976   El Campesinado y la Burocracia Estatal: Un Caso en Ecuador. Paper
          presented at the third meeting of the group on "Process of Social
          Articulation" (C.L.A.C.S.O.). Quito.
Murra, John
   1946   The Historic Tribes of Ecuador. In Julian H. Steward, ed., *Handbook
          of South American Indians,* vol. 2: *The Andean Civilizations.* Washing-
          ton, D.C.: Smithsonian Institution. *Bureau of American Ethnology Bul-
          letin* 143:785–822.
Nickel, Ben J.
   1965? *Along the Quichua Trail.* Smithville, Mo.: Gospel Missionary Union.
Peñaherrera de Costales, Piedad, and Alfredo Costales Samaniego
   1964   *El Concertaje de Indios y Manumisión de Esclavos.* Quito: Instituto Ecua-
          toriano de Antropología y Geografía, *Llacta* 17.
Poulantzas, Nicos
   1975   *Political Power and Social Classes.* London: New Left Books.
Proaño, Leonidas E.
   1974   *Concientizacion Evangelizacion Politica.* Salamanca: Ediciones Sígueme.
Reed, Gerardo
   1975   Los Evangélicos del Ecuador: Un Estudio Analítico. Unpublished
          manuscript. Quito: Iglesia del Pacto Evangélico del Ecuador.
Ribeiro, Darcy
   1973   *Fronteras Indígenas de la Civilización.* 2d ed. Mexico City: Siglo XXI.
Shanin, Teodor
   1971   Peasantry as a Political Factor. In Teodor Shanin, ed., *Peasants and
          Peasant Societies.* Baltimore: Penguin Books, pp. 238–63.
Turner, Victor
   1974   *Dramas, Fields, and Metaphors: Symbolic Action in Human Society.* Ith-
          aca, N.Y.: Cornell University Press.
Weber, Max
   1958   *The Protestant Ethic and the Spirit of Capitalism.* New York: Charles
          Scribner's Sons.
Westphal, Barbara
   1962   *These Fords Still Run.* Mountain View, Calif.: Pacific Press.
Whitten, Norman E., Jr. (with the assistance of Marcelo F. Naranjo, Marcelo
          Santi Simbaña, and Dorothea S. Whitten)
   1976   *Sacha Runa: Ethnicity and Adaptation of Ecuadorian Jungle Quichua.* Ur-
          bana: University of Illinois Press.
Willems, Emilio
   1967   *Followers of the New Faith: Culture Change and the Rise of Protestantism
          in Brazil and Chile.* Nashville, Tenn.: Vanderbilt University Press.
Williams, Raymond
   1977   *Marxism and Literature.* Oxford: Oxford University Press.
Wolf, Eric R.
   1966   *Peasants.* Englewood Cliffs, N.J.: Prentice-Hall.
   1969   *Peasant Wars of the Twentieth Century.* New York: Harper & Row.

19

Blacks in Ecuadorian Literature

Constance García-Barrio

Just west of the Andes, in the coastal riverine areas of the Pacific lowland rainforest-mangrove zone of northern Ecuador and southern Colombia, there is a vibrant, integrated Afro-Hispanic culture. Although the history of this area has been but touched upon (e.g. West 1957, Phelan 1967, Sharp 1968, Whitten 1974, Whitten and Friedemann 1974), one important documented factor (Cabello de Balboa 1945) which endures in oral history and in popular literature is that of the shipwreck of a slaver off the coast of Esmeraldas province, wherein blacks led by a *ladino*, hispanicized African, liberated themselves, forged inland from the Coast, encountered other peoples, created a new life, vigorously protected their freedom, formed the "Zambo Republic," and eventually walked to Quito to ally with the Spanish crown, on their own terms. According to the prominent Esmeraldeño writer Julio Estupiñán Tello (1967) in his quasi-history *El Negro en Esmeraldas*, the ship's cargo included 23 enslaved blacks who were bound for Peru. When the ship foundered on the reefs, it provided them with an opportunity for escape that they seized. Once blacks made their way inland and established themselves, their numbers grew. They intermixed with some Indian groups and fought continuously with others. Their settlement became haven and home for fugitive slaves and occasionally for Spaniards fleeing from the law.

The themes within Estupiñán Tello's small book include slavery (with Peru, never Ecuador, as destination for servitude); the idea of the "inland interior" as haven; intermixture with Indians (resulting in the racial-ethnic transformation to *zambo*); and the idea that the *zambo* haven could also serve as refuge for some Spaniards, provided they were renegades. These themes not only are part of the contemporary and historical cultural ethos of Esmeraldas but reflect common emphases in Afro-Hispanic literature throughout South America (see, e.g., Guillot 1961:243).

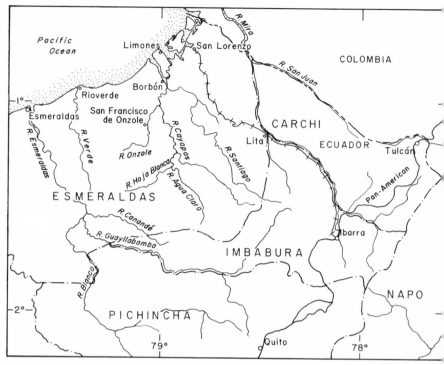

MAP 1 Esmeraldas Province

The Ecuadorian literature on Esmeraldas's geography, where blacks had their stronghold, portrays it as defying all pursuers bent on recapture of blacks or enforcement of slavery—one had to cross the Andes, hack a way through the jungle, and ford the "churning" Esmeraldas River. In this imagery the hot, humid climate producing a jungle alive with snakes and malaria-bearing mosquitoes defeated repeatedly the many attempts of colonial authorities to subdue the inhabitants. In such a portrayal credit is given to the putative inhospitality of the jungle for the dynamic expansion and maintenance of a viable Afro-Ecuadorian culture, rather than to the creative cultural adjustments made by the people themselves. Estupiñán Tello further stresses that for 300 years of colonial rule, coastal dwellers of African descent remained virtually self-governing.

The theme of prolonged separation of Esmeraldas from the bureaucratic controls of Quito is prominent in Estupiñán Tello's work, and it is well grounded in fact. Phelan (1967:19) tells us that as early as the seventeenth century " . . . a secure road across the Esmeraldas country would put the Kingdom of Quito in more rapid communication with Panama and Spain. An outlet on the coast of Esmeraldas would lend some geo-political reality to [the] pretention of the Quito tribunal's freedom from direct dependence on Lima." To elaborate on the theme of separation of Quito and Esmeraldas, frustration in expansion of the former, and autonomy and organization in the latter, Estupiñán Tello stresses the dual heritage of triumph and trouble in the early twentieth century. On the one hand, the separateness had protected the integrity and encouraged the maintenance of black *costeño* cultural distinctiveness[1] (*costeño*, of the Coast, is the primary term of self-identity for black people in this area). But on the other hand, it set in motion a cycle of ruinous relations between Quito and Esmeraldas. The government in Quito regarded the province as traditionally defiant and backward; it was reluctant to allocate funds for the needs of the area. Esmeraldeños, for their part, felt that the officialdom of Quito was insensitive to their problems and were predisposed to thwart the government whenever possible.

Many of the economic, social, and political relationships obtaining between *serranos* and *costeños*, and the bureaucratic Quiteño-lowland autonomous clashes and adjustments, are set forth in technical terms in Whitten (1965, 1974) and in analogous works for Colombia in Whitten and Friedemann (1974), Friedemann (1974), and Sharp (1977). In this paper I am concerned with the cultural expression of some of these phenomena as it takes shape within the written literature of Esmeraldas province. Literary works, of course, may describe information as seemingly minute as eating daily *verdes*, boiled plantains, as well as dramatize momentous events that can serve to rechannel and shape a nation's destiny. Although Reilly (1978:12) is correct in stating that "ethnic literature is not ethnography . . . though imaginative ethnic writing will help describe culture," both literature and ethnography are at their best when they serve to immerse the reader deeply in a web of particular events and facts only to have him emerge with the impression of having experienced something more universal. Though the presentation of particulars is evaluated for its own sake in ethnographic writing and is of little consequence in fictional literature, one of the most important effects of the best ethnographies is similar to that of other forms of literature—the ability to cause a heightened awareness of human experience which can transcend the specific content and context of its presentation.

Afro-Ecuadorian literature is of interest to social scientists and historians not only because it treats topics that concern all people at all times, but because themes are dealt with which have grown out of the writers' unique circumstance as Ecuadorian *costeños* of African, as well as indigenous and European, descent. In this paper I will sketch some of the dominant themes under rubrics which can relate the specific to the general: history, folklore, daily life and customs, racial identity–racial mixture, conflicts of culture, and commercial exploitation. My intent is to demonstrate the value inherent in analyzing Esmeraldeño literature itself, together with modern ethnographic portrayals. Finally, I will turn to my own observations of contemporary Esmeraldas and my experiences there as a black woman encountering for the first time discriminatory mechanisms within a setting where the ideology of racial mixture predominates.

CULTURAL THEMES IN ECUADORIAN BLACK LITERATURE

The viewpoint of outsiders looking in—the comments of noncoastal Ecuadorians about black coastal culture—was first treated in literature in *A la Costa* by Luís A. Martínez (1904). This novel describes the life of a middle-class family living in Quito toward the end of the nineteenth century. Illness, financial disaster, and a lack of determination undermine its members, one by one, forcing the son to go to Guayaquil to find work and save money so that his mother will not live her final days in poverty. There the protagonist encounters black people for the first time, and his impressions are profoundly negative. Where black characters are concerned, the book is a potpourri of stereotypes: brutalized black ex-slaves, the *mulato* as ignoble savage, and the seething sensuousness of women thought to have any black blood whatsoever. Edmundo Ribadeneira (1958:49–51), a leading literary critic, says: "The Ecuadorian social problem, with its double geographical framework of the highland and the coast, constitutes the essence and the meaning of *A la Costa*. . . . His trip [that of the protagonist] is really the confrontation of two worlds."

The first short stories about Afro-Ecuadorian lifeways appeared in *Los que se Van, Cuentos del Cholo y del Montuvio* (Carrión 1955), a collection of short stories written between 1928 and 1932 by Demetrio Aguilera Malta, Joaquín Gallegos Lara, and Enrique Gil Gilberto. The three writers were members of the *Grupo de Guayaquil*, to which two other writers belonged, José de la Cuadra and Alfredo Pareja y Diezcanseco: "five like a fist." The *Grupo* first fixed on the *cholo*, a pejorative term applied to persons of Indian descent, and the *montuvio*, an expression meaning backwoodsman (sometimes implying black blood), because these types gave their works the liveliness of local color. In time, however, the writers of the *Grupo* delved deeper than mere stereotypes to depict the poverty, futility, and mute anger in the lives of the poor *costeños* they described, and came to denounce the conditions that oppressed the *cholo* and the *montuvio*.

The main character in one story, "El Guaraguao," is " . . . a black with fine features and smiling lips who talked little" and who collects fine feathers to sell to Chinese merchants. Two scheming brothers, believing him to be well paid for the handsome plumes, kill him only to find that he had been paid a fraction of their value. Here murder is conjoined with the victimization of commercial exploitation. In another story, "Cuando Parió la Zamba," a beautiful woman of Indian and black parentage is married to a *negro*, black, but has a *blanco*, white, lover who has seen more prosperous times. When she announces that she is pregnant, the husband is pleased at the thought of having a little *negrito* while the lover wonders if he is really the father. Nine months later the midwife and the husband are shocked. The child is *ni negro ni amestizado*, "neither black nor mixed," but *blanco*. The midwife quickly explains to *la zamba*'s astonished husband that babies, like mice and foxes, are reddish and hairless when born and that it takes time for them to turn their proper color. The story ends in a barroom chat in which the *blanco* lover and a friend of his sympathize with the *zamba*'s difficult situation. "Cuando Parió la Zamba" is at once a comic and a serious view of the relationship between a man and his wife and of racial mixture. The *negro* husband looks foolish; he has taken pride in the prospect of fatherhood only to have his wife give birth to a child that could hardly be his. In other words, the "racial mixture" concepts *zambo* and *mestizo* serve to maintain the purity and separate stature of whiteness. This is evident in the midwife's assertion that, in time, proper (i.e., nonwhite) color will emerge. The *blanco* lover, on the other hand, feels satisfaction at having proved his manhood, even though he cannot boast without risking a confrontation with *la zamba*'s husband. Finally, one wonders about the audacity of the *zamba* herself. Given her apparent acceptance of the risk of becoming pregnant by her lover, the reader may consider several possibilities: she either has little regard for her husband, or affairs of this type are common and she expects conjugal and community tolerance.[2] In turn, such audacity signals a "tainting" of white *costeños* by black blood.

The stories by members of the *Grupo de Guayaquil* were written in the late 1920s and early 1930s. The later works of these writers are filled with strident protest. Chief among these is *El Negro Santander*, by Enrique Gil Gilberto (1968). The kernel of this story is the building of the railroad from Quito to Guayaquil. It is a bloody saga of exploitation, dynamite, and death. Many of the railroad workers are blacks from Jamaica, but some come from Esmeraldas. The construction bosses, who are white, arrange numerous artificial accidents to avoid paying wages and to rid the world of what they think of as human refuse. Also noteworthy is *Baldomera*, a novel by Alfredo Pareja y Diezcanseco (1938). Baldomera is a *mulata* who has the build and force of a combat tank and who perhaps embodies the potential strength of the downtrodden class to which she belongs. The Communist Party has an important place in this novel as organizer and mouthpiece of the exploited and deprived.

The social orientation of the *Grupo* authors made an impression on younger writers such as Adalberto Ortíz and Nelson Estupiñán Bass, who in the late 1930s began writing poetry about their surroundings. Ortíz has described Joaquín Gallegos Lara of the *Grupo de Guayaquil* as "mi maestro y mi amigo" (Walker 1977:188), and Estupiñán Bass has also spoken of the friendship and influence of the *Grupo* (Walker 1977:193). Further, both Estupiñán Bass and Ortíz acknowledge their debt to the Antillean poets Emilio Ballagas (Cuba, 1910–54), Nicolás Guillén (Cuba, 1902–), and Luís Palés Matos (Puerto Rico, 1899–1954), earlier portrayers of black life. While Palés Matos portrayed the black culture somewhat superficially and stereotypically with little else than pounding drums, leaping dancers, and shaking hips, Ballagas viewed protest as the crucial component of black poetry. However, the black theme represents no more than a phase in Ballagas's development as a poet. In his later works the lyric note prevails. Guillén's first collection of poems about black Cubans appeared in 1930 and proved a *coup de foudre* on the Havana literary scene. Guillén, the current president of the Union of Writers and Artists of Cuba, has continued to cultivate the black theme up to the present day.

Influenced by the *Grupo de Guayaquil*, the three Antillean poets, and their own Esmeraldas-born, racially mixed backgrounds, Estupiñán Bass and Ortíz launched a movement that has produced a wealth of literature which not only treats northern coastal blacks as worthy human beings but is rich in innovations of language and technique and in information about black coastal culture.

History

Slavery, and flight from it, is the first historical theme to be considered here, although scholars do not seem to agree about the impact of slavery on Esmeraldas. Estupiñán Tello writes that the effect of slavery on the province, a notorious stronghold for fugitive slaves, was relatively small. He says that in 1825 Simón Bolívar ordered a census of slaves in Ecuador, and that Esmeraldas had the lowest percentage in the country (Estupiñán Tello 1967:60). Walker (1977:41) presents quite a different view: " . . . seventy-five percent of the slaves in Ecuador lived in these three coastal provinces [Manabí, Guayas, Esmeraldas]." Perhaps because of the relatively low number of slaves and/or the wish to erase a regrettable chapter in the history of the province, slavery forms an infrequent theme. Mireya Ramírez (1975), in a collection of short stories called *Andarele*, includes several about life under slavery. One story, "Fragico," is about Lucha, a Mandinga slave, and Antonio, a Carabalí. The members of these two tribal groups were known to be antagonistic to one another, but, grouping all the blacks together, the master had sold Antonio's wife and decided to replace her with Lucha. Lucha is irritated by many of Antonio's habits and finally falls in love with Fragico (who had been given the Christian name "Francisco"), a runaway slave of her own group who is in hiding because he led a rebellion of slaves working in the Esmeraldas mines. Everyone believes that Fragico had met his death in the jaws of dogs used to crush the rebellion, but he escaped them and hid in the woods not far from the hut of Antonio and Lucha. Francisco becomes Lucha's lover and enjoys a comfortable arrangement until Antonio returns unexpectedly one day to find him in the hut. The sharp-witted Francisco explains that what Antonio is seeing is Francisco's ghost, that the real Francisco died in the mine melee. His ghost, he explains, has come to earth at the request of the Heavenly Father to search for meat for the hungry lot of little angels. He then bids Antonio and Lucha a fond good-bye. In this story the syncretism of European Christianity with African religion comes into play with the mention of ghosts and the Heavenly Father.

Syncretism is still more salient in another story by Ramírez, "A la Virgen y Los Demás." Here slaves left with an inept overseer see their chance to break the routine of work and whip. They slip a potion into the overseer's water, which leaves him in a stupor, and proceed to enjoy themselves. Since it is Holy Week, they decide that re-enactment of the Crucifixion will be a fine conclusion to their merry-making. The plantation chapel is the scene of the dramatization. Christ is portrayed by the skinniest slave while the priest is played by a short, fat man. The slaves intone sacred songs but substitute words of their own. Their liturgy goes: "The prettiest girl will be for the priest, Amen! Amen!" The owners and another overseer arrive at this moment and the slaves scatter, all but the Christ, who, firmly tied to the cross, blubbers over his bad luck. The scene is presented in a way that deprives it of pathos. The hapless Christ is comic, not tragic, like a movie character whose spectacular fall is calculated to evoke laughter.

Both stories end on a humorous note tinged with irony. In the first story the rebellion, the use of dogs, and the death of the slaves are overshadowed by the triangle of lovers. Francisco's cleverness and Antonio's gullibility hold center stage. In the second story the slaves seem to be passive, little more than light-hearted, light-headed children for whom punishment is normal. When comparing these stories to narratives about slavery by other contemporary Spanish American writers, "Fragico" and "A la Virgen y Los Demás" seem exceedingly mild. Mireya Ramírez does not tell of rape, murder, and mutilation as does the Cuban author Alejo Carpentier (*El Siglo de las Luces* and *El Reino de Este Mundo*) or the Venezuelan Ramón Díaz Sánchez (*Cumboto*). Mireya Ramírez's stories contribute to the popular Esmeraldeño image of slavery as an insignificant part of the past rather than a cruel indelible chapter in the nation's history.

Estupiñán Tello (1967:60) also states that the Ecuadorian government fixed 1854 as the date by which all slaves were to be freed. A tax was placed on gunpowder to raise money to compensate slave owners. The monies from the tax seem to have been insufficient and masters held on to their slaves. In many cases slaves were not freed until the mid-1860s. Further, in Ecuador, as in other Spanish American countries, a system of debt peonage developed. This system was known as *concertaje* in Ecuador, and it bound the *concierto* to his creditor as effectively as slavery had bound the servant to the master. *Concertaje* has received more attention in literature than slavery. The situation of the *concierto* is described in a novel by Nelson Estupiñán Bass, *Cuando los Guayacanes Florecían*. A hopeless debt is passed from parent to child: "They were *conciertos* from childhood. They were like a piece of furniture in doña Jacinta's hacienda. They grew up bound to the hacienda paying the debts of their dead parents" (Estupiñán Bass 1954:9).

Besides the period of *concertaje* (mid-1860s to 1890s), Estupiñán Bass's novel deals with another decisive moment in the history of Esmeraldas. From 1912 to 1916 coastal blacks made up the bulk of a rebel army led by Colonel Carlos Concha. Concha wanted to overthrow the government to avenge the death of the renowned liberal Eloy Alfaro, a political leader who had died at the hands of a mob in Quito. The blacks, rallying behind Concha's liberal standard and fighting in the jungle they knew so well, did not topple the Andean-based government, but they did succeed in bringing it to a standstill:

"The uprising of blacks, under the prestigious leadership of Colonel Carlos Concha, was kept up for four years, taking advantage of the deadly climate and impenetrable jungle where money and lives were spent to no purpose" (Reyes 1950:190). Adalberto Ortíz (1971:14) in a short story, "La Captura del Caudillo," records the battle song of blacks who fought with Concha:

> Carlos Concha is my father
> Who's come down from heaven
> If Carlos Concha dies
> Blacks will be left all alone.[3]

The war ended in a general amnesty in 1916, but the silent strife between highland and lowland Ecuador remains today.

Folklore

Just as Joel Chandler Harris put into literary form the animal stories he heard from slaves, charming all America with Br'er Fox and Br'er Bear, Esmeraldeño writers, familiar with coastal oral tradition, preserved *tío tigre*, Br'er Jaguar, and *tío conejo*, Br'er Rabbit, on the printed page.[4] A lesser known but equally pervasive motif that springs from West African folklore is that of the water creatures. In black folktales of Martinique and Guadalupe the *mama de l'eau* inhabits the rivers, while the *Mae d'agua* swims through the folktales of Brazil (Joel 1972, Pereda Valdes 1937). Adalberto Ortíz (1975:107), who has portrayed "La Madre del Agua" in his novels and short stories, comments on the survival of West African folk characters in South America: "It is interesting . . . to observe how some monsters of the forest, like the 'Tunda' in Esmeraldas or the 'Madre del monte' or 'Patica' in Colombia, similar to the 'Quimbungo' of the Bantus, were transplanted to the new Continent. Another of these fabulous beings is the water-mother . . . which has its equivalent in various Afroamerican regions."

The *tunda* mentioned by Ortíz is a malevolent water creature and a favorite of Esmeraldeño writers. A popular version of how the creature came to make its home in Esmeraldas refers to the early history of the province. As the story goes, the blacks who escaped from the shipwrecked vessel in the 1530s immediately began fighting with Indians occupying the land. After an especially fierce battle dying blacks and Indians did so much moaning and groaning that the noise reached hell and proved an intolerable nuisance to the devil. The devil decided that in the interest of his own peace and quiet he would have to exterminate both sides. So he went to Esmeraldas disguised as an African prince, Macumba. He craftily began by allowing the blacks to win, but his plans went awry when he fell in love with a beautiful young black woman. He was soon transformed from a dealer in fire and brimstone to a humble, hearth-bound husband. From the union of the devil with the lovely black girl a host of infernal creatures was born. One of this hellish brood is *la tunda*, a deformed black woman with huge lips and a club foot. *Tunda*, as a child of the devil, is unable to bear children herself and so has taken to robbing those of the black folk of Esmeraldas. *Tunda* is able to assume the appearance of a member of the family of a potential victim. She may look like a child's mother or a beloved aunt or older sister. Once *tunda* has her victims in the forest, she stuns them by breaking wind in their faces. After this the victim is entirely docile and is easily led to her lair. Wise parents don't allow children to go about without taking dogs with them, for the *tunda* apparition fears them and is frightened away. The *tunda* also fears the *bombo*, a large double-headed drum (Whitten 1974:100).

Although Esmeraldeño writers have breathed life into some West African spirits who people their pages, they also mention supernatural beings who don't seem to have West African roots. *La gualgura* is a chicken capable of growing to enormous proportions. *El bambero* is a tiny man whose head is disproportionately large but who, nevertheless, is just the right size to ride on the back of a boar. He carries a sack of medicinal herbs, including marijuana, on his back. It is his province to see that hunters never kill animals wantonly nor leave them to an agonizing death. *El riviel* is a frightening phantom. According to one account, the man who first became *el riviel* had been a fairly good person but far too fond of liquor. He went to the cemetery one night in a wine-drenched rage, challenged the dead, and burned the big crucifix in the cemetery. Angry at this sacrilege, the dead cursed caused him to have an accident in which he received a mortal wound. He died and went before St. Peter. St. Peter would not allow him to enter heaven because of his act of deep irreverence, yet he was not so bad that he deserved to go to hell. His unhallowed soul was made to wander until Judgment Day—or until he found a victim to take his place. A less Christian version of the condemnation of *el riviel* is found in Whitten (1974:100): "Before his death he went to the cemetery and cooked and ate a corpse. He saved the ashes from the corpse and drank them just before he died, thereby avoiding God's punishment. He is able to move freely in the world, on the sea, in Hell, and all parts of the sky and in other worlds. He is afraid of guns, the *atarraya* [a circular casting net], and the *bombo* and tries to trick the living into giving these to him."

Finally, there is reverence for a certain tree, called a Fernansánchez. In *Tierra Baldía* a character " . . . saw two Fernansánchez trees, with the last flowers of the season, of a violent dark rose color, and greeted them respectfully." He says to himself, "I don't believe in this, but they say that if you don't say hello to the tree, you get malaria" (Ramón 1958:24).

Daily Life and Customs

There are many novels and short stories which, in treating other themes, touch briefly on life in the rural Esmeraldeño household—the work, the food, the contents of the house, and the garden plot nearby. In *Once Cuentos Esmeraldeños* is a story by José Ortíz Urriola (1970), "Adan en el Paraíso," which summarizes the peaceful domestic routine of a family living in rural Esmeraldas. Strangers arrive at the home of Artemio Copete, and are greeted by his dark wife, *mujer color azabache*. Artemio, a tall black backwoodsman, treats them with reserve until one of them identifies himself as the son of an old friend. Once Artemio remembers them—and the male kinship bond—he outdoes himself in hospitality. Two chickens are killed and roasted for dinner. The use of fresh leaves for seasoning is described. There is hearty camaraderie among the men but the woman remains reticent and the children quiet and obedient. Artemio speaks plainly—and probably loudly since soft talking in these circumstances implies that secrets are being told—about where a woman's place is: " . . . in bed, in the kitchen . . ." (Ortíz Urriola 1970:42). When the guests leave the following day, they are given food for their long journey.

Just as the forest has its rustic etiquette, river life has its rituals as well. Nelson Estupiñán Bass (1960:127) tells in "El Gualajo" the story of a boy who must catch a certain kind of fish, a *gualajo*, to prove his manhood. His parents " . . . felt almost ashamed because Crispiano, to whom they had given a home since he was thirteen . . . still hadn't shown that credential of manhood." Also, the rivalry of black men living along the river is illustrated in this story using verse improvisation duels, whereby one man sings a stanza and his opponent must sing an appropriate rhymed response.[5] In the end Crispiano gets his fish and, with it, a new status in the community. Success in catching the fish indicates that he is now ready for the privileges and responsibilities of young adulthood.

A mainstay of the prosperity of the community is the *minga* or work cooperative (see Whitten 1974:164–65). Politics, kinship linkage, and economic wherewithal all converge on this institution. Thomsen writes about a man who wished to organize a *minga* to repair the roof of his house but could not do so until he had enough money to provide food and drink for the men who would work. "It was dishonorable to organize a *minga* without serving cane alcohol and food to the participants" (Thomsen 1969:176–77).

The *minga* and its manipulation form the core of "El Cinturón Maldito," an unpublished short story by Nelson Ortíz Estefanuto. One of the protagonists, Don Epaminondas, has been able to extract much from others and use it for his own gain. He has been especially adept at organizing *mingas*. In a self-congratulatory mood he thinks about " . . . the many mingas that were necessary to complete his magnificent mahogany-wood hacienda; he had promised the men that when the house was finished, he would begin construction of comfortable homes for everyone who had helped him for so many years." He becomes wealthy and achieves the position of mayor but reneges on his promise. Furthermore, he orders the destruction of a group of shacks on the outskirts of the city, known as *El Cinturón Maldito*, the black band, where very poor people live. A man who had co-operated with Don Epaminondas in countless *mingas* lived in one of the shacks. He already felt defrauded by Don Epaminondas's broken promise, but when he came home to find his shack smashed, he became outraged and set fire to Don Epaminondas's splendid house while the don slept peacefully inside. The fire consumes Epaminondas and his house.

"Un Disparo en las Tinieblas" is a short story by José Ortíz Urriola (1970:125–34). It is the age-old drama of adultery, sudden discovery of it by a spouse, and quick revenge. The drama is played out against the background of the *chigualo*, the wake for a dead child. In the words of Ortíz Urriola the *chigualo* is a " . . . ceremony . . . practiced primarily by *negros y mulatos* of the rural area of Esmeraldas" (for a full description see Whitten 1974:132–34). The activities during the *chigualo* are carried out with the desire to speed the unblemished souls of young children to heaven. Ortíz Urriola (1970:131) gives us this vivid description: "It was 10:00 P.M. and everyone was almost drunk. An old black woman, full of liquor . . . beat a drum with her open hand, indicating that they should form a circle to play some games typical of the event. Obedient, and lowering their thundering voices with laughter and dirty jokes—all of which was permitted at a child's wake—they began joining hands in a circle around her." The old woman began a chant and the others joined in:

> Little angel, go up to heaven
> Go on up to pave the road
> For when your godmother and godfather
> Pass that way.

The author, with apparent disapproval, refers repeatedly to the drinking at the *chigualos*, and his criticism is underscored by an unhappy ending. The merry-making ends abruptly when the father of the dead child, who has been on a trip, returns but can't find his wife because she and her lover have adjourned to the bushes. Some time passes before they become aware of the ominous silence in the adjacent house. They attempt to escape; a twig snaps, letting the husband know where they are hiding. He cannot see them clearly, but, guided by the snapping twig, he takes aim with his muzzle-loading shotgun; the story ends with the shotgun's blast.

Other customs and beliefs emerge in the course of the narrative. For example, the mother of a dying child attributes the cause of his illness to the evil eye, *está ojiado*. The story also sheds light on relations between men and women. Women, it seems, strive to confine men to the home while men thirst for freedom. This domestic tug of war is the theme of many coastal black songs and is dramatically enacted in the marimba dances (*currulao*), though not in the *chigualo* (Whitten 1974:108–23, 138–45). The mother of the protagonist advises him to stop running around and to marry, while his father urges him to have lots of women before settling down.

Finally, much information is given about the racial makeup of the characters. *Negros* and *mulatos* attend the *chigualo*. An old *negra* leads the festivities. The man whose wife is unfaithful is *el Mulato Polo Cangá* (Ortíz Urriola 1970:128). Fermina Canola, the unfaithful wife, is a *mulata alta* with regular features and full, provocative lips. Ignacio Quiñónez, the wife's lover, is described as both *negro alto* and *zambo*.

Racial Mixture–Racial Identity

In many works details about the racial background of characters is of secondary importance. In others, however, it forms the keystone. Reams of paper have been devoted to racial identity, a topic of Esmeraldas writers which has proven inexhaustible and even obsessive. *Juyungo*, a well-known, award-winning novel by Adalberto Ortíz, is in many ways the epic of Esmeraldas. There is in this tapestry of time and men, race and creed, a character named Antonio Angulo. Angulo, a *mulato*, belittles blacks and, ultimately, himself: "Under his impenetrable awning, Antonio Angulo felt separated from the rest of the world. He would move in among blacks. He too was black, to his sorrow. His black surname sometimes made him feel ashamed" (Ortíz 1943:78).[6] Antonio Angulo's feelings contrast sharply with those of the protagonist of *Juyungo*, Asensión Lastre. One critic comments: "Lastre . . . was a leader and a fighter, a proud man who rejected his slave heritage. Although Asensión hated white people who considered him inferior and who discriminated against . . . and exploited him, he saw that he could love white people and hate blacks, especially when the latter tried to take advantage of their own people" (Jackson 1976:101).

A short experimental theater piece by Nelson Estupiñán Bass also deals with the question of racial identity. In *La Otra* the protagonist, Olga, is a rich young black woman. In the opening scene she returns from a dance and finds Henry, a young white dandy, waiting for her. At the dance he had acted as if he didn't know her, but now, in the shadows of her doorway, he tries to make love to her. She spurns him and he leaves, but in the fierce monologue that follows she says: "This damn color is my curse! It's why Henry avoids me. It's only natural since he's white and the son of a gringo, he's ashamed to be with me" (Estupiñán Bass 1973:44). When Olga's raging subsides into fitful sleep, a black double and a white double emerge from her. They become locked in a mortal struggle for Olga's spirit. When the black double wins, it enables Olga to accept a black suitor.

Estupiñán Bass (1966) also treated the resolution of a black man's identity crisis in a novel, *El Último Río*. As Jackson (1976:107) says of the novel: "*El Último Río* explores a wide variety of racial feelings in Ecuador. While criticizing white racism and the cult-of-whiteness among black people, the author adds another dimension to his novel: the problem of greed that can drive a black man to enrich himself at the expense of his own people. . . . A final message becomes clear: all men are equal and must love one another if we are to get along in this world."

Another facet of racial mixture–racial identity is the position of the mulatto. In Ecuador, as in other places in the Americas, mulattoes often see themselves as members of a fraternity of uncertain identity. In Ecuador the confusion is multiplied: on the Coast mulattoes have usually been identified as members of the black community; in the

Sierra they are regarded as separate and distinct from blacks. Yet despite this confusion of identity, several Afro-Ecuadorians suggest that the inclusion of *mulato* characters who are wrestling with self-definition is simply a decorative element in a work, little more than a mere topic or so much literary tinsel. But at the 1977 Primer Congreso de la Cultura Negra de las Americas in Cali, Colombia, the ability of *mulato* writers to accurately portray black life was challenged by black spokesmen. Some *mulato* writers responded that they considered themselves black, that they lived and wrote from this perspective, and thus felt that there was no basis on which to challenge the authenticity of their work as black literature. Yet aside from this issue of the standpoint of the *mulato* writer and his critics, the persistent treatment of the *mulato* as a separate type must be pointed out. In "Torpedo," an unpublished story by Bolívar Drouet Calderón, the protagonist is described as a " . . . mulatto through and through." Self-preservation with minimal effort is his philosophy, the line of least resistance is his life line. The author seems to distinguish between the traits of this protagonist and those with which he would endow a black character.

The idea of *mejorar la raza*, improving the race—the strategy of marrying a white in order to have children of lighter complexion than oneself—is present in Afro-Ecuadorian literature as it is in the literature of most Spanish American countries where the number of people of African ancestry is significant. In one short story, "Los Amores de Fernand Muret" (Ortíz 1971:39–53), possession of a fair skin tips the scales in favor of one suitor of a much-courted *mulata*. The girl's mother, moreover, urges her to marry the blond, blue-eyed man whether or not she is in love with him. The girl's dusky (*muy oscura y mulata*) mother explains that she did her part by marrying the girl's father; he lacked many qualities she sought in a husband but he did have a light skin. She tells the girl that it's her turn now. On the day of the wedding the older woman thinks happily about blond or red-haired grandchildren (Ortíz 1971:47).

One of the most sensitive and thorough treatments of the *mulato* is found in *Juyungo*. Three representative *mulato* characters appear; one spurns blacks, one identifies with blacks, one agonizes in indecision:

> As a direct result of inducements to hide one's racial heritage if possible, Antonio Angulo, a *mulato*, becomes a "marginal man," completely unable to create a permanent and salutary sense of order in his crisis of racial loyalty. Nelson Díaz, the mulatto who does not hide his black parental stock, is relegated to the lower echelons of society. . . . In *Juyungo*, there is a scornful attitude [on the part of blacks] towards Max Ramírez because

this mulatto forsakes any association with blacks and their culture in order to experience upward social mobility. (Walker 1977:177)

Mulatos like Max Ramírez, who disavow black parentage to better their positions, are the most frequently mentioned and the most severely censured. In *Tierra Baldía* the boss of the stevedores is a "tough, loud *mulato*, who always carried a curved knife in his belt, and who wanted to show that it was not for nothing—that the Company had trusted him" (Ramón 1958:164).

Adalberto Ortíz (1973:63) speaks about his own mixed racial heritage and literature in *Tierra, Son y Tambor*:

> I am a mulatto, a child of mulattoes. It can be readily understood that as a result, all my literary work, in a certain sense, is fragmented or fragmentary, because it corresponds to the voice of a personality that is not very well defined or unified.

> Always spurred by the search, [my personality] moves toward a dichotomy, it goes groping like a blind man, touching on a variety of themes and styles, but it has none that are definite and characteristic. It seems to me that this is the tonic.

Conflicts of Culture

The commercial interdependence of coastal and highland provinces after the 1930s has meant contact between *costeños* and *serranos*. This contact has frequently been mutually disagreeable, if unavoidable, owing to cultural differences and historical circumstances. This old antagonism has often been treated by Esmeraldeño authors. Estupiñán Bass (1954:18) states, "Alberto Morcú remembered so many bad things that he'd heard about highlanders . . . that they were hypocrites, dirty, miserly and obsequious." An unpublished short story by Ortíz Urriola, "El Tercer Inquilino," begins dramatically with a group of black Esmeraldeños standing around a *serrano* who lies dead on the street. The *serrano*, a professor of sociology, had come to Esmeraldas to look for work. When he left home, reasonably sure of success, his little daughter had said, "You'll bring me a *negrito* so he can be my horsey." However, good fortune eludes him and he dies of hunger on the street as blacks mouth the words *serrano de mierda*, shitty highlander.

Black *costeños* can experience conflicts of culture even without venturing into the Andes. In the province of Esmeraldas there are two Indian tribes that live in proximity to blacks, the Colorado and the

Cayapa. The latter have been most frequently portrayed in literature. Blacks have acquired an evil name among the Cayapa, who refer to Afro-Ecuadorians as *juyungo*, howler monkey or devil. It is likely that this enmity grew, in part, from the competition of blacks and Indians for land and the livelihood derived from it. Barrett, who lived among the Cayapa from 1908 to 1909, describes the situation at that time: "The provincial and national governments recognize the rights of the Indian to full and peaceful possession of their territory, and have endeavored to protect them by enacting laws prohibiting the settlement of other peoples along the Río Cayapas. . . . The enforcement of these laws, however, has been quite another matter, for the Negroes, descendants of former slaves of Colombia and Ecuador, in later years have gradually worked their way up the streams" (Barrett 1925:37). More recent observations indicate that encroachment by blacks continues. Anthropologist Milton Altschuler (1967:46) states that " . . . Negroes often illegally harvest crops or, perhaps, plant their own on Cayapa-owned land. It is said that the Indian is always at a disadvantage in his dealings with Negroes because of the latter's readiness to engage in witchcraft and 'spoil' the land for the Indian owner."

In *Juyungo* a little black boy about ten or eleven years old runs away from home and, after a series of adventures, finds his way to a Cayapa village. At first his intrusion is seen with great disfavor, but gradually, because he is so young, there is reluctant toleration of his presence: "During the first days he felt uneasy . . . for the Cayapa hate blacks and also fear them. Very few strangers, and still fewer *gente de color* had been tolerated there for any length of time" (Ortíz 1943:25).

Another view of unfortunate relations between blacks and Indians is that presented by Hector Casierra Perlaza in his short story "Comecayapas." The ingredients of this narrative—ignorance of the customs of one's neighbors and the consequences of human foibles—are skillfully combined. In "Comecayapas" the sickly child of a Cayapa couple dies while the family is traveling away from home. In order to preserve the corpse until it can be buried near Punto Venado, their tribal home on the Cayapas River, the father treats the body in much the same way that smoked meat is prepared. As the couple journeys homeward with their dead son, they ask for shelter at the ranch of a prosperous but covetous *mulata*, Doña Secundina, and her husband. When the Cayapa stand at her door, Doña Secundina looks them up and down suspiciously. She silently compares them to her *compadre* Quilumba, an *indio del río Ónzoles* who had grown up among *morenos*.

Quilumba always brought game meat or produce to his *comadre* Secundina when he came to ask for shelter. These Cayapa were standing before her empty-handed. Nevertheless, Doña Secundina notices that as they arrange their bundles in the arbor where they have been told to sleep, the Indians seem to have packages that could only contain meat. They must be carrying it back to Punto Venado for the annual Cayapa tribal celebration, she reasons. During the night Doña Secundina and her goddaughter creep down to the arbor and steal one of the meat packets. The Cayapas move on the next day, and Doña Secundina and her family enjoy a hearty meal. Several days later the Indians return to ask for the missing leg of their son. When Doña Secundina denies having taken it, the Cayapa appeal to the local *teniente político* and the case stirs much interest in the community. *Indios, negros, y mestizos* crowd around the door of the room where the *teniente político* is interrogating Doña Secundina and her family. The husband gives no answers, for he knows nothing about it. Doña Secundina denies everything. Her goddaughter, however, under the *teniente político*'s relentless questioning, tells the truth. After that, people shout *Comecayapas*, "Cayapa-eater," whenever Doña Secundina or a member of her family appears. Some weeks later three bodies are found near the family ranch. The leg of one corpse, that of Doña Secundina, is missing. The story is based on an incident that actually took place.

Finally, a passage from *Juyungo* seems indicative of efforts to suppress, within city limits, one major manifestation of black culture—the marimba dance, or *currulao*. According to Whitten (1974:108): "Every settlement of 200 or more people has one marimba house, *casa de la marimba*, and every town has two or more marimbas placed in the older *barrios* of the community, as well as in the newly forming ones. In the rural scattered dwelling niche, there is normally a *casa de la marimba* available within four to six hours' canoe travel." In the novel *Juyungo* police officials issue an order stating that, "from this date on, it is strictly forbidden to hold marimba dances in the central parts of the city inasmuch as it constitutes an attack on order, morality, and the good customs of civilized people . . . " (Ortíz 1943:78). The words "good customs of civilized people" show that black lowland culture is not being judged on its own merit, or on its contribution to cultural adaptation to and transformation of the Pacific lowlands culture area (see, e.g., West 1957, Whitten 1974), but rather is constantly being measured, evaluated, and demeaned by an alien standard.

Commercial Exploitation

If injustices involved in conflicts of culture have claimed writers' attention, those resulting from commercial exploitation have also done so. Whitten describes the economic cycle that has become typical of the Pacific lowlands:

> The economic structure of the Pacific Littoral is based on the exploitation of forest and sea resources. Such exploitation is sporadic, best portrayed in any area, at any period of time, as a succession of boom and depression periods. For example, in different areas, at different times, there have been booms centering on gold, rubber, bananas, tagua, timber, fish, shellfish, and sometimes on secondary booms such as those brought about by road, railroad, and port construction, and by shipping and heightened commercial activity. (Whitten 1970:331–32)

The banana cycle has been the most compelling for writers, perhaps because when it began, cultivation and production were systematized for the first time so that the impact of the cycle was more immediate and dramatic.

Bolívar Drouet Calderón (1960:63–71), in "Embarque de Bananas," writes from experience. He worked as a fruit checker on banana boats for several years. One of the protagonists of "Embarque" is an old stevedore who, pressed by poverty, must go on working in spite of his age. He manages to do so until, in the course of carrying bananas, he is tossed an especially heavy load. He struggles under its weight for a moment, then lets out a sharp cry of pain. His back is severely injured, and the only means of supporting himself and his family within the banana "boom" economy is lost. The chain of commercial dependency in the coastal lowlands goes from the foreign capital interests, to absentee elite landowners[7] and the managerial and entrepreneurial white and *mestizo* upper class of the community, to the proletariat poor who depend on money for survival. The old stevedore in "Embarque" is a member of the latter group.

"El Bananero," by Adalberto Ortíz (1960), tells of a man who owns several acres of fertile land. It is not a large holding, but it provides a nice subsistence basis for him and his family. A representative from the banana company arrives and suggests that he could quadruple his earnings if he grew bananas. So the man rips out the ripening corn and thriving plantains and replaces them with the commercial bananas. At harvest time he takes the bananas to the company and is told that he has come late, that they have more fruit than they need, and they pay him but a pittance for his produce. He is ruined and is forced to sell his land in order to survive. The buyer is the international banana company, and soon the seller learns that dozens of others have lost their land in the same way. Adalberto Ortíz told me that he once read this story to an audience of Esmeraldeños and two men in it cried because, in listening, they relived vividly what had happened to them.

This current of the theme of exploitation has swelled into a literature of protest. A novel by Nelson Estupiñán Bass (1958) entitled— with razor-edge irony—*El Paraíso* emphasizes the participation of blacks in an uprising against a dictator. Also, in *Senderos Brillantes* Estupiñán Bass (1974) presents the imaginary Republic of Girasol (Esmeraldas), which is plagued by corruption. Much of it is the result of the influence of the "Associated States" (United States). The lush land and its dark people are ravaged by foreign business interests and corrupt compatriots. The novel is reminiscent of the Nobel Prize–winning *El Sr. Presidente* by the Guatemalan Miguel Angel Asturias (1964). *El Sr. Presidente* chronicles the fall from favor of the dictator's right-hand man, Miguel, *cara de angel*. Murder, torture, terror, and the dictator's anguished endless vigilance—these are the fruits of his government. This is also pointed out in *Senderos Brillantes*. Its publication proved all the more forceful because it coincided with an announcement by the government of Ecuador that Esmeraldas had been designated the first Ecuadorian oil port.

SUMMARY

Many works by Afro-Ecuadorian writers give us a clear view of black coastal culture. Racial mixture–racial identity, conflicts of culture, and commercial exploitation form a trilogy of crucial themes. If many works share common themes, they also share a common quality: exuberant sensuality and sexuality. This coastal warmth contrasts vividly with Andean coolness and distance. In works by Esmeraldeño writers one soaks up the scents and shadows of the forest and hears the cry of boatmen on every other page. Sexual encounters are frequent and sometimes violent.

Among these writers one also finds common patterns in the presentation and development of characters. Reilly (1978:5), when writing about ethnic literature in the United States, says much that is pertinent to the treatment of characters in works by Esmeraldeño writers:

> Ethnic motivation in literature yields a scheme for the arrangement or plot of imaginative ethnic prose: (A) A character is established in the context of

an . . . ethnic group. (B) That character conflicts with the facts of social organization as they are embodied in established patterns of power and discriminatory relationships. There is then a movement either to (C) Destruction of the character or (D) Character growth that transcends, in some manner, the historical-material facts of social organization.

Esmeraldeño writers, in their major works, have preferred (D), the outcome in which the protagonist ends with a keener sense of self-appreciation. Character growth is conspicuous in *Juyungo, La Otra,* and *El Último Río.*

In Esmeraldeño literature character growth means realization of the enormity of the injustice under which one labors. What this realization evokes is predictable: *anger.* One may be angry but unable to act, as in the case of the farmer who lost his land by trickery, or the old stevedore whose back is injured. In other cases anger compels action. In "Cinturón Maldito" the poor man, deceived by the wealthy Don Epaminondas, murders him. A violent act by one man is the individual analogue to social revolution, and revolution is often mentioned as the prescription to cure social ills.

Finally, one notes some recent trends in Afro-Ecuadorian literature. First, the need for political power and a desire to obtain a fair share of the wealth produced by the exploitation of natural resources have become paramount themes. Second, although not dealt with in this paper, poetry is beginning to emerge strongly among a new generation of writers. Perhaps this is because the short poem contains an idiom easily translatable into a song of protest. Such literature is utilitarian: it may reach and influence a greater number of people. It may also suggest that young writers are reaching an audience somewhat different from that of their predecessors.

ESMERALDAS TODAY—PERSONAL OBSERVATIONS

The black population of Ecuador is estimated at 7% to 10%, most of it concentrated in Esmeraldas province. There are also numerous indigenous peoples and a sizable population of European descent. Aware of this heterogeneity, I was curious about the degree of racial tolerance I might encounter, especially in Esmeraldas, where to look at the people was to see a kaleidoscope of phenotypes. I found that many Ecuadorians boast of their nation as a multiracial Eden, but on close inspection it seemed to me a somewhat troubled paradise. When I visited Esmeraldas in the summer of 1976, women on the street often pointed to my modest Afro and exclaimed *que pelo tan feo!* "what ugly hair!" Exposing kinky hair in that way was simply not

done. The reaction of these women was both amusing and sugges-
tive. Their comment implied that this particular negroid feature was
distasteful to them.

My husband, a native of Spain, and our two-year old son accompanied me on the trip. As a mixed couple, we evoked much curiosity.
I learned later that to find a white man actually married to a black
woman was proof that the age of miracles had not yet passed. When
we first arrived in Esmeraldas and were looking for a hotel, my husband saw a rooming house and asked the taxi driver to stop. The
baby and I remained in the taxi while my husband went to ask the
owner of the place, a fair-skinned woman who was sitting just outside the door, if there was a room available. The woman, an Ecuadorian, peered into the taxi and saw the baby and me. She then replied that if I was the maid, there was room for us. When my
husband answered that I was his wife, the woman said that all the
rooms were taken. When I mentioned the incident to one of the writers whom I interviewed, he explained that he was acquainted with
the woman, that she was not from Esmeraldas, that her attitude was
as unusual as it was regrettable. If this woman was from highland
Ecuador—I am not certain that she was—her ideas seem much less
surprising. Klumpp (1970) indicates that fair-skinned highlanders expect preferential treatment vis-à-vis their dark countrymen: "There
are stereotype expectations in highland Ecuador about how members
of different groups behave in interpersonal relations. . . . Buses in
highland Ecuador are a symbolic representation of the status differentials accorded to the various ethnic categories: 'whites' sit in the
very first row; a variety of mestizo types are found up toward the
front, middle and back; and Indians and Negroes occupy the last
rows of seats" (1970:259). Klumpp also observes that in stores, post
offices, and other government establishments blacks are usually
served after whites and *mestizos* who arrive later.

On another occasion I was told by a light-skinned woman who had
grown up in the lowlands that coastal blacks were proud of themselves, that it was just their color that they didn't like! She spoke with
great conviction, finding it perfectly compatible to take pride in one's
self yet reject an integral part of that self. Whether this woman's
statement reflected her own view of blacks or the feelings of the
blacks themselves, the conclusion that color matters, to her or to
them, is inescapable.

Besides evidence of the significance of color, the effect of development on the city of Esmeraldas powerfully drew my attention. In
1976 the Ecuadorian trans-Andes oil pipeline, which ends in Esme-

raldas, had just been completed. Outstanding was the number of foreigners and noncoastal Ecuadorians who were participating in the petroleum enterprise. The workers erecting the refinery were Japanese. A Chilean architect was designing the housing. Several English and Canadian engineers had been consulted, and American interest was clear in the signs along the beach bearing the names of U.S. oil companies. One must bear in mind that foreigners and nationals from other parts of Ecuador bring with them new values different from those held by coastal blacks (witness the rooming house incident). Moreover, the prestige attached to the positions that foreigners and noncoastal residents will have as entrepreneurs, managers, and technical advisors gives their way of looking at the world special weight. Their values will be more easily imposed. As Thompson (1972:152–53) points out, "It is not values that are important but the institutions they call into existence." It is probable that the values of the new coastal residents will call into existence institutions different from those with which black *costeños* have lived.

Dramatic change is already underway. In downtown Esmeraldas the ancient pleasure of listening to old story tellers is rapidly giving way to the more modern entertainment of the transistor radio and television. Money was recently spent to improve the water supply to the city, and plans are being made to expand port facilities. There is a small new American-style hotel, and construction of all types of edifices is underway. A small airfield has been completed and there are daily flights to Quito. The Motown sound is frequently heard on the juke box while groups of black marimba players are vanishing from the city, and the *currulao* itself seems to have disappeared except as an occasional tourist attraction. One must go to rural areas to hear the Afro-Ecuadorian music which, until just the last few years, was as vibrantly alive in the towns as on remote rivers (Whitten 1974).

Development in Esmeraldas, I found, meant all things to all men. Julio Estupiñán Tello, the owner of a modest hotel, was an advocate of new ideas and ways of living. In fact, he has written several short stories in which he urges the people of Esmeraldas to divest themselves of folk beliefs and other ideas which, he feels, are an obstacle to progress. One wonders if these stories reach the audience whose lives the author says he wishes to change, or whether they simply make the rounds in a small intellectual circle. By contrast, Tomás García, writer and bank teller, is distressed about the dwindling number of marimba bands in town. He spends his spare time building a band, training musicians, and then recording this "traditional" music. Still, what this music gains in recording—availability to a wider audience—it may lose in spontaneity. Nelson Estupiñán Bass, for his part, says that his major fear for Afro-Ecuadorian culture is that as the commercial importance of Esmeraldas increases, so will prostitution.

The fundamental question, it seems to me, is whether development will be planned in a way that will allow blacks to go on being vigorous participants in community life or whether it will make them marginal men. Whitten (1974) has written extensively on "black disenfranchisement" in northern Esmeraldas under the impress of developmental strategies. While black kinship groups in San Lorenzo once controlled the town, highland Ecuadorians who have come to take advantage of business opportunities are now assuming control. Grace Schubert, in the next chapter of this volume, brings us up to date on "modernization" in San Lorenzo, documenting the sharpening of racist constraints for black people there.

Time will answer the question of how much blacks will benefit from the growing economic importance of Esmeraldas province, but what is observable today is an attenuation of black culture in its capital city. Whitten explains that "non-black immigrants, the degree of upward mobility possibilities for blacks, national development strategies and activities, ethnic boundaries, and sheer police activity . . . " all contribute to the constraints facing black people there. He says further, "Esmeraldas is today the least characteristic town/city of the Pacific lowlands culture area in terms of traditional Afro-Ecuadorian, Afro-Colombian activities" (personal communication 1977). One wonders what distinctive features of Afro-Ecuadorian culture will remain, say, 50 years from now. Will a homogenization with "national" culture have taken place? Will the culture have been ransomed by the confinement of its bearers to a certain area in much the same way that some North American Indian cultures survive on the reservation? One may speculate endlessly. However, the word frequently has endured long after the culture has vanished. Black literature may become a treasury that will make the riches of Afro-Ecuadorian culture timeless.

NOTES

Acknowledgments: The research described in this paper was aided by a grant from the American Philosophical Society in 1976.

1. Estupiñán Tello (1967:77) notes that when the Ibarra–San Lorenzo railroad was built in 1950, railroad workers came upon a settlement of blacks where people lived "half-naked and spoke their own dialect." Thomsen

(1969:163) writes about a similar situation in *Living Poor*: "There is a village called Africa about twenty miles up the coast from Río Verde, a village of six grass houses and five hundred coconut palms. As you sail past the town and think of its name the village takes on an added freight of exoticness. It is a misplaced village, and it is completely outside history."

2. A passage from *Tierra Baldía*, a novel by Gonzalo Ramón (1958:110) about the blacks of Quinindé, a town in Esmeraldas, suggests that casual liaisons between white men and black women were common: "A few Ecuadorian whites have come [to the coast] as well as Germans, Italians, and Americans. They'll up and leave, just as they came, or they'll become acclimated here, mixing with our strong race, and the children will be *mulatos*, who'll feel as black as the rest of us . . . because if they think they're white, they're lost." The speaker's concern is thus not with illegitimacy but with racial identity.

3. This translation and all others in this paper are mine.

4. Duncan and Melendez (1974) discuss similar animal stories in the black oral tradition of Costa Rica, and Cabrera (1971) gives evidence of the vitality of animal stories among black Cubans.

5. This episode brings to mind a section of the Argentinian gaucho epic *Martín Fierro*, by José Hernández (1967:197–98). Originally published in 1872, the epic contains an adventure in which the hero, Martín Fierro, enters a duel of musical improvisation and lyric inventiveness with a black cowboy:

> Pinta el blanco negro al diablo,
> Y el negro blanco lo pinta;
> Blanca la cara o retinta,
> No hablo en contra ni en favor;
> De los hombres el Criador
> No hizo dos clases distintas.

6. Also, Estupiñán Tello (1967:57–60) explains that there are "ciertos apellidos esencialmente negros: Angulo, Ayoví, Caicedo, Coroso, Cuero Cangá, Lastre, Mina, Nazareno, Quiñónez."

7. Bitter remarks about absentee landowners are found in Ramón (1958): "[Cocoa] enriched many men who were living in France, like kings of cocoa, some of them never having seen their haciendas in this 'land of negros,' as they would call our country. . . ."

REFERENCES CITED

Altschuler, Milton
  1967 The Sacred and Profane Realms of Cayapa Law. *International Journal of Comparative Sociology* 8 (1):44–54.
Asturias, Miguel Angel
  1964 *El Sr. Presidente*. 4th ed. Buenos Aires: Editorial Losada.
Ballagas, Emilio
  1935 *Antología de la Poesía Negra Americana*. Madrid: Aguilar.
Barrett, Samuel A.
  1925 *The Cayapa Indians of Ecuador*. 2 vols. New York: Heye Foundation.
Cabello de Balboa, Miguel
  1945 Verdadera Descripción y Relación Larga de la Provincia y Tierra de Las Esmeraldas. In Miguel Cabello de Balboa, *Obras*, vol. 1. Quito: Editorial Ecuatoriana, pp. 5–55.

Cabrera, Lydia, ed.
1971   *Cuentos Negros de Cuba.* Havana: Ediciones Nuevo Mundo.
Carpentier, Alejo
1967   *El Reino de Este Mundo.* Barcelona: Editorial Seix Barral, S.A.
1969   *El Siglo de las Luces.* 5th ed. Mexico City: Compañía General de Ediciones, S.A.
Carrión, Benjamin, ed.
1955   *Los que se Van, Cuentos del Cholo y del Montuvio.* Quito: Casa de la Cultura Ecuatoriana.
Casierra Perlaza, Hector
1960   Comecayapas. In Alfredo Chaves, ed., *Antología de Cuentos Esmeraldeños.* Quito: Casa de la Cultura Ecuatoriana, pp. 183–93.
Chaves, Alfredo, ed.
1960   *Antología de Cuentos Esmeraldeños.* Quito: Casa de la Cultura Ecuatoriana.
Díaz Sánchez, Ramón
1960   *Cumboto.* 4th ed. Caracas: Colección Popular Venezolana.
Drouet Calderón, Bolívar
1960   Embarque de Bananas. In Alfredo Chaves, ed., *Antología de Cuentos Esmeraldeños.* Quito: Casa de la Cultura Ecuatoriana, pp. 63–71.
n.d.   Torpedo. Unpublished manuscript.
Duncan, Quince, and Carlos Melendez
1974   *El Negro en Costa Rica.* San José: Editorial Costa Rica.
Estupiñán Bass, Nelson
1954   *Cuando los Guayacanes Florecían.* Quito: Casa de la Cultura Ecuatoriana.
1958   *El Paraíso.* Quito: Casa de la Cultura Ecuatoriana.
1960   El Gualajo. In Alfredo Chaves, ed., *Antología de Cuentos Esmeraldeños.* Quito: Casa de la Cultura Ecuatoriana.
1966   *El Último Río.* Quito: Casa de la Cultura Ecuatoriana.
1967   Apuntes sobre el Negro de Esmeraldas en la Literatura Ecuatoriana. *Norte* 53:101–9.
1973   *Las Tres Carabelas—Poesía, Relato y Teatro.* Portoviejo: Editorial Gregorio.
1974   *Senderos Brillantes.* Quito: Casa de la Cultura Ecuatoriana.
Estupiñán Tello, Julio
1967   *El Negro en Esmeraldas: Apuntes para su Estudio.* Quito: Casa de la Cultura Ecuatoriana.
Friedemann, Nina S. de
1974   *Minería, Descendencia y Orfebreria Artesanal Litoral Pacífico (Colombia).* Bogotá: Facultad de Ciencias Humanas, Universidad Nacional.
Gallegos Lara, Joaquín
1946   *Las Cruces sobre el Agua.* Guayaquil: Vera & Cía.
Gil Gilberto, Enrique
1968   *El Negro Santander.* Guayaquil: Editorial "Claridad."
Guillén, Nicholás
1972   *Antología Mayor.* Mexico: Editorial Diógenes.
Guillot, Carlos Federico
1961   *Negros Rebeldes y Negros Cimarrones.* Buenos Aires: Fariña Editores.

Harris, Joel Chandler
1937   *Tales of Uncle Remus, Being Legends of the Old Plantation.* Mt. Vernon, N.Y.: Peter Pauper Press.

Hernández, José
1967   [1872] *Martín Fierro.* Barcelona: Artes Gráficas Medinaceli, S.A.

Jackson, Richard L.
1976   *The Black Image in Latin American Literature.* Albuquerque: University of New Mexico Press.

Joel, Miriam
1972   *African Traditions in Latin America.* Cuernavaca: Centro Intercultural de Documentación.

Klumpp, Kathleen
1970   Black Traders of North Highland Ecuador. In Norman E. Whitten, Jr., and John F. Szwed, eds., *Afro-American Anthropology: Contemporary Perspectives.* New York: Free Press, pp. 245–62.

Martínez, Luís A.
1904   *A la Costa.* Quito: Imprenta Nacional.

Ortíz, Adalberto
1943   *Juyungo.* Buenos Aires: Editorial Americalee.
1960   El Bananero. In Alfredo Chaves, ed., *Antología de Cuentos Esmeraldeños.* Quito: Casa de la Cultura Ecuatoriana, pp. 28–39.
1971   *La Entundada y Cuentos Variados.* Quito: Casa de la Cultura Ecuatoriana.
1973   *Tierra, Son y Tambor.* 5th ed. Quito: Casa de la Cultura Ecuatoriana.
1975   La Negritud en la Cultura Latinoamericana y Ecuatoriana. *Revista de la Universidad Católica* 3:97–118.
1976   *El Espejo y la Ventana.* Quito: Casa de la Cultura Ecuatoriana.

Ortíz Estefanuto, Nelson
n.d.   El Cinturón Maldito. Unpublished short story.

Ortíz Urriola, José
1958   *Un Disparo en las Tinieblas.* Quito: Casa de la Cultura Ecuatoriana.
1970–74 *Once Cuentos Esmeraldeños.* Esmeraldas: Casa de la Cultura Ecuātoriana.
n.d.   El Tercer Inquilino. Unpublished short story.

Palés Matos, Luís
1937   *Tuntún de Pasa y Grifería.* San Juan: Imprenta Venezuela.

Pareja y Diezcanseco, Alfredo
1938   *Baldomera.* Santiago, Chile: Ediciones Ercilla.

Pereda Valdes, Ildefonso
1937   *El Negro Rioplatense y Otros Ensayos.* Montevideo: Claudio García & Cía, Editores.

Phelan, John Leddy
1967   *The Kingdom of Quito in the Seventeenth Century: Bureaucratic Politics in the Spanish Empire.* Madison: University of Wisconsin Press.

Ramírez, Mireya
1975   *Andarele.* Quito.

Ramón, Gonzalo
1958   *Tierra Baldía.* Quito: Casa de la Cultura Ecuatoriana.

Reilly, John M.
    1978   Criticism of Ethnic Literature. *Melus: The Journal of the Society for the Study of Multi-Ethnic Literature of the United States* 5 (1):2–13.
Reyes, Oscar
    1950   *Breve Historia General del Ecuador*. 2 vols. 4th ed. Quito: Fray Jodoco Ricke.
Ribadeneira, Edmundo M.
    1958   *La Moderna Novela Ecuatoriana*. Quito: Casa de la Cultura Ecuatoriana.
Rout, Leslie B., Jr.
    1976   *The African Experience in Spanish America*. New York: Cambridge University Press.
Schyttner, Eugene
    1943   *Vida y Obras de Autores Ecuatorianos*. Havana: Editorial "Alfa."
Sharp, William F.
    1968   El Negro en Colombia: Manumisión y Posición Social. *Razón y Fábula* 8:91–107.
    1977   *Slavery on the Spanish Frontier: The Colombian Chocó 1680–1810*. Norman: University of Oklahoma Press.
Thompson, William Irvin
    1972   *At the Edge of History: Speculations on the Transformation of Culture*. New York: Harper & Row.
Thomsen, Moritz
    1969   *Living Poor: A Peace Corps Chronicle*. Seattle: University of Washington Press.
Walker, Michael Lee
    1977   The Black Social Identity in Selected Novels of Nelson Estupiñán Bass and Adalberto Ortíz. Ann Arbor, Mich.: University Microfilms. Ph.D. thesis, University of California, Riverside.
West, Robert C.
    1957   *The Pacific Lowlands of Colombia: A Negroid Area of the American Tropics*. Baton Rouge: Louisiana State University Press.
Whitten, Norman E., Jr.
    1965   *Class, Kinship, and Power in an Ecuadorian Town: The Negroes of San Lorenzo*. Stanford, Calif.: Stanford University Press.
    1970   Strategies of Adaptive Mobility in the Colombian-Ecuadorian Littoral. In Norman E. Whitten, Jr., and John F. Szwed, eds., *Afro-American Anthropology: Contemporary Perspectives*. New York: Free Press, pp. 329–44.
    1974   *Black Frontiersmen: A South American Case*. New York: Halsted (Wiley).
Whitten, Norman E., Jr., and Nina S. de Friedemann
    1974   La Cultura Negra del Litoral Ecuatoriano y Colombiano: Un Modelo de Adaptación Étnica. *Revista Colombiana de Antropología* (Bogotá) 17:75–115.

20

To Be Black Is Offensive: Racist Attitudes in San Lorenzo

Grace Schubert

What happens to a quiet, ethnically homogeneous if racially variable village when a new railroad brings in the outside world? One would expect radical change—and such there was in San Lorenzo, northern Esmeraldas, following the completion of the Ibarra–San Lorenzo line in 1957. By the time I came to this Pacific coastal town in 1972, I saw much more than that pre-1952 thatched-hut village of 500–700 *zambos* and *negros*, with two white families, described by Ferdon (1950:18). Here was a burgeoning town, now of over 5,600 inhabitants, racially variable and ethnically divided, with several growing industries and a wide variety of houses ranging from those constructed of poles and thatch to two-story dwellings of painted cement.

It would have been easy for me to draw generalizations from my first impressions. Highlanders would say, "I can tell you all about this place in an hour. You won't need more than two days to learn all there is to know about these [black] people." My stay was actually 20 months. During that time I found more than enough complexities in the socioeconomic system alone to command my attention for a much longer period.

My purpose here is to discuss one small facet of those complexities as reflected in the labeling and usage of racial categories in a changing political economy (see, e.g., Whitten 1974:197–98). I shall analyze both boundaries of categories and the correlation between changes in such boundaries and changes in socioeconomic systems. Evidence will be presented from an ethnosemantic point of view to establish further the decisive role of modernization (Poggie and Lynch 1974) in the heightening of racial barriers, an issue to which social scientists have repeatedly addressed themselves (see, e.g., Blalock 1967; Friedemann 1974; Kronus and Solaún 1973; van den Berghe 1967; Whitten 1970, 1974; Whitten and Friedemann 1974).

In order to do this, I shall first review briefly the history and cognitive categories of the two major ethnic groups chosen for this study, *blancos* from the Sierra and *negros* from the Coast. Then I will analyze the ways by which change has affected people grouped into these contrastive categories, the emergence of white dominance in the political economy, and the expression of this dominance in racist terms. Finally, I shall correlate political economic dominance with changes in cognitive categories from both points of view, focusing especially on the perspective of those grouped into the stigmatized black category.

SAN LORENZO—1965 AND BEFORE

The beginnings of a significant racial and ethnic mixture in San Lorenzo came between 1952 and 1957 during the construction of the Ibarra–San Lorenzo railroad, when "two distinct classes, both composed largely of highlanders, took up residence" there (Whitten 1965:31). Before this the town consisted primarily of blacks, with a few light coastal people and foreigners (Whitten 1965:25–27). The latter were drawn to the area by the promise of lucrative exploitation of gold, ivory nut (*tagua*), balsa, and bananas, all in demand on the world market at various times (Whitten 1974:74–75). The black population responded to the ebb and flow of these demands originating outside the native economy well before the railroad was even begun.

As opportunities stimulated by the world market presented themselves to the nonindigenous coastal people, they participated in a cash economy in return for securing the raw materials called for by foreign entrepreneurs. When this demand no longer existed, they adjusted by returning to their time-honored subsistence economy (Whitten 1968, 1974:8–9). Such readjustments were facilitated by the long-standing pattern of reciprocity in social relationships as the *costeños* of this area perceived them in terms of Afro-Hispanic culture.

Fundamental to all of this were the consanguineal, affinal, and fictive kin networks whose constituents usually were the potential partners for transactions. Obligations incurred were later reciprocated in exchanges that were culturally accepted and understood among blacks. In rural settlements day-to-day subsistence activities usually involved exchanges in kind—labor for labor, food for food (Whitten 1974:86–88).

"Outside" entrepreneurs would use this system through a black "network broker" who had a *jefe*, chief, of the *minga* indebted to him.[1] Such a chief had the ability to involve enough "debtors" to work with him in meeting the requests of the outsider, for example, in procuring lumber. The *jefe*, in turn, owed the workers cash or goods for their labor. Often the *jefe* would offer drinks to his workers, a ritual signaling his interest in potential future exchanges. A careful mental tally was kept, although the process gave an impression of informality. When the "busts" came along, the old subsistence type of exchange for kind rather than for cash was right there (Whitten 1974), making no transition necessary: cultural adaptability to the boom-bust economy within this Afro-Hispanic culture had become established.

A common practice was for men, especially *jefes* of the *minga* and network brokers, to have several consensual spouses. The men acquired more in-laws by doing this, thus increasing the number of possible partners for exchange and widening their base of operations. They did this partly by having one spouse or more take on an enterprise such as a store or a small farm. Diversification of this kind was a basic step toward upward mobility in the local socioeconomic hierarchy, mostly during "boom" periods (Whitten 1968; 1974:88–91, 168–69).

Summary of Racial and Ethnic History before 1965

With the building of the railroad and the wharf at its terminal, sustained contact with the Ecuadorian highlands was established. White and *mestizo* highlanders working for the Junta Autónoma agency responsible for railroad construction and maintenance were in charge of the land on either side of the railroad, an area amounting to the entire community at that time. This became a base for resentment and conflict with the local San Lorenzeños (Whitten 1965:30–31).

The construction of the railroad brought migrants from the highlands, from the Coast, and from Colombia, thus initiating a greater variety of racial and ethnic "types" and increased attention to phenotype in the affairs of San Lorenzo. Among the highlanders were those classified as white, *mestizo*, and Indian. Among the *costeños* and Colombians the distinctions were less clearcut: some were blacks, others were mulattoes of many varied phenotypic descriptions, and still others were white. For the purposes of this paper I must limit my focus to nonblack, nonindigenous highlanders, self-identifying as *blanco* and *serrano*, and the *costeños*, whom these *serranos* labeled *negro*.[2]

Even before the railroad was finished, highlanders had begun to reshape the growing village of San Lorenzo. Office buildings were built, electric power was installed in the center of town, and health services were inaugurated. The railroad physician later became the chief organizer of the best hospital in the province of Esmeraldas (Onofa 1973). Educational opportunities expanded in 1956 with the founding of a girls' primary school. A Catholic missionary took up permanent residence in the community in 1958, and the following year another arrived. These priests gave much encouragement to the development of the town.

After the building of the railroad, *serranos* came in even larger numbers. Although many left, others put down roots to stay. The latter worked primarily for the railroad and/or established businesses, some of them finding it to their advantage to marry into already successful light or dark coastal families, thereby gaining more knowledge of the local ropes (Whitten 1965, 1974).

For some coastal blacks the railroad construction brought more job opportunities. Demand for lumber was growing both in other parts of Ecuador and in other countries. Sawmills were built, and at first used a *minga* system to cut trees and transport the logs to the sawmills. Better transportation facilities helped entrepreneurs in San Lorenzo take advantage of this expanding demand, and the *minga* system and other wage-labor systems were used competitively through 1965. The export of other products (mussels, coconuts, mangrove bark) to the highlands was also facilitated by the railroad, creating further sources of cash income for both *serranos* and *costeños* (Whitten 1965).[3] Improved infrastructure was providing a base for continuing economic growth.

Those *serranos* who married into *costeño* families and took an interest in San Lorenzo had an influence on black lives. By the exertion of economic pressures such highlanders were able to impress their "community oriented" values upon certain blacks who were willing to conform to those preferences in various aspects of their lifestyle (Whitten 1965:95–111). *Serranos*, referring to *costeños*, would say to me, "If they would stop drinking, get married to one woman, wear shoes and clean clothes, be reliable, speak 'properly,' we'd buy from their store and lend them money more freely."

During the 1960s a relatively small number of *serranos* made a strong impact on the town's political economy and ethnic structure, thereby affecting black life there. Local upper- and middle-class[4] highlanders used their position and their money to change the lifestyle of about 20–25% of the blacks. Of this group 30–50% were middle class (Whitten 1965:46, 97, 163, 166). Some members of the latter grouping were network brokers and/or businessmen having contact with relatives through whom they still benefited from customary practices necessary for *minga* exchange (Whitten 1965:153, 164; 1968). Some blacks resisted the *serrano* influence; others played both sides for their family's advantage.

To understand why black reactions were so varied, we must remember how deeply rooted such traditions as drinking and having consensual spouses were in their lives. We have seen how commonly these practices were employed as mechanisms for economic mobility. Something so basic to the black way of life was not likely to be changed easily—and it wasn't. During this time the blacks were in control of the local situation (Whitten 1965:182) through the continuing effectiveness of the ramifying kinship networks through three generations. The pressure to conform to the new *serrano* ways affected the blacks' visible behavior in the presence of highlanders, but ties with the old family exchange systems continued.

RACIAL AND ETHNIC CATEGORIES: 1965

The imposition of one group's lifestyle upon another is certain to be reflected in expressions of their reciprocal perceptions. The introduction of *serrano* stereotypes in San Lorenzo by people holding what many blacks regarded as influential positions vis-à-vis the outside world led to the use of verbal labels reflecting altered perceptions of ethnic, social, and economic standing.

The coastal blacks in 1965 used *costeño*, meaning anyone from the Coast, to set themselves off from *serrano*, meaning anyone from the highlands. This distinction focused on the contrasting features of the highland and lowland lifestyles. Depending on the context, the term *serrano* could be relatively descriptive of natal region or could have pejorative connotations. The term *blanco* was applied to any white, light *mulato* (*mulato claro*), or upper- or middle-class *mestizo* who was held in some degree of respect. While *mulato* referred to a very light-skinned *costeño*, *cholo* designated a dark-skinned, straight-haired *costeño*. As we shall see, however, the tendency became much stronger to apply the more general term *moreno* to all *negros*, *zambos*, and *mulatos* who were not extremely light. Blacks preferred to use the term *moreno* as contrasted with *blanco*. In referring to one of his own color, a black would use *negro* descriptively or as a term of affection or insult, depending on the context (Whitten 1965:90–91). Used by nonblacks, however, *negro* was meant derogatorily for any black or dark *mulato*.

From the highland point of view, *costeño* meant anyone from the

Coast and *serrano* anyone from the highlands. *Blanco* was any middle- or upper-class *serrano* to whom respect was given. *Cholo* was used to designate a poor, phenotypic indigenous highlander and was also a derogatory term for a lower-class *mestizo*. A *costeño* with dark skin was considered *negro*, and *mulato* was any light-skinned person reflecting racial mixture (Whitten 1965:91–92).

These categories fall into three general groupings: those designating geographic origin and lifestyle, those labeling phenotypes, and those having class or pejorative ethnic implications. Later in this paper I give special attention to the two latter categories, but first I will consider the changing patterns of power relationships between socioeconomic elements in the town that was influenced so strongly by the railroad's coming.

SAN LORENZO: 1965–73

In the three-year period 1965–68 San Lorenzo experienced several changes in these elements—changes extensive enough to surprise Norman Whitten upon his return in 1968. Most important of these developments was the sharp decrease in the use of the *minga* system. It was largely replaced by the paying of cash wages on a periodic basis. Some black network brokers were displaced in competition with *serranos* (Whitten 1974:185, 189).

Invasions That Changed the Town

From 1965 to 1973 the number of highlanders increased sharply. In response to the founding of new primary and secondary schools, more *serrano* teachers came. Highlanders in business more than doubled during this period. They bought out several black businessmen and forced others out of business (Whitten 1974:186–89). By 1973 some *serranos* had expanded their power base to include lending money at a high interest rate and buying more land as it became available, especially in the center of town. Nevertheless, some of the founding coastal families have remained in the central area.

Other *serranos* got involved in the transport of mussels, *conchas*, gathered by women in the mangrove swamps. These *serranos* were in addition to one highlander and one coastal person who had been doing large-scale marketing of mussels and mangrove bark for at least five years. Furthermore, in 1970–73 some *costeños* started small businesses which transported and sold *conchas* along the Coast, competing strongly with the ambulant *serrano* merchants for mussels offered on the San Lorenzo market. These highland *comerciantes*,[5] laden with baskets of perishable foodstuffs, rode the *autocarril* from Ibarra to San Lorenzo and returned with sacks of *conchas*.

This latter marketing procedure was occasionally interrupted by breakdowns of the railroad, which lessened the supply of foods to which highlanders were accustomed and reduced the supply of plantains which remain a staple of the blacks' diet. Rural settlements as near as La Boca and San Javier de Cachabí shipped plantains to San Lorenzo by rail. Train failures were becoming progressively more critical as *serrano* and *costeño* populations grew. By the time I had been in the town for over a year, the breakdowns of the railroad had become more frequent and lasted up to a month (Zaldumbide 1974:17).[6]

The condition of the transportation system had much to do with the erratic pattern of prices in San Lorenzo stores. Even with regular deliveries from the highlands, blacks felt that *serranos* were overcharging them. Railroad delays and general scarcity of products made this matter worse. Sugar, for example, was often overpriced—grossly so during the scarcity in mid–1973.[7]

The growing white dominance of the San Lorenzo business community was not all *serrano*. In fact, the largest industrial development, a plywood factory which began production in 1971, was managed by a white man born in the United States. Its central office was in Guayaquil. Key personnel, mostly white *costeños* from Manabí and Guayas provinces, were recruited by a Guayaquil placement service. Although the factory was located outside San Lorenzo, most of the 190 unskilled workers were blacks residing in town. Many whites, including the manager, lived near the factory but would come to San Lorenzo for recreation.[8]

San Lorenzeños told me, "In 1970 the growth rate of San Lorenzo levelled off. There were few sawmills and they paid irregularly. The factory came to save this town." Blacks might be uncomfortable with the new disciplines of strict hours on a three-shift schedule and subservience to a nonblack foreman, but they liked the regular, dependable pay. It was the most mechanized institution in San Lorenzo to date and offered black workers another option for employment under white management.

Other factors were working toward increased financial security for long-term workers. Since this factory was known to pay wages regularly, store owners were more willing to grant its employees substantial credit. While all employees at all establishments were enjoying the benefits of the compulsory social security program of the Ecuadorian Institute of Social Security (IESS), the plywood factory and the *serrano*-managed sawmill established a commissary, making basic foods available to workers at a discount.

The Impact of Change

The impact of these changes upon San Lorenzo black *costeños* was profound. With the growth of the cash system, the *minga* system virtually disappeared, and the *jefe* role and network broker linkages between the lower class and the upwardly mobile became severely attenuated. Even more crucial has been the effect of this development on the role of consensual spouses. With the reduced function of in-laws in providing exchange partners, and a decline in the significance of spouses in male strategies for upward mobility, the position of women in the socioeconomic system has continued to change (Whitten 1974:193).[9]

In a sense, the focus of power passed from the network broker to the lumber entrepreneur with the direct hiring of workers. The entrepreneur was no longer as indebted to the network broker, nor was the *jefe* of the *minga*. In turn, even though the *jefe* could still recommend workers, they were not significantly indebted to him anymore. Formerly, indebtedness had been the basis for recruitment of workers. Now the exchange system, though still operating, was not the main factor in determining who would be hired for a given job. The power of the network broker to create asymmetrical indebtedness in an entrepreneur was greatly reduced, causing many blacks to lose a degree of access to strategic resources available through such contacts (Whitten 1974). These resources were still needed in the process of upward mobility, for which factory wages were rarely sufficient.

With the attenuation of their access to resources through social transactions within their Afro-Hispanic system, blacks had increased difficulty competing with *serranos*. Highlanders already had closer ties with the railroad and *serrano* businessmen, which meant greater facility in the transport of goods and more readily available credit from highland sources. *Serrano* businessmen took quick advantage of the new ready cash supply in the hands of rapidly growing numbers of workers, especially after the opening of the plywood factory. Had the *serranos* been more united as their numbers grew, they probably would have achieved an even greater dominance over the local political economy.

With many new attractive economic opportunities, particularly those offered at the plywood factory, changes began to come in the lives of some long-term black employees. Those who earned well above the minimum wage were able to move upward a rung in the local socioeconomic hierarchy by their conforming "community oriented" behavior, as before, but now also by acquiring new status symbols: tin roofs on their houses, jewelry and polyester clothing for their wives, new furniture, refrigerators. Schools were offering new opportunities for black children to compete, perhaps even with *serranos*, through their learning of mechanical and language skills.

Yet, with all these new options, more than half of the blacks living in town continued to cultivate subsistence farms. Some lacked birth certificates, the proper identification prerequisite for factory employment. Others were wage earners for a short time and then returned to subsistence farming because of its promise of greater security. Of those who were employed, many continued to maintain some form of tie with the old exchange system and agricultural pursuits, usually through relatives. San Lorenzeños estimate that with present extraction technology the wood from the forest might last another 10 to 30 years. When the wood gives out, they say, "We'll always have our land to go back to" (*Siempre hay la finca*). I got the impression that blacks are resourceful people who quite realistically assess what may well be anc 'her temporary boom and who determine not only how to be ready themselves, but also how to prepare their children for the commercial bust projected as the logical end to the lumber bonanza.

Developments in Racial Concept: 1965–73

The growing *serrano* stranglehold on the cash economy, their buying of strategic properties in the center of town, the imposition of their standards upon the blacks' lifestyle, plus many other elements—all contributed to the growing resentment toward *serranos* by *costeños*. It is true that some blacks who had money and connections outside San Lorenzo maintained certain power positions in the community. In 1973 the *teniente político*, the *registro civil*, and the customs official were black *costeños*. But *serranos*, in my view, largely controlled the *junta parroquial*, the major local governing body.

In response to economic and social pressures emanating from expansion of opportunity attendant upon "development," nonblack *serranos* and black *costeños* expressed increasingly their respective perceptions of each other in a dominance idiom predicated on *serrano* class-ethnic presumptions. As the *serrano* power base strengthened, the highlanders came to depend less on the blacks and to set themselves off as *blancos* in terms of the national class hierarchy, assigning those classed as *negro*—blacks that followed Afro-Hispanic practices—

to the very bottom (Whitten 1974:192). *Serranos* were thus more intensely projecting the imbalanced *blanco-negro* terminology as a replacement for the relatively balanced *serrano-costeño* set. The *blanco* label became increasingly desirable and almost advantageous for gaining higher positions in the political economy of town and region. Regardless of phenotype, a person with a great deal of money and power was regarded as being on the top rung, and therefore locally tagged *blanco* (or, in the case of a very dark person, *not* referred to as *negro*). Under no circumstances, though, would a phenotypic white *mestizo* be labeled *negro* because he was poor or lazy. If one lacked money and was not white, he or she still believed one could gain some advantage with even slightly lighter skin over darker competitors. *Blackness became increasingly offensive to nonblacks.*

Nowhere was the subject of blackness as being offensive more evident than in the arena of interspouse relationships. A repeated topic of conversation among blacks was the growing incidence of insults directed by a lighter mate toward a darker partner. Commenting on this, a black would say, "I want my child to marry someone his equal in skin color. Then there will be no reason for insults in that respect" (*Que mi hijo busque su igual. Así no se pueden insultar por el color*). Yet I heard this same black person say of someone else later, "She was lucky to marry light" (*Ella tenía la suerte de casarse con blanco*). One black woman summarized, "Although they may not admit it, most blacks want to marry lighter. To be black is offensive" (*Aunque no lo dicen, la mayoría de los morenos quieren casarse con alguien más blanco. Ser negro es como una ofensa*).

In 1968 most *serranos* were adding stereotypic, pejorative connotations to the category *negro*, such as lazy, dirty, stupid, ugly, even subhuman (Whitten 1974:192). In 1974 I saw and heard evidence of the occasional surfacing of these stereotypes in contexts of explicit verbal degradation of specific black people *because of their color*, not because of imputed or real behavior. I saw instances of this happening even in situations where black people were conforming to *serrano* behavioral preferences. For example, when one black woman, neatly dressed and clean, reacted with a questioning look to an exorbitant price quoted by a *serrano* storekeeper, he snapped, "There is no moreno more attractive than that dog!" (*No hay moreno más bonito que ese perro*).

But these extremely negative, racist statements were even more common under the pressure of private confrontations, as between family members. Through such insults, blacks were further "negrified" (*tratar de negro*), as the word *negro* was loaded with implications of inferiority in lifestyle. A darker partner in a marriage conflict was more than likely to experience verbal if not physical abuse because of the addition of a racial slur to the point at issue.

One *serrano* said to me, "With more education blacks will change. They act, realizing that they are inferior, yet they are proud. It's because of their color, the race itself" (*la raza misma es así*). Another commented: "The black race is lazy; it does not want to excel." Still another highlander told me, "The only hope for San Lorenzo is white in-migration." By 1973 the term *negro* used by a *serrano* not only meant black skin but also implied inferiority to the point of subhumanness.[10]

Such damaging *serrano* stereotypes of *negros* called forth understandably bitter responses by the blacks, clearly evident on a daily basis as they talked with one another. A *serrano*'s insults about physical appearance, for instance, would often cause a black to say to another black, "But he's not white" (*Pero él no es blanco*). *Serrano* statements about black ugliness were countered with examples of *serranos* whom they regarded as ugly. When *negro* lifestyle was stereotyped as lazy and dirty, blacks would say to each other: "The *serrano*[11] damages a *negro*'s reputation" (*El serrano estropea al negro*); "The *serrano* is useless [timid],[12] lazy, stingy, selfish" (*El serrano es cojudo, vago, cuñón, egoísta*); "He accumulates grime between his toes" (*Cria mugre en los pies*); "He is envious of the *moreno*. He doesn't want the *moreno* to rise" (*Serrano tiene envidia a moreno. No quiere que suben*). An occasional response which highlanders would find especially distasteful, if they heard it, would be the blacks' lumping together as *serrano* all who acted in a stingy, selfish manner.

Thus there developed a shift in the connotations associated with *serrano* when used by coastal blacks. It not only meant someone from the highlands with *serrano* lifestyle but also usually implied negative behavioral traits of that person: selfish, stingy, lazy, envious, one who treats blacks as inferior. Black San Lorenzeños were, however, quick to mention exceptions to the stereotype, thereby underscoring the categorical nature of the expanding negative ethnic class of *serrano*.

What the blacks said freely to one another was often edited for *serrano* consumption, depending on the blacks' goals and lifestyles. The goal promoting a *serrano-negro* interethnic encounter usually involved some favor that only a *serrano* could give at the time. The black woman who was insulted by the dog analogy needed a scarce product available from the highlander. She chose to "stretch the face" (*estirarse la cara*) to demonstrate to the *serrano* that she was not an uncouth, vulgar *negra grosera*. Holding her temper, she showed an aspect of behavior preferred by highlanders as she replied: "Don't talk to me about *morenos! Serranos* have it in for *morenos!*" (*De moreno no me hable. Serrano tiene pica a moreno*). Her detractor could now see her as a "tamed" *negra*, in comparison with other black people so abused who reacted more aggressively. Yet her demeanor in this encounter reflected her goal with the highlander to obtain a scarce good. Later she remarked, "I prefer to deal with a kind black instead of a white. A *negro* who works is worth more than a *serrano*" (*Que sea bién negrito. Negro educado que trata a uno con cariño en vez de blanco. Un negro que trabaja vale más que serrano*).

Other black people clearly transcended goal-oriented encounters and would return insult for insult. By this kind of behavior most *negros* were viewed as honest and forthright by other *negros* but as uncouth by *serranos*. But seldom did words lead to outright physical violence. A *serrano* informant admitted that certain *serranos* showed some constraint in such possible confrontations because of fear. The freedom to confront highlanders frankly seemed to stem from the occupational choice of some blacks. Instead of going into a type of employment requiring them to accept *serrano* ways, they chose less prestigious but more autonomous jobs in the forest or in the mangrove swamps.

Were we to graph these responses, another group would have to be placed at the opposite end of the scale from these straightforward blacks. Such persons represent the extreme of conformity to the *serrano* style. Usually they have married into *serrano* families, fitting in with highland ways, speaking "correctly" and "politely" by *serrano* standards. Some of these *costeños* have not only adopted the *serrano* regional accent, now despised in this area of the Coast, but refuse to turn it off when they address their old *costeño* friends. Those few who do this appear to symbolize full capitulation to *serrano* influence. However, even this degree of cultural capitulation has led not to the crossing of ethnic boundaries but rather to the creation of the anomaly of "blacks who act white."

The *serrano* denigration of blacks was reinforced by some light *costeños* who joined the racist chorus as they perceived the growing advantages of being lighter. Whitening (*blanqueamiento*; see, e.g., Whitten and Friedemann 1974) became "the thing." In 1973 it was a light *costeño* who was heard to say, "If you've got a *negro*, who needs a donkey?" (*Habiendo negro, para que burro*). Also contributing to the pressure to whiten were some of the few light in-migrants from Manabí and Guayas who echoed the same theme. One of them said,

"These *morenos* steal. It is a savage race" (*Estos morenos roban. Es una raza salvaje*).

When blacks would hear of something like this from a *manaba*, even one lighter than a *serrano*, they could still fight back by referring to a foreigner who was whiter than the *manaba*, or they could counter with a stereotypic remark about a *manaba*'s short temper and tendency to fight. This splitting of referents within the category *blanco* by those classed as *negro* is further illustrated by the black *costeño* use of the term *cholo* to emphasize still another division at the light end of the ethnic-phenotypic spectrum.[13] By 1973 *cholo*, as used by blacks, referred to someone with light skin and straight or slightly wavy hair. On occasions when they had to be more specific, some blacks labeled such phenotypes as "*cholo* from the coast," if even a bit darker-skinned, and "*cholo* from the highlands," if lighter, with stiffer hair. This latter designation fit most *serranos*, who intensely disliked being spoken of in this way. Tables 1 and 2 outline the designations described above.

TABLE 1. Meaning of Racial Terms from *Serrano* Point of View (1973).[1]

COLOR	CLASS
blanco = white	*blanco* = rich (white or black)
mestizo = mixed Indian and white (used very rarely)	(Rich black is verbally respected as *blanco*, but is referred to as *negro* behind his back.)
mulato = mixed black and white	
negro = black	*cholo* = poor white
	negro = poor black

ORIGIN	ETHNIC
serrano = born in highlands (now used less)	*serrano* = neat, polite, having regional accent of highlands
costeño = born on Coast	
manaba = born in province of Manabí	*cholo* = "hillbilly" from highlands with *serrano* regional accent
	costeño = inferiority associated with regional accent and characteristic demeanor
	negro = dirtiest, laziest, most uncouth

[1]Only for the purposes of this paper. Other cross-cutting category labels were used. See Schubert (1979).

TABLE 2. Meaning of Racial Terms from Black Point of View (1973).[1]

COLOR	CLASS
blanco = white	*blanco* = rich (white or black)
cholo[2] from the highlands (*serrano*) = yellowish white skin, straight "stiff" hair	(Rich black is treated by blacks with the respect given a *blanco*, yet they refer to him as "*moreno*, but rich.")
cholo[2] from the Coast = more yellowish skin, straight or slightly wavy hair	*negro* = poor black
moreno = brown skin	(Poor nonblacks are referred to as *serrano, cholo, blanco pobre*.)
negro = dark brown or black skin	

ORIGIN	ETHNIC
serrano = born in highlands (now used less)	*blanco* = white, polite, extravagant
costeño = born on Coast	*moreno* = straightforward, not presumptuous
manaba = born in province of Manabí	*costeño* = having regional accent of the Coast
	serrano = stingy, selfish, regardless of color, regional accent
	negro = fails to reciprocate at same class level

[1]Only for the purposes of this paper. Other cross-cutting category labels were used. See Schubert (1979).
[2]See note 13.

Space limits our ability to spell out the many ethnic divisions in this racial conflict. Briefly, it is a picture of white and black *serranos* (who are in conflict with one another; see, e.g., Klumpp 1970, Stutzman 1974) generally looking down on all *costeños*, with *costeños* usually hating (*tener rabia*) *serranos*, regardless of color. Light *costeños* pass part of their resentment on to dark *costeños* in terms of racial denigration. Responding to all this, coastal blacks insist that the entire set of their detractors is nothing but a mixed array of "less-than-whites," both physically and behaviorally. "Whites are more civilized than these colored ones" (*Blanco es más civilizado que estos de color*), they would say. I saw this as the reverse side of *blanqueamiento*, with the blacks turning the tables on *serranos* by using the highlanders' criteria for rating superiority to their own advantage.

In spite of such efforts among themselves to reverse the flow of

denigration, blacks in 1973 were keenly aware of the pervasive potential for insult whenever they dealt with anyone lighter than themselves. In my interviews with black informants I sought to determine
the depth of racist relations with nonblacks. These effects were difficult to determine; as strong as the possibility of insult might always
be, informants told me emphatically that they regarded the role of
race in their interactions as variable according to the personality of
each white *mestizo* with whom they dealt. If a lighter person did not
show respect for a darker person, even though they were of the same
socioeconomic status, race perception became important to the point
of overriding other considerations in structuring the relationship. On
the other hand, if there was mutual respect between two people,
black and white, of the same socioeconomic status, racial contrasts or
stereotypes were totally irrelevant, at least at the time. Later something might undermine that respect, and the racial boundary would
reappear. As one informant said, "The importance of color depends
on the behavior of each person." "Of course," she went on to say, "if
you're dealing with someone of your own color, at least you are sure
of mutual respect on that basis, regardless of what happens between
you" (*Por supuesto si es del mismo color no se puede insultar. En el color
hay respeto mutuo, sea como sea*).

When there is a lack of respect between whites and blacks, a complex and difficult question arises as to how different traits of the racist
stereotype are perceived to be relevant in explaining behavior. I cannot discuss this here, but in another study (Schubert 1979) I have
addressed myself to the details of that process. This is not to say that
other issues raised and examined in this paper are at all simple.
Blacks have not responded to *serrano* dominance (*blanqueamiento*) in a
single way; the range from capitulation to returned insults presents
many intermediate interactional and transactional intricacies. Even
within one person's evaluation, for instance, there is switching from
"It's good to be black" to "Lucky to marry white." Furthermore, in
the blacks' perception of whites, the scope has been extended from
simple *blanco* to *blanco, cholo, de color*. White Euro-American foreigners are the genuine *blancos* at one end of the scale, light *costeños* and
serranos at the other end, with *manabas* in the middle. It has been
possible merely to touch upon this involved picture.

What we see is a struggle for dominance that largely cuts across
any artificially contrived, simple black-white line. What may seem to
be a horizontal line is actually a slanting scale of color gradation. The
lighter-skinned person on that scale usually has the advantage in that
he can use insult more effectively. But the meaning of that insult for

the darker person varies as he pits one color against another to decide who is white enough to insult.

Whatever the complexities of the San Lorenzo scene that we might consider here or elsewhere, a single, underlying, ugly reality has come to infect the daily life of San Lorenzeños. Personal references in conversations seem almost invariably to begin with phenotypic designations. Moreover, within almost every black family there is widespread preoccupation with the possibility that the lighter color of a child's skin might hold the key to some eventual advantage.

As I listened for nearly two years to conversation after conversation saturated with this one theme, I couldn't help but think with regret of the apparent rapid deterioration of Afro-Hispanic culture in the area where its dynamic integration had been documented. But many blacks were looking ahead, not back. "Not for myself, perhaps, but for my child—or his child. Some day—maybe—we'll make it!"

CONCLUSION

On 24 August 1977 the First Congress of Black Culture in the Americas was held in Cali, Colombia. Although no one from San Lorenzo attended, spokesmen for the viable, if threatened, black culture of the Pacific lowlands from Esmeraldas, Ecuador, and from settings analogous to that of San Lorenzo in Tumaco and Buenaventura, Colombia, were there. Their voices joined with black spokesmen from Ibarra, Ecuador, and from the Cauca Valley, Chocó, and the Atlantic Littoral of Colombia to state forcefully the case for integrated black culture in numerous settings, on the one hand, and its fragmentation into intranational and international regions because of pervasive racism, on the other hand. Although themes in the congress varied widely (Organization of American States 1977), the Latin American black representatives were particularly oriented toward an appreciation of contemporary black cultures within their varied settings, and a condemnation of various forms of racism directed against black people or against manifestations of black culture in Latin American republics. Among the conclusions of the congress we find the following statement: "In Latin America racial discrimination is practiced in a manner that is deceitful, subtle, open or concealed" (*En la América Latina se practica la discriminación racial de manera solapada, sutil, abierta o encubierta;* Semanario Cultural 1977:12). The tendency in San Lorenzo, according to my observation in 1973, was for most racism to be expressed in less than open verbal confrontation in public, with such notable exceptions as the one involving the dog-

moreno reference. In most instances the *serrano* businessman would simply say in a curt and supercilious manner, "Take it or leave it!" without introducing a racial slur.

Even though racism in San Lorenzo is often subtle, it is nonetheless sufficiently pervasive to raise the question of the patterning of black identity and culture as a positive value in that area. The congress at Cali emphasized this in general terms: "Such discrimination uses different shades of skin color of the *negro* in order to effect the disappearance of the *negro* through the ideology of whitening as the search for the ideal person, in order to obtain better living conditions; and through this same mechanism, the political, economic, religious and family solidarity of black groups is destroyed" (*Semanario Cultural* 1977:12, my translation; cf. Jackson 1975).

In this paper I have attempted an analysis of the process by which *blanqueamiento* took hold progressively in San Lorenzo. Basic to this process was a sequence of developments in the political economy leading to *serrano* ascendancy and the enforcement of their ethnic presumptions. Many highlanders didn't have much when they came. "They came here with a sack of candies to sell," blacks would say, "and now they're rich. They came here to make themselves somebody" (*Llegaban aquí con un costal de caramelos y ahora estan ricos. Estos serranos venían para hacerse gente*).

As long as the Afro-Hispanic *minga* system was operating, *serranos* did only moderately well, but when workers came to be hired on a cash-wage basis, two changes took place in the socioeconomic system of the blacks. The extent of resources within the reach of the family network system was reduced, and, at the same time, the additional cash supply of the black workers was funneled more and more into *serrano* establishments. With this growth in income and with their more direct access to highland credit resources, the *serrano* businessmen soon outdistanced several of their *costeño* competitors.

It was in large part this economic success of the *serranos* that served as a springboard for strengthening their highland racist presumptions: (1) 1965–73: that blacks should respond to their covert incentive demand by conforming to the *serrano* lifestyle; (2) 1968–73: that white is better and black is ugly, lazy, inferior; (3) 1973: that (2) holds even though a black person conforms to *serrano* etiquette.

From their power position *serranos* now exert a white dominance over what was once a *costeño* village controlled by *morenos*. Over 50% of the highlanders had the freedom of option enjoyed by those in the middle and upper classes in the community. Black people's options are now more restricted, and freedom is reduced by powerlessness.

Their options in 1973 were: (1) insult *serranos* openly and retreat to the forest, maintaining autonomy at the bottom of the heap; (2) "stretch the face" and expose themselves all the more to the possibility of racial slurs; (3) marry white and possibly move up the socio-economic ladder, but compromise their ethnic identity through physical whitening.

Relief from these three unacceptable options emerged as children learned more skills in school. In the past blacks were often disqualified from jobs because of lack of skills. In 1973, for the first time ever, the possibility of their actively competing at higher economic levels on the basis of specific skills began to appear. With one less reason to push down blacks, *serranos* possibly will resort still more to color considerations in denigrating blackness or making employment decisions involving black people. Consequently, as younger blacks see education as an alternative way to move upward, as against marrying white, they will also discern how their competitiveness will probably bring out more explicit racism.

The future of most upwardly mobile blacks in San Lorenzo is clouded by the necessity of compromise, because of the offense of their being black. The lament of one woman continues to apply: "I can't help it that I have a black face" (*No es mi culpa que tengo cara negra*).

In the dominance battle which we have been highlighting in this study, blacks have had to struggle largely with verbal weapons, aired mostly among other blacks. Or they have chosen to work outside town in agricultural pursuits, in timber exploitation, or in mussel gathering. In either case their "weaponry" has not proven effective in this contention for dominance. Except for the progress of the better educated blacks and the indispensability of those engaged in the extraction of resources from the forest and swamp, they are losing the battle. It does not appear likely that hope will arise from within this paradoxical community. What hope might come from such outside sources as the Congress of Black Culture remains to be seen.

The social scientists mentioned earlier have analyzed similar dominance battles in other South American contexts. Kronus and Solaún (1973), relying largely on informant evaluation of random samples and their own analysis of visual data, have presented a structural interpretation of the relationship between modernization and non-conflictive racial adaptation in Cartagena, Colombia. Modernization and racism have not brought overt racial conflict to Cartagena or to San Lorenzo. However, the lack of open racial strife does not mean that there is not considerable hostility that is expressed in other ways, more readily apparent through data elicited through ethno-semantic techniques. A picture of a black woman and a lighter mate may represent visual data useful for certain purposes, but it doesn't clearly convey the possibility that the darker person might suffer a lifetime of swallowing racist denigration in order that her child might have the advantages of lighter skin. Adaptations of this kind, rather than pointing away from racism, can often demonstrate it in one of its most painful forms.

In seeking to determine the role of modernization in the expansion of racial barriers in San Lorenzo, it has been useful for me to compare what has happened there to developments in other areas. In his study of racism van den Berghe (1967) analyzed the racial situation in four countries, linking the dependent variable of race relations to independent variables characterizing economic and political infrastructure. These criteria include such structural factors as type of economy, division of labor, social stratification, and values. In the light of these elements he analyzed race relations in terms of two contrasting ideal types: paternalistic and competitive. Using this dichotomy, one might place each country on a continuum visualized from left to right, ranging from paternalistic to competitive. Brazil would be moving toward a more competitive position, characterized by more antagonistic, rather than benevolent, prejudice: in other words, toward the right.

Seeing San Lorenzo in the light of this typology of race relations, we might be inclined to place it to the left of Brazil on our "chart." Unlike Brazil (van den Berghe 1967:73–75), San Lorenzo has had little segregation in the customary sense. A casual view of the town reveals a black as *teniente político* in 1973, a black girl selected as queen of an all-community event, a black owning one of the most beautiful houses in the center of town. On the basis of these and similar observations, San Lorenzo might be moved leftward on our scale of racism, away from more aggressive forms of enactment of prejudice.

But the black view of whites forces us to move San Lorenzo slightly to the right of Brazil on our continuum. I say "slightly" because there are many parallels in the present racial situations in the two areas, the most outstanding of which is the emphasis on details of physical features. Yet a distinct contrast is seen in the application of color terms crossing class lines. In Brazil the importance of class outweighs that of color, moving in both directions on the socioeconomic ladder; in San Lorenzo, only upward. In both places a rich *negro* gets the treatment of a *blanco*. A Brazilian poor white is called *negro* (van den Berghe 1967:72). However, a San Lorenzo white remains white, even though poor.

This higher degree of racism in San Lorenzo can best be accounted for by recalling the later impact of the pre-existing categories in the national color-class hierarchy, a factor having little meaning in this isolated village before the coming of the railroad and even up to 1965. My purpose here has been to show that it was modernization, together with its resulting power in the hands of the *serranos*, that was the key to the successful invasion by this outside influence. It was not just the numbers of whites. Had they continued to be ambulant candy sellers, the story would have been very different. My black friends would say of *serranos*, "When they used to be out selling in the streets (after a rain), they'd sometimes fall—they didn't know how to walk in the mud!"

Some of those same people falling in the mud in the early 1960s were rich and presumptuous a decade later, yet there is no doubt that had they remained nothing but street sellers, in whatever numbers, *serranos* would not have come to express racism as they did in 1973. They would have had no platform from which to project the idea of blackness as being offensive.

That platform was provided by a change in the composition and balance of elements in the economic and social organization of the community. It is as though the construction of that elevated structure, like that of the railroad, began in the highlands, following the cuts in the mountains and requiring years to build. In time it was ready to convey, like a chute, what it also symbolized: the "gospel of civilization," that white is better and black is an offense. A crucial question for the future of San Lorenzo's blacks is, "How long will that platform last? When the lumber that built it gives out, will it begin to disintegrate, the way the railroad is already doing?"

NOTES

Acknowledgments: Fieldwork on which this paper is based was carried out during 1972–74. Financial support for the research was provided by a predoctoral fellowship from the National Institute of Mental Health (MH–546667–01) (CUAN) for which I am grateful. I wish to thank Arq. Hernán Crespo Toral, director of the Instituto Nacional de Antropología e Historia, in Quito, for initially allowing me to carry out my research and for encouraging me throughout the project. I am further indebted to the Ministry of Foreign Relations, the commander of the naval base at San Lorenzo, as well as to the *teniente político* and local government authorities for their permission and help. To the people of San Lorenzo who patiently explained aspects of their way of life to me, I owe a debt of gratitude. Their cooperation greatly facilitated the gathering of my data.

I thank Norman E. Whitten, Jr., for his insightful comments. Other valuable suggestions were made by Louisa R. Stark, A. W. Southall, and Arnold Strickon, to whom I am also grateful. Responsibility for the paper, including interpretations of Whitten's published and unpublished material as presented here, is strictly mine.

1. "Network broker" is an intermediary who has knowledge of the need of both outside businessmen and local workers and represents them to each other in the making of business contracts (Whitten 1974:163–66). *Minga* is a collective work system.

2. For the purpose of this paper I shall use *serrano* or "highlander" to indicate a white or *mestizo* highlander and "black" to designate a coastal black. See Schubert (1979) for a more complete discussion of most of the racial and ethnic terms current in San Lorenzo in 1973.

3. Even though the boom did not bust, some blacks did not give up their subsistence activities completely. They found that at certain times of the year they could earn more money by returning, if only temporarily, to their subsistence way of life (Whitten 1974:77).

4. Upper class in 1965 in San Lorenzo included professionals such as doctors and sawmill owners with incomes ranging from 5,000 to 3,500 sucres. Middle class included teachers, technicians, and businessmen having incomes of more than 1,000 sucres per month (Whitten 1965:47, 55).

5. Several highlanders who sold perishable goods were black *serranos* whom I discuss in Schubert (1979).

6. According to *El Comercio* (9 July 1974:9; 8 Sept. 1974:13) the railroad was out of commission for two months!

7. When an informant said, "San Lorenzo will progress when the ties of the railroad deteriorate and a highway is built," it made some sense to me, given the facility's checkered history. He continued, "That will bring us more sources of work." This man was one of many who favored the building of highways from Ibarra and from Esmeraldas to San Lorenzo. It was his strong conviction that only with the deterioration of the railroad might the completion of the highways be forced.

As of Dec. 1977, according to personal communication with informants, the road from Ibarra was built as far as Lita (cf. *El Comercio* 21 June 1974:11) and from Esmeraldas as far as Borbón.

8. A special company ship supplies the factory community with most of its needs and takes away its products.

9. I shall be focusing on this topic in forthcoming papers.

10. Subhumanness, *infrahumano*, is a term I heard several times, used by *serranos* to describe blacks. Whitten (1974) also reports such usage.

11. The term *blanco* is often used interchangeably with *serrano* to refer to upper- and middle-class *serranos*, especially when highlanders are present, since the term *blanco* is what *serranos* prefer. In all-black settings I heard *serrano* used most of the time.

12. A trait that blacks perceive to be reflected in *serrano* speech.

13. I must limit myself largely to the more specific features associated with these labels in everyday behavioral references. These same labels may be used to express other connotations when used at a more general level of contrast. For example, in this paper *cholo* is contrasted to *blanco*. Yet at a more general level a speaker may consider *cholo* as a subtype of *blanco*. See Schubert (1979).

REFERENCES CITED

Blalock, Hubert M.
	1967	*Toward a Theory of Minority-Group Relations.* New York: Wiley.
Bruner, Edward M.
	1974	The Expression of Ethnicity in Indonesia. In Abner Cohen, ed., *Urban Ethnicity.* London: Tavistock, pp. 251–80.
El Comercio (Quito)
	1974	Autoridades Inspeccionaron la Vía a Lita. 21 June:11.
	1974	Arrasados un Puente y Parte de Línea Férrea de Ibarra a San Lorenzo. 9 July:9.
	1974	Este Mes se Reanuda el Tránsito Normal en la Vía Férrea Ibarra–San Lorenzo. 8 Sept.:13.
Ferdon, Edwin N., Jr.
	1950	*Studies in Ecuadorian Geography.* Monographs of the School of American Research 15. Santa Fe, N.Mex.: School of American Research and the University of Southern California.
Friedemann, Nina S. de
	1974	Review of *Black Frontiersmen: A South American Case,* by Norman E. Whitten, Jr. *Revista Colombiana de Antropología* 17:261–63.
Jackson, Richard L.
	1975	"Mestizaje" vs. Black Identity: The Color Crisis in Latin America. *Black World* 24:4–21.
Klumpp, Kathleen
	1970	Black Traders of North Highland Ecuador. In Norman E. Whitten, Jr., and John F. Szwed, eds., *Afro-American Anthropology: Contemporary Perspectives.* New York: Free Press, pp. 245–62.
Kronus, Sidney, and Mauricio Solaún
	1973	Racial Adaptation in the Modernization of Cartagena, Colombia. In Robert E. Scott, ed., *Latin American Modernization Problems.* Urbana: University of Illinois Press, pp. 87–117.
Onofa, Luis
	1973	San Lorenzo: Un Sueño Convertido en Pesadilla. *El Tiempo* (Quito), 21 Dec.:12.
Organization of American States
	1977	*Primer Congreso de la Cultura Negra de las Américas.* Bogotá: Centro de Estudios Afro-Colombianos.
Poggie, John J., Jr., and Robert N. Lynch, eds.
	1974	*Rethinking Modernization: Anthropological Perspectives.* Westport, Conn.: Greenwood Press.
Schubert, Grace
	1979	"That's the Way It Is Here": An Ethnoscientific Approach to Racial Identity in San Lorenzo, Ecuador. Ph.D. thesis, University of Wisconsin, Madison.
Semanario Cultural
	1977	Primer Congreso de la Cultural Negra de las Americas. *Semanario Cultural: La Revista de el Pueblo* 70 (11 Sept.).
Stutzman, Ronald
	1974	Black Highlanders: Racism and Ethnic Stratification in the Ecuadorian Sierra. Ann Arbor, Mich.: University Microfilms. Ph.D. thesis, Washington University, St. Louis.

van den Berghe, Pierre L.
  1967   *Race and Racism: A Comparative Perspective.* New York: Wiley.
Whitten, Norman E., Jr.
  1965   *Class, Kinship, and Power in an Ecuadorian Town: The Negroes of San Lorenzo.* Stanford, Calif.: Stanford University Press.
  1968   Personal Networks and Musical Contexts in the Pacific Lowlands of Colombia and Ecuador. *Man: Journal of the Royal Anthropological Institute* 3:50–63.
  1969   Strategies of Adaptive Mobility in the Colombian-Ecuadorian Littoral. *American Anthropologist* 71:228–42.
  1970   Ecología de las Relaciones Raciales al Noroeste del Ecuador. *América Indígena* 30 (2):345–58.
  1974   *Black Frontiersmen: A South American Case.* New York: Wiley.
  1977   Brief Report for Afro-American Studies Program. Unpublished manuscript.
Whitten, Norman E., Jr., and Nina S. de Friedemann
  1974   La Cultura Negra del Litoral Ecuatoriano y Colombiano: Un Modelo de Adaptación Étnica. *Revista Colombiana de Antropología* (Bogotá) 17:75–115.
Zaldumbide, César
  1974   . . . No Nos Dejes Caer en Tentación, ni Permitas que Vivamos en San Lorenzo. *El Tiempo* (Quito), 2 Feb.:7, 17.

PART IV:
CULTURAL TRANSFORMATION,
ETHNICITY, AND ADAPTATION
IN THE ORIENTE

21

The Federación Shuar and the Colonization Frontier

Ernesto Salazar

This paper is intended to contribute to the understanding of the interethnic contact that has come about as a result of government-sponsored projects of colonization in the southern lowlands of Ecuador. The information gathered so far indicates that the Shuar Indians ("Frontier Jívaro" and "Interior Jívaro"; Harner 1972) are very concerned about the ever-growing colonization that is seriously threatening the existence of their culture. The Shuar offered relatively successful resistance to white penetration in the past, but since the beginning of the present century they have undergone strong acculturation through missionaries and colonists.

Confronted with a future that may bring only marginal integration into the national society, the Shuar have adopted new strategies to counteract the advance of the colonization frontier. These strategies have found their best expression in the establishment of the Shuar Federation (Federación de Centros Shuaras), which has been functioning since 1964. This organization represents a rather unexpected move on the part of the Shuar, considering the independence, individualism, egalitarianism, and even hostility among groups that have characterized Shuar social structure. In any case, the federation has shown that the Shuar are capable of great achievements, despite the discrimination with which they are faced in contemporary Ecuador.

The purpose of this paper is to describe the framework of the Federación Shuar and to analyze its meaning in the context of colonization in lowland Ecuador. Particular attention will be given to the factors involved in its formation, as well as to the possible explanation for the adoption of an administrative system that clearly differs from the traditional social organization of the Shuar.

THE COLONIZATION FRONTIER IN SHUAR TERRITORY

The Shuar, known ethnographically as the "Jívaro," live in the provinces of Morona Santiago and Zamora Chinchipe, in a roughly triangular territory delimited by the Pastaza River, the Andean cordillera, and the Ecuadorian-Peruvian boundary. According to Harner (1972) two "tribes" occupy this territory: the Untsuri Shuar, who live in the Upano and Zamora river valleys and part of the forest beyond Cordillera de Cutucú; and the Achuara Shuar, who inhabit the easternmost corner of Shuar territory, roughly east of the Pangui River, and across the border into Peru. Although, theoretically, the term "Shuar" refers to both Jivaroan tribes, in practice it is only applied to the Untsuri group or "Jívaro proper" (see Harner 1972 for ethnography of the Jívaro proper, Whitten 1976, 1978, for a different perspective with regard to the Achuara). The Upano Valley frontier group of Untsuri Shuara officially introduced the term on the occasion of the establishment of the federation. I will use the word "Shuar" in this restricted sense for the remainder of this paper. The term itself means "people"; the term "Jívaro" has clearly derogatory connotations in Ecuador, and the term "Shuar" is replacing it throughout the nation.

In order to understand the present situation of the Shuar vis-à-vis the colonist population, it is necessary to outline some developments that have taken place during the twentieth century in the southern lowlands of Ecuador. The major events directly affecting Shuar society are the permanent establishment of missionary orders, particularly Salesians and Franciscans, and the formation of a frontier system in Shuar territory.

The Salesian order came to Ecuador at the end of the nineteenth century and vigorously expanded its activities throughout the southern lowlands, establishing basic facilities such as schools, mission centers, and churches for colonists and Shuar alike. At the present time the Salesians maintain 13 mission centers, some of which (e.g., at Sucúa, Méndez, and Macas) have attracted relatively large populations of colonists during the twentieth century, thus becoming towns in their own right. Furthermore, this religious order has been entrusted with the administration of high schools, technical schools, and hospitals that the Ecuadorian government has established in the colonization frontier to provide assistance to both colonists and the native population. As a result of these activities, the Salesian order has gradually gained political power to the extent that it is, at present, the most influential institution in this area of the Oriente.

From the point of view of the Shuar, it can be said that the activities of the Salesian mission have been characterized by a paternalistic attitude and the negation of Shuar cultural values. The missionaries became convinced that, without their help, there could be no salvation for the Shuar because, as Father Barrueco (1968:44) put it, "the Indian mind suffers from a lack of foresight, character and decision to face problems . . . " (my translation).

In general terms, two strategies have dominated the expansion and success of the Salesian mission in Shuar territory. The first is the removal of Shuar children from their families to boarding schools under direct control of the missionaries. The second is the concentration of the sparse population in villages or hamlets, generally located near the mission center. These strategies are by no means a Salesian innovation but, rather, the standard procedure of missionaries to achieve effective control over the native population.

The Salesians' rationale for the establishment of boarding schools was the supposedly "low moral level" that they saw in Shuar families, which made the separation of children from their parents not only desirable but necessary (Barrueco 1968:42). In the boarding school Shuar children (boys and girls) grew up in a communal atmosphere, learning the values of the Catholic religion and western civilization. The acculturation process was long and intensive, for children did not leave the boarding school until they were old enough to choose a partner for marriage, who was usually a schoolmate. This type of marriage was often encouraged by the missionaries, who sometimes overlooked the fact that Shuar society prescribes cross-cousin marriage (Federación Shuar 1976:169). In any case, the married couple was acculturated enough so as to desire a permanent home near the mission center. Statistics for the late 1960s show that the Salesian mission was supporting 20 boarding schools with a total of 1,880 Shuar children (Barrueco 1968:57). Recently, however, the importance of these schools has decreased with the establishment of the federation, as I explain later.

A small group of approximately 3,000 Shuar living in the upper Zamora River valley is under the influence of the Franciscan missionaries. The so-called Vicariat of Zamora, given to the Franciscan order at the end of the nineteenth century, has been somewhat less successful than the Salesian Vicariat of Méndez. Driven out several times by the upper Zamora Shuar, the Franciscans could not establish themselves permanently until the early 1950s. Their strategies for the acculturation of the Shuar are similar to those adopted by the Salesians. The Ecuadorian government also finances several facilities, such as schools and hospitals, which are under the control of the

Franciscan mission. Presently, this religious order maintains 11 mission centers in the Zamora River valley, as well as five boarding schools sheltering about 250 children.

Generally speaking, recruitment of children for boarding schools was the hardest problem for both Salesian and Franciscan missionaries. Until a few years ago, at least in the case of the Franciscan mission, the usual procedure was kidnapping, an activity that often generated angry reactions from Shuar families. Also, as could be expected, kidnapped children were not always able to cope with this forced situation, and frequently fled the boarding school. Eventually, as acculturation intensified, boarding school children and even Shuar parents started bringing their little friends and relatives to the mission, thus obviating the problem of recruitment and actually facilitating rapid acculturation. Missionaries now claim that they have too many applicants, and admission to boarding schools has had to become selective.

Galarza Zavala (1973) has reported that the living conditions of the upper Zamora Shuar are more precarious than those of the Shuar controlled by the Salesians. In fact, it appears that the exploitation of the Shuar by the Franciscans has generated deep resentment in the native population toward the missionaries. This is somewhat less apparent among the Shuar of the Vicariat of Méndez, who hold the Salesians in rather high esteem. In any case, a fact that cannot be overlooked is that the religious mission in general has degenerated from a Christian religious enterprise into a Christian economic one. Both Salesian and Franciscan orders exploit for their own profit Shuar land entrusted to them by the Ecuadorian government as Shuar reserves. This land is worked gratis by young Shuar, and even children from the boarding schools, in exchange for education and shelter. Although the government supports the missionary orders that operate in the lowlands, there seems to be little control over expenditures. As a consequence, missions grow economically strong with state funds and Indian labor.

Besides Catholic missionary orders, there are other Christian missions working among the Shuar, although the number of adepts is not as large as those belonging to Catholic missions. The most important of these new institutions is the Gospel Missionary Union (GMU), with headquarters located in Macuma and serving about 5,000 Shuar. According to federation sources (Federación Shuar 1976:109), GMU missionaries have approached the cultural changes of the Shuar with greater anthropological concern than have other missionary orders, although certain restrictions imposed on them for religious reasons (prohibition on drinking *chicha*) have alienated the Shuar population.

Another major event that is directly responsible for the present situation of the Shuar is the wave of colonists that has invariably followed the missionary advance. Highlanders have been pouring into the lowlands since the beginning of the twentieth century, although the bulk of migration has been more apparent in the last 25 years because of governmental encouragement and propaganda. The area of colonization has been mostly confined to the strip between the eastern Andes and the fluvial network composed of the Upano, Namangoza, and Zamora rivers. However, colonists are gradually occupying the forest beyond the Sierra de Cutucú, which a few years ago was still considered a barrier to white penetration (see Harner 1972). The official involvement of the Ecuadorian government in the colonization of the southern lowlands started in the early 1960s through the establishment of the Centro de Reconversión Económica del Azuay, Cañar y Morona Santiago (CREA), a highland institution with its central office in the city of Cuenca. CREA is at present managing three projects of "semi-directed" colonization in Shuar territory, resettling hundreds of highland families in the lowlands.

It is apparent that the ever-increasing advance of the colonization frontier has become a serious threat to the interests of the Shuar population. Furthermore, the invasion of Indian lands, coupled with CREA's open bias toward the colonists, is gradually reducing their vital space. However, the Shuar are reluctant to become landless peasants; to protect their rights, they have formed a federation which, if successful, will eventually allow them to keep their land and their culture.

STRUCTURE OF THE SHUAR FEDERATION

The emergence of the Shuar Federation cannot be fully understood without considering the role played by the Salesian mission. It should be stated from the outset that this mission planned and carried out the establishment of the federation to counteract the continuous advance of colonization. The reasons for such a move on the part of the missionaries seem to be of an economic and religious nature. Galarza Zavala (1973:35) points out that colonization generated hostility between the colonists and the Shuar which could have led to the Indians' extermination or their retreat into the forest. This situation threatened the mission: in either case, it would have been deprived of converts and labor for mission lands. As a result, the missionaries sided with the Shuar against the colonists, who, in turn, often accused the Salesian fathers of obstructing the progress of the country by preventing them from penetrating Shuar reservations. The federation emerged as the culmination of a series of attempts on the part of the missionaries to protect the Shuar from the colonists.

The reaction on the colonization frontier to the establishment of the federation was, as could be expected, negative and even violent. As a result, the Salesian mission lost influence among a number of colonists, who, incidentally, have been accused of setting the fire that burned down one of the mission buildings in Sucúa in 1969 (Federación Shuar 1976:246). Under the circumstances the mission has opted to deny its participation in the establishment of the federation.

A factor which may have favored the creation of the Shuar organization is the change presently affecting the structure of missionary work. Young missionaries realized that the prevailing framework of the indoctrination process is ethnocentric, and essentially traumatic to the native population. The Second National Congress of Missions held in Quito in 1973 was openly critical of the traditional methods of evangelization, and stressed the need for a policy aimed at the safeguard of aboriginal cultures (Congreso Nacional 1973). Indeed, it appears that the mission has arrived at a turning point where the perpetuation of archaic schemes would be self-destructive. Consequently, a "new mission" has emerged which advocates that the Christian religion must adapt to the cultural values of the native population. Along this line, it could be said that the nativistic movement presently taking shape among the Shuar may be related, to some extent, to this new attitude on the part of the missionaries.

The first move toward unification started in the early 1960s in the town of Sucúa, apparently under Salesian auspices. Shuar families living around Sucúa decided to join efforts by establishing small administrative units called *centros*. These *centros* were largely autonomous, and the need to coordinate their activities led to the creation of the so-called Asociación de Sucúa, which was officially recognized by the government in 1962. At the same time informative meetings were held in other Shuar communities, and eventually new *centros* and *asociaciones* were established throughout Shuar territory. The success of this movement brought about the need for the formation of a higher-level administrative unit to control and coordinate the activities of all Shuar *asociaciones*. Thus the federation was born.

The Shuar Federation was established in January 1964 as an autonomous organization for the social, economic, and moral improvement of its members, and as a coordinating institution for colonization projects undertaken by the government (Federación Shuar 1974:3). In October of the same year the government approved the federation statutes and gave the Shuar organization official recognition.

The basic administrative unit of the federation is the *centro*, which is constituted by those individuals who have either signed its constitution act or applied subsequently for membership. An average *centro* is composed of 25–30 families, most of them related by marriage alliances. The first step in the establishment of a *centro* is to seek legal recognition from the Ministerio de Trabajo y Bienestar Social to allow it to function within Ecuadorian law. Only with official recognition can the *centro* be granted a territory of variable size, according to the number of families it includes. These features show that the Shuar *centro* represents a radical change from the traditional concept of Shuar community as defined by Harner (1972:77): "The interior Jívaro [Shuar] 'community' is a neighborhood of widely distributed households in which membership is not formally or usually very clearly defined and in which the abundance of land is accompanied by an absence of definitions or claims of territoriality." In any case, a link to the traditional neighborhood concept is still apparent in the distribution of households within a Shuar *centro*. A *centro* does not constitute a village, for its population is scattered following the characteristic settlement pattern of the Shuar. However, the structure of the *centro* seems to be designed for the specific purpose of giving the Shuar more of a sense of community than the neighborhood does. In the first place all *centros* have a square plaza with some structures built around it, namely the school, the chapel, the health center (actually a first-aid post), the teacher's house, and a few nearby houses that may be inhabited permanently by Shuar families. These features replicate, in incipient form, colonists' nucleated settlements (see, e.g., Whitten 1976).

In the second place each *centro* is managed by a council elected every two years by a general assembly composed of all the members of the *centro*. The maximum authority is the *síndico*, who works closely with the council in programs of social and economic development. In his position as leader of the community, the *síndico* has to be aware of the problems and needs of his *centro*, and to see that they are periodically reported to the Salesian mission center and higher officials of the federation. In order to stress the contrast with the traditional neighborhood, as well as the change operating in the Shuar concept of community, I would define a *centro* in the following terms: a political and administrative unit with a delimited territory, composed of a population with formally defined membership, and established under the authority of an elected council for the socioeconomic development of its members.

Since by its nature the *centro* is designed to meet the needs of the members only, there seems to be an implicit risk of isolationism which is counter to the aims of the federation. Consequently, to coordinate activities and to favor cooperation among the Shuar, all *centros* have been clustered into geographically wider administrative units called *asociaciones*. The number of *centros* grouped into one *asociación* varies from two to 15, with an average of eight *centros* per *asociación*. This latter unit is directed by a president, who usually lives in one of the mission centers located in his jurisdiction. The function of the president is primarily to see that the rules and policies issued by the federation are met by the *centros* under his authority.

Topping the hierarchy of administrative units is the *federación*, which coordinates the work of all *asociaciones* in Shuar territory. The legislative organism of the federation is the *asamblea general*, general assembly, consisting of three delegates for each *asociación*, plus one delegate for every *centro*. The assembly meets once a year in Sucúa to review the activities of the preceding year and set policies for the coming year. The management of the federation is a responsibility of the board of directors, which consists of eight members including the president and the vice-president of the federation, all of whom are elected for a two-year period. In order to ensure efficiency in the managing process, each member is assigned a particular task, such as colonization, health, education, or public relations. Matters of local nature that do not affect the federation as a whole may be resolved within the *asociación* by its president or within the *centro* by its *síndico*. Otherwise, all activities are managed from, or take place in, Sucúa, where the federation owns a modern building equipped with a radio station, a small library, and auditoriums for meetings and other social events.

The construction of this building was carried out by Italian volunteers and Shuar groups from Sucúa with 120,000 sucres of financial assistance from the government and a small token contribution of 1,000 sucres from the Salesian order. Ironically, the Salesian mission sold the land for the federation building to the Shuar for 40,000 sucres. This piece of land, along with others, was entrusted by the government to the Salesians in the name of the Shuar (Federación Shuar 1976:161).

At present, the Shuar Federation has 26,800 members distributed in 14 *asociaciones* and 138 *centros*, of which 118 are legally federated.

Most members belonging are Untsuri Shuar, including those living under the influence of the Franciscan mission. It is interesting to note that some groups of Achuara, traditional enemies of the Untsuri Shuar, have recently joined the federation. There is currently one Achuara *asociación* composed of two *centros*, and it is expected that more Achuara will join the federation in the near future.

The activities of the federation are financed through nonrefundable contributions from several institutions and Christian organizations, both Ecuadorian and foreign. According to federation sources, contributing institutions belong mostly to European countries, namely Holland (one), Germany (three), Switzerland (one), the Vatican (one), and Italy (one). In Ecuador financing has been channeled through the Ministries of Education, Health, and Industries (Federación Shuar 1976:128). A special area of federation financing deals with cattle development, carried out by virtue of contributions and loans from European, U.S., Ecuadorian, and international organizations.

There is, in Ecuador, some envious criticism from colonists and other indigenous organizations regarding the foreign aid received by the federation, but the Shuar claim that Ecuadorian banks are reluctant to extend credit to their organization. CREA, for example, is reported to extend credit to nonfederated Shuar for amounts greater than the federation can offer. The Banco Nacional de Fomento favors credit to individuals, but many Shuar are not eligible for loans owing to the lack of individual property titles. On the other hand, the same bank will not extend credit to a Shuar *centro*, *asociación*, or even the federation as a corporate group because it precludes, as a policy, loans to "federations" (Federación Shuar 1976:103). A small amount of money comes from the Shuar themselves; membership dues totaled 42,390 sucres in 1975, and salaried officials contribute 5% of their monthly wage to the treasury of the federation.

The Salesian mission never participates officially in federation activities, but its influence on the Shuar organization is strong. As a case in point, the mission has ruled that all administrative units must have "religious and moral counselors," usually missionaries or Shuar individuals with close ties to the mission. Similarly, *síndicos* are generally ex-pupils of the Salesian boarding schools. The trend is to put acculturated Indians in key posts within the *centros*. Arnalot (1978:43) points out that Shuar communities often elect mission-educated individuals as their authorities, at times only because they speak Spanish.

The general religious counselor and founder of the federation is the Salesian missionary Father Juan Shutka, whose time is almost completely devoted to the federation. Father Shutka maintains an office in the federation building, and the Shuar show a great deal of respect for him. It is apparent that his activities are not restricted to religious counseling alone. In fact, he seems to participate actively in the decision-making process of the Shuar organization. Indeed, Father Shutka can be considered the strong man of the federation, although lately his influence seems to have eroded. He does not keep daily office hours any longer, and there have even been attempts by Shuar individuals to oust him from the federation.

THE SHUAR FEDERATION AT WORK

The 14-year-old federation has been unusually successful in the struggle for Indian liberation in lowland Ecuador. Contrary to Father Barrueco's opinion, the Shuar have proved that they do have insight into the future as well as determination to survive the white nationalist and foreign invasion.

One of the first goals of the federation was to establish legal possession of the land, a crucial issue in terms of Shuar survival. Property rights in colonization lands are granted by the Instituto Ecuatoriano de Reforma Agraria y Colonización (IERAC), which is the official conveyor of land ownership according to Ecuadorian law.

At the federation's request, IERAC started working on legalization of Shuar property in the late 1960s. Titles were given to each individual nuclear family, making the whole operation extremely lengthy and cumbersome, since IERAC had to map family plots one by one. This situation prompted the federation to suggest that property titles be granted "globally" to each Shuar *centro*. It can be seen that this modification has a two-fold advantage for the Shuar: it speeds up the legalization of property, and it allows the *centro* to redistribute the land to federation families according to their size and needs. Furthermore, it offers fewer risks in terms of losing land to the colonists. In fact, under the old procedure the plots of Shuar land actually belonged not to the federation but to the family head who obtained the property title. As a result, this individual, as the legal owner of the land, could resell it to anyone. Needless to say, prospective buyers were likely to be colonists. However, under the global procedure a Shuar family receives a plot of land for its own use and can hold it indefinitely, but its sale is strictly forbidden without specific approval by the federation. In the event that a Shuar family wishes to relocate, the federation will take the necessary measures to provide them with a plot of land in a new location and to protect former land from colonist incursion.

IERAC has agreed to the Shuar request regarding the new procedure for the legalization of property, but the task is far from complete. Property titles have been granted so far to only 35 Shuar *centros* (Federación Shuar 1976:125), which means that most *centros* do not hold legal property. The amount of land granted to a *centro* depends largely upon the number of families affiliated and varies according to geographic location. A plot of land for a Shuar family may range between 30 and 70 hectares in size.

Another important concern of the federation has been the education of its members. The Shuar have strongly questioned the government educational system aimed at imposing on lowland Indians the values of western civilization (*Chicham*, May 1974). Consequently, the federation has undertaken the establishment of a school that would emphasize the revival of Shuar culture. To accomplish this goal, it has adopted a system of radio schools, *escuelas radiofónicas*, which broadcast educational programs. The Shuar radio school is designed to satisfy the educational needs of the whole population, providing instruction not only for elementary school children but for adults as well, since 34% of the Shuar population is still not literate (Federación Shuar 1976:72).

In 1972 the first Shuar radio station (HCSK or, as they call it, "Radio Federación") was inaugurated at the federation building in Sucúa. HCSK has several channels and is on the air 16 hours a day. Literacy courses are broadcast in the afternoon three days a week, while elementary school instruction is broadcast every day from 8:00 A.M. to 1:00 P.M. It is worth noting that HCSK is totally managed by Shuar personnel. The radio school is run by a permanent staff of ten Shuar teachers, *telemaestros*, who prepare and tape the lessons which are later delivered to the radio station for broadcasting. All Shuar *centros* are also provided with a teaching assistant, *teleauxiliar*, who plays the role of intermediary between the radio set and the children (or adults in the case of literacy courses). Teaching is done alternately in Shuar and Spanish.

Radio school teachers are required to have a high school diploma, while assistants need only to attend one of the training courses offered every summer at the federation building. Both teachers and assistants are paid employees, teachers receiving their salaries from the government and assistants from the federation (70 out of 214 assistants are now paid by the government). Recent statistics indicate that the federation maintains 138 radio schools serving approximately 3,500 children (Sainaghi 1976:86). The radio school system began in 1972 with instruction at the first-grade level, and has gradually increased its activities to include at present all six grades of Ecuadorian elementary school. The federation now plans to broadcast high school education.

Elementary education is mandatory among the Shuar. Parents who are reluctant to send their children to school are subject to a four-day confinement in jail, according to the statutes of the federation. Usually this matter is resolved between the assistant and the child's parents or by the president of the *centro*'s PTA.

The teaching staff has prepared textbooks especially designed for Shuar children attending the radio school, although instruction in upper grades follows the standard textbooks used in the rest of the country. The teaching process is supervised by both government and Shuar officials. Finally, the federation has a Shuar coordinator who holds regular meetings with teachers and assistants to solve problems and discuss improvements that could benefit the radio school.

An overall assessment of the radio school indicates that, so far, it represents the answer to the educational problem of the Shuar. The advantages of the radio school can be appreciated by a consideration of several features, some of them already outlined by the Shuar in a letter to the Minister of Education (*Chicham*, May 1974). By far the most important feature is that the radio school represents a Shuar effort to serve the Shuar. The spirit of cooperation that presently transcends the boundaries of households and neighborhoods is perhaps one of the greatest achievements of the federation. Furthermore, the radio school establishes uniformity and standardization in teaching, thus allowing Shuar children to transfer from one *centro* to another without noticeable detriment in terms of their educational progress. The Shuar school also has the advantage of being able to establish its own schedule according to the daily activities of the Shuar household. Unlike the missionary school, the Shuar radio school prevents long-term separation of parents and children. The establishment of a school in each *centro* has made education more accessible to Shuar children, who otherwise would have to travel long distances in order to attend the missionary schools. The Shuar radio school provides an introduction to Ecuadorian and international affairs, thereby preparing listeners to some extent for abrupt encounters with western civilization. The Shuar school is relatively inexpensive; according to Father Shutka, a Shuar child attending the radio school costs the government half the expense of his counterpart attending public schools elsewhere in the country.

The federation has seen that the radio schools teach in the Shuar language, and introduce Spanish gradually. There are also several subjects that the federation's Commission of Education has suggested be included in the Shuar educational programs, such as Shuar culture and mythology, Shuar grammar, comparative study of Spanish, and botanical and zoological subjects aimed at giving the child an accurate view of the tropical environment (Mashinkiash' 1976:79), which is rapidly being converted into cattle pasture.

The educational concern of the federation is not restricted to the radio school alone. It has also established a program of financial assistance for young Shuar willing to pursue their education in any large city of Ecuador. So far, the Commission of Education has financed, by means of a loan system, 140 high school students and 15 college students (Federación Shuar 1976:126). At the present time there are 46 Shuar holding high school diplomas and two holding university degrees.

The official publication of the federation is a bilingual Shuar-Spanish newspaper called *Chicham*, "Message," which appears irregularly. *Chicham* is devoted to accounts of the activities of the federation, as well as general information on such varied subjects as acculturation, government policies, and the situation of Indian groups in Ecuador and South America as a whole. The Shuar have already established contact with native American movements throughout the American continent. Furthermore, the federation has sponsored about 30 publications of different kinds, including scientific subjects (technology, social structure, and mythology of the Shuar), school books (literacy booklets and school texts), and religious works (prayer books, gospel translations). Particular attention must be drawn to the publication of the Mundo Shuar booklets, which represents the greatest effort so far to diffuse Shuar culture in printed form. The collection includes seven series of publications, each series covering a broad aspect of Shuar culture (e.g. ethnohistory, technology, linguistics). Authors include missionaries, white teachers, and Shuar intellectuals who contribute to the recently established Center for Documentation and Research on Shuar Culture. The collection as a whole is printed at the Salesian Publishing House in Quito, and is also directed by a Salesian priest, Father Juan Botasso. Mundo Shuar thus appears as a Salesian effort to rescue what is left of a rich culture that almost disintegrated as a result of more than half a century of Salesian administration of the Shuar people. The works so far published show, as could be expected, a varying degree of scholarship, but on the whole Mundo Shuar has been well accepted in the country, and promises to be an indispensable research tool for anthropologists interested in Shuar culture.

Turning from the subject of education, let us now consider the economic situation of the Shuar under the federation. In this regard, a major change has occurred with the shift from a subsistence to a market economy focused primarily on cattle raising, which is at present the only major source of income for indigenous people in the Amazonian lowlands of Ecuador. The management of the cattle industry is carried out by "development groups" which have been established in several Shuar *centros*. A cattle development group consists of at least 12 members of a particular *centro*. According to current regulations, these individuals have to work three days a week in cattle-raising activities. Acquisition of cattle is carried out through credit extended by the federation, which also provides technical assistance in veterinary medicine and agronomy, as well as related activities such as importation of prize cattle and artificial insemination. Profit is distributed among associates according to a system devised by the federation. Shuar officials have been encouraging the formation of cattle development groups, and the response has been favorable (in 1974 there were 40 development groups, but by 1976 there were 72). Recent statistics indicate that the federation has extended credit for a total of 7,437,200 sucres, which has been used for the purchase of 2,286 head of cattle (Knoblauch 1976:282). Reproduction has raised this figure to 3,394, which means a considerable profit for the *centros* involved in this program. The latter figure does not represent, of course, the total number of cattle in Shuar territory, for many Shuar have made individual acquisitions. Economic information for 1974 indicated, for instance, the existence of 7,672 head of cattle owned individually (*Chicham*, December 1974). It should be pointed out that the federation has started a program of marketing meat in Sucúa and Cuenca, thus making the cattle industry a promising economic activity, despite transportation problems and a shortage of technicians.

The high priority given by the federation to the cattle industry has resulted in socioeconomic advantages for the Shuar. Knoblauch (1976:267) points out that profit generated by cattle development groups has enabled many *centros* to allocate funds for improvement projects such as schools, airstrips, and potable water. At the same time the cattle industry has given the Shuar a sense of economic security and pride in their own achievements. Finally, through cattle raising the Shuar have found a way to prevent the government from expropriating their land. It is an IERAC policy that adjudicated land can be reclaimed if it fails to produce in a period of five years after its concession. By cultivating pastures the Shuar are able to keep their land.

The last, but not the least, concern of the federation is in the area of health. Kroeger and Ileckova (1976) report that the major problems affecting the Shuar population are a high infant mortality rate (14.5% in 1971) and malnutrition, particularly owing to low consumption of basic foods such as eggs, milk, and meat. Typically fatal diseases in Shuar children are measles, bronchitis, and parasite-induced diarrhea. Among adults, tuberculosis is becoming increasingly frequent as the colonization frontier advances further into Shuar territory. The federation maintains that government attention to Shuar health has been minimal, since medical care in lowland towns is largely a privilege of the colonist population. Consequently, the federation's Health Commission has established its own program with the help of the Salesian mission and the German Volunteers, both of which have organized training courses for health volunteers, nurses, and social workers. The emphasis of the Shuar health program is on preventive medicine, and fostering of hygienic habits is of primary importance. Information on health matters is provided by radio broadcasts and health workers who manage the program in each Shuar *centro*. First-aid kits provided by the federation are available in all *centros*. In the event of outbursts of contagious disease, each *asociación* has a special team of health officials to carry out vaccination campaigns. The entire health program is managed from the health center built by the federation in Sucúa. The Ministerio de Salúd provides technical assistance to the program.

INTERETHNIC FRICTION ON THE COLONIZATION FRONTIER

The establishment of the Shuar Federation curtailed, or at least severely limited, the colonists' access to Shuar land and labor. As a result, interethnic relations became quite tense in the late 1960s, particularly in Sucúa, where the federation building is located. As mentioned earlier, the colonists' resentment has been directed not only against the federation but also against the Salesian mission, which had a great part in the planning and organization of the federation. Salesian mission support of the federation can be considered to be the most positive contribution of the Salesians to the well-being of the Shuar. However, Salesian participation also has a negative side, for it has made the mission an influential force in Shuar affairs.

It is possible that Salesian intervention in the activities of the federation serves a positive purpose for intra-Shuar affairs, at least until the Shuar can assume complete control of their own destiny. But the present situation suggests that the mission may not relinquish its control over the Shuar. In fact, the federation as a whole has proved to be a most efficient instrument for the indoctrination "en masse" of the Shuar into Salesian and western ideology and cosmology. For instance, it is apparent that the radio school has greatly facilitated the missionary evangelical work, now being carried out by the Shuar themselves. The Salesian missionary Father Sainaghi (1976:77) clearly points out that radio programs are intended to be of "Christian inspiration," influencing its listening audience to adopt Christian ideas and "start thinking in a new way." Most indoctrination programs are broadcast in the Shuar language, in the interest of evangelizing the Indians faster and more effectively (for a list of programs see Sainaghi 1976:77ff.). The high potency of HCSK (one transmitter of 5 KW and another of 10 KW) allows the radio station to broadcast beyond Untsuri Shuar territory to other Jivaroan peoples such as the Achuara of Ecuador and Peru and the Aguaruna and Huambisa of Peru. This feature is of great importance, for it gives an idea of the harm that can be done to native lowland cosmology if the nature of penetration remains focused on evangelical conversion to new systems of thought.

It should be noted that, alongside the Shuar radio school, the Salesian mission has maintained the boarding school, which, from the point of view of the Shuar, is no longer necessary. Naturally, the mission has been under pressure to reduce boarding school recruitment, but there is a clear reluctance to close the schools altogether. Indeed, 14 years after the establishment of the Shuar Federation, the Salesian mission still operates 10 boarding schools sheltering 950 children (Federación Shuar 1976:50, Sainaghi 1976:86). It would appear, then, that the persistence of the boarding school represents a missionary strategy to maintain control of the Shuar population. To justify their continuation, the boarding schools have found it necessary to place emphasis on the formation of future leaders of Shuar communities. The legitimacy of this activity is questionable, however, in that the mission is taking upon itself the right to decide who will be the leaders of Shuar communities. It appears reasonable that the federation should be the only institution for the training of Shuar leaders. In this context, leadership training provided by the mission clearly reflects the Salesians' determination to keep a strong grip on the Shuar population. It is interesting to note that the federation sought for years to have the government institutionalize the radio schools as "public" schools, which would have made them free of religious interference. However, the Salesian mission managed to have them in-stitutionalized as *fisco-misional* schools, which means that the person-nel are paid by the government but the school itself remains under the direct control of the missionaries (*Chicham*, August 1977). It should also be noted that all radio school teaching assistants are reli-gious leaders faithful to the program of massive indoctrination set up by the Salesians (cf. Sainaghi 1976:85–86). All these features clearly indicate the strong control the Salesians exert over the Shuar popu-lation, particularly through the federation educational program and radio station.

The Shuar Federation regards missionaries as government agents because of the integration policies they advocate (Federación Shuar 1976:107). Indeed, the benefits that missionaries receive from the government make them unable to act otherwise. According to the document signed by President Velasco Ibarra (Velasco Ibarra 1955:7743), the Salesian mission enjoys the following benefits: tax exemption within the country, duty-free imports of any kind, financial assistance for boarding schools, financial assistance for the Salesian mission as a whole, free medical attention for missionaries in military hospitals, free trips in government planes, a monthly quota of free cargo trans-portation up to 300 kilograms of materials for mission centers, and salaries for missionaries devoted to teaching activities. In return, *the Salesians are obliged to "civilize and indoctrinate the savage tribes" of Shuar territory, to support and increase the founding of colonist and aboriginal settlements, and to carry out all the activities necessary to bring about these ends.* It is clear that the Salesian mission's duty is to carry out govern-ment policies of integration, which in plain language mean accultura-tion of the Shuar to western lifeways and assimilation into the na-tional society. It is not surprising that a few Shuar would like to see the Salesian mission ousted from the federation. These individuals belong to a small group of educated Shuar who feel that their people should be able to choose any religion they wish, or none at all if they so choose. However, as this group is a minority, it is unlikely that the federation will be emancipated from the mission's patronage, at least in the near future.

The Salesian mission may consider this somewhat negative view of its activities to be unfair, considering that its missionaries are usu-ally highly motivated individuals. Unfortunately, their religious fer-vor has often obscured the devastating effects of indoctrination poli-cies upon Shuar culture. It must also be pointed out that the Salesians are now aware of their mistake, and they are willing to correct the wrongs done to the Shuar. As a consequence, the Salesians have been recently advocating the revival of Shuar culture through a new approach, sometimes called the "new mission" strategy. The "new mission" aims to create a "native church" through the enhancement of Shuar culture elements that can be adapted to Catholic religious principles, and through the establishment of a native ecclesiastical hierarchy that would, theoretically, culminate in priesthood (Broseghini et al. 1976).

This strategy requires a complete reversal of indoctrination procedures. For instance, missionaries do not bring the natives to the mission center (as was the case with the traditional methods); instead, they live and work with the people in their own familiar environment. Furthermore, missionaries must acquire a profound knowledge of the aboriginal language and culture, particularly mythology, which, in a way, constitutes the infrastructure upon which Christian elements can be introduced (Broseghini et al. 1976, Sainaghi 1976). It is my opinion that the Shuar are already too acculturated in western ways to accept the idea of a native church. Moreover, many acculturated individuals feel that revival of their traditional culture, as advocated by the Salesians, is largely unnecessary. For the moment, they find it difficult to understand why they have to adopt, under Salesian pressure, Shuar culture elements and values that the Salesians themselves had eradicated from the native population during the past half-century.

From the point of view of the federation, dissociating forces are strong on the colonization frontier, as manifested by colonists' attitudes and white-biased activities of Ecuadorian institutions. There is an apparent feeling of frustration among colonists over the success of the federation. The extent to which this frustration has been felt is evident in the colonists' frequent criticism of the federation: "the Shuar are arrogant and rich," "federation officials misuse funds for personal profit," "the Shuar monopolize the land." Both Franciscan and Salesian missionaries have consistently tried to improve interethnic relations on the colonization frontier, but in general little has been accomplished. The basic issue is the manner in which the Shuar should be integrated into the national society. Ecuadorian nationals advocate complete assimilation, arguing that the Shuar should be "civilized" first, if they are to function in Ecuadorian *blanco* society. It is obvious that this position would not allow any indigenous values to be incorporated into, or accepted by, the national culture, for the *blanco* (civilized-national) versus *indio* (uncivilized-nonnational) cognitive dichotomy is part of developmentalist ideology. On the other hand, the Shuar position is also quite clear: there will be no integration if Ecuadorian society is not willing to accept the values of Shuar culture; development must take place within a pluralist setting which recognizes Shuar autonomy in decisions affecting their future.

Although the Ecuadorian government has given official recognition to the federation, its institutions have been operating in Shuar territory with colonist-oriented policies. Thus the Office of Vital Statistics, Registro Civil, became a problem for the Shuar when the government ruled that lowland Indians had to acquire the national identity card. The Shuar were eager to comply with the rule, but their I.D. cards had so many mistakes that they were practically invalidated. Fortunately, the federation was allowed to run its own I.D. card office, which has so far registered 17,000 Shuar and is now in the process of rectifying the cards erroneously made by government officials (Federación Shuar 1976:125).

Problems with IERAC occur frequently because this institution has been particularly slow to legalize Shuar property. The federation keeps a watchful eye on IERAC because of its colonization-oriented policies. However, on this matter the most frequent frictions arise between the federation and CREA. The Shuar are basically against CREA's projects, but at the same time they are aware that colonization has become an inevitable process. Consequently, they have decided not to oppose colonization per se, as long as they are not deprived of the necessary vital space to develop their own economy and culture. Federation officials have pointed out that CREA is either not aware of, or does not want to acknowledge, the very real physical and cultural presence of the Shuar in the lowlands. Indeed, CREA's reports hardly mention the Shuar, generally using low population figures to justify the no-man's-land status of Shuar territory. At present, there are three colonization projects being carried out in the southern lowlands and, curiously, not a single program has been established for the socioeconomic development of the Shuar. However, a clarification is necessary at this point. The present situation should not be completely attributed to CREA, as the Shuar themselves (presumably under Salesian pressure) have consistently refused to negotiate with CREA. Fortunately, the Shuar now realize that they are falling into isolationism, which was becoming detrimental to the federation because potential financial assistance from CREA was being lost. Coincidentally, the latter institution was undergoing some changes in colonization policies, particularly through more open-minded administrators. As the situation now stands, there are good indications that the federation and CREA may collaborate more closely in the near future. Last year, for instance, CREA gave two million sucres (over $80,000) to the federation to be spent in infrastructure works, and more interaction is expected between these antagonistic institutions.

The dissociating factors from the outside are counteracted within the federation by an increasing cohesiveness which, in the long run, will determine the success of the Shuar Federation. The federation pursues two main goals: the recognition of Shuar culture as a constitutive system of Ecuadorian society, and economic self-sufficiency as the basis for a development free of pressures and influences from the outside.

There are still a few thousand Shuar who, for various reasons, have not joined the federation, although efforts are being made to attract them. It is important to note that the Shuar living under the influence of the Gospel Missionary Union have established their own organization known as the Asociación Independiente del Pueblo Shuar del Ecuador (AIPSE) (see Taylor and Belzner, in this volume). The political and economic unit of AIPSE is the "cooperative," whose organization was at the beginning carried out by IERAC and is now controlled by GMU missionaries. There are at present 14 cooperatives with legalized property extended by IERAC for a surface area of 27,943 hectares (CREA 1976:42). In general terms, AIPSE has been less successful than the federation. Apparently the GMU cooperative system is limited in extent (it benefits 423 Shuar families only) and somewhat isolationist. Furthermore, the whole system is strongly oriented toward acculturation, particularly through a school program managed by whites (Federación Shuar 1976:109). In any case, both AIPSE and the federation appear to be a fine example of the disruptive effect generated by different religious beliefs in a culturally homogeneous population. We can see that in the case of the Shuar, Christian religion has promoted division instead of unity. Federation Shuar are Catholic, which is practically an unwritten requirement to be a member of the federation. On the other hand, AIPSE Shuar are evangelical Protestant, and somewhat more intransigent on religious matters than the federated Shuar. It is not surprising that religious beliefs have produced some friction among these Shuar groups, although the federation seems to have adopted a more mature attitude in the sense that it does not necessarily reject AIPSE Shuar for their religious beliefs. In fact, although not a part of the federation, the AIPSE Shuar are corporately affiliated with the federation.

CONCLUSIONS

This paper is an attempt to document the formation and activities of the Shuar Federation in the context of colonization in lowland Ecuador. It is known that the process of frontier settlement generates a series of strategies through which the parties involved in contact try to work out a physical and social adjustment to the new situation. However, no colonizing process can be fully understood without bearing in mind the fact that colonization frontiers represent the encounter of a technologically high energy-utilization society (the pioneers) with another possessing a low energy-utilization level (the native population). The nature of the societies involved in contact is a very important feature, for it makes possible the establishment of a colonialist relationship between the pioneers and the native population, usually involving forced acculturation of the latter by the former. Naturally, this relationship can only be possible when contact becomes more or less permanent, in other words, when a "frontier system" is established in the new territory. According to Wells (1973:6), a frontier system is a "dynamic social network" characterized by the following features: "1) one or more foci, 2) territorial expansion of the people from the focus, 3) direct contact by the expanding people with culturally distinct societies, and 4) the presence of a single communication network which links the various societies of the frontier system together."

In the light of this definition, the colonization frontier in the southern lowlands of Ecuador can be said to constitute a true frontier system with three foci represented by the highland towns of Riobamba, Cuenca, and Loja. The expansion of these foci into the lowlands has been marked by two distinct types of human migration: an early one characterized by squatters (spontaneous colonization), and a more recent one characterized by individuals participating in government-sponsored projects of colonization (semidirected colonization). As to the social background, most settlers are poor and lower-middle-class whites (actually *mestizos*), although recently Indian families have also resettled on the colonization frontier. In any case, through migration, the pioneer society came into contact with the native population of the lowlands, in this case with the Shuar, a tribal society with a tropical forest culture pattern. Interethnic contact has generated a communication network of economic and cultural nature, which has resulted in the imposition of the colonist population as the dominant society in the lowlands. The economic network has been established by means of western manufactured goods acquired by colonists at the highland foci of colonization and eventually passed to the Shuar in exchange for labor, land, and handicrafts.

The importance given by the Shuar to the technologically superior western goods has become the source of economic exploitation and dependence, intensified by the simultaneous acculturative process that the Shuar have undergone. It is interesting to note that, while the economic network flows both ways, that is, from the colonist to the Shuar and vice versa, the "cultural network" flows in only one direction, from the colonist to the Shuar. Colonists have not become acculturated; rather, it is their culture that is being imposed upon the Shuar people. The colonization frontier of contemporary eastern Ecuador represents a situation of "interethnic friction" inasmuch as one culture tends to reject the other (Cardoso de Oliveira 1972:79).

For more than half a century the Shuar have undergone the consequences of the colonialist expansion of the highland society into the lowlands. The expansion has now reached a critical point, aggravated by the lack of a consistent government policy aimed at the safeguard of Shuar culture. It is for this reason that the establishment of the federation constitutes in Shuar history a landmark in the struggle against complete assimilation by the national society.

The reader who is familiar with the ethnographic literature on the Shuar may have noticed that the structure of the federation differs clearly from the traditional social organization of the Shuar. It is indeed surprising that a tribal society with a cultural pattern of relatively independent households accepted a federated type of organization with centralized administrative procedures. I suggest that the federation emerged from the need to consolidate the current Shuar economic structure, which has been gradually encompassing wider segments of the native population. But it also appears that the structure of the federation is clearly related to the degree of acculturation attained by the Shuar.

Harner (1968) has pointed out that in the past few decades the economic network set up by the frontier system has practically embraced all Shuar territory, together with neighboring peoples such as the Canelos Quichua and Achuara. Western goods are distributed all over this region by means of trading partners and by Shuar individuals interested in becoming shamans (the acquisition of shamanistic power is bound up with trade for western goods). The booming trade in the southern lowlands has generated a tendency among Shuar men to become trade partners and shamans. Also, it has brought about the increasing need for safe travel across potentially hostile territory. Naturally prospective shamans and trade partners are reluctant to make long-distance trips to strange neighborhoods if their lives are in danger. Both missionaries and the military have contributed greatly to safe travel by quickly identifying and punishing alleged killers.

In short, the Shuar situation during the early 1960s was characterized by an active trade coupled with a declining frequency of feuding and warfare, and the advancing colonization frontier became a crucial issue for the continuing viability of Shuar culture and the survival of Shuar people. At this point, the Salesian proposal of establishing a federation was certainly a welcome idea, for such an organization offered the double perspective of consolidating the socioeconomic position of the Shuar and halting colonist encroachment on the land.

It appears that acculturation among the Shuar (particularly the Upano group, which is the promoter of the federation) has been extensive enough to favor the adoption of administrative structures characteristic of western institutions. Indeed, with the establishment of the frontier system, the Shuar became continuously involved in the administrative framework of Ecuadorian institutions. Although it is probable that the Salesian mission imposed the structure of the federation on the Shuar, it was always possible for the Shuar to reject such structure, had it proved operationally detrimental to their socioeconomic situation.

Despite the achievements of the federation, it can be said that the colonist society will continue to exert its dominance over the Shuar. And yet, should the government display a serious interest in the economic development of the Shuar and modify its colonization policies, the lowlands could become the setting of an unprecedented parallel development of both pioneer and Indian societies that would, eventually, lead the Shuar to a fair integration in Ecuadorian society. Unfortunately, nothing like this can be foreseen in the near future, for integration of native Amazonian peoples involves not only economic development but also a complete change of attitude on the part of the dominant society. This attitude change from denigration of everything *indio* to respect for indigenous cultures is unlikely under the social conditions of contemporary Ecuador.

As of now, the Shuar Federation seems to be struggling in a maze of contradictory forces. The ambiguity of government policies is helping the federation in some ways but preventing its development in others. The Salesian mission is advocating self-sufficiency for the Shuar but at the same time is attempting to keep steady control over the federation. Finally, a small group of Shuar intellectuals has become critical of the federation, questioning basic issues whose resolution is crucial for the future development of the Shuar organization. This new attitude has obviously created some confusion among the Shuar. Today, within the federation, there are Shuar favoring mission patronage and those against it, some who favor collaboration with CREA and those who refuse it, some who favor the revival of the traditional culture and those who want modernization. Indeed, the future of the federation itself is seen by many to lie in the prompt resolution of these contradictions.

A factor that must be clearly understood is the Shuar determination to survive as both an ethnic and a cultural entity. This factor is already felt in the rest of the country and, eventually, could make a difference if further constraints operate negatively for the Shuar. In fact, considered in a wider perspective, the Shuar Federation constitutes one of the most active and promising Indian movements in Ecuador. Although Ecuadorian Indians have not yet been able to present a unified front so as to become an influential force in Ecuadorian society, it is apparent that interindigenous communication has greatly increased in the last decades. In this context the Shuar experience represents an example to be followed, for the Shuar are, so far, the winners of a struggle where other Indian groups have failed. Indeed, in a national perspective the Shuar have become the potential leaders of a pan-Ecuadorian movement of Indian liberation.

NOTE

Acknowledgments: This chapter is a condensed, edited, and revised version of International Work Group for Indigenous Affairs, Document 28.

REFERENCES CITED

Arnalot, José
    1978   *Lo que los Achuar Me Han Enseñado*. Sucúa: Ediciones Mundo Shuar.
Barrueco, Domingo
    1968   *El Vicariato de Mendez a los 75 Años de su Fundación*. Cuenca: Editorial Don Bosco.
Broseghini, P. S., et al.
    1976   *La Iglesia Shuar: Nueva Presencia y Nuevo Lenguaje*. Sucúa: Ediciones Mundo Shuar, Serie B, fascículo 7.
Cardoso de Oliveira, Roberto
    1972   *A Sociologia do Brasil Indígena*. Rio de Janeiro: Ediçoes Tempo Brasileiro.

Congreso Nacional de Misiones
1973 *Por una Iglesia Ecuatoriana más Misionera y por una Iglesia Misionera más Ecuatoriana.* Quito: Editorial Don Bosco.
CREA (Centro de Reconversión Económica del Azuay, Cañar y Morona Santiago)
1976 *Colonización y Población Indígena en Morona Santiago.* Plan de Desarrollo Integral para las Provincias de Azuay, Cañar y Morona Santiago 6 (UN Project Ecu 74–005). Mimeographed. Cuenca.
Federación de Centros Shuar
n.d. *Chicham.* Organo Oficial de la Federación Shuar. Several issues. Sucúa.
1974 *Estatutos y Reglamentos de la Organización Shuar.* Sucúa.
1976 *Solución Original a un Problema Actual.* Sucúa.
Galarza Zavala, Jaime
1973 *Los Campesinos de Loja y Zamora.* Quito: Editorial Universitaria.
Harner, Michael J.
1968 Technological and Social Change among the Eastern Jivaro. *XXXVII Congreso Internacional de Americanistas, Actas y Memorias* 1:363–88. Buenos Aires.
1972 *The Jívaro: People of the Sacred Waterfalls.* Garden City, N.Y.: Natural History Press.
Knoblauch, Hans
1976 Evaluacion Sintética del Programa Ganadero de la Federación de Centros Shuar. In *Federación de Centros Shuar: Solución Original a un Problema Actual.* Sucúa: Federación Shuar, pp. 265–83.
Kroeger, A., and E. Ileckova
1976 *La Salud y la Alimentación.* Sucúa: Ediciones Mundo Shuar, Serie B, fascículo 5.
Mashinkiash', Rafael
1976 *La Educación entre los Shuar.* Sucúa: Ediciones Mundo Shuar, Serie B, fascículo 1.
Sainaghi, Ambrosio
1976 *El Pueblo Shuar-Achuar y su Evangelización.* Sucúa: Ediciones Mundo Shuar, Serie B, fascículo 6.
Velasco Ibarra, José María
1955 Facúltase al Sr. Ministro de Gobierno Celebre Contrato con el Representante de las Misiones Religiosas Salesianas. *Registro Oficial* 4 (939):7743–45, decreto 2153. Quito.
Wells, Robin F.
1973 Frontier Systems as a Sociocultural Type. *Papers in Anthropology* 14:6–15.
Whitten, Norman E., Jr.
1976 (with the assistance of Marcelo F. Naranjo, Marcelo Santi Simbaña, and Dorothea S. Whitten). *Sacha Runa: Ethnicity and Adaptation of Ecuadorian Jungle Quichua.* Urbana: University of Illinois Press.
1978 *Amazonian Ecuador: An Ethnic Interface in Ecological, Social, and Ideological Perspectives.* Copenhagen: International Work Group for Indigenous Affairs, Document 34.

22

From Scattered to Nucleated Settlement: A Process of Socioeconomic Change among the Achuar

Philippe Descola

The Jivaroan Achuar (also known as Achuara in Ecuador and Achual in Peru) inhabit the Upper Amazonian region drained by the Río Pastaza and the Río Morona and the inland tributaries of these two rivers. The ecology of these hunters and swidden horticulturalists is a transitional rainforest zone between the Ecuadorian *montaña* and the Peruvian lowlands. In Ecuador their population of about 2,000 persons is equally distributed on both sides of the Río Pastaza and its interfluvial area; they border the Canelos Quichua (Whitten 1976) on the north and northwest and the Jívaro proper, or Shuar (Harner 1972), on the south and southwest. Until a few years ago their reputed hostility had successfully prevented white penetration of their territory, even during the height of the Amazonian rubber boom which so affected some of their indigenous neighbors, especially the Zaparoans. Since the beginning of the seventies, however, several jungle airstrips have been opened in this area by Salesian and Protestant missionaries who are trying, with heavy economic inducements, to persuade the Achuar to cluster around these airstrips, give up their internal feuding, and dedicate themselves to cattle raising and breeding (see Taylor, in this volume).

Although cattle breeding still concerns but a very small fraction of the Achuar population, which otherwise maintains its characteristic cultural, social, and economic features, the traditional dispersed residential system is rapidly disappearing owing to the nucleation process initiated by Protestant and Catholic missionaries. The traditional Achuar peacetime settlement consists of a single polygynous nuclear family. During heavy feuding several households temporarily gather in the same fortified house for security reasons. The households, which were widely scattered in interfluvial areas or along the banks of a large river, are now being replaced in many areas by the *caserío*, seminucleated hamlet, wherein six to 12 families concentrate around a small airfield cleared in the jungle and try with considerable difficulty to adapt to village life as practiced, at times, in some places, by the Canelos Quichua (see Whitten 1976).

I will delineate and briefly analyze the different levels of ecological, economic, and social determinations combined in the Achuar process of material reproduction to study the factors of transformation that are affecting it. I give particular attention to the gradual passage from seminomadic scattered habitation to permanent nucleated settlements and the effects of this transformation on the process of acculturation.[1] This involves a critical discussion of current theoretical issues related to cultural ecology and an endeavor to test a specific methodological and theoretical approach, which stems from the seminal writings and tutorship of Claude Lévi-Strauss and Maurice Godelier.

ECOSYSTEM AND BIOSPHERE

In clearcut opposition to the Shuar and Canelos Quichua, the Achuar[2] occupy a truly amazonian biotope with altitudes varying between 400 meters (mesas and hills) and 250 meters (alluvial valleys), annual average isotherms superior to 23°C, and rainfalls ranging from 2,000 to 3,000 millimeters yearly. The Puyo area, for example, although no more than 100 kilometers from Achuar territory, has an altitude of over 600 meters and receives well over 5,000 millimeters of annual rainfall. From a phytogeographic standpoint, the natural Achuar habitat is the great *hylea amazonica* and not the tropical *montaña*, home of the Jívaro proper, whom Achuar typically call Muraya Shuar, "hill people." Within their area the Achuar occupy the terraces along a system of valleys oriented from the northwest toward the southeast, reserving the hinterland of hills and mesas as a hunting territory. The limit which separates the mesas system (brown soils of conglomerate clay and volcanic sandstone) from the hills system (red soils of sedimentary clay) divides the Ecuadorian Achuar territory approximately along the 77th parallel.

Within this valley system, however, one must clearly distinguish between two distinct microecotypes, the respective features of which are due to the different types of soils drained by the hydrographic network, thus entailing for the Achuar distinctive types of land occupancy. The Achuar occupy low terraces in the great alluvial basins where the aggrading rivers flow—Río Pastaza and the lower portions of some of its tributaries such as the Río Copataza, the Río Capahuari, the Río Ishpingu, or the Río Bobonaza. The alluvial volcanic soils called *shuwin nunka*, black soils, have a very high potential fertility. They also occupy the high terraces of degrading rivers originating in the mesas system—upper Río Capahuari and its tributaries, upper Río Bobonaza, upper Río Copataza, upper Río Conambo, and upper Río Corrientes. These are composed of red soils of ferralytic origin or of a mixture of red soils and sandy soils produced by the erosion of the hills and mesas. These two latter types of soils, known respectively as *keaku nunka*, red soil, and *nayakim nunka*, sandy soil, have a very low potential fertility (IGM 1978, and geomorphologist Georges-Laurent de Noni, personal communication). The Achuar north of the Río Pastaza simultaneously occupy both ecological niches and share sets of features characteristic of interfluve indigenous groups and typical of riverine groups (Lathrap 1968, Meggers 1974).

The specific differences between these two ecotypes entail important variations within the system of resources: the riverine habitat is distinguished by the high degree of fertility of alluvial soils, a concentrated fauna of large mammals roaming the riverbanks, rich aquatic resources, and, unfortunately, the pervasive presence of malaria. The interfluve habitat can be characterized by occupation of high, non-floodable, unfertile terraces, the absence of large aquatic mammals, a relatively low density of fish, very dispersed and predominantly tree-dwelling land fauna, and the absence of malaria (see Ross 1976:136–37 for the Peruvian Achuar).

This distinction between two ecotypes appears paradigmatically in native ideology. Within a shared mythical corpus the interfluve Achuar usually ascribe more importance to such supernatural beings as Amasank or Jurijri, associated with subterranean habitat in the hills and the hunting of monkeys, while riverine Achuar emphasize beings such as Tsunki, the water domain spirit, and stress the mythical feats of aquatic animals such as the anaconda or the nutria.[3]

The distinctive characteristics of the two ecotypes account for important differences in the horticultural productivity of pioneering slash-and-burn cultivation where old fallow plots are never used for new clearings. Variations of productivity between the two types of habitat will be clearly defined and related to the question of the degree of ecological determination of settlement patterns by horticultural techniques: are scattered habitat and the periodic relocation cycle really determined by the nature of tropical rainforest soils?

An answer to this question surely lies in the analysis of the agricultural carrying capacity, and specifically of the main staple crop, sweet manioc (*Manihot esculenta crantz*), since the latter in either solid or liquid form (manioc beer) accounts for nearly half the agriculturally produced intake in terms of weight. We are fully aware of the limits inherent in the concept of carrying capacity as a theoretical unit of measure of the critical threshold of environmental degradation (Sahlins 1972:42–51). Johnson (1974) has clearly shown that such a unit is ultimately meaningless as a theoretical factor. We will, therefore, use carrying capacity not as a strict measure of the possible density of a population within a given environment (which would overstress exclusive horticultural determination) but as a rough comparative framework which will enable us to refine the distinction between the two ecotypes and to show that, in the Achuar case, scattered habitat and periodic relocation cycles must be ascribed to factors other than soil impoverishment.

For the evaluation of horticultural carrying capacity, we have chosen to use the equations elaborated by Carneiro (1960) and to apply them to two households selected as test cases, both of them isolated and polygynous and both typical of each ecotype. The first one, an interfluvial household including ten persons over four years old, is situated on the Río Capahuari and has been exploiting the high nonalluvial terrace of this degrading river for three years. The second, riverine, household includes 13 persons over four years of age, is situated on the Río Pastaza, and has been exploiting the rich alluvial terrace of this aggrading river for the past five years.

Interfluvial Household: Quantified Data

Mean manioc productivity on 100 m² (based on a density sample of 66 plants/100 m² and an average weight of 2 kgs of husked root per plant) = 132 kgs.

Productivity by m² for the whole *chagra* (total cultivated surface of 28,260 m²) = 1.3 kg/m².

Productivity of the *chagra* = 37,303 kgs.

Average annual per capita consumption (on the basis of an average daily consumption per capita of 2.2 kgs) = 803 kgs of manioc.

The value of the variables in Carneiro's equations is:

A (area of *chagra* required to provide manioc for one person during one year): $A = 617$ m².

P (household population): $P = 10$.

Y (number of actual productive years for a *chagra* before it is abandoned): $Y = 3$.

R (number of years an abandoned *chagra* must lie fallow before it can be recultivated): $R = 25$.

T (total area of cultivable land with adequate soil and slope conditions within 15 minutes' walk from the household—calculated on the basis of field data and controlled through interpretation of aerial photos): $T = 600,000$ m².

Equation A—possible size of a permanent population in this locality given these factors:

$$P = \frac{\dfrac{T}{R + Y} \times Y}{A} = 104$$

The actual population being ten persons, this household exploits only 10.4% of its theoretical demographic potentiality of land occupancy when we consider only horticultural factors.

Equation B—smallest surface of cultivable land which would support the household on a permanently sedentary basis:

$$T = \frac{P \times A}{Y} \times (R + Y) = 57{,}586 \text{m}^2$$

This interfluvial household could thus maintain itself permanently on only 9.6% of the total cultivable land presently available within 15 minutes' walk.

Riverine Household: Quantified Data

Mean manioc productivity on 100 m² (based on a density sample of 90 plants/100 m² with an average weight of 2.5 kgs of husked root per plant) = 225 kgs.

Productivity by m² for the whole *chagra* (for a total cultivated surface of 16,550 m²) = 2.25 kgs/m².

Total productivity of the *chagra* = 37,237 kgs.

Average annual per capita consumption of manioc (on the basis of an average daily consumption per capita of 2.5 kgs) = 912.5 kgs.

The value of the variables in Carneiro's equations is:

$A = 405$ m².

$P = 13$.

$Y = 8$ (high fertility of alluvial soils allows *chagras* to be cultivated for a period of time sometimes exceeding ten years; the limiting factor in the riverine habitat is the great investment in feminine labor required by weeding rather than the impoverishment of the soil).

$R = 25$.

$T = 1,200,000$ m² (the cultivable land here is double that of the interfluve habitat; it is not limited by hills, the slopes of which are difficult to cultivate and subject to erosion and drainage).

Equation A—718 persons (possible size of a permanent population in this locality). The present population of the riverine household amounts to 13 persons; it thus exploits only 1.8% of its theoretical demographic potentiality of land occupancy when we consider only horticultural factors.

Equation B—21,718 m² (smallest surface of cultivable land which could support the household on a permanently sedentary basis). This household could thus support itself permanently on only 1.8% of the total cultivable land available within 15 minutes' walk.

It should be noted first that the difference of potential soil fertility in the two ecotypes introduces a remarkable disproportion in manioc output, since in order to produce almost equal theoretical annual quantities (37,237 kgs and 37,303 kgs), the interfluvial household needs 11,710 m² more (58%) cultivated land than the riverine household. Similarly, the interfluve household requires 212 m² more (65%) cultivated land to feed one individual with manioc for one year than the riverine household. Thus one of the immediate consequences of soil difference between riverine and interfluve ecotypes is the increase in investment of labor required by horticultural practices in the interfluvial habitat—felling more trees more often for the men, cultivating and weeding more extensive *chagras* for the women.

These results also tend to show the considerable underexploitation of horticultural resources in both ecotypes, either actually or potentially. At the actual level, if one compares the annual consumption of manioc (11,862 kgs for the riverine household and 8,030 kgs for the interfluve household) with the theoretical yearly output (37,237 kgs in one case and 37,303 in the other), it appears that the riverine household and the interfluvial household respectively consume only 32.0% and 21.5% of their potential manioc output. Even if one takes into account the somewhat speculative nature of these quantified extrapolations as well as certain restrictive ecological and cultural factors (overconsumption related to drinking feasts and interhousehold visits, rodent predation, and the continuous nature of the manioc cycle, which implies that all plants are not producing simultaneously), it nevertheless appears evident that the Achuar, in both ecotypes, systematically underexploit their actual horticultural resources. By leaving a major part of their production stored in the earth, it becomes an important surplus, always available but, to my knowledge, never actually used.

At a potential level the underexploitation of horticultural resources in both ecotypes is evident in that the riverine household exploits only 1.8% of its available arable land, while the percentage is 9.6% for the interfluvial household, an estimation very close to the 7% deduced from Carneiro's (1960) figures for the Kuikurú. Even if one considers these figures as merely a rough comparative framework for estimating actual and potential exploitation of horticultural resources, the disproportions they bring to light are such that they apparently exclude impoverishment of soil in the traditional mode of production as a determinant factor of Achuar settlement patterns. These patterns, again, are isolated residential units practicing periodic relocation every six to ten years.

In most cases household relocation occurs when the house itself is about to collapse. The palm roof thatch and hardwood posts deteriorate almost completely within a decade, and it is necessary to build a new house. A new house may be built nearby or at a new location rarely exceeding a day's walk or canoe trip from the old site. Criteria involved in the decision-making process vary greatly but include availability of game, fish, nuts, fruits, insects and their larvae, palms for thatch and poles, firewood, etc.; intensification of feuds requiring a tactical withdrawal from the enemies; or abandonment of the house following the death of the household head. All such factors are, in fact, structurally related and mutually reinforcing in the continuing social and ecological reproduction of the Achuar mode of production. Nonetheless, decrease of nonagricultural natural resources, and especially of protein sources, appears to be a determining factor in the cycle of periodical relocations of settlements from my observations and from the standpoint of indigenous interpretation.

This idea is not new. Many researchers (Carneiro 1970, Siskind 1973, Gross 1975, Ross 1976) have already criticized the misused preeminence of agriculture in the determination of settlement patterns. All emphasize that the critical determinant of settlement patterns is the limiting factor of adequate animal protein for nutritional purposes. Certain characteristics of tropical forest fauna—e.g. wide spatial distribution of the members of each species, low proportion of the animal biomass represented by large mammals and their vast nomadic areas—determine a low density of animal populations to which human predators must adapt. Among the Achuar, for example, 85% of the weight of the daily agricultural product is composed of various roots, tubers, and plantains which make up only one-fifth of the consumed proteins. The remaining four-fifths of protein are obtained mainly through hunting and fishing.

In recent years the dominant thesis among anthropologists developing and proclaiming a subfield of cultural ecology is that the procurement of animal protein represents a limiting factor for Amazonian societies. The scarcity of game implies not only low density of human populations but also a contingent series of adaptive cultural mechanisms to the regulation of these low densities. Examples of such adaptations include seminomadism, regular fissioning, polygamy, and inter- and intratribal feuds. In cultural ecological perspective these mechanisms would be explained through their regulatory role in the interrelations between human and animal populations.

STRUCTURAL CONSTRAINTS OF THE ECOSYSTEM ON THE SETTLEMENT PATTERN

Before analyzing in detail the influence of protein supply on the settlement pattern among the Achuar, let me state briefly the epistemological problem inherent in the explanatory value of simple ecological causality. Such causality seeks to establish the nature of social structure from a single ecosystem determinant. The determinant may be of productivity within slash-and-burn swidden agriculture, or it may be the limiting factor of protein supply. I am very skeptical about certain hypothetical ecological models such as the famous equation of Siskind (1973:226–27): scarcity of game equals scarcity of women through a metaphorical exchange of meat for sex, or the causal chain which makes polygamy and feuds among the Jívaro dependent upon the production of manioc *chicha* (Meggers 1975:159). These "demonstrations" are dependent upon a single postulate about the ecological milieu or about the infrastructure (scarcity of game for Siskind, *chicha* production as time-consuming, for Meggers), to account for a single corresponding element within the social structure (polygamy and feuds), without explication of the patterning of other elements within the social structure. For Meggers the simple causality is linear; for Siskind it is circular.

Use of a single ecosystem or infrastructure variable to explain social structure as a mere adaptive response is also unsatisfactory. Such an analysis implies that other elements of the social structure are the consequence of a single cause, but cannot tell us whether they are implicitly derived from this unique adaptive disposition or whether they are minor elements which do not pertain to the understanding of the functioning of the society. From a perspective of simple ecological causality, the use of Dravidian terminology among the Achuar, or the importance of formalized dialogues in their culture, is condemned to remain totally inaccessible to ecological analysis.

It is relatively easy to demonstrate hypothetically, at least, that an element of the social structure is adaptive to a dominant trait of the biotope. But such strictly ecological analyses do not, indeed cannot, show us the necessary causality of this adaptation. Therefore they do not explain why totally different social practices should be generated in two distinct societies through a similar technological exploitation of a similar ecosystem. The Piaroa in Venezuela (Kaplan 1975), for example, are apparently characterized by a process of production (division of labor and techniques of production), an ecosystem, and a social organization which are structurally similar to those of the interfluvial Achuar. But the Piaroa represent the symmetrical inverse of the Achuar with regard to the postulated adaptive disposition of polygyny and feuding. In fact, the Piaroa strive to maintain an institutionalization of peace in the relationships between endogamous groups as opposed to the institutionalization of war among the Achuar. They also practice an extremely restricted kind of polygyny as opposed to the generalized type typical of the Achuar.

The adaptive model of cultural ecology contents itself with the description of a process without demonstrating the causality and hidden logic behind it. By so doing, it renews the famous truism of functionalism[4] while asserting the tautology that a social structure is always adaptive to the ecosystem. It is, of course, clear that the societies under anthropological study are necessarily all adapted to their ecosystems unless their ecosystems or their social structures are too seriously changed by exterior influences. Otherwise, they would not have survived. The notion of adaptive disposition therefore represents a kind of "proof" *ab absurdam* where one contents oneself with demonstrating that which a society cannot do, if it is to survive, and then claims to have documented its adaptation.

The determination of social structure through the limiting factor of postulated game scarcity in the ecosystem of the tropical rainforest raises the more concrete problem of alternative protein sources. Scarcity of game is a limiting factor only if one chooses to draw one's proteins from hunting and fishing and not from vegetable sources. Ross (1976:3), who studied the Achuar of Peru, attributes the fact that

Amazonian societies in general, and the Achuar in particular, have not developed the cultivation of plants with high protein content, such as maize, kidney beans, or peanuts to "poor soils and greater labor demands." It seems doubtful that strictly ecological reasons are at the origin of such a presumptive choice, since the experience of the riverine Achuar shows that these plants, especially maize, are very productive and require very little labor input in their cultivation.

In the zones of low alluvial terraces it is not rare to see large *chagras* of maize (which is always cultivated in a separate *chagra*; manioc is mixed with other species in a polycultural swidden). These maize chagras sometimes *exceed* 5,000 square meters and are cultivated somewhat "for the sake of it." Corn does not figure in traditional Achuar diet and serves mainly to feed fowl. The work required to plant a *chagra* of maize is much less than that required to plant one of manioc. To plant maize, the Achuar neither clear the underbrush nor burn the clearing; seed is simply broadcast randomly into the bush.[5] Cultivation of maize, unlike other agricultural activities, is exclusively a male task, just as is hunting and fishing for large fish. The inversion of this relationship, which would intensify maize cultivation and simultaneously diminish the amount of time spent on hunting and gathering, would not subvert the sexual division of labor according to which men supply the essential proteins, a qualitative element, and the women the essential carbohydrate calories, a quantitative element.[6]

Kidney beans and peanuts are also very productive in the Achuar riverine habitat. They fix nitrogen, thereby improving soil fertility and creating a well-adapted protein source for this environment. Finally, we must note the extent of regular protein contribution to the traditional Achuar diet through gathering. For example, the palm weevil larvae can systematically replace meat and fish as principal protein supply during brief periods when hunting and fishing are not possible. Certain cultivated fruits such as chontaduro palm nutfruit (*Guilielma gasipaes*) are abuntantly consumed during five months of the year among the Achuar. At times, these foods supply up to 30% of the daily protein intake.

The marked preference among the Achuar for acquisition of animal protein through hunting and fishing reflects a deliberate cultural choice (quasi-universal among societies of Amazonia) rather than the result of a mechanistic determinism of the ecosystem. This cultural choice manifests itself in the value put on meat as food. This is true even to such an extent that the Achuar vocabulary distinguishes clearly among two different verbs for "to be hungry in general" and "to be hungry for meat." The human organism absorbs the calories, but it is first the taste, determined by a cultural logic of the senses, which orients the body toward one or another source of protein. The Achuar are therefore not ecologically "limited" by sources of culturally preferred animal protein, since in their absence, particularly in the riverine habitat, they could easily turn to abundant sources of vegetable protein which are actually underexploited.

Finally, it is extremely difficult to talk in general terms about scarcity of game as a specific limiting factor in a given region on the basis of a generalized, abstract "ecology of the tropical rainforest." The exact quantity of edible animal biomass potentially available within any microregion of a tropical rainforest, such as that of the Achuar, is unknown, and almost impossible to approximate in the absence of adequate studies and appropriate research techniques. It is thus rather cavalier to start out with an abstract postulate about the scarcity of game in order to deduce generalizations about the social structure. Lizot's (1977) extended, detailed studies among the Yanomamö, for example, demonstrate quite well that they are not faced with a chronic scarcity of game and that they are healthy and flourishing within their "critical threshold" of near scarcity (if this is really the case). Lizot's work totally invalidates Harris's (1974:102) polemical speculations where, in a mechanistic fashion, he seeks to explain feuding, infanticide, and male chauvinism and sexual brutality in this Amazonian society by postulating protein scarcity (see Sahlins 1978).[7]

Nonetheless, the ecological constraint on the consumption of proteins is an essential factor among the Achuar. This constraint is primarily manifest in the great dispersion of game, with important local variations between the riverine and the interfluvial habitats. This implies not a general scarcity of game but rather a scarcity for certain hunters at certain times. Since the Achuar have adopted hunting and fishing as production techniques for the procurement of a large part of their protein supply, this dispersion of game implies low human population densities to maximize production. The structural constraint of the ecosystem implies here an aspect of the mode of production, the density rate of human occupation, but not the totality of the social structure or even the settlement pattern—that is, whether it is dispersed or nucleated. Among the Achuar external sociological factors have certainly influenced habitat utilization. For example, low density and dispersed habitat were highly adaptive mechanisms against the intrusion of rubber gatherers in the nineteenth-century Amazonian rubber boom and also against epidemics of contagious diseases.

Each social and economic system produces its own mode of exploitation of natural resources and delimits specific norms for their regulated use. Thus each such system of norms constitutes an intentional economic rationality (Godelier 1968:279–93), i.e. a system of social rules which are consciously elaborated and applied in a fashion to satisfy, as best as possible, a range of socioeconomic objectives. This means that an ecosystem does not automatically generate, or determine, a device for adaptation. Rather, the possibilities offered by the environment are actualized through techniques of production within a process of maximization which can only make sense by reference to a hierarchy of needs and values which impose themselves on an individual within a specific society and which have their ultimate foundation within the structure of that society.

The low population density in a given territory comes about in Amazonia through two principal types of settlement patterns: dispersed residence and nucleated residence. Birth control is a complementary institution to limit population density. The latter does not exist among the Achuar except in the form of spacing of births, linked to the statistical effects of prolonged breast feeding on female fertility. However, this mechanism affects the population growth rate more than its dispersed or nucleated residential pattern. The Achuar death rate caused by feuding is probably more than 40% of the Achuar adult men. This does not really influence the population growth, though, in a society practicing polygyny and levirate (as is the case among the Achuar), for it is the biological reproductive capacity of women which is of importance here and not only the number of reproducers.

It appears that the limitations on human densities implied by the dispersion of game do not directly determine the type of population distribution over a territory, whether dispersed or nucleated. Rather, these limitations determine the type of control which a population exerts over a territory which permits it to maintain an optimum balance between human and animal populations. Aboriginal Amazonian populations have adopted different mechanisms for the regulation of territorial occupation which converge on maintenance of this balance and which are thereby "adaptive." However, each society adopts an original solution within the confines of its values, its social organization, and its techniques of production which permits it to exploit its habitat as effectively as possible. The Tukano groups, for example, trace the justification of specific stable localizations for specific unilineal sibs from mythology, and enact the mythical charter in ritual (Goldman 1963). Other Amazonian societies undergo processes of regularized fission; some are peaceful, as among the Piaroa (Kaplan 1975), and some are antagonistic, as among the Yanomamö (Chagnon 1968). All of these processes result in regularized decrease in habitat density at a specific rate.

The traditional Achuar form a series of endogamous areas divided into dispersed households whose composition varies between 10 and 30 individuals and which can in exceptional cases reach up to 60 people. Whether the households are totally isolated or whether they are found in aggregates of two or three, the distance between these households varies from one hour to a day's walk or canoe trip. Within the territory of each endogamous area intermarriages preferentially develop. Hence the area is occupied by a group of people who share close and direct relationships of consanguinity and affinity. The Achuar do not have unilineal descent groups nor do they have groups based on binding prescriptive rules of endogamy. The concept of endogamous area thus does not exist formally in indigenous ideology except through the general precepts which value marrying "close" over marrying "far"; the close marriage is a reproduction of the alliances of preceding generations, following the pattern of Dravidian marriage systems.

More than 60% of the marriages take place between related co-residents of the endogamous area. Exogamous marriages may occur through kidnapping women from a hostile endogamous area, or they may reflect a voluntary alliance with a neighboring endogamous area. In the eyes of every member of an endogamous group, newcomers continue to belong to their own natal kindred-based group, which is preferentially designated by the expression *winia shuar*, my people. When an individual marries outside his own endogamous group, he continues to use the phrase *winia shuar* exclusively for the members of his original endogamous group, not for his new affinal kindred-based group. This notion of an endogamous area thus constitutes a structure in the sense denoted by Lévi-Strauss: a principle of logical organization of Achuar society that is not directly represented by the indigenous people. Its presence and function, though, are reconstructed by the anthropologist and found to operate in the structuring of social organization.[8]

The backbone of these endogamous areas is usually an important river whose name characterizes membership in a group (*Kapawi shuar*, people of the Capahuari River). Although the dispersed houses in an endogamous area form a sort of continuum along the river and its tributaries which allows for a gradual transition from one endogamous area to another, the territorial distinctions between two areas are nonetheless quite precise. North of Río Pastaza there is a generally recognized no-man's-land of more than one day's travel between the two adjacent endogamous areas. Each of these endogamous areas is centered on the influence of a great man, famous warrior and/or powerful shaman, or a pair of great men, generally two brothers-in-law who exchanged sisters. The Achuar great man is very different from the traditional Melanesian big man; his prestige traditionally rests not on a clientele composed of kinsmen who are obligated through economic favors but rather on his skill and value as a warrior, together with his capacity to mobilize vast networks of alliance in times of conflict. The Achuar great man is a leader only in times of conflict, and he does not enjoy any particular economic or social privileges. He is thought of as representing the unity of the endogamous group, and the territory of a group often carries his name—*Mashient[a] nunkari*, the land of Mashient[a].

Intertribal conflicts with the Shuar (Jívaro proper) ceased about 15 years ago owing to mission penetration and influence. Conflict within an endogamous area is rare, since there are social mechanisms to prevent it. When a more or less open conflict does break out, the rift is almost always between a member of the endogamous area and an allied affinal resident. This type of individual conflict usually triggers an escalation of a conflict between groups in different endogamous areas. The male affine returns to his natal kindred in his original endogamous area to seek protection and refuge. As individual conflict escalates into group conflict, an attribution of collective responsibility is reciprocated between endogamous groups, and some instance preceding individual conflict is recalled. The most frequent pretext for conflict escalation is a brutal death attributed to sorcery. Assassination of an "innocent" member of the opposing group is frequent, and the concept behind it springs from this notion of collective responsibility. One does not take direct revenge on the person who precipitated the conflict, for he is most often hiding and inaccessible. Rather, revenge is taken on a member of his family, generally a consanguine, now accused of being co-responsible for the act triggering the immediate conflict.

The relationships between endogamous areas are usually either openly hostile or at best fraught with suspicion. The latter ambience obtains where there are repeated intermarriages. One of the results of this process of institutionalized hostility is to maintain "safe distances" between endogamous groups. The Achuar manage to maintain a no-man's-land between endogamous areas which serves as a territorial buffer. It appears, therefore, that the territoriality of each endogamous area is maintained through the endemic character of escalating group and individual conflicts. Territoriality itself, however, is not the cause of conflicts. Unlike the Yanomamö (Chagnon 1974:77), Achuar feuds do not intervene explicitly to maintain the sovereignty of a local group, which is, moreover, repeatedly dispersed throughout the endogamous area. The fact that the Achuar maintain a stable territoriality through intergroup feuds does not imply that war would have the nature of conquest of territory or of defense of territory. Social conflicts that trigger a war represent only the apparent form under which the maintenance of territoriality is hidden.

The endogamous areas vary considerably in their spatial, residential arrangements which promote accessibility to protein sources. In a riverine habitat, where fish are abundant, the endogamous units require only a relatively small hunting territory. In an interfluvial habitat, where game constitutes the principal resource for protein, the residential units are dispersed over a much larger endogamous area. Territory here refers to the forest through which the members of the endogamous area effectively travel and which they utilize. Territories of an endogamous area are not absolutely contiguous; there are also interstitial zones—no-man's-land—where no one claims exclusive rights to the use of resources. These interstitial zones are underutilized; they serve as parks for the preservation and reproduction of game.

If we analyze two endogamous areas with a more or less equal population, one situated in a riverine habitat and the other in an interfluvial habitat, it appears that the interfluvial territory is almost double the size of the riverine. This means that, given the density of 0.17 inhabitants/km^2 in a specific interfluvial endogamous area, the average individual disposes more than 6 km^2 of natural resources for his exclusive use, as opposed to 3 km^2 in the same case for an endogamous area in a riverine habitat. If one adds to that the greater rotational speed for *chagras* in an interfluvial habitat, one understands why the interfluvial zone should be characterized by an area of greater nomadism and dispersion of each residential unit. At the same time, the riverine habitat allows for greater household concentration and a quasi-permanent establishment of residential units. Despite these potentialities the riverine Achuar did not spontaneously adopt a permanent nucleated residence pattern. In fact, they maintained with great intensity the very cultural institutions (e.g. polygyny and feuding) which so many anthropologists associate with the interfluvial zones. According to the mechanistic cultural ecological school, these institutions are generated as adaptive dispositions owing to the scarcity of proteins in the interfluvial zone.

The endogamous area, as such, is not just a simple geographic conglomeration which includes the sum of the individual hunting territories of each of its members. It is also a social sodality which is activated in times of conflict and an ideological unity contributing to political stability. The social solidarity of each local group allows for the overall conservation of the ratio of human density owing to conflicts between endogamous areas. A series of transformations occurs according to which social sodality of the endogamous area promotes the ideological unity of its members in times of conflict. This, in turn, imposes a tactical distance between cognate endogamous areas and contributes indirectly to the maintenance of territoriality of each endogamous area. This territoriality results in a low density ratio for the whole of the Achuar region and consequently allows for the maintenance of an adequate territory for each residential unit and for each endogamous area.

These processes of social solidarity and ideological unity promoting territoriality do not disappear when the Achuar are artificially nucleated under mission influence. This is because household heads who form a nucleated center generally come from the same endogamous area. They preserve entirely their rights of utilization of the total endogamous area which they used to occupy in a dispersed habitat. The sum of the territories which were individually exploited by each member of the new nucleated center thereby forms a territory of exclusive rights of usage.

Control of the nucleated community is generally effected by domestic unit exploitation of its former hunting territory. This exploitation occurs as individuals of the domestic units go back and forth from the new *caserío* to the hunting territory, which may be located a considerable distance from the nucleated center. In such circumstances, a hunting hut and a small *chagra* are maintained at the center of the old individual territories to allow for hunting and gathering expeditions lasting several days. A series of highly respected rules protects the domestic unit's control over its hunting territory. These rules prohibit killing large game, fishing with piscicides, and felling palms in each acknowledged territory. The nucleation of a settlement within the habitat does not affect fundamentally the control which an endogamous group exerts over its territory. Nucleation even tends to reinforce control, since under the circumstances of a nucleated residential pattern, the rapid exhaustion of natural resources in the immediate vicinity of the *caserío* tends to reinforce the necessity of control over large territories for the community, especially in the case of the interfluvial habitat.

MODE OF PRODUCTION

The pronounced division of labor by sex among the Achuar refers to two distinct but complementary work processes: swidden horticulture, a quasi-exclusive female domain, and hunting and fishing for big fish, an exclusive male domain. The labor process of men can be thought of as an activity of *predation* (clearing gardens, killing game and fish) *within a natural ecosystem*, the forest. The labor process of women, on the other hand, must be conceived of as a *transformation of nature* (horticulture and food preparation) *which extends over an artificial ecosystem*, the clearing. Secondary productive activities such as gathering and fishing for small fish with piscicides belong to the domain of women and children; they do not invalidate the dual distinction of male-female labor processes.

The difference between predation of a natural ecosystem by men and transformation of an artificial ecosystem by women is very clearly marked in Achuar ideology. Men regularly retreat to the forest to acquire the vagrant soul, *arutam*, of an old deceased warrior. This soul allows the seeker who acquires it to regenerate himself as hunter and warrior, in which capacity his predation capacity is enhanced. For women the *chagra* is the object of their work and the source of their pride. Women take refuge in their *chagras* in times of social or domestic crisis. The *chagra* is the permanent habitat of Nunkui, the feminine spirit who presides over the harmonious development and the reproduction of the activities of horticultural transformation. These male and female labor processes bring into play two distinct levels of mediation of social relations in the process of production. The specific articulation of these two levels must be elucidated by an analysis of the social forms and conditions through which Achuar exercise control over their resources and their means of production.

Pioneering slash-and-burn swidden cultivation in the dispersed settlement is made possible through the abundance of disposable land which allows the Achuar to avoid cyclical, rotational clearing, fallow, and reclearing the same land. The choice of a *chagra* site includes such variables as soil, ground relief, erosion, absence of big trees, and proximity to the house: responsibility for making the choice falls to the male head of the domestic unit. Clearing is then done by the men of the household, including the head of the family, his adolescent unmarried sons, and, if there are any, his resident sons-in-law. The technique of clearing with an axe or a machete does not differ from the one described by Up de Graf for clearing with a stone axe among the Jívaro Antipa (Up de Graf 1923:203–4). After a preliminary clearing of the undergrowth, the small trees are first cut with a machete, and the big trees are then felled so that they drag along the mass of the small trees in their fall. After a period of up to two months, depending on climatic conditions, the men and women of the domestic unit begin the burning. Men pile up debris of dry branches and women stack and fire them. Thereafter the new *chagra* is exclusively the domain of women. The exception to this is the planting of special crops of plantain or maize which remain in effective control of men (although the harvesting is still done by women).

From the point of view of control over resources and means of production, horticultural labor processes remain within the sphere of the domestic unit. The *chagras* belong to the male head, who confers rights of usufruct to women of the household. Among the Achuar there is no concept of jurisdiction of property of nontransformed land; only the products of labor are subsumed under a rule of possession. The clearing is part of the household domain, owned and controlled by the household head; the *chagra* itself belongs to the women who work it. The Achuar household is self-sufficient with regard to its horticultural food supply; it exercises autonomous control over its resources, its means of production, and its products.

It is possible to invite kinsmen to help with the clearing of a *chagra*, but it is not necessary, and households, especially when very isolated, do not do it. There is no labor requiring cooperation between households, even in the construction of the great oval houses. Mutual, cooperative work parties undertaken between households respond to a social imperative, not to a technoeconomic one. Cooperative work presents an occasion for affirming interhousehold ties and alliances, to exchange news and gossip, and, above all, to have a drinking party to break the monotony of everyday life. The "tribal community" intervenes in the social reproduction of the means of labor through actual biological reproduction within the household, since the latter is dependent upon the circulation of women between households. This circulation is regulated and encoded within Achuar social structure and the system of kinship.

Fishing and hunting are male activities, the relative importance of which varies according to the ecotype. Fishing for small fish with piscicides is a collective activity of the household. Men hunt alone or are accompanied by one of their women to carry the catch. They may also use their well-trained dogs. All Achuar men know how to use the blowgun with great skill, and most of them also know how to make one. There are, however, very few who know how to make potent curare dart poison, which is preferably purchased from the Peruvian Achuar. The blowgun is economical and very effective for hunting arboreal animals. Muzzle-loading and breech-loading 16-gauge shotguns are also used, to a more limited extent. When the supply of ammunition and powder runs short, the Achuar save them for possible defense or warfare.

In the labor process of predation the domestic unit apparently controls the resources and the means of its reproduction within the core of the natural ecosystem which forms its territory.[9] Nevertheless, by contrast to the process of horticultural labor, maintenance of optimal, low-density man-animal ratios within a hunting territory depends not only on the domestic unit but also on the mechanisms of territorial regulation that prevail in endogamous areas. Control over the hunting territory by the domestic unit depends most of all on the maintenance of overall tribal territoriality. Maintenance of the domestic unit's hunting territory is then ultimately dependent, through a whole series of social mediations, on the institutionalization of intratribal feuding. Feuding is not a simple adaptive disposition to a limiting factor. Rather, it is—among other things—one of the hidden or disguised modes of reproduction of the domestic unit itself. Feuding as a non-apparent mode of socioeconomic reproduction is determinant precisely because the domestic unit has no direct control over its structural action. It is operative only through the mediation of the tribal group's social structures.

In distinguishing between these two labor processes and their respective functional conditions, I do not intend to make the same error as Terray (1969:132; 1977). He confuses the labor process with the mode of production and thus isolates two separate modes of production among the Gouro of the Ivory Coast. He distinguishes between a tribal-village mode of production tied to hunting and warfare, and a lineage mode of production based on agriculture. Among the Achuar there exist two labor processes with separate reproductive conditions. Their articulation takes place at distinct levels of the social relations of production. However, these two processes are complementary within a single mode of production. One finds here a symmetrically inverse situation to that found among certain agricultural lineage-based communities of Africa (Meillassoux 1975:57–71). There agriculture seems to be the determinant activity to which the other economic activities, especially hunting, are tied. Owing to its strategic situation, agriculture in these African communities gives shape to the overall social organization; membership in a lineage-based community conditions access to land. The community with its social rules and its kinship system determines for each domestic unit the framework and strict limits of the mode of appropriation of land and organization of labor. In a more "atomistic" society, such as that of the Achuar, where access to land is not tied to strict communal regulations, access to control over hunting territory through the mechanisms of spacing between endogamous areas seems to be the determining factor in structuring social relations.

The dual processes of production—female horticulture and male predation—influence both intentional and unintentional aspects of the relations of production of Achuar society. The intentional aspects are those which stem from the kinship and alliance system and which regulate the cooperation between the sexes through the concrete processes of social and biological reproduction within the domestic unit. The unintentional aspects, which are not represented in indigenous ideology, allow for an optimization of natural resources with respect to regulatory mechanisms of territoriality through mutual antagonism between endogamous areas.

The determinant character of predation activities in Achuar socioeconomic organization becomes crucial inasmuch as these activities and the conditions of their continuous reproduction determine the minimal requirements which shape the Achuar mode of production. Minimal requirements refer to a set of constraints (Godelier 1973:67–82) which, were they to be suppressed, would prevent the Achuar society from reproducing its mode of production in its traditional form. One can distinguish at least three such constraints here: (1) dispersion of the residential unit within the endogamous area, (2) social and ideological unity of the endogamous area, and (3) institutionalized antagonism between endogamous areas. These three types of internal constraints, which constitute pressures shaping the mode of production, delimit *social* conditions (not direct ecological conditions) of reproduction for the residential unit, for the endogamous area, and for the whole tribal group.

These three constraints form a system; they are in a state of permanent causal interaction. The first constraint signifies that each domestic unit may range freely over a territory to which it claims usufructory rights. However, the first constraint is contingent on the second, which represents the condition of the maintenance of these separate territories at the core of the endogamous area. In turn, the second constraint is maintained only if control over the endogamous territoriality is realized through the institutionalized antagonism between the endogamous areas. The second constraint, then, is contingent on the third, since feuding functions as social control only to the extent that it permits the aggregation of endogamous groups to form and solidify through conflict with cognate groups. Such formation of sodalities has no raison d'être without overt conflict with another such group.

Finally, let me point out that Achuar society is functional and reproductive not only because its social and cultural institutions are compatible with these constraints, which is thoroughly tautological, but because the institutions have a feedback effect on these constraints and thereby perpetuate them. This multifunctional causality avoids the trap of linear determinism of cultural ecology. It also allows us to give both a causal and a functional explanation of certain apparently minor or enigmatic institutions and, thereby, to account for the internal contradictions of traditional Achuar society.

Let us turn now to the socioeconomic transformations brought about by the progressive movement from dispersed to nucleated habitats. This sketchy portrayal of the system of constraints should allow us to evaluate the incipient modifications of the mode of production brought about by the recent introduction of new techniques of production.

SCATTERED AND NUCLEATED SETTLEMENT PATTERNS

I will briefly analyze here two factors of socioeconomic transformation affecting Achuar society prior to the present artificial process of nucleation: introduced technological change in the tools of production, and production for exchange to obtain western goods. About 40 years ago the Achuar first obtained steel tools, mostly machetes and fish hooks. Then they got firearms and, quite recently, axes and adzes. These technological changes brought about modifications in the nature of traditional male labor. They modified neither the work of women nor female productivity, since the steel machete is not a great deal more efficient than a split palm one for harvest and weeding.

Increased productivity of male labor is, by the way, not manifest as an increase in territory under cultivation, though male clearing of trees for a *chagra* is facilitated by the use of steel tools. Our Achuar informants agree with the accounts given by Harner (1972:198) that the cultivated areas were generally much more important *before* the introduction and spread of steel tools. The decrease in male subsistence predation and the introduction of steel tools allow men to invest part of their labor time in another type of predation activity oriented toward the market. This activity includes collecting commercially valuable animal hides (jaguar, ocelot, nutria, peccary), latex, cinnamon, and *kinguk* (*Phytelephas* sp.) fibers for Ecuadorian brooms. These items are then exchanged through the commercial traders for steel tools, shotguns, powder and shot, and for prestige items such as glass beads. More recently, brightly colored polyester clothes and transistor radios have entered the list of valued trade items.

The labor invested in the production of these exchange goods reproduces the conditions contributing to the decrease of traditional male labor. The amount of time taken from normal subsistence activities owing to the use of steel tools is spent precisely on activities directed toward the procurement of steel tools and other western goods. It appears then that there is neither a gain nor a loss of labor time, nor is there even a modification of the traditional sexual division of labor. The collection of marketable forest products is assimilated to the traditional work pattern of male predation. Overall, steel tools serve the same functions more efficiently than the old tools of production without altering the nature of traditional technological operations.

For different reasons, these two factors of transformation of the traditional work processes eventually bring about partial modification in the system. The first consequence of productive labor for cash gain and technological change in the mode of production is a faster rotation of *chagras*. It is more economical to clear a new *chagra* with steel tools than to weed an old one. Female labor declines with no increase in male labor, for the increase in the frequency of felling trees is offset by the decrease in time dedicated to felling. Steel tools are also the cause of overpredation of sectors of the ecosystem which fall in the sphere of the western market (*kinguk* palms, for example, are close to extinction in certain places), and of some sectors which fall into the traditional economy (some fruit-bearing trees are felled to collect the fruits more easily). There is also overpredation of large game and fish because of the increased efficiency of firearms and fish hooks and the marketability of hides.

The exchange system through which the Achuar obtain their steel tools is asymmetric in favor of the *comerciantes*; consequently, the Achuar are threatened by increasing dependency on Ecuadorian *comerciantes* who try to create an *enganche*, labor contract, system similar to the one found among the Achuar in Peru. By this method, manufactured objects are given to the Achuar to create debts which must be repaid with enormous quantities of natural products, the mone-

tary value of which is, in fact, far greater than that of the manufactured objects. This escalating debt forces men to spend more and
more labor time on collecting marketable goods. It also forces them
to rely increasingly on the female labor of the domestic unit to help
them gather these natural products. Clearly, the potential effects of
steel tools and the concomitant system of acquiring them through
overexploitation of the ecosystem, and "overproduction" in the
Achuar economy, are significant in the long run. In the short run,
though, we can say that use of steel tools by the Achuar has not yet
profoundly modified the traditional mode of production. Moreover,
the insidious, often "hidden" modifications are overshadowed by the
profound effects of residential and habitat nucleation and the introduction of cattle raising, which are taking place under Catholic and
Protestant missionary influence.

About two-thirds of the Achuar population north of the Río Pastaza is now concentrated, or about to be concentrated, in half a dozen
centros, as these nucleated communities are called. These *centros* relocate six to 12 domestic units around a small airstrip in the forest.
The Achuar region has, since colonial times, remained inaccessible
by conventional means of transportation. Today, single-engine,
STOL-type, mission-owned planes constitute links between distant
Achuar communities and the residential and administrative centers
of the missionary organizations. Although the remaining third of the
Achuar population still lives in traditional dispersed residential patterns, the isolated Achuar will soon be contacted by missionaries.

Anne-Christine Taylor discusses the process of *centro* formation under mission influence in the next chapter. Briefly, the Achuar are motivated to relocate and to construct a landing strip by the promise
made to them upon first missionary contact to give them cattle and
to provide them with a bilingual (Achuar-Spanish) school system for
their children. The Achuar hope to make great profit from the cattle,
and to use the profit to buy *all* of the new prestige goods for which
an artificial need has been created by *comerciantes*, including radios,
polyester clothing, and kerosene lamps.

I shall now offer a general overview of the consequences of residential nucleation and the introduction of cattle raising on the traditional mode of production, previously characterized by its system of
constraints. Residential nucleation poses a problem of apparent internal contradiction. On the one hand, I have argued that overall
population density within a territory is independent of the residential
form (dispersed or nucleated). But, on the other hand, I have isolated
as the first constraint on the traditional mode of production the dis-

persion and autonomy of each residential unit within each endogamous area. This contradiction is resolved when one realizes that constraint no. 1—as well as the other two constraints—is not generated
by simple ecological determinism but, rather, that it represents the
convergence of social factors of production. This constraint represents the
minimal condition under which the system of social relations can
continue to function without changing the existing relations of kinship, alliance, and power within the domestic unit, the endogamous
area, and the whole tribal entity.

Constraint no. 1 does not "prohibit" residential nucleation within
the traditional mode of production as a factor of ecological disequilibrium would. Rather, it treats the dispersion of the residential units as
a desirable mechanism for individual household identity and autonomy. Cognatic kinsmen must play a subtle game to meet reciprocal
obligations incurred with other households and to reconcile these obligations vis-à-vis other affinal and consanguineal groupings and alliances. Permanent nucleation within the traditional mode of production would generate social conflicts between domestic units owing to
the antinomy of obligations with respect to affinal and consanguineal
kin groups.

The second constraint—social and ideological unity of the endogamous area—is possible precisely because the residential units are
autonomous and dispersed. Cohabitation rapidly undermines this
constraint in the *centros.* One can summarize the interdependence of
these two constraints in this way: "To live happily, one must live
somewhat concealed." On the one hand, residences must be sufficiently close to maintain social unity of the endogamous area especially during conflicts against another endogamous area; but on the
other, they must not be so close as to tip the balance of "concealment"
and autonomy. Constant visiting generates conflicts such as adultery,
marital irregularities, accusations of sorcery, and encroachment on
hunting territories. Within the framework of the existing kinship system, it seems that an informal endogamous group can function only
if its members do not live together permanently. The unity of such a
group is essentially represented (as in the case of fortified houses) by
a series of processes of temporary alliance vis-à-vis another cognate
group.

There are two conditions by which residential nucleation need not
promote ecological disequilibrium. First, the residentially nucleated
members of an endogamous area must maintain the larger territory
for predation (as is the case in the *centros,* as we have seen). Second,
such residents must re-establish periodically their nucleated estab-

lishment at the interior of the endogamous area and/or factionalize and fission. This second condition characterizes the life of the Yanomamö *shabono,* "village-house." It is also present among the Achuar in the dispersed habitat when, in the course of a particularly bloody conflict, the dispersed elements of an endogamous area relocate themselves around a great man and construct a huge fortified house which may contain up to 60 people. In 1977, for example, an endogamous area of the lower Río Corrientes nucleated by splitting into two fortified houses which were seven hours' walk from one another. They were controlled by two allied great men involved in a serious conflict with another endogamous area. One of them contained over 46 people and the other protected a small group of temporary houses which contained 72 people. Among the Achuar this process of natural defensive nucleation never lasts for more than three or four years. Thereafter the huge fortified houses are abandoned as the most bloody phases of conflict end.

It should now be obvious that processes of nucleation within the traditional Achuar mode of production have fewer ecological consequences than social ones. A permanently nucleated Achuar settlement, relocating periodically inside its territory, would lead to a situation generating conflicts and fissions which would produce, in time, an atomization of the residential units, by the disintegration of internal solidarity within the endogamous area. Even in the present state of residential nucleation hunting and fishing have not notably diminished when compared to the situation in a dispersed residential pattern. Members of the *centros* continue to preserve the old territory of the endogamous area by means of traditional mechanisms, such as latent hostility or even open, armed conflicts with other endogamous areas (nucleated and dispersed). The current attempts at suppression of feuding (constraint no. 3), together with the sharp decrease of infant mortality owing to rudimentary western medical intervention, must produce a demographic explosion. This should result in an increase of population densities and a decrease of territorial control over the endogamous areas.

We find then, among the contemporary Achuar, a situation that involves progressive disappearance of constraint no. 1 (autonomy and dispersion of the residential units) juxtaposed to a gradual suppression of constraint no. 3 (institutionalized antagonism between endogamous areas) and an artificial reinforcement of constraint no. 2 (internal solidarity of the endogamous area). In the traditional mode of production constraint no. 1 does not prevent natural, temporary, fortified nucleation, but prohibits permanent nucleation to which the system of social relations is not adapted. The introduction of cattle raising, however, is a new and unadapted production factor which will alter this constraint in some fashion and give it an ecological content it did not initially have. Disregard of this constraint in the *centros* poses not only sociological problems but ecological ones as well. The permanent sedentary character of the *centros* and the future risks of a demographic explosion lead me to anticipate a progressive decrease of protein resources clearly apparent in the nucleated Shuar *centros* over the past 20 years. Above all else, land constitutes a limiting factor within the nucleated settlement–cattle complex system.

This problem of land shortage does not arise, as with the Shuar, from a threat of annexation of tribal territories through colonization. The Achuar are, for now, spared from this process. Rather, it arises from the simple fact of sedentarism in the *centros*. Construction of a landing strip, service buildings, schools, a house for the bilingual Shuar instructor, and a chapel represent considerable Achuar labor investments on the part of the members of the nucleated endogamous area. These cannot be repeated regularly, so the site of the *centro* becomes permanent.

The introduction of cattle raising contributes to the sedentary character of the nucleated settlement since, unlike the swidden *chagras*, a pasture becomes fixed once it is established. It is also necessary to constantly increase the pasture area, which begins with one hectare minimum per head of cattle but must increase as the herd increases and as the pasture's productivity decreases. The rotational periodicity of the swidden *chagras*, already accelerated through the use of steel tools, shortens, leaving a *chagra* in production for only two years before turning it into a pasture. The Achuar in such circumstances turn most old *chagras* into pastures, with severe ecological consequences for the interfluvial habitat. Once all of the flat land around the *centros* is transformed from *chagras* into pastures, the Achuar are left with graded hillside as the only available jungle source for new clearings. Some of these have a 50% incline and their red ferralithic soils have, at best, mediocre nutrients. The primary use of the red hillside soils guarantees decline in productivity (the plant roots cannot penetrate very deeply into the ground and are thus exposed to extensive erosion) along with an increase in labor time.

Permanent nucleated settlements and cattle raising tend to transform male labor from predator to cattleman, thus satisfying some missionaries' dreams of "reduction," *reducciones*. The Achuar stockman, from this perspective, lives in a village, is dependent on progressive capitalization, and is absorbed in productive tasks. Male labor time in the *centros* constantly increases. They clear more and more often, take care of the cattle, and sow pastures. They must also help maintain the landing strip and service buildings through regular, collective work, called *mingas*. Finally, they are forced to travel considerably greater distances in their hunting and fishing expeditions, to procure animal protein.

Even though the women do not undergo such profound changes in their productive activities, their labor time also increases in the *centros*. They must participate in certain communal labor tasks, such as weeding the landing strip. They must walk farther and farther to get to their *chagras*, which are pushed back beyond the area of the pastures. They also lose the help of their daughters, who must attend school (see Taylor, in this volume).

Residential nucleation and the introduction of cattle raising have greatly amplified factors of potential transformations which began with the introduction of steel tools. In the next chapter Taylor focuses directly on processes of radical change, which include raising cattle for market. Today subsistence economy in some Achuar villages is combined with a money economy which introduces, for the first time, western exchange values into the social life of household and kindred. The Achuar find themselves in a situation where the domestic unit is no longer completely autonomous, since it no longer controls all of the factors of production because continued access to cattle is tied to a credit system organized by the missionaries. Such Achuar households have also lost control over the consumption of their products: cattle are shipped out to a market operating under rules which are not comprehensible to the Achuar. The ultimate result of this process is illustrated by some Shuar communities in the Upano Valley. They engage only in cattle breeding and, having given up almost all subsistence production, find it more convenient to buy their food supplies from the whites than to invest labor in subsistence-oriented cultivation.

The disregard of constraint no. 1 and the introduction of cattle raising have, in effect, converted swidden horticulture into a limiting factor owing to the exhaustion of soils and the decrease of suitable land in the constantly expanding sedentary establishments where there is no fallow system left. In fact, the carrying capacity calculations made at the beginning of this paper (which indicate the possibility of higher human density rates than those presently existing in the Achuar *centros*) are predicated on a fallow system which is impossible to maintain if cattle raising continues in its present form (see also Macdonald, in this volume). Here, then, we see clearly the severe ecological consequences of the "cattle complex" so popular with the developers of the Oriente.

Development of cattle raising and the growth of nucleated settlements are part of a planned, national development program aimed at making the Oriente the nation's source of meat. This program is reinforced by a judiciary apparatus of the *Ley de Tierras Baldías*. Originally designed to fight the great haciendas of the Sierra and the Coast, the law stipulates that only effectively exploited land can be claimed by property titles (see Brownrigg and Macdonald, in this volume). Such a law cannot account for either the ecological parameters of the tropical rainforest or the limitations on existing adaptive cultural practices there (see Macdonald, in this volume, for a full discussion of these implications).

The threat to the Achuar *centros* engaging in cattle raising is the same one that all other eastern cattlemen face: nutrient depletion of the soil and progressive savannization. This depletion occurs when protective vegetation is cut over a large surface, exposing the fertile soil beds to the scouring action of sun and rain. The absence of a rainforest cyclical fallow system precludes nutritive reconstitution of the soil because the closed dynamic cycle of the ecosystem has been disrupted on several levels of vegetation. Even the rich alluvial soils are threatened and degraded by movements of cattle which trample the pasture, causing a rapid soil hydromorphy. This, in turn, gives rise to the formation of deep holes filled with stagnant water, precluding any subsequent cultivation whatsoever.

Once the processes of transformation of the traditional mode of production lead to an attenuation of constraint no. 1, with concomitant ecological and economic effects, the properties of constraint no. 2 are artificially reinforced as people who would otherwise be dispersed over the endogamous area are regrouped into *centros*. However, in spite of the pressures from the missionaries, the traditional social institutions continue to regulate interpersonal relations at this incipient stage. In the new environment characterized by new forms of production and the introduction of money, persistence of these traditional social institutions will exacerbate the centrifugal tendencies of each domestic unit (constraint no. 1). The Achuar experience great difficulties in trying to adapt themselves to the new *modus vivendi* of village life which, owing to the new constraints it constantly imposes, forces people to live in a system in which all of their values of individualism and independence are contradicted.

The Achuar in such circumstances are caught in a situation which constantly generates social fission. The generative force seems to be an apparently unsolvable contradiction between the postulated ideal of solidarity of kinsmen within an endogamous area, on the one hand, and the absence of any institutional basis—such as a uni-lineage or corporate group—on the other, which would facilitate the emergence of permanently nucleated residential groups with clearly established rights and obligations. While constraint no. 2 carries the ideological justification for temporary nucleation, it is contradicted by constraint no. 1 once nucleation is permanent. This contradiction between constraints nos. 1 and 2 generates conflict. The traditional mode of production allows for a system of contraction and dispersion of residential units. This traditional Achuar system is compatible with the institutional system, and people within it exploit alterna-tively the feasible extremes determined by both constraints. Once the concentration phase becomes permanent, however, as is now the case, the Achuar are faced with the danger of disintegration from internal conflicts.

It is clear that these internal structural conflicts, combined with the ecological limitations imposed by cattle raising and a nucleated sed-entary settlement pattern, can only provoke a new dispersion of the domestic units in the near future. This phenomenon is observable in the Shuar communities that were nucleated 20 years ago. Although informants generally describe out-migration as related exclusively to the constant dwindling of cultivable land and natural resources around the *centros*, it turns out that, at the root of almost every fis-sion, we find a latent or open social conflict which forces a domestic unit to re-establish itself at some distance from the *centro*. Domestic units which leave a *centro* maintain some sort of occasional contact with it to maintain access to western goods, to keep their children in school, and to ship their cattle to market. The dispersion radius, therefore, is sharply decreased.

Where the nucleated families in a traditional fortified house dis-perse spontaneously once the dangers of an attack are over, the fami-lies nucleated in a *centro* tend to disperse because they experience directly ecological, economic, and social pressures. The phenomena of nucleation and dispersion might appear to be similar, but they are really totally different processes subsumed by different modes of pro-duction and enacted within different institutional systems. The an-ticipated dispersion of the presently nucleated residential units in the Achuar *centros* cannot result in a new nucleation, as has always been possible within the traditional mode of production. If the introduc-tion of cattle raising continues at its present rate among the Achuar, the tendency to fission will become more and more aggravated in the *centros*, for fission represents the only viable solution for the domestic units to escape from the type of problems we have examined here. However, this constantly oscillating movement between population contraction and dispersion within an endogamous area can henceforth only end in a state of ultimate dispersion. It is then possible that, given the lack of possibilities for renucleation, Achuar society will be faced with the critical problem of sheer economic, social, and cultural survival.

NOTES

Acknowledgments: Fieldwork on which this paper is based was conducted among the northern Ecuadorian Achuar with Anne-Christine Taylor between Nov. 1976 and Aug. 1978. The research was supported by a grant from the Centre National de la Recherche Scientifique, a scholarship from the Foundation Paul Delheim du Collège de France, and two additional grants from the Ministère des Universités. In Ecuador, our investigation was sponsored by the Instituto Nacional de Antropología e Historia, and by the Department of Anthropology of the Catholic University of Ecuador, Quito. Both our papers were written in somewhat difficult conditions, while we were still in the midst of our fieldwork; hence we were unable to exploit our whole body of data. This accounts for the fact that, in the matter of economic quantifications, I sometimes fall back on rough estimates and restricted samples, adduced to demonstrate a set of tendencies rather than definitive conclusions. Further publications, however, will document the facts more fully.

1. The focus of this paper is the process of socioeconomic transformation of Achuar society; I thus deliberately omitted the study of various phenomena of cultural change owing to contact with mission organizations, which are the subject of the next chapter by Anne-Christine Taylor.

2. The ecosystem studied in this paper is more specifically that of the northern Pastaza Achuar, among whom we conducted most of our fieldwork; however, the general characteristics of this ecosystem are equally valid for the Achuar south of the Pastaza.

3. The same duality may be noted among the Campa of Peru (Varese 1966:35–37, Denevan 1974:94).

4. "To say that a society functions is a truism, but to say that everything in a society functions is an absurdity" (Lévi-Strauss 1958:17, my translation).

5. The Achuar data seem to contradict flatly the conclusions drawn by Harris (1971:495) from his study of the upper Orinoco swidden system: " . . . maize is more dependent than manioc on the efficiency of clearance and burning . . . (and) . . . the failure of the nutritionally more effective maize-dominated seed-crop complex to penetrate areas of traditional vegeculture in the South American tropical forest may be attributable to ecological as well as to cultural barriers."

6. In Pumpuentza (interfluvial habitat), Athens (1976) found a large number of mortars that he supposed were used to grind maize. Although this

hypothesis remains highly speculative, one may wonder whether the populations that formerly occupied this area did not rely more heavily on maize than is presently the case.

7. Marvin Harris attempts to forestall criticism on this point by declaring that warfare and fissions intervene as a mechanism before this critical threshold is reached. However, as he nowhere offers precise estimates of the ratio between animal biomass and degree of predation, this remains pure speculation on his part.

8. Karsten (1935:182–85) is the only author who explicitly underlines the endogamous character of neighborhood groups among the Jívaro, though the trait appears implicitly in Harner's and Stirling's works (Harner 1968, 1972:95; Stirling 1938:39).

9. Within the two work processes, however, certain technical tools of production (guns, fish hooks, steel implements) are not produced by the domestic unit, which must obtain them by trade, either with whites or with other native groups. In its relation to means of production, the domestic unit thus directly controls the means of labor and indirectly the technical factors of production.

REFERENCES CITED

Athens, Stephen
    1976   Reporte Preliminar sobre el Sitio de Pumpuentza. Unpublished manuscript. University of New Mexico.
Carneiro, Robert L.
    1960   Slash-and-Burn Agriculture: A Closer Look at Its Implications for Settlement Patterns. In Anthony F. C. Wallace, ed., *Men and Cultures*. Philadelphia: University of Pennsylvania Press, pp. 229–34.
    1970   The Transition from Hunting to Horticulture in the Amazon Basin. *Proceedings of the VIIIth International Congress of Anthropological and Ethnological Sciences* 3:244–48. Tokyo: Science Council of Japan.
Chagnon, Napoleon A.
    1968   *Yanomamö: The Fierce People*. New York: Holt, Rinehart and Winston.
    1974   *Studying the Yanomamö*. New York: Holt, Rinehart and Winston.
Denevan, William N.
    1974   Campa Subsistence in the Gran Pajonal, Eastern Peru. In Patricia J. Lyon, ed., *Native South Americans: Ethnology of the Least Known Continent*. Boston: Little, Brown, pp. 92–110.
Godelier, Maurice
    1968   *Rationalité et Irrationalité en Economie*. Paris: François Maspero.
    1973   *Horizon, Trajets Marxistes en Anthropologie*. Paris: François Maspero.
Goldman, Irving
    1963   *The Cubeo: Indians of the Northwest Amazon*. Urbana: University of Illinois Press.
Gross, Daniel R.
    1975   Protein Capture and Cultural Development in the Amazon Basin. *American Anthropologist* 77:526–49.
Harner, Michael J.
    1968   Technological and Social Change among the Eastern Jivaro. *Actas y*

Memorias del XXVII Congreso Internacional de Americanistas 1:363–88.
Buenos Aires.
1972   *The Jívaro: People of the Sacred Waterfalls.* Garden City, N.Y.: Natural
History Press.

Harris, David P.
1971   The Ecology of Swidden Cultivation in the Upper Orinoco Rain Forest, Venezuela. *Geographical Review* 61 (4):475–95.

Harris, Marvin
1974   *Cows, Pigs, Wars and Witches: The Riddles of Culture.* New York: Random House.

IGM (Instituto Geográfico Militar)
1978   Mapa Morfo-Edafológico de la Provincia de Pastaza. Quito: Ministerio de Agricultura y Ganadería—P.R.S.T.O.M.

Johnson, Allen
1974   Carrying Capacity in Amazonia: Problems in Theory and Method.
Paper read at the 73rd Annual Meeting of the American Anthropological Association, Mexico City.

Kaplan, Joanna O.
1975   *The Piaroa.* Oxford: Clarendon Press.

Karsten, Rafael
1935   *The Head-Hunters of Western Amazonas: The Life and Culture of the Jibaro
Indians of Eastern Ecuador and Peru.* Helsinki: Societas Scientiarum
Fennica, Commentationes Humanarum Litterarum 2 (1).

Lathrap, Donald W.
1968   The "Hunting" Economies of the Tropical Forest Zone of South
America: An Attempt at Historical Perspective. In Richard B. Lee
and I. DeVore, eds., *Man the Hunter.* Chicago: Aldine, pp. 23–29.

Lévi-Strauss, Claude
1958   *Anthropologie Structurale.* Paris: Plon.

Lizot, Jacques
1977   Population, Ressources et Guerre chez les Yanomami, Critique de
L'Anthropologie Écologique. *Libre* (Paris) 2:111–45.

Meggers, Betty J.
1974   *Amazonia: Man and Culture in a Counterfeit Paradise.* Chicago: Aldine-
Atherton.
1975   An Application of the Biological Model of Diversification to Cultural Distribution in Tropical Lowland South America. *Biotropica*
7 (3):141–61.

Meillassoux, Claude
1975   *Femmes, Greniers et Capitaux.* Paris: François Maspero.

Ross, Eric B.
1976   The Achuara Jívaro: Cultural Adaptation in the Upper Amazon.
Ann Arbor, Mich.: University Microfilms. Ph.D. dissertation, Columbia University.

Sahlins, Marshall
1972   *Stone Age Economics.* London: Tavistock.
1978   Culture as Protein and Profit. *New York Review of Books* 25 (18):45–53.

Siskind, Janet
1973   Tropical Forest Hunters and the Economy of Sex. In Daniel R. Gross,

ed., *Peoples and Cultures of Native South America*. Garden City, N.Y.:
Natural History Press, pp. 226–40.

Stirling, Matthew W.
  1938 *Historical and Ethnographical Material on the Jivaro Indians*. Washing-
        ton, D.C.: Bureau of American Ethnology, Bulletin 117.

Terray, Emmanuel
  1969 *Le Marxisme devant les Sociétés "Primitives."* Paris: François Maspero.
  1977 De L'Exploitation, Éléments d'un Bilan Autocritique. *Dialectiques*
        21:134–43.

Up de Graff, Fritz W.
  1923 *Head-Hunters of the Amazon: Seven Years of Exploration and Adventure*.
        New York: Duffield and Cie.

Varese, Stéfano
  1966 Los Indios Campa de la Selva Peruana en los Documentos de los
        Siglos XVI y XVII. Tesis de Bachillerato en Etnología, Universidad
        Católica de Lima.

Whitten, Norman E., Jr. (with the assistance of Marcelo F. Naranjo, Marcelo
        Santi Simbaña, and Dorothea S. Whitten)
  1976 *Sacha Runa: Ethnicity and Adaptation of Ecuadorian Jungle Quichua*. Ur-
        bana: University of Illinois Press.

23

God-Wealth: The Achuar and the Missions

Anne-Christine Taylor

Within the last decade the fiercely independent Achuar have come under the influence of two rival missionary organizations: the Catholic Salesian mission based in Macas and a joint group of Protestant evangelist sects, headed by the Gospel Missionary Union, based in Macuma. Both missions have fomented the creation of putative "independent" native organizations: Federación de Centros Shuar and Asociación Independiente del Pueblo Shuar del Ecuador (AIPSE) respectively. Both are heavily capitalized, replete with modern equipment including broadcasting networks that play an important role in their respective policies. The mission organizations are now the articulating mechanisms creating a hinge between the dominant mode of production of the national society, with its forms of exploitation specific to the tropical frontier areas, and the traditional Achuar tropical forest mode of production. The missions constitute the framework within which the factors of transformation presently affecting Achuar society are imbedded. Each organization has specific policies that produce somewhat distinct structural effects and engender partially distinct native ideological elaborations that, in turn, contribute to the incipient internal transformation of traditional social relationships.

The object of this paper is to describe and analyze some of the modifications within Achuar culture resulting from the missions' means of control over the Achuar. I will also describe briefly the economic, social, and ideological characteristics within traditional Achuar society that allow mission policies to take root within the very core of the culture. And I will address an apparent paradox: why do the Achuar, who seem to have a lucid though highly metaphoric vision of what these transformations imply, and who successfully resisted attempts at proselytization for nearly four centuries, now allow the missions to introduce irreversible and frequently painful changes that clearly herald a future of increasing alienation and domination?

Although the missions form the main front where the dominating and dominated modes of production meet, they are not the only locus of articulation. The Achuar have long been interacting with traders and with the Ecuadorian army. North of the Pastaza the army has indirectly affected the Achuar mode of production by limiting contact with the Peruvian Achuar, thereby constraining commercial traffic between Ecuador and Peru, and, through its Quichua garrison colonies, infectious diseases have been introduced and spread. Although south of the Pastaza, in Morona-Santiago, the army forced the Achuar and the Shuar to contribute collective labor, in Pastaza the Canelos Quichua colonies long established around the military garrisons provided whatever labor the army needed, and the northern Achuar were thus spared this form of exploitation. The Ecuadorian army has generally avoided direct interference in native Achuar affairs, particularly in conflicts and intergroup warfare. But the situation may change radically in the near future because of increasing military involvement in the process of colonization, as sanctioned by the *Ley de Colonización.*[1] Finally, it should be noted that the army plays a certain role in native beliefs, particularly in the field of shamanism: many (but by no means all) of the most reputed Achuar and Quichua shamans in the Bobonaza area are career soldiers or corporals, and their supernatural powers seem to be somewhat linked to their status as such and to their association with the army.

The Achuar have also long been in contact with itinerant *mestizo* traders, called *regatones* in Peru, *comerciantes* in Ecuador, particularly during the mini-rubber boom of 1940–45. However, the presence of rubber traders here does not seem to have had the disastrous effects entailed in other Amazonian areas, except as a factor in the spread of disease. The rubber traders during both booms relied on Achuar relays or intermediaries to obtain latex rather than on forced labor, and the trade rates appear to have been somewhat less scandalous than elsewhere; indeed, the Pastaza Achuar remember the period of the 1940s with fond nostalgia as an age of abundance. Nowadays a few traders based in Puyo or Montalvo deal in pelts and palm fiber collected by Indian labor, and a few Peruvian loggers exploit the local cedar, through native labor, in the southeastern area of Morona-Santiago. By and large, the labor extracted from the Achuar by the traders has been and is still minimal owing to poor communication and the difficulty of shipping the collected products. Catholic and Protestant missions have now begun to act as intermediaries for the traders. They are taking over the shipping and marketing of the products, and one may foresee, in view of the extensive network the missions have now established, the possibility of a sharp increase in native labor devoted to producing commercially exchangeable commodities. Control by the missions of previously existing commercial webs implies a transition from the labor exchange, labor contract (*enganche*) systems to cash payment, which, in turn, seems economically advantageous to the Achuar.

THE PROCESS OF MISSION IMPLANTATION

The implantation in Achuar territory of the Shuar mission of the Macuma began in the early 1960s, shortly before the Salesians initiated evangelization among the Achuar. In both cases the indigenous initiative of establishing contact, which put an end to 400 years of resistance to white penetration and evangelization, was taken by native "great men" or powerful shamans. These *uunt*[2] were influential and prestigious men who formed the nucleus of an endogamic area (see Descola, in this volume). Their motivation for articulating to mission strategy was to continue procuring indispensable manufactured goods which had long come from Peruvian sources prior to the 1941 conflict between Peru and Ecuador, and which became sharply reduced thereafter. The former web of interethnic trade was modified by the new international border, and the Achuar had to rely more on the missionized Shuar and, ultimately, on the missions themselves as purveyors of manufactured goods. The Achuar great men were also evidently attempting to reproduce the strategic alliances they once had with the rubber dealers which allowed them to control access to white goods and hence reinforce the networks of alliance they manipulated.

The first Protestant evangelist *centro* to be created is exemplary. It was established by Santiak, a very powerful Achuar great man who maintained formal trade relations[3] with a few evangelized Shuar in the Macuma area. At the missionaries' instigation, Santiak and his kin group built an airstrip, and the endogamous neighborhood which was focused on him nucleated in the new *centro*. During the sixties Santiak's airstrip was the only one in Achuar territory, and he enjoyed a quasi-monopoly on the new relations established with Macuma. Then, in 1966 or 1967, Santiak and several of his close kindred were killed during an Achuar raid. The *centro* again dispersed and the strip was abandoned. In the early 1970s the Achuar area on the middle Capahuari River nucleated, and an airstrip was built. Since then, at a few years' interval, nearly all the endogamous zones south and north of the Pastaza have nucleated. In every case the pattern is the same: a great man establishes contact with the mission, usually through Shuar trade partners; the mission, in turn, offers economic support on the condition that the group nucleate and build an airstrip.

The Salesians began making tours of evangelization in Achuar territory in 1962, and in 1968 a missionary settled permanently in Wichim, Morona-Santiago. Then, three or four years ago, the Salesians abandoned the system of permanent missions, and evangelizing priests among the Achuar began to travel constantly from one group to another. This Salesian strategy was probably taken to avoid monopolization of mission resources by one great man and his group to the detriment of others. During the middle 1970s the Federación Shuar, initially kept at a distance by certain missionaries who feared a brutal process of modernization under its influence, began to promote nucleated *centros* around airstrips among the Achuar, henceforth with the active support of the Salesian missionaries, now resigned to the necessity of integrating the Achuar into a powerful and united native organization. By 1978 most of the Achuar areas south of the Pastaza were nucleated, and the last areas of scattered habitat north of the Pastaza had been contacted by missionaries and had agreed to nucleate under the aegis of one or the other missionary organization.

During the early phase of this process the Protestant evangelists made far quicker progress than the Salesians, who refused initially to use planes and encourage the clearing of airstrips for fear of imposing a destructive cultural shock. Meanwhile, the Protestant evangelists actively encouraged Achuar demand for direct access to manufactured goods. Since the middle seventies Salesians, too, began to use all of the technical support at their disposal, and regained a good deal of territory. It seems now that the traditional preponderance of Protestants among the Achuar is losing ground to Catholics and the federation. The fierce rivalry between the missions initially offered the Achuar a margin of maneuver which they exploited strategically to obtain maximum advantages. But this margin is beginning to diminish in the older *centros* owing to the increased involvement in networks of trade and obligations specific to each mission.

WHY THE ACHUAR ACCEPTED MISSION ESTABLISHMENT

The reasons for the Achuar's initial acceptance of missionary penetration must be sought in a combination of three factors: the overwhelming importance of interethnic trade among this group, incipient transformations in the nature of political structures, and warfare and consequent migration for two decades prior to mission establishment. Unlike certain lowland groups, such as the Cashinahua (Kensinger 1975) or some of the Chaco groups, who obtained foreign goods through warfare and raiding (Clastres 1977), ethnohistorical evidence shows the Achuar to have been for centuries eager to obtain foreign goods through trade and, indeed, willing to create artificial scarcity within their own group to ensure the necessity of trade. This trade complex, and particularly the links forged with *regatones* since at least the beginning of this century, had long since established the need for manufactured goods and paved the way for missionary penetration. When the pre-existing trade web was dismantled as a consequence of the 1941 international conflict, the Achuar, in order to maintain their trade complex, had no choice but to initiate contact with new sources of foreign goods.

Although trade with whites and access to manufactured goods had not altered the traditional mode of production, since the Achuar still indirectly controlled their technical factors of production, the trade complex was beginning to affect traditional political relations. Some great men had added control over white goods to the base of their power, and had initiated a process whereby they integrated an economic dimension to their position, a process that was to be generalized and considerably amplified by the missions. Thus, prior to the establishment of the religious organizations, the political status of a few great men already depended to a limited extent on privileged access to white goods. To maintain their position, they were obliged to seek the means to reproduce the economic component of their power. This explains, I think, the decisive role played by great men in establishing contact with the missions.

The last factor is more contingent, and concerns the intensity of warfare and migration in the two decades prior to mission establishment. By all native accounts, intergroup warfare and consequent migration between roughly 1940 and 1960 were exceptionally intense. This engendered an acute need for guns and ammunition, and thus reinforced Achuar dependency on means of access to manufactured commodities. At the same time the spread of firearms and the violence of feuding (linked to a combination of historical factors I cannot detail here) led to a situation wherein traditional warfare, as the Achuar explicitly recognize, was getting out of hand. At a rough estimate, well over 50% of the adult males in that generation were killed in feuds, and the Achuar frequently refer to this period as one during which "we were ending," by which they clearly mean that the rate of Achuar mortality was menacing their very survival. This apocalyptic atmosphere was favorable to mission implantation: intergroup trade was difficult, particularly for refugee groups in remote areas, access to guns was essential, and the intensity of killing, apparently well beyond anything the traditional pattern of warfare could account for, probably made the Achuar receptive to the claims of manifestly powerful white groups who offered protection and stressed "peace."

The combination of these three factors accounts for the manner by which the Achuar initiated contact and attempted to reproduce a pre-established model of sociopolitical relations with whites, treating the missionaries initially as merely another ethnic variety of purveyors of manufactured goods. The economic and political features of this process explain the initial success of the Protestant evangelist mission, whose base was strategically located in an area where most Pastaza Achuar had long since established formal trade relations with the local Shuar population.[4]

The methods of implantation of the Catholic and Protestant missions were somewhat distinct. Among the evangelists the clearing of an airstrip was a preliminary condition to the process of mission acculturation. It thereby implied a clearcut decision on the part of the Achuar to henceforth engage in direct and sustained contact with the white world. Among the Salesians the process was more gradual and allowed the Achuar greater possibilities of tactical maneuver and a certain familiarity with forms of behavior characteristic of the missionaries. These variations in the methods of implantation point to important differences, at the ideological and administrative levels, between the two missions. Among the Protestants, control is remote; evangelist missionaries very rarely visit the Achuar *centros*, and then only very briefly. It is also highly centralized and based on the energetic fostering of economic dependency through mechanisms I will describe in due course. The Salesian system, by contrast, is characterized by a much higher degree of direct contact with the Achuar of a few itinerant missionaries thoroughly familiar with Achuar language and behavior, and by a greater degree of decentralization. The Salesians also made an initial, rather unsuccessful effort to dissociate Christianity, technology, and economics, while the Protestants link them inextricably. These differences between the missions account for partially distinct native attitudes and ideological elaborations vis-à-vis each mission organization.

THE MISSIONS' MECHANISMS OF CONTROL

In addition to residential nucleation (see Descola, in this volume) the major innovations introduced by both organizations are cattle raising and breeding, mission control of access to manufactured goods, and formal education. These four factors are the main instruments of mission control over Achuar economy, society, and ideology.

Cattle and the Political Economy

According to the Achuar themselves, the prospect of acquiring cattle as a source of revenue was the main incentive for settling in *centros* and accepting the tutorship of the missions. Cattle are in fact now the main source of cash among the Achuar, at least in the older *centros*, and they are also the main commodity denoted by the native concept of *yus kuit*, "God-wealth." God-wealth is that purveyed by the mission and associated with Christian proselytization.

Wage labor is still sporadic and limited, though north of the Pastaza most adult men have contributed at least a few months of work to the *kumpánia*, Amoco and other petroleum exploration companies. A handful of Achuar worked in the coastal provinces; all returned after a year at most and resumed their traditional mode of existence. The money thus earned was sometimes invested in cattle but far more often in consumer goods such as radios and clothes that were rapidly reinvested in the traditional *amigri* or shamanistic trade circuits (see Harner 1972). Wage labor did not, then, entail a process of capital accumulation.

Cattle raising and breeding, however, is definitely causing incipient capital accumulation. In Shuar Federation territory cattle raising stemmed essentially from the necessity of effectively occupying and legally maintaining a maximum amount of land in the face of IERAC and CREA policies (see Salazar, in this volume). The process culminated in the development of a large-scale cattle program which now menaces the very land it was initially meant to protect. This program was extended to the Achuar a few years ago. According to federation policy (Salazar, in this volume; Federación de Centros Shuar 1976), the *centros* are encouraged to form communal *grupos de desarrollo ganadero*, and a large injection of credit extended by the federation allows them to acquire *gramalote* seeds and large quantities of cattle. There are now about 200 cattle in Achuar federation territory, most of them concentrated in the two oldest *centros*, Pumpuentza and Wichim. Despite the federation's cooperative charter, most cattle are individually appropriated.

The introduction of cattle through the AIPSE, by contrast, had little to do with land claims. Cattle were introduced explicitly to foment individual accumulation of capital profits as a means of acquiring consumer goods such as clothes, radios, and medicine. The specific rationale was to set the Achuar on the path to "civilization." Development of cattle breeding in the Protestant centers is still incipient; of the six evangelist *centros* north of the Pastaza, only two have any cattle at all, and two dozen head is the total number between them as of August 1978. Cattle are nearly always purchased in Macuma, and most native people participate in the AIPSE system. In this system a Shuar or the mission itself gives an Achuar a calf, and then takes about half of the profits when the grown animal is slaughtered. This rental or cattle-share system spares the initial owner the work of expanding cleared pasture land and usefully diffuses such pasture land out of the Macuma area. Among the Protestant Achuar there is no communal or cooperative property; appropriation is strictly individual.[5]

In both the federation and AIPSE systems the slaughtered cattle are immediately shipped out by plane and sold at market towns such as Puyo or Sucúa. One head of cattle is worth 3,000 to 7,000 sucres there, and the missions calculate profits against the shipment flight. The cost of meat flights averages 1,500 sucres for most Achuar *centros*. Macuma keeps firm control over the entire process, by its monopoly over access to cattle, transportation, and sale, while the federation controls the Shuar's own program somewhat independently of the Salesians. The Achuar themselves have no control whatsoever over these economic processes.

Despite their distinct ideological concerns and forms of administration, the differences between the two organizations are more a matter of degree than of kind with respect to cattle commerce. The effects of the cattle-based political economy are far more drastic, however, in the federation *centros* than in the AIPSE ones. Despite the frankly capitalist, individually accumulative aspects of the latter program, it is as yet on such a small scale that the effects are relatively limited.

Some of the consequences of the introduction of cattle among the Achuar, specifically the ecological changes and the fundamental modification of the traditional mode of production linked to nucleation, have been detailed in Descola's paper; I am concerned here with another facet of the process: the transformation of traditional political relationships.

The individual appropriation of new factors of production establishes an incipient economic inequality that directly affects the form and content of social relations of a political nature. The great men who initiated contact with the missions are usually the first to receive cattle from the missions. Their loyalty to one or the other mission organization is essential to keep their endogamous nucleating kin group in the missions' orbit, and it is rewarded with economic privileges. This bond of loyalty, constantly fed by the missions, takes on an aspect of economic dependency. The power of the great men, previously based primarily on a combination of personal prestige and the capacity to manipulate vast networks of alliance, is juxtaposed to a radically different economic base.

The mission-induced inflation of the economic base of the great men's power has allowed them to acquire large quantities of manufactured goods. This privileged access to white wealth now unfolding among the Achuar automatically places great men in the position of purveyors of new means of production and prestige values within their *centros*, a position which greatly reinforces their former status.[6] They provide their kin with new commodities, but their kin usually cannot repay them in kind and thereby remain permanently in debt to them. The great men, by adding a completely new economic dimension to the base of their power, add bonds of economic dependency to the traditional system of kinship-based political relations. Just as they become dependent on the mission, so too do their endogamous kindred come to depend on them.

As more and more domestic units receive cattle directly from the missions, economic dependency on the great men weakens, but it does not disappear. The great men have a head start in the process and will continue to accumulate and hence maintain the gap between themselves and the rest of their kin group. The great men are now exploring new means of maintaining and expressing their power. One of these means seems to be the manipulation of the new *cargos* introduced by the missions. These *cargos* involve holding formal "office" (e.g. president, secretary, *vocal*) within the nucleated settlement, the offices being the formal linkages with the missions and the indigenous organizations. The *cargos* themselves seem to be inspired partly by the Ecuadorian central bureaucracy and partly by ancient Andean models. Protestant missionaries, Catholic missionaries, Shuar Federation officials, and development specialists seem equally attracted to, and attached to, this model. Initially, the great men shunned these new forms of political authority, and they were invariably occupied by semimarginalized youths (who were, however, dependent upon a great man) with some experience working for the missions. Today in the older *centros* these *cargos*, particularly that of *presidente*, are being sought after by traditional or aspiring great men, who add heretofore unknown political dimensions to their power (e.g. the giving of direct orders) as their phase of exclusive economic privilege begins to wane.

Trade and Commerce

Trade is an obsessive preoccupation among the Achuar; rates and objects of exchange are a constant subject of conversation, and travelers often form the impression that Achuar trade merely for trade's sake. Achuar society is criss-crossed by a dense web of trade relations, and there is a constant flow of commodities within the endogamous group, between endogamous areas, and between the Achuar as an ethnic unit and their jungle Quichua and Shuar neighbors. At the territorial and intertribal level these trade relations were, and still are to a certain extent, based on local specializations. The northern Achuar excelled in the manufacture of blowguns and traded them north to the Canelos Quichua and south to the Morona Achuar; curare and glass beads from Peru were channeled west toward the Shuar; shotguns and salt came from the Shuar and flowed east, and so on. This local specialization was itself based either on a quasi-monopoly over certain natural products with restricted geographic distribution (e.g. specific palms, salt, latex, pigments for ceramics) or on the monopoly of access to certain manufactured goods (steel tools, rifles, shotguns, black powder, shot, and glass beads).

A crucial aspect of trade relations among the Achuar is the tremendous value attached to goods from "outside": outside the territorial group, outside the tribe, and the more "exotic" the more highly valued. Moreover, the prestige attributed to "foreignness" applies equally to material and symbolic values, a point to which I shall return. This aspect of Achuar ideology appears to be structural rather than contingent and due to recent historical factors. It offers the missions a foothold for penetration and constitutes a vital point of asymmetric articulation. Both missionary organizations have capitalized on these factors and have progressively created or gained control over channels of access to white goods. Their interference with, or manipulation of, native trade circuits has entailed fundamental economic and ideological transformations.

The federation and the Salesians are attempting to suppress recourse to *mestizo* intermediaries, to permit fair access to the national market economy. Toward this end, they have begun to establish local sources of manufactured goods within each *centro* or within easy reach of them, in the form of cooperative *tiendas*, small shops, that provide the Achuar with consumer goods such as cloth, radios, batteries, and production tools such as machetes, fishing tackle, and hunting implements. Both organizations promote the sale of short-wave radio sets, since radio transmission is for both an important element of propaganda. These *tiendas* are stocked by plane through the mission networks. The multiplication of local sources of manufactured goods in the federation centers is beginning to replace the traditional trade relations with the Shuar and Peruvian Achuar, and those between endogamous zones as well. Consumer goods and traditional exchange values still circulate to some extent, but the *amigri*-type relations, by losing their former economic importance, are gradually losing a good deal of their strength. Furthermore, the circulation of cash, fairly plentiful now in some Achuar federation *centros* because of the cattle program, also erodes these relations. Finally, the Salesians themselves now maintain a virtual monopoly on the trade of Italian glass seed beads, *shauk*, which formerly came westward from Peru. This quasi-monopoly of the highly valued beads, believed to be of celestial origin by the Achuar, is a great asset to the Salesians. Many Achuar explicitly (though privately) invoke easier access to the beloved *shauk* to justify joining the federation or shifting their allegiance from the Protestant AIPSE to the *Sucúa Pátri*, Fathers of Sucúa.

The federation officials appear to be aware of the socioeconomic effects implied by articulation to the national market economy, that is, the breakdown of intergroup relations and incipient stratification based on economic inequality. However, the federation's hyper *desarrollista* attitude, the advanced degree of acculturation of the Shuar proper (whence all the federation leaders stem), and their own increasing and inevitable involvement in the national economy entrap them in contradictions (see Salazar, in this volume). In spite of themselves, the federation and the Salesians are today engendering among the Achuar an increasing dependency on imported goods and increasing dependency on the organizations that control access to these goods.

The basic aim of Protestant evangelist policy is quite clearly to integrate the AIPSE Achuar and Shuar into the national market at whatever cost. In Protestant evangelist ideology the capitalist market is both natural and divinely sanctioned, and does not imply inequality *per se*. According to Protestant economic doctrine in its most naive form, the market itself is fundamentally equilibrated, and apparent injustices are merely transitional phenomena destined to disappear with the onset of technological "progress." Evangelist methods differ markedly from those of the federation and Salesians. Macuma has, until recently, concentrated on controlling and intensifying the traditional web of trade relations centered on the Shuar of its surrounding area, who obtain manufactured goods from the mission shop. Nearly all Pastaza Achuar have *amigri* in Macuma, and many had them before the mission settled there. These *amigri* relations have been reinforced by the mission, whose radio and air service greatly facilitated communication, and the flow of goods into and out of Macuma has enormously increased in volume. Through this trade network flow traditionally valued goods such as dogs, blowguns, curare, and jungle products, most of these coming from the Achuar; from the Shuar flow consumer goods bought for barter purposes at the mission shop. The mission also controls the still important trade of native salt, another highly valued item produced by the Mangosiza Shuar and redistributed through Macuma networks. Rather than create new channels of access to white goods, the Protestant mission has thus chosen to reinforce and control the traditional trade network centered on Macuma, and modify its content rather than its form. This centralized control is based on personal relationships of dependency on, and loyalty to, mission workers and highly evangelized Shuar. The nature of the trade network now radiating out of Macuma accounts for limited circulation of cash in the evangelist area and for the persistence of traditional forms of trade relations there.

Among the Pastaza Achuar, most adult men have also long had *compadrazgo* or *amigri* bonds with Montalvo *mestizo* traders who were formerly the main purveyors of manufactured goods of Peruvian origin.[7] Within the past two years, however, the Protestant mission has begun to modify this ancient network by sending native evangelist highland *comerciantes* by plane into the Achuar *centros* to facilitate direct access to consumer goods wherever cash is available. This project has so far met with limited success, since cash is still scarce and the prices are the same as in Montalvo. Furthermore, the Achuar are unwilling to enter into impersonal market relationships which no longer constitute exchange, as they know it, but a form of transaction the terms of which escape their control and their understanding.

Both Protestant and Catholic missions have begun to act as intermediaries for the Montalvo and Puyo traders in the commerce of palm fiber and cinnamon. In the *centros* where cattle breeding has become important and time-consuming, this mission move has had little effect, since, despite the new incentives, men involved with cattle and their pastures have little time to devote to collecting activities. In those *centros* where cattle are still scarce or nonexistent, however, there has been a sharp increase in labor devoted to the trade in tropical products. The intensive exploitation of natural resources has begun to engender territorial conflicts, particularly *within* the endogamous group. Unless cattle raising and the "sedentarizing" bond it implies counterbalance this commercial gathering, the stepped-up commerce radiating out of Puyo and Montalvo will undoubtedly cause new forms of land appropriation and engender hitherto unknown types of conflict.

Formal Education

In the Salesian-controlled areas the Achuar have generally escaped the mission boarding school system (see Salazar, in this volume) that has so affected the Shuar proper. Children are today taught through the bilingual education radio program elaborated and set up by the federation. The lessons are prepared by federation *telemaestros* who have completed their secondary studies, usually in the Salesian boarding school, and daily transmitted by radio from headquarters in Sucúa. In each *centro* a *teleauxiliar*, who is supposed to be a member of the *centro* where he is teaching, explains and supervises work in the *centro* school. In fact, since there are still very few bilingual and literate Achuar, these *teleauxiliares* are usually Shuar, trained in the mission boarding school. The auxiliary teachers are given brief training seminars every year in Sucúa, under the aegis of the federation and the Salesians. The Protestant evangelists, by contrast, never tried to impose boarding schools, except on a very small scale in Macuma, and from the start they established bilingual schools within each *centro*. Teachers are either Macuma Shuar, with a low degree of formal schooling, or, increasingly in Pastaza province, Napo Quichua recruited in a well-established Quichua evangelist *centro*. This is an odd system, since Achuar-Quichua bilingualism is not generalized among all northern Achuar, and very few children know Quichua. Moreover, unlike the Canelos Quichua (Whitten 1976a and b, 1978), Napo Quichua do not know Achuar. These Shuar and Quichua teachers are always dedicated evangelists, and serve as preachers in the *centros* where they teach. They are trained at the Summer Institute of Linguistics' main base in Limoncocha during yearly summer sessions. The bilingual education programs are recognized by the Ecuadorian Ministry of Education and are to a certain extent bound by the programs and directives issued by the ministry.

The introduction of formal schooling implies direct effects on work processes and on traditional modes of socialization. It stresses, for example, the removal of unmarried girls' labor from the work force and so has considerable impact on the feminine sphere of production. Most Achuar women try to keep at least one of their daughters at home, since the bond between mother and daughter is a very powerful one, and women need their daughters' company and help. Swidden gardens are the essential female domain, and transmission of basic feminine technical and symbolic knowledge revolves around it. Formal schooling also interferes, though to a lesser extent, with the boys' acquisition of the highly complex hunting techniques and general knowledge of the jungle world that life in the tropical rainforest demands.

Formal education is the institution which instills the ideology bred, consciously and unconsciously, by the missionary organizations. This ideology, in turn, is more or less receptive to the values characteristic of the dominant national ideology. The explicit or implicit messages transmitted by the teachers draw their efficacy from the signs flaunted by the teachers of "a successful approach" to the white world. Success is explicitly tied to accumulation of wealth in consumer goods, accumulation of money, mastery of written and spoken Spanish, etc. This putative profitability of association with the spheres of white power gives teachers an important status that enables them to play a vital role in many fields beyond their competence. In fact, they do play a key role in most of the processes of indigenous cultural transformation through contact. This is especially notable in the institutional organization of the nucleated *centros* where teachers unofficially help elect appointees to the organization's *cargos*, formally divide the *centro* into "private" plots allotted to each household, and organize collective tasks to maintain airstrip, public buildings, and the like. A clear indication of both the teachers' status and of the Achuar's awareness of their strategic position lies in the fact that great men or aspiring great men frequently offer them daughters in marriage. The point of this prestation is to transform the teachers into dependent sons-in-law, an asymmetrical relationship that in the traditional system implies a lengthy period of submission to the wife's father.

The teachers' influence, as vehicles and models of acculturation, works at distinct levels. The most vital of these, perhaps, for the Achuar are the insidious alterations in patterns of behavior, such as newly acquired food habits, conjugal relationships, and parental relations. These alterations imply a radical, if tacit, subversion of native cognitive categories. For example, Achuar women view the wealth in consumer goods exhibited by the teachers' wives as the result of a superior symbolic knowledge, and the unusual public demonstrations of conjugal affection exhibited by the teachers as the effect of a magical power of seduction. Intense interest in such putative symbolic superiority of the teachers' wives blinds the Achuar women to the latter's increasing alienation. These wives, in fact, suffer very real loss of symbolic participation in the ordering of the swidden, household, and rainforest universe, and come to live in an affectively sterile world.

Both male and female Achuar also share the widespread belief that Shuar and white women take better care of their children. Achuar women are, overall, the social, economic, and symbolic "reproducers" of life. The belief in Achuar inferiority in this respect seems to be a metaphoric expression of the women's awareness that they now lack the necessary symbolic tools to continue playing their full, traditional roles in a changing world, and prefigures not only the isolation and alienation awaiting them as women but the waning of a whole way of life. In fact, teachers' wives and Shuar women, in general, have easier access to, and a greater familiarity with, white medicine and western hygiene and their babies have a lower rate of mortality; this is perceived by the Achuar women to indicate greater symbolic power through association with the white world, and they thereby give considerable weight to the models of behavior these women introduce.

Housing, too, is an aspect of Achuar life into which teachers intrude. The traditional Achuar house is a cultural microcosm of the universe, a locus of dense symbolic markers endowed with a highly complex structure. Many teachers, however, have assimilated the whites' repugnance for this kind of house, a horror rooted in fantasies of savage promiscuity within the *jivaría* coupled with the dread induced by dispersed habitat which lies beyond the pale of a village and its nucleated warmth and security. The Achuar house is thus for many whites an emblematic image of *salvajismo*, forest savagery. The introduction of a new architectural model, now also common among jungle Quichua, was initially imposed by the Dominican missionaries. Its primary aim is to isolate the conjugal pair from its children, on the one hand, and kindred, on the other, by segmenting the house into "bedrooms," kitchen, and public sectors. This division of space is completely at odds with the traditional Achuar model, as it is with the Canelos Quichua one (Whitten 1976a), which is based on a purely symbolic division between male and female sectors. The new model, particularly vaunted by the Protestant evangelist teachers, implies considerable modification in the nature and function of intrahousehold relationships. Children are increasingly cut off from their parents' technical and symbolic knowledge, informally trans-mitted, in a traditional setting through public discussion of dreams, the telling of myths, and the ordinary conversations that flow through a house at night and in the very early hours of the morning. Women are also increasingly relegated to, and isolated in, a separate kitchen cut off from the public or social male sector. The sad culmi-nation of this process may be seen in highly acculturated Shuar *cen-tros*, where the men, in *colono*-style houses, occupy the vacant scene of modernity, while the women in these homes live in a kitchen-hut often built as a reduced model of a traditional house, and are thereby relegated symbolically to a meaningless "primitivity," the traditional complementarity between male and female spheres a fading memory.[8] The weight of white prejudice against traditional houses is much stronger in Protestant *centros*, particularly north of the Pastaza. In the federation centers the determined efforts of a few missionaries who have come to appreciate and understand Achuar architecture has in some measure offset the influence of these prejudices.

At the level of the explicit content of education, and the official mission ideology transmitted by the teachers, the differences be-tween the Protestant and Catholic organizations are far more clear-cut. The Salesian mission stresses the value of traditional culture and endeavors to relate the content of modern, nationalist education to traditional Shuar lifeways. This effort, however, is contradictory, as the Achuar are exposed to Shuar culture as digested by the Salesians and reassimilated by the federation *maestros*. The educational pro-duce, although crafted with high valuation on traditional Shuar cul-ture, is, of course, neither Achuar culture nor even authentic Shuar culture. Moreover, the relatively rationalist or "scientific" world view shared by the Salesians and imposed by the Ministry of Education is at odds with the native world view. The conception of causality and cosmological order implicit in this "scientific" world view has had very little impact so far, but in the long run, combined with and rein-forced by other factors of change, it will progressively undermine traditional accounts of the universe.

Another contradiction may be detected in the methods of formal education, wherein the basic technique is collective, based on rote assimilation and wholly cut off from the adult world. By contrast, traditional Achuar individual teaching, based on example, observa-tion, and the personal transmission of techniques of symbolic control and supernatural powers, is utterly alien to western pedagogy. It is questionable whether traditional content, transmitted through nontraditional media, really contributes to the maintenance of native values; the media, above all, allow the constant social manipulation of native ideology that keeps traditional representations alive and meaningful. Finally, the militancy of the *telemaestros* and the federation leaders is by no means always shared by the local auxiliaries who work in Achuar territory. These *teleauxiliares* lack the formal training that allows the *maestros* and leaders to intellectualize and, up to a point, utilize, white culture, in white terms, and so they tend to perpetuate attitudes formerly imposed by the Salesians and prejudices absorbed uncritically from the white world. Just as the Shuar were not long ago the "savages" of the missionaries, the Achuar have now become the "savages" of the Shuar. The Achuar within the Salesian-federation system are thus to a certain extent victims of an educational system and a set of values and attitudes sincerely repudiated by most present-day missionaries.

Among the Protestant evangelists, by contrast, there is very little contradiction between implicit and explicit messages, and education quite openly implies the rejection of traditional values. Through radio propaganda and formal education the Protestants explicitly aim at suppressing certain fundamental social characteristics of Achuar culture such as polygyny, shamanism, warfare, the consumption of *chicha*, dancing and drinking feasts, and even ritual speech, which is felt, rightly, to be a manifestation of indigenous spiritual power, and as such discouraged. Of these prohibitions, the only ones that seem to be truly effective up to now are those pertaining to dancing and drinking feasts, probably because these were always somewhat explosive and tension-fraught affairs. In a nucleated setting such occasions could generate situations of conflict incompatible with *centro* unity. Achuar pliancy in the face of this prohibition is thus a self-imposed repression—the Protestant prohibition is effective because it is linked to a critical internal contradiction attendant on nucleation. Although the Achuar are not yet prepared to give up all the other practices forbidden by the missionaries, white disapproval does weigh heavily on their minds and accounts for certain attitudes toward conversion.

In addition to denigrating Achuar culture, the evangelist teachers exalt the virtues of hard work, technological development, and personal capital accumulation. They amalgamate these values in the vague but much-bandied concept of *adelantamiento*, progress. The intercultural clash is further aggravated, in the case of Quichua teachers, by the infusion of native ethnocentric prejudice, sanctioned by and sometimes confused with evangelical attitudes. The Protestant evangelist teachers' message is constantly repeated at school, during religious services, and in conversations with *centro* members. It clearly illustrates a confused synthesis of three different dynamics: access to the white national and international world, christianization, and rejection of Achuar values. This ideology is actively inculcated to the teachers at Limoncocha during the summer training sessions.[9] I do not mean to imply, however, that native evangelist teachers are wholly submissive to mission policies and ideas. I do mean to stress that their possibilities of contestation are rather limited. The level of education of the missionaries themselves and their anti-intellectual prejudices do not lead them to encourage advanced or even adequate education for Indian youths. And the evangelist *maestros* generally have a level of education far inferior to that of the federation teachers, so that, unlike the latter, they cannot use the tools of a modern education to "white" means of action. A certain political awareness is, however, emerging within the ranks of evangelist *maestros*. Thus far, this political contestation is limited to the occasional refusal to comply with certain missionary demands. Its current form of incipient protest, expressed through claims such as "they make money from us" or "we do their work for them," is rooted in an inchoate perception of the exploitative aspects of the mission-native relationship by which native maneuvers to extract greater benefits from the mission are justified. The Pastaza missions, aware of this discontent, have been trying to co-opt the native organizations that are springing up as a result of native frustration, particularly among semieducated christianized Indians, and thus short-circuit and subvert their potentially explosive character. Among the "acculturated," putatively christianized groups whence the native teachers stem, coherent protest does take place at other levels, notably in mythology, ritual, and shamanism, inaccessible to direct white manipulation.

INDIGENOUS INTERETHNIC RELATIONS AND MISSION CONTROL

In the course of the preceding paragraphs a feature common to both Protestant and Catholic missions should have emerged: both rely heavily on native ethnic groups adjacent to the Achuar—the jungle Quichua and the Shuar proper—to further their policies. The manner in which the missions put these neighboring groups to use is conditioned by the past history of interethnic relations, which are, in turn, partially modified according to mission needs. A brief examination of the nature of these relations, both past and present, is now in order.

Achuar-Shuar

The relationships between Achuar and Shuar, as with all relations within the Jivaroan cultures, were until recently forged through institutionalized warfare and hostility. A warrior ethos was apparently common to the whole Jivaroan group—including Maina, Huambisa, Aguaruna, as well as Shuar and Achuar. The ideological specificities of each group in this respect are complementary, and probably form a coherent transformational system which remains to be described and analyzed. These relations should not be conceived of, in my opinion, as a negation of exchange or its converse aspect, "the issue of an unfortunate or failed transaction" (Lévi-Strauss 1943:136), but rather as a specific modality of exchange, expressed in the idiom of violence. To put it succinctly, Jivaroan subgroups exchanged deaths to ensure the symbolic reproduction of their own units.[10] The same notion of violent reciprocal exchange underlies representations linked to hunting, which is closely associated, symbolically (and generally in terms of systematic inversion), to warfare. Hunting is assimilated to warfare against the animal spirit populations, whereas warfare is assimilated to predation through the warrior's stipulated identity with a jungle predator.[11] We seem, then, to have the equation *hunting:culture acting on nature::war:nature acting on culture.* This equation reflects the symmetric inversion characteristic of many Achuar representations.

Jivaroan exchange of violence (both of death and of women, through abduction) by no means excluded "normal" trade, both of commodities and of women, but rather included them and endowed them with particularly structured features (Harner 1972). These features have been progressively modified, owing, on the one hand, to the disequilibrium in the intertribal trade network and, on the other, to acculturation of the Shuar and the consequent disappearance of head-taking raids. Contemporary trade relations are stripped of the warfare practices and a large part of the bellicose ideology that formerly included them. Achuar trade relations are currently based on the Shuar's proximity to white commodities and their presumed greater familiarity with mechanisms of acquisition of these goods. However, an imagery of violence still strongly permeates these trade relations. One such Shuar in Achuar territory stated his insecurity succinctly by telling us: "we feel like hostages here." The underlying ideology of violence is also manifest in the rigid control which Achuar fathers-in-law exercise over their Shuar sons-in-law, the constant accusations of sexual misconduct and "woman stealing" that

are directed at Shuar by Achuar, and the pervasive tension and frequent rows that erupt between Achuar and Shuar brothers-in-law.
The hostility that permeates these relations is further complicated by
the incipient infiltration of Shuar in Achuar land, owing to demographic expansion and increasing *colono* pressure on Shuar territory.
In light of these factors the bestowing of Achuar women on Shuar
men may be seen as a reluctant but necessary alliance, the counterpart of which is access to white goods and techniques of control. The
Shuar position, however, lies exclusively in their greater proximity
to, and familiarity with, the white spheres, and not in different techniques of supernatural control. Their techniques of symbolic manipulation as applied to the white world are only quantitatively superior
to, not qualitatively different from, those of the Achuar. The Shuar
position is thus essentially that of economic mediator and they are
used as such, consciously or not, by the missions. Their influence
and their margin of maneuver are circumscribed and conditioned by
the stringent control the Achuar attempt to impose on them, and by
the systematically emphasized cultural "distance" between the two
Jivaroan subgroups.

Achuar–Jungle Quichua

The relation between the Achuar and the jungle Quichua is wholly
distinct and forms a different constellation, quite independent from
the intra-Jivaroan war complex. Whereas the Shuar appear essentially as necessary mediators in the flow of white *material* commodities, the Quichuas are above all mediators in the flow of white *symbolic* powers, manipulated essentially through shamanistic networks.
The supernatural powers of the Shuar are basically identical to those
of the Achuar, but more developed and amplified through assimilation of certain white techniques, owing to their greater familiarity
with the latter. The jungle Quichua, however, have qualitatively distinct and specific powers. This complex of differential cosmic power
also implies trade, but of a somewhat different nature. The Shuar
and Achuar traded goods and women with each other in exchange
for material wealth. They both also traded goods and women with
the jungle Quichua in exchange for supernatural commodities. A remarkable trait of this complex is that while Shuar and Achuar remain
linguistically and ethnically clearly separate and distant, Achuar/Qui-
chua relations are characterized by extraordinary lability and fluidity.
Ethnic boundaries are much more imprecise and fluctuating, under-
played rather than emphasized, and phenomena of transculturation

and bilingualism that allow individuals to slide in and out of groups whose social structures are markedly different (though the structure of their ideology is in many ways similar) are very common among the northern Achuar.

This peculiar type of interethnic relation is linked to the specific nature of jungle Quichua culture, forged by centuries of white domination, which, while being apparently wholly submissive to the dominant society, has developed extremely subtle techniques of ideological resistance, based on the *Alli Runa/Sacha Runa* polarity: *Alli Runa* is the white man's Christian Quichua, pliant to the dominance of *mestizo* society and Dominican authority which the Quichua have been confronting for centuries. *Sacha Runa*, steeped in supernatural power based on techniques of symbolic manipulation that seek to control white power by integrating it to complex traditional paradigms, remains invisible to and hidden from the white world. A fuller description of the fascinating and complex oscillation of this Janus-faced native group is far beyond the reach of this work, and may be found in the studies the Whittens have devoted to it (Whitten 1976a, 1976b, 1978; Whitten and Whitten 1978; D. Whitten, in this volume).

To put it in somewhat simplified terms, jungle Quichua societies form species of multilayered transformational mechanisms. Whites generally see them as a civilizing influence able to bring the Jivaroan and Auca *bravo* Indians to submit to "decent" attitudes and behavior, whereas the indigenous groups such as Achuar and Shuar interact with the *Sacha Runa* side, with its highly developed techniques of symbolic manipulation.

Jungle Quichua cultures are thus double-edged instruments in social transformation. They derive their prestige from their supernatural powers, and this very prestige adds enormous weight to the influence of the cultural models they transmit. I take many of these models to be the result of advanced forced acculturation and white pressure. Therefore, if I am correct, Quichua culture is a potentially effective tool of national domination and penetration, and this fact accounts for, and justifies, the intensive use which Catholic and Protestant missions have long made of these native peoples. On the other hand, the missions are evidently wholly ignorant of what ultimately accounts for the efficacy of the Quichua's "civilizing" influences—the symbolic power diverted from the white universe. Therefore, the missions remain entirely unaware of the possibilities of ideological resistance which this jungle Quichua power also implies (see Whitten 1978).

Mission Ideology and Indigenous Ethnicity

Before exploring Achuar ideological elaborations in the face of missionary penetration, some further comments on the mission organizations themselves and their underlying ideological differences are required. In this paper I have consistently linked the Salesian mission to the Shuar Federation. This could be misleading but is justified vis-à-vis the Achuar, who make no distinction between the *Sucúa Pátri* and the federation. Indeed, they assume that the former entirely run the latter. Whether or not this is generally true is a moot point. However, the Achuar's own view seems to reflect the local situation accurately. The missionaries at work among the Achuar are, in effect, the main links to the federation and are the purveyors of its policies. They are the local federation counselors and can act as buffers between the Achuar and the Shuar Federation. The fact that the Salesians were able, if only for a brief time, to isolate the Achuar from the federation is a sure sign of their narrow control over federation policies and administration in this particular area.

The Salesian mission has undergone profound transformation in the last few years. The pastoral crises highlighted in the mission conferences at Melgar (1969), Iquitos (1971), and Manaus (1975) that followed the Vatican II Concile led to a major reorientation of mission policies through the progressive abandonment of permanent missions and the oppressive structures they implied (boarding schools, exploitation of native labor). Pastoral and liturgic reform took place following the widespread adoption of the principle of divine incarnation and the consequent Christian adaptation of native ritual.[12] Although former Salesian structures and attitudes still carry weight (there is yet a strong conservative faction within the mission), and although there are many points beyond which Catholic doctrine simply cannot adapt to native value systems (e.g. to the Achuar's attachment to warfare and polygyny), it is clear that the Salesian mission nowadays is a far cry from the traditional, fiercely conservative, fundamentally paternalist Latin American Roman Catholic mission. The latter traits are still characteristic, however, of the Dominican mission of Canelos, now centered in urban Puyo. Until recently this mission was in charge of all native groups including the Achuar in southern Pastaza province, a fact that contributed to Protestant evangelist penetration in the area.[13] While the Salesians did not want to upset established territorial mission prerogatives and take over Dominican fiefs, the Protestants, untroubled by such considerations, moved in with a vengeance. The Dominican presence, highly sporadic among the Achuar, seems to have left very little mark on them, beyond the belief that Hell is located in the Tungurahua volcano (an idea now used by the Protestant evangelists) and the appearance of a new figure in the supernatural bestiary, the Pátri Titipiur, an evil, bearded, black-booted spirit dressed in white that feeds on the livers of sleeping people.

The sociological and ideological background of the Protestant evangelist mission is entirely different from the Catholic one. It is based in a sectarian-egalitarian fundamentalist tradition of individualism and rural community-based democracy. These features, combined with its greater structural compatibility with native social systems and its latent anti-Latin and strong anti-Catholic prejudice, can and do make it appear as a countermodel to, or an instrument of protest against, dominant national and nationalist structures. This implicit element of protest helps to account, along with messianic traits, for overwhelming evangelist success in situations of intolerable social oppression (see Ribeiro 1971). Among the Achuar, stress owing to national pressure has not yet reached this critical degree, but it is sufficient to ensure this feature of evangelism a certain echo among the Indians, particularly in Pastaza province. The potential political implications of Protestant evangelism are immediately deflected and offset, however, by other aspects of its ideology which transform it into a semimessianic and ultimately conservative ideology. The midwestern and southern U.S. fundamentalism typical of the Macuma mission is characterized by the exaltation of routinized physical labor and success in capital accumulation as a sign of divine favor, and by an emphasis on direct recourse to God in mundane affairs. In their eyes, poverty and misfortune are born not of social conditions but of a lack of faith. Despite the Protestant evangelists' antiscientific bias, they rely strongly on industrial technology, a product which they regard as deriving from man's divinely inspired natural ingenuity. Social progress is linked to individual efforts at economic growth through an appeal to divine intervention. These notions lead them to consider all values opposed to or outside these beliefs as fundamentally non-Christian or anti-Christian. They are Satan-inspired.[14]

These attitudes are, of course, applied to the traditional culture of the Achuar, whose religious beliefs terrify the evangelist missionaries. They consider Achuar culture to be an oppressive system that maintains the natives themselves in a state of permanent spiritual terror. This characteristic fundamentalist attitude justifies the cultural destruction of native groups, since, in good faith, destruction is the only way to liberate them from Satan's grip and save the individual souls of converts. Moreover, a strong infusion of militaristic values leads them to consider evangelical proselytization as a Holy War against Evil (Evil here includes all nonevangelist values and life-styles), a theme that is constantly emphasized and diffused in popular biblical imagery, hymns, and religious radio programs.

As might be expected, then, the interaction between native beliefs and variant Christian doctrines is by no means entirely similar among Catholic-evangelized and Protestant-evangelized Achuar. The articulation is more complex and syncretic among the former; sharply polarized, asyncretic, and incipiently messianic among the latter. Paradoxically, at a deeper level, certain Protestant evangelist notions closely tally with native conceptions. However, the differences in these contrasting ideologies are, for the time being, largely hidden by and subordinate to native ideological productions vis-à-vis the white world that are common to both groups. In the long run, though, as the social context changes, these differential effects should come to be more and more marked.

GOD-WEALTH: THE IDEOLOGICAL ROOTS OF MISSIONARY PENETRATION

There is no doubt that conversion to Christianity is taken by the Achuar to mean, if not subordination, at least a markedly one-sided alliance with the white man's world. Christian proselytization is, for them, both the means and the symbolic model of a situation of cultural domination. For example, obedience to God means coming to terms with all missionaries and to whites in general. They are clearly aware that unrestricted access to the white world implies the rejection of most of their traditional values, particularly in the Protestant evangelist sector. There the alternative is dramatically stark. On one side, there is Christianity on mission terms, or Paradise, which the Achuar equate with access to white spiritual domains and hence access to white-controlled wealth. On the other side, there is rejection of mission domination, or Hell, which is equated with white hostility and the loss of most means of access to indispensable white wealth and its techniques of control. The choice between polar alternatives is, for them, clear and agonizing. Achuar men often told us that they hesitate to accept baptism for fear that traditional social demands such as active familial defense involving killing would lead them to commit sin in terms of the new value system. Such sin, in turn, would cause the loss of their cows and destine them to Hell. They prefer, they clearly say, to remain true Achuar, and to keep what wealth they have accumulated, rather than risk rejection by the missionaries and thereby loss of the little they have gained. This solution, however, implies renouncing white techniques of obtaining more wealth. In effect, the Achuar are in a "double bind" (Bateson 1972:271ff.). One may wonder why the Achuar take conversion (or its rejection) so seriously, and why they do not simply simulate formal adhesion to mission canons while privately sticking to their traditional beliefs and lifestyles.

The answer to this question has been suggested implicitly throughout this paper and it must now be explicitly restated. If the Achuar are vulnerable to missionary ideological penetration, it is ultimately because of certain characteristics of their own ideological system. For them, the efficacy of white Christianity is manifest in the technological power and the wealth of the missionaries. These assets, in turn, are perceived by the Achuar as being the result of techniques of supernatural control. The doctrine of poverty rigorously observed by the Salesian missionaries has, in this respect, little influence on them, since the Achuar tend to suspect that the fathers' efforts to dissociate religion and wealth is simply a manifestation of white duplicity. As for the Protestants, they do nothing to separate the production of wealth from religious practices, since they have thoroughly internalized this "Protestant ethic and spirit of capitalism" themselves.

In Achuar society this Protestant ethic is superficially congruent with the traditional conception that technical mastery is rooted in symbolic mastery. For example, a woman's capacity to reproduce culturally transformed nature through agriculture and animal husbandry depends directly on the nature of her relationship to Nunkui. This relationship is mediated by a set of simultaneously technical and symbolic observances such as fasting, singing, and respecting various prohibitions. This native conception of reproductive labor is projected onto the white world. Accordingly, white wealth is produced either by specialists whose privileged relation to the supernatural enables them to make airplanes, radios, and guns, or by people such as the missionaries who are endowed with such exceptional supernatural powers that they can "produce" all manufactured goods. During our fieldwork the Achuar systematically pursued the first theme, asking repeatedly "who is the man who builds planes," "does he have a beard," and so on. They also frequently questioned us to determine the range of goods the missionaries were able to conjure up, and which, the Salesians or the Protestants, was inferior in this respect. At the mythic level the Achuar express these notions by giving credit for blanket reproduction of foreign goods to Jurijri, an underground, hill-dwelling, polyglot spirit population closely associated with monkeys and, at a deeper level, with whites. Experiences in working for wage labor has not affected the traditional concept of reproductive work. The Achuar simply dissociate the levels of job execution and symbolic control, the latter remaining in the hands of the owner/directors of the *kumpánia*.

The religious practices of the missionaries are viewed by the Achuar in the same light as they view their own symbolic practices in the production of material values. Many Achuar, particularly the great men, adopt typical missionary public behavior: they pray ostensively, simulate mastery of reading, and sing hymns. The ritual care with which they imitate and reproduce these activities testifies to their efforts to assimilate foreign symbolic techniques which, they say, are the keys to the reproduction of white manufactured wealth.

Another basic tenet of Achuar thought is that supernatural power is an exchangeable commodity. The missionaries—both Protestant and Catholic—seemingly refuse to transmit their symbolic powers and to relinquish their monopoly on foreign wealth on native terms. The Achuar do, however, include these very missionaries in imaginary networks of symbolic and material exchange.[15] The Achuar's frustration in the face of the missionaries' refusal to comply with these expectations, and their apparent reluctance to hand over the whole goods, accounts for certain superficial cargo cult (Burridge 1969, Jarvie 1964) traits, conjoining demands for exchangeable, material "god-wealth" with conspicuous display of Christian-style religiosity. This trait is particularly developed among the Protestant Achuar, probably because of the evangelists' continued insistence on the direct relationship between material wealth and overt, ostensive religious practice.

At a deeper level, the Achuar also attempt to bypass missionary mediation and to tap white spiritual power sources directly through shamanistic manipulation. The shaman, *uwishin*, is a specialist in symbolic relations with the outside, as opposed to the great man, *uunt*, who specializes in relations within the endogamous area. Shamans mediate symbolic bonds and seek to control other groups, particularly the whites; ultimately, it seems, shamanistic power is derived from sources *outside* the group, and the more remote the source, the stronger the power.[16] Nowadays such power is derived primarily from white spheres. Let me explain this last source. The ideological basis of prestige and value ascribed to foreignness is today epitomized by the "white world." The spirit domains, notably that of Tsunki (the water domain), tapped exclusively by shamans, are consistently associated with aspects of the white world familiar to the Achuar. For example, Tsunki live in aquatic cities where they travel by car; however, they are seated on turtle carapaces, the traditional spirit seat of Tsunki. Tsunki spirits are in fact frequently described as "white people." Thus Achuar shamanism seems to be, among other things, a means of capturing and appropriating white power from Tsunki underwater spirit domains.

This level of shamanistic power and its symbolic exchanges constitute the critical feature of articulation between Achuar and jungle Quichua. But shaman power and its basic cosmology may also be the root of eventual alienation. By ascribing to white spheres a superior capacity to manipulate supernatural forces, it could validate and canonize the overwhelming force of white power, proof of which rests, according to the Achuar, in the foreigner's capacity to produce infinite wealth. At the same time, Achuar shamanism also carries a potentiality of resistance. By incorporating white power to their own traditional paradigms, they may use this very power to oppose national domination and alienation and express on-going ethnic identity and strength. In the shamanistic domain ethnocide and ethnogenesis are inextricably bound and expressed.

NOTES

Acknowledgments: Fieldwork on which this paper is based was conducted among the northern Ecuadorian Achuar with Philippe Descola between Nov. 1976 and Aug. 1978. This research was supported by a grant from the Centre Nacional de la Recherche Scientifique, a scholarship from the Foundation Paul Delheim du Collège de France, and two additional grants from the Ministère des Universités. In Ecuador, our investigation was sponsored by the Instituto Nacional de Antropología e Historia, and by the Department of Anthropology of the Catholic University of Ecuador, Quito.

1. The projected *Ley de Colonización* invokes national security as its fundamental preoccupation (*La Colonización de la Región Amazónica Ecuatoriana*, Obra Nacional 1977:30), and proposes that the armed forces take over temporary management of the process of colonization in the Oriente (ibid., art. 31, p. 43).

2. This term, meaning literally "old and big one," is roughly equivalent to the Shuar *kakaram* (see Harner 1972).

3. I refer here to the *amigri* bond, a ritually initiated trade relation that establishes a close tie between partners implying mutual hospitality, protection, and cooperation (see Harner 1972:125–33 for a full description).

4. The Macuma area was formerly occupied by the Achuar. The Shuar probably began moving into this territory sometime between 1900 and 1930,

and had taken it over by 1940. Intertribal warfare was very intense in this area, but it did not prevent the forging of trade relations; indeed, among the Jivaroan groups intertribal trade and war relations often coincided.

5. The Protestant mission has fomented cooperatives among the Shuar; however, it has not encouraged them among the Achuar. The Macuma missionaries seem to think that the Achuar are too individualistic and not yet sufficiently "developed" to cope with this type of organization.

6. Insofar as the great men's power was closely linked to warfare, the waning of intertribal conflict and internal feuding was bound to affect their position. Economic power is to some extent a substitute for war-derived power. In this respect both the missionaries' and the great men's interests neatly coincide.

7. Until recently very isolated, Montalvo was founded in the 1920s by a nucleus of *comerciante* families intimately involved with the northern Achuar. The founding families consider themselves as the "civilizers" of the Achuar, who in turn used them to procure goods, to deal with the authorities, and to intercede with the military. Montalvo is also the seat of very intense shamanistic activity.

8. I wish to make it clear that I am not advocating a return to the traditional system of relations between the sexes. Achuar women are quite definitely dominated by men, and their life is by no means a free and easy one. However, the emancipation of native women emphatically need not emulate the imposition of men/women relations characteristic of frontier *colono* society, in which the degradation and ideological oppression of women are certainly greater than among the Achuar.

9. The possible political function of the SIL through the division of native communities and the "defusing" or deflecting of social tensions, particularly in the Sierra, has been frequently suggested. This aspect of their work, though beyond the scope of this paper, should be kept in mind.

10. This is *not* to say that institutionalized warfare within cultural units should be reduced to an expression and actualization of native representations. Here, however, I am concerned with the manner in which interethnic bonds are conceptualized and internalized by native groups, and the manner in which these underlying theories infuse present-day interethnic relationships. These native theories should not, however, be confused with scientific explanation of hostility and warfare within and between Jivaroan groups.

11. These two linked sets of paradigms are very easily elicited from the hunting songs and the war songs. The material on which these ideas are based has not yet been published. It will be further analyzed and published in future works.

12. The Catholic principle of divine incarnation holds that God is present since the beginning of time in all native religions. The role of evangelization is merely to reveal this presence. An exposition of this theological trend may be found in the Mundo Shuar fascicules devoted to religious problems, particularly in Botasso, Botasso, and Münzel (1979).

13. A recent agreement between the Salesians and the Dominican mission has led to a take-over by the Salesians of the Pastaza Achuar who were formerly under Dominican jurisdiction.

14. Although M. Münzel's short analysis (Botasso, Botasso, and Münzel 1979) of the contrast between the two missions among the Shuar proper had

not yet appeared when I wrote this paper, his conclusions are strikingly similar to mine.

15. A remarkable example of this inclusion in imaginary networks may be found in the Salesian missionary José "Chuint" Arnalot's diary (1978). He describes a matrimonial transaction involving a Catholic-baptized Achuar girl and a "heathen" Achuar boy. For theological reasons the Salesians were strongly opposed to the union. The parents of the youths dealt with the *padres* exactly as though they were the "fathers" of the Catholic girl. The Achuar created an imaginary network of kinship around the missionaries and treated the latter as if they were seeking traditional compensation for an alliance they did not agree to.

16. Shamanistic power is included in a "Chinese box" structure: minor shamans manipulate a limited symbolic and territorial space but, as one moves up the hierarchy, this shamanistic space becomes ever wider. This type of logical structure, involving widening series of enclosed domains that refer to a common paradigm, can be found in other fields of the native symbolic system. For example, the territorial basis of the Arutam, Nekas Wakani, and Emesak spirits (see Harner 1972) respectively is structured along the same lines.

REFERENCES CITED

Arnalot, José
    1978   *Lo que los Achuar Me Han Ensenado.* Sucúa: Ediciones Mundo Shuar.
Bateson, Gregory
    1972   *Steps to an Ecology of Mind.* New York: Ballantine Books.
Botasso, D., J. Botasso, and M. Münzel
    1979   La Iglesia Shuar: Interroyantes y Perspectivas. Sucúa: Ediciones Mundo Shuar.
Burridge, Kenelm
    1969   *New Heaven, New Earth: A Study of Millenarian Activities.* New York: Schocken Books.
Clastres, Pierre
    1977   Malheur du Guerrier Sauvage. *Libre* 2:69–109.
Federación de Centros Shuar
    1976   *Solución Original a un Problema Actual.* Sucúa.
Harner, Michael J.
    1972   *The Jívaro: People of the Sacred Waterfalls.* Garden City, N.Y.: Natural History Press.
Jarvie, I. C.
    1964   *The Revolution in Anthropology.* London: Routledge and Kegan Paul.
Kensinger, Kenneth
    1975   *The Cashinahua of Eastern Peru.* Providence, R.I.: Haffenreffer Museum of Anthropology.
Lévi-Strauss, Claude
    1943   Guerre et Commerce chez les Indiens D'Amérique du Sud. *Renaissance* 1 (fasc. 1 and 2).

Obra Nacional
  1977   *La Colonización de la Región Amazonica Ecuatoriana*. Quito: Ministerio de Agricultura y Ganadería.
Ribeiro, Darcy
  1971   *Fronteras Indígenas de la Civilización*. Buenos Aires: Siglo XXI.
Sahlins, Marshall
  1963   Poor Man, Rich Man, Big Man, Chief: Political Types in Melanesia and Polynesia. *Comparative Studies in Society and History* 5 (3):285–303.
Salazar, Ernesto
  1977   *An Indian Federation in Lowland Ecuador*. Copenhagen: International Work Group for Indigenous Affairs, Document 28.
Whitten, Dorothea S., and Norman E. Whitten, Jr.
  1978   Ceramics of the Canelos Quichua. *Natural History Magazine* 87 (8):90–99, 152.
Whitten, Norman E., Jr.
  1976a (with the assistance of Marcelo F. Naranjo, Marcelo Santi Simbaña, and Dorothea S. Whitten). *Sacha Runa: Ethnicity and Adaptation of Ecuadorian Jungle Quichua*. Urbana: University of Illinois Press.
  1976b *Ecuadorian Ethnocide and Indigenous Ethnogenesis: Amazonian Resurgence amidst Andean Colonialism*. Copenhagen: International Work Group for Indigenous Affairs, Document 23.
  1978   Ecological Imagery and Cultural Adaptability: The Canelos Quichua of Eastern Ecuador. *American Anthropologist* 80 (4):836–59.

24

Twenty Years of Contact: The Mechanisms of Change in Wao ("Auca") Culture

James A. Yost

For centuries that area in the Ecuadorian Oriente bounded by the Napo and Curaray rivers has been regarded as dangerous to travel into and impossible to inhabit. The reason is that various indigenous groups have occupied the territory and resisted incursions by outsiders. Since the turn of the century this area has been recognized as the homeland of the "Aucas," who have been credited with all of the hostilities that have occurred there since the entrance of Europeans into Amazonia. Although not completely accurate, this is largely true for the past 50 years.

"Auca" is a Quichua word which I take to mean "savage" or "barbarian"; it is used by the Canelos Quichua to refer to any number of non-Quichua–speaking native peoples of Amazonia (Whitten 1976:12, 30; 1978:41). Recent national Ecuadorian usage applies the name to a single group who call themselves "Waorani" or "the people." (The term "Wao" which will also be used in this discussion is the singular form "person" as well as the adjectival form.)[1] Linguistically, examination of extensive wordlists representing many South American language families has demonstrated no congeners for the Wao language (Peeke 1973:3, 4).

HISTORY OF CONTACT

The history of contact with the Waorani has been marked by violence and exploitation. The earliest reference to them in the late 1600s indicates that the initial peaceful contact with them ended seven years later in violence (Blomberg 1957:60). Later attempts to contact them were frustrated in some cases by Wao timidity and in others by their hostility. The atrocities of the rubber gatherers throughout Amazonia in the late nineteenth century are well documented (Jouanen 1977:166), and the Wao accounts of their relationship to the outside world indicate that they were not exempt from these atrocities.

The scant published history available demonstrates that even attempts at peaceful contact were marred by seemingly innocent acts which, although not intended to be hostile or antagonistic, were interpreted by the Waorani as such. Up de Graff (1923) and Blomberg (1957:161) both took food from "abandoned" gardens which were, in fact, not abandoned but part of the Wao swidden subsistence system in which each family maintains several *quehuencori*, gardens, at great distances from each other, migrating cyclically from one to the other. None are in any sense abandoned, and food taken from one is stolen food. Similarly, the common practice of entering "abandoned" Wao houses and taking goods stored there (Blomberg 1957:18) constituted an offense, particularly when the house was merely vacated because of the intruder's presence.

Spearing forays made by the Waorani against outside groups were answered with retaliatory punitive raids such as the one in 1920 in which 80 Waorani were reportedly killed and several taken prisoner (Blomberg 1957:55). Because of the confusion surrounding the name "Auca," it is likely that the Waorani at times suffered for killings done by other groups. In spite of the long history of isolation, 17% of the Wao fates recorded in genealogies extending back as far as five generations were a result of being shot or captured by *cohuori*, non-Waorani.

The activities of petroleum exploration companies in Wao territory date back to the early 1940s, when Royal Dutch Shell Oil Corporation conducted geological surveys in the area, and continue to the present. While policies regarding contact with the Waorani have varied from company to company, and from time to time within a company, the Waorani apparently saw no need to change their policy of relationship with the oil companies; both sides lost people to the other. Until the 1950s contact between Wao culture and outside cultures was characterized by individualism and hostility; except for Wao acquisition of steel tools through raids, very little diffusion of traits between the cultures occurred.

The recent contact process, recorded in detail by Wallis (1960, 1973) and Elliot (1957, 1958, 1961), has been both sustained and peaceful. It began in 1958 when Elisabeth Elliot of Christian Missions in Many Lands and Rachel Saint of the Summer Institute of Linguistics (SIL) accompanied the Wao woman Dayomé to the Tehuéno River to try to locate her relatives from whom she had fled following a spearing raid

11 years earlier. They located a small group of 56 people, the Gue-quetairi, living on the lower Tehuéno, thereby initiating the process of a sustained, peaceful contact with the Waorani (see Map 1).

At the time this contact was made there were four groups of Wao-rani totaling about 500 people scattered over approximately 8,100 square miles (.06 persons per square mile). Although having close kin ties, the groups were hostile to one another and to all outsiders and therefore took great effort to conceal their locations. None of the groups was certain how many other groups of Waorani actually ex-isted or where they lived. Disruptive raids had scattered some out of contact with their relatives and resulted in capture for others.

One small group of approximately 50 fugitives from such a raid joined the Guequetairi soon after the missionaries had moved to the Tehuéno. The majority of the raided group, the Piyémoiri (104 indi-viduals), had retired to the area embraced by the upper Tiputini and Tivacuno rivers, and it was there that they were located by SIL over-flights and then contacted by the Guequetairi in 1968. They joined the group on the Tehuéno, swelling the already doubled population to over 200. At this time, responding to a request by the Waorani, the Ecuadorian government established a protectorate zone of approxi-mately 620 square miles on the Curaray River. A year later the Bai-huairi, who had been living near the lower Tiguino, were located and contacted in the same manner, and they moved into the protectorate, increasing the population there to 300.

Then again in 1970, using aircraft and dropping radio transmitters to isolated Wao groups, SIL effected contact with the Huepeiri, a re-mote group who had been separated from the Tehuéno group by a raid nearly four decades earlier. They had taken refuge on the Gabaro River (tributary of the Nashiño), joining a few Waorani there whose ancestral ties could be traced only tenuously. Beginning in late 1971 and continuing over the next five years, members of that group also relocated in the protectorate, bringing the total population there to nearly 500 and leaving fewer than 100 outside that territory.

Thus, in a matter of a few years, the Waorani were subjected to a tremendous expansion of their social environment. This expansion, or increase in scale (Berreman 1978), occurred in two forms simulta-neously. In one form it was Wao society confronted with an internal population increase stemming from a variety of causes including the cessation of several practices—spearing raids, hostilities with *cohuori*, and infanticide. But beyond that was an increase in the density of the existing population through concentration in a reduced area. The dis-persed settlement pattern was transformed as the previously isolated local groups moved into a territory less than one-tenth the original size.

The second form of scale increase which occurred was the movement of Wao society into lasting relationships with the external world. As the Waorani ended their hostilities with the *cohuori*, they began making visits to outside communities, and *cohuori* began entering Wao territory for a wide variety of reasons. This type of increase in scale—the increase in continuous relationships between two cultures—had just begun to accelerate when the data for this paper were gathered.[2]

In this paper I will explore the impact of these forms of scale increase upon Wao culture and social relations, giving special attention to those variables of the contact situation and those internal to Wao culture which facilitated this expansion of scale.

AGENTS OF CHANGE

The agents of change among the Waorani cover a wide variety of individuals and groups, including missionaries, other indigenous groups, oil company crews, tourists, journalists, scientists, and estranged Waorani. Two groups, the Summer Institute of Linguistics and Wao cultural brokers, will be discussed here because of their significant role in the change process during the last two decades. It should be noted, however, that other change-producing agents, particularly tourists and oil companies, are gaining in significance at an alarming rate.

Summer Institute of Linguistics

There can be little doubt that the entrance of the two missionary women and Dayomé in 1958 was critical in establishing the atmosphere which allowed the changes that have transpired since. That the missionaries and Dayomé were tolerated, much less able to have any impact, was a result of several factors. First and most obviously, the missionaries were accompanied by someone who had originated from the group they were contacting. Second, they were women, and therefore not threatening to the physical security of the Waorani, since women are not supposed to kill. Third, they had knowledge of and experience with the outside world, which the Waorani were curious about but feared. Fourth, their message offered the chance of escape from the stresses which plagued the Waorani most, the fear of the *cohuori* and of their enemy groups. In addition, the missionaries and Dayomé were all very strong, highly motivated individuals, a trait which gave them an edge in the diffuse egalitarian system of Wao social relationships. The importance of these traits will become more apparent as the discussion proceeds.

After Elisabeth Elliot departed from Tehuéno in 1961, Rachel Saint, a member of the linguistically oriented missionary organization SIL, whose stated goal is to see portions of the Bible translated into the world's languages, was joined by other SIL personnel in succeeding years. Rosi Jung, from Germany, began in 1969 to assist in the increasing demands for medical aid; Pat Kelley, a Canadian, joined them in 1972 to coordinate literacy work; and Catherine Peeke, who has lived in Tehuéno periodically since 1962, pursued the linguistic analysis. Then, in 1973, SIL requested that I conduct an anthropological study of the Waorani. Through the years care has been taken by SIL not to have all of these researchers in the village at the same time (Yost 1979).

A significant role of the personnel of SIL, in addition to being the principal motivating force behind the initial Wao contact, has been to provide a model for interaction with *cohuori*. One of the correlates of extension of scale is insecurity in interpersonal relationships, since only parts of the total social identity of an individual are known. According to Berreman (1979:232), in small-scale societies "villagers interact in terms of their total identities on a personal basis with others who know them well." In large-scale societies the opposite is the case; ambiguity regarding status and role is high. Across vastly disparate cultural boundaries, such as the one examined here, that ambiguity and its concomitant insecurity are intensified. It is true that today the Waorani still exhibit high levels of anxiety in interacting with *cohuori*, but the sustained presence of SIL personnel has reduced this considerably from what it was in years past. Through their continued interaction with SIL people, the Waorani reduced their long-standing fears of the *cohuori* and learned, to a limited extent, to predict *cohuori* behavior and thereby to carry on social and commercial transactions with other *cohuori*. The presence of SIL personnel became the principal vehicle in increasing scale for Wao society. This has been true not only for Waorani seeking greater access to the outside but also for outsiders seeking access to the Waorani. The SIL model has demonstrated to outsiders, tourists in particular, that it is "safe" for them to visit Wao territory.

Wao Cultural Brokers

It is probably safe to say that were it not for individuals like Dayomé, a peaceful, enduring contact with the Waorani would not exist today. During the years of the internal vendetta it was not uncommon for Wao women to flee Wao territory to escape the threat of death, and to join a Quichua-speaking group.[3] There they learned the ways and language of the Quichuas and married Quichua men. After Dayomé returned and convinced her relatives to stop killing *cohuori*, these women also returned and, with their children, assumed important roles as cultural brokers. Three of the present-day villages are strongly influenced by these women, and the other villages rely upon those three for much of their communication with the *cohuori*.

AREAS OF CHANGE

It is a well-known fact in anthropology that change proceeds at differential rates within a culture. The dynamic interaction of three sets of variables—the internal structure of Wao culture, the structure of the contact situation, and the nature of increased scale itself—has produced change in some areas of Wao culture and resistance to change in others.

Demographic Change

The traditional Wao settlement pattern has been semipermanent sedentarism (Beardsley et al. 1956) with an interesting twist. While the Waorani are planting and harvesting their manioc in one location, manioc which they have planted in another location is maturing. When they have completed harvesting in the first location, they move on to the second, which is usually a day or two away from the first. After harvesting and replanting there (a process taking three to four months), they move on to a third location. When they have finished harvesting and planting in the third location, the gardens in the first location are ready to harvest, so they return there and begin the cycle anew. This not only disperses their utilization of the land over a wider area but also acts as a means of defense against raids. The smaller gardens and the lower intensity of trail use within a given area make it more difficult for raiding groups to locate housing sites. Also, when a raid does occur, the raided group can flee to a location where food is available.

The housing pattern is also adapted to defense. Within a single house, which for obvious reasons is often positioned on a hill, an older man lives with his wife or wives and all of their unmarried children as well as their married daughters with their husbands and children. Anywhere from a few minutes to an hour away a brother of the old man will likely live with his extended household. These neighborhood clusters of closely related kin provide less vulnerability through dispersal, but still make close kinsmen available when needed. Half a day or so from the first neighborhood cluster is likely to live another neighborhood cluster of people not so closely related to the first. Although this group is an ally of the first, it is not so closely related as the brothers and therefore maintains a little more distance. The major groups of Waorani existing at the time of the 1958 contact with the SIL were each composed of these neighborhood clusters dispersed throughout their respective areas, as indicated on Map 1.

The factors which influenced the Tehueno group's attempts to contact the other groups, their traditional enemies, were varied and complex. At this point it is difficult to sort out the truly significant motivators from those which were just later adjunct spin-offs of the contacts. Wallis (1973) documents the desire of both the Waorani and SIL to avoid confrontations between hostile Waorani and oil exploration crews, and of the desire of both to evangelize the other groups. In addition, the Waorani were anxious to re-establish contact with relatives who had been separated by raids.

Apart from the economic advantages of surrounding oneself with numerous kin, there was the matter of marriage. Marriage is prescribed bilateral cross-cousin marriage, and the small groups were experiencing a lack of proper potential spouses. Contact with other groups would ensure marriages for the children. Also, if the groups could be contacted and convinced that there was a guarantee of peace in the protectorate, possibly the vendetta could be ended once and for all. The threat of impending retaliation against the Tehueno group could be ended, and spouses could be obtained without risk.

This matter of spouses cannot be overestimated. After initial contact with the Gabado group, they soon began relocating in Tehueno. Since the distance separating the two groups is so great and since no trails connecting the area were known, SIL began relocating the Gabaro people by flying them in their airplanes at the request of the Waorani. The process was a slow one; every few months a nuclear family was flown to Tehueno after relatives there had prepared manioc gardens for the newcomers. I objected to this relocation system,

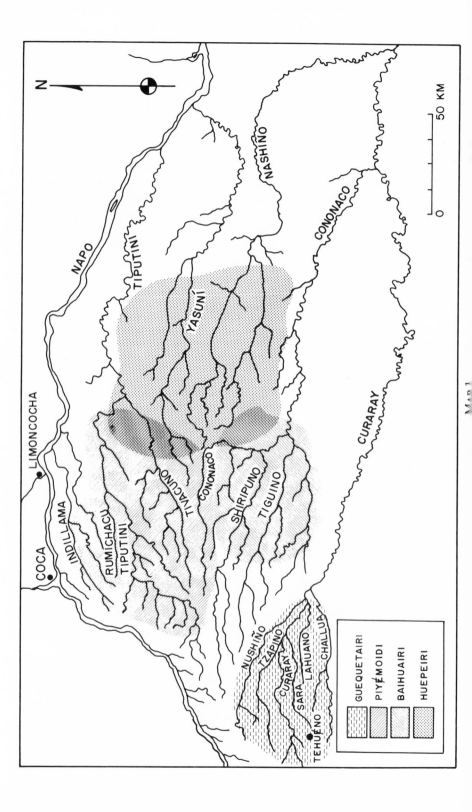

MAP 1

arguing, first, that the Waorani should not evacuate their lands and, second, that it put the new groups in a vulnerable position as they became obligated to their upriver relatives for feeding them. I was roundly corrected by the Waorani involved. It was one of the two times that I have been threatened by the Waorani; they wanted to relocate to obtain spouses, and any efforts to hinder them in this provoked their anger.

Once the groups were contacted and joined the Tehuéno group in the protectorate, a number of demographic changes began. First, the very fact of relocating reduced the territory covered by 500 people from over 8,000 square miles to 620 square miles. This greatly increased the intensity of interaction between groups and individuals. But beyond that, the Tehuéno group insisted that new groups entering the protectorate live near the airstrip where they could be observed and peer pressure in its myriad forms could be exerted to ensure that the newcomers would not begin spearing again. This, of course, concentrated the population in an even smaller territory.

Thus, for a time following the relocation of the Piyémoiri and the Baihuairi into the protectorate, the traditional pattern of settlement was disrupted. The new groups felt particularly vulnerable. They were not completely convinced of the peaceful intent of the Guequetairi and were ill at ease in their new location. Even though they were equal in number to the Guequetairi, they were at a distinct disadvantage because they were unfamiliar with the territory and because they had no crops of their own. This, reinforced by the Tehuéno group's felt need to keep the new people close by for observation and indoctrination, also contributed to the pressure for the new groups to live in more concentrated settlements.

However, as they learned to cope with their new environment, the new groups gained confidence. As their own gardens matured, they began to move away from the Tehuéno area, eventually dispersing over the entire protectorate. Considerable mixing occurred as people from the separate groups established new residential groups, particularly those who had been separated from their families by spearing raids earlier but were now able to reunite. Small population centers developed on the Tzapino, Nushiño, Curaray, and Tehuéno Rivers, each composed primarily of members from one of the original major groups but bolstered with individual families from others (see Map 2).

The process of dispersal, which began around 1972, continues today, particularly as the Waorani lose their fear of the *cohuori* and move

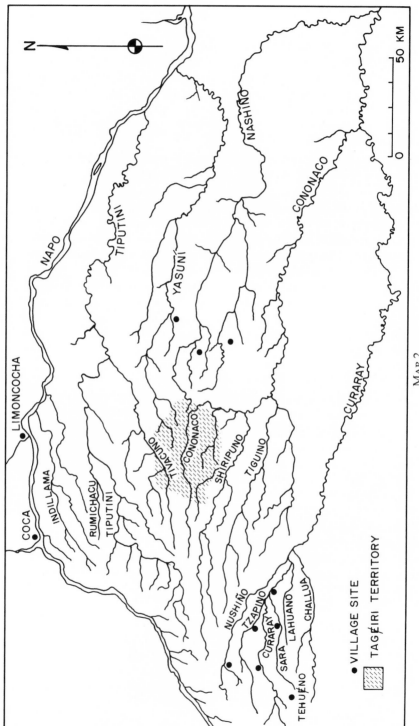

MAP 2

N

50 KM

0

NAPO

LIMONCOCHA

COCA

INDILLAMA

RUMICHACU

TIPUTINI

TIPUTINI

TIVACUNO

CONONACO

SHIRIPUNO

TIGUINO

NUSHIÑO

TZAPINO

CURARAY

SARA

LAHUANO

TEHUEÑO

CHALLUA

YASUNI

NASHIÑO

CONONACO

CURARAY

● VILLAGE SITE

▨ TAGÉIRI TERRITORY

to the perimeter of the territory to increase their access to goods coming in from outside their culture. For a number of years the Waorani obtained *cohuori* goods almost exclusively by means of SIL flights into and out of the Tehuéno airstrip, because they feared contacting the *cohuori* directly. But in 1975 the SIL began to change its policy by limiting more stringently goods flown in. The Waorani responded by seeking other sources for *cohuori* goods, and population dispersal accelerated. The attraction of such goods as western clothing, aluminum pots, shotguns, cartridges, and steel tools, which had originally kept them clustered near the airstrip, became a significant motivation for dispersal to other points.

Other demographic consequences of the contact process relate to mortality. Of the reported deaths spanning up to five generations only two individuals purportedly died of natural causes in old age.[4] Forty-four percent of the deaths were a result of intratribal spearing, and 5% were due to infanticide. Seventeen percent were a result of *cohuori* shootings and captures; snakebite accounted for another 5% and illness 11%.

The contact process has had a profound impact upon all of these. The cessation of revenge spearings and infanticide, the end of the general practice of shooting Waorani, the introduction of modern medicines to counter introduced diseases and to treat snakebite, and the availability of aircraft to transport seriously injured Waorani to hospitals have all contributed to an increase in the Wao population in the past 20 years. During the period of my study there were five deaths and 38 live births in a population of 525. The resulting average annual rate of increase for the three years is 2.2%, a good indicator of the demographic changes the Waorani are experiencing.

Scale, in many instances, is a direct expression of demography. The internal scale increase the Waorani have experienced is an outgrowth of two demographic processes outlined here: population redistribution and decreased mortality. When the newly contacted groups of Waorani began relocating in the protectorate, they were subjected to an increase in scale, the consequences of which are enduring. Not the least of these consequences is the altered ecology of the territory. The Waorani know well, and state clearly, that the game and fish resources are exhibiting the pressures of overutilization. They are beginning to comment on the scarcity of quality cultivable land as they are forced to shorten the fallow time of their *quehuencori* swidden, manioc gardens, in some areas.

Technological Change

Even before peaceful contact was established, the Waorani were making raids upon *cohuori* to obtain steel axes and machetes. Similarly, two Wao women, who traveled to Arajuno in 1957 to observe the *cohuori*, proposed to Elisabeth Elliot that he accompany them to the Tehuéno River where they would build an airstrip so the plane could bring not only food and visitors but also "gifts" for which the Waorani could trade (Elliot 1961:63).

Today the Waorani expend a great amount of time and energy in their preoccupation with *cohuori* technology. This is evidenced in numerous ways, but a couple of examples will suffice. In 1975 the Waorani at Tsapino, deep inside the protectorate, asked me to come inspect an airstrip they had just constructed. They were quick to explain that they had built it so the airplanes could bring them outside goods and an outside teacher. Also, in some areas, such as Gabaro, pursuit of *cohuori* technology has assumed features which, superficially at least, are reminiscent of *cargo* cults of Oceania. For example, simple rituals imitating certain activities which occur at an oil camp are enacted, and songs are sung about helicopters. The Waorani do this to attract the oil company helicopters which occasionally do drop in with gifts of axes, machetes, clothes, aluminum pots, and rubber boots.

When the first missionaries entered with Dayomé to spend an extended period with the Waorani, they planned to take only those goods essential to their work (Elliot 1961:104). However, three factors hindered the realization of this principle. First, the pervading Wao motivation to obtain *cohouri* goods put the missionaries under extreme pressure to provide them, if they were to enjoy the extended stay there which they planned. Second, because the primary determinant of interpersonal relationship in most small-scale societies is kinship, and because "kin relationship" for the Waorani is defined in terms of a name, a stranger is quickly named (thereby decreasing the insecurity over status and role assignment which accompanies an extension of scale). Once the individual is named, she/he enters the system of formal relationships and is then expected to abide by the corresponding rules of obligation. The rule of obligation here is clear: *cohouri* people have access to *cohouri* goods, so they must provide them for their Waorani relatives. Third, although Dayomé was Wao and had been socialized into Wao culture, she had also learned to appreciate such items as aluminum pots and blankets available to the jungle Quichua and perhaps had become dependent upon them. According to Elliot (1961:146), "Dayuma, accustomed to the facilities of civilized transportation, took a dim view of a three day trip into our jungle home." It was she who sustained the airstrip construction, in large part to help maintain her access to the outside. But her possession of *cohuori* conveniences made her vulnerable; to live in harmony with her relatives, she was obligated from the start to provide the same possessions for them. When a person has a blanket, it is his to keep and use, but if he can acquire another, he must give one to a requesting kinsman. To do otherwise is a serious breach of propriety. It was possible for the two *cohuori* missionary women to renege on their obligations but impossible for Dayomé to do so. The principle of keeping *cohuori* goods at a minimum was undermined in that "minimum" for the *cohuori* invariably meant "extra" to the Waorani.

Most of the technology has had little negative impact thus far; the two notable exceptions are dynamite, obtained by trading with jungle Quichua or oil company workers, and DDT, purchased on occasion from malaria sprayers. Both are used to catch fish. The DDT, when dumped into the rivers, acts as a substitute for the native poisons, but with insidious consequences of ecological degradation. The impact of the dynamite is even more obvious. Areas that had heavy fish concentrations when I began my research in 1974 are now almost devoid of fish (Yost 1978). The most disruptive aspect of foreign technology—differential access to it—will be discussed at length in the section on political change.

An area of technology that is very instructive, because it represents some of the important dynamics occurring in current Wao society, is clothing. Although the Waorani traditionally wore only the *kome*, G-string, for decades they have stolen clothes in raids to use for adornment and display (Blomberg 1957:38). When Dayomé returned to her people in 1958, she wore the clothing she had learned to wear among the *cohuori*. Undoubtedly, simple emulation of Dayomé and the two missionary women provided a certain amount of the initial motivation to wear clothing, but, beyond that, Dayomé had learned that the Quichuas in this area are very sensitive about clothing, citing the lack of it as the primary definition of savagery (Carolyn Orr, personal communication; Theodore Macdonald, personal communication). The disdain she encountered while living on the hacienda as a young girl had become deeply imprinted. She returned to Tehuéno as a Quichua woman determined not to be regarded as a savage animal (Elliot 1961:94). She has communicated this to the Waorani, so that they are now painfully aware of the outside attitude toward them. The sense of status deprivation created by this communication has helped push the Waorani to attempt to emulate the lifestyle of the surrounding lowland Quichua. They want to be thought of as human beings by the Quichua and go to great lengths to identify with them. Clothing and removal of the traditional ear labrets signal that identification, communicating especially to the Quichua who hunt Wao territory that they are not part of an uncontacted hostile group and, therefore, should not be shot on sight.

In summary, the Waorani wanted and actively sought outside technology and consumer goods. Access to these goods was greatly intensified by the continued presence of the missionary women and Dayomé, who were bound by the Waorani system of reciprocity to supply such items, which, in time, became a symbol of identification with the outside world.

Social Change

A trait list of Wao technology, past and present, would make it appear that precipitous change resulted from Wao contact with the high-energy-consumption, industrial cultures and their attendant technology and consumer goods. However, closer examination of earlier descriptions of Wao culture, of the more isolated groups of Waorani, and of data available in the Wao life histories make the changes that have occurred appear superficial. While the Waorani have taken what technology they could from the outside, their social structure has remained essentially intact.

It would be reasonable to expect that congregating traditionally hostile groups into a smaller territory would precipitate either conflict or significant changes in the structure of social relations. In part, the reason this did not occur lies in the very nature of an increase in scale. Berreman (1978:231) has shown that an increase in scale is an increase in density of communication, that is, of interaction. This increased communication between the newly congregated Wao groups was a deterrent to hostility, since face-to-face relationships developed with individuals who were previously unknown or known at best through reputation. As I have shown elsewhere (Yost 1979), spatial distance and lack of communication between the various local groups served to keep anxiety high. When the density of communication or interaction was increased, the activities of the separate groups became more visible to one another, making them generally less suspect to one another and also reducing the possibility of a surprise move on the part of one against another. In addition, interpersonal relationships and transactions developed as kinship relationships were traced and retraced. The corresponding sense of ramifying obligation was thereby allowed to be manifest through a material flow, making peer pressure more effective as a social control mechanism.

Another significant variable was the structure of Wao social relations manifest in the kindred. Scheffler (1966), Keesing (1971), and Goodenough (1970:58) have documented the flexibility of the kindred in enabling people to adapt to changing circumstances. Kindreds are egocentric-based social units (Yengoyan 1973:164) which allow fluidity in membership. The right to belong to a given group is defined by kinship, but the actualization of that right varies according to such circumstances as shared residence in a common locale and contextuality. With regard to the latter, a given ego may claim his relationship with one set of kin in one type of activity but claim his relationship with another set in a different type of activity.

At the time of missionary contact the members of each Wao local kindred could trace their relationship to most individuals in the other groups through known links by going back no more than two ascending generations. The only exception to this was a small group of approximately a dozen *huarani*, "others," living among the Gabaro group. The close historical connections between the various groups and the nature of bifurcate merging kinship terminology gave rise to the feature which allowed Wao mobility: almost everyone in ego's generation is treated either as a sibling, as a spouse (or potential spouse), or as an affine.

Therefore, in the concentration and redistribution of the population, individuals gained a tremendous amount of flexibility. They found themselves among others who were at the same time strangers, enemies, and relatives, and could take advantage of the ambiguities and anomalies, contradictions and complementarities, inherent in the situation. Considerable mixing occurred between the groups for various reasons. In some instances close relatives who had been separated by earlier raids or kidnappings were able to renew their ties; in other instances pressures from some individuals seeking to increase their influence or the size of their groups convinced others to join them; in still others the desire to assure future marriage possibilities for children prompted realignment of kin ties; and, finally, attraction to those who had greater access to outside goods induced some to shift their residence to a different group. This shifting involved choice of community, not household composition. The extended family is the unit which realigns, not individuals from within a given household, although that has occurred for a few individuals. It is difficult to determine the degree to which this shifting, which continues today, is an artifact of the contact situation and the degree to which it reflects past tendencies (which are documented). The central point here is that the flexibility inherent in kindred structure facilitated adjustment to an increase in scale.

There is one area of social change resulting from scale increase that is beginning to give evidence of conflict—that of Wao marriages to lowland Quichua men and women. Wao women who have established their leadership among Wao groups after living on haciendas most of their lives urge Waorani to marry Quichuas. By arranging the marriages, they receive benefits from the Quichuas, including material goods as well as prestige. The Wao reaction to such marriages has been mixed; some view it as the opening of new avenues of relationship to the outside, but many are openly bitter about the consequent demands for hunting and fishing rights in Wao territory made by the dozens of new Quichua relatives. The concomitant increase in scale implied by these marriages is just beginning to be realized as some Waorani now feel free to spend considerable time with their Quichua affines in nearby towns, and the Quichuas, in return, feel free to spend time among the Waorani on hunting and fishing expeditions. That further changes are inevitable from this is reflected in Berreman's (1978:299) analysis that "interaction among more and different people increases the number of novel situations, and the likelihood of the 'conjunction of differences' which leads to innovation."

Political Change

The traditional pattern of Wao authority was one typical of much of Amazonia: egalitarianism with situationally defined leadership (Wilson and Yost 1979). Contrary to popular belief, the Waorani had no "chiefs." Apart from the very limited authority which an older person had over a younger, or a male over a female, the existence of individuals who have widespread influence is an artifact of the contact situation.

When Dayomé returned to her people in 1958, she had two new assets: a knowledge of the *cohuori* and their ways, and favorable relationships with those *cohuori*. These two qualities immediately gave her power that no other Wao had ever experienced. As the repository of knowledge of the *cohuori*, she became the crucial link, or cultural broker, between the Waorani and the *cohuori*. Through her influence and that of the missionaries, the Waorani overcame their fears of the outside and slowly began seeking trade relationships with the *co-huori*, particularly with the lowland Quichua at Arajuno.

In time, other Wao women who had fled to the *cohuori* years before also began returning to the tribe when they were convinced that the internal hostilities had truly ceased. They too returned with the same advantages that Dayomé had acquired, particularly the ability to speak Quichua and a very limited amount of Spanish. This ability made it possible for them to act as the intermediaries in most contact situations.

The result of such cultural brokerage and the mediation of "Quichuaized" women between Waorani and *cohuori* was the establishment of a more generalized form of leadership than the situational leadership which had prevailed before. The women were sought out more and more as the intensity of contact increased until, eventually, they exerted influence in areas other than relationships with the *co-huori*. They were also able to do this through their control of the flow of goods and services into the tribe from the outside. In addition, they were able to do it because the newly contacted groups were moving into the protectorate and were in a very vulnerable position. They had no crops and did not know the territory well enough to hunt it efficiently. Consequently, they were forced to rely upon relatives for manioc and meat for a number of months, becoming deeply obligated to them. The Waorani who had learned the hacienda system of debt servitude made the most of the opportunity and "called in" their debts in the form of protracted labor obligations or Wao artifacts which the brokers could exchange on the tourist market for *cohuori* goods. Some of these, in turn, were given to the debtors to intensify and protract their obligation.

As the new groups began to move into the protectorate, competition for the following of the new groups arose between the women. When the new arrivals were confident enough to move off, some split off from the Tehuéno group in the pattern of fissioning so common throughout Amazonia, forming allegiances around one or another of these women. By the very nature of the system of reciprocity, which controls so much of social relationships, these "followers" became deeply obligated to the women who aided them in initially securing *cohuori* goods from the Quichuas, tourists, oil searchers, missionaries, or anyone else they might contact. Outsiders continue to reinforce this situation by seeking out the "chiefs" (anyone who can communicate with them in Quichua or Spanish) for their transactions.

Although in the past Wao men attempted to develop a following primarily through the prestige of hunting abilities and exploits in warfare, both men and women could gain influence by obligating others in the system of generalized reciprocity (Sahlins 1965:147) which characterized Wao relationships. This system was by nature dynamic and oscillating. Individuals were continuously gaining ground over others through obligation, only to lose the advantage at a later date, so that no single individual gained an extreme advantage over others. If a person wanted something that another had, he simply requested it by invoking his rights as defined by kinship, and an exchange of goods or services took place over a period of time, with no one becoming deeply indebted to anyone else.

However, the introduction of large quantities of trade and consumer goods that only a few were able to obtain by virtue of specialized abilities transformed the system of reciprocity into an artifice of power structure. Those with access to the scarce resources employed these resources in the manner typical of Melanesian "big man" leadership where the big man uses ". . . a calculated disposition of his wealth, which puts people under obligation to him and constrains their circumspection" (Sahlins 1965:22). The pressures resulting from the externally induced differential access coalesced with the fluid system of social relationships to intensify the system of reciprocity, moving the egalitarian structure toward a ranked one (Fried 1967). The intensification of an existing pattern within the traditional system transformed much of Wao political structure from egalitarianism and situational leadership to a consolidation of authority.

Here a qualification must be added; not everybody is involved in the movement toward social ranking through asymmetric exchange of scarce resources. Those older males who are stronger and more assertive have withdrawn from the influence of the female brokers, maintaining only limited contact with them and seeking their own avenues of outside contact. Also, there is high motivation on the part of many of the younger men to learn Quichua and/or Spanish. They recognize the potential of these languages for them within the Wao system as well as within the *cohuori* systems. If they can accomplish their goals, gaining independence in their relationships with the outside, there is a chance the Wao system will reverse its trend, returning toward a more egalitarian base; of course, the system will never return to the level at which it began, for it is now embedded in a larger national and international economy, society, polity, and ideology.

Cosmological Change

As in other areas of Wao life, there were aspects of the belief system that facilitated acceptance of new elements. The most significant of these is that Wao beliefs are not highly systematized, and even though the culture has always been fairly homogeneous from group to group, cosmology has been debated and takes on several variant forms. Alternate explanations for phenomena are accepted with little real concern by the great majority of people, and little effort is made to harmonize new data or interpretations with the old. In most cases, rather than syncretize the Christian and indigenous systems, the new is just accreted to the old. Following this process, the concepts of Christ and God were introduced and accepted as spirit beings who are more powerful than the evil spirits who can be sent to cause harm.

Undoubtedly, the greatest appeal of the teachings of Dayomé and the missionaries has been the injunction to stop killing one another. The promise of an afterlife of peace had little appeal, since the indigenous system already taught that everyone would experience that, but the hope that the revenge killings might cease had great appeal. Even today one is overwhelmed with the primary function of the weekly "church" gatherings: the reinforcement and reassurance that no one will begin spearing again. A great deal of anxiety regarding spearing is expressed in these gatherings, particularly when some individuals refuse to attend, thereby failing to reassure others that they have no intention of reinstituting the killings.

But the reduction and virtual elimination of the spearing threats began to be felt in the area of social control. Previously, the threat of uncontrolled anger erupting into violence acted as a means of social control, but with that threat greatly diminished mechanisms of social control became problematic. The solution was, again, intensification of an existing pattern through the utilization of a new vehicle for expression. As in the past (Elliot 1961:145), the Waorani remain very open and uninhibited about challenging someone who has violated the behavior code. If it is a clearcut case of transgression, people openly band together in their verbal flogging of the transgressor, who, if nothing else, is inundated by sheer numbers alone. To bolster this pattern, the authority of Huéngongi, the creator, is invoked. What began as Huéngongi's injunctions against revenge killing was extended into most of the other social values to the point that now "Huéngongi says" is often simply an expression of one person's desire to influence another's behavior. To the great majority of Waorani, what it is that Huéngongi may do is uncertain, although it is possible that he may cause one to be snakebitten or become ill. For some it carries the implication that Huéngongi will be manipulated against offenders just as an evil spirit would. Whatever the interpretation, "Huéngongi says" has become an expression of peer opinion. What on the surface appears to be religious sanction turns out to be social pressure, a position many anthropologists have maintained for years.

Subsistence

In spite of the technological changes which have occurred, the subsistence-based economy remains essentially unchanged. A few Wao men have joined the oil company crews in the past two years to earn money and, more important to them, to learn about the *cohouri*. The impact upon the basic patterns of subsistence, however, has been minimal, primarily because few have done this, and those who have remained for short periods. The main impact of this activity is upon the wives and families of the men who go; they have no one to hunt meat for them or to clear the forest for manioc gardens while the men are away.

The trading relationships the Waorani have cultivated with numerous sources have provided them not only with the *cohouri* goods they are seeking but also with an education regarding the workings of the *cohouri* market system. Very few, however, have attempted to extend the monetary system among their own peers.

MECHANISMS OF CHANGE

In seeking an explanation for the processes underlying the visible changes in Wao culture, two primary processes emerge—substitution and intensification. The process of substitution, where elements from the contacting culture replace indigenous elements because of their functional equivalence or near equivalence, has been adequately covered in anthropological literature for many years. The substitution of aluminum pots for clay ones, clothing for feathers, antibiotics for *Banisteriopsis*, or the control of the flow of goods for physical prowess are just a few of the examples of substitution in Wao culture.

The process of intensification, on the other hand, has been less fully developed in the literature. It involves an increase in emphasis of a given trait or pattern to the point that the pattern appears to undergo transformation. Thus the intensification of one oscillation in a cycle of reciprocity lays the basis for further intensification and, ultimately, for the movement of the entire system to a new state, as, for example, when an egalitarian system gives way to a consolidation of power and transforms into a system of ranked statuses of differential access to valued resources. Although both substitution and intensification depend heavily upon existing features internal to the system that is changing, I maintain that the process of intensification is more directly an outgrowth of the internal structure than an imposition of external features. Among the Waorani, elements or patterns arising from intensification take their shape almost entirely from the existing structure, whereas those arising from substitution are heavily dependent upon the shape they had in the external culture from which they came. Intensification is more likely to involve complex patterns of relationship of elements, whereas substitution is more likely to involve simple elements.

An examination of the data outlined in the previous sections also reveals that Wao culture was characterized by forces in dynamic tension. The ties of kinship pulled toward unity and harmony between the various local descent groups, but geographical distribution and separation pushed toward suspicion and hostility. The obligations generated by the system of reciprocity induced one to share to avoid being stigmatized as selfish, but also deterred one from asking for too much too often because of the need to reciprocate later. Past hostilities of outsiders against Waorani and the belief that *cohouri* are cannibals pushed the Waorani to avoid and fear the *cohouri*, but the desire to escape the internal vendetta and an intense curiosity about the *cohouri* motivated some to seek contact with them. All through the culture lines of stress such as these kept the system oscillating within fairly well-defined boundaries. But the increase in scale which the system began to experience two decades ago put pressures upon certain of these lines of tension, causing them to exceed normal boundaries and to move the system to a new state. In some cases change was effected because existing tensions were reduced. In others existing tensions were increased, and in still other instances new tensions were created.

An example of the first instance, change produced through the reduction of existing tensions, can be seen in the relationship of the various local groups following relocation. When geographical separation was reduced, the resulting increase in communication and interaction lowered the suspicion and hostility between the groups, and the existing forces contributing to unity moved into prominence.

The existing tension between forces for unity and forces for disunity was reduced. In another instance, though, the introduction of *co-houri* technology and differential access to it increased the existing tensions between sharing and requesting, resulting in the beginnings of a rank system. In the final case, that of changes produced by the creation of new lines of tension, the arrival and continued presence of *cohouri* in Wao territory introduced new types of tensions as the Waorani had to determine how to relate to them. This has been accentuated more recently by the variety of types of *cohouri* who are entering the area, each with his own distinct purpose and mode of interaction.

Thus the internal forces operating in Wao culture interacted with the change-producing stresses established by the increase in scale with all its manifestations. Once the hostility to the outside world was alleviated, or at least reduced, scale increased. An important aspect of scale observable from the Wao data is its generative capability. An increase in scale gives impetus to further scale increases through the changes caused by the initial increase. When the missionary women entered Wao territory with Dayomé, their presence constituted an increase in scale for the Wao society. But it also gave rise to changes in the culture such as the end of the notion that all *cohouri* are cannibals, and the development of a sense of trust in the *cohouri*. These changes encouraged extended contact with more *cohouri*, increasing scale even further. The new level of scale produced even greater changes, and the process continues on.

One of the consequences frequently associated with an increase in scale, particularly across cultural boundaries, is a sense of deprivation and disorientation culminating in demoralization (Berreman 1978). The Waorani have not experienced this, in great part because they have acquired access to the goals they have thus far sought, primarily the possession of *cohouri* goods and the use of modern medicines. The most extreme changes that have occurred in Wao culture are those pertaining to political relationships, but these changes have not resulted in disorientation because *the goods controlled within the transformed political arena are not essential to survival*. The subsistence-based economy remains essentially unchanged. The land base and its resources are still available to all using traditional methods, *giving all equal access to life-sustaining necessities*. In essence, the Waorani still have considerable control over their lives. As Lingenfelter (1977:116) and Berreman (1978) have both documented, as long as a group has access to the rewards it seeks, the frustration, disorganization, and anomie of the modernization process can be averted.

EPILOGUE

Although this paper is based upon data gathered from 1974 to 1977, return trips in 1978 and 1979 demonstrated that a number of tendencies outlined above have intensified drastically, thereby increasing the extension of scale dramatically. Most noticeably, the tension between those forces contributing to dependence on the female cultural brokers and those forces contributing to independence has intensified. As more individual Waorani have developed their own avenues of relationship with the outside world, the Quichua/Spanish-speaking women have had to expand their efforts to counter the leveling effect of the tendencies toward egalitarianism in relationships with the outside.

Of the forces contributing to independence from the female cultural brokers, the employment of Waorani by oil companies working in Wao territory is the most conspicuous. Whereas fewer than ten men had worked for oil companies prior to 1977, by late 1978 33 men, or 27% of the work-eligible male population in the proctectorate, had gone out to work on at least one occasion, and many on several occasions. By late 1979 this percentage had grown to 60%, thus bringing a significant number of outside influences into the area, not the least of which is large quantities of money. More than that, it has given those men experience with the outside world that they previously lacked. This direct experience includes living by the work ethic and monetary exchange system of a market economy, observing *cohuori* behavior, interacting with large numbers of *cohuori* from various cultural backgrounds, using advanced *cohuori* technology, and eating *cohuori* foods. All of these experiences have stimulated a desire for more direct interaction.

In addition, a few single women, 13 thus far, have gone to the surrounding towns such as Tena to work as domestic servants for the *blancos* living there. Most work for room and board only, receiving little or no wage in return for their labor. In one instance a family took their daughter to Puyo to work, but has been unable to get her back for nearly a year now. Negative experiences such as these are likely to keep the number of Wao women who go outside to work from increasing greatly. In such a situation males could gain an advantage over females, thereby weakening the egalitarianism between the sexes that currently exists in most areas.

In addition to the rush to work on the outside, there is a general movement toward establishing *compadrazgo* relationships with Quichua in surrounding towns such as Tena, Arajuno, Pano, and the military base at Curaray. By late 1979 80% of the married couples in the protectorate had *compadrazgo* ties among the Quichua, some with as many as nine *compadres*. Compared with the 14% that had *compadres* in 1977, this number is astounding—a powerful index of the interaction that is beginning to take place between the Waorani and the outside. What this means for the Waorani is a place to stay during trips to the outside, someone to act as an intermediary in transactions, and the opportunity to observe outside ways in a nonthreatening environment. For the Quichua it means a source of smoked meat and fish plus hunting and fishing privileges in Wao territory. The shortage of jungle meat in many areas of the Oriente has stimulated large-scale exportation of smoked meat from Wao territory to the surrounding towns. Two or three times a week Waorani carry several hundred pounds of smoked meat and fish to their *compadres* who have become the middlemen in the system.

Thus the dyadic relationships between *compadres* have facilitated and encouraged the movement of Waorani to the outside and the movement of Quichuas into Wao territory. But beyond that, they have brought a new element of peer pressure to bear on Wao behavior. Both Waorani and Quichua operate on the face-to-face level typical of small-scale societies, and the *compadre* relationships are a manifestation of that principle across cultural boundaries. Most important, the land squeeze which is being felt in the more populated areas of the Oriente is prompting some Quichua to use the *compadrazgo* system to pressure their Wao *compadres* to give or sell them land in the protectorate. In a face-to-face society one of the most serious accusations that can be made is that of being selfish, and several of the *compadres* from Arajuno are informing the Waorani that they are being selfish by not sharing the protectorate land with them. The fact that some Waorani are considering these requests even though their own Wao relatives are incensed at the suggestion demonstrates the degree to which some Waorani have come to identify with the Quichua culture, thereby making Quichua peer pressure effective among Waorani.

To counter the various kinds of threats of independence from their brokerage hegemony, the women who previously controlled all access to the outside have had to take more extreme measures. One of these is to try to attract the tourist industry which "discovered" the "Aucas" in 1976. During 1976 from 250 to 300 tourists hiked the 12-hour trail from Campana Cocha to Nushiño to see the "savages." In an attempt to keep from losing her following to that village, one of the female brokers had a trail opened from Ahuano to her newly established village of Toñémpade on the Curaray. The huge recent upsurge in Ecuadorian tourism accommodated her, and in 1979 groups of three to eight persons visited Toñémpade twice a week. This not only keeps the broker's followers at Toñémpade to observe the *cohuori* tourists but also reinforces the hegemony, since the tour guides advertise the tour as a trip to see the "Auca Queens" and pay only those "Queens" for services, food, etc. while in the Wao villages. Even those villages that do not particularly want or like tourists are getting them too as the guides continue to seek more "savage"-looking groups to attract more tourists. An unfortunate but predictable result of the tourism has been widespread illness carried in by the tourists, and the death of two people in the latest epidemic.

Another measure the brokers use to attract a following is to persuade Quichua school teachers to come to live and teach in a village. The two Wao women who have succeeded in getting them use strong pressures to convince other Waorani that they should move to their villages to attend school to learn Spanish. The implications of this for the Waorani go beyond just learning to read or write. In both instances the school teachers have not been enthusiastic, to say the least, about encouraging traditional Wao ways. In the two villages where they teach, people are beginning to take a derogatory stance toward their own language and customs, led by the female brokers who now openly demonstrate their orientation to Quichua culture and their disdain for Wao culture. On one occasion they burned reading materials written by Wao authors from another village because "the Huao language is no good."

Finally, efforts to arrange Quichua-Wao marriages have intensified, particularly among the female brokers who receive great benefits from the arrangements. This is putting even greater pressure on some Waorani to give their new Quichua relatives land from the protectorate, thereby increasing the strain in relationship between those Waorani who want to maintain Wao culture, language, and territory and those who want to become Quichua.

Complicating all of these tensions between the *cohuori* orientation and the Wao orientation are the number of agencies, private and governmental, who have taken an active and aggressive interest in the Waorani, particularly as word is spreading that the "Aucas" are no longer killing outsiders. For example, at least four separate agencies and organizations are currently vying for the opportunity to train Waorani as health workers. Other agencies are attempting to implement more Spanish-speaking schools and various community development projects among the Waorani.

In summary, the process of scale increase began slowly, with Wao-rani operating under the rules of small-scale society. For a number of years their orientation to the outside was primarily dependent upon personal relationships they developed with SIL people living among them. Then, stimulated by the leadership of female cultural brokers, they began to expand their orientation to the outside, still depending upon certain key individuals to act as intermediaries. Now in many ways they are freeing themselves from dependence upon the female cultural brokers, operating more as individuals on their own behalf, but they are at the same time beginning to look more outwardly, in some cases to the point of attempting to deny their own heritage and take on that of the surrounding Quichua.

The implication of all of this in expansion of scale is best elucidated through an example. As I wrote this, I received word that the group living on the Nushiño River who first attempted to develop intensive relationships with the outside, who first received tourists in great numbers, and who got the first Spanish-speaking school have gone to Tena hoping to "live forever as *cohuori*." That they will return is fairly certain, but most likely with the sense of deprivation and frustration that Berreman (1978) has described. One hopes that sense will be momentary. Their options are not all cut off as long as they have their land and its resources to return to. The burning question right now is whether they can, or will, hold onto their land.

NOTES

Acknowledgments: I am indebted to Norman E. Whitten, Jr., Kathleen Fine, C. Roderick Wilson, Glen Turner, Catherine Peeke, Pat Kelley, and Mary Ruth Wise for their suggestions and criticisms, which have strengthened this paper and challenged my thinking. Of course, none of these is to be held responsible for errors or weaknesses in the paper, and all views expressed are my responsibility. In addition, I would also like to express my gratitude to the Summer Institute of Linguistics, under whose auspices this research was conducted.

1. The orthography used here is based upon Spanish orthography, except that the phonetic value of *é* is [æ] and *e* is [I]; in the case of the people's self-identifying name, Wao-Waorani, I am using *W* rather than *Hu*. Nasalization is phonemic on Wao vowels, but has been omitted here.

2. The data for this paper were gathered during the period Jan. 1974 through Apr. 1977, when I lived with my family in the Wao village of Te-huéno. Numerous visits, of two weeks or more each, were made to all other Wao groups except the Tagéiri, a family of fewer than a dozen individuals roaming the headwaters of the Cononaco River.

3. Slightly over 5% of the Waorani recorded in genealogies extending back as far as five generations fled to the outside never to return.

4. Even these two are subject to skepticism. I had recorded a third individual who, according to a number of Waorani, had also "died, becoming old." Then one day someone let it slip that "because he had gotten so old, they speared him, threw him in the river, and he died." I am now quite suspicious of the other two "natural" deaths.

REFERENCES CITED

Beardsley, R. K., et al.
 1956 *Functional and Evolutionary Implications of Community Patterning.* Seminars in Archaeology, ed. Robert Wauchope. Memoirs of the Society for American Archaeology 11.
Berreman, Gerald D.
 1978 Scale and Social Relations. *Current Anthropology* 19 (2):225–45.
Blomberg, Rolf
 1957 *The Naked Aucas: An Account of the Indians of Ecuador.* Trans. F. H. Lyon. London: George Allen & Unwin Ltd.
Elliot, Elisabeth
 1957 *Through Gates of Splendor.* New York: Harper & Row.
 1958 *Shadow of the Almighty.* New York: Harper & Row.
 1961 *The Savage My Kinsman.* New York: Harper & Row.
Fried, Morton
 1967 *The Evolution of Political Society: An Essay in Political Anthropology.* New York: Random House.
Goodenough, Ward H.
 1970 *Description and Comparison in Cultural Anthropology.* Chicago: Aldine.
Jouanen, J., S.J.
 1977 *Los Jesuitas y el Oriente Ecuatoriano: Monografia Historica, 1868–1898.* Guayaquil: Editorial Arquidiocesana.
Keesing, Roger M.
 1971 Descent, Residence and Cultural Codes. In L. R. Hiatt and C. Jaywardena, eds., *Anthropology in Oceania: Essays Presented to Ian Hogbin.* Sydney: Angus and Robertson, pp. 121–38.
Lingenfelter, Sherwood
 1977 Socioeconomic Change in Oceania. *Oceania* 48 (2):102–20.
Peeke, Catherine M.
 1973 *Preliminary Grammar of Auca.* Norman, Okla.: Summer Institute of Linguistics.
Sahlins, Marshall
 1965 On the Sociology of Primitive Exchange. In Michael Banton, ed., *The Relevance of Models for Social Anthropology.* New York: Praeger.
 1968 *Tribesmen.* Englewood Cliffs, N.J.: Prentice-Hall.
Scheffler, H. W.
 1966 Ancestor Worship in Anthropology: Or, Observation on Descent and Descent Groups. *Current Anthropology* 7:541–51.

Up de Graff, Fritz W.
1923 *Head Hunters of the Amazon*. Garden City, N.Y.: Garden City Publishing Co.
Wallis, Ethel E.
1960 *The Dayuma Story*. Old Tappan, N.J.: Spire Books.
1973 *Aucas Downriver*. New York: Harper & Row.
Whitten, Norman E., Jr.
1976 (with the assistance of Marcelo F. Naranjo, Marcelo Santi Simbaña, and Dorothea S. Whitten). *Sacha Runa: Ethnicity and Adaptation of Ecuadorian Jungle Quichua*. Urbana: University of Illinois Press.
1978 *Amazonian Ecuador: An Ethnic Interface in Ecological, Social, and Ideological Perspectives*. Copenhagen: International Work Group for Indigenous Affairs, Document 34.
Wilson, C. R., and James A. Yost
1979 The New Amazons: From Equality to Dominance. Paper delivered to the American Anthropological Association symposium "Women's Roles in Traditional and Modernizing Societies," Cincinnati, Ohio.
Yengoyan, Aram A.
1973 Kindreds and Task Groups in Mandaya Social Organization. *Ethnology* 12 (2):163–77.
Yost, James A.
1978 Variables Affecting Land Requirements for Tropical Forest Horticulturalists: Some Policy Implications. Paper delivered to the Second International Conference on Amazonia, Madison, Wis.
1979 *El Desarrollo Comunitario y la Supervivencia Etnica: El Caso de los Huaorani, Amazonía Ecuatoriana*. Quito: Instituto Lingüístico de Verano, Cuadernos Etnolingüísticos 6.

25

Ideation as Adaptation: Traditional Belief and Modern Intervention in Siona-Secoya Religion

William T. Vickers

In western culture "religion" is a semantic domain that is commonly conceptualized as the order of phenomena having to do with spirituality, supernatural belief, ritual sanctity, and cosmology. One of the time-honored tasks of the social sciences has been the analysis of the functions of religion in social, psychological, and economic terms. This tradition is so ingrained that no introductory text of sociology, psychology, or anthropology would be complete without some discussion of the theories of Marx, Freud, Weber, Tylor, and Frazer as they pertain to religion.

Although Marx (1964 [1848]) saw religion as rationalizing existing economic inequalities in class-stratified capitalist societies, and Weber (1958 [1904]) emphasized the role that Calvinist ideology had in the formation of the Protestant "work ethic," relatively few anthropologists have made detailed studies of the economic and ecological implications of religion. Even Julian Steward (1955), whose "method of cultural ecology" laid the groundwork for modern ecological studies in anthropology, tended to treat religion as an epiphenomenon in his classic analyses of the Great Basin Shoshone and the northeastern Algonkians and Mundurucú (Murphy and Steward 1956).

More recently, anthropological studies such as those by Rappaport (1968) on the ritual cycle of the Tsembaga-Maring of New Guinea and Harner (1977) on Aztec human sacrifice have attempted to interpret religious practices in terms of processes of ecological adaptation. Although the specific adaptive models postulated by ecological anthropologists may be debated (cf. Price's 1978 critique of Harner's sacrificial hypothesis), a central thesis of this paper is that religious systems do not exist on the level of symbolic abstraction alone, but are fundamental components of human adaptation.

Rappaport's Tsembaga study reveals the adaptive attributes of the religious system of a given ethnic community as it interacts with its habitat and other ethnic communities manifesting similar levels of technology and ideational systems. By contrast, the present paper focuses on an interethnic contact situation in which competing cultural, religious, and socioeconomic systems confront one another. Specifically, this case involves contact between a community of Amazonian Indians who are the bearers of a traditional culture and world view, and members of a foreign missionary organization and the national society of Ecuador. In this paper "religion" is not viewed in strictly symbolic or moralistic terms but is interpreted as an adaptive "mechanism" for two competing socioeconomic systems. The traditional ideological system of the Siona-Secoya Indians is interpreted as having behavioral consequences that promote a dispersed settlement pattern, thereby enhancing the stability of the subsistence ecology. The data presented will indicate that the changes brought about by missionary activity do not merely represent a battle for the minds and souls of the Siona-Secoya, but are the harbingers of a technological and social transformation which must be understood in terms of its economic and political context. The opening of the Oriente regions of Ecuador represents a competition for land and resources involving many players, including oil companies, colonists, agricultural and commercial entrepreneurs, and the expanding populations of lowland Indian groups. This paper will analyze both traditional and new religious orders in terms of their adaptive attributes in the distinctive ecological and economic systems of the aboriginal society and the nation.

THE SIONA-SECOYA

The Siona-Secoya Indians are a tropical forest people who live on the Aguarico, Eno, and Cuyabeno rivers in northeastern Ecuador (see Map 1). They are related linguistically and culturally to the Siona, Makaguaje, and Coreguaje Indians of Colombia and to the Secoya and Angotero Indians of Peru. All of these peoples are members of the Western Tucanoan linguistic family. As of 1975 the population of the Siona-Secoya in Ecuador was 283, and the population of related Western Tucanoan speakers probably did not exceed 1,400 individuals (Langdon 1974:13). Steward (1949:663) estimated that the aboriginal population of the Western Tucanoans was 16,000.

The native settlement pattern of the Siona-Secoya is one of scattered residential groups whose nuclei are formed by patrilineal, patrilocal extended families. Each group is associated with particular

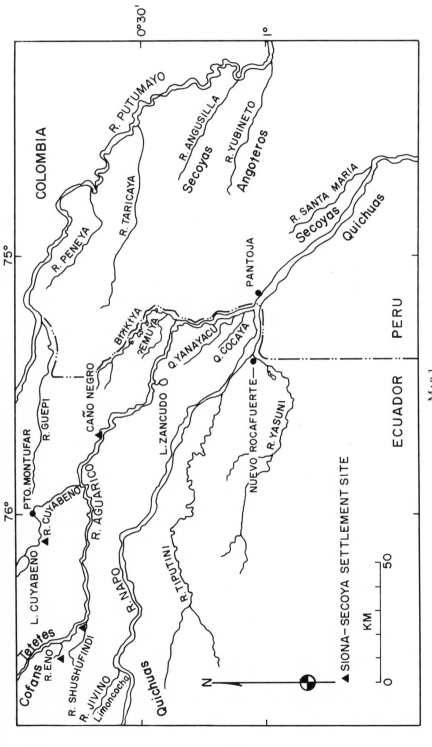

MAP 1

rivers or sections of rivers. Before the intrusion of outside influences, the actual settlements were hidden and could not be seen from the courses of the major rivers such as the Napo and Aguarico. Typically, the villages were located on smaller streams that provided the domestic water supply. On the basis of rather fragmentary reports Steward (1948:742) concluded that the Western Tucanoans did not possess canoes in aboriginal times, but the evidence for this is by no means conclusive. Regardless, the Indians were able canoeists by the mid-1600s and continue to be so today. In modern times the Siona-Secoya have moved their settlements to the banks of the rivers.

The subsistence of the Siona-Secoya is based on shifting cultivation, hunting, fishing, and collecting. Their cultivars include both "sweet" and "bitter" manioc, maize, plantains, peach palm (*Guilielma gasipaes*), breadfruit, caimito (*Chrysophillum cainito*), achira (*Canna edulis*), papaya, yams (*Dioscorea* spp.), and sweet potatoes (*Ipomoea batatas*) among others.[1] The broad outlines of Western Tucanoan horticulture are similar to those of many other tropical forest groups; plots in the forest are felled at the beginning of the dry season (November–December in this part of the Amazon Basin) and are burned and planted prior to the onset of the rainy season in February. The cropping cycle in a given garden extends over two to three years and then secondary growth claims the plot. Normally, a new garden is made each year so that old, intermediate, and new plots exist contemporaneously. This provides the household with the widest possible range of garden products, for some cultivars are slow to mature (e.g. some varieties of manioc, plantains, and fruit trees), whereas crops such as maize may be harvested within 90 days of planting.

Hunting is an important activity in Siona-Secoya society. The most important species taken include peccaries (*Tayassu tacuaju* and *T. pecari*), monkeys (*Lagothrix* and *Alouatta*), tapir, agoutis, armadillos, and birds such as guans (*Penelope* spp.) and curassows (*Mitu* sp.). Hunting is conducted year round and provides important sources of protein in the Siona-Secoya diet. Fishing is more variable than hunting because it is affected by seasonal fluctuations in water levels and by the varying limnological characteristics of the rivers and streams that flow through the Siona-Secoya territory. On many of the rivers fishing is little practiced during the rainy season, but some of the smaller rivers and streams are fished year round. Aquatic hunting and collecting are also practiced, and involve the taking of caimans, manatees, and river turtles and their eggs. As in fishing, the rivers vary in the degree to which they present habitats for these species.

As a consequence of the temporal and spatial variations in resource availabilities, the Siona-Secoya diet is subject to differing emphases according to the seasons and settlement locations. Some settlements, such as those on the Cuyabeno River, depend more upon riverine resources than hunting. In villages with established gardens collecting provides a small proportion of the total diet (less than 5% of the calorie intake). Nevertheless, certain collected plant products such as the fruit of the *Mauritia* palm make important contributions to the diet on a seasonal basis. The collection of forest fruits and nuts assumes greater importance when people engage in treks through the forest or have immature gardens following the relocation of a village. Finally, wild food collection is important in a qualitative sense because it gives the diet additional variety and essential nutrients such as vitamins.

Although the Siona-Secoya do engage in extended hunting and fishing trips from time to time, the vast majority of these activities take place within a half-day's journey of any given settlement (a distance of about 15 kilometers). This area may be viewed as a range which is directly exploited for subsistence purposes. Studies at the village of San Pablo (Shushufindi) on the Aguarico River during 1973–75 indicate a size of approximately 225 square kilometers for this zone of primary exploitation. The fringe of one settlement's zone does not border on that of another settlement, however, because settlements are spaced a full day's journey or more apart.[2] The land beyond the immediate exploitation range may be viewed as fallowed territory into which the settlement may move in the future. The manifest explanations for settlement relocations are varied and may allude to a declining subsistence base in the old range or may be linked to social or supernatural factors. In a broad sense, therefore, each residence group may be viewed as being associated with a particular geographical area or territory within which it makes periodic moves from one specific settlement site to another every 5–20 years.

THE TRADITIONAL RELIGIOUS COMPLEX

In hunting and gathering and simple horticultural societies cultural institutions and domains are less specialized than in advanced agricultural and industrial societies. Generally, there are fewer people, fewer cultural elements, and less functional compartmentalization of statuses and roles. Although Siona-Secoya culture presents the ethnologist with a rich intellectual and linguistic tapestry, the confluence of religious, social, political, and economic functions makes these domains less discrete than in modern technological societies.

Shamans and Headmen

The central figure in Siona-Secoya residential groupings is an elder male who serves as the headman and shaman. The headman-shaman status combines the roles of head of household, religious practitioner, healer, protector, and savant. The native term for headman-shaman is /ĩnti ba'ikɨ/, which is glossed as "this person who lives." The Siona-Secoya explain that this term implies that the headman-shaman lives "better," by which they mean that his behavior more perfectly approximates the ideal norms of the society.

Although the basis of the residential groups consists of a man, his wife, their married sons, and their wives and children (i.e. the patrilineal, patrilocal extended household), some headmen attract additional households to their settlements by virtue of their charismatic qualities and shamanistic prowess. The curative power of a great shaman is the greatest assurance of protection from illnesses deriving from supernatural forces. There is an underlying tension in the relations between neighboring settlements because of sorcery accusations among the various shamans. Except for certain accidental deaths, virtually all fatalities of past and present generations are attributed to the malevolent actions of neighboring shamans (i.e. shamans from other settlements which are known to the local community, although not necessarily the closest ones). House sites are relocated following these deaths because memories of the deceased render places "sad."

Although all headmen are shamans, not all shamans are headmen. To become a respected shaman, an individual must undergo an apprenticeship and then develop his abilities over a period of years. He must also demonstrate the correct attributes of asceticism, generosity, concern for the well-being of others, and dignified bearing. Most of all, he must demonstrate proficiency in conducting the *yagé* ceremony, in experiencing *yagé* visions, and establishing contact with supernatural beings. (*Yagé* is the Siona-Secoya term for hallucinogenic plants of the genus *Banisteriopsis*.)

The use of *yagé* and the other hallucinogenic plants in the Siona-Secoya pharmacopoeia is very important and highly ritualized. It is believed that such vision-producing substances are a medium through which contact may be made with supernatural realms and beings. The experienced shaman also undergoes physical transformation and soul flight via the medium of *yagé*. Many aspirants fail to achieve full shamanistic status because they do not experience visions of sufficient intensity or lack the discipline to continue the strict regimen of fasting, sexual abstinence, and physical isolation required of apprentices.

The Siona-Secoya universe consists of multiple layers of existence, including an underworld, the world of the present reality, and several celestial realms. These layers are inhabited by various ancestral spirits, mythological culture heroes and antagonists, spirit helpers, demons, and animal spirits and their keepers. The relationship between these beings and the Siona-Secoya is of extreme importance, for the latter believe that many of the significant events in their lives are caused or influenced by supernatural intervention. Included among these is success in hunting and fishing; more important, the supernatural sphere is the source of illness and death, which are attributed to the harm done by the spirit helpers of evil sorcerers.

The Siona-Secoya term which comprehends "disease" is /dawu/. It is contrasted with a polar concept /wahí/, which implies life and well-being. The opposition of /wahí/ and /dawu/ is a fundamental postulate of Siona-Secoya thought and constitutes the basis of a complex logical system (Langdon 1974). While it is not within the scope of this paper to discuss these complex semantic domains in detail, it is useful to provide several illustrations of recognized illness syndromes among the Siona-Secoya to support the relationships that will be suggested in the analysis. Three of the many syndromes are described briefly below:

1. /ʔɨsɨ dawu/, sun illness. This illness is caused when a sorcerer pierces the chest of his victim with a "sun dart." The sorcerer enlists a spirit helper to carry the dart to the victim where it cuts the heart "like a bullet." The dart can travel great distances in an instant. The victim feels great pain, vomits blood, and dies quickly.

2. /ma oma dawu/, red frog illness. This illness is likewise caused by a sorcerer's dart, but in this case a "red frog" dart is utilized. The victim does not die rapidly, but lapses into a deathlike coma and occasionally may gasp, "Ah . . . ah . . . ah." Soon the body begins to rot but the soul lingers on. If the condition of the victim does not improve, he or she may be buried alive.

3. /ʔaíro baī dawu/, forest people illness. The /ʔaíro baī/ are small spirit beings that live in the forest canopy.[3] At the request of a sorcerer they may produce vapors on a forest trail. These are invisible but stretch across the path like a spider's web. The person who walks through the vapors experiences severe nausea and vomiting, but will not die if he is treated by a friendly shaman.

Although these examples are not exhaustive, they indicate how objective symptoms such as chest pain, coma, and nausea are ex-

plained within an internally consistent theory of disease. Specific illnesses are diagnosed by local shamans and are blamed on distant
shamans who are perceived as sorcerers. The diagnosis and treatment of disease occurs within the setting of communal *yagé* ceremonies which are conducted in special ceremonial huts away from the
village proper. The hallucinogenic medium enables the curing shaman to visualize the source of the illness and to intervene in the activities of the sorcerer's spirit helper.

As individuals go through life experiencing a number of illnesses,
viewing the illnesses of kin and neighbors, and hearing of the illnesses of past generations, a corpus of information concerning shamans and sorcerers is built up. In some cases the resentments deriving from past deaths among one's family and community become so
exacerbated that individuals engage in revenge killings of suspected
sorcerers. These histories are well known to the older members of all
the settlements and are passed on to younger generations. They explain much of the fear and distrust felt by the members of one settlement toward those of another.

Ideation as Adaptation

In order to understand the relationship between Siona-Secoya "religion" and "ecology," it is necessary to consider the essential or minimal conditions of the system under analysis. These include (1) the
environmental baseline: the tropical forest and riverine habitats and
their associated resources; (2) the human baseline: a resident human
community; and (3) the technological baseline: subsistence based on
horticulture, hunting, fishing, and collecting with basic hand tools
and no extrapersonal sources of energy for work.

Given these conditions, it is possible to make hypothetical statements about the relationships between the elements of the system.
These are presented as postulates rather than as statements of fact
because no program of research in the Amazon to date has been extensive enough to systematically test each of the suggested relationships by the method of controlled comparison. Nevertheless, the
postulates are not entirely deductive, for they are suggested by observations made during 18 months of quantitative and qualitative
field research on Siona-Secoya subsistence.[4] The most useful aspect
of the postulates is that they may serve as working hypotheses for
future research.

The first general theorem describing the system is: Subsistence efficiency tends to be inversely related to population density. The sim-

plest quantitative expression of "subsistence efficiency" is the ratio of output calories (yield) to input calories (labor and materials invested). However, it is important to recognize that calories are but one dimension of subsistence. A diet of 2,500 calories, for example, may or may not contain adequate nutritive components such as proteins, fats, vitamins, and minerals. Both the qualitative and quantitative aspects of subsistence must be borne in mind. Nevertheless, "subsistence efficiency," as here defined, is a useful and operationalized concept. The first theorem stated above is derived from the following postulates:

1. All other conditions being equal, horticultural yields (in a given area) per unit of labor are inversely related to the length of cultivation.

2. All other conditions being equal, hunting yields (in a given area) per unit of labor are inversely related to the rate of hunting.

3. All other conditions being equal, fishing yields (in a given area) per unit of labor are inversely related to the rate of fishing.

4. All other conditions being equal, collecting yields (in a given area) are inversely related to the rate of collecting.

If these postulates describing the ecological relationships of the Siona-Secoya are accurate, it then becomes valid to derive such statements as "A low population density is adaptive" and "A dispersed settlement pattern is adaptive." As employed here, the term "adaptive" refers to any behavior or process that tends to increase the efficiency of subsistence or the reproductive chances of the population, or which promotes the stability of the subsistence and reproductive systems by mediating between demands and resources (i.e. by contributing to the maintenance of the resource base).

The second general theorem is: Subsistence efficiency is positively related to periodic movement. It is based on the following postulates:

1. All other conditions being equal, horticultural yields per unit of labor increase when a population moves from an old settlement site to one where cultivation has been absent or the land fallowed.

2. All other conditions being equal, hunting yields per unit of labor increase when a population moves from an old hunting territory to an area where human predation on fauna has been absent.

3. All other conditions being equal, fishing yields per unit of labor increase when a population moves from rivers that have been fished to rivers that have not been fished.

4. All other conditions being equal, collecting yields per unit of labor increase when a population moves from an old collecting territory to an area where collecting has been absent.

If these postulates are correct, it is valid to derive the statement "The periodic movement of settlements is adaptive."

Although the religious complex of the Siona-Secoya is interpreted as promoting settlement dispersion and relocation, it is important to make the point that the manifest explanations for all settlement relocations are not linked to religious factors. Any number of explanations may be given to account for settlement movements. Among these may be references to "boredom" with the old site, a desire to move closer to kin, or factors relating to subsistence, such as declining hunting yields or a scarcity of cultivable lands. Regardless of the manifest explanation for a move, a relocation tends to increase the efficiency of subsistence when all other factors remain equal. Hence movement has a latent ecological function which may or may not be independent of its manifest explanation. Nevertheless, manifest explanations based on supernatural or religious factors do constitute one of the most significant sets of rationalizations given to account for the movement of settlements.

It is also important to note that settlement relocations do not occur only when the resources of an inhabited site have been exhausted. It is difficult to conceive of a situation where the multiple resources of a given area would be depleted simultaneously. Such a situation would make for a very slow recovery of the fauna and flora. It is far more adaptive for settlement relocations to occur prior to the point of environmental exhaustion. It should be noted that some ethnologists (e.g. Chagnon 1968a, 1968b), who have observed village movements in the Amazon taking place despite apparently abundant resources at the old sites, have taken these observations as evidence that the typical tropical forest pattern of semipermanent villages is not based on ecological factors.

MODERN RELIGIOUS TRANSFORMATIONS

The Siona-Secoya have been introduced to several external religious influences since the Spanish conquest of the New World. The Franciscans contacted their Western Tucanoan ancestors briefly during the seventeenth century, but a *cedula real* issued in 1683 assigned the Aguarico and Napo region to the Jesuit order. The Jesuit effort among the "Encabellados" (the term used to designate the Western Tucanoans of the Aguarico and Napo rivers) lasted from 1709 through the 1760s. The missionaries trekked through the forests and endured considerable hardships in order to locate the various *encabellado* settlements (cf. Chantre y Herrera 1901). They then used their powers of persuasion and promises of iron tools to coax the Indians into moving to sites along the banks of the Napo and Aguarico. The Jesuit plan was to form *reducciones*, "reductions," where the scattered Indian groups would be combined, thus simplifying the work of the missionaries considerably. However, the headmen of some of the groups insisted on making settlements that were independent of those of the other groups, citing fears of sorcery. The missionaries assented, viewing this compromise as a temporary necessity.

During the eighteenth century 17 Jesuit missions were established among the *encabellado*. These missions were quite unstable, however, because the Jesuits were few in number and had to travel between the missions continuously and therefore could not maintain control over the Indians who left for hunting and collecting expeditions, or whenever illness, sorcery accusations, or other tensions developed. By the mid–1700s the *encabellado* missions had experienced several uprisings and epidemics and were on the decline. Charles III's order of 1769 expelling the Jesuits from South America sealed their fate. It was not possible to elicit any oral history pertaining to the Jesuit missions from the Siona-Secoya living today. Nevertheless, they do have a rich oral tradition which focuses on the events of mythical times. One must conclude that the Jesuit contact was too sporadic to make a significant impact on the precepts of Siona-Secoya thought. Indeed, only one of the Jesuits, Padre Martín Iriarte, was said to have been fluent in the language of the Indians (Chantre y Herrera 1901:398).

Other missionaries were to come to the Siona-Secoya in the twentieth century. In the mid-1950s members of the Summer Institute of Linguistics (SIL) made contact with a group living on the Cuyabeno River, and a missionary-linguist and his family subsequently established a mission outpost there. A few years later a Catholic priest from Spain arrived and worked in the settlement for about a year and a half before departing. The work of the SIL among the Siona-Secoya has continued to the present and constitutes the major external influence on their way of life.

The SIL presence in Ecuador is not due to chance, but comes as the result of a contract with the Ecuadorian Ministry of Public Education. This contract charges the SIL with the responsibility of studying the native languages and "developing a program of practical, patriotic and moral services" in each tribe in which they work (SIL 1969:3; my translation from the Spanish). In prosaic terms, these services include the establishment and operation of bilingual schools, the training of native teachers to staff the schools, the writing and publication of textbooks in the native languages, medical assistance, agricultural extension, and miscellaneous services such as giving classes in carpentry and typing. The SIL also provides transportation and communications services through its Jungle Aviation and Radio Service (JAARS) division, but the primary function of this branch is to meet the logistical needs of the mission outposts. The philosophy of the SIL is to offer certain of these services, such as health care and transportation, on a fee basis so that the Indians will learn how to handle Ecuadorian currency. Although the cash income of the Indians is small and derives primarily from the sale of jaguar and ocelot skins, they do gain some supplemental income by selling artifacts to a SIL store which markets them to visitors and tourists, and by working at miscellaneous tasks for the missionary-linguist.

The modern mission activities are not occurring in isolation, for the period since the arrival of the SIL has been one in which Ecuador has sought to establish control and an official presence in its long-neglected eastern regions. Although the *audiencia* of Quito once ruled over vast areas of the Upper Amazon Basin, Ecuador's inability to colonize these lands led to large losses of territory to Peru and Colombia during the national period. The pre-eminent event in this process was the Ecuadorian-Peruvian war of 1941, which resulted in the loss of more than 200,000 square kilometers of national territory (Martz 1972:69). Both the war and the subsequent Protocol of Río de Janeiro at which the dispute was arbitrated were national humiliations for Ecuador. In spirit, Ecuador refuses to acknowledge the territorial losses to Peru as being permanent; all official and textbook maps include the full eastern region as national territory, with the Río Protocol boundary labeled as such. The slogan "Ecuador has been, is, and will be an Amazonian nation" appears on official stationery and billboards around the country.[5]

Official government policy has called for the colonization of the Oriente for many years; in fact, this has traditionally been viewed as the safety valve that would someday relieve the demographic pressures that were building in the intermontane valleys of the Sierra. The main catalysts for the settlement of the Oriente, however, have come from the activities of foreign corporations searching for oil. The first highway into the Oriente was constructed during 1936–47 in conjunction with unsuccessful explorations carried out by Royal Dutch Shell (Hegen 1966:123). The route led eastward from Ambato to Puyo and gradually was extended northward to Napo, Tena, and Archidona. The area along this highway was the first major area of colonization in eastern Ecuador, and Puyo, with a population estimated to be 10,000 in 1972 (Whitten 1976:249), is the major city of the entire region. In the early 1970s a northern road into the Oriente was constructed by a Texaco-Gulf consortium following the route from Quito eastward to the old colonial town of Baeza, and then on to the Lago Agrio oilfield on the Aguarico River before turning south to Coca on the Napo River. Settlement of the land along this highway has been very rapid, although not without hardship for the would-be pioneers who were attracted to the lands opened by the road (cf. Bromley 1972). Within the past three decades the Oriente has passed from the status of an isolated national backwater to that of a dynamic and expanding national frontier. This is the context in which the modern missionization of the Siona-Secoya is taking place.

Missionization

The SIL has a tripartite organization which includes the Wycliffe Bible Translators (WBT), the Summer Institute of Linguistics (SIL), and the Jungle Aviation and Radio Service (JAARS). Some critics (e.g. Hart 1973) have alleged that this structure is a cover which allows the organization to appeal to religious contributors in the United States, yet pass as a scientific and service organization in other nations. The SIL's counterargument is that WBT, SIL, and JAARS are simply functional departments of the organization. Regardless of this controversy, it is true that the SIL tends to emphasize its linguistic and educative functions when dealing with Ecuadorian officials and news media.

The field activities of the SIL are multifaceted and include:

1. A bilingual education program which includes the training of native teachers, the preparation of native language texts, and logistical support for the schools.

2. A program of linguistic analysis whose primary goal is the production of Bible translations, but which also leads to scientific publication in some cases.

3. The establishment of a health care delivery system which includes village-level health workers, a base camp infirmary staffed by two professional nurses, and access to regional and national hospitals.

4. A program of agricultural extension involving the introduction of new cultigens and domesticated animals such as pigs, cattle, goats, and chickens.

5. The introduction of new technology and a ready supply of tools and other items such as machetes, axes, knives, shotguns and ammunition, fishing gear, sewing machines, radios, etc.

6. The introduction of a "rational" economic system which includes a national monetary currency, the concept of cash payment for goods and services rendered, and the concepts of credit and debt.

7. The encouragement of a nucleated settlement so that the formerly dispersed population can form a "community" of participants for the school and other mission and government programs.

8. The introduction of Protestant religious and moral precepts, artifacts, and rituals including the Bible and other religious literature, hymns, religious tape recordings, services, baptisms, and conferences. The moral precepts include prohibitions against the consumption of traditional hallucinogenic and psychotropic substances, alcoholic beverages including native manioc and maize *chicha* and purchased cane alcohol, sexual promiscuity, and nudity.

9. The introduction of national symbols such as the Ecuadorian flag and anthem, and nationalistic concepts pertaining to the rights and obligations of citizenship, national history, and national holidays.

The strategy employed by the SIL in its program of attempted social and cultural change is to recruit and train indigenous leaders who are independent of the old shamanistic traditions. The educational system is the vehicle for selecting, training, and giving status to new Indian leaders. The new leadership status is that of the teacher in the bilingual school. The most likely candidates for teacher training are those youths who are bright, have the patience to pursue academic activities, and are receptive to the missionary presence. It is interesting to note that these are also the attributes that shamans seek in their apprentices. In fact, the head teacher at Shushufindi told me that when he was a boy he had looked forward to the day when he would enter into an apprenticeship under his father's brother, who is a renowned headman-shaman. A SIL newsletter describes the recruitment of this individual for his teaching post:

As the years went by ——— listened to what (the missionaries) told him of the only true God Who lived in Heaven, the God Who is all powerful, mightier than the spirits the Secoyas fear so much. But the teaching was so different from what the Secoyas knew. "It is one thing that we believe, and another thing that you teach me," ——— said to the translators. "Two are not right; one is wrong. Which is it?"

Soon the translators realized ——— would make a good teacher. Simple books in the Secoya language were prepared and a small school was started for the children in the village. ——— loved to teach, and even after school hours he stayed to help anyone who wanted to learn. . . .

——— kept thinking about God. One thing bothered him—If it was true about the One, all-powerful God, why did only two people believe in

Him? Then one summer he was flown in a small JAARS plane to the Indian Teacher Training Course at Limoncocha, Wycliffe's jungle base in Ecuador. During his three months of training he met many people who believed in the one God. All summer he read the Bible in Spanish, and at the end of summer he believed, and surrendered himself to the Living God. Now his life began to change. . . .

Today ——— is still teaching school in the little village . . . and leading his people to know more of the things of the Lord. (SIL n.d.)

At the Limoncocha teacher training courses the teacher candidates receive pedagogical training from Ecuadorian educators supplied by the Ministry of Public Education. The curriculum of these annual institutes emphasizes Ecuadorian history and geography and incorporates national symbolic and ritual content in daily flag-raising ceremonies and the singing of the national anthem. All of these activities are likewise performed in the village schools when the teachers return to give classes on the local level. A SIL brochure outlines the role of the teacher in the following terms:

The bilingual teacher carries progress to the community:
* teaches the children
* gives literacy classes to the adults
* is concerned with improving the hygiene and health conditions
* assists in the introduction of new livestock
* is the bearer of civilization
* is the spiritual leader of the community
One hundred Indian Bilingual Schools will be necessary to give the jungle Indians the opportunity to leave their ignorance and illiteracy for a level of life that they need in order to be useful Ecuadorian citizens. (SIL 1968; my translation from the Spanish)[6]

Once an individual has achieved the status of teacher, he has become a central figure in the interactional patterns of the community. He spends considerable amounts of time with children from most of the households in the community, and organizes communal support for the maintenance of the schoolhouse and grounds. He also oversees the distribution of supplies and goods which are sent to the schools from Limoncocha. These include gifts of food such as cooking oil, rice, and flour in addition to the more mundane school supplies.

Because of his relatively advanced educational level, fluency and literacy in Spanish, and experience in the outside world, the teacher occupies a position that is intermediate between that of his fellow villagers and the larger national society. Owing to these factors, he tends to be the individual who mediates the relations between the world of the village and the world of the nation. This role is not inconsequential to the Siona-Secoya, for few of them speak good Spanish and they tend to be uncertain and tentative in their dealings with outsiders. Most villagers see the teacher as a spokesman who can articulate their needs and desires to the military personnel, government officials, and other outsiders who visit or are otherwise involved in activities that impinge on their lives. Hence the teacher serves as the gatekeeper to educational opportunities and certain material goods and as the cultural broker between the Siona-Secoya and the nation.

Some critics of the SIL–Ministry of Public Education assume that religious instruction and proselytization are a regular feature of the classroom. This is not the case at San Pablo, where the curriculum followed is the one prescribed by the ministry; it emphasizes traditional subjects such as reading and writing, arithmetic, history, and geography. Nor are religious services held in the schoolhouse. *Cultos*, as the services are called, are held in a thatched church constructed in 1978 (previously they were held in private houses).

Although there is a formal separation of "church" and "state" in the bilingual schools, there are certain relationships that tend to link the new religion and education. Principal among these is the fact that the SIL missionary-linguists select the teacher candidates who receive advanced training. Students who are unreceptive to the missionary and Christianity stand little chance of becoming teachers. The SIL-selected and trained teachers usually become the religious leaders of the Christian converts in their communities. During 1973–75 the senior teacher at San Pablo was very serious about this role and presented a regular series of Protestant-style services complete with a sermon and the communal singing of hymns which had been translated into Secoya. In 1979 the *cultos* were being directed by the teacher's brother, who had been elected "president" of the community. These services are well attended by both converts and by others who have not formally declared themselves to be "believers," *creyentes*. The nonbelievers who attend the services appear to appreciate them for their social and entertainment value, and wear their best clothing and ornaments and paint their faces for these occasions. They mix easily with their kin and fellow villagers who are "believers."

As indicated above, the distinction between believer and nonbeliever does not rest upon the criterion of church attendance. Rather, the Siona-Secoya are instructed that true believers are those whose new faith leads them to make certain changes in their lifestyles. That is, a profession of Christian faith must be validated by some attempt to "lead a Christian life." The SIL missionary-linguists view traditional practices as being in conflict with the Christian way at a number of points. Specific behavioral changes which indicate that the members of a household have given up "pagan" ways include when:

1. They stop using psychotropic substances and cease to attend the *yagé* ceremonies conducted by shamans.

2. They no longer prepare or consume fermented *chicha* or purchase the cane alcohol sold by river traders.

3. They no longer smoke tobacco.

4. They refrain from extramarital sexual affairs.

5. They dictate that their children must marry individuals who are believers.

At the beginning of the field research upon which this paper is based (September 1973) the community of San Pablo was split fairly evenly among those households that had accepted the believer lifestyle and those which had not. In March 1974 the SIL missionary-linguist arranged for a lay pastor from a Protestant hospital in Quito to come to the village for a series of sermons over a one-week period. This "revival" concluded with the mass baptism of 53 Siona-Secoya in the Aguarico River. This was nearly a third of the settlement, and members of nearly every household had stated their intentions to become believers. The degree to which the 1974 baptisms represented an enduring commitment to the believer lifestyle is unknown at the present time, but between 1977 and 1978 ten households of predominantly unconverted Sionas fissioned from San Pablo and moved to locations on the Aguarico River near the mouth of the Eno River.

Ideational Change as Nationalization

Some observers view the missionization of indigenous peoples in terms of mentalistic concepts and lament the destruction of native symbolic systems which they appreciate for their complexity and exotic nature. Miller (1974) argues that missionaries are "agents of secularization" who, despite their religious message, introduce naturalistic explanations for many phenomena formerly attributed to supernatural forces (e.g. naturalistic concepts of disease etiology are proposed to replace native medical theories). According to Miller, the presence of missionaries leads to a decline in the overall supernatural explanation of events and therefore "secularizes" the native population. The central point of this paper, however, is that the interface between the Indians and the missionaries is not simply a competition between two religions or world views. Rather, it is merely the cutting edge of a competition between two very different socioeconomic systems.

The SIL and Ministry of Public Education programs among the Siona-Secoya represent a comprehensive effort to shift their ideology, alter their settlement pattern, restructure their subsistence activities, and modify their social organization within the context of an expansionist, development-oriented national society. All nation-states seek to extend control over their citizenries, and their degree of success in doing this is referred to as the level of "national integration" achieved. Often ethnic and linguistic differences are viewed as barriers to development which must be overcome. Tribal peoples must be "civilized" because "savages" are an anachronism at best and a national embarrassment at worst.

Even though the Ecuadorian government espouses prodevelopment policies, it does not control fully the complex processes of population growth, expanding use of land, and resource exploitation. Decrees made in Quito often bear little relation to events in the expanding frontier regions of the nation. One example of this occurred in 1970–72 when spontaneous colonization along the Quito–Lago Agrio highway proceeded so rapidly that the government colonization program became an *ex post facto* phenomenon. Government services have always been scarce or absent in most areas of the Oriente. The contract between the Ministry of Public Education and the SIL is based on the reality that the missionary organization has the professional manpower, technical expertise, and financial resources to bring education to people who would not otherwise receive it. This institutional relationship has several trade-offs for both parties. The mission receives diplomatic access to Ecuador, a legitimization of its activities, and access to potential converts. In exchange, the government receives assistance in extending its control over the frontier areas of the nation and technical expertise and manpower in such areas as health care delivery, education, communications, and transportation. In effect, the nation draws more citizens under its hegemony in exchange for allowing a certain portion of its population to be exposed to missionary influences.

The fact that the SIL is completely dependent upon its relationship with the government helps to explain why the organization seeks to avoid political controversy in its operations. The mission has a public relations officer and strives to maintain an effective liaison with government officials. This involves carrying officials on inspection tours of Limoncocha and the outlying posts, acknowledging government support in its publications, supporting government projects via the JAARS transportation and communications network, and even providing technical advice on the maintenance of aircraft belonging to some nonmilitary government ministries.

Criticism of the SIL does appear from time to time, however, as in February 1965 when a series of critical articles appeared in the Quito and Guayaquil newspapers (cf. *El Universo* 1975, *El Tiempo* 1975, *Ultimas Noticias* 1975a and 1975b). These were stimulated by individuals who alleged that the SIL had denied them entrance into Indian communities. The subsequent articles accused the SIL of enslaving the Indians and stealing their lands. When these criticisms surfaced, the initial reaction of the government appeared to be noncommittal; i.e., it did not issue any press releases to clarify the status of the SIL in Ecuador. Rather, the Ministry of Public Education sent an observer to investigate SIL's activities in the various field sites where the organization is active. I was present at San Pablo when this official visited there 19 February 1975. He was flown on the SIL Helio-Courier (a light plane especially adapted for short takeoffs and landings), given a tour of the village, and then taken to the schoolhouse where the bilingual teacher directed the students in the singing of the national anthem in Secoya and Spanish. Following this, the investigator conducted an oral examination of the students by asking them questions in history and giving them simple problems in arithmetic. After the examination one boy recited a poem entitled "Mi Bandera es de Tres Colores," "My Flag Is of Three Colors." That afternoon the investigator flew back to Limoncocha. Since the SIL has continued its Ecuadorian operations to the present, it seems reasonable to assume that the results of the investigation were favorable or at least were insufficiently damaging to lead to the revocation of their government contract.

From a structural point of view, the position of the government is far stronger than the SIL's in controversies such as the one outlined above. The government can approve or disapprove of the SIL's activities, or can affect an air of judicial detachment pending investigation. But rhetorical condemnations of the SIL alone are naive because they are based on the assumption that its operations are those of an autonomous organization. In fact, the government is equally involved because it has employed the SIL as an agent of nationalization and development.

It is interesting to note that the government of Brazil recently issued an order calling for the expulsion of the SIL (*Time* 1978). Although the missionaries have not yet been forced out of the country, they have been pulled out of their tribal locations. In Brazil, however, there exists a government agency, the Fundação Nacional do Indio (FUNAI), which administers Indian affairs. The fact that FUNAI and the SIL worked among the same Indians and shared a common, but somewhat different, concern about their status instituted a structural situation in which the probability of policy conflicts was increased. Until 1978 there was no bureaucratic entity in Ecuador that was comparable to FUNAI and whose mandate overlapped with the SIL to any significant degree. In 1978 a new agency called Instituto Nacional de Colonización de la Región Amazónica Ecuatoriana (INCRAE) was instituted. The policies of this agency currently appear to be much more pro-Indian than the older and still extant Instituto Ecuatoriano de Reforma Agraria y Colonización (IERAC). Discussions with SIL and INCRAE personnel during June–August 1979 indicate that the two organizations have cooperated in sponsoring an indigenous leadership conference held at the SIL base camp at Limoncocha. SIL has also flown INCRAE field staff to a number of tribal locations for discussions concerning the problems faced by the native communities.

IDEATION IN COMPETING SOCIOECONOMIC SYSTEMS

This paper has described how the attempted replacement of the Siona-Secoya ideational system by Christian precepts is associated with the imposition of a new economic, social, and political order. Table 1 summarizes and contrasts several of the major attributes of the traditional and national systems. Here "religion" has the very significant function of modifying Indian behavior so that it becomes more integrated with the dominant national socioeconomic system. In contrast, the analysis suggests that the aboriginal "religion" is consistent with a distinctive subsistence system which involves the exploitation of the tropical forest and riverine habitats with a preindustrial technology based on shifting horticulture, hunting, fishing, and collecting. It is postulated that the belief system promotes settlement dispersion and movement because it identifies neighboring villages as the sources of disease and death. The conclusion is that "religion" is a major dynamic in both the aboriginal and national economic orders because it serves as an adaptive mechanism that orients human behavior to the material conditions of each system. The larger process of national encroachment on Indian lands is one of cultural evolution in which cultural systems with the technology to tap greater sources of energy displace systems with smaller energy bases.

TABLE 1. Some Characteristics of the Traditional and National Socioeconomic Systems Relative to the Siona-Secoya.

Traditional Socioeconomic System

Scope:	The Siona-Secoya and neighboring Indian groups
Technology:	Shifting cultivation, hunting, fishing, and collecting
Strategy:	Subsistence
Social Structure:	Egalitarian, with the headman-shaman as the first among equals
Ideational Component:	Native religion places emphasis on local autonomy and security; the projection of hostilities to other groups promotes a dispersed settlement pattern and complements the stability of subsistence

National Socioeconomic System

Scope:	National and international capitalist spheres
Technology:	Industrialism, intensive agriculture
Strategy:	Development and profit
Social Structure:	Specialized social statuses and class stratification
Ideational Component:	Mission religion attempts directed cultural change to "prepare" Indians for transition from native system to national system by promoting nucleated settlements, suppressing "pagan" beliefs and practices, instituting formal education, indoctrinating to national symbols and ideology, training new leaders to serve as cultural brokers, and instructing in "rational" economics and intensified production techniques

AN IMPLICATION FOR NATIONAL POLICY

From a humanistic and ethical perspective, it is most reasonable to argue for the protection of Indian culture and territory. From a strictly scientific point of view, it is evident that the demographic and territorial expansions of industrializing nations have rarely been thwarted by concerns for the cultural integrity and well-being of sparsely settled minority groups. When once remote Indian groups are contacted by missionaries, it is but the first step in a transformation process that is as economic and political as it is "religious." The members of the SIL are aware of this and state that their multifaceted program is designed to give the Indians a period of adjustment before they bear the full brunt of the advancing frontier. As one missionary said, "We want to give them a little time in which they can learn to defend themselves."

Despite the government view that Indians who become "civilized" will enjoy a higher level of material and moral existence, there are few indicators which suggest that the standard of living of the Indians will be enhanced under the modern system. In fact, some prominent theorists have suggested that the opposite effect is more likely (cf. Harris 1977, Whitten 1976). Certainly none of the Indian groups will retain all of their former territories, for much of these have already been lost. A more pressing issue is whether native peoples will be able to maintain enough land and resources to support present and future generations. In 1977 IERAC presented the Siona-Secoya with the title to 7,043 hectares of land between the Eno, Aguarico, and Shushufindi rivers.[7] The land deeded to the community incorporates house sites and gardens on the south bank of the Aguarico between the Eno and Shushufindi, as well as a small amount of forest which has been utilized for hunting and collecting but is now nearly depleted of game. The grant does not include house sites and extensive gardens on the north banks of the Eno and Aguarico, and house and garden sites on both sides of the Aguarico downriver from the mouth of the Shushufindi. It also fails to include a significant proportion of the lands which the Siona-Secoya have traditionally used for hunting.

The present grant does provide slightly more than 100 hectares of land per household in 1979, and some colonists in the region point out that this is double what they receive from IERAC and that it is "more land than the Indians know how to use." While a superficial analysis may suggest that each Siona-Secoya household does not use 100 hectares for cultivation purposes, it totally ignores the fact that this amount of land is hopelessly inadequate for hunting, fishing, and collecting and does not provide adequate raw materials for basic needs such as canoes (which are made from scarce cedar trees) and house thatch. Furthermore, the 100 hectares per household will be drastically reduced within several generations given the current rate of population growth among the Siona-Secoya. As of June 1979 the western boundary of the present land grant had already been settled by colonists, precious trees were being illegally cut by white profiteers from Lago Agrio, and a prized hunting ground on the south bank of the Shushufindi River was being destroyed by a multinational firm named Palmeras del Ecuador which was bulldozing 9,850 hectares of forest to create an African palm plantation to produce cooking oil for the domestic market. In order for Siona-Secoya culture to survive, the government must act to recognize legitimate native claims for title to more land within the Aguarico River basin. The Siona-Secoya are painfully aware of their deteriorating situation; in

August 1979 they began to organize an appeal to INCRAE for the official recognition of their claim to a larger portion of their traditional territory.

A question for the Ecuadorian government to ponder is whether the national interest will better be served by an attempt to reduce all remote ethnic groups to the common denominator of a homogeneous rural population bearing a generalized *mestizo* culture, or by an attempt to develop policies that will permit a degree of cultural diversity. The government of Ecuador has wisely instituted measures to ensure the survival of the fauna of the Galápagos Islands. Is the survival of unique human cultures of less significance? Native peoples cannot be isolated like museum specimens, but they deserve the legal safeguards afforded to other citizens, including the protection of land rights and the right of cultural self-determination within the social fabric of the nation.

NOTES

Acknowledgments: Research in 1973–75 was supported by fellowships from the Henry L. and Grace Doherty Foundation and the National Institute of Mental Health (1Fol MH 58552–01). The Instituto Nacional de Antropología e Historia under the directorship of Arq. Hernán Crespo Toral provided the Ecuadorian affiliation for the research. Follow-up fieldwork during June–Aug. 1979 was made possible by a grant from the Florida International University Foundation, Inc.

1. A more detailed analysis of Siona-Secoya horticulture and a list of cultigens may be found in Vickers (1976).

2. This pattern was also described by the Jesuit missionaries who worked among the Western Tucanoan ancestors of the Siona-Secoya during the eighteenth century (cf. Chantre y Herrera 1901).

3. The term /ʔaíro baĩ/, forest people, is also used to refer to the Tetetes, a nearly extinct Western Tucanoan group that was last reported on the Paca Yacu, a northern tributary of the Aguarico River (Robinson 1971).

4. A quantitative analysis of the various subsistence activities of the Siona-Secoya is found in Vickers (1976, 1979).

5. "El Ecuador ha sido, es, y será país Amazonico."

6. The original Spanish text reads:

El maestro bilingüe indígena lleva el progreso a la comunidad:
* enseña a los niños
* da clases de alfabetización a los adultos
* se preocupa por mejorar las condiciones de higiene y salud
* ayuda a formar nuevas ganaderías
* es portador de la civilización
* es el líder espiritual de la comunidad
Serían necesarias unas 100 Escuelas Bilingües Indígenas para dar opor-

tunidad a los indígenas de la selva para salir de su ignorancia y del analfabetismo a un nivel de vida que ellos merecen para que sean ciudadanos Ecuatorianos útiles para toda buena obra.

7. During 1974 and 1975 there were several discussions between SIL personnel, the Siona-Secoya, and myself concerning the need for the native community to obtain legal title to its lands. I contacted IERAC personnel in the main office in Quito in Jan. 1974, but was told that their surveying crews were inadequate to keep up with the needs of the colonists in the Lago Agrio–Coca area and that the Indians had a very low priority because they were still isolated and had "ample lands." I also contacted the director of the U.S. Peace Corps in Ecuador concerning the possibility of using Peace Corps surveyors to map Siona-Secoya lands, but was informed that their personnel were involved in a long-term project among the Shuar and were not available. In 1975 the SIL flew several surveyors to San Pablo, but they did not accomplish much work in the few days they visited the community. In Dec. 1976 the SIL linguist-missionary working among the Siona-Secoya mobilized the community to clear a trail between the Eno River and a northern tributary of the Shushufindi River known locally as Dráwïaya; he proposed that this line should form the western boundary of the communal lands. Finally, in 1977 IERAC topographers visited the community and established the boundaries of the present 7,043-hectare holding between the Eno, Aguarico, and Shushufindi rivers.

REFERENCES CITED

Bromley, Ray
    1972 Agricultural Colonization in the Upper Amazon Basin: The Impact of the Oil Discoveries. *Tijdschrift voor Economische en Sociale Geografie* 63:278–94.

Chagnon, Napoleon A.
    1968a *Yanomamö: The Fierce People.* New York: Holt, Rinehart and Winston.
    1968b Yanomamö Social Organization and Warfare. In Morton Fried, Marvin Harris, and Robert Murphy, eds., *War: The Anthropology of Armed Conflict and Aggression.* Garden City, N.Y.: Natural History Press, pp. 109–59.

Chantre y Herrera, José
    1901 *Historia de las Misiones de la Compañia de Jesús en el Marañón Español.* Madrid: Imprenta de A. Avrial.

El Universo (Guayaquil)
    1975 El Instituto Lingüístico de Verano no Cumple Propósitos en Región Oriental. 28 Jan.:11.

El Tiempo (Quito)
    1975 Acusaciones contra el Instituto Lingüístico. 17 Feb.: pagination unknown.

Harner, Michael J.
    1977 The Ecological Basis for Aztec Sacrifice. *American Ethnologist* 4:117–35.

Harris, Marvin
    1977 *Cannibals and Kings.* New York: Random House.

Hart, Laurie
  1973   Story of the Wycliffe Translators: Pacifying the Last Frontiers. *NACLA's Latin America and Empire Report* 8 (10):15–31.
Hegen, Edmund Eduard
  1966   *Highways into the Upper Amazon Basin: Pioneer Lands in Southern Colombia, Ecuador, and Northern Peru.* Gainesville: Center for Latin American Studies, University of Florida.
Langdon, E. Jean
  1974   The Siona Medical System: Beliefs and Behavior. Ann Arbor, Mich.: University Microfilms. Ph.D. thesis, Tulane University.
Martz, John D.
  1972   *Ecuador: Conflicting Political Culture and the Quest for Progress.* Boston: Allyn and Bacon.
Marx, Karl
  1964 [1848]   *Selected Writings in Sociology and Social Philosophy.* Ed. T. B. Bottomore and Maximillian Rubel. Baltimore: Penguin.
Miller, Elmer S.
  1974   The Christian Missionary, Agent of Secularization. In Patricia J. Lyon, ed., *Native South Americans: Ethnology of the Least Known Continent.* Boston: Little, Brown, pp. 391–97.
Murphy, Robert, and Julian H. Steward
  1956   Tappers and Trappers: Parallel Process in Acculturation. *Economic Development and Change* 4:335–55.
Price, Barbara J.
  1978   Demystification, Enriddlement, and Aztec Cannibalism: A Materialist Rejoinder to Harner. *American Ethnologist* 5 (1):98–115.
Rappaport, Roy A.
  1968   *Pigs for the Ancestors: Ritual in the Ecology of a New Guinea People.* New Haven, Conn.: Yale University Press.
Robinson, Scott S.
  1971   El Etnocidio Ecuatoriano. Reprint from *La Situación Actual de los Indígenas en America del Sur.* Montevideo: Editorial Tierra Nueva; Mexico City: Universidad Iberoamericana.
Steward, Julian H.
  1948   Western Tucanoan Tribes. In Julian H. Steward, ed., *Handbook of South American Indians,* vol. 3: *The Tropical Forest Tribes.* Bureau of American Ethnology Bulletin 143:737–48.
  1949   The Native Population of South America. In Julian H. Steward, ed., *Handbook of South American Indians,* vol. 5: *The Comparative Anthropology of South American Indians. Bureau of American Ethnology Bulletin* 143:655–68.
  1955   *Theory of Culture Change: The Methodology of Multilinear Evolution.* Urbana: University of Illinois Press.
SIL (Summer Institute of Linguistics)
  1968   *Tres Lustros entre las Tribus Indígenas de la Selva Ecuatoriana 1953–1968.* Quito.
  1969   *La Obra Civilizadora del Instituto Lingüístico de Verano entre los Aucas.* Quito.
  n.d.   *Tribal-gram* 6. Santa Ana, Calif.: Wycliffe Bible Translators, Inc.

Time
    1978   Beyond Babel: Wycliffians Practice Phonetics So They Can Preach
            the Gospel. 9 Jan.:65.
Ultimas Noticias (Quito)
    1975a   Denuncian que Instituto Lingüístico busca Dividir a Comunidades
            Indigenas. 17 Feb.:1.
    1975b   Ministro de Educacción Ordenó Examinar Labor de Instituto
            Lingüístico de Verano. 18 Feb.:5.
Vickers, William T.
    1976   Cultural Adaptation to Amazonian Habitats: The Siona-Secoya of
            Eastern Ecuador. Ann Arbor, Mich.: University Microfilms. Ph.D.
            thesis, University of Florida, Gainesville.
    1979   Native Amazonian Subsistence in Diverse Habitats: The Siona-Se-
            coya of Ecuador. In Emilio F. Moran, ed., *Changing Agricultural Sys-
            tems in Latin America*. Studies in Third World Societies, Publication
            7. Williamsburg: Department of Anthropology, College of William
            and Mary, pp. 6–36.
Weber, Max
    1958 [1904]   *The Protestant Ethic and the Spirit of Capitalism*. New York: Scrib-
            ner's.
Whitten, Norman E., Jr. (with the assistance of Marcelo F. Naranjo, Marcelo
            Santi Simbaña, and Dorothea S. Whitten)
    1976   *Sacha Runa: Ethnicity and Adaptation of Ecuadorian Jungle Quichua*. Ur-
            bana: University of Illinois Press.

26

Music, Modernization, and Westernization among the Macuma Shuar

William Belzner

Music has been shown to be one of the most conservative elements of culture (see, e.g., McAllester 1954, Merriam 1967). Long after economic, political, religious, and other social institutions have allegedly "degenerated" or even disappeared in a westernizing or modernizing[1] context, music retains many of its traditional features. It must, therefore, embody elements of continuity within a culture, even as that culture undergoes dramatic transformation. The nature of these elements of continuity in the musical system of the Shuar in the area around the evangelical mission at Macuma, and the importance of these elements for understanding Shuar responses to the current acculturative situation there—both musical and nonmusical—will be the subjects of this paper.

The literature on musical change suggests various ways of viewing music within a culture confronting increasing western influence (see, e.g., Irvine and Sapir 1976, Katz 1970, Nettl 1978b, Neuman 1976). All of these approaches have as their basic, if often implicit, premise the divisibility of music-in-culture into sound, behavior, and concept (see Merriam 1964:32–35).

A study of musical sound takes as its focus the organizational principles of the sound itself. One must ask, for example, such questions as: what tonal resources are available to the individual performer; what are the various types of units on which classes of music are based; how are these musical units combined; what is the degree of allowed variation of a piece of music? The structural principles of the musical repertoire can then often be seen to mirror structural principles operating in other domains of culture. Music, in a sense, comments on these organizational principles of a culture by such processes as imitation, inversion, reversal, and any number of other types of structural transformations. An analysis which seeks the replicating structural principles is likely to provide access to significant culture-wide forms and processes that might not otherwise be easily abstracted from divergent activities and institutions.

A study of musical behavior starts with the premise that music is a component of culture, occurring in certain contexts and serving certain explicit and implicit functions within these contexts. An analysis of musical behavior can especially illuminate such features as the rules of social group formation, interaction, and disintegration; significant divisions of space and time within ritual settings; and degrees and qualities of sacralization and secularization. Such an analysis provides a productive approach to some of the cultural values which suggest the underlying ethos of the culture.

The study of music-as-concept is not so easily characterized. Traditionally, this most significant part of the study of music consisted of exegetical statements, if they existed, of what music is, how it originated, what it does, and other such broad and problematic, not to say ethnocentric, questions. With the increased attention paid by anthropologists and ethnomusicologists in recent years to the creation and manipulation of symbols, and the refinement of structuralist methodology by Claude Lévi-Strauss, a study of musical concept has come to imply a search for the basic cognitive paradigms (and rules of relationship between these paradigms) that limit and shape musical thought and action (see, e.g., Robertson–de Carbo 1976). Such an approach does not rely on native exegesis, except as this exegesis serves as one behavioral manifestation of the schemata abstracted by the analyst in the model-building process. Used in this sense, one can see that music-as-concept is the epistemological root of musical sound and behavior. One cannot merely list these root paradigms (see, e.g., Turner 1974) and their rules of combination and then claim "explanation." For an analysis to be explanatory of the musical system as a whole we must show how the cognitive organizational principles embodied in these paradigms and their combinations shape what has been called cultural ethos (see, e.g., Bateson 1936, Honigmann 1947). The structure created by these methods must be related to the patterns of affect and value characteristic of the culture—its ethos—for the structure to have any meaning.

The perspective on music outlined above will form the conceptual organization of the ensuing analysis. I will show that contemporary Shuar responses to the westernizing and modernizing pressures now occurring in Macuma are contained in nuclear, unelaborated form in their musical conceptual system and acted out within the values shaping their traditional ethos.

assistance of various garden spirits in making the garden grow well. War songs, supposedly no longer sung but still known to many Shuar women, were sung before and during a war raid to assure the safe return of the men.

Other musical contexts about which the data are contradictory or altogether lacking in the literature with regard to their classification as *nampesma* include songs or chants sung at *tsantsa* feasts celebrating the taking of a head, women's initiation-marriage feasts, and victory feasts after a war. None of these now occur in the Macuma area according to my Shuar informants. In eliciting these responses, though, I may have obtained no more than "public imagery" of ignorance. Recordings of war victory songs and *tsantsa* feast songs do exist in the large collection of Shuar music at the Macuma radio station, dating from after 1973, and Arnalot (1978) frequently mentions the continuing blood feuds and associated ceremonies among the Shuar and Achuar just east of Macuma.

Shuar music is characterized by a tritonic "scalar" structure, utilizing most frequently what we would call the third and fifth above a "tonic." The range is quite variable, though rarely less than a fifth nor more than a fifth above the octave. The general melodic contour is descending, as is common with most native American music. The "tonic" often occurs as an extended ostinato or drone figure. There is often a marked underlying pulse, though the rhythm is quite variable. A dual metrical pattern seems ubiquitous in all Shuar music. Songs are formed by variation of small motives of limited tonal material, generally following the incomplete repetition form so common in North American indigenous music. Inés Muriel (1976) finds a strong correlation between the occurrence of certain melodic motivic forms and certain rhythmic patterns. George List (1963) finds that certain melodies (with variable texts) occur exclusively in one or another class of *nampesma*.

Songs within a class seem to be organized into tune types or tune families. I find that some songs identified as love songs, for example, sounded melodically very similar, though sung to different words in each version. Macuma Shuar explained this by stating that, since these songs were generally learned from one particular person, it was only to be expected that they sound similar. They recognized some songs as melodically similar and some as melodically different, but stated clearly that melodic correspondence is of little importance. The texts, they insisted, are the differentiating feature from song to song within a class. There seemed to be great freedom in text choice, and improvisation or on-the-spot extemporization of the text seemed perfectly acceptable, especially with the songs sung in public on secular occasions. As long as the melody follows the general phrase contour and principles of motivic combination and sequencing associated with the particular class of music and tune type or family of which the song is a member, textual and motivic variation is freely allowed.

While most songs are sung or performed by single individuals, ensemble performances do occur. War songs are sung by groups of women; some public songs are sung by groups of women during social dances (though more often each woman sings her own song to her male partner at the same time as other women sing their particular songs); occasionally a group of men may perform together on flutes, again on social occasions. In all of these cases, each individual performer sings or plays one motivic segment (a combination of two or three motives into a musical phrase or line) with apparently little concern for when and what others are singing or playing. The only referent feature for each performer seems to be an underlying pulse, occasionally marked by the beating of the *tampur* or the rattling of the *makich* or *shakap* produced by the women as they dance, but often not marked by any instrument. Even in these cases of group performance, then, the importance of the individual performer outweighs such values as ensemble blend, metrical or rhythmic consistency, and melodic invariability. Musically, subordination of the individual to group interaction is not valued.

The musical system of the Macuma Shuar is best understood as structured by a paradigm of public versus private and sacred versus secular musical behaviors. The differing contexts in which men and women perform function as points of articulation for the relationships between these four categories. *Nampesma* are primarily performed on secular occasions, both public and private, and only secondarily on sacred occasions where direct manipulation of either beneficent or maleficent power is the desired goal. Its realm is that of cultural manipulation of the power of positive or negative supernature toward desired cultural goals.

In the case of secular *nampesma* performance, the underlying functions are almost exclusively oriented toward the values of family solidarity, economic increase and independence, general social (including sexual) fusion, and easing of inherent social tensions. Sacred *nampesma* performances, by contrast, deal with the realm we call "religious," serving such functions as power acquisition and manipulation of this power toward strictly individual (often antisocial or anticultural) goals. These two contrasting functions are, of course, never entirely separable. Any performance of *nampesma* functions in both ways, differing considerably, though, in the degree of emphasis on one or the other function. This distinction will be seen to be important for an understanding of the types of change now occurring in Macuma and Shuar responses to these changes.

WESTERNIZATION AND MODERNIZATION OF THE MACUMA SHUAR: CHANGE OR CONTINUITY?

The most significant locus of change in traditional Shuar culture around Macuma is the mission. Though it has been in existence for over 30 years, its effect on the local Shuar was relatively minimal until regular flights from Shell became established. Beginning then, about 15 years ago, large amounts of building materials, machinery (including a jeep—in an area without roads), medicines, and foodstuffs were flown in to support the missionaries and their families. The radio station, electrical generating station, houses, infirmary, and other buildings were built with local Shuar assistance. Some older Shuar still recall their surprise and curiosity at so large an undertaking.

Attracted by the apparent economic advantages of association with Protestant evangelical Christianity, a number of Shuar began to relocate their houses on the outskirts of the mission community. Two groups of people formed this first wave of Shuar to settle near Macuma: young couples, often with children just reaching school age, who sought the economic and religious power believed offered by association with the missionaries; and family groups involved in intra-Shuar blood feuds. Both groups were acting in ways consistent with traditional Shuar values. Young men just beginning their adult lives traditionally sought access to material goods and religious power; they obtained the former by developing a network of *amigri* trading relationships and the latter by purchasing shamanistic power (see Harner 1972). The mission seemed to simplify the process of power acquisition by offering both forms of power. Indeed, the brand of evangelical Christianity preached by the local missionaries inextricably linked economic and religious power (see Taylor, in this volume). Families involved in blood feuds, often fearing retaliation for a previous killing, traditionally associated themselves with a big man, *kakaram*, willing to offer them protection. This protection involved them in a series of debts and obligations to the big man. The mission served the same function: it offered protection in exchange for certain obligations that appeared minimal, on the surface. This first migration reached its peak approximately ten years ago.

Eventually, the number of people surrounding the community exceeded the carrying capacity of the available land within the predominant rotating swidden-mulch system of cultivation. The missionaries saw that the Shuar would be forced either to become economically dependent on them or to move back to areas of the forest where adequate land was still available. While strongly desiring the access offered by community nucleation, the mission could not afford to support large numbers of people. Their solution was to build schoolhouse-church buildings in two nearby areas of some population density (the hamlets of Achuensa and Amazonas) and to lend money through the association for the purchase of cattle and grass cuttings. Previously unusable swidden land near the mission headquarters could thus be used for cattle grazing. In these ways the missionaries tried to provide a means for both continued nucleation and economic independence.

Instead of contributing to these goals, however, this conversion to a cash economy has led to increasing Shuar difficulties. The only mode of transport for the dressed beef to the Shell-Puyo market is by mission plane, for which they must pay the standard pound-weight fare. Once in Puyo, they are subject to the prices offered by local meat buyers. The Shuar feel that these meat buyers cheat them, knowing they can't very well fly home with the meat if the offered prices are too low. The actual cash profit is, therefore, very low. The Shuar also found out that continued planting of the land with *gramalote* led to ultimate, irreparable depletion of the land's resources. After a few years of use the land would grow nothing. Beginning approximately five years ago, this situation led to community fragmentation, with many of those living near Macuma moving back to their former lands and returning to their traditional swidden-mulch system. This pattern of community fission has since spread to the two hamlets. Now very few houses are occupied in the central zones of Macuma, Achuensa, and Amazonas.

The missionary response to this disaffection was to focus more carefully on understanding the Shuar mind in the continuing attempt to improve their methods of religious conversion without the encumbrance of these economic dfficulties. Music is seen quite specifically as one tool of great value in the process of conversion of traditional Shuar concepts and values into Protestant evangelical Christian terms.

The missionaries are quite explicit about the role of music in the accomplishment of this overriding goal. The development of a corpus of traditional songs with Shuar texts expressing Christian concepts—

an indigenous hymnody—is their immediate goal. They are concerned with expressing fundamental Christian concepts in forms that will be immediately comprehensible to the Shuar. One missionary with some musical training has gone so far as to write a paper entitled "On Developing an Indigenous Jivaro Hymnody" that deals with the methodology of cross-cultural study of music. This project, according to the missionary, was directly motivated by the dislike the Shuar have of the hymnal that has been in use for about 20 years. This small hymnal is a collection of Shuar language texts on Christian themes sung to an odd collection of familiar western hymn tunes, including "Rock of Ages," "Onward Christian Soldiers," and "Silent Night."

During a Shuar church service in Achuensa it was clear that the hymns violate almost every structural and functional pattern of traditional Shuar music. They are sung in unison by the entire congregation, which consists of three or four young men and ten to 15 women and children. The missionaries had apparently made an attempt to teach the singers to harmonize, but they were able to do so only at the octave and occasionally at the fifth. Guitar accompaniment sometimes provided a chord ground having little or no tonal relationship to the piece being sung. The deliberate, invariable meter and long phrase lengths are likewise alien to traditional Shuar music. The texts, written by a longtime missionary with the help of an SIL linguist, ignore the inflection patterns of sung Shuar. The Shuar seem to universally dislike these songs and often privately disparage them.

The second, immediately observable, change in the musical system is the popularity of the guitar among the young men between the ages of 15 and 25. This is most likely due to the playing of Latin popular music by the radio stations received in the area. These young men, all educated in the Macuma schools since the advent of the radio station, have begun acquiring inexpensive guitars on their occasional visits to Puyo or Macas. The missionary with musical training has recently (the first class was in July 1978) instituted guitar classes for these young men. They are taught to tune their guitars and to play simple chord progressions. Their goal is to be able to sing and play the pop songs they hear on the radio. Success seems to be minimal. The missionary is besieged by requests to retune the guitars of those he taught the week before. Many seem to care little at all whether their guitar tuning matches their singing. Most of these young men seem to lose interest in playing their instruments within a few weeks, though they carry them about everywhere they go as a symbol of their ability to act out *blanco* roles.

The role that these western musical phenomena play in Shuar culture can best be seen by examining the different uses of traditional Shuar music and western-derived music on the local radio station.

Programming for the musical portions of the morning and evening sessions is chosen by the chief announcer, who is also the vice-president of the association, a thirty-year-old man deeply committed to preservation of traditional Shuar culture. In addition to consulting with the missionaries on general programming, he actively seeks out the opinions of other Shuar on his musical choices. He finds that most women of all ages and men above the age of 30 prefer to hear traditional Shuar music; most young men from age 15 to 25 prefer Latin pop, especially the very popular Ecuadorian-Colombian *cumbia* genre; a very few older women, usually widows, specifically request hymns. He draws his final programming choices from an extensive collection of Shuar music tape-recorded *in situ* by both the missionaries and members of the Education Committee of the association, a small collection of Latin pop music records, and a few miscellaneous records and tapes ranging in content from Shuar hymns and English-language Christmas carols to Sousa marches and western popular show tunes.

During a given day's programming, Shuar music and western-derived music seem to occur in distinct but consistent contexts, in approximately equal amounts. All of the various types of music occur during any given program; only the percentage of each type varies with the program. From 4:30 to 7:30 P.M. is considered "prime time," the time with the largest Shuar audience. This is the time when *saludos* and *comunicaciones*—greetings, arrivals and departures, death announcements, recent weddings, messages of interest to the general Shuar community—are broadcast. Shuar music predominates, both as a boundary marker and as an interludic element between announcements. Some western-derived music is also played, usually short phrases of Latin or North American popular instrumental pieces. For example, an instrumental version of the theme of "Jesus Christ Superstar" and a similar instrumental version of "Rudolph, the Red-Nosed Reindeer" are both frequently used. Rarely is an entire piece of music—Shuar or western—played during this segment of the programming.

Following the *saludos*, the musical interlude will consist either of a series of Shuar hymns or a series of Latin-derived soft rock pieces or phrases. In the former case the daily religious lesson will follow. In the latter case approximately a half-hour of popular Latin rock, mostly *cumbia*, will be played. In general, then, the type of music played signals the nature of the ensuing program, musical and otherwise. Programs of specifically Shuar interest will be signaled by the increased (though not exclusive) incidence of Shuar music; programs dealing with the mission and general Christian themes will be signaled by Shuar and Christian hymns (including Christmas carols); Ecuadorian national (*mestizo, blanco*) themes will be signaled by Latin-based or indigenous Andean music.

DISCUSSION AND CONCLUSIONS

What emerges from these data is the impression that the Shuar are able to clearly differentiate the values and behaviors appropriate to *blanco* culture from their traditional conceptual and behavioral system. The Macuma Shuar are, indeed, effectively bicultural and cross role boundaries with ease, subtlety, and with full cognizance of what they are doing, what they want, and how to get it. Sometime in the past the Shuar perceived potential benefits from an alliance with the missionaries. These perceived benefits were primarily economic in nature, but to acquire them involved acceptance of a whole range of ideological and consequent social changes. The Shuar learned how to act out these new sets of roles while never losing their traditional values. When time proved that the values and benefits offered by *blanco* culture were specious and required radical and perhaps irrevocable change of traditional Shuar operating paradigms, they effectively rejected the types of westernization and modernization offered by the missionaries.

The Shuar, it seems, knew exactly what they rejected and why. Their fundamental concern with the acquisition and control of power—a lifelong activity for Shuar men especially—provided the initial impetus for their involvement in the forms of *blanco* culture offered by the missionaries. The association, in Protestant evangelical doctrine, of the sacred and economic was something already deeply rooted in traditional Shuar culture, seen most clearly in the process of acquiring shamanistic power (see Harner 1972). When experience proved that the missionaries' ethos would ultimately undermine the most basic values of Shuar culture without offering access to a power that would allow them the same degree of control over their lives in *blanco* culture as they have in their traditional culture, they opted to remain Shuar. They retain their ability to operate in known segments of *blanco* culture, and are still willing to accept those parts of it perceived to be of benefit to them. The association, for instance, represents a phenomenon requiring the acting out of *blanco* roles for benefits directed to the Shuar.

Musically, we can be even more specific about this process. Using Nettl's (1978a) schema of musical change, several microprocesses can be differentiated. Most fundamentally, it can be seen that the traditional and nontraditional musical systems are entirely separate and incompatible, a fact mirrored in most other areas of Shuar-*blanco* interaction. No westernization or syncretism has occurred in the traditional musical system, and only a modicum of modernization can be seen in the addition of new musical genres: hymns and Latin popular music. Even these genres have limited impact on the Shuar as a whole, appealing only to specialized groups at certain periods of their lives or in contexts seen to offer some psychological or material benefits to specific segments of Shuar society.

The process of community nucleation and subsequent disillusionment and fragmentation discussed above is also reflected in musical developments. Many Shuar with whom I spoke lamented the loss of certain songs and instrumental genres caused by contact with the mission over the past ten to 20 years. They worry over this perceived impoverishment and fear that their children will not learn Shuar music as they themselves did, by direct transmission. This expression of imminent loss of musical repertoire led to an effort by AIPSE to record as much traditional music as possible, a task they began in earnest about eight years ago. This artificial preservation had, then, no goal other than preserving a part of culture feared to be disappearing. In typical Shuar fashion they soon saw a way to use a *blanco* institution, in this case the local school, for furthering Shuar purposes. Many local Shuar began pushing for the teaching of Shuar songs in the school. This is now beginning to occur, supported by both the association and the missionaries.

It is probably not possible to ever fully explain why particular peoples confront external, especially western, influences in the unique ways that they do. I have tried to provide a very broad statement of what has occurred and is now occurring, and a sketch of the historical and cultural settings in which these changes have taken place. The basic conceptual paradigm underlying the musical system of the Macuma Shuar—that of public versus private and sacred versus secular domains of interaction—is itself grounded in the complex symbolic matrix of acquisition and control of the flux of power. This conceptual paradigm facilitated the inclusion of western-derived genres and contexts of music within Shuar culture. The genres were presented in contexts that were seen by the Shuar to involve an extension of the traditional power-oriented paradigms to encounters with purveyors of *blanco* culture. When experience showed that these western genres and contexts actually threatened the values basic to their traditional ethos and offered little in return, they were rejected by the Shuar. Where *blanco* music was seen to subordinate independence and self-sufficiency, and to provide no context for the manipulation of the forms of power so central to Shuar culture, this music and its attendant contexts became unimportant in daily Shuar life except as phenomena signaling roles or topics particular to Shuar-*blanco* interaction.

This flexibility of Shuar role assumption probably has its roots in the most basic organizational principles of Shuar epistemology. Some sort of mechanism that allows both this flexibility and remarkable cultural continuity must exist at the very base of Shuar culture. It would seem to be apparent that the people of any culture have a dominant way of organizing their sense perceptions into a world view. Implied in this perhaps obvious statement is the belief that this underlying epistemology has certain features that distinguish it from the dominant epistemologies of other cultures; there are undoubtedly many different ways of organizing perception and manipulating the symbols generated by these various epistemological systems (see Maruyama 1974, 1977, 1978). The way knowledge is organized would seem to determine, or at least strongly influence, how the culture members respond to external influences. How one goes about uncovering the significant features of a people's epistemology is still a basic problem. Maruyama (1978) has given us a starting point in his linkage of epistemic qualities with aesthetic domains such as spatial and temporal organization, typological classification, and architectural preferences. Further categories can be abstracted by looking at the symbolic complexes associated with the domains of music-as-concept.

This is precisely the method I have tried to use in this examination of the confrontation between the culture of the Macuma Shuar and *blanco* culture. The mechanism that seems to generate the previously discussed paradigms that underlie both the marked continuity of traditional Shuar values and their ability to function successfully within *blanco* culture can be illustrated by briefly examining one of the central elements of Shuar cosmology.

The Shuar, like their neighbors to the north, the Canelos Quichua, have a symbolic complex involving as one of its elements the spirit Tsungui (Sungui, in Quichua). This symbol, more paradigmatic than unitary, has various referential associations. Tsungui (Sungui) is both spirit of the river and world representation of the whole hydrosphere (see Whitten 1976, 1978). From these two associations it can be seen that Tsungui, as a symbol, contains itself. That is, Tsungui, as the spirit of the river, is a part of the larger representation of the whole world as a hydrosphere. Both are called Tsungui, differing only in the level of representation. Tsungui, the river, in combination with other hydrospheric elements such as rain, generates Tsungui, the whole world as water-related phenomena. Tsungui, for the Shuar, as with the Canelos Quichua (Whitten 1976, 1978, 1979), is the source from which shamanic power derives (see also Harner 1972; Taylor, D. Whitten, in this volume).

This leads me to posit a self-generating dialectic as a key feature of Shuar epistemology, leading me further to suspect that the Shuar would generally respond to intrusion of elements of *blanco* culture by expanding the affected traditional paradigm(s) to include the kinds of roles appropriate to the interaction between the traditional and intrusive cultures (see Whitten 1978; Taylor, D. Whitten, in this volume). This is just what has occurred. It is seen most clearly in the musical behavior of the Macuma Shuar, but I suspect that further study will show it to be true across the entire range of interactions between Shuar and *blanco* cultures.

NOTES

Acknowledgments: The fieldwork on which this paper is based was carried out in the summer of 1978. Funds for this research were provided by the Department of Anthropology at the University of Illinois at Urbana-Champaign, as part of their Summer Research Grant program. Special thanks are due to Bruno Nettl and Norman E. Whitten, Jr., for their help in developing and refining the ideas contained in this paper. Thanks, too, to Bruce Miller, Chris Waterman, and Bill Westcott for discussions that helped me clarify many points developed here.

1. As used in this paper, westernization and modernization are not synonymous. Following Nettl, modernization is defined as "the adoption and adaptation of Western technology and other products of Western culture, as needed, simultaneously with an insistence that the core of cultural values does not change greatly and in the end does not match those of the West." Westernization, by contrast, refers to the "simple incorporation of a society into the Western cultural system" (Nettl 1978a:127).

2. The almost ubiquitous lack of an indigenous word or concept of music that parallels the western concept is just one of several difficulties confronted by the ethnomusicologist studying humanly organized sound among South American cultures. These problems are well summarized in Carol Robert-

son–de Carbo's article (1976) on the Mapuche *tayil*. Much analysis of sound classification among these cultures needs to be done before the various problems can be solved.

REFERENCES CITED

Arnalot, José
  1978   *Lo que los Achuar Me Han Enseñado.* Sucúa: Ediciones Mundo Shuar.
Bateson, Gregory
  1936   *Naven.* Stanford, Calif.: Stanford University Press.
Drown, Frank and Marie
  1961   *Mission to the Headhunters.* New York: Harper.
Federación de Centros Shuar
  1976   Instrumentos Musicales. Mundo Shuar, serie C, 7. Sucúa.
Harner, Michael J.
  1972   *The Jívaro: People of the Sacred Waterfalls.* Garden City, N.Y.: Natural History Press.
  1973   Music of the Jívaro of Ecuador. Notes and Introduction to Ethnic Folkways Record FE 4386. New York: Ethnic Folkways.
Honigmann, John J.
  1947   *Culture and Ethos in Kaska Society.* New Haven, Conn.: Yale University Publications in Anthropology 40.
Irvine, Judith T., and J. David Sapir
  1976   Musical Style and Social Change among the Kujamaat Diola. *Ethnomusicology* 20 (1):67–86.
Karsten, Rafael
  1935   *The Head-hunters of Western Amazonas: The Life and Culture of the Jibaro Indians of Eastern Ecuador and Peru.* Helsinki: Societas Scientiarum Fennica, Commentationes Humanarum Litterarum 2 (1).
Katz, Ruth
  1970   Mannerisms and Cultural Change: An Ethnomusicological Example. *Current Anthropology* 11 (4–5):465–75.
List, George
  1963   Music in the Culture of the Jíbaro Indians of the Ecuadorian Montana. *Premeria Conferencia Interamericana de Ethnomusiocología.* Washington, D.C.: Pan American Union.
McAllester, David
  1954   *Enemy Way Music: A Study of Social and Esthetic Values as Seen in Navaho Music.* Cambridge, Mass.: Papers of the Peabody Museum of American Archaeology and Ethnology 41 (3).
Maruyama, Magoroh
  1974   Paradigmatology and Its Application to Cross-Disciplinary, Cross-Professional, and Cross-Cultural Communication. *Cybernetica* 17 (2 and 3):136–56, and 237–81.
  1977   Heterogenistics: An Epistemological Restructuring of Biological and Social Sciences. *Cybernetica* 20 (1):69–86.
  1978   Epistemologies and Esthetic Principles. *Journal of the Steward Anthropological Society* 8 (2):155–68.

Merriam, Alan P.
  1964   *The Anthropology of Music.* Evanston, Ill.: Northwestern University Press.
  1967   *Ethnomusicology of the Flathead Indians.* Viking Fund Publications in Anthropology 44.
Muriel, Inés
  1976   Jívaros del Ecuador. *Folklore Americano* (Bogotá) 21:141–58.
Nettl, Bruno
  1978a   Some Aspects of the History of World Music in the Twentieth Century: Questions, Problems, and Concepts. *Ethnomusicology* 22 (1):123–36.
  1978b   (Ed.) *Eight Urban Musical Cultures.* Urbana: University of Illinois Press.
Neuman, Daniel
  1976   Towards an Ethnomusicology of Culture Change in Asia. *Asian Music* 7 (2):1–5.
Robertson–de Carbo, Carol
  1976   Tayil as Category and Communication among the Argentine Mapuche: A Methodological Suggestion. *Yearbook of the International Folk Music Council.*
Stirling, Matthew W.
  1938   *Historical and Ethnographical Material on the Jívaro Indians.* Washington, D.C.: Bureau of American Ethnology, Bulletin 117.
Turner, Victor
  1974   *Dramas, Fields, and Metaphors: Symbolic Action in Human Society.* Ithaca, N.Y.: Cornell University Press.
Whitten, Norman E., Jr.
  1976   (with the assistance of Marcelo F. Naranjo, Marcelo Santi Simbaña, and Dorothea S. Whitten). *Sacha Runa: Ethnicity and Adaptation of Ecuadorian Jungle Quichua.* Urbana: University of Illinois Press.
  1978   Ecological Imagery and Cultural Adaptability: The Canelos Quichua of Eastern Ecuador. *American Anthropologist* 80 (4):836–59.
  1979   (with the assistance of Julian Santi Vargas, María Aguinda Mamallacta, and William Belzner). *Soul Vine Shaman.* Monograph accompanying record produced and distributed by Neelon Crawford. Urbana, Ill.: Sacha Runa Research Foundation, Occasional Publication 5.

27

Ancient Tradition in a Contemporary Context: Canelos Quichua Ceramics and Symbolism

Dorothea S. Whitten

To the contemporary adventurer willing to endure jumbo jets and luxury hotels, the Ecuadorian tourist market offers a variety of trophies worthy of a prominent place on the coffee table, bookcase, or wall, and of many recountings of the perils and delights of shopping in foreign lands. Few travelers realize the depth of tradition behind the production of some forms popularly regarded as tourist or folk arts (Graburn 1976, Litto 1976). In contrast to highly commercialized sierran weaving, discussed by Salomon (in this volume) and Casagrande (1977), this chapter deals with a little known and poorly understood ceramic manufacture which is deeply rooted in ancient Amazonian tradition (Lathrap 1970). Canelos Quichua ceramics are currently gaining in the commercial, tourist market and consequently facing pressures to bend to modern technical production.

During the autumn of 1964 my husband and I attended the Fifth Congreso Indigenista Interamericano in Quito, and naturally took time to search for tourist trophies. In two or three gift shops we encountered for the first time some well-turned, thin-walled pottery with delicate decorations, black and terra cotta lines and figures against a buff background. Shopkeepers professed ignorance about the source of this pottery or vaguely said it was from "the Oriente"; it was labeled by the glaring misnomer of "Jívaro pottery" and sold at almost dime-store prices, from $1.00 to $5.00. A popular book published several years later (Scheller 1971) reflected the same lack of knowledge or confusion. A map located the ceramic-making area in the province of Morona-Santiago, yet the text described the ceramics in Quichua terms and identified the makers as the "Jíbaros del Oriente" who were said to live along banks of the Bobonaza River (north of Morona-Santiago, in the province of Pastaza). This compounding of Quichua and "Jíbaro" groups, who have distinct pottery-making techniques (cf. Harner 1972 and Whitten 1976), seemed to represent a tradition that omitted Quichua-speaking peoples from nationally recognized ethnic groups and overlooked their territory as a locus of genuine indigenous culture (see Editor's end note, p. 33).

We returned to Ecuador in 1968 and again found scattered pieces of this pottery in the same Quito gift shops. In the interim we had learned that similar pottery (called Geeváro, after Jívaro) had reached the St. Louis art market from some undetermined area of South America, but we had no knowledge of other U.S. distribution. The 1968 trip included extensive traveling throughout the Ecuadorian Oriente to select an area for future research. In the town of Puyo perusals of shops and conversations with natives from nearby areas indicated that this was the geographic locus of this pottery. Much credit was given to local Peace Corps volunteers for their efforts to encourage increased production and marketing as a source of indigenous income, and the shops reflected this drive in crowding fine bowls next to crude ashtrays, all sold for a pittance. As we traveled north to Puerto Napo, Tena, Archidona, and Misahuallí, down the Napo River to Ahuano, and then flew south to Macas and Sucúa, it became clear that we had left the area of this pottery-making tradition. When one went east, into the Bobonaza River area, to such sites as Canelos, Pacayacu, Sarayacu, Teresa Mama, Montalvo, or north to Curaray, fine pottery manufacture of this distinct style not only continued but appeared to be flourishing.

Currently these ceramics, appropriately labeled "Canelos Quichua," are sold in a number of fine gift shops in Quito at very respectable prices, from $10.00 to $75.00 for bowls and figurines, $150.00 to $300.00 for large storage jars. One gallery and two shops in Puyo specialize in the sale of ceramics; in these and smaller shops selling only a few pieces, prices are comparable to those in Quito. Several factors contribute to the growth of a national market for the ceramics: increased tourism, restrictions on export of archaeological artifacts, and emerging recognition of the aesthetic quality of the ceramics with proper accreditation to the Canelos Quichua as manufacturers.[1] Contemporary appreciation, however, competes with the historical *lack* of recognition of Canelos Quichua indigenous culture, and this apparent exclusionist attitude far exceeds the bounds of art and artifacts. Absence of dramatic characteristics no doubt is associated with national ignorance: Canelos Quichua do not wear feathers in their noses, do not go naked, do not wear long black robes, and do not spear missionaries.[2] Without such distinguishing characteristics to reinforce national stereotypes of "true Amazonian natives," how can

they be their own people? It follows that if they do not exist stereotypically as a people, they cannot possibly be the makers of such fine
ceramics. This seems to involve political as well as aesthetic judgments operant in the context of the viewers, as Graburn (1978) has
discussed.[3]

If we concede that there is growing awareness, at least within some
art circles, of the Canelos Quichua as a viable indigenous culture,
which in turn allows the ceramics to be judged by aesthetic values,
we face the problem: judged as *what*? Functional items, made for
mundane and ceremonial purposes, and decorated in traditionally
symbolic yet individually expressive ways, they are "inwardly directed arts" which persist as "traditional or functional fine arts" (Graburn 1976:5–6), in spite of a changing environment. It must be emphasized here that these ceramics serve very well the purposes for
which they are made, but they are much too fragile to be utilitarian
in other settings. They may cradle a plant or a dried flower or feather
arrangement, but they are primarily of aesthetic, decorative service
to the outside world. These limitations apparently enhance appreciation of the egg-shell-like quality of the ceramics in the eyes of many
people, but response to an expanding market thus far has stimulated
production of exquisite as well as crude ceramics, and both can be
found in the homes of potters and in shops.

The future of Canelos Quichua ceramics as a distinct form clearly
depends upon its enduring significance within Canelos Quichua culture. Whether it becomes an extinct art form, endures in a traditional
mode, or takes on some form of acculturated art (Graburn 1976:4–5)
will also depend upon the nature of external acceptance and the consequent pressures placed on Canelos Quichua art by the burgeoning
market economy for "primitive art" and ethnic or folk handicrafts. To
understand current cultural meaning inherent in Canelos Quichua
ceramic manufacture, and its symbolic significance in daily life and
ritual events, it is necessary to sketch aspects of a remarkable continuity and of an equally remarkable adaptability. Accordingly, we will
note the environmental pressures endured by the Canelos Quichua
over the past century, their adaptations, and the integration of their
artistic expression and ethnic coherence.

TRADITIONAL CERAMICS AND SYMBOLISM

Before sunrise, Laica sat down on a split bamboo mat and reached for the
cool, damp clay at her side. She had dreamed of water, and of her husband, Taruga, trekking north to hunt game for the coming annual cere-

mony. Pungent smoke from the glowing wood fire penetrated the swirling, chilly pre-dawn mists rising from the surrounding jungle hills. She relaxed as she studied the handsome faces of her children—Aida, at 14 the oldest daughter still at home, Hugo and Virgilio, 11 and 9, and the three younger ones. She concentrated on her dream visions, seeking to integrate them with her vast environmental knowledge. Segments of mythic episodes came swiftly to mind, and from them she selected images to guide her pottery making: Quilla, the roguish moon; Jilucu, moon's sister-lover; Nunghuí, master spirit of garden soil and of pottery clay; and *palu*, the dart-like snakebite of shamanistic death. The images became more vivid as she recalled songs about them and softly repeated these to her children, while thinking of what she would create: a half-moon in the form of a cornet, a pregnant Potoo (*Nyctibius*) bird, drinking bowls with her special designs, and a joined pair of deadly bushmasters, mouths open to strike.

Her special array of ceramics would be completed on the eve of Taruga's return, when he would drum the thunder of Amasanga, forest spirit, to begin the ritual which would join souls she imparted to the ceramics with those of people and with soil and water spirits.

This contemporary pottery-making scenario belongs to an ancient Upper Amazonian tradition being maintained in the face of cataclysmic change by the Canelos Quichua-speaking peoples of east-central Ecuador. Their very hilly rainforest habitat ranges from the eastern base of the Andes to the low hill-and-swamp ecosystem near the present border of Peru. Annual rainfall averages 200 inches.

Natives of this habitat have experienced numerous intrusions since the sixteenth century. Prominent in recent history are the Amazonian rubber boom of the late nineteenth century; Royal Dutch Shell oil explorations in the 1930s; sugar plantation development and consequent colonization in the late 1930s; Peruvian invasion of Ecuadorian Amazonian territories in the 1940s; development of national infrastructure of roads, towns, and schools from the 1950s into the present; establishment and expansion of tea plantations, with more colonization, from the late 1950s; and return of oil explorations during the 1960s and '70s. Today, in areas such as Puyo, indigenous peoples have been dislodged from earlier home sites and have resettled in a jungle territory ringed by plantations. As the town of Puyo continues to grow as a trade center and mecca for commerce and colonization, wastes of the urban process are dumped into once crystal rivers. Roads cut through virgin jungle have destroyed native habitation sites, driven out game, and brought lingering clouds of diesel fuel exhaust. Roman Catholic missions, endeavoring for three centuries to save native souls, now concentrate on the increasing colonist population, while continuing to minister their blessing to natives at periodic ceremonies.

In this changing environment the Canelos Quichua, like other indigenous peoples of the Ecuadorian moist tropics, strive to maintain rational continuity with their ancient traditions while seeking a firm position for their expanding population. The 10,000 Canelos Quichua, many of whom are intermarried with neighboring Achuara Jivaroans, practice swidden horticulture on one-two-hectare plots. The basic crops—manioc, plantain, taro, sweet potato, maize, and peanuts—grow to three vertical layers of vegetation, a replication of the natural forest ecosystem which provides a continuous canopy to break and diffuse rainfall, filter sunlight, and provide an undersoil root lattice to retard leaching of vital nutrients. The basis of this horticultural system is strategic use of forest matter to provide necessary nitrogen, potassium, and phosphorus through natural, organic decomposition. Before the soil becomes exhausted, men fell trees to create another plot, allowing the first to return to forest. The people complement their carbohydrate resources and vegetable protein with animal protein acquired through fishing and hunting, and collecting of insects and larvae, land snails, tortoises, turtles, bird and reptile eggs, and river crustaceans.

Their dietary staple is *asua, chicha*, a gruel-like drink made from masticated cooked manioc, sometimes with sweet potatoes or taro added. This food drink, rich in carbohydrates, also contains vegetable proteins which are increased through fermentation.

The subsistence base of the Canelos Quichua is integrated with their social organization through a cosmology expressed in beliefs stressing continuity through descent, alliance through marriage. Horticulture of manioc exemplifies the fundamental male-female division of labor: men clear land; women plant manioc, considered a "woman's crop." Women are responsible for harvesting but may receive help from men; making *asua* is strictly woman's work. Women also maintain the Upper Amazonian tradition of making decorated pottery for storing and serving *asua* and blackened pottery for a variety of cooking and serving uses. Embedded in the pottery-making tradition is the symbolism which communicates and evokes the fundamental integration of ecosystem knowledge, personal experience, familial integrity, and ideology.

Basic to their ideology is a learning process through which knowledge and vision are integrated. The Canelos Quichua refer to knowledge as specific information they may acquire from any source. Vision comes primarily from dreams, and the Canelos Quichua seek to understand their dream mechanisms. It is important to awake after dreaming, to sift the jumble of images into an analyzable symbol system relating past knowledge to present observed behavior. A flash of insight in which one realizes the relation of dream content to previous knowledge also provides vision.

The Canelos believe in a biosphere of spirits; the master ones are Amasanga, forest spirit, Nunghuí, pottery clay–garden soil spirit, and Sungui, water spirit. The spirit world is the visionary world. To enter this world, *huanduj*, the powerful *Datura* (*Solanacea brugmansia* sp.) hallucinogen is used. This propels the taker directly into the spirit world where continuous series of visual and sensory episodes are experienced for six to twelve hours. The return to the waking, human world is characterized by simultaneous interaction within normal surroundings and recurring hallucinations for one to three days. During this period the seeker sees both human world and spirit world; the former endures as the latter fades away.

To attain another level of vision, shamans employ *ayahuasca*, soul vine (*Banisteriopsis* sp.), to allow them to travel between the human and spirit worlds. *Ayahuasca* is thought to induce a dreamlike reality which mediates the human domain of dream vision and the spirit domain of *Datura* vision. Through the knowledge-vision dynamic, embedded in a continuous learning process, ancient custom and knowledge are transmitted.

The ceramic tradition, carried on and transmitted only by women, reflects this synthesis of knowledge and vision. Girls and young married women learn basic techniques of hand building, painting, and firing from their own or their husbands' mothers, but one's decorative style develops as she gains more knowledge and vision of her world. Once or twice during her lifetime a woman may seek a deeper vision of the spirit universe by taking *Datura*.

Husbands play an important auxiliary role in the pottery tradition by helping to mine clay and by acquiring special stones used to burnish and to make dyes. Mining itself is exciting, challenging, grueling. Once or twice a year a small group of related women with their husbands and children walk for a day or more through the rugged hilly terrain to a clay pit or riverbank, the site ostensibly known only to them. There they probe to find the right consistency of fine, nearly pebble-free clay. They then dig with hands, machetes, and sticks to build a supply which adults can carry. Mounds of soaking wet clay— up to 100 pounds for a woman, 150 for a man—are wrapped in fresh leaves to be lugged home on their backs with the aid of tump lines.

During mining the women and men talk animatedly, their stories and jokes punctuated by ringing laughter. An undercurrent of excitement buoys them as they watch carefully for special stones to turn up in newly dug clay or under the water. Particularly prized are the smooth, water-polished stones, certain textured rocks, and mineral ore fragments which yield black and red dyes used to decorate pottery. Some stones are said "to live"; they are believed to contain a spirit which facilitates the merger of earth and water. To test its living substance a man exhales on the stone; if it retains moisture condensation, it "lives."

Small, smooth spirit stones are valued for burnishing—of drum heads by men, of pottery by women. Textured and polished rocks, believed to contain the enduring souls of deceased shamans, are used to "accompany" a man endeavoring to integrate vision and knowledge through his own learning process. One who discovers a special stone may quickly pocket it or may memorize its position and leave it in the earth or water, evoking his memory of it when its spirit is sought.

After the exhausting trek home the potter stores mounds of clay in damp leaves to let it age for at least three days. When she is ready to begin production, she separates the clay into manageable lumps and plasters some against the split palm or bamboo house walls to dry, while she wedges the others one at a time. She continues to alternate the wedging and drying processes, adding a little water when necessary to keep a consistent dampness, until the clay is free of tiny pebbles and feels uniformly workable to her. No substance is required or used to temper the fine clay. Many women then "rest" the clay under water for a few more days, but some do not take the time to do this. Finally, the potter separates the prepared clay into small chunks, kneads them, and rolls out a number of coils 12 to 18 inches long and one-half to three-quarters inch in diameter on a turtle-shaped wooden board carved by her husband. A daughter usually helps to prepare the clay and also to build up a supply of coils.

To begin a *mucahua*, the traditional drinking bowl, the end of a coil is rolled into a small circle which is pressed flat against the board to form the base. Walls are built up by pinching the coil against the base and then continuing the pinching process of coil against coil. The bowl may be held in the palm of one hand, or kept on the board, as two or three more coils are pressed into position, one at a time. When the walls are several inches high, the woman smooths the coils by swift upward strokes of her fingers, carefully supporting the opposite side of the wall with her other hand. After evening the walls she selects one of her smooth calabash scrapers according to desired size and slant of its curvature and, again with swift circular upward movements, thins, widens, and shapes the walls as she scrapes and paddles the clay. She then puts the pot aside on a split bamboo mat or rack to dry as she repeats the process on her next *mucahua* (Kelley and Orr 1976).

A daughter or daughter-in-law normally joins the woman to produce the modest assortment needed for household use. Such help signals serious apprentice status. If the intent is to produce a large volume of pottery for use in an upcoming ceremony, sisters may work together along with their daughters and daughters-in-law. The mood is initially quiet as they think of songs about the spirit inspirations of their creations. They say that the songs come to them in bird-like warbling melody and sometimes point out that birds mediate between the domains of forest, water, and soil. As work proceeds they talk more, sharing news of recent events, discuss prospective marriage alliances for their children, and joke about clandestine love affairs. Younger children hang around to watch, sometimes making a small animal figure out of a ball of clay, then rolling it up and making another animal. Occasionally the women take an *asua* break to relieve the fatigue of sitting for hours on cold earthen floors with scant bamboo covering.

When the first *mucahua* is dry enough to hold new coils, the potter levels the top by biting all around it, spitting out small pieces of clay as she goes. Biting produces a remarkably even wall top and serves to score and moisten it for joining the next coil. Finishing the coiling, scraping, and paddling, she again evens off the top by biting and then smoothes her teeth marks with a scraper, fingers, and sometimes a moistened maize leaf.

A *tinaja* (Spanish, called *asua churana manga* in Quichua) is a large decorated jar used to store the fermenting manioc mash. The potter uses the same techniques, but with heavier coils, to make a *tinaja*, which may be over two feet in diameter. It must be strong enough to store ten to 20 gallons of *asua* which will be placed in it weekly for five to ten years. The potter builds up part of a *tinaja*, completes more *mucahuas*, and, while they dry, turns her attention to creating some figurines from which to serve *asua* during special ceremonies. By a method of coil sculpturing, she may fashion fish, reptiles, crustaceans, insects, nuts or fruits, animals, or birds. A circular snake, for example, is made by joining coils which have been curved into split-tube shapes, then cutting into this cylinder to insert and join the head (or heads), tail, and spout which have been hand sculptured. Representation of human or spirit figures is rarer, but occurs. Examples include the form of a brave "cougar man" who dances and drums at ceremonies, the forest spirit himself or the spirit of garden soil and pottery clay, an oil company worker, or a masked wrestler seen on a cinema poster. Rarer still is a replication of an ancient human burial urn adorned with four versions of a human head, each decorated as an Achuara Jivaroan dressed for a festive occasion.

Before the design is painted, each ceramic piece must be air-dried a day or so until quite firm. It is then covered with slip—clay thinned to a creamy consistency—usually white but sometimes pink or red. It is again air-dried until leather hard, then burnished with a smooth "living" stone.

Just as women decorate their faces and bodies with red and black domesticated vegetable paints—*Bixa orellana* and *Genipa americana* respectively—they employ the spirit masters' black and red colors, derived from rocks, to paint designs on the *asua* storage and serving bowls. A multicolored spectrum, with red predominant, is believed to represent the domain of Sungui, master spirit of water life. Black and red, conceptualized as discrete colors, are manifestations of Nunghuí, master spirit of garden soil and pottery clay. *Asua* itself is regarded as a special merger of garden root crop and water, a merger symbolized by placing the black and red design upon white, pink, or red slip which has been burnished by a water-polished stone. To men and women alike, the *mucahua* and *tinaja* are the greatest artistic accomplishments of their culture, and also signal its continuity of past, present, and future.

Now that a number of pieces are drying and others are underway, the woman (typified as Laica in the opening paragraph) checks her assembled decorating equipment. She sorts her precious rock dyes, attained from many sources and kept hidden since her last pottery manufacture. She chooses the rocks that will yield various shades of red, black, and white when powder scraped from them is mixed with water. She makes delicate brushes, fastening small locks of her own and her daughters' hair to little sticks for several different size tips. Each brush is named according to its color-specific and size-specific purpose. She prepares the rock dyes in a stone vessel, hollowed by years of grinding, then settles down on the floor to paint her special designs on the first *mucahua*, thinking of songs which relate mythic episodes to her contemporary household microcosm.

First, she follows the tradition of adorning the bowl with *mama churana*, the primary female motif represented by a heavy red line. She may know of several hundred base designs for *mama churana*, but she will choose from about 30 of her favorites, any one of which may be used to symbolize different things. One zig-zag design, for example, may represent a winding river, Sungui's domain, or Nunghuí manifested as a harmless brown snake. Sometimes especially skilled women cover the entire slipped bowl with a red paint on which they add their white *mama churana* primary design.

Next, and again traditionally, she emphasizes the *mama churana* design with fine black lines, *aisana*, representing male embellishment. These lines are painted either parallel to, surrounding, or radiating from the base red or white design. The name *aisana*, derived from the word for "drawing together," signals a complex set of associations of husband-wife and brother-sister relationships. Fundamental to these relationships are combined concepts of warmth, togetherness, and ultimate continuity of male and female clan essence through women.

The decorations a woman paints on her ceramics are traditional in color and base design, but the choice and presentation of certain motifs express her individual integration of knowledge with vision. During the burnishing and decorating processes a woman imparts three souls to each ceramic piece. The first is that of Nunghuí, garden soil and pottery clay spirit. The burnishing stone, itself a representation of Nunghuí's domain, carries strong toad and frog symbolism of transformation, basic to acquisition of male shamanic power. This impartation also includes a tinge of the power of Sungui, water spirit master. The second soul, that of the woman herself, represents her synthesis of knowledge, vision, and technique acquired through the process of learning. The third soul derives from the woman's household, which is regarded as a microcosm of the enduring biosphere because of the particular integration of interpersonal relationships, mythically embedded traditions, and spirit forces.

Immediately after decorating the last *mucahua*, the potter stokes a fire within the intersection of three logs, usually kept smouldering in her kitchen, and pushes them closer to make the right size fire. A firing frame is made by chipping out the bottom of an old pot to form an opening slightly smaller than that of the rim of the *mucahua* to be fired. She sets the frame upright over the logs and then places the newly painted *mucahua* inside it, inverted, over the hole. She preheats the *mucahua*, covers it with warm ashes, adds hotter ashes and glowing sticks, often murmuring, "It's strong!" She adds more wood to the fire's center, blows lightly, and returns to decorating the last few figurines.

At the peak of the fire, usually occurring in 25–30 minutes, temperatures of slightly over 1,500°F are reached. Coals and *mucahua* glow vibrantly. Within 35 minutes the firing frame is removed with a pair of machetes held tonglike, placed on the floor, and the still glowing pot removed in the same manner and gently lowered to a log stool, a leaf on the floor, or an old tin can. The potter now picks up a wad of *shinquillu*, a tree resin, and tests it against the hot *mucahua*. The resin first sizzles and smokes, but it soon melts and adheres to the surface as the woman quickly lacquers the entire bowl. The shiny resin deepens the colors, some transformed by firing, to their permanent intensity. The *mucahua* is complete, but still too hot to touch. It rests while the potter continues her work.

After two or three days a woman has a full production process in operation; she moves from building to slipping and burnishing to decorating to firing different pieces, intuitively synchronizing her and her helpers' timing of each motion. Several *mucahuas* shine with new resin, a huge *tinaja* is ready to receive its neck, and more bowls are drying after their white slipping. Three or four figurines are also decorated and ready to be fired. Because her large assemblage must be fired soon after the painted decorations dry, the potter prepares an additional fire outdoors, in a cleared area. She places the figurines on four-inch bamboo staves and then stacks a close-fitting crate of more bamboo, bits of split palm, and other household firewood around and over the clay figures. The fire, set off with a burning stick from the kitchen fire, smoulders, gradually catches, and reaches a roaring climax in about 15 minutes, when it registers 1,500 to 1,800°F. All the wood is consumed in about 30 minutes, when the potter lifts the first glowing figurine from the coals; helpers remove the remaining figurines, and all are coated with resin while sizzling hot. If a woman has made only a couple of figurines or small pots, she will probably fire them inside, using the hot ash technique she always uses for the *mucahuas*. The big *tinajas* are fired outside in the same manner as the figurines. Small *tinaja*-shaped pots, used for storing feathers and secret things, are decorated and fired as figurines.

Black cooking ware, *yanuna manga*, and serving-eating ware, *callana*, present an interesting contrast to painted ceramics. Cooking ware include an impressive array of forms, each with a name for its special use: pots to cook manioc, fish, meat, capsicum, *ayahuasca* (*Banisteriopsis caapi*), *huayusa* (*Ilex* sp.), and curare dart poison are some of the more distinctive examples. The bowls made to serve manioc, plantain soup, fish, and meat also vary in form and elaboration. Hand coiling techniques are also used to build black ware, which have thicker walls than *mucahuas*. Thumb-print corrugation and fingernail incision are common, and sometimes stick punctation is added. No slip is applied to black ware; burnishing varies. If there is continuous rain, the pot may be hung over the household fire to speed drying. When hard and dry, it is fired outdoors in an upright position, using the bamboo crate technique. This firing may darken the outside but not the inside walls. To make the inside shiny black, the bowl is rubbed with one of several leaves, such as taro or sweet potato; the sap serves as an oxygen-reducing medium. The pot is then inverted directly over a built-up household fire which produces volumes of smoke and then high heat. The pot emerges from this second firing smokey black outside, glistening black inside. More exterior blackening occurs as the pot is used, while the interior loses some of its sheen because of food absorption during cooking.

Ceramic manufacture for major ceremonies is the most concentrated, voluminous time of production but not the only one. Pottery may be made at various times, according to the needs of, and demands upon, the potter. Life-cycle status contingencies significantly influence a woman's ceramic work. A young woman, still adolescent by U.S. standards, may show a florescence of skill in executing intricate designs as she approaches marriage. Once married, her energies are spent in raw survival chores of homesteading a new plot of land with her husband; then come the children, with attendant duties. During this period of intensive maintenance activity, a woman usually "keeps her hand in" by making what pottery she needs, but most simply do not have time for really creative production. Her children grow, her garden plot matures, and eventually she can devote thought and energies to making ceramics once again. By now she has incorporated the surge of youth with the demands of existence and the visions of spirit worlds. If she chooses to apply herself to ceramics—and not all women do—the products will reflect her integration of life experiences.

A few women achieve remarkable results with their ceramics because their creativity derives, in part, from special relationships with powerful spirits. As previously discussed, the core of male shamanic power is the possession of cumulative, integrated knowledge and vision, through which the shaman relates and manipulates spiritual and profane domains. The female counterpart of special power is, similarly, possession of this fabric of knowledge and vision, through which women gain insight into powerful spirits. Those so equipped express the relation of domains through their production of exceptional ceramic pieces, and this is particularly apparent among women who are daughters, sisters, and/or wives of shamans. Occasionally, a young betrothed girl transcends time-acquired skills to turn out incredible works, a feat that seems to occur when the engaged couple both have shamanic connections. Such extraordinary figurines or finely painted *mucahua*s are recognized by other potters and by men as *sinchi*, strong or powerful, a quality equated with beauty. These figurines might take the form of a cayman, symbolic of ancient peoples' ability to traverse the water domain, or of a fer-de-lance, representing shaman-directed spirit attack, or an anaconda, a symbol of the water spirit master manifested through the spirit domain of *Datura*. The songs these women sing when making pottery and during ceremonies signal a synthesis of shaman and spirit powers never reached by the majority of culture bearers.

Canelos Quichua ceramics are used continuously in daily life. Upon waking, a woman stokes up the smouldering fire, procures water from a nearby stream, and boils it quickly. She takes a handful of freshly fermented manioc mash from her *tinaja*, puts it in the *mucahua*, and mixes it with hot water. Still mixing the gruel with her fingers, she walks to her husband and serves him the tangy, yeasty drink. He softly blows on it, then drinks. As they drink *asua* in these pre-dawn hours, men and women exchange what they "saw" just before wakening and seek to separate and integrate observations drawn from the day's encounters with the night's dream resortment. Mythic images of forest, soil, and water spirits are evoked by the designs on the bowls from which they drink. By reference to these images they reaffirm their own strength and purpose, resolving yesterday's problems and reaching today's decisions.

As the day wears on the Canelos continue to serve and to drink *asua* within their houses, on their jungle plots, or in the forest. Although calabashes and aluminum bowls are readily available, the Canelos Quichua still prefer to use their hand-made ceramics to serve and store *asua*.

Men making long jungle treks or canoe trips carry one or two delicate *mucahua*s with them. Women choose particular *mucahua*s to serve guests. The more important the guest, the finer the piece of serving ware. Today, near Puyo, where national and foreign intrusion is intense, a woman may deny that she uses ceramic serving ware if she regards a visitor as a potential threat to household or clan integrity.

PUYO: THE URBAN AMBIENCE

Puyo, the capital of the province of Pastaza, presently has an estimated 10,000–12,000 residents. Earliest colonists, seeking refuge from economic oppression and natural disasters in their sierran homelands, walked down ancient trade routes or perhaps rode a donkey along the precipitous banks of the Pastaza River into the Oriente to find the village of Puyo, a scattering of native houses around the Dominican church mission buildings. Under the thrust of national expansion and exploitation of natural resources, road construction pushed slowly from the Sierra into the Oriente, each completed section bringing in more traders, explorers, and colonists. The settlement of the early 1900s grew into a village and ultimately into a bustling frontier town following two major events: completion of the last lap of the road to Puyo in 1947, and a population shift from Shell to Puyo when Royal Dutch Shell Oil Company ceased operations and withdrew from Shell-Mera in 1950 (Gillette 1970; Casagrande, Thompson, and Young 1964).

As migrant traders became resident merchants, truckers were needed to bring supplies from the highlands to the expanding sugar plantations and to return lowland products of *trago* (see Ekstrom, in this volume), *panela* (crude brown sugar), cinnamon, and broom fibers to markets. The void left by the first petroleum exploration company was filled by Protestant evangelist missionaries and military groups whose presence was felt from their base in Shell, eight miles from Puyo. Establishment of canton headquarters and later the provincial capital, construction of private, commercial, and governmental buildings, and infrastructural development created needs for personnel.[4] Services demanded still more specialized supporting services, growth built upon growth. The displacement of natives by newcomers was virtually complete by 1955, when the last dozen or so "holdout" Runa families moved into *comuna* territory (Whitten 1976). By our first visit to Puyo in 1968, only one old indigenous woman lived in town, where she continued to store *asua* in large undecorated *tinajas* and to serve her visitors from beautiful but chipped *mucahuas*, the last her eyes would let her make.

During the early 1970s Puyo and Shell were staging areas for another wave of petroleum exploration, concluding in 1975 amid contradictory rumors that companies would soon return, that nothing was found, and that wells were found but capped for future use. This economic input and withdrawal created a distinct boom-bust atmosphere, especially among merchants overstocked in English gin. But underneath this flashy economy was steady growth which became apparent as the government freed money, based on new national oil riches, for loans for construction (commercial and private) and for developing businesses, particularly agricultural ones. Instead of one national and one local bank in 1968, there were three national governmental banks by 1977. As regional offices of national agencies expanded services, they required even more personnel to keep up with the necessary paperwork.

The growth of local bureaucracy added a clerical and managerial element to the now old-line colonist merchant class, the existing upper class by local standards of occupation, wealth, and community prestige. More medical and legal professionals found their ways to Puyo to meet the needs of a growing monied clientele. Constant expansion and improvement of roadways, increased availability of motor vehicles, and greater volume of communication and trade with highland urban centers worked together to produce the single largest occupational force, that of professional drivers of trucks, buses, taxis.[5] Not only are the chauffeurs licensed, which in this case validates a certain level of literacy and special training, but they are, almost to a man, members of the provincial chauffeurs' union, which in turn is affiliated with the national chauffeurs' union. They represent a powerful political force locally and a potential force nationally in times of crisis. To the old-line status criteria of occupation, wealth, and community prestige now must be added education (including occupational training), professional status, and corporate power.

The population growth rate of the Oriente from 1950 through 1974 far outdistanced that of the nation as a whole and those of sierran and coastal areas. Within the Oriente rural growth exceeded urban, and the urban growth pattern showed a large increase in age groups under 15 and over 65.[6] Nationally during this same period educational attainment was considerably higher for urban than for rural populations; in the Oriente both primary and secondary school enrollment was almost double that of the nation. Interpretation of these statistical trends was borne out by our observations. Puyo was the educational center of Pastaza province, with parochial and public schools serving growing numbers of urban children as well as many others who continued their education in town following the six grades offered by their home rural schools. There was also a technical *colegio* and a public night school which gave adults and working school-age children a chance to learn the basics they otherwise missed.

The accelerated tempo of modernization is reflected in a number of material concomitants. Wooden buildings were replaced by concrete ones, and the frontier look of portico-covered sidewalks gave way to the modern scene of multiple-storied buildings connected by a maze of power and telephone lines. In 1968–71 one generator supplied electric power to the town for two early morning hours and four hours in the evening, if it did not break down. A generator-run water pump frequently broke down too, and *no hay agua, no hay luz*, were often heard cries. Garbage collection consisted of an open-back dumptruck, operated by a driver, a pick-up man, and an advance man who ran in front of the truck, ringing a bell to warn residents to put their garbage out on the streets, lest the containers be dumped and stolen if put out prematurely. By 1972 a new generator produced a strong and generally uninterrupted power supply, and both power and water operations have continually improved. The big news in sanitation, by 1977, was the replacement of the old garbage truck by a modern hydraulic truck, operated by the same three men, minus the bell.

Striking changes could be seen in the commercial scene during the 1970s. General stores, which had long supplied outlying plantations with basic food products, aluminum pots, shotguns, tools, hardware, fishhooks, and dynamite, added transistor radios and phonographs, all types of plastic housewares, and imported cosmetics. Stores specializing in appliances, veterinary and agribusiness supplies, and prefabricated building supplies sprang up. Typewriters, cameras, several brands of sewing machines, foam rubber mattresses, and mass-produced clothing were displayed everywhere. Refrigerators became more than a front-room prestige item as electricity improved and ultimately led to such phenomena as cold beer and cokes, refrigerated milk and cheese, and butcher shops open all day instead of from only 6:00 to 7:00 A.M. Electric ovens and chicken-broiling rotisseries opened new dimensions in local bakery and restaurant businesses. Glaring traffic lights had replaced policemen at every major intersection by 1978. Television sets, including many color ones, were offered for sale a couple of years before the relay system reached Puyo. Once the relay was completed, television was to be seen in stores, bars, and barber shops all over town, with absolutely any program or test pattern watched by small, transfixed clusters of people.

The central market is the hub of weekend activity. Here permanent stalls and *kioskos* are surrounded by makeshift booths; hawkers spread everything from used clothes, tools, medicines, and switchblades to new enamel pots and pans along sidewalks and advertise their wares over loudspeakers to compete for the crowd's attention. National music blares out of jukeboxes in open-front saloons, where groups of men discuss the week's activities over rounds of beer. The Saturday morning scene of frantically unloading produce and goods brought in atop buses from Ambato is reversed on Sunday afternoon, while taxis wheel in and out to pick up homeward-bound passengers, many unable to navigate on their own feet. Except for motor traffic, a day-after sense of calm prevails on Monday, when banks, government offices, and many stores are closed. By Tuesday the town is in full swing again, everything is open, and the pervasive traffic continues.

Just as Puyo is dependent on other parts of the country for supplies, trucked in from Ambato, so it is the purveyor of goods to the small colonist towns which have grown up on its periphery. Transport of goods is accompanied by human activity, of course, and the traffic pattern reflects the seemingly constant motion of people and exchange of goods. Crowded buses rumble in and out over the cobblestone streets from 3:00 A.M. till midnight or 1:00 A.M. Trucks, taxis, microbuses, and small pick-ups come and go at all hours; military and a growing number of private vehicles circle through town, and occasionally the ambulance or the new police van sets out with siren screaming. Air traffic out of the nearby base at Shell dropped noticeably at the withdrawal of petroleum explorations, but military and missionary flights soon picked up to about 40 take-offs and landings a day. Many of these planes are not seen from town because their flight paths direct about 75% of them south of Puyo, over *comuna* territory, where they are accurately identified as Twin, Push-Pull, Buffalo, Caribou, or Cucaracha by the experienced eyes of the indigenous inhabitants.

There is no element of the preceding overview of Puyo that does not involve the Canelos Quichua in some way. Because there was no way to maintain traditional lifeways in an incipient urbanizing milieu, an option to remain in town would have required almost total, sudden change. We view the Canelos' withdrawal from town to *comuna* as a rational flight from domination to maintain self-integrity, an adaptation which allowed them cultural independence while they continued exchange patterns which have existed with missionaries and colonists from early times into the present (Whitten 1976:235–36). *Compadrazgo* ties have been maintained over two and three generations, and to these ritual ties with nonindigenous people have been added legal, contractual bonds. No longer content with pasturing cattle of colonists, Puyo Runa have been buying cattle with their own earnings from sale of produce, petroleum company wages, and, more recently, loans from the National Development Bank, Banco Nacional de Fomento. Some Runa men and women continue their elementary or secondary education in night school, and a few attend the vocational school, usually supporting themselves by a part-time job in town. In at least two cases a young man's school expenses are supported, in part, from his mother's sale of fine ceramics, which may net her from $40.00 to $120.00 per month. Many Runa, weary of being underenumerated and overlooked, respond to government pressure for citizen registration by meticulously recording marriages, births, and deaths, sometimes spending hours or days at the registration office while they await acceptance of old baptismal records.

On weekends Runa come to town to trade, selling *naranjilla* (*Solonacea quitoensis*), ipecac, fiber, and other jungle products, and buying salt, sugar, or perhaps school clothes for a child. Women may sell a few pieces of pottery, or they may give them to patrons as insurance against future return favors. Men may try to sell a headdress or drum used at a recent ceremony, and some are now carving wooden animals to sell to tourists. Puyo Runa come to visit with their children who work and board in town in order to attend school; they visit with patrons, with other Runa, with Shuar, with *gringo* tourists, and they come just to see who else is in town that day. As they congregate before a store front to watch the bikini-clad contestants for the "Miss Ecuador" title, one wonders if they remember early (and successful) missionary efforts to garb them in western clothes. Their presence in town is so commonplace that an observer is apt to think of the *comuna* as a dormitory suburb and to forget that its nearest boundary is an hour or two's hard trek away, and that many *comuneros* must walk four to six hours to reach that boundary.

Puyo Runa participation in the modern world is manifest in their options to assume national styles in speech, clothing, sports, music, and dance without relinquishing their own language or musical tradition. This has been more true of men than women until the last few years, but now women are displaying more aspects of nonindigenous lifestyles in their "town persona." This is seen in increasing Quichua-Spanish bilingualism, in seeking more education, in wearing slacks or pants suits, and in dancing to national popular music. When possible, wives of *comuna* soccer teams accompany their mates to games (both local and in the Sierra) to form an exuberant cheering section. The ostensible blend of Runa into the contemporary Puyo setting leads many outsiders to declare that the "natives have disappeared," an assumption that might vanish if they were present during the 12th of May celebrations.

Doce de Mayo, 12th of May, the official founding day of Puyo, is the major civic and social event of each year. It is celebrated by barrio dances and contests for queen, speeches, and exhibits. It culminates in a parade, an indoor musical revue topped by presentation of the queens, and two dances, one a free street dance, the other an indoor ticket-only affair. The day begins at 4:00 A.M. with one long burst of military machinegun fire. The opening salvo is repeated an hour later with short bursts all around Puyo, and by loud explosions of blank hand grenades. At exactly 5:00 A.M. the National Police Band of Quito plays the national anthem and then begins to walk through the streets playing sierran *San Juanitos*, stopping to play *costeño cumbias* before homes of prominent citizens who reward the players with glasses of *trago, canelazos*, and whisky. By daylight, every mother in town is dressing her children in their parade costumes, while small groups of men put finishing touches on floats. Houses have been freshly painted, new clothes are donned, and the weeks of preparation are over; it is time to take places in line or as spectators.

Runa from near Puyo and from more distant areas flood into town. Some have come a day or two early to trade or register new babies, and have spent the night in cheap *pensiones* or a community room provided by a church. Others leave their own or relatives' homes before dawn and walk two or three hours to reach town by 7:00 or 8:00 A.M. The pattern is repeated by colonists from the surrounding hinterland and villages.

The parade is Puyo on display, reflecting every status, age, and national ethnic gradient in the makeup of the town or nation. Leading off are directors of the local Red Cross, the most prestigious men in town, marching shoulder to shoulder in their black wool suits and red neckties and sweating profusely under the Amazonian sun. They are followed by the National Police Band of Quito and then miles of school children, each class costumed to represent some segment of the national sierran, coastal, or less frequently Oriente ethnic heritage. School classes are interspersed with bands and units from the Police Band of Quito, with queen-bearing floats from each barrio, with the adult night school classes, and with some lowland indigenous groups stereotypically dressed and clearly labeled so as to leave no doubt of their identity as nonnationals. Phony costumes notwithstanding, a true badge of Runa identity may be seen in the beautiful *mucahuas* some women carry, or in the two-faced figurine the young queen bears as she marches with her people. She carefully holds the obvious sun-face motif toward the crowd while keeping the private, mythically symbolic tree mushroom (*ala*) side toward her body.

The military establishment at Shell, including the band, and the entire *Batallón de la Selva* conclude the parade to a tune which always sounds to me like "Yankee Doodle Dollar." All available jeeps and trucks roll through town while military planes buzz the central plaza where participants and spectators have assembled. There, from the balcony of the Dominican school building, the crowd is addressed by the president of the republic who, through 9 August 1979, is also head of the armed forces.[7] The president is flanked by the Dominican bishop of Puyo and the diocese of Canelos, the bishop's top aides, the provincial governor, and the top-ranking town officials. The annual review of the parade and address to the people by the president and his allies symbolically and dramatically reassert that Puyo has become a civilized city in a nationalist state, and that the fate of the citizens is in the joined hands of the Catholic church and the state.

Doce de Mayo may be seen as a time of heightened contact between indigenous and nonindigenous groups, for civic and church organizers invite people from indigenous areas to exhibit their ceramics and other crafts and to take part in the parade. This includes an opportunity to perform before the review stand, an occasion Runa use to make their presence known to national leaders. They may do this by presenting a fine *mucahua* to a government official or serving him *asua* from a ceramic portrayal of Amasanga, or perhaps they enact a short dance which appears stereotypically "native" to onlookers but evokes imagery of the powers of the master water spirit for the performers. In 1978 a rain shower sent the officials scurrying for cover after one such dance. Even preparation for their participation generates asymmetrical interaction patterns, for the organizers instruct the Runa in what to wear and how to perform to look "authentic." Organizers also assist native marchers in making banners to carry showing the public that they are bona fide *indígenas* from specific areas. If their performance is considered effective, townspeople congratulate the organizers and even compliment the anthropologist who is identified with the Runa. Backstage, after the presentation of the queens, including a young queen from a *comuna* group, natives mingle with townspeople and watch Puyo elites drink toasts to one another, and only to one another.

Later, distinctions melt into the night as everyone strolls through the streets, stopping to listen to the blaring electronic sounds of imported musical groups, to exchange *trago* and *canelazo* drinks with *compadres*, and to make friends of old enemies. Next to the bandstands middle-class youths of Puyo seem to form a solid mass of motion, bobbing up and down to *cumbia* and disco beats; on the edges of the crowd Runa and Shuar youths perform the same gyrations while their parents watch and study them from the sidelines. Runa think about this scene and wonder about the future as they walk back to their jungle homes the next day.

Dorothea S. Whitten

PUYO RUNA CULTURAL INTEGRITY

Once or twice a year, in their own *caseríos*, the Canelos Quichua hold ceremonies which symbolize the relationship of their enduring culture to a changing world.[8] In this ceremony metaphoric expression inherent in the ceramic tradition is constantly manipulated vis-à-vis perceived intrusions stemming from religious and political pressures and from ecosystem transformation. The date for the ceremony is arranged with a priest from Puyo or Canelos who will come to say Mass and perform any marriages or baptisms awaiting benediction. Then previously designated *priostes* and their families start traditional preparations. Groups of men symbolically "invade" remote jungle areas where dangerous *jurijuri* spirits control the spirits of resident game. There they hunt for tapir, peccary, deer, and monkey and fish for large catfish; game is smoked in the forest and carried home about two weeks after the hunters' departure. During the men's absence women gather to make a large array of ceramics, often taking over the entire household since they need to produce extra *tinajas* as well as dozens of *mucahua*s, *callana*s, and figurines. Here each potter makes a cultural statement related to her private world of dreams, to the intraindigenous world of shared mythology, and to perceived alterations caused by national intrusions. Such statements, reflected in the totality of each array, are shared by the women in their continuous interaction. They also bring in great piles of manioc from their jungle gardens; as the communally made *asua* ferments in new, old, and borrowed *tinajas*, they chop weeds from the plaza with machetes, sweep their homes, and ready themselves for the hunters' return.

Preparations are complete once the hunters safely return, describe their recent adventures, and distribute the smoked meat and fish. Friends and relatives from all parts of the *comuna* and from more distant areas gather in the large homes chosen to house the ceremony. The three-day ritual begins with men beating drums, producing a resonance which signals the thunder of forest spirit Amasanga. Their steady drumming continues as the men slowly circle in the center of the *priostes'* houses. Guests, seated side by side on low benches around the perimeter, are served *asua* by several women. The server holds the large *mucahua* firmly to the drinker's mouth while he or she braces a hand against it and gulps down the yeasty brew. Movement intensifies as more people arrive and women rush back and forth to refill *mucahua*s and serve everyone repeatedly. One or two men play a transverse flute while dancing, and a powerful shaman plays a six-hole vertical flute. Women pause to serve the drummers and respond to an invitation to dance. As the drummer or flute player strides toward a woman, she moves backward and sideways in birdlike hops as she sways her head and shoulders from side to side, her long black hair swinging about her face. The dancers reverse their direction and repeat their back-and-forth pattern for only a few minutes. Then the woman ceases her dance to Nunghuí and resumes serving *asua*, while the man rejoins the other circling drummers and flute players to continue beating the sound of rolling thunder which makes everyone "dream and reflect."

Women pour gallons of *asua* into the mouths of participants and intentionally spill and throw much of the substance on them. To increase the subtlety of this *asua* baptism, women serve from animal and fish figurines made with an extra, hidden opening which they uncover to release a dribble or stream of *asua* on the drinker. Continuous drumming plus a deluge of *asua* call forth imagery of the encompassing power of water spirit Sungui, whose presence is evoked to express resistance to further destruction of the Upper Amazonian ecology. As the ceremony moves toward a crescendo, a prestigious *prioste* is served *asua* from a ceramic trumpet made by his sister who decorated it with symbols of their shared, shamanic ancestry. Then she refills it and presents it to a strong Runa man known for his *palanca*, "leverage," vis-à-vis some religious, political, or commercial outsider. The recipient drinks from the trumpet's bell and then accepts the trumpet as a gift; he blows it repeatedly to mimic the call of *yami*, the trumpeter swan, a sound which evokes thoughts of mutual Runa suffering in the face of externally imposed punishment. Women serve still more *asua* from figurines in the form of fish, symbolic of Sungui's domain, or in the shape of reptiles, symbolic of Amasanga, Nunghuí, and Sungui, or perhaps in a merged starmushroom (*ala*) image representing clan continuity and the regeneration of ancient Runa ancestral siblings. Before the arrival of the Dominican priest, women decorate the rustic altar with fresh flowers placed in ceramic bowls and with candles stuck into the spouts or mouths of ceramic figurines. As they do this, they think of the mythic segments of their cultural statements to be juxtaposed to Christian chalice, wafer, and wine. For his part in this juxtaposition, a man may hang a drum next to the church's bell.

It is usual for the priest and his coterie to arrive on Sunday, the last day of the ceremony, to give Mass and stay through the *camari*, feast. The last two days of the ceremony may be attended by specially invited *compadres*, a few local dignitaries, and some public workers seizing the opportunity to present their newest program to a large assemblage of Runa. A coincidental scheduling error turned one ceremony we attended in 1972 into an arena of competing outside interferences which reinforced the ritual arena of ceremonial enactment. Because of an ecclesiastical conflict on the given Sunday, the priest came to the Canelos' ceremony on Saturday, unannounced, and called everyone to Mass. Angry because the on-going soccer game kept too many people away, he rescheduled Mass for 10:00 A.M. the next day, under threat of withdrawing all church affiliation if people failed to attend. Later that day public health workers appeared at the ceremony to preach the necessity of receiving polio vaccine. They informed everyone that the oral vaccine would be given the next day, in Puyo, between 10:00 and 11:00 A.M., and *at no other time*. The forced choice between risk of polio and loss of the church as benefactor was very real. Because most wanted the priest's presence at their ceremony, they opted to continue ceremonial activity through Sunday. Before he left the ceremony, the priest was given a ceramic representation of Amasanga and asked to keep it in the church. The priest was flattered by the gift from his "flock"; the Runa, in turn, were pleased that an image of their jungle spirit master would represent them in the outside sphere of Dominican power. Had the public health workers come to them, they said, they would have accepted the vaccine and presented each worker with some ceramic imagery of the enduring strength of the Runa biosphere.

Images which express cognizance of recent environmental intrusions are also brought forth on the final day of ceremonial enactment. A woman may don a ceramic hardhat, shaped like those worn by petroleum company workers but decorated with an ancient reptilian design. Another serves guests *asua* from a pottery jukebox complete with the name of the colonists' weekend saloon; its principal anaconda motif, symbolizing Sungui, escapes no one. As men and women drink *asua* from these ceramic representations of a changing world, they think of the pre-dawn song of the *paspanchu* bird, which to them means, "evil is coming but I am ready to meet it." Men dance with women while playing this song on their flutes; women sing out songs coming to them from spirits, distant people, and souls of deceased relatives and ancestors. By confronting the new with the ancient, the Canelos Quichua seek to maintain their sense of order in a radically changing environment.

While Canelos Quichua culture is a repository of ancient symbolism, enacted in ceremonies and portrayed in ceramic design, it is not "pristine." Its bearers move between two worlds, maintaining their

cultural identity while rationally incorporating some aspects, and rejecting others, of a changing environment and social order. Their balance between two worlds is reflected in their ceramics, which remain
essentially traditional but not unchanging. To date, we have not seen
significant evidence that stereotypic predictions are occurring: potters are neither deserting their hand-made wares for convenient plastic and metal utensils, although these are used, nor are they directing
all their energies into producing "arts of acculturation" (Graburn
1976:5).

The volume of ceramics available on the 1980 tourist market is as
extensive as it is varied. It reaches the market primarily by means of
brokers (some indigenous, some not) who buy from potters and sell
to dealers, tourists and/or collectors, rather than through an influx of
tourists to the pottery-making areas. The potters demand—and receive—good prices and do not appear to object to this unobtrusive
method of marketing their products as an important supplement to
their family incomes. Their response to increased demand reflects
their essential adaptability and results in ceramic products designed
to accommodate a range of tourists' budgets and tastes.

Materials and techniques of production remain basically unchanged; the few attempted short-cuts by use of commercial paints
and glazes obviously fail to replicate natural dyes and resins. Stylist-
ically, the greatest changes are in form, similar to the Shipibo-Conibo
responses to tourism described by Lathrap (1976:109–205) as "miniaturization" and "reduction in complexity of design." Miniaturization
of *tinajas* began several years ago in response to a market demand for
transportable replicas of the beautiful but large storage jars, which
frequently measure two to three feet in diameter and height.[9] The
miniaturization trend continues in the production of ubiquitous
forms representing birds, insects, animals, and even shamans'
stools. Inexpensive and easily slipped into a purse or bag, many of
these items reduce hand coiling to its lowest level, such as a tiny coil
overlapped once to become a snake, although they are still "properly," traditionally fired and decorated.

"Reduction in complexity of design" is seen primarily in the increased production of effigy pots (figurines) without serving spouts,
which transforms them into nonfunctional, purely decorative, and
very popular tourist items. This stylistic device must be seen in relation to a market audience, however, for some women make spoutless
animal forms to amuse a child or to use as a familiar through which
to sing messages to an estranged husband, and traditional effigy
forms with serving spouts are still made for ceremonies.

In general, overall execution and decoration of *mucahua*s are of a higher quality in 1980 than in 1968. Indeed, this form has achieved a high art status among some nationals who collect and decorate their homes with exquisite (and expensive) Canelos Quichua bowls instead of (or in addition to) pre-Columbian ones. The range from folk junk through traditional-functional fine arts to collectible fine art is recognized by the potters themselves, as exemplified by the statement, "These pieces of garbage-clay are for tourists who want them; these beautiful *mucahuas* are for my house, and some are for sale at a high price to someone who appreciates them."

The Puyo Runa groupings of the Canelos Quichua culture are clearly aware of the aesthetic quality of their ceramics. They have long given them as gifts to prestigious visitors to their region, and they are pleased with the current value of their pottery in the tourist market. They continue to make fine ceramics for their own household and ceremonial use and to make extras of this quality for sale, while at the same time expanding production of innovative tourist products. It is impossible to predict how long they can continue their ceramic tradition in the face of ecological, economic, and social pressures to change. Their ceramic tradition is a graphic and metaphoric expression of cultural continuity and adaptation. Its disappearance, or a departure to an introduced ceramic technology, will in my opinion signal the demise of the heart of Canelos Quichua culture.

NOTES

Acknowledgments: Portions of this research were funded by a National Science Foundation grant (GS–2999) between 1972 and 1974. I am indebted to Hernán Crespo Toral for sponsoring my research in Ecuador through the auspices of the Instituto Nacional de Antropología e Historia and the Museo del Banco Central del Ecuador. The general ethnography of the Canelos Quichua, including sections on ritual, social structure, and Puyo Runa adaptability, is given in Whitten (1976), and elaboration of the symbolism appears in Whitten (1978). Sections of this paper were written in collaboration with Norman E. Whitten, Jr., and are reprinted here by permission of *Natural History Magazine*.

The paper could not have been written without the basic *ricsina*, encouragement, and critical help of Norman Whitten, but I accept responsibility for any errors in interpretation. I am also grateful to Janet Dougherty, Dave Grove, Charlie Keller, and Rick Thompson for commenting on an earlier version of this paper, and to Bill Belzner, Joe Brenner, Ginger Farrer, Kathy Fine, and Liz Franck for comments and suggestions on the revised version. For a number of years, Olga Fisch has graciously encouraged and aided the Whittens' involvement with Canelos Quichua ceramics and I thank her deeply, for both of us. And I am indebted to many *profesoras de cerámica*, especially Faviola Vargas Aranda, Celia Santi, María Grefa, Blanca and Lola Santi, Clara Santi Simbaña, Teresa Santi Maianchi, Antonia Aguinda, Ascencióna Canelos, Soledad Vargas, Olimpia and Elsa Santi, and Apacha Vargas.

1. Growing recognition has been in part due to the efforts of the Sacha Runa Research Foundation (see Whitten and Whitten 1977, 1978).

2. Patzelt (1973) documents all such colorful "Hijos de la Selva Ecuatoriana" while completely omitting lowland Quichua groups.

3. Although Graburn (1978) addresses his experiment to judgment of commercial art, his analysis seems applicable to the art form discussed in this paper.

4. For detailed description of the growth and development of Puyo, see Gillette (1970).

5. By 1979 IERAC (Instituto Ecuatoriano de Reforma Agraria y Colonización) had 30–50 field representatives working out of Puyo; the Banco Nacional de Fomento, Banco Nacional de la Vivienda, and the Caja de Credito had about 40 professional-level employees. The "choferes" numbered about 150, with 450 enrolled in their training course in Puyo.

6. Statistical data and trends are based on the report by Saunders (n.d.).

7. The 28 Apr. 1979 return to civilian presidency did not alter the pageantry of control described here.

8. For a full explication of the ceremony see Whitten (1976:165–202).

9. We refer to actual miniatures of *tinajas*, made expressly for sale to tourists. These are not to be confused with the existing form of *sicuanga manga*, toucan pot, a small *tinaja*-shaped jar traditionally hung secretly in the rafters of the great oval houses, and still used by women to store feathers, seed beads, and other special substances.

REFERENCES CITED

Casagrande, Joseph B.
1977   Looms of Otavalo. *Natural History Magazine* 86 (8):40–59.
Casagrande, Joseph B., Stephen I. Thompson, and Philip D. Young
1964   Colonization as a Research Frontier: The Ecuadorian Case. In Robert A. Manners, ed., *Process and Pattern in Culture: Essays in Honor of Julian H. Steward*. Chicago: Aldine, pp. 281–325.
Gillette, Cynthia
1970   Problems of Colonization in the Ecuadorian Oriente. M.A. thesis, Washington University, St. Louis.
Graburn, Nelson H. H.
1976   Introduction: The Arts of the Fourth World. In Nelson H. H. Graburn, ed., *Ethnic and Tourist Arts: Cultural Expressions from the Fourth World*. Berkeley: University of California Press, pp. 1–32.
1978   "I like things to look more different than that stuff did": An Experiment in Cross-Cultural Art Appreciation. In Michael Greenhalgh and Vincent Megaw, eds., *Art in Society: Studies in Style, Culture and Aesthetics*. New York: St. Martin's Press, pp. 51–70.

Harner, Michael J.
1972 *The Jívaro: People of the Sacred Waterfalls.* Garden City, N.Y.: Natural History Press.

Kelley, Patricia, and Carolyn Orr
1976 *Sarayacu Quichua Pottery.* Dallas: SIL Museum of Anthropology, Publication 1.

Lathrap, Donald W.
1970 *The Upper Amazon.* New York: Praeger.
1976 Shipibo Tourist Art. In Nelson H. H. Graburn, ed., *Ethnic and Tourist Arts: Cultural Expressions from the Fourth World.* Berkeley: University of California Press, pp. 197–207.

Litto, Gertrude
1976 *South American Folk Pottery.* New York: Watson-Guptill Publications.

Patzelt, Erwin
1973 *Hijos de la Selva Ecuatoriana.* Guayaquil: Colegio Alemán Humbolt.

Saunders, John
n.d. Population Change in Ecuador. Manuscript submitted to Joseph B. Casagrande, ed., *Handbook of Ecuador.*

Scheller, Ulf, ed.
1971 *Artesanía Folclórica en el Ecuador.* Guayaquil: Colegio Alemán Humbolt.

Whitten, Dorothea S., and Norman E. Whitten, Jr.
1978 Ceramics of the Canelos Quichua. *Natural History Magazine* 87 (8):90–99.

Whitten, Norman E., Jr.
1976 (with the assistance of Marcelo F. Naranjo, Marcelo Santi Simbaña, and Dorothea S. Whitten). *Sacha Runa: Ethnicity and Adaptation of Ecuadorian Jungle Quichua.* Urbana: University of Illinois Press.
1978 Ecological Imagery and Cultural Adaptability: The Canelos Quichua of Eastern Ecuador. *American Anthropologist* 80 (4):836–59.

Whitten, Norman E., Jr., and Dorothea S. Whitten
1977 Report of a Process Linking Basic Science Research with an Action Oriented Program for Research Subjects. *Human Organization* 36 (1):101–5.

Afterword

Norman E. Whitten, Jr.

> "Only the clash of ideas can ignite the light of truth."[1]
> Jaime Roldós Aguilera, president of the Republic of Ecuador.

> "It is important that society comprehend its indomestizo roots."[2]
> Osvaldo Hurtado Larrea, vice-president of the Republic of Ecuador.

In 1979, just as this book manuscript underwent its final revision, a radical governmental change occurred. The political pendulum swung left and, in a free run-off election administered by the military, the people of Ecuador overwhelmingly elected Jaime Roldós Aguilera as president and Osvaldo Hurtado as vice-president, resoundingly defeating the military's own chosen candidate, Sixto Durán Ballén Cordovez. Thus ended nine years of military dictatorship. The new era began with accelerated centralization, and ethnic mobilization, presaged by the first official pronouncement of the president, soon became a key mechanism to "demarginalize" the majority of Ecuadorians. The first year of Roldós's presidency bore witness to severe splits within his own party. A series of crises occurred, including legislative deadlocks, legislative dissolvement and restructuring, students' manifestations, and even a near-paralyzing transportation strike. The crises seem to be based on the pragmatic assessment by peoples in many walks of Ecuadorian life, that the rich are getting richer, the plight of the poor may by worsening, and an eclipse of the OPEC-fueled light of development is occurring.

As the petroleum boom created a new epoch of industrial wealth, strengthening tremendously the power of the state (e.g. Drekonja 1980), the interminable clash of contradictory principles also sparked an enlightened, publicly expressed, political ideology. During his first year in office Roldós announced policies aimed at a radical reorientation of the distribution of petroleum revenues and guaranteed human rights, including for the first time the right to vote and the right to literacy for *all* people (see *El Comercio*, 20 June 1980:A-1). Roldós not only promised that the winds of change would sweep coastal, sierran, and Amazonian Ecuador but also emphatically asserted his desire to see Ecuador's emphasis on liberation of humans from the bondage of the past and from the tyranny of the near present ramify throughout the hemisphere.

The clash of principles in political ideology to become public during the past year is that which the authors of this book have constantly uncovered and described. Moreover, the intellectual and analytical styles and positions taken by the authors of this work—which range from ritual revelation (Salomon) to structural Marxism (Taylor and Descola), and from "materialist" (Vickers, Macdonald) to "idealist" (Stutzman)—are replicated in the public analyses and positioning of Ecuadorian commentators. As the nation entered a phase of intensive public debate over its own essentialist and epochalist (Geertz 1973 [1971]:240–49) dynamic character, the president launched a program that emphasized the positive values of ethnically pluralist unity aimed at "demarginalization" of the nation's diverse peoples. Within this dimension of political ideology and praxis, ethnic mobilization became a key linkage between political-economic centralization and cultural, social, ethnic, and economic diversification. The promise of corporate power, and in some cases economic wherewithal, is now being offered to those involved in movements of ethnic surgency.

Roldós and Hurtado took office on Ecuador's independence day, 10 August 1979. During his inaugural address the president, in an unprecedented display of ethnic awareness, spoke for a brief period in Quichua.[3] He first stated forcefully, "We will not work in vain as in the year past; we will pull together." Then, after asking rhetorically whether he spoke for only the wealthy, only the literate, he answered, "No! I speak for all people who live in this country." And then he named these people: "those of the Oriente from whence the sun rises—Shuar, Waorani, Secoya, Siona, Cofán [he had already made it clear, by speaking in Quichua, that he included all peoples speaking that language in the Sierra and the Oriente]—to where it sets, the *occidente*," again naming first two groups of indigenous peoples there (Colorado and Cayapa), clearly including them in his list of Ecuadorians. Then, still speaking Quichua, he named the rest of the Ecuadorians to whom his message was addressed: "the thousands and thousands of people who live united within our mother land, with the white people, with the black people, with all, including those who come from distant countries" (*El Comercio*, 11 August 1979:A-1).

As Roldós continued to construct an administrative policy based on a plank of ethnic diversity and awareness, his vice-president began to speak publicly of a unified and central "cultural policy" reminiscent of that proclaimed by the earlier deposed nationalist military dictator, General Rodríguez Lara (see Whitten 1976; Stutzman in this volume, Chapter 2). This cultural policy focuses on *indomestizaje*, an ideology of ethnic amalgamation that stresses the rediscovery of "true" Ecuadorian man perceived as an original synthesis of pristine indigenous culture with transformed European ethos and world view. While the public, ideological stance of both Roldós and Hurtado challenges a doctrine of white supremacy, Roldós's position incorporates the *blanco* along with the *negro* into a nation of diversity wherein suffrage to all should be extended equally. Hurtado's position, seemingly in contrast with that of Roldós, perpetuates the deeper conflict between ethnic synthesis and ethnic pluralism.

Indomestizaje today reflects a genuine interest on the part of many urban and rural Ecuadorians to come to grips with a revitalized view of culture history that accepts not only the indigenous side of the *mestizo* as equal to the European but also the *Ecuadorian indigenous* (as opposed to Incaic-imperialist) contribution to ethnic amalgamation as a viable, national heritage. *Indomestizaje* omits the African side of the triangular paradigm (as discussed by García-Barrio and Schubert), and indigenous peoples themselves may be required to recognize that they have emerged from ancient cultural roots now claimed by a modern republic that has excluded their own participation. As such, native autonomy and cultural distinction are tied by nationalist ideology to political articulation within the centralizing nation-state.

Throughout Ecuador in 1979 and 1980 one encounters a surgency of pro-nationalist feeling, together with the sense that nationalization is still not working well. Some of the strongest statements made recently by indigenous leaders stress the sheer fact of continuing native existence, adaptability, intelligence, and inner power. Such leaders espouse an interest in their distinct culture history and in the cultural future of the modern nation. Roldós's statements today are striking human nerve bundles in many places, under many circumstances; the resulting cross-ethnic synapses seem to be generating new intercultural respect and awakening an interest in continuing differentiation in many areas. *Indomestizaje*, as a political ideology of cultural policy, seems to interfere with Roldós's vision of a diverse people drawn together in common national pursuits. It also interferes with the process of transcultural communication that such a cognitive drawing together generates.

At this time (October 1980) the policy and praxis promulgated by President Roldós would appear to be incompatible with the rhetoric and programmatic recommendations of Vice-President Hurtado. Although each deals with a concept of unity for Ecuador's peoples, their messages, when received, contradict one another. Roldós's vision is of a national unity forged in appreciation of genuine diversity, devoid of a cultural or ethnic "center"; the messages attributed by the media to Hurtado focus on the exclusionist dream of an all-inclusive *indomestizo*. The contradiction represented by the dual concepts of political ethnicity, within the praxis of ethnic pluralism and ethnic mobilization vis-à-vis nationalist consolidation, generates familiar surface tensions that ramify into all programs of planning for development within the new regime.

Whether or not my analysis of intrapolicy contradiction turns out to be correct, two facets of the new ideology of nationalist political-economic consolidation can be identified as *ethnic mobilization* and a *cultural policy of indomestizaje*. They are complemented by a third, *mystic commitment to bureaucratic service* (*El Comercio*, 3 June 1980:A-1).

Faced with overwhelming, first-hand evidence of developmentalist failure in Amazonian, sierran, and coastal Ecuador, proponents of right, left, and center political positions began, by mid-1978, to openly question and publicly challenge the heretofore nearly undisputed "good" bound up in the values expressed as "Democratic-Capitalist-Developmentalist-Progress." Arguments similar to that presented by Marcelo Naranjo (Chapter 3) were introduced and elaborated by social scientists and politicians of many political persuasions. By 1980 the slogan that "Ecuador will be the Brazil of the Pacific" changed to the president's dramatic message of the "atrophy of developmentalism" (*El Comercio*, 30 December 1979:A-1). Roldós called for a national transcendence of the oppressive barrier imposed by the programs of lethargic progress initiated and directed by his uniformed forebears. With no political, economic, or technological strategy available to move the nation from its recognized dependency on foreign exports and imported consumer goods, Roldós asked all employed Ecuadorians—especially those in the areas of education and public administration—to assume a countenance of dedicated, religious, near "mystic" commitment to their routine jobs. According to this position, revitalized commitment to administrative and educational service could psychically energize economic and political developmentalism, and facilitate the channeling of new developmental vitality into the redistribution of revenues to Ecuador's diverse peoples.

Lest such mystic commitment to bureaucratic service seem fanciful, one must only remember the web of sinecures throughout the developmental agencies in Ecuador (see Whitten, Chapter 4), as well as a reflected and reified ethnic/class hierarchy within such development agencies. By drawing on religious metaphors for intrabureaucratic service, Roldós seems bent on communicating directly with those who must implement policies, if any plan is to become transformed from ideological rhetoric to developmental program.

The rhetoric of sustained revitalization within the new regime is not confined to bureaucratic services; it also addresses a concept of economic, social, cultural, and ethnic margins and the positive forces to be released by the transcendence of such demarcated barriers (*El Comercio*, 23 December 1980:A-1). This *transcendence of marginality*, the fourth identifiable facet of political ideology within Roldós's party, relates the creative potential produced by centuries of peripherality to the creative potential inherent in centralized bureaucracy. Both center and periphery must together transcend the limits of oppression to effect a genuine developmentalism with true redistributive capacity.

In 1980 the very people discussed in the preceding chapters are being viewed increasingly not only as oppressed and marginalized but also as a cultural reservoir for centralized resurgence. This reservoir seems to be analogous to the multilayered heavy crude oil that is so terribly expensive to extract from its matrices of shale. Release of the creativity born of marginality, according to this ideological facet, cannot be accomplished by tapping the culture and producing a "gusher." Great expense and even novel technology are seen as prerequisites to empower cultural liberation.[4] For the first time in my experience in Ecuador, there are public pronouncements being made by strongly pro-nationalist spokesmen that there is something embedded in indigenous cultures, in black cultures, in *cholo* cultures—a residual, inchoate, potential wealth of creativity—that can help the very people forced to live at low economic levels, or in a situation of exclusion from political participation, to transcend their circumstances. In such rhetoric, there is more than an occasional pronouncement that the cultural knowledge that can help the "marginalized" survive, can also help the nation to transform itself and break the ties of dependency that marginalize the whole. Remember, here, I am discussing facets of *emerging nationalist ideology*; I am not developing a "theory of marginality."

The new revitalization of ethnic awareness and ethnic mobilization initiated by Roldós's insistence that the clash of ideas should *saltar la luz de la verdad* has, in some instances, sought to unite dedicated commitment to service in the central bureaucracies with a growing mystique of marginality. Tempting though it may be to view the ideological forces restructuring the national responses to acknowledged dependency as unique and internally generated, such ideology may also flow directly from western neocolonialism and contemporary dependence on modern neocolonial powers.

The fervor for bureaucratic reform and assistance offered to "bona fide ethnic movements" manifest by some Ecuadorian agencies over the past two years is matched by stepped-up assistance programs originating in the most industrial nations, including the United States, Canada, England, and Germany among the more prominent. Each organization, in turn, promulgates facets of ideological confrontation that are communicated to Ecuador's distinct peoples in various ways. People identified as bearers of "genuine" ethnic cultures by national and international agencies are more likely to come into sustained contact with programs initiated outside Ecuador than are peoples not so tagged or identified. As the nation strives ideologically to transcend dependency by stressing the creativity of marginality, those in so-called marginal positions could become dependent upon outside support to press their cases for quasi-independence within Ecuador's tightening political sovereignty and control of economic resources.

The crossing of thresholds, however, is nothing new to most Ecuadorians; novel solutions to unforeseen problems seem characteristic of many of the people described in this book. The commonly expressed, simplistic assertion that is now favored by many nationalist spokesmen that indigenous Ecuadorians are being influenced unduly by outside forces—and thereby losing the distinctive Ecuadorian character of their pristine or syncretic indigenous existence at the very moment of its emergence—is denied by recent events. For example, stress has long been placed on the segmental, nonhierarchical, egalitarian qualities of social organization of the indigenous peoples of the Oriente. Building upon the characteristic tropical forest features of these social orders, new federation formations, somewhat like that described in Chapter 21 by Ernesto Salazar and alluded to by Descola, Taylor, and Belzner, have emerged elsewhere in Amazonian Ecuador and in Esmeraldas province. In spite of the seemingly crucial need for operating capital, one such new organization recently refused economic help not only from the governmental agencies of Ecuador but from a prominent international "self-help" foundation as well.

We usually think of transcendence as an overcoming of thresholds imposed by constraints. But incentives, too, must be "overcome" if an organization is to map its own destiny. Incentives, like constraints, may be viewed as limens that define an organization's hierarchical and vertical position vis-à-vis other organizations. By transcending nearly overwhelming constraints, and by transcending new sets of incentives (e.g., large amounts of money for ecology-altering and po-litical economy–altering "projects"), indigenous peoples in the Ama-zonian provinces are currently generating a segmental structure of interfederation alliances bound by nonhierarchical and hierarchical linkages.

As North American, European, and Ecuadorian self-help and de-velopment agencies joust with one another over control of these in-dividual organizations, and lament the supposed lack of internal or-der within each, a larger unity born of segmental articulation is emerging. Internal segmentation of each identifiable surgent organi-zation (or "survival vehicle"—Adams 1981) combined with the new movement toward "confederation," creates a barrier against external control. Moreover, the increasing visibility of the new federations and their alliances—however internally segmented they may be (or appear to be according to sets of imposed criteria for "organization")—facilitates direct communication between federation leaders and the central administration or its major bureaucratic office holders. Devel-opment of agency brokerage institutions is somewhat curtailed, and native autonomy is at least partially maintained by the proliferation of native brokerage in this situation of escalating segmental articula-tion (or segmentation and rearticulation).

In the face of *real* ethnic mobilization, itself independent of but coterminous with a policy of its encouragement by the Roldós admin-istration, the planning arms of the central administrative bureaucracy are faced with some hard decisions. To respect cultural and ethnic diversity is one thing; to plan for it is quite another. While the former draws on enlightenment and transcultural enrichment, the latter can lead to apartheid-like policy or programs. For example, a recent plan discussed publicly by the Ecuadorian Instituto Nacional para la Co-lonización de la Región Amazónica Ecuatoriana (INCRAE) desig-nated indigenous territories within each of the four provinces of the Oriente. The plan included regulations that would restrict indige-nous peoples to allotted lands within culturally reserved territories.

Given the segmental nature of indigenous organizations, and their dependence, in part, on cross-territorial linkages through marriage supported by bilingualism, such an "enlightened" policy could be as destructive of native autonomy as that of large-scale colonization into indigenous territory.

Thus far the segmental nature of nationalist bureaucracy itself has kept such programs from becoming established, while at the same time chipping away at ethnic unity by presenting a myriad of access channels for articulation to sources of national growth. One of the most fascinating aspects of this process of bureaucratic segmentation face to face with the segmented unity of ethnic surgency is the way by which ideologically grounded metaphoric "leaps" can be made by actors in one arena to a situation existing in another.

For example, oppositions in the national system abound; they are communicated day by day through the press, across the airwaves, and increasingly via television. One prominent opposition is seen as Ecuadorian unity versus internal pluralism; another is Ecuadorian sovereignty in the face of adjacent territorial claims; a third is Ecuadorian autonomy versus dependency on external capital, technology, and models for development. Within the indigenous system of the Oriente, to continue to draw our illustrations from this focal zone of nationalist "concern," clearcut sets of oppositions exist within and among identifiable ethnic groups (Canelos Quichua, Quijos Quichua, Achuar, Shuar, Waorani, Cofán, Siona-Secoya) together with cross-cutting alliances among segments of groups formed by clans (or kindreds) or segments of recognizable kin groupings. Another indigenous oppositional process is that of egalitarianism versus hierarchy, and a fifth is that of external adjudication versus internal resolution of disputes. Each of these sets of oppositions is expressed symbolically as an allusive paradigm of cultural perseverance forged increasingly into ideologies, on the one hand, and by quite concrete, pragmatic, environmental management programs in radical contrast to ones promulgated by developers, on the other. These systems of oppositions provide adaptational templates, the dialectical deployment of which continuously generate novel solutions to emergent constraints and incentives. Pragmatic and symbolic polarization, social oppositions, cultural antagonisms, and ideological clashes cannot be understood in terms of sheer surface manifestations, as most of the analyses in this book demonstrate. For example, much of the contemporary rhetoric about "indigenous versus national" sets of clashes must be taken to be no more—but certainly no less—than a collective national and indigenous confrontational exegesis for integrated sets of deeper conflicts and contradictions that have existed for centuries.

It is at this point that we must return to the premises of critical anthropology that I raised in the Introduction and that many authors have drawn upon to frame their analytical contributions (Whitten pp. 22-23). Critical anthropology favors ethnography as a theory-generative endeavor and takes its *forte* to be the empirical description—a thick one, of course (see Geertz 1973:3–30)—of aspects having relevance for a nation-state and its subject peoples, as well as an ability to uncover and analyze unrecognized relationships that undergird enduring structures and adaptive versatilities. Such holism leads critical anthropology to the often antagonistic arena where debate over "the consequences of political-economic control over people's lifestyles, lifeways, and life chances" generates pervasive salience. But critical anthropology may treat such debate itself as an interpretable, penetrable exegesis of an oppositional process, not as a one-dimensional polarity within which one must take sides. To extol virtues of critical analysis rather than to champion immediate advocacy is not to assert that critical anthropology is "value free," for it surely is not. As stated in Chapter 1 (p. 23):

> . . . it regards centralized control over either cultural variety or cultural homogenization as an infringement upon human freedom. [It] . . . accepts, admires, and seeks to illuminate the inner *integrity of a cultural system*—the *structure*—without assuming that it is "functioning on its own," without assuming "retention" from past systems, without assuming "isolation" from larger environing systems, and without assuming "marginality" to a larger system. It accepts *cultural adaptation* without assuming accommodative or assimilationist tendencies, and it accepts *cultural pluralism* without assuming any need for centralized imposition of segmental order . . . it assumes that *cultural transformation* . . . may take place at any level of any system at any time. . . . Finally, it assumes that cultural transformation and *social reproduction* must be considered within a unified frame of reference.

A key to the analytic power of critical anthropology lies in the notion of a universal, dynamic, reality-constructive process utilized by all peoples situated, however variously, in multiple social and ethnic groupings, confined in myriad ways by ethnic, social, racial, or political stereotyping, "strung together" by transacted bonds that ramify through and across aggregates, groups, and categories, and "fractured" by inevitable breaches, rifts, retaliations, and other processes of social differentiation. Peoples everywhere not only "react" to exigencies in their material, social, and spiritual environments; they forever draw things together by relating the known to the unknown. Iconic and arbitrary isomorphisms—imperfect though they will inevitably be—among related and unrelated domains of experience are universally developed into communicable paradigms (e.g. Turner 1974, Landsberg 1980). The resulting *correspondence structures*—keys to both radical adaptability and structural perseverance, to nationalist consolidation and ethnic surgency—provide what Clifford Geertz (1966, 1973:93–94) calls "models of" reality. Before pursuing this line of reasoning in contemporary Ecuador, let me try to make clear why the concept of *universality* of correspondence structuring is so vital (see, for background, Lévi-Strauss 1966, Firth 1973, Geertz 1973, Leach 1976, Sperber 1975, Moore and Myerhoff 1977).

Anthropology has long given at least lip service to a human universal called "psychic unity." By the use of this concept we affirm the powerful assertion, grounded in extensive research, that peoples everywhere have the same abilities to comprehend the universe, through the vehicle of their own languages. Psychic unity as an anthropological "doctrine" was a motivating intellectual force in combating racism, imperialism, and oppression based upon biological evolutionism applied to "progress toward civilization." To assert the mere ability, however, is not enough; it leaves us with a rash of neoracisms born of neocolonial mentality. In one imperialist mode, it may be argued that people must be "taught" the nature of their own lifeways, including the system of oppression within which they are embedded. In the alter imperialist mode, it may be argued that people must be "taught" to become members of the State, to "renounce" their distinctive lifeways.

The creative synthesis between these neocolonial antitheses is to teach peoples how to become citizens while at the same time teaching them to restore their own lifeways. Failing to understand the universality of correspondence structur*ing*, neocolonial thesis and antithesis and the enlightened synthesis all seek to control peoples' models of reality. By so doing, neocolonial ideologies, even in their enlightened manifestations, seek to deprive humanity of its fundamental unity in diversity. This unity lies in the perpetuative dynamic wherein peoples themselves are seen as forever generating "models of" reality.

If, as contemporary ethnography in its critical dimensions makes clear, all human groupings are equally capable of generating correspondence structures within their own languages (and by use of the vehicle of other languages, even in pidgin or creole forms, as well), then it becomes imperative to understand that interpretation of a situation leading to "comprehension" is not something that must be learned over long periods of time. Rather, some form of comprehension—however frustratingly exotic or "wildly wrong" the set of correspondences framing it may appear to one from a different cultural or contextual synthesis—should be near-*instantaneous*. If we consider for a moment the revelatory nature of the North Quito *yumbada* discussed by Salomon in Chapter 5, my meaning should be clear. Where power is felt, I submit, human groupings have mechanisms for revealing its nature and for transmitting its revealed form, as well as symbolic mechanisms for transcendence of the barriers thereby imposed. In settings of radical change human groupings structure their response to altering (and alternating) fields of force and reflexively relate, reveal, and encode their dynamic "selfhood" to the thresholds and boundaries that flourish.

Let us now consider briefly correspondence structuring in Ecuador. Materials in this book constantly demonstrate that Ecuadorians in all walks of life have a "model of" the Waorani, a "model of" blackness, a "model of" *blanco-indio* and *blanco-negro* asymmetry. Take the Waorani as an exemplar here. Ecuadorian elites and bureaucrats have a fairly "clear" (if totally erroneous) perspective of these native peoples, one that includes their alleged ferocity, their alleged eating of raw meat, their alleged absence of horticultural skills, their alleged matriarchy, and the alleged inevitability of their imminent disappearance in the face of "modernization" or "civilization." The Canelos Quichua and Quijos Quichua, too, have models of these people, that vary considerably in terms of territory, exchange relations, and the like. To understand one of the jungle Quichua models of "*aucaness*," or to comprehend the model of "being savage" promulgated by the director of IERAC or INCRAE, it is essential to come to grips with the deeper set of mutually reinforcing, sometimes reciprocal, *oppositions* that may give rise to *both* the jungle Quichua "models of" *and* the nationalist "models of" these "Auca" peoples. The Waorani, too, have "models of" the *cohouri* (non-Waorani) that are built reflexively out of known domains and immediate experience, as Yost demonstrates. To render such models in terms of a diffusionist dribble of traits or an acculturative flow of traits, or to posit evolutionary stages in model construction as necessary to Waorani adaptability, is to miss the fundamental point of their own creative, constructive endeavor.

The jungle Quichua models of the Waorani generally stress the *auca* character of non-Quichua speakers that begins with the non-Andean feature, "to be of" the tropical forest (*sacha manda*). Here *auca*ness is a *shared feature* of self-assertive adaptability to a known habitat. "Auca" becomes mildly pejorative in Quichua reflexively vis-à-vis territoriality when jungle Quichua peoples speak of "Auca territory," *auca partimanda*. Runa then qualify the "Auca" designation, if the actual inhabitants are well known, using another ethnic term acceptable to those living there if hostilities have not recently erupted. But vis-à-vis nationals such as church personnel or development officers, jungle Quichua differentiate themselves completely from *auca*ness, encoding national sets of oppositions as they "play with" (*pugllana, pugllangahua*) an alter paradigm. In such play, ideas coalesce into a cross-ethnic, communicable, "external template" that represents a "model of" a people so as to "fit them," however stereotypically, into a larger system of ideas that we call *ideology*. Geertz's (1973 [1964]:219) statement about ideology is an apt one with regard to recent developments in Ecuador: "It is when neither a society's most general cultural orientations nor its most down-to-earth 'pragmatic' ones suffice any longer to provide an adequate image of political process that ideologies begin to become crucial as sources of sociopolitical meanings and attitudes."

Let us see if we can "read" ideological rhetoric as a text. To do so, we need a few orienting concepts drawn from philosophy and literary analysis (Pepper 1942; Burke 1954, 1966; Black 1962; Boyd 1977). The concepts are having a sort of "run" these days in anthropology (e.g. Fernandez 1969, 1974, 1977; Leach 1976; Sapir 1977; Sapir and Crocker 1977), perhaps because they allow us to cut through our own stereotypic viewpoints to achieve critical insights into rapid cross-cultural and cross-ethnic communications during periods of radical change. In such settings peoples' thoughts seem to jump, leap, and rebound in *consistent* ways. So, let us take our analytical mode from writers who themselves seek to explain mental leaping and jumping in a consistent manner. Writing of the highly improbable "relationship" between squashes and human sexual relations, Norrman and Haarbert (1980:2) define a couple of key notions quite clearly: ". . . to gain a fuller understanding of the nature and function of one textual element one can study either its relation to the other elements, and particularly the neighboring ones, in the same text (its syntagmatic relations), or its relation to elements that are the same, or similar, or *likely to occur in a corresponding position* in other texts (its *paradigmatic* relations)" (emphasis added; see also Leach 1976, Sapir and Crocker 1977).

An Ecuadorian national model of consistent and enduring syntagmatic associations can be presented as a set of asymmetric contrasts, as follows:

national	indigenous (or black)
developmental	resistant
progressive	backward
white	Indian (or black)
urban	jungle (*not* "rural," in Ecuador. To be rural is to be oriented *toward* urban. Jungle is the antithesis of urban; it is to be oriented away from the urban.)
Christian	heathen
hierarchical	egalitarian
controlled	free
civilized	savage
educated and adultlike	ignorant and childlike
bureaucratic	segmental
dependent on development	independent of development
light	dark

The oppositions listed above constitute mutually reinforcing elements in syntagmatic chains. Each column is bound by metonymy, which simply means here that one expects the associations to be linked to one another in a "consistent" way. The statement "Civilized people are educated, they are national, and they are white, not Indian," illustrates such consistency. To move from left to right or right to left in a row is to initiate a process leading to paradigmatic patterning, which, in turn, provides the cognitive mechanisms for heightened status awareness ("to be black is offensive") and also for symbolic inversions, reversals, and various complex associations ("I am a Quito [urban] Runa [Indian]").

The above list of paired oppositions itself cannot constitute a paradigm, for the contrast sets merely reflect one another asymmetrically and "obey" rules of consistency that "order" them. These linked, contrasting, paired metonymic chains provide the *orienting constructs* (e.g. Ortner 1973) upon which metaphoric predication works. To understand ethnicity and cultural transformation in contemporary Ecuador, three features of the above contrast sets must be understood. First, those *in control of resources* reinforce the asymmetry in the contrast sets, driving a wider and wider wedge between those groups, classes, categories, or aggregates of people tagged as representative remnants of right-column qualities, and the other Ecuadorians, often seen as marginal to the qualities listed in the left column, and regarded as "held back" by the persistence of indigenous and black traits. Second, those *in control of resources* seek to construct "models *for*" (hereafter "*plans for*") social reality. Such models are actual blueprints for "development" of social groupings, the specifications of which are to be read just as one would read plans for bridge building. But where "models of" social reality are universal, "*plans for*" *social reality generally emanate directly from the power structure of the expansionist state.* The third factor in understanding the "models of" Ecuadorian reality, beyond those of control and "plans for," is that of *reflexivity in the oppositional process.*

Let us return to the jungle Quichua and nationalist development. To understand paradigmatic structuring by national developers and by Runa, Shuar, or Achuar in Canelos Quichua territory, it is necessary to first understand the *pairing of national oppositions vis-à-vis indigenous oppositions.* Some of the specific public national oppositions (left, below) that are metaphorically shaped by indigenous people predicating them upon their own partially structured and partially inchoate oppositions (right, below) may be used by nationals and by indigenous peoples to exacerbate and adjudicate internal conflicts within specific indigenous territories. Some of the indigenous oppositions (right, below) are also alluded to by nationals making metaphoric leaps from specific, structured, publicly stereotyped oppositions (left, below), when they seek to "understand" (that is, construct "models of") and control (construct "plans for") indigenous society. Such society is usually viewed by nationals in terms of ramifying conflict seen as preventing indigenous integration not only into the nation-state but also into the genuine emergence of indigenous "self-awareness" as a distinct cultural segment of a plural nation.

National Oppositions	*Indigenous Oppositions*
Ecuadorian national unity/ Ecuadorian ethnic diversity	indigenous/non-indigenous
sovereignty/territorial loss	civilized indigenous or national indigenous/savage indigenous
dependency/autonomy	language group A/language group B
OPEC wealth/national poverty	ethnic group A/ethnic group B
society of classes/dual society	alliance A/alliance B
standardized development/ maintenance of uniqueness	clan A/clan B
Andean-coastal opposition/ Amazonian synthesis	equality/hierarchy
centralized power/regional power and autonomy	ordinary person/shaman
hierarchy based on Brazilian model/egalitarianism cutting across hierarchy	federated/nonfederated
Oriente as synthesizer/ Oriente as marginal	dependency on national development/access to resources beyond national control

Obviously, the national oppositions as portrayed in the left column do not (and cannot) pair logically with those listed in the right column. Nonetheless, people who receive even glimmers of these distinct sets of oppositions constantly construct "symbolic bundles" of metaphoric-metonymic correspondences based upon sets of oppositions drawn from both columns. While the left column set remains relatively invariant throughout the nation, the right column sets vary tremendously. Analogic leaps of one sort or another are facilitated by the syntagmatic chains sketched on p. 788 above. Even when absurd, such models for reality may spark powerful, "consciousness-raising," reflective reconsiderations of the nature of society itself.

For a local example, very familiar to me, a Runa man may discuss the sets in the left column with a mixed Runa-Achuar group drinking in a Puyo saloon on Sunday morning. Every member of the drinking group is thinking about previous Achuar-Runa hostilities, exchange of shaman power, and the cross-cutting ties of Runa-Achuar inter-marriage. Every member is at the same time "practicing" nationalist urban acceptable behavior, and using the practice session to gloss over past antagonisms while constructing new ideological motiva-tions for exchange and alliance. At another table, in the same saloon, a mixed Ecuadorian–North American–British group discusses surface tensions reflecting the oppositions in the right column, each striving toward a demonstration of new sensitivity to the issues of indigenous persistence and the "problems" remaining if native peoples are to enter the mainstream of Ecuadorian life but preserve their essential, indigenous character. In the process of the latter discussion, Puyo residents themselves may set forth a new opposition, that of *oriental* (of the Amazonian territory) versus *nacional* (of the nation as sierran-coastal synthesis) and construct their own awakening of a novel right column–left column paradigm by proclaiming the province of Pas-taza's capital to be neither sierran-coastal nor indigenous. In such a paradigm Pastaza is national but *of* the Oriente. Oriente is no longer synthesis of Coast-Sierra but a new, surgent antithesis to each. The Oriente itself here emerges as a pluralized synthesis of strong indige-nous and strong frontiersman characteristics, the pluralism surgent in terms of regional "awareness."

The "national oppositions" available for paradigmatic construction are regularly set forth in the press, in popular magazines, over the radio, and in scholarly debate. The indigenous oppositions them-selves emerge in contexts ranging from shamanic performance to in-digenous-nonindigenous meetings and are communicated back and forth from indigenous to national settings. Each set, *qua* set, is seen in many contexts as confounding, obfuscating, or confusing the alter set. This is a process of reproduction of oppositions with symbolic and pragmatic dimensions. Through reproduction, coherence is gen-erated in settings of radical change. The coherence is pluralist in char-acter, but the pluralism allows for many creative metaphoric-meto-nymic symbolic bundles that define new boundaries while revealing their ideologically spurious nature.

We have now worked our way from the Quiteño pinnacle of Ecua-dorian power structure and the ideology emanating from it to a Puyo saloon and the paradigmatic imagery generated there. Four salient facets of new political ideology and praxis that flow downward from national policy include *ethnic mobilization,* a *cultural policy of indomes-tizaje,* a *mystic commitment to bureaucratic service,* and a *transcendence of marginality.* Further down the power pyramid—at the hinge, so to speak, between urbanized bureaucratic control and the forest of indigenous dissidence (in Puyo, capital of Pastaza province where the national pyramid is replicated in microcosm)—we have applied criteria of critical anthropology to identify several key processes. These have been discussed in terms of *power* (including control of resources and control of social constructs of oppositional asymmetry), *correspondence structuring,* and *opposition structuring.* The logical structure of nationalist control, when revealed in a system of ethnic surgency, appears culturally as a syncretism. We have tried to demonstrate that oppositional sets are constructed syntagmatically and paradigmatically into creative and powerful syncretisms, the bases for which have long existed. The syncretic reflexivity inherent in the oppositional process reveals structural asymmetries to those feeling the effects of control. Revealed structural asymmetry, then, generates aesthetic, ethical, moral, or pragmatic subversion of the elegant formation of any given paradigm based upon the division of human beings into superior and inferior categories, classes, sets, or aggregates.

   With the growth of the nation-state, diverse peoples have tended toward centralization and a oneness of common purpose, while at the same time tending toward diversity and fragmentation (e.g. Geertz 1973 [1963, 1964, 1966, 1971]; Young 1976; Adams 1975, 1977, 1981; Wolfe 1979; Wolf 1979). There is no reason whatsoever to nourish the belief that this phenomenon is in any way paradoxical, contradictory, or representative of a strange, unusual, or exceptional human condition. It is "a historical process as concrete as industrialization and as tangible as war" (Geertz 1973 [1971]:243). The papers presented in this book, by and large, illustrate the absurdity of treating diversity and uniformity as analytical opposites. To do so is to invoke a myopic and unidimensional nationalist ideological paradigm of cultural standardization in the process of political-economic centralization that much modern ethnography—bolstered by the flow of world events—emphatically denies. It is to misunderstand the fact that both nationalism and ethnicity have essentialist and epochalist dimensions and that correspondence structuring in the face of increasing, decreasing, or oscillating power inevitably reveals a paradigm of oppression while motivating a "subversive" antithesis. Such constructions and revelations may imperfectly cloak or mask "reality," of course. But the path to humanistic or scientific understanding does not lie in raising the question as to the exact relationship between ideology and "reality." Rather, it lies in the critical appraisal of the ebb and flow of dialectical and transactional processes wherein cultural transformation and social reproduction of oppositions may be understood within a unified frame of reference.

The impulse to dichotomize the phenomena of ethnic/cultural diversity and political-economic centralization as separable spheres of analysis is amplified not only by nationalist rhetoric but by social scientific folly. Social scientific folly exists, for example, when something called "integrationist theory" is pitted against "pluralist theory" in situations such as the Ecuadorian one. The banal hypothesis that the nation must be tending more toward integration *or* toward pluralism at a given time is set forth within each theory, and then "tested" to see which side wins the academic debate over surface manifestations and their sophisticated measurements.

Critical anthropology's endeavors to break through such masks of objectivity are tied to its ability to transcend the paradox of its own peculiar existence. As Marshall Sahlins (1977:14) puts it, ". . . the conflict between the symbolic and the pragmatic is a kind of original, founding contradiction, reproducing itself across all the other oppositions that have carried anthropology from one theoretical moment to the next" (see also Sahlins 1976:55). The political rhetoric and the social scientific folly are best considered as surface manifestations of a series of impulses stemming from the "founding contradiction" of western epistemology applied to society. Bureaucratic planners, great *caudillos*, and critical analysts of modern nations alike seek to subvert this polarity. Unfortunately, however, its amplification is enhanced by the even more embedded contradiction, also described by Sahlins (1977:27), where "the oppositions on each side of the proportion are realized historically by their engagement with distinctions on the other side."

To say *plus ça change, plus c'est la même chose* may be to utter a platitude here, but it nonetheless conveys a sense of the new transformation of Ecuadorian stability born of segmental oscillation in a system of increasingly centralized bureaucratic control. Intercultural systems (Drummond 1980) within an increasingly pyramidal power structure interdigitate in novel ways. As a monolithic form of government becomes ever stronger, the putative "subversions" (or multivocalic protests) of the culturally and ethnically distinct are nourished as they are bounded, and they diversify as they draw closer together. In such situations one expects "prophetic breaks" to occur with greater and greater frequency ". . . when seemingly fundamental social principles lose their former efficacy, their capacity to operate as axioms for social behavior, and new modes of social organization emerge, at first to transect and, later, to replace traditional ones"

(Turner 1974:248). Roldós's rise to democratic power, and his endeavor to enfranchise all of Ecuador's peoples, could well be seen structurally as a "prophetic break" itself forecast by the continuous replication of systems of opposition. The forecast cannot, however, tell us whether charismatic leadership will develop in the break; nor can it tell us who, if anyone, will emerge with a communicable, prophetic paradigm.

Ecuador today is, to use the phrase of Hernán Crespo Toral in the Foreword to this work, "truly unique." But the themes and transformations that constitute its structure emerge as "familiar" to Andeanists, South Americanists, Latin Americanists, analysts of Third World nations, or—if one reflects on them at length—to students of any nation-state in the contemporary world. In its uniqueness Ecuador is also characteristic of the processes of "world society." No unidimensional "integrationist versus pluralist" or "idealist versus materialist" stultifying polarity can help to understand these processes. Unidimensional analytic strength embedded in such fashionable academic polarities leads to sophisticated confusion. Reality must be faced as it exists in modern Ecuador, as part of "today's world," at surface, middle-range, and deep levels. By studying the founding polarities of contemporary nations in depth and in breadth, anthropology could pass over its *own* constraining limens and contribute critically to the breaking of neocolonial mentality. Such analytical rupture is crucial to our understanding of infrastructural, social structural, and ideological transformation in contemporary nations.

The deep, longitudinal study of ethnicity and cultural transformation in modern Ecuador has led many of us in this book to develop our critical powers of analysis by describing remarkable continuities and transformations within a unified national frame of reference that itself is challenged continuously by an equally unified process of ethnic perseverance.

On 24 May 1981 — Ecuador's Independence Day — President Jaime Roldós Aguilera, his wife, Martha Bucarám de Roldós, members of his cabinet, and his aides lost their lives in a plane crash in the southern part of the country. The same day, Osvaldo Hurtado assumed the office of the presidency. Roldós's last public words, delivered in a speech in Quito an hour before he boarded the military plane for his ill-fated trip to Loja, were: ". . . *Ecuador amazónica desde siempre y hasta siempre . . . ¡Viva la Patria!* (El Comercio, 31 May 1981:A2). On 1 June, the National Chamber of Representatives elected the late president's brother, León Roldós Aguilera, to serve as vice-president of Ecuador.

NOTES

Acknowledgments: In preparing this Afterword I am consciously influenced by the writings of Richard N. Adams, James W. Fernandez, Clifford Geertz, John Gulick, the late John J. Honigmann, and Victor Turner in anthropology, and by Karl Marx and Max Weber for critical social thought and action-oriented analysis, respectively. The glue that binds the theories and perspectives that motivate this interpretative analysis is the insistence on the concrete, empirical nature of the flow of human events, together with an analytical modality capable of treating human beings and their aggregations as the bearers and creators of cultural systems.

I am indebted to Mary-Elizabeth B. M. Reeve for her assistance during the writing of this Afterword, and to Sibby Whitten, Janet Dougherty, Edward M. Bruner, John Stewart, Ronald Stutzman and Jane Adams for their critical commentary on various drafts. Discussions with Marcelo F. Naranjo and María Isabel Silva helped clarify some of my own inchoate thoughts with regard to one facet of nationalist ideology in the new administration. Sibby Whitten contributed greatly to my reconsideration of the "concrete" in Ecuadorian rhetoric both during the summer of 1980 and while I worked on this Afterword. All faults in analysis and failures to communicate are mine.

1. *El Comercio,* 27 Jan. 1979:A-1, A-15. The context of this statement lies in Roldós's need to defend himself against an attack from the renowned populist Asad Bucaram, who helped Roldós get elected initially (see the diagrams on pp. 8 and 9 of the Introduction, and the discussion of *caudillismo* there to help understand this constant threat of attack from the politically close, and thereby to ally with the politically distant), while at the same time defend the ideology that would allow such attack to escalate.

2. *El Comercio,* 25 Apr. 1980:A-1. Vice-President Hurtado made this statement during the ceremony issuing the first three volumes of the "Pendoneros" series of books about Ecuador, published by the Instituto Otavaleño de Antropología with a subsidy from the Banco Central del Ecuador. A segment of the Introduction to this book, together with Chapters 2 through 5, is now in press for publication as a separate volume in this series. The fact that our essays in the vein of critical anthropology are being published in this series underscores the sincere praxis of the *choque de las ideas* promulgated by the Roldós administration, and given concrete form through such organizations as the Museos del Banco Central and the Instituto Otavaleño de Antropología.

3. Here is the relevant portion of the text (*El Comercio,* 11 Aug. 1979:A-16):

Kunan punchaka, mana pushaita japinchik. Kunanka, tukui runakuna pushaita japinchikmi. Uakin millai runakunamanta pushaita japishpa, tukui makipura imatapish rurashpa kausakrinchikmi.

Kunanka, pikunaman rimani? Mishukunamalla? Iachakkunamanlla? Mana. Nukaka, tukui kai llaktapi kausak runakunamanmi rimani. Inti iluksina llaktapi kausak runakunaman: shuara, uaukrani, sikiua, siuna, kuphanman, tukui urkupi kausak runakunaman; intichinkana llaktapi runakunaman: puka, kaiapaman; tukui kastillakunaman; tukui uaranak uaranka runakuna nukanchik Mama llaktapi kausakukkunaman; jurak runakunaman, iana runakunaman, karu llaktamanta shamushka runakunamanpish.

4. The exhibition entitled "Arte y Marginalidad" that opened in Quito at the new Museo de Artesanías on 12 Oct. 1980 is but one illustration of the process to which I refer.

REFERENCES CITED

Adams, Richard N.
  1975 *Energy and Structure: A Theory of Social Power.* Austin: University of Texas Press.
  1977 Power in Human Societies: A Synthesis. In Raymond D. Fogelson and Richard N. Adams, eds., *The Anthropology of Power.* New York: Academic Press, 387–410.
  1981 The Dynamics of Societal Diversity: Notes from Nicaragua for a Sociology of Survival. *American Ethnologist* 8 (1):1–20.
Black, Max
  1962 *Models and Metaphors.* Ithaca, N.Y.: Cornell University Press.
Boyd, Richard
  1977 Theory Constitutive Metaphors. Paper presented at the Conference on Metaphor and Thought, September, University of Illinois, Urbana.
Burke, Kenneth
  1954 *Permanence and Change: An Anatomy of Purpose.* 2d ed. Los Altos, Calif.: Hermes Publications. (Originally New York: New Republic, 1935.)
  1966 *Language as Symbolic Action.* Berkeley: University of California Press.
Drekonja, Gerhard
  1980 Ecuador: How to Handle the Banana Republic Turned Oil State. *Boletín de Estudios Latinoamericanos y del Caribe* 28 (June):77–94.
Drummond, Lee
  1980 The Cultural Continuum: A Theory of Intersystems. *Man* (n.s.) 15 (2):352–74.
Fernandez, James W.
  1969 *Microcosmogony and Modernization in African Religious Movements.* Montreal: McGill University Centre for Developing Area Studies, Occasional Paper 3.
  1974 The Mission of Metaphor in Expressive Culture. *Current Anthropology* 15 (2):119–45.
  1977 The Performance of Ritual Metaphors. In J. David Sapir and J. Christopher Crocker, eds., *The Social Use of Metaphor.* Philadelphia: University of Pennsylvania Press, pp. 100–131.
Firth, Raymond
  1973 *Symbols: Public and Private.* Ithaca, N.Y.: Cornell University Press.
Geertz, Clifford
  1963 The Integrative Revolution: Primordial Sentiments and Civil Politics in the New States. In Clifford Geertz, ed., *Old Societies and New States.* New York: Free Press, pp. 105–57.
  1964 Ideology as a Cultural System. In David Apter, ed., *Ideology and Discontent.* New York: Free Press, pp. 47–56.
  1966 Religion as a Cultural System. In Michael Banton, ed., *Anthropological Approaches to the Study of Religion.* London: Tavistock, pp. 1–46.
  1971 After the Revolution: The Fate of Nationalism in the New States. In Bernard Barber and Alex Inkeles, eds., *Stability and Social Change.* Boston: Little, Brown, pp. 357–76.
  1973 *The Interpretation of Cultures.* New York: Basic Books.
Landsberg, Marge E.
  1980 The Icon in Semiotic Theory. *Current Anthropology* 21 (2):93–95.

Leach, Edmund R.
   1976   *Culture and Communication: The Logic by which Symbols are Connected.*
          New York: Cambridge University Press.
Lévi-Strauss, Claude
   1966   *The Savage Mind.* Chicago: University of Chicago Press. (Original
          French version, Paris: Plon, 1962.)
Norrman, Ralf, and Jon Haarbert
   1980   *Nature and Language: A Semiotic Study of Cucurbits in Literature.* Lon-
          don: Routledge and Kegan Paul.
Moore, Sally Falk, and Barbara G. Myerhoff, eds.
   1977   *Secular Ritual.* Amsterdam: Van Gorcum, Assen.
Ortner, Sherry
   1973   On Key Symbols. *American Anthropologist* 75:1338–46.
Pepper, Stephen
   1942   *World Hypothesis: A Study in Evidence.* Berkeley: University of Califor-
          nia Press.
Sahlins, Marshall
   1976   *Culture and Practical Reason.* Chicago: University of Chicago Press.
   1977   The State of the Art in Social/Cultural Anthropology: Search for an
          Object. In Anthony F. C. Wallace et al., eds., *Perspectives on Anthro-
          pology 1976.* Washington, D.C.: American Anthropological Associa-
          tion, Special Publication 10, pp. 14–32.
Sapir, J. David
   1977   The Anatomy of Metaphor. In J. David Sapir and J. Christopher
          Crocker, eds., *The Social Use of Metaphor.* Philadelphia: University of
          Pennsylvania Press, pp. 3–32.
Sapir, J. David, and J. Christopher·Crocker, eds.
   1977   *The Social Use of Metaphor.* Philadelphia: University of Pennsylvania
          Press.
Sperber, Dan
   1975   *Rethinking Symbolism.* Cambridge: Cambridge University Press.
Turner, Victor
   1974   *Dramas, Fields, and Metaphors: Symbolic Action in Human Society.* Ith-
          aca, N.Y.: Cornell University Press.
Whitten, Norman E., Jr. (with the assistance of Marcelo F. Naranjo, Marcelo
          Santi Simbaña, and Dorothea S. Whitten)
   1976   *Sacha Runa: Ethnicity and Adaptation of Ecuadorian Jungle Quichua.* Ur-
          bana: University of Illinois Press.
Wolf, Eric R.
   1967   *Peasant Wars in the 20th Century.* New York: Harper & Row.
   1979   Convergence and Differentiation in World Capitalism. Paper pre-
          sented at 78th Meeting of the American Anthropological Associa-
          tion, Plenary Session: The Emergence of a Global Society, Cincin-
          nati.
Wolfe, Alvin W.
   1979   Introduction. Paper presented at 78th Meeting of the American An-
          thropological Association, Plenary Session: The Emergence of a
          Global Society, Cincinnati.
Young, Crawford
   1976   *The Politics of Cultural Pluralism.* Madison: University of Wisconsin
          Press.

Index

Notes on Contributors

LINDA SMITH BELOTE and JIM BELOTE teach in the Social Sciences Department of Michigan Technological University, Houghton. They have co-authored several articles on Saraguro lifeways.

WILLIAM BELZNER is a graduate student in anthropology at the University of Illinois, Urbana, currently completing research among the Shuar, Achuar, and Canelos Quichua.

RAY BROMLEY, who teaches in the Centre for Development Studies at the University College of Swansea, University of Wales, is currently visiting professor at Syracuse University. Among his numerous publications are *Development and Planning in Ecuador* (1977) and *Casual Work and Poverty in Third World Cities* (edited, with Chris Gerry, 1979).

LESLIE A. BROWNRIGG is president of AMARU IV, Washington, D.C. She has published several articles on Ecuadorian cultures and processes of development.

JOSEPH B. CASAGRANDE is professor of anthropology and director of the Center for International Comparative Studies at the University of Illinois, Urbana. In addition to his edited books, *Some Uses of Anthropology* (with Thomas Gladwin, 1956) and *In the Company of Man* (1960), his publications include various articles and chapters on Ecuadorian society.

MURIEL CRESPI is affiliated with the Department of Anthropology, Brown University. Her interests in Ecuadorian hacienda and community structure and change have led to several articles.

HERNÁN CRESPO TORAL is director of the National Institute of Anthropology and History and of the Museums of the Central Bank of Ecuador, Quito.

PHILIPPE DESCOLA is affiliated with the Ecole des Hautes Etudes en Sciences Sociales, Paris, where he lectures on economic anthropology. He is currently completing his doctoral dissertation on Achuar economy and social structure.

J. PETER EKSTROM is associate professor of anthropology at Southwestern at Memphis. Research on colonization was preceded by community development work in the Sierra and research in the Oriente.

KATHLEEN FINE is a graduate student at the University of Illinois, Urbana, and is currently completing field research on black-Indian ethnic relations in the Quito area.

NIELS FOCK is professor of anthropology at the University of Copenhagen, Denmark. He has produced monographs and articles on diverse Amazonian and Andean peoples.

CONSTANCE GARCÍA-BARRIO teaches at Albright College, in Reading, Pa. She has published several articles on blacks in the history and literature of Spanish America.

THEODORE MACDONALD, JR., is project director for Cultural Survival, and is a postdoctoral fellow at Harvard University. He has recently edited *Amazonia: Extinction or Survival?* (in press for publication in 1982).

DEWIGHT R. MIDDLETON is associate professor of anthropology at the State University of New York, College at Oswego. He has authored several articles based on his coastal Ecuadorian research.

BLANCA MURATORIO teaches in the Department of Anthropology and Sociology at the University of British Columbia, Vancouver. Her research on indigenous peasants in relation to capitalism has led to new research among other indigenous peoples of Ecuador's eastern and western rainforests.

MARCELO F. NARANJO is research associate in anthropology at the University of Illinois, Urbana, and professor of anthropology at the Catholic University of Ecuador, Quito. He is editor (with José Pereira V. and Norman E. Whitten, Jr.) of *Temas sobre la Continuidad y Adaptación Cultural Ecuatoriana* (1977).

ERNESTO SALAZAR is associated with the Museums of the Central Bank of Ecuador. Although primarily an archaeologist, he has also undertaken applied social research in Ecuador. He is currently doing research on colonization in the Chiguaza region (CREA's Upano-Palora project).

FRANK SALOMON is visiting assistant professor in anthropology and Latin American studies at the University of Illinois, Urbana, and the author of *Ethnic Lords of Quito in the Age of the Incas* (1978). On-going research includes ethnological and archaeological dimensions of indigenous Ecuadorian cultures.

GRACE SCHUBERT is project associate with the Institute for Research on Poverty at the University of Wisconsin, Madison. Her study of ethnicity began among blacks on the northwest coast of Ecuador and continues with blacks and other minorities in the United States.

SUSAN C. M. SCRIMSHAW is assistant professor in the School of Public Health, University of California, Los Angeles. She has published a number of papers based on Ecuadorian research, and has continued her research on culture and reproduction in Guatemala and Los Angeles.

Louisa R. Stark is professor of anthropology at the University of Wisconsin, Madison, and president of the Foundation for Inter-Andean Development, Madison. She is the author of *El Quichua de Imbabura* (with Lawrence A. Carpenter, 1973), *El Quichua de la Sierra Ecuatoriana* (1975), and *Diccionario Español-Quichua/Quichua-Español* (with Pieter Muysken, 1977).

Ronald Stutzman is assistant professor of anthropology at Goshen College, Goshen, Ind. He is currently preparing a book on black and *cholo* ethnicity in north Ecuador.

Anne-Christine Taylor is affiliated with, and teaches at, the Ecole des Hautes Etudes en Sciences Sociales, Paris, where she is now completing her doctoral dissertation on Achuar ethnohistory and change.

William T. Vickers is assistant professor of anthropology at Florida International University, Miami. He has published a number of papers on the human ecology of the Amazon and edited *Social Science Education for Development* (with Glenn Howze, 1978).

Dorothea S. Whitten is research associate in the Center for Latin American and Caribbean Studies, University of Illinois, Urbana, and co-founder of the Sacha Runa Research Foundation, Urbana. In addition to articles on medical care delivery and art style, she is co-designer of exhibitions on "Art and Technology from Ecuador's Rainforest."

Norman E. Whitten, Jr., is professor of anthropology at the University of Illinois, Urbana, editor of the *American Ethnologist*, and president of the Sacha Runa Research Foundation, Urbana. His books include *Class, Kinship and Power in an Ecuadorian Town* (1965), *Afro-American Anthropology* (edited, with John F. Szwed, 1970), *Black Frontiersmen* (1974), and *Sacha Runa* (1976).

James A. Yost is affiliated with the Summer Institute of Linguistics, Quito and Limoncocha, through the auspices of which he continues his research and publication on Waorani lifeways in contexts of radical change.